Swimming Even Faster

Swimming Even Faster

The updated and expanded edition of *Swimming Faster*

Ernest W. Maglischo

Arizona State University

Mayfield Publishing Company

Mountain View, California
London • Toronto

To my wife, Cheryl—I could not have completed this difficult task without her help and encouragement.

Library of Congress Cataloging-in-Publication Data

Maglischo, Ernest W.
Swimming even faster / Ernest W. Maglischo.
p. cm.
Rev. ed. of: Swimming faster. c1982.
Includes bibliographical references and index.
ISBN 1-55934-036-3
1. Swimming—Training. 2. Swimming—Physiological aspects.
I. Maglischo, Ernest W. Swimming faster. II. Title.
GV838.T73M33 1993
797.2′1—dc20 92-41324
CIP

Manufactured in the United States of America

10

Mayfield Publishing Company
1240 Villa Street
Mountain View, California 94041

Sponsoring editor, Erin Mulligan; developmental editor, Sylvia Stein Wright; production editor, April Wells-Hayes; copyeditor, Andrea McCarrick; text and cover designer, Richard Kharibian; art director, Jeannie M. Schreiber; art editor, Robin Mouat; illustrators, Natalie Hill and Willa Bower; manufacturing manager, Martha Branch. The text was set in 10/12 Times Roman and printed on 45# Penntech Penn Plus by R. R. Donnelley.

Acknowledgments and copyrights appear at the back of the book on page 755, which constitutes an extension of the copyright page.

Swimming Even Faster is a revised edition of *Swimming Faster*, © 1982 by Mayfield Publishing Company.

PREFACE

When the first edition of this book was published, I expected to sell six copies, one to each member of my immediate family. I was pleasantly surprised that it was so well received throughout the world, and I'm honored that so many knowledgeable persons felt it was worth reading. The book apparently filled a void. It had been some years since Doc Counsilman's excellent texts on the science of swimming were published, and members of the swimming community must have been eager for someone to provide a more recent survey of swimming research. Now it is nearly a decade since the first edition of *Swimming Faster* appeared. Since then, volumes of additional research have been published. I have attempted to compile the pertinent research for the 1980s in this edition. It is not a book that most of you will read from cover to cover. It has been written as a reference for readers to gather information on particular problems that may confront them.

This edition, like the old, is divided into three parts. The order has been changed, however: Part I deals with training; Part II, with stroke mechanics; and Part III, with special topics, such as pacing, warm-up, strength training, flexibility exercises, and nutrition.

The section on training begins with a discussion of basic physiology, so far as the muscular, circulatory, and respiratory systems are concerned. It also includes a description of energy metabolism. This should provide readers with the background information necessary to understand and evaluate the applications to training that are discussed later in the book.

The next group of chapters on training are presented in an entirely new way. Hardly a paragraph has survived intact from the first edition. To be sure, much of the information from that edition is still applicable and has been included here, but it is presented in what is, hopefully, a more understandable format. One of the most important changes has been in the terminology used to describe the training process. The terms *aerobic* and *anaerobic* have been replaced with *endurance* and *sprint*. These are the terms used by coaches and trainers throughout the world, so it seemed more appropriate to communicate in that language rather than the language of the scientific community. The five forms of training from the first edition have been replaced with these two forms. The other forms have not been eliminated, however. Most are included among the various subcategories of endurance and sprint training. These changes in terminology should not confuse those of you who have read the earlier edition. At the same time, I hope it will make it easier for first-time readers to understand the training process.

In addition to terminology changes, there are three important differences in emphasis and two changes in the procedures for training. The first difference in emphasis has evolved from a greater understanding of the anaerobic threshold theory of endurance training. This theory was in its infancy at the time the first edition was written, and only a small section was included. Volumes of research have been published since that time, most of them favorable to this concept. Consequently, a much larger number of pages have been devoted to this important theory of training.

The second difference in emphasis concerns maximum oxygen consumption. Apparently, this measure is not as important to endurance performance as was once believed. Most research now shows that the anaerobic threshold is more highly related to performance than maximum oxygen consumption.

The third difference in emphasis involves the training of buffering capacity. There was some doubt that training could improve buffering capacity at the time of the first writing. Since that time, however, several reports have shown that buffering capacity can be increased with training and that it has a significant effect on improving performance. The method for improving buffering capacity was called *lactate tolerance training* in the first edition; this term is also used in this edition.

The first important change in the procedures of training involves a realization that the ATP-CP system — or nonaerobic system as it is referred to in this edition — plays an insignificant role in nearly all competitive swimming events. The effects of increased muscular power were mistaken for contributions from this system. It is true that the quantities of ATP and CP and the speed of their energy-releasing reactions can be increased in muscles after training. However, the amounts of each of these energy-supplying chemicals and their enzymes are so miniscule to begin with that even large percentage increases would only improve swimming speed by a few tenths of a second. Consequently, the effects of training on the nonaerobic system probably has less to do with improving performance than do the increases in muscular strength and power that accompany the training of this system.

A second major difference in the training scheme concerns methods for increasing the rate of anaerobic metabolism. Only one category, lactate tolerance training, was described for this system in the first edition. It has since become apparent that better results can be achieved with two categories of sprint training: the first, lactate tolerance, is for the training of buffering capacity; the second involves improving the rate of energy release from the anaerobic system. Methods for increasing the rate of energy release are identified as lactate production training in this edition.

I have studiously avoided presenting training information in a cookbook format in this edition, just as I did at the time of the first writing; data are presented from both sides of controversial issues. However, I have taken positions on issues where I felt competent to do so. Readers, of course, are free to accept or reject those positions based on their experience and analysis of the research data presented.

The approach to swimming propulsion has been changed considerably in Part II. Bernoulli's theorem has not been used to explain propulsion; instead, Newton's action-reaction principle has been invoked. I have come to believe that the original concept of pushing water back to go forward is the major element in swimming propulsion. Although Bernoulli's principle undoubtedly operates, its role in propulsion is probably minor compared to Newton's action-reaction principle. Swimmers do not need to push their hands and feet directly back to push water back. The action-reaction principle also operates when swimmers displace water back with sculling movements that follow complex, three-dimensional paths.

Several technical changes are included in the chapters on stroke mechanics. Since writing the first edition, I have had the opportunity to participate in research with members of two U.S. Olympic swimming teams, in 1984 and again in 1988. As a result, we have information that was unavailable earlier on the stroke techniques used by world-class swimmers. For one thing, the undulating (or what is presently known as the *wave-style*) breaststroke has been more widely accepted since this book was first published. An important propulsive phase of the back crawl stroke has also been uncovered.

Much of Part III remains the same, although the techniques for warming up have changed somewhat. The advice on pacing has not changed, but new splits for recent world records are listed. The chapter on strength and flexibility was, in my opinion, the weakest part of the first edition. Hopefully, I have been more thorough and informative this time around.

Most of the information on nutrition is the same. One important change, however, is the elimination of methods for measuring body composition. An overconcern with body composition may be encouraging eating disorders, such as bulimia and anorexia nervosa, in a small but significant number of competitive swimmers, so measuring it is no longer recommended.

Through talking with coaches from various levels of competitive swimming I learned of some glaring omissions in the first edition, which, hopefully, have been rectified this time around with the addition of many new sections. The largest new section is about seasonal planning. We have learned that it is not enough to simply include the "correct" types of training in a season; they must be placed strategically and interchanged periodically with periods of rest and recovery for swimmers to achieve their best results *at the proper time in the season*. The practice of planning seasons around macrocycles, mesocycles, and microcycles is described in detail to help systematize the training process.

A greatly expanded section on age group training is also included in this edition. This is probably the most important phase of a swimmer's career because it is the time when the foundations are laid for future success. The patterns of growth and development in children are described, and some suggestions are provided for using this information to structure the training of age group swimmers.

A section on training females and Masters swimmers is also included in this edition. Problems that are unique to or more prevalent among female athletes, such as menstrual disorders and anemia, are discussed. The process of aging and its effect on training and performance are also described.

A section on altitude training has been added to this edition because it has become an important part of the program of many swimmers throughout the world during the last decade. The value of this procedure is debatable, so both sides of the issue are presented. Some suggestions from experts on altitude training are also provided for those who wish to use them.

Stroke rate measuring is another new topic in this edition. It provides an excellent means for evaluating training, stroking efficiency, and pacing. Some methods for measuring these rates and using the information to improve performances are discussed. Drills that can help in this process are also described.

Special thanks are due to Carol Tait-Remen for her thoughtful review of an early version of this manuscript.

I hope this book will be received as well as the previous edition. I hope, also, that the information helps athletes swim even faster.

CONTENTS

Chapter 25 Diets for Training and Competition 663

Part I

TRAINING

The first two chapters review exercise physiology as it relates to the training of competitive swimmers. This should provide readers with background information that supports the methods of training that are presented in the following chapters. The major sections of the first two chapters are concerned with energy metabolism and the structure and function of skeletal muscles. Circulation, respiration, and hormonal functions are also described.

The causes of fatigue and how it can be delayed are the topics for Chapter 3. The remaining chapters of Part I are concerned with the application of this information to the training process. Chapter 4 begins with a discussion of the principles of training. This is followed by a description of the anaerobic threshold theory of training. Procedures for endurance and sprint training are described in Chapter 5.

How to find the proper balance for all of the various types of training that swimmers need is the topic for Chapter 6. Chapter 7 is a catchall for several of the special forms of training that were not included in Chapter 5. The values of controversial methods, such as hypoxic, high-intensity, and altitude training, are discussed. Several of the most popular types of training sets are also critiqued.

Blood testing has become quite widespread since the first edition of this book was published. That topic is covered in Chapter 8. The majority of coaches throughout the world do not have access to blood testing, so several other methods for prescribing training paces and monitoring training progress are also explained.

Yearly and seasonal planning are the topics for Chapter 9, and procedures for weekly and daily planning are discussed in Chapter 10. Entire chapters are devoted to tapering and overtraining because of their importance to performance. Tapering is covered in Chapter 11 and overtraining in Chapter 12.

Throughout this section, every effort has been made to present the information in such a way that it can be applied to the training of all swimmers, regardless of age, sex, or level of ability. Nevertheless, readers will have many questions about special populations of competitive swimmers. So, the final two chapters of Part I are devoted to special training procedures for age group swimmers (Chapter 13) and for female and Masters swimmers (Chapter 14). References for the information in all of these chapters are included at the end of the book.

CHAPTER 1

Energy Metabolism and Swimming Performance

Swimming from one end of a pool to the other is made possible by the contractions of muscles. Muscular contraction, in turn, is achieved through the release of energy stored in chemical compounds within the body. Energy provides the power for swimming; without energy, muscles could not contract. This chapter describes the physiological mechanisms that provide energy for muscular contraction. The totality of the processes of supplying energy is called *metabolism*. During the past two decades, information about energy metabolism has been largely responsible for improvements in training methods, and it is therefore important that serious students of training understand the metabolic process.

This chapter begins with a description of energy and proceeds to a discussion of the physiological mechanisms that make it available to the muscles for contraction.

ENERGY AND ITS SOURCES

Energy is usually defined as the capacity to do work. The ultimate source of our energy is the sun, which radiates energy to the earth. When that energy strikes plants, it is transferred to them and stored as chemical energy through photosynthesis. When we eat these plants or the flesh of animals that have eaten them, we take the energy into our bodies and store it for later use. Energy is stored in plants and animals as carbohydrates, fats, and proteins.

We also store energy in our bodies in combination with certain chemicals. We transform the chemical energy to electrical energy for the transmission of nerve impulses and to mechanical energy for powering the work of muscular contraction. *The speed of sprinters and the ability of middle-distance swimmers and distance swimmers to maintain a certain pace are determined by the body's capacity to release chemical energy and transform it into mechanical energy for work.*

Because energy availability is *the* factor that governs the speed and pace of swimmers, the purpose of training should be to make more energy available to the muscles at faster rates. Training does this through a process called *adaptation.* When swimmers continually expend large amounts of energy at rapid rates during training, their body stores more substances that contain energy and releases it more rapidly when it is needed during races. In other words, the body's physiological mechanisms adapt to the specific demands that are placed on them so that more energy is available to perform more work with less fatigue.

A *calorie* is a measure of energy, and the caloric content of foods indicates the amount of energy we receive from them. A *kilocalorie* contains 1,000 calories. The term *Calorie,* with a capital "C," is a method for expressing a kilocalorie; *calorie,* with a lowercase "c," identifies the smaller calorie units. One thousand calories is equal to one Calorie (or one kilocalorie), which is equal to 426.85 kg/m of work (3,087.4 ft/lb).

STORAGE FORMS OF ENERGY IN THE BODY

Energy is stored in our bodies in combination with the following chemical substances: *adenosine triphosphate (ATP), creatine phosphate (CP), carbohydrates, fats,* and *proteins.* All of these substances are formed by combinations of chemical molecules.

Adenosine Triphosphate (ATP)

ATP consists of a protein molecule—adenosine—and three molecules of phosphate. Figure 1-1 illustrates the chemical structure of ATP. The diamond-shaped symbols connecting the four components represent energy. That energy binds the four smaller molecules together to form the larger ATP molecule. The bonds between these molecules are sources of chemical energy waiting to be used.

ATP is the only source of energy in the body that can be used for muscular contraction. All the other energy-containing chemicals are used to recycle ATP. Our muscles contain amounts of ATP that are so small that they can be depleted in the first few seconds of exercise. Because ATP cannot be supplied to working

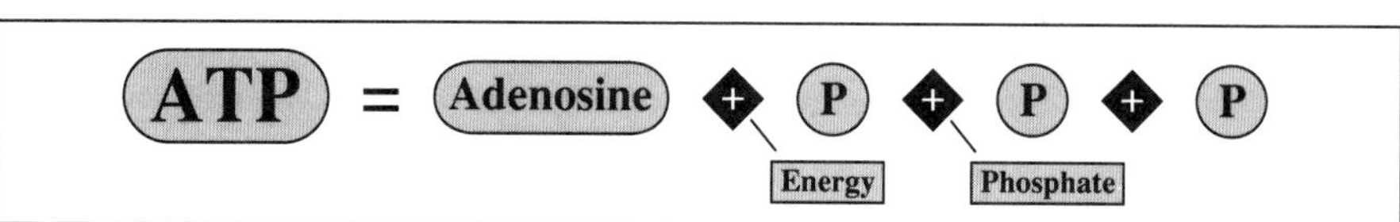

Figure 1-1. The chemical structure of adenosine triphosphate.

muscle fibers from other parts of the body, it must be recycled immediately by other sources of energy stored inside those same muscle fibers. These sources are the remaining four chemicals: creatine phosphate (CP), carbohydrates, fats, and proteins. Enzymes begin breaking these substances down immediately at the onset of exercise so that their energy will be instantly available for recycling ATP. They recycle ATP at different rates of speed, however, the rate being largely determined by the number of intermediate steps they must undergo before their energy is released. The following ranking reflects their rates for recycling ATP:

1. Creatine phosphate
2. Carbohydrates
3. Fats and proteins

Creatine Phosphate (CP)

This chemical provides the most rapid source of energy for ATP recycling. As its name implies, it is composed of one molecule of creatine and one of phosphate. The molecules are bound together by energy (see Figure 1-2).

Unfortunately, the amount of CP that can be stored in the muscles is also quite small, only enough to maintain muscular contraction for about 10 to 15 seconds of all-out effort (Gollnick & Hermansen, 1973). After that, the CP supply is nearly depleted and the muscles must get the energy and phosphate they need to recycle ATP from carbohydrates, fats, and proteins.

Carbohydrates

These foods are made up of simple sugars and starches, which supply the energy for all body functions, including thinking and exercise. Glucose is the simple sugar that is used for ATP recycling. Foods that contain simple and complex sugars and starches are reduced to glucose during the digestive process and enter the bloodstream, where they are carried to the cells of the body.

Muscle Glycogen Glucose that enters muscle cells is stored there as glycogen. Muscle glycogen consists of a chain of glucose molecules.

When exercise begins, the glycogen stored in muscles is converted back to glucose. That glucose is then metabolized in a long and complex chain of events termed *glycolysis*. Energy for ATP recycling is released at several points along the chain. The energy from muscle glycogen can be made available more rapidly than other carbohydrate forms because it is stored in the muscles and does not need to be transported to them. Consequently, muscle glycogen is the primary source of

Figure 1-2. The chemical structure of creatine phosphate.

energy for ATP recycling in all but the very shortest swimming events. It is also the next fastest source for ATP recycling after CP.

Liver Glycogen and Blood Glucose The blood and liver also contain supplies of glucose that can be mobilized and transported to the muscles when needed for energy. Blood glucose is more commonly called *blood sugar.* It is glucose that is poured into the blood from the stomach during the digestion of foods. At rest, it is transported to the muscles and the liver, where it is stored as glycogen. When swimmers are training, glucose that was circulating in the blood can diffuse into the muscle cells and enter the metabolic process without first being converted to glycogen.

The glucose that enters the liver is stored as glycogen. Liver glycogen must be converted back to glucose before it can be transported to the muscles and used to supplement their glycogen supply, however. Another important function of liver glycogen is to maintain an adequate blood glucose supply to the brain and other nervous tissues. Nerve cells, like other cells in the body, use glucose for energy, but, unlike muscles cells, they cannot store it as glycogen. Therefore, they need a constant supply via the circulation.

Blood glucose and liver glycogen play almost no role in supplying energy during competition. The rate of speed called for in swimming races is so fast that the muscles must rely almost entirely on muscle glycogen for ATP recycling.

Liver glycogen and blood glucose can supplement muscle glycogen during endurance exercise, although they cannot replace the latter substance entirely. The process of converting liver glycogen to blood glucose and transporting it to the muscles is too slow to provide all of the energy for ATP recycling at fast, or even moderate, swimming speeds. So, both liver glycogen and blood glucose can serve only as supplements, not substitutes, for muscle glycogen. Nevertheless, the role they play is very important because they allow swimmers to do more work before muscle glycogen becomes depleted.

Both blood glucose and liver glycogen play another important role by replacing muscle glycogen during the recovery period following exercise. This allows swimmers to replace this energy source between training sessions.

Fats

Fats are also an important source of energy for ATP recycling during exercise. One gram of fat contains more than twice the energy of an equal quantity of carbohydrate. Additionally, there is enough adipose tissue on the bodies of most athletes to supply energy for several days of training. Nevertheless, carbohydrates are the preferred fuel during exercise because the release of energy from fat is a slow process and it cannot replace ATP fast enough to sustain anything but slow to moderate swimming speeds.

As mentioned, fat can only be metabolized aerobically, and this process involves additional transport time from its storage depots—adipose tissue—to muscles, where it must enter Krebs cycle (see p. 12) before it can be metabolized for energy. Thus, although the oxidation of fatty acids supplies abundant energy, it is released so slowly that swimmers could not sustain an adequate pace during races if this were the only source, or even the primary source, for ATP recycling. Consequently, energy from fat can supplement, but cannot replace, glycogen as a source for ATP recycling during training.

In competitive swimming, the essential role of fat metabolism is to supply energy for ATP replacement during training. It can provide a significant amount of energy during long repeat sets that are swum at moderate speeds. This reduces the rate of muscle glycogen use and delays fatigue.

Athletes can use two sources of fat during exercise: (1) adipose tissue that is stored beneath the skin and (2) fat molecules that are stored within muscles. Adipose tissue supplies about one-half of the free fatty acids used during exercise. The other half is furnished by fat stored in the muscle cells. Fast-twitch and slow-twitch muscle fibers do not use fat at equal rates of speed (see p. 25). Slow-twitch fibers are best suited for metabolizing fat because they have a greater blood supply and can transport it to the muscles more rapidly and because they have more mitochondria, where fat from both the circulation and muscles can be metabolized. The rate of fat metabolism in slow-twitch muscle fibers has been estimated to be ten times greater than in their fast-twitch counterparts (Brooks & Fahey, 1984). Consequently, distance swimmers, who generally have a higher percentage of slow-twitch fibers, burn more fat (and less muscle glycogen) for energy during training. Thus, it may take longer for distance swimmers to deplete their muscle glycogen supply. This may be one reason why they seem to tolerate training better than sprinters.

Proteins

Proteins are synonymous with strength because they are the basic structural element of muscles. They are also one of the most important buffers in the body. Accordingly, they play a role in regulating the balance between acidity and alkalinity of body fluids — acid-base balance — during exercise.

In addition to their other functions, proteins can donate small amounts of energy for recycling ATP during exercise. However, like fat, the release of energy from protein is a slow, aerobic process. Protein metabolism is, in fact, the slowest and least economical method for recycling ATP.

ENERGY METABOLISM: THE THREE STAGES

The term *metabolism* has been used several times in the preceding discussion without completely defining it. It is the process of storing and releasing energy from chemical nutrients. An understanding of energy metabolism is necessary to comprehend the roles that various types of repeat sets, land drills, cycle programs, and other facets of training play in the adaptation process.

The two broad categories of metabolism are *aerobic* and *anaerobic*. We all presume to understand them; however, they are much more complex than the usual definitions "with oxygen" and "without oxygen" imply. Before we describe aerobic and anaerobic metabolism, we will discuss a third phase — *nonaerobic metabolism*.

Nonaerobic Metabolism

This phase of the metabolic process refers to the rapid recycling of ATP from the breakdown of CP. The process has commonly been referred to as anaerobic because it does not require oxygen, but I prefer to use the term "nonaerobic" to differentiate it from the phase of metabolism that involves the anaerobic breakdown of glucose and the formation of lactic acid. The ability to distinguish between these two phases of the metabolic process has important implications for understanding their respective roles in swimming races and training.

When a nerve impulse stimulates a muscle fiber to contract, the protein filaments of that fiber—myosin and actin—combine. They activate an enzyme *actomyosin ATPase*. This enzyme, with water, causes one of the phosphate bonds to be split from the ATP molecule. In the process, the chemical energy in the phosphate bond is released and converted, in part, to mechanical energy that can be used by the muscle fiber to perform the work of contraction. This process is illustrated in Figure 1-3. It is very rapid and does not limit the force that a swimmer can exert. The amount of force is regulated by the number of fibers that are contracting at one time in a muscle.

When ATP releases energy for muscular contraction, it also loses one of its phosphate molecules. Consequently, the substance remaining after the breakdown of ATP is termed *adenosine diphosphate (ADP)* because it now contains only two phosphate molecules (see Figure 1-4).

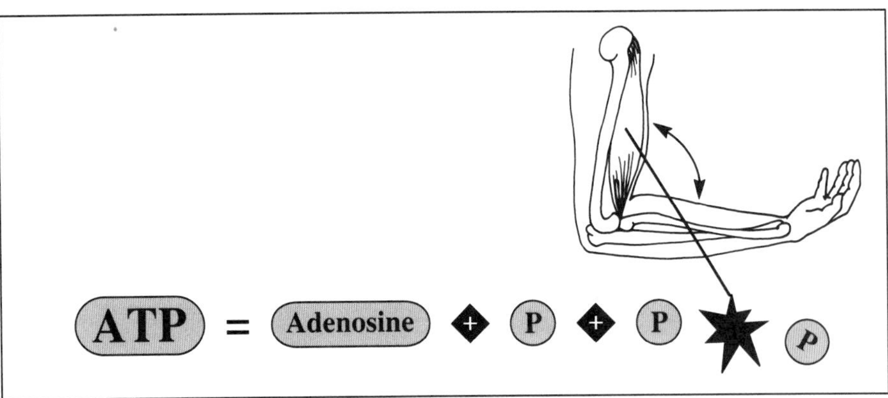

Figure 1-3. The release of energy from ATP.

Figure 1-4. The chemical structure of adenosine diphosphate (ADP).

The breakdown of one molecule of ATP liberates 7.3 Calories of chemical energy. Some of this is converted to mechanical energy and used by the muscles for contraction, and the rest is converted to heat energy.

The percentage of the total energy used for work determines efficiency. For example, when a swimmer's efficiency is listed as 14 percent (a typical efficiency for front crawl stroke swimming, Pendergast et al., 1978), it means that only 14 percent of the chemical energy released is used for the work of muscular contraction. The remaining 86 percent is converted to heat energy.

The substance remaining—ADP—must be recycled to ATP very rapidly for exercise to continue. Remember, there is only enough ATP in muscle cells to fuel muscular contraction for a few seconds.

The recycling of ATP requires replacement of the phosphate and free energy that were lost. The most rapid method for doing this is through the splitting of CP. The phosphate and energy needed for recycling can be made available in one step when this substance is used (see Figure 1-5). ATP can be replaced so rapidly from the breakdown of CP that neither the rate nor the force of muscular contraction will be reduced. The bond that connects creatine and phosphate is broken, so that both energy and phosphate are freed. The phosphate and energy combine with ADP to replace that which was lost so that a new ATP molecule can be formed. After 10 to 15 seconds, when the supply of creatine phosphate is nearly depleted, the processes of anaerobic and aerobic metabolism become the principal sources for ATP replacement.

Anaerobic Metabolism

This phase of the metabolic process refers to the first eleven steps in the breakdown of glycogen in a process known as *glycolysis*. The process happens very rapidly and can supply energy for ATP replacement almost as quickly as it is supplied by CP. The steps involved in anaerobic metabolism, as well as the enzymes involved, are listed in Figure 1-6.

In most cases, the process begins with the conversion of muscle glycogen to glucose, a procedure that is catalyzed by an activated form of the enzyme *phos-*

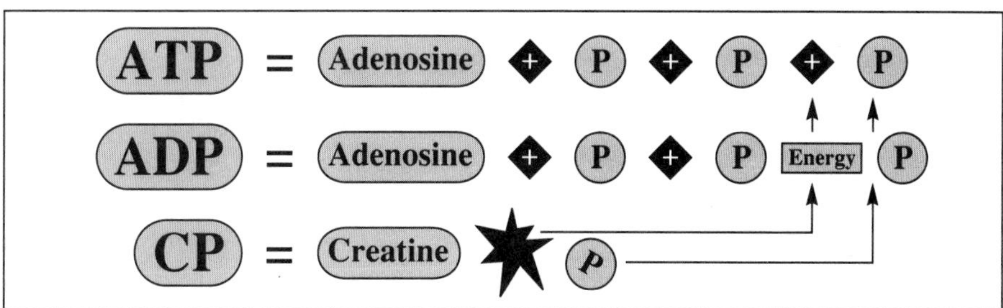

Figure 1-5. The replacement of ATP from creatine phosphate.

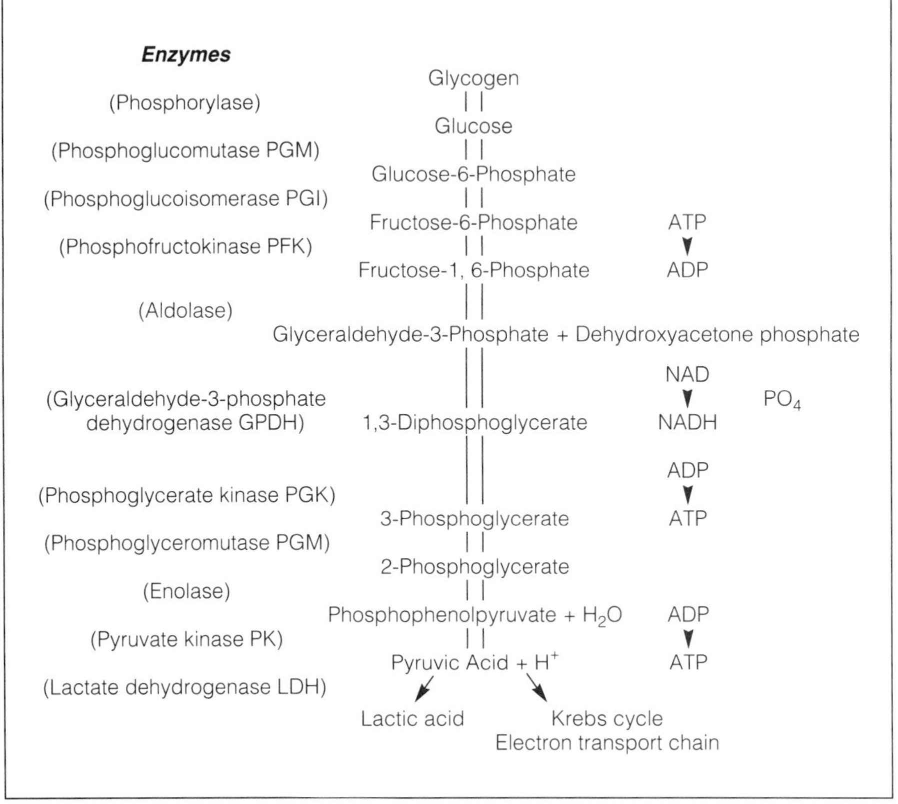

Figure 1-6. Anaerobic metabolism.

phorylase. After this initial step, the metabolism of glucose proceeds through ten additional stages, ending with the formation of pyruvic acid from phosphophenolpyruvate. This procedure is catalyzed by the enzyme *pyruvate kinase*. All of these reactions take place in the protoplasm (cytoplasm) of the muscle cell and do not require oxygen. Another of the important enzymes in this process is *phosphofructokinase (PFK),* because it plays a major role in regulating the rate of anaerobic metabolism.

Hydrogen ions (H^+) are also released continuously from glucose when it is metabolized. These are electrically charged atoms that contain energy in the electrons ($^+$) they carry. When pyruvic acid and hydrogen ions combine, they form *lactic acid*. This reaction is catalyzed by the enzyme *lactate dehydrogenase (LDH),* particularly the muscle form of that enzyme.

Lactic acid is an intermediate product of glucose metabolism and is produced when some of the by-products of that process are not metabolized aerobically. Consequently, it is the end product of the anaerobic phase of metabolism. The accumulation of lactic acid in muscles is thought to be a principal cause of fatigue during swimming races because of its effect on pH.

pH is a measure of the balance between the acidity and alkalinity of fluids. A neutral condition is identified with a value of 7.0. Alkaline fluids have a pH that is greater than this, and fluids that are acidic have a lower pH. We are concerned with the pH of fluids contained within muscle cells (intracellular fluid).

When the human body is at rest, the acid-base balance of intracellular fluids is neutral. That is, they have a pH of 7.0. This balance will be upset toward the acidic side when lactic acid is produced during exercise. When muscle pH falls below 7.0, a person is said to be suffering from *acidosis*.

A swimmer's speed will be affected when the fluids within his or her muscles become acidic. The rate of ATP recycling will slow when muscle pH falls below 7.0, with this restraint becoming progressively more severe as it continues to decline. Because it will be impossible for athletes to contract their muscles rapidly and forcefully, their speed will decline.

At fast speeds, the accumulation of lactic acid will lower muscle pH well below 7.0 in less than 60 seconds. This is why 100 distances are the upper limit for all-out sprint events. It will take longer to reduce muscle pH when athletes swim longer races at slower speeds. Nevertheless, acidosis will ultimately cause fatigue when the accumulation of lactic acid exceeds its rate of removal from muscles.

Fortunately, the body can remove some of the lactic acid so that acidosis can be delayed. This happens when lactic acid diffuses out of the muscles and into the blood, where it can be carried to other parts of the body. Some of the lactic acid can even diffuse into fibers within the same muscle group that are not contracting. This process removes lactic acid from working muscle fibers, where the pH is declining, and takes it to other tissues where the pH is normal and additional lactic acid is not being produced. This reduces the rate of fatigue in the working muscles without adversely affecting the other tissues to which the excess lactic acid is taken.

Lactic acid is removed from the tissues during recovery by converting it back to pyruvic acid and hydrogen ions. From there, it can be converted back to glycogen and stored for later use or it can enter the aerobic phase of metabolism and be converted to carbon dioxide and water.

Another way of delaying fatigue is for the body to produce less lactic acid. All of the pyruvic acid and hydrogen ions released during the anaerobic phase of metabolism do not necessarily have to combine to form lactic acid. The metabolic process can continue in at least two other directions after these two substances are formed and before they combine to make lactic acid. The major direction is through aerobic metabolism. A secondary pathway is through the formation of *alanine*.

Aerobic Metabolism

This phase of the metabolic process refers to the remaining steps in glycogen metabolism, ending with the production of carbon dioxide and water. Hundreds of steps are involved in this process.

When glycogen is metabolized aerobically, the step producing lactic acid is skipped. Instead, by-products of pyruvic acid and hydrogen ions are metabolized to carbon dioxide and water. Consequently, acidosis is delayed because lactic acid is not produced.

Aerobic metabolism has two phases: Krebs cycle (also known as the citric acid cycle) and the electron transport chain. Pyruvic acid is metabolized to carbon dioxide in Krebs cycle. Hydrogen ions are metabolized to water in the electron transport chain.

Krebs Cycle Some of the pyruvic acid that was formed during anaerobic metabolism is prepared for entry into Krebs cycle by joining with coenzyme A (A stands for acetic acid) to form *acetyl coenzyme A (acetyl-CoA)*. From there, the acetyl-CoA enters Krebs cycle, where it will ultimately be metabolized to carbon dioxide and water. Within Krebs cycle, acetyl-CoA joins with oxaloacetic acid to form citric acid—the same citric acid found in citrus fruits. The breakdown of citric acid then takes place in a whirling, circular fashion until the acetyl-CoA is dissociated to carbon dioxide and hydrogen ions. The remaining oxaloacetic acid continues through to the starting point, where it picks up more acetyl-CoA to begin the cycle again. A diagram of Krebs cycle is shown in Figure 1-7.

A large number of enzymes regulate Krebs cycle, the most important of which are also shown in Figure 1-7. Endurance training increases the activity of these enzymes so that more pyruvic acid can be taken into Krebs cycle during each minute of exercise so that even less lactic acid is produced at race speeds.

The Electron Transport Chain The hydrogen ions that were formed during anaerobic metabolism must also be removed if fatigue is to be delayed. It is the hydrogen ions in lactic acid and not the lactic acid per se that reduces muscle pH.

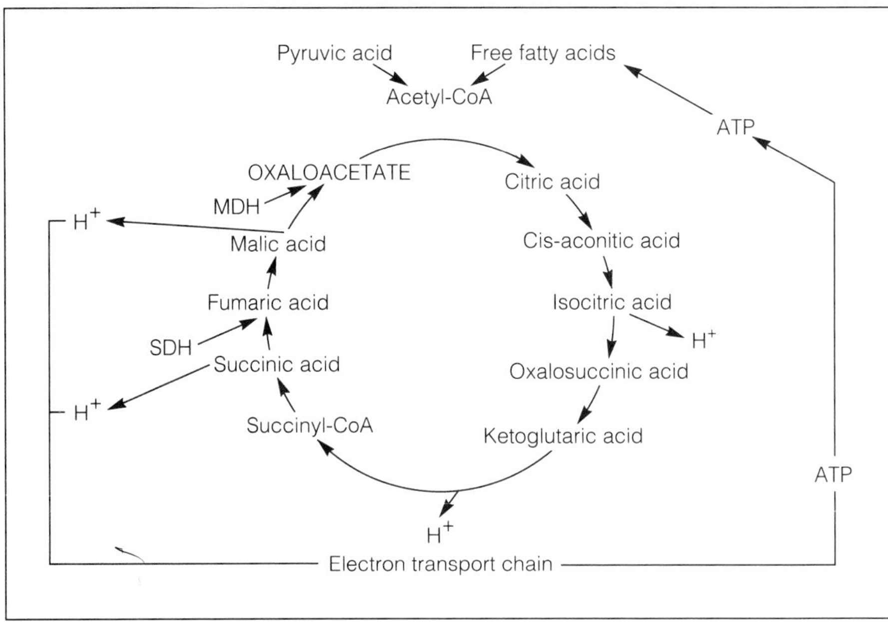

Figure 1-7. Krebs cycle. (Adapted from Costill, 1978, pp. 233–48.)

Therefore, it is important to remove as many hydrogen ions as possible during exercise so they do not combine with pyruvic acid to form lactic acid and lower muscle pH.

A schematic of the electron transport chain is shown in Figure 1-8. In this process, hydrogen ions combine with oxygen to form H_2O. The hydrogen ions are prepared for entry into the electron transport chain by combining with another coenzyme—*nicotinamide adenine dinucleotide (NAD^+)*—to form NADH. Still another coenzyme—*flavin adenine dinucleotide (FAD)*—can also pick up hydrogen ions, forming FADH in the process. Both NADH and FADH are then taken to the electron transport chain, where they are passed through it in bucket brigade fashion by a series of enzymes called the *cytochromes*. Cytochromes are composed of iron and protein. The iron (ferric) portion can remove the hydrogen ions from

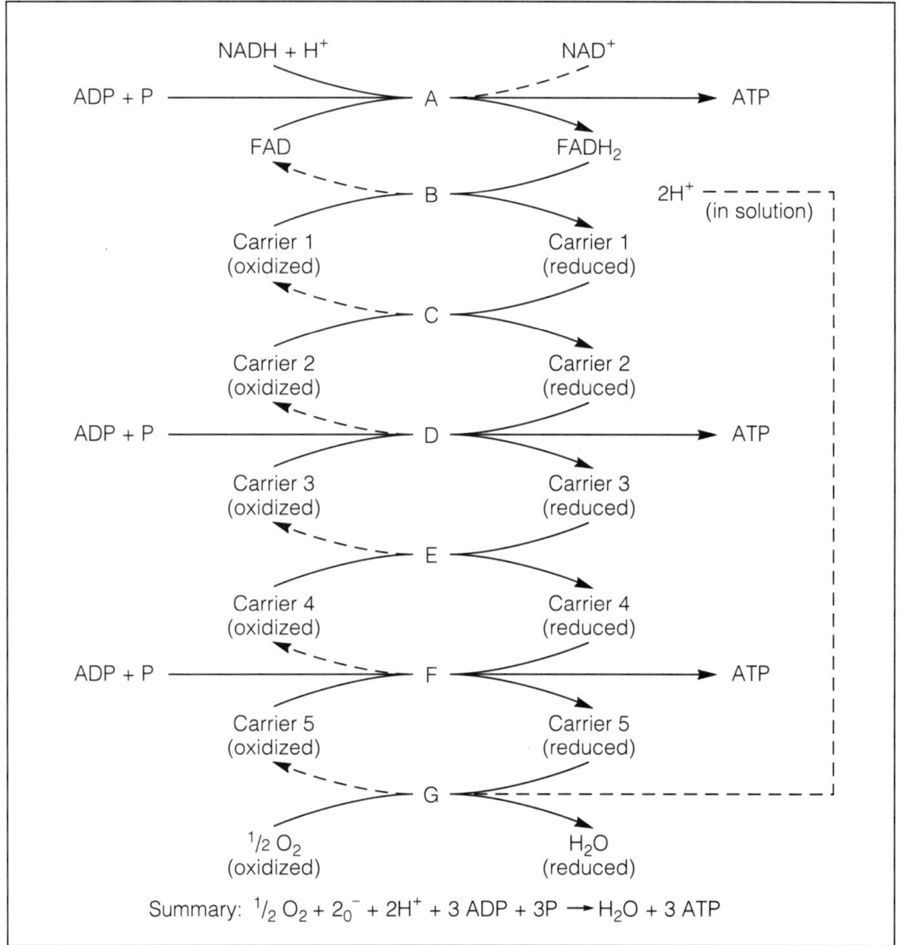

Figure 1-8. The electron transport chain. (Adapted from Lamb, 1978.)

NADH and FADH and transfer them to the next cytochrome in the chain. This frees the remaining NAD^+ and FAD to return for more hydrogen ions. The energy connected to hydrogen ions is released from the electrons at several points of transfer along the chain and bound to ADP to form ATP. The remaining hydrogen combines with oxygen to form water. Over 90 percent of the recycling of ATP takes place in the electron transport chain.

The Role of Oxygen in Aerobic Metabolism Because it is the final acceptor of hydrogen in the electron transport chain, oxygen regulates the rate of energy release from aerobic metabolism. The rate at which NAD^+ and FAD can be made available to remove hydrogen ions from muscles depends on the availability of oxygen for releasing the hydrogen molecule from NADH and FADH. When more oxygen is available, a greater amount of hydrogen is dissociated from NADH and FADH, so that more NAD^+ and FAD are freed to return and "gather" more hydrogen ions.

When oxygen is not available in sufficient quantity to accept all of the hydrogen that was released during exercise, the entire process of aerobic metabolism will back up so that the rates of entry of pyruvic acid into Krebs cycle and of hydrogen ions into the electron transport chain are slowed. When this happens, the hydrogen ions that could not find NAD^+ and FAD to combine with will instead combine with excess pyruvic acid to form lactic acid.

Unlike anaerobic metabolism, which can proceed in the cytoplasm of muscle cells, the only place where aerobic metabolism can occur is in the *mitochondria* of those cells. Mitochondria are rod-shaped bodies that are embedded within the cytoplasm (protoplasm) of muscle cells.

The mitochondria must have oxygen to perform their function, and that oxygen is transported to them by a protein substance called *myoglobin* that is in the cytoplasm of muscle cells. Oxygen diffuses through the cell membrane, where it is picked up by myoglobin and transported to the mitochondria. Figure 1-9 is a

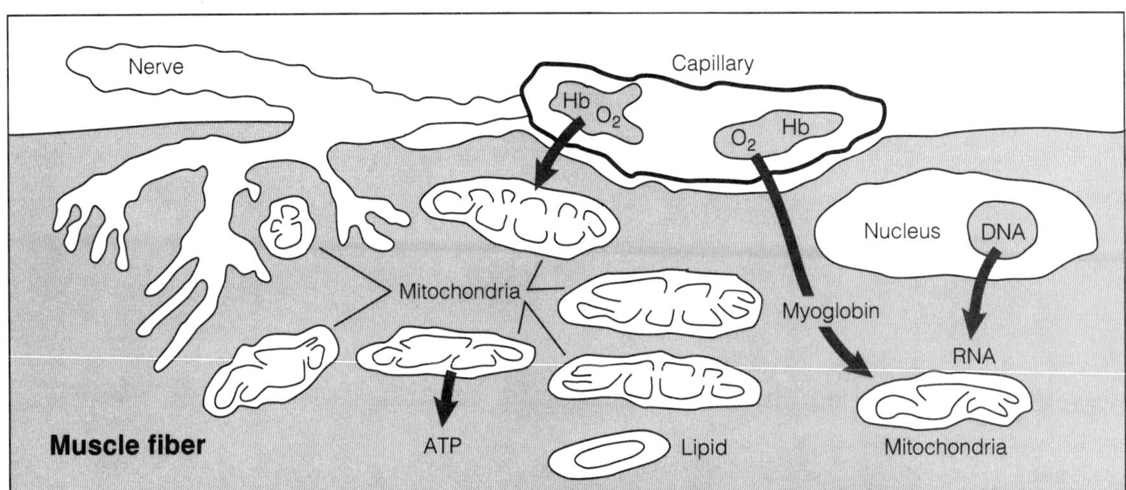

Figure 1-9. A muscle fiber, showing the path of oxygen diffusion from capillaries to mitochondria. (Adapted from Edington & Edgerton, 1976.)

schematic drawing of a muscle fiber, showing the location of mitochondria. It shows the oxygen diffusing into the muscle cell from capillaries, after which it is transported to the mitochondria by myoglobin. The aerobic endurance of swimmers is in part determined by the size and number of mitochondria they possess. Those swimmers with large and numerous mitochondria will have more little chemical factories for performing aerobic metabolism, so they will not fatigue so quickly.

The Alanine Pathway This is the second pathway that acts to reduce the production of lactic acid. In this process, some of the pyruvic acid and hydrogen ions formed during anaerobic metabolism bind with ammonia to form alanine instead of combining to form lactic acid. The alanine is then transported to the liver, where it can be converted back to glucose and "poured" into the blood to replenish the muscles' energy supply.

Fat Metabolism In addition to glycogen, fat and protein can also be metabolized aerobically so that their energy and phosphate can be used to reform ATP. However, these substances must first be converted to an intermediate by-product of glycogen metabolism so that they can enter Krebs cycle. Fats must be converted from *triglycerides* to *free fatty acids* for this purpose.

Triglycerides are the storage form of fat in the body. They are split to *glycerol* and three molecules of *free fatty acids* by the enzyme *lipase*. The free fatty acids are transported by the blood to working muscles, where they can be absorbed and transported to the mitochondria. They enter the mitochondria with the aid of another enzyme, *carnitine transferase (CT)*. From there, they are converted to acetyl-CoA in a process called *beta oxidation*. The conversion to acetyl-CoA is catalyzed by the enzyme *acetyl-CoA synthetase*. Once converted to acetyl-CoA, the free fatty acids are metabolized to carbon dioxide via Krebs cycle in the same way as glycogen. One hundred and forty-seven molecules of ATP can be formed from each fatty acid molecule once it enters Krebs cycle (McArdle, Katch, & Katch, 1981).

Protein Metabolism During exercise, certain amino acids—principally alanine—are released from working muscles and transported by the blood to the liver, where they are converted to glucose. That glucose is then released into the blood and delivered back to the working muscles. This process is known variously as the *alanine-shuttle,* or *glucose-alanine cycle*. Other amino acids that play a similar, though less pronounced, role in supplying energy are *glutamate* and *aspartate*.

Energy Metabolism During Slow, Medium, and Maximum Swimming Speeds

This whole process of metabolism is analogous to filling a tank with fluid until it overflows. Figures 1-10*a*, 1-10*b*, and 1-10*c* may help clarify this process.

Assume that the aerobic phase of metabolism is represented by the large tank and that the smaller overflow container attached to it represents anaerobic metabolism. The breakdown of glycogen and the formation of pyruvic acid and hydrogen ions are represented by the large spigot. The large container has a small spigot at

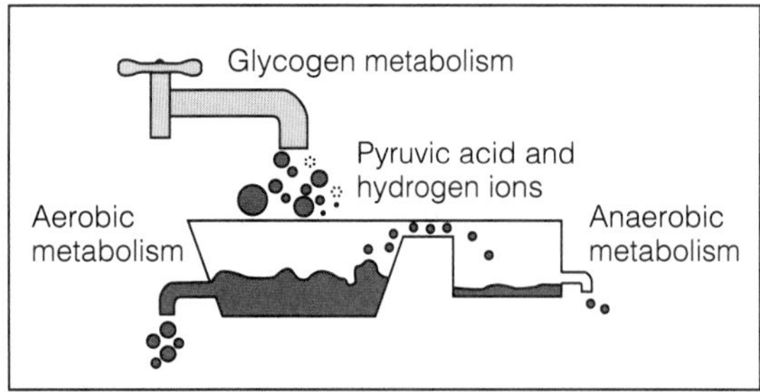

Figure 1-10*a*. Energy metabolism at slow speeds.

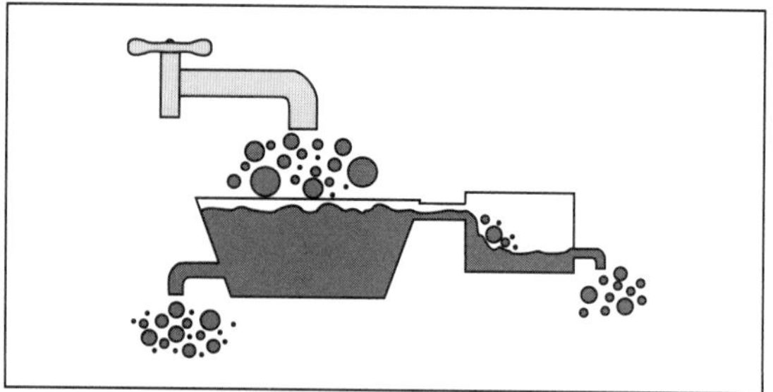

Figure 1-10*b*. Energy metabolism at fast, but not maximum, speeds.

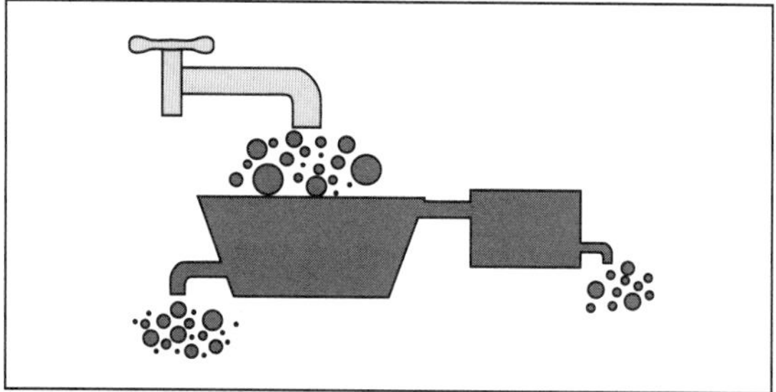

Figure 1-10*c*. Energy metabolism at maximum speeds.

the bottom, but its maximum rate for emptying is slower than the maximum rate at which it can be filled by the larger spigot. The overflow tank also has a small spigot for emptying (into the bloodstream), but its maximum rate of emptying is also slower than the maximum fill rate.

At slow speeds, the fluid (pyruvic acid and hydrogen ions) is poured into the large tank only slightly faster than it can be removed, so the tank fills very slowly (see Figure 1-10*a*). This represents easy swimming, where the rate of aerobic metabolism is not maximal, as shown by the fact that the large container is not filled. The excess pyruvic acid and hydrogen ions combine to form a small amount of lactic acid that splashes into the overflow container while the larger container is being filled. However, it can be removed from the overflow container as fast as it pours in, so the athlete should be able to continue at this pace for as long as he or she has glucose, fat, and protein available to supply the energy needed to recycle ATP.

At medium speeds, the larger (aerobic) container becomes filled and the pyruvic acid and hydrogen ions back up into the overflow container, forming lactic acid (see Figure 1-10*b*). The rate of removal in the anaerobic container nearly matches the rate of accumulation, however, so that it does not fill completely. Consequently, very little lactic acid accumulates in the muscles and acidosis does not occur. This speed represents an overload of aerobic metabolism. It does not represent maximum swimming speed, however. The athlete can still swim faster by using anaerobic metabolism until the smaller container becomes filled.

A maximum swimming speed is illustrated in Figure 1-10*c*. In this case, the breakdown of glycogen is so rapid that the capacities of both the large tank and the overflow tank are exceeded. Acidosis causes fatigue rather quickly at this speed because of the rapid accumulation of lactic acid in the overflow tank. That fatigue is apparent because the swimmer is forced to slow his or her speed to one that matches the rate of emptying so that the capacity of the overflow tank is not exceeded.

The effects of training can also be illustrated by these containers. For example, the time required to fill the large tank depends on the rate fluid is flowing into it versus the rate it is emptying. Training can increase the rate of emptying from the large container by increasing the speed of aerobic metabolism. This, in turn, reduces the amount of lactic acid that pours into the overflow container so that it does not fill as quickly. When this happens, we say that training has reduced the rate of lactic acid accumulation.

Training can also increase the rate of emptying from the overflow container so that it does not fill so rapidly. This training effect is stated as an increase in the rate of lactic acid removal from muscles. When these mechanisms are improved, athletes are able to swim faster and longer before acidosis occurs in their muscles.

Energy Metabolism Summarized

Figure 1-11 may make the three phases of metabolism easier to understand. The nonaerobic system is shown at the top, with ATP supplying the energy for muscular contraction, after which it is recycled by CP. The anaerobic system, in the middle, shows the breakdown of glycogen to pyruvic acid. Some of the pyruvic acid combines with hydrogen ions to form lactic acid. Some of that lactic acid remains in the muscles, yet a sizable portion diffuses out of the muscles into the blood, where it is carried to the heart and liver.

A portion of the remaining pyruvic acid combines with ammonia to form alanine, and the rest enters Krebs cycle, after first combining with coenzyme A to form acetyl-CoA.

The hydrogen ions that remain are also metabolized aerobically. They enter the electron transport chain after combining with NAD^+ and FAD to form NADH and FADH.

In Krebs cycle, the acetyl-CoA goes through a large number of steps before it is finally converted to carbon dioxide. In the electron transport chain, the hydrogen ions are stripped from NADH and FADH and oxidized to water. This frees additional NAD^+ and FAD to return and gather more hydrogen ions.

Figure 1-11 illustrates the metabolism of an athlete who is swimming at a submaximum speed. That speed is, nevertheless, fast enough to overload the aerobic system. This can be seen by the fact that the containers representing both Krebs cycle and the electron transport chain are full. A small amount of lactic acid is being produced in the muscles, as indicated by the shaded area in the container labeled muscles, because the rate at which hydrogen ions are being released is

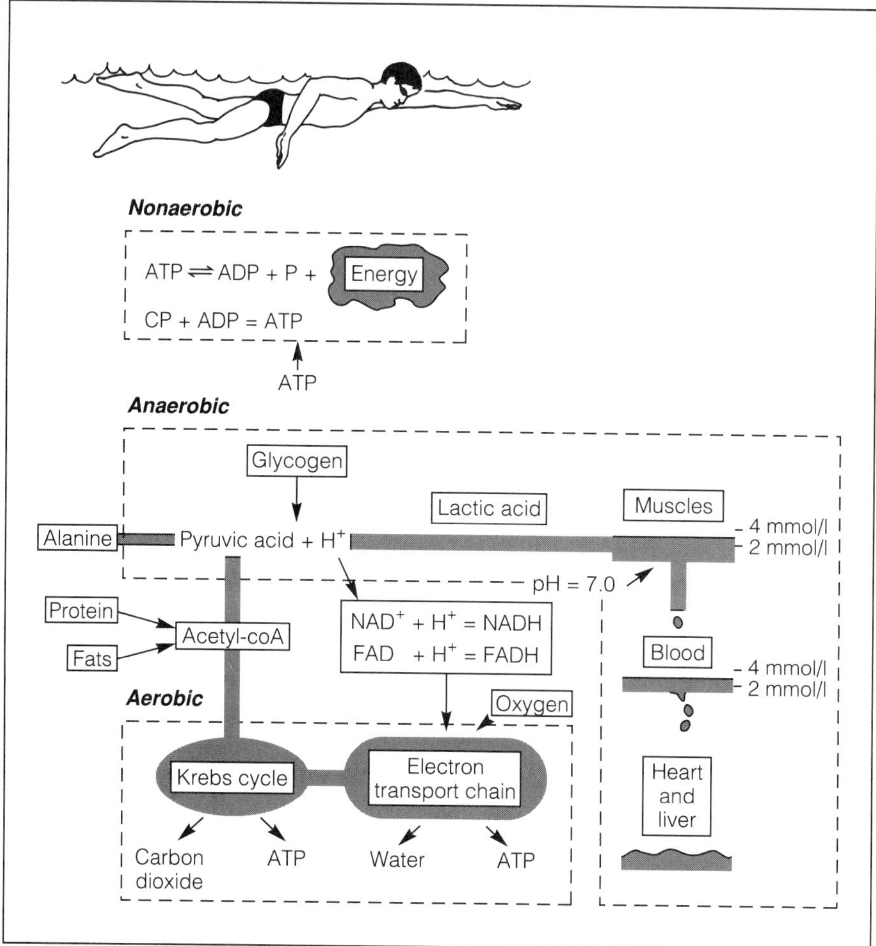

Figure 1-11. The metabolic process.

slightly faster than the rate at which they can be transported into the electron transport chain. This small amount of additional lactic acid in the muscles indicates that aerobic metabolism is overloaded. If it were not, the aerobic system would speed up so that the additional hydrogen ions and pyruvic acid could be metabolized aerobically and the formation of additional lactic acid could be avoided. The amount of lactic acid being produced is well within the athlete's capacity, as indicated by the submaximum level of 3.0 mmol/l of lactic acid in the container labeled muscles and by the fact that the acid-base balance of the muscles is maintained at a neutral pH of 7.0. The circulatory system helps to maintain this low level of lactic acid by diffusing the lactic acid into the bloodstream and carrying it away from the site.

When athletes swim at speeds that overload aerobic metabolism *without* accumulating large amounts of lactic acid, they are said to be training at the *anaerobic threshold*. Some experts feel that training at the anaerobic threshold improves aerobic endurance as fast and as much as it can possibly be improved. Furthermore, they believe that training faster may cause athletes to become overtrained.

THE EFFICIENCY OF AEROBIC VERSUS ANAEROBIC METABOLISM

It is considered more desirable to recycle ATP aerobically than anaerobically for two reasons: (1) because aerobic metabolism results in the replacement of more ATP and (2) because acidosis does not occur during aerobic metabolism.

The anaerobic metabolism of one molecule of glycogen produces only four molecules of ATP. The energy from two of these is used to operate the anaerobic process, providing a net of only 2 ATP molecules that can supply energy for muscular contraction. In the aerobic process, one molecule of glycogen provides enough energy to replace 36 molecules of ATP. Anaerobic metabolism produces lactic acid and, consequently, acidosis. On the other hand, the aerobic process produces carbon dioxide and water, which can easily be removed from the body without causing fatigue.

Unfortunately, aerobic metabolism cannot supply all of the energy for ATP recycling during swimming races or even during fast training repeats. The process is too slow. Hundreds of steps are needed before that energy can be released. Aerobic metabolism can supplement the energy provided by anaerobic metabolism in these situations. The amount of supplementation will be less in shorter races because more rapid speeds are required, and it will be greater in longer races, in which the pace is somewhat slower. *One of the most important functions of training is to increase the rate of aerobic metabolism so that this process can make a greater contribution to the ATP supply in all races.*

THE INTERACTION OF NONAEROBIC, ANAEROBIC, AND AEROBIC METABOLISM DURING EXERCISE

Various swimming events are commonly referred to as either aerobic or anaerobic, giving the false impression that the phases of metabolism are separate and that they occur in sequence, with the next phase beginning at the instant the preceding phase has been completed. For example, a common belief is that nonaerobic metabolism supplies all of the energy for muscular contraction during the first 10 to 15 seconds of work. Anaerobic metabolism supposedly takes over for the next 1 or 2 minutes, after which all of the energy is supplied by aerobic metabolism. This is an oversimplification of the actual sequence of events. Actually, all three phases of the metabolic process operate from the first moment of exercise. The only difference is in the relative contribution from each phase. That contribution depends on the speed and the distance of the swim. In sprints, the major contributors are the nonaerobic and anaerobic phases. Aerobic metabolism proceeds too slowly to meet all, or even most, of the rapid demand for energy in these events. Nevertheless, a small amount of the energy for sprinting is supplied by aerobic metabolism. The aerobic contribution becomes greater as the distance increases and/or the athlete swims at a slower speed. Because they are completed at slower average speeds, the major portion of energy for ATP recycling comes from aerobic metabolism in distance races and submaximum repeat sets in training.

The energy donated by muscle glycogen and by blood glucose and fat during aerobic metabolism is also influenced by distance and swimming speed. During long swims or repeat sets, where the pace is maximum or nearly so (greater than 85 percent of maximum), nearly all of the energy comes from glycogen stored in the working muscle fibers. At slower speeds, both fat and blood glucose provide a greater percentage of the energy. Blood glucose supplies 20 to 30 percent of the energy for endurance training by some estimates (Brooks & Fahey, 1984) and 30 to 40 percent by others (Felig & Wahren, 1975). Fat metabolism probably supplies between 30 to 50 percent of the total energy used during typical two-hour training sessions (Ahlborg, Hagenfeldt, & Wahren, 1974) but only negligible amounts during competition. Only small amounts of energy — 5 to 15 percent — are derived from protein when sufficient muscle glycogen is available (Brooks & Fahey, 1984; Felig & Wahren, 1971). Carbohydrates and fats are the preferred sources of energy for muscular contraction so that protein can be spared to rebuild tissue and enzymes. Therefore, protein becomes a significant source of energy for exercise only when the glucose supply is low. The danger in using excessive amounts of protein for energy lies in the fact that swimmers could literally catabolize their own muscle tissue. They would lose power and endurance if that were to happen.

A trained athlete's body always tries to recycle ATP in the most economical manner. That is, it uses aerobic metabolism to the greatest possible extent allowed by the speed of the race or repeat. Within the aerobic process, fat contributes as much energy as the metabolic rate permits.

The Contributions of Each Metabolic Phase to Swimming Races and Practice Repeats

It is common to refer to sprints as anaerobic events and distance races as aerobic. However, these characterizations are not completely accurate; as explained earlier, all of the different phases of the metabolic process are operating at once in all races. For this reason, it would probably be more accurate to describe the various race distances as mostly aerobic or mostly anaerobic.

The values in Table 1-1 estimate the contributions of the different phases of metabolism during competition and training. The aerobic phase of metabolism is subdivided into two phases — glucose metabolism and fat metabolism — to differentiate the roles played by these two substances in supplying energy. Notice that the various races are listed by competition times and distances in the upper part of this table. Sprint and anaerobic repeats are listed by distance and send-off times in the lower section. Also in the lower section, aerobic repeats are listed by set length. The data are presented in this way so that the information can be adapted for swimmers of any age and level of ability.

In the upper portion of the table, the percentage contributions for each energy system that are listed opposite each race distance apply only to experienced

Table 1-1. Relative Contributions of Each Phase of Energy Metabolism to Various Swimming Races and Practice Repeats

Competition Times	Most Common Race Distances	Percentage of Nonaerobic Metabolism	Percentage of Anaerobic Metabolism	Aerobic Metabolism: *Percentage of Glucose Metabolism*	Aerobic Metabolism: *Percentage of Fat Metabolism*
10–15 sec	25 yd/m	80	20	Neg.	Neg.*
19–30 sec	50 yd/m	50	48	2	Neg.
40–60 sec	100 yd/m	25	65	10	Neg.
1:30–2 min	200 yd/m	10	60	25	Neg.
2–3 min	200 yd/m	10	50	40	Neg.
4–6 min	400 m–500 yd	5	45	50	Neg.
7–10 min	800 m	5	30	60	5
10–12 min	1000 yd	4	25	65	6
14–22 min	1500 m–1650 yd	2	20	70	8
REPEAT SETS					
Types and Distances	Send-Off Times				
Sprints					
10–15 yd/m	1–2 min	90	10	Neg.	Neg.
25 yd/m	1–2 min	75	20	5	Neg.
Anaerobic					
50 yd/m	3–5 min	30	60	9	1
100 yd/m	5–10 min	20	60	18	2
200 yd/m	8–12 min	12	45	40	4
Aerobic	*Set Length*				
	15–20 min	10	20	65	5
	30–40 min	Neg.	5	75	20
	50–60 min	Neg.	2	70	28
	90–100 min	Neg.	1	30	70

*Neg. = Negligible

senior-level swimmers. They can be misleading when directed at age group and Masters swimmers and to athletes of less than average ability. For swimmers in these categories, competition times are more accurate than distances for reflecting the way their bodies use their various sources of energy. For example, a 10-year-old athlete who swims 100 m in 1:50.00 probably derives energy from the four metabolic phases in approximately the same proportions as a 22-year-old who swims 200 m in the same time. For these reasons, the relationships between race and repeat distances and the contributions from each energy source can only be used as a guide for experienced teenage and senior swimmers. The relationship between swimming time and energy use is more accurate for preadolescents, older Masters swimmers, and competitors with limited experience.

Where races are concerned, the nonaerobic and anaerobic phases of metabolism supply most of the energy for events of 25 to 50 yd/m (events requiring 10 to 30 seconds). Anaerobic metabolism is the major contributor for race distances of 100 and 200 yd/m (events lasting 1 to 3 minutes), although the role of aerobic metabolism becomes increasingly more important at the 200 distance. Both anaerobic and aerobic metabolism contribute substantially to the energy supply in races of 400 m and 500 yd (4 to 6 minutes of swimming). The amount of energy supplied nonaerobically and by fat metabolism is negligible at these distances.

The aerobic metabolism of glycogen is the chief source of energy for races of 800 meters to 1,650 yards, although anaerobic metabolism contributes one-fourth to one-third of the energy for these distances. The roles of nonaerobic and fat metabolism are, once again, negligible.

Where sprint repeat sets are concerned, nonaerobic and anaerobic metabolism supply most of the energy for sprints of 25 yd/m and less. Anaerobic metabolism is the major source during fast swims of 50 and 100 yd/m. The energy for fast repeats of 200 yd/m is obtained almost equally from aerobic and anaerobic sources, with muscle glycogen as the primary source of fuel.

Endurance repeat sets can be swum at any distance. The time required to complete the set is the factor that determines the relative contributions from the various sources of energy. Assuming that these sets are swum at the fastest possible average speed—those that require 15 to 20 minutes to complete—a considerable amount of muscle glycogen is used. The energy from this source is derived from both aerobic and anaerobic processes. The contributions from fat (and blood glucose) become significant after the first half hour, when the muscles' glycogen supply is dwindling. After one hour of training, muscle glycogen will be so depleted that fat and blood glucose supply the major portion of the energy for ATP recycling. The energy for speeds that are slow to moderate comes primarily from fat and blood glucose, regardless of the time needed to complete the set.

CHAPTER 2

Muscular, Circulatory, Respiratory, and Hormonal Responses to Exercise

The metabolic events that provide energy for fast swimming occur in the muscular system. The circulatory and respiratory systems are responsible for delivering oxygen and other nutrients to the muscles so that metabolism can proceed. The endocrine system also plays an important part in this process. These four physiological systems are the topics for this chapter.

THE MUSCULAR SYSTEM

There are three types of muscles in the human body: smooth muscles located in various organs, cardiac muscles in the heart, and skeletal muscles that are connected to the bones. Contractions of skeletal muscles produce the force that makes it possible to move the limbs through the water.

Skeletal muscles contract when they receive a message from the nervous system in the form of an electrical impulse. When a muscle contracts, it shortens, pulling the end where it is attached—the insertion—toward the other end—the origin. Muscles appear to contract in total, although the shortening really occurs in only a portion of the fibers of each muscle.

Large muscles, like the biceps, consist of thousands of tiny fibers arranged in bundles called *fasciculi* that are wrapped in connective tissue. Each fiber is a single muscle cell. It is about as thick as a human hair and can vary in length from a few millimeters to several centimeters. Figure 2-1 shows a muscle consisting of bundles of fibers. The fibers are arranged in groups called motor units.

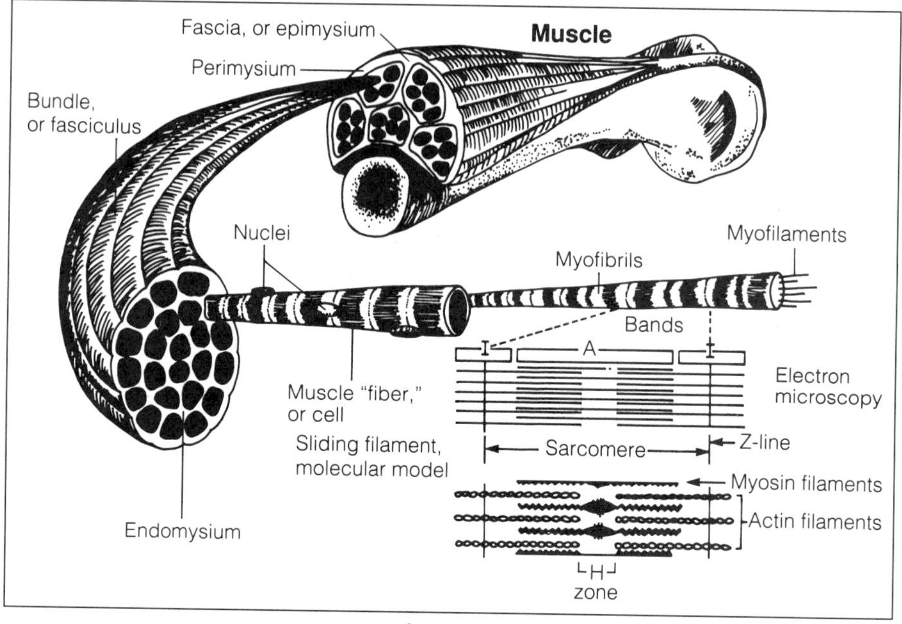

Figure 2-1. A muscle, showing individual muscle cells and the arrangement of actin and myosin within them. (Wilmore & Costill, 1988)

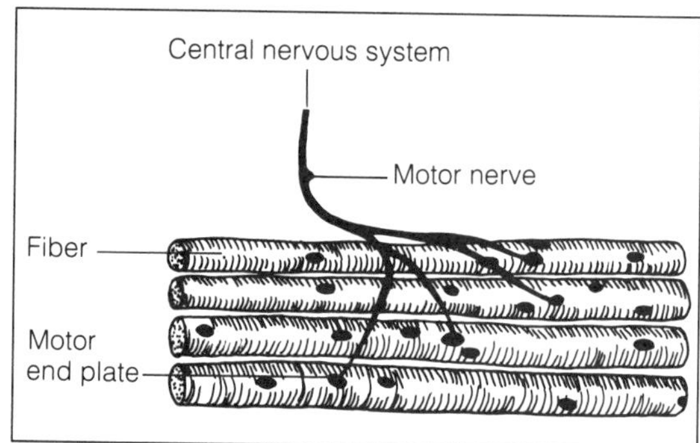

Figure 2-2. A motor unit, showing the nerve twig, its branches, and all the muscle fibers they connect with. (Fox & Mathews, 1981)

A motor unit is pictured in Figure 2-2. Each motor unit is served by a single nerve that branches to all of the fibers in the unit. So, each muscle fiber has a nerve ending that relays messages from the nervous system, which tells it to contract. Any impulse that comes over that nerve causes all of the fibers in a motor unit to contract at once. This is known as the all-or-none law. When a nerve impulse travels to a motor unit, it will cause all of the muscle fibers within that unit to contract if it is strong enough. None of them will contract if it is not.

The contractile force of an entire muscle is determined by the number of its motor units contracting at any moment. Only a few motor units (a few hundred fibers) will contract when the demand for force is low during easy swimming. Nearly all of the motor units in a muscle will contract at once when the demand for force is high, as in sprinting.

We learn from experience how much force is needed to perform certain jobs. The nervous system stimulates the appropriate number of motor units when we perform this work. This precise pattern of muscle fiber stimulation is called *motor unit recruitment*.

One way that we maintain work for a long time is to rotate the effort among groups of motor units so that some muscle fibers contract while others rest. When contracting fibers become fatigued, muscle fibers that have been resting are recruited to replace them so that the desired amount of force can be maintained.

Most experts believe that we never use all of the motor units in a muscle at one time, even during maximum efforts. The nervous system inhibits us from doing so, because the force would be so great it might snap our bones. In the rotation process, however, we may eventually use all of the motor units within a muscle.

The speed with which fibers can be recruited and the number that can be stimulated at any one time is probably an important determinant of an athlete's potential for sprinting. Also, the pattern of recruitment probably has an effect on maximum speed. That pattern of recruitment determines whether motor units from many different muscles and from different areas within each muscle can contract in a sequence that provides the desired amount of force at the right time and at the most effective angle of pull.

Motor unit recruitment patterns probably affect our endurance as well. That is, if the pattern is efficient, fewer motor units will be used at a particular swimming speed and more will be available to rotate in later.

Slow-Twitch and Fast-Twitch Muscle Fibers

Humans have two categories of fibers in the skeletal muscles of their body. These are known variously as slow-twitch, red, or Type I fibers, and fast-twitch, white, or Type II fibers.

Fast-twitch (FT) muscle fibers contract rapidly (30 to 50 times per second). Slow-twitch (ST) muscle fibers contract at slower rates (10 to 15 times per second). Another important difference between the two fiber types is in their capacity for endurance and power work. ST muscle fibers have more endurance because of their greater capacity for aerobic metabolism. They have more myoglobin, two to five times more mitochondria, more fat, and a greater concentration of aerobic enzymes than their FT counterparts (Costill, Fink, & Pollock, 1976; Howald, 1975; Keul, Doll, & Keppler, 1972; Pette & Staudte, 1973). Conversely, they have a lower capacity for nonaerobic and anaerobic metabolism because of their smaller concentrations of CP and anaerobic enzymes.

FT muscle fibers possess more CP and more anaerobic enzymes. Furthermore, they contain 12 percent more protein (FT fibers are usually larger than ST fibers), more calcium (calcium triggers muscle contraction), and greater buffering capacity (Keul, Doll, & Keppler, 1972; Lamb, 1978; Pette & Staudte, 1973). Obviously, FT fibers have a much greater capacity for nonaerobic and anaerobic metabolism. On the other hand, their capacity for aerobic metabolism is lower than that of ST fibers. The ATP and glycogen content of the two fiber types are similar (Gollnick & Hermansen, 1973; Pette & Staudte, 1973).

The larger amounts of myoglobin in ST muscle fibers gives them their red appearance (myoglobin has a reddish pigment). FT fibers are white (actually, light pink) because they contain less myoglobin.

The discovery of these fiber types resulted from a muscle biopsy technique pioneered in Sweden (Bergstrom, Hermansen, Hultman, & Saltin, 1967), which made it possible to determine the proportions of the two types of fibers within the muscle, the size of the fibers, their glycogen, ATP, and CP contents, and the activity of a wide assortment of enzymes. This technique has also allowed researchers to study directly the effects of exercise and training on muscles, rather than inferring those effects from gas and blood analysis.

The muscles we use to move our limbs usually contain a mixture of FT and ST fibers. This mixture can vary considerably from one person to another, even within the same muscle group. For the majority of the population, muscles contain approximately 50 percent of each fiber type. However, there is a small number of persons whose muscles contain a much greater proportion of one fiber type than another. For example, the percentage of ST muscle fibers in the deltoid muscle can be as high as 80 percent for one swimmer and as low as 20 percent for another (Costill, 1978). These percentages are probably inherited and do not change appreciably from birth to death.

There has been speculation that an athlete's potential for sprint or endurance performance is, to some extent, determined by the predominant type of fiber contained in certain muscles. Athletes with an unusually high percentage of FT muscle fibers have a greater potential for sprint events because they have more fibers that can deliver energy both nonaerobically and anaerobically. However, these same persons are at a disadvantage in endurance events. They have only a small number of ST fibers and, therefore, a reduced ability to deliver energy aerobically. The reverse is true for athletes with an unusually high percentage of ST fibers. They have an aptitude for endurance events but are ill equipped for sprinting because they have fewer fibers that can deliver large amounts of energy anaerobically. Because most athletes' muscles have approximately equal percentages of FT and ST fibers, they can choose the events they wish to participate in. This is probably why research has shown that the percentages of FT and ST muscle fibers have limited value for predicting the outcome of particular races, unless those races are at extreme ends of the sprint-endurance spectrum (Campbell, Bonen, Kirby, & Belcastro, 1979; Komi & Karlsson, 1978).

Success in swimming races, with the possible exception of the 50, requires that significant amounts of ATP be recycled from both anaerobic and aerobic metabolism. Consequently, athletes with approximately equal proportions of each fiber type are best equipped to excel. Any advantage possessed by a sprint swimmer with a high percentage of FT fibers could be overcome by superior training and better propulsive efficiency on the part of swimmers with nearly equal proportions of the two fiber types. While a high percentage of ST muscle fibers should help in distance races, that advantage could also be overcome by excellent training and good stroke mechanics. Clearly, swimmers would gain little, if any, useful information about their potential from muscle biopsies. That information might even be detrimental if it caused them to think that their potential was limited to certain race distances when in reality no such limitation existed.

Although endurance training can increase the capacity for aerobic metabolism in both FT and ST muscle fibers, trained FT fibers never reach the level of aerobic capacity that can be attained in trained ST muscle fibers. Conversely, sprint training will increase the anaerobic capacity of both types of fibers, although ST muscle fibers never achieve the level of trained FT fibers.

Subgroups of Muscle Fibers Experts have identified subgroups within the FT group of human muscle fibers. They have been variously labeled in two ways: (1) as Type IIa, IIb, and IIc fibers, and (2) as FTa, FTb, and FTc fibers. The latter terms are used throughout this text.

In addition to anaerobic capacity, the FTa fibers have more aerobic capacity than either the FTb or FTc fibers. The FTb muscle fibers are also anaerobic in nature but have little capacity for aerobic metabolism. The significance of FTc fibers is not known, but there is speculation that they may be fibers that are in transition from FT to ST populations, or vice versa (McArdle, Katch, & Katch, 1991).

With biopsy techniques, the various fiber types and subtypes can be identified by their ability to accept stains, which indicates the quantities of aerobic and anaerobic enzymes they possess. When a stain is used to identify aerobic capacity, the ST fibers stain darkest because they contain a large concentration of aerobic enzymes. FTa fibers stain lighter because they do not. When a stain is used to identify anaerobic capacity, the FTb fibers stain darker than their FTa counterparts because the former possess more anaerobic enzymes. FTc fibers stain lightest of all. A sample of muscle tissue that has been stained for aerobic and anaerobic capacity is shown in Figure 2-3. The properties of the various fiber groups are listed in Table 2-1.

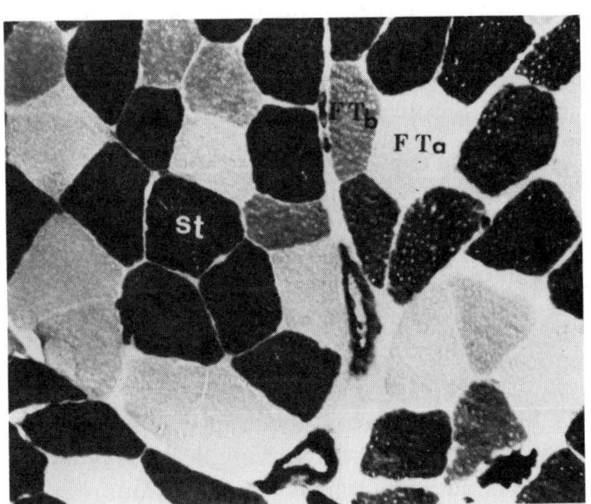

Figure 2-3. An electron micrograph of a muscle, showing the locations of ST, FTa, and FTb muscle fibers. The darkest-stained fibers are the ST fibers, which have been stained for the presence of aerobic enzymes. The medium-stained fibers are the FTb fibers, and the white fibers are FTa fibers. The subject's muscle contains 43 percent ST fibers, and 57 percent FT fibers. Of the FT fibers, 35 percent have been classified as FTa fibers, and 25 percent as FTb fibers. FTc fibers are not shown in this sample.

Table 2-1. Properties of FT and ST Muscle Fibers

Property	FTa	FTb	ST
Contractile speed	fast	fast	slower
Capacity for anaerobic metabolism	greater	greater	less
Capacity for aerobic metabolism	less	least	greatest
Size*	larger	larger	smaller
Aerobic endurance	less	least	greatest
Power	greater	greater	less
Mitochondria	less	least	most
Capillaries	less	least	most
Anaerobic enzyme activity	greater	greater	less
Aerobic enzyme activity	less	least	greatest
ATPase activity	greater	greater	less
CPK activity	greater	greater	less
Glycogen content		no difference	
ATP content		no difference	
CP content	more	more	less
Fat content	less	less	more
Protein content	more	more	less
Myoglobin content	less	least	most
Calcium content	more	more	least
Buffering capacity	greater	greater	least

*FT fibers are larger in the average person. This relationship can easily be changed with training. Well-trained endurance athletes usually have larger ST fibers, while the FT fibers of sprint- and power-trained athletes are even larger than those found in the average population.

FTa fibers have more aerobic capacity than either of the other two subtypes of FT fibers because they contain more and larger mitochondria, more myoglobin, and greater activity of aerobic enzymes. They also have more capillaries around them. They may be members of the FT group that have adapted to endurance training by storing more myoglobin and increasing mitochondria, and the FTb subgroup may be FT fibers that have not yet adapted to endurance training. Evidence that training may cause a conversion of FTb to FTa fibers has been presented by Costill et al. (1976), who found only 2.2 percent FTb fibers in the gastrocnemius muscles of distance runners. Likewise, Houston (1978) reported that a group of trained kayakers had only 8.5 percent FTb fibers in their biceps but 13 percent FTb fibers in the vastus lateralis muscles of their legs.

Can FT Fibers Be Converted to ST Fibers? There has been speculation that FT fibers can be converted to ST fibers, and vice versa, with training. It is thought that such conversion occurs through the FTc population, which is in transition from FT to ST types (Jansson, Sjodin, & Tesch, 1978). Further, it is believed that this conversion occurs as a result of long-term endurance or power training. Studies on this matter have been contradictory to date. Conversions were suggested in a cross-sectional study, where the percentages of FTc, FT, and ST muscle fibers were compared between children and adults (duPlessis et al., 1986). Longitudinal studies have not supported this claim, however. MacDougall and his colleagues (1984) did not find any change in the percentage of FT and ST muscle fibers among a group of subjects after six months of weight training. In addition, they found no difference in the percentages of FT and ST muscle fibers in the triceps and biceps of elite bodybuilders and untrained subjects, even though the bodybuilders had been training regularly for six to eight years (MacDougall, Sales, Alway, & Sutton, 1984).

Another possibility has been raised that training changes the proportions of FT and ST muscle fibers through the growth of new fibers, a process known as *hyperplasia* (Gonyea, Ericson, & Bonde-Peterson, 1977; Green et al., 1984). Recent studies do not support this position, however (Gollnick, Parsons, Riedy, & Moore, 1983; Gollnick, Timson, Moore, & Riedy, 1981; Timson, Bowlin, Dudenhoeffer, & George, 1985).

Although this matter remains unresolved, the bulk of evidence suggests that training will not convert ST to FT muscle fibers, and vice versa. It also appears doubtful that the total numbers of FT or ST muscle fibers can be increased by training.

Using ST and FT Muscle Fibers During Work A common misconception is that swimmers use FT muscle fibers when they sprint and ST fibers when they swim distance events, but this is not an accurate portrayal of the way these two fiber types are used. ST muscle fibers do most of the work at slow speeds, and both types of fibers contract during faster swims.

Fiber use depends on the force required in muscles, not the speed of the effort nor the distance of the swim. The pattern of muscle fiber recruitment during work is shown in Figure 2-4, which depicts the so-called *ramp effect* of muscular contraction. Only ST muscle fibers contract when the force required is light to moderate.

FT fibers do not begin contracting until the force is moderate. The numbers of FT fibers contracting also increase as the demand for force goes up. Within the FT group, the FTa muscle fibers carry most of the load, until the required level of force is near maximum. Then, the FTb fibers rotate in. All fiber types will be contracting when maximum force is exerted.

This progressive order of recruitment occurs because the FT fibers need a higher level of nervous stimulation to contract (Henneman & Olson, 1965). FT fibers are innervated by large neurons that can only be stimulated when the demand for force is great. Conversely, ST fibers are connected to smaller neurons that are easily excited. They tend to be used in preference to FT fibers at low levels of effort (distance swimming); whereas at high levels of effort, they are used in addition to the FT fibers (Costill, 1978).

Although both fiber types are activated when athletes swim at near-maximum speeds, the FT fibers provide most of the energy, not because they contract faster but because they can release more energy anaerobically. This is why FT muscle

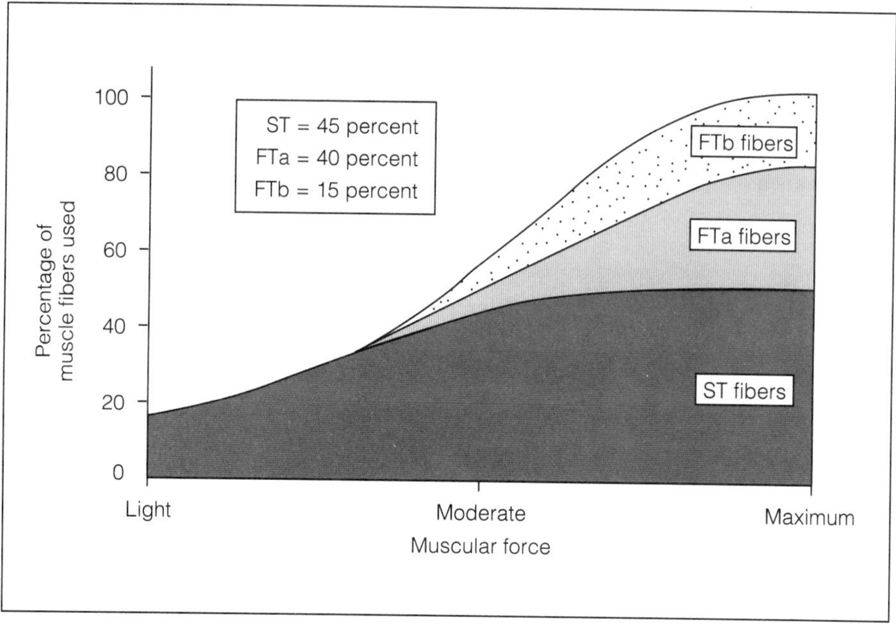

Figure 2-4. The ramp effect of muscle fiber recruitment.

fibers are the first to lose their glycogen during fast swimming. ST fibers are depleted first during long, slow, continuous swims or sets of repeats.

The amount of glycogen that is used within each fiber type can be determined from biopsies taken before and after a bout of exercise. The fiber type that has lost more of its glycogen will be the one that supplied most of the energy for ATP recycling. Research shows that FT muscle fibers are depleted of glycogen first during sustained efforts of 70 to 90 percent of maximum. ST fibers lose their glycogen first during slower swims.

Figure 2-5 shows the pattern of glycogen depletion during alternating days of high- and low-intensity swim training in a study by Houston (1978). On the low-intensity day, swimmers completed 6.1 km of freestyle swimming at a moderate pace. The repeat distances varied from 50 to 400 m, with short rest periods. On the high-intensity day, the swimmers warmed up with five 200-m swims at a low intensity. They then swam and kicked 1.5 km of long rest repeats at distances of 25 to 100 m. Those repeats were swum at near maximum speeds. More ST than FT fibers were depleted or partially depleted of glycogen on the low-intensity day, while the ST and FT fibers were depleted equally during the high-intensity day.

Another interesting aspect of fiber recruitment patterns is the manner in which one type of fiber will assist the other when fatigue sets in. Due to their greater propensity for anaerobic metabolism, FT muscle fibers usually become acidotic before their ST counterparts. When this happens, more ST motor units rotate in to maintain the required force. Unfortunately, they are not able to supply anaerobic

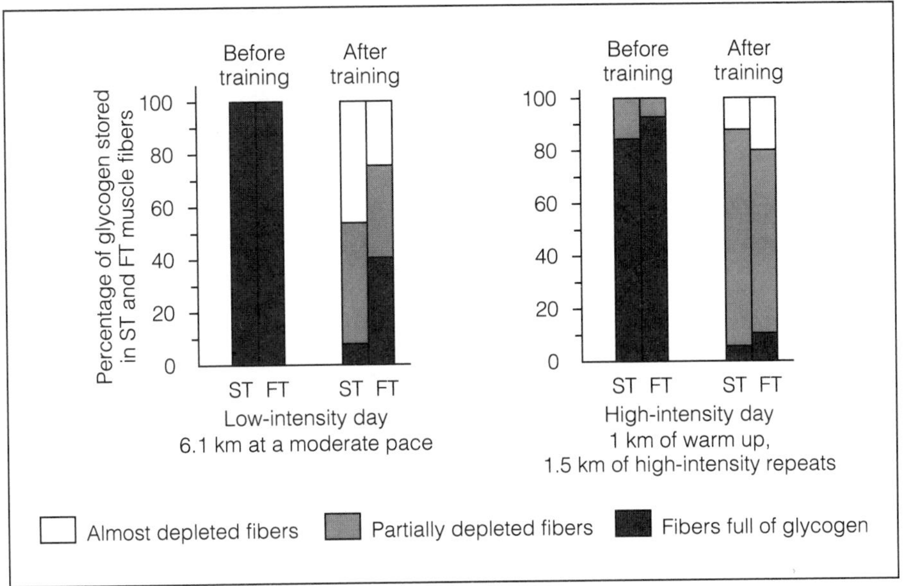

Figure 2-5. The effects of sprint and endurance swimming on muscle glycogen use in ST and FT muscle fibers. (Houston, 1978)

energy as rapidly, and some force is lost. On the other hand, when ST fibers become depleted of their glycogen supply during long, slow swims, FT fibers rotate into the activity to supply the energy needed, thus allowing swimmers to maintain their desired pace for several additional minutes. That pace will slow in time, however. Because the capacity for aerobic metabolism is lower in FT muscle fibers, swimming speed must be slowed to prevent the production of lactic acid and acidosis.

THE CIRCULATORY SYSTEM

The purpose of the circulatory system is to transport blood throughout the body. This is an important function because blood carries oxygen, glucose, and other nutrients to the tissues and takes lactic acid and carbon dioxide away from them. The circulatory system is essentially like the recirculating filtering system of a swimming pool. The heart is the pump, and the arteries and veins are the pipes going to and from the pool (muscles), respectively. The blood is like the water that is pushed out to the pool after being cleaned and then returned from the pool for further cleaning. A schematic drawing of the circulatory system is shown in Figure 2-6.

The left side of the heart pumps blood out to the muscles and other tissues of the body via the arteries and arterioles, which are like branching sets of pipes that continue to get smaller in diameter until they reach their destinations in the tissues.

Arteries are the large branches, and arterioles are the small vessels that extend from them. Arterioles end in capillaries, which are the smallest vessel units that surround the individual muscle fibers.

The blood delivers oxygen, glucose, and other substances to the capillaries. From there, these substances diffuse into the muscles. Blood then leaves the tissues via these same capillaries after picking up carbon dioxide, lactic acid, and other waste products of metabolism after they have diffused out of the muscles. The blood travels through venules to veins and back to the right side of the heart, where it is pumped to the lungs through arteries. In the lungs, carbon dioxide diffuses out

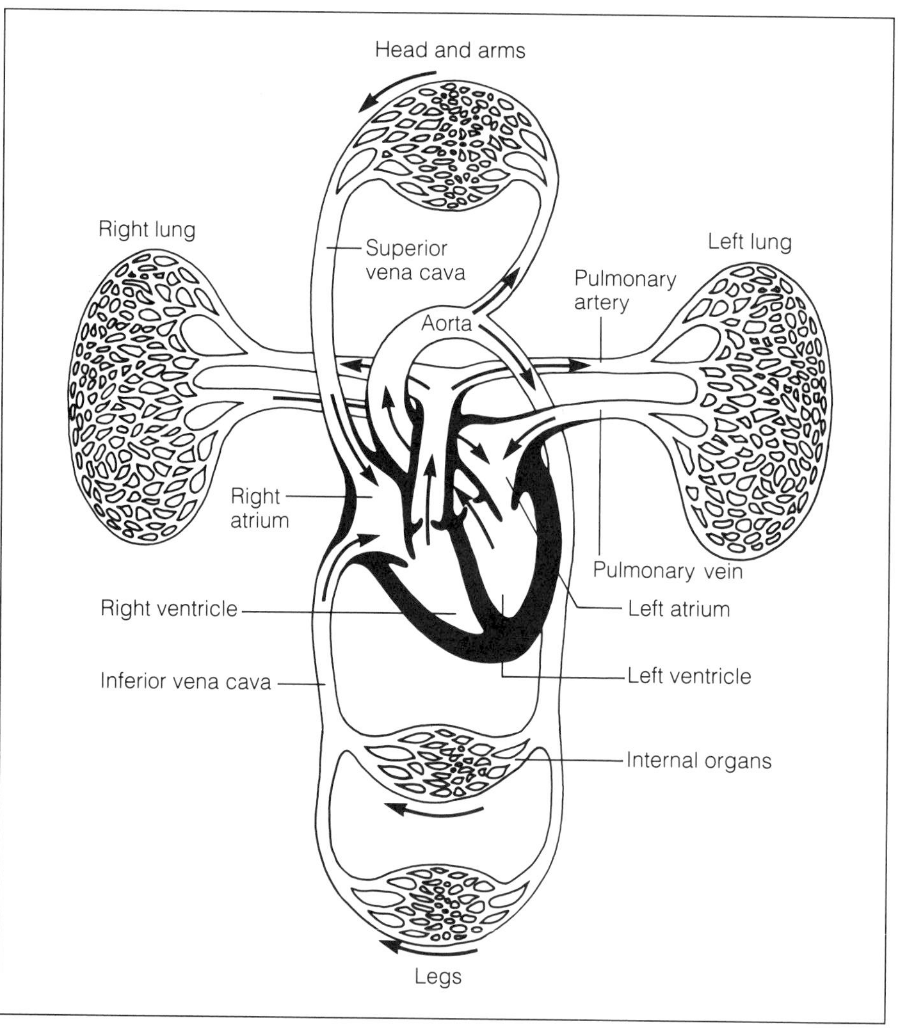

Figure 2-6. The circulatory system, showing the path of blood flow through the body. (Wilmore & Costill, 1988)

to the alveoli and is exhaled while inhaled oxygen diffuses from the alveoli into the blood. The blood flows from the lungs to the left side of the heart through venules and veins, and the process begins again. Venules begin at the capillaries, branching to the larger venules and finally becoming large veins that carry blood back to the heart.

There are several terms that describe the functions of the circulatory system: (1) heart rate, (2) stroke volume, and (3) cardiac output.

Heart Rate

The *heart rate* refers to the number of times the heart beats each minute. Simultaneous contractions of both the right and left sides of the heart (the ventricles) are counted as one beat. Resting heart rates are in the neighborhood of 60 to 80 beats per minute (bpm) for most persons. The resting heart rates of trained athletes tend to be lower than those of nonathletes, frequently between 30 to 50 bpm. The resting heart rate declines with training because the heart becomes stronger and can push more blood out with each beat. Consequently, fewer beats are needed to supply the quantity required by the human body at rest.

Each of us has a maximum heart rate; that is, our hearts do not beat faster than a certain number of times per minute. This is probably a protective mechanism that keeps the heart from beating so fast that there would not be enough time for it to fill with blood between beats. An average maximum heart rate for teenagers and young adults is 200 bpm. The typical range of maximum values is 180 to 220 bpm.

Stroke Volume

The amount of blood that is pushed out of the heart with each beat is known as the *stroke volume*. A normal range of values at rest is between 60 and 130 milliliters per beat (ml/b). These amounts can increase to between 150 and 180 ml/b during exercise. The values cited refer only to blood pumped from the left side of the heart. An equal amount of blood is also being pumped from the right side simultaneously. The stroke volumes of athletes are greater than nonathletes, which explains why they have a lower resting heart rate. They can supply the same amount of blood by pushing more out with each beat.

The reductions in heart rate that happen at rest and during submaximum swims after training are excellent indicators that an athlete's stroke volume has increased. This is one reason for monitoring resting and exercise heart rates during training.

Cardiac Output

Cardiac output is the amount of blood ejected from the heart (left side) per minute. It is calculated by multiplying the heart rate by the stroke volume. A normal cardiac output at rest is 5 liters per minute (l/min). Untrained athletes can increase this amount fourfold during exercise. On the other hand, trained athletes can increase their cardiac output by a factor of 6 or 7. Values of 30 and 35 l/min are not unusual after training (see the box at the top of page 34).

Typical Cardiac Output Values for Trained and Untrained Persons

Cardiac Output for Trained Athletes

At rest: 40 bpm × 100 ml/b = 4,000 ml/min, or 4 l/min

During exercise: 200 bpm × 150 ml/b = 30,000 ml/min, or 30 l/min

Cardiac Output for Untrained Persons

At rest: 80 bpm × 60 ml/b = 4,800 ml/min, or 4.8 l/min

During exercise: 200 bpm × 100 ml/b = 20,000 ml/min, or 20 l/min

Cardiac Output During Submaximum Exercise The cardiac outputs of trained and untrained persons are similar at rest and during submaximum swimming. The major difference between the two is that trained persons supply their blood with a *lower heart rate* and *greater stroke volume*. This means that, during submaximum exercise, a trained athlete's heart does not need to work as hard to supply the same quantity of blood per minute. An example of the effect of training on the cardiac output during submaximum efforts is provided by the calculations in the following box. Before training, the cardiac output of 20.0 l/min was supplied with a higher heart rate (170 bpm) and a lower stroke volume (118 ml/b). After training, the athlete's heart rate declined by 20 bpm and his stroke volume increased by 16 ml/b; thus, his cardiac output was being supplied more efficiently. There was also a greater reserve of heart beats available so that the cardiac output could be increased at maximum swimming speeds.

Cardiac Output During Maximum Exercise Trained athletes have a much greater cardiac output than untrained persons during maximum efforts. The major

The Effect of Training on Cardiac Output at Submaximum Swimming Speeds

Note: At a swimming speed of 1:15.00 per 100 m, the swimmer's cardiac output was approximately 20 l/min. Before training, his cardiac output was supplied by a higher heart rate of 170 bpm and a lower stroke volume of 118 ml/b. After training, it was supplied by a heart rate of 150 bpm and a stroke volume of 134 ml/b.

Before Training

170 bpm × 118 ml/b = 20.1 l/min

After Training

150 bpm × 134 ml/b = 20.1 l/min

adaptation that causes an enhancement of the cardiac output during maximum efforts is an increase in the stroke volume. An increase in cardiac output at maximum efforts provides a greater oxygen and glucose supply to the muscles and enables larger amounts of lactic acid and carbon dioxide to be transported away from them.

The best training for improving maximum cardiac output is not known. We do know, however, that maximum stroke volumes are achieved at low levels of effort. This is because the heart's filling time decreases when it is beating rapidly. Thus, although the cardiac output is greater at fast speeds, the stroke volume will be lower. This effect is illustrated in the following box. The stroke volume for this athlete was 130 ml/b at a heart rate of 130 bpm. This resulted in a cardiac output of 16.9 l/min. When she swam faster, her heart rate increased to 180 bpm but her stroke volume declined to 110 ml/b. Nevertheless, her cardiac output increased nearly 3 l/min to 19.8 l/min.

The Effect of Increased Swimming Speed on Heart Rate, Stroke Volume, and Cardiac Output

Note: During easy swimming, the swimmer's heart rate is 130 bpm and her stroke volume is 130 ml/b, resulting in a cardiac output of 16.9 l/min. At a faster speed, her heart rate increases to 180 bpm and her stroke volume declines to 110 ml/b. Nevertheless, her cardiac output increases 3 l/min to 19.8 l/min.

Easy Swimming

130 bpm × 130 ml/b = 16,900 ml = 16.9 l/min

Swimming at a Faster Speed

180 bpm × 110 ml/beat = 19,800 ml = 19.8 l/min

There are other aspects of circulatory function that increase with training and, thereby, improve performance potential. These include (1) an increase in the number of red blood cells, (2) an increase in the total amount of blood in the body (blood volume), (3) an increase in the number of capillaries, and (4) an improvement of blood shunting.

Red Blood Cells and Blood Volume

Trained athletes generally have more blood and a greater number of red blood cells than untrained persons (Astrand & Rodahl, 1977).

Red Blood Cells Where training is concerned, an increase in red blood cells is important because they contain *hemoglobin,* which is an iron-containing protein substance that allows oxygen to be carried in the blood. Thus, the accompanying increase in hemoglobin should increase the quantity of oxygen that can be carried in the blood. One of the reasons that athletes train at high altitudes is to increase hemoglobin. This is also the reason for blood doping (reinfusing an athlete with his own blood before competition).

A reduction in the normal hemoglobin concentration of blood reduces oxygen consumption and lessens endurance. This condition is known as *anemia*.

Blood Volume The fluid in blood increases relatively more with training than does hemoglobin. This is good because the additional fluid prevents the extra hemoglobin from causing the blood to thicken (become viscous). Greater viscosity slows the rate of blood flow, which could conceivably reduce the oxygen and glucose available during exercise.

There is little information available about the best way to increase hemoglobin and blood volume with training. Logically, however, endurance training should be best for this purpose because it produces a sustained demand for oxygen in the tissues, which should stimulate an increase in blood volume and hemoglobin.

Capillaries

Every muscle fiber is surrounded by capillaries. Their location is shown in Figure 2-7. Figure 2-7*a* shows how the capillaries branch off arterioles and venules into muscles. Figure 2-7*b* shows the arrangement of capillaries around individual muscle fibers.

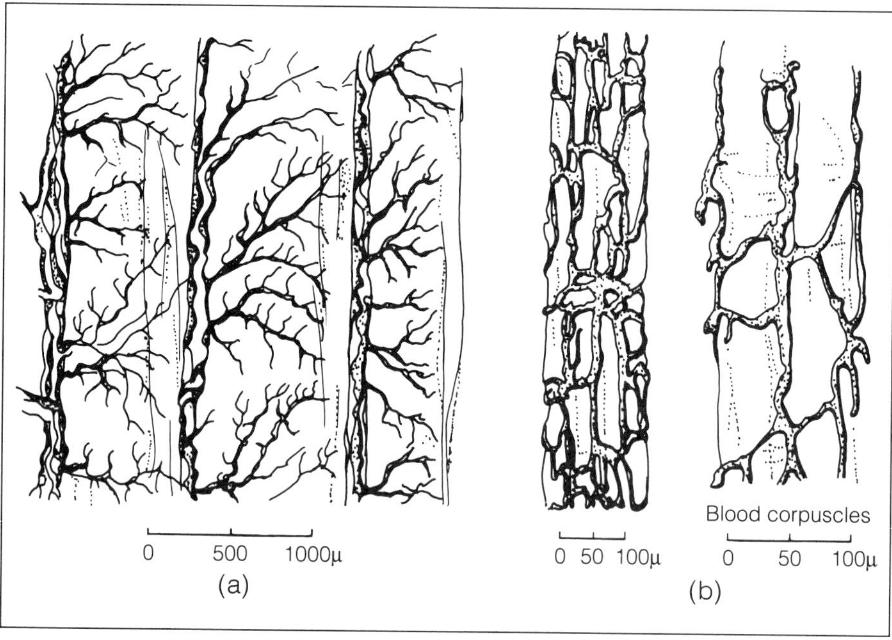

Figure 2-7. The arrangement of capillaries around muscle fibers.

The exchange of oxygen and nutrients for waste products takes place between muscles and capillaries during exercise. Oxygen and glucose diffuse out of the capillaries into the muscles, and lactic acid and carbon dioxide diffuse out of muscle cells and into the capillaries. Capillaries are quite small and can admit only one molecule of these substances at a time. So, an increase in the number of capillaries around muscle fibers should allow the delivery of more oxygen and the removal of more waste products during exercise. An important effect of endurance training is that it increases the total number of capillaries surrounding muscle fibers and, thus, increases the diffusion rates of nutrients and waste products (Carrow, Brown, & Van Huss, 1967; Hermansen & Wachlova, 1971).

Blood Shunting

This is, perhaps, the most important training effect for improving performance because it causes the most substantial increase in blood flow during exercise. The human body contains about 5 l of blood. At rest, the total volume is equally distributed to all tissues. During exercise, however, shunting increases the amount of blood being sent to the working muscles and reduces its supply to nonworking muscles and other tissues. For example, at rest, only 15 to 20 percent of the total blood volume goes to the skeletal muscles; however, during exercise, that amount increases to 85 or 90 percent of the total (Mathews & Fox, 1976). This has the effect of supplying more blood where it is needed so that more oxygen and other nutrients are furnished to the muscles and more waste products are carried away from them.

Blood shunting happens because the arteries that supply the working muscles dilate (get larger) while those that serve inactive areas of the body constrict (get smaller); thus, greater quantities of blood flow through the larger arteries, where the pressure and resistance to flow is less, and less blood flows through the constricted arteries.

No discussion of the circulatory system would be complete without mentioning blood pressure.

Blood Pressure

Blood that is flowing through vessels exerts pressure on the walls of those vessels. This pressure is measured by the number of millimeters it makes a column of mercury rise. Two types of measurements are used: (1) when the heart beats and (2) when the heart rests between beats. The pressure in vessels when the heart beats is called *systolic* because the heartbeat is called a *systole*. The pressure between beats is called *diastolic* because the rest period of the heart is termed a *diastole*. Typical resting systolic and diastolic blood pressures are 120/80 mm Hg, respectively.

Blood pressure, particularly systolic pressure, could increase to dangerous levels during exercise because of the large increase in the amount of blood flowing through vessels per unit time. Luckily, the vessels are elastic and stretch to reduce the pressure exerted on them. Nevertheless, systolic pressure will rise to values in excess of 200 mm Hg when work is strenuous. Increases in diastolic blood pressure are not so dramatic because the amount of blood in the vessels subsides somewhat between beats. Under normal conditions, it generally increases to only 100 or 110 mm Hg during exercise.

Endurance training reduces both systolic and diastolic blood pressure at rest and during submaximum exercise. This is probably due to improved elasticity in the blood vessels.

THE RESPIRATORY SYSTEM

The two primary purposes of respiration are to provide the body with oxygen and to remove carbon dioxide. This process makes life possible, for we could not live more than a few minutes without oxygen. A less-known, but important, function of respiration is to regulate the acid-base balance of the blood. The respiratory system consists of the mouth and nose, the pharynx, the lungs, the bronchiole tubes, and the alveoli, which are surrounded by capillaries. The anatomy of the respiratory system is shown in Figure 2-8.

The inhalation phase of respiration allows us to take oxygen out of the air and into our body. Carbon dioxide and some water vapor is removed during the exhal-

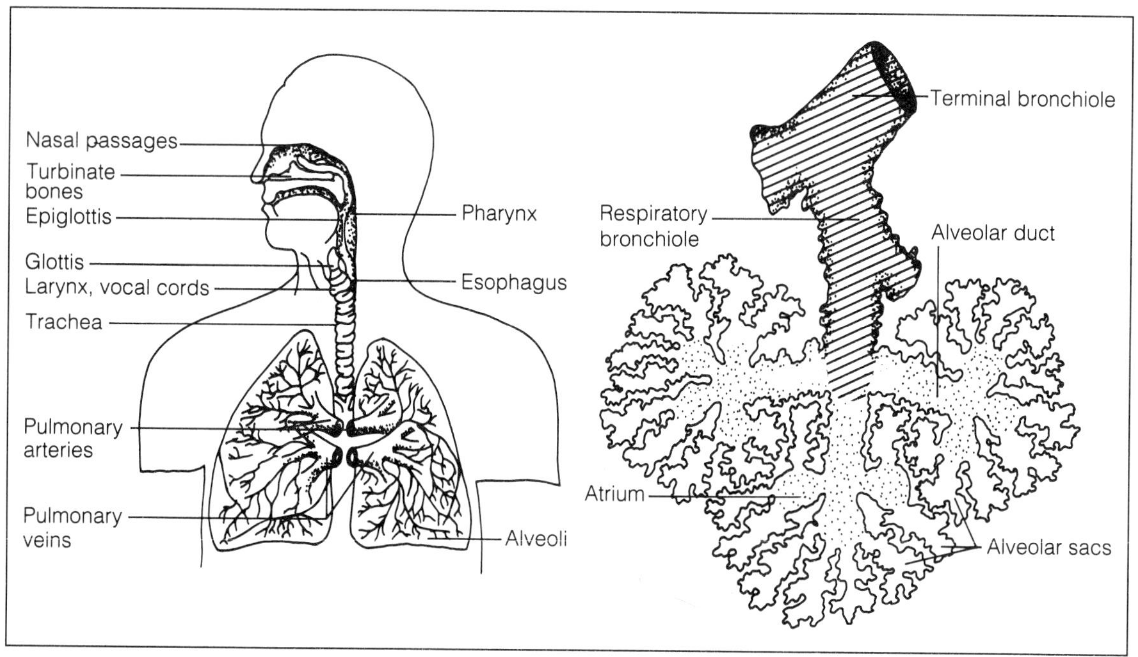

Figure 2-8. The anatomy of the respiratory system.

ation phase. Air is taken in via the nose and mouth. It travels down the pharynx, or windpipe, through the bronchiole tubes, into the bronchioles of the lungs, and lastly to the alveoli. The alveoli are small balloonlike sacs at the ends of the bronchioles that are surrounded by capillaries. Oxygen diffuses from the alveoli into the bloodstream via the pulmonary capillaries. Carbon dioxide diffuses in the opposite direction.

At sea level, the air we breathe is made up of 21 percent oxygen and 79 percent nitrogen, with a negligible amount of carbon dioxide (0.03 percent). While resting, we normally consume between 0.25 and 0.30 liter of oxygen per minute (l/min).

The term for the amount of air exchanged per breath is the *tidal volume*. The amount of air exchanged per minute is termed the *minute volume*. The tidal volume is between 500 to 700 ml of air per breath, and we breathe 12 to 15 times per minute. This provides a minute volume of 6 to 10 l/min of air. The breathing rates can increase from 40 to 60 breaths per minute during exercise, and the tidal volume can increase somewhere between 2.0 and 4.0 l per breath. This will provide a minute volume of 100 to 140 l/min of air for nonathletes. Trained athletes can exchange 150 to 180 l/min of air, because training increases their tidal volume.

With training, athletes tend to adopt a maximum breathing rate that provides the greatest minute volume with the least effort. Most do this naturally. They learn to breathe slower and deeper during exercise, but not so slow and deep that they increase the work of breathing unnecessarily. Swimmers learn this skill particularly well because they must regulate their breathing to match their stroke rhythms. During exercise, the enhanced minute volume increases the amount of oxygen consumed to 2 and 3 l/min for average, nonathletic females and males, respectively.

Oxygen Consumption and Swimming Performance

The term for the amount of oxygen that a person uses during one minute of exercise is $\dot{V}O_2$. The maximum amount of oxygen that a person can consume during one minute of exercise has been termed *maximum oxygen consumption*, or $\dot{V}O_2max$. Much has been made of the importance of $\dot{V}O_2$max to endurance performance.

An athlete's oxygen consumption is measured by calculating the amount of oxygen she exhales in one minute and subtracting that value from the amount inhaled. $\dot{V}O_2$max is calculated by measuring oxygen consumption during repeated intervals of exercise at progressively faster speeds. The number of bouts are continued until a plateau is reached at which a further increase of speed does not cause an additional increase in oxygen consumption. When that happens, the athlete has reached her maximum ability to consume oxygen.

One aspect of oxygen consumption that is difficult for many people to understand is that the maximum rate is reached when athletes are swimming at slower than maximum speeds. The capacity for anaerobic metabolism is what makes it possible for them to continue swimming faster after they have reached their maximum limit of oxygen consumption. Athletes continue supplying energy by producing lactic acid, even though the oxygen supply is inadequate. Those increased speeds can only be maintained for a short time, however, because lactic acid will accumulate in the muscles and cause acidosis.

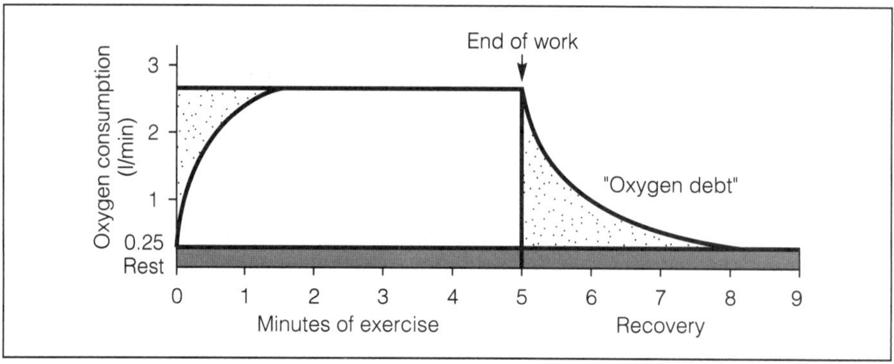

Figure 2-9. Results of a typical test of $\dot{V}O_2$max. (Astrand & Rodahl, 1977)

Each of us has a finite ability to consume oxygen during exercise. That ability can be increased somewhat by training, although the amount of increase is determined by heredity. The $\dot{V}O_2$max of gifted female swimmers has been measured beyond 4 l/min; their male counterparts can consume more than 5 l/min of oxygen at maximum rates. The results of a representative test for $\dot{V}O_2$max are illustrated in Figure 2-9. It typically takes 1 to 3 minutes for oxygen consumption to increase to a maximum value. That value is approximately 2.7 l/min.

Oxygen consumption can be misleading when expressed in liters per minute because it is biased toward large persons. Large athletes usually have a higher $\dot{V}O_2$max than those who are smaller simply because they can exchange more air per minute. This does not mean that they are supplying more oxygen to their muscles, however. The supply depends on the amount of oxygen available to each kilogram of muscle tissue, and larger people have more muscles to supply.

For this reason, $\dot{V}O_2$max is often expressed relative to body size. In this method, oxygen consumption is expressed according to the number of milliliters of oxygen a person can consume per kilogram of body weight during each minute of exercise (ml/kg/min). The procedure for converting an absolute oxygen consumption value to a relative value is shown in the following box. Here, the person weighing 70 kg has an absolute $\dot{V}O_2$max of 4.2 l/min. In other words, that person is consuming

The Procedure for Converting an Absolute $\dot{V}O_2$max Value to a Relative Value

$\dot{V}O_2$max = 4.2 l/min = 4,200 ml/min

Weight = 70 kg (154 lbs)
Relative $\dot{V}O_2$max = 60 ml/kg/min
4,200 ml ÷ 70 kg = 60 ml/kg/min

4,200 milliliters of oxygen per minute. Dividing the person's absolute oxygen consumption by his weight yields a relative value for $\dot{V}O_2$max of 60 ml/kg/min.

Expressing $\dot{V}O_2$max relative to body weight provides a more realistic method for comparing the oxygen supply of different-sized athletes. For example, a person who weighs 70 kg (154 lb) and consumes oxygen at 4 l/min will have a lower relative $\dot{V}O_2$max than someone who has an identical absolute capacity for oxygen consumption but weighs only 65 kg (143 lb). The former would have a relative $\dot{V}O_2$max of 57 ml/kg/min (4,000 ml ÷ 70 kg), yet the value for the latter person would be greater, at 61 ml/kg/min (4,000 ml ÷ 65 kg).

Average values for relative $\dot{V}O_2$max are 35 and 45 ml/kg/min for women and men, respectively. World-class female and male swimmers have been tested as high as 66 and 80 ml/kg/min, respectively (Van Handel et al., 1988).

For many years, the capacity to consume oxygen maximally was considered the most valid measure of an athlete's ability to perform in endurance events. We believed that a person who could supply more oxygen to his body during every minute of exercise would be able to get more energy from aerobic metabolism. Thus, he would fatigue at a slower rate because he would be less dependent on anaerobic metabolism. This concept has been challenged in recent years. Research has shown that $\dot{V}O_2$max was not as highly related to success in endurance events as we once thought.

The fractional percentage of $\dot{V}O_2$max that can be used without producing fatigue seems to be more highly related to performance in endurance events than $\dot{V}O_2$max. The fractional utilization of $\dot{V}O_2$max is illustrated in Figure 2-10. Another aspect of oxygen consumption that may also play an important role in performance concerns the ability to swim certain submaximum speeds with a lower oxygen requirement — a phenomenon that has been termed *swimming economy.* The relationship of these two components of oxygen consumption and performance is the subject of the next two sections.

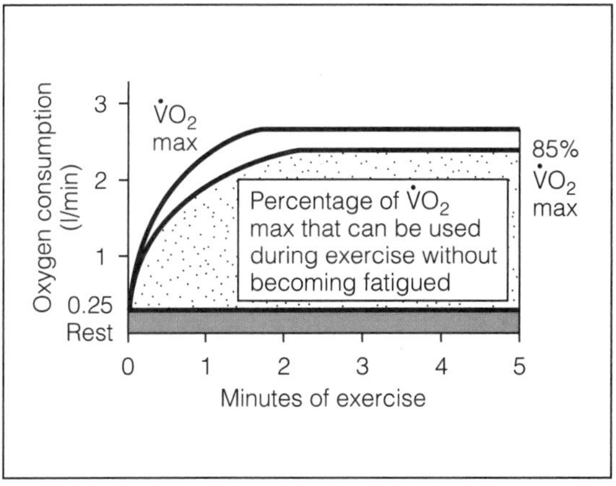

Figure 2-10. The fractional utilization of $\dot{V}O_2$max.

Percentage Utilization of $\dot{V}O_2max$ This measure of endurance performance refers to an athlete's ability to perform at a given percentage of $\dot{V}O_2max$ without becoming fatigued. The purpose is to find the fastest speed that athletes can maintain without accumulating an excess amount of lactic acid. In other words, it is the fastest speed they can maintain aerobically, known popularly as the *anaerobic threshold*.

Athletes who can swim at a high percentage of $\dot{V}O_2max$ without accumulating large amounts of lactic acid in their muscles have an advantage over those who simply have high $\dot{V}O_2max$. This fact may be difficult to comprehend, because, theoretically, swimmers with a high maximum rate *should* be able to consume more oxygen at any percentage of maximum than those with a lower $\dot{V}O_2max$. Such a relationship between a high $\dot{V}O_2max$ and performance does not seem to exist in real life, however. Apparently, the ability of some athletes to swim at a higher percentage of maximum outweighs the advantage of a large $\dot{V}O_2max$ in others. The calculations in the following box illustrate how a swimmer with a smaller $\dot{V}O_2max$ could actually swim a faster pace than his teammate with a greater $\dot{V}O_2max$.

A Comparison of Percentage Consumptions of Oxygen for Two Swimmers with Different $\dot{V}O_2max$ Values

Swimmer A

$\dot{V}O_2max$ = 60 ml/kg/min

Swimmer A can swim at 92 percent of maximum without becoming fatigued; therefore he can consume oxygen at a rate of 55.2 ml/kg/min.

$60 \times .92 = 55.20$

Swimmer B

$\dot{V}O_2max$ = 65 ml/kg/min

Swimmer B can swim at 75 percent of maximum without becoming fatigued; therefore, he can consume oxygen at a rate of only 48.75 ml/kg/min.

$65 \times .75 = 48.75$

Swimmer A has an advantage where endurance is concerned. Although his $\dot{V}O_2max$ is only 60 ml/kg/min, he can swim at 92 percent of that maximum without becoming fatigued. By contrast, swimmer B, with a higher $\dot{V}O_2max$ of 65 ml/kg/min can only swim at 75 percent of that value without becoming fatigued. If both were swimming at a speed at which the oxygen cost were 58 ml/kg/min during a race, we would expect that swimmer B would fatigue earlier than swimmer A because his oxygen cost would be well above his ability to swim aerobically. Swimmer B would go into oxygen debt at a rate of approximately 9 ml/kg/

min, yet swimmer A's oxygen debt would accumulate at a rate of approximately 3 ml/kg/min.

Although $\dot{V}O_2max$ stops increasing after the first six to eight weeks of each season, a swimmer's ability to use ever-greater percentages of his or her $\dot{V}O_2max$ without incurring acidosis can continue to increase for much longer periods. For untrained persons, the highest fractional utilization of $\dot{V}O_2max$ that will not cause fatigue is usually between 50 and 70 percent of maximum. Training can improve this value to between 75 and 90 percent of maximum. As with $\dot{V}O_2max$, heredity seems to play a role in determining the highest percentage of maximum that some athletes can reach.

Swimming Economy Swimming economy is a measure of the oxygen needed to swim at certain submaximum speeds. Swimmers who use less oxygen at a certain velocity are considered more economical than those who use more. Figure 2-11 shows a swimmer being tested for swimming economy.

The oxygen consumed during a swimming economy test can be reported in two forms: (1) as milliliters of oxygen consumed per kilogram of body weight for each meter swum ($mlO_2/kg/m$) and (2) as a percentage of $\dot{V}O_2max$ for each speed. The first index considers the energy cost of swimming relative to body size. The second

Figure 2-11. An athlete being tested for swimming economy at the U.S. Swimming's International Center for Aquatic Research in Colorado Springs, Colorado.

Table 2-2. Swimming Economy Measures for World-class U.S. Swimmers

	Economy Measures			
	Women		Men	
Velocity	*$mlO_2/kg/m$*	*Percentage of $\dot{V}O_2max$*	*$mlO_2/kg/m$*	*Percentage of $\dot{V}O_2max$*
1.2 m/sec	28	49	36	53
1.4 m/sec	52	77	53	91
1.6 m/sec	67	118	72	106

expresses the oxygen cost relative to each swimmer's $\dot{V}O_2max$. Average values for world-class swimmers are listed for several swimming velocities in Table 2-2. They are from a study by Van Handel and associates (1988).

Relative to body size, the average values for females and males were 28 and 36 $mlO_2/kg/m$, respectively, at a velocity of 1.2 m/sec; 52 and 53 $mlO_2/kg/m$ at a velocity of 1.4 m/sec; and 67 and 72 $mlO_2/kg/m$ at a velocity of 1.6 m/sec.

There was a considerable amount of variation in the economy measures among this group of international-level athletes. The range between the least and most economical swimmers was 20 mlO_2/m. The most economical swimmer in the sample had values of 25 $ml/O_2/kg/m$ at a velocity of 1.2 m/sec; 40 $mlO_2/kg/m$ at 1.4 m/sec; and a projected value of 55 $mlO_2/kg/m$ at 1.6 m/sec. The least economical swimmer in the group had values of 47 $mlO_2/kg/m$ at 1.2 m/sec; 60 $mlO_2/kg/m$ at 1.4 m/sec; and a projected value of 72 $mlO_2/kg/m$ at 1.6 m/sec. Even at the world-class level, some athletes swim much more efficiently than others.

Expressed as a percent of $\dot{V}O_2max$, the oxygen requirement for swimming at 1.2 m/sec was 53 percent for the male and 49 percent for the female world-class swimmers in this group; at 1.4 m/sec, 77 percent and 91 percent, respectively; and at 1.6 m/sec, 106 percent and 118 percent. The percentage values for women were always higher than those for men at the fastest two velocities, probably because women were swimming closer to their maximum speeds.

Van Handel and his coworkers (1988) reported a significant negative relationship of -0.625 between measures of swimming economy and performance for 400-m freestyle swims. The relationship was negative because a lower economy corresponded to a faster time. This relationship accounted for approximately 39 percent of the difference in the performances of these swimmers. In other words, 39 percent of the difference in effort among this group of freestyle swimmers was due to the amount of oxygen they needed to swim at certain speeds. The low relationship between swimming economy and swimming success is not surprising; a survey of research on the relationship between economy and running performance was also inconclusive (Bune, Heller, Sprynarova, & Zdanowicz, 1986).

At the present time, the best use for measures of swimming economy may be to determine whether stroke changes are beneficial. An athlete's potential for performance has probably improved when a change in mechanics results in less oxygen being consumed at fast, but submaximum speeds.

The Oxygen Debt At one time, the oxygen debt was the most popular concept in exercise physiology. It was believed that athletes breathed faster and deeper for a short time after exercise in order to repay the oxygen the body needed but could not get during the exercise. That additional oxygen was thought to be used for the purpose of metabolizing the lactic acid produced during exercise.

Figure 2-9 illustrates the concept of the oxygen debt as extra oxygen consumed during the recovery period following exercise. The oxygen debt was actually determined by measuring the extra oxygen consumed during the recovery period following exercise. The oxygen consumed during the exercise and the oxygen debt were then summed to determine the oxygen requirement of the exercise. The results were then used to quantify the aerobic (oxygen consumed during exercise) and anaerobic (extra oxygen consumed during recovery) components of the exercise. Many tables listing the percentage of energy supplied from aerobic and anaerobic sources in various events were based on these calculations. This method of quantifying metabolism proved to be inaccurate, however, because it oversimplified a very complex process.

It has never been possible to equate the additional amount of oxygen consumed during recovery with the elimination of lactic acid produced during the exercise for several reasons. For one, studies showed that some lactic acid was always being produced during slow work, even when there was no extra oxygen consumed during recovery. For another, in cases where additional oxygen was consumed during recovery, it usually continued long after lactic acid levels had returned to normal. Finally, there were cases where blood lactic acid levels remained elevated during recovery long after oxygen consumption had returned to normal resting levels (McArdle, Katch, & Katch, 1991).

There has been a recent resurgence of interest in using a modification of the oxygen debt theory to quantify the aerobic and anaerobic components of work. The original concept has been modified in two ways, however. First, the term *oxygen deficit* has replaced *oxygen debt* because it more accurately portrays what is being quantified—that is, the oxygen used during recovery. Second, the oxygen deficit is calculated rather than the oxygen requirement.

To measure the oxygen deficit, the oxygen requirement of a particular bout of strenuous exercise is first extrapolated from measurements of oxygen consumed during short bouts of that exercise at the same rate of effort. Next, the oxygen consumption is measured during the actual exercise bout. Finally, the oxygen deficit is calculated by subtracting the oxygen consumed during the exercise from the calculated oxygen requirement.

Although not perfect, the newer concept of calculating the oxygen deficit provides a potentially more precise means of quantifying the aerobic and anaerobic components of various types of exercise.

Vital Capacity and Pulmonary Diffusion

Both of these terms are often encountered in the literature on respiration. *Vital capacity* refers to the total amount of air that can be exchanged with one breath. *Pulmonary diffusion* concerns the rate of oxygen diffusion from the alveoli into the blood.

Vital Capacity Much was made of the importance of vital capacity in early writings under the mistaken assumption that persons who could exchange more air with each breath could also consume more oxygen. In truth, the relationship of vital capacity and $\dot{V}O_2max$ expressed in liters per minute is high, but that relationship has little to do with performance. It occurs primarily because of the association between both of these measures and body size. Large persons generally have a greater vital capacity and maximum rate of oxygen consumption. On the other hand, the relationship of vital capacity to $\dot{V}O_2max$ expressed relative to body size is low. This probably explains why a large vital capacity has not been associated with superior performance.

Many athletes practice deep-breathing exercises to increase their vital capacity. These exercises probably serve no useful purpose. They do not improve vital capacity and would not improve performance, even if they did.

Pulmonary Diffusion The pulmonary-diffusing capacity of trained swimmers is generally greater than that of untrained persons. Nevertheless, this measure has a negligible relationship to performance. A large pulmonary-diffusing capacity would not necessarily mean that an athlete had a greater oxygen supply. That would depend more on how well the athlete had trained her circulatory and muscular systems to deliver and use the oxygen that was made available.

Respiration and Acid-Base Balance

The respiratory system plays an important role in acid-base balance during exercise by assisting in the buffering process. An increased respiration rate will remove more carbon dioxide from the body, which in turn will facilitate the combining of hydrogen ions and bicarbonate so that blood pH does not drop so rapidly. This, in turn, should cause more hydrogen ions to diffuse out of the muscles and into the blood so that the rate of acidosis in muscles is reduced as well.

There is no known training effect that improves the role of the respiratory system in maintaining acid-base balance beyond simply breathing more efficiently during exercise. That adjustment should happen as a normal consequence of training.

Second Wind and a Stitch in the Side

Second Wind This is a feeling of relief that occurs after exercise has become strenuous. Whereas breathing was labored and the work felt painful before, breathing becomes easier and the work more tolerable after athletes experience a second wind. The reasons for this reduction in effort are not known. The early distress may be associated with the temporary use of anaerobic metabolism until oxygen consumption has increased and aerobic metabolism is providing a larger percentage of the energy for work. There is some support for this notion in the fact that second wind only occurs during endurance efforts.

Second wind usually occurs when athletes are just beginning their training program after a long layoff. Well-trained athletes rarely experience this phenomenon, probably because their circulatory system adjusts more rapidly after they become conditioned.

Stitch in the Side Swimmers experience this as a sharp pain in the side, just underneath the lungs. Although no scientific proof is available to explain the occurrence of a stitch in the side, the popular theory is that a temporary lack of oxygen occurs in the diaphragm or intercostal (breathing) muscles during endurance efforts. That oxygen deficiency is believed to occur because the circulatory and respiratory systems adjust too slowly. Like second wind, stitches in the side are usually experienced by athletes who are poorly conditioned, and they disappear once the athletes become trained.

THE ROLE OF HORMONES

Hormones are chemical substances produced in the endocrine glands, which are secreted directly into the bloodstream, where they travel to cells and attach themselves to receptor sites in these cells. Hormones, because they travel in the blood, can reach and affect all tissues of the body. Cells contain between 2,000 and 10,000 receptor sites, where specific hormones can attach themselves and perform their functions. Of particular concern to coaches and athletes are those functions involved with (1) enhancing the energy supply during exercise and (2) replacing that energy during recovery.

Hormones are not poured into the blood at a constant rate. They are released in bursts when stimulated by certain events. The secretion of hormones is regulated largely by the autonomic (unconscious) nervous system. It has two parts that are known as the *sympathetic* and *parasympathetic* nervous systems. The sympathetic nervous system regulates energy mobilization for exercise through the well-known "fight or flight" reaction. The parasympathetic system governs the replacement of fuels during recovery. The most prominent hormones are listed in Table 2-3.

The Effect of Training on Hormones

The general effect of training on hormones is to reduce their rate of secretion during exercise. This mediates the effect of hormones so that exercise can continue longer without energy imbalances taking place. An example of the effect of training on some of these hormones may help you to understand their effect on performances in practice and competition.

Training reduces the fall of insulin during exercise, which has the effect of maintaining a higher blood glucose level over a longer period. This will reduce muscle glycogen use during exercise, allowing athletes to train more intensely for longer periods. Similarly, after an athlete becomes well trained, glucagon and the catecholamines epinephrine and norepinephrine will respond less actively during exercise; consequently, the rate of glycogen use will decrease and the rate of fat metabolism will increase.

Table 2-3. Hormones and Their Functions

Location	Hormone	Function
Pancreas	Insulin	Stimulates glucose and free fatty acid uptake by cells.
	Glucagon	Stimulates release of glucose from the liver. Also encourages formation of glycogen from protein in the liver.
	Somatostatin	Decreases the secretion of insulin and glucagon.
Adrenal glands		
Medulla	Epinephrine (adrenaline)	Stimulates breakdown of muscle glycogen and triglycerides. Also stimulates heart rate, nerve impulse conduction, and muscle contraction.
	Norepinephrine	Stimulates heart rate and blood flow by raising blood pressure. Stimulates release of free fatty acids from adipose tissue.
Cortex	Cortisol	Stimulates release of amino acids from muscle and free fatty acids in adipose tissue.
	Aldosterone	Regulates sodium retention and, thus, water and electrolyte balance.
Pituitary gland		
Anterior	Growth hormone	Stimulates tissue building and fat metabolism.
	Thyroid-stimulating hormone	Controls the amount of thyroxin produced and released by the thyroid gland.
	ACTH (adrenocorticotropic hormone)	Stimulates release of adrenal hormones.
	Follicle-stimulating hormone (FSH)	Initiates growth of follicles in the ovaries and promotes secretion of estrogen from the ovaries.
	Luteinizing hormone (LH)	Promotes secretion of estrogen and progesterone and causes the follicle to rupture, releasing the ovum.
Posterior	ADH (antidiuretic hormone)	Stimulates water retention and reduces urine output.
Thyroid gland	Thyroxine	Increases cell metabolism, thereby increasing oxygen consumption, fat and glycogen breakdown, and tissue repair.
	Calcitonin	Controls calcium concentration in blood.
Parathyroid gland	Parathormone	Stimulates bone growth through its effect on calcium. Also responsible for development of strong teeth.
Gonads	Testosterone	Stimulates tissue building and repair.
	Estrogen	Promotes development of female sex organs. Provides for increased fat storage. Assists in regulating the menstrual cycle.
	Progesterone	Assists in regulating the menstrual cycle.

CHAPTER 3

Causes of Fatigue and Training Effects That Can Delay It

The causes of fatigue are the focus of the first part of this chapter. The training effects that help delay fatigue are covered in the second part.

THE CAUSES OF FATIGUE IN COMPETITION AND TRAINING

Fatigue can be defined as a reduction in swimming speed. It is a natural outcome of competition and cannot be prevented, only delayed. The reasons for this reduction in speed are not the same for each race distance. Accordingly, accurate definitions of fatigue must take into consideration the event being contested.

Fatigue occurs in events as short as 25 m when athletes cannot maintain maximum speed for the entire distance. They slow down despite the fact that they do not suffer pain nor become exhausted. Swimmers in events of 1,500 m suffer fatigue when they cannot maintain a desired pace and must finish the race at a slower speed. Obviously, athletes experience different types of fatigue in these two races. Both types are, in turn, different from the exhaustion and pain that occurs at the end of long sprint races. Additionally, each of these forms of fatigue is also different from the heavy, sluggish feeling that swimmers experience when they don't have enough energy to swim fast in training.

Theories about the causes of fatigue fall into four categories:

1. Depletion of the muscles' ATP and CP supplies.
2. An inadequate rate of anaerobic metabolism.

3. Reduced rates of energy release from ATP, CP, and muscle glycogen, resulting from a low muscle pH. In this case, fatigue is caused by the accumulation of lactic acid (acidosis).
4. A reduced rate of anaerobic metabolism caused by low muscle glycogen levels.

Depletion of ATP and CP

Depletions of the chemical sources of energy—adenosine triphosphate (ATP) and creatine phosphate (CP)—have been proposed as the reasons for fatigue in sprints. It appears, however, that only CP depletion may be involved, and then only for 25 and 50 sprints. ATP can be replaced as long as there is glucose, fat, or protein available. Consequently, the muscles' ATP supply is never depleted, even after long, exhausting competitions, not to mention sprints (Sahlin, Harris, Nylind, & Hultman, 1976).

However, a reduction in the muscles' CP supply can reduce the rate of ATP recycling, which, in turn, will slow the rate and force of contraction in muscles, so that sprint speed can no longer be maintained. The CP supply in muscles declines in two stages. It drops rapidly during the first 5 to 6 seconds of effort and then more slowly for the remainder of the race. The contractile rate is undoubtedly reduced after the initial rapid decline in CP, as the muscles try to prevent depletion of CP by turning to glycogen. This is probably an internal protective mechanism to maintain the muscles' CP supply. Continued sprinting after 5 or 6 seconds will deplete the CP supply further, so that it will be almost gone within 10 to 15 seconds. After this, the major source of energy for ATP recycling will be the anaerobic breakdown of muscle glycogen. This process is slower because it involves eleven steps rather than one, so speed will decline even more.

Inadequate Rates of Anaerobic Metabolism

When the CP supply is nearly exhausted, the rate of anaerobic energy release is probably the factor that determines how fast athletes can continue to swim in sprints. Energy from anaerobic sources is obviously important to 50 sprinters during the last 5 to 10 m of their races, when the CP supply is nearly depleted. It plays an even more prominent role in 100 sprints because they are longer. Less known is the role that anaerobic metabolism plays during the final sprint of longer races. A swimmer's ability to deliver energy anaerobically largely determines how fast he or she will sprint over the final 30 to 50 m. Since the end product of anaerobic metabolism is lactic acid, an athlete's capacity to deliver energy from this source is also commonly referred to as the *lactate production rate*.

It might seem unusual to include a slowing of this rate as a cause of fatigue, because it does not really slow athletes down. It simply prevents them from swimming as fast as they would like to. The lactate production rate can be increased through proper training, although heredity probably sets a limit on the amount of improvement that is possible.

Acidosis (Low Muscle pH)

Despite opinions to the contrary (Brooks & Fahey, 1984; Sapega, Sokolow, Grahm, & Chance, 1988), most experts believe that acidosis is the major cause of fatigue in all swimming races longer than 50 m. When the rate of anaerobic metabolism is high and pyruvic acid combines with hydrogen ions to form lactic acid, muscle pH will drop from its neutral state of 7.0 to an acidic level, setting in motion a chain of events that will progressively reduce muscle contractile speed. A reduction of contractile speed will reduce athletes' stroking force, and they will slow down. At very low pH values (6.5 to 6.8), anaerobic metabolism is almost nonexistent and swimmers can only operate aerobically, so they must swim at very slow speeds. The reasons why progressive acidosis reduces the rate of anaerobic metabolism follow:

1. The amount of calcium needed for muscular contraction will increase. Calcium activates the coupling of myosin and actin filaments within muscle fibers, causing them to contract. When more calcium is needed, it will take longer to activate these enzymes and the rate of contraction will be reduced.

2. The rate of activity of the enzyme ATPase will be reduced. This enzyme regulates the release of energy from ATP. When the activity of that enzyme is reduced, energy will be released from ATP at a slower rate and muscular contractile speed will become slower.

3. The rate of activity of the enzyme phosphofructokinase (PFK) will be inhibited. This enzyme is believed to be one of the chief regulators of the rate of anaerobic metabolism. A reduction in its activity will slow the rate of anaerobic metabolism and, consequently, the rate of muscular contraction. It has been found to be almost inactive at a pH of 6.4 (Danforth, 1965).

4. The rate of lactic acid removal is slower (Hirche et al., 1975). Acidosis produces a symbiotic relationship between the rates of lactic acid production and removal. An increase of lactic acid lowers pH, which reduces the removal rate and leads to more rapid accumulation of lactic acid in the muscles and a further lowering of pH. The muscles will, undoubtedly, try to protect themselves by reducing the rate of lactic acid production when this happens.

5. Acidosis produces pain that will cause some athletes to slow down. Although the sharp, burning pain of acidosis tests the willpower of most athletes, some continue on in spite of it. Others may not be willing to endure it, and they will slow their speed to prevent a further drop in muscle pH. Still others may become frightened when the pain begins too early in a race, and they may slow their pace unnecessarily in the middle only to find that they have lost more ground than they can make up in the final stage of the race.

Some athletes and coaches mistakenly believe that the fatigue is entirely psychological and can be controlled by a willingness to tolerate the pain of acidosis. A low muscle pH can produce physiological, as well as psychological, effects that will reduce speeds, however. Pain tolerance, by itself, is not sufficient to ensure success in competition. It certainly helps athletes perform better; nevertheless, they must also deal with the physiological effects of acidosis, and these cannot be willed away. Swimmers cannot maintain an adequate speed when their muscle pH falls to 6.8 or less, no matter how much they may want to. Athletes must train their bodies to delay the physiological causes of acidosis. No amount of willpower or desire will allow them to reach their potential without such training.

Low Muscle Glycogen Levels

Glycogen is the only chemical that can supply energy for recycling ATP anaerobically once the muscles' CP supplies are nearly depleted after the first 10 to 15 seconds of effort. Accordingly, muscle glycogen makes it possible to maintain a competitive pace for any race distance beyond 50 m. When the supply of glycogen is low, the muscles must rely on the fat and protein that is stored within them and the fat and glucose that are delivered by the blood. More time is needed to get energy from these sources, making it impossible to maintain competitive speeds when they are used. Consequently, it is very important to have an adequate amount of glycogen stored in muscles when maximum or near-maximum efforts are needed. Normal levels of muscle glycogen are usually sufficient to supply energy for 1 to 3 hours, depending on the rate of work (Costill et al., 1973). Consequently, the only time glycogen depletion should affect competition is when the glycogen in muscles is low to begin with. In this regard, low muscle glycogen levels could affect the rate of lactate production in mid-season competitions, when training may be depleting glycogen faster than it is being replaced from day to day. The rate of lactate production should not be affected detrimentally when swimmers are well fed and have had a few days of rest to replace their muscle glycogen, however. For this reason, swimmers should play it safe by reducing the rate of work and increasing the amount of carbohydrates they eat for 2 or 3 days before important mid-season meets.

Training is a different matter. Athletes' muscles can become nearly depleted after one or two training sessions. When this happens, the muscles will try to conserve this valuable source of energy by utilizing fat and protein for energy. Under these conditions, the rate of anaerobic metabolism will be less than optimum and it will be difficult for athletes to swim fast in practice. Muscle glycogen can be nearly depleted by long, intense training sessions of 1 hour or more (Beltz et al., 1988; Houston, 1978). There is also conclusive proof that it can be nearly depleted by successive days of intense training (Costill et al., 1988). In most cases, 24 to 48 hours are required to replace the muscle glycogen used during extended training.

The symptoms of fatigue that swimmers experience from muscle glycogen depletion differ from those involving acidosis. The pain is not sharp and intense. Instead, swimmers experience a dull, heavy, lethargic sensation. These swimmers often don't believe they are fatigued. They think they are lazy or depressed. They will be able to swim long sets at slow to moderate speeds in training, with no noticeable symptoms, because much of the energy for ATP recycling can be supplied by stored fat at those speeds. It is only when they try to swim fast that they will become exhausted, because there will not be enough glycogen available to supply energy at the faster speeds.

The Causes of Fatigue Summarized by Event

25 and 50 Events In these events, fatigue is manifested by an inability to maintain a high rate of speed. It is not caused by muscle acidity and pain, because both events are too short to depress muscle pH to the level required to produce severe acidosis. This is evidenced by the fact that blood lactate concentrations after 50 races are only 50 to 75 percent of maximum. There are two causes of fatigue in these events: (1) a depletion of the muscles' CP supply, and (2) an inability to operate anaerobic metabolism rapidly enough.

100 and 200 Events The ability to maintain a fast pace in these events is probably limited by the inhibiting effect that acidosis has on the rate of anaerobic metabolism. Improvements in aerobic and anaerobic metabolism will reduce the rate of acidosis. Aerobic metabolism reduces acidosis by reducing the rate of lactic acid production and its rate of removal from muscles. Anaerobic metabolism reduces acidosis by improving buffering capacity. Pain tolerance may also play a role with some swimmers. Furthermore, as in the shorter races, increased rates of lactic acid production will increase maximum speed.

Loss of muscle glycogen should not play a role in fatigue in these or shorter events unless the muscles are nearly depleted before the events begin. Their duration is too short to deplete muscles that have adequate supplies of glycogen.

CP does contribute energy for these events. Nevertheless, an increase in the muscles' supply should only delay acidosis by a few tenths of a second, at best. Therefore, swimmers in 100 and 200 events can make better use of their time by working on improving aerobic and anaerobic metabolism so that they can reduce the rate of acidosis.

Middle-Distance and Distance Races Acidosis is also the principal cause of fatigue in these races and is reduced best by improving the rate of aerobic metabolism.

Race distances of 400 m and greater are too long for swimmers to survive primarily on the energy supplied by nonaerobic and anaerobic metabolism. Therefore, success will accrue largely from the ability to supply energy aerobically.

Once again, a normal muscle glycogen supply will be sufficient to provide the energy needed to swim these events, even 1,500 m. A supply that is less than adequate could affect performance detrimentally, however. The muscle CP supply has no bearing on delaying fatigue or improving performance in these events. The amount of energy contributed from this source is minor. The causes of fatigue at various race distances are summarized in the box on page 54.

TRAINING EFFECTS THAT CAN DELAY FATIGUE

Now that the causes of fatigue have been identified, the important issue becomes how training can delay fatigue. The training effects that do this for each phase of the metabolic process are discussed in the following sections.

The Causes of Fatigue at Various Race Distances

25 and 50 Events

1. CP depletion
2. An inadequate rate of anaerobic metabolism

100 and 200 Events

1. Acidosis
2. Pain tolerance

Middle-Distance and Distance Events

1. Acidosis
2. Pain tolerance

Nonaerobic Training Effects

Many publications, including the first edition of this textbook, have stressed the importance of the nonaerobic system for improving sprint speed, but that importance has probably been overstated. CP does provide a more rapid source of energy for recycling ATP than is supplied by the anaerobic metabolism of muscle glycogen. However, the supply of CP is so small that it cannot do this for any significant period of time. CP is the principal source of energy for ATP recycling only during the first 4 to 6 seconds of exercise (Hasson & Barnes, 1986). The contributions of glycolysis (the anaerobic metabolism of muscle glycogen) are almost as great at 10 seconds and twice as great by 30 seconds of exercise (Serresse, Lortie, Bouchard, & Boulay, 1988). Consequently, the nonaerobic system contributes only a small amount of energy in all races over 50 yd/m.

The effects of training on the ATP and CP supplies are also misleading. Although the quantities of these energy-containing chemicals have been shown to increase with training (Houston & Thomson, 1977; Karlsson, Nordesjo, Jorfeldt, & Saltin, 1972; MacDougall, Ward, Sale, & Sutton, 1977), that increase is so minor that it would only improve speed by a few hundredths of a second, at best. Sprinters are the only athletes that would profit from these increases. They could improve their times by a few tenths of a second. However, they could increase their speed more by concentrating on improving muscle power and stroke efficiency. Training of this type, by its very nature, involves the nonaerobic system, so ATP and CP supplies will increase as a byproduct. Muscular power should be the primary focus of sprint training. Improvements of muscular power result from two principal training effects: (1) increases in muscle size and strength and (2) improvements in the speed and accuracy of muscle fiber contraction patterns during exercise (*muscle fiber recruitment* patterns).

Increased Muscle Strength, Power, and Recruitment Patterns In addition to improved stroke mechanics, increased muscle strength, power, and recruitment patterns compose the major training effects that will increase swimming speed. Resistance training is an excellent medium for improving muscle strength. However, it must be coupled with in-water sprint training, because stroking power will only be improved by muscle fiber recruitment patterns that employ the proper fibers in the correct sequences of motion (Sale, 1986).

Anaerobic Training Effects

Anaerobic capacity refers to those mechanisms that recycle ATP through anaerobic metabolism and those that allow persons to tolerate the accumulation of lactic acid. There are three types of improvements of anaerobic capacity that will make swimmers faster: (1) increasing the rate of anaerobic metabolism (lactate production), (2) increasing buffering capacity, and (3) improving pain tolerance.

Increasing the Rate of Anaerobic Metabolism The maximum swimming speed that athletes can reach is probably limited by their stroke mechanics, their muscular force, and their muscular power. The last of these will be affected by the maximum rate of anaerobic metabolism which can be improved with proper training (Cunningham & Faulkner, 1969; Karlsson, Nordesjo, Jorfeldt, & Saltin, 1972; Robinson & Harmon, 1941; Saltin et al., 1976).

The rate of lactate production is probably limited by the activities of enzymes that regulate anaerobic metabolism. If that rate could be improved, the most likely mechanism for doing so would be through an increase in the activity of these enzymes.

The most important enzymes of anaerobic metabolism are:

1. *Phosphorylase,* which regulates the breakdown of glycogen to glucose.
2. *Phosphofructokinase (PFK),* which governs the conversion of fructose-6-phosphate to fructose-1.6-phosphate.
3. *Pyruvate kinase (PK),* which is involved in the conversion of phosphophenylpyruvate to pyruvic acid.
4. *Lactate dehydrogenase (LDH),* which mediates the conversion of pyruvic acid to lactic acid.

Of these, the three that have received the most attention are phosphorylase, PFK, and LDH. Until recently, PFK was thought to be the enzyme most responsible for controlling the rate of anaerobic metabolism. Recent studies involving nuclear magnetic resonance imply that phosphorylase may play a greater role than was once thought, however (Chance et al., 1983).

Training appears to increase both the quantity and activity of many of these enzymes (Costill, Fink, & Pollock, 1976; Costill, 1978). Sprints are particularly good for this purpose.

In general, training-induced increases of anaerobic enzymes have not been as great as those reported for the enzymes of aerobic metabolism. Most of these have ranged between 2 and 22 percent. A surprising result has been that the activity of some enzymes is actually decreased by aerobic training (Baldwin, Winder, Terjung, & Holloszy, 1973; Holloszy, 1973). These data point to the possibility of an antagonistic relationship between aerobic and anaerobic training. This controversy will be covered in Chapter 5.

Increasing Buffering Capacity Buffers are alkaline substances that can absorb hydrogen ions when they dissociate from lactic acid. By doing so, they change the strong lactic acid to a weaker acid so that its effect on muscle pH is not so great. For example, with efficient buffering, a 10-fold increase in lactic acid only causes an 8 percent decrease in pH (Keul, Doll, & Keppler, 1972). An increase in buffering capacity allows swimmers to produce more lactic acid with less reduction in muscle contractile speed. By buffering lactic acid, they are able to maintain a fast pace for a longer time before acidosis becomes severe.

Buffers are found in the blood and in the intracellular fluid of muscle cells. The two most important substances are sodium bicarbonate and sodium phosphate, collectively known as the alkaline reserve.

Some of the amino acids within muscles may also serve as buffers. They provide free radicals that combine with hydrogen ions to form water. Little is known about these free radicals at the present time. However, it has been estimated that 50 percent of all buffering is accomplished by amino acids (Hultman & Sahlin, 1980).

Blood hemoglobin also serves as a buffer for hydrogen ions. It prevents a drop in blood pH so that more hydrogen ions will diffuse out of muscles. Respiration, another potent buffering system, has already been discussed.

Buffer systems can react almost immediately at the beginning of exercise to prevent drops in muscle pH. Consequently, a swimmer's buffering capacity is probably very important to success in 100 and 200 races. The speeds required in these races are so fast and the duration so brief that most of the energy must come from anaerobic metabolism. There is simply not enough time to consume a sufficient amount of oxygen to reduce the rate of lactic acid production to any great extent.

Buffering capacity is improved best by anaerobic training, while endurance training does not seem to have any effect. In two studies, athletes in sprint events had greater than average buffering capacity, while endurance-trained athletes were no different from untrained persons in buffering capacity (McKenzie et al., 1983; Sharp, Costill, Fink, & King, 1983).

Improving Pain Tolerance Because some athletes are unwilling to tolerate the pain of acidosis, they may reduce their speed more than necessary. Athletes who can tolerate more pain should be able to compete closer to their true physiological limit.

We do not know why some athletes tolerate pain better than others. It is most certainly tied to their desire for success. As such, pain tolerance may be a function of motivation and not amenable to training. It is possible that athletes can become less sensitive to pain when they subject themselves to it periodically in training.

Aerobic Training Effects

Aerobic capacity can be defined as the ability to do work without interference from anaerobic metabolism. This does not mean that lactic acid is not being produced. It simply means that it is being removed from the muscles almost as fast as it is produced.

The training effects that will improve the contribution of aerobic metabolism to the energy supply during competition are many and complex. Nevertheless, they fit neatly into two categories: (1) those that reduce the rate of lactic acid production and (2) those that increase the rate of lactic acid removal from muscles.

It could be argued that the ability to remove lactic acid from working muscles is not a part of aerobic metabolism. I have included it here because the mechanisms involved in improving lactate removal are enhanced by aerobic endurance training. Two additional results of such training, while not essential to competition, are important because they increase the ability to do more work in practice; they are: (3) an increase in the amount of muscle glycogen stored in muscles and (4) an increase in the use of fat for energy.

Reducing the Rate of Lactic Acid Production Opinions among researchers differ as to whether training can reduce the rate of lactic acid production (Donovan & Brooks, 1983; Favier, Constable, Chen, & Holloszy, 1986). This controversy has important implications for training. If that rate is *not* changed with training, there would be no need to concern ourselves with training aerobic metabolism. We would focus, instead, on training only those mechanisms responsible for removing lactic acid from muscles once it had been produced. However, if the rate of lactic acid production can be reduced, our training should also include procedures that would improve the oxygen supply to muscles.

It seems logical that the rate of lactic acid production can be reduced by increasing the rate of aerobic metabolism. Increases of aerobic enzyme activity, oxygen consumption, and mitochondrial size and number after training support this belief. These adaptations are all important to reducing that rate.

All of the training effects that reduce the rate of lactic acid production provide, as a common denominator, an increase of oxygen to the muscles. The training-induced adaptations that should increase the oxygen supply and the rate of aerobic metabolism in muscles are:

1. An increase in capillaries around individual muscle fibers, which will bring more oxygen in close proximity to the muscle fibers where it can diffuse into them.

2. Improvements of blood shunting to those muscles that are being used to perform work so that more blood and, thus, oxygen reaches the capillaries.

3. An increase in the quantity of myoglobin in muscles so that, once the oxygen diffuses into muscle fibers, it can be transported across the cells to the mitochondria.

4. An increase in the size and number of mitochondria in muscles to provide more and larger areas for receiving oxygen and performing aerobic metabolism.
5. Increases in the activity of the enzymes that regulate aerobic metabolism in the muscles.

Two additional mechanisms may be involved in reducing the rate of lactate production: (6) the conversion of pyruvic acid to alanine through the glucose-alanine cycle and (7) an increase in the number of hydrogen ions that enter the electron transport chain by means of the malate-aspartate shuttle.

An increase of muscle capillaries Research has shown that endurance training will increase muscle capillaries (Brodal, Ingjer, & Hermansen, 1976; Carrow, Brown, & Van Huss, 1967; Hermansen & Wachlova, 1971). Endurance-trained athletes were found to have 50 percent more capillaries around their muscles than untrained persons (Wilmore & Costill, 1988). Some of this effect may be hereditary. Nevertheless, an increase of 15 percent after 8 weeks of training was shown in one study (Klausen, Anderson, & Pelle, 1981).

These capillary increases are specific to the muscle fibers used in training. Therefore, swimmers can only increase capillarization around muscle fibers that are trained. Many other circulatory adaptations are general in nature; that is, they involve the heart and large arteries that serve all areas of the body. These adaptations can be produced by any type of endurance exercise and can benefit any other type of work. For example, an increase in stroke volume that is produced from running can benefit athletes when they swim. Capillaries are different, however. They will not increase around a muscle fiber unless the demand for oxygen in that particular fiber is greater than its supply. By the same token, capillaries are an integral part of the structure of muscle fibers and cannot be borrowed from one to serve others. In other words, running may improve capillarization around the leg muscles, but it will do very little for the arms. Swimmers are best advised to do most of their aerobic training in the pool to ensure that they increase the capillaries around the muscle fibers they will use in races.

Blood shunting Training will increase that proportion of the total amount of blood that flows to working muscles during maximum efforts (Clausen 1973; Keul, Doll, & Keppler, 1972; Saltin 1973; Simmons & Shepard, 1972). Improvements of blood shunting are probably produced best by endurance training at fast speeds because the greatest quantities of blood are redistributed to working muscles during long, intense swimming.

Myoglobin This is the iron-containing protein in muscles that gives them their reddish color. It serves two functions: (1) to transport the oxygen that diffuses in from the blood across the cell to the mitochondria and (2) to store small amounts of oxygen in the muscle cells. The storage function is generally considered insignificant because the total amount that can be stored by all of the muscles in the body is only about 240 ml.

Although training has been reported to increase the myoglobin content by 80 percent in the muscles of rats (Pattengale & Holloszy, 1967), recent research with human subjects has failed to validate this effect. For example, Svedenhag and coworkers (1983) could not produce an increase of myoglobin in a group of human subjects after eight weeks of training.

Regardless of these results, the door should not be closed on myoglobin increases with training. It seems reasonable to assume that a substance that serves such an important function during exercise would be amenable to increases with proper training. It would, therefore, be a good idea to consider myoglobin increases as one of the important outcomes of endurance training and to plan programs to encourage this effect until evidence to the contrary is overwhelming.

Mitochondrial changes Mitochondria are the small "chemical plants" in muscle cells where aerobic metabolism takes place. Muscle fibers contain many mitochondria, and they increase in both size and number with training (Kiessling, Piehl, & Lundquist, 1971; Morgan et al., 1971). Increases of 60 percent have been reported after endurance training.

Mitochondrial increases help in one very important way to reduce the rate of lactic acid production. With more mitochondria available, there are a greater number of locations where aerobic metabolism can take place within each muscle fiber. This makes more energy available from that source during each minute of exercise. This effect (and, perhaps, an increase in myoglobin) probably accounts for trained athletes being able to use a larger percentage of their $\dot{V}O_2$max without increasing lactic acid production.

Increases of aerobic enzymes When mitochondria increase in size and number, the quantities of aerobic enzymes within them also increase. This change causes aerobic metabolism to proceed at a faster rate due to the larger quantities of enzymes available to run the process.

The enzyme that is believed to play the most important role in regulating the rate of aerobic metabolism is succinate dehydrogenase (SDH). Increases of 39 to 95 percent have been reported after endurance training (Costill, 1978; Eriksson, Gollnick, & Saltin, 1973; Gollnick et al., 1973a). Other mitochondrial enzymes that increase with training are citrate synthase (Baldwin et al., 1972), aconitase, isocitrate dehydrogenase, x-ketoglutarate dehydrogenase, and malate dehydrogenase (Holloszy, Oscai, Don, & Mole, 1970). The activities of enzymes of the electron transport chain have also been shown to increase with endurance training (Gollnick et al., 1973a).

The enzyme hexokinase is unique in that it is involved with anaerobic metabolism yet appears to increase most through endurance training (Morgan et al., 1971). Hexokinase regulates the breakdown of glucose-6-phosphate to fructose-6-phosphate. This process takes place early in the anaerobic phase of metabolism, just after glucose enters the muscles. So, an increase in the activity of this enzyme probably improves endurance by increasing the amount of blood glucose that can be taken up by the muscles. In one study, the hexokinase activity of endurance-trained rats increased between 30 and 170 percent (Baldwin et al., 1973).

The glucose-alanine cycle This process can reduce lactate production by removing some of the pyruvic acid that was produced during anaerobic metabolism before it can combine with hydrogen ions to form lactic acid (Felig & Wahren, 1971). The pyruvic acid combines with ammonia to form the protein alanine. Alanine is then transported to the liver, where it can be converted to glucose and stored as glycogen or poured back into the bloodstream and carried to the muscles to be used for energy. Interestingly enough, this cycle functions during short sprints as well as endurance events (Weicker et al., 1983).

The glucose-alanine cycle has been estimated to supply between 10 and 15 percent of the total energy requirement during training (McArdle, Katch, & Katch, 1981). Studies suggest that the conversion of glucose to alanine is a trainable response. Brooks and Fahey (1984) reported an increased use of alanine after training. Activity of the major enzyme that regulates this reaction, alanine transaminase, was also found to increase with training (Mole, Baldwin, Terjung, & Holloszy, 1973).

The malate-aspartate shuttle This mechanism can reduce the rate of lactic acid production by removing some hydrogen ions before they combine with pyruvic acid. It begins in Krebs cycle, where aspartic acid is formed in the process of converting malic acid to oxaloacetic acid. As part of this conversion, hydrogen ions are released from NADH so that they can enter the electron transport chain. Once the hydrogen ions have been released, the NAD^+ that remains is free to pick up other hydrogen ions before they combine with pyruvic acid to form lactic acid.

The major enzymes of this process—aspartate transaminase and malate dehydrogenase—have been reported to increase as much as 60 percent in humans after endurance training (Holloszy, 1975). So, the malate-aspartate shuttle may also play a small, but important, role in reducing lactic acid production during exercise.

Increasing the Rate of Lactic Acid Removal from Muscles

Lactic acid that is removed from working muscle fibers will not be available to reduce pH. Consequently, athletes can supply more energy anaerobically and, thus, faster without creating severe acidosis when lactic acid can be removed from muscles rapidly. Any training effects that increase the rate of lactic acid removal should play a major role in improving performance. That role will be greater in longer races because there is more time to remove lactic acid. Although smaller in magnitude, the effect will also be significant in shorter races. In fact, it may be the most important aerobic training effect in 100 and 200 races.

Several factors mediate the rate of lactic acid removal from muscles. Many of them involve central circulatory mechanisms that pick up the lactic acid and transport it away from muscles. Lactic acid may also be removed by diffusing from working muscle fibers to those that are resting within a single muscle group. Some possible mechanisms for circulatory removal and diffusion of lactic acid between muscle fibers are described in the next sections.

Removal of Lactic Acid by the Circulatory System An improved cardiac output should increase the rate of blood flow so that each red blood cell can pick up lactic acid, take it elsewhere, and return for more, in less time. This effect should operate only during maximum efforts. Training has not been shown to increase cardiac output at submaximum rates of speed.

Because stroke volume is reduced at fast speeds, and because it is such an important component of cardiac output, some experts have suggested that both can be improved best by training at slow speeds, where stroke volume is maximum or near maximum. This suggestion makes good sense. Astrand & Rodahl (1977) showed that training speeds between 50 to 60 percent of maximum should be ideal for this purpose. The effects of such training on stroke volume can be monitored by charting swimmers' heart rates at these speeds. Their heart rates will decrease when their stroke volumes increase.

Improved blood shunting should also increase lactate removal during maximum efforts. Although not definite, it is likely that this mechanism also operates when athletes are swimming at submaximum rates of speed.

Additionally, an increase in muscle capillaries should definitely increase lactic acid removal during both maximum and submaximum swims. An increase of muscle capillaries provide a greater surface area for diffusion at any speed.

An increase of cardiac output is a central effect that can be produced by endurance training of any type. Improved blood shunting and capillarization are peripheral effects that can only be enhanced in the muscles used in training. Therefore, swimming will be more beneficial for these effects than nonswimming forms of exercise.

Lactic Acid Removal by Muscle Fibers Although improvements of circulatory function should play a major role in improving lactic acid removal, they are not the only mechanisms in this process. Another mechanism may be the diffusion of lactic acid from working muscle fibers to adjacent resting fibers within the same muscle.

It is well known that only a portion of the fibers within a muscle are working at any one time; a sizable number of inactive fibers are also present. These fibers have lower concentrations of lactic acid; thus, the pressure gradient will favor the diffusion of lactic acid out of the working fibers and into those that are inactive. This will provide a very rapid removal route because the fibers are in such close proximity that the diffusion distance is minimal. Once inside those fibers, lactic acid can be oxidized or converted to glucose. In the meantime, the concentration of lactic acid will reduce in working muscles and, consequently, delay acidosis. Brooks (1986) has estimated that, at least, 50 percent of the lactic acid produced during exercise diffuses into adjacent fibers. So, this mechanism probably plays a very important role in removing lactic acid during exercise.

The amount of lactic acid that diffuses from working to resting fibers is determined by: (1) the ratio between working and resting fibers, (2) the difference in lactate concentrations between them, and (3) their proximity. The final two are probably not amenable to training. The ratio can be changed by improving stroke efficiency. The number of fibers that are contracting at any one time are influenced by the skill of the swimmer. Swimmers with good propulsive efficiency and few extraneous movements probably use fewer muscle fibers to produce a particular speed. This leaves more resting fibers available to pick up lactic acid.

It seems logical that the repeats designed to improve the rate of lactate removal should be fast enough to produce a reasonable amount of lactic acid in the muscles, thus creating the need to transport it away from them. On the other hand, the swims should not be so fast that swimmers become exhausted within a few minutes, otherwise the duration of the repeats will not be sufficient to produce the desired training effect. Swimming at or just above the anaerobic threshold should be best for this purpose, because aerobic metabolism is overloaded and anaerobic metabolism causes lactic acid to accumulate at a slow, but steady rate.

The training effects that improve aerobic capacity are summarized in the following box.

ADAPTATIONS THAT IMPROVE THE ABILITY TO TRAIN

There are two training effects that improve the ability to train: (1) an increase in muscle glycogen storage and (2) an enhanced rate of fat metabolism. They are important to success, because when athletes can train longer or more intensely, they stand a better chance of producing adaptations that improve their competitive performances.

Training Effects That Improve Aerobic Capacity

A Reduced Rate of Lactic Acid Production

This effect is largely a result of the following adaptations:

1. Increased capillarization around working muscle fibers
2. Improved blood shunting
3. Perhaps an increase in muscle myoglobin
4. Increases in the size and number of mitochondria in working muscle fibers
5. Increased activity of the enzymes that regulate aerobic metabolism
6. Improved function of the glucose-alanine cycle
7. Improved function of the malate-aspartate shuttle

An Increased Rate of Lactic Acid Removal from Working Muscle Fibers

1. Increased removal by the circulatory system, which occurs through the following adaptations:
   a. Improved cardiac output
   b. Improved blood shunting
   c. Increased capillarization around working muscle fibers
2. Increased removal by the diffusion of lactic acid to nonworking muscle fibers

Table 3-1. Training Effects That Improve Aerobic, Nonaerobic, and Anaerobic Capacities

Physiological Mechanism	Untrained/ Trained	Percentage of Improvement
Aerobic Training Effects		
Glycogen storage, mmol/g wet muscle − 1	85/120	40–50
Number of mitochondria		90–100
Mitochondrial size		200–300
Aerobic enzymes		39–95
Maximum stroke volume, ml/b	120/180	40–50
Maximum cardiac output, l/min	20/30–40	50–75
Resting heart rate, bpm	70/40	−40–50
Maximum heart rate	190/180	0–5
Blood volume, l	5/6	20–30
Hemoglobin, g/kg-1		15–20
Muscle capillaries		40–50
Blood shunting		25–50
VO_2max, ml/kg/min	40–50/60–80	30–40
Lactate production		−28–50
Rate of fat metabolism		15–20
Nonaerobic Training Effects		
ATP, mmol/g wet muscle	5/6	10–15
CP, mmol/g wet muscle	17/18	2–5
Anaerobic Training Effects		
Peak lactic acid, mmol/l	12/14	10–20
Buffer capacity		30–40
Anaerobic enzymes		2–20

Increased Muscle Glycogen Storage

Muscle glycogen provides the major source of fuel for all swimming events longer than 50 m. With a short rest and good diet, there is usually enough glycogen stored in muscles to provide the energy needed for swimming races. Training is a different matter, however. Swimmers are frequently low in muscle glycogen when they train hard for several days in a row without a break.

One important effect of endurance training is an increase in the amount of glycogen that muscles can store. Increases of 40 to 60 percent are not uncommon (McArdle, Katch, & Katch, 1981; Wilmore & Costill, 1988). This amount can be increased another 50 percent or more for a short time through carbohydrate loading, although it is doubtful that carbohydrate loading will benefit swimmers in training or competition, because no more than a normal amount of muscle glycogen is needed even in the longest swimming races.

Increased Fat Metabolism

The release of energy from fat metabolism is too slow to meet the demand for ATP replacement during competitions. It can supply a substantial amount of energy during training, however.

One very important effect of endurance training is to increase the amount of energy that can be provided from fat during practice repeats. Before training, the percentage of the total energy furnished by fat is between 35 and 40 percent. This amount will increase to 50 to 60 percent after training (Holloszy et al., 1986).

An increase in fat metabolism will reduce the use of muscle glycogen so that more will be available for faster repeats later in the same or subsequent sessions. An increase in fat metabolism also reduces muscle glycogen use from day to day, so swimmers can train faster twice a day for several days at a time. The best form of training for improving fat metabolism is to swim long sets of repeats on very short rest intervals (5 to 15 seconds). These swims should be completed at moderate speeds, where the aerobic metabolism of fat can provide a significant portion of the energy needed.

The effects of training on each phase of metabolism have been summarized in Table 3-1. Typical improvements with training are indicated in percentages. Average values for untrained and trained persons are also listed, where they are known.

CHAPTER 4

Training Principles and the Anaerobic Threshold

The previous two chapters were concerned with the *why* of training. The purpose of this and all of the chapters that follow in Part I are to describe *how* to train. Information from the preceding chapters is applied to suggest training procedures based on scientific information. The first part of this chapter includes discussions of the principles of training. The anaerobic threshold theory of training is covered in the final part.

PRINCIPLES OF TRAINING

There is no one best way to train the energy systems of the human body, but all training programs must follow certain principles to be successful: (1) adaptation, (2) overload, (3) progression, and (4) specificity.

The Adaptation Principle

The purpose of training programs is to produce metabolic, physiological, and psychological adaptations that allow swimmers to perform better. The term *adaptation* pertains to changes that occur in response to training. One example of the adaptation process is an increase in muscle mitochondria, which takes place as follows. When training increases the demand for aerobic energy, the number and size of muscle mitochondria increase, so that these "chemical factories," where aerobic metabolism takes place, become larger and more numerous. This enables an athlete to provide more energy from aerobic metabolism so that he can swim farther without becoming fatigued.

The adaptation process occurs when the tissues are stimulated maximally, or nearly so. This stimulation will cause some *catabolism,* or breaking down of tissues, during the work itself. However, those tissues will rebuild larger, stronger, and more functional during the recovery period if sufficient nutrients are available. The repair process is called *anabolism*. There must always be a balance between the catabolic and anabolic processes during training. If training is not sufficiently intense to cause some catabolism, there will be no stimulation for rebuilding. On the other hand, if the rate of catabolism exceeds the rate of anabolism, the athlete's physiological systems will deteriorate over time, as will his performance.

There are at least three steps in the adaptation process:

1. Creating the need for more energy with training
2. Providing the proper nutrients to build and repair tissue
3. Providing athletes with enough rest to build and repair tissue

Finally, once the adaptation process has been completed, it will be necessary to increase the duration and/or intensity of training to create further adaptations. This brings us to the next two principles of training: overload and progression.

The Overload Principle

The basis of this principle is that adaptations take place only when the demands of training are greater than the usual demands made on a particular physiological mechanism, in other words, when the particular mechanism is *overloaded*. For example, when training creates a demand for greater than normal amounts of aerobic metabolism, muscle mitochondria will increase in size and number in order to meet that demand.

This principle, although simple in definition, is quite complex in application because while the demands of training must be sufficient to stimulate adaptation, they cannot be too great or the training effect will be lost through injury or overtraining. If the amount of overload exceeds the tolerance of a particular physiological system, that system will simply break down.

The Progression Principle

A particular training load will only remain an overload until the swimmer adapts to it. At that point, the intensity and/or duration must be increased before any further adaptations will happen. The step-by-step process of increasing the overload is called *progression*.

Figure 4-1 illustrates the importance of overload and progression in the training process. It depicts changes in the blood lactic acid content of a treadmill runner over a training period of approximately 50 days. A reduction of blood lactic acid at a particular speed is a good indicator of improved aerobic capacity. Notice that reductions took place only when training speeds were progressively increased.

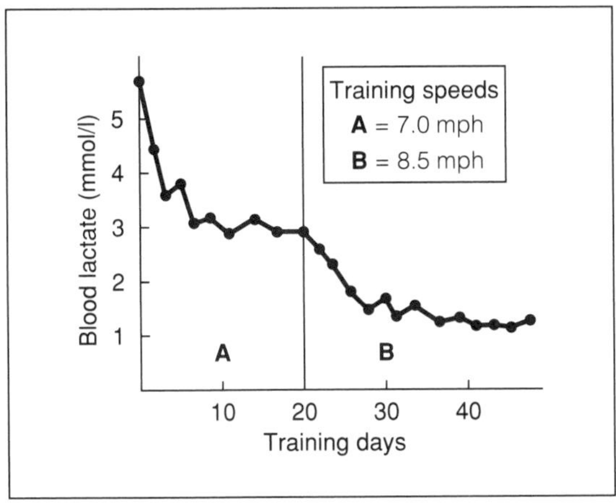

Figure 4-1. The effect of overload and progression on aerobic endurance as measured by decreases in blood lactic acid. (Adapted from Astrand & Rodahl, 1977)

The runner portrayed in Figure 4-1 began on day 1 running at a speed of 7.0 mph. You can see that the lactic acid content of his blood decreased from slightly more than 5 mmol/l to less than 3 mmol/l after only 10 days of training at that speed. Obviously, running at 7.0 mph was an overload during the first 10 days of training. Notice, however, that blood lactic acid did not decrease further over the next 10 days (day 10 to 20) of training at that same speed because the athlete's aerobic system had adapted to running at 7.0 mph and this speed no longer represented an overload. Another significant reduction in blood lactic acid occurred when the running speed was increased to 8.5 mph after day 20. Once again, that reduction took place during the first 10 days (day 20 to 30) at the new speed and was followed by a plateau over the next 20 days (day 30 to 50) of running.

This graph clearly shows that athletes, including swimmers, cannot train at the same speeds week after week and expect to continue improving their aerobic capacity, or other capacities for that matter. They must gradually increase their training speeds throughout the season to provide a progressive overload.

The principles of overload and progression can be applied by manipulating the three variables of interval training:

1. The speed of swimming repeats, also referred to as training *intensity*.
2. The number of repeats, also referred to as training *volume*.
3. The rest interval between repeats, also referred to as training *density*.

Overload and progression can be applied by increasing one or more of these variables while maintaining the others at their usual level. For example, increasing swimming speed without reducing volume or density will provide overload and progression. An increase in volume with no change in speed or density will do likewise. Finally, density can be increased when the rest intervals between repeats are reduced while speed and volume remain unchanged. Training programs should include deliberate progression plans. Systematic increases in training intensity, duration, and density will produce greater amounts of adaptation with less risk of injury.

The Specificity Principle: A Different Interpretation

Like overload, the *specificity principle* is straightforward in definition but complex in application. This principle states that the physiological processes improved most by training will be those that are stressed most.

Problems can arise when coaches translate this principle too narrowly, misinterpreting it to mean that athletes should swim only at competition speeds so that the demands of training will be identical to those of competition. While this is certainly one form of specific training, it is not the only, nor even the most important form. Truly specific training includes swimming at speeds that will progressively overload all of the various phases of the metabolic system that supply energy for the replacement of adenosine triphosphate (ATP) during races.

While race-speed swimming will train the nonaerobic, anaerobic, and aerobic systems to provide energy in approximately the same proportions as supplied in competition, *only the dominant energy system will be overloaded sufficiently to produce a maximum training effect*. The other energy systems may not be overloaded optimally and will, therefore, not improve as much as they might with another form of training. This, in turn, will not allow the other systems to make the contribution to the energy supply during races that they might otherwise make.

The anaerobic system will be the one improved most when swimming at race speed is the dominant form of specific training while the other systems will be cheated. For example, the anaerobic system is stressed most by underdistance, race-speed repeats simply because a great deal of the energy required to swim at these speeds comes from that system in most races. On the other hand, the aerobic system will not receive the stimulation it needs to adapt maximally if most of the major sets are swum at race speeds in training because the accumulation of lactic acid will produce fatigue before swimmers have completed enough mileage to encourage the desired training effects.

The nonaerobic system also will not receive sufficient stimulation for maximum improvement by swimming at race speed, for a different reason, however. Training speeds need to be faster than those in competition to overload this system.

A broad interpretation of specificity should include at least three modes of training: (1) training that is specific to competition speeds (race-speed training), (2) training that is specific to muscle fibers, and (3) training that is specific to energy systems.

Training That Is Specific to Energy Systems A large number of studies endorse this type of specificity. Figure 4-2 illustrates the results of one of these. The three graphs depict the effects of both sprint and endurance training programs on the three energy systems. Figure 4-2*a* shows the effects of these two programs on the ATP-CP reaction, or nonaerobic system. Notice that the sprint training program improved this system most, while endurance training improved it only slightly. The relative effect of sprint and endurance training on blood lactic acid content is shown in Figure 4-2*b*. A reduction in lactic acid was produced most by endurance training and least by sprint training. As we discussed, a reduction in blood lactic acid accumulation reflects improved aerobic capacity. Finally, Figure 4-2*c* shows the effects of sprint and endurance training on the maximum amount of lactic acid that

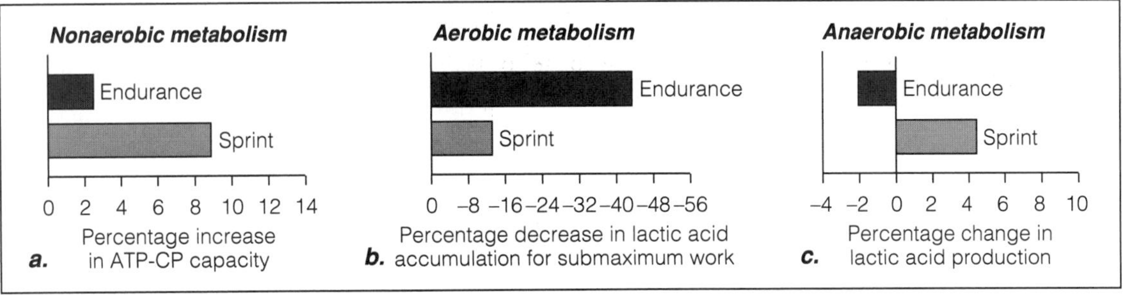

Figure 4-2. Effects of sprint and endurance training on the nonaerobic (*a*), aerobic (*b*), and anaerobic (*c*) energy systems. (Fox & Mathews, 1981)

can accumulate in the blood after exercise. An increase in this amount is a desirable anaerobic training effect because it shows that athletes can produce more lactic acid before becoming fatigued. This effect is produced only by sprint training. It is interesting that endurance training actually reduced the quantity of lactic acid that accumulated in the blood. This result indicates the possibility that an athlete's capacity for anaerobic metabolism may be reduced by endurance training. This possibility has important implications for training and will be discussed more thoroughly in Chapter 5.

Training That Is Specific to Muscle Fibers *Central* training effects refer to changes that take place in the central circulatory and respiratory systems. The effects will be the same regardless of the exercise performed and can be transferred to other forms of exercise. *Peripheral* training effects, on the other hand, occur only in and around the muscle fibers that are exercised. These training effects are specific to the muscle fibers used and are only transferrable to other activities where those same fibers do the work.

Proponents of cross-training (for example, running for swimmers) point to the importance of central training effects. However, studies using muscle biopsies to assess differences of physiological capacity between trained and untrained muscle fibers within the same person offer convincing evidence that peripheral training effects are more important. These studies have shown consistently that only the fibers that are used in training increase their (1) mitochondrial size and number, (2) myoglobin content, (3) glycogen, ATP, and CP storage, (4) aerobic, nonaerobic, and anaerobic enzyme activities, (5) capillary density, (6) buffering capacity, and (7) protein content.

This was shown convincingly in a study where subjects trained only one leg on a bicycle ergometer. The results are shown in Figure 4-3. Notice that, after training, the lactic acid concentration decreased markedly in the trained leg but only slightly in the untrained leg. The small improvement in the untrained leg probably resulted from central circulatory and respiratory adaptations, while the much greater decrease in lactic acid concentration in the trained leg was undoubtedly due to some of the peripheral training effects mentioned in the previous paragraph.

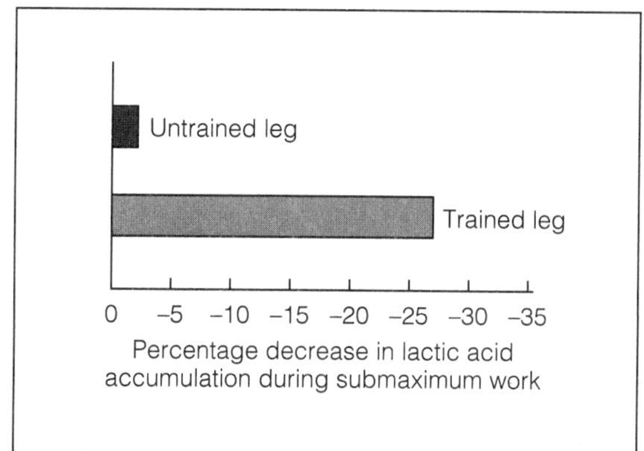

Figure 4-3. Comparison of aerobic training effects on a trained and untrained leg. (Fox & Mathews, 1981)

Additional studies have supported these results (Glina et. al., 1984; Hardman & Williams, 1983; Loftin, Boileau, Massey, & Lohman, 1988), showing clearly that the major adaptations to training are peripheral, that is, occurring only in muscles that are exercised. This means that swimmers cannot depend entirely on nonspecific training of the central circulatory and respiratory systems for top performance. They cannot hope to become conditioned for maximum performance unless they use the same muscle fibers in training that they will use in competition.

In light of the results of these studies and the many other works corroborating them, it seems clear that swimmers must do most of their training in the water. It also seems reasonable to recommend that they swim a large percentage of their training mileage in their main stroke or strokes. This is the only way that they can be sure of training the muscle fibers they will use in races. The amount of overlap in muscle use is probably greater between swimming strokes than between trained and untrained limbs. Nevertheless, we cannot assume that all of the muscle fibers used in swimming butterfly, for example, will be trained when we swim freestyle. Although the armstrokes are very similar for these two competitive styles, butterflyers sweep their hands out rather than down at the beginning of the underwater armstroke, and they also sweep their hands in to a greater extent. Because of these differences, it is reasonable to assume that swimmers utilize some muscle fibers in butterfly that are not called into play when they swim freestyle. There is even less similarity between the movement patterns in backstroke and breaststroke.

Another important point about specific training is that athletes must swim repeats at all levels of endurance and sprint training when they use these strokes. This will ensure that all phases of the metabolic system receive adequate stimulation within their muscle fibers. A swimmer's performance can only be as good as the weakest link in his or her muscle fiber chain.

How Specific Should Training Be? Let's recap the four points of view about training specificity that were presented in the previous discussion.

1. The major adaptations that improve performance take place in the muscular system. Adaptations in the respiratory and circulatory systems, while prob-

ably contributing to improvements in performance, are not as important as those that are produced in the muscles.

2. Only muscle fibers that are used in training will adapt maximally.
3. Swimming a particular stroke in training is the only sure way to produce adaptations in all of the muscle fibers that are used for that stroke.
4. Athletes should do both endurance and sprint training in their major strokes.

The evidence that athletes should train specifically seems irrefutable. Yet, the experiences of many athletes and coaches have caused them to take the opposite position. That is, swimmers will perform best when they do not swim their main stroke too frequently. We all know of swimmers, particularly butterflyers and breaststrokers, who swam well after doing most of their training with freestyle. Likewise, we have all had the experience of training swimmers in one stroke, only to have them perform much better in another stroke. The purpose of this section is to offer some thoughts on this seeming conflict between scientific evidence and practical experience.

I suspect that there may be at least two reasons why some athletes swim slower when they train extensively in a particular stroke. The first is that some of the muscle fibers involved in swimming that stroke may become overtrained. A second possibility is that athletes may use the wrong balance of training for those fibers. In either case, the trained fibers lose some of their aerobic and anaerobic capacities and the athletes will swim slower with that stroke. In contrast, their performances in other strokes might be very good because other fibers that have not been overtrained or mistrained are heavily involved.

The same idea may apply to different race distances. When swimmers overtrain or mistrain a particular phase of the metabolic process, they may swim slower in events where that particular phase is dominant. On the other hand, they may swim well at other distances where the metabolic process plays a minor role. For example, there have been many times when a swimmer who trains for distance events performs poorly in such races but posts a lifetime best in the sprints.

I realize this explanation is highly theoretical. Nevertheless, the evidence for training specificity is so compelling that some form of overtraining or mistraining seems the only possible explanation for lack of improvement when swimmers train specifically.

I have two recommendations for applying the principle of specificity adequately, without overdoing it.

1. Assuming a season of 24 weeks, swimmers should probably concentrate on mixed-stroke training (or freestyle training for nonfreestylers) during the first 8 to 12 weeks. They should concentrate on their main stroke(s) during the middle 6 to 10 weeks. Perhaps 60 to 70 percent of their total yardage should be performed in that style as kicking, pulling, and swimming repeats during that time. The swimmers should taper during the final 3 to 5 weeks.

2. Swimmers should swim stroke-specific sets for all energy systems. For example, butterflyers should not swim their endurance sets in freestyle and their sprint sets in butterfly. Many training programs use the front crawl stroke for nearly all of the endurance training sets. Butterfly, backstroke, or breaststroke are only swum in race-specific or sprint sets. The aerobic capacity of some muscle fibers may be neglected in these programs. Athletes must swim some endurance sets in their main stroke if they want to improve the aerobic capacity of all the muscle fibers they will use in competition.

THE ANAEROBIC THRESHOLD THEORY OF TRAINING

In the mid-1970s Dr. Alois Mader (Mader, Heck, & Hollmann, 1976) introduced a theory of endurance training that was different from the methods we were then using. The major difference between his and earlier theories was the idea that aerobic endurance could be improved best by training at speeds where aerobic metabolism was overloaded but anaerobic metabolism was not occurring at a rapid rate. Accordingly, the term anaerobic threshold became associated with this theory. The significance of the anaerobic threshold is that it identifies the best speed for endurance training. Mader believed that aerobic endurance could be improved as rapidly as possible with less likelihood of becoming overtrained when athletes swam at the anaerobic threshold.

The term *anaerobic threshold* was an unfortunate choice for this phenomenon. It gives a different impression from the one Mader intended. Persons who are new to this concept generally misinterpret it to mean that athletes should train at speeds where anaerobic metabolism begins. Actually, some anaerobic metabolism occurs at rest. In this sense, then, there is no speed where anaerobic metabolism begins. Anaerobic threshold, in popular use, really represents the speed where aerobic metabolism and lactate removal mechanisms are operating at near-maximum capacity and lactic acid is not accumulating in the muscles rapidly enough to produce acidosis.

Because the term *anaerobic threshold* does not accurately portray the metabolic events that take place, researchers have proposed more descriptive names. Some of the most popular have been *onset of blood lactate accumulation (OBLA)* (Sjodin & Jacobs, 1981), *lactate threshold* (Ivy et al., 1987), *lactate breakpoint* (DiVico, Simon, Lichtman, & Gutin, 1989), and *maximum lactate steady state (Maxlass)* (Griess et al., 1988).

The terms *lactate threshold* and *Maxlass* probably come closer to identifying Mader's original concept. Nevertheless, the name *anaerobic threshold* has achieved popular acceptance among athletes and coaches. Therefore, I will use that term when referring to this balance point, except where Maxlass seems more appropriate. It should be understood that both terms, as used here, refer to the same physiological phenomenon: *They identify the slowest training speed where aerobic metabolism is maximally overloaded, as indicated by the achievement of a balance between the rate of entrance of lactic acid into the blood and the rate of removal of lactic acid from the blood.*

Blood Testing

Another of Mader's important contributions to the study of exercise was his proposal to use blood lactic acid, rather than oxygen consumption, to measure the overload on aerobic metabolism. His belief was that the amount of lactic acid in an athlete's blood would increase rapidly when the capacity of the aerobic system to supply energy for muscular contraction had been exceeded. The linear increase in blood lactic acid showed that the rate of entry of lactic acid into blood had exceeded its rate of removal. In other words, lactic acid was being produced faster than it could be removed. Mader reasoned, therefore, that the swimming speed just before this linear increase was the optimal pace for endurance training. At that speed, the aerobic metabolic processes were being overloaded at near maximum levels while anaerobic metabolism was operating at a minimal rate. Consequently, athletes would be able to stress aerobic metabolism for long periods of time without becoming fatigued from acidosis. As a result, they should be able to do more endurance training each week and month of the season without risking overtraining.

Anaerobic threshold represents the same phenomenon that was designated by the fractional utilization of maximum oxygen consumption ($\dot{V}O_2max$), although the methods for assessing it are different. Mader's method for monitoring training according to the anaerobic threshold concept has become known by the term *blood testing,* and it works in the following manner.

Since much of the lactic acid produced during exercise diffuses out of the muscles and into the blood, it is possible to estimate the amount of anaerobic metabolism occurring in muscles by measuring the content of lactic acid in blood. This simple procedure requires taking a small sample of blood (5 to 25 microliters) from the ear or fingertip and measuring the amount of lactic acid (see Figure 4-4).

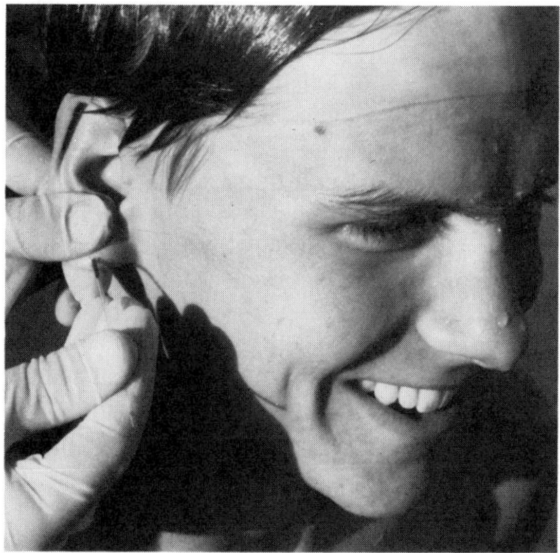

Figure 4-4. Swimmer Tom Glass having a sample of blood taken from his ear lobe after a time trial.

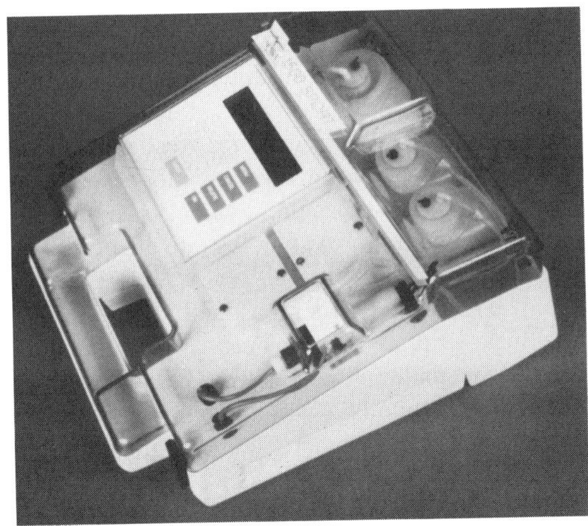

Figure 4-5. A Yellow Springs Model 1500 sport lactate analyzer. Twenty-five microliters of blood can be injected into the machine, and the quantity of lactic acid in that blood will be displayed on the digital readout.

Several machines have been developed that quickly and accurately measure the quantity of lactic acid in small samples of blood (see Figure 4-5). The blood sample is injected into the machine, and the quantity of lactic acid is read from the digital readout.

These samples are collected and analyzed after each of several swims at progressively faster speeds, and the results can be graphed to show an athlete's blood lactate response to exercise.

The Blood Lactate Response to Exercise

Figure 4-6 depicts the typical response of blood lactic acid to progressively faster speeds. The blood lactate content is registered on the vertical axis in millimoles per liter of blood (mmol/l). A millimole is equal to 1/1,000 of a mole. A mole is equal to the molecular weight of lactic acid in grams. Time is registered in minutes and velocity (m/sec) on the horizontal axis. This graph does not show the results of a typical blood test. Graphs of that type will be presented later in Chapter 8. The graph in Figure 4-6 is used simply to clarify the blood lactate response to exercise.

We will assume that the athlete is completing a continuous swim, beginning at a very slow speed, and that we can monitor his blood lactic acid levels continuously during the swim. His speed is increased 0.10 m/sec (approximately 5 seconds per 100 meters) every 5 minutes until fatigue occurs.

The tracing does not begin at zero on the vertical axis because a small amount of lactic acid is present in the blood even at rest. In this case, that amount is 1.00 mmol/l. The blood lactate content for most persons is between 0.80 and 1.50 mmol/l at rest, so this figure is within normal limits.

In the first 5 minutes, while swimming at 1.10 m/sec (1:30 per 100 m), there was a slight increase of lactic acid for the first minute. It then decreased to resting levels during the remaining 4 minutes. The initial rise occurred because lactic acid

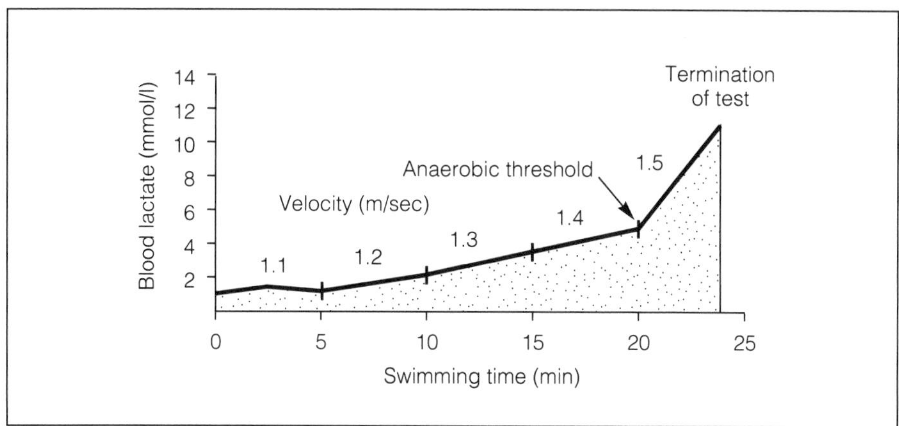

Figure 4-6. The blood lactate response during exercise.

was accumulating in the blood until the rates of aerobic metabolism and lactate removal caught up with the energy demand. After that, the oxygen supply was adequate to supply the needed energy and no more lactic acid accumulated in the muscles. The reduction in anaerobic metabolism plus an increased rate of removal from the blood caused the lactic acid concentration to return to the resting level of 1.0 mmol/l. Thus, the energy required to swim at this speed was well within the subject's aerobic capacity. No significant amount of anaerobic metabolism was required.

During the next 5 minutes, the increase in swimming speed to 1.20 m/sec (1:23.00 per 100 m) caused a gradual accumulation of blood lactate so that the level reached 2 mmol/l by the end of the period. Further, gradual increases were seen at 1.30 m/sec (1:17.00 per 100 m) and 1.4 m/sec (1:11.00 per 100 m) during the next two 5-minute periods. Blood lactic acid concentrations reached 3 mmol/l and 4 mmol/l during each of these periods of increased swimming velocity. The subject's capacity for aerobic metabolism was not exceeded, despite the fact that the lactic acid level of the blood was elevated during each successive increase of velocity. The gradual nature of the increases showed that the rate of anaerobic metabolism was minimal and/or that lactic acid was being removed from the muscles and blood almost as fast as it was being produced. Consequently, muscle pH was probably not being affected. This athlete could swim at these speeds for long periods without becoming fatigued. The anaerobic threshold had not been exceeded.

This situation changed during the fifth 5-minute period. The rate of increase became so rapid when the swimming velocity was elevated to 1.50 m/sec (1:06.00 per 100 m) that blood lactic acid climbed linearly during that work period. The lactic acid content of the subject's blood increased from 4 to 10 mmol/l quickly, and the resulting acidosis caused fatigue before the 5-minute work period could be completed. A large amount of energy was obviously being supplied by anaerobic metabolism because the rate of accumulation of lactic acid in the blood was far greater than its rate of removal. This linear increase of lactic acid shows that the athlete's anaerobic threshold had been exceeded.

The anaerobic threshold was reached at a swimming velocity of 1.40 m/sec in the example shown in Figure 4-6. This is inferred from the fact that blood lactate was still increasing gradually during the 5 minutes when he swam at 1.40 m/sec, while it rose rapidly from 4 to 10 mmol/l during the next 5-minute period, when his speed increased to 1.50 m/sec. Thus, in the case of this athlete, the optimal speed for endurance training (anaerobic threshold) would be at a velocity of 1.40 m/sec, which corresponds to a swimming speed of 1:11.00 per 100 m.

Where Is the Anaerobic Threshold Located?

Experts have not been able to agree on the location of the anaerobic threshold. In Figure 4-6, it was proposed to occur at a blood lactate concentration of approximately 4 mmol/l, where a linear increase in blood lactic acid took place. However, others believe that the anaerobic threshold is closer to a concentration of 2 mmol/l, where the first increase of blood lactic acid above resting levels occurs. Still others believe that it occurs at a different blood lactate for each person, the so-called individual anaerobic threshold. Other methods for identifying the anaerobic threshold have involved designating some fixed lactate increase above resting (Simon, Segal, & Jaffe, 1987) or a particular rate of increase above resting (Keul et al., 1979; Simon et al., 1981).

Contrary to the opinion expressed above, Kindermann and associates (1979) believe a blood lactate concentration of 2mmol/l represents a second threshold that they have termed the *aerobic threshold*. They believe it identifies the minimum training speed that will produce an endurance training effect, although it is not the optional velocity for this purpose.

Ten years of experience with blood testing have shown me that training at the individual anaerobic threshold is superior to training at some fixed value. Fixed thresholds, such as 2 or 4 mmol/l, tend to underestimate the optimal pace for some athletes while overestimating it for others.

While all of these "thresholds" have very high positive relationships with performance, relationships between individual anaerobic thresholds and performance have generally been higher than those for fixed thresholds of 2 and 4 mmol/l. They have ranged between 0.91 and 0.98 in several studies (Farrell et al., 1979; Hagberg & Coyle, 1983). On the other hand, relationships have ranged between 0.85 and 0.95 for fixed thresholds. The methods utilizing a fixed increase of blood lactate above resting and a particular rate of increase above resting have not been studied adequately at this time.

Questions and Criticisms About the Anaerobic Threshold Theory of Training

There is considerable controversy about the anaerobic threshold theory and the blood testing procedures for identifying it. Some of the controversial aspects are discussed in the following sections.

Does It Work? At the heart of the controversy is a concern that training speeds at the anaerobic threshold are not fast enough to overload aerobic metabolism. These speeds are generally slower than race pace and do not allow athletes to consume oxygen at maximum rates. Consequently, some experts doubt that they are sufficiently intense to improve performances. Earlier theories of endurance training stressed that the optimal training speeds for improving endurance were those where $\dot{V}O_2max$ occurred. These training speeds were considerably faster than those recommended by Mader. Recent studies have tended to confirm Mader's beliefs, however. Several have shown that the relationship between the anaerobic threshold and performance is much higher than the relationship between $\dot{V}O_2max$ and performance (LaFontaine, Londeree, & Spath, 1981; Sjodin, 1982; Sjodin & Jacobs, 1981; Sjodin, Schele, & Karlsson, 1982). In fact, Troup and Daniels (1986) and Montpetit and coworkers (1987) found no relationship between $\dot{V}O_2max$ and performance among a group of competitive swimmers. Similarly, Gullstrand and Holmer (1983) reported no increases of $\dot{V}O_2max$ for a group of athletes over several years of training, even though their performances continued to improve.

What proponents of $\dot{V}O_2max$ training failed to take into account was that athletes cannot maintain $\dot{V}O_2max$ speeds for very long without becoming fatigued. Consequently, the volume of training that could be performed at these speeds is not sufficient to produce maximum adaptations in aerobic metabolism.

The anaerobic threshold concept of training seems to be a valid method for determining the minimum training speed that will overload aerobic metabolism, because once the anaerobic threshold has been reached, any further increases in training speeds cause a linear increase in lactic acid. That increase signals one or both of the following events which indicate that a near-maximum rate of aerobic metabolism has been reached:

1. The maximum rate of entry of pyruvic acid and hydrogen ions into the aerobic phase of metabolism (the citric acid cycle) has been exceeded. As a result, these chemicals accumulate rapidly in the muscles, where they are converted to lactic acid.
2. The maximum rate of elimination of lactic acid from the muscles and blood has been exceeded because the rate of entry of lactic acid into the blood is now obviously greater than its rate of removal from the blood.

Do Blood Lactic Acid Values Provide Valid Estimates of the Metabolism Taking Place in Muscles? Although this matter is controversial, there is a reasonable body of research that indicates a linear relationship between muscle and blood lactate at mild to moderate levels of exercise. Several researchers have reported a high positive relationship of 0.91 between muscle and blood lactate at concentrations below 4 to 5 mmol/l (Jacobs & Kaiser, 1982; Jorfeldt, Juhlin-Dannfelt, & Karlsson, 1978; Robergs, Chwalbinska-Moneta, Costill, & Fink, 1989). After reaching concentrations of 4 to 5 mmol/l, muscle lactic acid tended to increase, while blood lactic acid concentrations plateaued. The results of the study by Jorfeldt and associates are shown in Figure 4-7. The bulk of evidence suggests that increases in blood lactic acid do represent elevated muscle lactate production.

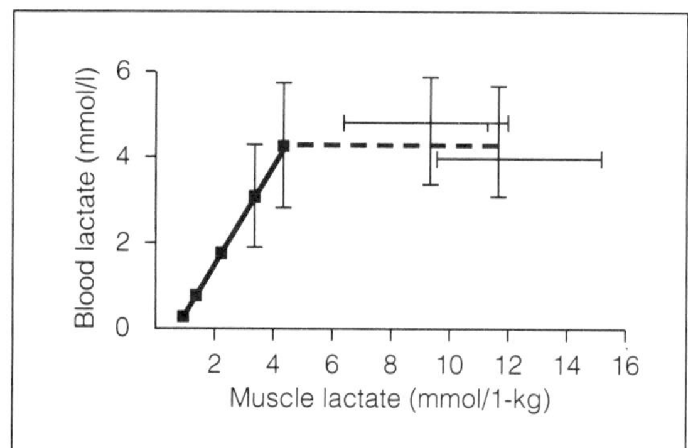

Figure 4-7. A comparison of muscle and blood lactic acid concentrations during exercise. (Jorfeldt, Juhlin-Dannfelt, & Karlsson, 1978)

Because increases of blood lactic acid seem to parallel muscle increases, it seems worthwhile to continue using blood testing to monitor training. Considering the ease with which blood lactic acid can be measured, compared to muscle lactate and oxygen consumption, it is certainly the most convenient method for evaluating metabolic happenings during training and competition.

Will Frequent Training Above the Anaerobic Threshold Hurt Endurance? A growing number of studies suggest that the answer to this question is yes. My experience as a coach leads me to agree. For example, Madsen and Olbrecht (1983) have reported that athletes who trained at speeds that produced blood lactate concentrations in the neighborhood of 6 mmol/l (which was probably above the anaerobic threshold for most) exhibited a deterioration of aerobic capacity. Hollmann and coworkers (1981) reported that subjects who trained for 6 weeks above the 4-mmol/l threshold did not improve their aerobic capacity. Heck and his associates (1985) reported similar results when subjects trained for 20 weeks at speeds above the fixed 4-mmol/l threshold. Mikesell and Dudley (1984) also reported that runners who did their endurance training at fast speeds lost aerobic capacity.

These studies suggest that aerobic capacity can deteriorate if an athlete trains too frequently above the anaerobic threshold. There are two principal reasons why this might happen. First, high rates of oxidation cause the accumulation of free radicals during endurance training. Free radicals, in turn, can damage the DNA and other structures of muscle cells, causing a loss of aerobic endurance (see Chapter 12 for a more complete discussion of free radicals).

Some coaches frequently complain that athletes will be training too slow if they swim at anaerobic threshold speeds, but nothing could be further from the truth. Training at the anaerobic threshold is one of the most difficult things a swimmer can do if the set has been constructed properly, that is, when it requires about 20 to 30 minutes to complete and is swum on short rest intervals. Athletes must put forth maximum efforts to swim at their anaerobic thresholds for that length of time.

The second reason that aerobic capacity can deteriorate is that intense training reduces the quantity of endurance work that can be accomplished. When training sets are completed above the individual anaerobic threshold, a steady increase of muscle lactate occurs, which reduces pH and causes fatigue within 10 to 20 minutes. Once swimmers become fatigued, it will probably require 10 to 30 minutes of easy swimming before muscle pH will be normalized and another intense set of repeats can be performed (Hermansen & Osnes, 1973). So, the actual volume of effective endurance training is usually reduced by swimming above the anaerobic threshold. The athlete who trains above the anaerobic threshold will typically spend a small amount of time swimming fast and a large amount of time swimming slow. Slow speeds are usually inadequate and fast repeats are too short to overload aerobic metabolism. Gullstrand (1985) has presented evidence that overtrained athletes experience a reversal of one important aerobic training effect. That is, their mitochondria actually decrease in size and number. It is possible that training too frequently with high levels of oxidation in the muscles causes this decrease in mitochondrial size and number and possibly other deteriorations that reduce aerobic capacity.

Admittedly, the evidence is far too scarce to be conclusive at this time. Nevertheless, the idea that training above the anaerobic threshold too often can reduce aerobic capacity fits with my experiences as a coach. I have seen athletes get worse when they did so. I have also seen the performances of those swimmers improve when they incorporated more threshold training into their programs.

Should Swimmers Compete in Training? Another frequent complaint is that threshold swimming takes the competition out of training. Each athlete repeats at his or her individual threshold pace without trying to match the speed of those who are repeating faster. Is this the way they should train, or will they become better competitors by racing with other swimmers in practice? This is an easy question to answer. Swimmers should compete with one another *but only in certain phases of their training*. Those phases are during sprint repeats and other high quality sets. They should not compete during threshold training. They will improve their aerobic endurance faster by training at speeds approximating their individual anaerobic thresholds, and they can train to compete in quality sets designed to improve anaerobic capacity.

Swimmers who adhere to an individual system of progressive overload in endurance training should not despair that they will never catch faster competitors. In fact, training at one's individual anaerobic threshold will usually improve a swimmer's aerobic capacity at a much faster rate than the usual hit-and-miss approach. The result will be that careful swimmers will pass many undertrained and overtrained competitors late in the season even though those swimmers had faster thresholds earlier.

Athletes should also understand that the anaerobic threshold only reflects the capacity for aerobic metabolism, not success in races. Although the performances of a swimmer will certainly improve when his or her anaerobic threshold improves, a fast anaerobic threshold does not guarantee success in competition. Many times, a swimmer with superior anaerobic capacity, pacing ability, and/or competitive ability can outswim competitors with faster anaerobic thresholds. This is especially true at distances of 200 m and less. Aerobic capacity accounts for only 60 to 70 percent of the performance at this race distance. So swimmers who are training more slowly than their competitors during endurance sets should not despair that they cannot beat those teammates, and they should be willing to race them during quality sets.

CHAPTER 5

Endurance and Sprint Training

According to the interpretation of training specificity I have proposed, it follows that two broad categories of training are needed by all swimmers: (1) *endurance training* for improving aerobic metabolism and (2) *sprint training* for improving anaerobic metabolism and power. These categories have been traditional parts of swim training for years. There are several subtypes of training within each category that may be new to some readers, however.

The categories of training are different from the ones described in the first edition of this textbook. The difference is more in terminology than substance. Training procedures are referred to by different names in this edition: *overload training* replaces *maximum oxygen consumption* ($\dot{V}O_2max$) *training; threshold endurance training* replaces *anaerobic threshold training;* and the procedures for *lactate tolerance training* include swimming at *race pace*. The changes in terminology were made in order to present the training process in more accurate and understandable terms.

ENDURANCE TRAINING

The purpose of endurance training is to improve aerobic capacity, allowing athletes to swim faster with less reliance on anaerobic metabolism so that lactic acid will accumulate at a slower rate, and acidosis will be delayed. Athletes who are endurance trained will be able to swim at a faster average pace through the first three-

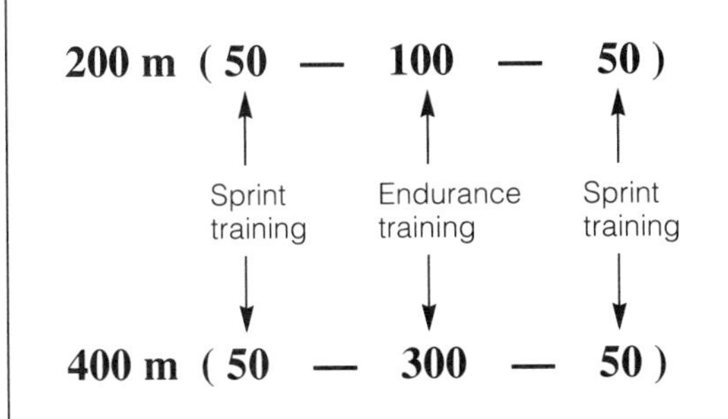

Figure 5-1. Relationship of the two forms of training to swimming races.

quarters of most races and still have the energy to sprint fast at the end. Endurance training is important for athletes in all events of 100 yd/m and longer. Sprint and endurance training play important and different roles in races. Those roles are illustrated for distances of 200 and 400 m in Figure 5-1. Sprint training is needed for getting races out fast, with less effort in the first 25 to 50 m, and for bringing them back fast in the last 25 to 50 m. The purpose of endurance training is to help swimmers maintain a faster average pace through the middle of the race without becoming overly fatigued. Since the contributions of sprint training are greatest only in the first and last 25 to 50 m of races, the importance of endurance training increases as the race becomes longer.

Levels of Endurance Training

Training at speeds that correspond to the anaerobic threshold is the most effective way to improve aerobic capacity. However, a good program of endurance training must also include other efforts at both slower and faster speeds.

The reason for swimming some repeats slower than anaerobic threshold speeds is quite compelling. *It is not physically possible to train at anaerobic threshold speeds day after day*. The main energy source at anaerobic threshold speeds is muscle glycogen, and it becomes impossible to train fast when muscle glycogen is nearly depleted. Typical, two-a-day training sessions that include 4,000 to 6,000 m at anaerobic threshold paces will reduce the muscles' glycogen supply by nearly 80 percent (Costill, Maglischo, & Richardson, 1992). It will then require 24 to 48 hours to replace it before similar sets can be swum again. So, although training at the individual anaerobic threshold may be the most effective way to improve aerobic metabolism, the muscles' glycogen supply will only permit such training for one or two sessions in a row before depletion becomes so severe that swimmers are forced to swim slower. At slower speeds, fat becomes a principal energy source and the rate of muscle glycogen replacement will exceed its rate of use, so the muscles will be able to replace their supply.

The preceding explanation may bring two questions to mind: (1) Why can't athletes swim fast while using fat for energy? and (2) Why not rest instead of swim on days when muscle glycogen needs replacing?

The answer to the first question was supplied in Chapter 1. Fat metabolism can only proceed aerobically, and that process is slower than the aerobic metabolism of glycogen. Several additional steps are required to change fat to a substance that can enter Krebs cycle. Consequently, fat metabolism cannot recycle adenosine triphosphate (ATP) rapidly enough to support anaerobic threshold speeds. Those speeds will only be possible if the swimmers draw heavily on muscle glycogen.

The answer to the second question is that slow swimming can improve aerobic capacity, although at a slower rate. Nevertheless, when muscle glycogen is nearly depleted, athletes must settle for these benefits or none at all. Although resting will allow muscle glycogen to be replaced faster, this advantage must be weighed against the loss of conditioning that might result from training only a few days each week. It is better to train at less-than-maximum efforts than not to train at all.

Many benefits can be gained from training while muscle glycogen is being replaced. Drills can be practiced to improve strokes, starts, and turns. Stroke volume and other central circulatory and respiratory adaptations can be achieved by swimming slower than anaerobic threshold speeds. Additionally, all aspects of aerobic metabolism can probably experience some improvement even though, as mentioned, the extent of the overload will not be optimal.

In addition to swimming slower during certain times of the week, there are also times when swimmers should train slightly above threshold speeds, because training at that level provides a combined aerobic-anaerobic mix of energy metabolism that is similar to that which takes place in most races. Training slightly above the threshold, because it duplicates the aerobic-anaerobic conditions of competition, may be the most effective form of training for producing the important muscular adaptations that improve performance. This may be particularly true during periods when athletes plateau and can't seem to improve their race times. During these periods, swimming slightly above the threshold may provide the training overload that will reduce the production of lactic acid and/or increase its removal during races so that muscle pH does not decline as rapidly as before.

Considering the benefits, you may wonder why swimmers shouldn't do all of their endurance training above the anaerobic threshold. There are two reasons:

1. Swimming above an athlete's present anaerobic threshold includes a large component of anaerobic metabolism. Aerobic endurance may deteriorate if this type of training is used too frequently.
2. Because of the large anaerobic component, the volume of swimming that can be done above the anaerobic threshold will be inadequate for effective endurance training.

Training at speeds that are faster than the anaerobic threshold should be viewed as a supplement to, not a substitute for, regular endurance training.

Based on the previous discussion, athletes should use three levels of endurance training: the level below threshold speeds is referred to as *basic endurance training;* the second is *threshold endurance training;* and the level beyond threshold speeds is termed *overload endurance training*. These three levels are also referred to in this text by the following terms:

1. End-1 (basic endurance training)

2. End-2 (threshold endurance training)
3. End-3 (overload endurance training)

Threshold Endurance Training (End-2) The purpose of this level of endurance training is to improve aerobic capacity at the fastest possible rate without overstressing a swimmer. This is the most effective type of endurance training that a swimmer can perform. To do it effectively, however, the athlete must know the swimming speed that corresponds to his or her individual anaerobic threshold. The best method for determining this speed is blood testing. Unfortunately, it is not possible for many swimmers and coaches to use blood testing because it requires expensive equipment. For this reason, several methods for estimating the anaerobic threshold that require only a pace clock will be presented in Chapter 8.

One of the reasons why threshold endurance speeds are so effective is that they require contractions of both the fast-twitch (FT) and slow-twitch (ST) fibers in muscle groups. Thus, these speeds improve the aerobic capacity of both fiber groups, whereas only ST fibers are affected at slower speeds.

The following box provides some guidelines for constructing threshold endurance sets. Any repeat distance can be used for this purpose, even 25s. The speed, rest interval, and total distance of the set determine the training effect more so than the repeat distance. Repeat sets are listed both by the time required for completion and the repeat distance so that they can be adapted for swimmers of any age or ability level.

Guidelines for Constructing Threshold Endurance Sets

1. Set distance: 2,000 to 4,000 yd/m for senior swimmers, or 25 to 40 minutes for others
2. Repeat distances: any distance from 25 to 4,000 yd/m
3. Rest intervals: 10 to 30 seconds
4. Speed: individual anaerobic threshold speed, or maximum effort over the distance of the entire set
5. Suggested mileage per week: 12,000 to 16,000 yd/m

For best results, the total distance of the set should require 25 to 40 minutes to complete. Senior swimmers can usually finish 2,000 to 4,000 yd/m in this time. Age group, older Masters, and inexperienced athletes can probably swim between 800 and 3,000 yd/m in 25 to 40 minutes, depending on their age and ability level.

The send-off times should provide 10 to 60 seconds of rest between repeats. The shorter rest periods (10 to 30 seconds) should be used for repeats of 200 yd/m and less, and the interval may be slightly longer for longer swims. Up to 1 minute of rest can probably be allowed for repeats of 800 yd/m and longer without interfering with the training effect, although it is not necessary to rest for this length of time.

Repeat speeds should be sufficient to overload aerobic metabolism in both the FT and ST muscle fibers. These will be speeds that correspond to each swimmer's individual anaerobic threshold. For most swimmers, these speeds will produce blood lactic acid concentrations between 3 and 5 mmol/l. It is not really necessary to equate repeat speeds with blood lactic acid concentrations, however. If athletes complete these sets at the fastest possible average speed, they will be swimming near their individual anaerobic threshold. The set is too long to permit them to swim faster than anaerobic threshold speeds, because if they swim faster the increased rate of lactic acid accumulation would cause acidosis after the first 10 to 20 minutes.

The major source of energy for ATP recycling will be muscle glycogen at threshold speeds. Working muscles usually lose 50 to 70 percent of the muscle glycogen they have stored when swimmers complete one of these sets. Therefore, each set or two should be followed by 1 to 1½ days of training at reduced speeds or duration. For this reason, athletes will probably not be able to swim much more than 12,000 to 16,000 yd/m per week at threshold intensities.

Overload Endurance Training (End-3) Athletes swim slightly above their individual anaerobic threshold in this type of endurance set. As mentioned, this form of training is very specific to the actual metabolic conditions encountered in races. It is also an excellent form of training for improving $\dot{V}O_2max$. Guidelines for constructing overload endurance sets are listed in the following box.

Guidelines for Constructing Overload Endurance Sets

1. Set distance: 1,500 to 2,000 yd/m for senior swimmers, or 20 to 25 minutes for others
2. Repeat distances: 25 to 2,000 yd/m
3. Rest intervals: 30 seconds to 2 minutes
4. Speed: 1 to 2 seconds per 100 yd/m faster than threshold speeds, or the fastest possible average for the entire set distance
5. Suggested mileage per week: 4,000 to 6,000 yd/m

My experience has been that athletes can maintain these speeds for only 20 to 25 minutes. Consequently, the optimal distance for overload endurance sets is between 1,500 and 2,000 yd/m for senior swimmers. Several researchers have reported similar results (Madsen & Lohberg, 1987; Stegmann & Kindermann, 1982). The time frame of 20 to 25 minutes is a better guide than yardage for determining the optimal length for overload endurance sets where younger swimmers, older swimmers, and those with less ability or experience are concerned.

Any repeat distance from 25 yd/m up to continuous swims of 2,000 yd/m can be used for this purpose. The send-off times should provide for rest intervals that are similar to those of threshold sets, only slightly longer. Twenty seconds to 1 minute is good for distances less than 400 yd/m, and 1 to 2 minutes can be used for longer repeat distances.

For most swimmers, overload endurance training speeds correspond to those that produce blood lactic acid concentrations of 4 to 6 mmol/l, although values of 3 to 5 mmol/l may be more suitable for some well-trained endurance swimmers. A simpler method for estimating the proper pace is to subtract 1 to 2 seconds per 100 yd/m from threshold endurance training paces.

Overload endurance training is very strenuous and cannot be used too frequently or aerobic capacity may deteriorate from overtraining. For this reason, I suggest that senior swimmers complete only 4,000 to 6,000 yd/m per week at this intensity. The total for age group swimmers should be revised downward to 3,000 to 4,000 yd/m because of their slower training speeds.

The rate of muscle glycogen depletion will be very rapid when swimming at overload endurance speeds. However, the sets are usually too short to cause complete depletion, unless the amount stored was low to begin with. Accordingly, overload endurance sets should not be attempted when low muscle glycogen levels are suspected.

Basic Endurance Training (End-1) Basic endurance sets provide a period of time when the rate of glycogen use is reduced below the rate of repletion so that the muscles can replace the glycogen used during threshold and overload endurance sets, while maintaining a training intensity that will improve some aspects of aerobic capacity. Both fat and muscle glycogen supply the energy for ATP recycling at this intensity. Fats provide perhaps 50 to 60 percent of the total, depending on the length and average speed of the set (Holloszy et al., 1986).

Another interesting aspect of basic endurance training concerns the selective depletion of FT and ST muscle fibers. Most of the work will be completed by ST fibers, providing time for even faster repletion of their FT counterparts.

An important training effect of basic endurance swimming is an increase in the rate of fat metabolism during exercise. When more of the energy for threshold and overload endurance swimming comes from fat, it produces a "sparing effect" on muscle glycogen, thus reducing the depletion of that substance. Consequently, athletes will be able to train more often at threshold speeds or faster without becoming glycogen depleted. In one study, muscle glycogen depletion during 1½ to 2 hours of cycling was 42 percent less after 12 weeks of endurance training while fat use was nearly doubled (Hurley et al., 1985). It is a good idea to stress basic endurance training early in the season so that swimmers can improve their rate of fat metabolism. This improvement will not benefit races directly, because fat metabolism is not an important source of energy during competition. The advantage lies in the fact that by sparing muscle glycogen swimmers will be able to train longer and more intensely later in the season. This should improve the magnitude of the aerobic and anaerobic training effects involving glycogen metabolism and lactic acid removal. Those effects will improve performance in competition.

Basic endurance training should be used extensively during the first 3 to 6 weeks of each new season. It should comprise perhaps 50 to 60 percent of the yardage devoted to endurance training during this time. Once the rate of fat metabolism has been increased, the percentage of this form of training can be reduced to 30 or 40 percent of the total. Threshold and overload training should be increased to cover the remaining 20 percent. Guidelines for constructing basic endurance sets are listed in the following box.

Guidelines for Constructing Basic Endurance Sets

1. Set distance: 2,000 to 10,000 yd/m for senior swimmers, or 20 to 120 minutes for others
2. Repeat distances: any repeat distance can be used
3. Rest intervals: 5 to 30 seconds
4. Speed: 2 to 4 seconds per 100 slower than threshold endurance speed

The proper speeds for these sets range from the speed at which the first rise in blood lactate above the resting level is noted (the aerobic threshold) up to the speed that is comfortably below a swimmer's individual anaerobic threshold. For most persons, that will be between blood lactic acid concentrations of 1 and 3 mmol/l. Another method for determining the proper range of repeat speeds for this level of endurance training is to add 2 to 4 seconds per 100 yd/m to threshold endurance speeds. My experience has been that, for most swimmers, this addition provides an intensity that is above the aerobic threshold and below the anaerobic threshold.

Set distances can range anywhere from 2,000 yd/m up to the maximum amount of time available for training during a particular session. A minimum set length of 20 minutes is probably required to achieve a significant endurance training effect. The maximum time can be as long as the motivation of the swimmer permits. The daily mileage for basic endurance training can be swum as a long, continuous set, or several shorter sets of repeats can be strung together for swimmers who don't like long sets.

Any repeat distance can be used from 25 yd/m up to and including swims of 10,000 yd/m or more. Send-off times should be very short, allowing no more than 5 to 30 seconds of rest between repeats. Longer rest intervals are not necessary at submaximum speeds, and they simply waste time. Furthermore, short rest intervals such as these also encourage swimmers to train below their individual threshold. Costill and coworkers (1988) have shown that athletes tend to swim faster (and burn more muscle glycogen) when rest intervals are increased to 60 seconds (and when the repeat distances are less than 200 yd/m).

SPRINT TRAINING

There are two main purposes for sprint training: (1) to increase sprinting speed so that swimmers can take races out faster and (2) to improve buffering capacity so that swimmers can maintain their speed in spite of accumulating lactic acid. The three most trainable mechanisms that will improve sprinting speed buffering capacity are: (1) stroke mechanics, (2) muscular power, and (3) anaerobic metabolism. Muscular power and anaerobic metabolism are discussed in this chapter. Stroke mechanics will be covered in Part II.

Muscular Power

Increases in muscular power make it possible for swimmers to apply more force to the water during each second of swimming. Muscular power can be increased by improving muscle size and strength and by improving muscle fiber recruitment patterns during swimming. The most accepted way to improve muscular size and strength is through resistance training, such as heavy weight training, circuit training, and the swim bench. These topics will be covered in Chapter 24. Swimming drills that can increase power are discussed in this chapter.

Anaerobic Metabolism

The importance of anaerobic metabolism to sprinters is unquestioned, because their speeds could not be maintained without high rates of glycolysis. To review, the amount of time that athletes can sustain high rates of anaerobic metabolism is limited by the amount of lactic acid they can accumulate before acidosis occurs.

Three Roles of Anaerobic Metabolism in Swimming Races Anaerobic metabolism plays three roles in improving sprint speed. The three together are often referred to as *anaerobic capacity.* The first role concerns the rate of lactic acid production in muscles. When that rate is increased by training, ATP can be recycled faster by glycolysis, making more energy available for muscular contraction. The end result will be that swimmers can maintain a near-maximum sprint for several additional seconds after their creatine phosphate (CP) supply has been nearly depleted in the first 5 to 10 seconds of a race.

The second role is to reduce the effect of lactic acid accumulation on muscle pH so that swimmers can use the energy from anaerobic metabolism to swim faster for a longer time before acidosis occurs. This process is known as *buffering*. Buffers convert the strong lactic acid to a weaker acid that does not reduce muscle pH so much. This makes it possible for swimmers to recycle more ATP through anaerobic metabolism before acidosis becomes severe.

The third role is to increase athletes' tolerance to pain. This allows them to push on toward their physiological limit rather than backing off too early. The same repeats can be used for training buffering capacity and pain tolerance. Repeat distances need to be adjusted somewhat for improving the rate of anaerobic metabolism, however. The three roles of anaerobic metabolism are listed in the following box.

Three Roles of Anaerobic Metabolism for Improving Sprint Speed

1. To increase the rate of lactic acid production
2. To improve buffering capacity
3. To improve pain tolerance

Three Types of Sprint Training

A combination of the roles played by muscular power and anaerobic metabolism points to the necessity for three types of training for improving sprint speed:

1. *Lactate tolerance training (Spr-1)*—for increasing buffering capacity and tolerance to the pain of acidosis
2. *Lactate production training (Spr-2)*—for increasing the rate of anaerobic metabolism
3. *Power training (Spr-3)*—for increasing the amount of muscular power that swimmers can apply when sprinting

Each of the three types of sprint training is discussed in the following sections. Because sprint training has not been studied as extensively as endurance training, most of the information presented is based on personal experience and the application of related research.

Lactate Tolerance Training (Spr-1) Lactate tolerance training operates principally through increasing buffering capacity in the muscles and blood and by improving tolerance to the pain of acidosis. Buffers react with lactic acid and weaken it by reducing the number of hydrogen ions it contains, thus lessening the effect of lactic acid on pH. In other words, the quantity of lactic acid that accumulates does not produce the same degree of acidosis it normally would. When buffering capacity is improved, swimmers are able to maintain a fast rate of lactic acid production longer before a decline of pH reduces this rate and causes them to slow down.

Recent research has left no doubt that buffering capacity is a trainable mechanism. Sharp and coworkers (1986) improved buffering capacity an average of 37 percent in a group of subjects who trained anaerobically. This resulted in a 22-percent increase of work output (anaerobic capacity) in a test of high-speed cycling to exhaustion. The average amount of lactic acid in the subjects' leg muscles (vastus lateralis) was 19 percent greater upon retesting after training, proving an increase in buffering capacity. At the same time, muscle pH was not as low as it had been when the subjects were tested before the training program began.

The subjects trained for 8 weeks, 4 days per week. They did eight 30-second all-out rides on a bicycle ergometer, resting 4 minutes between each ride. Figure 5-2 shows the results of this study. Notice that the amount of lactic acid in the subjects' legs increased from an average of 20 to nearly 25 mmol/kg following

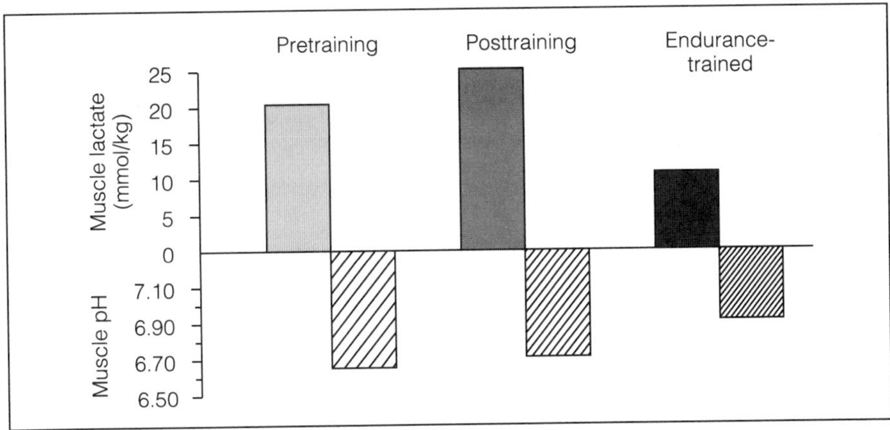

Figure 5-2. Effect of anaerobic training on muscle lactic acid content and pH. (Adapted from Sharp, Costill, Fink, & King, 1986)

training, yet the decline in pH was only 6.70 after training versus 6.65 prior to training.

Another method for improving anaerobic capacity may be through increasing psychological tolerance to the pain of progressive acidosis. I use the word "may" because the way an individual athlete reacts to acidosis could be a matter of motivation and, thus, not really amenable to training. On the other hand, some research suggests that pain tolerance can be trained. Hays and coworkers (1984) believe that they were able to improve the pain tolerance of rats with hard swim training. After training, the rats stayed on a hot plate (55°C) longer before jumping off. Perhaps in a similar manner, humans who test the limits of their tolerance to the pain of acidosis may be training themselves to ignore, or tolerate, that pain. As a result, they can persevere at speeds where they might have previously slowed down.

Constructing repeat sets for lactate tolerance training Lactate tolerance repeats should be swum very fast, and they should be long enough to produce severe acidosis. Acidosis should provide the stimulus needed for increasing muscle and blood buffers. Of course, the pain associated with acidosis should also furnish the requisite stimulus for improving tolerance to that pain. Research shows that the best distances for this purpose are between 75 and 200 yd/m. They produce the highest levels of lactic acid in the blood. Each swim should be at maximum or near-maximum speed. This category of training can also serve as race-pace training because it is challenging, but possible, to swim at race speed for underdistance repeats (repeats that are one-quarter to one-half of the race distance).

The rest intervals should be long enough to restore muscle pH to normal or near-normal values before another repeat is attempted at the same intensity. Rest periods of 5 minutes or longer should suffice for this purpose (Krukau, Volker, & Leisen, 1987; Troup, Bradley, Hall, & Van Handel, 1985). Swimmers should probably not be expected to do more than three to six such swims in a training session. This recommendation is supported by the work of Gollnick, Armstrong et al. (1973), which showed that FT muscle fibers were becoming depleted after four to six all-out rides on a bicycle ergometer and that ST fibers were being called upon increasingly to provide the energy for ATP recycling. Their subjects had undoubtedly reached the point of diminishing returns for improving anaerobic metabolism after the sixth ride.

Repeats of 25 and 50 yd/m can also be used for lactate tolerance training if they are performed on short rest intervals and in sets of three to eight. Although these distances are too short to produce severe acidosis during each swim, the cumulative effect of three to eight such swims will produce severe acidosis if the rest interval is so short that the pH is not restored to a normal level between repeats. Three to six sets of these repeats are probably optimal for any single training session. The athletes should be given time to recover between each set by swimming easy for 10 to 20 minutes.

Although research has not disclosed the optimal weekly mileage for lactate tolerance training, my suggestion is that athletes swim no more than 2,000 to 3,000 yd/m per week at this level. Four hundred to 600 yd/m per week would probably be adequate for young age group swimmers (less than 11 years old).

Broken swims are one excellent method for improving buffering capacity. Races are another form of lactate tolerance training. Competitions should be calculated as part of the weekly mileage assigned to this form of training. Suggestions for constructing lactate tolerance sets are summarized in the following box.

Guidelines for Constructing Lactate Tolerance Sets

1. Set distance: 300 to 1,000 yd/m
2. Repeat distances: 75 to 200 yd/m; 25s and 50s can also be used in sets of 2 to 12 repeats. 3 to 6 sets are optimal.
3. Rest intervals: 5 to 15 minutes between longer repeats; intervals of 5 to 30 seconds are optimal between shorter repeats that are done in sets.
4. Speed: as fast as possible
5. Suggested mileage per week: 2,000 to 3,000 yd/m

Dangers of excessive lactate tolerance training Lactate tolerance training is very stressful, both physically and mentally. The amount of muscular force required is quite high. This, together with the severe acidosis it produces, may cause some transient damage to muscle tissue, which will require time for repair and regeneration (Hagerman et al., 1984). The emotional content of lactate tolerance training is also much higher than for any other form of training. A great deal of motivation and psychological endurance are required to withstand the pain of acidosis on a regular basis. Sometimes, the anxiety associated with failing to swim fast in this form of training can be overwhelming. Some athletes become depressed, lose their appetites, and experience insomnia, among other manifestations of distress. For these reasons, sessions that contain major lactate tolerance training sets should be alternated with basic endurance swimming to provide time for recovery and regeneration.

Extensive use of lactate tolerance training should also be put off until the final 6 to 8 weeks of a season to prevent athletes from becoming saturated with it. Some lactate tolerance training should be performed earlier in the season, however. It will prevent large reductions in the rate of anaerobic metabolism during periods when endurance training is being stressed. Major sets of lactate tolerance training should only be performed once or twice per week in the early part of the season and two to three times per week (including meets) later.

Lactate Production Training (Spr-2) The major goal of lactate production training is the exact opposite of the one sought through endurance swimming. With endurance training, the primary purpose is to *reduce* the rate of lactic acid accumulation. The goal of lactate production training is to *increase* the rate of lactic acid production. This paradox is illustrated in Figure 5-3.

The roles played by each of these two conflicting training methods can be explained best in the context of races. The first portion of any race (except the 50) should be paced at something less than maximum speed in order to reduce anaerobic metabolism so that the rate of lactic acid production and, consequently, acidosis can be delayed until near the end of the race. Endurance training is the best procedure for this purpose. Once swimmers reach the final 50 to 30 yd/m of a race, however, they should forget about pacing and sprint as fast as possible. Their rate of anaerobic metabolism will determine their maximum speed during this final sprint, and that rate should be increased most by lactate production training. *During this time, their ability to produce lactic acid becomes more important than restraining its accumulation*. Paradoxes such as this one make the training process difficult, but challenging to understand.

Controversy exists over whether the rate of lactate production can be improved by training. Those who believe that this ability can be improved point to the appearance of increased levels of lactic acid in the muscles and blood of athletes after training. Those who disagree believe that these increases reflect only greater accumulation of lactic acid in the muscles and blood and not a faster rate of production in muscles. They think that improved buffering in the muscles and increased rates of lactic acid movement into the blood allow trained athletes to start

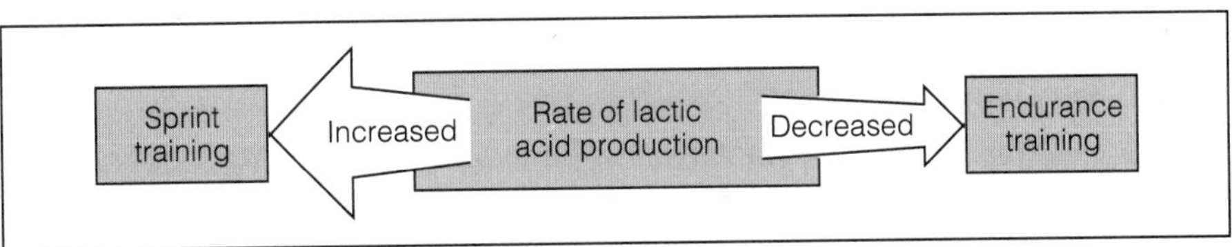

Figure 5-3. Paradoxical effects of endurance and sprint training on lactic acid production.

their final sprint earlier and maintain it longer. By doing so, the total *amount* of lactic acid produced in their muscles becomes greater over the course of a race, even though their *rate* of production does not increase. I agree with those experts who believe that the rate of lactic acid production can be enhanced by sprint training. Some suggested methods that might accomplish this purpose are outlined below.

Training to increase the rate of anaerobic metabolism, like all training methods, should include the principles of overload, progression, and specificity. Unlike endurance training, there are no optimal repeat speeds for this form of sprint training. Overload is applied by swimming lactate production repeats as fast as possible. Progression results from increasing the speed or volume of these repeats throughout the season. Athletes can apply the principle of specificity by swimming their major stroke(s) frequently in training.

There is a considerable amount of overlap between the effects of lactate production training and lactate tolerance training. Both improve all of the trainable aspects of anaerobic capacity. The difference between them concerns the degree to which they improve each aspect. Buffering capacity and pain tolerance are trained best by using long sprints. Short sprints should improve the rate of lactate production best.

The rate of anaerobic metabolism is most rapid when swimmers sprint as fast as possible and when muscle pH is maintained within normal limits (pH 7.0). Long sprints reduce this rate because they reduce muscle pH below 7.0 and the resulting acidosis inhibits the activity of the enzyme phosphofructokinase (PFK) (Danforth, 1965; Relman, 1972; Ui, 1966). PFK is the chief enzyme responsible for a fast rate of anaerobic metabolism. Long sprints and long anaerobic sets of repeats produce acidosis. Swimmers learn quickly to pace their way through long anaerobic sets so that they can complete them before becoming exhausted. Consequently, athletes swim lactate tolerance repeats with less-than-maximum rates of anaerobic metabolism either because they are pacing or because their muscle pH has dropped below 7.0.

For the reasons just cited, high-speed swims of 25 to 50 yd/m are probably better suited for lactate production training than longer distances because they demand high rates of lactate production but are not long enough to cause severe acidosis (Hellwig, Leisen, Mader, & Hollman, 1988; Song et al., 1988), which usually takes 40 to 50 seconds of maximum effort. The usual blood lactic acid levels after swims of 25 or 50 yd/m are 4 to 5 mmol/l and 8 to 9 mmol/l, respectively, because these events take between 9 and 30 seconds for most swimmers. Accordingly, the speeds that athletes can achieve for 25s and 50s are fast enough to overload anaerobic metabolism and the time is short enough that severe acidosis does not take place and inhibit that process early in the set. Repeats of 75 yd/m are also appropriate for senior swimmers, although they border on being too long for age group swimmers.

Constructing repeat sets for lactate production training As indicated, the best repeat distances are 25 and 50 yd/m, and they should be swum at very fast speeds. The send-off times should provide enough rest to remove a large amount of lactic acid so that acidosis does not occur after a few repeats. Rest intervals of 1 to

3 minutes should be sufficient. It is probably best to keep the rest intervals at the low end of this range for 25 repeats. This will prevent complete restoration of the muscles' CP supply so that most of the energy for recycling ATP has to come from glycolysis and the production of lactic acid.

The optimal length for lactate production sets is probably between 200 and 600 yd/m. Acidosis will creep up slowly and reduce swimming speed and, consequently, the training effect if the sets are much longer than this. Two or three sets of lactate production training can be completed in one training session. Ten to 20 minutes of easy swimming and kicking should be used for recovery between each set.

Senior swimmers and older age group swimmers should probably do about 2,000 to 3,000 yd/m of lactate production training per week. The range for young age group swimmers (under 11 years old) is probably 600 to 800 yd/m per week. The guidelines for constructing lactate production sets are summarized in the following box.

Guidelines for Constructing Lactate Production Sets

1. Set distance: 200 to 600 yd/m per set; 1 to 3 sets per training session
2. Repeat distances: 25, 50, and 75 yd/m
3. Rest intervals: 1 to 3 minutes
4. Speed: As fast as possible; at least 5 seconds faster than threshold pace
5. Suggested mileage per week: 2,000 to 3,000 yd/m

Power Training (Spr-3) Power training increases the muscular power that swimmers can exert at fast speeds. Because *power* refers to the rate of work, it is concerned with both *stroking rate* and *stroking force*. Stroking force is very difficult to measure accurately, so it is usually assessed by calculating a swimmer's stroke length. Stroke rates can be measured by one of several methods.

In its simplest terms, improving sprint speed is a matter of improving stroke length while maintaining stroke rate, or vice versa. If swimmers can increase their average stroke rate for a particular race distance *without reducing their average stroke length,* they will sprint faster. Conversely, their time will also be faster if they improve their average stroke length over the distance of a race *without reducing their average stroke rate*.

Stroke rate and stroke length A stroke rate is usually expressed according to the number of stroke cycles a swimmer takes each minute (stroke cycle/min). Stroke length is calculated as the number of meters the swimmer's body moves forward during each stroke cycle (m/stroke cycle). The relationship between stroke rate and stroke length is a negative one. That is, stroke length tends to decrease as stroke rate increases, and vice versa. Nevertheless, the best swimmers generally cover more distance with each stroke cycle at a competition stroke rate (Craig, Skehan, Pawelczyk, & Boomer, 1985; Letzelter & Freitag, 1983). Males, on the average, have a longer stroke than females, although stroke rates for males and females are nearly the same for a particular race distance (Letzelter & Freitag, 1983).

Time and effort are required to monitor stroke rate and stroke length, but it is time and effort well spent. The following box shows that even small improvements of one or two stroke cycles per minute or increases in length of a few hundredths of a meter per stroke will result in large improvements of time. The influence of the start is disregarded to make the calculations easier to understand.

The Effect of an Increase of Stroke Rate on Swimming Speed

Before Training

Stroke rate = 60 strokes cycle/min

Stroke length = 1.75 m/stroke cycle

60 stroke cycle/min = 1.00 sec/stroke cycle

1.75 m/stroke cycle ÷ 1.00 sec/stroke cycle = 1.75 m/sec

50 m ÷ 1.75 m/sec = 28.51 sec

After Training—Stroke Rate Increased to 62 Stroke Cycle/Min

62 stroke cycle/min = 0.97 sec/stroke cycle

1.75 m/stroke cycle ÷ 0.97 sec/stroke cycle = 1.80 m/sec

50 m ÷ 1.80 m/sec = 27.77 sec

After Training—Stroke Length Increased to 1.80 m/Stroke Cycle

60 stroke cycle/min = 1.00 sec/stroke cycle

1.80 m/stroke cycle ÷ 1.00 sec/stroke cycle = 1.80 m/sec

50 m ÷ 1.80 m/sec = 27.77 sec

The swimmer in this example has pretraining values of 60 strokes cycle/min and a stroke length of 1.75 m/stroke cycle. Therefore, her time for 50 m calculates to 28.51 (50 ÷ 1.75). The calculations show that her time would improve to 27.77 if her stroke rate could be increased to 62 stroke cycle/min with no loss of stroke length. Alternatively, an improvement in length to 1.80 m/stroke cycle with no loss of stroke rate would also produce a time of 27.77.

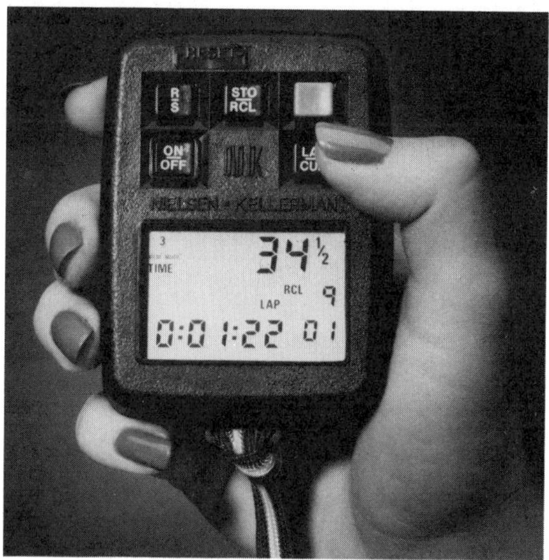

Figure 5-4. This watch doubles as a stopwatch and stroke rate counter. It is capable of storing any combination of 12 split times or stroke rates.

Stroke rates can be calculated with several stopwatches presently on the market. One of the best, pictured in Figure 5-4, is a combination stopwatch and stroke rate counter that is manufactured by the Neilsen-Kellerman Company. The stroke rate counter is pressed when the swimmer's hand enters the water to begin a stroke cycle and is pressed again when the cycle is completed. The watch will convert the time for the stroke cycle to stroke cycles per minute and display it immediately on the digital readout. For greater accuracy, several cycles can be counted and the watch will average them.

One way of counting stroke rates with a regular stopwatch is to time two or more stroke cycles. The formula provided in the following box can then be used to convert this figure to stroke cycles per minute. Three stroke cycles were counted in this example, and the time was 3.2 seconds. Thus, the swimmer was stroking at a rate of 1.067 seconds per stroke, which is equal to 57 stroke cycles per minute.

Procedure for Calculating Stroke Cycles Per Minute with a Stopwatch

The swimmer completed 3 stroke cycles in 3.2 seconds

3.2 seconds ÷ 3 stroke cycles = 1.067 stroke cycles per second

60 seconds ÷ 1.067 stroke cycles per second = 57 strokes per minute

Stroke length is more difficult to calculate. The effect of the start or pushoff must be eliminated to get an accurate measurement of the distance that swimmers travel with each stroke cycle. The most accurate procedures are (1) to count the number of stroke cycles between the flags or (2) to measure the distance traveled in one stroke cycle.

Drills for improving stroke rate and stroke length Stroke counting during timed sprints is one of the best ways to work on increasing stroke rate and stroke length. Drills for increasing stroke rate should emphasize covering the repeat distance in less time with a more rapid stroke rate *and no increase in the number of strokes*. Drills for increasing stroke length should emphasize covering the distance in less time with fewer strokes *and no change in stroke rate*.

Careful monitoring is important, because if stroke length increases are accompanied by decreases in stroke rate, the time for the repeat may not improve significantly, even though fewer strokes are taken. Correspondingly, when stroke rate increases are coupled with decreases in stroke length, more strokes will be taken, and the time may not improve. The relationship of changes in stroke rate and stroke length to time and number of strokes taken during repeats is summarized in Table 5-1.

Drills for improving stroke rate or stroke length may be done slowly in the learning stage. They must be swum at competition stroke rate as soon as possible, however, if a swimmer expects to cover more distance per stroke in races.

A good drill for improving stroke rate and stroke length is a game called *swolf,* which stands for a combination of "swimming" and "golf." Athletes swim at a particular repeat distance (25 or 50 yd/m) while counting their strokes. Their times are noted, and the two measures—number of strokes and time for the swim—are combined for a score. A lower score indicates improvement. Once they have established a base score, they can use any one of several variations on the game to improve the relationship between stroke rate and stroke length.

1. They can try to swim faster with fewer strokes. This should encourage an increase in stroke length.

Table 5-1. The Influence of Changes in Stroke Rate and Stroke Length on Repeat Times and the Number of Strokes Taken During Repeats

Stroke Rate	Stroke Length	Effect on Number of Strokes Taken	Effect on Time per Pool Length
Desirable Effects			
Increase	No change	No change	Faster
No change	Increase	Fewer	Faster
Undesirable Effects			
Decrease	No change	No change	Slower
No change	Decrease	More	Slower
Questionable Effects			
Increase	Decrease	More	May be slower, faster, or no change
Decrease	Increase	Fewer	May be slower, faster, or no change

2. They can try to swim faster with no increase in the number of strokes. This should encourage an increase in stroke rate.

Higher scores on these drills, of course, reflect unwanted effects, such as slower times due to either (1) an increased stroke rate and a decreased stroke length or (2) an increased stroke length and a decreased stroke rate.

In another simple drill, time is held constant and the distance traveled per stroke cycle is measured. Measuring the distance covered in 10 seconds in the middle of a long course pool is excellent for this purpose. The goals are (1) to cover more distance with no increase in stroke rate (in which case stroke length has improved) or (2) to cover more distance with a faster stroke rate (showing that stroke length has not deteriorated). If the stroke rate increases but the distance covered does not, stroke length has decreased. Correspondingly, if the distance traveled and stroke rate remain unchanged for a given time, stroke length has not increased.

Another good drill is to swim underdistance repeats at race speed while trying to take fewer strokes. A base score should be established on the first repeat. Then the athlete can try to swim the same time with fewer strokes or a faster time without increasing the number of strokes. This drill can also be done by counting stroke rates. The athlete should try to swim the same time with a slower stroke rate or a faster time without increasing the stroke rate. Any of these changes will mean that the swimmer has increased his or her stroke length.

Drills designed to improve the relationship between stroke rate and stroke length should be done when athletes are both rested and fatigued. Faster swimmers not only cover more distance with each stroke early in a race, they lose less distance per stroke as fatigue sets in later in the race (Weiss et al., 1988). In other words, stroke length tends to become shorter when swimmers fatigue, but the most successful swimmers shorten their strokes the least, so drills that emphasize maintaining stroke rate and length when fatigued serve an important function.

Constructing repeat sets to improve muscular power Several additional types of repeat sets will improve muscular power. They do not require counting stroke rate and stroke length, although their effect will be improved if both are monitored.

Repeats of 5 to 12½ yd/m are the best distances for increasing muscular power. Swimmers can be encouraged to exert more force against the water during these swims than they do at any other time in training, thereby overloading the mechanisms responsible for increasing muscular power. Distances of 25 and 50 yd/m can also be used and will serve the dual purpose of training muscular power and the rate of anaerobic metabolism.

Each repeat should be done at maximum speed. Swimmers should probably not be expected to do more than five to ten such repeats at a time. Athletes tend to swim somewhat slower when the number of repeats is increased too much beyond this range. They can swim several sets of repeats per training session, provided a rest period of 10 minutes or longer is allowed between each set to recover from any progressive acidosis that may have taken place.

The rest intervals between repeats should be 30 seconds to 1 minute for sprints of 15 yd/m and 2 to 3 minutes for 25s and 50s. Swimmers can rest longer if they like. This will not reduce the training effect. The most important consideration is that the rest interval not be too short. Short rest periods do not allow sufficient time to remove most of the lactic acid produced during the swim. Consequently, a stacking effect takes place with each subsequent swim, which will ultimately lead to acidosis and a reduction in swimming speed.

Swimmers should be cautioned not to thrash when they sprint. Their stroke rate should be at least as fast as that which they intend to use in sprint races, and they should constantly try to increase their stroke length during these repeats *without reducing their stroke rate*.

Unlike lactate tolerance training, power training should not cause pain or a loss of speed. Both signal that the swimmer is no longer overloading muscular power; the set is not achieving the desired purpose and should be terminated.

Although the *rates* of glycogen use and lactic acid production are higher with power sets than with any other form of training, the actual time athletes spend sprinting is too short to seriously deplete glycogen or allow large amounts of lactic acid to accumulate. Consequently, swimmers can probably do some sprinting during every training session, even when muscle glycogen is low. Senior athletes who specialize in the sprints should probably swim 1,500 to 2,000 yd/m of these repeats per week; 600 to 1,000 yd/m per week should suffice for middle-distance and distance swimmers. The guidelines for constructing power sets have been summarized in the following box.

Guidelines for Constructing Power Sets

1. Set distance: 200 to 300 yd/m; 1 to 2 sets per training session
2. Repeat distances: 10 to 50 yd/m
3. Rest intervals: 30 seconds to 5 minutes
4. Speed: maximum or near-maximum
5. Suggested mileage per week: 1,500 to 2,000 yd/m

Active Recovery Versus Passive Recovery During Sprint Sets

Several studies have shown that recovery is faster when subjects exercise moderately instead of resting passively (Belcastro & Bonen, 1975; Bond et al., 1987; Davies, Knibbs, & Musgrove, 1970; Hermansen & Stensvold, 1972). The term for moderate exercise during the recovery process is *active recovery,* and the term for sitting or lying quietly is *passive recovery*. In one study (Belcastro & Bonen, 1975), the recovery rate was 100 percent greater at 5 minutes and 400 percent greater at 20 minutes when a group of runners jogged as compared to another group that lay down or sat beside the track during the recovery period.

Similar results from another study, contrasting active and passive recovery methods, are shown in Figure 5-5. The subjects in the passive recovery group sat quietly after a series of exercise bouts to exhaustion. Members of the active recovery

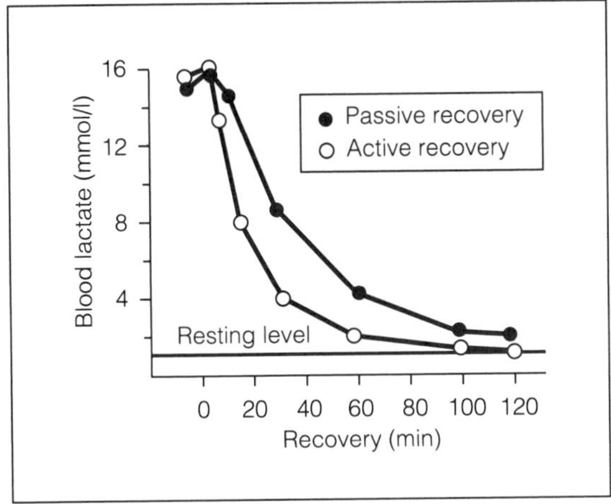

Figure 5-5. The effects of active recovery and passive recovery on the removal of blood lactic acid. (Wilmore & Costill, 1988)

group continued to run easily at a rate requiring 50- to 60-percent effort. You can see that the active recovery group lowered their blood lactic acid levels nearly twice as fast as the passive recovery group.

Light exercise is superior to rest during recovery periods because a faster rate of blood flow is maintained. Thus, more lactic acid can be removed from muscles in less time. At lower levels of effort, including complete rest, the rate of removal is slower. If the effort is too high, however, additional lactic acid will be produced.

Studies have been conducted to determine (1) the best mode of exercise and (2) the proper intensity for active recovery. Regarding the mode of exercise, it was clearly shown that swimmers recover faster when they swim during recovery as opposed to performing some nonspecific exercise (Krukau, Volker, & Leisen, 1987). Easy swimming brought blood lactate back to one-half its resting level in approximately 6 minutes after a fast 200 time trial. The time was 13 minutes when the subjects used easy cycling as their mode of active recovery.

Where intensity is concerned, Hermansen and Stensvold (1972), among others, have shown that work performed at efforts between 50 and 70 percent of $\dot{V}O_2max$ causes more rapid recovery. It apparently means little to swimmers when the optimal rates of effort for active recovery are reported as percentages of $\dot{V}O_2max$, however. Cazorla and coworkers (1983) identified these rates in more practical terms and reported that swimmers recovered more than twice as fast when they swam at 60 to 75 percent of their maximum speed for 100 m. Another interesting aspect of this study was that the swimmers recovered just as quickly when they chose their own pace. It seems, therefore, that coaches do not need to be concerned about the level of effort that swimmers use during active recovery. They will intuitively select a speed that is adequate for this purpose.

Special Forms of Sprint Training

The types of sprint training presented in this section all require an accessory device that increases or reduces resistance. They fall into three general categories: *sprint-*

resisted swimming, sprint-assisted swimming, and *land resistance training*. None of these procedures can take the place of short sprints at very fast speeds for improving muscular power. Some are good supplements, however. Others have limited value, and still others are valuable only if certain precautions are taken. Sprint-assisted and sprint-resisted training are discussed in the following sections. Land resistance training will be discussed in Chapter 24.

Sprint-Resisted Training The most popular forms of sprint-resisted training are tethered swimming and swimming against surgical tubing. Sprinting with hand paddles, swimming with shoes and clothes to add resistance, and towing objects down the pool are other methods in popular use. Recently, two devices have been developed that allow swimmers to perform types of weight lifting in the water. They are the Power Rack and the swim wheel.

The major advantage of sprint-resisted training is that it requires athletes to use more muscular force to overcome additional resistance. All methods of sprint-resisted training have one serious drawback, however. Although the additional resistance encourages swimmers to stroke with more force, it also alters their stroke mechanics and body position. They take slower and shorter strokes, they kick deeper, and they tend to thrash and swing their body from side to side (Maglischo et al., 1984). It is no wonder that research on the effects of these and other methods of sprint-resisted training has not reported improvements of swimming speed (Good, 1973; Hutinger, 1970; Ross, 1973). Nevertheless, certain types of sprint-resisted training can be beneficial if careful attention is paid to stroke rate and stroke length. If the stroke rate remains near competition level and athletes attempt to maintain their stroke length, stroking power will be maximized while minimizing undesirable effects on mechanics and body position.

Stroke length will decline somewhat during sprint-resisted swimming, but there is usually little danger that the strokes of experienced senior swimmers will deteriorate from sprint-resisted drills, *provided they do not try to swim the same way in races*. Senior swimmers' strokes become "grooved" by the large amount of free swimming they do during their careers and are not likely to be changed by small amounts of sprint-resisted training.

Inexperienced swimmers are another matter, however, because they are more prone to carry over to competition some of the counterproductive efforts for increasing stroking force they may use in sprint-resisted training. Consequently, if coaches choose to use sprint-resisted training with such swimmers, they should balance it with equal or greater amounts of free sprinting in which careful attention is given to swimming correctly.

Tethered swimming, partially-tethered swimming, towing, and drag suits Ropes and surgical tubing usually provide the resistance for tethered and partially-tethered swimming. Some swimmers wear special belts with pockets or "drag suits" with cups that are designed to catch water and increase resistance to forward motion. Still others tow objects like a bucket at the end of a rope up and down the pool. All of these methods are potentially dangerous but can be used to increase muscular power, the rate of lactate production, and lactate tolerance if certain precautions are taken.

The work time for swims aimed at increasing muscular power should be 5 to 15 seconds. One of the best drills with surgical tubing is to sprint for 5 to 10 seconds while using a very high stroke rate (60 to 70 stroke cycle/min). Six to ten such repeats in sets of one to three should be excellent for increasing stroking power. Send-off times of 1 to 2 minutes are ideal, with 5 to 10 minutes of easy swimming between sets.

The work time should be 20 to 30 seconds when the goal is to increase the rate of lactate production. Four to eight repeats should be adequate. Rest intervals between repeats should be 1 to 3 minutes.

In all three of these methods, stroke rate should be checked to make sure that swimmers are training at competition rate or faster *while at the same time trying to maintain the greatest possible stroke length*. Swimmers should be cautioned to stroke smoothly and to keep their body in a streamlined position.

When sprint-resisted swimming is used to improve lactate tolerance, the work time should be 45 seconds to 2 minutes, with rest intervals of 5 to 10 minutes during which the athletes swim easily. Three to six repeats are recommended. The swimmers will not be able to maintain a competition stroke rate. Nevertheless, they should try for the fastest possible rate during the period of work. They should also try to improve on that average throughout the season. This is the weakest use for sprint-resisted training and is really not recommended. Stroke deterioration will be more severe than in any other type of resistance training. On the other hand, free swimming can provide the same training effect without the potential damage to stroke mechanics.

Because tethered swimming efforts are very difficult and stressful, they should be done sparingly. They should also be calculated as part of the sprint mileage each week so that the balance of training is not upset.

Swimming with shoes and clothes Swimming against the resistance supplied by shoes and clothes has no place in the training program. This type of sprint-resisted training reduces stroke rate and stroke length and causes a loss of streamlining that cannot be prevented. In addition, chances of improving muscular power are minimal because athletes swim at such slow rates. About the only possible benefit is the sense of ease and speed experienced after removing these items; however, that could be a false sensation because it does not translate to faster times and, most likely, has no bearing on improving sprint speed.

Sprinting with hand paddles Although hand paddles increase the amount of water resistance swimmers must overcome, they also increase the surface area of the hand, making it possible for athletes to swim faster and, thereby, perhaps increase muscular power. Furthermore, swimmers may reap some of the benefits of sprint-assisted training that are detailed later in this chapter.

Sprinting with hand paddles is a potentially valuable aid for increasing sprint speed. Careful attention must be paid to the stroke rate, however. It should be at least equal to the competition rate. Speeds should be faster than when the same repeats are swum without hand paddles to ensure that the swimmers are working at a maximum to near-maximum rate of stroking power. A slower stroke rate and time will mean that a swimmer is simply substituting surface area for force. Muscular power will not be increased by swimming this way.

Any of the repeat sets suggested for power training can be performed with hand paddles. The only disadvantage to this type of training is the possibility of exacerbating the symptoms of tendinitis. That is a big disadvantage. Swimmers with a history of shoulder problems should be cautious about using this method. They should discontinue it at the first sign of shoulder pain.

The Power Rack and Swim Wheel The Power Rack (see Figure 5-6) consists of a stack of weighted plates that can be wheeled to poolside. Swimmers don a harness and lift the plates over a double pulley system as they sprint down the pool. The distance they can travel is limited to approximately 12 yd by the travel height of the plates.

The Swim Wheel (see Figure 5-7) is made up of a large wheel with a rope that connects to a belt worn by swimmers. There is a small axle inside the large wheel.

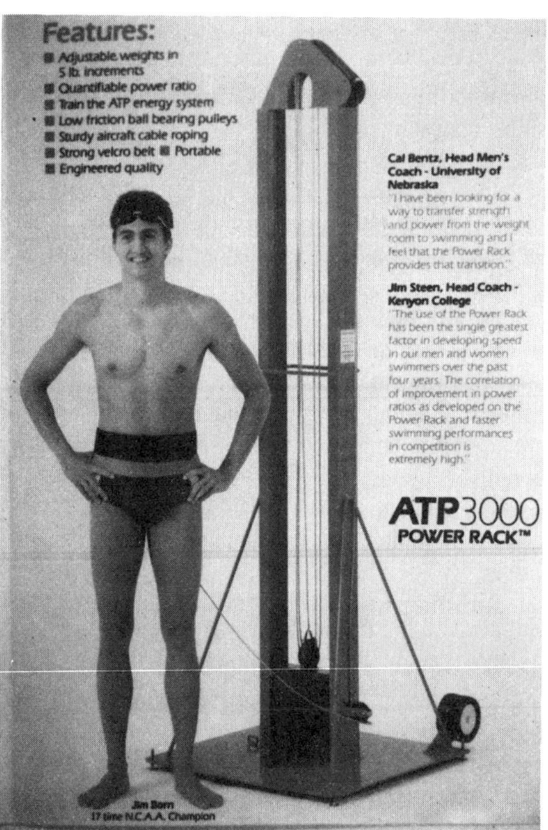

Figure 5-6. The Power Rack (Total Performance, Inc.).

a

b

Figure 5-7. The Swim Wheel was invented by Bob Mertz while he was a student at California State University, Bakersfield. Figure 5-7*a* shows Derek Robinson getting ready to swim down the pool. The wheel is mounted on the fence behind him with a bucket of diving bricks sitting on the deck. Figure 5-7*b* shows him swimming down the pool while lifting the bucket.

The rope from the axle is connected to a bucket of diving bricks that the athletes lift as they swim down the pool. The bucket is lifted by the resistance rope winding up on the axle as athletes pull the harness rope out on the large wheel. The rope on the large wheel is long enough to permit athletes to swim 25 yd before the bucket is raised to its maximum height of 8 ft. The advantage of the Swim Wheel over the Power Rack is that it allows swimmers to sprint against resistance for a greater distance.

The advantage that both of these methods have over tethered and partially tethered swimming is their ability to apply overload and progression. Power can be calculated for swimmers because the weight, the distance it is lifted, and the time required to lift it can all be measured accurately. Additionally, these variables can be manipulated over time so that the power swimmers exert in training can be increased progressively. The two simplest methods for applying progression are to lift the weight faster or to lift more weight without losing speed.

Training sets for both of these devices should probably include four to ten swims performed in one to three sets. Rest periods between repeats should be in the neighborhood of 1 to 3 minutes, with 3 to 10 minutes of easy swimming between sets. Effort should be maximum and stroke rate should be monitored during these forms of training. It should be close to competition rate. Because research has shown that power and the rate of application are closely linked (Moffroid & Whipple, 1970), it would be a mistake to lift large amounts of resistance with a slow stroke rate. The force would not be available at a fast stroke rate. Athletes should first establish the desired stroke rate for their event and then add enough resistance so that they cannot quite maintain that rate. They should then train with that amount until they can consistently equal or surpass the desired stroke rate, after which they should increase the resistance and begin a new training cycle.

Although stroke mechanics are undoubtedly changed somewhat by the added resistance of the Power Rack and Swim Wheel, the effect should not be of the same magnitude as produced by tethered and partially-tethered swimming. The swimmers can travel down the pool more smoothly because they are not being pulled back as they would be by surgical tubing.

Sprint-resisted training need not be used more than three times per week for 4 to 8 weeks of each season. It can be used infrequently throughout the rest of the season. A period of 4 to 8 weeks provides plenty of time to maximize stroking power. On the other hand, overuse leads to saturation and a reduction of motivation.

Sprint-Assisted Training Sprint-assisted training methods were developed to counteract the major disadvantages of sprint-resisted training — slow turnover rates and detrimental changes of stroke mechanics. They were first used in track after coaches found that sprint-resisted methods were causing runners to shorten their stride length and reduce their stride rate (Dintiman, 1984). The results were so impressive that Eleanor Rowe, Don Lytle, and I (1977) decided to study the effects of sprint-assisted training with swimmers. Swim fins were the best method of sprint-assisted training we could think of at the time, even though we were aware of the possible changes in stroke mechanics and timing that would occur when swimmers used them. As it turned out, our concerns were unfounded. The results of the study are listed in Table 5-2.

Two groups of 7- and 8-year-old male and female competitive swimmers were matched according to their best time for a 25-yd freestyle. They were then sprint trained for 8 weeks. The swimmers in both groups followed a typical program of mixed training that was identical in all respects but one. The experimental group wore fins for a set of fifteen 25-yd freestyle sprints that were done three times each week. They were encouraged to swim each 25 faster than their best unassisted time. The control group also swam these sprints, but without fins. They were encouraged to swim each repeat within 90 percent of their best competitive time. All subjects were trained in the same pool at the same time and by the same coach.

Following completion of the training period, the swimmers were again timed for a 25 yd of freestyle in competition. Both groups improved significantly. This

Table 5-2. A Comparative Study of Sprint-assisted Training Using Swim Fins

Comparison of Control Group Pretraining and Posttraining Times			Comparison of Experimental Group Pretraining and Posttraining Times		
Subject	*Pretraining Times*	*Posttraining Times*	*Subject*	*Pretraining Times*	*Posttraining Times*
1	16.90	17.00	1	17.00	16.70
2	21.60	21.40	2	21.60	21.90
3	17.90	17.80	3	18.00	17.40
4	17.60	17.10	4	17.60	15.90
5	22.90	22.70	5	22.80	22.80
6	17.90	17.80	6	17.80	17.50
7	17.70	17.50	7	17.70	17.00
8	17.20	17.10	8	17.10	16.80
9	20.20	19.90	9	20.10	19.00
10	27.10	27.00	10	27.30	26.50
11	17.90	17.80	11	17.90	17.20
12	16.90	16.80	12	16.80	16.30
13	17.70	17.90	13	17.80	17.20
14	17.80	17.80	14	17.90	17.80
Mean time	19.09	18.97	Mean time	19.10	18.57
Standard deviation	2.92	2.90	Standard deviation	2.95	3.04
*t**	2.71		*t*	4.01	
Level of significance	.01		Level of significance	.005	

**t* is the score for a t-test, which compares the means and standard deviations for two sets of scores.

Source: Adapted from Rowe, Maglischo, & Lytle, 1977.

result was not unexpected because both the control and experimental groups had been sprint trained. The important finding was that the average 25-yd freestyle speed of the experimental group improved significantly more that that of the control group. The control group improved an average of 0.12 second, yet the average improvement of the experimental group was 0.53 second. The 0.41-second difference in improvement between the two groups was significant.

Two other methods of sprint-assisted training can be equally effective. Surgical tubing is used in the first, but opposite from the way it is used in sprint-resisted training. Athletes swim *with* the stretched tubing rather than against it. An adjustable belt made of webbing is attached to 20 to 25 ft of thin-walled surgical tubing (see Figure 5-8). The tubing is tied to the end of the pool *below water level* so that it will not cause injury if it should break. Wearing the belt, swimmers walk or swim down to the other end of the pool, stretching the tubing as they go. They then swim back as fast as possible. The stretched tubing will pull them back, assisting them to swim faster than they could without it.

Figure 5-8. Amon Emeka getting ready for sprint-assisted training using a surgical tubing belt.

One reason why this form of sprint-assisted training is so effective is because swimmers automatically increase their stroke rate while performing it. Some also increase their stroke length. In one study (Maglischo, Maglischo, Zier, & Santos, 1985), three of six swimmers voluntarily increased their stroke lengths during this type of sprint-assisted training, yet stroke lengths were shorter for the remaining subjects. All of the subjects increased their stroke rates.

To achieve maximum benefit, swimmers should be cautioned to maintain a normal stroke length during this form of sprint-assisted training. Stroke rate should also be checked frequently to be certain that the swimmers are working on this component as well.

As with sprint-resisted efforts, sprint-assisted training tends to change the stroke mechanics of swimmers. In this case, however, the changes are generally beneficial rather than detrimental. We found that the stroke mechanics of several butterflyers changed for the better during sprint-assisted efforts as compared to their free swimming butterfly styles (Maglischo, Maglischo, Zier, & Santos, 1985). Some dropped their elbows less at the catch, and those who tended to push up or let go of the water early during the final upsweep portion of their underwater armstroke exhibited more hyperextension at the wrist joints and a longer sweep upward.

Another method for sprint-assisted training that is a lot of fun is swimming with the current. Swimmers set up a current in the pool by pushing the water in one direction with kickboards. One by one, they push off the wall or dive into the water and sprint one length in the direction the water is traveling. Athletes can swim some phenomenal times using this method. It is a good procedure for sprint training because their stroke rate increases while their stroke length remains the same or increases.

Sprint-assisted repeats are constructed similarly to the guidelines presented earlier for power training sets. Distances of 25 yd/m are best, although 50 m can be used in long-course pools. The optimal number of repeats should probably be in the neighborhood of four to ten, with rest intervals that are long enough to remove most of the lactic acid produced during the swim. One to three minutes is recommended. Sprinters should probably do some form of sprint-assisted training two or three times per week during that portion of the season when sprint training is emphasized; 1 or 2 days per week should suffice during other parts of the season. Middle-distance and distance swimmers can probably do this type of training once or twice per week all season long.

CAN ENDURANCE TRAINING HURT SPRINTING SPEED?

Several reports in the literature have raised the possibility that endurance training can reduce anaerobic capacity and, therefore, sprinting speed. For example, Lindinger and colleagues (1990) found that the lactate production rate of rats was reduced by 24 percent after 4 weeks of endurance training. Dudley and Djamil (1985) reported a reduction in maximum force (peak torque) at fast velocities of leg extension after endurance training, and Sharp and associates (1986) found that endurance-trained cyclists had a lower rate of lactate production than untrained persons.

Fitts and associates (1989) conducted a very interesting study in which the effect of endurance training on the contractile speed of individual muscle fibers was measured. The subjects were a group of male collegiate competitive swimmers who were subjected to 10 days of intense endurance training in which their normal daily yardage was nearly doubled from 5,000 to approximately 9,000 yd. Muscle biopsies were taken from the deltoid muscle just before and immediately after the training period. These researchers reported a significant reduction in the size of the subjects' FT muscle fibers, which was believed to be due to increased protein catabolism. The most important result, however, was a reduction in the contractile speed of FT muscle fibers by more than 50 percent. Their results are illustrated in Figure 5-9.

Although these results support the position that endurance training will reduce sprinting speed, the question is far from resolved. There are an equal number of works that have reported improvements in both capacities during combined training. For example, Hickson and associates (1988) reported improvements in anaerobic capacity of 11 to 13 percent among a group of subjects in a study that combined strength and endurance training. Jacobs, Sale, and MacDougall (1987) reported similar results in a study in which subjects strength trained both legs but endurance trained only one leg. Improvements of muscle size and anaerobic enzyme activity were similar in both legs. Nelson and associates (1984) and Sharp and coworkers (1989) also reported that simultaneous endurance and sprint training did not impair sprint training effects.

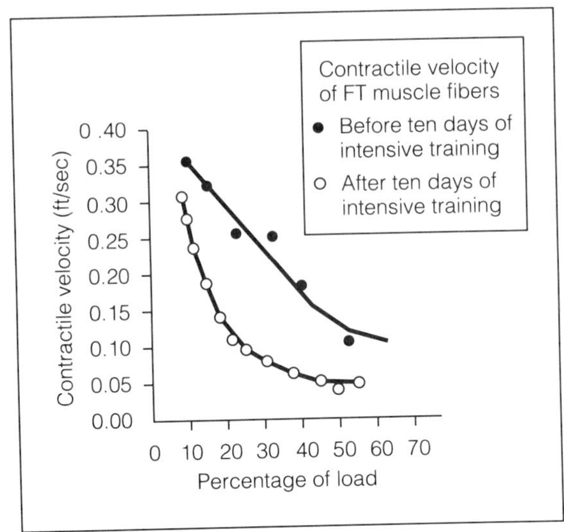

Figure 5-9. Effects of 10 days of intensive endurance training on the contractile speed of FT muscle fibers. (Adapted from Fitts, Costill, & Gardetto, 1989)

Although the matter is controversial, I remain convinced that endurance training can reduce anaerobic capacity. During 10 years of blood testing, I have watched peak blood lactate values decline during periods of heavy endurance swimming. I realize that this, in itself, does not prove a reduction in anaerobic capacity, because endurance training causes a number of adaptations that can reduce the amount of lactic acid diffusing from muscles into the blood without reducing the rate of anaerobic metabolism. Nevertheless, when a reduction in peak lactate is coupled with poor performance in sprint events, it seems reasonable to suspect that a reduction of anaerobic capacity has taken place.

Endurance training may not have had a detrimental effect on anaerobic capacity in the studies cited above because untrained persons were used as subjects. Untrained persons tend to improve quickly in all aspects of performance during early training (as do swimmers who start a new season after a layoff). It is only later in the season, when the rate of improvement slows down, that reductions of anaerobic capacity seem to occur. Perhaps anaerobic capacity does not begin to decline for several weeks after athletes commence endurance training.

What about the flip side of this question, Can an imbalance of sprint training reduce aerobic capacity? Once again, research is controversial. The preponderance of studies report no reduction in aerobic capacity when persons are trained with sprints or when endurance and sprint training are combined (Hickson et al., 1988; Jacobs, Sale, & MacDougall, 1987; Loy & Segel, 1988; Luthi et al., 1986; MacDougall et al., 1987; Sale et al., 1988; Sharp, Ness, Hackney, & Runyan, 1989). However, the results of a few studies have suggested detrimental effects (Jacobs, Esbjornsson et al., 1987; Nelson et al., 1984; Tesch, Hakkinen, & Komi, 1985).

Because this issue remains unresolved, it is probably a good idea to reduce the quantity of sprint training (and overload endurance swimming) when tests of aerobic capacity indicate endurance has deteriorated.

CHAPTER 6

Training Balance

Some coaches and athletes believe that the value of training programs should be judged according to the number of yards or meters swum each day. Others assert that training mileage can be reduced with no loss of endurance if athletes simply swim their repeats at faster speeds. Neither position is correct in this controversy of quality versus quantity training. A good program must have a balance of slow, medium, fast, and superfast swimming. It is this balance, more than total mileage or training speeds, that determines the magnitude of the training effect.

Three aspects of training contribute to a balanced program: (1) the duration of training, (2) the frequency of training in days per week, and (3) the intensity or speed of training.

TRAINING DURATION

Most of the research bearing on this issue has involved rats rather than humans. Nevertheless, it has provided valuable information. Harms and Hickson (1983) reported that increases in measures of aerobic capacity were 40 to 70 percent greater when rats were trained for 2 hours per day as opposed to 40 minutes. These researchers trained their group of rats on a treadmill 6 days per week for 14 weeks. Their results were compared to those of an untrained control group. The markers used to reflect changes in aerobic capacity were the quantities of citrate synthase (CS), succinate dehydrogenase (SDH), and myoglobin in the rats' muscles. Performance times for an endurance run to exhaustion were also compared between groups.

As a result of this study, Harms and Hickson (1983) concluded that exercise duration appears to have a more direct and stronger influence on mitochondrial adaptations and, thus, aerobic endurance than intensity of training.

Studies by Baldwin and coworkers (1973) and Fitts and associates (1975) have also found that 2 hours of training are superior to shorter durations for improving aerobic capacity. The available research suggests that at least 2 hours of daily training are needed for maximum improvements of aerobic capacity. I use the words *at least* because studies have not been conducted using longer durations.

TRAINING FREQUENCY

The frequency of training is also important in a balanced program because each additional day of training allows swimmers to log more miles per week. In this regard, Hickson (1981) reported that rats who were trained 6 days per week improved considerably more on measures of aerobic capacity and *running time to exhaustion* than did rodents that had been trained for either 2 or 4 days per week. Training speeds and daily training duration were the same in all groups.

For the rats training 6 days per week, running time to exhaustion was 136 percent greater than for the group training 2 days per week (100 versus 236 minutes) and 34 percent greater than for the group training 4 days per week (176 versus 236 minutes). The group training 4 days per week improved 76 percent more than the rats training 2 days per week on this measure (100 versus 176 minutes).

The group training 6 days per week was also superior to the other groups where measures of aerobic capacity were concerned. They showed improvements that were 12 to 55 percent greater than those for the group training 2 days per week on these measures. They also improved 8 to 30 percent more than the group training 4 days per week on these measures. The range of improvements between the groups training 2 days per week and 4 days per week were 4 to 30 percent in favor of the latter group. The results suggest that athletes must train in excess of 4 days per week for maximum results.

TRAINING INTENSITY

The study by Harms and Hickson (1983) that was mentioned in relation to training duration also addressed the topic of training intensity. These researchers trained three subgroups of rats on a treadmill for 40 minutes per day, 6 days per week, for 14 weeks at speeds of 11 m/min, 22 m/min, and 44 m/min. The effect of different training intensities was also studied by Dudley and associates (1982). They trained rats at six different speeds: 10, 20, 30, 40, 50, and 60 m/min. Rats have three distinct types of muscle fibers: ST, FT red, and FT white. The ST fibers have similar characteristics to the ST fibers of humans. FT red fibers are similar to the FTa fibers of humans; they have a reasonable amount of aerobic capacity. The FT white fibers of rats are like the FTb fibers of humans; they have good anaerobic capacity but are limited in their ability to do work aerobically. Both groups of researchers reached similar conclusions about the effects of training intensity on these three types of fibers. Results from these two studies are summarized in Table 6-1.

The results of both studies agreed on the following points:

1. The aerobic capacity of slow-twitch (ST) muscle fibers was improved most by training that was moderate in intensity.
2. The aerobic capacity of the rats' fast-twitch (FT) red muscle fibers (FTa in humans) were trained equally well at moderate or high work intensities.
3. The aerobic capacity of the rats' FT white fibers (FTb in humans) responded best to increases in the intensity of training.

In the study by Dudley and coworkers, the aerobic capacity of ST muscle fibers improved linearly up to a speed of 30 m/min. A speed of 30 m/min is equal to an oxygen consumption of 80 to 85 percent of $\dot{V}O_2max$ for rats. This is similar to the range where the anaerobic threshold occurs in most humans.

The FT red muscle fibers of the rats also improved significantly up to a speed of 30 m/min. The rats who trained at faster speeds did not show any greater improvement. Their values were not significantly lower than the group that trained at 30 m/min, however.

Table 6-1. The Results of Two Studies on the Effect of Different Training Speeds on the Aerobic Capacity of Rat Muscle Fibers

	Running Speed (m/min)					
Measure	*10/11*	*20/22*	*30*	*40/44*	*50*	*60*
Running Time to Exhaustion (min)	127*	314*		569*		
Citrate synthase (CS)	Percent Increase					
FT red muscle fibers	33%*	49%*		72%*		
FT white muscle fibers	13%	29%		48%*		
ST muscle fibers	30%*	35%*		30%*		
Succinate dehydrogenase (SDH)						
FT red muscle fibers	17%*	36%*		68%*		
FT white muscle fibers				negligible		
ST muscle fibers				negligible		
Myoglobin						
FT red muscle fibers	7%	11%		17%		
FT white muscle fibers				no change		
ST muscle fibers	15%*	6%		6%		
Cytochrome C						
FT red muscle fibers	21%*	37%*	47%*	47%*	42%*	47%*
FT white muscle fibers	0	0	40%*	80%*	90%*	180%*
ST muscle fibers	17%*	23%*	39%*	31%*	15%*	7%

*Significant improvement

Sources: Adapted from Dudley, Abraham, & Terjung, 1982; Harms & Hickson, 1983.

Contrary to the results with other fiber types, aerobic capacity did not increase in the FT white muscle fibers of the rats until the running speed reached 30 m/min. After that, their aerobic capacity continued to increase linearly, with the greatest improvement occurring at the fastest running speed, 60 m/min. The intensity of this speed is estimated to be equivalent to efforts of approximately 120 percent of $\dot{V}O_2max$.

The results of Harms and Hickson concurred with those of Dudley and coworkers. The aerobic capacity of ST muscle fibers and FT red fibers was improved at moderate running speeds, and the aerobic capacity of FT white muscle fibers was increased most at faster speeds. In the study by Harms and Hickson, only the 44-m/min running group increased the CS activity of their FT white muscle fibers significantly above that of an untrained control group. Thus, in agreement with the results of Dudley and associates, it appears that the intensity of training must be above the anaerobic threshold to improve the aerobic capacity of FT white muscle fibers.

The most important result from the study by Harms and Hickson was the improvement in running time to exhaustion. This is the proof of the pudding where performance is concerned. A linear relationship was found between this measure and training speed. The rats who trained at 44 m/min outperformed the 11-m/min and 22-m/min groups by a whopping 348 percent and 81 percent, respectively, on this test. They ran nearly 7½ hours longer than the 11-m/min group (569 versus 127 minutes), and 4⅓ hours longer than the 22-m/min group (569 versus 314 minutes). The group that ran at a speed of 22 m/min outperformed the 11 m/min group by 147 percent (314 versus 127 minutes). A running speed of 44 m/min corresponds to a training intensity of 100 percent of $\dot{V}O_2max$.

These results point to the need to include some overload endurance training in a program for the purpose of improving the aerobic capacity of the FTb muscle fibers. The ST and FTa fibers can be trained reasonably well with mixtures of basic and threshold endurance repeats.

If these results can be applied to humans, training duration, frequency, and intensity are important to the training process in the following ways:

1. Because FT muscle fibers are not used very much at slow speeds, endurance repeats should be swum at moderate to fast speeds to improve aerobic capacity. Speeds in the neighborhood of 60 to 70 percent of maximum are probably required to activate the FTa fibers, and speeds above the anaerobic threshold are needed to improve the aerobic capacity of FTb muscle fibers.

2. Long, slow swims or repeats in the neighborhood of 50 to 60 percent of maximum can be used to train ST fibers while providing a recovery period for their FT counterparts, which are not activated to any great extent at these slow speeds.

3. The anaerobic capacity of both FT and ST muscle fibers is probably improved best by sustained sprints.

The remainder of Chapter 6 is concerned with three topics: (1) optimal training mileage, (2) the balance of training with respect to recommended mileage for each level of endurance and sprint training, and (3) special procedures for training butterfly, backstroke, breaststroke, and individual medley swimmers.

TRAINING MILEAGE

The research on training duration and frequency only tells us that endurance athletes should train a minimum of 2 hours per day for 5 or 6 days per week. However, most serious competitive swimmers train well in excess of this amount at the present time. Some athletes have been reported to train in excess of 20,000 yd/m per day, and reports of weekly mileages of 80,000 to 100,000 yd/m are not uncommon (Maglischo & Daland, 1987). Many coaches and researchers have been seeking an optimal figure for training mileage that provides maximum benefits with the least expenditure of time.

Research with runners has a bearing on this matter because it suggests an optimum that may apply to swimmers as well. It has been reported that 60 to 90 miles of running per week improved aerobic capacity as much as it could be improved (Costill, 1986). It would require 1½ to 2½ hours per day, 6 days per week for most runners to complete this range of miles, which agrees closely with the research by Harms & Hickson (1983) that was cited earlier.

In swimming terms, the optimal running mileage of 60 to 90 miles is equal to between 30,000 and 50,000 yd/m of weekly training. This was calculated by using the four-to-one rule for converting running to swimming mileage. That is, a trained runner can run four times as far as a trained swimmer can swim in the same amount of time. Unfortunately, improvements of $\dot{V}O_2max$ were used as the criterion measure for these runners instead of the anaerobic threshold. Nevertheless, this research agrees closely with the optimum I have calculated by empirical means.

I took the approach of calculating the mileage for each level of endurance and sprint training according to the amounts that could probably be tolerated by athletes, based on the opinions of expert coaches and what we know about glycogen depletion and replacement. It equalled between 28,000 and 69,000 yd/m weekly, a figure that is surprisingly close to the optimal range suggested from running studies. These calculations were based on training once or twice per day, 6 days per week. The addition of mileage for warming up and swimming down brought this weekly total somewhere in the range of 40,000 to 90,000 yd/m per week (see Table 6-2).

These figures are offered only as suggestions. It is impossible to substantiate their accuracy. Research is inconclusive, and the training of swimmers is generally based on outdoing the successful club across town or across the world rather than

Table 6-2. Suggested Minimum Weekly Mileage for Each Type of Training

Form of Training	Meters per Week
Endurance	25,000 to 60,000
Sprint	3,500 to 9,000
Weekly training mileage	28,500 to 69,000
Warm-up and swim-down (2,000 per session)	12,000 to 24,000
Total weekly mileage	40,500 to 93,000

on physical needs. The debate about optimal training mileage will probably continue for a long time.

THE BALANCE OF TRAINING

Probably more important to swimming success than the total mileage completed per day, per week, or per season are the relative proportions of training that are done at each of the endurance and sprint levels. Discovering the proper training balance will be a major direction for research in the next decade. In the absence of current research on this topic, I have provided some estimates based on experience and interpretations of related studies. Age, sex, ability level, individual differences in physiological makeup (such as the relative percentages of FT and ST muscle fibers), and the events in which athletes compete make it impossible to do anything but generalize about training balance, however.

The estimates for each training category are listed in two forms: (1) as percentages of the total weekly mileage and (2) as total weekly mileage. Percentages are the most convenient form for communicating the balance of training, but they can give a false impression when the weekly mileage is outside the usual range of 40,000 to 80,000 yd/m per week. Figures for weekly mileage furnish more accurate estimates for programs that are outside this range. They are particularly useful for comparing the programs of distance and sprint swimmers. Sprint swimmers may appear to do a similar percentage of endurance training as distance swimmers. However, their weekly mileage is usually one-half to one-third less than that of distance swimmers; thus, the total amount of their endurance mileage is significantly less.

The mileages in yards and meters that have been suggested for endurance and sprint training are, in my opinion, necessary to success in international competition. The ranges are quite large in some categories. Narrowing them is impossible because successful swimmers have trained at both ends of these ranges.

The following categories have been used to express the balance of training:

1. Mileage devoted to warming up and swimming down
2. Mileage devoted to kicking
3. Endurance training mileage subdivided into values for basic, threshold, and overload endurance training
4. Sprint training mileage subdivided to reflect the amounts of lactate tolerance, lactate production, and power training

Suggestions for training balance have been summarized in Table 6-3 in terms of mileage per week for each training category. Percentages of the total mileage per week are also presented for each category. These figures generally apply to swimmers training for events from 200 to 400 m. Each of the categories is discussed in the following sections.

Warming Up, Swimming Down, and Kicking

Approximately 12 to 15 percent of the weekly mileage should be devoted to warming up before and swimming down after each training session. In most programs, this

Table 6-3. Suggested Weekly Mileage and Percentages for the Various Levels of Sprint Training and Endurance Training

Training Category	Total Yards/Meters per Week	Percentage of Total Mileage per Week
Warm-up and swim-down	6,000–12,000	12–15
Kicking	6,000–12,000	12–15
Endurance Training	22,000–58,000	50–60
Overload (End-3)	4,000–6,000	5–10
Threshold (End-2)	6,000–10,000	10–15
Basic (End-1)	12,000–40,000	30–40
Sprint training	4,000–8,000	8–12
Lactate tolerance (Spr-1)	1,500–3,000	3–5
Lactate production (Spr-2)	1,500–3,000	3–5
Power (Spr-3)	1,000–2,000	2–3

comprises 6,000 to 12,000 yd/m per week, depending on whether swimmers are training once or twice per day. Similar percentages and weekly mileages are usually devoted to kicking, although there is a wide variation in this category from program to program.

Endurance Training

Endurance training should comprise between 50 and 60 percent of the weekly total, with distance swimmers at the high end of that percentage and sprinters at the low end. Within the endurance category, 15 to 25 percent of the weekly mileage should be in the form of threshold and overload training. A significantly greater proportion—30 to 40 percent—of the weekly mileage should be performed at basic endurance speeds.

It is impossible to recommend minimum or maximum mileages for basic endurance training on a physical basis. Because much of the energy is provided by fat metabolism, swimmers should have adequate amounts of energy in their muscles for any weekly distance they wish to swim. Their only restriction would be the time they have available for training. Consequently, a range of 12,000 to 40,000 yd/m per week is suggested, based on time considerations only.

Optimums for the other levels of endurance training can be suggested based on what we know about the time course for muscle glycogen use and replacement. Obviously, swimmers can only train at the threshold and overload levels when they have adequate supplies of muscle glycogen. As we discussed in Chapter 2, swimmers can complete only two threshold or two overload endurance sets before depleting muscle glycogen, after which they will require 1 or 2 days to replace it. So, the muscle glycogen supply can probably only support three or four threshold or overload sets per week. Each set should be 1,500 to 4,000 yd/m in length for a weekly total of between 10,000 and 16,000 yd/m.

Sprint Training

Eight to 12 percent of the mileage should be devoted to sprint training. In this case, sprinters should be at the high end of the range and distance swimmers at the low end. Lactate production and lactate tolerance training should each comprise 3 to 5 percent of the weekly total. The remaining 2 to 3 percent should be done as power training.

Because research on sprint training is minimal, the best information we have on mileage and frequency comes from the experiences of successful coaches. They seem, overwhelmingly, to recommend distances between 400 and 800 yd/m for lactate production sets. The optimal range of distances for lactate tolerance sets is probably between 600 and 1,200 yd/m per set. They also recommend that lactate production training and lactate tolerance training be conducted no more than two to four times per week (Maglischo & Daland, 1987; Paulsson, 1984; Wilke & Madsen, 1983). The mileage covered in competitions should be counted as lactate tolerance training in the weekly total.

Sprint training makes large demands on anaerobic metabolism and probably requires some recovery time from day to day. One reason may be that some transient muscle damage occurs. Perhaps this is why athletes respond best when they have at least 24 hours of rest between sprint sets.

This rest period may also be needed to replace glycogen in the FT muscle fibers. Both Jacobs (1981) and Cheetham and associates (1986) have reported that one 30-second maximum effort reduced muscle glycogen 25 percent, while Thomson and coworkers (1979) reported that 50 percent of their subjects' FT muscle fibers were completely emptied of glycogen after five 1-minute maximum efforts.

Power training is even more poorly researched than the other two levels of sprint training; however, experience has taught the great sprint coaches in track and field that 4,000 to 5,000 m of sprinting per week is optimal, with no more than 1,000 to 2,000 m in any one session (Dintiman & Ward, 1988). This translates to a range of 1,000 to 1,300 m of weekly sprint training for swimmers. On the other hand, most successful swim coaches recommend 2,000 to 3,000 m of power training per week, with only 200 to 600 m being completed during any particular training session. Perhaps track athletes do less power training than swimmers because of the greater chance of trauma that accompanies maximum efforts on the track. Power sets should probably be swum only three to five times per week for best results. Accordingly, the recommended combined total for these three types of sprint training is between 4,000 and 8,000 yd/m per week.

SPECIALIZED TRAINING FOR DIFFERENT EVENTS AND STROKES

As mentioned, the information in Table 6-3 applied to the training of middle-distance swimmers. The next series of topics are concerned with adapting this general scheme of training for swimmers in different events and strokes.

Once swimmers reach the senior level, their training must be specialized by event and by stroke. It is probably better if swimmers do not specialize during their formative years, however. Specialized training for sprinters and distance swimmers is discussed in this section. Some suggestions for training swimmers who specialize in a particular competitive stroke are also provided as well as some advice for training individual medley swimmers. Training age group swimmers will be covered in Chapter 13.

Sprinters

A sprinter is defined as a swimmer whose major events are at distances of 50 and 100 yd/m. Muscular power and anaerobic endurance are musts for these swimmers. Although sprinters need endurance training, they must be careful not to overdo it. Nevertheless, some endurance training is necessary because a good aerobic base will allow sprinters to train more intensely later in the season. Endurance training will increase the quantity of muscle glycogen so that more and longer sprint sets can be completed without becoming exhausted. Additionally, endurance training will shorten recovery time between practice sets and between training sessions. Finally, in 100-yd/m events, the contribution of increased aerobic capacity to improved performance will be almost equal to that of increases in muscular power and anaerobic capacity. The contribution of oxygen consumption to the energy supply for 100 events has been estimated to be in the neighborhood of 35 to 40 percent (Serresse, Lortie, Bouchard, & Boulay, 1988). The contribution of aerobic capacity may be even greater, however, because an improvement in the mechanisms that remove lactic acid from muscles should play a significant role in delaying acidosis.

The difficulty in training sprinters is maintaining the proper balance between endurance and sprint training so that aerobic capacity can be increased adequately without significant losses in muscular power and anaerobic capacity. How much endurance mileage is too much? is a question that cannot be answered at this time. Even if it could, the answer would probably be somewhat different for each athlete. A minimum can be suggested by calculating the mileage sprinters probably need to produce a reasonable amount of improvement at each level of endurance training. That minimum would be approximately 20,000 to 30,000 yd/m per week.

The next step is to alter the proportions of the various types of endurance training to include more basic endurance swimming and less threshold mileage. Although some threshold training is needed to train the FT fiber population, the total amount of such training should be reduced from that of middle-distance and distance swimmers so that their speed of contraction and anaerobic capacity can be maintained at a reasonable level. Overload endurance training should be maintained at recommended levels to be certain that all of the FT muscle fibers gain some endurance.

Senior swimmers who specialize at the 50- and 100-yd/m distances should increase their sprint training mileage to between 9,000 and 12,000 yd/m per week. The intensity or speed of their sprint training is far more important than the quantity, however.

The amount of endurance training at threshold should probably be reduced to approximately 3,000 to 6,000 yd/m per week. Overload endurance training should be maintained at 3,000 to 6,000 yd/m per week. Basic endurance mileage should also be reduced to, perhaps, 15,000 to 20,000 yd/m per week. The amount of warm-up and swim-down mileage should probably increase to between 10,000 and 15,000 yd/m per week. The amounts of lactate production, lactate tolerance, and power training should each be increased to approximately 3,000 or 4,000yd/m per week. Table 6-4 gives a breakdown of suggested weekly mileage for sprinters by each form of training.

Sprinters should spend more time on kicking than distance swimmers because they use their kick so much more in their races. The major emphasis should be on improving the endurance of leg muscles, because freestylers tend to relax their legs during most of their endurance and even some of their sprint training. Consequently, they must do special sets of endurance kicking to be certain that the aerobic capacity of their leg muscles is maximized. Although some sprint kicking drills are useful, sprinters should be able to improve the anaerobic capacity and the power of their leg muscles by kicking hard during full stroke sprint training.

Sprinters generally have slower threshold paces than those of swimmers of comparable ability in other events. You can expect sprinters to repeat between 3 and 5 seconds slower per 100 than middle-distance and distance swimmers on endurance sets. They also have lower heart rates when they swim at threshold speeds (generally in the range of 150 to 170 bpm), and they swim at lower percent efforts (usually in the range of 70 to 80 percent of maximum speed).

Although sprinters may be slower in endurance repeats, their greater power and speed should allow them to excel during sprint training. They can be expected to swim high-speed 50 repeats 6 to 8 seconds faster than the speeds they maintain for the same distance in threshold endurance sets. Times in fast 100 repeats may be 10 to 12 seconds faster than their threshold paces.

Sprinters should spend more time on resistance training than other swimmers. On land, this training can take the form of weight training, circuit training, or swim bench training. The emphasis should be on improving muscular power and anaer-

Table 6-4. Suggested Minimum Weekly Training Mileage for Sprinters

Form of Training	Yards/Meters per Week
Basic endurance (End-1)	15,000–20,000
Threshold endurance (End-2)	3,000–6,000
Overload endurance (End-3)	3,000–6,000
Lactate tolerance (Spr-1)	3,000–4,000
Lactate production (Spr-2)	3,000–4,000
Power (Spr-3)	3,000–4,000
Weekly training mileage	30,000–44,000
Warm-up and swim-down	10,000–15,000
Total weekly mileage	40,000–55,000

obic endurance. Some exercises should incorporate a small number of maximum efforts. Four to 12 repetitions for three to six sets are recommended. In others, the emphasis should be on training for approximately 20 to 40 seconds for three to five sets. In the water, stroke rates should be similar to or faster than the stroke rates these swimmers will use in races. Stroke rate and stroke length should be monitored carefully, with the swimmers always conscious of (1) trying to maintain competition stroke rate and (2) maintaining the greatest possible stroke length without reducing that rate.

Sprinters can train twice per day without becoming overtrained. In fact, it may even be advantageous for them to do so because they must become trained to swim fast in preliminary and final heats during competitions. The balance between the types of training is a much more important consideration than the number of training sessions per week.

Distance Swimmers

Distance swimmers must maximize aerobic capacity, even if it means compromising muscular power and anaerobic capacity somewhat. Consequently, they should swim more mileage per week than swimmers in shorter events. Some of that additional mileage should be in the form of threshold training and overload endurance training, although most will be at the basic endurance level. The mileage per week for distance swimmers should probably be in excess of 60,000 yd/m.

The amount of threshold and overload endurance training should be increased approximately 20 percent over that recommended for middle-distance swimmers. That means an increase of 3,000 to 4,000 yd/m per week for these two types of endurance training. Most of that increase should occur during the competitive period. This will encourage further improvements of aerobic capacity at a time when it is beginning to plateau. Suggestions for the weekly mileage in each form of training are provided for distance swimmers in Table 6-5.

Table 6-5. Suggested Minimum Weekly Training Mileage for Distance Swimmers

Form of Training	Yards/Meters per Week
Basic endurance (End-1)	30,000–50,000
Threshold endurance (End-2)	8,000–12,000
Overload endurance (End-3)	4,000–8,000
Lactate tolerance (Spr-1)	3,000–4,000
Lactate production (Spr-2)	3,000–4,000
Power (Spr-3)	1,000–2,000
Weekly training mileage	49,000–80,000
Warm-up and swim-down	10,000–15,000
Total weekly mileage	59,000–95,000

Distance swimmers will have faster threshold paces than swimmers of comparable ability in other events. You can also expect distance swimmers to train at a somewhat higher heart rate and percent effort than other swimmers during endurance sets.

Distance swimmers should not avoid sprint training. On the contrary, they should sprint train regularly to minimize the loss of anaerobic capacity that may be brought on by greater quantities of endurance swimming. Although minor in comparison to aerobic capacity, anaerobic capacity plays an important role in distance races. One estimate places the percentage contribution of anaerobic capacity at 14 percent in events lasting 15 to 20 minutes (Darabos, Bulbulian, & Wilcox, 1984). That contribution can probably be doubled for events of 400 m and 500 yd. The total mileage for sprint training should be the same as recommended for middle-distance swimmers in Table 6-3, although the percentage will be less because of their increased weekly mileage.

Distance swimmers will not be able to improve on their endurance repeat times as much as middle-distance and sprint swimmers when they swim sprint sets. Unlike sprinters, distance swimmers may only be able to sprint 50-yd/m repeats 3 to 5 seconds faster than their threshold paces for that distance. Times for fast 100 repeats may only be 6 to 8 seconds faster than threshold paces.

The value of heavy-resistance land training is questionable for distance swimmers. Their events do not require great power, and this form of training may interfere with their attempt to improve aerobic capacity. The decision as to whether to include dryland weight training or circuit training in the programs for distance swimmers will remain a matter of individual preference until more research is available. These programs should never be included at the expense of adequate training mileage, however.

Training for Events Other Than Freestyle

Athletes must swim their major strokes frequently in training to ensure that the muscle fibers used in a particular stroke become trained. Further, these strokes must be swum at all levels of endurance training and sprint training so that the various energy systems in these muscle fibers are stimulated to adapt maximally. For these reasons, backstroke, breaststroke, and butterfly swimmers should not spend most of their time swimming freestyle. Freestyle training can be emphasized for all swimmers during the early season. After that, however, swimmers should spend at least 4 to 6 weeks stressing endurance training in their specialties and an additional 4 to 6 weeks emphasizing sprint training in that same stroke or strokes.

Athletes should swim more than half of their training mileage in their specialty during the second half of the season. They should swim a minimum of two sets per week in each of the following types of training: basic endurance training, threshold endurance training, and lactate production training. They should also swim at least one set each of overload endurance repeats and lactate tolerance repeats in their main stroke each week. Freestyle swimming can be done in most, but not all, basic endurance sets. Athletes should perform nearly all of their kicking mileage in their specialty for reasons that will be given later.

Specific training methods for three of the four competitive strokes and the individual medley are the topics of the next four sections.

Backstroke Large teams and crowded training conditions have discouraged many athletes from swimming backstroke in training. This is unfortunate and should be remedied. Coaches should encourage backstrokers to swim their specialty for a sizable portion of both their endurance and sprint training. Backstroke flags should be up at every training session to encourage them to do so.

Backstrokers should spend more time in kicking drills than front crawl swimmers. The fact that nearly all world-class backstrokers use a six-beat kick (rather than the two- and four-beat kicks used by a sizable number of freestyle swimmers) attests to the need for an effective backstroke kick. The kick probably contributes more to propulsion in backstroke because the swimmer's supine position allows for a longer propulsive upbeat of the legs than is efficacious in the front crawl.

The principal emphasis of kicking drills should be on improving the aerobic endurance of leg muscles. Like freestylers, backstrokers tend to relax their legs when they swim endurance sets; when they do so, the aerobic capacity of their leg muscles suffers. Nevertheless, backstrokers should be discouraged from using broken-tempo kicks to save energy in endurance sets.

Backstrokers also need to do some sprint kicking; however, the speed of full-stroke sprint swimming requires a strong kick, so swimming backstroke sprints alone should be sufficient for improving the anaerobic capacity of their leg muscles.

Proper kicking mechanics should be stressed continually. Coaches should maintain a watchful eye to make sure that backstrokers are kicking correctly. One remedy when they are not is to use flexibility exercises to improve their ankle extension ability.

Butterfly Many coaches and swimmers harbor the misconception that they should not swim butterfly for long distances in training. Nothing could be further from the truth. Butterflyers need aerobic endurance in the muscle fibers they use, and there is no guarantee that freestyle swimming provides this. Muscle fiber involvement, although similar, is not exactly the same in both strokes.

They must be careful not to overdo the endurance training, however. Butterfly is a very rigorous stroke because of the large fluctuations in velocity that occur within each stroke cycle. This tends to invoke anaerobic metabolic processes at slower relative speeds; thus, the probability for upsetting the balance between aerobic and anaerobic training and becoming overtrained is increased for swimmers who swim long butterfly sets. Fortunately, the mechanics of the front crawl and butterfly strokes are more alike than those of any other two competitive strokes, so butterflyers can build some endurance with freestyle training.

The kick is equally important to swimmers in the butterfly stroke. Consequently, butterflyers must have good aerobic endurance in their leg muscles, excellent ankle extension ability, and good kicking mechanics.

A common belief is that butterflyers should refrain from swimming this stroke when their mechanics deteriorate. This misconception precludes many athletes from swimming butterfly during endurance sets and probably reduces their potential for improving aerobic capacity. A certain amount of stroke deterioration has to be expected during endurance sets, but that should not cause any serious mechanical problems. Swimmers are capable of discriminating between distance and sprint butterfly swimming. The fact that their mechanics deteriorate on long sets does not mean that they will also deteriorate during races, provided they concentrate on swimming correctly in all types of sets.

The idea of swimming butterfly in long endurance sets should not be carried to extremes. Coaches should pick a reasonable starting distance for endurance sets— one that swimmers can accomplish with only moderate difficulty. That distance should be increased week by week until athletes are spending at least 20 to 30 minutes swimming butterfly sets on short rest. Those sets should be done two to four times each week.

A variety of methods can be used to achieve this building process, such as swimming long sets of short distance repeats. Swimmers will be able to maintain better mechanics with frequent but short periods of rest. Another method is to combine one-arm and two-arm butterfly swimming. For example, repeats in which swimmers take two or three strokes with the right arm, two or three with the left arm, and then two or three with both arms for the length of the set are very good for swimming distance butterfly. One-arm and two-arm butterfly swimming can also be alternated by lengths. The same is true of freestyle and butterfly swimming and butterfly swimming and kicking. The goal in these sets should always be to increase the amount of full-stroke butterfly swimming.

Swimmers on high mileage programs should be able to swim 20 to 30 percent of their training yards/meters using butterfly without reducing their potential training adaptations. They should be sure to maintain a minimum of 8,000 to 10,000 yd/m per week of endurance butterfly swimming during the middle of the season. It is also a good idea for butterflyers to use the dolphin kick, rather than the flutter, in most of their kicking mileage.

Breaststroke All that has been said about the importance of kicking in backstroke and butterfly goes double or triple for the breaststroke. Breaststrokers should kick as much as their knees will stand. The potential for knee problems makes it necessary to administer kicking mileage with the dual considerations of improving leg endurance and preventing sore knees. Because the legs provide so much propulsion in this stroke, full-stroke swimming can reduce the amount of kicking needed by breaststrokers. So, when the potential for sore knees forces a choice between kicking or swimming breaststroke, swimming is the better choice. The leg muscles will be involved and the training effect on the whole body will be greater.

Unlike swimmers in other strokes, breaststrokers tend to relax their arms, rather than their legs, when they swim endurance sets. Consequently, full-stroke swimming will improve the aerobic and anaerobic capacity of the leg muscles, but the muscles of the upper body may be neglected somewhat. It is a good idea, therefore, to include a substantial amount of endurance pulling in the training programs of breaststrokers. This will keep the aerobic capacity of their upper body muscles at maximum levels. They should use the breaststroke pull in these sets.

The practice of pulling with a dolphin kick should be discouraged, except during stroke drills. Breaststrokers with weak pulls may compensate by letting their kicks do most of the work. Accordingly, the training stimulus on the arm muscles may remain too low for optimal adaptations of aerobic metabolism.

Breaststrokers generally do not deemphasize their armstroke during sprint sets, so sprint pulling is usually not required in these sets. Nevertheless, if coaches suspect that some breaststrokers are not using their arms fully during sprint swimming, it would be a good idea to include sprint pulling sets.

The energy demands of swimming breaststroke are even greater than those of butterfly because swimming speed decelerates so much during the recovery phase of each stroke cycle. Consequently, breaststrokers require a great amount of effort to accelerate their body forward after each recovery. For this reason, breaststrokers tend to produce more lactic acid at slower speeds, and, like sprinters, their anaerobic thresholds are slower relative to their best times. Therefore, they generally swim at a lower heart rate and percent effort than middle-distance and distance freestyle swimmers during threshold sets.

Even though their stroke requires a great deal of energy to swim, breaststrokers, unlike butterflyers, should not reduce their specialty training below 50 percent during the middle of the season. They need adequate specific mileage at all of the various levels of training to improve the three energy systems in their muscles. When sore knees make it impossible to swim breaststroke, a sizable amount of the full-stroke swimming can be replaced by breaststroke pulling and butterfly swimming. The similarity between the butterfly and breaststroke armstrokes is so great that breaststroke swimmers with weak armstrokes would be well advised to swim a lot of butterfly in training.

Individual Medley Swimmers in the individual medley must spend a considerable amount of time swimming all four competitive strokes, and they must include all levels of training in each stroke, although they do not need to stress each form of training to the same extent in every stroke.

The major training requirements for butterfly are to develop aerobic endurance and easy speed because it is the first stroke swum in these races. The individual medley swimmer wants to be able to take both 400 and 200 races out reasonably fast without becoming fatigued. This suggests the need for lots of stroke work, lactate production training, power training, and endurance training in butterfly. Lactate tolerance training is not so important because the butterfly segment of the race should be swum at a submaximum speed.

The premium is on endurance for the backstroke and breaststroke segments of 400 individual medley races because these strokes must be swum efficiently at submaximum speeds with the least involvement of anaerobic metabolism. Swimmers should focus on endurance sets, particularly at the threshold and overload levels.

Both endurance and easy speed are needed for the backstroke and breaststroke segments in 200 individual medley races. Some lactate production and power training should be included for swimmers at this distance. A small amount of lactate tolerance training is also needed in the breaststroke. Muscle pH will decline during this split, and an improvement of buffering capacity can offset the rate of oncoming acidosis.

Both lactate production training and lactate tolerance training are needed to swim a fast freestyle segment in both individual medley races. The main line of defense against impending acidosis will be an increase in buffering capacity. An improvement in the rate of lactate production will also help athletes to swim faster in spite of the acidosis they are experiencing.

Endurance repeats should consist primarily of straight sets, in which athletes swim one stroke for at least 1,200 to 2,000 m before changing over. This must be done to provide an adequate stimulus for improvements of aerobic capacity. The practice of changing strokes every 50 to 400 yd/m may not provide enough time to stimulate the aerobic mechanisms in certain muscle fibers.

Most lactate production and lactate tolerance repeats should be done in a similar manner, although the length of the sets will be considerably shorter—300 to 600 yd. The stimulus for an increase in muscle and blood buffers should be greater if a particular stroke is swum for several repeats before changing over.

In spite of what was just said, repeat sets utilizing more than one stroke in individual medley order are not without their benefits. They help swimmers improve their ability to change from one stroke to the next without losing rhythm. Many athletes tend to swim too fast immediately after changing strokes and slow down later when they realize the pace is too fast. Individual medley swimmers must learn to maintain an even pace during both the backstroke and breaststroke segments of their races so that the rate of acidosis does not accelerate too early.

Sets in which several repeats are done in each style in individual medley order are excellent changeover drills. The rest intervals between these repeats generally should be short, although they can be lengthened during the freestyle repeats to encourage faster swimming. The emphasis should be on swimming the first three strokes aerobically and the final stroke anaerobically. Repeat sets where two strokes are swum in succession, such as butterfly-backstroke, backstroke-breaststroke, breaststroke-freestyle, are also excellent changeover drills.

Individual medley swimmers need to develop strong butterfly, backstroke, and breaststroke kicks. The breaststroke kick is the most important because a weak breaststroke kick is usually the reason why many athletes cannot swim a good individual medley. In addition to its positive effect on the breaststroke leg of the race, a good breaststroke kick can allow swimmers to rest their arms somewhat for the freestyle leg. Swimmers in these events also need efficient butterfly and backstroke kicks, although these kicks should be deemphasized somewhat during the race to conserve energy for the breaststroke and freestyle segments that follow.

CHAPTER 7

Special Forms of Training

$\dot{V}O_2max$ (maximum oxygen consumption) and race-pace training were not included among the categories described in Chapter 5 because the intensity of overload endurance training is adequate for improving $\dot{V}O_2max$ and because lactate tolerance training can be done at race pace. I recognize, however, that some coaches and athletes prefer a scheme that directly addresses these two categories of training, so they are discussed briefly in this chapter. Other types of training that are in popular use are also commented on. They are broken swimming, hypoxic training, marathon training, fartlek training, and cross-country running.

Recently, it has been suggested that training with low mileage and short repeats of 25 and 50 yd/m can improve endurance as well as longer distances and repeats. This method, termed *high-intensity training,* is also discussed. Training at high altitude is the last topic covered in this chapter.

$\dot{V}O_2$max TRAINING AND RACE-PACE TRAINING

$\dot{V}O_2$max Training

The following suggestions are provided for constructing repeat sets to increase $\dot{V}O_2max$.

1. The best repeat distances for senior swimmers are between 300 and 600 yd/m. These distances provide enough time to reach and maintain $\dot{V}O_2max$ so that a training effect can take place. Age group swimmers can probably achieve the same effect at distances of 100 and 200 yd/m, provided the repeats take 3 to 6 minutes to complete.

2. The send-off times should allow for rest periods of 1 minute or longer between repeats, which will allow swimmers to maintain a speed that will produce $\dot{V}O_2$max, while shorter rest periods may force them to swim at some percentage of that maximum (Beltz et al., 1988).

3. The optimal number of repeats is probably between three and eight. This is because high levels of oxygen consumption can only be maintained for 8 to 12 minutes before acidosis makes it impossible to continue at the proper speed.

There is a considerable anaerobic component to $\dot{V}O_2$max training, even though it is thought of primarily as a form of aerobic endurance training. Consequently, it cannot be used too frequently. One or two sessions per week should be optimal.

The proper speeds for $\dot{V}O_2$max training are difficult to determine. They usually correspond to those that produce blood lactic acid levels that are 4 to 5 mmol/l above the individual anaerobic threshold. For most persons, this is in the range of 8 to 10 mmol/l. Percent efforts of 85 to 95 percent of lifetime bests and ratings of perceived effort in the 8-to-9 range are also reasonable indicators.

Race-Pace Training

Swimming at race pace is a valuable form of training for the following reasons:

1. It can improve the interaction between nonaerobic, anaerobic, and aerobic metabolic processes so that energy will be supplied in the most economical manner during races.
2. It provides a highly motivating environment because swimmers try to equal or surpass the pace of present races.
3. Athletes can train to swim with the best combination of stroke length and stroke rate under competition-specific conditions.
4. It provides an excellent method for pace training.

The most important aspect of a race-pace set is the speed of the repeats. For this reason, the repeat distances should be one-fourth to one-half the race distance so that swimmers can approximate their paces for the final portions of races. One way to apply progression to these sets is to increase the average speed from present to desired race pace during the course of the season.

The send-off time for race-pace repeats should be as long as is required to maintain race speed. It should be the shortest interval that will allow swimmers to do so, however. Another excellent means of progression is to gradually reduce the send-off times throughout the season. The ideal set distance is between 800 and 1,200 yd/m.

This form of training is very demanding and should probably not be done more than once every week or two. Swimmers soon become saturated with it, and the repeats lose their motivational value. Some guidelines for constructing race-pace sets are provided in Table 7-1.

Table 7-1. Guidelines for Constructing Race-Pace Repeat Sets

Interval Training Variable	Guidelines
Set distance	800 to 1,200 yd/m
Repeat distance	Any distance that will cause the athlete to be challenged when swimming at race speed; usually one-half to one-fourth of the race distance, except for the 1,500/1,650, where repeats of 200 or less are usually required
Rest interval	The shortest period that will allow the swimmer to maintain race speed

SAMPLE REPEAT SETS

Repeat Distance	Number of Repeats	Rest Interval
For 50 events:		
12½s	1–3 sets of 6–8	20–30 seconds between repeats; 2–3 minutes between sets
25s	1–3 sets of 4–8	30 seconds–1 minute between repeats; 2–3 minutes between sets
For 100 events:		
25s	1–4 sets of 6–12	15–30 seconds between repeats; 3–5 minutes between sets
50s	6–16	30–45 seconds
For 200 events:		
25s	3–5 sets of 12–20	5 to 10 seconds between repeats; 3–5 minutes between sets
50s	2–4 sets of 8–10	20–30 seconds between repeats; 3–5 minutes between sets
100s	8–12	45–90 seconds
For 400/500 events:		
50s	20–40	10–20 seconds
100s	10–15	30–45 seconds
200s	4–8	1–3 minutes
For 1,500/1,650 events:		
50s	30–60	10 seconds
100s	15–30	10–20 seconds
200s	10–15	30–60 seconds
400/500	2–3	2–5 minutes

POPULAR TRAINING METHODS

Broken Swimming

Broken swimming is a form of interval training in which a particular race distance is separated (broken) into several parts. These parts are repeated in sequence with a short interval of rest (5 to 10 seconds) between each. Afterward, the total time, minus the rest periods, is compared to a swimmer's best time for the distance. For example, a 200-m race could be broken into four 50-yd swims with 5 to 10 seconds' rest between each. If the swimmer averaged a time of 30 seconds for each 50, her time would be 2:00.00 for the broken 200.

Broken swimming is a very motivating form of training. Athletes enjoy swimming a broken 200 in 2:00.00, whereas a time of 2:10.00 for an unbroken 200 repeat is not nearly as exciting. Fast elapsed times are possible during broken swims, because the short rest periods allow for the replacement of some CP and the removal of a small portion of the lactic acid that has accumulated.

Broken swimming is also an excellent way to learn pacing. Swimmers can check their pace after each part of the swim and can try various methods of pacing to see which works best for a particular race distance. Some ways to separate race distances for broken swimming are listed in Table 7-2.

Table 7-2. Constructing Broken Swims

Race Distance	Segment	Rest Interval (seconds)
50	2 × 25	5–10
100	4 × 25	5–10
	25 – 50 – 25	5–10
	2 × 50	10–20
200	4 × 50	5–10
	50 – 100 – 50	5–10
	8 × 25	5
	50 – 100 – 25 – 25	5–10
	100 – 50 – 50	5–10
	2 × 100	10–30
400/500	4 or 5 × 100	10–20
	8 or 10 × 50	5–10
	200 – 100 – 100	20–30
	200 – 50 – 50 – 50 – 50	10–20
	100 – 200 – 100	20–30
	100 – 200 – 50 – 50	10–20
	200 – 100 – 100	20–30
	200 – 200 – 50 – 50	20–30
1,500/1,650	15 × 100	10–20
	16 × 100 + 5	10–20
	30 × 50	5–10

Anaerobic metabolism supplies a good deal of the energy for broken swimming. Therefore, this form of training should not be used more than once or twice per week. Blood tests have shown that swimmers reach near-maximum values for blood lactic acid when the elapsed times of their broken swims exceed their season best performances. Therefore, broken swims should be included in the lactate tolerance category in the weekly calculations of the different kinds of training. The only exception would be broken 50s, which are a form of lactate production training.

Hypoxic Training

Hypoxic training refers to swimming a repeat distance with a restricted breathing pattern. Swimmers may breathe only once every second, third, or fourth stroke cycle. The original purpose of this method of training was to simulate swimming at high altitude. Proponents thought that reducing the breathing rate would also curtail the oxygen supply and create the same kind of hypoxia that takes place at high altitudes.

We know now that this assumption was incorrect. Hypoxia refers to a reduced oxygen supply in blood and body tissues, and several studies have shown that the oxygen supply to the tissues is not reduced by hypoxic training (Craig, 1978; Dicker, Lofthus, Thornton, & Brooks, 1980; Stager, Cordain, Malley, & Stickler, 1985; Stanford, Williams, Sharp, & Bevan, 1985; VanNess & Town, 1989; Yamamoto, Mutoh, Kobayashi, & Miyashita, 1985). Although small reductions in alveolar oxygen were reported in some studies, they were not sufficient to simulate high-altitude conditions.

Nevertheless, hypoxic training enjoys considerable popularity, perhaps because it produces other, as yet unidentified training effects. It may also be that the difficulty of swimming with restricted breathing appeals to coaches and athletes because of the effort and discipline it requires.

We do know that hypoxic training produces a condition called *Hypercapnia,* which is an increase of carbon dioxide in the alveolar air. Hypercapnia produces a strong drive to breathe. In fact, when swimmers are having difficulty holding their breath during races, it is the increase of carbon dioxide, not a reduction in oxygen, that causes them to feel starved for air. Accordingly, hypoxic training can condition athletes to hold their breath so that they are able to reduce the number of breaths they take in races. For this reason, hypoxic training should be a valuable training aid for freestyle sprinters and butterflyers. Backstrokers may also gain an advantage from hypoxic training if they use the underwater dolphin kick in races.

Marathon and Fartlek Training

Athletes swim long distances continuously during marathon and fartlek training. (*Fartlek* is a Swedish word that means "speed play.") The major difference between the two methods is that the pace of the swim is constant in marathon training, and it is varied in fartlek training. Both methods of training are excellent for improving aerobic capacity.

Marathon and fartlek swims should take a minimum of 15 minutes to complete; 30 or more minutes is preferable. These forms of training generally serve the same purpose as basic endurance training; however, fartlek training can also be used to improve anaerobic capacity when sprints are mixed with slower recovery swims.

Some experts feel that these types of continuous training are far superior to interval training for improving endurance. Although the relative values of continuous and interval training have been debated for many years, the argument is academic for swimming coaches, because they have long since settled on interval training as the predominant work form because it affords greater control over the intensity of training, and the principles of overload and progression can be applied in a more systematic manner. Nevertheless, it is wise to include some marathon and fartlek swimming in every training program, because long continuous swimming may encourage aerobic adaptations that are in some ways superior to interval training.

Running and Swimming

Running and other land activities, such as running stairs, have become common early-season activities in many swimming programs because many coaches and athletes believe that these procedures enhance the training effect beyond that of simply swimming. Although running will produce central adaptations that can make a small contribution to general endurance, the peripheral adaptations that improve performance most will be very different between the two training mediums.

Running will train the circulatory and respiratory systems, causing improvements in cardiac output, stroke volume, tidal volume, and pulmonary diffusing capacity, which will improve oxygen delivery during swimming. It will also produce peripheral adaptations in the leg muscles, such as increases in capillarization, blood shunting, and mitochondria. However, for reasons explained in Chapter 4, it will not produce any significant peripheral training effects in the muscles of the upper body that swimmers use most.

The rationale for including running in the training of swimmers was originally based on research in which subjects achieved higher heart rates and higher rates of oxygen consumption by running than by swimming (Holmer, 1974). Holmer's work was misinterpreted to mean that running was superior to swimming for improving aerobic endurance. However, it really demonstrated the principle of specificity, because most of the subjects were not trained swimmers. It went unnoticed that Holmer also reported that trained swimmers achieved higher heart rates and $\dot{V}O_2$max values when swimming.

Other studies have repeatedly supported the position that oxygen consumption is improved best by specific training (Magel et al., 1975; McArdle et al., 1978; Pechar et al., 1974). In one of these, Magel and his associates (1975) swim trained 15 men for 1 hour per day and 3 days per week over a 10-week period. The subjects' $\dot{V}O_2$max values were measured before and after training, both while swimming and while running on a treadmill. Swimming $\dot{V}O_2$max increased 11 percent, and swimming times to exhaustion increased 34 percent. The subjects showed no improvement on the running $\dot{V}O_2$max tests.

Although running can be used as a supplemental form of training, swimmers should never substitute running for swimming. Any swimmer who substitutes running for swimming should understand that the results will be inferior to those he could achieve if the same time and effort were expended in swim training.

Running stadium steps is another activity that has been used as a supplement to swim training. However, although it may improve explosive power in the legs, it can be very dangerous; there is the obvious danger of falling. Furthermore, the stress placed on knee and hip joints also presents an ever-present danger of injury, particularly for females.

High-Intensity Training

David Salo (1986) has suggested that training at fast speeds for only 3,000 to 3,500 yd/m per day may be as effective for improving performance in sprint and middle-distance events as the high-mileage programs presently in use. This method has become known as *high-intensity training*.

Many coaches and swimmers see this method as an alternative to traditional training programs that require more time and effort. That assumption is doubtful, however. Support for this theory has been drawn from the results of isolated training cases in which swimmers improved their season-best and lifetime-best performances after high-intensity training. These swimmers' improvements do not support the superiority of high-intensity training; instead, they simply validate the value of training. The most important question is whether high-intensity training is equal to or better than higher-mileage, traditional programs for accomplishing these tasks.

Salo cited a study by Dudley and coworkers (1982) in support of the superiority of high-intensity training. Two pieces of supporting evidence from this study follow:

1. Dudley and associates postulated the existence of a *duration threshold* of 60 minutes for improvements in aerobic capacity. A duration threshold means that the aerobic capacity of muscles could be increased maximally in this amount of time and that additional time spent in training would not enhance the rate of improvement.

2. The aerobic capacity of fast-twitch (FT) muscle fibers could only be improved by swimming at fast speeds. These researchers reported that an intensity of 80 percent of $\dot{V}O_2max$ (about 90 percent of maximum speed) was required to produce adaptations in FT red muscle fibers and that even faster speeds were required to improve the endurance of FT white fibers.

It was a mistake to interpret the results of this study to mean that high-intensity swimming is required to improve the aerobic capacity of FT muscle fibers. An intensity of 80 percent of $\dot{V}O_2max$ falls near the anaerobic threshold for most well trained athletes. Ivy and associates (1987) also showed that both slow-twitch (ST) and FT muscle fibers of humans were recruited extensively at speeds that were 23 percent below the anaerobic threshold. Consequently, it should not be necessary to swim faster than basic or threshold endurance speeds to improve the aerobic capacity of FT muscle fibers.

The only groups of FT muscle fibers that might require faster speeds would be the FTb fibers of humans. However, Harms and Hickson (1983) suggested that too much emphasis on improving the aerobic capacity of FTb muscle fibers may interfere with the overall endurance training effect when they stated, "Faster running speeds are needed to elicit further responses by white fibers (fast twitch); but this would be possible only at the expense of dramatically reducing training duration and consequently reducing the red fiber mitochondrial adaptations."

Like other researchers, Dudley and associates (1982) did not find that high-speed training was needed to improve the aerobic capacity of ST muscle fibers. They also reported that the aerobic capacity of ST muscle fibers was increased to maximum at speeds below 80 percent of $\dot{V}O_2$max and did not increase further when the intensity of training was increased. These results were supported in works by Fitts and colleagues (1975) and Harms and Hickson (1983). It was also important to note that Dudley and associates ended their report by stating, "Our data should not be interpreted to mean that short-term intense training is necessarily adequate preparation for prolonged endurance-performance."

The concept of a duration threshold of 60 minutes for improving aerobic capacity is also challenged by the results of other researchers. Fitts and coworkers (1975) and Harms and Hickson (1983) have shown a direct relationship between training duration and improvement of aerobic capacity with work lasting up to 2 hours. In the latter study, the authors reported that the aerobic capacity in the ST muscle fibers of rats trained for 40 minutes per day at running intensities equalling 100 percent of $\dot{V}O_2$max was only half of that of rats trained for 2 hours per day at slower running speeds.

Studies contrasting improvements between two matched groups are needed to advance our understanding of the training process and guide us toward the establishment of a duration threshold for swim training, if, indeed, one exists. Even better would be a design in which one limb or set of limbs was trained with high-intensity work while the other was trained with a traditional program.

High-Altitude Training

The 1968 Olympic Games in Mexico City generated a considerable amount of interest in high-altitude training. A surprising finding was that many athletes, particularly distance runners, improved their sea-level performances in competitions immediately following the games (Karikosk, 1983). These results convinced some coaches and athletes that training at high altitudes could enhance performance at sea level. Not all experts were convinced of this benefit, however. Some researchers have cited improvements in aerobic capacity and performance at sea level following periods of actual or simulated high-altitude training (Balke, Nagle, & Daniels, 1965; Bannister & Woo, 1978; Daniels & Oldridge, 1970; Dill & Adams, 1971; Faulkner, Daniels, & Balke, 1967), yet others have reported no improvement (Buskirk et al., 1967; Faulkner et al., 1968; Reeves, Grover, & Cohn, 1967; Saltin, Grover, et al., 1968). There is even evidence of impaired performance after high-altitude training (Rahkila & Rusko, 1982).

Despite these conflicting results, swimming coaches throughout the world are making increasing use of high-altitude training in their preparation for major competitions. A survey of coaches from eight countries at the 1987 European Championships (Maglischo & Daland, 1987) revealed that all were conducting one or two high-altitude training camps per year for their swimmers. The only physiological reason they could provide for doing so was that training at high altitude increased red blood cells. However, all were emphatic that experience had shown that swimmers perform better at sea level after training at high altitudes.

The following sections deal with what happens to athletes physiologically when they train at high altitude and the probable performance-enhancing training effects they receive. Finally, some suggestions for training above sea level are offered, as well as some precautions that should be taken.

Immediate Physiological Effects of High-Altitude Training The first thing a swimmer senses upon training at high altitude is that there seems to be less oxygen in the air. Actually, the percentage of oxygen in the air is the same as at sea level—21 percent. The amount of oxygen available to swimmers is reduced, however, because the pressure of air is gradually reduced as you travel higher above sea level. The lower air pressure causes less oxygen to be driven into the lungs. This sets up a chain reaction that reduces the oxygen entering the blood and, finally, the muscles. Table 7-3 outlines the differences in barometric pressure, atmospheric pressure of oxygen, blood oxygen saturation, and $\dot{V}O_2max$ between sea level and altitudes of 2,300 and 4,300 m.

Barometric pressure refers to the total pressure of atmospheric air, including oxygen. The portion of barometric pressure that is exerted by oxygen is the atmospheric pressure of oxygen. The percentage of oxygen saturation of blood, in column four, refers to the proportion of oxygen in the blood relative to the total amount it can hold. The fifth column shows the percentage of sea-level $\dot{V}O_2max$ that is retained at various altitudes. Notice that the barometric pressure declines as the altitude increases, which, in turn, reduces the atmospheric pressure of oxygen and causes a reduction in $\dot{V}O_2max$.

The reduced pressure of oxygen in the atmosphere at high altitudes does not present a great problem when athletes are resting or during easy swimming. Humans respond by breathing faster to increase the total amount of oxygen brought into their lungs and by increasing the rate of blood flow so that more oxygen can be absorbed into the bloodstream per unit time. This permits them to maintain an adequate oxygen supply even though their respiratory and circulatory systems must work somewhat harder to do so.

Table 7-3. Effects of Altitude on Oxygen Consumption

Altitude	Barometric Pressure	Atmospheric Pressure of Oxygen	Percentage of Oxygen Saturation of Blood	Percentage of Sea Level $\dot{V}O_2max$
Sea level	760 mm Hg	159 mm Hg	97	100
2,300 m (7,500 ft)	586 mm Hg	123 mm Hg	92	83
4,300 m (14,000 ft)	446 mm Hg	94 mm Hg	85	73

The work these systems must do to supply oxygen to the tissues increases considerably when athletes swim at moderate to fast speeds. As a result, the oxygen supply becomes inadequate at much slower speeds at high altitudes as compared to sea level. This, in turn, increases the rate of anaerobic metabolism at slower speeds; thus, swimmers fatigue sooner. Accordingly, swimmers reach their anaerobic thresholds at slower speeds, and the increase of lactic acid production causes a concomitant fall in muscle pH that would not take place at sea level when swimming at these same speeds.

$\dot{V}O_2$max declines approximately 8 percent for every 1,000-m (3,300-ft) increase in altitude above 700 m (2,300 ft) (Grover, Weil, & Reeves, 1986). Decreases of approximately 18 percent (Adams, Bernauer, Dill, & Bomar, 1975) and 27 percent (Maher, Jones, & Hartley, 1974) have been reported at 2,300 m (7,500 ft) and 4,300 m (14,000 ft), respectively. These reductions decreased endurance performances by 17 to 20 percent at 2,300 m and between 25 and 45 percent at 4,300 m above sea level.

Long-Term Physiological Adaptations to Altitude Training The most important long-term physiological adaptations take place in the circulatory and muscular systems. Regarding circulatory adaptations, the oxygen-carrying capacity of the blood is enhanced by an increase in red blood cells. The principal reason for this is an increase in the hemoglobin concentration of the blood so that there is more "material" available to transport oxygen. Hemoglobin is an iron-containing protein in red blood cells that serves as an oxygen carrier. When more oxygen is carried in the blood, the pressure, or *driving force,* for diffusion of hemoglobin into the muscles is greater. Karvonen and associates (1986) reported a significant increase of 7 percent in red blood cells for a group of high-altitude-trained sprinters. The members of a control group that trained at sea level did not improve on this measure.

The increase of hemoglobin at high altitude is accompanied by a loss in blood volume. This increases the viscosity of blood and could conceivably reduce its rate of flow, so that the advantage gained in red blood cells would be offset by sluggish circulation. However, blood volume increases to normal upon return to sea level, and there is no reduction in the rate of flow.

Once oxygen enters the muscle fibers, it must be transported across the cells to the mitochondria, where it can be used in aerobic metabolism. That is the job of myoglobin—an iron-containing protein that absorbs oxygen. Increases in the myoglobin concentration of muscles after high-altitude training have been reported in the literature (Sharrat, 1982; Weihe, 1967). Such findings may point to a very significant advantage to high-altitude training, because large increases of myoglobin have not been found in humans after training at sea level (Jansson, Sylven, & Nordevang, 1982; Svedenhag, Henriksson, & Sylven, 1983).

Other physiological adaptations to high-altitude training that have been reported in the literature are increases in mitochondria (Lahiri, 1974; Taguchi, Hata, Itoh, & Itoh, 1984), an increase in the number of capillaries around muscle fibers (Terrados et al., 1988), increases in the activity of aerobic enzymes (Weihe, 1967), and increases of $\dot{V}O_2$max (Daniels & Oldridge, 1970). However, all of these adaptations also take place during sea-level training, so some experts believe that high-altitude training does not provide an advantage. Indeed, many studies have reported no changes in these physiological measures after training at high altitudes (Adams, Bernauer, Dill, & Bomar, 1975; Daniels, Troup, & Telander, 1989; Karvonen, Peltola, & Saarela, 1986; Young et al., 1984).

Unfortunately, few studies have compared the effects of high-altitude and sea-level training on the anaerobic threshold. One that did, however, involved competitive swimmers (Daniels, Troup, & Telander, 1989). Six national-level and junior-national-level competitors were trained at 2,000 m (6,500 ft) above sea level for 4½ weeks. Their results were compared with those of a control group that trained at sea level with the same relative workload. Upon returning to sea level, the high-altitude-trained swimmers showed a greater reduction in blood lactate and oxygen consumption during submaximum swims than did the control group. Both measures point to an improvement of the speed required to reach the anaerobic threshold. There was no difference between high-altitude-trained and sea-level-trained groups on improvements of $\dot{V}O_2max$. All tests were conducted within 2 to 5 days after returning to sea level. Unfortunately, neither the differences in values for the various physiological measures nor the levels of significance were reported. Perhaps the most important result was that the high-altitude group recorded more personal best performances than the sea-level-trained group in races at the 1987 Olympic Festival competition held shortly after they returned to sea level.

Although most of the attention has been focused on changes in aerobic capacity, there is some evidence that certain adaptations of anaerobic capacity may be enhanced by high-altitude training. Principal among these are increases of muscle and blood buffering capacities. Wyndham and coworkers (1969) reported an improved tolerance for acidosis in runners after high-altitude training. Mizuno and associates (1990) reported a 6-percent increase in buffering capacity after 2 weeks of training at 2,700 m above sea level. They suggested that this was responsible for an average improvement of 17 percent in short-term running time to exhaustion.

High-altitude training may be an effective method for increasing muscle buffering capacity because of the following reasons:

1. Athletes typically breathe faster and deeper at high-altitudes than at sea level. This causes an increase in blood pH. The body responds to this increase by excreting bicarbonate, which lowers both the alkalinity and buffering capacity of the blood. This effect, in turn, may trigger a supercompensating increase of blood buffers upon return to sea level.

2. Identical swimming speeds produce higher muscle lactate values at high altitudes than at sea level. This may encourage an increase in muscle buffering capacity beyond that which can be achieved at sea level.

The results of research regarding performance improvements at sea level after high-altitude training have been inconclusive. Neither Karvonen and associates (1986) nor Terrados and coworkers (1988) were able to report any significant differences in performance between groups trained at high altitudes and those trained at sea level. The subjects were sprint runners in the former study and cyclists in the latter. In the study by Terrados and associates, the high-altitude-trained group improved cycling time to exhaustion by 33 percent, but the group trained at sea level improved only 22 percent. However, the difference between the high-altitude-trained and sea-level-trained groups was not statistically significant.

Although few in number, some researchers have even reported evidence that high-altitude training can impair performance. Rahkila and Rusko (1982) reported mixed results for a group of six skiers who trained for 11 days at an high-altitude of 2,600 m (8,500 ft). Two skiers improved their performance, two performed equally as well as before, and two did much worse.

Where high-altitude training is concerned, we have a classic example of the conflict between researcher and practitioner. Researchers have presented a collection of inconclusive and contradictory evidence. On the other hand, coaches increasingly are using high-altitude training to prepare swimmers for major competitions. Are these coaches intuitively correct or guilty of misjudgment? Until this question can be answered conclusively, athletes would be well advised to include some high-altitude training in their preparation. The preponderance of evidence indicates that this form of training is at least as effective as training at sea level, and there are a number of studies and a large volume of anecdotal data that suggest it may be even more effective. However, those few cases that cited poorer performance make it imperative that athletes who engage in high-altitude training do so in a well-planned and cautious way.

Questions About High-Altitude Training There are several questions about high-altitude training that need to be answered before an effective program can be constructed.

What is the most effective altitude for training? In order to improve performance at sea level, experts suggest training at altitudes 1,500 to 2,500 m (5,000 to 8,000 ft) above sea level (Karikosk, 1983). To train for competitions that will be conducted at some predetermined altitude, it is best to train at that altitude or some similar distance above sea level.

How long should athletes train at high altitudes? The optimal length is between 2 and 3 weeks, with most experienced coaches and researchers recommending the latter time period (Karikosk, 1983; Maglischo & Daland, 1987; Sharrat, 1982). This is in keeping with results showing that increases of red blood cells tend to occur after 3 weeks of training above sea level (Grover, Weil, & Reeves, 1986).

Another recommended method is to alternate two 7- to 14-day phases of high-altitude training with 5 to 11 days of sea-level training (Karikosk, 1983). This procedure is probably designed to incorporate periodic breaks from high-altitude training to reduce the possibility of overstressing athletes.

How many times per year should athletes train at high altitudes? Most experts suggest two to four high-altitude training periods per year, with each major competition preceded by one of these training periods. Kutsar (1983) suggests that sprinters train at high altitudes for 2 weeks twice a year and that distance swimmers train for 2 weeks four times per year.

How soon should athletes return to sea level before important meets? The suggested time span ranges from 16 to 21 days; 5 to 15 days seems to be too short a period to reacclimate and produce good performances. Nevertheless, Karikosk (1983) observed that some of the physiological effects of high-altitude training were diminished and performances were noticeably reduced after 3 weeks at sea level.

Training should be reduced for 2 to 3 days after returning to sea level in order to facilitate reacclimation. The increase in available oxygen causes swimmers to feel very strong after returning, and they tend to overwork if not watched carefully.

Suggestions for Training at High Altitudes Athletes should be in good condition before going to high altitudes; otherwise, much of their time will be wasted gaining adaptations that could have been produced just as easily at sea level. The program should be conducted in three stages. The first stage is for adjusting to the stress of high-altitude training. It should last 3 to 4 days for experienced senior swimmers, although young athletes may require 7 to 10 days. Daily training mileage should be roughly one-third to one-half of normal sea-level values during the adjustment stage. The work should consist of easy swimming, kicking, and pulling at basic endurance speeds that have been adjusted for the distance above sea level. These adjustments will be most accurate if they are based on a blood test or some other method for determining training speeds that is conducted at the high-altitude site. Monitoring heart rate and perceived effort can also be done if other methods for prescribing training are not appropriate. Heart rates of 130 to 150 bpm are recommended for endurance training, as are ratings of 5 to 6 on the modified Borg scale (see pp. 164–165).

The second stage should last 2 to 4 days for senior athletes and 5 to 8 days for younger swimmers. Daily training mileage should gradually increase until it reaches normal sea-level values by the end of this period. Most of the swimming should continue to be performed at basic levels, with short sets of more intense swimming introduced near the end of this stage.

Training mileage should be at normal sea-level values during the third stage, which should begin approximately 1 week after arrival at high altitude. Threshold and overload endurance training, lactate production, lactate tolerance, and power training should be added to the basic endurance mileage in approximately the same proportions recommended for sea-level training. The following box summarizes the recommendations for these three stages of high-altitude training.

The Three Stages of High-Altitude Training

Stage 1 — Adjustment (3 to 4 days): one-third to one-half of normal sea-level values

Stage 2 — Build up (2 to 4 days): build to normal sea-level values by the end of this stage

Stage 3 — Full training: normal sea-level mileage, with training speeds and send-off times adjusted for altitude

An athlete's first attempt at high-altitude training should *never* precede a major competition. A swimmer needs previous experience with high-altitude training at less important times of the season to learn how to train properly. Inexperience with high-altitude training may cause many athletes to attempt to swim as fast in practice as they did at sea level. This could result in fatigue, sickness, or injury before the end of the training period. Consequently, it is imperative that careful control be exercised over training speeds.

A blood test or some other test for prescribing training speeds should be conducted soon after the adjustment phase is completed to establish repeat times for the high-altitude training environment. If it is not feasible to conduct a test, there are some correction factors that can be employed. A rule of thumb for adjusting training times for altitudes of 2,000 to 2,500 m (6,000 to 8,000 ft) is to add 2 to 3 seconds per 100 yd/m to sea-level training times. The addition of 3 to 5 seconds per 100 is recommended at higher altitudes.

Precautions for Training at High Altitudes Swimmers experience greater stress at slower speeds, so they can easily become overtrained at high altitudes. This may go unnoticed until too late because many of the usual markers used to monitor training responses may not apply at high altitudes. The three most common methods used to evaluate training—heart rates, repeat times, and blood lactate concentrations—can be misinterpreted easily if the effects that high-altitude training exerts on them are not understood.

Changes of heart rates, repeat times, and blood lactate concentrations during high-altitude training Maximum heart rates will generally be 5 to 10 bpm lower at 2,000 m above sea level. The difference may be as great as 20 bpm at higher altitude. Although a reduction in maximum heart rate is experienced by most sea-level athletes who train at high altitudes, it should be mentioned that there are some who maintain their sea-level maximum (Reeves, Grover, & Cohn, 1967; Saltin, Grover, et al., 1968).

There is no confusion concerning the effect of high altitudes on heart rates during submaximum swims. They will increase by perhaps 15 to 20 bpm as compared to the same speeds at sea level.

Blood lactates follow a similar pattern to the one described for heart rates. There are reports of decreases in maximum blood lactate values at altitudes of 4,000 m (13,000 ft) and higher (Klausen, Dill, & Horvath, 1970; Dill & Adams, 1971). Peak values tend to remain about the same at lower altitude levels (Adams, Bernauer, Dill, & Bomar, 1975; Karvonen, Peltola, & Saarela, 1986). Blood lactate values for submaximum swims will be approximately 1 to 2 mmol/l higher at high altitudes as compared to equivalent speeds at sea level (Terrados et al., 1988).

Finally, times for maximum and near-maximum repeats will be 6 to 10 seconds slower per 200 m at altitudes of 2,000 to 4,000 (6,500 to 13,000 ft). The box opposite summarizes this information.

Mountain sickness Athletes frequently develop symptoms commonly referred to as *mountain sickness* when they train at high altitudes. They may feel

Changes in Heart Rates, Blood Lactates, and Swim Times at High Altitude

Heart rates:

Maximum — 5 to 10 beats lower at 2,000 m above sea level
Submaximum — 15 to 20 beats higher for same sea level speeds

Blood lactates:

Peak values — Lower at 4,000 m and above
Submaximum efforts — 1 to 2 mmol/l higher for similar sea-level times

Swim times:

6 to 10 seconds slower per 200 m at 2,000 to 4,000 m above sea level

weak and complain of dizziness. Other symptoms are headaches, nausea, and, in severe cases, vomiting. Furthermore, they may experience a loss of appetite, have difficulty sleeping, and even show some signs of depression. Severe or persistent symptoms such as these indicate that the training load is being increased too rapidly.

Diet Many athletes have been reported to lose weight during high-altitude training (Adams, Bernauer, Dill, & Bomar, 1975; Dill & Adams, 1971; Karvonen, Peltola, & Saarela, 1986). As mentioned earlier, nausea, loss of appetite, and even vomiting sometimes occur during adjustments to training above sea level. The reduced oxygen supply, combined with inexperience and exuberance, may cause some swimmers to deplete their muscle glycogen at an accelerated rate compared to sea-level training (Heigenhauser & Lindinger, 1986), causing them to lose weight. For this reason, it is imperative that athletes match their caloric intake to the number of calories they expend in training. Their diets should consist of foods that are high in carbohydrates and low in fats to encourage more rapid replacement of liver and muscle glycogen supplies. It is also advisable to increase the protein content slightly if particular athletes tend toward a vegetarian diet. Their diets should also be supplemented with B-complex vitamins, vitamin C, and pantothenic acid to combat stress.

CHAPTER 8

Blood Testing and Other Methods of Monitoring Training

The effective administration of endurance training requires accurate monitoring of changes in aerobic and anaerobic capacities as well as carefully controlling training speeds. Blood testing is the most precise method for doing this at the present time; however, this procedure is not without its pitfalls. Furthermore, most coaches do not have the equipment, funds, time, or expertise to use blood testing. That is why other, more practicable methods must be found.

This chapter describes some methods for blood testing, as well as other methods of estimating training speeds that do not require any special equipment. Please do not skip the section on blood testing even if you do not intend to use it. You will understand why the other procedures work if you know how they relate to the results of blood tests.

BLOOD TESTING

Tests to locate the anaerobic threshold all have one thing in common: they measure the content of blood lactic acid after each of a series of time trials at progressively faster speeds. The lactic acid content is then graphed opposite the swimming speeds. Figure 8-1 shows the results of one of the most popular blood tests.

The athlete swam six 300-m freestyles, with 1 minute of rest between each swim. The time for the first swim was set so that it would be well below the athlete's anaerobic threshold. The time for each succeeding swim was reduced by approximately 5 seconds, and the last swim was a maximum effort. A resting blood sample was taken after the warm-up and before the first swim. Figure 8-1 shows that the

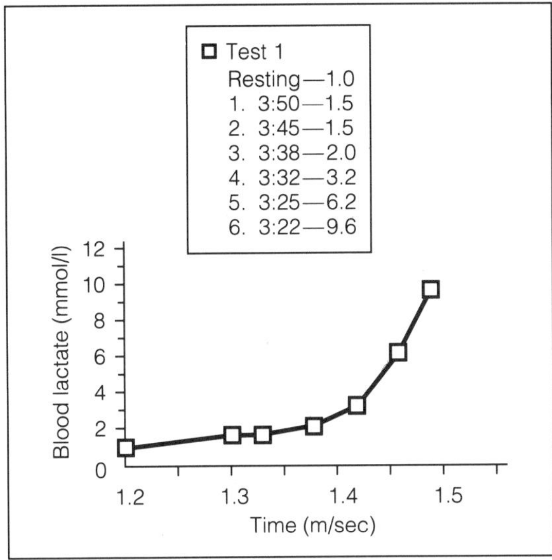

Figure 8-1. Results of a typical blood test.

content of lactic acid in that sample was 1.00 mmol/l. Blood samples were also taken during the rest interval after each of the first five swims. Samples were taken at 1, 3, 5, 7, and 9 minutes after completing the sixth swim to ensure that a maximum lactic acid concentration was detected. Muscle lactic acid continues to diffuse into the blood for several minutes after maximum and near-maximum efforts until an equilibrium exists. After that, blood lactic acid will decline because the amount pouring out of the muscles has diminished. So, several blood samples must be taken at regular intervals after these efforts until the level declines in the blood. Only by using this procedure can trainers be sure of measuring the maximum concentration of lactic acid in an athlete's blood after exercise.

Times are shown in meters per second on the horizontal axis so that they can be converted to other distances. The times for these swims, given in minutes and seconds, and the blood lactate concentrations are listed at the top of the graph for easy reference.

The first 300-m swim was completed in 3:50.00 seconds, and the lactic acid content of the swimmer's blood was measured at 1.50 mmol/l. The time for the second swim was 3:45.00, with a blood lactate of 1.50 mmol/l. The lactic acid content was 2.00 mmol/l and the time was 3:38.00 for the third swim. The figures were 3.20, 6.20, and 9.60 mmol/l for the final three swims, respectively. This last figure was the maximum value for the last swim. The times were 3:32.00, 3:25.00, and 3:22.00, respectively.

Notice that there was no increase of blood lactate from the first to the second swim, despite the fact that the time for the second swim was 5 seconds faster than the first. The speeds for these swims were below the athlete's aerobic threshold. In other words, they were well within his or her capability for supplying energy aerobically.

Blood lactate increased between the second and fourth swims (1.5 to 3.2 mmol/l). This increase suggested that aerobic metabolism was becoming overloaded because lactic acid was accumulating in the blood faster than it was being removed. The athlete's anaerobic threshold was exceeded after the fourth swim, at a speed of 3:32.00 for 300 m.

It would have been easy to mistake the increase between swims 3 and 4 for the anaerobic threshold. However, the slope of the line provides the clue that the maximum lactate steady state had not been exceeded until after the fourth swim. The slope of line was still curvilinear between swims 3 and 4 and did not become linear until after swim 4. This linear increase shows that the rate of blood lactic acid accumulation was maximal.

From the information provided in Figure 8-1, we can estimate that the athlete's individual anaerobic threshold was exceeded at a speed in the neighborhood of 3:32.00 for 300 m. That speed is equal to a velocity of 1.42 m/sec (300 ÷ 212 seconds). Another method for determining this velocity is to drop a straight line down from the point where the increase of lactic acid becomes linear.

The advantage of expressing the threshold velocity in meters per second is that it can be easily translated to speeds for other repeat distances. For example, the pace for 100 m would be 1:10.50 (100 ÷ 1.42 m/sec). I will refer to this speed more simply as the *threshold pace*.

An even simpler method to convert the threshold pace for 300 m to 100 m is to divide by 3 (212 seconds ÷ 3 = 1:10.60). Longer distances become multiples of this basic pace. For example, the threshold pace for 400-m repeats would be 4:42.40 (1:10.60 × 4).

Paces for various repeat distances that are calculated by either of these methods become the optimal speeds for threshold endurance training. They can be adjusted for basic and overload endurance training by adding 2 to 4 seconds per 100 m for the former and by subtracting 1 to 2 seconds per 100 m for the latter. The minimum speed for basic endurance training can also be taken as the velocity in meters per second at which the concentration of blood lactic acid first increases above resting. The velocity for overload endurance training will be approximately 1 to 2 mmol/l above the concentration at which the anaerobic threshold occurs. Once again, the velocity in meters per second can be determined by dropping a vertical line from either of these lactate values until it intersects with the horizontal axis.

Blood tests should be administered every three to four weeks to establish new training paces and to determine if athletes are improving their aerobic capacity. Figure 8-2 contains both the results of the blood test in Figure 8-1 and a second test administered four weeks later. Notice that for every swim the blood lactic acid concentrations during the second test are lower at the same relative speed than they were during the first test. As a result, the lactate velocity curve for the second test shifts to the right and downward with respect to the first test. A shift in this direction is an excellent result, because it reflects that the swimmer's aerobic capacity has improved. His or her ability to swim the same speeds (or faster) with lower blood lactic acid concentrations during the second test means that the energy supplied by aerobic metabolism was greater and, conversely, that the amount supplied anaerobi-

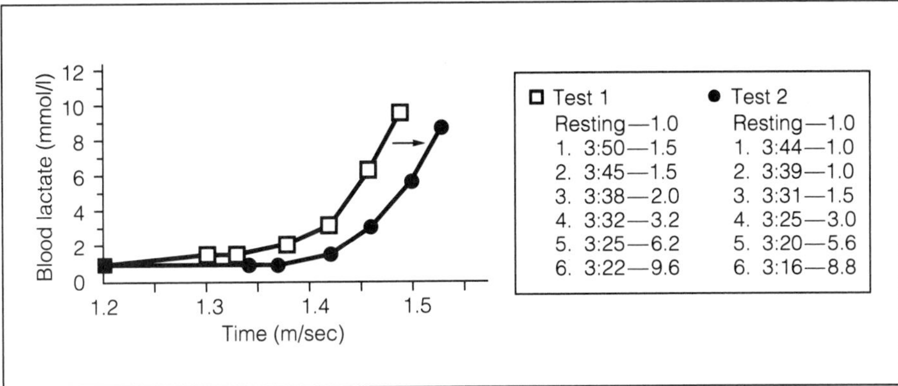

Figure 8-2. Results of two blood tests taken four weeks apart.

cally had decreased. Because of these improvements, the swimmer should experience a slower progression of acidosis (fatigue) at the test speeds and all faster speeds, including race speeds.

Swimmers should establish a faster range of speeds for the three levels of endurance training when their lactate velocity curves shift to the right, thus applying the principle of progression. Results of the second test in Figure 8-2 show that the new threshold pace will be 1.46 m/sec, or 1:08.50 for 100 m (3:25.5 ÷ 3). The athlete in Figure 8-2 would no longer be overloading aerobic metabolism if he or she continued to swim threshold sets at a velocity of 1.42 m/sec.

This type of testing lets athletes know when they are ready to train faster. Progression that occurs in concert with an athlete's ability to adapt physiologically to the demands of training should be safer and more effective. The blood test described here is very good for evaluating changes in aerobic capacity and prescribing training speeds.

USING BLOOD TESTS TO IMPROVE TRAINING

Blood tests can be used to improve training in four general ways (the first two have already been mentioned): (1) to prescribe training speeds, (2) to monitor training progress, (3) to diagnose weaknesses in the training program, and (4) to compare the potential for performance of one athlete with that of another.

Prescribing Training Speeds

One method for predicting training speeds at the individual anaerobic threshold was described in the previous section. Other methods use fixed threshold levels at 2 and 4 mmol/l. A test for determining the 4-mmol threshold is described first because it has been the most popular.

The 4-mmol Threshold Mader and colleagues (1976) suggested using a fixed blood lactate value of 4 mmol/l to identify the anaerobic threshold because of research showing that most athletes could maintain training speeds corresponding to 4 mmol/l for approximately 30 minutes. At faster speeds and correspondingly higher levels of blood lactic acid, athletes became exhausted within 5 to 15 minutes, yet at slower speeds and lower blood lactate levels they could maintain the effort for 60 minutes or longer without distress. Mader reasoned, therefore, that training speeds would be too fast to maintain an adequate duration of aerobic stimulation at higher blood lactate levels. By the same token, they would be too slow to overload aerobic metabolism maximally at lower levels.

Mader developed the so-called *two-speed test* to identify the swimming velocity corresponding to the 4-mmol threshold. In this test, athletes swam two 400-m time trials, with approximately 20 minutes of rest between each. The first swim was at 85 to 90 percent of maximum speed so that a blood lactate in excess of 4-mmol/l would be produced. The second time trial was a maximum effort. Blood samples were taken at 2-minute intervals for 9 to 11 minutes during the recovery period between each 400-m swim so that the peak lactic acid concentration would be revealed. The test data are shown in Figure 8-3. The line connecting the results of the two swims was extended downward until it intersected with a horizontal line extending from the 4-mmol level. A vertical line was dropped from this point to the horizontal axis, and the threshold pace (in meters per second) was identified by the intersection of those two lines.

One important administrative feature of this test is that the speed of the first swim must be sufficient to produce a blood lactic acid concentration of 4 mmol/l or higher. The slope of the lactate velocity curve should be maximum above this level, and the line connecting these two swims should be straight rather than curvilinear, so that the speed that will produce a blood lactate of 4 mmol can be determined by extending it vertically downward from the 4 mmol/l level.

The main weakness of using a fixed value such as 4 mmol to prescribe training speeds is that it may underestimate the individual anaerobic threshold for some

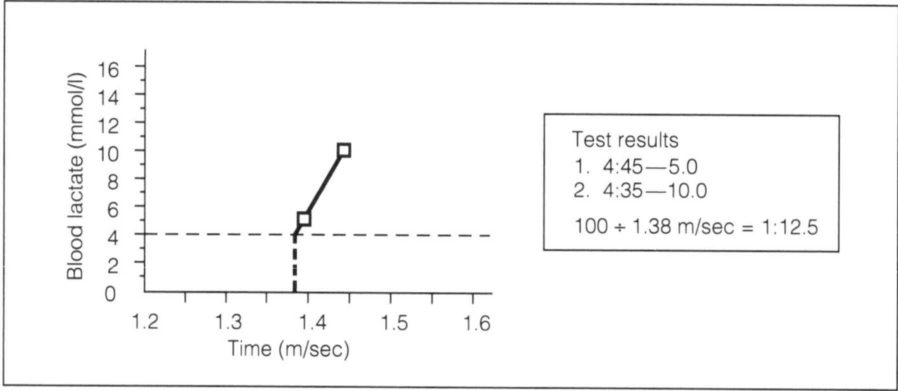

Figure 8-3. Results of a two-speed test.

athletes and overestimate it for others. Consequently, those with higher thresholds may not stress aerobic metabolism sufficiently enough to produce maximum improvements, yet those with lower thresholds may become overtrained by swimming above the threshold speed too often. The best this procedure can do is approximate the speed at which each swimmer's maximum lactate steady state occurs.

The literature is filled with studies that are skeptical of using the fixed 4-mmol threshold to prescribe optimal endurance training speeds. For example, Stegmann and Kindermann (1982) found that 15 of 19 rowers became exhausted in 12 to 16 minutes when they tried to work at speeds corresponding to their 4-mmol thresholds, and Yoshida and associates (1987) reported that subjects were only able to exercise for 15 minutes at 4-mmol speeds.

These results suggest that training speeds corresponding to the fixed 4-mmol threshold are, for many athletes, too fast for effective endurance training. There are also data suggesting that some athletes have individual anaerobic thresholds that are above blood lactate concentrations of 4 mmol/l (Jones & Ehrsam, 1982; Stegmann & Kindermann, 1982).

There are data that suggest that speeds corresponding to a blood lactate concentration of 4 mmol/l can be too slow for athletes whose individual anaerobic thresholds are above the 4-mmol level. One of the rowers in the study by Stegmann and Kindermann (1982) had an anaerobic threshold that coincided with a blood lactic acid concentration of 6.1 mmol/l. Consequently, he was able to complete 50 minutes of work with ease at speeds corresponding to the 4-mmol level. Jones and Ehrsam (1982) reported that one of their subjects was able to work for 1 hour at a steady blood lactate concentration of 10 mmol/l.

Although most swimmers can probably train safely at speeds that produce blood lactate concentrations of 4 mmol/l, those who have a threshold that is significantly below or above that value are best advised to train near their individual anaerobic threshold. Aerobic capacity may be enhanced because they will be able to train longer without fatigue and there will be less chance of overtraining.

The Individual Anaerobic Threshold An individual anaerobic threshold may be either above or below those speeds corresponding to a blood lactate concentration of 4 mmol/l; indeed, individual anaerobic thresholds ranging from 1.3 to 6.8 mmol/l have been reported in the literature (McLellan & Jacobs, 1989; Stegmann & Kindermann, 1982). Experience of more than ten years of blood testing has shown that the 4-mmol threshold approximates the individual anaerobic threshold for only 50 to 60 percent of the swimmers I have trained. The anaerobic threshold occurs at significantly lower values for another 20 to 30 percent, and it occurs at some lactic acid concentration above 4 mmol/l for the remaining 10 to 20 percent.

Other attempts to develop methods for determining the individual anaerobic threshold have included:

1. *The Simon threshold* (Simon, Segal, & Jaffe, 1987). In this test, the individual anaerobic threshold corresponds to a speed that increases blood lactic acid 1.5 mmol/l above the resting level and that produces an angle of inclination of 45 percent.

2. *The lactate-turnover threshold.* This test is based on the rate of increase of lactic acid above resting; it is the point at which 1 mmol of lactate increase equals 1 cm and 0.10 m/sec of increase in swimming speed equals 2 cm.

The lactate-turnover threshold corresponded best to the maximum speed that could be maintained during a 30-minute swim in a study comparing it with the Simon threshold and the 4-mmol threshold. Speeds calculated from the Simon threshold and the 4-mmol threshold were faster than the lactate-turnover threshold (Weiss et al., 1988).

The Maximum Lactate Steady State (Maxlass) Another type of individual anaerobic threshold that has shown promise for prescribing the optimal pace for endurance training has been termed the *maximum lactate steady state,* or *Maxlass* for short. The maximum blood lactate concentration and training speed that can be maintained for a lengthy period of time — that is, 30 minutes or more — corresponds to Maxlass. Griess and associates (1988) have presented a method for determining Maxlass. First, the test requires producing a high level of blood lactate, followed by a series of five to six 300-m swims at gradually increasing speeds. Their belief was that normal recovery would cause blood lactate concentrations to decrease at test speeds below Maxlass and to increase when it had been surpassed. In other words, a swimmer who began the series of 300-m swims with a high level of blood lactate would experience a decrease in that level until she reached a speed at which the rate of entry of lactic acid into the blood exceeded its rate of removal. Then the concentration would rise, signaling that Maxlass had been exceeded.

A sample of the results from such a test are shown in Figure 8-4. The athlete first completed two maximum-effort 50-m swims, with a 10-second rest interval between each. A blood sample was taken and analyzed after 8 minutes of rest following the second 50-m swim. The blood lactic acid concentration for that sample was used as the initial value for the series of 300-m swims. In this case, it was 9.6 mmol/l. Next, a series of five 300-m swims were completed at progressively faster speeds. The first swim was at a slow speed, with the time for each

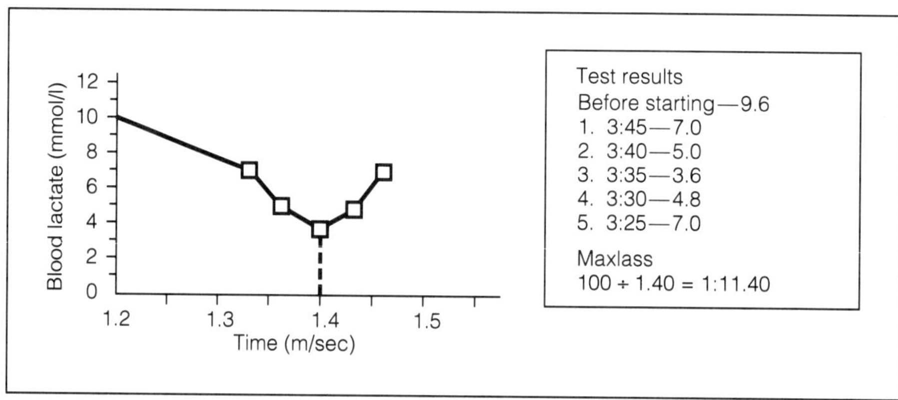

Figure 8-4. Results of a Maxlass test.

succeeding swim increased by 6 seconds. Blood samples were taken immediately after each of the 300-m swims.

Maxlass is identified by the dotted vertical line at a speed of 1.4 m/sec. The fact that blood lactate increased from 3.6 to 4.8 mmol/l after the fourth swim reflected that the rate of lactic acid entry exceeded its rate of removal at this point. Thus, the authors reasoned that Maxlass had been reached on the third swim.

Although this procedure seems a reasonable one, Olbrecht and coworkers (1988) have questioned its validity. They first determined Maxlass for 15 swimmers according to the method of Griess and coworkers. They then had the athletes swim a series of five 400-m swims on each of three successive days. On the first day, the 400s were swum at the supposed Maxlass speed as identified by the method of Griess and associates. The athletes swam the set of 400s at both slower and faster speeds during the next two days. All but two of the swimmers were able to maintain a steady or slightly declining level of lactic acid in their blood at faster speeds than those that had been predicted to produce Maxlass. It would not have been possible to do this if the test results had, in fact, predicted their *maximum* lactate steady state accurately. The authors concluded, therefore, that the Maxlass test of Griess and associates identified a lactate steady state but not *the maximum* lactate steady state. The accuracy of this test remains to be proven. It should be mentioned also that the accuracy of the test presented in Figure 8-3 has not been proven either.

Problems Associated with Using Blood Tests to Prescribe Training Speeds A problem with prescribing training paces from blood tests is that speeds corresponding to individual or fixed anaerobic thresholds at some particular test distance do not always produce the same effect at other distances. The same holds true when rest intervals between repeats are lengthened or shortened. Olbrecht and coworkers (1985) found that the velocity at the fixed 4-mmol threshold had to be corrected for repeat distances that were less than the test distance of 400 m so that the same intensity of effort could be maintained. Rest intervals had to be corrected for the same reason. These correction factors were reported in a publication by Madsen and Lohberg (1987) and are listed in Table 8-1 for those readers who might be interested in using them. Correction factors for the two-speed test are provided for both male and female swimmers. They are also shown for some of the most popular repeat distances and for rest intervals of 10 and 30 seconds.

Table 8-1. Correction Factors for Adjusting 4-mmol Threshold Speeds

		Repeat Distances			
Sex	Rest Interval	*400s*	*200s*	*100s*	*50s*
Females	10 seconds	100.0%	101.5%	103.0%	110.0%
	30 seconds	100.5%	102.5%	106.5%	114.0%
Males	10 seconds	99.5%	101.5%	103.0%	108.0%
	30 seconds	100.5%	102.5%	108.0%	115.0%

Source: Madsen & Lohberg, 1987.

Another source of error can occur when subsequent blood tests are given at different times of the day. Athletes' lactate velocity curves tend to shift to the right from morning to afternoon. According to the results of Olbrecht and coworkers (1988), athletes tend to swim faster in the afternoon with no increase in blood lactic acid. This means that training speeds prescribed from tests taken in the afternoon would need to be slowed somewhat for morning training, and vice versa.

Recommended Blood Testing Protocols Apparently, there is at present no method for determining the individual anaerobic threshold that is 100 percent accurate. All of the tests described give reasonable approximations, however. I recommend the 6 × 300 test that was presented in Figure 8-1 and the Maxlass test. Both tests are easier to administer and interpret than the Simon threshold and lactate-turnover threshold tests. I have been satisfied over the years with the 6 × 300 test. On the other hand, the Maxlass test seems to be a reasonable procedure that warrants careful consideration.

If the increase in speeds is carefully controlled, it should be possible to locate the individual anaerobic threshold within a range of 1 or 2 seconds per 100 with either test. Experience has shown that the progressive 300s test also requires fewer corrections for prescribing training speeds at other repeat distances; 50 and 100 repeats generally have to be swum approximately 1 to 2 seconds faster than the 100 pace predicted from the 300-m swims. Swims of 800 yd/m and longer should be swum 1 to 2 seconds slower than the predicted pace per 100.

Other excellent blood testing protocols involve swimming sets of eight 100-m repeats, eight 200-m repeats, and six 400-m repeats. The sets of 100 and 200 repeats provide the best information for training sprinters, while the set of 400 repeats provides the most accurate data for middle-distance and distance swimmers. These protocols have the advantage of producing a smooth lactate-velocity curve that represents training status at both the aerobic and anaerobic ends of the curve and several points in between. Sample blood testing protocols for these distances are shown in the box opposite.

Blood tests should only be conducted under the safest sanitary conditions so the possibility of spreading the AIDS virus is reduced. Different sterilized lancets should be used for each puncture and athletes should clean their hands with a sterile gauze pad after each test. Test administrators should wear rubber gloves and these gloves should be cleaned with a disinfectant after taking each blood sample.

Verifying the Results of Blood Tests It should be apparent from the previous discussion that care should be exercised when using blood tests to find the individual anaerobic threshold. For this reason, I would suggest that any attempts to prescribe training speeds from blood tests be followed by verification tests in which the athletes swim their prescribed threshold pace for a few long sets of repeats. The repeat sets should be 2,500 to 4,000 m for good senior swimmers, or they should take 25 to 45 minutes to complete for age group swimmers and swimmers of lower ability. The rest interval should be similar to the usual practice interval for endurance repeat sets. The repeat distances should be both shorter and longer than the test distance and should encompass the usual range of distances used in training.

Blood Testing Protocols

8 × 100 Protocol

1. Swim 3 × 100 with one minute rest between each at 75% effort. Rest 3 minutes. Take blood sample between 2nd. and 3rd. minutes
2. Swim 2 × 100 with 1 minute rest between each at 85% effort. Rest 4 minutes. Take blood sample between 3rd. and 4th. minutes
3. Swim 1 × 100 at 90% effort. Rest 6 minutes. Take blood sample between 4th. and 5th. minutes
4. Swim 1 × 100 at 95% effort. Rest 20 minutes. Take blood sample between 5th. and 6th. minutes
5. Swim 1 × 100 at 100% effort. Take blood sample between 5th. and 6th. minutes

8 × 200 Protocol

1. Swim 3 × 200 with 1 minute rest between each at 75% effort. Rest 3 minutes. Take blood sample between 2nd. and 3rd. minutes.
2. Swim 2 × 200 with 1 minute rest between each at 85% effort. Rest 4 minutes. Take blood sample between 3rd. and 4th. minutes.
3. Swim 1 × 200 at 90% effort. Rest 6 minutes. Take blood sample between 5th. and 6th. minutes.
4. Swim 1 × 200 at 95% effort. Rest 20 minutes. Take blood sample between 5th. and 6th. minutes.
5. Swim 1 × 200 at 100% effort. Take blood sample between 5th. and 6th. minutes

6 × 400 Protocol

1. Swim 3 × 400 with 1 minute rest between each at 85% effort. Rest 3 minutes. Take blood sample between 2nd. and 3rd. minutes.
2. Swim 1 × 400 at 90% effort. Rest 6 minutes. Take blood sample between 5th. and 6th. minutes.
3. Swim 1 × 400 at 95% effort. Rest 20 minutes. Take blood sample between 5th. and 6th. minutes
4. Swim 1 × 400 at 100% effort. Take blood sample between 5th. and 6th. minutes

If a particular swimmer cannot complete one of these verification sets, the speed of the repeats is obviously faster than his or her present individual anaerobic threshold speed. If it can be completed easily, it is below that intensity. Those swimmers who complete a set but have difficulty doing so are probably training very near their Maxlass and can use the results of their blood tests with assurance.

Swimmers who cannot complete the verification set can find their "real" threshold pace by completing similar sets at gradually slower speeds on successive days until the fastest speed is found at which they can complete the set. That speed can be used as the basis for prescribing endurance training at other distances.

Swimmers who can complete the verification set easily should use the opposite procedure. That is, they should swim similar sets at gradually increasing speeds until they fail to complete them. The speed of the last set they complete will probably approximate their individual anaerobic threshold.

These verification tests may seem burdensome because of the large number of sets required to determine the real threshold pace. They are worth the time, however. As stated before, when athletes train at the threshold pace that is right for them, they will improve faster with less risk of overtraining. Verification sets also serve as good endurance training vehicles. Furthermore, their experimental nature provides a purpose that makes practice more interesting. Fewer verification sets will be needed to determine the real threshold pace when you get to know the relationship between a particular swimmer's blood test results and his or her ability to train at the paces predicted by that test.

Monitoring Training Progress

Training progress can be monitored by comparing the results of one blood test to another. For example, Figure 8-2 shows a shift to the right in the lactate velocity curve in a subsequent test. This is a desirable result, indicating that aerobic capacity is improving.

What about the opposite effect, a curve that moves to the left during a subsequent test? In Figure 8-5, the swimmer's times were nearly the same for each swim on the second test as compared to the first. However, blood lactate levels were consistently higher. When the blood lactic acid concentration increases with no corresponding increase in swimming speed, it reflects that the swimmer's aerobic capacity has worsened. He is supplying less energy through aerobic metabolism and must rely on anaerobic metabolism to a greater extent at all but the slowest test speeds. This will undoubtedly cause him to fatigue earlier in races.

Once a shift to the left is found, a coach must quickly remedy the situation, or the swimmer, very likely, will not perform well at the end of the season. The advantage of monitoring training in this way is that a coach can correct training

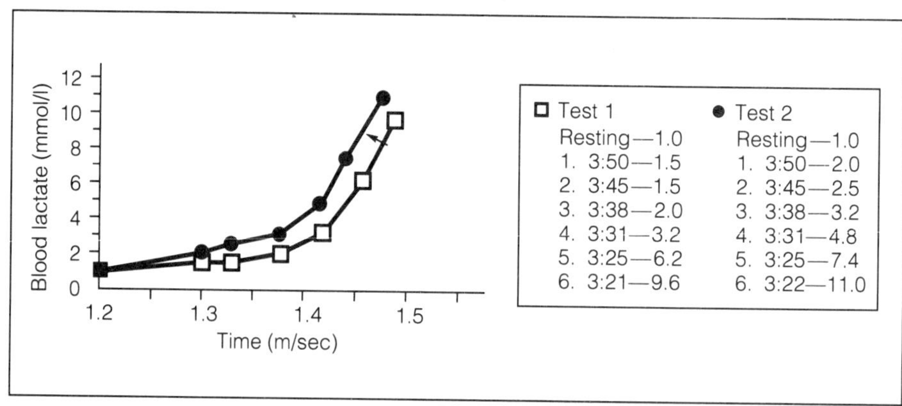

Figure 8-5. A lactate-velocity curve that indicates a loss of aerobic capacity.

problems almost immediately as they occur during the season. This will improve a swimmer's odds of performing better in the most important meets at season's end.

False Shifts in the Lactate Velocity Curve Research has shown that glycogen depletion can shift the lactate velocity curve to the right even when there has been no real improvement in aerobic capacity (Ivy et al., 1980). This is because athletes who are low in muscle glycogen must burn larger amounts of fat for energy. Because fat can only be metabolized aerobically, less lactic acid will be produced in the muscles at a particular swimming speed; therefore, less lactic acid will appear in the blood. Consequently, the lactate velocity curve will shift to the right even though there has been no change of aerobic capacity. In one study (Busse, Maassen, & Boning, 1987), glycogen depletion produced a shift to the right in the lactate velocity curve that implied a 24-percent improvement in aerobic capacity even though the ability to do aerobic work had been reduced by 13 percent. Drinking caffeine before testing will also cause an increase of fat metabolism, which will produce a false shift to the right.

One way to avoid misinterpreting shifts of the lactate velocity curve is to have athletes attempt at least one near-maximum swim during the test. Fast swimming requires a substantial amount of anaerobic metabolism that can only occur in the presence of adequate supplies of muscle glycogen. When muscle glycogen supplies are low, the effort to swim fast may be so great that athletes cannot or will not do so. Their attempt at a maximum effort will probably produce a slow time and low blood lactic acid concentration. Although this point may fall below the corresponding swim on a previous test, it will probably signify a substantial depletion of muscle glycogen rather than an improvement of aerobic capacity.

An example of a false shift to the right in the lactate velocity curve is shown in Figure 8-6. In test 2, blood lactic acid concentrations were lower at similar submaximum speeds during the first five swims as compared to test 1. This caused the lactate velocity curve to shift to the right on the first five swims of test 2. The tip-off that this was a false shift occurred when the athlete was too fatigued to attempt the sixth swim of the second test.

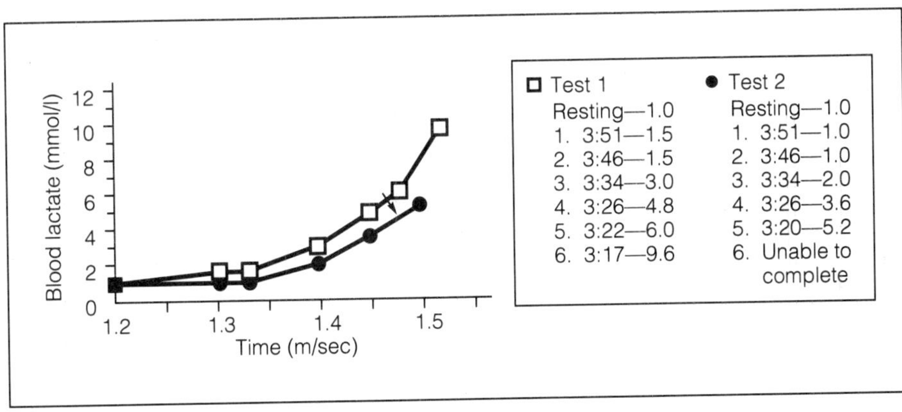

Figure 8-6. A blood test showing a false shift to the right.

A good way to test for false shifts is to have the athlete attempt a swim at the previous maximum speed. If she cannot do this, as was the case here, she may be partially glycogen depleted. In this case, the athlete should not attempt to train at the speeds indicated by the second test. Instead, she should look for the breakpoint in the curve (where blood lactate began to increase linearly) and use that speed as her threshold pace for prescribing training. The breakpoint will usually identify the individual anaerobic threshold accurately, even when the curve shifts falsely (McKenzie & Mavrogiannis, 1986). The linear increase of lactic acid will simply begin at a lower lactate level. Nevertheless, the speed it corresponds to should mark the point at which Maxlass exists. Figure 8-6 shows that the velocity corresponding to the breakpoint of the second curve was similar to that of the first—1.40 m/sec. This demonstrates that the swimmer's aerobic capacity had not changed even though the second curve shifted to the right.

Hard endurance training just prior to testing can also cause a false rightward shift in the lactate velocity curve (Fric et al., 1988; McKenzie & Mavrogiannis, 1986), possibly because the training caused some degree of glycogen depletion. For greater accuracy, athletes should probably reduce their training volume and intensity for two or three days prior to blood testing.

What about the opposite effect? A curve displaying a false shift to the left could conceivably occur if an athlete's muscle glycogen levels were high during the present test but had been partially depleted on a previous test. A false shift of this type is shown in Figure 8-7. Notice that the blood lactic acid concentrations during the slower swims are approximately the same during the glycogen-depleted (test 1) and glycogen-repleted (test 2) tests. The curve shifted to the left during the glycogen-repleted test, when the speed of the swims was sufficient to require a considerable contribution from anaerobic metabolism. In this case, the blood lactate concentration was relatively higher than on the previous test. Higher blood lactic acid concentrations that occurred only during the faster swims may be one indication that the movement to the left was a false indicator of reduced aerobic capacity.

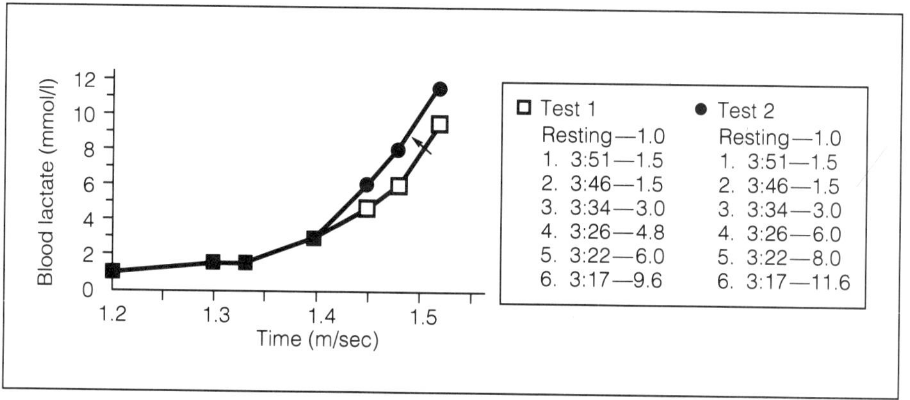

Figure 8-7. A blood test showing a false shift to the left.

Reducing training for two or three days prior to each testing period will also avoid this mistake. Athletes will be able to restore their muscle glycogen so that the levels are approximately the same each time they test.

Blood tests that are administered during the taper are most likely to show a false shift to the left because the muscle glycogen stores of swimmers are usually repleted during this time, whereas they may have been partially depleted during earlier parts of the season. A few researchers have reported finding shifts to the left during the taper (Gullstrand, 1984; Sharp, 1984). These results were interpreted as losses of aerobic capacity from a taper that was too long, too easy, or both. I suspect, however, that the leftward shift of the lactate velocity curves was due more likely to glycogen repletion. The swimmers were probably partially glycogen depleted during earlier tests and had increased their storage of glycogen to normal or supranormal levels during the taper.

The following suggestions are given for avoiding false interpretations of shifts in the lactate velocity curve:

1. Provide swimmers with at least three days of easy swimming before each test.
2. Conduct subsequent tests at approximately the same time of day.

Diagnosing Weaknesses in the Training Program

Deficiencies in training can be spotted by comparing the shape of the lactate velocity curve from one test to the next. That is, the shape can suggest that swimmers are doing too much of one kind of training—sprint or endurance—and not enough of another. Suppose, for example, that the second test produced a curve like the one in Figure 8-8. This curve shifted to the right during the slower swims (swims 1 to 3) and moved to the left during the faster swims (swims 4 to 6).

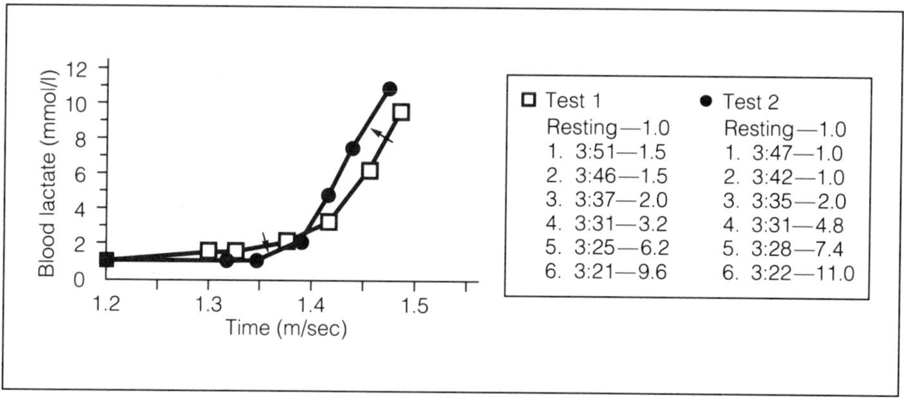

Figure 8-8. A blood test showing, perhaps, a loss of aerobic capacity at faster speeds.

It is very difficult to make accurate interpretations of training progress from complex movements of the lactate velocity curve such as those shown in Figure 8-8. The best that can be said is that this swimmer may have been doing either too much or too little training above his anaerobic threshold. A review of his training program during the previous month should pinpoint the probable cause.

Figure 8-9 shows another complex shift of the lactate velocity curve. It shifted slightly to the left during the three slower swims and to the right during the three faster ones. Notice also that the length of the curve increased. That is, the athlete was able to achieve a faster time and higher blood lactic acid level on the final swim of the second test. A curve such as this probably reflects a slight loss of aerobic capacity at slower speeds and a sizable improvement in aerobic and anaerobic capacities at faster speeds. This result is desirable, particularly in the later stages of a season, when the major meets are approaching. The swimmer graphed in this figure has an ability to swim at race speeds with less reliance on anaerobic capacity during most of the race as indicated by the lower blood lactate concentrations in the middle of the range. An improved anaerobic capacity is also manifested by the faster speed and higher lactate level on the final swim. This swimmer should have a strong finishing kick in the final 50 m of her races.

Aerobic capacity can be better at faster speeds and worse during slower swims because the curve reflects different aspects of aerobic capacity. The actual aerobic metabolism of glycogen might be slightly less efficient, as represented by the shift to the left, at slower speeds. On the other hand, the removal of lactic acid might be enhanced at faster speeds.

One of the most common shifts in the lactate velocity curve is shown in Figure 8-10. In this case, the curve moved to the right during the second test. Notice, however, that the speed of the final swim was slower and that the blood lactic acid concentration following that swim was not so great as in the first test. Two possible explanations for a shift of this nature are:

1. The swimmer did not try as hard on the final swim.
2. The swimmer's anaerobic capacity had worsened.

If it can be determined that the swimmer made an honest effort on the last swim, the low maximum value indicates that his ability to produce lactic acid may have deteriorated.

If an athlete's anaerobic capacity has declined, this trend should be reversed and sprint training should be emphasized. Reversing the trend also requires reducing both the quantity and quality of endurance training for a short period.

Some loss of anaerobic capacity usually occurs when large volumes of endurance training are being performed. Consequently, *some sprint training should be conducted throughout the entire season to reduce the loss of anaerobic capacity that usually accompanies an emphasis on endurance training*.

Comparing Potential Performances

The final use for lactate velocity curves is to compare the performance potential of one swimmer with another, the assumption being that an athlete who swims faster with lower blood lactic acid levels should be faster in races. That assumption is

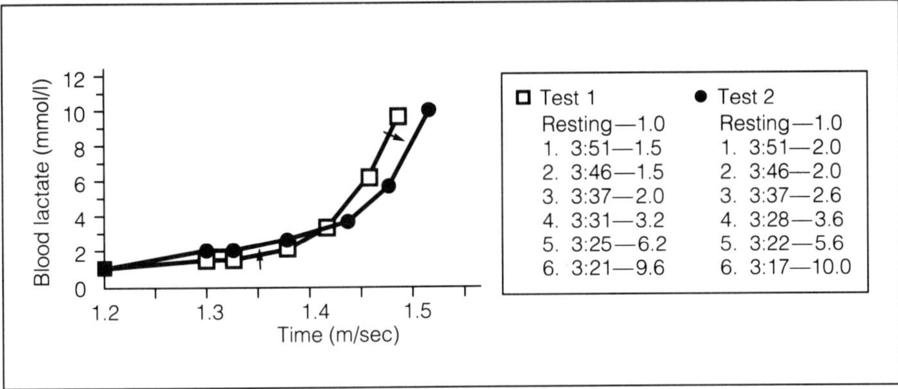

Figure 8-9. A blood test showing, perhaps, a loss of aerobic capacity at slower speeds.

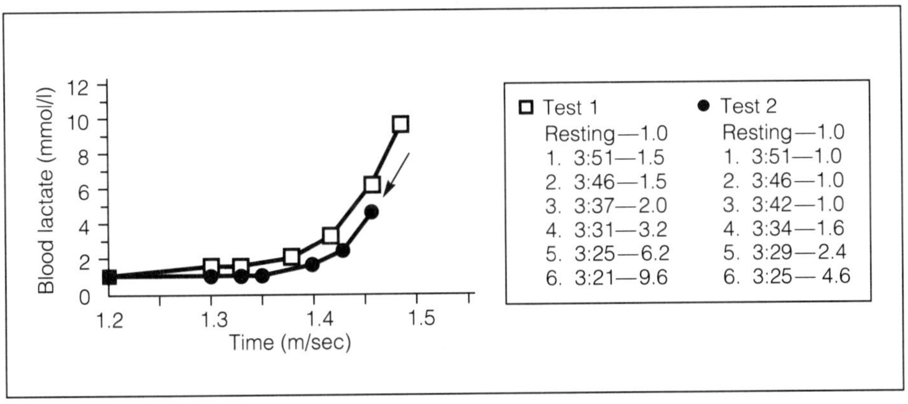

Figure 8-10. Blood test showing a possible loss of anaerobic capacity.

justified for heterogeneous groups of swimmers. Caution should be exercised when making judgments among members of homogeneous groups, however. Sharp and associates (1984a) compared the lactate velocity curves for members of the 1984 U.S. Olympic team with those of non-Olympic college swimmers. The Olympians had significantly faster velocities at the 4-mmol threshold. The Olympic males averaged 1.54 m/sec, versus 1.44 m/sec for the non-Olympic male collegians. For women, the difference was 1.47 m/sec for the Olympians, versus 1.29 m/sec for the non-Olympians. These differences were significant.

I would recommend caution when using lactate velocity curves to compare the performance potential of more homogeneous groups of athletes. Although the relationship between performance and both fixed and individual anaerobic thresholds is quite high, it accounts for only 80 percent of the differences in times for events of 400 m and longer and only 60 percent of the differences for events of 100 and 200 yd/m. Both percentages leave a considerable portion of the performance unaccounted for. So, it would be difficult to predict which of two swimmers would win if they had similar performance times, even if one had a faster individual anaerobic threshold.

MONITORING TRAINING WITHOUT BLOOD TESTING

Monitoring endurance training is important to the success of swimmers, and blood testing is certainly the best method for doing so. Blood testing is not always possible, however; most coaches lack the equipment and, with large teams, the time to administer tests. There is also the danger of contracting the AIDS virus if sterile conditions are not maintained during testing. These two reasons make it imperative that other, less complex and less expensive methods be found to monitor training and prescribe endurance training speeds.

The time-honored methods that we coaches have used to monitor training are (1) with a stopwatch or pace clock and (2) through intuition. There are several ways to use the concepts of blood testing with these tools for monitoring training and prescribing training speeds. They all have certain weaknesses (as does blood testing). Nevertheless, they provide quantitative and qualitative data about certain aspects of training that can assist us in making better judgments. Some of the best tests are presented in the sections that follow. Some popular procedures that are not so accurate are discussed later in this chapter.

The T-30 Test

Developed by Olbrecht and his associates (1985) from the Institute for Sports Medicine in Cologne, Germany, this test consists of swimming either a 30-minute or 3,000-m time trial. The swim should be a maximum effort and evenly paced from start to finish. The results are then converted to an average speed per 100 m by dividing the distance swum in 100s by the time in seconds. The following box illustrates this procedure. In this case, the swimmer completed a 3,000-m swim in

Procedures for Administering the T-30 Test

3,000 Swim time = 35 minutes (2,100 seconds)

Pace per 100 m = 2,100 ÷ 30 = 1:10

Pace for other repeat distances = 1:10 × distance in 100s

Example time for 400 m: 1:10 × 4 = 4:40

Correction factors: 200s = T-30 time − 2 seconds
100s = T-30 time − 1.5 seconds
50s = T-30 time − 1 second

Source: Olbrecht et al., 1985.

35 minutes (2,100 seconds), which calculates to an average speed per 100 m of 1:10 (2,100 ÷ 30 = 70 seconds).

Olbrecht and coworkers found that the average speed for a T-30 swim corresponded very closely to the pace that produced a blood lactic acid concentration of 4 mmol/l as determined from a typical blood test. I suspect, however, that it corresponds even more closely to each swimmer's individual anaerobic threshold, because swimmers should not be able to swim above their individual anaerobic threshold for 30 minutes without a severe loss of speed during the later stages of the swim (Stegmann & Kindermann, 1982). The average speed for a T-30 test probably does not differ significantly from the 4-mmol speed, because, for most swimmers, the individual anaerobic threshold lies between values of 3 and 5 mmol/l. Consequently, the T-30 test provides an accurate method for prescribing endurance training that does not require blood testing.

The threshold pace calculated from this test can be used to prescribe training at other repeat distances and at other levels of endurance training. Other repeat distances are simply multiples of the threshold pace. For example, if 1:10 is the threshold pace calculated from a T-30 test, 300 repeats would be swum at speeds approximating 3:30 (3 × 1:10), while 800 repeats would be swum at 9:20 (8 × 1:10). Paces for basic endurance training can be determined by adding 3 to 4 seconds per 100 yd/m to the threshold pace, and paces for overload endurance training are calculated by subtracting 1 to 2 seconds per 100 yd/m.

The authors of the T-30 test found that multiples of the threshold pace were only accurate for repeat distances of 300 m and longer and for rest intervals of 10 to 20 seconds. At shorter distances and longer rest intervals, the multiples needed to be adjusted somewhat. Correction factors for repeat distances of 200 m and less are listed in the preceding box.

The T-30 test is practical for senior swimmers of reasonable ability as it was described. It can be adapted easily for younger and older swimmers and those with less ability. The important factor to remember when making adaptations is that the test distance should require approximately 30 minutes to complete. One procedure that could be used when adaptations are required is to chart the distance swum in 30 minutes and calculate the threshold pace by dividing 30 minutes by the distance in 100s. Another procedure is to establish a test distance, such as 2,000 or 2,500 m, that would take approximately 30 minutes to swim.

The major advantage of the T-30 test over other, noninvasive methods is that it has been proven to be a valid indicator of the swimming speeds required to attain Maxlass. Another important advantage is that it should be a valid indicator for all swimmers, even those with anaerobic thresholds that are above and below the 4-mmol level. The disadvantages of the T-30 test follow:

1. Swimmers must make an honest effort, or the test results will not be accurate. The calculated threshold pace will be too slow to reach Maxlass if athletes do not swim at 100-percent effort during the test. Consequently, they will not be swimming at their real individual anaerobic threshold when they train at these paces.

2. Substandard efforts will also provide inaccurate information about changes of aerobic capacity. Less effort on subsequent tests can give the false impression that aerobic capacity has not improved. Conversely, a 100-percent effort following a previous substandard swim will give a false impression of improved aerobic capacity.

3. The test does not lend itself to estimating the threshold pace of butterfly and breaststroke swimmers. The distance is too long for most athletes to swim butterfly well, and many breaststrokers may not be able to complete the test at maximum effort because of knee pain.

The problems with substandard efforts can be avoided when athletes are properly motivated and understand the importance of the test. Butterfly and breaststroke swimmers may need to use the next procedure.

Predicting Threshold Paces with Repeat Sets

This simple procedure consists of swimming a long set of repeats on short rest. Research with the T-30 test showed that athletes cannot swim much longer than 30 minutes above their individual anaerobic threshold. Therefore, the maximum average speed for a set of repeats that takes approximately this amount of time to complete should correspond closely to their threshold pace. Accordingly, the set should take from 25 to 40 minutes to complete, and the rest intervals should approximate those that are typically used in endurance training, usually between 10 and 30 seconds. The best repeat distances for this set are between 200 and 400 yd/m because the estimated threshold pace can be converted with reasonable accuracy for the usual range of practice repeat distances.

We tested this method for estimating the threshold pace and found it to be reasonably accurate (Maglischo, 1989). A group of athletes swam fifteen 200-yd repeats, with a send-off time that provided 10 to 15 seconds of rest between swims. The subjects were asked to swim the entire set at the fastest possible average speed, with no more than 2 to 4 seconds difference per 200 from the fastest to slowest repeat in the set. They were given three practice trials before testing to help them learn what they were capable of achieving. Blood lactic acid samples were collected immediately after the eighth and the fifteenth repeats. These were compared to the subjects' most recent blood tests (5 × 300) to determine how closely their average speed and blood lactic acid concentration corresponded to those identifying their individual anaerobic threshold.

Statistical analysis showed that there was no significant difference between their average time for the 200 repeats and their threshold pace for 200-yd repeats. The difference between their blood lactate values during the set of 200s and their threshold values were also not significantly different. The results are listed in Table 8-2.

Repeat distances of 30 × 100 yd, 6 × 500 yd, and 4 × 800 yd on short rest (10 to 30 seconds) were used to verify the threshold paces calculated from this set of 15 × 200-yd repeats. The verification procedure was carried out in two stages. In the first stage, the athletes swam the sets at their threshold pace that was predicted from the set of repeats. Blood samples were taken at the completion of the set or at the time of failure and were analyzed for lactic acid content.

Table 8-2. Comparison of Threshold Paces Calculated from Blood Tests and a Set of 15 × 200

Subject	Average for 200 Swims	Blood Lactate	Threshold Pace from Blood Test	Blood Lactate
1	2:26.00	4.5	2:30.00	3.0
2	2:24.00	4.5	2:24.00	3.3
3	2:14.00	2.0	2:14.00	2.5
4	2:14.00	3.9	2:16.00	3.5
5	2:20.00	4.2	2:24.00	3.0
6	2:20.00	2.4	2:16.00	4.2
7	2:10.00	5.7	2:14.00	2.5
8	2:18.00	3.6	2:18.00	3.0
9	2:20.00	3.0	2:20.00	3.0
10	2:16.00	4.2	2:16.00	2.1
11	2:10.00	3.0	2:11.00	2.5
12	2:20.00	4.5	2:20.00	3.8
13	2:24.00	4.8	2:25.00	3.8
14	2:20.00	5.7	2:24.00	4.0
15	2:08.00	4.2	2:09.00	3.0
16	2:14.00	3.5	2:14.00	3.8
17	2:16.00	3.9	2:20.00	2.8
18	2:28.00	5.1	2:30.00	4.2
19	2:16.00	3.6	2:16.00	2.0
20	2:06.00	3.3	2:08.00	3.0
21	2:26.00	4.5	2:26.00	4.0
22	2:16.00	4.8	2:18.00	4.1
23	2:21.00	4.2	2:24.00	3.3
24	2:10.00	3.0	2:08.00	2.5
25	2:04.00	4.2	2:06.00	3.8
26	2:10.00	3.6	2:16.00	3.0
27	2:16.00	1.5	2:14.00	2.0
28	2:28.00	3.9	2:28.00	4.0
29	2:16.00	4.8	2:18.00	4.0

Source: Maglischo, 1989.

Twenty-six of 33 swimmers were able to complete the sets at their threshold pace. Blood lactate measures were at or near those corresponding to their individual anaerobic threshold for those who made the entire set. Those values were between 3.3 and 4.8 mmol/l. Most of the failures came in the set of 800s. It appeared that the threshold pace predicted from the set of 15 × 200 needed to be increased by 1 to 2 seconds per 100 for repeats of this length and longer.

The purpose of the second verification procedure was to determine if the threshold paces that had been determined from the swim test were producing Maxlass.

The athletes were asked to complete the same 3,000-yd sets of repeats on short rest at an average speed that was 2 to 3 seconds per 100 yd faster than their predicted threshold pace. They were told to complete the sets even if they could not maintain their prescribed pace. They were also told to have a blood sample taken when they could no longer maintain the pace within 2 seconds per 100 of the prescribed time or when they completed the set.

Only 10 of 32 swimmers were able to complete the set at their prescribed pace. All of these athletes swam 100 repeats. The range of blood lactic acid levels for those who failed were 2.7 to 8.4 mmol/l at the time of failure, and the range for those who completed the set of 30 × 100 were between 2.4 and 4.8 mmol/l.

These results showed that the test set identified the swimming speeds that produced Maxlass for the vast majority of the swimmers in the group. Apparently, however, those speeds need to be adjusted for repeats of 100 yd/m and less. Ten of 12 swimmers were able to complete the set of 30 × 100 at a speed faster than their threshold pace. The athletes generally swam 2 to 3 seconds faster and remained within the usual range of blood lactic acid concentration at which the individual anaerobic threshold is found. This means that the threshold pace predicted from the set of 200s should be reduced 2 to 3 seconds per 100 when swimming repeat distances of 100 yd/m and less.

A test set of this type is an accurate method for prescribing threshold paces, with some slight reductions for repeat distances of 100 yd/m and increases for repeats of 800 yd/m and longer. The advantages of test sets over other methods for prescribing training speeds are several. For one, no breaks in training are needed for test administration. Threshold paces can be established from typical sets in regular training sessions. Once determined, they can be adjusted for other distances, rest intervals, and levels of endurance training. Another important advantage of this method over the T-30 test is that it can be used by butterfly and breaststroke swimmers. A third advantage is that test sets of repeats can be adapted easily for use with age group and older Masters swimmers. Simply change the number and/or distance of the repeats and the rest intervals to fit the ability levels of the swimmers. The rules of thumb for adapting test sets follow:

1. The test set should require 25 to 40 minutes to complete.
2. The rest interval should be short, 30 seconds or less. An example of a test set for younger swimmers would be fifteen or twenty 100-m repeats on a send-off of 1:50. This set should suffice for a group of 9- to 10-year-old swimmers who generally repeat 100s in 1:25 to 1:40.

The Swimming Step Test

The swimming step test was recently developed to identify swimming speeds that produce Maxlass. The advantage to this test is that it reduces the probability that lack of effort will invalidate the results. The test consists of swimming several short sets of repeats at progressively faster speeds until an athlete can no longer complete a set at the prescribed pace. We chose sets of 5 × 200 on a send-off time that allowed 10 to 15 seconds of rest between repeats. The first set was swum at a slow speed that was known to be below the athlete's Maxlass (individual anaerobic threshold). The average speed per 200 was increased by approximately 4 seconds for each succeeding set. The starting speed was set so that swimmers would be able to complete at least three sets before they failed. (The starting speed must be estimated the first time the test is administered but is easy to figure for subsequent tests.) Failure was defined as being unable to swim at the prescribed speed for the previous set. Defining failure in this way improved the accuracy of the test results and prevented athletes from stopping prematurely when they missed the pace by only 1 or 2 seconds.

The test administrator was responsible for recording the average speed for each set and the number of the repeat at which the swimmer failed in the final set. The threshold pace was estimated from these data in the following manner. If failure occurred late in the final set, a swimmer's threshold pace was taken to be the average speed of the previous set. If failure occurred during one of the first two repeats in the final set, the threshold pace was listed as the swimmer's average time from two sets earlier.

The assumption behind this method of selecting the threshold pace was that swimmers who failed late in a set probably exceeded their Maxlass during that set. Consequently, their threshold pace was probably the time of the previous set. On the other hand, athletes who failed early in a set probably exceeded their Maxlass during the previous set. Therefore, their threshold pace was the time of the set before that (two sets before failure occurred).

The results of two step tests are shown in the following box. They should help clarify the procedure for estimating threshold pace. Swimmer A had a threshold pace of 1:12.00 for 100 m. He failed during the fourth repeat of the third set of 200s, so his threshold pace was the average speed of the previous set (2:24) corrected to 100 m. Swimmer B failed in the first repeat of the fourth set, so his threshold pace was the average speed of the second set (2:24), which, corrected to 100 m, was also 1:12.00.

Results of Two Swimming Step Tests

The Swimming Step Test (Sets of 5 × 200 with Rest Intervals of 10 to 15 Seconds)

Swimmer A	Swimmer B
Set 1—2:28—completed	Set 1—2:28—completed
Set 2—2:24—completed	Set 2—2:24—completed
Set 3—2:20—failed on fourth repeat	Set 3—2:20—completed
	Set 4—2:16—failed on first repeat
Aerobic pace is 1:12.00 for 100 m.	Aerobic pace is 1:12.00 for 100 m.
2:24. + ÷ 2 = 1:12.00	2:24. + ÷ 2 = 1:12.00

The validity of this procedure was tested by comparing the threshold paces for a group of 38 male and female collegiate swimmers from a typical blood test (5 × 300) with the paces predicted from a swimming step test. The blood test was administered first, and the Maxlass test was carried out two days later. The relationship was calculated at a highly significant 0.94. This relationship showed that the swimmers' individual anaerobic threshold could be estimated accurately with the swimming step test.

The swimming step test can be adapted for younger swimmers and swimmers of less-than-average ability by applying the following rules:

1. Each repeat should require 1½ to 3 minutes to swim.
2. Each set of repeats should require approximately 10 minutes to complete.

Thus, younger and slower swimmers could use 3 × 200 or 4 or 5 × 100 sets for this purpose (assuming an average speed of 1:30 or slower per 100).

The test may also need to be adapted for butterfly swimmers, who have difficulty swimming multiple 200 repeats. We have used sets of 5 × 100 with 15-second rest intervals for this purpose and have found them satisfactory for prescribing training speeds.

The major advantage of the swimming step test is that it reduces the likelihood that substandard efforts will affect the results. You can be reasonably certain that swimmers have given a maximum effort when they swim to failure. One disadvantage is that it is not possible to pinpoint the exact speed at which the Maxlass pace was surpassed. The best you can do is estimate the pace within a range of 2 seconds per 100 yd/m. However, this is not a serious disadvantage. It is often just as difficult to estimate the threshold pace from breakpoints on the lactate velocity curve.

Another disadvantage is that it becomes difficult to monitor changes of aerobic capacity late in the season. The rate of improvement tends to decline after the middle of the season, and a 2-second error range per 100 may be too large to pinpoint small improvements or decrements. In this case, the number of repeats an athlete can complete in the final set (assuming it is attempted at the same average speed as during previous tests) is probably a good guide for interpreting changes of aerobic capacity. If more swims can be completed before failure, the swimmer has probably improved her aerobic capacity, even though the calculated threshold pace did not change. Conversely, the opposite effect has probably occurred if she completes fewer repeats.

The swimming step test is still in the developmental stage. Although it is accurate in its present form, there may be several features that could be adjusted for even better results. Other repeat distances, numbers of repeats, and send-off times need to be tested.

Cruise Intervals

The cruise intervals test, developed by Dick Bower, has achieved a considerable degree of acceptance because it can be easily administered and adapted to swimmers of all ages and ability levels. The early version required swimming a set of 5 × 100 on the fastest possible send-off time. The swimmer then added 5 seconds to the send-off time to determine his or her cruise interval. For example, a swimmer who completed a set of 5 × 100 on 1:05 would have a cruise interval of 1:10 (1:05 + 5) for 100 repeats. The goal of swimmers in an endurance practice set of, say, 20 × 100 on 1:10, would be simply to make the interval. They could do this by swimming slower than 1:05 per 100 but not slower than 1:10. Swimmers were, in fact, encouraged to swim at slower speeds—for example, 1:06 to 1:08—in order to encourage aerobic adaptations without becoming overtrained.

Cruise intervals can also be used to determine send-off times for other distances. Longer repeat distances were simply multiples of the cruise interval time for 100s. For example, the cruise interval for a set of 200s would be 2:20; for 500s, 5:50.

The latest version of the test is longer in order to improve its accuracy for predicting endurance training speeds. In this version, athletes swim a set of 15 × 100 on the shortest possible interval. The cruise intervals for various repeat distances are then determined in the same manner as described in the previous paragraphs.

The cruise interval test is believed to predict the threshold pace for endurance training. We tested the validity of this belief by testing 12 male university competitive swimmers (Firman & Maglischo, 1986). We found each swimmer's cruise interval using the 5 × 100 test. Following that, we asked them to swim a set of 20 × 100 on their calculated cruise interval send-off times. Their average speed was recorded for each repeat and compared to their threshold pace, which had been calculated from blood testing just a few days earlier. Samples of blood lactate were also taken near the end of each cruise interval set to determine concentration values being produced by the swims.

The cruise speeds were generally slower than the threshold paces that had been determined from blood testing. Blood lactate concentrations were somewhat above the threshold level for 5 of the 12 subjects and at or near the threshold for the remaining 7. Our conclusion was that although the cruise speeds approximated the threshold pace, blood lactate concentrations suggested that some of the athletes may have been swimming above their individual anaerobic threshold. This may have been because the rest intervals were generally less than 5 seconds.

Bower (1985) has recently suggested that the test interval plus 10 seconds might be more effective for endurance training than adding only 5 seconds to that figure. The Firman and Maglischo results support that contention. Adding 10 seconds will probably slow the cruise speed enough to allow most swimmers to train at or slightly below their threshold. The original procedure of adding 5 seconds to the test results is probably good for prescribing the paces for overload endurance training. According to our results, it will encourage swimmers to train at or just above their individual anaerobic threshold.

Bower (1985) has also proposed the addition of cruise^{+} and cruise^{-} intervals to the training program. In cruise^{+} swimming, an additional 5 or 10 seconds is added to the cruise interval to allow swimmers to repeat at a lower intensity. This intensity probably corresponds to the basic level of endurance training. Cruise^{-} repeats have the opposite purpose. Two to 10 seconds are subtracted from the cruise interval to force the swimmers into repeating at more intense efforts. Cruise^{-} repeats are probably similar to overload endurance and lactate tolerance intensities.

The major advantage of cruise intervals is that they provide an easily understood and administratively feasible structure for endurance training that encourages each swimmer to train in the individual range of endurance speeds that is best for him. Furthermore, this method for individualizing training can be accomplished in a crowded pool with a large and diverse group of swimmers.

Another advantage is that the test needs little, if any, adjustments for use with swimmers of different ages and ability levels. All of the other tests that have been described require some adjustments for these groups.

The primary disadvantage of cruise intervals is that they may not be precise enough to maximize the effects of endurance training. Cruise intervals do not identify the threshold pace, only a range in which it probably falls. Also, there is no guarantee that longer repeats, which are multiples of the cruise interval speeds for 100s, will overload aerobic metabolism to the same extent that it was overloaded by the shorter swims. It is possible, therefore, that some swimmers may undertrain and others may overtrain on a steady diet of cruise intervals. There will be less danger of this happening if the training program includes a variety of send-off times that include not only the cruise interval but also cruise$^+$ and cruise$^-$ intervals.

The Modified Borg Scale

The Borg scale was originally developed to monitor training during cardiac rehabilitation. Patients were taught to equate work intensities to a number on a scale. Researchers found that their patients learned to monitor the intensity of training quickly and with acceptable accuracy when they used this procedure (Bellew, Burke, & Jensen, 1983; Purvis & Cureton, 1981).

It occurred to me that swimmers could be taught to monitor the intensity of their training in the same way. The original Borg scale rated exercise intensity from 1 (easy) to 20 (extremely hard). It seemed that a scale that was graduated from 1 to 10 would serve the same purpose; therefore, the Borg scale was adapted as shown in Table 8-3. The exercise intensities and probable training effects corresponding to each number on the scale are listed in the various columns.

Swimmers must first be familiar with the physical and mental sensations associated with swimming below, at, and above their anaerobic threshold before they can use this scale effectively. That can be accomplished by establishing their threshold pace with one of the tests described previously. Then, they should swim some repeat sets that are both faster and slower than this pace while trying to assign a rating of perceived effort from this scale. For example, for most swimmers, repeats that are at or near their present anaerobic threshold should feel like an intensity of 7 to 8 (7 early in the set, 8 later). Overload endurance sets should probably begin at an intensity corresponding to 8 and progress to 9, and basic endurance sets would begin at a rating of perceived effort of 3 and progress to 6. Sets that are designed for race pace, VO_2max, and sprint training should always be at a rating of perceived effort of 9 or 10.

This adapted Borg scale has the advantage of being a very convenient and easy procedure for prescribing training intensities. Training according to a rating of perceived effort also allows swimmers to compensate for periodic variations in physiological capacity. Perhaps the most important advantage is that it allows

Table 8-3. The Modified Borg Scale

Rating	Perceived Effort	Probable Training Effect	Level of Training
10	Extremely difficult	Improves anaerobic metabolism	Lactate tolerance
9	Very difficult	Improves anaerobic capacity and and VO_2max; intensity is above the present anaerobic threshold	Lactate tolerance End-3
7–8	Hard but manageable	Overloads aerobic metabolism; work at or slightly below the present anaerobic threshold	End-2
5–6	Moderate effort	Improves aerobic capacity while providing some relief from intense training	End-1
3–4	Easy	Maintains aerobic endurance while recovering from intense training	End-1
1–2	Very easy	Is useful for warming up and swimming down	

motivated swimmers to progress at their own pace rather than according to some preselected test schedule. That is, they can increase their training paces when they feel capable of doing so, rather than waiting for new test results to tell them when to do it.

The major disadvantage of this method is its lack of quantification in the form of paces for training. Poorly motivated and supermotivated swimmers may frequently train too slow or too fast. Without actual training speeds for guidance, poorly motivated swimmers will overestimate the intensity of their repeats, and supermotivated swimmers will generally underestimate them.

Descending Sets

Descending sets (or progressive, if you prefer) are those where repeat times become gradually faster from the beginning to the end of the set. Although this method is not really a test for determining threshold paces, it can, nevertheless, be a very effective form of training because athletes can swim at several aerobic and anaerobic levels along the lactate velocity curve during one set. This type of training has the advantage of holding the swimmer back in the early repeats so that a reasonable amount of endurance swimming can be accomplished before fatigue sets in. There is the additional advantage of ensuring that some training occurs at most of the various endurance levels even when a particular swimmer's threshold pace is not known. Figure 8-11 illustrates the probable metabolic effects of a descending set of 10 × 200.

The swimmer begins the set at a speed of 2:14 and quickly increases her speed so that the majority of the repeats are swum between 2:12 and 2:10. As you can see, this speed is near her anaerobic threshold, although she may not know it. The final

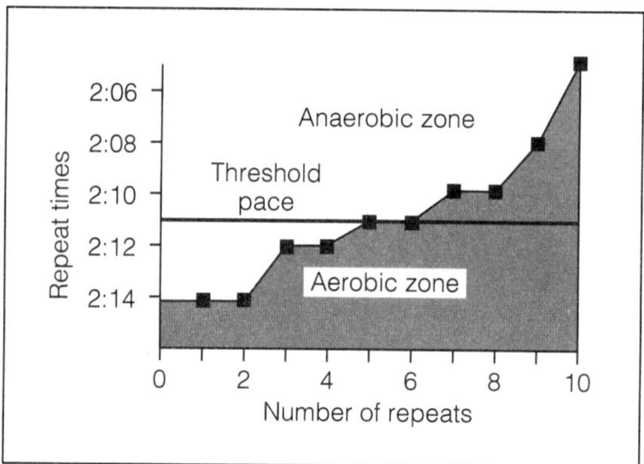

Figure 8-11. The physiological effect of a descending set of 10 × 200 on short rest.

two repeats are swum at 2:08 and 2:05, which is well into the anaerobic range. Thus, within one set, this swimmer performed a small amount of basic endurance training, a large amount of threshold training, and a small amount of sprint training. This is the best way to train when a swimmer's threshold pace is unknown. Most motivated athletes swim the majority of the repeats near their present anaerobic threshold when they complete descending sets.

The disadvantage of descending sets relates to their lack of precision. Athletes may spend too much time swimming at one aerobic level and too little at others. Conversely, when the sets are short (less than 2,000 yd/m), motivated athletes may be encouraged to swim in the overload endurance zone. Thus, swimmers may spend too much time in the basic endurance zone when sets are very long or too much emphasis is placed on descending down to very fast speeds.

Descending sets that are designed for the basic endurance level should probably encourage swimmers to improve their times by 6 or more seconds per 100 throughout the course of the set, with most of that improvement coming in the final few repeats. When sets are designed for the threshold level, the difference between the slowest and fastest times should probably not be greater than 2 to 4 seconds per 100 and the set should be 2,000 yd/m or longer. The difference between repeats should probably be only 1 to 2 seconds per 100 on overload endurance sets.

Heart Rate Profiles

The primary use for all of the methods described in the previous sections has been to prescribe speeds for endurance training. Sharp, Vitelli, Costill, and Thomas (1984) have suggested a method for monitoring changes in aerobic capacity that could be used in conjunction with these tests. It involves counting heart rates and comparing them to swimming speeds. These two measures are used to construct a graph on which heart rates are plotted on the vertical axis and speed is plotted on the horizontal axis.

The data for the graphs are gathered by having subjects complete at least two time trials, which should be swum at speeds corresponding to efforts of approximately 90 and 100 percent of maximum. Twenty minutes of rest are taken between each time trial. Three 15-second heart rate counts are taken after each swim. The first count is taken at 15 seconds after the swim has been completed; the second, at 45 seconds; and the third, at 90 seconds. The three counts are summed and plotted against swimming velocity, which can be expressed in seconds, meters per second, or yards per second. Swims of 200 yd were used when developing this test, although any distance could be used, as long as it does not change from one test to the next.

A similar test can be repeated at a later time for monitoring purposes. The results should be plotted on the same graph so that they can be compared with earlier test data. The procedures for administering the test for a heart rate profile is summarized in Figure 8-12. A heart rate profile is displayed in Figure 8-13.

The developers of the test believed that rightward shifts in the heart rate velocity profile reflected changes in aerobic capacity like those from blood tests. To test this hypothesis, Sharp and his coworkers (1984) compared the heart rate profiles and blood test results for a group of swimmers over the course of a season. The subjects were 12 members of a university swim team who were tested during the early, middle, and late portions of the season. Heart rates were counted after each swim and graphed opposite swimming velocities according to the methods shown in Figures 8-12 and 8-13. Blood samples were also collected after each swim. These samples were taken at 1, 3, 5, 7, and 9 minutes after each time trial to determine the highest blood lactic acid concentrations. The blood lactate and swimming velocity values were also graphed for the subjects so that shifts in their lactate velocity curves could be compared with their heart rate velocity profiles. The results of this comparison are displayed in Figure 8-14.

Both profiles shifted to the right from the first test (T1) to the second test (T2) and from the second test to the third test (T3). It is interesting that they showed the same relative shift and that the slopes of the lines for the lactate velocity and heart rate velocity were very similar. The authors concluded that heart rate profiles were capable of sensing changes in performance capacity similar to those identified by lactate velocity profiles.

1. Swim two time trials with 20-minute rest intervals between each. Distances can be 100 to 400 yd/m. The first swim should be at 90 percent effort; the second, at 100 percent effort.

2. Take three 15-second heart rate counts after each time trial: the first at 15 seconds postswim, the second at 45 seconds postswim, and the third at 90 seconds postswim. Sum these and graph with swim times.

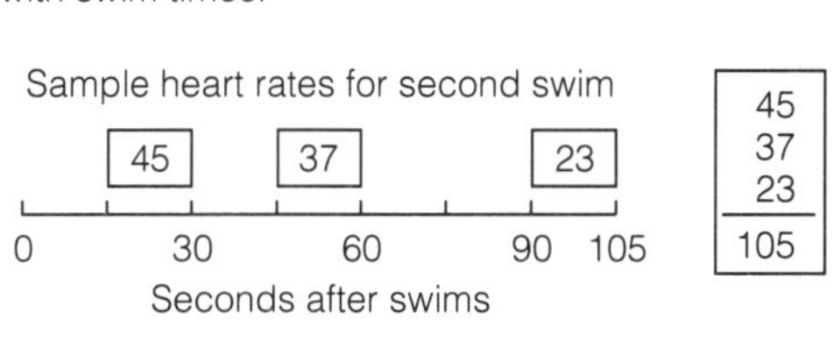

Figure 8-12. Protocol for collecting data for a heart rate profile.

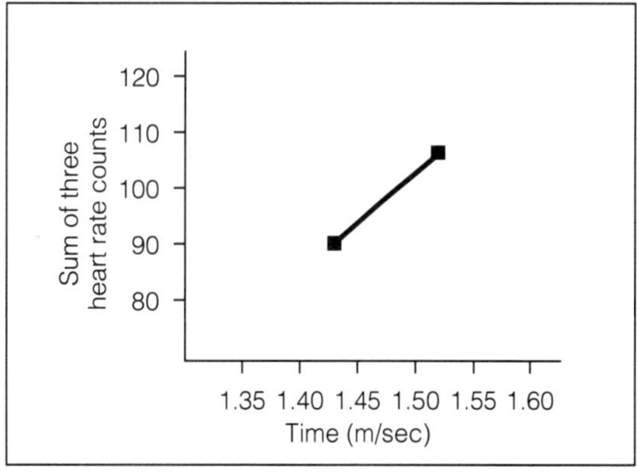

Figure 8-13. A heart rate profile constructed from two 200-m time trials.

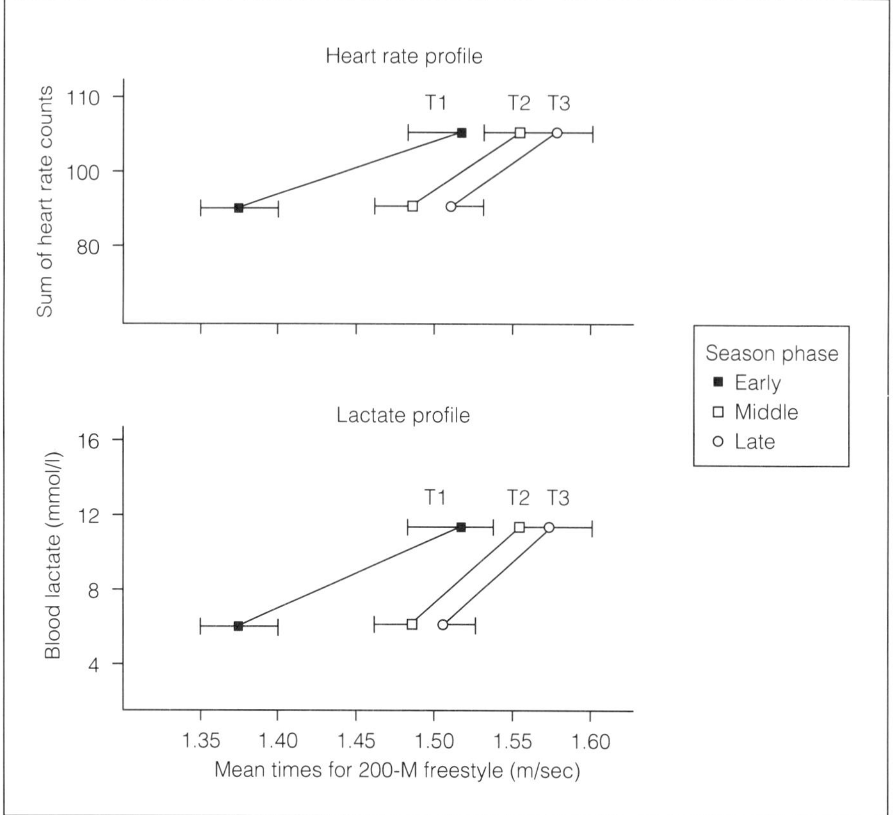

Figure 8-14. Comparison of heart rate and lactate profiles during one swimming season. (Sharp, Vitelli, Costill, & Thomas, 1984)

It seems that heart rate profiles provide an excellent alternative to blood testing for monitoring training progress. The test developers noted, however, that the heart rate profiles of some subjects tended to show more variation than their lactate profiles. They concluded, therefore, that the former method was not as reliable as the latter. Nevertheless, the ease of administering these tests, when compared to blood testing, provides all coaches with an inexpensive, accessible, and valuable tool for monitoring training. Heart rate profiles cannot be used to prescribe training speeds, however, nor can they be used to monitor weaknesses in a training program.

Methods That Have Questionable Value

Several tests in common use have not proven to be very accurate for monitoring training or prescribing training speeds. They are discussed in the following sections.

The Conconi Test Conconi and his associates (1982) developed a test that used heart rate counting rather than blood lactic acid concentrations to predict speeds at the anaerobic threshold. This test has been adapted for several sports, including swimming. The swimming test consists of a long continuous swim that begins at a slow speed and increases by two or three seconds after each 50 m until the intensity is well beyond the athlete's anaerobic threshold (Cellini et al., 1986). Heart rates are continuously monitored with a transducer or telemetric device that can be used in the water (the Heart Corder 232 system, Sport Tester TM PE 3000).

The test developers believed that a line expressing the relationship between increases in heart rate and increases in swimming speed would be linear below the anaerobic threshold and that the line would become nonlinear after the threshold had been exceeded. The speed at which the line becomes nonlinear is called the *deflection velocity* and is supposedly equivalent to the subject's threshold pace. Figure 8-15 shows the results of a swimming Conconi test for one subject. Notice the rather sharp change in direction of the heart rate velocity curve at a swimming speed near 1.30 m/sec and a heart rate of 158 bpm.

The results of several research studies have questioned the accuracy of the Conconi test for predicting threshold training speeds. The test failed to identify the individual anaerobic threshold or some fixed threshold with any degree of consistency in studies involving running (Coen, Urhausen, & Kindermann, 1988; Tiberi et al., 1988), cycling (Coen, Urhausen, & Kindermann, 1988; Heck et al., 1988; Ribeiro et al., 1985), and arm cranking (Kruger, Mortier, Heck, & Hollmann, 1988). Additionally, most of the researchers reported that test results were not easy to interpret accurately. Deflection velocities were not visible in 20 to 50 percent of the subjects' heart rate velocity pairings. They also found that it was difficult to determine the deflection velocity in at least an additional 20 to 30 percent of the cases.

Heart Rates and Percent Efforts Because better methods were not available, I recommended heart rates and percent efforts for prescribing training speeds in the first edition of this text. There are now so many more precise ways to obtain this information that these estimates are no longer needed.

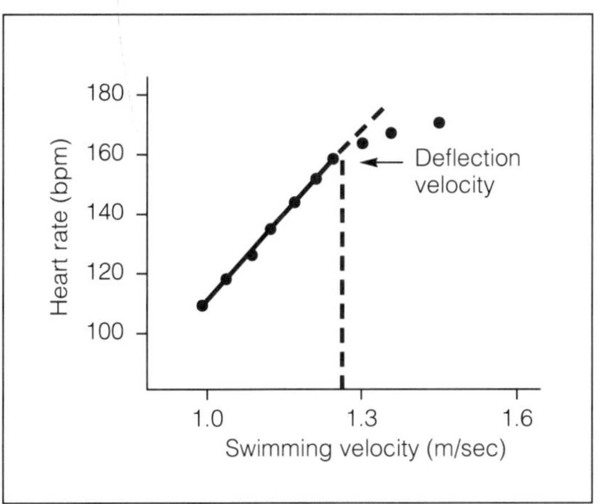

Figure 8-15. Results of a Conconi test. (Cellini et al., 1986)

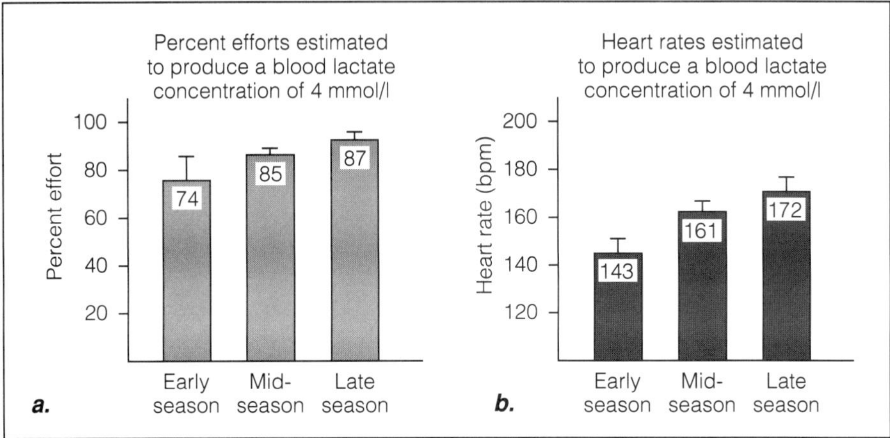

Figure 8-16. Percent efforts and heart rates that will produce a blood lactate concentration of 4 mmol/l.

The information in the two graphs in Figure 8-16 illustrates the margins of error that could exist when heart rates and percent efforts are used to prescribe training speeds. They show the results of six weeks of training on the percent efforts (Figure 8-16*a*) and heart rates (Figure 8-16*b*) required to reach the 4-mmol threshold. The range of percent efforts required to reach the 4-mmol threshold was 64 to 85 percent among the subjects early in the training period. Although that range became smaller later, there was still a rather large difference of 12 percent in the efforts required for the swimmers to reach their 4-mmol thresholds. The range of heart rates was just as great—approximately 15 bpm—and did not change throughout the training period.

These data show that the percent efforts and heart rates for threshold training could not be predicted for each individual swimmer with reasonable accuracy. They could only be prescribed in ranges that were so large that a sizable number of athletes would be training too slow to produce a maximum improvement of aerobic capacity and others would be swimming so fast that they might become overtrained. Additionally, athletes could not train at one particular heart rate or percent effort throughout the season and expect to overload aerobic metabolism. They would need to progressively increase both throughout the season. The problem comes in knowing when and how much to increase them.

Because of tradition, many coaches will choose to use heart rates and percent efforts to monitor training despite their lack of precision. The data in Table 8-4 are presented for this reason. They show the range of percent efforts and heart rates that should approximate the 4-mmol threshold for most athletes at different points of the season.

TESTS OF ANAEROBIC CAPACITY

We have many tests for monitoring aerobic capacity but very few for anaerobic capacity. Anaerobic tests are desperately needed, because a loss of anaerobic ca-

Table 8-4. Range of Percent Efforts and Heart Rates Required to Reach the 4-mmol Threshold at Various Times of the Swim Season

Season Phase	Percent Efforts	Heart Rates
Early season	70–80	130–150
Mid season	80–90	150–170
Late season	85–95	160–180

Note: These percent efforts are based on lifetime-best performances. If you prefer to base them on season-best times, these efforts should be 3 to 5 percent greater.

pacity can be devastating to swimmers in events of 400 m and less. Some tests that are available are described in the following sections.

Blood Tests

At present, the best method for monitoring anaerobic capacity is to measure maximum blood lactate concentrations after races in competition. When lower values are coupled with poor performances, a swimmer may be overtrained (provided, of course, that races are swum at maximum effort). Some loss of anaerobic capacity is probably a necessary consequence of the endurance mileage required to improve aerobic capacity, but a swimmer's ability to recycle ATP anaerobically should return during the taper.

Nevertheless, it may also be advisable to monitor an athlete's maximum blood lactate values during the season. The loss of anaerobic capacity should not be so great that it cannot be regained before important meets, or swimmers will go into competition without the kick needed to win close races. Monitoring can be done by collecting blood samples after races in competition. Blood samples should be taken every one to two minutes for approximately ten minutes following competition to assess peak lactate values. Low peak blood lactate values coupled with slow performances are a cause for concern because they indicate the possibility that an athlete may be experiencing too great a loss of anaerobic capacity.

Hellwig and associates (1988) have suggested another procedure for monitoring changes of anaerobic capacity that may have merit. They used blood testing to monitor the speeds needed to produce a blood lactate concentration of 6 mmol/l. A significant relationship of 0.75 was calculated between this measure and maximum speed in competition. According to their results, improvements in the speed that produces a blood lactate concentration of 6 mmol/l should result in improved performance. By the same token, a loss of speed at this lactate level may signal a loss of anaerobic capacity.

Repeat Sets

Both of the methods for monitoring changes of anaerobic capacity described in the previous section suffer from the same disadvantages mentioned for other forms of blood testing. For this reason, coaches need other means to gain the same information. Monitoring the effects of sprint training with sets of repeats can be an excellent substitute for blood testing if the sets are constructed properly and administered correctly.

Sets such as 6 to 8 × 50 on a one-minute send-off, 4 to 6 × 75 on a two-minute send-off, and 3 to 5 × 100 on a send-off of three to ten minutes should be ideal for this purpose. The send-off times I have recommended are not critical. They can probably be lengthened or shortened without affecting the validity of the test. They should not be different from one test to the next, however, nor should the distances or numbers of repeats be changed.

The test set should be repeated once every three to four weeks. If the average speed for the set declines, anaerobic capacity may be deteriorating. As indicated earlier, some loss of speed should probably be expected during periods of intense endurance training. It is important, however, that this loss not be too great, or there will not be enough time to regain an adequate level of anaerobic metabolism during the final two to four weeks of the season when the athlete is tapering. Every attempt should be made to structure training so that athletes achieve their best averages in sprint test sets just before they begin tapering for the most important competitions of the season.

These sets should not be used to prescribe training speeds. There is no way to do this accurately, nor is it necessary to do so. Sprint training should always be completed as fast as possible.

Other Tests of Anaerobic Capacity

Rohrs and coworkers (1989) have suggested a tethered swim test that they believe relates to sprint swimming performance. It requires a 30-second maximum effort against some known amount of resistance. They reported correlations of 0.66 with 100 events and 0.78 with 50 events.

Some of you may be familiar with the Wingate test of anaerobic capacity. I would not recommend its use. Although a few studies have shown a relationship between scores on this test and sprint performance, most indicated that its validity is questionable (Jacobs et al., 1983) or that it is too nonspecific to be used for measuring the anaerobic capacity of athletes in different sports (Ferris, Pizza, Wygand, & Otto, 1989; Tamayo et al., 1984).

TESTS OF SWIMMING POWER

Although the swim bench has often been used for this purpose, research has shown that the relationship between swim bench scores and sprinting speed is not very high among homogeneous groups of athletes (Sharp, 1986). Consequently, scores on the swim bench are not good measures of swimming power. The relationship is much higher when stroking power is measured in the water. Costill, King, Thomas, and Hargreaves (1985) showed this when they adapted the control mechanism from a biokinetic swim bench to record stroking power in the water. The rope was replaced with a steel cable. Swimmers attached one end of the cable to their waists by means of a harness, and they were able to sprint 25 yd against the resistance supplied by the various settings on the control mechanism. The output from the control mechanism was connected to a chart recorder so that the swimmers' mean and peak power outputs could both be measured. The control mechanism calculated stroking force multiplied by the swimming distance and provided a reading of work done in kiloponds per meters; the speed of paper moving through the chart recorder allowed these researchers to include time in this equation so that they could measure power in kilopond-meters per second.

When power was tested in this way, a very high relationship with swimming speed was found to exist even among homogeneous groups of athletes. Costill, King, Thomas, and Hargreaves (1985) reported a significant negative relationship of −0.68 between stroking power measured in the water and sprint speed. The correlation was negative because swimmers with the highest power scores had faster times for sprints. On the other hand, the relationship between stroking powered measured in the water and power measured on land was a nonsignificant 0.34.

These results suggest that the force and power athletes can generate during 25 yd of sprint swimming is very important to success in sprinting. They further suggest that the amount of force swimmers can apply with each stroke also has a very close connection with speed. It would seem wise, then, at least for swimmers in events of 50 yd/m to 400 m and 500 yd, to engage in activities that improve muscular power.

These results show that in-water measurements against resistance are the most accurate way to monitor stroking power. The Power Rack and Swim Wheel are excellent devices for this purpose (see pp. 102–103). They provide accurate ways to measure (1) the amount of weight lifted, (2) the distance it is lifted, and (3) the time required to lift it. With these figures, the power generated can be calculated by using the formula in the following box.

Another method for estimating changes in stroking power is to time swimmers for four to six 25-yd/m sprints on a three-minute rest interval (a two-minute interval could also be used). An improvement in average time suggests that an athlete's stroking power has probably increased. Conversely, an inability to maintain a previous average time suggests that stroking power has probably declined.

Sample Calculations for Stroking Power

1. Weight lifted: 20 kg (44 lb)
2. Distance lifted: 2.5 m (8 ft, 2 in)
3. Time required to lift weight: 10.80 sec

Stroking power for 25 yd = 4.63 kg/m/sec

$$\frac{20\text{ kg} \times 2.5\text{ m}}{10.80\text{ sec}} = 4.63\text{ kg/m/sec } (33.41\text{ ft/lb/sec})$$

CHAPTER 9

Planning Yearly Training Programs

Planning a swim season requires separating the training year into smaller, more manageable units that emphasize the development of certain characteristics. Planning should focus on producing systematic adaptations that will bring swimmers to their peak at the time of their most important meets. When a program is planned correctly, all of the levels of training that were described in the previous chapters can be incorporated in the proper proportions and administered at the appropriate times of the season.

The first step in planning the training year is to decide how many times swimmers will shave and taper for important meets. This will establish the number of seasons within the training year. Next, each season should be divided into phases with very specific objectives. Finally, each of these season phases should be subdivided into shorter phases that provide for systematic progressions in training mileage and/or intensity.

Planning of this type has been termed *periodization*. The seasonal phases and subphases are popularly known as *macrocycles, mesocycles,* and *microcycles*. As used here, macrocycles refer to the major phases within each swimming season that usually last 6 to 12 weeks. Mesocycles are subphases of macrocycles that can last 2 to 4 weeks. A microcycle is the weekly structure of training. This chapter is concerned with yearly and seasonal planning. Weekly and daily planning will be covered in the next chapter.

TRAINING METHODS

The first step in planning any training year is to decide which training methods to include. The following is a list of methods that most senior swimmers use at sometime during the season:

1. Strength training
2. Power training
3. Flexibility training
4. Endurance training
5. Speed training, including race-pace training
6. Stroke drills
7. Starts and turns
8. Pace training
9. Race strategy training
10. Psychological training

This list represents most of the important aspects of training, although it is by no means complete. All of these training methods should be included in every training phase, with varying degrees of emphasis depending on the time of the season.

YEARLY PLANNING

Most coaches divide the training year into two or three seasons, depending on the number of times they wish to shave and taper for important meets. Others separate the year into five macrocycles, or miniseasons.

A Two-Season Yearly Plan

This is the most popular approach to yearly planning. The training year is separated into short-course and long-course seasons:

1. Short-course season — September to March (30 weeks)
2. Long-course season — April to August (20 weeks)

The short course, or winter season, culminates in a major national or international competition sometime in March or April. The long course, or summer season, ends with a meet of equal or greater importance in August. The swimmers are usually given one or two weeks for rest and recuperation between seasons.

A Three-Season Yearly Plan

A three-season yearly plan is divided into three seasons:

1. Fall season — September to December (16 weeks)

2. Winter season — January to April (15 weeks)
3. Summer season — May to August (16 weeks)

Once again, the swimmers usually take a break of one or two weeks between each season. Coaches who like to shave and taper for an important meet in December or January prefer this plan.

A Yearly Plan with Five Macrocycles

In this plan, the training year is partitioned into five 10-week macrocycles. A two-week break from training is provided in late August or early September to complete the year. This plan was made popular because it was used by Vladimir Salnikov when he set world records in the distance events and became the first man to break 15 minutes for 1,500 meters. One way to space five macrocycles throughout the training year follows:

Macrocycle 1 — September to November
Macrocycle 2 — November to January
Macrocycle 3 — January to mid-March
Macrocycle 4 — Mid-March to late May
Macrocycle 5 — Late May to mid-August

Progression in the Yearly Plan

It is important to program systematic increases of training volume and intensity into the plan for each season and each phase of the season. Whatever the yearly plan, the volume and intensity of training should reach a peak during the phase of the season that contains the most important meet.

Most programs do not plan adequately for progression because they are structured like the example in Figure 9-1. Here, the swimmers build to their maximum weekly mileage and intensity during the first 4 weeks of the season and then remain at that level for 10 to 20 weeks before tapering. The typical effect on performance of this linear increase in training mileage and intensity is also shown in Figure 9-1. Race performances will generally improve rapidly to within 2 or 3 percent of previous lifetime bests during the first 4 to 6 weeks of each new season. After that, they will plateau until swimmers taper, when race performances may improve only slightly from previous best performances.

Figure 9-2 illustrates a superior method of progression. It is planned so that a series of phases progressively increase in intensity and/or volume throughout the season in staircase fashion. Recovery periods are placed between each phase to provide some rest and adaptation so that the next phase can be performed at a higher level of effort.

Notice that the workload in Figure 9-2 surpasses that of Figure 9-1 during the second half of the season due primarily to the improvements occurring during the recovery periods. The additional work that the swimmers in Figure 9-2 are able to do later in the season should cause them to respond to the taper with an improvement

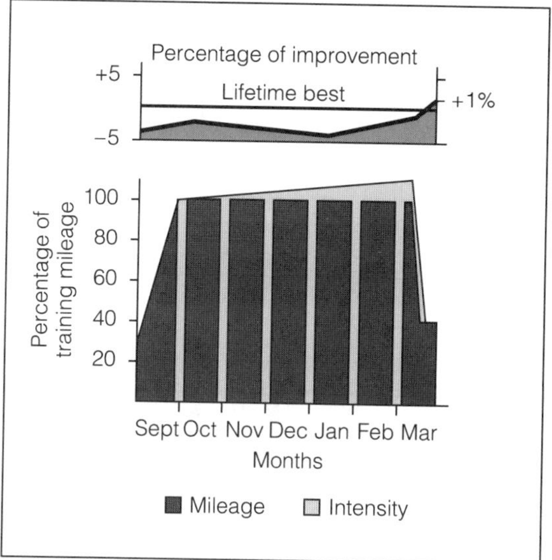

Figure 9-1. A linear progression plan for a typical training season.

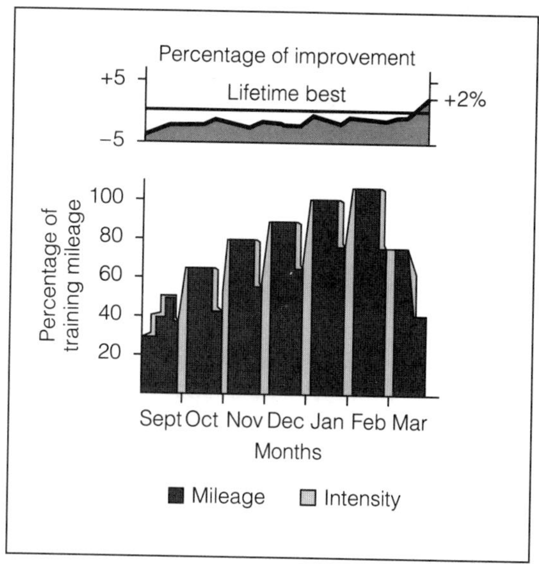

Figure 9-2. A staircase progression plan for a typical training season.

in performance that exceeds their personal bests by considerably more than the swimmers in Figure 9-1.

These illustrations are theoretical and were used only to illustrate the probable response of swimmers to these two systems of progression. Although there is no guarantee that actual swimmers will respond better to a staircase method of seasonal planning, scientific evidence and expert opinion suggest that they will.

Biquarterly and Quarterly Progression Plans

This method refers to programming a system of progression into two- and four-year plans that coincide with the dates for the World Swimming Championships and the Olympic Games. The purpose is to bring swimmers to a peak of performance at the proper times in their careers. An example of a biquarterly progression plan is displayed in Figure 9-3. The largest volumes and intensities of training occur during the years when the World Swimming Championships and the Olympic Games are held. Training volume and intensity are reduced somewhat during the off years.

An example of another quarterly plan is illustrated in Figure 9-4. It has been designed to bring swimmers to a peak for the Olympic Games. Volume and intensity are increased each year in a staircase manner and reach their peak during the Olympic year.

Another quarterly plan that may have some merit is displayed in Figure 9-5. In this case, the peak in training volume takes place during the year preceding the Olympic Games. Volume is then reduced somewhat during the Olympic year so that training intensity can be increased in order to enhance the likelihood of swim-

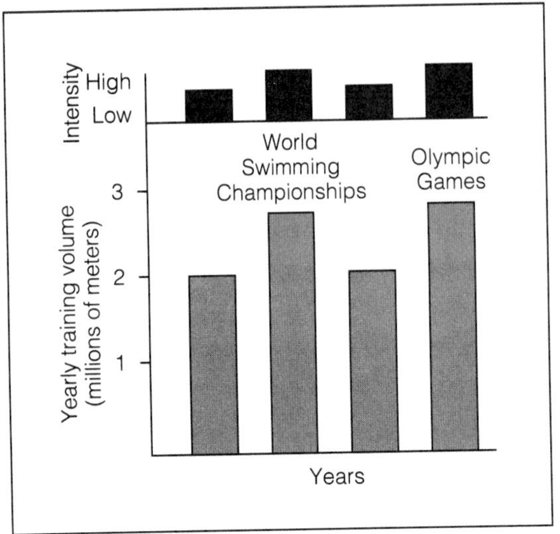

Figure 9-3. A typical biquarterly plan with increased volume and intensity during World Swimming Championship and Olympic years.

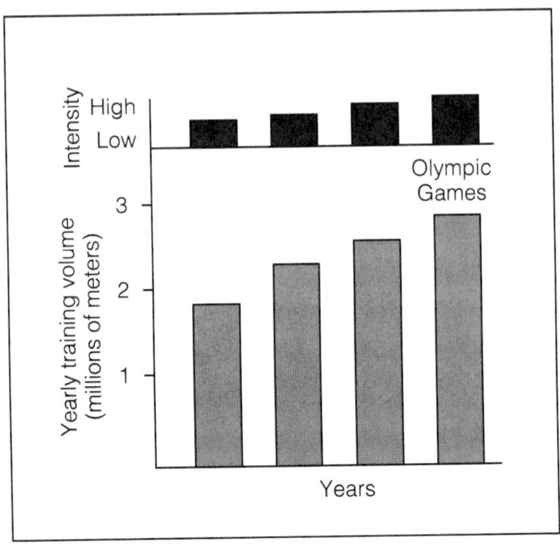

Figure 9-4. A staircase quarterly plan with greatest mileage and intensity during the Olympic year.

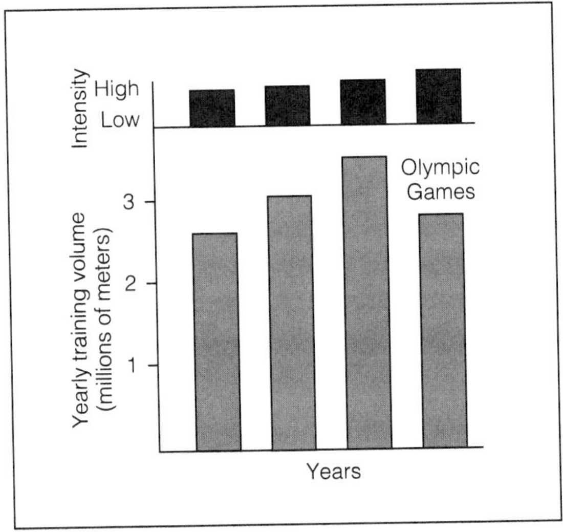

Figure 9-5. A quarterly plan with reduced volume and increased intensity during the Olympic year.

ming faster during the Olympic year and to reduce the possibility of becoming exhausted from training.

SEASONAL PLANNING

Once the year has been divided into seasons, the next step is to separate each season into phases, or macrocycles. Each of these phases should have different goals in terms of the adaptations sought and the kinds of training used to produce them. Each macrocycle should be further subdivided into mesocycles that provide a systematic plan of progression for that seasonal phase.

Season Length

What is the optimal number of weeks for a season? In one of the few studies to address this question, Denis and associates (1982) trained five subjects on a bicycle ergometer for 40 weeks. The subjects trained for 1 hour a day, 3 days per week. Workloads were adjusted every 10 weeks according to heart rate responses and to the results of 1-hour endurance tests that were performed at 85 to 90 percent of maximum oxygen consumption ($\dot{V}O_2max$).

$\dot{V}O_2max$ did not improve after the first 10 weeks. Average values increased from 3.40 to 3.59 l/min during the first 10 weeks but did not change appreciably after that. This result was expected, because we know that $\dot{V}O_2max$ does not increase any further after 6 to 10 weeks of training. However, both the individual and 4-mmol anaerobic thresholds improved significantly up to 30 weeks but failed to improve thereafter. The total amounts of improvement were 14 and 15 percent in the individual and 4-mmol thresholds, respectively. It should be mentioned that most of these increases took place during the first 20 weeks of the study. The increase was 11 percent for the individual anaerobic threshold over that time. The 4-mmol threshold was increased to its maximum value of 15 percent during the same period.

The subjects also improved in their ability to do work. Those improvements corresponded to changes in both the individual and 4-mmol anaerobic thresholds. Workloads improved significantly for 20 weeks and then plateaued for the remainder of the training period. Changes in the anaerobic threshold, expressed as a percentage of $\dot{V}O_2max$ that could be utilized without incurring acidosis, are listed in Table 9-1. This study provides evidence that the optimal training time for adaptations in aerobic capacity is between 20 and 30 weeks.

The Duration of Macrocycles

Bompa (1983) and Harre (1982) suggest that the optimal duration of a particular macrocycle is between 6 and 12 weeks. Swimmers tend to plateau after this unless a major change in training methods is introduced. These radical changes are referred to by Bill Boomer as "organized confusion of the body . . . [wherein] you don't give the body a chance to get used to what you're doing" (Laughlin, 1989).

Table 9-1. Changes in the Anaerobic Threshold during 40 Weeks of Endurance Training

	Anaerobic Threshold Expressed as a Percentage of $\dot{V}O_2max$
Week 1	72
Week 10	77
Week 20	83
Week 30	82
Week 40	83

Source: Denis et al., 1982.

A Typical Seasonal Plan

Seasons can usually be divided into four phases for which I will use the following terms:

1. The general endurance period
2. The specific endurance period
3. The competition period
4. The taper period

General Endurance Period This phase should last six to ten weeks when conditions permit. The emphasis should be on improving general aerobic capacity, strength, flexibility, stroke mechanics, starts and turns, and resistance to psychological stress. Swimming should consist primarily of stroke drills, pulling, and kicking at basic endurance speeds. The amounts of threshold and overload endurance training should gradually increase throughout this phase until they reach the percentages that were recommended for them in the previous chapter. Approximately 60 percent of the weekly mileage should be of the endurance type, with 20 percent of that amount at the threshold and overload levels.

Some sprint training should be included with all three levels represented. The suggested amount is approximately 5 percent of the weekly total. This is an excellent time to include water polo in the training program. It provides an enjoyable form of sprint training.

Athletes should swim all strokes and repeat distances in training with no emphasis on their specialties. This is also true of sprinters, although they should not be expected to do as much mileage as middle-distance and distance swimmers are doing late in this phase.

Three to four hours per week should be spent on dryland training in order to increase the size and strength of all the major muscle groups. If they wish, distance swimmers may forego dryland training in favor of swimming additional mileage each week. They may also substitute stroke-specific land circuit training for heavy-resistance training. The circuit should be aimed at improving muscular endurance for their 500/400 events.

Stretching exercises should be conducted daily, with major emphasis on the joints of the ankles, lower back, and shoulders. This is the time for instructions on stroke techniques and for diagnosing the strokes of swimmers on videotape. Various forms of psychological training can also be conducted such as visualization and relaxation drills.

Specific Endurance Period This phase should last between 8 and 12 weeks, when time permits. The emphasis remains on improving endurance. This amount of time, together with the time spent on endurance training in the general endurance period, will provide the 20 or more weeks needed to train the aerobic system for peak performance.

The major difference between the specific endurance period and the general endurance period is that a great deal of the endurance training should be done in the swimmer's specialty stroke(s)—perhaps 50 to 60 percent. Endurance training mileage should reach its highest level during this phase, and more endurance mileage should be done at the threshold and overload levels. Mileages for both should increase by approximately 5 percent.

Stretching exercises should be continued. The emphasis on dryland resistance training should shift to fast repetitions that are designed to produce muscular power. Most of the dryland training should consist of stroke-simulated exercises at competition turnover rates during the last portion of this phase. Some resistance training should also be done in the water. In-water, sprint-assisted training can be introduced at this time, although the majority of this type of training should be saved until the next phase. The amount of sprint training should also double to 10 percent.

Psychological training can continue; however, the emphasis should shift toward personal conflicts that may interfere with training and performance. Swimmers should perform visualization and relaxation drills on their own.

Sprinters should train with less mileage and greater average intensity than swimmers in other events during this phase. They should also move into the next macrocycle—the competition period—2 or 3 weeks before athletes who swim longer events. Distance swimmers should discontinue dryland training in favor of swimming more mileage per week.

Competition Period This is the period of the season when most of the important competitions should be scheduled. It is also the time when the emphasis of training should shift from endurance to sprinting for all but distance swimmers. The stress should be on race-pace training, lactate production training, lactate tolerance training, and power training, with enough endurance training to maintain the improvements that were made during the previous two phases. Distance swimmers should follow a similar pattern, except that their race-pace training should be more at threshold endurance and overload endurance levels.

There is no consistent body of research that indicates the optimal duration for training anaerobic capacity and muscular power. However, the experiences of most coaches suggest that four to eight weeks is optimal (Paulsson, 1984; Wilke & Madsen, 1983). Accordingly, the competitive period is generally scheduled for the final four to eight weeks prior to the beginning of the taper.

Weekly mileage should be reduced perhaps 25 percent to allow for longer rest intervals and faster swims. Lactate production and lactate tolerance training should be increased about 5 percent.

Sprinters should be using sprint-assisted training, race-pace swimming, lactate production and lactate tolerance training, and power training to a greater extent than other swimmers. Distance swimmers should be doing less sprint training and more overload endurance training than swimmers in other events. Because overload endurance repeats are swum above the anaerobic threshold, they will be more specific to the combined aerobic-anaerobic nature of distance races than shorter anaerobic swims.

Flexibility training should continue, although the amount can be reduced to a maintenance level. Dryland training should consist of stroke-simulated circuit training exercises that are designed to increase muscular power. They can be done on land or in the water.

Because swimmers will be competing in more meets during this period, it is an ideal time to stress race strategies. No further changes in stroke mechanics should be suggested, except for those swimmers who are making very serious mistakes. Athletes want to feel that they are swimming fast without having to decrease their effort to incorporate new techniques. They want to be able to concentrate more on the competition and less on their styles. The only exception to this suggestion is that swimmers should continue to concentrate on swimming as economically as possible. They should always be conscious of training with the combination of stroke length and stroke rate that puts them on pace with the least expenditure of energy. They should also concentrate on maintaining that combination when they are fatigued near the end of races and fast repeats. Furthermore, they should concentrate on finishing strong in all races and practice repeats.

Taper Period The final phase of each season is the taper—a period of reduced volume and intensity that should last two to five weeks. The taper is so important and complex that it will be covered in detail in Chapter 11.

Personalizing the Seasonal Plan Coaches must always be ready to make adjustments to any plan for certain situations and certain swimmers; for example, seasons that are shorter due to facility availability or administrative edicts. Family vacations, academic and personal commitments, illnesses, or injuries may cause swimmers to be absent at times when important training overloads are scheduled. Failure to adjust seasonal plans accordingly will cause inferior results. Regardless of the restrictions imposed, an effective seasonal plan should include the four phases described earlier, although the amounts of time given to each may differ from the ideal situation described previously.

The first step in designing a personalized seasonal plan is to determine the date of the season-culminating meet. The next step is to count backward from that meet. Count back 3 to 5 weeks for the taper phase and then an additional 4 to 8 for the competition period. The remaining number of weeks become the general and specific endurance periods, which can be divided in any way that seems appropriate. If fewer than 16 weeks are available for these last two periods, at least 6 to 8 of those weeks should be set aside for specific endurance training, with the remainder assigned to the general endurance phase. If the number of weeks is too short for an adequate general endurance period (less than 4 weeks), the coach may wish to reduce the taper and competition periods to provide some additional time. However, I don't suggest reducing the competition period to less than 4 weeks or the taper period to less than 2 weeks.

Integrating Seasonal and Yearly Plans

The two following boxes provide examples of how seasonal plans can be integrated into two-season and three-season yearly plans. Because it was necessary to adjust the two-season and three-season examples to the typical training year, the length of

Suggested Macrocyles for a Two-Season Training Year

Short-Course Season 29 Weeks	One-Week Break	Long-Course Season 20 Weeks	Two-Week Break
General Endurance Period September to November—9 weeks		April to May—6 weeks	
Specific Endurance Period November to mid-January—10 weeks		May to mid-June—6 weeks	
Competition Period January to March—6 weeks		June to mid-July—5 weeks	
Taper Period March to April—4 weeks		July to August—3 weeks	

Suggested Macrocyles for a Three-Season Training Year

Fall Season 16 Weeks	Two-Week Break	Winter Season 15 Weeks	One-Week Break	Summer Season 16 Weeks	Two-Week Break
General Endurance Period September to October—4 weeks		January to February—3 weeks		May—3 weeks	
Specific Endurance Period October to November—6 weeks		February to March—5 weeks		May to July—6 weeks	
Competition Period November to December—4 weeks		March—4 weeks		July to August—4 weeks	
Taper Period December to January—2 weeks		April—3 weeks		August—3 weeks	

the various periods of each season do not always correspond to the durations recommended earlier.

In the three-season training year, the winter season is the shortest. However, swimmers will have a good endurance background from the fall season, so the duration of the general endurance period can be shortened to 3 weeks, and the other seasonal phases can be scheduled within recommended time frames.

Earlier in this chapter, we outlined a yearly plan consisting of five 10-week macrocycles and a two-week break at the end of the training year. This plan involves structuring each of these macrocycles into five 2-week mesocycles. Different aspects of training should be emphasized during each mesocycle, and the volume or intensity of training should be changed to encourage a systematic progression in training adaptations. Figure 9-6 is an example of one of the 10-week macrocycles used by Salnikov during the season when he set world records in the 400 and 1,500-m freestyles.

Speed and technique training were emphasized during the first mesocycle, when stroke mechanics were evaluated and corrected. Weekly training mileage was approximately half of what it would be later during the peak phase of this macrocycle. The intensity of training was also low, with most of the swimming at what I would consider to be a basic endurance level. Swim training was not stroke specific, and all strokes were included in the training sessions. Dryland training was stressed during this period. Salnikov spent two hours per day, four days per week doing exercises that included weight training, the swim bench, and flexibility training.

The development of strength and power were emphasized during the second mesocycle. A rigorous program of circuit training was used that included weights and swim bench devices. The time devoted to dryland training was increased to

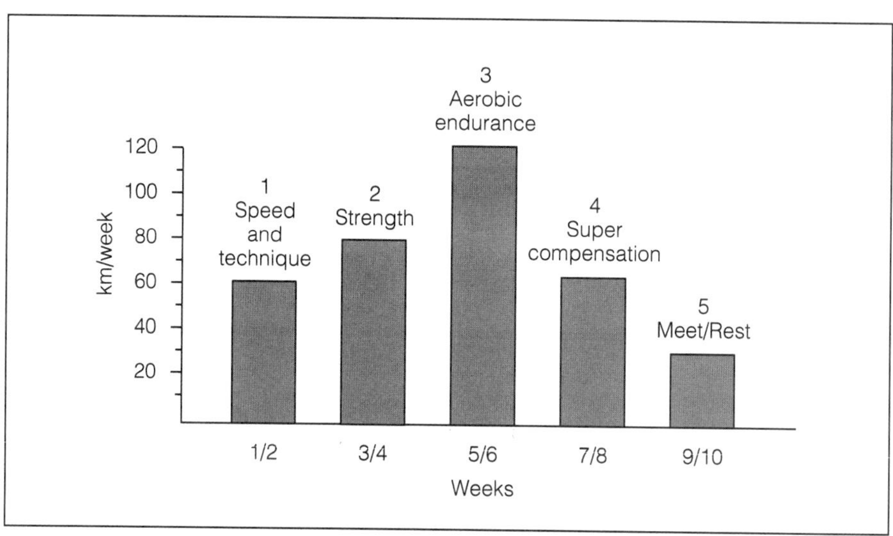

Figure 9-6. The plan for one of the five macrocycles used by Vladimir Salnikov during the training year. (Adapted from Koshkin, 1984).

approximately two hours per day, six days per week. Tethered swimming against surgical tubing was also used to develop strength and power, and flexibility training was continued. Swim training mileage escalated to approximately 70 percent of the maximum weekly value that would be reached later in the most intense phase of the macrocycle. Intensity was not a major concern with most of the mileage performed at a basic endurance level. Much of the swimming was done with hand paddles and tubes. The mileage devoted to kicking was increased during this mesocycle.

The third mesocycle was the most intense. The goal was to produce a large increase in aerobic endurance. Training mileage reached a peak of 88 to 120 km per week. The intensity of swimming was also increased at all levels of training; however, most of that training was at threshold speeds or slightly slower. Dryland training was reduced to the level of the first mesocycle.

The purpose of the fourth mesocycle was supercompensation. The mileage and intensity of training were reduced to allow recovery without a loss of conditioning. Weekly mileage dropped back to the level of the first mesocycle; however, intensity was maintained at a somewhat higher level. All levels of training were included in the weekly plan, although the sets were considerably shorter than they had been during the third mesocycle. Dryland training was reduced to approximately one hour per day.

The purpose of the fifth mesocycle was to rest and recuperate. An important meet was usually scheduled near the end of it. Training mileage reached its lowest level, with most of it in the form of easy swimming. Dryland training was discontinued, although stretching remained part of the daily training. These 2 weeks were used as a rest period preceding the start of the next macrocycle.

Which Plan Is Best? The value of these yearly plans is probably determined more by the way they fit the schedule of a particular swimmer, team, or country than by anything inherent in their structure. Compared to the three-season and five-macrocycle plans, the two-season year fits the nature of present-day swimming competition best because each season culminates with one of the most important meets of the year. This plan also allows the duration of each macrocycle to be in the optimal range for the greatest improvement of a particular metabolic system, whereas the number of consecutive weeks that can be devoted to a particular type of training becomes shorter as the year is sectioned into more parts.

The three-season plan suffers from the fact that less time is devoted to endurance training and more time to tapering. Nevertheless, it can be a good plan for swimmers who like to make their qualifying standards early in the season so that they need only shave and taper once in the last 4 to 6 weeks before an important competition.

The five-macrocycle plan also has some advantages. It allows for greater variety in training and more periods for rest and supercompensation. The constantly changing emphasis of training should allow for greater adaptation with less danger of overtraining. On the negative side, a five-macrocycle plan requires that swimmers train conscientiously throughout the entire year. The total volume of aerobic training may not be sufficient to reach a peak performance if they decide to skip one or two macrocycles or if they train erratically during one or two.

Mesocycles

Mesocycles are periods within season phases during which the volume and intensity of training remain similar. The recommended duration for mesocycles is between two and four weeks. Several studies have shown that this is the optimal length of time during which a particular intensity or duration of training can be used effectively. Hickson, Hagberg, Ehsani, and Holloszy (1981) found that human subjects who trained by running and cycling made significant reductions in heart rates and blood lactate concentrations for standardized submaximum workloads (a measure that corresponds to the anaerobic threshold) for up to three weeks before plateaus occurred. After that, they did not improve further until their training intensity was increased. These results agree with those of Gaesser and Poole (1988), who observed a 53-percent reduction in blood lactate for a standardized workload after three weeks of training. In both studies, the major improvement took place in the first two weeks of the training period, with only minor changes occurring in the third and fourth weeks. Swimmers' bodies apparently adapt to a particular intensity of training very rapidly. After that, further improvements are not likely to take place unless some form of progression is introduced.

Three to four weeks may be the optimal length for mesocycles, but shorter and longer periods can also be used effectively when required by the logistics of different yearly plans. A recovery period of three to seven days should be included in each mesocycle. The major adaptations to a particular level of work probably take place during this time. Figure 9-7 illustrates this phenomenon for a four-week mesocycle. It is adapted from the classic cycle of supercompensation proposed by Yakolev (Harre, 1982).

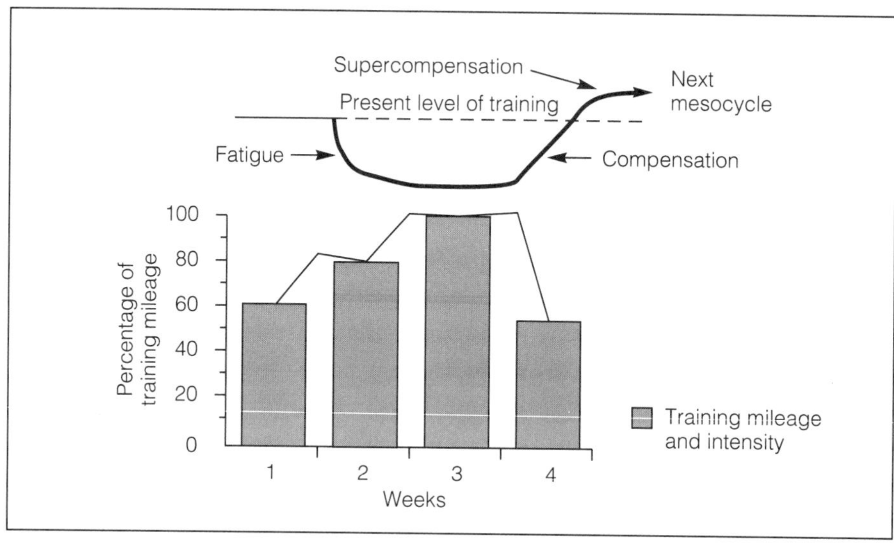

Figure 9-7. Yakolev's theory of supercompensation.

Intense training is conducted for three weeks and is followed by a one-week recovery period. The workload during the first three weeks should be great enough to cause fatigue, which may result in some degree of physiological breakdown coupled with poor performances. This is indicated by the small line graph at the top of Figure 9-7. Coaches should not be concerned about this fatigue unless it is unusually severe. It is probably needed to stimulate adaptations that occur during the recovery week (Pfeiffer, 1988).

The workload should be reduced in both volume and intensity during the recovery week to provide the rest that will encourage training adaptations to occur. The recovery days should not be times of complete rest, however. The intensity and volume of training should be designed to maintain the level of performance reached during the present mesocycle without causing further fatigue.

Mesocycle Construction There are literally thousands of ways to construct mesocycles, but they generally fall into three broad categories: *staircase, constant,* and *integrated*. The staircase mesocycle was illustrated in Figure 9-7. In a constant mesocycle, the same volume of training is maintained throughout the hard training weeks. The proportions of endurance and sprint training are also held constant throughout the mesocycle, and the intensity is increased slightly with each succeeding week. Figure 9-8 is an example of a constant mesocycle that lasts four weeks, with three weeks of high-volume training and one week for rest and recovery. This is generally referred to as a 3 + 1 mesocycle.

An integrated mesocycle is shown in Figure 9-9. It consists of two weeks of emphasis on endurance training, followed by one week of sprint emphasis. The final week is for rest, recovery, and adaptation. This is referred to as a 2 + 1 + 1

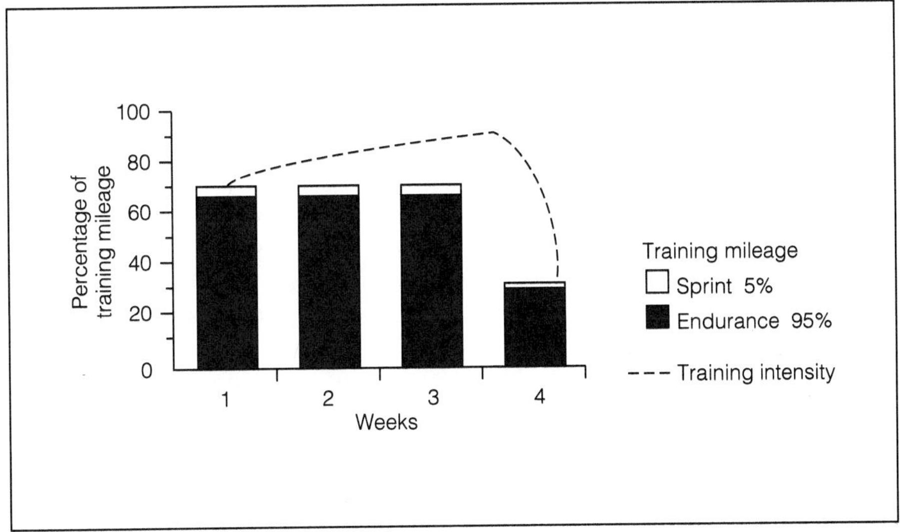

Figure 9-8. A constant mesocycle using a 3 + 1 structure.

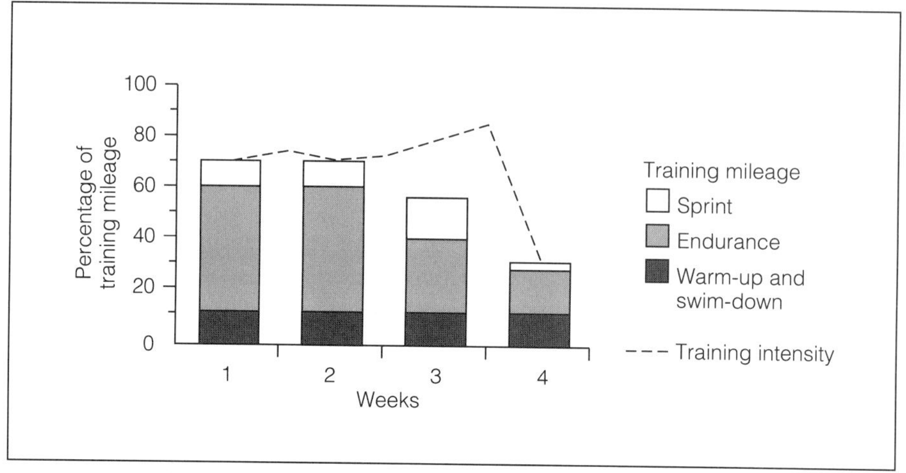

Figure 9-9. An integrated mesocycle using a 2 + 1 + 1 structure.

design. The intensity is gradually increased during the first two weeks of endurance training and reaches its peak during the sprint week. The volume of training is reduced during that week to permit longer rest intervals and faster swimming.

An integrated design such as this could also be planned for a five- or six-week period. Endurance would be stressed during the first two or three weeks. Then, one or two weeks would be assigned to sprint training before the week of rest and recovery would begin.

Mesocycle Progression Regardless of the way mesocycles are constructed, the best results will occur when some system of progression is employed when going from one mesocycle to the next. Each succeeding mesocycle should be higher in volume or greater in intensity than the preceding one.

An example of progression is presented in Figure 9-10. It shows two constant mesocycles that stress endurance training. The volume of training increases during the second mesocycle to provide a progressive overload. Similar increases should take place during each subsequent mesocycle.

Each succeeding mesocycle should continue to escalate in training volume and intensity until the maximum volume is reached sometime near the end of the specific endurance period. After that, training volume should be reduced and intensity increased during the competition period. Bompa (1983) suggests that swimming speed should be increased between 3 and 6 percent with each succeeding mesocycle.

Planned progression is one of the best ways to ensure that swimmers reach their physiological peak at the right time of the season. It also helps to avoid plateaus and overtraining. Progress should be slower at first when mesocycles are constructed in this manner. Swimmers will ultimately reach higher levels of adaptation and, consequently, better performances.

Another example of mesocycle progression is illustrated in Figure 9-11. A staircase method is used in which the volume of training increases for each corresponding week during the subsequent mesocycle.

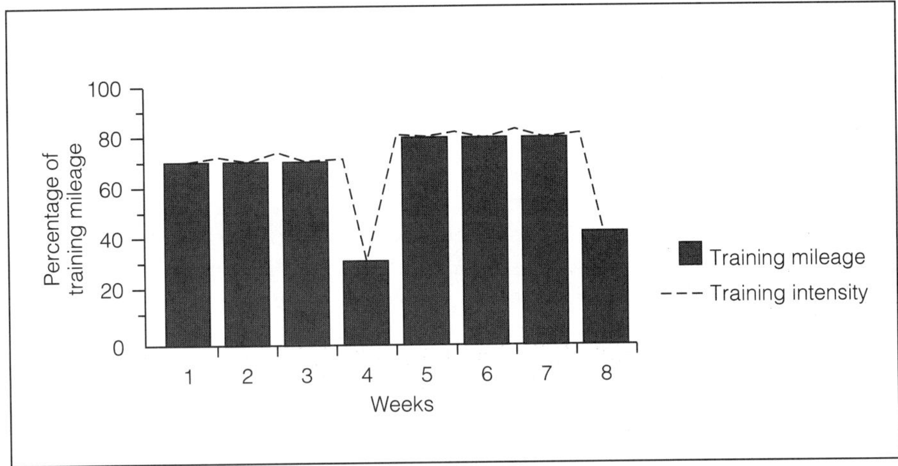

Figure 9-10. Two constant mesocycles showing progression in intensity and volume.

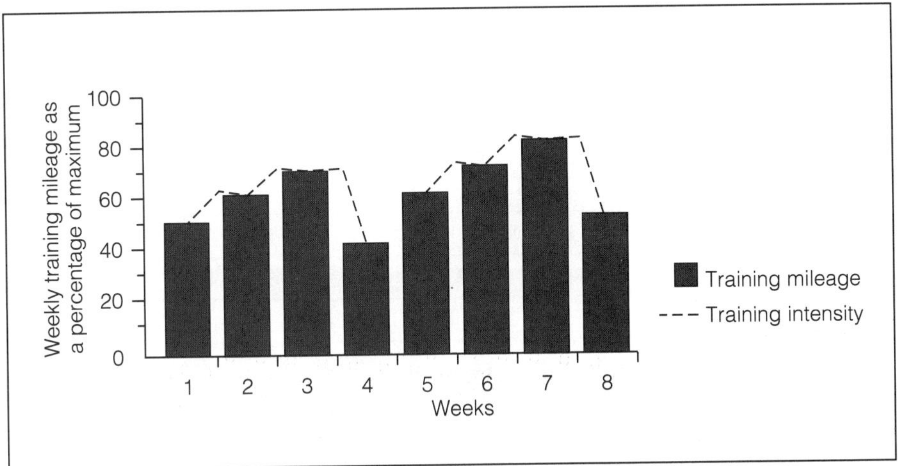

Figure 9-11. A system of consecutive progression using staircase mesocycles.

During the first mesocycle, mileage progresses from 50 percent of the maximum weekly total for a particular season to 70 percent at the end of three weeks. Following the recovery week, mileage for the first week of the second mesocycle is below 70 percent of maximum, but it is greater than it was for the corresponding week of the previous mesocycle (50 percent at week 1). Training volume during the second mesocycle then increases by 10 percent each succeeding week until the recovery week begins. Notice that mileage during the recovery week does not drop as much as it did in the previous mesocycle. In fact, the volume and intensity are as high as they were during the first week of the first mesocycle. The recovery week should not be a taper period.

Seasonal Planning Summarized

The illustrations in Figures 9-12 and 9-13 show forms that can be used for seasonal planning. Each of the plans are described in detail as examples of how the information in this chapter can be used in constructing seasonal plans. There are times in each example when I have purposely deviated from general guidelines to show how adjustments can be made to accommodate different training circumstances.

A short-course season plan is illustrated in Figure 9-12. The types of training

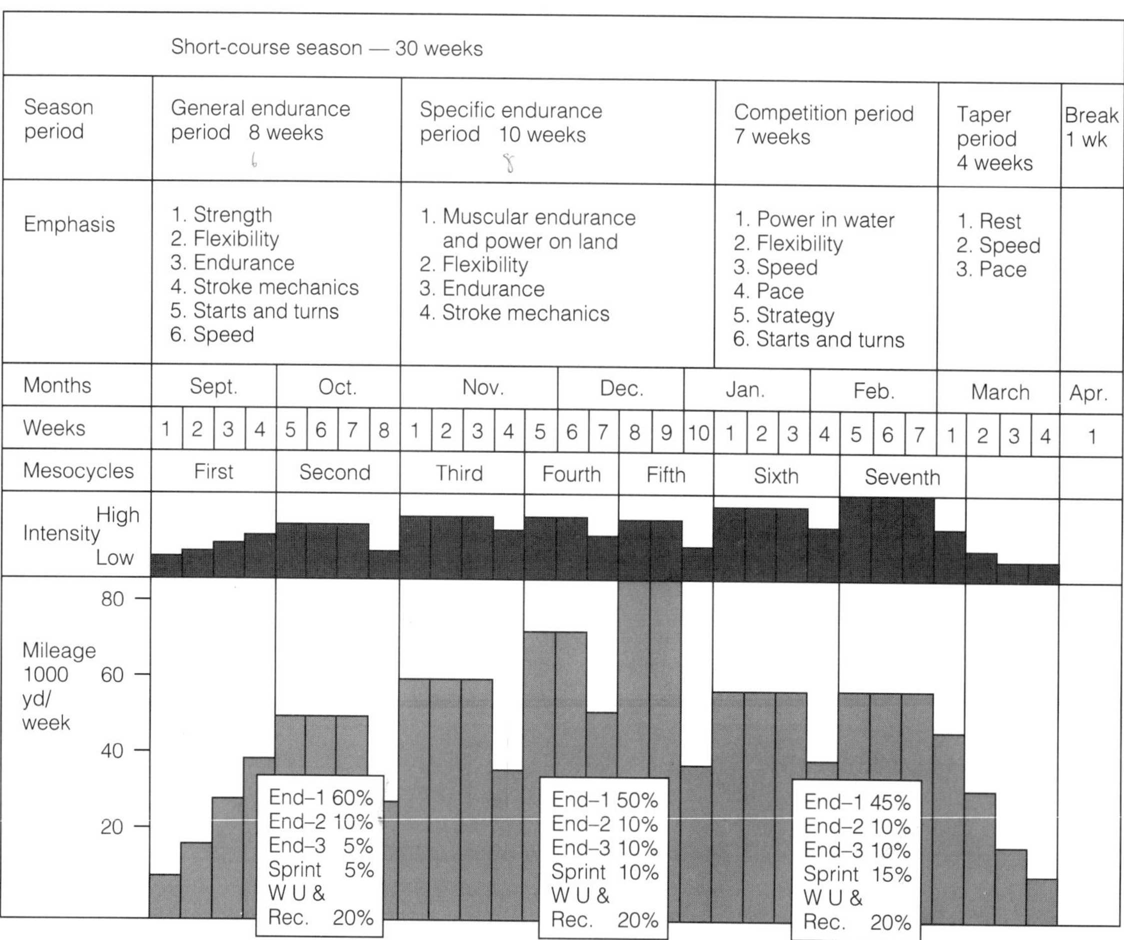

Figure 9-12. Sample plan for a short-course season.

stressed during each phase of the season are listed near the top of the chart; the intensity of training is charted from low to high in the middle of the chart; and the total volume of training is charted in the bottom segment. The percentages for each type of training are also listed.

In this short-course season, the general endurance period encompassed 8 weeks, during which endurance training was emphasized. This period was partitioned into two 4-week mesocycles with a 3 + 1 design. A staircase progression in training volume and intensity was used during the first mesocycle because the swimmers had just returned from a break. Constant mesocycles were used throughout the remainder of the season until the taper period. Volume and intensity were increased during the second, third, and fourth mesocycles until the competition period, when volume decreased and intensity continued to increase.

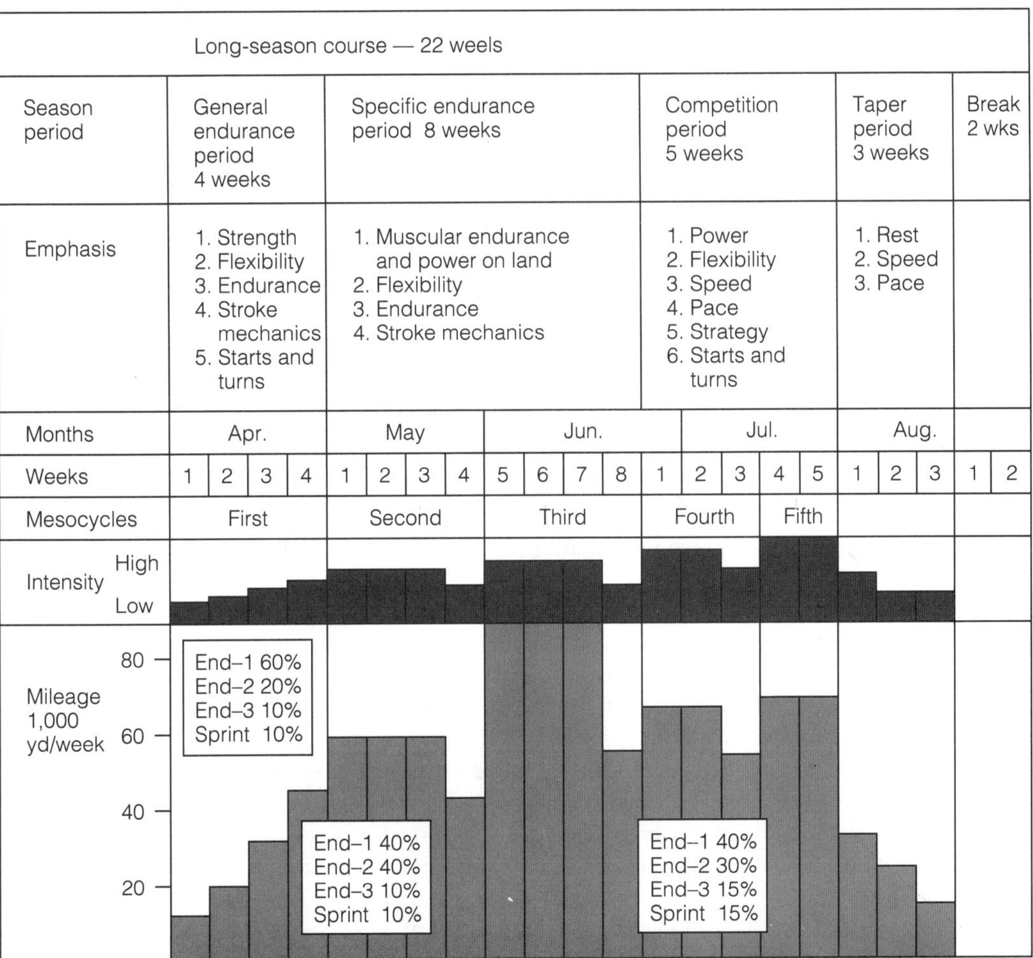

Figure 9-13. Sample plan for a long-course season.

General strength training, flexibility training, stroke mechanics, and the techniques for starting and turning were stressed during the general endurance period. Most of the endurance training was done at the basic level (End-1) to improve fat metabolism and to prepare swimmers for more intense endurance training later.

The specific endurance period was 10 weeks long. The mesocycles were planned around the Thanksgiving and Christmas holiday seasons, when swimmers were on vacation from school and had more time for training. The recovery weeks were scheduled to fit practices around family gatherings and other holiday responsibilities.

Flexibility continued to be stressed during the specific endurance period. However, the emphasis with land resistance training shifted toward power and muscular endurance. Specific endurance training was stressed, and most athletes swam at least half of their mileage in their major stroke(s), with the exception of butterflyers. The maximum weekly mileage for this season phase was reached during the last mesocycle of the specific endurance period. More endurance swimming was performed at the threshold level (End-2), and the mileage devoted to basic endurance training remained approximately the same because total mileage had increased. Overload endurance (End-3) and sprint training mileages were increased slightly.

The competition period lasted 7 weeks. It was sectioned into one 4-week mesocycle with a 3 + 1 design and one 3-week mesocycle. The recovery week that would generally follow the second mesocycle actually became the first week of the taper period. The emphasis changed from endurance training to sprint training during the competition period, and training intensity reached its highest level. The volumes of overload and sprint training were increased accordingly. Total mileage was reduced somewhat to accommodate longer rest intervals, and volumes of basic and threshold training were reduced to maintenance levels so that athletes could concentrate on quality swimming.

Flexibility was still an important feature of the land training program, but land resistance training was discontinued. It was replaced with power training drills in the water, using sprint-resisted and sprint-assisted training. Pace and race-strategy training were stressed, and starts and turns were emphasized in preparation for the important meets that were coming up.

The taper period was 4 weeks long, during which training volume and intensity were reduced slightly to provide for recovery and adaptation *with no loss of endurance*. Further reductions in volume and intensity continued during each of the next three weeks. After the culminating week of the season, the swimmers were given a 1-week break before beginning the long-course season.

A sample structure for the long-course season is outlined in Figure 9-13. The long-course season in this case lasted 22 weeks. The general endurance period was reduced to 4 weeks because this season was shorter than the short-course season. The general endurance period was constructed as one staircase mesocycle to prepare the swimmers for the longer mileage and stroke-specific work of the next period.

The specific endurance period was set at 8 weeks, which were sectioned into two 3 + 1 mesocycles. The emphasis was on improving aerobic capacity in the swimmers' major stroke(s).

The competition period, which lasted 5 weeks, was structured into two 2 + 1 mesocycles, with the recovery week of the second mesocycle becoming the first week of the taper period. The taper period lasted 3 weeks. After the major meet of the season, swimmers were given a 2-week break before beginning the next short-course season.

EVALUATING PROGRESS THROUGHOUT THE TRAINING SEASON

The motivation of swimmers will be greatly increased if they have goals for each mesocycle of the season and if their progress toward these goals is evaluated. The following categories of tests can be used for this purpose:

1. *Strength* One-repetition maximum lifts and stroke-simulated pulls on a swim bench are excellent for evaluating changes in strength. Progress on standard strength training exercises can also be monitored.

2. *Power* Simulated arm pulls on a swim bench, swimming against resistance in the water, and times for 25 sprints are all tests that can be used for evaluating power. In-water swimming against some type of measuring device provides the best test of all because it evaluates power in actual swimming movements.

3. *Body composition and flexibility* Methods for measuring flexibility will be described in Chapter 24. Body composition measurements can be used to evaluate increases in muscle tissue. *They should not be used to measure body fat.* The reasons for this statement will be discussed in Chapter 25.

4. *Aerobic capacity* Blood tests or any of the other noninvasive methods that were described in Chapter 8 can be used to evaluate aerobic capacity. Times on standardized endurance repeat sets can also be used.

5. *Anaerobic capacity* Measures of peak blood lactate and shifts in lactate speed curves that occur above 6 mmol/l are excellent measuring devices for anaerobic capacity. Some of the noninvasive swimming sets that were described in Chapter 7 can also be used.

6. *Speed* Sprints of 10 to 25 yd are the most direct means for evaluating speed. The 10-yd sprints should be done between flags to give swimmers a chance to accelerate to top speed before they are timed.

7. *Stroke mechanics* Repeated videotaping is a good way to evaluate stroke changes. Another good method is to chart changes in stroke length at competition stroke rates. Procedures for doing this were discussed in Chapter 5.

8. *Starts and turns* These can be evaluated through videotaping. Timing swimmers' starting and turning speeds for short distances is another excellent method for evaluating these techniques.

9. *Pacing* Swimmers can complete broken swims or underdistance repeats at various speeds to test their sense of pace.

All of these components do not need to be evaluated after each mesocycle. Only those that are being stressed or the ones that are considered to be very important at that time of the season need to be measured.

BREAKS FROM TRAINING

As indicated earlier, there should be breaks of one to two weeks between each major season of the training year. Swimmers generally feel drained after the major competition of a season, and they look forward to some time away from training to rest and pursue other interests. One to two weeks will provide time for rejuvenation while not being so long that the swimmers will lose a significant amount of conditioning.

Problems arise when swimmers take training breaks that last four weeks to nine months. Layoffs this long are not uncommon for summer recreational swimmers

Table 9-2. Effects of Detraining on Various Physiological Measures of Aerobic Endurance, Anaerobic Endurance, and Muscular Power

Measure	Percentage of Loss with Detraining	Time for Loss (Weeks)	Sources
Aerobic capacity ($\dot{V}O_2max$)	7	2	Coyle, Martin, & Holloszy, 1983
	16	12	Drinkwater & Horvath, 1972
Anaerobic threshold	17	12	Coyle et al., 1985
	8–10	4	Costill, Fink, et al., 1985
Muscle glycogen	39	4	Costill, Fink, et al., 1985
Aerobic enzymes	10–50	2–6	Wilmore & Costill, 1988
	40	8	Coyle et al., 1985
Stroke volume	12	4	Coyle, Martin, & Holloszy, 1983
Capillarization	14–25	1–7	Klausen, Anderson, & Pelle, 1981
Anaerobic capacity	50	3	Troup, 1989c
Anaerobic enzymes	0	4	Costill, Fink, et al., 1985
	0	12	Coyle et al., 1985
Strength and power	7–13	1–4	Costill, Fink, et al., 1985
	68	12	Graves et al., 1988
Performance	2 (3 sec over 200 m)	1	Troup, 1989c
	6 (8 sec over 200 m)	3	Troup, 1989c
Flexibility	100	4	Maglischo, 1990

and for some high school and college athletes. They cannot be recommended for serious swimmers; all of the training adaptations gained during the previous season will have dissipated by the beginning of the next season. The swimmers will then have to spend most of their time playing catch-up; that is, the major portion of the season will be spent regaining lost adaptations rather than building on those they had already developed. The detrimental effects of breaks in training have been demonstrated in several studies and are listed in Table 9-2.

It appears that athletes lose 7 percent of their $\dot{V}O_2$max capacity within 12 days after they stop training (Coyle, Martin, & Holloszy, 1983). This loss increases to approximately 16 percent within three months (Drinkwater & Horvath, 1972) and returns to pretraining levels within three to four months after athletes stop training (Brynteson & Sinning, 1973).

The anaerobic threshold also deteriorates rapidly. Blood lactate concentrations following a 200 swim at 90-percent effort have been reported to increase 2 mmol/l within the first week of detraining and 5.5 mmol/l after four weeks (Neufer et al., 1988).

Translated to swimming performance, these decrements in aerobic capacity probably account for a three-second increase in time for 200 m in just one week and an approximate eight-second increase after three weeks. Those were the results reported by Troup (1989c) during a detraining study with high-level competitive swimmers. Once lost, it may require six to eight weeks to regain these endurance training adaptations (Saltin, Blomquist, et al., 1968b).

Sprinting speed does not seem to be affected as much by breaks in training. Nevertheless, swimmers do lose some of their ability to exert force against the water. This may go unnoticed if tests of strength and power are conducted only on land. Figure 9-14 shows the relationship between stroking power measured in the water and on land during periods of reduced training. Notice that the swimmers' land scores continued to improve during four weeks of detraining and that their

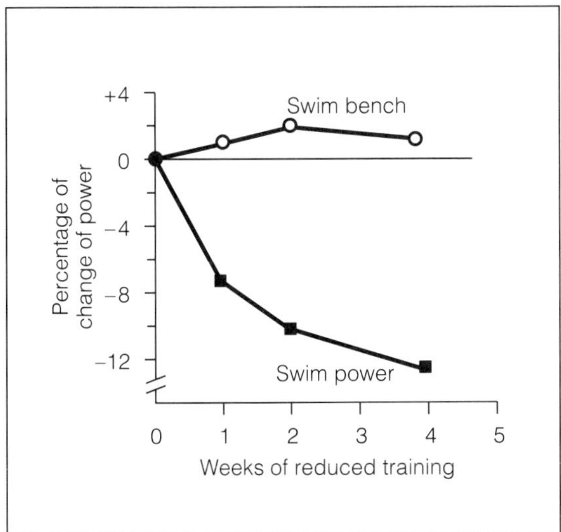

Figure 9-14. The effect of reduced training on power measured on land with a biokinetic swim bench and measured in the water with a swim-resistance control unit of a biokinetic swim bench. (Costill, King, Thomas, & Hargreaves, 1985)

water scores decreased. These swimmers were losing power in the water that was not being detected by the land test. However, the reduction in swimming power may have had more to do with loss of "feel" for the water than actual reductions in muscular strength and power.

Lactate production does not seem to be affected detrimentally by detraining. Many athletes achieve maximum blood lactate values that are as high or higher than those achieved during the regular season (Maglischo, 1988). There are also reports of increases in the activity of anaerobic enzymes during detraining (Coyle et al., 1985). These increases may be one reason for the rebound in sprinting speed that is sometimes noted when training in the water is reduced but not suspended entirely. The effect of detraining on muscle buffering capacity is not known, although experience suggests that it probably declines. Flexibility is lost quite rapidly and decreases to pretraining values within four weeks of detraining (Maglischo, 1990).

Unfortunately, losses of muscle tissue and increases of body fat seem to be the rule, rather than the exception, during training breaks. Over several months of training, swimmers' appetites become conditioned to a high level of caloric intake, which they tend to maintain during breaks, when their body no longer requires as many calories. Some athletes may gain 10 to 20 pounds during three to six months away from training. The situation may be worse than the scale indicates, however. Swimmers may actually gain 20 to 35 pounds of fat and at the same time lose 10 to 15 pounds of muscle tissue. As a consequence, they will spend nearly half of the next season returning to their previous body composition.

It should be obvious that swimmers who are serious about performing well should not take long breaks from training. They should understand that the best way for them to maintain a reasonable level of endurance is to swim. Although central circulatory-respiratory capacity can be maintained by most types of land activities, swimming is required to maintain the physiological capacities of the swimming muscles. Loftin and associates (1988) demonstrated this by comparing the effects of arms-only training on the aerobic capacity of both the arms and legs. Arms-only training resulted in an 80-percent increase in work output during arm cranking but only an 18-percent increase for the legs during cycling. Research by Glina and coworkers (1984) reported much the same results in a similarly designed study.

These results indicate that swimmers who train only with running, cycling, or other leg-dominant activities during breaks will probably lose some aerobic endurance in the muscles of their upper body. There will probably be some loss of power and anaerobic capacity, as well. Consequently, swimmers should do a sufficient amount of swim training in their off-season to prevent significant losses of upper-body endurance and power.

Swimming for three or four days per week should be sufficient to prevent large losses of aerobic and anaerobic endurance. However, the training must be adequate in duration and intensity. According to Houmard and associates (1989) and Hickson and coworkers (1982), daily mileage should be maintained above 50 percent of usual training levels. This means that most swimmers can safely reduce their training mileage to between 3,000 and 6,000 yd/m per day.

The intensity of training must also be maintained near normal season levels. Threshold and overload endurance training and anaerobic and sprint training should be included in approximately the same proportions as suggested for regular training. The absolute quantity of each should not fall below two-thirds of normal season levels.

Swimmers would be wise to swim their major strokes during most of this period of reduced training. This will help prevent losses of endurance in the muscle fibers that are most important to their performances.

Athletes should also engage in strength and flexibility training that exercise the muscles and joints involved in swimming. Strength training will prevent losses of muscle tissue, while stretching exercises will prevent decrements in range and ease of motion.

The caloric needs of reduced training should be calculated, and swimmers should be provided with some nutritional counseling that will help them reduce their caloric intakes to their new levels of expenditure. It would be a good idea to check body composition periodically to estimate the extent of muscle loss and fat gain.

Regardless of what has just been said, there will always be athletes who do not wish to swim during their training breaks. Playing water polo would be the next best thing for them to do. They would continue training in the water, with intensities ranging from aerobic to sprint speeds. Swimmers who do not wish to play water polo should be advised to participate in mixed programs that include leg-endurance activities (such as running, cycling, or skiing) and arm-endurance activities (such as rowing or rope climbing). Additionally, they should participate in activities that require power and anaerobic capacity (such as basketball, tennis, volleyball, handball, racquetball, and circuit training). They should spend at least two days per week doing activities that are endurance oriented and an equal amount of time in some activities that involve power and anaerobic endurance. These athletes should continue both weight training and flexibility training. Furthermore, they should receive nutritional counseling and have their body compositions checked periodically.

CHAPTER 10

Weekly and Daily Planning

Once a seasonal plan has been constructed, the planning of weekly and daily training programs becomes the next order of business. This chapter provides some suggestions for doing so.

WEEKLY PLANNING

First and foremost, all of the levels of endurance and sprint training should be included in the weekly training program, with two general guidelines:

1. At least two major sets should be swum at each endurance and sprint training level every week.
2. These sets should be scheduled so that adequate time is allowed for the replacement of muscle glycogen.

Regardless of the energy system targeted by a particular level of training, there will always be some overlap with others. Therefore, all systems will be getting some daily stimulation, even if major sets for particular energy systems are only performed twice each week. The training effect can be improved, however, if one or two levels of training are targeted during a particular mesocycle and three or four major sets are scheduled at those levels each week.

Muscle Glycogen Levels and Their Importance to Planning

As mentioned earlier, muscle glycogen is an important source of energy for training. Some studies have demonstrated that the working capacity of athletes is reduced when muscle glycogen is nearly depleted (Bergstrom, Hermansen, Hultman, & Saltin, 1967; Costill, Bowers, Branam, & Sparks, 1971; Kirwan et al., 1988), yet other studies deny this effect (Lamb et al., 1990; Simonsen et al., 1991). However, there seems to be no disagreement about the fact that training performance is better when muscles have an adequate supply of glycogen. It becomes important, therefore, to know which types of training deplete muscle glycogen most and which can be used during recovery periods.

Threshold and overload endurance training are the levels that cause the greatest depletion. Fat provides a greater portion of the energy for recycling adenosine triphosphate (ATP) during less intense basic endurance swimming, resulting in a lower rate of muscle glycogen use. Although the *rate* of glycogen use is highest during sprint training, the sets are shorter; therefore, the *amount* of muscle glycogen used is less than that used in longer threshold and overload endurance sets. Table 10-1 summarizes the results of several studies on muscle glycogen depletion during various types of exercise. Notice that muscle glycogen was depleted more

Table 10-1. Muscle Glycogen Depletion during Exercise of Different Types, Intensities, and Durations

Exercise Type	Percentage of Muscle Glycogen Depletion	Sources
Anaerobic Exercise		
1. One 30-second maximum effort on a bicycle ergometer	25	Jacobs et al., 1983
2. One 30-second maximum run	25	Cheetham, Boobis, Brooks, & Williams, 1986
3. Six 1-minute maximum efforts on a bicycle ergometer	40*	Gollnick, Armstrong, Sembrowich, et al., 1973
4. 2,200 m of high-intensity 25-m and 100-m repeats	35**	Houston, 1978
Aerobic Exercise		
1. Six 500 swims with 1-minute rest between swims	54	Costill et al., 1988
2. Thirty 100 swims with 20-second rest between swims	69	Costill et al., 1988
3. Twelve 500 swims with 1-minute rest between swims	62	Costill et al., 1988
4. Sixty 100 swims with 20-second rest between swims	85	Costill et al., 1988
5. 9,000 m of short-rest repeats at distances from 50 m to 400 m	62	Houston, 1978
6. 30-km run	60***	Costill, Gollnick, et al., 1973
7. 2 hours of cycling	75	Bovens, Keiser, & Kuipers, 1985

*Approximately 50 percent of FT fibers were depleted, and 20 percent were partially depleted. Only 25 percent of ST fibers were depleted, and 5 percent were partially depleted.

**Approximately 25 percent of FT fibers were depleted, and 70 percent were partially depleted. Ten percent of ST fibers were depleted, and 85 percent were partially depleted.

***Seventy percent of ST fibers were almost completely depleted, and 25 percent were partially depleted. Forty percent of FT fibers were partially depleted.

than twice as much by long bouts of aerobic exercise than by shorter anaerobic efforts.

The data in Table 10-1 suggest that most swimmers could only complete 6,000 to 8,000 yd/m of threshold or overload endurance training before depleting a significant amount of muscle glycogen. Because 24 to 48 hours of recovery time are needed to recover from such depletion, swimmers should alternate endurance sets of these types with basic endurance or sprint sets throughout the week, making certain that they do no more than 6,000 to 8,000 yd/m at these training levels without providing a recovery period.

Figure 10-1 is an example of what probably happens to muscle glycogen if swimmers complete too many threshold and overload endurance sets in a row. For each day of the week, the "AM" bar illustrates the amount of glycogen in the muscles before training commences on that day; the "PM" bar illustrates the amount remaining in the muscles after training is completed on a particular day.

The rate of muscle glycogen use exceeds the rate of replacement during the first three days of the week, causing a significant amount of depletion by the beginning of the fourth day. After that, it is doubtful that athletes could train intensely until they had rested for one or two days.

As Figure 10-1 illustrates, athletes are probably capable of swimming intense endurance sets at the threshold and overload levels only four days of each week, with the remaining three days set aside for muscle glycogen replacement. Athletes should continue to train during the recovery days, however. They can swim at other levels of endurance and sprint training without any serious interference with the rate of muscle glycogen replacement.

Basic endurance sets are an excellent form of endurance training for recovery days. Although some glycogen is used for energy during basic endurance swim-

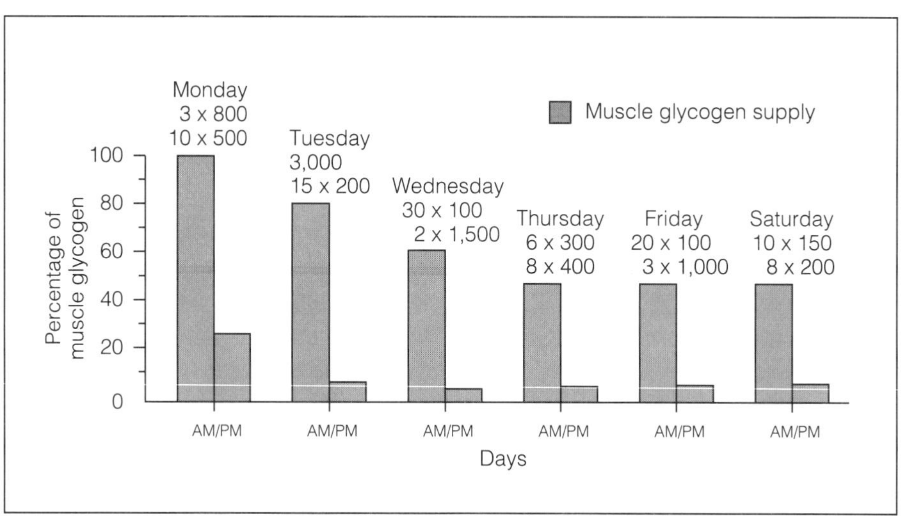

Figure 10-1. An example of muscle glycogen depletion during one week of hard training.

ming, the slower speed should allow enough energy to be provided by fat metabolism that the rate of glycogen repletion will exceed its rate of use. The net result should be a significant increase in the muscle glycogen supply by the next training day.

All three levels of sprint training can also be scheduled during recovery days. Typical sprint training sets should deplete only 25 to 30 percent of the glycogen stored in muscles. Because 50 percent or more of lost muscle glycogen can be replaced in 12 hours, the rate of replacement will exceed the rate of use so that a net increase is evident by the following day.

Figure 10-2 illustrates how adequate replacement of muscle glycogen can take place when threshold endurance (End-2) and overload endurance (End-3) sets are alternated with basic endurance (End-1) and sprint sets throughout the week. In this example, the basic endurance and sprint sets are scheduled for Tuesday and Thursday, and the swimmers rest on Sunday. Accordingly, the rate of muscle glycogen use is less than its rate of replacement on those days, allowing swimmers to restore the supply in their muscles on Monday, Wednesday, and Friday. This will make it possible for athletes to swim at threshold and overload speeds on those three days. With this plan, swimmers could also schedule a threshold or overload set for Saturday because they get to rest on Sunday.

Sample Weekly Plans

The next two sections outline some examples for structuring weekly training programs for teams that train twice per day and teams that train once per day. These sections also explain the rationale for training level placement so that the myriad possibilities for other weekly plans will be apparent.

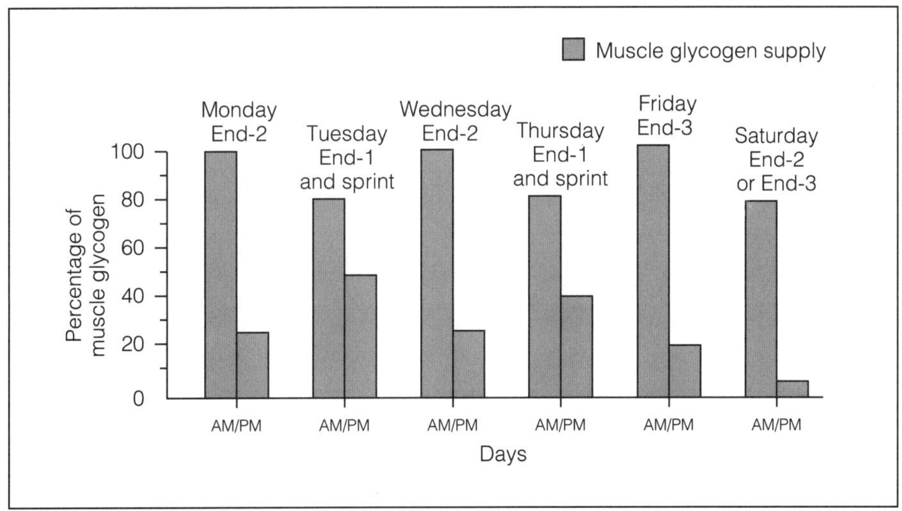

Figure 10-2. An example of how proper cycling of the various training levels can provide adequate time for muscle glycogen replacement during the training week.

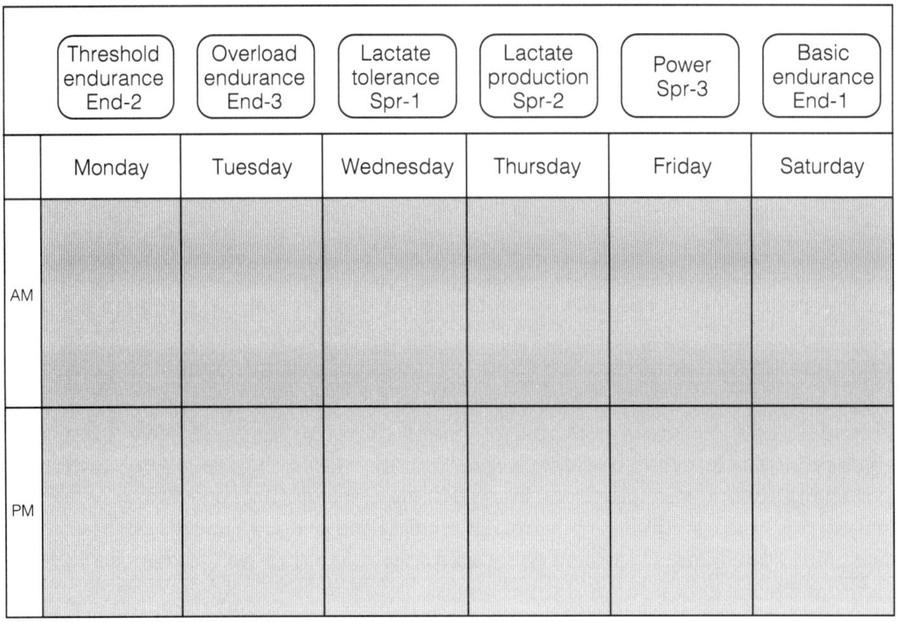

	Threshold endurance End-2	Overload endurance End-3	Lactate tolerance Spr-1	Lactate production Spr-2	Power Spr-3	Basic endurance End-1
	Monday	Tuesday	Wednesday	Thursday	Friday	Saturday
AM						
PM						

Figure 10-3. A sample diagram for weekly planning.

Planning for Two Training Sessions Per Day Figure 10-3 shows a blank worksheet for placing the various levels of training in a typical training week with two sessions per day Monday through Friday and one session on Saturday. Overload and threshold training should be positioned first because they use more muscle glycogen. The other levels of training should be positioned around them to allow time for muscle glycogen replacement. Two methods of placement can be used. In the first method, one threshold or overload set can be scheduled every 24 to 36 hours; this is referred to as an *alternating method*. In the second method, two sets of threshold or overload training can be scheduled in succession before providing 36 to 48 hours for recovery; this is called the *combined method*.

Alternating method Figures 10-4, 10-5, and 10-6 illustrate one method for cycling the various levels of training using the alternating method. The threshold and overload endurance sets are scheduled for Monday afternoon, Wednesday morning, Thursday afternoon, and Saturday morning in Figure 10-4. This arrangement permits 32 hours of recovery between each set.

Lactate production, lactate tolerance, and sprint, or power, sets can then be placed as shown in Figure 10-5. Two lactate production sets are scheduled: one on Monday afternoon and the other on Thursday afternoon. Both of these follow the endurance sets on those days. One lactate tolerance set is also scheduled for Saturday morning after the overload endurance set. These sets are placed in this manner to allow more complete rest on Tuesday, Wednesday afternoon, and Friday. They could also be placed on those days, however.

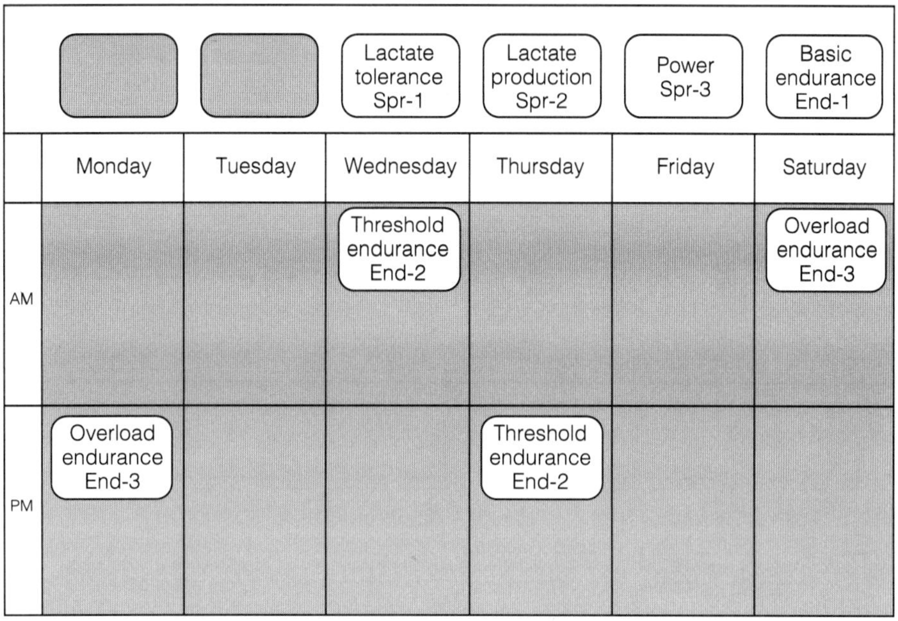

	Monday	Tuesday	Wednesday	Thursday	Friday	Saturday
			Lactate tolerance Spr-1	Lactate production Spr-2	Power Spr-3	Basic endurance End-1
AM			Threshold endurance End-2			Overload endurance End-3
PM	Overload endurance End-3			Threshold endurance End-2		

Figure 10-4. Placement of threshold endurance and overload endurance training using an alternating method for weekly planning.

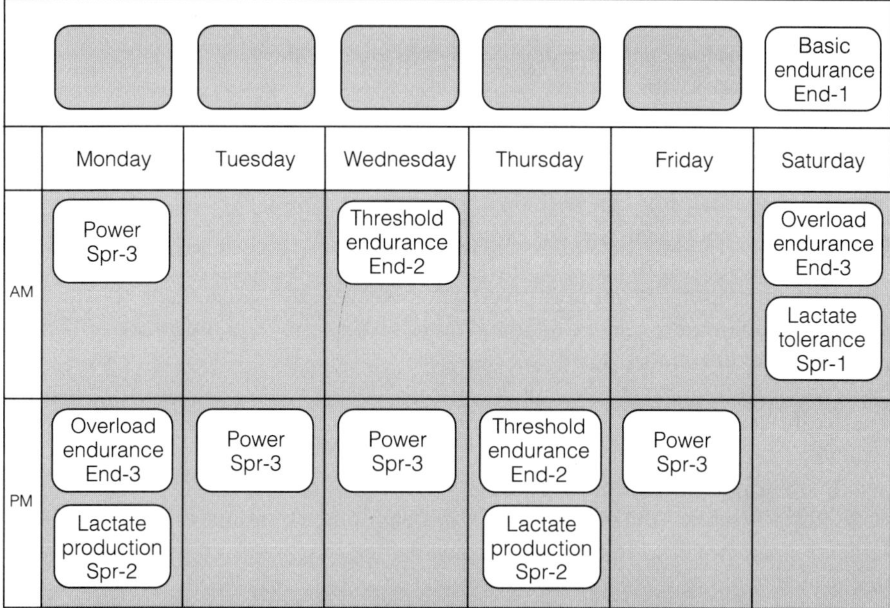

Figure 10-5. Placement of lactate production, lactate tolerance, and power (sprint) sets using an alternating method for weekly planning.

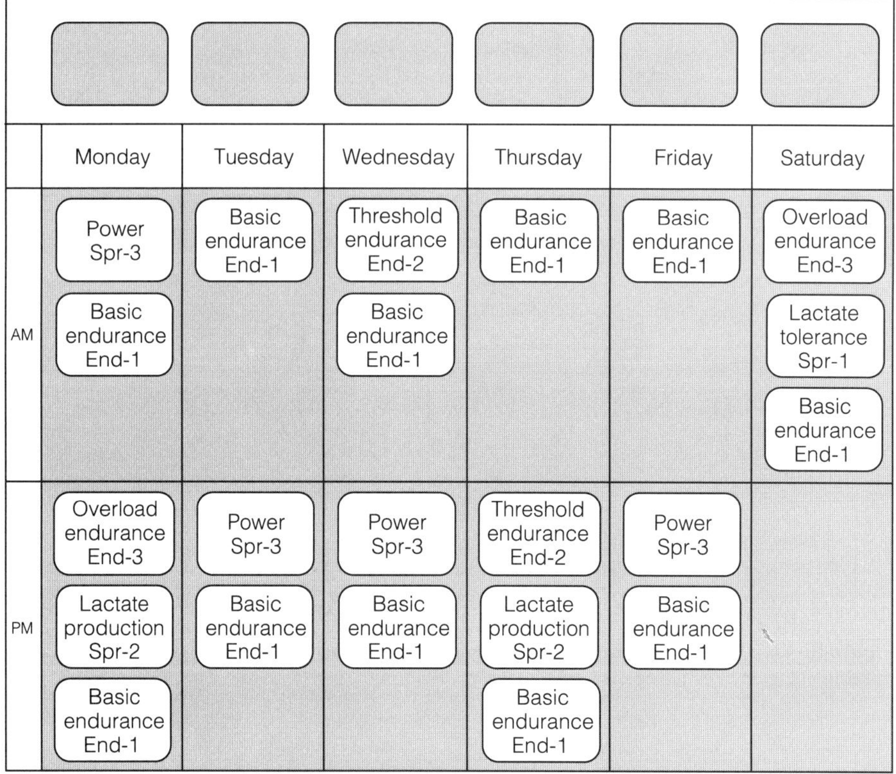

Figure 10-6. Placement of basic endurance training using an alternating method for weekly planning.

Power sets should be placed at times when muscle glycogen is at least partially replaced so that athletes can swim fast. In this case, four power sets are scheduled for Monday morning and Tuesday, Wednesday, and Friday afternoons. They could be placed in any of the other sessions because they are not stressful and will not use a significant amount of muscle glycogen; however, this placement was chosen because the swimmers may be encouraged to sprint faster when they are not doing any other intense training during that session.

Scheduling major power sets in this manner does not preclude the use of shorter power sets (100 to 300 yd/m) during other sessions. Specialty sprint work such as sprint-assisted and sprint-resisted training can also be placed anywhere in the weekly program without causing problems.

Figure 10-6 shows the placement of basic endurance training in the weekly plan. Athletes should swim at this level each day, but the longer sets should be scheduled on days when major threshold and overload sets are not being done.

Combined method Figure 10-7 illustrates an example of a combined method for placing the six levels of training in a weekly plan. Three major threshold sets

	Monday	Tuesday	Wednesday	Thursday	Friday	Saturday
AM	Threshold endurance End-2	Basic endurance End-1	Basic endurance End-1	Threshold endurance End-2	Basic endurance End-1	Overload endurance End-3
	Basic endurance End-1			Basic endurance End-1		Lactate tolerance Spr-1
						Basic endurance End-1
PM	Overload endurance End-3	Lactate production Spr-2	Threshold endurance End-2	Lactate production Spr-2	Power Spr-3	
	Basic endurance End-1	Power Spr-3	Power Spr-3	Basic endurance End-1	Basic endurance End-1	
		Basic endurance End-1	Basic endurance End-1			

Figure 10-7. Cycling the various levels of training using a combined method for weekly planning.

and two major overload sets are positioned in groups of two so that swimmers have 32 to 48 hours to recover before these levels of endurance training are used again. The additional recovery time is needed because muscle glycogen should be nearly depleted after 5,000 to 8,000 yd/m of endurance swimming at or above the threshold level (Costill et al., 1988).

The threshold sets are placed during the morning sessions on Monday and Thursday and on Wednesday afternoon. The overload sets are scheduled for Monday afternoon and Saturday morning. The first recovery period of the week extends from Tuesday morning until Wednesday afternoon; the second, from Thursday afternoon until Saturday morning.

Two major lactate production sets are placed on Tuesday and Thursday afternoon, and one lactate tolerance set is scheduled for Saturday morning. This arrangement provides swimmers with at least 24 hours of recovery after the two consecutive endurance sets before these serial sets are attempted.

Power sets need to be scheduled carefully when the combined method is used. In this example, they are positioned on Tuesday, Wednesday, and Friday afternoon so that athletes have time to recover somewhat from their endurance training before attempting them. The power sets could also be placed on Monday and Wednesday afternoon preceding the threshold sets because there should still be enough glycogen in the muscles at this time to support fast speeds. It would be a bad idea to schedule them after the second set of threshold endurance training on Monday or

Thursday morning because muscle glycogen might be so low that the swimmers could not muster enough speed to swim the repeats with any quality.

The combination of overload and lactate tolerance sets on Saturday morning should not be a problem. Both the overload and lactate tolerance sets are shorter than the usual threshold set; therefore, the combination should only deplete muscle glycogen by 60 to 70 percent, after which swimmers will have approximately 40 hours (Saturday afternoon and all day Sunday) of complete recovery before beginning another week of training.

Once again, some basic endurance training is part of every training session, with the major sets scheduled during times when other endurance sets are not being done.

Adjustments for sprinters and distance swimmers Sprinters should include more sprint training in their programs. Figure 10-8 shows one method for adjusting an alternating weekly plan to do this. The threshold set that was scheduled for Wednesday morning in Figure 10-6 is replaced with lactate production and lactate tolerance sets in Figure 10-8. This plan has five power sets — on Monday and Thursday morning, and on Tuesday, Wednesday, and Friday afternoon.

Athletes in distance events need to add more threshold and overload endurance sets, as shown in Figure 10-9. Using Figure 10-7 as a starting point, an overload set is added on Friday afternoon. It could also be a threshold set. That placement comes at a time when there should be a normal amount of glycogen in the muscles.

	Monday	Tuesday	Wednesday	Thursday	Friday	Saturday
AM	Power Spr-3 Basic endurance End-1	Basic endurance End-1	✓Lactate production Spr-2 ✓Lactate tolerance Spr-1 Basic endurance End-1	✓Power Spr-3 Basic endurance End-1	Basic endurance End-1	✓Overload endurance End-3 Lactate tolerance Spr-1 Basic endurance End-1
PM	Overload endurance End-3 Lactate production Spr-2 Basic endurance End-1	Power Spr-3 Basic endurance End-1	Power Spr-3 Basic endurance End-1	Threshold endurance End-2 Lactate production Spr-2 Basic endurance End-1	Power Spr-3 Basic endurance End-1	

Figure 10-8. Adjusting an alternating weekly plan for sprinters.

	Monday	Tuesday	Wednesday	Thursday	Friday	Saturday
AM	Threshold endurance End-2 Basic endurance End-1	Basic endurance End-1	Basic endurance End-1	Threshold endurance End-2 Basic endurance End-1	Basic endurance End-1	Overload endurance End-3 Lactate tolerance Spr-1 Basic endurance End-1
PM	Overload endurance End-3 Basic endurance End-1	Lactate production Spr-2 Power Spr-3 Basic endurance End-1	Threshold endurance End-2 Power Spr-3 Basic endurance End-1	Lactate production Spr-2 Basic endurance End-1	Overload endurance ✓ End-3 Power Spr-3 Basic endurance End-1	

Figure 10-9. Adjusting a combined weekly plan for distance swimmers.

Planning for One Training Session Per Day Swimmers who train once per day are not as likely to become glycogen depleted because they get 24 hours of complete rest between each session. Nevertheless, it is probably a good idea to use alternating or combined weekly plans to ensure adequate muscle glycogen replacement. Even though these swimmers train fewer times per week, they should make certain that they include two or three threshold sets and one overload set in their weekly plan. They should also swim two lactate production, one or two lactate tolerance, and one or two power sets each week.

Alternating method Figure 10-10 illustrates an alternating method for swimmers who train five days per week and swim a meet on Saturday afternoon. The threshold and overload sets are scheduled for Monday, Wednesday, and Friday afternoon. Lactate production sets are placed on Tuesday and Thursday afternoon, and the meet on Saturday afternoon is labeled as a lactate tolerance set. Power sets are scheduled for Monday, Tuesday, and Thursday afternoon. They could be scheduled for Monday, Wednesday, and Friday with equal effectiveness.

Combined method Figure 10-11 is an example of a combined weekly plan for training one session per day. The threshold and overload sets are placed on Tuesday, Wednesday, and Friday afternoon. Lactate production training is placed on Monday and Thursday afternoon, and the meet on Saturday afternoon is designated as lactate tolerance training. Power training is placed on Monday, Tuesday, and Thursday, when the muscle glycogen supply should be adequate for fast swimming. It is

	Monday	Tuesday	Wednesday	Thursday	Friday	Saturday
PM	Threshold endurance End-2 Power Spr-3 Basic endurance End-1	Lactate production Spr-2 Power Spr-3 Basic endurance End-1	Overload endurance End-3 Basic endurance End-1	Lactate production Spr-2 Power Spr-3 Basic endurance End-1	Threshold endurance End-2 Basic endurance End-1	Lactate tolerance Spr-1

Figure 10-10. An alternating weekly plan for one training session per day.

	Monday	Tuesday	Wednesday	Thursday	Friday	Saturday
PM	Lactate production Spr-2 Power Spr-3 Basic endurance End-1	Threshold endurance End-2 Power Spr-3 Basic endurance End-1	Threshold endurance End-2 Basic endurance End-1	Lactate production Spr-2 Power Spr-3 Basic endurance End-1	Overload endurance End-3 Basic endurance End-1	Lactate tolerance Spr-1

Figure 10-11. A combined weekly plan for one training session per day.

not scheduled for Wednesday because muscle glycogen may be low after threshold endurance sets on that day and the preceding day.

Adjustments for sprinters and distance swimmers Sprinters can increase their sprinting mileage by replacing one threshold or overload endurance set with two sprint sets. Monday would be a good day with the alternating method shown in Figure 10-10 because the swimmers would not have sprint training three days in a row. Tuesday would be a good day with the combined method shown in Figure 10-11.

Distance swimmers can add more endurance training to the alternating method shown in Figure 10-10 by adding a second overload endurance set on Monday or Friday and reducing the amount of basic endurance swimming on the chosen day. It would be difficult to add any additional threshold or overload endurance sets to the combined example in Figure 10-11.

DAILY PLANNING

The most important consideration in planning daily training sessions is determining the best order for the various types of training. That order should encourage athletes to swim each set of repeats at the most effective intensity. Some guidelines for daily planning follow:

1. Power and lactate production training should usually be placed early in the session before swimmers are too fatigued to swim fast.
2. Lactate tolerance, threshold endurance, and overload endurance repeats should usually be placed late in the training sessions.

Substantial threshold sets will hinder athletes from swimming fast in subsequent sets because of a loss of muscle glycogen. Lactate tolerance and overload endurance sets, even when they are not substantial, are very fatiguing. They cause differing degrees of acidosis that require 15 to 30 minutes of recovery before athletes are capable of swimming another set of repeats at fast speeds. Accordingly, sets of these types should always be followed by 10 to 30 minutes of recovery or basic endurance training before additional fast swims are attempted.

The following box outlines a recommended plan for one-session training. It is designed primarily to improve aerobic capacity and includes some lactate production and power training.

A Sample Daily Training Plan

1. *Warm-up*
   Swim 300 m
   Pull 300 m
   Swim 4 × 50 on 1 minute

   800 m
2. *Lactate production training*
   6 × 50 on 3 minutes
   Swim easy 150 m between each 50

   300 m of lactate production training
   750 m of recovery swimming
3. *Stroke drill*
   10 × 100 on 2 minutes
   (25 right, 25 left, 100 both)

   1,000 m of basic endurance swimming
4. *Basic aerobic set*
   2 × 1,000 on 12 minutes

   2,000 m
5. *Kick*
   6 × 200 m on 4 minutes

   1,200 m
6. *Overload endurance set*
   8 × 200 on 2 minutes, 45 seconds

   1,600 m
7. *Recovery set*
   4 × 200 m on 2 minutes, 45 seconds
   (Start at a basic endurance speed and swim each 200 slower until recovered.)

   800 m of recovery swimming

TOTAL = 8,450 m

The session begins with a warm-up of 800 m done in segments of two 300s—one swimming, one pulling—and four 50-m repeats on a send-off time of one minute. Swimming speed should progress to a basic endurance level during the 300 repeats so that the warm-up serves a training purpose as well. The 50s should be descended to a reasonably fast speed so that body temperature rises.

A lactate production set is placed next so that swimmers can sprint before they become too fatigued. This is followed by a stroke drill that serves the dual purpose of allowing swimmers to work on their stroke mechanics while recovering from the previous set.

The next set consists of 2,000 m basic endurance swimming to improve endurance without causing extreme fatigue. It is placed early in the training session so that athletes do not swim too slow and use it for recovery purposes. That might easily happen if this set were placed after one of the more intense repeat sets that comes later.

The next set consists of 1,200 m of kicking to improve leg endurance. The kicking is done at a basic endurance level so that athletes can swim the next set with good quality.

The main set for this session is eight 200-m swims at an overload endurance level. It is placed late in the session so that the resulting acidosis and fatigue do not interfere with the earlier sets. It can be positioned earlier if it is followed by a long recovery set so that swimmers have time to reduce the acidosis before they swim fast again. The final segment of the training session is 800 m of easy swimming to aid recovery.

The placement of repeats in this sample daily training plan is very sound physiologically and should be followed for planning most daily training sessions. However, as with all general plans, there are times when deviations are warranted. For example, it is a good idea, on occasion, to swim two intense anaerobic sets in the same session to improve pain tolerance and mental toughness, particularly if swimmers are not permitted time to recover completely between sets. This training can be strategically advantageous when a swimmer must take a race out faster than usual and then "hang on." It may also improve a swimmer's ability to swim several events in one meet.

CHAPTER 11

Tapering

Prior to 1960, it was believed that the most intense training of the entire season should be performed in the few weeks preceding the most important meet. We know now that a period of reduced training called *tapering* results in much better performances. This chapter focuses on some theories and procedures for tapering.

TYPES OF TAPERS

The process of resting two to five weeks for season-ending meets is called a *major taper*. Swimmers commonly improve their season best performances by 3 to 4 percent after a major taper (Costill, Maglischo, & Richardson, 1991). The usual practice is to plan for one major taper per season, although some coaches and athletes prefer to taper two or more times during a single season. Experts suggest that athletes plan only two to four major tapers in a single training year (Bompa, 1983). This is logical advice, because tapering for two to four weeks several times per year can cause swimmers to lose valuable training time. Five major tapers per year added to the breaks required for mental and physical regeneration will reduce yearly training time by nearly 50 percent.

Many seasonal plans also require the scheduling of *minor tapers* (a short rest period of one week or less) and *retapers* (a second taper following a major taper). A minor taper is used when a good performance is needed early in a particular season—for example, to qualify for a more important meet later in the season. A retaper is used when one important meet is followed closely by another—that is, within three to five weeks of the first competition.

Coaches have conflicting opinions about the advisability of minor tapers. Some feel that they interfere with training and prevent swimmers from reaching peak performances at the end of the season. Others feel that occasional minor tapers are good for swimmers, both physiologically and psychologically. Minor tapers provide an opportunity to recover and adapt physiologically, and swimming in a less-fatigued state can improve a swimmer's confidence and motivation.

Because of the increase in the number of major meets per season and the difficulty of qualifying for those meets, the process of retapering is becoming increasingly important. Although it was previously believed that swimmers could maintain a taper for only a few days each season, the proliferation of major meets has shown that they can maintain peak performances over a considerably longer period of time. It has been suggested that the duration of one peak in performance can be maintained for seven to ten days without additional training (Ozolin, 1971, cited in Bompa, 1983) and that two or three peaks can be achieved within one to two consecutive months if there is time available for training between each peak (Matveev, Kalinen, & Ozolin, 1974). It should be stated, however, that a solid background of training is essential for the maintenance of peak performances. Swimmers who train on a yearly basis are able to maintain peak performances longer, and they are able to peak more times in a short period than those who train for only part of the year.

WHAT ARE THE PHYSIOLOGICAL CHANGES THAT PRODUCE A TAPER EFFECT?

A mystique surrounds the taper because we know so little about the physical changes that produce its effect. Some experts attribute a major portion of the taper effect to supercompensation of the muscle glycogen supply. Although glycogen supercompensation has been shown to improve performances in endurance running events (Bergstrom, Hermansen, Hultman, & Saltin, 1967), the same effect is not likely in our sport, however, because the duration of the running events far exceeded those of competitive swimming races. Additionally, high levels of muscle glycogen are not required in swimming events because they are too short for any significant depletion to occur. Consequently, it is doubtful that the performances of swimmers would be enhanced by glycogen loading. Furthermore, this rationale does not explain why swimmers require one or more weeks to produce a taper effect; two to three days of rest are adequate for glycogen loading to take place in muscles.

A second reason advanced for the taper effect has been a supercompensating effect on selected physiological processes. Although, this explanation is vague, it may, nevertheless, be the best one available at the present time. A supercompensating effect that enhances power could occur in muscles. Large increases of muscular power have been noted during tapers (Troup, Plyley, Sharp, & Costill, 1981). The same could be true for anaerobic capacity, because higher levels of blood lactate have been noted after performances when athletes were tapered (Maglischo, 1989a,

1989b). In fairness, it should be mentioned that several swimmers have posted good performances during tapers without showing significant increases of muscular power, while others have not improved despite the fact that their maximum blood lactate values increased. This is why it is so difficult to pinpoint the reasons for the taper effect. Regardless, improvements in power and anaerobic capacity seem the most reasonable explanation for the taper effect at the present time.

Figure 11-1 illustrates this theory. The three sections represent a swimmer's aerobic, anaerobic, and nonaerobic capacities. For demonstration purposes, these capacities have been equated with times for 200-m freestyle to show their relationship to performance. When stacked one on top of the other, the combined height of the three sections reflects the athlete's total physiological capacity and best performance for 200-m freestyle at different times during the season. This swimmer's total capacity made it possible for him to swim 1:55.00 for 200 m at the beginning of the season. In this example, training increased the swimmer's total physiological capacity to the point where he could swim 200 m in 1:45.00 by the end of the season. This improvement resulted principally from an improvement in aerobic capacity during the first three quarters of the season and an improvement in anaerobic capacity late in the season.

Although research is controversial on this issue, I believe aerobic capacity increases at the expense of anaerobic and nonaerobic capacities during most of the swim season. A reduction of endurance training and an increase of sprint training later in the season then sets the stage for improvements in nonaerobic and anaerobic capacities, which are maximized when the athlete rests during the taper. In Figure 11-1, the antagonistic effects of endurance training on anaerobic and nonaerobic capacities are represented by the relatively flat inclines during the middle and late

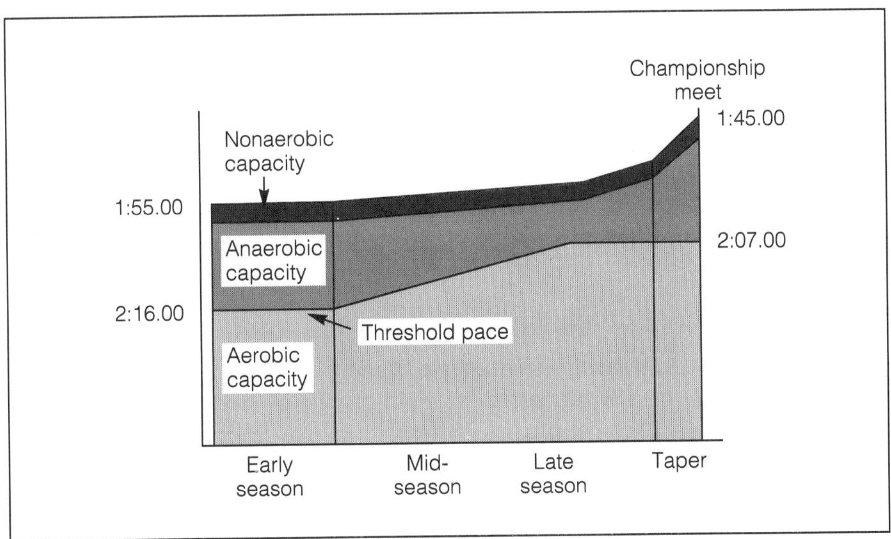

Figure 11-1. A theoretical pattern of physiological progress during a swimming season.

portions of the season. An improvement in aerobic capacity is illustrated by a steeper incline. When sprint training is stressed late in the season, it results in a partial recovery of anaerobic and nonaerobic capacities by the end of regular training and a supercompensation during the taper, when endurance training is reduced to a maintenance level. The net result is that the combined total of the three capacities reaches its highest level at the end of the taper, and the swimmer achieves a lifetime-best performance.

The taper, then, may be a time when a swimmer's anaerobic capacity and muscular power return to early season levels or, perhaps, supercompensate. If aerobic capacity has not declined, increases in the other two capacities should allow the athlete's total physiological capacity to be at its highest point, and he will be able to swim better than he has at any other time of the season. This theory illustrates the importance between the balance of work and rest during the taper. Athletes must rest long enough to regain or supercompensate power and anaerobic capacity and, at the same time, train sufficiently to maintain the improvements in aerobic capacity they achieved earlier in the season.

BALANCING WORK AND REST DURING THE TAPER

How much training is needed to maintain training adaptations? Research indicates that athletes lose conditioning quickly when they stop training completely (Saltin, Blomquist, et al., 1968). However, swimmers can maintain training adaptations with considerably less work than was needed to produce them. Decreases of 7 to 50 percent in certain physiological capacities have been cited after only one week of inactivity (Costill, Fink, et al., 1985; Costill, King, Thomas, & Hargreaves, 1985; Coyle, Martin & Holloszy, 1983; Klausen, Anderson, & Pelle, 1981; Neufer et al., 1988). Yet other research has shown that athletes were able to maintain training adaptations and performances for up to five weeks with 35- to 50-percent reductions in workload (Hickson et al., 1982; Houmard, Kirwan, Flynn, & Mitchell, 1989; Troup 1989c).

Aerobic capacity seems to be the most difficult aspect of performance to maintain during the taper. It requires precise combinations of training duration, intensity, and frequency. There are several pieces of research that can provide some guidance in determining the best combination of the three for maintaining endurance.

Maintaining Training Effects during the Taper

A study by Troup (1989b) suggests that maintaining training frequency and speed are more important than duration for the maintenance of training effects. He exposed three groups—each containing six senior national-level swimmers—to different forms of reduced training over a period of five weeks. Their results were compared to those of a control group that continued training normally during this period. Groups that maintained a training frequency of six days per week and swam at least 12 to 15 percent of their training mileage above their anaerobic threshold maintained their performances best. This was true even when the duration of daily training was reduced by two-thirds, from 3 hours to 1 hour per day. The groups that reduced their training frequency by two-thirds, from six to two days per week, showed the greatest loss in performance even though they maintained the same daily training times and speeds. From these results, Troup suggested that training adaptations could be sustained if the number of training sessions were maintained at four to six per week and if 10 to 15 percent of the training mileage were at speeds above the anaerobic threshold. According to the results of this study, swimmers could reduce training duration to 60 minutes daily without losses of performance.

A series of studies by Hickson and associates (Hickson & Rosenkoetter, 1981a; Hickson et al., 1982; Hickson et al., 1985) support some of Troup's observations. Performances worsened for groups of subjects who reduced their training speeds by one-third and two-thirds. The group that reduced training speed by one-third showed a 21-percent reduction in running and cycling time to exhaustion (184 minutes before versus 145 minutes after). The group that reduced training speed by two-thirds was 30 percent worse (202 minutes before versus 141 minutes after). These researchers also showed that endurance could be maintained with a 35-percent reduction in training duration, provided weekly training frequency was maintained at six days per week. Endurance was also maintained for events lasting 2 minutes or less when training duration was reduced by 68 percent, but performances in longer events were 10 percent worse. Hickson and colleagues also reported that performances for events lasting 5 minutes and less could be maintained when training frequency was reduced from six to four days per week as long as training speed was at normal levels and training duration was maintained at 60 minutes per day.

There are two additional studies concerning reductions in training mileage and its effect on aerobic capacity that may shed some light on the relationship of that variable to maintaining endurance. Houmard and associates (1989) did not find any decrements in performance or in tests of aerobic capacity when training mileage was reduced 50 percent for ten days.

Neufer and his helpers (1988) reported a significant increase in blood lactate of 1.8 mmol/l following a standardized 200-yd swim after training mileage had been reduced by approximately 80 percent for four weeks. The normal weekly total of 54,000 yd (9,000 yd per day, six days per week) was reduced to 9,000 yd (3,000 yd per day, three days per week). It is unfortunate that maximum tests of endurance and sprint performance were not included in this study. However, evidence that performance would probably have worsened was provided by measures of stroke rate and stroke length taken during the subjects' standardized 200-yd swims. Stroke length decreased during each week, declining by a total 4 percent (2.54 to 2.45 m/stroke) by the fourth week of reduced training. These results suggest that maintenance of endurance training effects requires that training volume be reduced no more than 35 percent, that training frequency be maintained at 4 to 6 days per week, and that training speeds be maintained at normal levels for each category of training.

Most of the detraining effects mentioned in the previous paragraphs are concerned with aerobic capacity. Adaptations in both muscular power and anaerobic capacity seem to increase when endurance training is reduced during the taper.

However, significant losses of both can occur if training is reduced too much over too long a period. Intensity seems to be the key to maintaining these qualities. It seems that both anaerobic capacity and power can be maintained rather easily if swimmers occasionally sprint fast during the taper. Strength gains have been maintained for up to 12 weeks by training only once per week, provided the training was near previous maximum values (Graves et al., 1988), and anaerobic capacity has been maintained for up to 15 weeks when training mileage was reduced by two-thirds (Hickson et al., 1982) and when training frequency was reduced to two sessions per week (Hickson & Rosenkoetter, 1981b).

According to the results of these studies, swimmers should engage in sprint training at least twice per week during the taper. They should maintain the intensity of their sprint training at near-normal levels and the daily duration within one-third of the usual amount.

Table 11-1 summarizes the results of several studies on the maintenance of training effects during the taper.

GUIDELINES FOR TAPERING

Some of the suggestions provided in this section are based on studies cited earlier in this chapter; however, because many aspects of the tapering process have not been studied adequately, most of the guidelines have been drawn from personal experience.

A major taper should last two to three weeks, following a two-week pretaper period. The purpose of the pretaper is to help coaches assess the level of fatigue for each swimmer and structure the actual taper period to provide the proper balance of rest and work.

Table 11-1. Summary of Research on the Maintenance of Training Effects

	Minimum Amounts of Training That Can Be Performed Without Affecting Performance	
Training Variable	*Sprint and Middle-Distance Efforts (4 to 6 minutes)*	*Distance Efforts (1 to 3 hours)*
Daily mileage	50 to 60 percent	65 percent
Weekly frequency	4 days per week	4–6 days per week
Intensity		
Mileage swum above the anaerobic threshold	50 percent of usual	10–15 percent
Reduction of usual endurance training speeds	33 percent	not more than 1/4

Sources: Hickson, 1981; Hickson & Rosenkoetter, 1981b; Hickson et al., 1985; Houmard, Kirwan, Flynn, & Mitchell, 1989; Neufer et al., 1988; Troup, 1989c.

The Pretaper

Athletes should reduce training mileage and intensity somewhat during these two weeks, but not to taper levels. If athletes are swimming 9,000 yd/m or more, the mileage should probably be reduced by 15 to 20 percent. Athletes who are training once a day for 5,000 or 6,000 yd/m should remain at that mileage and reduce their usual basic endurance training intensity by approximately 2 to 3 seconds per 100 yd/m. The speed of threshold and overload sets should remain at normal season levels, although the mileage at these levels should decrease somewhat. The quantity, but not the quality, of sprint training should be reduced as well. Swimmers who are training twice a day should continue to do so. Athletes should cut back on land-resistance and flexibility training to maintenance levels; two to three sessions per week should be adequate. Those who are training once a day should continue with five or six sessions per week.

It is important that swimmers understand that they are merely trying to maintain their aerobic training effects from this point on. A common mistake is to respond to a reduction of training mileage by increasing training speed. This is not a good idea because it will delay the recovery and supercompensation processes.

Coaches should evaluate the recovery of swimmers at the end of each pretaper week. Swimmers who are responding well will become more energetic by the end of the first week. They may also perform better in meets. These swimmers can safely stay on the same program for another week. Swimmers who do not seem to be recovering during the first week should reduce their mileage and intensity considerably and begin their taper during the second week of the pretaper period. The program should be like the one described below for the first week of the taper.

The Taper Period

This phase of the season should last approximately three weeks. The reduction in training mileage and intensity should be gradual during this time so that swimmers do not risk losing endurance while they are recovering. Table 11-2 outlines the general plan for tapering senior swimmers. It applies to swimmers who have been training a minimum of once per day, five to six days per week.

Week 1 Swimmers who were training once per day during the season should maintain training frequency at the normal level. Those who were training twice per day may safely reduce the number of training sessions by two or three over the week.

The morning session should be shortened to 2,000 or 3,000 yd/m, with most of the mileage in the form of recovery and basic endurance swimming and kicking, pulling, and stroke drills. If possible, coaches should schedule morning training at the same time the preliminary heats will be held. This will help reorient swimmers' biological time clocks to competition times and provide some additional rest by beginning training later than usual in the morning. By the same token, the second session of the day should be held at the time of the finals, if it is practical to do so.

Table 11-2. Training Frequency, Mileage, and Intensity during the Taper

Daily Sessions	Frequency (Sessions per Week)	Mileage	Intensity
Pretaper (2 weeks)			
2 per day	10–12	7,000–9,000	Reduce 10 percent
1 per day	5–6	5,000–7,000	Reduce 10 percent
Taper period			
Week 1			
2 per day	10–11	6,000–8,000	Reduce 10 percent
1 per day	5–6	4,000–5,000	Reduce 10 percent
Week 2			
2 per day	8–10	4,000–6,000	Same as previous week
1 per day	5–6	3,000–4,000	
Week 3			
2 per day	daily until meet begins		Warm up only
1 per day	daily until meet begins		Warm up only

Coaches should set aside three afternoon sessions for maintaining aerobic endurance, with one set of threshold or overload endurance swims placed during each of these sessions. That set can be 1,200 to 2,000 yd/m. The remainder of the daily endurance mileage should be in the basic endurance category. Basic endurance sets should not exceed 2,000 yd/m except for distance swimmers, who may, on occasion, increase their basic endurance sets to 3,000 yd/m or more.

Coaches should include two short lactate tolerance or lactate production sets during this week. The athletes may swim as fast as possible on these repeats. One or two broken swims, a short lactate production, or an equally short lactate tolerance set can be used. Sets such as 4 to 6 × 50 with 2 to 3 minutes' rest, or 3 to 4 × 100 with 2 to 5 minutes' rest, are ideal for this purpose.

Scheduling a short set of sprint swims during two mornings of this week should keep athletes in the habit of swimming fast early in the day. A few sprints of 10 to 25 yd/m should also be done in the afternoon. Swimming four to six 25s should suffice for these sets.

Swimmers should warm up well before each training session and swim down for 800 to 1,200 yd/m afterward. Stretching should continue to precede each practice period. Swimmers should discontinue dryland resistance training. There are many who may not agree with this last piece of advice; however, research suggests that strength and power on land will actually increase during the taper for a period of at least 15 days with no further training (Costill, King, Thomas, & Hargreaves, 1985). Sprinting should provide an adequate stimulus for maintenance of strength and power in the water.

The only exception to the plan I have just outlined concerns swimmers who show signs of being overly fatigued at the end of the pretaper period. Their anaerobic capacity and muscular power are probably still depressed, and they may require a major reduction in training mileage for them to recover to near-normal levels. Consequently, it would be advisable to reduce their training mileage and intensity drastically during the first week of the taper. They should train only once per day for 3,000 to 4,000 yd/m, with most of that training in the form of warming up and basic endurance swimming. They should practice stroke drills and work on starts and turns. These athletes should swim one or two threshold sets totaling no more than 1200 yd/m each during the week. Some power training should be done during two or three days, but only one short lactate production or lactate tolerance set should be performed during the week.

Week 2 The plan suggested for this week is almost identical to the preceding one, except that training mileage should decline further to between 4,000 and 5,000 yd/m per day. Swimmers who are training twice per day can reduce training frequency by an additional one to two sessions per week. Those reductions should come in the morning sessions. Swimmers training once per day should continue at their usual weekly frequency of five to six sessions per week.

Athletes should swim 1,200 to 2,000-yd/m in the morning and only 3,000- to 4,000-yd/m in the afternoon. Most of that mileage should continue to be in the form of warming up and basic endurance swimming in sets of 1,500 to 2,000 yd/m. Swimmers should complete threshold or overload endurance sets of 1,200 to 2,000 yd/m two times during this week.

Distance swimmers can increase the mileage of their threshold sets to 2,000 or 2,500 yd/m. They should also swim longer basic endurance sets; 2,000 to 3,000 yd/m per set should be adequate. Sprinters should reduce their endurance training drastically during this week. They can swim the two threshold sets and some sprint sets, and the remainder of their mileage should consist of warm-up swimming and stroke drills.

All athletes should swim two short sprint sets during this week. These sets can consist of one or two broken swims, four to six 50s, or three to four 100s. Maximum efforts should not be required, but the swims should be fast enough to increase the rate of lactate production near maximum, even though peak levels of blood lactic acid will not be reached. Athletes should also swim 100 to 200 yd/m of 25- and 50-yd/m sprints at least twice during this week. Stretching before each session should continue so that athletes maintain the greatest possible range of motion.

Those swimmers who seemed to be overly fatigued during the previous week should return to the regular taper program this week if they are showing signs of recovering. Their mileage can even be increased somewhat beyond that of the others. They should continue with the program outlined for week 1 if they do not seem to be recovering.

The Final Week Swimmers should only warm up during the first three or four days of this week if the major meet begins midweek. If the meet begins late in the week, the duration and intensity of training should be similar to that described for week 2 until swimmers are within three days of the meet. Athletes can safely reduce training for the final three days prior to the meet. It is not possible to lose endurance in this time unless the taper has already been too long, and the additional rest may restore or supercompensate anaerobic capacity and muscular power more completely.

Warm-up should be similar to the one athletes will use in meets, including sprints and/or pace work. If they have been training twice per day, swimmers should warm up twice per day. Swimmers training once a day should stay on that schedule. Ideally, warm-ups should occur at the same time of day that the meet will be held. Daily training mileage is inconsequential during the final three days.

Table 11-3 lists the suggested daily distances for each type of training by week for the pretaper and taper. Swimmers should focus a considerable amount of attention on perfecting starts, turns, and relay starts during the taper. They should practice starts and turns at least every other session. Pace training should also be a priority. Athletes should swim underdistance repeats until they can duplicate their ideal pace for races within 0.20 to 0.50. They should also practice swimming with the most efficient combination of stroke rate and stroke length. It may not be realistically possible for athletes to swim at ideal race speeds when they are unshaved. However, they can practice under race-like conditions if they duplicate the correct stroke rate for each of their events during pace training.

Coaches and athletes should also spend some time discussing meet and race strategy. Swimmers should be advised about warming up properly, particularly under the crowded conditions they will encounter at most major meets. They should be cautioned to spend 15 to 20 minutes swimming down after all races so that they will recover more quickly and completely. Some discussions should be held concerning the strategy for swimming preliminaries and finals with regard to such matters as the difficulty in qualifying for the finals and the lane positions swimmers prefer if they qualify. Swimmers should also be concerned with the race plans they will use against certain competitors in the finals.

A good portion of the swimmers' warm-ups, swim-downs, and basic endurance training should be in the form of stroke drills. They should also concentrate on

Table 11-3. Suggested Set Length for Each Type of Training during the Taper

Form of Training	Pretaper	Week 1	Week 2	Week 3
End-1	5–8 × 2,000–2,500	5–8 × 1,500–2,000	5–8 × 1,500–2,000	Negligible
End-2 and End-3	3× 1,200–2,000	3 × 1,200–2,000	2 × 1,200–2,000	Negligible
Lactate production	2 × 200–400	2 × 200–400	1–2 × 200–400	Negligible
Lactate tolerance	1 × 200–400	1 × 200–400	1 × 200–400	Negligible
Power	3–4 × 200–300	3–4 × 200–300	3–4 × 200–300	Negligible
Dryland	Reduced	Discontinued throughout taper		
Flexibility	Continued throughout pretaper and taper			
Pace	2–3 × 300–400	2 × 200–300	1–2 × 200–300	2–3 × 100–300

using the best possible mechanics in all of their pace, sprint, and intense endurance swimming. The fatigue of hard training sometimes causes swimmers' strokes to deteriorate somewhat, so the taper is an excellent time to polish their techniques. However, major stroke changes should *not* be attempted during the taper. Coaches will be gambling if they try to introduce a change in stroke technique over a short time. Although performance may improve if swimmers are able to incorporate a change, the more likely result is that the change will have a detrimental effect. Swimmers will not be able to compete at 100-percent effort if the change confuses or inhibits them such that they must hold back to control a newly learned stroke technique.

Oversprinting Many swimmers make the mistake of sprinting too much during the taper. They do so, perhaps, because they feel good or because they hope to gain confidence with some fast swims. Whatever the reason, too much swimming at high levels of muscle lactate may send swimmers into competition with a tendency toward excessive lactic acid production at slower speeds. In other words, their anaerobic thresholds may be slowed somewhat. This, in turn, will cause them to fatigue earlier in races.

If sprint training has been administered in adequate amounts throughout the season, rest—rather than additional fast swimming—is needed. It will provide the recovery or possible supercompensating effects of anaerobic capacity and muscular power that will prepare swimmers for a season-best performance.

Weight Gains Swimmers should reduce their caloric intake slightly during the taper to prevent the accumulation of excessive fat tissue. A slight weight gain of two to four pounds should be expected, however. Many swimmers are somewhat dehydrated during the season from chronically low muscle glycogen levels. The replacement and supercompensation of muscle glycogen that occurs during the taper will cause them to rehydrate or even superhydrate. Their body will store approximately three grams of water for every gram of glycogen they deposit (Wilmore & Costill, 1988), and their muscle glycogen levels may supercompensate to two or three times their normal limits (Bergstrom, Hermansen, Hultman, & Saltin, 1967). Thus, the first two to four pounds of weight gain will come primarily from additional water storage and not an increase of adipose tissue. However, continued weight gain beyond this level should be avoided.

Psychological Factors The success of tapers may be related to psychological factors as much if not more than physiological factors. For a taper to have its full effect, swimmers must believe that they are going to swim well. The axiom "Performance is 90 percent mental and only 10 percent physical" probably underrates the physiological contributions to performance in one context and the psychological contributions in another. Poorly conditioned athletes cannot will themselves to peak performances. However, once athletes are well conditioned, their success probably depends 100 percent on their state of mind.

The uncertainties of the taper, particularly whether swimmers feel they are getting too much or too little rest, can create anxieties that may erode confidence.

Swimmers will look to their coaches for support and guidance. They need to be convinced that their training programs have been successful and that all signs indicate that they are going to swim well. Leading experts around the world are unanimous in their advice that coaches must remain calm and exude an attitude of confidence during this time. However, that does not mean that coaches should lie to swimmers if the taper is not proceeding as expected. Coaches should tell swimmers if the taper is not on schedule and offer advice to remedy the situation so that swimmers can feel confident that things will be alright.

Good performances on paced or broken swims will give swimmers confidence during the taper. Good scores on evaluative measures such as blood tests, tests of power, sprints, and measures of stroke length and stroke rate will have the same effect.

However, caution must be exercised in using these evaluative measures. Some swimmers do not perform well on them. For some unknown reason, there are athletes who swim very poorly during a taper but often swim very well at meets. I suspect that such swimmers realize intuitively that they must reduce swimming intensity during the taper in order to restore muscular power and anaerobic capacity, so they hold back, often without realizing what they are doing. Regardless of their reasons for swimming poorly, results of evaluative swims and tests would only cause worry and send them into the meet lacking confidence.

Individualizing Tapers The taper is the most individual time of the year. Humans are so complex that myriad factors can affect the balance between work and rest that can produce an outstanding performance. Age, sex, event length, the volume of previous training, and individual abilities to recover from hard training all influence the balance between work and rest that is required to produce an outstanding performance. Following is a list of some of the more common individual adjustments required during the taper.

1. Older swimmers seem to need more time to recover.
2. Females seem to need less time than males to recover.
3. Distance swimmers should generally maintain a greater volume of training because they cannot afford to lose aerobic capacity.
4. Sprinters frequently need to reduce their training volume more while increasing the length of their tapers to ensure that power and anaerobic capacity are maximized.
5. Swimmers who train 10 or 11 months during the year seem to recover faster than those who train only a few months during the year.

The previous list makes it clear that the time needed to produce a taper can differ from one person to the next. The art of the taper is in knowing (1) how much to reduce the workload without losing aerobic capacity and (2) how long it will take to restore anaerobic and nonaerobic capacities for each individual swimmer. There are as many different responses to a taper as there are athletes on a team. For this reason, the general plan presented in the previous sections may need to be individualized for certain swimmers. Be prepared to change that plan for any swimmer who is not responding well. In these cases, personal experience must be your guide in determining what changes should be made.

Preparing Swimmers for the Competition Site Swimmers should be prepared for all of the possible problems that could occur at the meet site. Crowded pools, long lines to get into the meet or dining hall, different styles of food preparation, different time zones, inadequate gutter systems, gutters with flush walls, poor visibility on turns, poor starting block construction, and shallow pools are some of the most common, unnerving circumstances that can be encountered at meet sites. Swimmers will have confidence in their preparation if they know that all of these eventualities have been considered. When possible, plan to arrive at the site a few days early so that swimmers can adjust to their different surroundings.

Different Tapers for Men and Women? The experiences of many coaches have led them to conclude that men require longer tapers and greater reductions of training mileage and intensity than women and younger males. To my knowledge, this belief has not been investigated in a controlled scientific study. It may be accurate, nonetheless. Millard and associates (1985) have reported higher creatine phosphokinase (CPK) levels in men than women following heavy training, even though both sexes swam the same workouts. Elevated levels of CPK suggest that the training caused greater muscle damage in men than women. Accordingly, women may require a shorter recovery period than men because they have less muscle damage to repair. Women may be best advised to continue training with somewhat greater intensity than men during the first week of the taper period. This suggestion should only be followed by women in middle-distance and distance events and only then if they have reacted favorably to the pretaper period.

The Retaper

The training procedures used during a retaper will depend on the length of time before the next major competition. If it is two or three days, swimmers should simply continue to rest. If it is a week, they should rest for two days after the previous meet, train moderately for two days, and then rest again. If it is several weeks, swimmers should resume training at a pretaper level until one week before the next meet.

Swimmers should retaper by training at basic endurance levels for two or three days following a major competition in which athletes swam shaved and tapered. The swimmers will be drained emotionally and physically from the competition, and swimming at these speeds will help them recover while preventing losses of aerobic capacity. No sprint training should be done during this period beyond a few 25s or 50s. Training should be conducted once per day. Daily mileage is not important; a reasonable amount would be 2,000 to 4,000 yd/m.

Following this recovery period, swimmers should begin training in a manner similar to that described for the pretaper period. The purpose of their training is to *maintain* aerobic and anaerobic endurance, so they should not risk becoming overly fatigued by training extra hard. Swimmers can return to dryland training, but they should keep it to a maintenance level. Swimmers who are accustomed to training twice per day should resume that schedule; those who have been training once per day should stay with that program.

If the time between meets is three to four weeks, daily mileage for two of those weeks should be maintained between 7,000 and 9,000 yd/m for swimmers training twice per day and 5,000 to 6,000 yd/m for those training once per day. After that, swimmers should taper in the manner described for week 2 and the final week of a major taper.

All swimmers can remain at 5,000 to 7,000 yd/m per day for the first week if the intervening time between meets is only two weeks. They should resume tapering during the second week, following the schedule described for the final week of a major taper.

All levels of training should be included during the period of moderate training that precedes the next taper. Threshold endurance training can be conducted two or three times per week, with set distances of 2,000 to 3,000 yd/m. One or two sets of lactate tolerance training should be sufficient, with set distances between 400 and 600 yd/m. Lactate production and power sprinting can be maintained at a frequency of three to five days per week for 200 to 300 yd/m per set. One set of overload endurance training should be conducted per week, with set distances of 1,200 to 1,500 yd/m. The remainder of the training mileage should be at a basic endurance level.

Athletes should be able to maintain their performances for up to five weeks on the retaper program I have outlined. If the time between meets is longer than this, it would be wise to return to regular training until the swimmers are within two or three weeks of the next competition. At this time, they should taper according to the guidelines for the final two weeks of a major taper.

Minor Tapers

Minor tapers usually last two to five days. They are used to achieve good performances in an early-season or midseason meet. Swimmers usually do not shave for these meets, so their performances should not be as fast as they will be later. The recovery weeks of mesocycles should be planned to coincide with minor tapers so as not to interfere with regular training. Five to seven minor tapers could be scheduled into the recovery weeks for the mesocycles of a season without affecting training volume or intensity. Swimmers should not rest completely during minor tapers because, as mentioned in Chapter 9, training adaptations can be lost in as few as six days of inactivity (Klausen, Anderson, & Pelle, 1981).

There seem to be two methods for implementing a minor taper. The first is to reduce training mileage dramatically for two to five days. A daily total of 3,000 to 4,000 yd/m is most commonly used for this purpose. The second method is to reduce training intensity while maintaining mileage near normal levels. Sprinters should probably use the former method for minor tapers so that they can sprint fast. The latter method is best suited for middle-distance and distance swimmers to prevent a significant loss of endurance.

Reducing training intensity without significantly reducing training mileage is best accomplished by reducing the quantities of sprint training and overload and threshold endurance training. The bulk of training will then be at the basic endurance level for maintenance of aerobic capacity.

TRAINING IMBALANCES AND HOW THEY AFFECT THE TAPER

It is common for swimmers to blame an inadequate taper for poor performances at season's end. However, it has been my experience that poor performances are caused more often by training imbalances that occurred during the regular season. Specifically, swimmers may do too much or too little intense endurance training during the season. Figures 11-2 and 11-3 illustrate examples of these two training imbalances. Figure 11-2 shows the result of an overemphasis on intense endurance training during the season. Notice that aerobic capacity continued to improve throughout the season. However, nonaerobic and anaerobic capacities were depressed so much that the swimmer was not able to recover to normal levels in the time provided for the taper. As a result, the athlete's performance in competition, although a season-best, was not as fast as the one shown in Figure 11-1 (1:48.00 versus 1:45.00).

Figure 11-2 also shows that a few extra weeks of rest restored those capacities to normal so that the athlete was able to swim faster (1:47.00) in a postchampionship competition. This happened despite the fact that he lost some aerobic capacity

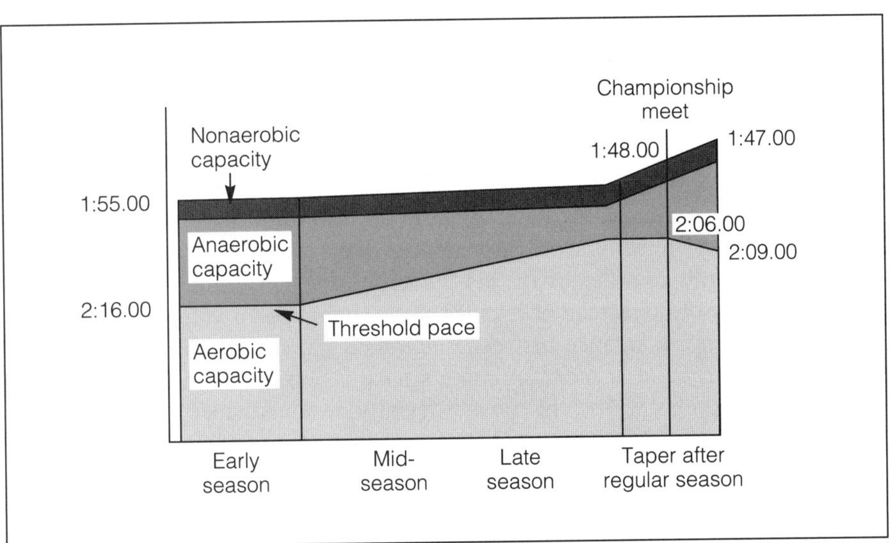

Figure 11-2. The result of an overemphasis on endurance training.

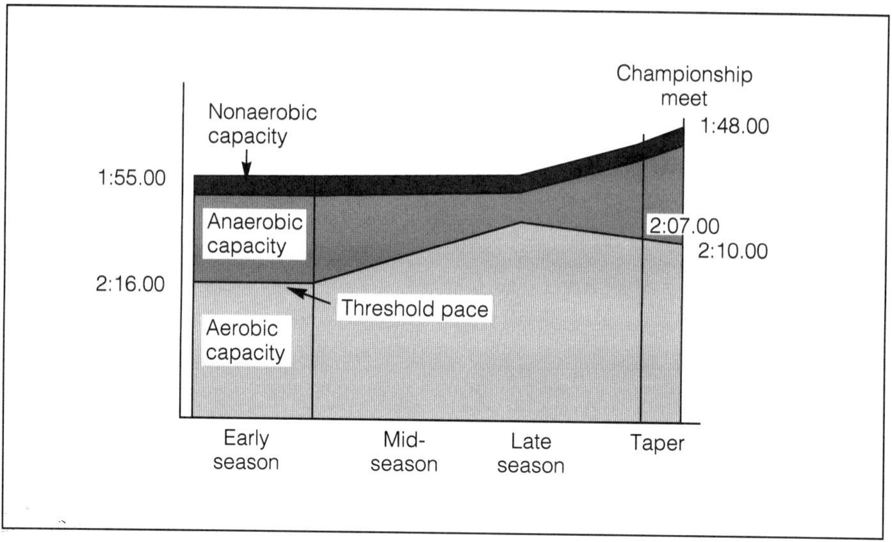

Figure 11-3. The result of an underemphasis on endurance training.

during those weeks, as indicated by an increase in his threshold pace from 2:06 to 2:09. His time improved, nonetheless, because that loss was offset by increases in his anaerobic and nonaerobic capacities so that his total capacity was greater than it had been at the championship meet. We can only speculate on how much faster he would have swum if the three capacities had peaked at the same times. I cite this example because we have all coached athletes who surprised us by swimming well in unimportant meets after they stopped training. This example may explain why they were able to do so in spite of the fact that their training was curtailed beyond that needed to maintain endurance.

The opposite problem, an underemphasis on endurance training, is illustrated in Figure 11-3. Here, both the volume and intensity of endurance training were decreased too much in the second half of the season, and the swimmer lost aerobic capacity. This is indicated by the change in his threshold pace from 2:06.00 to 2:09.00. Although anaerobic and nonaerobic capacities increased considerably, their improvement was offset by the loss of aerobic capacity, and the athlete in this example swam 1:48.00 instead of 1:45.00 in the championship meet.

When the delicate balance between endurance and sprint training is managed well during the regular season, swimmers have a better-than-average chance of tapering well. When it is not, the most efficiently designed taper may not result in a good performance.

CHAPTER 12

Overtraining

Overtraining is the term used to identify a condition that appears when athletes' adaptive mechanisms have been stressed to the point of failure. Athletes may create excessive stress by exceeding their tolerance to a particular form of training by using it too frequently. Excessive stress can be due to the cumulative effects of inadequate nutrition or insufficient time for rest and recovery. Anxiety caused by crises in athletes' emotional lives can also be a potent stressor. When excessive anxiety combines with the demands of normal training, adaptive mechanisms can fail.

Stress should not be avoided in training, however. Quite the contrary. Frequent and progressive doses of specific forms of stress are required to stimulate physiological systems toward optimal levels of adaptation. It is only when that stress exceeds an athlete's tolerance that it becomes counterproductive. When that happens, the consequences of training shift from their usual anabolic (building-up) effects to those which are catabolic — in other words, the stress tears athletes down.

It is difficult for even the most knowledgeable coach to design a training program that will not overstress some members of a team during the course of a season. Morgan and his associates (1987) reported that 10 percent of collegiate male and female swimmers became seriously overtrained at some time during their careers.

Unfortunately, cases of overtraining are more frequent among the most highly motivated athletes because they are always trying to exceed their limits. One of the saddest experiences in all of sports is to see a dedicated athlete fail after making countless sacrifices in the pursuit of success.

The basis for overtraining was presented several decades ago by Hans Selye (1956) in his famous discourse on the stress syndrome. He proposed that stress affects persons in both specific and general ways. The specific reactions are different, depending on the nature of the stressor, but the general reactions to stress are similar for all living things. Therefore, any specific stressor affects not only a certain physiological system but also every other system. Accordingly, when a number of stressors act on the body at once, their cumulative effect can cause failing adaptation, even though no single stressor is, by itself, excessive.

Selye theorized that the resources for dealing with stress come from a store of general adaptation energy. He believed that the size of that store was finite and determined by heredity. Figure 12-1 shows the relationship between the store of general adaptation energy and the energy supply for swimmers' activities. The most common specific stressors that act on all swimmers are training, academic demands, social demands, anxiety, and illness and injury.

As shown in Figure 12-1, the reservoir of general adaptation energy flows downward, replacing energy that is lost daily from each of the specific stores. This reservoir is, in turn, replaced by rest and good nutrition.

Selye believed that it was possible for the general adaptation energy supply to become depleted, or nearly so, when (1) the requirement from any specific activity became inordinately high, (2) when the demand from several areas increased unexpectedly, or (3) when energy was not being replaced adequately through diet and rest.

In support of this theory, athletes frequently display symptoms of overtraining when there is a sudden and dramatic increase in training volume or intensity. By the same token, they often exhibit symptoms of overtraining after sudden and dramatic increases in the demands from other stressors. For example, the performances of athletes are usually somewhat worse during examination periods. Likewise, they have difficulty training at usual levels when an emotional crisis occurs, such as a disagreement with friends or parents. Athletes who attend an inordinate amount of social functions and/or participate in a large variety of outside activities

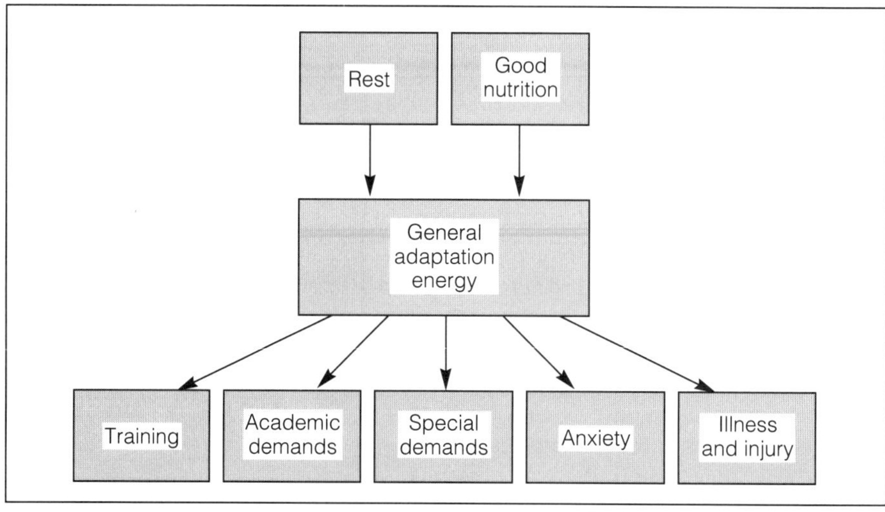

Figure 12-1. Selye's general adaptation theory as applied to swimmers.

frequently do not get enough sleep or quiet time to replace energy. Finally, athletes whose *diets* do not contain enough calories or the proper proportions of nutritious foods are more likely to become overtrained for the same reason.

It is unfortunate that the term *overtraining* has become associated with this condition. The connotation is that athletes are training too much. In reality, Selye's theory implicates many other causative factors. Athletes can and should engage in large volumes of training if they are given sufficient recovery time, if they consume enough of the right kinds of calories, and if they can manage outside stresses. They must overload each energy system on a frequent basis with very intense and challenging swimming sets while providing enough time for rest and recovery so that the stress does not become intolerable.

SIGNS OF OVERTRAINING

Table 12-1 lists the symptoms associated with overtraining. All of these are also common reactions to training and competition. It is only when they seem exaggerated or persist longer than usual that overtraining should be suspected.

Performance Symptoms

The first sign that coaches and athletes should notice is *poor performances* in meets and in training. Athletes may show signs of being overtrained when they swim consistently slower in training over several days or when their performances in meets are very poor over a few weeks. Signs such as a higher heart rate for a particular time, complaints of fatigue during moderate-speed swims, and an inability to swim sets at or beyond threshold paces without becoming unusually fatigued all point to overtraining.

Physical Symptoms

The most common symptom is a loss of weight that cannot be explained from dietary habits or training volume. Swimmers will normally lose some weight during

Table 12-1. Symptoms of Overtraining

Performance	Physical	Psychological
Slower times in meets and training	Loss of weight	Depression
	Joint and muscle soreness	Irritability
	Allergic reactions	Insomnia
	Loss of appetite	Anxiety
	Head colds and sinusitis	Withdrawal
	Nausea	Difficulty concentrating
	Lack of energy	Loss of confidence

the first weeks of the season; however, their weight should stabilize after that. Consequently, sudden weight losses during the middle of the season warn that overtraining may be imminent.

Swimmers will also routinely lose one to three pounds from the beginning to the end of training days. Most of this weight loss is dehydration caused by sweating and loss of muscle glycogen. Both the fluid and muscle glycogen should be replaced, or nearly so, by the next morning. Posttraining weight losses that are not replaced after two or three days may signal the possibility of overtraining.

Muscle and joint soreness is normal during the early weeks of training, following sessions of supramaximum effort during any phase of the season, and whenever a new form of training is added to the program. However, overtraining should be suspected when athletes complain of sore muscles or joints in the middle of the season after normal or subnormal training. Not all athletes who complain of sore shoulders or knees are overtrained however. Some may be suffering symptoms of overuse and should use other training methods until these symptoms are relieved. Complete rest may be required, however, when these symptoms persist during work that is usually not severe enough to cause soreness and when other signs of overtraining are present.

Swimmers who tend toward allergic reactions will usually demonstrate these symptoms when they are overtrained. Hives, rashes, head colds, and stuffy noses are the most common signs and may occur at unusual times or may be unusually severe when athletes are overtrained.

Swimmers may complain that they have no energy when they are overtrained. These complaints may be associated with a loss of appetite. With the close association between a lack of energy and nutrition, you might assume that overtrained athletes would eat more than usual. However, that is not the case; they generally lose interest in food and do not feel hungry in spite of the fact that they may be losing weight.

Emotional Symptoms

The association between athletes' physical and emotional reactions to overtraining is so intertwined that it is impossible to separate the two. It appears that some negative disturbances in an athlete's disposition are a normal response to intense training (Morgan et al., 1987). It is only when these disturbances become unusually severe and persistent that overtraining should be suspected.

Raglin and Morgan (1989) and Morgan and associates (1987), citing research spanning more than ten years, have stated that overtraining is nearly always accompanied by depression and anxiety. This reaction is interesting in light of the fact that mild exercise has been shown to have the opposite effect (Morgan, 1985). Athletes who are overtrained may become unusually irritable. They may appear uptight and show signs of having difficulty concentrating at practice and at other times during the day. Their manner may suggest a loss of confidence, and they may withdraw from social gatherings. In practice, they may prefer to swim by themselves in an empty lane. Additionally, they may avoid interacting with teammates by arriving just before practice and leaving immediately afterward. They may also experience insomnia. They may have difficulty getting to sleep, and, when they do sleep, they may toss and turn or wake up several times during the night.

Overtraining should be suspected only when these symptoms seem exaggerated relative to the training effort and/or when they persist over several days. Unfortunately, when these symptoms become noticeable, the swimmer will have already entered a state of failing adaptation. Nevertheless, the condition will not be too severe to correct.

TYPES OF OVERTRAINING

There seem to be two categories of overtraining. The first of these has been described by Israel as being *inhibitory* (1963, cited in Bompa, 1983). The second category of overtraining could be termed *excitatory* because it seems to be intimately related to the emotional content of the competitive environment.

Inhibitory Overtraining

The causes of inhibitory overtraining are not known. It may be related to a reduction of the muscles' energy supply, causing the body to shut down so that energy can be replaced, or it may be caused by the accumulation of certain by-products of oxidation, *free radicals*.

Diagnosing Inhibitory Overtraining The difficulty in diagnosing inhibitory overtraining is that the intense symptoms of irritability, nausea, allergic reactions, and so on may not be present or, if present, may go unnoticed until they are very severe. Additionally, athletes may be performing well in endurance sets; but the telltale clue appears when these swimmers try to sprint, swim time trials, or race in sprint and middle-distance events and are unable to swim very much faster than they do in endurance sets.

Athletes suffering from inhibitory overtraining will also complain of fatigue that is associated with a heavy feeling in their muscles during training, rather than the acute pain they feel following intense sprint efforts. The former is an indication that athletes are lacking in muscle glycogen, while the latter is a normal consequence of acidosis following fast swims. Athletes may also express that they do not feel tired but that they can't swim any faster.

In my experience, an inability to swim well at threshold speeds and faster is the best indicator that inhibitory overtraining is imminent. It will be particularly difficult to diagnose with distance swimmers, because the difference between their endurance training and maximum effort speeds is not as great as it is for sprinters and middle-distance swimmers. Diagnosis is further complicated by the expectation of slower competition times during midseason, when athletes are competing tired. Some distance swimmers become so well trained aerobically that they can swim very well in competition even when tired. It is only after they taper and their performances do not improve very much that it becomes evident that something went wrong in the training process. It will be too late to salvage the season by this time.

Middle-distance and sprint swimmers are also susceptible to inhibitory overtraining, even though they generally swim fewer meters per day in training. Most have a greater percentage of fast twitch (FT) muscle fibers, so they tend to swim more anaerobically in training. Consequently, their daily glycogen use could conceivably be greater than that of distance swimmers.

Causes of Inhibitory Overtraining Although controversial, recent research suggests that inhibitory overtraining may very well be due to the accumulation of free radicals during endurance training. Free radicals are groups of atoms that remain after the process of oxidation has been completed. An abundance of free radicals can damage the DNA and other structures of muscle cells, causing loss of aerobic and anaerobic endurance, power, and speed. Free radicals are produced during both rest and exercise; however, the rate of production is greatly increased during endurance training, when high rates of oxygen consumption are required. When large numbers of free radicals accumulate, the rate of tissue damage may exceed the rate of repair, resulting in the deteriorations in performance that are associated with the phenomenon of overtraining.

A group of vitamins and provitamins that are collectively known as *antioxidants* can help defend the tissues against the ravages of free radicals. The principal antioxidants are vitamins C, E, and the provitamin beta-carotene. In sufficient quantities, these substances will quench free radicals before they damage muscle cells. However, when swimmers are subjected to daily bouts of intense endurance training requiring high rates of oxygen consumption, the production of free radicals will exceed the quantity of antioxidants available to eliminate them, and the rate of tissue damage will exceed the rate of repair.

Supplementing the diet with vitamins C and E and beta-carotene can reduce the accumulation of free radicals during training and, in so doing, reduce the incidence and severity of inhibitory overtraining. Supplementing the diets of athletes with 1,000 I.U. of vitamin E and 1,000 mg of vitamin C reduced tissue damage by 25%.

Recommended antioxidant supplementation for swimmers in heavy training is 400 to 1,000 mg of vitamin C, 400 to 1,000 I.U. of vitamin E, and 5,000 to 8,000 I.U. of beta-carotene daily. These amounts will not produce toxicity, not even with the fat-soluble vitamin E and vitamin A (which is derived from beta-carotene).

Another principal cause of overtraining may be the progressive depletion of muscle glycogen that occurs over several days or weeks of training. When muscle glycogen is low and energy is needed for training, athletes' muscles react (1) by consuming their own protein material for energy (Anderson & Sharp, 1990) and (2) by inhibiting anaerobic metabolism.

An increase in protein use could be particularly damaging. Research shows that both muscle hypertrophy (Goldspink, Garlick, & McNurian, 1983; Laurent & Milward, 1980) and mitochondrial size and number (Booth & Holloszy, 1977) are regulated by an increase in the protein supply of muscles. Consequently, an increase in muscle protein catabolism should, at the very least, interfere with improvements of muscular power and aerobic capacity and, at worst, cause a reversal of these training effects. In other words, athletes could literally cannibalize their own muscle tissue for energy.

It may be difficult to accept that muscles will consume their own protein material for energy during training. However, this effect was reported in a study by Anderson and Sharp (1990). They reported an increase in protein use when muscle glycogen was depleted between 33 and 55 percent. Several other studies have also shown an increase in protein catabolism during heavy training, although muscle glycogen levels were not measured in these works (Dohm, Williams, Kasperek, & van Rij, 1982; Refsum, Gjessing, & Stromme, 1979; Tarnopolsky, MacDougall, & Atkinson, 1988). Indirect evidence of protein loss has also been presented in other studies. The mitochondria of athletes' muscles, which are composed of protein, became smaller and less numerous when training was excessive (Arcos et al., 1968; Gullstrand, 1985). Evidence also comes from diet studies in which daily caloric intake was inadequate to replace muscle glycogen. Muscle protein loss was reported in one study in which subjects trained for two hours per day while their daily caloric intake was reduced by 1,000 calories (McMurray, Ben-Ezra, Forsythe, & Smith, 1985).

You might be wondering why fat is not consumed for energy in preference to protein when muscle glycogen supplies are low. It is because low muscle glycogen levels seriously limit the transfer of energy from fat, even when large amounts are available in the body (McArdle, Katch, & Katch, 1991).

When free fatty acids are converted to acetyl-CoA, they must combine with oxaloacetic acid to enter Krebs cycle and be oxidized. Oxaloacetic acid is produced primarily by glucose metabolism. Thus, there must be sufficient glucose available to produce oxaloacetic acid before fat can be metabolized in Krebs cycle. The significance of this observation is that swimmers will not be able to metabolize fat for energy when their muscle glycogen and blood glucose supplies are low. Consequently, they will have to rely on protein in their muscles for this purpose, in which case they will lose endurance and power.

Costill and his associates (1988) have presented evidence that connects low muscle glycogen levels to overtraining. They subjected twelve well-conditioned male collegiate swimmers to ten days of training at a daily average mileage of 9,000 m. Four of these swimmers showed signs of overtraining during the training period. They had difficulty finishing the sessions and were not able to maintain their usual training speeds. The remaining six swimmers appeared to tolerate the training with no unusual disturbances in function.

Although several physiological measurements were collected, the only one that differentiated the four swimmers who were having difficulty from the others was a low level of muscle glycogen. After ten days, their muscle glycogen levels, measured before training, were approximately 40 percent lower than those of the other subjects. The six swimmers who were able to tolerate the increased training maintained high levels of muscle glycogen from the beginning to the end of the training period.

It was interesting to note that diet analyses showed that the four swimmers who were having problems in training consumed approximately 1,000 fewer calories per day than they were expending. In contrast, the caloric intake of the six swimmers

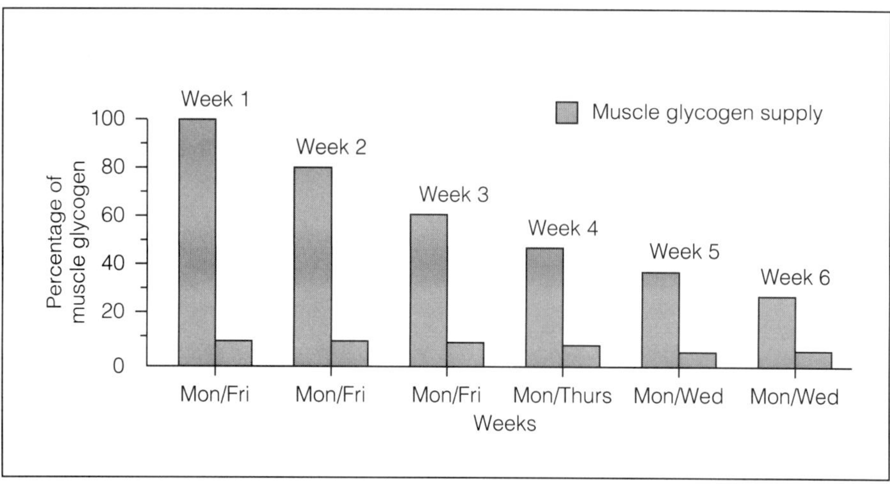

Figure 12-2. The probable effect of six weeks of training on progressive glycogen depletion.

who tolerated training matched their daily caloric output. Training was obviously not the culprit that caused poor performances for four of the swimmers. It was a diet that was inadequate in calories.

Figure 12-2 illustrates how a gradual depletion of muscle glycogen could cause inhibitory overtraining after several weeks of training. In this example, the demands of training and an inadequate intake of calories and carbohydrates prevent complete replacement of muscle glycogen from day to day and week to week. Consequently, there is a gradual depletion of muscle glycogen until it is only 50 percent of normal by the end of week 5. Muscle glycogen supplies are typically depleted by 60 to 85 percent in two hours of training (Costill et al., 1988; Houston, 1978); therefore, when swimmers begin a training day with a 50-percent deficit, it will not take very long to reach a point where the metabolism of protein may be accelerated. If this pattern continues for two or more weeks, the loss of muscle protein could become so severe that swimmers become overtrained.

I should make it clear that it is not necessary to deplete 100 percent of the glycogen from a particular muscle group before accelerated protein use might occur. In studies where up to two-thirds of the muscles' glycogen supplies were depleted, approximately 23 to 60 percent of those fibers were found to be completely empty (Gollnick, Armstrong, et al., 1973; Kirwan et al., 1988).

It should be mentioned that the work of other researchers does not support this theory of progressive muscle glycogen depletion. In studies with rowers (Simonsen et al., 1991) and swimmers (Lamb et al., 1990), several days of intense training and low caloric intake did not show a detrimental effect on performance. Muscle glycogen levels were not measured in these studies, although the intensity of work combined with the daily caloric restrictions should have been sufficient to cause near depletion. The fact that glycogen depletion did not impair performance in the swimming study may be explained by the fact that the authors compared the training times of these athletes to their usual practice performance levels, which may have been achieved during periods of near depletion. Support for this contention comes from the fact that the authors reported that athletes on high-carbohydrate diets performed better than usual and better than their counterparts who were on normal diets.

Excitatory Overtraining

This form of overtraining is characterized by the "fight or flight" reaction—that is, swimmers become agitated, hostile, and/or withdrawn. Control for these processes resides in the sympathetic portion of the autonomic nervous system. Excitatory overtraining comes on more rapidly than inhibitory overtraining and seems to be precipitated by excessive amounts of high-intensity swimming or emotional upset. However, we cannot dismiss the impact of other nontraining stressors on this type of overtraining. I can attest to this, having suffered symptoms of overtraining each season even though I was only watching the swimmers train. I'm sure many coaches can identify with this reaction.

Diagnosing Excitatory Overtraining Athletes who suffer from excitatory overtraining persistently display several of the symptoms listed in Table 12-1.

Causes of Excitatory Overtraining Excessive amounts of high-intensity training, anxiety, and competition from outside stressors are most commonly mentioned as causative factors for excitatory overtraining. The anxiety from having to produce maximum efforts in training each day and competing in a large number of meets can be emotionally fatiguing, particularly if an athlete is high strung. This may be why Miller and Mason (1964) reported a relationship between training intensity and symptoms of overtraining.

Athletes who become overinvolved in outside activities often display symptoms of excitatory overtraining even when training is not intense or excessive. The paradox in all of this is that the persons who are most susceptible to excitatory overtraining are often the ones most likely to get involved in too many activities.

Some experts have suggested that the cause of excitatory overtraining may result from the competition between nerves and muscles for a limited glucose supply. Nerve cells cannot store glycogen, so, they have first call on the blood glucose supply. High-intensity swimming or emotional upset could cause these cells to demand more frequent refilling, which could, in turn, reduce the supply of glucose available to muscle fibers.

RELIEVING OVERTRAINING

The problem with prescribing recovery procedures for overtraining is that we do not know exactly from what swimmers must recover. The most likely candidates are muscle glycogen depletion and damaged and lost muscle tissue. However, the problem could reside with some other physical dysfunction, or it could be emotional in origin.

Three to seven days of recovery training is usually sufficient to reduce the symptoms of excitatory overtraining (Urhausen, Kullmer, & Kindermann, 1987) when the condition is due to a sudden and pronounced increase of stress in one or more areas of an athlete's life. Recovery is quite different for the athlete who develops a case of inhibitory overtraining. A recovery period of two or three weeks to three months may be required. Morgan and coworkers (1987) have reported on a number of swimmers who required several weeks to return to normal mood states after becoming overtrained. They also reported on others who never fully recovered during four to six weeks of rest.

When possible, athletes should stay in training while recovering from overtraining. Complete rest would lengthen the recovery process because athletes would become deconditioned. Swimmers can lose 7 to 10 percent of their aerobic capacity and 10 to 12 percent of their muscular power over a four-week period (Neufer et al., 1988). Once lost, swimmers require several weeks of regular training to regain these physiological adaptations.

Another reason for continuing training is to help athletes maintain a hopeful and positive outlook. Athletes who are most susceptible to overtraining are conscientious, hard working, highly motivated, and unusually anxious about their performance. Being away from the pool will only increase their anxiety, causing them to feel that they are falling behind.

Even though athletes should stay in training during the recovery process, both training volume and intensity should be reduced, and most of the training should be at the basic endurance level. A maximum of 4,000 to 6,000 yd/m is probably the ideal daily mileage. Swimming at recovery speeds and basic endurance levels will act as a catharsis that should hasten the regeneration of muscle and nerve tissue. Endurance can be maintained by one weekly set each of threshold and overload endurance training. Sets of 1,000 to 2,000 yd/m should be sufficient.

Anaerobic endurance and muscular power can be maintained with a few short sprint sets each week that are designed merely to stimulate anaerobic metabolism and not to exhaust swimmers. One lactate tolerance and one or two lactate production sets per week at 200 to 500 m should suffice for maintaining anaerobic capacity. Several weekly power sets of 200 to 300 m should be completed to maintain muscular power. Training frequency should be reduced to once per day to provide more time for rest, recovery of muscle glycogen, and regeneration of muscle tissue.

The condition may be very severe if an overtrained swimmer is not showing strong signs of recovery within one week. In this case, the swimmer should be excused from training for one week, after which training should begin again. Once they resume, the bulk of that training, except for a few sprints, should be done at the basic endurance level until the symptoms of overtraining have disappeared.

Athletes who become overtrained because of emotional stressors should be given some time away from training, even though excessive work is not the precipitating factor. They should use the free time to resolve whatever personal conflicts they might have. Heart-to-heart talks with instructors, friends, and parents may be in order. These swimmers should also use the time to catch up on neglected schoolwork, chores, and club duties that may have been creating excessive stress. They may also need to talk with the coach and other swimmers whom they respect if anxiety about performances has been causing their emotional unrest.

Coaches should pay close attention to rest and diet when swimmers are trying to recover from either excitatory or inhibitory overtraining. Swimmers should make every effort to sleep a minimum of 8 hours per night. Scheduling periodic 30-minute or 1-hour rest periods once or twice during the day is also a good idea. Swimmers' diets should contain (1) an adequate number of calories, (2) extra amounts of complex and simple carbohydrates, and (3) adequate amounts of vitamins and minerals. They will need to correct deficiencies in all of these areas before they can recover.

All of the procedures outlined for relieving overtraining have been summarized in the following box.

Relieving Overtraining

1. Reduce daily training mileage to 4,000 to 6,000 yd/m.
2. Train once per day.
3. Swim 80 percent of training mileage at the basic endurance level.
4. Rest away from the pool.
5. Resolve conflicts that may be adding stress.
6. Increase carbohydrate intake.
7. Check for vitamin-mineral and caloric deficiencies.
8. Take a one-week break from training if the condition is severe.

PREVENTING OVERTRAINING

The fact that swimmers become overtrained does not necessarily mean that they will perform poorly at the end of the season. Personal experience has shown that many swimmers who followed the recovery procedures outlined in the previous section went on to post personal-best times. Nevertheless, it is always preferable to avoid overtraining than to cure it once it develops. The chances of becoming overtrained can be reduced by customizing training programs to each individual swimmer's lifestyle and capacity for handling work and other stressors. Individualized programs require that coaches possess a knowledge of athletes and their reactions to training that comes only after a few years of working together. Complicating matters, there is a limit to the amount of customizing that can be done in a group framework. A certain amount of conformity is usually necessary because of crowded pool conditions, limited training hours, and personal jealousies.

Incorporating recovery periods into weekly, seasonal, and yearly training programs is one method for reducing the incidence of overtraining. Weekly cycles, such as those described in Chapter 10, should be constructed with a careful eye toward providing 24 hours or more between each session or two of intense endurance training for the replacement of muscle glycogen. Mesocycles should be constructed to provide three to seven days of reduced training after each two to four weeks of intense effort to provide time for the body to catch up with the needed repair in muscles. A one- or two-week break should be given after each season of the training year so that athletes can recover emotionally from the letdown that often follows intense effort over a long period.

Perhaps the most important thing that athletes can do to reduce the possibility of becoming overtrained is to maintain a diet that has enough calories to support the work being performed. Their diet should contain 500 to 600 grams (g) of complex carbohydrates daily, or, to be more specific, 10 g of carbohydrates per kilogram (kg) of body weight (Sherman & Maglischo, 1991). Such a diet will replace muscle glycogen in half the time of typical diets. To put this into terms that are easier to understand, 2,000 to 3,500 of the calories athletes consume each day should be in the form of carbohydrates. Table 12-2 provides more exact figures for various-sized athletes.

Drinking carbohydrate solutions during training sessions may also help prevent the glycogen depletion that precedes most cases of overtraining. Some products on the market are premixed, and others are in powder form and are mixed with water to make a 10-percent solution. These solutions should be kept beside the swimmers' lanes, where athletes can drink them whenever they feel thirsty during practice. The glucose in these drinks will maintain the swimmers' blood glucose at a higher level so that more will be transported into the muscles, where it can be used for energy during training. These drinks will provide glucose for energy when muscle glycogen supplies may be low and, thus, should reduce the rapid combustion of muscle protein that could lead to overtraining.

Finally, preventing overtraining also requires anticipating and reducing the effects of other stressors in the swimmers' lives before they accumulate to disruptive levels. Training should be motivating, but the atmosphere should not be so high pressured that swimmers are continually anxious about their performance. Swimmers must be educated that the training process is full of peaks and valleys and that they should focus on the peaks without becoming overly concerned with the valleys. Coaches should strive to keep the effort high and the anxiety low during intense training sessions. Cycling the emotional intensity of these sessions with periods of more relaxed training can also help.

Athletes frequently take on more responsibilities than they can handle during training. Coaches should counsel swimmers to reduce their outside responsibilities;

Table 12-2. Recommended Daily Carbohydrate Consumption for Athletes of Various Sizes

Weight (pounds)	Total Daily Caloric Intake	Daily Carbohydrate Intake
100	2,800	1,800
150	4,200	2,700
200	5,600	3,650

however, they should also be sensitive to some outside commitments that swimmers may have and be willing to give them a few days off on occasion to catch up on schoolwork and get their affairs in order. The suggestions for preventing overtraining are summarized in the following box.

Preventing Overtraining

1. Provide 24 to 36 hours of basic endurance and sprint training after every day or two of threshold and overload endurance training.
2. Provide three to seven days of recovery training after every two to four weeks of hard training.
3. Prescribe a high-carbohydrate diet.
4. Provide carbohydrate solution during training sessions.
5. Reduce other sources of stress or reduce training when additional stress is anticipated.
6. Don't allow athletes to become overextended by taking on too many responsibilities.

DIAGNOSING OVERTRAINING WITH PHYSICAL TESTS

Researchers have generated a considerable amount of interest in finding physiological markers that can identify athletes who are overtrained before the condition becomes severe. Attempts have included measures of oxygen consumption, blood lactate, heart rate, stroke rate, muscular power, anaerobic capacity, blood pressure, ECGs, white blood cells, muscle enzymes, hormonal changes, urinary and blood proteins, and psychological mood states. However, none of these methods has proven entirely accurate, and some tests are expensive and complicated to administer and evaluate.

Oxygen Consumption

The most reliable indicator of overtraining may be a deterioration of swimming economy. In other words, swimmers may require more oxygen to swim a particular speed. Costill (1986) reported on a cross-country runner who required 14 percent more oxygen to run at a particular submaximum speed when he became overtrained. His oxygen cost was 49 ml/kg/min for a submaximum run at the time of his best competitive performance, but it increased to 56 ml/kg/min later in the season when his performance deteriorated. Miller and colleagues (1989) also reported decreases in economy for a group of swimmers who were overtrained.

The difficulty in diagnosing overtraining by measuring oxygen consumption is that economy tends to decline when athletes are training hard. Consequently, criteria need to be established that differentiate the amount of decline that signals overtraining from the normal decline that occurs during training. Additionally, measuring oxygen consumption requires expensive equipment and an experienced operator to administer and evaluate tests.

Blood Lactate

Like the previous test, measuring blood lactate concentrations is an expensive and complicated test to administer, yet it provides another method for diagnosing changes in swimming economy. A swimmer may be overtrained (1) when blood lactate concentrations increase at certain submaximum speeds, (2) when speeds are slower at a particular blood lactate concentration, or (3) when large reductions in blood lactate concentrations are present following maximum-effort swims at slower speeds.

However, glycogen depletion is one factor that could cause a misdiagnosis of overtraining. Lower blood lactate concentrations may occur at submaximum and maximum speeds when athletes are glycogen depleted. Thus, they may appear to be improving their aerobic capacity when they are, in reality, becoming overtrained (Frohlich, Urhausen, Seul, & Kindermann, 1988).

There is a study that may help readers make judgments about diagnosing overtraining from blood tests. Tegtbur and associates (1988) showed that speeds at the anaerobic threshold needed to be corrected for reductions in peak blood lactate values before the former could be used to diagnose the effects of training. In other words, if a particular swimmer exhibited a reduction of 15 percent in maximum blood lactate, the velocity at the anaerobic or some fixed threshold needed to be increased by 15 percent before it would accurately reflect the athlete's threshold pace. If that increase resulted in a slower threshold pace than was achieved on previous tests, the swimmer might be overtrained.

Conversely, the lactate velocity curve could shift to the left for athletes who were rested and had a large amount of glycogen stored in their muscles if the muscles had been depleted of glycogen on previous tests (Busse, Maassen, & Boning, 1987). Consequently, swimmers might appear to be overtrained when they are not.

Maximum-effort swims may provide the best method for diagnosing overtraining from blood lactate concentrations. Overtrained athletes will have similar or lower maximum blood lactate concentrations and slower swims than they had on previous tests. Maximum blood lactate values require some degree of interpretation to improve their accuracy for diagnosing overtraining, however. They will normally be reduced somewhat during periods of emphasis on endurance training. Therefore, coaches need to assess the degree of peak blood lactate reductions in order to distinguish overtraining from a normal training-induced reduction.

Increases in resting blood lactate concentrations have also been used to indicate overtraining. However, some swimmers will have normal resting blood lactate concentrations when they are overtrained. Nevertheless, resting values of 2.5 to 4 mmol/l (normal is 1 mmol/l) give reason to suspect overtraining. Resting blood lactate measurements should be taken before training and after swimmers have rested for five or ten minutes. This will reduce the possibility of contamination from other activities the swimmers may have engaged in before arriving at the training site.

Heart Rate

The heart rate profile (Sharp, Vitelli, Costill, & Thomas, 1984) that was described in Chapter 8 can also be used to diagnose overtraining. Unlike the two previous tests, heart rate profiles require no expensive equipment and are easy to administer and evaluate.

A swimmer may be overtrained when his or heart rate is higher at a particular submaximum speed. The heart rate of the cross-country runner in the study by Costill (1986) increased by 24 bpm (18-percent increase) for the same submaximum running speed when he was tested in an overtrained state.

Another useful method is to record exercise and recovery heart rates during a standardized set of training repeats. The possibility of overtraining should be investigated when the heart rates are consistently higher for those sets.

Researchers have also used resting heart rates to diagnose overtraining. The literature reports increases of 6 to 10 bpm to be associated with overtraining (Dressendorfer, Wade, & Schaff, 1985; Stray-Gunderson, Videman, & Snell, 1986). As is the case with resting blood lactate, an athlete who exhibits a large increase in resting heart rate is probably overtrained. However, not all overtrained athletes show an increase in resting heart rate. Athletes should rest quietly for five or ten minutes before counting their resting heart rate to improve the accuracy of this measure.

Recovery heart rates may also be good markers of overtraining. When athletes require longer to recover from a standard-speed submaximum swim or set of repeats, overtraining should be suspected. The validity of this method will be improved if the speed of the swim is sufficient to elevate the heart rate to a near-maximum level. The swimming and recovery times should be standardized. One to three minutes of recovery is sufficient for well-trained athletes. Although the heart rate may not return to normal in this time, the amount of reduction will provide a good indication of a swimmer's state of fatigue. Slower recovery by 8 to 10 bpm may be an indicator of overtraining.

Figure 12-3 illustrates the changes in resting, exercise, and recovery heart rates that may occur when an athlete becomes overtrained. Notice that under normal training conditions the values for a well-trained athlete are 70 and 140 bpm for resting and for submaximum swimming speed and that the values are 120 and 100 after one minute and two minutes of recovery, respectively. When overtrained, the same athlete may show a 10-bpm increase in resting heart rate (80 bpm) and a 20-bpm increase in exercise heart rate (160 bpm). Recovery heart rates may be approximately 10 bpm higher at one and two minutes after exercise.

Stroke Rate

An excellent and easy measure for identifying overtraining that has not received much attention is an increase in stroke rate. Recent research infers that a stroke rate change may be a very accurate method for spotting overtraining because athletes who become less efficient have to swim a particular race speed with a higher stroke rate to compensate for a shorter stroke length. That race speed has to be reasonably fast to provide enough stress to require compensation. Weiss and coworkers (1988) showed that speeds above the anaerobic threshold are sufficient for this purpose.

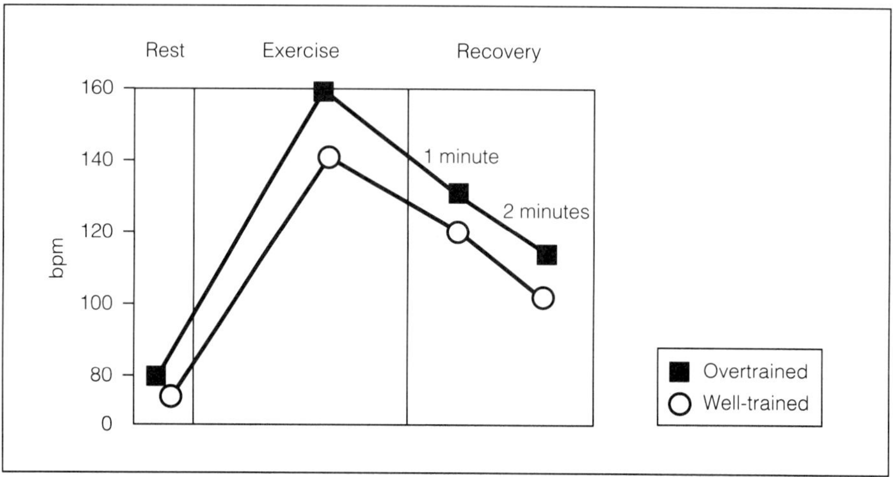

Figure 12-3. The effect of overtraining on resting, exercise, and recovery heart rates.

Stroke rates can be used to diagnose overtraining by selecting a swim of 200 to 500 yd/m at a speed in the neighborhood of 85 to 95 percent of an athlete's best time so that the anaerobic threshold is exceeded. Athletes may be overtrained when they require a significantly faster stroke rate to complete the test distance at the prescribed speed.

The difficulty in making a completely reliable determination from this measure is that some loss in stroke length and a concomitant increase in stroke rate will probably occur during periods of hard training and between the beginning and end of weeks during which a steady depletion of glycogen has occurred. Therefore, the results will be more accurate if the test is administered after athletes have had a few days' rest. Coaches will have to rely on their judgment and experience to distinguish normal training-induced stroke rate increases from those that suggest overtraining.

Muscular Power and Anaerobic Capacity

Some persons have speculated that power and anaerobic capacity decline when athletes become overtrained. Therefore, tests such as one repetition of a weight-lifting exercise with maximum resistance, one pull on a swim bench, or a vertical jump have been proposed for diagnosing overtraining. However, the validity of these tests is doubtful. They are too short to reflect major changes in swimming performance and, except for the swim bench test, are not specific to swimming. Performing sets of 50 or 100 swims would be a better method. Swim bench pulls may also be used if the test duration is between 20 and 40 seconds. Tests of this length make greater demands on anaerobic metabolism and may be more sensitive to the overtrained condition.

Blood Pressure

There were indications in a study by Kirwan and associates (1988) of a pronounced rise in resting diastolic blood pressure when athletes were having difficulty tolerating training. Although not conclusive, their results suggest that increases in resting diastolic pressures of 10 mm Hg may signify overtraining.

ECG Tracings

Three decades ago, Carlile (1966) suggested that overtraining was accompanied by distorted T-waves in electrocardiographic (ECG) tracings. However, the validity of this measure was questioned when, in a later publication, Carlile and Carlile (1978) reported that many swimmers who were clearly overtrained had normal ECG tracings.

Figure 12-4 illustrates normal and distorted T-waves. The abnormal T-wave in Figure 12-4*b* is inverted. It is representative of the form the ECG tracing took for Australian swimmers who showed signs of overtraining in Carlile's initial study.

A change in the T-wave is one of the most important indicators of mild abnormalities of cardiac muscle fibers, which can result from several causes, including infections, overstimulation of cellular metabolism, glandular dysfunction, and changes in the acid-base balance in the body (Guyton, 1964). These causes suggest that an inverted T-wave could be a normal response to hard training or to illness rather than an indication of overtraining.

White Blood Cells

Some persons have suggested that a high white blood cell count can identify athletes who are overtrained (Schubert, 1977). That conclusion is doubtful because white

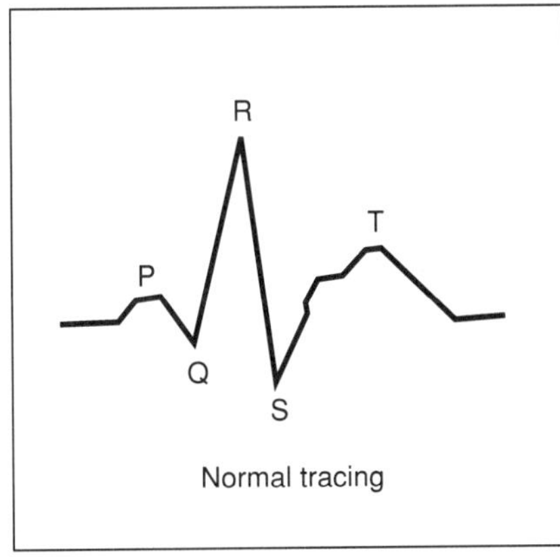

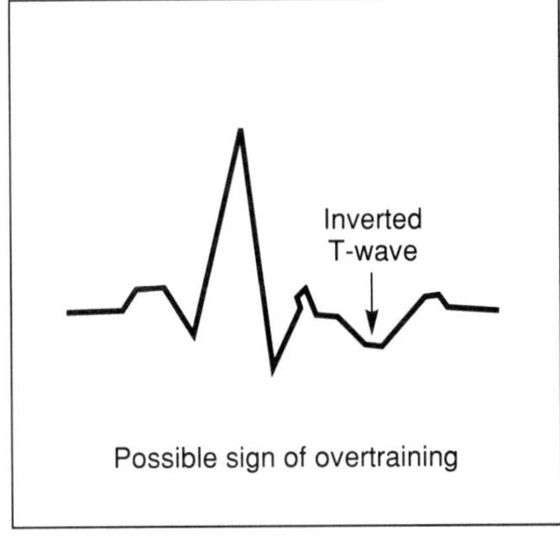

Figure 12-4. A normal ECG tracing and one that may indicate overtraining.

blood cell counts usually increase as a normal response to exercise (Lamb, 1978). The normal value for humans is 7,000 white blood cells per cubic millimeter of blood, but this figure can fluctuate considerably because it is measured relative to blood volume, which frequently changes during training.

Muscle Enzymes

The enzymes creatine phosphokinase (CPK), serum glutamic oxalic transaminase (SGOT), and lactate dehydrogenase (LDH) have been mentioned as indicators of overtraining. They are generally found inside muscle cells and are believed to signal tissue damage and, consequently, overtraining when they escape into the blood in unusually large quantities.

The validity of this conclusion must also be questioned. There is mounting evidence that tissue damage and subsequent repair are normal parts of the training process. Consequently, any increase of enzymes in the blood that accompanies such damage may be a normal response to hard training rather than a sign of overtraining. Normal training-induced increases of these enzymes must be differentiated from those that are abnormal before they can be used for diagnosing overtraining.

Millard and associates (1985) have suggested such a criterion measure for the enzyme CPK. Figure 12-5 shows the results of their study with male and female collegiate swimmers in which resting CPK values tended to drop after several weeks of training. The values for men decreased from approximately 210 international units per liter (iu/l) to 80 iu/l over five months. The decline was less pronounced for women—from 100 to 60 iu/l. They suggested, therefore, that CPK levels that

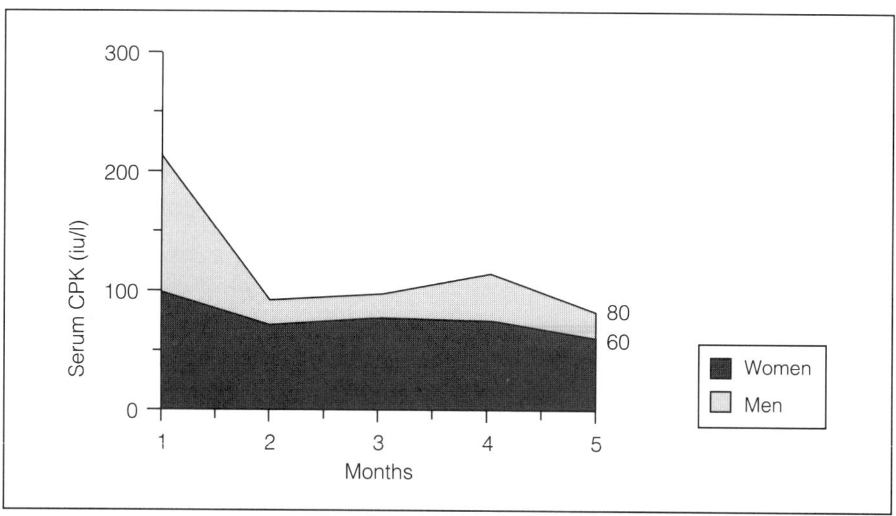

Figure 12-5. Effects of training on resting levels of serum CPK. (Millard, Zauner, & Reese)

were substantially above 120 iu/l for men and 90 iu/l for women in hard training may signal overtraining.

Hormones

Two groups of hormones have been implicated in overtraining. The first is cortisol, which is secreted by the cortex of the adrenal gland. Its function is to aid in the maintenance of normal blood glucose and free fatty acid levels. The second group consists of the catecholamines epinephrine (adrenalin) and norepinephrine. Epinephrine stimulates blood flow, oxygen consumption, and the breakdown of glycogen. Norepinephrine increases heart rate and blood pressure.

The normal response to training is that secretions of cortisol and the catecholamines are reduced for a standardized workload (Winder et al., 1979). Because of this, some experts have speculated that higher-than-normal blood levels of these hormones may signal overtraining. Cortisol is one hormone that has received considerable attention. O'Connor and his coworkers (1989) reported that a high resting level of cortisol was significantly related to overtraining. The results of Kirwan and associates (1988) suggest otherwise, however. They reported that an increase of cortisol was a normal response to hard training and could not be used to identify overtrained athletes.

Urea and 3-Methylhistidine

There is an assumption that an increased rate of protein breakdown signals the point at which further training will cause a loss of muscular adaptations. Several techniques are used to determine the rate of protein breakdown.

Measurements of the *urea* content in blood, sweat, and urine have been used because of the relationship between urea content and the rate of protein catabolism. Nitrogen is excreted from the body when proteins are consumed for energy, and the major portion of that nitrogen is excreted as urea. Therefore, an increase of urea above some normal training level has been touted as an excellent sign that an athlete is either overtrained or will soon become so.

Some question the validity of this method. The body has many additional sources of protein besides those in muscle tissue; thus, any estimates of muscle loss from protein catabolism could be in error, because a sizable portion of the protein could be coming from sources outside of muscles (Brooks, 1987; Wolfe, 1987). Nevertheless, muscle urea represents 80 to 90 percent of the nitrogen excreted when protein is metabolized. Furthermore, over 60 percent of all protein in the body is found in the muscles (Ballard & Tomas, 1983). Consequently, any measure of whole-body protein consumption during exercise should provide a sensitive measure of increases of protein catabolism occurring in muscles.

Urea concentrations in the blood are probably better than those in sweat and urine for measuring protein catabolism, because the quantities in sweat and urine are subject to much greater fluctuations under normal conditions than urea in the blood (Wolfe, 1987). Normal levels of blood urea are in the range of 16 to 21 milligrams per deciliter (mg/dl). Troup (1989a) suggested that concentrations of 30 mg/dl and greater may signal accelerated muscle protein catabolism.

Young and Munro (1978) proposed that 3-methylhistidine is another measure of protein catabolism because it is a by-product of the metabolism of the muscle proteins myosin and actin. They suggested that an unusually large amount of 3-methylhistidine in the body (assessed from urine samples) reflects excessive muscle protein catabolism.

The validity of this measure has also been questioned because studies have reported increases (Dohm, Williams, Kasperek, & van Rij, 1982), no change (Horswill et al., 1988), and decreases (Radha & Bessman, 1983) in 3-methylhistidine after intense training. Dohm and colleagues (1985) showed that these conflicting results were due to the time of sampling. In three separate experiments, they showed that 3-methylhistidine excretion decreased immediately after exercise, followed by a prolonged increase. Three-methylhistidine, if measured at standard times following exercise, shows promise for diagnosing overtraining, because, as stated earlier, most of the increases that occur during exercise should reflect protein catabolism in muscle cells. Unfortunately, the technology for administering this test is not available to the average swimming coach.

Psychological Mood States

Morgan and his coworkers have used a test called the Profile of Mood States (POMS) to spot overtrained athletes. The test was developed by McNair, Lorr, and Droppleman (1971). It consists of 65 items that measure levels of tension, depression, anger, vigor, fatigue, and confusion. Vigor is considered a positive mood state, so it is scored positively. The other five are labeled negative mood states, so high scores are assigned a negative value. A composite score is computed by subtracting the score on vigor from the sum of the five negative scores. The composite score is multiplied by 100 to eliminate the negative values, and the resulting positive number reveals whether an athlete is lacking in interest and vigor or has an optimistic outlook on life. High scores reflect a tendency toward depression, lack of interest, and energy; low scores manifest an optimistic outlook.

Morgan and his coworkers administered this test to 186 male and female swimmers over a period of four years. During each year of testing, unusually high scores on the POMS test were characteristic of swimmers whom coaches considered to be overtrained based on performances in training and competition. The POMS test was able to identify between 74 percent of the male and 89 percent of the female swimmers who were considered to be overtrained (Raglin & Morgan, 1989).

The POMS test was used as one of the markers for overtraining in a study by Morgan and associates (1988) concerning the effect of a sudden increase in training mileage. Figure 12-6 illustrates the results for the six swimmers who tolerated the training well (responders) and the four who did not (nonresponders). You can see that, although scores increased for both groups, the four nonresponders who were having difficulty with the training program increased their scores significantly more.

Judging from these results, the POMS test may be a valuable tool for diagnosing impending overtraining. A survey of the literature suggests that absolute POMS

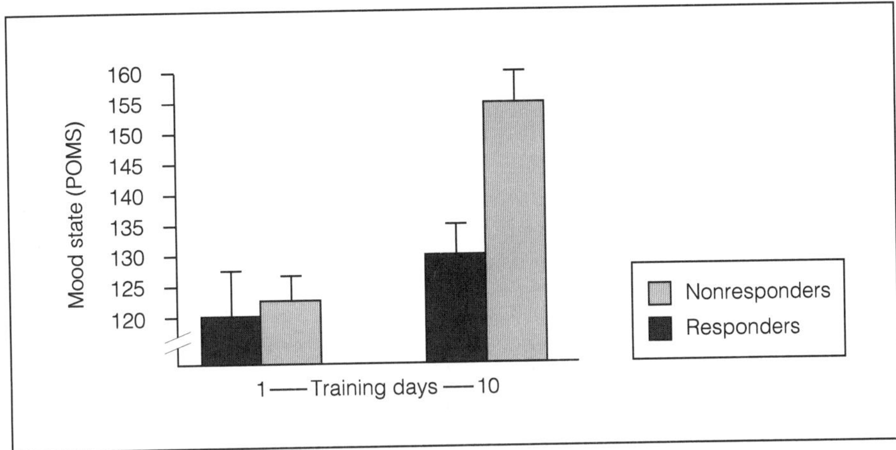

Figure 12-6. The effect of 10 days of intensified swim training on POMS test scores. (Adapted from Morgan et al., 1988)

scores above 150 or relative score increases greater than 25 percent signify that overtraining may be imminent.

Although the POMS test identifies athletes who are more depressed than average, high scores should not be considered symptomatic of clinical depression. High scores mean only that an athlete may be overtrained and may require some rest and recovery. This test should not be used to predict serious psychological disturbances. When coaches advise a particular swimmer to seek professional help, it should be based on disruptive changes in that athlete's behavior, not the results of a psychological inventory.

A Brief Review of Tests for Diagnosing Overtraining

Certain markers can provide us with quantifiable methods that can improve our ability to diagnose overtraining before it becomes too severe. However, none is 100 percent reliable. The best of these methods are the following:

1. *Oxygen consumption* Increased oxygen consumption at some standard submaximum speed seems to be a very good indicator of overtraining. Some criteria should be established to differentiate the normal fatigue caused by an increase in training from the debilitating fatigue of overtraining to improve the accuracy of prediction from this measure. One suggestion is to permit a few days of recovery time before administering a swimming economy test. Then, only the overtrained swimmers will show decrements in performance. On the negative side, this test requires expensive equipment and an expert to administer and evaluate it.

2. *Blood lactate* This is also a very reliable measure if administered correctly. When athletes swim slower at a particular blood lactate concentration or when they swim the same time with a higher concentration, they may be overtrained. Once again, swimmers should be given a few days of rest to reduce the transitory effects of hard training and muscle glycogen depletion. The test should include a maximum-effort swim for more accurate interpretation of the results. Like measures of oxygen consumption, the disadvantage of blood lactate tests is that they require expensive equipment and an experienced operator.

3. *Resting blood lactate* This test may not identify all of the overtrained athletes on a team; however, those who show a high resting blood lactate concentration in the neighborhood of 2.5 to 4 mmol/l are probably overtrained. Nevertheless, this test also requires expertise and expensive equipment.

4. *Heart rate* Heart rate profiles, resting heart rates, recovery heart rates, and heart rates during standard-speed swims can all be used to spot the onset of overtraining. A higher rate at rest or during standardized swims indicates that an athlete may be overtrained. A slower recovery to normal may signal the same condition. Heart rate measures are somewhat more erratic than measures of swimming economy and blood lactate. Consequently, they may not be as reliable. On the positive side, they require no expensive equipment and are easy to administer and evaluate.

5. *Stroke rate* This is probably the easiest measure of all to use for identifying overtraining. It may also be the most reliable, particularly if combined with a measurement of stroke length. When athletes must stroke faster to swim a standard time, there is a good possibility that they are in need of some rest and recovery or they may soon become overtrained. The reliability and validity of these measures for diagnosing overtraining have not been investigated at this time, but they show great promise for this purpose.

5. *CPK* Once the season is underway, large increases in CPK may be a reliable sign of overtraining. These tests also require equipment and expertise, however.

6. *Urea and 3-methylhistidine* These may be the best methods for early diagnosis of overtraining. A large increase in blood urea implies an increased rate of muscle protein use. When that happens, athletes may lose endurance and muscular power. Unfortunately, the technology for administering this test is not available to the average swimming coach.

7. *The POMS test* This may be a very good instrument for identifying overtraining if norms can be established for normal and extranormal increases with hard training. Coaches must be able to distinguish between the normal reduction in positive outlook that accompanies an increase in training mileage and a movement toward depression that signals overtraining.

CHAPTER 13

Age Group Swimming

Age group swimming continues to be one of the most popular forms of athletic participation for boys and girls because it is both physically and experientially rewarding. Age group swimming was also one of the first sports to demonstrate that children could train with the same intensity as adults and that females could train with the same volume and intensity as males. While many were debating whether intense training was dangerous for children, we swimming coaches were watching them flourish with hard training. Still, there are many misconceptions and myths surrounding the reactions of children to training. Some of these are discussed in this chapter. This chapter (1) describes some of the important physical changes that take place as children grow toward adulthood, (2) discusses the implications of these changes for training, and (3) answers some of the questions that are asked most frequently about the training of age group swimmers.

GROWTH AND DEVELOPMENT

Children grow rapidly during their preadolescent years; however, their rate of growth accelerates even more markedly during puberty. Girls usually reach puberty between the ages of 11 and 13; boys experience a growth spurt somewhat later between the ages of 13 and 15 (Brooks & Fahey, 1984).

Physiological Changes

Bones Bone growth continues up to and sometimes beyond 20 years of age for boys but is usually completed during the late teenage years for girls. Bone growth occurs at the ends of bones in the epiphyseal cartilages and growth plates. These are areas of incomplete bone closure where additional matrix can accumulate to increase the length of the bones.

Training has no influence on the maximum length that bones will reach at the time of closure. It does, however, increase bone width and density, providing bones with greater resistance to stress and reducing the potential for breakage. These increases in width and density are influenced greatly by the direction of the pull that contracting muscles exert on bones; thus, bones adapt specifically to the activities children engage in. This information has two implications for training children. First, children should engage in a wide variety of activities so that their bones are more resistant to stress in all directions of motion. Second, early training as an age group swimmer should prepare athletes to withstand greater training loads when they are senior swimmers.

Because bone closure does not begin until puberty, there has been some concern that heavy resistance training before or during adolescence could cause injuries to the growth plates that could ultimately result in less growth. This issue is discussed later in this chapter.

Muscles Muscle growth follows a similar pattern to that of bones. Muscle fibers increase in size, but not number, throughout childhood and adolescence (Saltin & Gollnick, 1983). Boys experience an accelerated increase in muscle hypertrophy at puberty, which is probably due to a tenfold increase in their production of testosterone. Girls' muscles also continue to increase in size until adulthood, but there is no growth spurt at puberty. Muscle size reaches a peak between the ages of 16 and 18 in females and between 18 and 22 in males. After this time, the amount of muscle tissue remains relatively stable until ages 30 to 40, unless altered by exercise and diet.

Increases of muscle size cause yearly improvements of strength and power in males and females, with peaks reached at about age 16 for women and between the ages of 20 and 30 for men (Beunen & Malina, 1988). The rate of increase in muscle strength and power accelerates at puberty for boys but not for girls. The absolute strength of girls is about half that of boys throughout childhood and adulthood.

The pattern of increase in power is different for boys and girls as they grow toward maturity. Boys can increase muscular power in their arms and shoulders by as much as 200 percent between the ages of 10 and 20 and by an additional 125 percent by age 30 if they continue regular training (Inbar & Bar-Or, 1986). For girls, strength tends to increase by similar percentages up to age 13 or 14 (Beunen & Malina, 1988). At that time, arm strength declines and leg strength continues to increase up to age 17 or 18.

The percentages of FT and ST muscle fibers in boys and girls appear to be very similar to that of men and women. These percentages are listed in Table 13-1. A review of several studies showed that adults had, on the average, 52 percent ST and

Table 13-1. Percentages of FT and ST Muscle Fibers in Male and Female Adults and Children

Category	Percentage of ST Muscle Fibers	Percentage of FT Muscle Fibers
Men		
Average	52	48
Range	13–98	(not provided)
Distribution of FT fibers		32 FTa, 16 FTb
Women		
Average	52	48
Range	32–69	(not provided)
Distribution of FT fibers		32 FTa, 16 FTb
Boys		
Average	53–56	42–47
Range	37–69	44–63
Distribution of FT fibers		22 FTa, 20 FTb
Girls		
Average	46–56	42–54
Range	32–60	
Distribution of FT fibers		22 FTa, 20 FTb

Source: Bell, MacDougall, Billeteter, & Howald, 1980; duPlessis et al., 1986; Saltin & Gollnick, 1983.

48 percent FT fibers. The FT muscle fibers were distributed 32 percent FTa and 16 percent FTb fibers (Saltin & Gollnick, 1983). Similar values were reported for 6-year-old boys and girls by Bell and associates (1980)—56 percent ST, 22 percent FTa, and 20 percent FTb.

As stated in Chapter 2, some experts have speculated that FTc muscle fibers, which are more prevalent in youngsters than adults, are undifferentiated muscle tissue that can become either FT or ST fibers according to the demands made on them (duPlessis et al., 1986). If true, this would mean that children could change their inherited percentages of FT and ST muscle fibers by engaging in a preponderance of distance or sprint training from an early age. Although this matter is still controversial, the most reliable information suggests that the type of early training youngsters undertake will *not* change the percentages of FT and ST muscle fibers. Consequently, age group swimmers should be able to perform large amounts of mixed training without reducing their potential for events at either end of the sprint-endurance spectrum.

Body Fat Fat cells can accumulate in the body from before birth to death. In females, the amount of fat usually increases from approximately 10 or 12 percent of body weight at birth to 25 percent during young adulthood. Most of that increase occurs after puberty, when estrogen levels increase.

The percentage of body fat for boys remains fairly stable throughout childhood and into adulthood. It increases 3 or 4 percent during childhood, from 10 percent to approximately 15 percent, recedes 2 or 3 percent during puberty, and then, on the average, increases 2 or 3 percent early in adulthood (Saris et al., 1985). Exercise greatly affects the amount of fat that a person carries. Thus, the body fat of age group swimmers is generally only 1 or 2 percent lower than children in the normal population. The difference between trained and untrained adults is usually much greater.

Respiration Lung volumes increase up to the age of 20 to 30 (Wilmore & Costill, 1988). As children grow, the amount of air they can move into their lungs and back out again increases from about 40 l/min at age 6 to between 110 and 140 l/min at maturity. The smaller minute volume that children exchange has no bearing on their ability to train, however. Their smaller bodies do not require as much oxygen.

Circulation The maximum heart rates of young children are higher than those of adults. They are generally between 200 and 210 bpm from ages 6 to 14 (Saris et al., 1985). After that, they drop to the typical range of 185 to 205 bpm seen in adults. A child's faster heart rate partially compensates for a smaller stroke volume. A child's heart is smaller, so less blood is pumped out per beat.

Oxygen Consumption The amount of blood pumped from a child's heart per minute (cardiac output) does not equal that of adults; therefore, a child's absolute VO_2max will be less than that of an adult. Values for boys increase steadily from an average of 1.46 l/min at ages 6 to 8 to 3 or 4 l/min at maturity. The increase is not so great in girls, going from an average 1.2 l/min at ages 6 to 8 to 2 or 3 l/min between the ages of 14 and 16. Growth is the main reason for these marked increases. The heart and lungs get larger and the muscle mitochondria more numerous, so they can process more oxygen per minute. Oxygen consumption remains fairly stable for both sexes throughout their early adult years.

These differences in absolute VO_2max between children and adults are inconsequential to training. A child has a smaller body and does not need as much blood to supply it adequately with oxygen and nutrients. The relative oxygen consumption of children is the same as for adults when expressed in terms of the milliliters of oxygen they consume per kilogram of body weight per minute of exercise (ml/kg/min). This is true even with children as young as 6 years old. Some boys have been measured at a relative VO_2max near 80 ml/kg/min—a value that rivals that of older international-level male competitors.

The average values for females expressed both absolutely and relative to body weight are, on the average, lower than those for males from childhood throughout life, presumably because men have a larger heart, a greater volume of blood, and more hemoglobin in their blood. Girls who are not training may actually lose some of their VO_2max capacity after puberty because of their rapid weight gains.

The Anaerobic Threshold Comparisons between children and adults are not very numerous on this measure of endurance capacity because its importance to performance has only recently been discovered. The anaerobic thresholds of preadolescents and adolescents have been similar to those of adults in the few studies in which they were measured (Bunc, Heller, Sprynarova, & Zdanowicz, 1986;

Reinhards, Mader, & Hollmann, 1987). Furthermore, there is no difference between boys and girls if the workload at which the anaerobic threshold occurs is expressed relative to their performance or to VO_2max (Macek & Vavra, 1985).

There is some evidence that the anaerobic threshold declines from age 6 to 14 for females and after maturity for males who are not training (Weyman, Reybrouck, Stijns, & Knops, 1985). Adults cannot work as close to maximum without becoming fatigued as they could when they were younger. The reasons given are a decrease in the activity of the aerobic enzyme succinate dehydrogenase (SDH) and an increase in the anaerobic enzyme phosphofructokinase (PFK).

Anaerobic Capacity Although some researchers dispute the claims for lower anaerobic capacity in children (Cumming, Hastman, McCort, & McCullough, 1980), evidence overwhelmingly suggests that it is less than that of adults. The anaerobic capacity of children is lower than that of adults, even when it is measured relative to their size. The peak blood lactates of children ages 6 to 11 are less than half those of adults. They can increase over 50 percent from age 8 to maturity. This has been equated to increases of between 200 and 300 percent in the ability to do anaerobic work.

Anaerobic capacity increases at the time of puberty, with maximum blood lactate increasing between the ages of 12 and 13 until it reaches a normal adult level at 14 or 15. Although the average maximum blood lactate of teenagers is reported to be similar to that of adults by ages 14 to 15, some adults can reach values of 18 to 20 mmol/l, yet most teenagers cannot go beyond 14 mmol/l until they are 17 or 18. There seems to be no difference in the peak blood lactates that can be achieved by males and females at any age. Table 13-2 lists the average values and ranges for blood lactate concentration in children of various ages and adults.

Children also have less glycogen stored in their muscles and less creatine phosphate (CP) (Bar-Or, 1985). The enzyme PFK, which has a major influence on the conversion of glycogen to lactic acid, is less active as well (Eriksson, Gollnick, & Saltin, 1973). With less CP and glycogen available and a lower activity of PFK, a smaller anaerobic capacity for children is very likely.

Table 13-2. Peak Blood Lactate Values for Children Ages 6 to 15 and for Adults

Age Group	Average Peak Blood Lactate Values	Range of Peak Blood Lactate Values
6–7	5 mmol/l	4–6 mmol/l
8–9	8 mmol/l	6–10 mmol/l
10–12	10 mmol/l	7–12 mmol/l
13–16	12 mmol/l	8–14 mmol/l
Adults	12 mmol/l	8–16 mmol/l

Sources: Cunningham & Paterson, 1988; Saris et al., 1985; Suurnakki et al., 1986; Tanaka & Shindo, 1985.

Acidosis is not as severe in children, which provides further evidence of their reduced anaerobic capacity. On the average, pH is generally .10 to .20 unit higher for 8-year-olds than for adults. The difference declines at a rate of .01 to .02 pH unit per year until it reaches adult values by age 18 (Kindermann, Huber, & Keul, 1975).

With less anaerobic capacity, the difference between the aerobic capacity of children and their total physiological capacity is not as great as that for adults. This means that children can train much closer to their maximum speeds without becoming fatigued.

Performance Changes

Motor Ability This measure of skill improves with age in children as the nervous system matures and develops. The myelin sheaths around nerve fibers must be completely formed before maximum rates of nerve impulse conduction can be achieved.

Boys tend to increase steadily on tests of motor ability from age 6 to 17. On the other hand, nonathletic females plateau at the time of puberty. An increase of body fat is the physiological reason usually given for their lack of progress after this time. However, athletic females continue to improve in motor ability after puberty, indicating that the reduction of physical activity that commonly takes place among teenage females may have more to do with their lack of progress in motor ability than any measure of physiological maturity.

Mechanical Efficiency Children tend to be less efficient than adults when they work. This is evidenced by the fact that children must work harder to produce a particular submaximum effort than an adult (Bunc, Heller, Sprynarova, & Zdanowicz, 1986; Krahenbuhl, Morgan, & Pangrazi, 1989). If a child and adult were swimming at the same rate, the child would require more energy to do the work, even if that rate were only moderate for both of them. The superiority of adults in mechanical efficiency is probably due to improved motor coordination and greater skill from years of training. This is another good reason for beginning training in a particular sport at a young age.

Table 13-3 provides a summary of the similarities and differences between children and adults and between girls and boys on certain physiological and performance measures.

Early Maturers Versus Late Maturers

Some children mature earlier than others, and the increased muscle tissue of early maturers generally gives them a performance advantage over their late-maturing competitors. This advantage usually disappears after puberty, however. In fact, boys who mature earlier may be at a disadvantage later because they tend to be shorter and more muscular at maturity (Brooks & Fahey, 1984). A less-streamlined body type would be disadvantageous to swimmers unless the increased water resistance were balanced by greater muscular strength and power. Girls who mature earlier tend to be shorter and have smaller upper body musculature—two factors that could also limit their performance.

Table 13-3. Summary of Physiological Data on Children as Compared with Adults and between Boys and Girls

Measure	Comparison with Adults	Comparison between Boys and Girls
Aerobic capacity	No difference	Girls are approximately 11 percent lower in VO_2max than boys
Muscular strength	Children are 75 to 80 percent lower; even when expressed relative to body weight, the values for children are 20 to 40 percent lower than for adults	Girls are 50 percent weaker than boys on the average
Anaerobic capacity	Children are 60 to 70 percent lower	No difference between boys and girls
Motor ability	Children are slower and less coordinated	No known difference, although girls are more flexible and believed to learn skills faster

Late maturers usually exceed the performance of early maturers on measures of muscular power (Beunen & Malina, 1988), anaerobic capacity (Paterson & Cunningham, 1985), and aerobic endurance (Kemper, Verschuur, & Ritmeester, 1986). So, although early maturers tend to perform better in the age groups, their late-maturing competitors have an excellent chance of passing them at puberty.

IMPLICATIONS FOR TRAINING

Endurance Training

Children are capable of training as long and as strenuously as adults. In fact, they may be better equipped for such training if it is maintained at a pace that is relative to their ability. Research shows (1) that children are capable of supplying their body with as much oxygen as adults and (2) that they are capable of training nearer their personal maximum speed without becoming fatigued.

The only negative aspect of age group endurance training is that children do not swim as economically as adults. Therefore, they fatigue earlier if they try to work at the same absolute effort as older swimmers. There is no difference, however, if the effort is at the same relative level. In other words, children can swim repeats at, say, 85 percent of their best time as easily as adults; however, if they tried to swim those repeats at 85 percent of an *adult best time,* they would fatigue much sooner.

Endurance Training Mileage The endurance mileage suggested for senior swimmers can be adapted to the ability of age group swimmers. Table 13-4 lists recommended distances for each age group from 7/8 up to 13/14. These distances have been calculated by equating the relative times required to complete endurance

Table 13-4. Suggested Weekly Mileage (in Yards/Meters) for Each Level of Endurance Training for Age Group Swimmers

Age Group	Basic Endurance (End-1)	Threshold Endurance (End-2)	Overload Endurance (End-3)
7/8	1,500–2,000	1,000–2,000	400–800
9/10	3,000–5,000	2,000–3,000	1,000–2,000
11/12	6,000–8,000	4,000–6,000	2,000–3,000
13/14	8,000–12,000	6,000–9,000	2,000–3,000

repeat sets for children of each age group and typical senior swimmers. These are not recommendations for beginning swimmers. The distances apply to athletes who have been training for a year or two and who possess the basic swimming skills to train adequately. The ranges for basic and threshold endurance training have been made deliberately large to account for the wide ranges in the ability of youngsters.

Seven- and 8-year-old swimmers should train 3–5 hours per week. They should swim two or three threshold endurance sets per week with each set averaging 500 to 1,000 yd/m. They should also complete an equal or greater amount of basic endurance swimming, with most of that mileage in the form of stroke drills, swimming, pulling, and kicking. Coaches should schedule one or two overload endurance sets per week, with the length of each set at approximately 400 to 500 yd/m. This training should require between three and five hours per week.

Weekly mileage should be stepped up for the 9/10 age group, and training time should be increased to between five and seven hours per week. Once again, swimmers should complete two or three sets of threshold endurance training per week, with each set covering 1,000 to 1,500 yd/m. A slightly greater amount of basic endurance training should be done on a daily basis. Coaches should also schedule one or two overload endurance sets each week at an optimal length of 500 to 1,000 yd/m.

Training should become much more serious when children enter the 11/12 age group. They can train 7 to 10 hours per week. Mileage should double to between 6,000 and 8,000 yd/m per week for basic endurance training and 4,000 to 6,000 yd/m per week for threshold endurance training. Swimmers should complete two or three sets of threshold swimming per week, with each set averaging 1,500 to 2,000 yd/m. Coaches should schedule basic endurance swimming every day in sets of 1,000 to 2,000 yd/m and in the form of occasional long swims of 30 minutes to 1 hour. One or two overload endurance sets should be included each week, with the length of each between 1,000 and 1,500 yd/m.

When swimmers reach the 13/14 age group, they will be training almost like senior swimmers. Females will have passed puberty, and training will become a much more important factor in their success. Although males will continue to improve through growth, they will be competing in longer events, and additional training should play a greater role in their success than it had in the past.

Swimmers in the 13/14 age group can begin training twice per day, or, if preferred, they can accomplish suggested minimum training distances by training two hours per day for five or six days each week. Athletes should swim two to three threshold sets each week, with each set between 2,000 and 3,000 yd/m. Basic endurance training should be done in sets of 1,000 to 2,000 yd/m each day. Coaches should schedule long swims once or twice per month because of the difference in aerobic stimulus they provide. One or two sets of overload endurance training should be completed each week, with each set at 1,000 to 1,500 yd/m.

In all age groups, the send-off times on endurance sets should provide similar amounts of rest as for senior swimmers—that is, between 10 and 30 seconds for most repeats. Rest intervals can be increased to 1 minute on overload sets at repeat distances of 100 yd/m or longer in the younger age groups and 200 yd/m or longer in the older age groups. *Children do not need more rest than adults during their repeats.*

Monitoring Endurance Training The concept of training according to the anaerobic threshold is as valid for children as it is for adults. Heck and coworkers (1987) found no real difference between adults and children regarding the blood lactate concentrations corresponding to the anaerobic threshold. For most, the concentrations were between 2.5 and 5 mmol/l. Of course, the age group swimmers swam slower at these concentrations than senior athletes.

As with adults, blood testing is not necessary to effectively monitor the training of youngsters. Coaches can use any of the methods that were described in Chapter 8. Of these, The T-30 test is convenient and reasonably accurate, although the distance will need to be scaled down from 3,000 yd/m to one which requires approximately 30 minutes for a particular age group. The swimming step test is also very good, although it is quite rigorous for very young children. Repeat sets of 5 × 50 could probably be used to monitor training for the 7/8 age group. Sets of 5 × 100 would suffice for the 9/10 age group. For the 11/12 age group, the repeat distance should be 200 yd/m with a minimum of four repeats per set. The test for the 13/14 age group should be identical to the one suggested for senior swimmers.

Although less accurate, heart rate measures can be used to monitor training if they are adapted for the physiological differences between children and adults. Up to age 13, children's maximum heart rates are approximately 5 to 10 bpm higher than those of senior swimmers. Accordingly, heart rates should probably range between 160 and 190 bpm during threshold endurance sets and between 140 and 160 bpm during basic endurance training.

If coaches use percent efforts to monitor training, they should remember that children can repeat much closer to their maximum speed than adults because their anaerobic capacity and muscular power are less than those of adults. Figure 13-1 illustrates the relationships of aerobic, anaerobic, and nonaerobic capacities for an age group swimmer and a senior swimmer. The threshold pace for children is closer to their maximum speed than it is for adults as is shown by the age group swimmer in Figure 13-1, who has a threshold pace for 200 yd/m that is very close to 90 percent of maximum speed (2:18.00 versus 2:05.00). The figure for the senior swimmer is closer to 85 percent (2:07.00 versus 1:50.00). Although hypothetical,

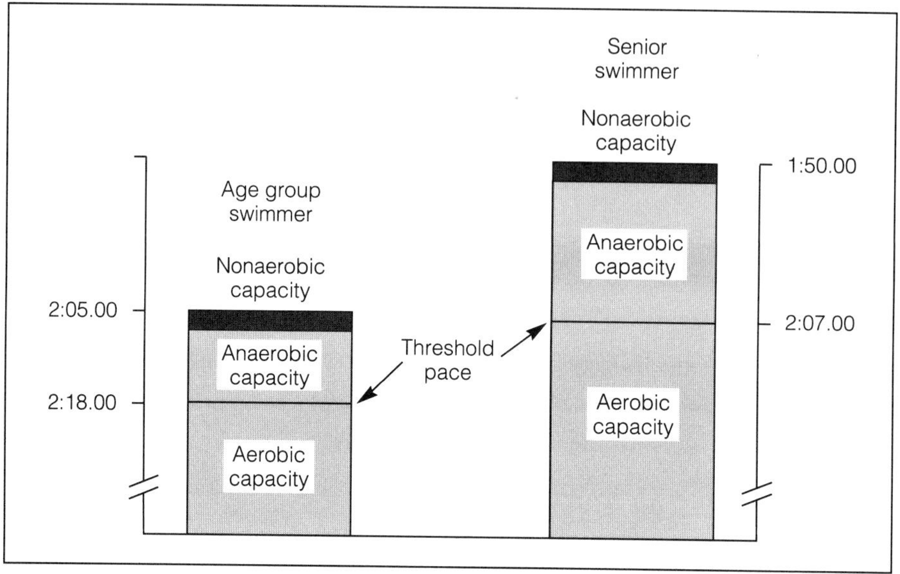

Figure 13-1. The difference in anaerobic capacity between an age group swimmer and a senior swimmer.

this example is probably an accurate representation of the differences in percent efforts between adults and children on measures of the anaerobic threshold.

Given the lesser anaerobic capacity of children, they should probably repeat threshold sets between 85 and 95 percent of their best time for a particular distance. Overload sets should be done between 90 and 95 percent of their best time.

Endurance Trainability There is a common misconception that children are so active in normal play that they come to the training environment already in peak physical condition and that, therefore, they do not improve with training. This is absolutely untrue. Children are trainable. They improve similarly to adults when training programs are administered according to sound principles of overload, progression, and specificity.

$\dot{V}O_2$max has been shown to improve between 7 and 26 percent in studies in which normally active children were subjected to adequate endurance training (Rowland, 1985). This is similar to the improvement rate of adults, which has been measured at between 5 and 25 percent in various studies. Additional evidence of the value of training came from the fact that the anaerobic thresholds of trained children ages 8 to 15 were 21 to 30 percent faster than those of untrained, but normally active youngsters (Tanaka & Shindo, 1985).

Sprint Training

The anaerobic capacity of children is also trainable. Performances of trained children are usually 5 to 10 percent better than untrained children on anaerobic tests, even when those tests do not require different levels of skill. In one study, children improved their performances on a measure of anaerobic capacity by 10 percent after training, yet an age-matched control group improved a nonsignificant 1.4 percent during the same time period (Rotstein, Dotan, Bar-Or, & Tenenbaum, 1986). So, although anaerobic capacity increases to some extent with the normal growth of children, training can enhance that improvement considerably. There appear to be no differences in the way that girls and boys react to anaerobic training (Bar-Or, 1989).

The fact that anaerobic capacity can be improved should not be taken to mean that age group swimmers should engage in more anaerobic training than senior swimmers. Lactate tolerance and lactate production training should be used sparingly, because the effect is the same as for senior swimmers. Very little lactate production and lactate tolerance training is needed to produce maximum improvements, yet in large amounts, they are stressful and can lead to significant overtraining.

Coaches sometimes go overboard with anaerobic training because most of the events that age group athletes swim rely heavily on this energy system. This may produce good results quickly, but it will not help swimmers in the long run. Age group swimmers need a good base of skill and endurance training to succeed later in their careers.

Mileage Swimmers should complete sprint sets three to five times per week. Two or three of those should be lactate production sets. Four to twelve 25s or 50s would be good for lactate production training at any age. The rest intervals between these repeats should be one to three minutes—similar to those recommended for senior swimmers.

One or two sets of lactate tolerance training should be enough to improve buffering capacity. Distances of 50 to 100 yd/m are best for this level of training. The number of lactate tolerance sets can also be reduced if swimmers are competing in a meet during the week.

Power sprints should be done three to five times weekly for short periods of time. Cross-pool sprints and 25s are the best forms of power training at any age, including childhood. The usual games and relays that coaches include in training to keep it interesting for children are adequate for this purpose.

Age group training should include sprint-assisted and sprint-resisted training, which are fun and help improve swimmers' muscular power. Age group programs should also include measures of stroke rate and stroke length, using some of the drills that were mentioned in Chapter 5. Children should learn to sprint from an early age because the habits they develop then will stay with them for the rest of their careers.

Strength and Power Training

One of the common myths concerning strength training is that children are incapable of improving muscular strength until puberty. Ample evidence suggests that training enhances the development of muscular strength in children beyond the yearly increases in muscle size and strength that accompany normal growth. Improvements of strength after resistance training were reported to be 100 percent

(Blimpkie et al., 1988) to 400 percent (Sewall & Micheli, 1984) greater than those of age-matched preadolescent control groups. Resistance was also shown to improve strength more than normal growth when groups of preadolescents were matched according to physiological age rather than chronological age (Bar-Or, 1989).

Despite the fact that strength can be increased, gains in muscle size are not nearly so evident in youngsters as they are in adults who use resistance training. This is probably because children have lower levels of the anabolic hormone testosterone in their bodies. At puberty, a nearly tenfold increase in this hormone greatly enhances the capacity of boys to add muscle size with resistance training. The same is not true of females, however. They have lower levels of circulating testosterone throughout life and can never increase muscle tissue to the same extent as males.

Because strength and muscular hypertrophy are related, you may wonder how children can improve the former and not the latter. The answer is probably because most of their strength gains are due to the learning of lifting techniques. Their nervous system becomes more efficient at recruiting more muscle fibers at faster rates. This points up the need to include stroke-simulated resistance training for youngsters, because much of their improvements in strength seem to be due to improved movement patterns. Swim benches, trolleys, stretch cords, and tethered or partially tethered swimming are good examples of methods that age group swimmers can use. A general, nonspecific program of resistance training is certainly desirable to improve the potential of muscles to produce force. However, coaches should not neglect specific programs, which will probably produce greater benefits for youngsters.

As you would expect, the muscular power of children is also trainable. In one study, a group of preadolescent boys improved 14 percent, yet performance decreased by a nonsignificant 1 percent in a control group that did not train (Rotstein, Dotan, Bar-Or, & Tenenbaum, 1986).

Should Children Lift Weights? This is one of the most controversial topics concerning the training of children. In the past, most experts advised against weight training because of the possibility of injuring the growth plates of the bones that were not fully closed. However, recent reports have suggested that the incidence of injury is no greater in children than in adults during weight training. Further, these reports indicated that most of those injuries were minor and did not involve the growth plates in adolescents (Benton, 1983; Brady, Cahill, & Bodnar, 1982; Gumbs, 1982; Ryan & Salciccioli, 1976) or preadolescents (Sewall & Micheli, 1984; Weltman et al., 1986). An interesting observation in this regard, is that preadolescents may be more resistant to injuries of the growth plates than adolescents because growth plates are actually stronger and more resistant to stress before puberty (Micheli, 1988b).

It seems that children can participate in weight training programs and gain strength from them. The potential for injury and permanent bone damage is as low for children and teenagers as it is for adults who participate in weight training programs, provided, of course, that these programs are well designed and well supervised. Of the few injuries that occur in weight training programs — whether for adults or for children — most are caused by dropping weights, lifting weights improperly, and trying to lift very heavy weights for a small number of repetitions. Consequently, programs for children should observe the same safety rules recommended for any resistance training program. In fact, it is probably best to take an ultraconservative approach because children are adventurous and programs are not always well supervised.

Rather than use free weights, children should train on weight machines, isokinetic devices, and other modes of resistance training that can be used without the risk of dropping weights. Their weight training programs should not include maximum lifts because they encourage improper lifting techniques and increase the likelihood of injuring joints and muscles.

Special sets involving very heavy resistance for a small number of repetitions are not recommended, for the same reasons. Age group swimmers should definitely follow a system of progression. A program in which a child progresses from 8 to 12 repetitions before adding additional weight is preferred because it will increase strength while ensuring that the resistance is only moderately heavy. This will protect children from attempting lifts that are beyond their present capability and are potentially dangerous. The number of sets — one to three — should be the same as recommended for adult resistance programs.

Overhead lifts such as military presses, behind-the-neck presses, and others should be avoided because they increase the risk of shoulder injuries. Back injuries are most likely to occur with exercises for the thighs and calf muscles because these exercises require large amounts of resistance; consequently, age group swimmers should perform these exercises from a seated position to lessen the potential danger.

A resistance training program for children should include all of the major muscle groups of the body, with an emphasis on those that are most important to swimming fast. Coaches should also remember to include stroke-simulating exercises.

AGE GROUP SWIM TRAINING: DOES IT GIVE CHILDREN AN ADVANTAGE LATER?

The research is meager and inconclusive on this question. Some experts feel that exposing children to a broad spectrum of movement experiences encompassing many sports will provide a foundation of general motor skills that can be used to achieve success in a particular sport later in life. On the other hand, others believe that training for a specific sport from an early age will develop more efficient movement patterns and also encourage changes in physiological systems that favor performance in that particular activity. I agree with the second position; however, specific sports training should not be emphasized to the exclusion of other normal childhood activities.

Swim training at an early age will develop bones and muscles that are more resistant to the specific stresses of aquatic sports. There is even the possibility, although remote, that the distribution of FT and ST muscle fibers might become more favorable. Starting early also allows athletes more time to perfect the skills of swimming. It would be worthwhile to start early for this reason, if for no other.

It should be mentioned that, although swim training at an early age may provide an advantage, it is not essential to success. There are swimmers who have made it to the top of international competitions who did not start training until the age of 15 or 16. There is probably no minimum age to begin training that will ensure success, nor is there a maximum age beyond which success will be unattainable. It seems, however, that most world-class swimmers begin training at least by age 10. For this reason, the chances of success are probably better if youngsters are given some exposure to the sport before their teenage years.

SUGGESTIONS FOR TRAINING IN THE VARIOUS AGE GROUPS

The recommendations in the following sections are based on the position that swim training should be only one of many enjoyable activities that children engage in. The time they spend in training should not be so excessive that it crowds out other growth-enhancing and enjoyable experiences.

6/8 Age Group

Children in this age group can progress nicely by training three to four times per week for approximately 45 minutes to 1 hour per session. This includes time for warming up and swimming down.

The major emphasis in their training should be on enjoyment and the mastery of stroke mechanics. Training should continually shift between the excitement inherent in mastering skills and the fun and games of racing and socializing with friends. Dryland training should consist of mild stretching and, perhaps, resistance training with stretch cords, calisthenics, or swim benches.

Children in this age group can commit to training 11 or 12 months out of the year, but they should feel free to take breaks of one day to several weeks when they desire. Meets should only be held every few weeks, and the competitions should be short, requiring no more than a few hours to complete.

9/10 Age Group

Everything that was said about the 6/8 age group applies equally to children in this age group. Their training mileage should increase, but only because they are capable of repeating faster in practice. The one difference is that training should become somewhat more structured; on occasion—perhaps once or twice per week—it should resemble the striving-for-excellence training that is expected of older swimmers. Children in this age group should occasionally perform sets and distance swims that really challenge their mind and body and coaches should encourage swimmers to take pride in making an honest attempt to complete them.

11/12 Age Group

Training should become even more structured and more intense when swimmers move up to this age group. Swimmers should participate in practice sessions five days per week for 1½ to 2 hours per session. Children in this age group should make a commitment to attend most, but not all, of these sessions. Their training should appear very much like that of senior swimmers, although it will be shorter and contain less mileage. More emphasis should be placed on athletes' striving to become better swimmers, with a great deal of the enjoyment of training coming from attempting to meet challenges. Coaches must select these challenges carefully and gear them to the ability of the individual swimmer so that these challenges are difficult but achievable. Coaches should balance this kind of motivated training with occasional weekly sessions of relaxed fun and games, which swimmers were accustomed to in the previous age group training. Above all, coaches and swimmers should equate success in training and competition with striving rather than achieving.

Eleven- and 12-year-old swimmers should be encouraged to train during the entire year, but they should also be given two or three weeks off at the completion of the winter and summer season. The number of meets can increase to include some weekend competitions during the summer months; however, most competitions should continue to require only part of a morning or afternoon, and the schedule should be such that children have well over half of their weekends free each year. Coaches can initiate a formal dryland training program that includes resistance training, or they can continue to use stretch cords, swim benches, and calisthenic-type exercises.

13/14 Age Group

Training volume should take another quantum leap upward for this age group. Everything that was said about the training of 11- and 12-year-old swimmers applies, only more so. I would not recommend that swimmers in this age group train twice per day, except during the summer months. Training volume and intensity should be similar to that of senior swimmers during each session, but athletes should swim fewer sessions per week. Their training should encompass 2 to 2½ hours per session, with the opportunity to train six days per week available but not required. The schedule of meets should provide for at least half of swimmers' weekends to be free each year, and swimmers should be given two- or three-week breaks between the winter and summer seasons.

Some teenagers in the 13/14 age group, particularly females, will progress so fast that they will already be swimming in national and international competitions. They may be swimming at the peak of their career, although coaches may not be aware of that fact at the time. It would be wrong to hold these swimmers back when they might be ready to achieve at their highest levels. For this reason, I suggest that these unusual athletes be permitted to train with the senior swimmers on the team.

15/18 Age Group

All swimmers who wish to should be training like senior competitors when they enter this age group. However, that does not mean that they must train two sessions per day, six days per week, and eleven months out of each year. Swimmers should make the decision as to how many days and months they train each year and how many hours they train per day. Swimmers and coaches can use the information provided in the previous chapters to structure training programs.

FREQUENTLY ASKED QUESTIONS ABOUT AGE GROUP TRAINING

Certain questions about age group training have been asked by each new generation of parents and coaches. Although a few can be answered conclusively, only informed opinions can be provided for most.

When should children start to specialize in a stroke or range of events? Probably not before the ages of 12 to 14. Athletes are not physiologically ready for specialization during their childhood and early teenage years. This is shown by the fact that relationships between performance and specific physiological capacities are not high (Rotstein, Dotan, Bar-Or, & Tenenbaum, 1986; Thorland et al., 1988). In other words, performance is generally related more to age and level of maturity than to physical measures such as $\dot{V}O_2$max and the anaerobic threshold. A large, early-maturing youngster will probably outswim a smaller, late-maturing competitor for any distance, given adequate levels of training for both.

Children are not physiologically ready for specialization, nor is it possible for coaches and parents to guess with any reasonable degree of accuracy which stroke(s) or event(s) they will swim best later in life. Consequently, children's options should be left open by training in all strokes and at a variety of distances. That kind of training should continue until they are between the ages of 12 and 14.

Are there any permanent disabilities that can arise from participation in age group swimming? The most serious problem that may arise is tendinitis in the shoulders and knees. Researchers estimate that nearly 50 percent of all swimmers suffer tendinitis in one or both of these joints at some time during their career (Dominguez, 1980; Greipp, 1985; Kennedy & Hawkins, 1974). If these overuse injuries go untreated, they can become chronic and plague a swimmer for the rest of his or her life. There should be no permanent ill effects if they are treated promptly and properly.

There is a misconception that hard training will stunt growth or cause an athlete to develop disproportionately. Quite the contrary. Training encourages growth and, as I mentioned earlier, enhances physical development.

Swimming is, perhaps, the most symmetrical of all sports and, for this reason, is a very desirable mode of exercise for young children. Both sides of the body are used equally, and both the arms and legs are required to work at high levels of effort. The large shoulders in some world-class female swimmers and the large legs and toed-out duck walk of male and female breaststrokers are not due to training in the sport. They are more likely genetic endowments that have helped these particular swimmers become successful.

Is participation in competitive sports damaging to the psychological and moral development of young athletes? There has been very little research done in this area, and the few results that are available have been contradictory. The competitive environment has the potential to aid or detract from good psychological development and strong moral values. Inherently, it is neither good nor evil but has the potential to be either. It can be an atmosphere in which children learn the values of dedicating themselves to a task and the need for cooperating with others to achieve a goal; it can also be a place where they learn to hide behind excuses for poor performance and view each competitor as an enemy. Children can take from the competitive environment a love of testing themselves against standards and worthy opponents, or they can learn to view competition as frightening and potentially damaging to their self-esteem. They can also come to realize that nonattainment of a goal is not failing but rather a form of success, if the goal is worthy and the effort to achieve it sincere; conversely, they can see goal setting as frightening and not to be attempted without an unfair edge or a ready excuse for failure.

Whether children react positively or negatively to the competitive environment will be due largely to the influence of the adults involved. Parents and coaches are responsible for the climate in which the child trains and competes. Hopefully, they will structure that environment so that children (1) gain confidence in their ability to meet challenges, (2) learn that achievement and fun are not mutually exclusive, (3) come to view themselves as having unique qualities that give them a special value, (4) become independent thinkers who can disagree with others without becoming overly argumentative, (5) learn to cooperate with others toward a common goal despite their differences, (6) learn that winning is not "winning" unless it is accomplished within the rules, (7) learn to take responsibility for their actions, (8) learn to accept and give help when it is needed, and, finally, (9) look back on their competitive experience with fond memories.

Why do some children leave competitive swimming at an early age? It has been estimated that nearly four out of every ten nationally ranked age group athletes drop out before they reach the usual age of senior competition for their sex — that is, age 14 for women and 18 for men. This is true of most age group sports and is not confined solely to competitive swimming (Rutenfranz, 1985). The reasons for this high rate of attrition are not known, although most people believe that pressure and high training volumes cause some athletes to burn out at an early age. I doubt that training volume is the reason why these young competitive swimmers leave the sport. Misplaced pressure is probably the culprit, although training volume may be involved indirectly.

Age group swimmers often doubt their chances for success when they fail to improve or when rivals pass them as they get older. In addition to this loss of confidence, their expectations and the expectations of others generally cause them to endure intense emotional pressure. That pressure can be self-induced or created by an overly critical or anxious coach or parent. It is probably this pressure that causes swimmers to retreat from the sport.

Experience has shown that most swimmers remain highly motivated if they feel their chances for success are good. However, motivation seems to wane when they feel those chances are remote. The paradox of age group sports is that success usually goes to the early maturer. Yet studies have shown that the late-maturing person generally ends up with greater physical abilities. It is no wonder, then, that some of our best senior athletes were not highly ranked as age group swimmers.

If this assumption is accurate, we need to find ways to encourage the late-maturing child even though he or she may not be the fastest swimmer on the team. We also need to help the swimmer who has had early success cope with occasional failures as a teenager without losing confidence or motivation.

EXERCISE-INDUCED ASTHMA AND OTHER MALADIES THAT SOMETIMES AFFLICT AGE GROUP SWIMMERS

Exercise-Induced Asthma

Approximately 12 to 15 percent of the general population suffers from exercise-induced asthma (Afrasiabi & Spector, 1991). It occurs when physical activity causes the air passages in the lungs (the bronchial tubes) to constrict. This reduces a child's ability to move air into and out of the lungs, thus reducing the oxygen supply. Symptoms can include coughing, shortness of breath, tightness in the chest, fatigue, and stomachache. Attacks may last several minutes. About 30 to 40 percent of children with exercise-induced asthma experience another attack three to six hours after training (so-called *late-phase asthma*).

It is generally agreed that exercise-induced asthma occurs because the respiratory passages constrict when they become dry and cool. Because atmospheric air is dryer and cooler than air in the lungs, the latter gives up a large amount of heat and moisture to humidify inhaled air. Although this does not cause problems for most, it may trigger attacks for those who are susceptible to exercise-induced asthma.

The stimulus that triggers such attacks is not known. Heredity undoubtedly plays a role. Allergies may also trigger asthma attacks or cause the attacks during exercise to become more frequent and severe (Katz, 1989). Attacks of exercise-induced asthma can also be exacerbated by pollution and secondhand smoke.

One theory that has been proposed to explain exercise-induced asthma is that some individuals have nerve receptors that are unusually sensitive to temperature changes, which become irritated when the temperature cools, causing the smooth muscles in the bronchial walls to contract.

Another theory involves the mast cells, which are located in the bronchial tubes. They release chemical compounds called mediators when they become irritated, which can cause contraction of the smooth muscles in the bronchial tubes, swelling of the mucous membranes, or production of mucus in the airways.

Swimming is one of the activities recommended for asthma sufferers. Swimmers are continually breathing air that has been heated and humidified by the water; consequently, the atmospheric air in swimming pools does not cool or dry the airways as much once it enters the swimmer's lungs.

Exercise-induced asthma can be controlled and does not preclude athletes from intense training or competitive success. U.S. athletes with a history of asthma won 41 medals at the 1984 Summer Olympic Games in Los Angeles, including Nancy Hogshead, who won a gold medal in the 100-m freestyle (McCarthy, 1989).

Training actually produces certain adaptive mechanisms of the airways that allow asthma sufferers to perform well in spite of their affliction. Studies have shown that asthmatics respond to training with improved ventilation and oxygen consumption the same as other athletes (Afrasiabi & Spector, 1991).

Athletes who suffer from exercise-induced asthma can use a variety of medications to prevent or reduce the incidence of attacks. Inhaling beta agonists such as albuterol or metaproterenol or cromolyn sodium 15 minutes before exercise have been shown to be 80- to 95-percent effective for preventing attacks, and they produce no harmful side effects (Gong, 1992; Katz, 1986). These medications should be prescribed by a doctor after a thorough examination.

Older swimmers who suffer from exercise-induced asthma have usually learned how to deal with the situation. Many keep inhalers at poolside and use them periodically during training. It has been my experience that teenage and college-age asthmatic swimmers have no limitations in training. They are able to perform the same as others on long endurance and intense sprint sets. Young swimmers who experience these attacks may require special handling, however, because they may be anxious about the effects that exertion can have on their breathing. They may be frightened and unsure of their ability to train and compete, so they should not be pushed to go beyond what they believe to be their limit until they have gained more confidence. They should be permitted to dictate the length and intensity of their training. Attempts at progressing beyond their usual limit should occur only with their approval.

Following are some guidelines for training swimmers who suffer from exercise-induced asthma (Gong, 1992):

1. Take physician-prescribed medications on a regular basis to control asthmatic symptoms.
2. Use an inhaler 15 minutes before the start of training.
3. Warm up thoroughly for 10 to 15 minutes before attempting any intense swimming.
4. Swim down for 10 to 20 minutes after training to avoid rapid thermal changes in the airways.

Some asthmatic swimmers may claim that chlorine exacerbates their condition. This is probably a manifestation of their insecurity about training rather than a "true" allergic reaction, because allergies to chlorine are very rare.

Diabetes Mellitus and Epilepsy

Persons who suffer from either of these conditions can train, provided they are under the care of a physician and take certain precautions.

Diabetes Mellitus Diabetes mellitus is usually caused by an inability of the body to produce sufficient quantities of insulin. As a consequence, diabetics have difficulty getting glucose from the blood into their muscles, where it can be used to supply energy for exercise. This condition is known as hypoglycemia.

Coaches who work with diabetic swimmers must be aware of the symptoms and immediate treatment for hypoglycemia. The disease can take several forms, so the family or a physician will need to supply this information. The usual symptoms are dizziness, loss of judgment, loss of coordination, and incoherence. Diabetics should immediately terminate exercise when some or all of these symptoms appear, and they should receive the necessary treatment immediately.

Training can have very beneficial effects for the diabetic. Exercise encourages the uptake of glucose by muscle cells and, by doing so, it can help diabetics reduce their need for insulin.

Epilepsy Exercise, even when very intense, will not precipitate an epileptic seizure. Nevertheless, an attack can occur during training just as it can at any other time of day. Epileptic children should be under the care of a physician, and they should be receiving medication to control their condition. They can train with no restrictions when these conditions are met. A coach should consult the swimmer's physician to learn what to do in the rare event that a seizure should take place.

CHAPTER 14

Female Swimmers and Masters Swimmers

Many of the issues surrounding age group training are also debated with regard to training female swimmers and Masters swimmers. The answers are generally the same. They can train just as long, just as intensely, and just as frequently as young adult males. Nevertheless, both groups have special needs that should be provided for in order to maximize their progress in training. The similarities and special needs of these two groups are the subjects of this chapter.

FEMALE SWIMMERS

Of the many misconceptions about women in sports, the most prevalent have been (1) that women could not train as strenuously as men, (2) that training was masculinizing, and (3) that female athletes reached their potential for performance between the ages of 12 and 15. These myths have been dispelled largely during the last 10 to 15 years. With the passage of Title IX, there has been a huge increase in the number of females that have competed in organized sports programs at the high school and college levels. As a result, it has been demonstrated that women can tolerate hard training equally as well as men and that they do not lose their femininity in the process. It has also been shown that they can improve their performance well into adulthood.

Although the general public has only recently been made aware of the misconceptions about women in sports, swimming coaches have known they were untrue for more than three decades. Training for men and women has been similar in swimming since the 1960s. It is fortunate for women and for our sport that the coaches of that era were smart enough to disregard the cautions of so-called experts.

Unfortunately, there are still places in the world where these misconceptions continue to exist. Many countries do not allow women to compete in the longer events, and their influence has kept the women's 1,500-m freestyle off the Olympic program even though women of all ages are competing in swims of over 2 miles in triathlon competitions.

Although the programs for women should generally be identical to those of men, there are some physiological differences between the two sexes that need to be understood in order to plan and evaluate the training of women more intelligently. The problem is in separating "real" differences from those that are not real. Many supposed differences between the sexes are due to nothing more than the difference in average size. Frequently, the different capacities cited for men and women are often no greater than those for larger and smaller men. In most cases, the overlap in the range of scores for the two sexes is so great that average values become meaningless. The scores for women on many tests of physical capacity may often exceed those of some men, even though the peak and average values for men are greater than those achieved by women.

To complicate matters even more, some of the differences between men and women that I cite may be outdated before this book is published. Considerable evidence suggests that differences in physical capacity and performance between men and women are narrowing as the number of genetically talented females entering competitive sports increases. For example, the difference between the winning times in the 400-m freestyle for men and women was 16 percent in the 1924 Olympic Games. That difference was still 12 percent in 1984. The gap between the performances of men and women in this event narrowed more in the following 4 years than in the previous 60 years; the difference was only 7 percent at the 1988 Olympiad. Another interesting fact is that in 1979 a woman swam the 800-m freestyle faster than the world record for men in 1972 (Wilmore & Costill, 1988). Only time will tell if the performances of women can match or exceed those of their male contemporaries in certain events.

No matter how similar to men's the training of women should be, women have special training needs. Women must contend with menstruation, which raises many questions about the possible harmful effects of training on the reproductive process. Women are also more prone to certain dietary deficiencies that can affect their performance and their health. Two of these are osteoporosis and anemia. A third, anorexia nervosa, results from inadequate caloric intake.

The physiological makeups of men and women are contrasted in the first section of this chapter, followed by a comparison of the responses of the two sexes to training. The final sections on female training are concerned with irregularities of the menstrual cycle, pregnancy, and other special considerations for female athletes such as osteoporosis, anorexia, and bulimia.

The Physiology of Female Athletes

Body Fat There appear to be no differences in body composition between males and females until some time between the ages of 12 and 14. At puberty, females' ovaries develop and the secretion of the hormone estrogen begins. Estrogen increases bone growth for approximately 2 years, after which most women reach their maximum height. At the same time, males begin to secrete testosterone and experience a growth spurt of considerably greater magnitude, which continues into their 20s.

Estrogen also stimulates the development of female secondary sex characteristics. The hips begin to broaden, the breasts develop, and the amount of body fat increases. As a result of these changes, the average female, when compared to the average male, is 13 cm (5 in) shorter and 14 to 18 kg (30 to 40 lb) lighter. Her lean body weight (bone and muscle tissue) is 18 to 22 kg (40 to 50 lb) less, and she has 3 to 6 kg (7 to 13 lb) of additional fat.

The average difference in body fat between nonathletic men and women is 9 percent (15 percent versus 24 percent, respectively). A similar difference also exists between male and female competitive swimmers, although the percentage for each sex is considerably different. Heusner (1985) reported that the average body fat percentages for male and female members of the 1984 U.S. Olympic Swimming Team were 10 percent and 18 percent, respectively. The range for males was 8 to 12 percent, and for females it was 15 to 21 percent. It was interesting that those male and female athletes with lower percentages of body fat did not necessarily outperform members of the same sex with higher percentages. Apparently, more fat weight does not seem to hinder the performance of a female swimmer as long as her body fat percentage is no greater than a critical value of approximately 20 percent. Perhaps this is because additional fat causes the body to float higher so that any increase in water resistance that might be caused by the excess tissue is negated by improved buoyancy up to a certain level (20 percent).

It is an unsolved mystery why the body fat percentages of female swimmers are generally greater than those of female distance runners. Female distance runners generally have a range of body fat between 12 and 16 percent, which is unusual because both swimmers and runners train with similar relative volumes and intensities. Swimmers also tend to consume fewer calories than runners relative to their body size. The results of one study (Jang et al., 1987) showed that a group of female swimmers were in a negative caloric balance during training, yet an age- and activity-matched group of female runners maintained a positive balance. When expressed relative to body size, the smaller runners were consuming six calories per kilogram more than the swimmers. These data indicated that the female swimmers should have been more lean than the runners, yet they were generally carrying 6 more kilograms (13 lb) of fat on their body than the runners (14 kg versus 8 kg).

The reasons are not known for the differences in body fat percentages between these two groups of athletes. There may be something inherent in the training of runners and swimmers that encourages the preservation of body fat in the latter. On the other hand, these differences could be a product of natural selection. Larger females may gravitate toward a sport like swimming, in which the water supports their body. Conversely, women who are more lean may engage in sports like distance running in which they can be successful because they have less body weight to propel.

Although swimmers carry more body fat than runners, they do not appear soft and flabby. Their bone structure and musculature are generally larger, and they have a lean and firm look even though they may carry more body fat.

Muscle Tissue The muscle fibers of men are approximately 30 percent larger than those of women, although differences of only 15 percent have been found between endurance-trained males and females (Drinkwater, 1984b). Women also tend to have fewer fibers in their muscles than men. However, there is a considerable overlap in the ranges of the two sexes. In one study, the number of muscle fibers in the biceps of trained men and women were 350,000 and 320,000, respectively. The range for men was 280,000 to 400,000, and for women it was 240,000 to 380,000 (Nygaard, 1980, 1982). You can see, then, that some women have more muscle fibers in the same muscle group than some men.

The proportions of fast twitch (FT) and slow twitch (ST) muscle fibers are, on the average, similar for men and women. The percentage distribution is also similar between men and women in the same range of events. That is, both female and male sprint swimmers tend to have a predominance of FT muscle fibers, and women who specialize in distance events, like their male counterparts, generally have a greater proportion of ST muscle fibers.

Although the distribution of FT and ST muscle fibers are approximately equal, more males than females tend to have extreme types of fiber distribution. Men at extreme ends of the range have as many as 98 percent ST muscle fibers and as many as 87 percent FT muscle fibers. The range for women was much smaller; it was between 72-percent ST and 63-percent FT muscle fibers (Saltin & Gollnick, 1983). This suggests that a slightly greater percentage of men than women are at extreme ends of the spectrum where the potentials for speed and endurance performance are concerned. This should not limit the performance of women in sprint or distance events because the range of swimming events is less broad than those of other sports. So, the athletes who succeed in sprint swimming are those who tend to have a preponderance but nonextreme proportion of FT muscle fibers, and those who perform best in the distance events display the opposite tendency. It means, however, that fewer females than males will be either drop-dead sprinters or distance swimmers who cannot sprint at all.

Although body fat has little effect on performance as long as it is within normal ranges, the muscle weight of women has considerable influence. In a study involving 248 female competitive swimmers, Stager and Cordain (1984) reported a significant negative relationship between lean body weight and 100-yd swim times. The relationship was negative because the times became faster (lower) as lean body weight increased.

Strength and Muscular Power Women have, on the average, only half the strength of men in their upper body. The absolute strength of their leg muscles is only 25 to 30 percent less than that of men, however, and their leg muscles are actually stronger relative to their size.

Strength is usually expressed in absolute values or in relationship to body weight (strength/kg). Both measures are biased in favor of men. Differences in the strength of men and women need to be compared relative to muscle weight (strength/lbw, or strength per kilogram of lean body weight), to determine if they are inherent or due only to the fact that women are generally smaller and have more body fat. When this is done, the scores for men and women are generally equal, although the leg muscles of women tend to be slightly stronger than those of men. In one study, the leg press strength of women was 4 percent greater than that for men when expressed relative to lean body weight (Hoffman, Stauffer, & Jackson, 1979). These results reflect that there is really no difference between men and women in the quality of their muscle tissue, only in the absolute quantity. Men are generally stronger and more powerful than women only because they have larger muscles, not because their muscle structure is inherently superior.

Regardless of this fact, women are still at a disadvantage in swimming events that require strength and power because they carry more body fat relative to their total weight. Although strength per kilogram of muscle weight is an accurate way › compare the strength of the muscle fibers of men and women, it is strength per logram of total body weight that reflects the power available for swimming fast. this basis, the average power of women is generally less than that of men.

ibility Women seem to have greater joint flexibility than men at any age. is some belief that women have an advantage in learning all sports or physical including swimming techniques, because of greater flexibility. There is no research to validate this belief, although it is supported by the personal ions of many.

ugh more flexible, the joints of women are not as strong as those of men. ntly, some experts believe that the potential for injury may be greater in quiring strength and power. This is another area that is underresearched; doubt the accuracy of this observation. It would seem that the bones, nd tendons of females should be relatively as strong as those of men. he joint structures of women are smaller should not make a difference, uscular force is applied against them. Consequently, women's joint ld be able to withstand the pull exerted on them by muscles equally men. Both resistance training and endurance training increase and ve tissues and make bones more dense. Accordingly, they should e resistant to joint and bone injuries rather than increase their em.

experts have speculated that a woman's maximum heart rate (Brooks & Fahey, 1984), yet no differences have been reported b Costill, 1988). Submaximum heart rates should be the same at ts, so the range of values used to monitor training intensity sho nen and women.

Aerobi spects of aerobic capacity that are compared are oxygen consum nd the anaerobic threshold, muscle glycogen, and fat metabolism.

Oxygen consumption and the anaerobic threshold The highest recorded $\dot{V}O_2$max for a female athlete was 77 ml/kg/min and for a male was 94 ml/kg/min. Both athletes were cross-country skiers (Wilmore & Costill, 1988). At maturity, the relative $\dot{V}O_2$max of the average woman is only 70 to 75 percent that of the average man.

Although the average $\dot{V}O_2max$ for women is less than that of men, the overlap between males and females is so great that the aerobic capacity of some females on every team will exceed that of some males. The range of $\dot{V}O_2max$ values for female members of the 1984 U.S. Olympic Swimming Team was 50 to 66 ml/kg/min, and for males it was 57 to 80 ml/kg/min (VanHandel et al., 1988a). So, you can see that some female members of the team had greater $\dot{V}O_2max$ values than some male Olympians.

The average difference between men and women in $\dot{V}O_2max$ is accounted for primarily by size. Men tend to have a larger heart, greater blood volume, and more hemoglobin in their blood. Consequently, they can eject a greater amount of blood and transport more oxygen and other nutrients during each minute of exercise. They also have greater lung volume.

Interestingly, men and women of similar ability use the same amount of oxygen when swimming at a particular speed. However, because their maximum ability to consume oxygen is usually less than that of men, women tend to work nearer their maximum at that speed. It should be expected, therefore, that women fatigue more quickly when they try to swim at the same speed as men of similar relative ability. The responses of men and women are very similar when they swim at the same relative speeds; thus, women can work at the same percentage of their $\dot{V}O_2max$ as men without becoming fatigued.

Women reach their anaerobic threshold at the same range of blood lactate values as men — approximately 2 to 5 mmol/l. However, the absolute anaerobic threshold speeds of women differ by approximately 5 percent from those of men (Sharp, Vitelli, Costill, & Thomas, 1984b). This amounts to a difference of approximately 3 or 4 seconds per 100 yd/m.

Muscle glycogen Women's muscles are capable of storing as much glycogen as those of men. Their smaller muscle size means a smaller total quantity, although the amount of glycogen per unit of muscle tissue is the same as for men. Women are also capable of increasing glycogen supply to the same extent as men through training. In fact, women also respond to endurance training with the same percentage improvements in cardiac output, oxygen consumption, and muscle enzymes as do men (Eddy, Sparks, & Adelizi, 1977).

Fat metabolism One aspect of the endurance training response that has received a lot of attention concerns the ability of women to use fat for energy during exercise. Women improve in this ability equally to men with training. However, because fat tends to make up a greater percentage of their total body weight, some theorize that women are inherently better suited than men for competition at long distances. Others have even speculated that women could ultimately surpass men in events at ultramarathon distances because they can utilize more fat for energy and, thus, not deplete their muscle glycogen supplies so rapidly.

The validity of this theory was tested by Costill and his associates (1979), using 13 male and 12 female distance runners. Members from each sex were matched according to $\dot{V}O_2max$ capacity, fiber type percentages, and training mileage. Researchers found that fat use was nearly identical for men and women at the same relative running speed (70 percent of $\dot{V}O_2max$). These results infer that there is no difference between men and women in their potential to perform ultralong endurance exercise.

Anaerobic Capacity The ability of women to do work that requires a large anaerobic component, such as races from 50 to 200 yd/m, is approximately 17 percent less than that of men (Medbo & Burgers, 1990). This, once again, is due principally to women's smaller muscle size. However, the relative amounts of anaerobic enzymes are the same in the muscles of males and females, and women respond to training with percentage enzyme increases similar to men's.

Although sparse, the small amount of research that is available suggests that training does not improve the buffering capacity of women as much as that of men. Medbo and Burgers (1990) reported a 16-percent increase for men after six weeks of sprint training, yet women improved only 5 percent on the same program. Surprisingly, the effects of training on the rate of lactic acid production were similar for both sexes. Both the male and female subjects in this study improved their rate of anerobic energy release by 10 percent.

Peak blood lactate values have been reported to be slightly less for women in some publications and equal to those of men in others. The sprinting of women should not be affected detrimentally, even if their maximum blood lactate concentrations are somewhat lower. Women have fewer and smaller fibers than men. Consequently, with fewer fibers to produce lactic acid, their rate of production may be equal to or greater than that of men even though the total quantity of lactic acid in the blood is less.

The anaerobic training procedures described in this book for senior swimmers are equally applicable for women. It is not necessary to reduce intensity, volume, or frequency for females. Women should not neglect anaerobic or power training. Those who compete in events from 50 to 200 yd/m need anaerobic capacity and power to reach their peak in these events.

Table 14-1 (page 276) summarizes the comparisons of physical characteristics for male and female athletes that were discussed in the preceding section.

Physiological Implications for Training

Although there are physiological differences between men and women, most of them do not have important implications for training. Women are as capable as men of training long and intensely. They can train with the same weekly and daily mileages, repeat sets, and rest intervals.

Training speeds for women and men can be prescribed with equal effectiveness from blood tests or any of the other methods for prescribing training speeds that were described in Chapter 8. Shifts in women's lactate velocity curves can also be interpreted in the same way they are interpreted for men.

Women cannot be expected to swim as fast as men of *similar relative ability* in training. However, they can certainly be expected to swim as fast as men with similar race times and faster than men with slower times.

Some experts have stated that endurance swimming should comprise a greater percentage of the training for women (Maglischo & Daland, 1987) — 65 percent for women as compared to 50 percent for men. The reason for this suggestion may be

Table 14-1. Physical Characteristics of Female Athletes Compared to Males

Measure	Differences Between Men and Women
Height	On the average, 13 cm shorter for women
Muscle tissue	On the average, 18 to 22 kg less for women
Body fat	On the average, 3 to 6 kg more for women
Percentage of body fat	On the average, 9 percent higher for women
Proportions of FT and ST muscle fibers	Similar for men and women
Strength	Absolute strength is 50 percent less for women in upper body; 25 to 30 percent less in lower body. Relative strength is similar for both sexes
Flexibility	Greater for women
$\dot{V}O_2max$	25 to 30 percent less for women
Muscle glycogen	Similar for men and women, although women have a smaller total because they have less muscle tissue
Fat metabolism	Similar for men and women
Anaerobic capacity	On the average, 17 percent less for women

related to the fact that women have less force available. Thus, compared to men, they may need to rely more on aerobic capacity at all race distances. Consequently, they may need more endurance training to improve that aerobic capacity.

Contrary to this recommendation, it would seem that the most important training effects women should seek are those that increase muscular strength and power. It is in these areas, rather than in measures of endurance, where women's scores fall most behind those of men. Therefore, improving strength and power should provide the fastest route to major improvements in performance, particularly because the majority of competitive swimming events require power.

The fact that females might profit from additional attention to strength and power training should not conflict with the recommended balance between endurance and sprint training that was described in Chapter 6. The quantities of lactate tolerance, lactate production, and power training that are needed to improve anaerobic capacity and muscular power are quite small, so the recommended amounts of these types of training need not differ greatly between men and women. The point to be made is that females should concentrate on making the best use of their anaerobic and power training because of the importance of power to their performances.

The Trainability of Female Athletes

Early studies reported that women did not improve power as much with training as did men. I suspect, however, that women were not required to overload to the same extent as men in many of these studies. Recent studies have contradicted earlier results, showing that women respond as well as men to weight training and other forms of resistance training. In fact, in some of these studies, the percentage gains for women were greater than for men (Cureton, Collins, Hill, & McElhannon, 1988).

Another common misconception is that strength training does not cause women's muscles to increase in size as much as men's. Contrary to this notion, Cureton and associates (1988) reported no differences in the amount of muscle tissue gained by men and women after strength training. However, there is no need to be concerned that women will develop big muscles from weight training. There are only a small number of persons in the general population, male or female, who possess the genetic predisposition to build large amounts of muscle tissue through resistance training. Remember also that female swimmers perform a large amount of endurance work concurrently with their strength training, which tends to reduce body fat and muscle bulk.

It should be mentioned that women are no more susceptible to injury from resistance training than men. Accordingly, they can train with heavy weights and maximum efforts in well-constructed, properly supervised resistance programs.

Special Training Considerations for Female Swimmers

Although the volume and intensity of training should be similar for both sexes, women must contend with certain unique physiological responses that may require special adjustments. Among these are menstruation and pregnancy. Oral contraceptives can also affect performance. Furthermore, conditions such as osteoporosis, anemia, anorexia, and bulimia are much more prevalent among women than among men.

Menstruation The major issues concern the effects of training on the beginning of menstruation, missed menstrual periods, painful menstruation, and the effect of menstruation on performances.

Delayed menarche Training seems to delay the commencement of menstruation, or *menarche*. Whereas most females have their first menstrual period between the ages of 12 and 13, athletic girls do not menstruate until six months to one year later. Some have even reported that their first menstrual flow did not happen until they were 16 or 17 (Rogol, 1988).

There also seems to be a relationship between the ability of female athletes and the age of menarche. Higher-level performers report the greatest delay of first menstrual flow. In a study involving 345 female competitive swimmers, the mean age at menarche was 13.4 years, yet those swimmers in the group with the fastest times achieved menarche at ages 15 to 16 (Stager & Cordain, 1984).

Several theories have been advanced for the delay of menarche in female competitors. The most accepted theory indicates natural selection as the cause. Late-maturing girls have greater potential for athletic performance, so they are found more frequently training for competitive sports.

There seem to be no short-term or long-term complications from delayed menarche. Nevertheless, because most athletes experience their first menstrual flow by age 17, it would be prudent to consult a physician if a particular competitor did not have her first menstrual flow by age 18.

Amenorrhea and oligomenorrhea More incidences of missed periods occur in the athletic population than in the nonathletic population. The occurrence of irregular periods, where menstrual flow is interrupted for two to six months, is called *oligomenorrhea*. When menstruation stops for periods of six months to several years, the condition is termed *amenorrhea*. Some female athletes believe that amenorrhea means that they cannot become pregnant. However, amenorrhea cannot be depended on as a form of birth control, because some women have reported becoming pregnant during time spans when they were amenorrheic (Wells & Plowman, 1988).

The incidences of amenorrhea and oligomenorrhea have been reported to be between 12 and 45 percent in various athletic groups. In contrast, only 2 to 3 percent of nonathletic women have reported experiencing amenorrhea, and 10 to 12 percent have indicated irregular menstruation over shorter time spans (Drinkwater, 1984a). Sanborn and colleagues (1982) reported that 12 percent of swimmers surveyed were or had been amenorrheic at some time in their career. Stein and associates (1983) reported an incidence of 50 percent for shorter-term menstrual irregularities in another group of swimmers.

Amenorrhea is more common among younger athletes than among older ones. Baker (1981) reported a 67-percent incidence of amenorrhea in a group of runners who were 29 years old and younger, yet only 9 percent of those over 30 were currently having menstrual irregularities.

Several explanations have been proposed for the unusually large incidence of amenorrhea and oligomenorrhea among groups of female athletes. Excessive training has been cited as one possible cause. However, neither training volume, frequency, nor intensity has shown any relationship to the occurrence of these menstrual irregularities in most studies (Baker, 1981; Feicht et al., 1978; Sanborn, Martin, & Wagner, 1982; Schwartz et al., 1981; Shangold & Levine, 1982).

Of the other explanations, the *critical fat theory* has received the most attention. This theory was put forth by Frisch and colleagues in several publications (Frisch & Revelle, 1971a, 1971b, 1971c; Frisch & McArthur, 1974). These researchers proposed that 17 percent body fat was required for menarche and that 22 percent was required for the maintenance of normal menstrual function. Members of the scientific community have largely dismissed the critical fat theory; however, low body weight and body fat have been implicated in so many cases of disturbed menstrual function that many experts continue to believe that there is a causal relationship even though there may not be any critical level for such disturbances.

The information in Table 14-2 negates the existence of a relationship between training mileage, critical fat, and menstrual irregularities. The figures are from a study by Rogol (1988) involving female distance runners who were experiencing irregular menstrual flow. They were placed in groups according to weekly training mileage and years of training. The data demonstrate considerable variances among the subjects in each group on all measures, making it difficult to identify any as the cause for their disruption in menstrual function.

Table 14-2. Characteristics of Amenorrheic Distance Runners

Years of Training	Training Mileage (km/week)	Number of Menses per Year	Percentage of Body Fat	Weight (kg)	Height (cm)	Age at Menarche
6	20–35	0–1	14.5	48	163	13
2	30–40	1–2	13.6	49	162	14
5	30–54	1–2	16.7	59	167	14
10	40–70	0–1	11.2	62	161	17
15	40–60	2–3	16.7	55	162	17
Nonathletes		11–13	24.0	63	168	13

Source: Adapted from Rogol, 1988.

Another, more plausible explanation implicates the rate and amount of weight loss as precipitating causes. Amenorrheic runners have been reported to lose more weight from training than runners who were having regular menstrual periods, and it has been speculated that a 33-percent loss of body fat or a 10- to 15-percent weight loss may interrupt the menstrual cycle (Wells & Plowman, 1988).

A relationship between rapid weight loss and menstrual irregularities may have to do with a reduction in the hormone estrogen. Estrogen is formed in adipose tissue and is required during the follicular phase of the menstrual cycle in order for ovulation to take place. It has been proposed that a rapid or large loss of body fat could reduce the amount of estrogen being produced and, thus, interrupt the normal occurrence of menstrual flow. In this regard, low estrogen levels have often been reported in groups of highly trained female runners (Wells & Plowman, 1988).

Although there is evidence to support the rapid weight loss theory, it is not accepted by all. Some researchers believe any relationship between rapid weight loss and interrupted menstrual function is coincidental because both are controlled by the same areas of the brain—the hypothalamus and the pituitary gland.

Another popular notion is known as the *energy drain theory*. Proponents believe that females do not ovulate during training because the body senses that the stress of exercise does not leave it with enough energy to reproduce.

A final theory has to do with protein in the diet. Diets that are deficient in certain amino acids have been found to alter neurotransmitter substances that affect the secretion of hormones necessary for ovulation. Supporters of this theory point to a greater incidence of menstrual irregularities among vegetarians. In one study, 82 percent of women with interrupted menstrual flows were vegetarians (Brooks, Sanborn, Albrecht, & Wagner, 1984). Vegetarians are obviously more at risk for protein deficiencies because they have more difficulty getting all of the essential amino acids without eating a wide variety of foods.

Despite these many theories, it is not surprising that the causes of menstrual irregularities remain a mystery. The female reproductive system is extremely complex, being under the influence of several glands and a large number of hormones. At the present time, the only thing we know for sure is that any swimming team has several female members who will experience irregular menstruation at some time during their career. Fortunately, the condition seems to correct itself during periods of reduced training or breaks in training, and there do not seem to be any long-lasting deleterious effects on menstrual function (Rogol, 1988).

Dysmenorrhea Painful menstruation is termed *dysmenorrhea*. It is the most common form of menstrual disorder in the general population of women. Most female athletes experience dysmenorrhea several times during their career, although the condition seems to be less common among female athletes than nonathletic women (Brooks & Fahey, 1984). Several over-the-counter medications can provide some relief from the symptoms of headache, nausea, backache, and abdominal cramps that are associated with this condition. It should be the athlete's choice to train or rest when the symptoms of dysmenorrhea occur.

Menstruation and performance Female athletes frequently want to know if they should train and compete when they are menstruating. That should also be the personal choice of each female athlete. No known dangers to health or safety are associated with training and competing during menstruation, although some athletes may experience discomfort when they do so.

Another question that is often asked concerns whether or not female athletes can swim faster during certain times of the menstrual cycle than others. Research shows a very small improvement of performance for about 15 days during the postmenstrual period (Hall-Jurkowski, Jones, Toews, & Sutton, 1981). The difference is so slight, however, that the effect on performance could easily be nullified by motivation or several of the other myriad factors involved in performing well.

Training is another factor that can reduce the variability in performance between the different stages of the menstrual cycle because it seems to reduce reactions to the hormonal fluctuations associated with those stages (Clement et al., 1985). Interestingly, women have set world records during every stage of the menstrual cycle (Brooks & Fahey, 1984).

Pregnancy There are two prominent myths surrounding this topic. To dispel them: female athletes *can* train and compete in the early stages of pregnancy, and they *can* improve on their performance after childbirth. Training during pregnancy prevents athletes from becoming entirely deconditioned and helps them maintain a level of muscle strength that may reduce the time spent in labor. However, training should be reduced in volume and intensity during pregnancy in accordance with the recommendations of a physician.

Women who are in good physical condition spend less time in labor than those who have become deconditioned (Wong & McKenzie, 1985). They also require less medication and have fewer cesarean sections (Kaufman & Hall, 1985). Well-conditioned women also have fewer stretch marks because they have less fat around their abdomen and because their well-conditioned stomach muscles reduce the amount of stretching (Brooks & Fahey, 1984). Sensible training during pregnancy also seems to have a positive effect on the unborn fetus. The weights of newborn babies are significantly higher for trained women (Kaufman & Hall, 1985).

Women have won Olympic medals during the early stages of pregnancy. In general, however, pregnant athletes are not able to perform as well in competition. Women can improve their performance after pregnancy, as has been shown many times by Olympians and Masters swimmers.

Oral Contraceptives The use of oral contraceptives presents no immediate problems for training or competition; however, it can precipitate certain dietary deficiencies that will ultimately harm performance. Deficiencies and marginal levels of vitamin B_6 (pyridoxine), folacin (another of the B-complex group), B_1 (thiamine), B_2 (riboflavin), and B_{12} (cobalamin) have been reported in women who were using oral contraceptives (Wells, 1985). For this reason, daily supplements of 5 to 10 mg of vitamin B_6, folacin, B_1, B_2, and B_{12} are recommended.

Osteoporosis This is a condition that weakens bones, making them more susceptible to injury. Osteoporosis is the twelfth leading cause of death in the U.S. and over 700,000 fractures due to osteoporosis are reported among women each year (Loucks, 1988).

Most of us think of bones as inert, unchanging structures. In fact, they are composed of living material that is continually being replaced by the foods we eat each day. The major structural substances that require continual replacement are calcium, phosphate, and carbonate. Under normal circumstances, these substances are deposited faster in the bones than they are reabsorbed, so that bones grow larger and more dense until age 35 in both women and men. The process tends to become reversed in women at approximately age 50, when estrogen levels decrease during menopause.

Recently, a number of studies have shown an accelerated rate of loss in bone mineral content among young amenorrheic women (Cann, Martin, Genant, & Jaffe, 1984; Drinkwater et al., 1984; Lindberg et al., 1984; Marcus et al., 1985). Women in this group commonly show low levels of estrogen, which are thought to be involved in their rapid loss of bone mineral content. Drinkwater and colleagues reported a 14-percent loss of bone minerals from the spines of a group of amenorrheic runners. Although the runners were in their mid-20s, their bones had the mineral content of 50-year-old women.

The most important nutrient for preventing bone mineral loss seems to be calcium, and deficiencies of this mineral have become widespread in recent years. The national Health and Nutrition Examination Survey (HANES) reported that over one-half of the female population was consuming insufficient amounts of calcium each day (Wilmore & Costill, 1988). The incidence and severity of calcium deficiencies appear to be even greater among teenage females. Surveys by the U.S. Public Health Service from 1971 to 1974 and then again in 1976 show that the average calcium intake of females declined steadily during that decade. The latter survey showed that the average calcium intake of women had fallen more than 25 percent below the recommended daily allowance (RDA) of 800 mg and that teenagers in the sample were consuming 30 percent less calcium than the RDA. One explanation for these findings was that many females were reducing their daily caloric intake and substituting diet soft drinks for calcium-containing fluids in an attempt to remain thin. Calcium needs are met rather easily when athletes consume 3,000 calories per day or more. Unfortunately, many females are not ingesting this amount.

An intake of 1,500 mg/day of calcium has been recommended for females at risk for calcium deficiencies (Martin & Houston, 1987). It is probably advisable for female swimmers to supplement their diets with at least 1,000 mg of calcium per day. However, this may not solve the problem because calcium absorption is not always adequate from supplements. For this reason, athletes should make certain that their diets contain adequate amounts of calcium-rich foods, such as milk and other dairy products. Skim milk is recommended because it has less fat and fewer calories.

Anemia This is a condition in which the number of circulating red blood cells is reduced. The corresponding loss of hemoglobin seriously diminishes an athlete's aerobic capacity and probably reduces her anaerobic capacity as well.

Blood hemoglobin carries oxygen to the muscles, where it is absorbed by diffusion, and it carries carbon dioxide to the lungs for expulsion. A reduced blood hemoglobin content is thus accompanied by a reduction in the oxygen supply. Such a reduction would cause an endurance athlete's respiratory and circulatory systems to work faster to supply the oxygen needed during exercise. This would be reflected by a faster heart rate and higher blood lactate concentrations at submaximum training speeds and by an athlete's inability to maintain her usual pace in fast training swims and endurance races. The amount by which performance would worsen would depend on the amount of hemoglobin lost.

Low levels of hemoglobin may also affect anaerobic performance by reducing the removal of carbon dioxide from muscles. Accordingly, any reduction in the hemoglobin supply would reduce the amount of carbon dioxide that could be transported to the lungs per minute. Carbon dioxide acts as a buffer by transporting away hydrogen ions (H^+) that are produced in the muscles during exercise. Thus a reduction in the rate of carbon dioxide removal should also reduce the rate of H^+ removal, causing acidosis to occur earlier in muscles.

The iron content of an athlete's body seems to have a direct effect on the amount of stored hemoglobin. Hemoglobin molecules continually undergo destruction and rebuilding in the blood. The main structural ingredient of hemoglobin is the mineral iron. When iron is in short supply, the rate of hemoglobin reformation is reduced and the supply diminishes.

A woman's need for iron is greater than that of a man because of the blood lost during menstruation each month. That amount has been estimated at 150 ml, which corresponds to an additional iron loss of 75 mg/month (Schottelius & Schottelius, 1973). This amounts to an average daily iron loss of approximately 1.5 mg, although the majority of this loss occurs for only a short period each month. One report placed 76 percent of the women surveyed below the RDA for iron intake (Newhouse & Clement, 1988). For this reason, an RDA of 18 mg of iron is suggested for women, yet an RDA of only 10 mg is recommended for men.

Recent research suggests that iron deficiencies are more prevalent among female athletes than once believed. Risser and coworkers (1988) reported that 31 percent of the female athletes they studied were iron deficient. Selby and Eichner (1985) reported iron deficiency in 14 percent and low iron stores in 43 percent of the female swimmers they surveyed.

One reason for this considerable incidence of iron deficiency may be that many females, including female athletes, do not consume sufficient quantities of iron by dietary means. The average American diet contains about 6 mg of iron per 1,000 calories. Consequently, females who eat fewer than 3,000 calories per day (and many do) take in less than 18 mg of iron daily.

Another problem is the poor absorption of iron. Estimates of the amount of iron absorbed range from 6 to 20 percent of the total amount consumed. The type of food eaten greatly influences the rate of absorption. The iron found in meat, fish, and poultry is of the higher-grade *heme* variety, which is more readily absorbed than that found in vegetable sources. Thus, vegetarians should have a more difficult time absorbing the iron they need. In a study that compared vegetarian and meat-eating runners, the vegetarian group absorbed 25 percent less iron and had lower ferritin levels than the runners who included meat in their diets (Snyder, Dvorak, & Roepke, 1987). Regardless of these findings, recent reports show a trend toward vegetarian diets among athletes (Pate et al., 1986; van Erp-Baart et al., 1989).

Many experts believe that the risk of anemia is greater among both male and female athletes because both expend more iron in training. Exercise increases the need for protein in muscle tissue, some of which may be supplied by transferring the protein in hemoglobin to the interior of the muscle cell (McMurray, Ben-Ezra, Forsythe, & Smith, 1985; Yoshimura, Inone, Yamada, & Shiraki, 1980). In addition, a significant amount of iron appears to be lost in sweat each day, with estimates as high as 1 mg/hour (Consolazio et al., 1963; Veller, 1968). Another way that athletes can lose iron is through blood in the feces. Small amounts of blood appeared in the feces of up to 30 percent of a group of distance runners after competition (Stewart et al., 1984). The additional iron these athletes lost through gastrointestinal bleeding was calculated at 2 mg/day.

Athletes are often unaware of the progressive development of anemia until it is very advanced. Anemia develops in stages, and performance may not suffer until the last stage, when hemoglobin loss becomes quite severe. Iron is absorbed from the intestine by a substance called transferrin and transported to the blood and then to the liver, spleen, and bone marrow for storage in the form of ferritin. When there is a need for iron to replace red blood cells, the ferritin is released from these areas and circulates into the blood once again.

In the first stage of anemia, blood ferritin is low, but iron and hemoglobin are normal. In the second stage, ferritin is minimal. In this situation, the absorption of iron and, consequently, the storage of iron is decreased; however, hemoglobin remains normal. The hemoglobin content of the blood decreases significantly in the final stage, when the quantity of stored iron becomes insufficient to supply the material needed to reform this blood protein. This is when serious decrements of performance take place. Hemoglobin levels below 11.5 g/dl (grams per deciliter) for women and 13.5 g/dl for men classify them as anemic (Ruud, 1990).

If impending anemia can be diagnosed early, before the iron stores are depleted, athletes can recover rather quickly with no loss of performance. However, several weeks of recovery will be required if athletes progress to the final stage of anemia without receiving treatment. Measurements of blood hemoglobin are not satisfactory for early detection. As mentioned, hemoglobin does not decrease until the condition is quite advanced, and, by then, the athletes' performances will have deteriorated to the point that a test will not be necessary to tell them that something is wrong. The levels of circulating blood (serum) ferritin are most often used as an early indicator because decreases in these levels usually occur in the second stage of impending anemia. Furthermore, iron deficiency is the only condition that causes a decrease in ferritin. Exercise, infections, and inflammations all cause a temporary increase. Persons with ferritin levels that are below 20 ug/dl are presumed to be iron deficient, and values below 10 ug/dl require immediate medical treatment. Normal serum ferritin levels range from 50 to 100 ug/dl (Rudd, 1990).

The possibility of swimmers' developing anemia is certainly sufficient to require preventive measures, the most common of which is iron supplementation. Iron supplements in the amount of 100 mg/day should suffice for most. This amount has been found to increase iron storage and endurance in athletes who were iron deficient (Lamanca & Haymes, 1989). Athletes on vegetarian diets get their iron from sources that do not provide as great absorption; consequently, they may need to supplement their diets with 300 mg of iron per day. Supplementing with more than five times the RDA may seem excessive, but it is probably a good precaution until we know more about the iron needs of athletes.

Athletes should know that it would be a mistake to depend on supplements to supply all of the iron they need because of the aforementioned low absorption rate from supplements. For this reason, their diets should also contain adequate amounts of meat, fish, or poultry. Good sources of dietary iron for vegetarians are green leafy vegetables, fruit, eggs, enriched breads, and cereals.

Vitamin C promotes iron storage, yet antacids, carbonates, phosphates, tannins, and oxalates do not; therefore, it is probably a good idea for athletes to supplement their diets with vitamin C and to reduce their intake of antacids, soft drinks, and tea.

Acetylsalicylic acid, a chemical that is found in many painkilling products like aspirin, promotes gastrointestinal bleeding and, consequently, iron loss. Athletes should be advised against using painkillers and anti-inflammatory drugs that contain this ingredient.

Some experts have denied the need for iron supplements by pointing to the fact that they have not improved performance in some studies (Newhouse, Clement, Taunton, & McKenzie, 1989; Schwarzkopf, McKenzie, Tatham, & Keller, 1986). Subjects in those studies may have been in only the first or second stage of deficiency, so their normal performance may not have deteriorated. There is no doubt that iron supplementation will improve the performance of late-stage anemic athletes. This has been shown time and time again in studies in which persons with severe iron deficiencies were identified, tested, and then retested after recovery (Lamanca & Haymes, 1989; Rowland, Deisroth, & Kelleher, 1987).

Although iron supplementation may improve performance in athletes who are competing in the final stages of anemia, it is not a "supersupplement" that will cause athletes to improve who are not anemic. Megadoses of iron are not recommended for this reason and because they may be potentially dangerous.

Anorexia and Bulimia The danger and extent of these conditions have only been recognized during the last 10 or 15 years. *Anorexia nervosa* is a condition in which caloric intake is reduced to starvation levels in order to lose weight. When this condition goes unchecked for a long time, anorexics can lose so much tissue and body fluid that death from heart failure becomes a real possibility.

Bulimia nervosa is a cyclic condition in which periods of severe caloric restriction are alternated with periods of binge eating. These binges are often followed by induced vomiting. Bulimic behaviors can cause internal injuries, particularly to the lining of the stomach. Bulimics are also prone to develop into full-blown anorexics, with the attendant dangers of excessive weight loss and heart failure.

Females are most likely to develop into anorexics during or immediately following puberty, when their fat weight increases markedly. This is a critical time when insensitive treatment can have a disastrous effect. Placing too much emphasis on becoming lean or reaching a particular body fat percentage may be just the push that brings latent tendencies for anorexic and bulimic behaviors to the surface. Remarks about changes in body proportions and about fears that training causes females to become too muscular may also provide the negative stimuli that can increase the severity of these conditions.

The desire of anorexics and bulimics to lose weight apparently results from a strong psychological need to exert some control over their lives, which, in turn, is caused by deep-seated and unresolved conflicts. Frequently, these persons are the superdedicated, "perfect" students or athletes who want to do everything right. Anorexic and bulimic behaviors are usually accompanied by feelings of guilt and depression that can be so debilitating as to require psychological counseling.

One of the paradoxes of these conditions is that anorexic athletes do not recognize how thin and weak they have become. Although their unusual weight loss may be quite noticeable to others, they see themselves as overweight and in need of fewer calories. Because of the gradual nature of the weight loss, the condition may go unnoticed by parents, coaches, and teammates who see the athlete daily. That is why it is so important to watch for early symptoms. The most common symptom is an obsession with weight and appearance that seems to dominate the athlete's conversation. Table 14-3 lists other anorexic symptoms such as excessive use of laxatives, diuretics, and diet pills.

Some experts believe that many potentially anorexic and bulimic personalities join teams in order to use heavy training as a form of weight control (Weight & Noakes, 1987; Yates, Leefkey, & Shisslak, 1983). There is no doubt that the incidences of these two behaviors are at least as prevalent among groups of female athletes as they are in the general female population.

Dummer and colleagues (1987) surveyed the eating patterns among 955 male and female competitive swimmers between the ages of 9 and 18 and reported that 15 percent of the girls and 4 percent of the boys admitted to at least one of the pathogenic behaviors associated with anorexia and bulimia. Some of the swimmers in the survey acknowledged having used such severe weight control measures as diet pills and self-induced vomiting as early as age 9. Eating disorders associated

Table 14-3. Methods Used by Teenage Swimmers Who Tried to Lose Weight (n = 399)

Method	Percentage of Girls Using Method (n = 268)	Percentage of Boys Using Method (n = 131)
Smaller meals	77.7	70.3
Skipping meals	62.9	45.5
Calorie counting	44.4	27.4
Special diets	29.4	17.3
Fasting	27.0	16.4
Sauna or steam baths	18.0	17.3
Drinking less	11.8	8.2
Vomiting	12.7	2.7
Diet pill use	10.7	6.8
Spitting	1.5	13.5
Laxative use	2.5	4.1
Diuretic use	1.5	2.8
Other	24.2	28.3

Source: Dummer et al., 1987.

with anorexia and bulimia were even more prevalent when the responses of only teenage girls were considered; in that population, 25 percent acknowledged pathogenic behaviors associated with eating disorders. The authors of this study suspected that the actual number of subjects of any age or sex with eating disorders may have been higher because of the natural reluctance to admit to eating disorders. Data from the study by Dummer and associates (1987) are shown in Table 14-3.

Another surprising aspect of this survey was that the subjects' reasons for wanting to lose weight generally had nothing to do with competitive swimming. By far the most common reason given by the respondents was a desire to improve their appearance. When asked what prompted them to want this change, they responded most often that they had received verbal or nonverbal messages that they were overweight from parents (54 percent), brothers and sisters (35 percent), or friends (29 percent). I'm happy to report that the number of coaches who contributed to this problem was very small; only 18 percent of the swimmers (n = 172) indicated that coaches were strict about their weight or had expressed some concern about it.

Many of the swimmers had misperceptions about their weight. Although 43 percent of the girls perceived themselves as overweight, only 13 percent could be considered overweight according to the body weights they listed.

This study by Dummer and associates (1987) demonstrates that the incidence of reported pathogenic eating disorders is sufficiently large for us to be concerned. Tendencies that at the very least could lead to reduced growth and at worst could result in early death appear to be affecting a sizable number of participants in our sport, particularly teenage females.

For their part, coaches would be wise to refrain from using weight charts, overemphasizing the importance of leanness to performance, and making sarcastic comments about weight gains. They should also be very careful in their handling of the information provided by tests of body composition. Body fat estimates of 15 to 20 percent can sound excessive to female teenagers, even though they are below average for the general population of females.

MASTERS SWIMMING

Aging is usually accompanied by an increase in body fat and by losses of aerobic capacity, muscle size, strength, power, speed, coordination, and flexibility. The rate of change is approximately 5 to 10 percent for each decade after age 20 or 30. That is the bad news. The good news is that training can slow the rate of decline. It is not certain to what extent training can reduce this decline. However, with increasing participation in Masters sports, including swimming, older athletes are providing an excellent group of subjects for studying the effects of continued high-level training on the aging process. The results thus far show that training can arrest the aging process to a considerable extent (Pollock et al., in press).

You need only attend a Masters meet to dispel many of the myths about the inevitable effects of aging on physical ability and appearance. With proper training, the rate of decline is imperceptible during middle age and slows considerably during the senior years. This says nothing of the emotional uplift participants receive from continuing to be physically active and competitive. Although many Masters swimmers begin training to improve their health, they continue because of the challenge of competition.

Effects of Aging on Physical Capacity

Table 14-4 (page 288) lists values by age group for some of the typical physiological decrements nonathletes experience with increasing age. These values can be compared with values for training groups that are discussed later in this chapter in the section that discusses the effects of training on the aging process.

Aerobic capacity declines by approximately 30 to 40 percent between the ages of 20 and 65 (Wilmore & Costill, 1988). This is due primarily to a decrease in the stroke volume and a reduction in the maximum heart rate. Both the size and number of muscle fibers decrease after ages 20 to 30, with the greatest loss occurring in the FT fiber group (Brooks & Fahey, 1984). The rate of loss in strength is approximately 5 percent per decade in men after age 40. That loss begins shortly after puberty for inactive women.

Most persons also gain 0.2 to 0.8 kg (0.5 to 2 lb) of body fat each year after ages 20 to 30 (McArdle, Katch, & Katch, 1981). Accordingly, a large number of men and women double or triple the amount of fat in their body by age 60. An inactive lifestyle also accelerates a loss of bone mineral content, particularly in postmenopausal women. Joints become less stable, and flexibility declines markedly, thus increasing the risk of fractures and joint injuries as people grow older.

There is a loss of active nerve cells and an approximate 10-percent loss in nerve conduction speed with age. This means that movement times and reaction times become slower.

Table 14-4. Effects of Aging on Physical Measures for Untrained Persons

	Age						
Function	*20*	*30*	*40*	*50*	*60*	*70*	*80*
Percentage of basal metabolic rate			−2	−5	−10	−15	−18
Percentage of VO_2max		−5	−15	−25	−30		
Heart rate (bpm)			180	170	160	150	140
Percentage of stroke volume			−10	−15	−25		
Percentage of cardiac output			−10	−15	−25	−30	
Blood pressure (mm Hg)	120				130		
Percentage of vital capacity		−2	−10	−15	−20	−30	−45
Body weight (kg)		+1	+4	+7	−2		
Percentage of body fat							
Men	15			20	28	30	
Women	25			30	40		
Peak blood lactate (mmol/l)	12			10.5	9		
Percentage of strength							
Men			−5	−10	−15		
Women		−5	−10	−15			

Cardiovascular Disease

Many of the decrements in physiological capacity mentioned above can increase the risk of developing several diseases. The most common is cardiovascular disease, which is the leading cause of death in the United States, beginning at age 30 for men and 40 for women. It accounts for nearly 50 percent of all deaths. One particular form of cardiovascular disease—coronary artery disease—accounts for nearly 30 percent of all deaths each year.

Coronary artery disease refers to the blockage of the vessels within the heart. It is caused by an increased deposit of fat (plaque) and scar tissue on the inner walls of arteries. This condition is known as *atherosclerosis* and causes a narrowing of the arteries and a reduction in the blood supply to affected tissues. The arteries most commonly affected are the small ones in the heart and in the brain. When they are partially blocked, blood flow may be slowed to the point of clotting, which also terminates the flow of blood to tissues and may cause a *thrombosis*. When arteries are severely but not completely blocked, persons may experience chest pain and shortness of breath during exercise (or even at rest). This is called *angina*.

The process of plaque formation begins before birth and continues throughout life, so people of all ages have some plaque accumulating in their arteries even though, in most cases, it is not severe enough to be labeled as heart disease. It is the rate of accumulation that determines the age at which a first heart attack may occur. That rate is apparently influenced most by heredity and next by a combination of so-called risk factors that include smoking, unusually large amounts of fat in the diet, excessive weight gain, *lack of physical activity,* and tension and anxiety. All of these risk factors are so interrelated that scientists have found it impossible to rank them according to the severity of danger that each one presents. For example, persons who do not exercise regularly are frequently overweight and sometimes in occupations that cause stress and anxiety.

Cholesterol is a form of fat that has recently received a lot of attention. It is found in great quantities in many diets around the world and is the principal fatty ingredient of plaque. Excessive cholesterol in the diet is believed to be a precipitating cause of atherosclerosis. Screening clinics have sprung up in shopping malls where people can have their blood cholesterol measured in 15 or 20 minutes. These tests are good for spotting unusually high levels of cholesterol that require more careful examination. They do not tell the whole story, however.

Cholesterol is carried in the blood in combination with two types of proteins—low-density lipoproteins (LDLs) and high-density lipoproteins (HDLs). HDLs are the "good" lipoproteins because they help cholesterol travel through the arteries without hardening and becoming attached to their inner walls. LDLs are the "bad" lipoproteins because they encourage cholesterol to harden and adhere to the interior of vessel walls, reducing the flow of blood through them. High-circulating levels of LDLs have been associated with progressive atherosclerosis in many studies.

Both types of lipoproteins are found in differing amounts in the blood of humans. Thus, it is possible for a person to have a normal total cholesterol count and be at high risk for coronary heart disease because of an abnormally high level of LDLs. Likewise, a person can have a somewhat elevated total cholesterol count but be at low risk of heart disease because the majority of fat is carried by HDLs. Inexpensive blood tests are becoming available that measure not only total cholesterol but also the HDL-C and LDL-C fractions, so, screening procedures will probably improve in the future. Until then, it is a good idea to have a more complete blood analysis if a screening shows that your total cholesterol level is even slightly elevated. You may get good news, or, then again, the risk may be greater than you supposed.

Reducing cholesterol in the diet is, of course, one of the major ways to reduce the risk of contracting coronary artery disease. Although the effects of exercise are still debated, it, too, seems to help by encouraging the metabolism of cholesterol so that less is circulating in the blood and by increasing the fraction of HDLs that reduce the deposit of cholesterol on artery walls.

Effects of Training on the Aging Process

One of the best studies on the effects of training and aging was conducted by Pollock and his associates (1987). They followed a group of Masters track athletes between the ages of 50 and 82 for ten years. During that period, 11 of the athletes continued to compete, maintaining a high level of training. Thirteen dropped out of competition but maintained a reduced level of training. The group that remained in competition kept their aerobic capacity at nearly the same level for the length of the study.

$\dot{V}O_2$max values were, on the average, 54.2 ml/kg/min at the beginning of this longitudinal study and 53.3 ml/kg/min ten years later. During that same time span, the $\dot{V}O_2$max values for the noncompetitors dropped from 52.5 to 45.9 ml/kg/min. This represented a 13-percent decline in ten years, which is very close to the rate expected from normal aging. It appears, then, that the effects of aging can be delayed for several decades if training volume and intensity are maintained. A small amount of training, although better than no training at all, will not delay these effects as greatly, however.

Another, cross-sectional study suggested that Masters athletes can maintain a considerable amount of aerobic capacity for several decades. Two groups of competitive runners were matched according to training and performance in a 10-km run. One group consisted of runners between the ages of 23 and 29, and the other group was made up of athletes between the ages of 53 and 63. The $\dot{V}O_2$max values for the older Masters runners were 90 percent above those of a group of age-matched, older nonathletes. However, the older Masters athletes' values were between 9 and 19 percent lower than those of the younger athletes, suggesting that some decline takes place with advancing age even if athletes continue to train extensively (Hagberg et al., 1985).

Training can reduce by at least 50 percent the normal muscle loss and presumed strength loss that accompany aging (Mitchell, Brynes, & Mazzeo, 1989). Changes in speed and reaction time appear to be specific to the sport for which a person is training. Masters athletes who continue to train in a particular sport seem to retain speed and reaction time in the skills of that activity (Suominen et al., 1980).

Effects of Training on Masters Swimmers

Contrary to popular belief, out-of-shape Masters athletes can make dramatic improvements with training, and their rates of improvement in strength and aerobic capacity can be similar to those of younger athletes. Hagberg and associates (1989) showed that a group of men and women between the ages of 70 and 79 responded to training in the same manner as younger athletes over 26 weeks of endurance and strength training. Members of both groups improved their oxygen consumption by an average of 22 percent and their strength between 9 and 18 percent. In another study, the rate of improvement of $\dot{V}O_2$max was similar for a group of younger adults between the ages of 24 and 28 and for a group of older adults ages 63 to 67 (Evans et al., 1987).

Several additional studies have shown that older persons can improve their muscular strength and muscle size at the same rate as younger persons. Subjects between the ages of 60 and 70 increased their strength between 33 and 48 percent on various tests in one study (Brown et al., 1988) and 102 and 172 percent in another (Frontera et al., 1987). Muscle size increased between 10 and 27 percent in both studies, and most of this increase took place in the FT muscle fibers, which are the fibers that atrophy and disappear in the greatest number during aging.

Effects of Aging on Swimming Performance

Performance in both sprint and middle-distance events (if you consider 200 m a middle-distance event) recedes at a rate of approximately 1 percent per year between the ages of 25 and 85, based on the records posted by athletes in the various age groups. This same rate of decline takes place in both men and women and amounts to an increase in time of approximately 2 seconds per 50 and 10 seconds per 200 during each decade. Figure 14-1 shows the changes of swimming velocity for each age and sex group for 50- and 200-m freestyles.

The data in Figure 14-1 represent average decrements in performance. It should be made clear, however, that many Masters swimmers continue to improve their performance during middle and old age; however, the extent of their improvement depends on their ability to improve stroking skill, training intensity, and/or racing ability.

Effects of Training on Longevity

For some of us, it is not enough to retard the aging process; we want to reverse it. Unfortunately, exercise is no fountain of youth. Barring accidents or disease, the age at which we will die is probably influenced more by heredity than any other factor. There is a strong possibility that regular training can reduce the number of early deaths due to accidents and disease, however.

Holloszy and his colleagues (1985) compared the life spans of rats that were active throughout their lives to those that were inactive. The number of rats who died early was greater in the inactive group. More of the active rats lived to old age. However, the active rats died at about the same time as the inactive rats who managed to live to old age. Thus, although regular training may not increase your life span beyond that of your parents and grandparents, it may reduce the possibility that you will die from some other cause at an earlier age.

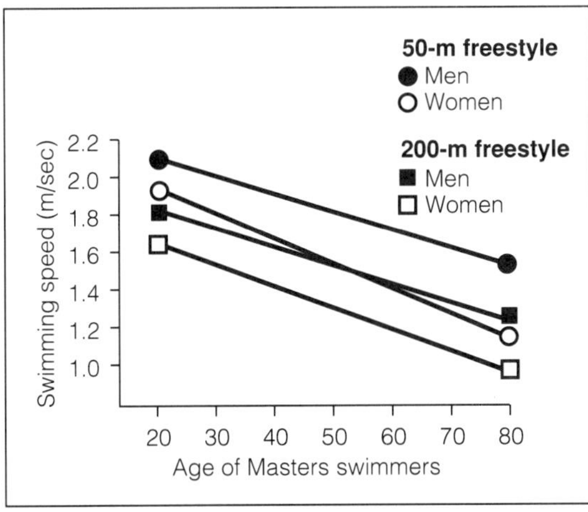

Figure 14-1. Effects of aging on swimming performance. (Wilmore & Costill, 1988)

Training Masters Swimmers

Volume and Intensity Masters swimmers do not need to be any more cautious in their training than younger swimmers, *unless they resume training after several years of inactivity*. Persons who are entering the sport after layoffs of two decades or more should have a thorough physical examination to determine the extent of atherosclerosis and osteoporosis and any other effects of inactivity that may require special precautions during training. Once cleared, Masters swimmers can train as long and as intensely as their time and motivation permit. They are no more susceptible to overexertion or injury than younger athletes, provided they are given time to adjust to the training load.

Masters swimmers can, if they wish, train up to the same optimal mileage range and intensities discussed in Chapter 6. However, they can probably get by on less training, because their competitors, with equally busy schedules, are also swimming fewer meters per day. Two hours of training per day are recommended for producing good results on a busy schedule, although one hour per day is certainly sufficient to compete at a high level.

The daily mileage needed for optimal training decreases as Masters swimmers move into the later age groups, because they will be swimming slower in training. Consequently, they can achieve the same training effects with less mileage. If they continue to swim for the same number of minutes per set, the training effects should be similar even though the repeat sets are shorter. That same statement applies to swimmers of all ages.

Workout Construction and Monitoring All of the various levels of sprint and endurance training should be used in the approximate proportions suggested for senior swimmers in earlier chapters. There is a possibility that Masters swimmers may need more endurance training, however. Losses of muscle tissue and slower times for certain events will cause them to rely more on aerobic metabolism for energy.

Stroke drills, kicking, and pulling should be included in the training programs of Masters swimmers. They can benefit similarly from these as can younger competitors.

The repeats used for training Masters swimmers can be the same as those used for every other age group. The send-off times should be adjusted to the age and ability of the swimmers so that they provide rest intervals of 5 to 30 seconds on most repeats and 30 seconds to 1 minute on longer or more intense endurance sets. Longer rest periods of 3 to 7 minutes should be used in some sprint sets.

The anaerobic threshold concept of training is equally applicable to Masters swimmers as to younger groups. Their anaerobic thresholds occur at the same relative efforts as those of younger swimmers. Any of the procedures for prescribing training speeds and for monitoring training that were described in Chapter 8 can also be used with Masters swimmers.

The previous statement, however, should be qualified where heart rate is concerned. Training speeds may have to be adjusted downward somewhat in the upper age groups. As indicated previously, the maximum heart rate tends to decline by 10 bpm during each decade after age 30. Masters swimmers may need to adjust the range for threshold endurance swimming by about 10 beats per decade. By age 50 it is between 130 and 150 bpm for most swimmers.

Masters swimmers who are in their 40s and 50s have a range of maximum heart rates between 160 and 200 bpm, depending on the rate of decline. This range becomes considerably larger after age 60. Peak rates as high as 200 bpm and as low as 105 bpm have been reported in the literature (Brooks & Fahey, 1984). Although several previous years of regular training should reduce this variability, it is probably necessary to base training heart rates on individual maximums rather than on averages when swimmers reach this age.

Sprint training should be included in the programs for Masters competitors. Once again, the proportions should be similar to those recommended for younger swimmers. The types of repeat sets should also be the same. Short sprints that are designed to improve stroking power should not be neglected; they are very important to Masters athletes for maintaining their power, skill, and speed near previous levels. Endurance swimming is not intense enough to maintain these qualities.

It is a good idea for Masters swimmers to include dryland resistance training for the same reasons. It may be more important for them than for any other group of swimmers. Resistance training retards the normal decrease in size and number of muscle fibers, particularly FT muscle fibers. Executing at least a portion of their resistance training at fast speeds may also help Masters swimmers maintain nerve conduction speed.

Although swimming probably maintains flexibility, a supplemental program can provide an additional safeguard against possible reductions and a vehicle for regaining any range of motion that might have been lost during inactive periods. The flexibility of Masters swimmers can improve dramatically in a short time. Munn (1981) reported increases of 8 percent in the shoulders and 48 percent in the ankles after only 12 weeks of supplemental flexibility training.

Part II

STROKE MECHANICS

Competitive swimming is a unique sport. Athletes compete while suspended in a fluid medium, and they must propel their body by pushing against a liquid rather than a solid substance. Water offers less resistance to swimmers' propulsive efforts than the ground that runners push against, yet water offers considerably greater resistance to the forward progress of swimmers. For these reasons, and others, the usual applications of the laws of motion do not always apply. This has made it difficult to determine how swimmers apply certain physical laws to propel their body through the water more efficiently. How they generate propulsion and reduce resistance is the focus of Part II.

Chapter 15 discusses ways that swimmers can reduce their resistance to forward motion. The scientific term for water resistance is *drag,* and Chapter 15 describes the various types of drag that swimmers must deal with.

Gaining an understanding of swimming propulsion has been a lengthy process that is far from completed. Experts have advanced many theories through the years, and each new hypothesis increases our knowledge of the mechanisms involved. Chapter 16 summarizes the history of propulsive theory and discusses the elements of propulsion, such as limb direction, angle of attack, and limb velocity. Chapter 17 concerns the application of these elements of propulsion and describes several additional physical principles that are common to all strokes. Hopefully, these two chapters will provide readers with the knowledge to analyze stroke mechanics from the standpoint of their propulsive characteristics and to correct swimmers' strokes without affecting their individuality.

Each of the competitive strokes is described in Chapters 18 through 21: the *front crawl stroke* (most commonly referred to as the *freestyle*) is the topic of Chapter 18; the *butterfly,* Chapter 19; the *back crawl,* or *backstroke,* Chapter 20; and the *breaststroke,* Chapter 21. Starts and turns are described in Chapter 22, the final chapter of Part II.

RELATIVE MOTION

When swimmers move through water, they exert forces against the water that set it in motion. Some of these forces propel the body forward, and others hold it back. Although swimmers move forward through the water, the effect of these forces are usually described as though swimmers were motionless and the water were moving past their body. This method of describing the movement of water is referred to as *relative motion*.

The concept of relative motion has been used extensively in descriptions of swimming because it makes it easier to understand the forces being exerted by the swimmer against the water as well as those that are being exerted by the water against the swimmer. It is an accurate way to describe the forces that are operating, because the difference in speed between the body and the water is the same whether swimmers are moving forward or the water is moving backward. Therefore, the same laws of motion apply because the movement of the swimmers and the movement of the water are relative to one another. Scientists have made many important breakthroughs in the study of aerodynamics and hydrodynamics by suspending scale models of objects in wind tunnels or water channels and forcing air or water past them. This was, in fact, the method used by the Wright brothers to study the potential of wing shapes for flight.

CHAPTER 15

Resistance

Coaches and swimmers tend to focus most of their attention on stroke mechanics yet neglect the resistive forces that hold them back. This is unfortunate because swimmers can improve performance considerably by reducing water resistance.

Water has a very profound retarding effect on objects moving through it. It is 1,000 times more dense than air, so when the body pushes forward against the water, the water pushes back against the body. The term for the resistance of water to a swimmer's movements is *drag*. *Drag forces always act opposite to the direction a swimmer moves*. When a swimmer moves forward, the relative motion of water will be backward, resisting the swimmer's movement through it.

The importance of reducing drag can be conveyed by the following example. Suppose a swimmer applied an average of approximately 15 kg (33 lb) of propulsive force with each armstroke as she swam down the pool. Suppose also that her body encountered an average of approximately 10 kg (22 lb) of resistive drag. Her net propulsive force per armstroke would be 5 kg (11 lb). She would need to increase this net propulsive force to swim faster. This could be accomplished by increasing propulsive force or by reducing resistive drag. The sample calculations in the following box illustrate these effects. They show that a swimmer can achieve the same increase of net propulsion by increasing propulsive force 2 kg, by reducing resistive drag by 2 kg, or by using some combination of the two.

Increases of propulsive force require improved mechanics and training to increase stroking power. This process can take several weeks. Drag can be reduced in a few minutes by orienting the body differently. An understanding of the ways in which drag can be reduced first requires a knowledge of the characteristics of water flow.

Effects of Increasing Propulsive Force and Reducing Drag on Net Propulsion

Propulsive force (PF) = 15 kg
Resistive drag (RD) = 10 kg
Net propulsion = 5 kg

Net propulsion can be increased by:

1. Increasing propulsive force

   17 kg PF − 10 kg RD = 7 kg NP

2. Reducing resistive drag

   15 kg PF − 8 kg RD = 7 kg NP

3. Some combination of the two

   16 kg PF − 9 kg RD = 7 kg NP

CHARACTERISTICS OF WATER FLOW

Laminar and Turbulent Flow

Water consists of hydrogen and oxygen molecules that tend to flow in smooth, unbroken streams until they encounter some solid object that interrupts their movement. These streams are packed one on top of the other, thus the term *laminar flow*. The water is said to become *turbulent* when this smooth flow is interrupted. The water molecules break away from their laminar streams, rebounding from one another in random directions. Water molecules that have become turbulent will intrude on other laminar streams, causing an ever-widening pattern of turbulence that is visible as white water at the surface.

Laminar flow has the least resistance associated with its movement because all the water molecules are traveling in the same direction at a uniform speed. Turbulent flow, on the other hand, creates much greater resistance to movement because of the pressure increase due to the wildly whirling water molecules.

Figure 15-1 illustrates laminar and turbulent flow. Laminar streams are represented by the straight lines, and turbulence is depicted by the swirling lines. As the swimmer moves forward, he opens a "hole" in the water for his body to pass through. Thus, when the swimmer's body pushes against oncoming laminar streams of water molecules, those streams become turbulent. The water molecules rebound wildly in all directions—some backward, others upward or downward, and some are carried along with the swimmer for a short time due to friction

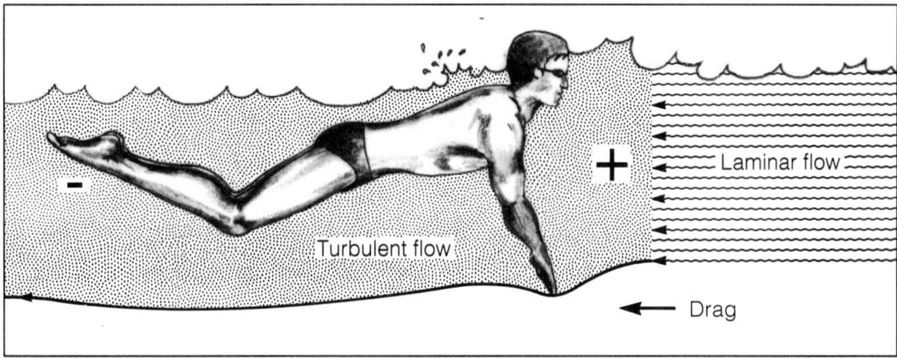

Figure 15-1. Turbulence caused by a swimmer's body moving into laminar streams.

between the water and his body. The turbulence continues until the swimmer's body has passed through a particular section of water. After that, the water will fill in behind him, and laminar flow will be reestablished.

The swirling water in front and to the sides of a swimmer will increase the pressure in those areas relative to the pressure behind his body, where the flow has not yet filled in. (This is indicated in Figure 15-1 by the + sign for high pressure in front of the swimmer and the − sign signifying lower pressure behind him.) This pressure differential will slow the swimmer's forward speed.

The drag encountered by a swimmer is directly proportional to the amount of turbulence he creates. Water will be mildly turbulent when only a few laminar streams have been disturbed. The pressure differential and, thus, the retarding effect, will be considerably greater when there is a large amount of turbulence.

Eddy Currents

As mentioned, the holes that swimmers open do not fill in immediately once the swimmers have passed through them. What remains is an area similar to a partial vacuum, where only a small number of water molecules are swirling wildly. The whirling molecules in this area are called *eddy currents*. They are illustrated by the swirling water behind the swimmer's legs in Figure 15-1. Because of the small number of molecules present in this area behind the swimmer, the pressure of the water is low even though the water is turbulent. The combination of increased pressure in front and reduced pressure behind the swimmer augments the pressure differential from front to back, causing a further retardation of forward speed. In effect, the swimmer is pushed back by the high pressure area in front of him and pulled back by the low pressure area behind him.

The area of eddy currents will be larger and will require longer to fill in if the pattern of turbulence is great; consequently, the retarding effect on the swimmer's forward speed will be greater. Conversely, the retarding effect will be less if the pattern of turbulence is less, because the area where eddy currents are present will be smaller and will be able to fill in more rapidly.

When a swimmer "drags" off another in training or competition, she follows closely behind a leading swimmer and strokes in the "pocket" of whirling eddy currents of the leader. The pressure immediately in front of the trailing swimmer is higher than the pressure in the pocket behind the leading swimmer, creating a suction effect that pulls the trailing swimmer along. Thus, the trailing swimmer is able to maintain her speed with less effort.

Swimmers can save energy by dragging behind teammates in the same lane during a practice session. They can also reduce their energy cost by moving to the side of the lane, where they can drag off a competitor in an adjacent lane.

CHARACTERISTICS OF SWIMMERS THAT AFFECT DRAG

Three of the most important factors responsible for the turbulence that swimmers create are (1) the shape that swimmers present to the water, (2) the orientation of their body in the water, and (3) their speed of movement.

Effects of the Shape and Orientation of the Swimmer's Body

Regarding shape, tapered objects encounter less resistance than objects with squared corners and convoluted shapes. Figure 15-2 illustrates this effect. Both objects have exactly the same surface area, but one is tapered at both ends and the other is rectangular. The object in Figure 15-2*a* has less drag. The tapered front allows the direction of water molecules to change very gradually as the object passes through them. Consequently, these molecules disturb only a small number of adjacent streams and the pattern of turbulence is kept to a minimum. The tapered rear allows the water molecules to fill in almost immediately after the object passes through, so the small area of eddy currents in back will dissipate rapidly.

The shape of the object in Figure 15-2*b* will create considerably more drag because its front presents a flat surface to the wall of water, causing the object to encounter several streams of molecules at one time. Because the surface is flat, the molecules cannot continue to move forward around the object, so they rebound back from the front surface, where they collide with molecules from other streams. This creates a wide pattern of turbulence that increases pressure in front of the object and retards its forward movement.

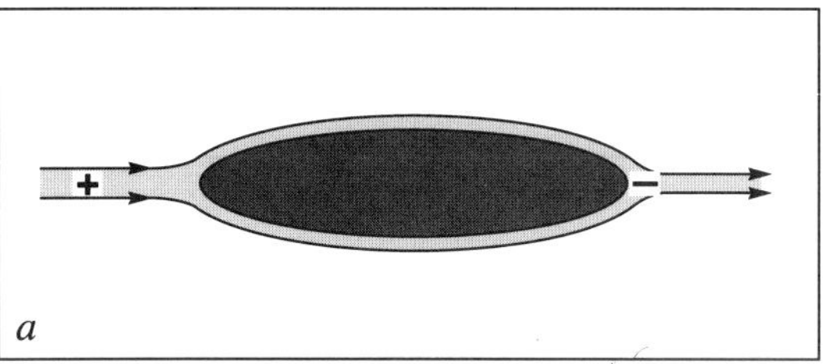

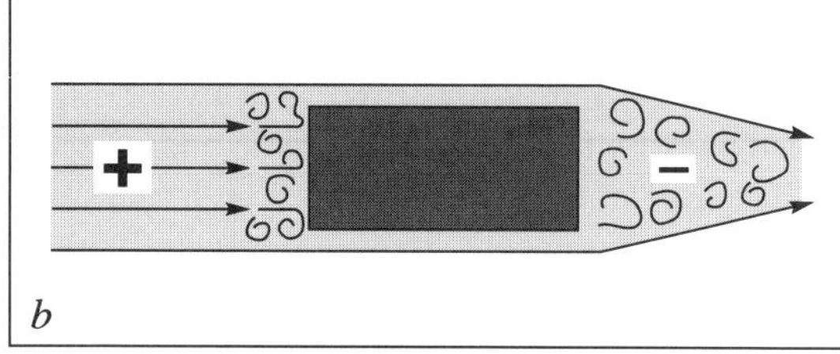

Figure 15-2. The effect of shape on drag.

The squared rear of the box keeps the streams of molecules separated for a longer time after it passes through. This increases the low-pressure area of eddy currents behind, which, in turn, increases the pressure differential between the front and rear of the object so that its forward movement will be retarded even more.

It should be obvious from the illustrations in Figure 15-2 that the ideal form for reducing drag is bullet-shaped (or fish-shaped). Boats, cars, airplanes, and other objects that travel through air and water have become increasingly tapered over the years in an effort to simulate that form because it presents the least amount of resistance against air and water. Unfortunately, compared to a fish, the human body is larger and has flatter surfaces. Furthermore, swimmers cannot remain in a static, bullet-shaped position as they move through the water. They change positions constantly, presenting a variety of different shapes to the oncoming water flow. Nevertheless, the fastest swimmers maintain the most streamlined positions as they assume these various shapes; slower swimmers do not.

Regarding the body's orientation to the water, drag is usually increased when swimmers are less than horizontal with the surface and when they wiggle from side to side. This is because they take up more space than necessary, causing them to interrupt a greater number of molecular streams.

The space that swimmers occupy in the water has both horizontal and lateral components. The horizontal component concerns the depth of their body. The lateral component refers to the space that they occupy from side to side.

The swimmer in Figure 15-3*a* takes up less space than the swimmer in Figure 15-3*b* because his entire body remains nearly horizontal with the surface. That swimmer moves through a much smaller column of water than the one in Figure 15-3*b*, whose body inclines down from front to rear. The latter swimmer attempts to carry his head and shoulders high in a hydroplaning position, causing him to

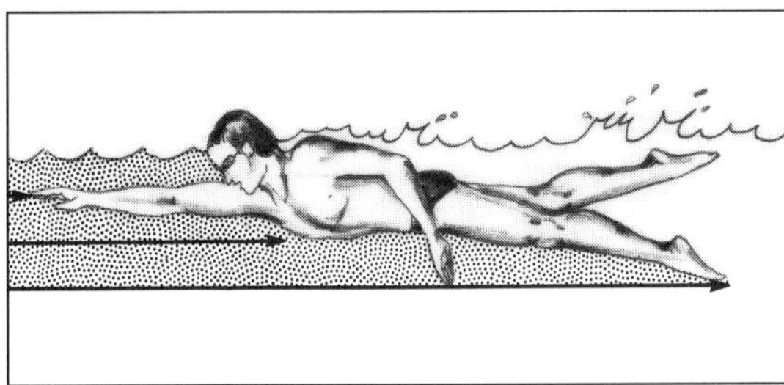

a

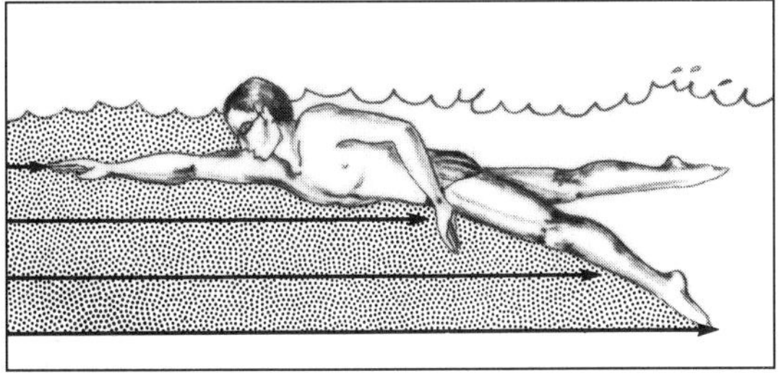

b

Figure 15-3. The effect of the space swimmers take up in the water on drag.

kick deeper and, in turn, increasing the inclination of his body so that more streams of water molecules are interrupted. He also encounters more drag simply because he must push his body forward against more water. With few exceptions, *swimmers should try to remain as horizontal as possible when they move through the water*.

The need to create large propulsive forces does not permit athletes to stay perfectly horizontal as they swim down the pool, however. Their body positions constantly change throughout each stroke cycle. Freestyle and backstroke swimmers must roll their body from side to side to gain propulsive force, and breaststroke and butterfly swimmers need to move their body up and down in an undulating manner for the same reason. Although these movements increase drag, they increase propulsion even more. In order to swim fast, athletes must balance the need to stay horizontal with the need to apply propulsive force. It is possible for them to go overboard in either direction. Swimmers can move their body around too much in their desire to apply propulsion and, thus, increase drag relatively more than they increase propulsion. By the same token, attempting to remain too horizontal can reduce propulsion relatively more than it reduces drag. Suggestions for striking the proper balance between these two aspects of swimming propulsion are provided in the chapters on each competitive stroke (Chapters 18 through 21).

Effect of Speed

When swimmers increase their speed, they create more friction and turbulence and, thus, increase their drag. The effect of speed is so potent that doubling forward velocity will quadruple drag.

The effect of speed may seem academic, because it would be foolish for an athlete to swim slow and lose races simply to reduce drag; however, this effect demonstrates the wisdom of pacing. An athlete who swims the first half of a race at a slower speed than an opponent should expend less effort to overcome drag. If the swimmers are nearly equal in ability, the one who paces the early part of the race should be able to win by finishing faster than the more fatigued competitor.

TYPES OF DRAG

Swimmers must contend with three categories of drag. They are *form drag, wave drag,* and *frictional drag*. The following box summarizes these types of drag and their causes.

Three Categories of Drag and Their Causes

Form drag—Caused by the size and shape of swimmers' bodies as they move forward through the water

Wave drag—Caused by the waves that swimmers make

Frictional drag—Caused by friction between the swimmers' skin and water molecules that come in contact with it

Form Drag

This type of drag is a product of the "form" that a swimmer's body takes as it moves forward through the water. It would be more correct to say "forms" because, as mentioned earlier, the shapes that the body presents to the water change constantly throughout each stroke cycle.

Observations of world-class swimmers suggest that there are certain body types that create less form drag. Swimmers with wide shoulders and tapered hips and thighs should have an advantage in this regard. However, swimmers with other body types should not despair; they can reduce form drag by controlling the orientation of their body to the water. Clarys (1979) found no relationship between body shape and drag measured during actual swimming.

Horizontal Alignment Reducing form drag is a matter of remaining as horizontal as possible without reducing propulsive force and, insomuch as possible, orienting the body so that all contours taper gradually from front to back. Swimmers should strike a compromise by kicking deep enough to propel their body forward but not so deep as to unnecessarily increase the area they take up. In butterfly and breaststroke, swimmers must strike a compromise between excessive undulation and moving their body up and down enough to stroke and breathe properly.

Figure 15-4 (p. 304) contrasts good and poor horizontal alignment for three of the four competitive strokes (the front crawl stroke was illustrated in Figure 15-3).

Drag is also increased when swimmers kick too deep and pedal their legs. Figures 15-5*a* and 15-5*b* (p. 305) show a butterfly swimmer and a breaststroke swimmer who are kicking too deep. In Figure 15-5*c*, a backstroke swimmer is pedaling, or pushing forward against the water with his thighs, during the upbeat. These rapid, alternating, pushing motions of his legs will have a devastating effect on his forward speed.

Lateral Alignment Excessive lateral motions of the body will push forward and sideways against the water and increase drag. Lateral alignment can only be disrupted in the front and back crawl strokes, where the alternating movements of the arms and legs have the potential to move the body through the water in a wiggling, snakelike manner. Figure 15-6 (p. 306) shows top views of front crawl swimmers with good and poor lateral alignment. The swimmer in Figure 15-6*a* is streamlined, and the swimmer in Figure 15-6*b* is wiggling excessively from side to side. These side-to-side movements cause the swimmer in Figure 15-6*b* to take up much more space in the water than the other. Additionally, the side-to-side movements of her body cause her to push water forward. Both actions increase drag dramatically.

Figure 15-7 (p. 306) illustrates underneath views of two backstroke swimmers with good and poor lateral alignment. The backstroke swimmer in Figure 15-7*b* has poor lateral alignment because he enters his hand across his head toward the opposite shoulder. This causes his body to swing from side to side, increasing turbulence and drag. The swimmer in Figure 15-7*a*, with good lateral alignment, keeps her body aligned by rolling from side to side.

Rolling Early research in which swimmers were towed through the water flat on their stomachs and sides indicated that flat positions created less form drag (Coun-

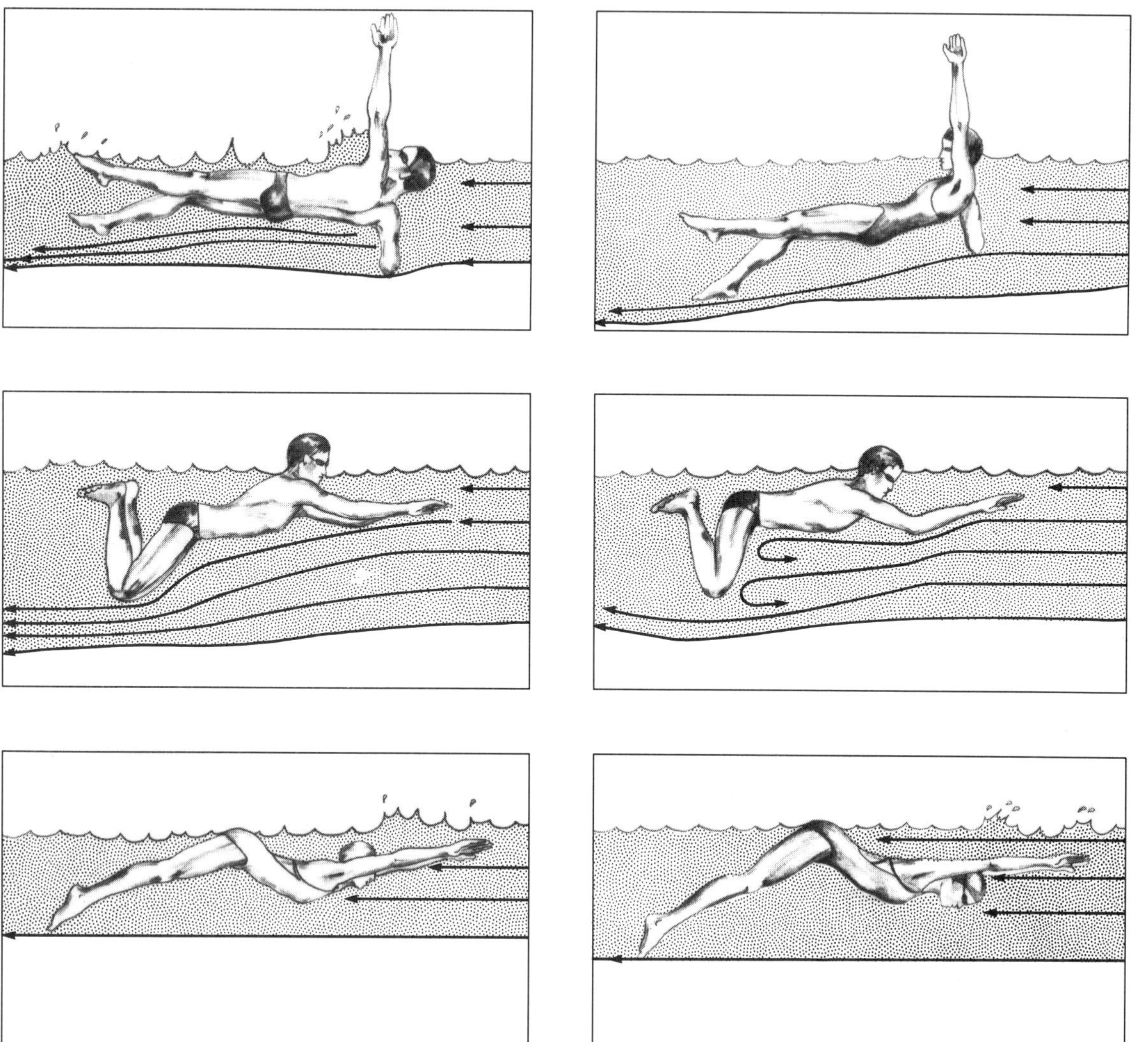

Figure 15-4. A comparison of good and poor body positions in three of the four competitive strokes. The swimmers on the left illustrate good alignment; the swimmers on the right, poor alignment.

silman, 1955). This caused many swimmers and coaches to reason that athletes should keep their body as flat as possible while swimming the front and back crawl strokes. However, nothing could be further from the truth. Swimmers in the front and back crawl strokes really don't have a choice between rolling and swimming flat. Their choice is to roll or to wiggle, because in both strokes one arm is always traveling down through the water while the other is traveling up. Because a swimmer's body is suspended in the water, it is naturally pulled from side to side by these

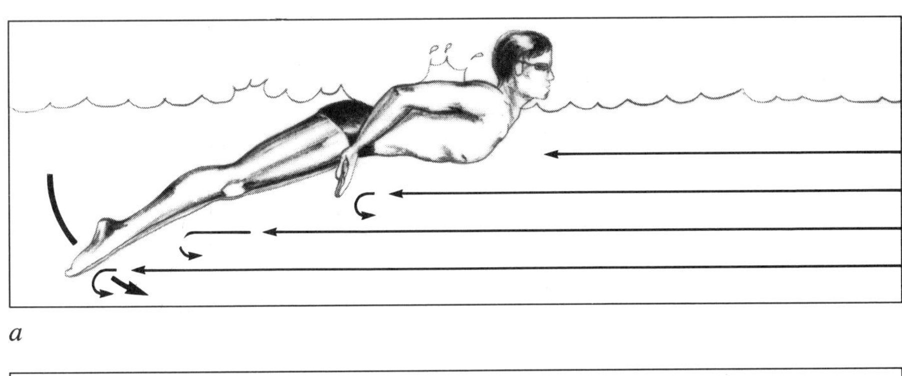

a

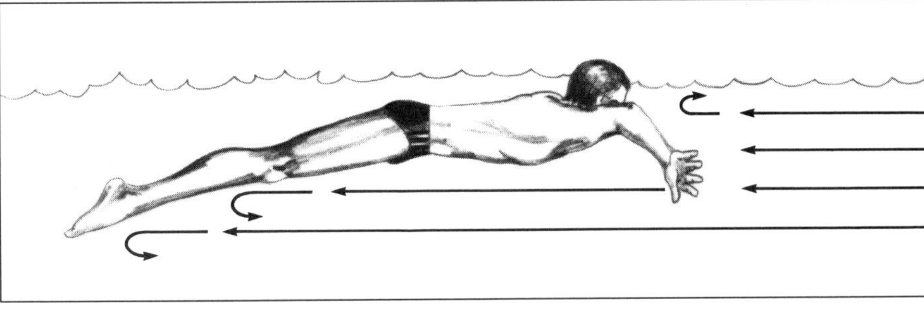

b

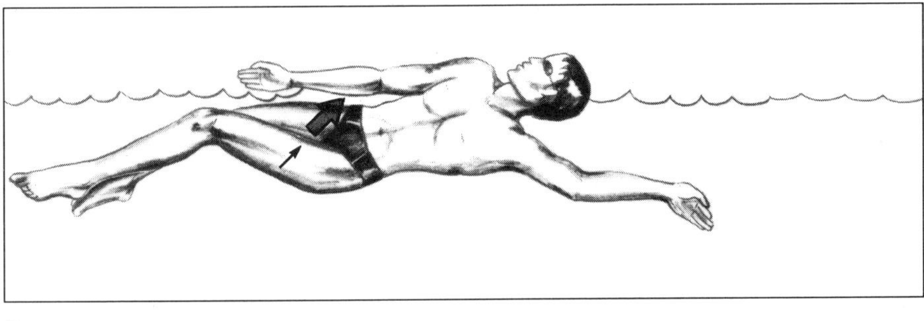

c

Figure 15-5. The effect of kicking motions on form drag.

vertical movements of the arms. Any attempt to remain flat would interfere with this natural rotation, causing the suspended body to move in lateral directions.

Figure 15-8 (p. 307) shows swimmers at the point of maximum roll in their respective strokes. As you can see, their bodies are rotated nearly 45 degrees from the horizontal. They will roll an equal amount to the other side during their next armstrokes.

Rolling aids swimming speed in a number of ways that are outlined in the box on page 307.

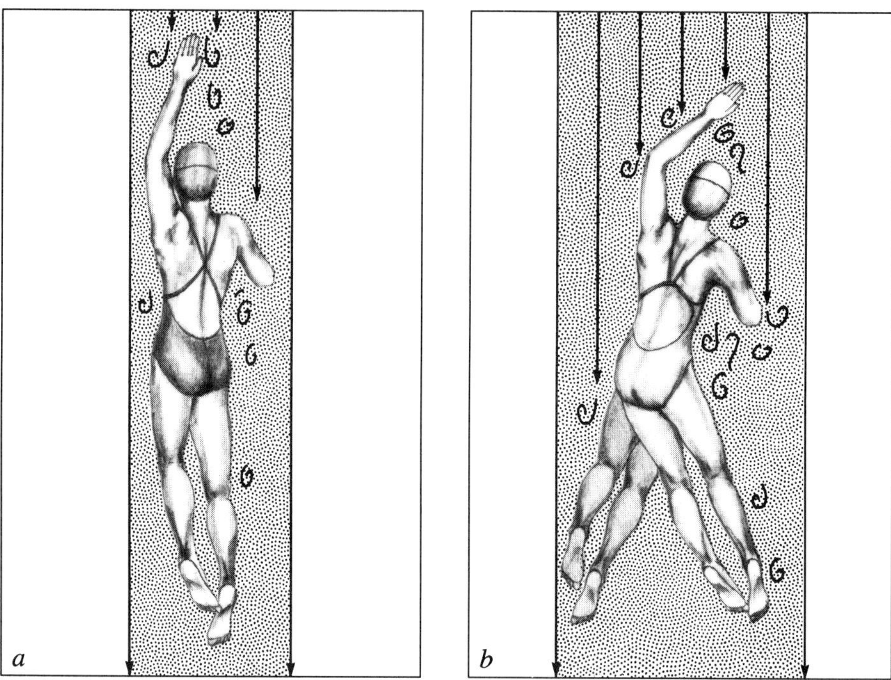

Figure 15-6. The effect of excessive side-to-side body movements on drag in the front crawl stroke.

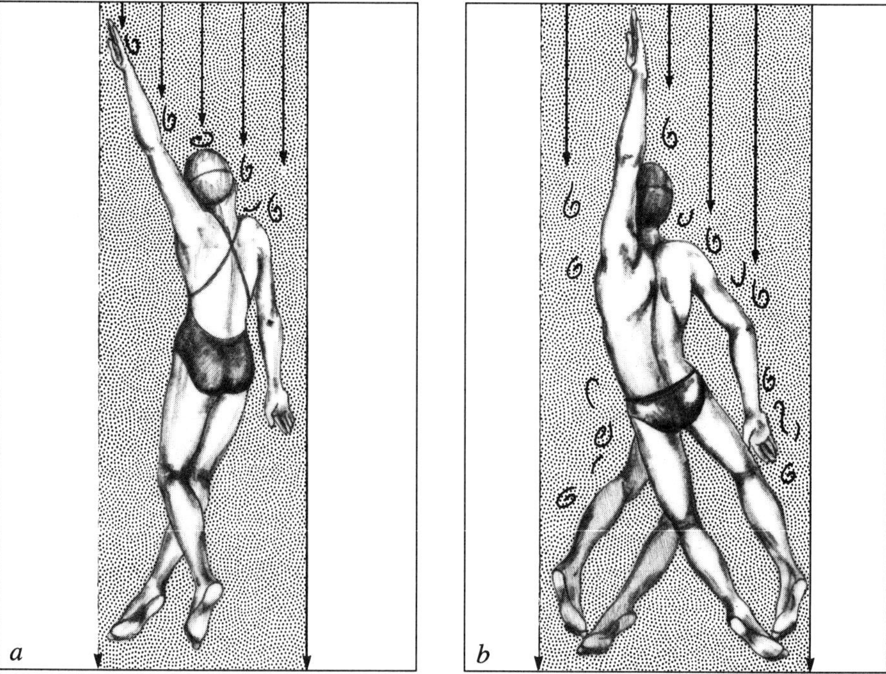

Figure 15-7. The effect of excessive side-to-side body movements on drag in the back crawl stroke.

a

b

Figure 15-8. A front crawl swimmer (*a*) and a back crawl swimmer (*b*) at the point of maximum roll during their respective stroke cycles.

How Rolling Can Increase Swimming Speed

1. By placing the arms in better position to deliver propulsive force
2. By allowing diagonal kicking, which helps stabilize the trunk during alternating arm movements
3. By minimizing lateral movements of the trunk and excessive lateral movements of the legs

Wave Drag

This form of drag is caused by turbulence at the surface of the water. We are all aware that some pools have more waves than others because of poor construction and/or inadequate lane lines. Athletes' performances are usually worse when they compete in these "slow" pools. Waves of this origin are beyond the control of competitors, so they should be negligible to the outcome (but not the time) of the race because they affect all swimmers equally. Swimmers do have some control over the waves they produce with their own movements through the water, however.

The most common form of wave drag is created by bow waves, which press back against swimmers' bodies and slow their forward speed. Bow waves can be created by the head and trunk as they move forward, to the side, or up and down. Figure 15-9 (p. 308) shows a bow wave building up in front of a backstroke swimmer.

Swimming speed has a potent effect on wave drag, just as it did on form drag. Bow waves swell with increases in swimming speed because of the wall of water rising in front of the swimmer. These waves exert such a powerful restraining effect that drag increases by a factor of eight when swimming speed doubles (Northrip, Logan, & McKinney 1974).

Figure 15-9. This backstroke swimmer is shown with a bow wave in front of him.

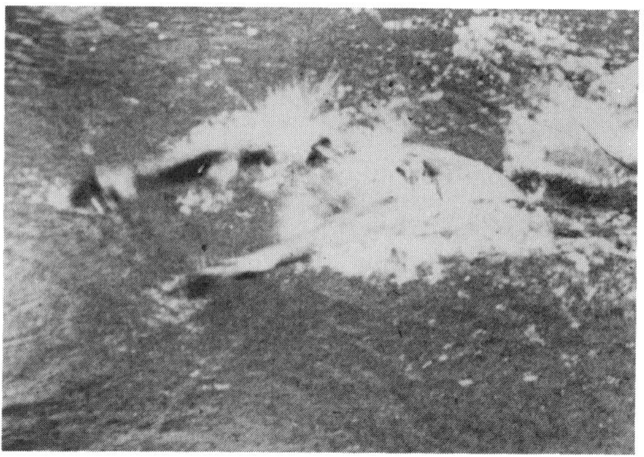

Figure 15-10. A butterfly swimmer creating wave drag with her recovery movements.

Wave drag also increases when swimmers push their limbs or body forward or to the side against the water. When swimmers drag their arms across the surface or smash them into the water, they push waves of turbulent water forward that finally swell and push back against them. The retarding force is even greater when swimmers recover their limbs forward underwater because of the increased surface area presented to the water. Even diagonal underwater sculling movements, which should be propulsive, can retard forward speed if they displace water in some direction other than back.

Figure 15-10 shows one way that recovery movements can increase drag. The butterfly swimmer is dragging her arms through the water on the recovery. A swimmer who pushes her arms forward through the water in this manner will have her speed reduced by 30 percent within 1/16 second. This reduction of forward speed, when multiplied by several strokes over the length of a race, can have a devastating effect on performance.

Backstroke and freestyle swimmers frequently create wave drag when they push the back of their hand forward during their entry into the water. It is far better for the hand to enter on its side. This reduces the frontal surface area presented to the water.

Frictional Drag

As swimmers move forward, friction between their skin and the water causes some of the molecules to be carried along with them. Once they begin moving, the friction between these molecules and those in the adjacent laminar stream pull that layer along with the swimmers as well. This pattern continues layer by layer until, at some distance from the body, the amount of friction is not sufficient to cause any binding effect.

The laminar streams that are carried along with swimmers are referred to as the *boundary layer,* which can increase turbulence in the following manner. The backward flow of the water molecules in the boundary layer reverses when friction causes them to be carried along with the body. Accordingly, these molecules collide with others in front, which, in turn, rebound into the paths of adjacent laminar streams and cause a widening path of turbulence. The boundary layer is said to have separated when turbulence occurs. Because of the turbulence created, drag increases considerably in areas where the boundary layer has separated.

Figures 15-11*a* and 15-11*b* show the way boundary layers react to frictional forces. Figure 15-11*a* shows the actual movement of fluid past a sphere that has been immersed. Notice the area of turbulence at the right side. This is where the boundary layer has separated. Figure 15-11*b* depicts the way this separation occurs. The surface of the spheroid in the drawing creates friction, which causes a boundary layer of fluid to reverse directions and travel with it. The water molecules in that boundary layer collide with others immediately in front and to the sides, creating a

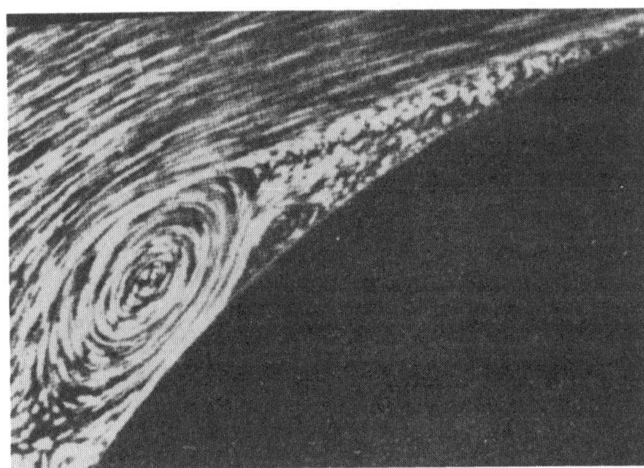

a

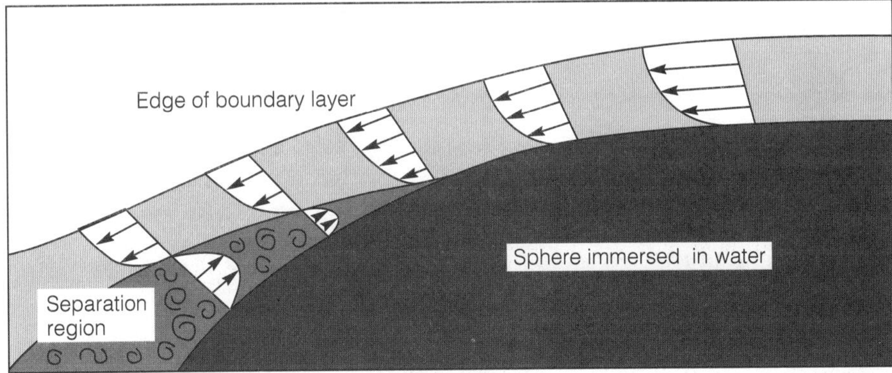

b

Figure 15-11. The effect of frictional drag on the boundary layer. Figure 15-11*a* shows the actual movement of fluids around an immersed sphere. Figure 15-11*b* depicts the reason for the increasing turbulence of that fluid.

pattern of turbulence that finally causes the boundary layer to separate from the surface of the sphere at some distant point.

Some experts have stated that frictional drag is negligible on a swimmer's body, because humans are so poorly streamlined (as compared to aquatic mammals) that wave drag and form drag cause the boundary layer to separate almost immediately when water starts moving around the body (Clarys, 1979). However, Hay and Thayer (1989) conducted a study that disputes this opinion. They were able to study the pattern of water flow around the body by attaching one end of small plastic strips (tufts) to swimmers. When the swimmers were filmed, the waving motion of the tufts demonstrated the direction in which the water in the boundary layer was moving. These researchers concluded that a boundary layer did exist on some areas of the body as the swimmer moved forward through the water. Figure 15-12 shows a butterfly swimmer with tufts. The tufts that are flowing back on the swimmer's trunk and those that are flowing opposite the downward direction her legs are moving indicate laminar flow. Those that are not flowing opposite the direction the swimmer's trunk and limbs are moving are turbulent.

The principal factors that influence the amount of frictional drag exerted on objects are (1) the surface area of the object, (2) the velocity of the object, and (3) the roughness of its surface. Swimmers have no control over surface area. Likewise, speed can only be controlled to the extent that swimmers can pace the early portions of a race. That leaves surface smoothness as the only source of frictional drag that can be controlled most easily.

Obviously, smooth surfaces cause less friction than rough surfaces. This may explain why swimmers almost universally improve their performance when they

Figure 15-12. A swimmer wearing tufts. (Reproduced from Hay & Thayer, 1989)

wear low-friction swim suits and when they shave down before important contests. However, not everyone agrees that these improvements cause reductions in frictional drag. Some feel that shaving down and wearing skin suits have become "big meet" rituals that coincide with good performances but don't cause them. Another popular theory is that shaving down improves kinesthetic sensitivity so that swimmers are able to stroke more efficiently.

Sharp and Costill (1989) have presented evidence suggesting that shaving down does reduce frictional drag. They tested a group of swimmers with identically paced submaximum swims before and after shaving. There were nine days intervening between test periods. When shaved, the swimmers completed their paced swims with significantly lower blood lactate values and greater stroke lengths, indicating that they used less effort to complete the swims after shaving down. The average blood lactate values for the group were 8.48 mmol/l before and 6.74 mmol/l after shaving. The average stroke length increased from 2.07 m per stroke cycle before shaving to 2.31 m per stroke cycle afterward. The control group did not improve on either measure.

Both the experimental and control groups of swimmers were also given a tethered swim test in which the energy cost was assessed by measuring oxygen consumption during several incremental stages of work. This test was used to study the possible kinesthetic effects of shaving down on performance. Frictional drag should be negligible during tethered swims because swimmers do not move through the water. Consequently, if the swimmers improved their performances on the tethered swim after shaving down it would most likely be due to improved kinesthetic feel.

The experimental swimmers did not reduce their energy cost for the tethered swimming tests after shaving down, which would seem to rule out better kinesthetic feel as a reason for their reduced efforts on the paced swims they had performed earlier. Thus, a reduction of frictional drag seemed the logical cause for the lower blood lactate concentrations and the increase in the average distance traveled during each stroke cycle after shaving down.

As part of this study, Sharp and Costill (1989) also measured the rate of deceleration following a push-off before and after shaving down. They used a special device called a velocity meter for this purpose, which is shown in Figure 15-13*a* (p. 312). The velocity meter is used to measure linear velocity during free swimming. It consists of a harness of fine steel wire that is pulled over a generator as swimmers travel down the pool. The voltage output from the generator wheel is fed through a voltage divider in an analog-digital converter, which measures linear velocities in meters per second.

In this study, the swimmers pushed off the wall while wearing the harness, and they glided out until their velocities fell below 1 m/sec. The rate of decline was measured between velocities of 2 m/sec and 1 m/sec, which is the usual range of swimming speeds in races. The rate of decline was significantly less rapid after shaving, causing the authors to speculate that frictional drag had been reduced by shaving down. The results of these studies indicate that there may be sound physiological reasons for shaving down.

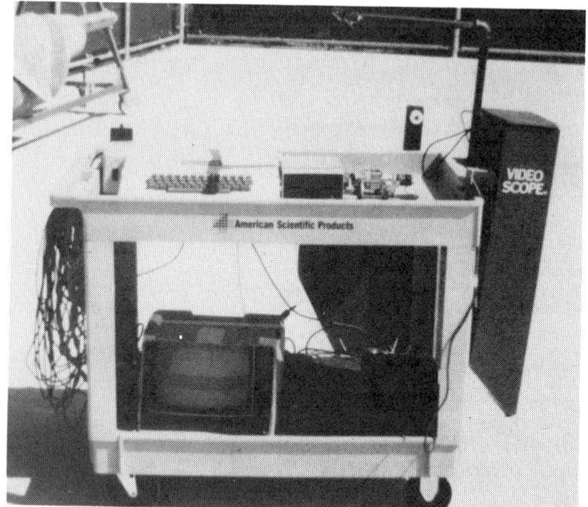

a

b

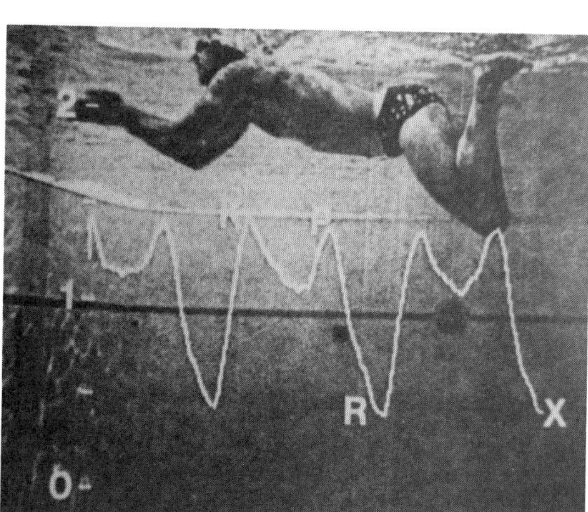

c

Figure 15-13. The velocity meter is a device that was developed by D. L. Costill and Gary Lee at the Human Performance Laboratory at Ball State University, Muncie, Indiana. The idea was borrowed from a prototype developed by Dr. A. Craig from the University of Rochester. The computer, VCR, and coach scope are shown in Figure 15-13*a*. Figure 15-13*b* shows the reel on the deck being controlled by Mike Heard. The swimmer, Rick Graves, has the harness around his neck. Figure 15-13*c* shows a sample tracing for the breaststroke provided on the video tape.

CHAPTER 16

Propulsion

At this point in time, we have only theories concerning the laws of motion that govern swimming propulsion. These theories are presented in the first part of this chapter. The second part discusses three important aspects of stroking and kicking that can increase propulsion: limb direction, angle of attack, and velocity.

THEORIES OF SWIMMING PROPULSION

Early attempts to describe the propulsive movements of competitive swimmers likened swimmers' arms to oars or paddlewheels. The stroke pattern for the front crawl was thought to resemble the one shown in Figure 16-1. Swimmers were taught to keep their arm straight and to move it in a semicircular pattern, like the sweep of a paddle wheel, during the propulsive phase of their stroke. However, underwater observations revealed that swimmers were actually bending their arms during the underwater phases of the various competitive strokes. These observations led to the first modern-day attempts to apply scientific principles to swimming propulsion—the introduction of the several drag theories of propulsion.

Propulsive Drag Theories

The Push-Straight-Back-To-Go-Forward Theory J. E. Counsilman (1968) and C. E. Silvia (1970) introduced this theory of propulsion in two separate publications. They believed that *Newton's third law of motion* was the principal physical

Figure 16-1. The paddle-wheel theory of propulsion.

law that swimmers applied to propel their body forward. This basic law of motion states that *for every action there is an equal and opposite reaction*. In more specific terms, when swimmers push water back, the water exerts a force of equal magnitude that pushes them forward.

Both men had noticed that swimmers alternately flexed and extended their arms during the propulsive portions of their armstrokes, and they reasoned that this was done so that the swimmers could push water back horizontally over a long distance and, in so doing, push their body forward farther and faster. According to this theory, the hand was used like a paddle to push back against the water. It was believed that swimmers directed water back in the first third of their underwater armstroke by gradually flexing their arm and that they continued moving it directly back by extending their arm during the final third. At the time, proponents advised that any deviation from this backward direction of the arm would cause the body to veer off in some other direction, increasing resistance and reducing propulsion. Figure 16-2 shows a stroke pattern according to what has become known as the

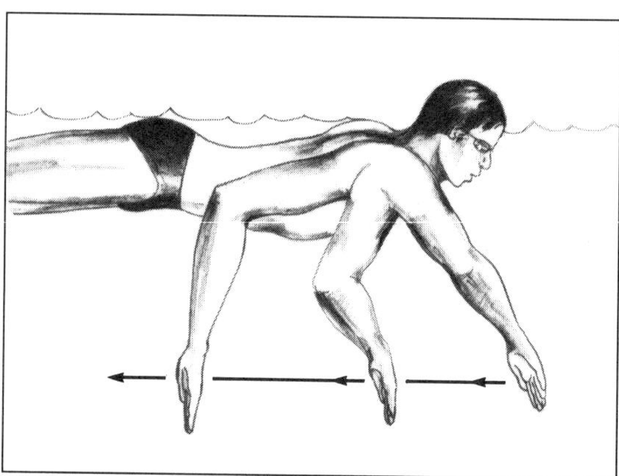

Figure 16-2. The propulsive drag theory of propulsion.

propulsive drag theory. The first half of the underwater armstroke was termed a *pull;* the second half, a *push*.

The Weaving-Back Theory Counsilman and Silvia's theories were widely accepted and influenced the teaching of stroke mechanics throughout the world for many years. However, at a later time, Counsilman, using underwater photography, noticed that the hand did not travel straight back under the body. Instead, it followed a weaving-backward path. Counsilman reasoned that swimmers stroked in this way so that they could move large amounts of water back for short distances instead of moving a small amount of water back over a long distance. This observation resulted in a modification of the original propulsive drag theory, and swimmers were advised to move their hand in *S*-like paths under and to the side of their body. The underneath view in Figure 16-3 shows a stroke pattern for the freestyle according to the *weaving-back* theory of drag propulsion.

The rationale behind abandoning the straight-back pull in favor of S-like motions is that the former required more effort to accelerate water that was already moving backward than would be required to accelerate quiet or slowly moving water. This is because a particular armful of water gains momentum once it has been accelerated back, and swimmers are not able to continue pushing against it with the same force unless they accelerate their arm speed beyond the backward

Figure 16-3. A freestyle swimmer, shown from an underneath view, moving her hand in an *S*-like propulsive pattern according to the weaving-back theory of propulsion.

speed of the water. However, by changing the direction of their arm, skilled swimmers can find "new" or undisturbed water to push against, once they have accelerated a previous armful of water back. This saves energy because swimmers can gain more propulsion with less muscular force and because it increases the range of motion during the propulsive phase of swimmers' armstrokes. Thus, the advantages of diagonal stroking motions are as follows:

1. Less force is required to accelerate water back.
2. Propulsive force can be applied over a greater distance.

Lift Theories of Propulsion

Although his theories were widely accepted throughout the world, Counsilman was not satisfied that he had discovered the "true" nature of swimming propulsion, so he continued his investigations of hydrodynamics. In 1971, he and Ronald Brown reported the results of a landmark study that revolutionized the teaching of stroke mechanics (Brown & Counsilman, 1971).

These two men filmed swimmers wearing lights on their hands while swimming in a darkened pool. The stroboscopic effect of the light flashes that appeared on the developed film showed the underwater paths of swimmers' hands during the four competitive strokes. The unique thing about these patterns was that they were displayed relative to the water instead of a swimmer's body, which is how all patterns had been displayed previously. Brown and Counsilman showed that the propulsive movements of swimmers' hands and arms were largely made in lateral and vertical, rather than backward, directions. The swimmers seemed to be propelling their body forward by sculling in and out and down and up rather than by pushing their arms straight back or in weaving-backward patterns under their body.

Since Counsilman and Brown first presented their findings, several other researchers have provided evidence that substantiates the observation that swimmers use sculling motions for propulsion (Barthels & Adrian, 1974; Plagenhoff, 1971; Schleihauf, 1974, 1978). The study by Counsilman and Brown was honored as the most important biomechanical research of the 1970s and is a credit to the authors, particularly Doc Counsilman, who has been the major contributor to our knowledge of competitive swimming in this generation.

A typical freestyle stroke pattern drawn relative to the water is shown from a side view in Figure 16-4. You can see that the swimmer's right hand actually leaves the water ahead of the point where it entered and that the amount that his hand moves backward is minimal relative to its motion downward and upward.

Contrary to some opinions, these results do *not* support the weaving-back theory. If that theory were accurate, arm movements would be primarily backward, with just enough lateral and vertical movement to find undisturbed water to push against. Research in which stroke patterns were drawn has consistently shown that the patterns for all competitive styles contain a preponderance of sculling movements (Barthels & Adrian, 1974; Belokovsky & Ivanchenko, 1975; Brown & Counsilman, 1971; Czabanski & Koszyczyc, 1979; Hinrichs, 1986; Luedtke, 1986; Maglischo et al., 1986; Plagenhoff, 1971; Reischle, 1979; Schleihauf, 1978; Schlei-

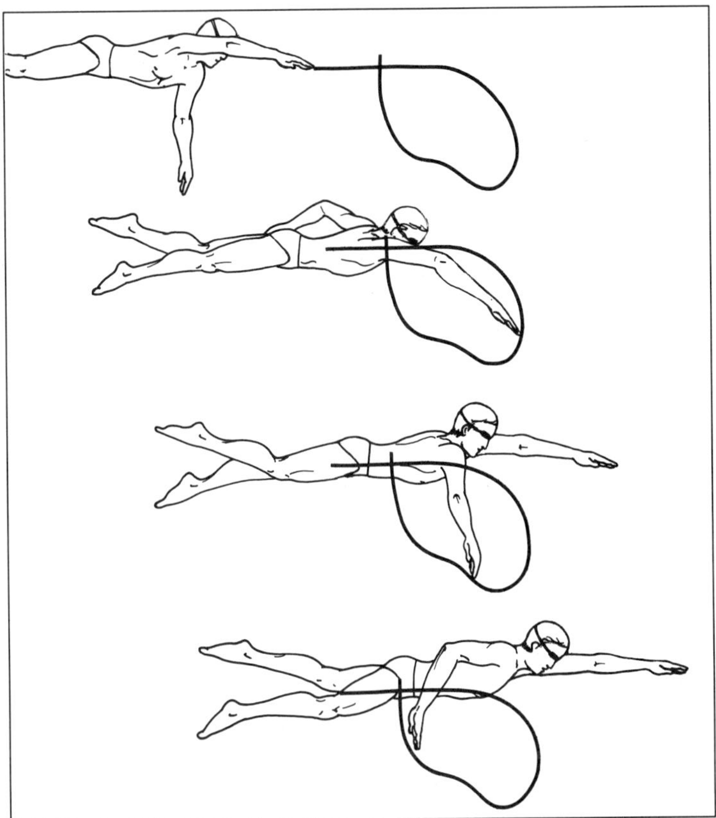

Figure 16-4. A freestyle stroke pattern drawn relative to a fixed point in the pool. (Adapted from Schleihauf, 1978)

hauf et al., 1984). The backward movement of swimmers' arms were minimal relative to the lateral and vertical sweeps. Consequently, the weaving-back theory does not supply a complete understanding of swimming propulsion. Nevertheless, the idea of finding "still" water to push back has merit. Swimmers probably do change directions periodically so that they can find undisturbed water to move back even though they don't push their arms back to any great extent. If this sounds confusing, read on. The nature of swimming propulsion may become clearer in the next section.

Bernoulli's Theorem Brown and Counsilman (1971) proposed that the swimmers' sculling motions were propulsive because they generated *lift force*. Daniel Bernoulli was a Swiss scientist who first identified the inverse relationship between the velocity of fluid flow and pressure. In other words, pressure is lower when a fluid velocity is rapid, and it is higher when the fluid velocity is slow. *Bernoulli's theorem* was used to explain the way lift force was produced.

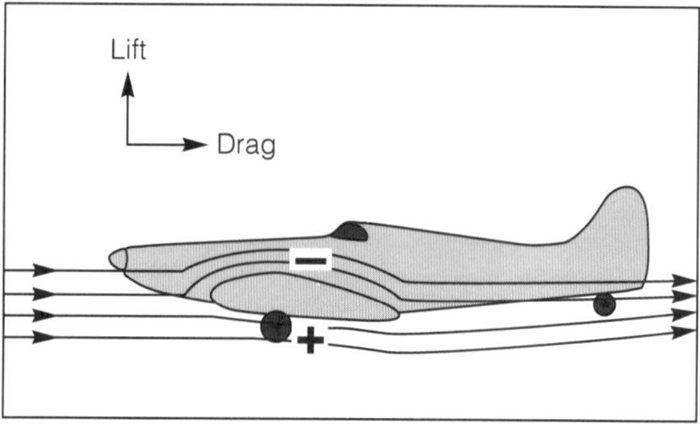

Figure 16-5. An example of lift force.

Bernoulli's theorem can best be described by explaining how a lift effect is produced by airplane wings. Figure 16-5 illustrates this effect. When an airplane travels forward, the relative motion of the air stream immediately in front of the wing is backward, exerting a drag force opposite to the direction in which the airplane is moving. The wing must split the streams of air to pass through them. Consequently, some of the streams pass over the top of the wing while others pass underneath. This motion is shown by the small arrows representing the relative flow of air in Figure 16-5.

Wings are shaped so that the air traveling over the top is accelerated relative to the air flowing underneath. The upper surface is rounded and, thus, longer, compared to the underside, so the air flowing over the top must accelerate to reach the other side of the wing at the same time as the air underneath. The increase in flow causes a reduction of pressure on the top of the wing relative to that underneath. Because objects tend to move from areas of higher to lower pressure, this pressure differential pushes the airplane upward and keeps it aloft. The upward force exerted by that pressure differential is termed *lift,* and, as you can see, *it is always exerted perpendicular to the direction of drag force*.

Counsilman and Brown suggested that the human hand was shaped like a wing and could be used to produce lift in a manner similar to that produced by airfoils. Figure 16-6 illustrates swimming propulsion according to Bernoulli's theorem. It shows an underneath view of a butterfly swimmer as his hands sweep back and in under his body. This motion creates a drag force in the opposite direction — out and forward. That force is indicated by the drag vector in Figure 16-6.

Because the hands are traveling inward, the relative direction of water flow will be out over his hands from the thumbs toward the little fingers. According to Bernoulli's theorem, the water flowing over the longer upper surfaces of the swimmer's hands (illustrated by the small arrows above the swimmer's left hand in Figure 16-6) will be accelerated so that it reaches the little-finger sides at the same time as the water flowing underneath the hands (illustrated by the large arrow underneath the left hand in Figure 16-6). Consequently, the pressure of the water is lower above the hands, where it is traveling faster, compared to the pressure underneath, where the flow is slower. This difference in pressure is indicated by the + and − signs below and above the swimmer's left hand in Figure 16-6. The pressure differential between the palm and knuckle sides of the hands is believed to produce

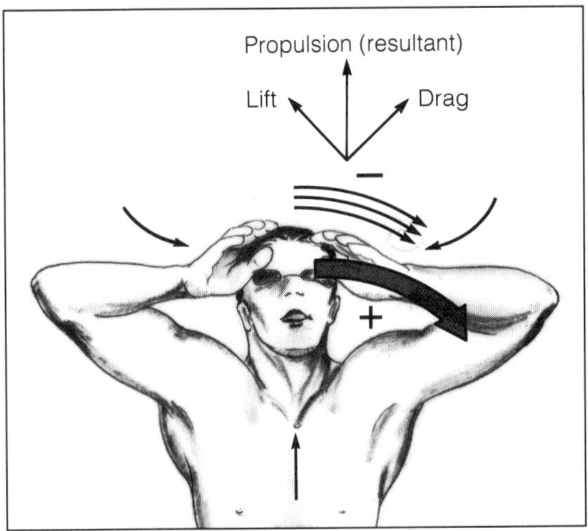

Figure 16-6. The application of Bernoulli's theorem to swimming propulsion.

a lift force that acts in the direction shown by the lift vector. The lift force and the drag force are believed to combine to produce a resultant force that accelerates the swimmer's body forward. (Remember the perspective of this illustration is from underneath, so the resultant vector that is pointing up actually represents force in a forward direction.)

This lift theory of propulsion has gained wide acceptance during the past two decades because it provides a scientific rationale for the sculling motions that swimmers obviously use for propulsion. However, I will indicate later that Newton's third law of motion may play a greater role, although not in the manner described relative to propulsive drag theories. I would like to describe one additional propulsive theory before doing that.

The Vortex Theory of Swimming Propulsion Cecil Colwin has proposed a theory of swimming propulsion that is based on the formation and shedding of vortices (Colwin, 1984, 1985a, 1985b). Not surprisingly, this proposal has become known as the vortex theory of swimming propulsion.

Although most swimming researchers have studied swimming propulsion from the point of view of the athletes' stroking motions, Colwin has also studied water movements and their effect on propulsion. He has proposed that efficient swimmers use two types of propulsion; *foil* and *fling-ring*. In general, he believes that foil propulsion takes place in the first half of the underwater armstroke and that the fling-ring mechanism is used most often to produce propulsion in the second half.

Foil propulsion This type of propulsion is a result of the lift forces produced by circulating water flow in a *bound vortex,* which is a mass of rotating fluid that circulates around a foil. Figure 16-7 shows the manner in which a bound vortex is formed by the flow of water around a foil. Some of the water passing underneath the foil curls around at the back end and begins circulating upward and backward, forming a starting vortex. This happens because the pressure is lower on the

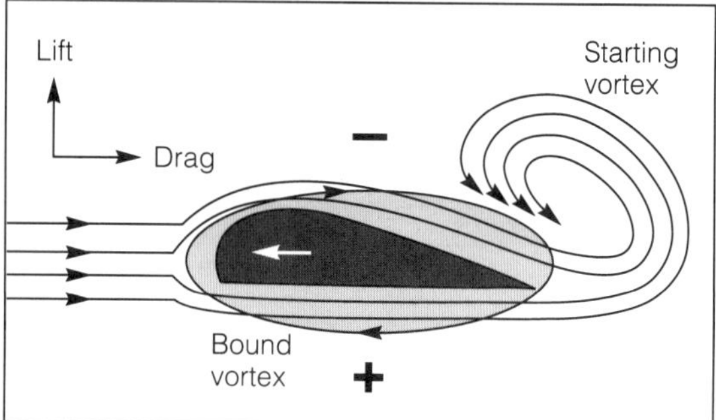

Figure 16-7. The formation of a bound vortex around a foil and its effect on producing lift forces and subsequent propulsion.

upperside of the foil, causing the water coming from underneath to flow upward and backward. That water then mixes with the water flowing over the top of the foil and begins flowing in a backward direction. This reversal produces a bound vortex of equal strength that circulates around the foil in a clockwise direction.

The bound vortex reacts with the fluid flowing past the foil to further lower the pressure on the upper surface and add to the increase of pressure on the underside. This happens because the rotating fluid in the bound vortex travels in the same direction as the adjacent fluid over the upper side, so it causes that fluid to travel faster, reducing its pressure. The vortex moves in an opposite direction to that of the fluid on the underside, which has the effect of slowing the rate of water flow and increasing pressure underneath. Accordingly, the pressure differential between the upper (−) and under (+) sides of the foil are augmented and the magnitude of the lift force is increased. That lift force then combines with the drag force, and the resultant force propels the swimmer forward.

Colwin has proposed that bound vortices can be formed around swimmers' hands in a similar manner, and thereby generate propulsive force. The creation of a bound vortex is dependent on a steadily circulating fluid flow. Skilled swimmers are believed to establish this steady flow by carefully orienting their hands at the beginning of the underwater armstroke. Once it is established, swimmers maintain the bound vortex by careful acceleration and orientation of their limbs so that the fluid does not break away from them.

Fling-ring propulsion The maintenance of a bound vortex is impossible in certain phases of the competitive strokes, particularly near the end of the underwater portions of the butterfly and freestyle armstrokes and during the downbeats of the butterfly and flutter kicks. Rapid changes of direction cause the boundary layer of fluid to break away during these phases. When this happens, a condition of nonsteady flow is created, where lift propulsion is no longer effective. This is when the fling-ring mechanism may come into play.

The butterfly swimmer in Figure 16-8 illustrates the mechanism for fling-ring propulsion during the downbeat of the dolphin kick. Colwin believes that the rapid change of direction from up to down at the top of the kick creates a pressure differential between the underside of the legs (where the pressure is greater) and the upperside (where it is lower). The resulting separation of the air-water boundary,

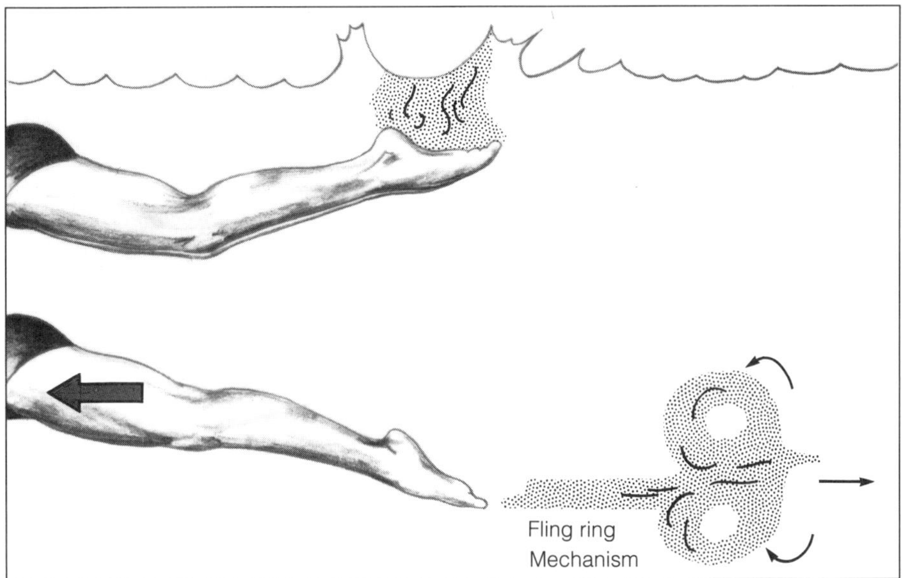

Figure 16-8. An example of the fling-ring mechanism of swimming propulsion in the dolphin kick. (Adapted from Colwin, 1984)

in turn, establishes a bound vortex around the feet. The rapid acceleration of the feet during the subsequent downbeat causes the vortex to be maintained until the swimmer's feet stop moving momentarily at the end of the downbeat. At that time, the fluid in this bound vortex is rapidly shed backward. The backward movement of water, in turn, creates a counterforce that propels the swimmer forward.

As mentioned, the fling-ring mechanism may also provide propulsion during the end of the underwater armstrokes in butterfly and freestyle. This phenomenon is illustrated by the freestyle swimmer in Figure 16-9. He is completing the final upward sweep of his armstroke. In this case, the swimmer changes the direction of his hand movements rapidly from in to out. In the process, he carries a bound vortex that is shed backward as his hand speed decelerates just before reaching the surface.

The vortex theory is really an extension of the lift theory. There are many problems associated with its validation however, just as there have been with other theories. The major problem is determining whether swimmers can actually establish bound vortices around their hands and feet. The flow around a swimmer's hands and arms is usually only visible immediately after entry, when some air has been trapped by them. Skilled swimmers usually lose the air before beginning the major propulsive phase of their stroke, so the direction of water flow is not visible and cannot be studied during these important propulsive movements. It is worth noting, also, that the inclination of a propelling hand and arm does not seem to be very important to propulsion in this theory. This does not fit with the precise and

Figure 16-9. The fling-ring mechanism in freestyle propulsion. (Adapted from Colwin, 1984)

very similar angles of attack that swimmers have been demonstrated to use during propulsive phases of their strokes (Luedtke, 1986; Maglischo et al., 1986; Schleihauf, 1978; Schleihauf, Gray, & DeRose, 1983; Schleihauf et al., 1988; Thayer et al., 1986). Nevertheless, this theory is deserving of consideration and may lead to a better understanding of the way swimmers use lift forces for propulsion.

Back to Newton: Another Interpretation of Lift Theory

Each new theory has contributed to our present understanding of swimming propulsion, although none has been able to explain all aspects of it. Nevertheless, the diagonal stroke patterns that swimmers use lead me to accept propulsive lift as the most probable explanation for swimming propulsion. I doubt that Bernoulli's principle is the primary mechanism producing that lift, however. The application of Newton's third law of motion probably plays a much greater role.

Bernoulli's principle suggests that small changes in the shape of the hand should cause large changes in lift. If this were true, swimmers would not have to angle their hands when they stroked them through the water. They could simply utilize their foil shape to produce lift and the resultant forces. However, research and personal observations have shown that swimmers generate more propulsive force when they move their hands through the water at certain precise angles of attack (Hinrichs, 1986; Luedtke, 1986; Maglischo et al., 1986; Schleihauf, 1978, 1986; Schleihauf et al., 1988).

You can test for yourself the relative importance of angle of attack versus shape by putting your hand out of the window of a moving car. If you angle it down from front to back, your hand will be pushed up immediately. You will feel little effect, however, if your hand remains perfectly flat, at a zero-degree angle of attack, no matter how much you curve it.

I am not disputing the fact that Bernoulli's principle may play a role in the production of lift forces. However, its role is probably minor. By contrast, an explanation that is based on Newton's third law of motion probably represents a more accurate description of the most important propulsive mechanisms swimmers use—that is, *swimmers must push water back to go forward.*

Perhaps the principal reason for rejecting Newton's law of action-reaction in favor of Bernoulli's principle was the discovery in the early 1970s that swimmers stroke diagonally rather than straight back. This caused us to search for another explanation, and we settled on Bernoulli's principle. We had interpreted Newton's law too narrowly, believing that swimmers had to push their arms and legs *directly back* to push water back. We failed to appreciate that swimmers could also accelerate water back with diagonal stroking motions by orienting the hand and arm in such a way that they caused the relative flow of water to be displaced back.

Figure 16-10 shows how swimmers can accelerate water back with diagonal motions during midstroke in the front crawl stroke. An underneath view of a freestyle swimmer is shown as he sweeps his hand in under his body. The swimmer's hand is traveling back and in, as indicated by the solid black arrow behind it. The relative flow of water starts under the hand in the opposite direction—that is, out and forward, as indicated by the first half of the shaded arrow as it approaches

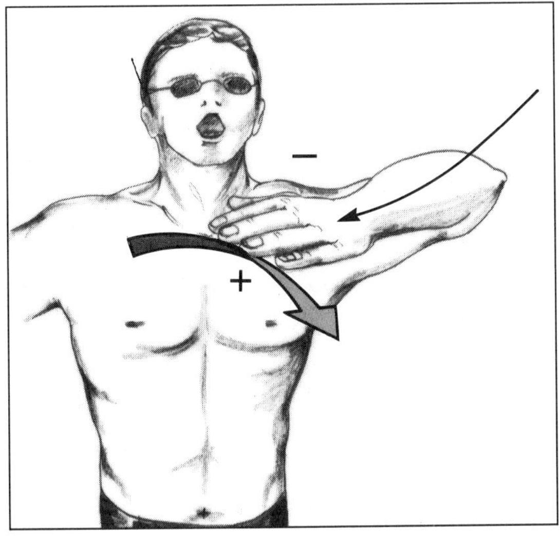

Figure 16-10. A method for displacing water back with diagonal stroking motions.

the thumb side of the swimmer's hand. Notice that his hand is angled (pitched) in so that the thumb side is slightly higher than the little-finger side. This angle causes a change in the relative direction of water flow as it passes under the swimmer's hand toward the little-finger side. The water is displaced back, as shown by the change in direction of the shaded arrow, as it passes under the swimmer's palm. The backward force imparted to the water should, in accordance with Newton's third law of motion, produce a counterforce of equal magnitude that will propel the swimmer's body forward.

Bernoulli's principle may also be operating in Figure 16-10. However, the pressure differential between the upper (−) and underside (+) of the hand and the lift and resultant forces are probably more related to the angle of attack and the resulting backward displacement of water it produces than they are to an acceleration of fluid flow over the knuckles.

What I have described is similar to the way in which propellers work. Outboard motors make use of a rotating propeller that has three blades. Each is inclined back from its leading to trailing edges as illustrated in Figure 16-11. As they rotate in circular paths, the leading edge of each blade "bites" into the water, displacing it back for a short time as the blade passes through from leading to trailing edges. This makes it possible for the propeller to drive a boat forward even though it is rotating laterally.

I believe that swimmers use their hands like a rotating propeller. Their hand forms a new blade each time they change its direction during an underwater armstroke. They can use that hand like two or more blades, depending on the stroke being swum.

Figure 16-12 shows a front crawl swimmer using her hands and arms like rotating propeller blades. In the first propulsive sweep, (Figure 16-12*a*), the swimmer sweeps her right hand and arm in under her body at midstroke. In Figure 16-12*b*, she sweeps her left hand out and up in the final third of the underwater armstroke. The leading edge of her hand is the thumb side, and the trailing edge is the little-finger side in Figure 16-12*a*. The little-finger side is the leading edge and the thumb side is the trailing edge of the hand-arm blade in Figure 16-12*b*.

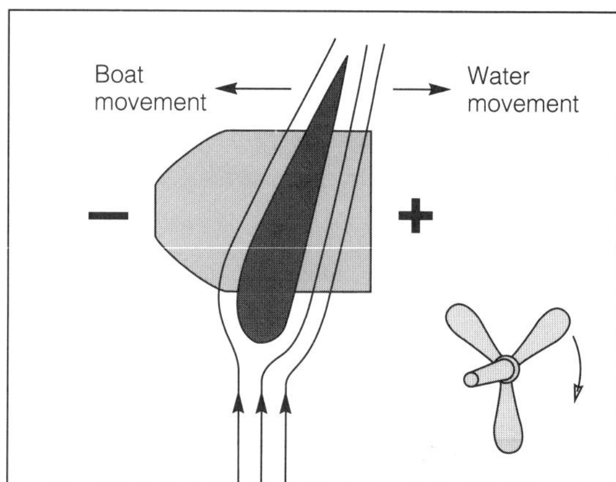

Figure 16-11. An example of propeller propulsion.

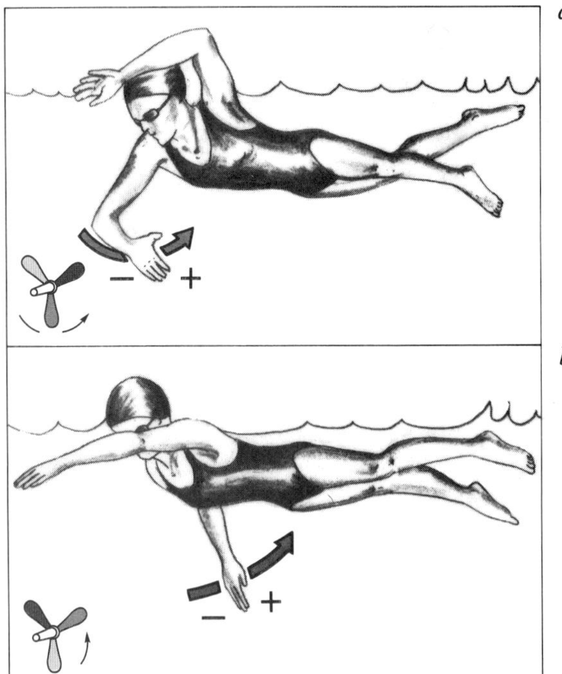

Figure 16-12. Similarities between the hand movements of a swimmer during the front crawl stroke and the rotating blades of a propeller. In Figure 16-12*a*, the swimmer sweeps her hand in, up, and back. In Figure 16-12*b*, she sweeps her hand out, up, and back.

As mentioned earlier, one of the reasons swimmers must change the directions of their arms and hands periodically throughout the underwater armstroke is to get away from water that has already been accelerated and to find "new," undisturbed water to push against. Another reason why a propulsive motion cannot continue indefinitely in any one direction is that friction will finally cause the boundary layer of water around the arms and hands to break away. This will cause turbulence and a reduction of propulsive force.

DIRECTION, ANGLE OF ATTACK, AND VELOCITY

The arms and legs are major propelling agents in swimming, and they achieve that propulsion with diagonal sculling motions. There are three important aspects of the movements of swimmers' limbs that determine the effectiveness with which they can accelerate water backward during these diagonal sculling motions. They are, *direction, angle of attack,* and *velocity*.

The directions in which swimmers' limbs move can be learned from stroke patterns, and their angles of attack can be determined from the inclinations of their limbs. Velocity refers to the speed of their hands and feet as they travel through the water. The following box summarizes this information.

Three Aspects of Limb Movement That Are Important to Swimming Propulsion

1. Direction — determined from stroke patterns
2. Angle of attack — determined from the inclination of swimmers' hands and feet
3. Velocity — speed of hands and feet

Direction

Stroke patterns are the best way to visualize the direction of the propelling movements that swimmers make with their arms and legs. These patterns can be expressed in two ways: (1) relative to the water and (2) relative to the swimmer's body. Patterns drawn relative to the water help us understand the way movements of swimmers' limbs affect the movements of water. They provide the most accurate representation of propulsion because, in the final analysis, *it is the effect that swimmers' limbs exert on the direction of water flow that determines the amount of propulsive force they can produce*. The second way to depict stroke patterns is relative to a swimmer's moving body.

Figure 16-13 shows an underneath stroke pattern for a front crawl swimmer depicted in both ways. The pattern is drawn relative to the water in Figure 16-13*a* and relative to the body in Figure 16-13*b*. These patterns depict the movements of the swimmer's middle finger. Notice that in both cases her hand follows an *S* pattern. It sweeps out, in, and out, again. The lateral motions appear considerably greater in Figure 16-13*a*, yet the backward movements of the swimmer's hand appear greater in Figure 16-13*b*.

The pattern in Figure 16-13*b* is deceiving because it makes it appear that the swimmer's body remains stationary while her hand travels back. Accordingly, it appears that her hand moves back more than it actually does. Because the pattern is elongated, the magnitude of her lateral movements also appears to be less than it actually is. These inaccuracies notwithstanding, the pattern in Figure 16-13*b* is the better teaching tool. Patterns drawn in this manner are good vehicles for teaching stroke mechanics. They are excellent for communicating the directions of stroking motions to swimmers because athletes tend to visualize their stroking motions relative to their body rather than relative to the water. As a result, they learn faster when the motions are presented in this way.

Teaching swimmers with relative patterns like that shown in Figure 16-13*b* will not cause athletes to swim incorrectly. When they move their limbs correctly relative to their body, they will also stroke correctly relative to the water. For example, if the swimmer in Figure 16-13*b* were moving toward the top of the page, as she would if she were actually swimming, her body would travel forward more and her hand would travel backward considerably less. In fact, the pattern she would produce would be identical to the one in Figure 16-13*a*.

For teaching purposes, stroke patterns that are drawn relative to a swimmer's body are illustrated in the chapters discussing each stroke (Chapters 18 through 21).

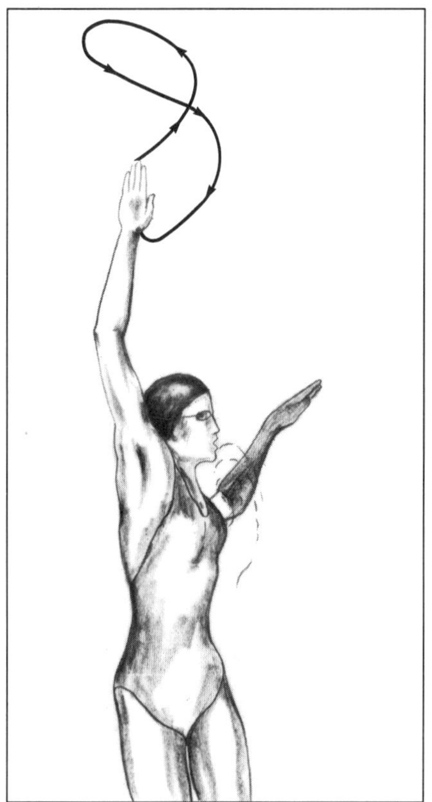

a

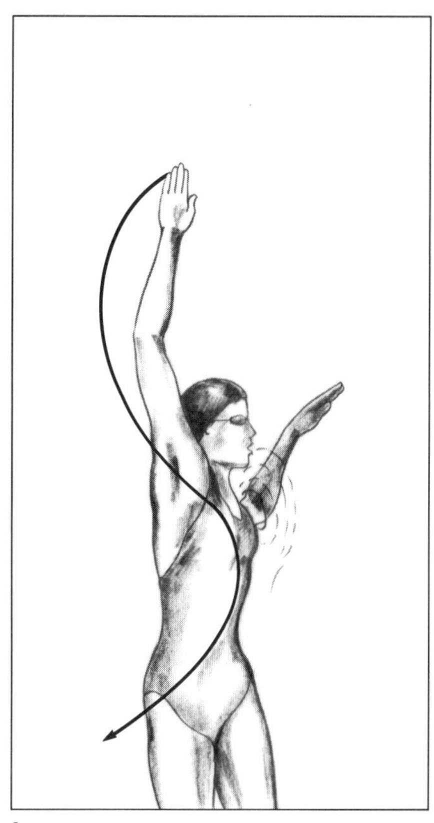

b

Figure 16-13. A comparison of stroke patterns drawn relative to the water (*a*) and relative to the swimmer's body (*b*). An underneath view of the front crawl stroke is shown.

For now, we'll concentrate on stroke patterns that are drawn relative to the water because they depict the "true" directions of swimmers' limbs.

Figure 16-14 (p. 328) illustrates front, side, and underneath patterns for the four competitive strokes. They were drawn from films of world-class athletes swimming at competition speeds. Figure 16-14*a* shows a front view of the front crawl stroke; Figure 16-14*b*, a side view of the backstroke; Figure 16-14*c*, an underneath view of the butterfly; and Figure 16-14*d*, a front view of the breaststroke.

Notice that, in all four competitive strokes, the swimmers' hands travel in predominantly lateral and vertical directions. It is interesting that world-class swimmers use sculling motions, because most of them were taught to swim in the early 1970s, when the propulsive drag theory was popular. They seem to have learned intuitively to use diagonal sculling rather than backward paddling motions. Additional evidence about the superiority of sculling motions has been provided by Reischle (1979), who reported that the best swimmers exhibited the least backward hand movements in their strokes.

You can see from the side and underneath views in Figure 16-14, that there is some backward motion in these stroke patterns. Some backward movement of the

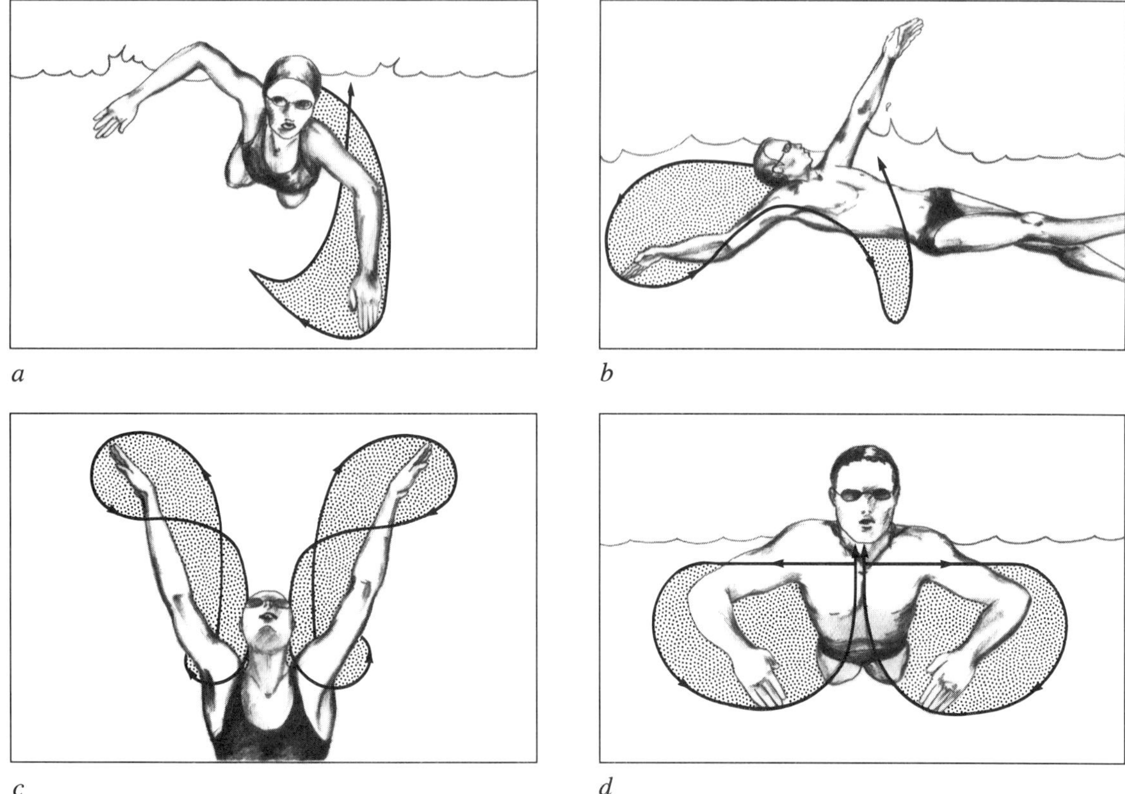

Figure 16-14. Patterns for the four competitive armstrokes drawn relative to the water.

limbs is probably needed to ensure that optimal amounts of water are displaced backward. Although water can be displaced backward by moving the limbs only in lateral and vertical directions, our research has shown that more propulsion is gained when the limbs travel diagonally so that some backward motion is included in the movement (Luedtke, 1986; Maglischo et al., 1986; Schleihauf et al., 1988).

Another interesting observation about these stroke patterns is that swimmers make major changes in the directions of their hands two or more times during the underwater portions of each competitive stroke. The purpose of these changes is probably so that swimmers can find undisturbed water that they can displace backward once a previous section of water has been accelerated to the rear.

The patterns of a particular stroke are very similar for all swimmers, although each athlete will have something unique about his or her pattern that distinguishes it from those of other swimmers. A useful analogy might be to think of a particular stroke pattern as a handwritten letter of the alphabet. Although each swimmer will write that letter differently, it will still be recognizable and will not be so different from the writing of others that it could be mistaken for another letter of the alphabet.

In the same way, every swimmer has a stroke pattern that is somewhat different from that of every other swimmer, yet the patterns for one competitive stroke are so similar from swimmer to swimmer that they could not be confused for that of another stroke. We can learn the directions in which swimmers' arms and hands should move in each competitive style by studying similarities in the stroke patterns of several world-class swimmers.

The Law of Inertia All of the stroke patterns described in this section were circular in nature. This is because swimmers use less muscular effort to change directions when they stroke in curvilinear paths. The physical principle they follow is involved with Newton's first law of motion — the law of inertia. According to this law, an object moving in one direction has inertia that must be overcome before that direction can be changed. When the motion is linear, a great deal of muscular force is required to stop the inertia of a hand and arm that are moving in one direction and accelerate them in a new direction. However, when the motion is curvilinear, the hand and arm can continue moving at a reasonable velocity as it changes directions so that no sudden stops or starts are required. In this way, inertia in one direction can be overcome gradually and the change to a new direction can be effected with less muscular effort.

Another reason why curvilinear stroke patterns are superior to linear patterns involves their effect on the alignment of the body. With linear stroking motions, the sudden "braking effect" when a hand and arm change directions will create a force of equal magnitude in the opposite direction. That force will be transferred to a swimmer's suspended body and will force it out of alignment. This loss of alignment will, of course, increase drag and reduce forward speed.

Figure 16-15 (p. 330) compares the effect of curvilinear and linear changes of direction. The backstroke swimmer in Figure 16-15*a* sweeps his hand in a curvilinear path as he makes the transition from sweeping down to sweeping up at midstroke. The circular motion of his arm should aid in overcoming the arm's downward inertia as it changes directions to move upward. It should also reduce the magnitude of reactive force that could disrupt his body alignment.

The swimmer in Figure 16-15*b* makes the transition from down to up in a more linear manner. That is, he sweeps his arm almost directly down and then directly up. As a result, the downward motion of his arm has to be stopped before it can change directions and start up. The amount of muscular force required to stop the hand's downward motion and then accelerate it up should be considerably greater than that used by the other swimmer. In addition, the counterforce causes the swimmer in Figure 16-15*b* to bounce up and down. It pushes his head and trunk up during the braking action of the downward hand motion and then pulls him down as the hand accelerates up. This is one reason why some backstrokers' heads bob up and down when they swim.

Angle of Attack

The angle of attack is the angle formed by the inclination of the hand and arm (or leg and foot) to the direction it is moving. Figure 16-16 illustrates a two-dimensional

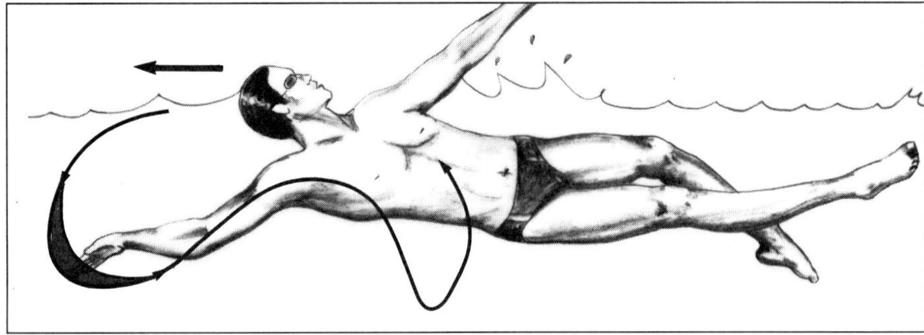

a

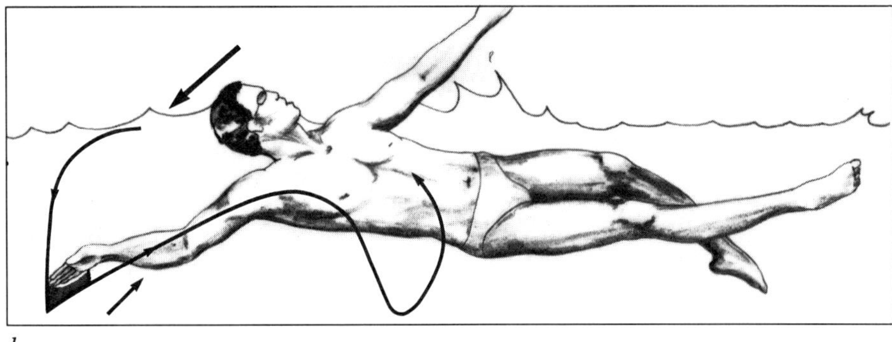

b

Figure 16-15. The effect of curvilinear and linear stroking motions in backstroke.

angle of attack for the hands of a breaststroke swimmer from underneath and side views.

The swimmer moves his hands out and down to the catch. That direction is indicated by the arrows above his hands in both views. The angle of attack is the angle formed by the arrow that represents the direction in which his hands are moving and the line showing the inclination of his palms. In Figure 16-16*a*, his palms are pitched out back at an angle of attack of 35 degrees. From the side (Figure 16-16*b*), you can see that they are pitched down and back at an angle of attack of 40 degrees to the direction in which his hands are moving.

The hands, when angled in this manner, can be likened to hydrofoils for purposes of understanding the forces they create. The movement of a foil through fluid is identified by its leading and trailing edges. In Figure 16-16*b*, the thumb side of the swimmer's hands is called the *leading edge* because it is the first part to encounter undisturbed streams of water as it sweeps down. The little-finger side is the *trailing edge* because it is the last part of the hand-foil to have contact with that water. Identifying these edges is important in understanding how stroking movements can change the directions of water and, in doing so, impart force to it.

The palm and rear portion of the arms are always the underside of the hand-foil in swimming propulsion. The leading edge can be the fingertips, wrist, thumb side,

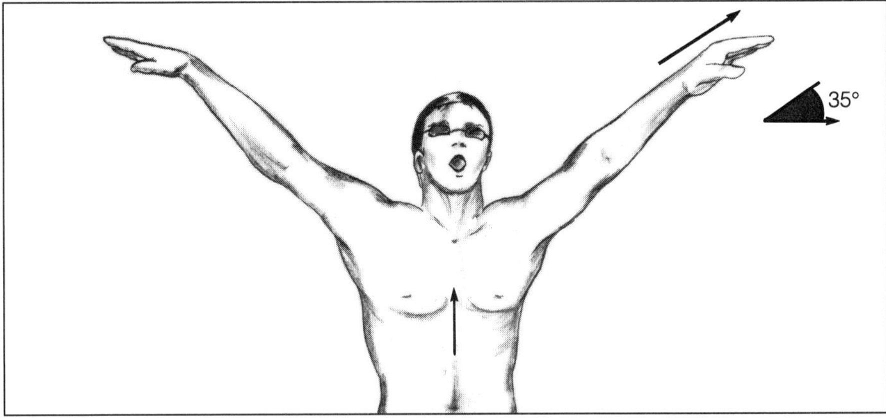

a

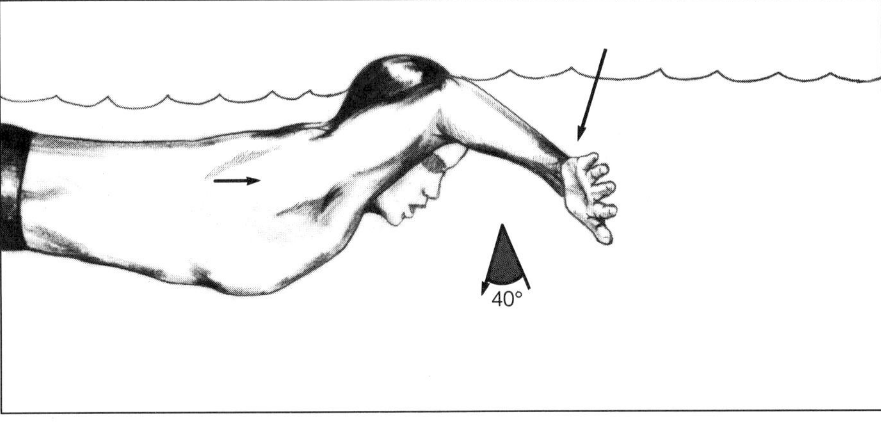

b

Figure 16-16. Underneath and side views of a breaststroke swimmer showing how the angle of attack of the hands is measured at the catch.

or little-finger side at various times during the underwater armstrokes of the four competitive styles. In certain cases, the elbow can also serve as the leading edge of the arm-hand foil unit.

Unfortunately, angles of attack can only be shown in two dimensions. Consequently, the 35- and 40-degree angles of inclination shown in Figure 16-16 do not represent the "true" three-dimensional angle of attack the swimmer is actually using during this phase of the stroke. The direction and inclination of the hands must be assessed from two views that encompass all three planes of motion before an accurate angle of attack can be calculated.

The angle of attack has great significance to the production of propulsive forces. Propulsion is diminished if the angle of attack is too great or too small. Information gained from studying foils that were suspended in wind tunnels supports this observation. The coefficient of lift curve in Figure 16-17 demonstrates the importance of using an optimal angle of attack. It shows the amount of lift created by foils when they were suspended at various angles of attack and air was forced by them. Because air is technically a fluid, objects obey the same laws of motion in air that they would if suspended in water. Consequently, we can be confident that the behavior of air and water would be the same at the angles of attack shown in Figure 16-17.

The coefficient of lift curve shows that the amount of lift is enhanced with increases in the angle of attack of a foil up to 40 degrees. After that, lift decreases steadily as the angle approaches 90 degrees. Lift force disappears entirely when the foil is perpendicular to the flow of air.

Figure 16-18 illustrates why lift forces increase and decrease with changing angles of attack. Swimmers' hands have been substituted for airfoils to show the application of this information to swimming propulsion. The hands are shown from an underneath view as though they were sweeping in under the swimmer's body at midstroke in the butterfly. The hands are sweeping in with angles of attack of 0, 40, 70, and 90 degrees. The amount of lift force is minimal when the angle of attack is 0 degrees. This is because the swimmer's hands pass through the water without displacing it backward to any great extent. Thus, there is only a small counterforce to propel the swimmer forward. This is illustrated by the small pressure differential between the palm and knuckle sides of the swimmer's hand. Swimmers commonly sweep their hands underneath their body in this manner at midstroke in the mistaken belief that they are pushing water back with their palms. In fact, they are pushing against the water with the thumb edge.

Propulsive force increases considerably when the angle of attack approaches 40 degrees. This is because a considerable amount of backward force is imparted to the water as it passes under the swimmer's palm from the leading (thumb side) to the trailing (little-finger side) edges. You can see that the angle of attack causes the water to be pushed down for a short time as it passes under the palm. This slows and compacts the streams of water molecules passing under the palm so that the pressure increases. The large pressure differential between the palm and knuckle sides of the hand results in a large lift force that acts perpendicular to the direction in which the palm is moving. Even more important to the magnitude of this pressure differential is the fact that the backward displacement of water produces a counterforce that propels the swimmer forward. The angle of attack shown here is probably very close to the ideal that swimmers should use when sweeping their hands under their bodies.

Propulsive force is reduced considerably when the angle of attack approaches the perpendicular. The palm presents a surface that is too flat when it is pitched at 70 degrees. Consequently, the effect of the leading edge is lost and the water cannot change directions gradually. When water strikes the flat surface of the palm in many places at once, the effect is not unlike throwing a bucket of fluid against a wall. Some of the molecules squirt wildly away from the hand in random directions, and a good portion of the remaining water molecules reverse their motion. This reaction is illustrated by the reversal of two of the streams striking the palm at 70 degrees in Figure 16-18.

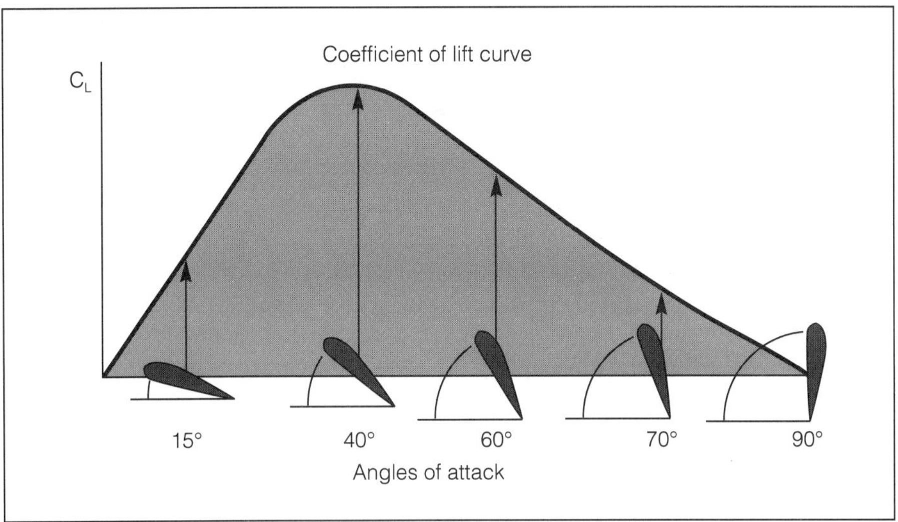

Figure 16-17. A coefficient of lift curve for foils suspended in a wind tunnel. (Adapted from Schleihauf, 1978)

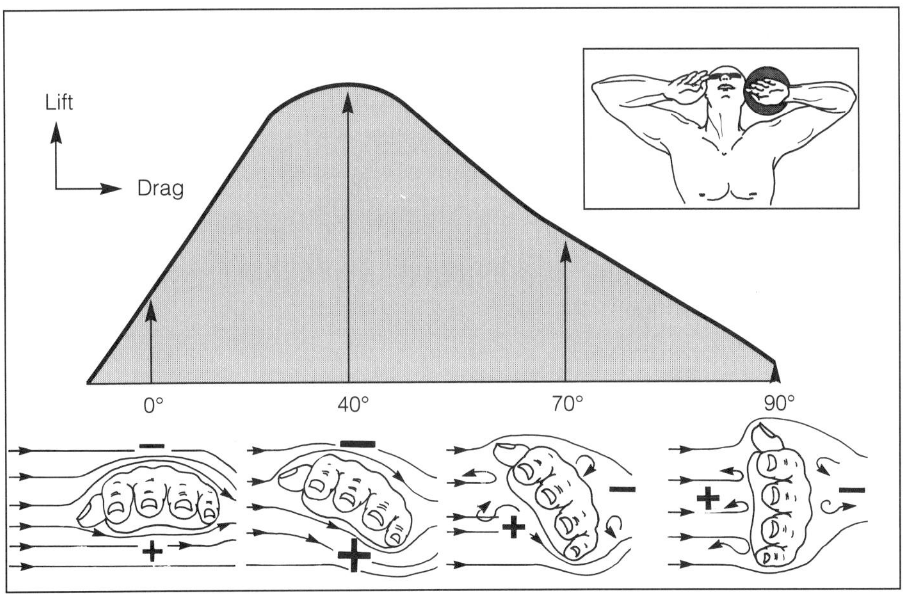

Figure 16-18. The effect of angle of attack on water movement during swimming.

In addition, the boundary layer of water molecules passing over the top of the hand breaks away and becomes turbulent because it can't make the large change of direction required to follow the contour of the hand from leading to trailing edges. The increase of turbulence reduces the pressure differential and, consequently, the lift force. At this angle of attack, the counterforce is exerted outward more than forward because of the reversal in water flow. Thus, much of the force the swimmer produces with his hand movements is wasted by pushing his body to the side.

This loss of propulsion is even greater when the palm is perpendicular to the direction in which it is moving. In this case, the hand acts like a paddle that pushes water in. There is no leading or trailing edge, only the large, flat surface of the palm pushing sideward against several streams of water molecules simultaneously. This angle of attack can be used for propulsion when swimmers' hands are traveling back but not when they are traveling down, up, in, or out. Regardless, it is not the preferred method of propulsion for world-class swimmers.

Schleihauf (1978) has conducted research that supports the fact that angles of attack are important to swimming propulsion. He studied the effects of different angles of attack on lift by suspending plaster models of a human hand in a water channel. The water was forced past the hands at flow velocities similar to the hand speeds measured during competitive swims. He demonstrated a coefficient of lift curve for the hands that was similar to the one shown for foils in Figure 16-17. The following were among the most significant findings he reported:

1. The coefficient of lift increased steadily up to an angle of attack of 40 degrees and then decreased as the angle approached 90 degrees. Angles of attack between 20 and 50 degrees had very high coefficients of lift. The coefficient of drag increased as the angle of attack approached 90 degrees.
2. Having the fingers together or no more than ⅛ inch (.32 cm) apart was superior to finger spreads of ¼ inch (.64 cm) and ½ inch (1.27 cm) for producing lift.
3. Separating the thumb from the hand by a small amount produced more lift than a wide thumb spread.

Based on these observations, swimmers should use angles of attack between 20 and 50 degrees during most phases of their underwater armstrokes (and perhaps during kicking). This range of angles is most effective for producing propulsive force because it permits an *edge* of the hand to move into undisturbed water and displace it back gradually under the palm as the remainder of the hand passes through it. Where propulsion is concerned, it is important that the leading edge be just what its name implies, a small, tapered surface that will not displace a section of water too radically as it starts through it. This will prevent the water from becoming turbulent. Then the hand, if it is inclined slightly in the right direction, can impart some backward force to the water.

The most common mistake swimmers make is to present a flat surface to the water. In other words, they use their hands like paddles rather than hydrofoils by pitching their limbs at angles of attack that are nearly perpendicular to the direction in which they are moving. As you saw in Figure 16-18, when a large surface of the hand pushes against several streams of water molecules simultaneously, the direction and speed of the water will be altered radically and turbulence will occur. Swimmers can propel themselves forward with these large angles of attack *if* their hands push back against the water; however, turbulence will reduce the amount of propulsion they can produce as compared to sculling motions. Swimmers' bodies will be pushed out of alignment, and their forward speed will be reduced dramatically if they push their hands in, out, up, or down at these large angles of attack, however.

Air Bubbles The search for optimal angles of attack can be aided by observing the air bubbles behind the hands of swimmers, at least during the first third of their underwater armstroke. Many coaches have noticed that world-class swimmers have fewer air bubbles around their limbs than swimmers of lesser achievement. Air bubbles indicate turbulence and a concomitant loss of propulsive force. They signal that swimmers are using the wrong combination of direction and angle of attack. The two freestyle swimmers in Figure 16-19 show good and poor patterns of turbulence.

After entering the water, the swimmer in Figure 16-19*a* has correctly changed the direction and speed of his arm movements as he moves his hand down into the catch position. Consequently, the bubbles of air he trapped under his palm at entry pass away from it, showing that he has moved his hand and arm into undisturbed water by the time he begins to apply propulsive force.

The swimmer in Figure 16-19*b* has a pattern of turbulence around his hand at the catch because he attempted to apply propulsive force almost from the time his hand entered the water. He began pushing his hand down and back almost immediately after entry. He accelerated his hand speed and did not change its direction or angle of attack from entry to catch. Consequently, the water behind his hand remains turbulent, with bubbles of trapped air still swirling around it at the catch.

Air bubbles can be seen around the hands and arms of all swimmers between the entry and catch positions of the butterfly, backstroke, and front crawl. These do

a

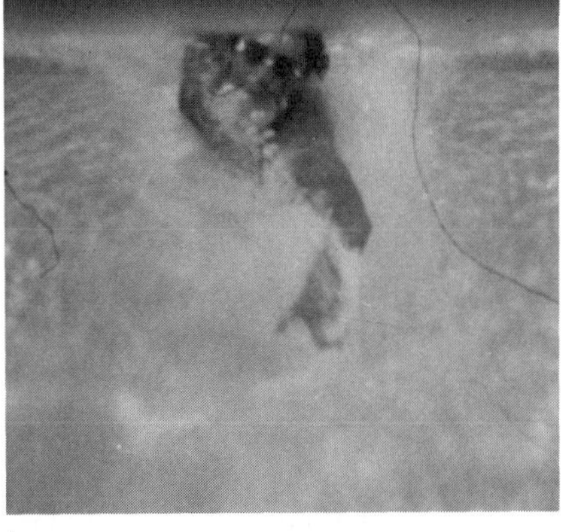

b

Figure 16-19. Turbulence created by air bubbles around the hands.

not indicate faulty stroke mechanics. However, when this turbulence remains after the propulsive phases of the strokes begin, it is a dead giveaway that swimmers are stroking incorrectly. They must change the direction in which their hands are moving, their angle of attack, or both to correct the problem.

The Relationship between Direction and Angle of Attack There is an intricate relationship between the direction in which limbs move and their optimal angles of attack for propulsion. Although all swimmers use diagonal sculling motions, some swimmers' motions are more diagonal than others. Swimmers' stroke patterns that incorporate a large degree of diagonal motion should be most effective with the angles of attack recommended earlier—20 to 40 degrees. Swimmers' stroke patterns that incorporate more backward motion will probably be effective with angles of attack that are closer to perpendicular. Schleihauf (1978) reported that good swimmers use angles of attack as slight as 15 degrees and as great as 73 degrees during various phases of the four competitive strokes.

Figure 16-20 illustrates the stroke patterns for freestylers Bruce Furniss and Jim Montgomery. You can see that Montgomery uses a pattern that incorporates less sculling than Furniss. As reported by Schleihauf (1978), his angles of attack were also closer to the perpendicular, ranging between 48 and 74 degrees for most propulsive phases of the armstroke. Conversely, Furniss used more diagonal strok-

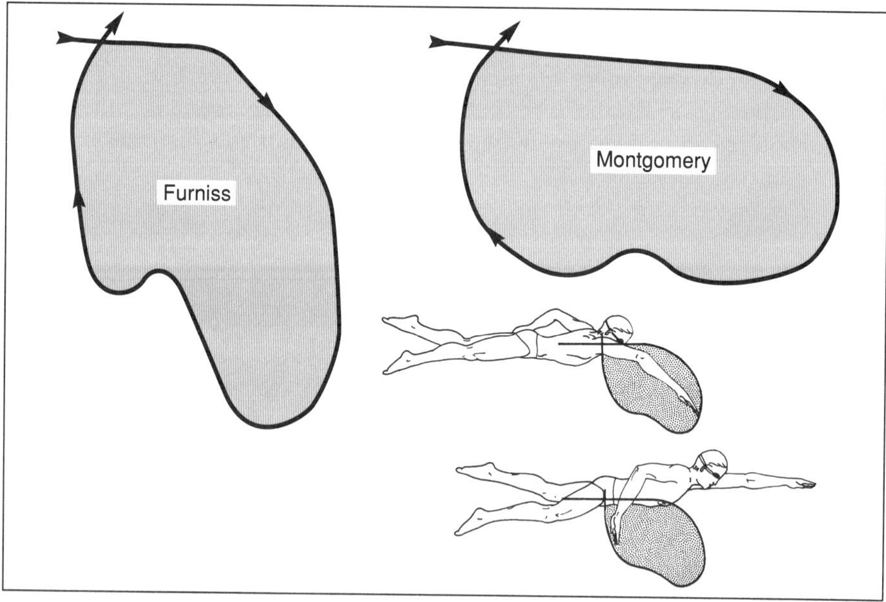

Figure 16-20. Stroke patterns for two former world-record holders, Bruce Furniss, a former world-record holder for the 200-m freestyle, and Jim Montgomery, a former world-record holder for the 100-m freestyle. (Adapted from Schleihauf, 1978)

ing motions and his angles of attack were smaller (20 to 37 degrees) during every phase of his underwater armstroke.

Because great swimmers have used both methods, it is not possible to validate one as superior. I suspect, however, that the style used by Furniss is more efficient because it incorporates more diagonal sculling motions. Accordingly, he should be able to attain a particular swimming speed with less hand acceleration and muscular force.

Research on Angles of Attack There have been many attempts over the years to determine the ideal angles of attack for swimming propulsion. The issue has not been an easy one to resolve. Measuring angles of attack three-dimensionally is a complicated and laborious procedure that is fraught with difficulty. Nevertheless, it has been attempted by several researchers over the years (Hinrichs, 1986; Luedtke, 1986; Maglischo et al., 1986; Schleihauf, Gray, & DeRose, 1983; Schleihauf et al., 1984, 1988; Thayer et al., 1986). Measurements must be taken from matching frames of film or videotape that were recorded simultaneously from two different perspectives. The difficulty in getting precise measurements lies in the fact that they are taken from tiny images of the hands, arms, feet, or legs that appear in these frames. To make matters worse, these images are often partially obscured by turbulence. For these reasons, reports of the angles of attack used in swimming can only be considered as estimates.

A team of researchers, including this author, attempted to ascertain the best angles of attack for producing propulsive force while swimming the front crawl stroke (Maglischo et al., 1986). The subjects were eight distance freestylers who were all members of the 1984 U.S. Olympic Swimming Team. There were four males and four females who were filmed while swimming at race speed. We reported that angles of attack between 30 and 46 degrees were most effective during the propulsive phases of their strokes. Swimmers who used angles of attack between 50 and 70 degrees did not accelerate their bodies forward as rapidly during these phases.

Another approach to this problem has been to deduce the optimal angles of attack from measurements taken on foils in wind tunnels and water channels. Wood (1978) used a wind tunnel and plaster models of swimmers' hands and forearms to perform a series of studies similar to the ones conducted by Schleihauf (1978) that were mentioned earlier. His findings were generally the same concerning the effects of different angles of attack on the coefficients of lift and drag. One interesting aspect of Wood's research was that he used three different directions of water flow across the hand. The most effective angles of attack were between 55 and 60 degrees when the water was flowing across the hand from the thumb to the little finger, as water flows when swimmers sweep their hand in underneath their bodies at midstroke. The largest coefficients of lift occurred between angles of 15 and 35 degrees when the flow of water was directed from the little finger to the thumb, as it flows when swimmers sweep their hands out and up during the final portion of the underwater stroke in freestyle and butterfly. In the final series of experiments, the water was forced across the hand from fingertips to wrist, in the direction it would travel as swimmers sweep their hands out or down at the beginning of the underwater portion of the four competitive strokes. In this case, the optimal angles of attack were between 50 and 55 degrees.

It is obvious that the issue of angles of attack in swimming is a complicated one that is far from being resolved. Data from wind tunnels and water channels indicate that angles between 20 and 60 degrees are most effective for producing lift forces. Measurements on swimmers seem to favor angles of attack in the range of 30 to 40 degrees.

This information on angles of attack may seem academic because swimmers are constantly changing the orientation of their hands to the water each time they change directions during their underwater armstrokes. Thus, the sensation they receive is one of constantly changing angles of attack, even though they may simply be rotating their hands to attain the same angle in a new direction that was used during a previous stroke phase. Nevertheless, it should be easier for swimmers to find the correct angle of attack for a particular stroke phase if they know the approximate angle of inclination they should be trying to achieve. The following information should simplify a swimmer's search for the optimal angles of attack.

1. The hands (and feet) should always be inclined slightly in the direction they are moving.
2. A degree of inclination that is midway between 0 and 90 degrees will put swimmers very close to the proper angle of attack for a particular stroking movement.
3. Each major change of direction by the hands (and feet) will require a change in their direction of inclination (pitch).
4. Swimmers need to be conscious of which side of the hand (or foot) is the leading edge and which is the trailing edge with each change of direction.

If they follow these suggestions, swimmers with that nebulous phenomenon we call "feel for the water" will probably happen upon the proper combination of direction and angle of attack that is best for a particular stroking motion. These guidelines should also help swimmers with a poorly developed feel for the water come closer to achieving the proper angles of attack than they would without guidance.

One of the best ways to learn how the limbs should be moved through the water is to study underwater videotapes of world-class swimmers in slow motion. Look for the following:

1. The directions in which their hands and feet are inclined during each phase of the various strokes.
2. When and how these directions change as the swimmers pass from one phase of an underwater armstroke to the next.

Hand and Foot Pitch and Angle of Attack The terms *pitch* and *angle of attack* are often used interchangeably when referring to the direction in which limbs are inclined. Consequently, it is important to make a clear distinction between them. Pitch refers to the direction in which the hands and feet are facing. The angle of attack is the number of degrees at which they are inclined in a given direction.

Figure 16-21 illustrates the most common hand and foot pitches used in competitive swimming. The butterfly swimmer in Figure 16-21*a* has his hands pitched out. That is, his palms are facing away from his body to some extent. This hand pitch is used at the beginning of the underwater armstrokes for butterfly and breaststroke. The swimmer in Figure 16-21*b* also has his hands pitched out. This pitch is used in the first portion of the underwater armstrokes for the front crawl and back crawl. The swimmer in Figure 16-21*c* has his hand pitched in toward his body. This hand pitch is used at midstroke in all four of the competitive styles. The swimmer in Figure 16-21*d* has his hand pitched out. This pitch is used during the final portion of the front crawl and butterfly strokes.

The butterfly swimmer in Figure 16-21*e* (p. 340) has her feet pitched up. This pitch is used during the downbeats of the dolphin and flutter kicks. It is also used during the upbeat of the backstroke kick, although, in this case, the pitch of the swimmer's feet would have to be described as *down* because the swimmer is in a

Figure 16-21. The most common hand and foot pitches in competitive swimming.

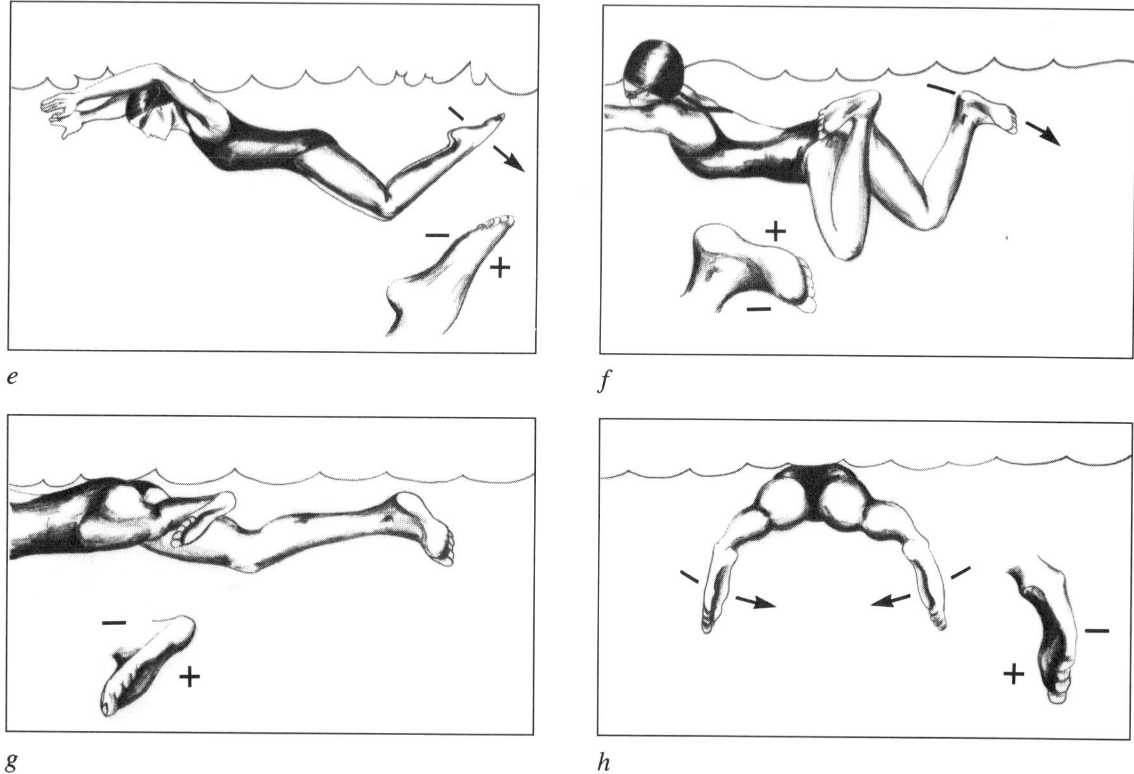

Figure 16-21. (continued)

supine position. The feet of the breaststroke swimmer are pitched out in Figure 16-21*f*, down in Figure 16-21*g*, and in in Figure 16-21*h*.

Velocity

Counsilman and Wasilak (1982) investigated the relationship between limb velocity and swimming speed and reported that the best swimmers accelerated their hands from the beginning to the end of their underwater armstroke. Later research by Schleihauf (1986) showed that this concept was accurate but oversimplified. Swimmers did not accelerate their hands smoothly from start to finish. Rather, hand speed was accelerated in pulses, decreasing and then increasing with each major change of direction during their underwater armstroke. The fastest velocities usually occurred during the final propulsive portion of an underwater armstroke, as Counsilman and Wasilak had stated.

Figure 16-22 shows a typical hand velocity pattern during freestyle swimming. The vertical axis shows the swimmer's velocity in meters per second. The time to complete each stroke phase is shown in hundredths of a second on the horizontal axis. The curved graph lines at the top show the changes in his hand velocity

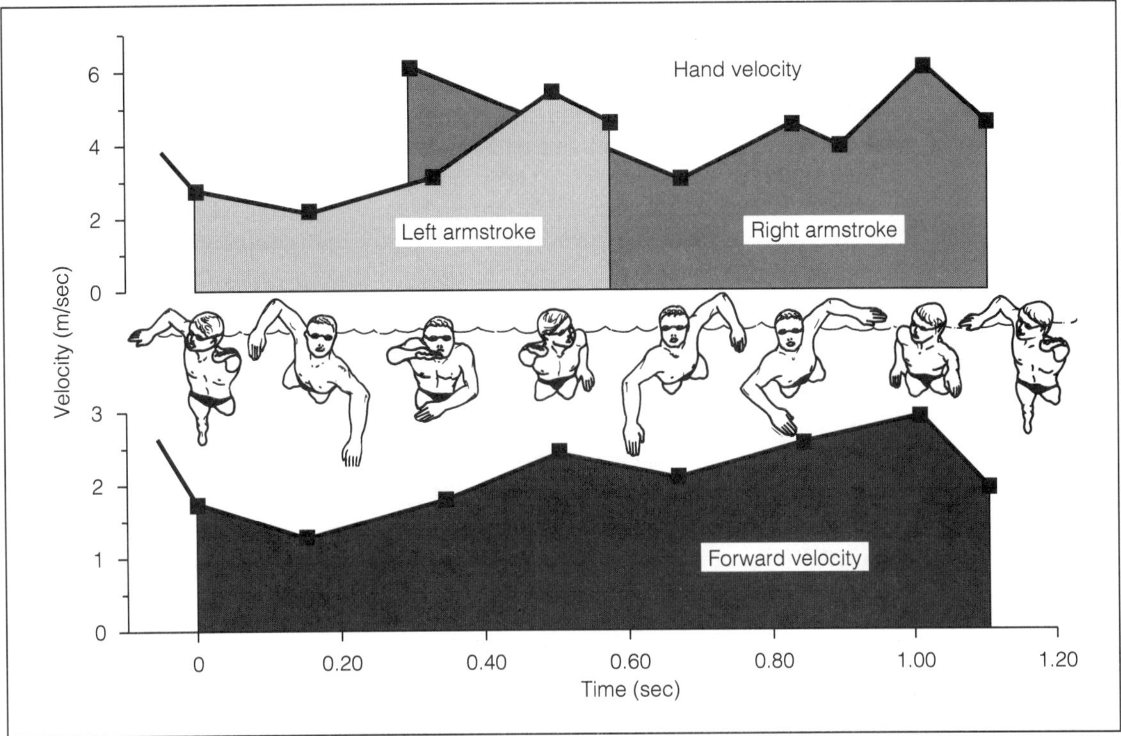

Figure 16-22. A typical hand velocity pattern for the front crawl stroke.

throughout one underwater stroke cycle. The swimmers drawn in the middle of the graph show which portion of the stroke is being completed. The bottom graph displays his forward velocity.

The velocities measured are those taking place in diagonal directions during the underwater stroke of his left and right hands. As such, they are three-dimensional in nature, having backward, sideward, upward, and downward components. They should not be confused with the backward speed of his hand or its speed in some other direction. This graph represents the actual velocity of his hands in their planes of motion. The tips of the middle fingers were used as the references for hand velocity, and he was swimming at 100 m speed.

His pattern of pulses in hand velocity were as follows. The speed of his left hand decreased after entry until the catch was made. His hand velocity accelerated, although not maximally, during the first propulsive sweep, as it traveled in under his body. This was followed by another acceleration of hand velocity when he swept his hand toward the surface. His left hand decelerated near the surface as he released pressure on the water and started his recovery. A similar pattern occurred during his right armstroke. Notice that accelerations and decelerations of his hand velocities corresponded very closely to like changes in his forward propulsion.

The hand velocity pattern in Figure 16-22 is typical of those for the remaining three competitive strokes. In all cases, swimmers accelerate and decelerate their hands in pulses each time they change directions during the stroke. Counsilman and Wasilak (1982) reported maximum hand velocities in the range of 4.5 to 6 m/sec (14 to 20 ft/sec). Schleihauf and coworkers (1988) reported velocities in the same range for world-class freestyle sprinters.

There is probably a precise relationship between hand speed and angle of attack that should be used during each phase of the four underwater armstrokes. Apparently, swimmers consciously maintain some submaximum hand velocity until the final portion of the armstroke. They probably do this to conserve energy. Perhaps, over the course of a race, it is not possible to maintain maximum hand speed for each complete underwater armstroke.

As you would expect, swimmers accelerate their hands more in sprints than longer races. Also, females generally do not attain maximum velocities as great as those attained by males (Maglischo et al., 1986).

As indicated previously, a swimmer's diagonal stroke pattern is a combination of movements in horizontal, lateral, and vertical directions. An examination of velocities for each of these components can shed additional light on the mechanisms swimmers use to produce propulsive force because during a particular stroke phase, the major propulsive effort is probably made in the directional component where the hands are moving most rapidly. These component hand velocities can also elucidate the way that swimmers initiate changes in direction. The direction showing the greatest increase is probably the initiator.

Figure 16-23 shows directional components of hand velocities for a world-record holder in the butterfly. It is a very complicated graph so let me explain it carefully. The athlete is swimming butterfly at 200-m speed. The directional components for a particular stroke phase are enclosed in a bar. A swimmer is drawn above each bar, showing the particular stroke phase. Rectangles represent hand velocity for the horizontal (forward-back) component of velocity; triangles indicate lateral (in-out) hand velocity; and circles denote hand velocity for the vertical (up-down) component. The line through the middle of the graph separates the two directions represented by each of these components. Backward hand speeds for the horizontal component are shown above this line; forward hand speeds, below this line. For the lateral component, inward hand velocity is represented above the line, and outward velocity is represented below. For the vertical component, upward hand velocity is shown above the line; downward velocity, below. The actual direction in which the hands are moving during each stroke phase are printed in the appropriate symbol, and the placement of these symbols indicates how fast the swimmer's hands are traveling in those directions.

Now, to describe the directional velocities. The swimmer's hands travel forward, up, and in shortly after entering the water (see bar A of Figure 16-23). That direction changes quickly to forward, down, and out, as the hands travel to the catch (bar B). Her hands gradually decelerate in all directions during this time. Their velocity in an outward direction appears to predominate during this part of the stroke, however.

Her hands accelerate in, back, and down after the catch, as she sweeps her arms under her body at midstroke. They accelerate down faster than any other direction

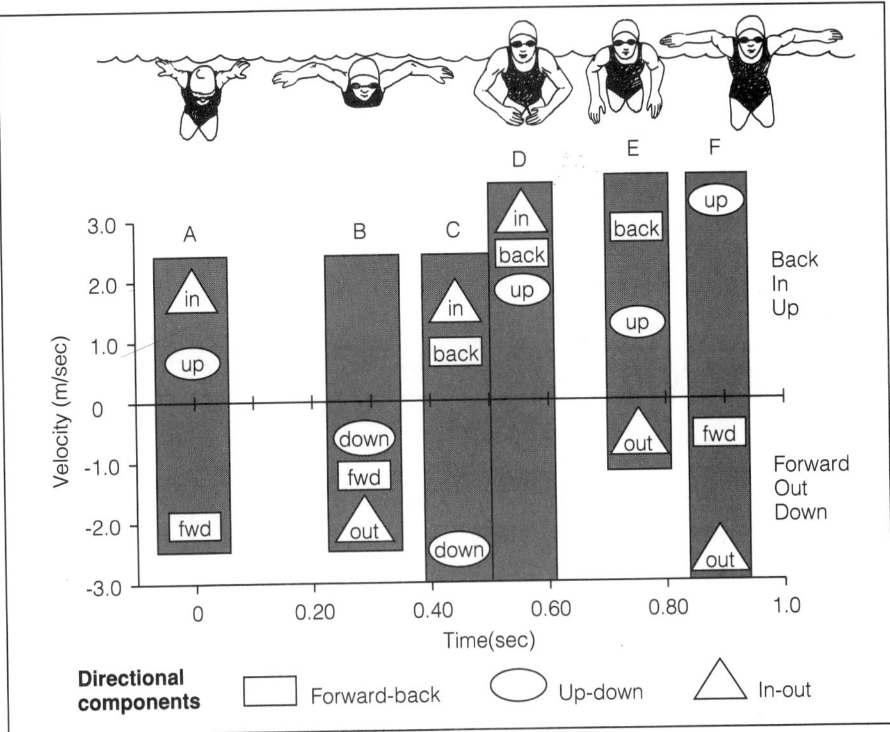

Figure 16-23. Directional components of hand velocity for Mary T. swimming butterfly.

during the first half of the sweep under her body (bar C), so that is probably the direction that supplies most of the propulsion. In the second half, they move at nearly equal speeds in all directional components (see bar D). However, the fact that the inward speed of her hands is slightly greater shows that this is probably the major propulsive direction during this sweep.

The principal change of hand direction is from in to out during the first part of the final sweep toward the surface (bar E). Hand speed also accelerates somewhat in a backward direction.

The upward and outward velocities of her hands accelerate markedly through the final portion of this sweep as they near the surface (bar F). They also begin moving forward before they leave the water, showing that the swimmer does not try to maintain propulsive force all the way to the surface. She actually begins to recover her arms before they leave the water.

Directional velocities like these offer additional support to the notion that the major propulsive motions of swimmers are in diagonal rather than backward directions. They also support the need to make major changes in hand direction periodically during the armstroke. This information will be applied to swimmers' stroking movements in the next chapter.

CHAPTER

17

Propulsive Fundamentals

The purpose of this chapter is to make some practical applications of the information on propulsion that was presented in Chapter 16. The basic sweeps that are common to all strokes are described first. The propulsive motions of the legs are discussed next, followed by some conjecture on how the body might contribute to propulsion. Finally, this information is summarized by suggesting some fundamentals of propulsion.

STROKING: A DIFFERENT TERMINOLOGY

The commonly used terms *pull* and *push* seem obsolete in light of the fact that swimmers use diagonal sculling motions rather than paddlelike pushes. That is why I suggested a more descriptive terminology in the first edition of this book. I use the term *sweep* because it conveys the propellerlike nature of these stroking motions. A prefix is attached to this term to describe the direction of the sweep; however, the selection of a prefix is complicated because each sweep has three different directional components. In naming each sweep, I selected the prefix that best communicates the nature of a particular motion. The most dominant of the three directional components is usually the prefix. However, in some cases, movements in directions of less magnitude are used because they seem to communicate the nature of a particular sweep best.

Let me cite one example to clarify the method for selecting these prefixes. The swimmer in Figure 17-1 is midway through the initial underwater sweep in the front

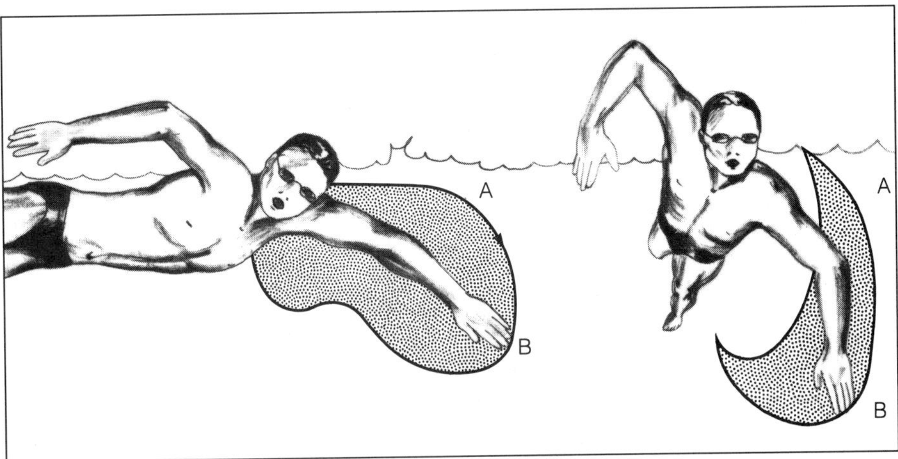

Figure 17-1. The downsweep in the front crawl stroke.

crawl stroke. His stroke pattern is shown from both front and side views so that all directional components are visible. In the sweep (A to B) his arm travels diagonally down, out, and forward. The downward motion predominates, so the movement is called a *downsweep*.

The Four Sweeps in Swimming

After studying films and video tapes for several years, it became clear that the propulsive movements of competitive swimmers' arms could be reduced to four basic sweeps. The rules governing a particular stroke sometimes cause these sweeps to appear different from stroke to stroke because the swimmers' arms move in somewhat different directions. Nevertheless, an examination of the way the arms displaced water back revealed that the nature of certain sweeps were remarkably similar from one stroke to the next.

The four basic arm sweeps have been termed *outsweep, downsweep, insweep,* and *upsweep* and are summarized in the following box. They are summarized here but will be described in detail in the chapters on each competitive stroke.

The Four Basic Arm Sweeps Used by Competitive Swimmers

1. Outsweep—the initial underwater sweep in the butterfly and breaststroke
2. Downsweep—the initial underwater sweep used in the front crawl and back crawl
3. Insweep—the second sweep used in all competitive strokes
4. Upsweep—the final sweep of the front crawl and butterfly

Outsweep The outsweep is the initial underwater movement in the breaststroke and butterfly. It is illustrated in Figure 17-2. The outsweep is not a propulsive movement but is, instead, used to move swimmers' hands and arms into position for the catch.

Downsweep Front crawl and back crawl swimmers use a downsweep to begin their underwater armstrokes. Figure 17-3 depicts the downsweep as it is used in these strokes. It is also *non*propulsive.

Insweep The insweep follows the downsweep in the front crawl and the back crawl, and it follows the outsweep in butterfly and breaststroke. It is the first major propulsive sweep in three of the four competitive strokes. There is a corresponding movement in the back crawl but it is termed an upsweep because the swimmer is supine and the arm travels up more than in during this motion. Nevertheless, the way that propulsion is produced during the upsweep of the back crawl is identical to the insweep in all respects but direction. The insweep for a front crawl swimmer

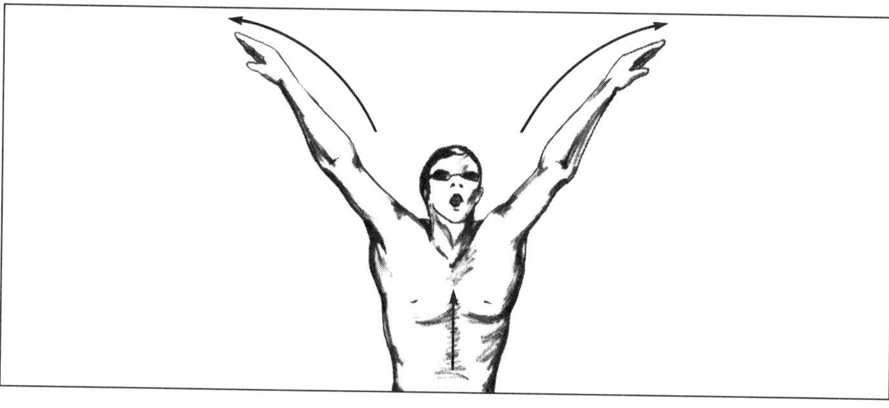

Figure 17-2. The outsweep as used in the butterfly and breaststroke.

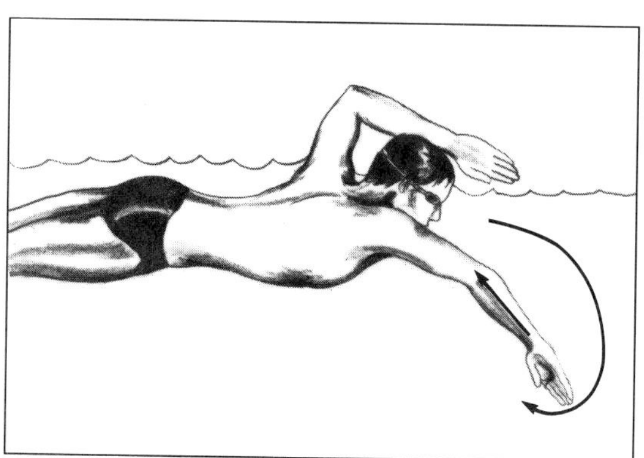

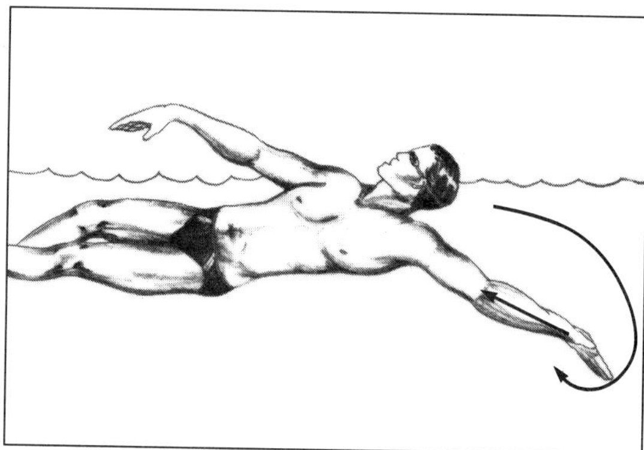

Figure 17-3. The downsweep in the front crawl and back crawl.

was used to describe propeller propulsion in Chapter 16 (see Figure 16-10). Figure 17-4 shows the insweep as used in butterfly and breaststroke.

Upsweep The upsweep follows the insweep in the front crawl and butterfly strokes. (There are actually two corresponding movements in the backstroke that will be described in Chapter 20.) Figure 17-5 illustrates the upsweep during front crawl swimming from side and front views.

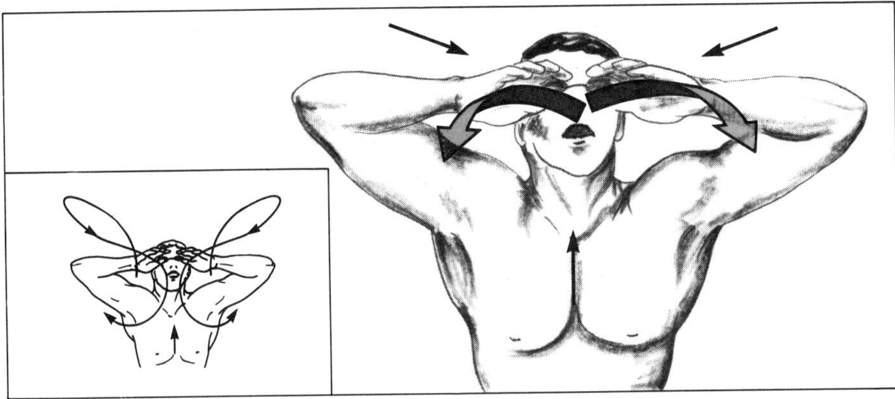

Figure 17-4. The insweep as used in the butterfly and breaststroke.

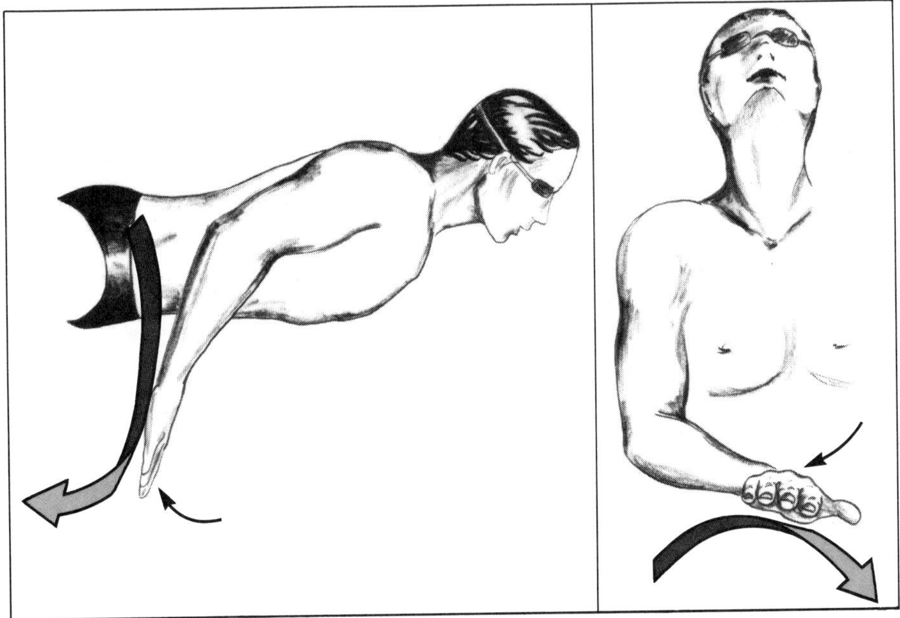

Figure 17-5. The upsweep as used in the front crawl stroke. Side and underneath views show how water can be displaced back by the outward and upward sweep of the hand during this phase of the underwater armstroke.

The Catch Is All-Important to Fast Swimming

The *catch* is the point during the underwater armstroke where propulsion begins. Most swimmers mistakenly believe that the catch should be made immediately after their hands enter the water in three of the four competitive strokes. In breaststroke, some swimmers believe that it starts immediately when they begin sweeping their hands out to the sides. This mistake causes one of the most common stroke problems in competitive swimming—the *dropped elbow*. Actually, in all strokes, propulsion begins about one-third of the way through the underwater armstroke. The arm(s) should travel out or down approximately 40 to 50 cm and be flexed through a range of 30 to 40 degrees at the elbow before the catch is made. Swimmers require this length of time to get their arms positioned to displace water back.

Figure 17-6 shows when propulsion begins in the front crawl. The data were collected from filming Matt Biondi swimming at 100-m speed. Schleihauf's method for calculating propulsive force was used (Schleihauf, Gray, & DeRose, 1983). Force is expressed in kilograms on the vertical axis. Time, in hundredths of a second, is displayed on the horizontal axis. A side view stroke pattern is drawn at the top of the graph marked in hundredths of a second to illustrate how much propulsive force is being produced during each phase of the armstroke.

Notice that Biondi does not begin to apply propulsive force until his hand is near its deepest point and nearly one-third of the way through the underwater portion of the stroke. This is because his hand must travel down that distance before the arm can be positioned so that it is facing back. Likewise, swimmers in the

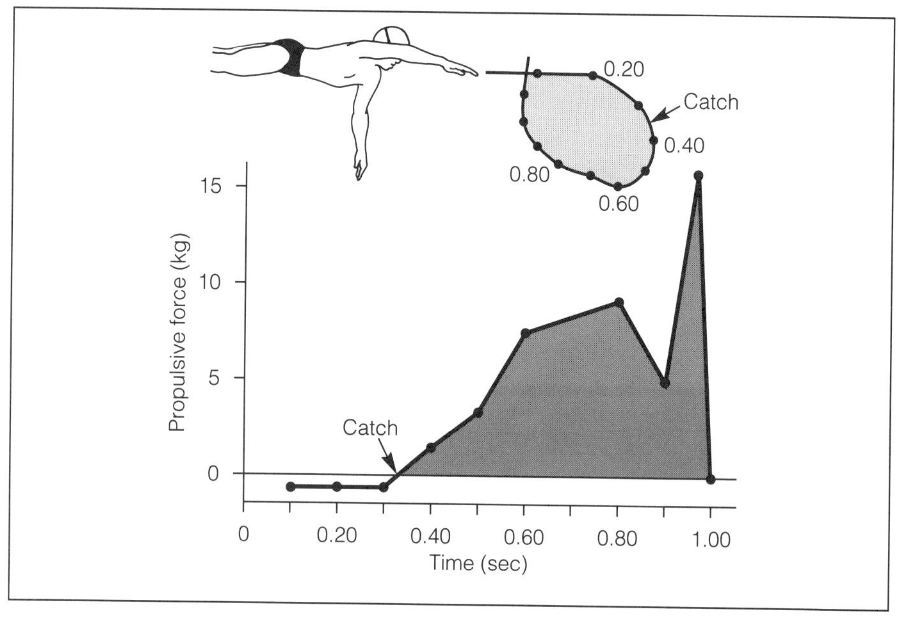

Figure 17-6. A propulsive force graph for Matt Biondi, world-record holder in the 100-m freestyle and 1988 gold medalist in five events.

remaining three competitive strokes should not apply propulsive force until they are approximately one-third of the way through their underwater stroke cycles. The catch is important because the succeeding propulsive phases of the stroke will be less effective if it is not made correctly.

Figure 17-7 shows the position of the hand and arm at the catch in the front crawl stroke. Coaches frequently refer to this position as a *high elbow* for obvious reasons. *Swimmers should not attempt to apply propulsive force until their arms are in this high-elbow position.* Any attempt to do so will only reduce their forward speed.

The High Elbow Doc Counsilman first made us aware of the importance of the high-elbow position in his excellent book *The Science of Swimming* (1968). At the time, we believed that swimmers used the high elbow to place their arms in position to push back through the water. We know now that a high elbow permits the arms and hands to displace water backward more effectively as swimmers scull them in lateral and vertical directions. The high-elbow position is important to fast swimming because *until the arm is facing back, the swimmer cannot displace water back effectively.*

Perhaps the most common mistake in swimming is to begin the propulsive phase of the armstroke before a high-elbow position has been achieved. If the elbow is not above the arm when the catch is made, water will be pushed down, not back. Figure 17-8 shows a front crawl swimmer with a dropped elbow. This drawing illustrates why this is such a serious stroke defect. With his elbow down, the underside of the swimmer's forearm is oriented nearly perpendicular to the direction it is traveling, causing him to push water down rather than displace it back. The swimmer mistakenly believes that he is pushing water back because his wrist is flexed and his hand is facing back.

In butterfly and breaststroke, a high-elbow position must be achieved by sweeping the hands *out* and down. Because swimmers cannot roll their body to the side in these strokes, their hands must sweep outside their shoulders before they can orient their arms back against the water.

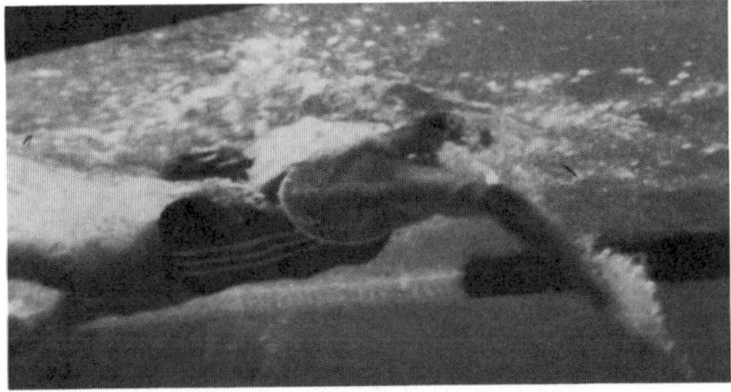

Figure 17-7. A side view of a front crawl swimmer showing the arm depth and the high-elbow position at the catch.

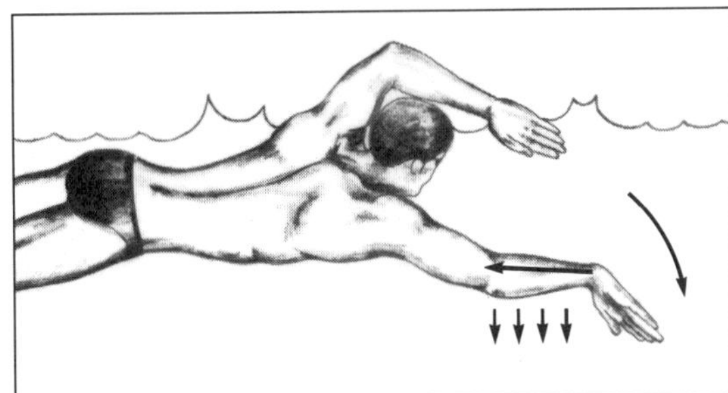

Figure 17-8. The dropped elbow in front crawl swimming.

Why is the dropped elbow so prevalent among slower swimmers? Many coaches believe that the dropped elbow is due to lack of strength. I doubt the validity of this observation. More likely, it is because these swimmers attempt to push their arms back too early in their underwater armstrokes. Swimmers are most likely to drop their elbow during the downsweep of the freestyle and backstroke and during the outsweep of the butterfly and breaststroke. *They must be coached to wait until these phases of the strokes have been completed before they start applying force.*

The fastest swimmers do not drop their elbows because they do not try to apply force until they reach the catch position. They have learned, through instruction or intuition, to wait until their arms are deep enough or wide enough to achieve a backward orientation to the water. When they take the time to do this, their elbows ride up above their hands so that they achieve the high-elbow position.

Arm and Hand Alignment at the Catch An important point to make about the catch is that swimmers must align both their forearms and hands before attempting to apply propulsive force. The front crawl swimmer in Figure 17-7 has her arm aligned properly. You could draw a straight line from the tip of her middle finger to the tip of her elbow. This allows her to use her forearm and hand like a rotating hydrofoil during the propulsive phases of the stroke. If her hand were flexed excessively or her forearm were facing down, a portion of this foil effect would be lost. It would be like trying to fly with a broken wing.

Chronic Shoulder Pain (Tendinitis)

One of the most serious medical problems facing competitive swimmers is tendinitis in the shoulder region. It has even been nicknamed swimmer's shoulder because of its prevalence in our sport. At the very least, chronic tendinitis reduces swimmers' performances. At worst, it can cause them to leave the sport prematurely. Many swimmers can prevent tendinitis or reduce its severity if they follow this advice: *They should not try to get their elbows up and push their arms back at the same time.* Many swimmers are taught to make a "quick" or "early" catch so that they can begin pushing water back almost immediately after their hands enter the water. Friction on the ligaments and tendons of the shoulder joints can be quite severe when swimmers stroke this way. Figure 17-9 shows the locations of these structures.

The most common cause of chronic shoulder pain is when the proximal head of the humerus (the long bone of the upper arm) rubs across the supraspinatus tendon, the biceps tendons, and the coracoacromial ligament (Kennedy, 1978). Medial rotation of the shoulder joint increases the likelihood of this friction occurring. The most severe medial rotation takes place when swimmers try to push their elbows up while pressing their hands back. In doing so, the head of the humerus thrusts forward in close proximity to the ligamentous structure of the shoulder joint where it is more likely to come in contact with this structure as it rotates forward and down.

Medial rotation will be less intense if the downsweep of the front crawl is performed correctly—that is, by sweeping the arm and hand down, with no attempt

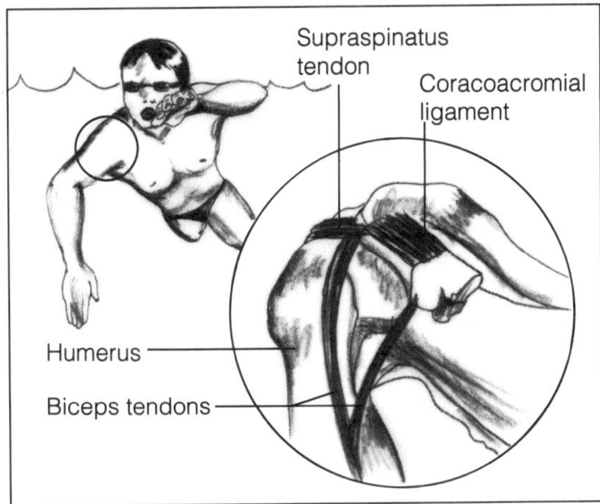

Figure 17-9. Structure of the shoulder joint.

to push them back, until the high-elbow position has been reached. The head of the humerus will not be thrust forward so vigorously against the ligaments of the shoulder if the catch is made this way. You can feel the difference for yourself. Hold your arm in front of you at shoulder height. Then push your shoulder forward while pressing your hand down and back. You should feel a twisting strain in your shoulder joint as the head of the humerus moves forward and rotates down. Next, start with your arm outstretched. Reach forward and down with your hand until your elbow and shoulder naturally ride up above it. The sensations of twisting and strain should be considerably reduced because the head of the humerus does not thrust forward as much when it rotates.

A similar experiment will produce the same result using an outsweep. In this case, reach your hands *forward* and out to the catch position to avoid friction. You will feel more strain if you try to pull your hands back while pushing your elbows up above them. Many swimmers with a history of severe tendinitis have experienced little or no shoulder pain by learning to catch before they push their hands back.

Teaching Swimmers to Use Sweeps

Experienced swimmers sometimes find it difficult to grasp the concept of using their hands like foils. This is particularly true if they were taught to use them like paddles early in their careers. Novice swimmers should be taught to use sweeps before they develop bad habits. Sculling drills can aid both groups in this purpose.

Books on synchronized swimming are good sources for these drills, or you can devise some of your own. There are three sculling drills that I have found to be particularly effective. They are called the front scull, middle scull, and rear scull drills. Each drill should be performed with pull buoys or tubes wrapped around the ankles. Swimmers will learn sculling motions faster if they do not rely on their legs for propulsion.

Front Sculling Drill Figure 17-10 illustrates the mechanics of this sculling drill. In a prone position with arms extended overhead, swimmers scull their hands out and in simultaneously, trying to propel their body forward while doing so. They should find this rather easy to do with very little practice. The emphasis is on extending the arms slightly on the way out and flexing them as they scull in. The motion is made in a continuous figure-eight pattern, with the arms sculling out and back to a catch position (see Figure 17-10*a*) and then sculling inward and forward to begin another cycle (see Figure 17-10*b*).

The palms of the swimmers' hands face down when they start the scull out. They rotate out during the scull out and then rotate in during the scull in. The fingertips are the leading edges of the hands on the scull out and the thumb sides are the leading edges on the scull in. Caution swimmers against pushing back too much during these sculls. They will do this if the continuous figure-eight nature of the scull is not emphasized. The purpose of this drill is to teach swimmers to catch properly before beginning the insweep. A variation on the drill can be done by sculling the hands in until they cross at the wrists.

Middle Sculling Drill Figure 17-11*a* shows the swimmer at the end of the outsweep of the scull, and Figure 17-11*b* shows her at the end of the insweep. The

a

b

Figure 17-10. The front sculling drill.

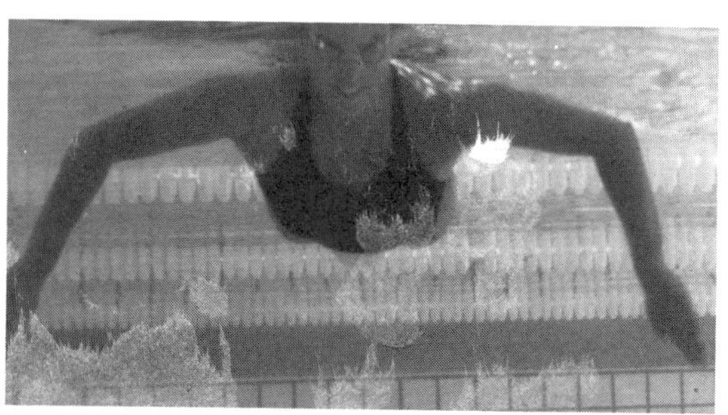

a

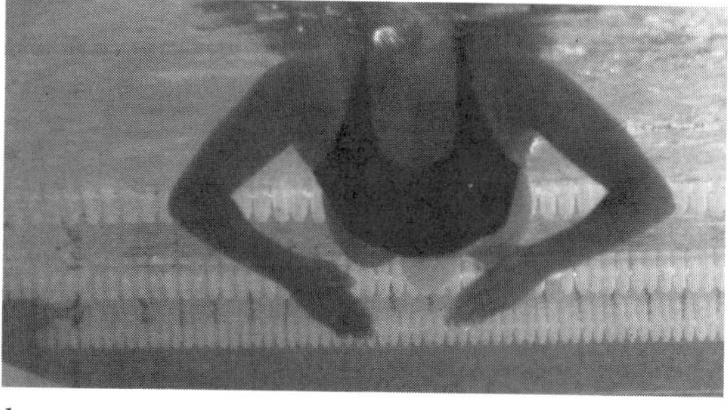

b

Figure 17-11. The middle sculling drill.

purpose of this scull is to teach swimmers how to do the insweep of the front crawl, butterfly, and breaststroke.

The swimmer is face down, once again. This time her arms are under her shoulders with her elbows out to the side. Her hands scull in and out directly under her shoulders. She extends her arms on the outsweep and flexes them on the insweep. Her palms rotate out during the outsweep and in during the insweep. Her arms come together or cross underneath her chest on the scull in. They should not be fully extended on the scull out. The little-finger sides of her hands are the leading edges during the scull out and the thumbs the leading edges during the scull in. The scull in is the portion that relates to competitive swimming, so athletes should emphasize propulsion from the scull in by adding some backward motion to it. The scull out should include some forward motion to return their hands to a position for the next scull in.

Rear Sculling Drill This drill is excellent for teaching swimmers the upsweep. Figure 17-12*a* shows the swimmer during the scull in. Figure 17-12*b* shows her at the end of the scull out. The scull out is similar to the upsweep of the front crawl and butterfly. The scull in is used to return the hands for another scull out.

From a prone position, the swimmer's arms are back under her waist and flexed at the elbows. Her wrists are aligned with her forearms so that both are facing in (see Figure 17-12*a*). From this position, the swimmer sculls her hands out and back and then in and forward in an alternating manner. Her arms extend slightly on the scull out and flex slightly on the scull in. They should not extend completely, however, or the swimmer's arms will not be oriented properly. Her palms rotate out on the scull out and in on the scull in. The little-finger sides of the swimmer's hands are the leading edges on the scull out and the thumb sides the leading edges on the scull in. Swimmers should emphasize the scull out, because it is similar to the propulsive upsweeps of the front crawl and butterfly armstrokes.

You'll find that swimmers can be taught the armstrokes of the competitive strokes very quickly once they have mastered these drills. After the catch position, the underwater armstroke of the front crawl consists of the inward portion of the middle scull and the outward portion of the rear scull. The butterfly armstroke consists of a gentle front scull out to the catch, followed by the inward portion of

a *b*

Figure 17-12. The rear sculling drill.

the middle scull and the outward portion of the rear scull. The breaststroke armstroke is made up of a gentle front scull out to the catch, followed by a middle scull in.

THE ROLE OF LEGS IN SWIMMING PROPULSION

The legs were not believed to be a significant propulsive agent in most competitive strokes when the propulsive drag theory was popular, because it was argued that, except in breaststroke, the feet and legs moved up and down rather than back through the water. We realize now that water is displaced back by upward and downward movements of the legs just as it is by vertical movements of the arms.

Swimmers should be able to accelerate their body forward with the flutter and dolphin kicks in much the same manner that a dolphin is propelled by the vertical movements of its tail (fluke). In fact, we know that the kick propels swimmers because we watch it happen every day in kicking drills. Figure 17-13 shows how the downbeat of the dolphin kick can propel a swimmer forward. The small black arrow shows that the swimmer's feet sweep almost directly down during the downbeat. With the knees bent and the toes pointed up, her lower legs take on the characteristics of a hydrofoil, with her knees as the leading edge and her toes the trailing edge.

With her knees flexed at the start, the angle of attack of her lower legs causes the backward displacement of water as her legs sweep down. The relative direction of water flow is opposite to the downward motion of her legs, causing that water to be displaced back as it travels upward from her knees toward her feet. Gradual extension of her legs maintains that backward force on the water until her legs are nearly extended. At that time, her legs push down on the water at an angle of attack that is near perpendicular so that they lose their propulsive effect and their major effect is to push the swimmer's hips toward the surface. Her feet, however, can still propel her forward if she has an adequate range of motion at the ankles. Figure 17-14 shows why. The swimmer in Figure 17-14*a*, who can extend her feet through a large range of motion, should be able to maintain an effective (upward) angle of attack with her feet for a longer portion of the downbeat. With the feet facing up,

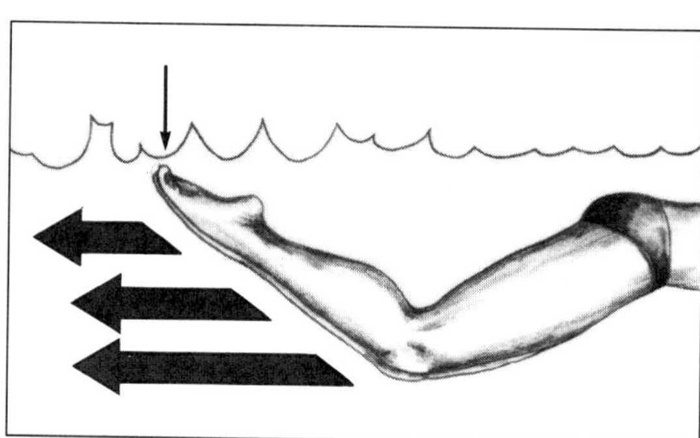

Figure 17-13. Propulsion during the dolphin kick.

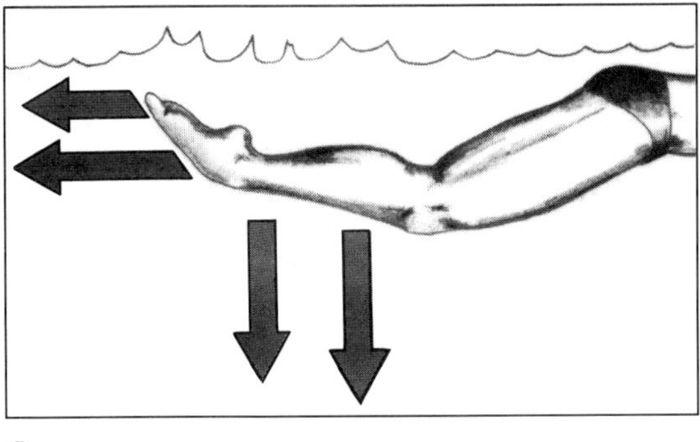
a

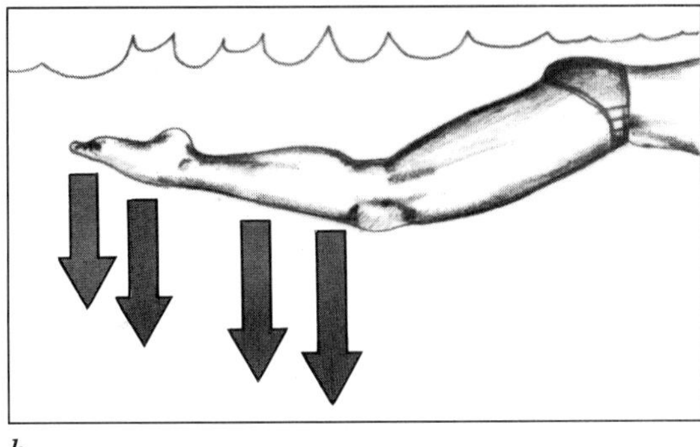
b

Figure 17-14. The importance of ankle extension ability to kicking.

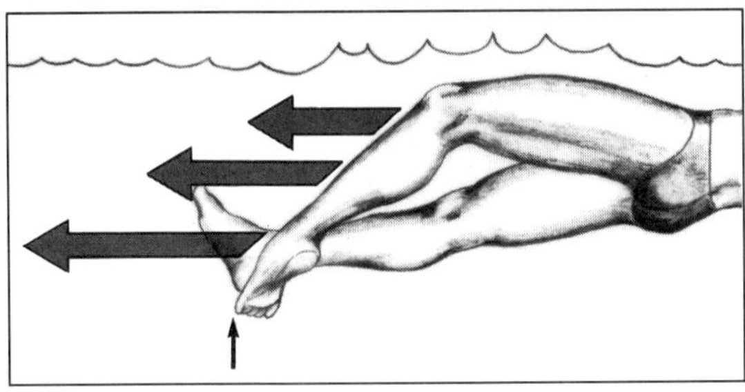

Figure 17-15. Propulsion during the upbeat of the back crawl flutter kick.

the angle of attack is such that the water can continue to be displaced back as it flows upward from the swimmer's ankles to her toes, even though her legs are perpendicular to the water flow and pushing down.

The swimmer in Figure 17-14*b* has less ability to extend her feet at the ankles. As a consequence, her feet face down long before her legs are extended. Because her feet are nearly perpendicular to the water flow, this swimmer pushes water down, not back, with her feet and her legs near the end of the downbeat.

Another propulsive mechanism that may be operating in the dolphin and flutter kicks is the fling-ring mechanism proposed by Colwin (1984, 1985a, 1985b), which was described in Chapter 16. In this mechanism, swimmers carry water down with their legs and then *fling,* or accelerate, it back when their legs reach extension and make the sudden change from downbeat to upbeat.

The propulsive mechanisms described for the downbeat of the dolphin kick should be equally effective in the flutter kick of the front crawl stroke. The corresponding movement in the back crawl stroke is an upbeat. Figure 17-15 shows how propulsion is probably produced during this motion. In this case, the lower leg kicks up (and laterally), with the knee flexed and the foot extended down and in (pigeon toed). With this orientation, water can be displaced back from the leading edge (the knee) to the trailing edge (the toes) as the swimmer extends his leg during the upbeat.

Support for the kick as a propelling agent comes from two sources. Watkins and Gordon (1983) found that a group of 33 male and female competitors could only pull at 90 percent of full stroke sprint speed when they were not kicking. The swimmers' legs were supported by pull buoys while they swam the front crawl stroke.

The most convincing work has been completed by Hollander and his associates (1988). They used a *MAD* (measuring active drag) system to measure propulsive force while swimming and pulling. Figure 17-16 illustrates the MAD system.

It consists of a series of adjustable pads mounted on underwater poles. The pads are placed in a series down the length of the pool so that swimmers can reach forward, grip a pad, and push back against it one arm after the other as they swim down the pool. The pads are attached to a force transducer that is interfaced with a computer to measure the force applied to each pad. Because there is no slippage when the swimmer pushes against the pad, all of the force measured is propulsive. Consequently, none is lost or used for stabilization.

These researches tested 18 male and female national- and Olympic-level swimmers under two conditions: (1) while swimming the full stroke (arms and legs) at maximum speed and (2) while pulling (arms only) at maximum speed with their legs supported by a pull buoy. The mean force produced during full-stroke swim-

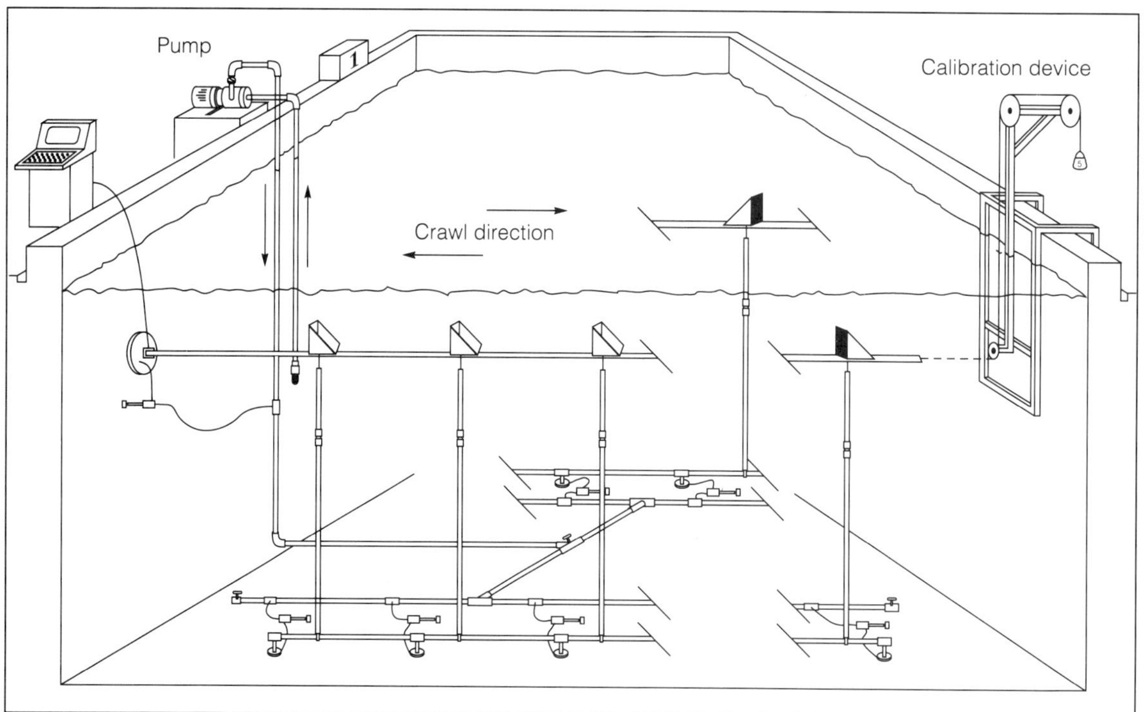

Figure 17-16. A schematic of the MAD system. (Reproduced from Toussaint, 1988)

ming was, on the average, approximately 12 percent greater. They concluded that the additional force was supplied by the kick because the arms were not capable of stroking any more efficiently.

It is interesting to note that they found a range of kicking effectiveness between −6 to +27 percent among the group of swimmers. Most swimmers obviously derived force from their kicks, yet there were a few (3 subjects) whose kicks actually reduced their propulsive force.

Four Leg Sweeps

There are four basic leg sweeps used by competitive swimmers. The dolphin and flutter kicks are composed of a *downbeat* and *upbeat*. In the breaststroke, the leg movements are best described as an *outsweep* and *insweep*. The propulsive mechanics of the downbeat (upbeat of the backstroke) were described in the preceding paragraphs. The upbeat (downbeat in backstroke) is described here. The outsweep and insweep of the breaststroke will be described in Chapter 21.

Upbeats are probably not propulsive. Figure 17-17 shows why. It depicts a butterfly swimmer during the upbeat of the dolphin kick.

Kick patterns that were drawn from films of athletes swimming at competitive speeds show that their feet travel up *and forward* during the upbeat. Their legs should be completely extended while this is taking place, which produces a perpendicular angle of attack that pushes water up. The feet hang loosely from the ankles and are maintained in a natural position, midway between extension and flexion, during the upbeat. This places them at a small angle of attack relative to the direction in which they are traveling, so little if any water is displaced back by them as they travel up.

If the upbeat were made with great force, it would push the body down and decelerate forward speed. However, if made gently (as it probably is), the upbeat stabilizes the body. It keeps it from being pushed up by the downward movements of the arms.

Support for the nonpropulsive nature of the upbeat can be drawn from the work of Ungerechts (1983). He showed that, in butterfly swimming, the legs kicked down 63 percent faster than they kicked up.

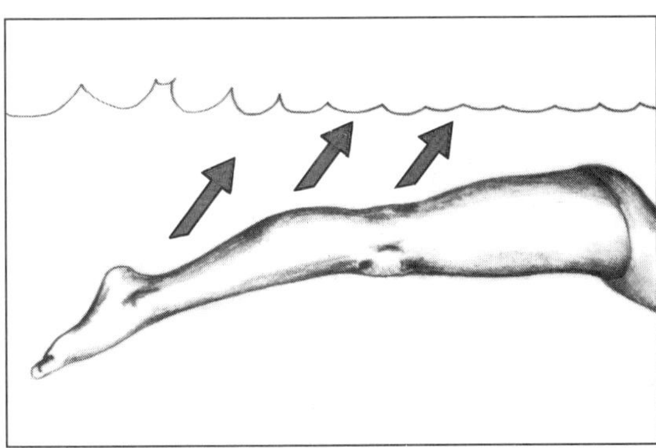

Figure 17-17. The upbeat of the dolphin kick.

The upbeat probably serves three purposes, none of which is propulsive: (1) it probably stabilizes the trunk; (2) it improves streamlining by bringing the legs up in line with the body during a portion of the stroke cycle; and, of course, (3) it brings the legs up into position for the next downbeat. The downbeat of the backstroke is probably nonpropulsive as well.

Swimmers who bend their legs too much during the upbeat create the problem illustrated in Figure 17-18. The swimmer's legs are moving in the direction of the arrow on his foot. That is, they are traveling up and forward. This has the effect of pushing water up and forward, which will push his hips down and decelerate his forward speed. The upbeat should be a rebound motion assisted by an extension of the hips, and *it should be made with the legs straight*.

THE ROLE OF THE BODY IN SWIMMING PROPULSION

Most explanations of swimming propulsion involve only the arms and legs. However, several experts have speculated that the trunk contributes to propulsion during the undulating movements of the butterfly and breaststroke (Kreighbaum & Barthels, 1985; Persyn, Vervaecke, & Verhetsel, 1983; Ungerechts, 1983; Van Tilborgh, Willens, & Persyn, 1988).

Figure 17-19 shows the way in which body undulation *might* contribute to propulsion in the butterfly. In Figure 17-19*a,* the swimmer is piked at the waist as she completes the downbeat of her first dolphin kick. Figure 17-19*b* shows her trunk lowered with her back arched as she completes the upbeat of that same kick.

It is possible that butterfly swimmers accelerate water back with their trunk as their hips drop from position *a* to position *b*. This possibility is represented by the arrows showing the direction of water movement in Figure 17-19. Water is trapped in the pocket formed by her trunk and thighs when she is in position *a,* and that water may be accelerated back when her trunk and hips come down to position *b*. Her legs move up and out of the way at the same time so that they do not interfere with the backward flow of water.

The reason water would be accelerated back rather than down as her hips drop is that her trunk and hips drop down in a sequential manner as she travels *forward*. At the same time, the relative flow of water is up and back in the opposite direction. With her body flowing down and forward sequentially, it may act like a foil with each segment, maintaining an angle of attack that gradually displaces each segment of the water back as her trunk passes down through it from chest to hips.

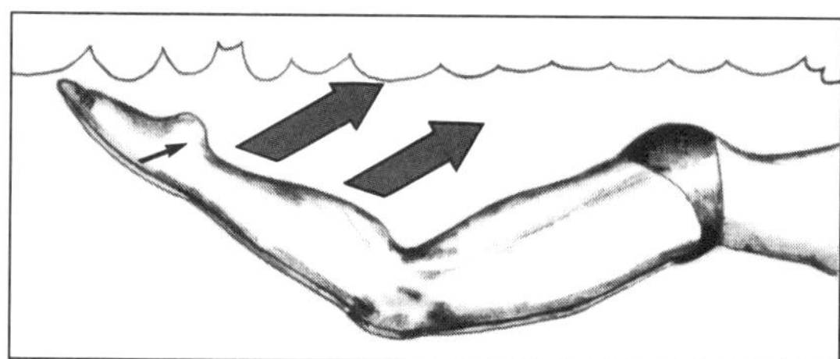

Figure 17-18. The mistake of bending the legs too much during the upbeat of the dolphin kick.

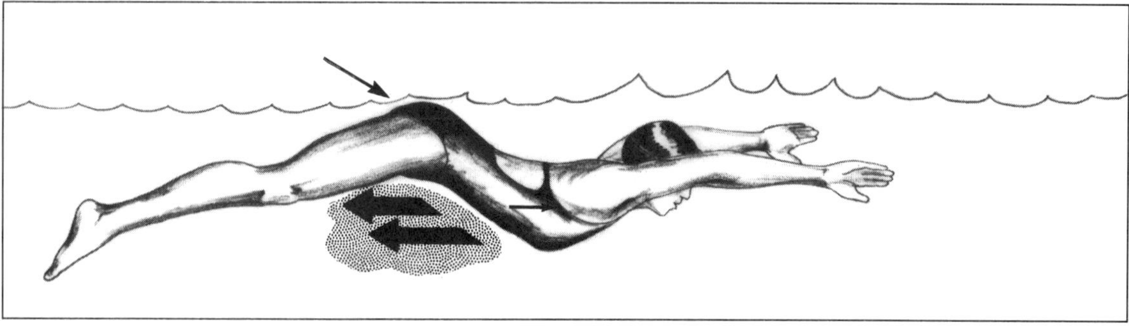

a

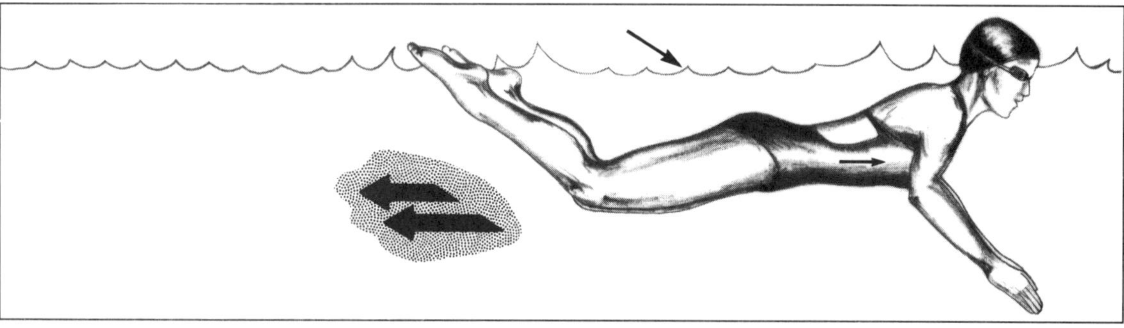

b

Figure 17-19. Undulating motions of the body during butterfly and their possible propulsive effects.

Many butterfly swimmers say that they make a conscious effort to push their chests down as they reach for the catch, which is the phase of the stroke cycle when this body-foil mechanism would take place. Thus, they may be dropping their chests to accelerate water back with their trunks.

Observing the way that some sea animals swim is justification for this theory (Lighthill, 1969; Ungerechts, 1983). Figure 17-20 (p. 360) illustrates how fish use their bodies for propulsion. Fish accelerate water back as they undulate through it. The sideward sweeps of a fish's tail cause the middle of its body to move to the side in the opposite direction. This forms a concave surface where water is trapped (see Figure 17-20*a*). That water accelerates back when the fish sweeps its tail to the opposite side (see Figure 17-20*b*). The backward movement of water results in a counter force that propels the fish forward.

Swimmers who use an undulating style in the breaststroke may also contribute to their forward propulsion with these body movements, although probably not to the same extent as butterflyers. Figure 17-21 (p. 360) shows a "dolphin-style" breaststroke swimmer in a piked position as he completes the propulsive phase of his kick (Figure 17-21*a*) and with his hips dropped during the first half of his armstroke (Figure 17-21*b*).

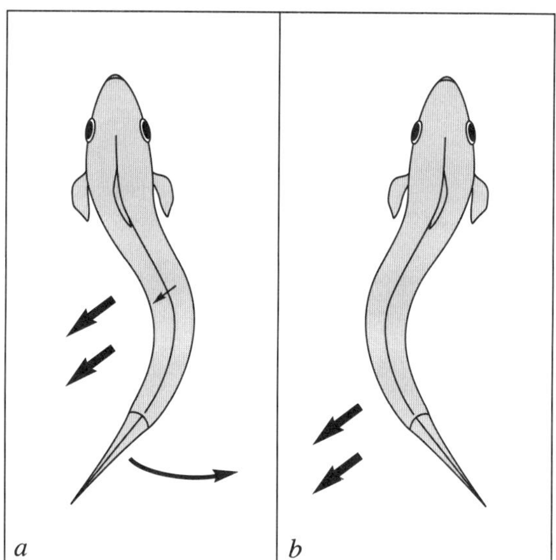

Figure 17-20. Fish propulsion.

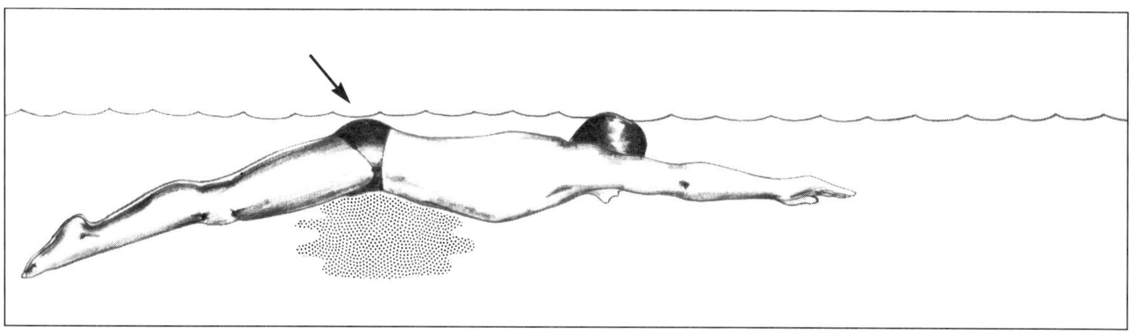

a

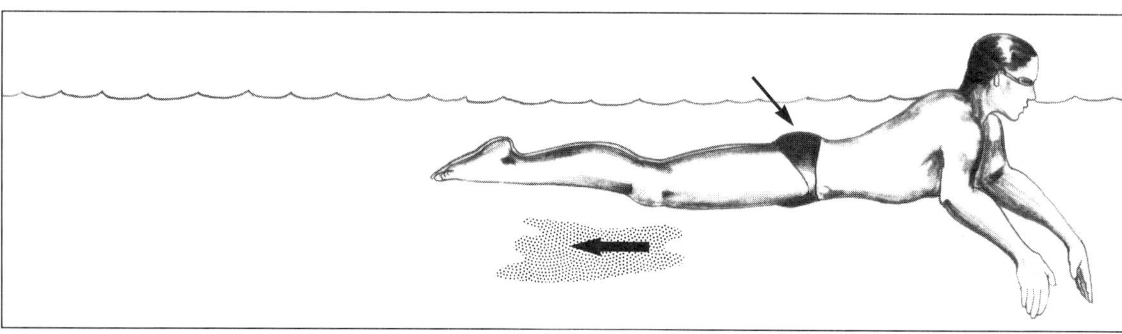

b

Figure 17-21. Possible body propulsion in dolphin-style breaststroke.

Van Tilborgh and his coworkers (1988) have reported a greater propulsive impulse during the hip drop for a dolphin-style breaststroker than for eight other subjects who did not use the dolphin style. These researchers theorized that the impulse was due either to a longer propulsive phase of the armstroke or reduced form drag. However, as shown, swimmers may have accelerated water back with the undulating movements of their trunk.

Swimmers who choose to incorporate some undulation in their breaststroke must be careful not to overdo it. Excessive undulation increases form drag and causes a longer period of deceleration between the time breaststrokers complete the propulsive phase of their kick and begin propulsion with their arms.

These examples certainly do not provide conclusive evidence that the undulating movements of the body contribute to propulsion. The possibility deserves further study, however.

GUIDELINES FOR SWIMMING PROPULSION

Much of the material presented in this chapter has been theoretical and technical. Swimmers need simpler instructions. The following list presents some guidelines for swimming propulsion in terms that make the information more useful to coaches and swimmers.

1. *Always wait until your elbows are above your hands before applying force.* The most common mistake novices make is to try to overpower the water at the beginning of the underwater armstroke. They try to apply force when their arms are facing down on the water. The first third of every underwater armstroke should be a gentle search for a catch. That catch should not be made until the forearms are facing back against the water, and that does not happen until swimmers' elbows are above their hands.

Remember also, that swimmers should reach down and/or out while their elbows are riding up above their hands. They should not try to push their elbows up and their hands back or they may develop tendinitis in their shoulder joints. The arm(s) should flex approximately 30 to 40 degrees while searching for the catch. An additional 40 to 50 degrees of elbow flexion should take place during the insweep (upsweep in backstroke) that follows.

2. *Always stroke in diagonal directions.* Swimmers should never try to push their hands and arms directly back. Rather, they should always sweep them back diagonally.

3. *Always incline the hands slightly in the direction they are stroking.* The correct angle of attack can be approximated for a particular sweep if swimmers' palms are inclined slightly in the direction they are moving. They should seldom be inclined more than 45 degrees in that direction, however. The palms should not be used like paddles to push water back.

4. *There should be two or more major changes in direction during each underwater armstroke.* Swimmers should not try to push their hands straight back from the beginning to the end of an underwater armstroke. Sweeps that are only mildly diagonal are also not very effective. The changes in limb direction should be major in order to find undisturbed water that can be accelerated back once a previous section of water has been displaced back.

5. *Hand speeds should gradually accelerate from the catch to the end of each underwater armstroke.* Swimmers' hands accelerate in pulses during the underwater armstroke, slowing as they make the transition from one sweep to the next and then accelerating to the next point of transition. Nevertheless, their hands should never reach maximum velocity until they are near the end of the propulsive phase of a single underwater armstroke. A simple way to teach the concept of acceleration is to have swimmers gradually increase their hand speed from the catch to the end of an underwater armstroke. Stroking this way will naturally result in pulses as swimmers' hands change directions during the various phases of their underwater armstroke. Furthermore, this will discourage swimmers from making the common mistake of accelerating their hands too rapidly early in the stroke.

6. *Hands and forearms should be aligned during the propulsive phases of most underwater armstrokes.* The tendency to overflex or hyperextend the wrists is one of the most common errors swimmers make. This reduces the foil characteristics of the hands and arms and creates turbulence, which reduces swimmers' propulsive efforts. You should be able to draw a straight line from the tip of the elbow through the fingertips during most propulsive phases of the underwater armstrokes. The only exceptions to this rule occur during the final stages of the freestyle, butterfly, and backstroke. At these times, the wrists are hyperextended for best results.

7. *Always keep the hands pitched out until they pass underneath the elbows during the insweep.* Swimmers who pitch their hands in too early during the insweep lose propulsive force because their angle of attack becomes too perpendicular before the sweep ends. This same guideline can be applied to the upsweep at midstroke in the backstroke. Only here the hand sweeps up instead of in. In the first upsweep of the backstroke, the hand should remain pitched down until it passes the elbow during its upward path. At that point, the hand should rotate up until it is pitched up slightly at the end of the upsweep.

8. *Propulsive efforts should cease when the hands pass the legs on their way to the surface.* Another of the most common mistakes that swimmers make is to try to push against the water until their hands reach the surface. The combination of direction (forward) and angle of attack (near perpendicular) of their hands exerts a braking effect on forward speed when they do this.

CHAPTER 18

Front Crawl Stroke

The front crawl stroke, or freestyle, has evolved into the fastest of the four competitive styles. One stroke cycle consists of a right and left armstroke and a varying number of kicks. This chapter uses the following order of topics to describe the front crawl:

1. The armstroke
2. Stroke patterns
3. The flutter kick
4. Timing between arms and legs
5. Body position and breathing
6. Hand and body velocity patterns
7. Common mistakes
8. Drills
9. Breathing patterns

ARMSTROKE

The underwater armstroke consists of three diagonal sweeps: a downsweep, an insweep, and an upsweep. The entry and stretch and the release and recovery are additional parts of the armstroke that are described in this section. Figures 18-1 and 18-2 show underwater sequence photos for the front crawl from a side view and from a front view, respectively.

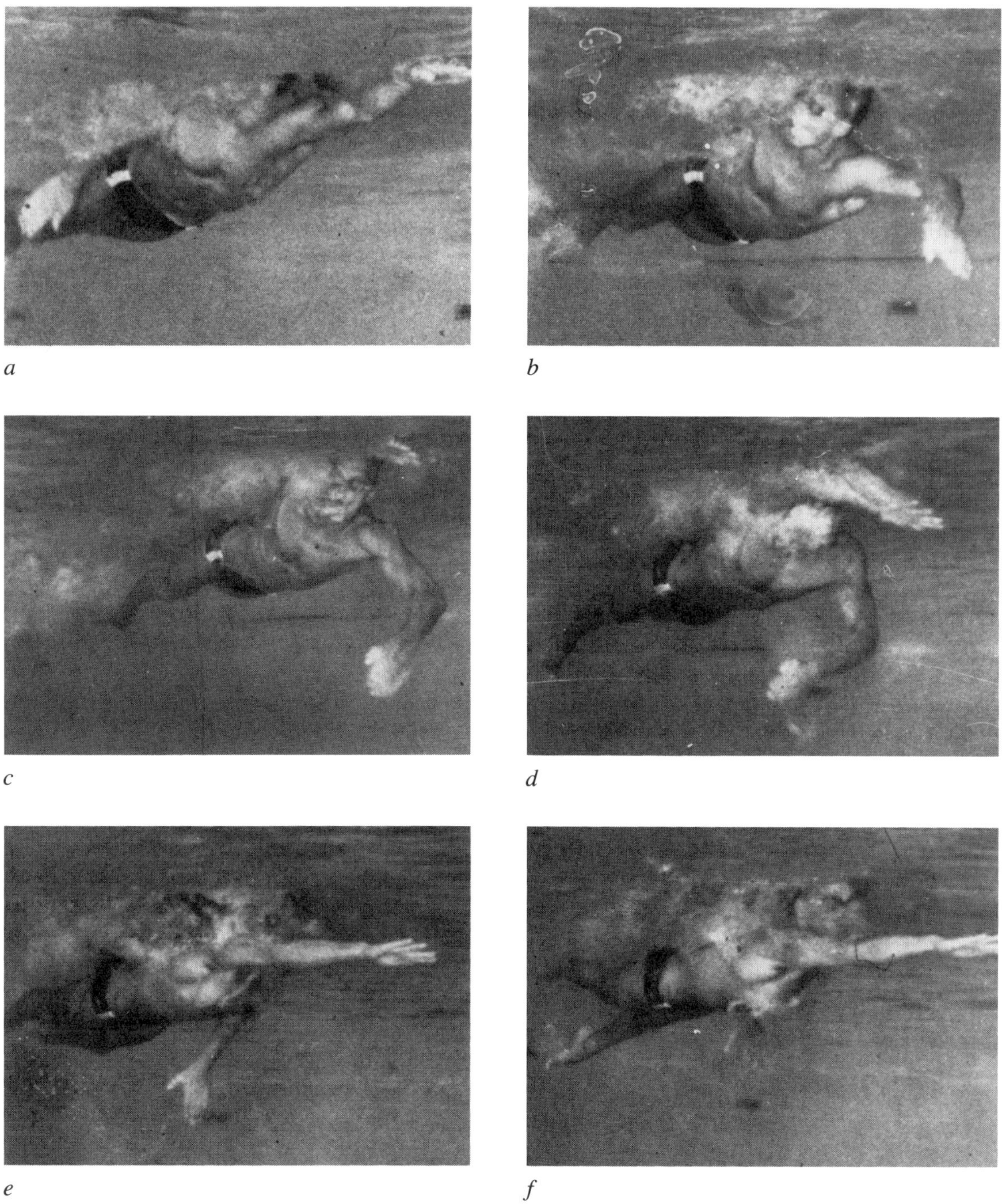

a *b* *c* *d* *e* *f*

Figure 18-1. Side-view underwater sequence of Rowdy Gaines swimming the front crawl stroke. Gaines was the gold medalist in the 100-m freestyle at the 1984 Olympic Games.

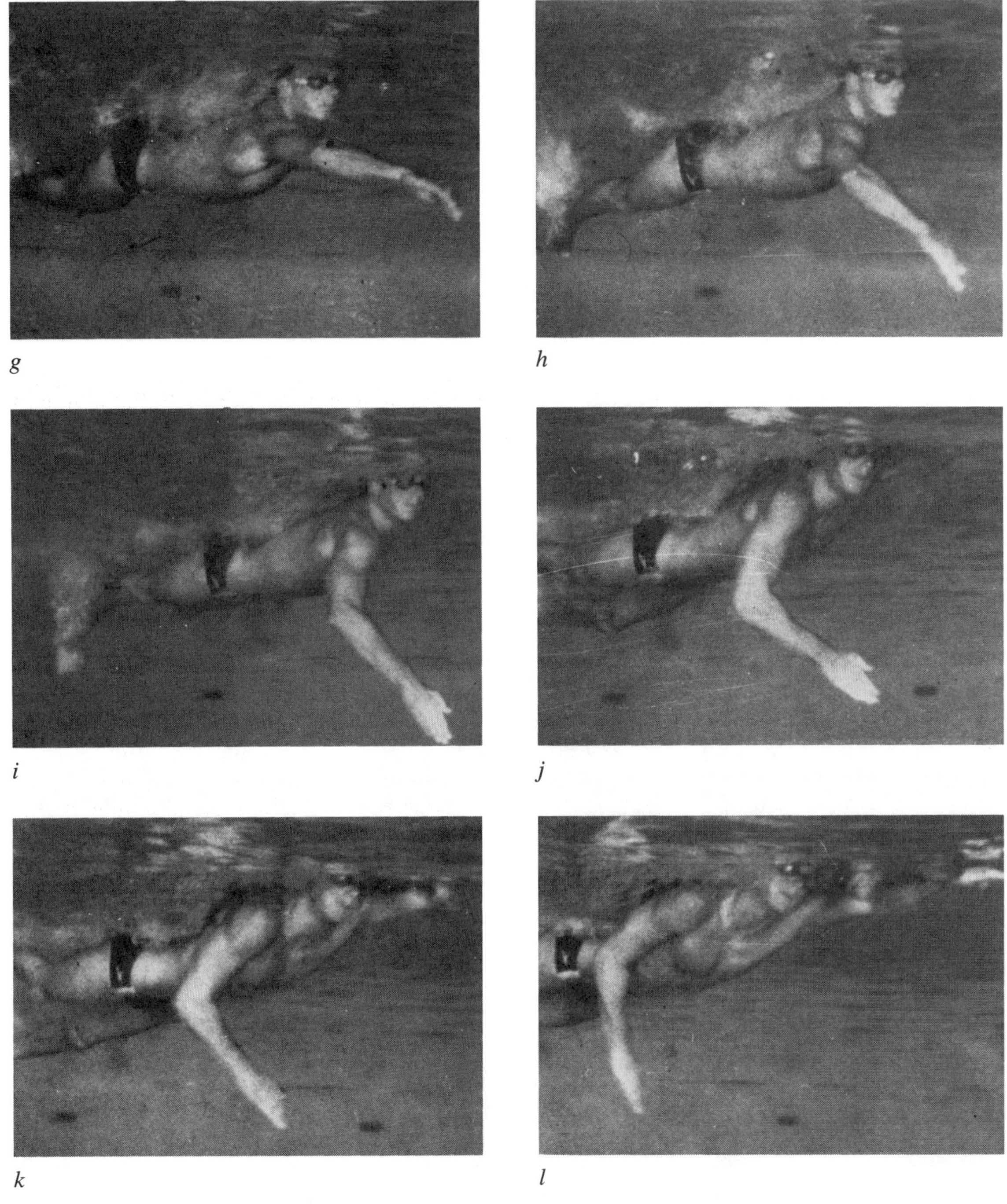

g *h*

i *j*

k *l*

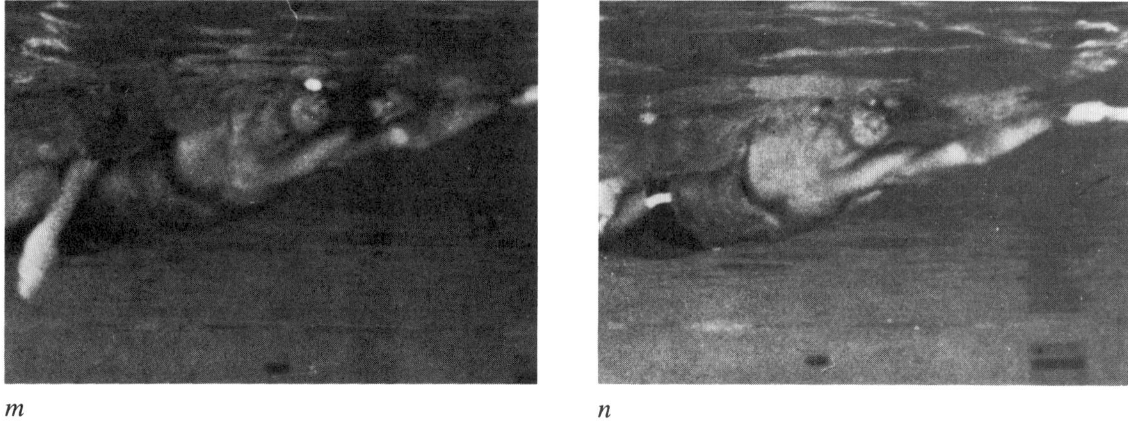

m *n*

Figure 18-1. (continued)

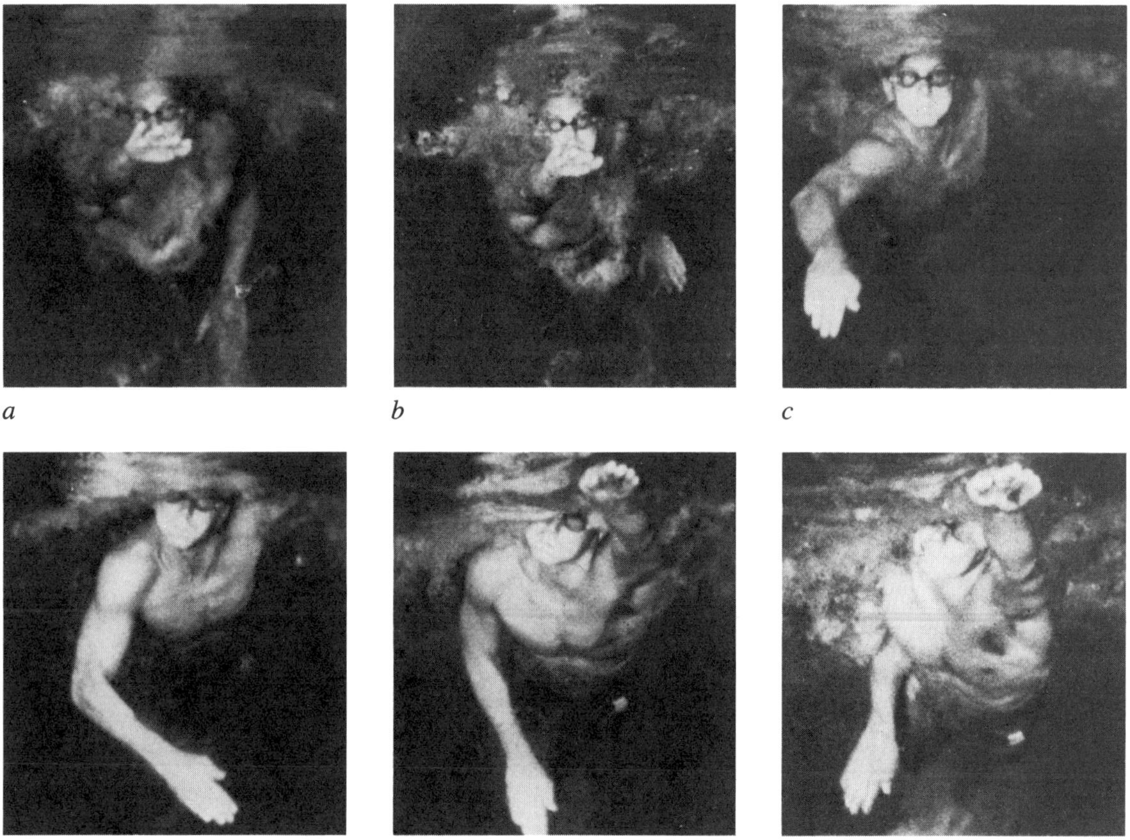

a *b* *c*

d *e* *f*

Figure 18-2. Front-view underwater sequence of Rowdy Gaines swimming the front crawl stroke.

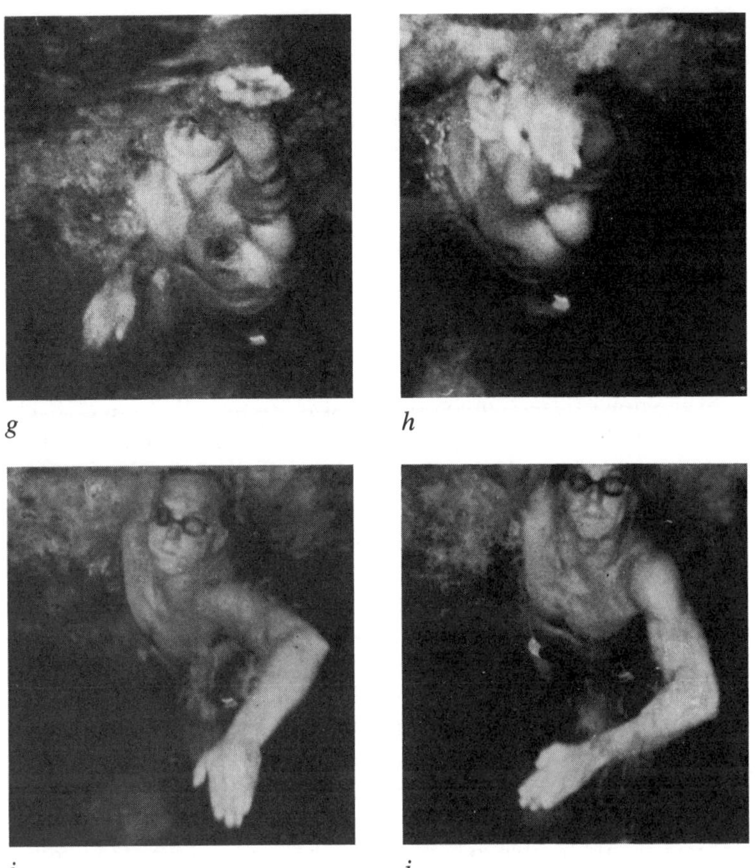

g *h* *i* *j*

Entry and Stretch

Underwater views of the entry and stretch of the swimmer's right arm can be seen best from a side view in Figures 18-1*c* through 18-1*f*. Figures 18-2*d* through 18-2*g* show these portions of the armstroke for the left arm from a front view.

The entry should be made forward of the head and between the middle of the head and the tip of the shoulder on the entry side (see Figure 18-2*e*). The swimmer's arm should be flexed slightly and the palm should be pitched out as it enters. The fingertips should be the first part of the arm to enter the water (see Figure 18-1*c*). After that, the arm can slide into the water through the same hole opened by the hand.

After entering the water, the arm should extend forward just under the surface, with the palm rotating down until it faces down at the end of the stretch. This phase of the armstroke is called a stretch rather than a glide because the arm does not stop moving forward. The swimmer's hand produces wave drag as it pushes forward through the water, so the hand should slip into the water on its edge, with a minimum of turbulence, and stretch forward gently in a streamlined position.

Swimmers should not attempt to apply force immediately after their hand enters the water because the other arm is midway through its propulsive phase and the efforts of the arm in front would interfere with those of the arm behind. For this reason, the entering arm should remain between the middle of the head and the tip of the shoulder and stretch directly forward so that it presents a streamlined shape to the water that acts somewhat like the bow of a ship.

Hand velocity should decrease from the entry throughout the stretch until the arm is simply pushed forward by the body near the end of the other arm's propulsive phase. The stretch should be timed so that the arm nears complete extension as the other arm finishes the propulsive phase of its underwater armstroke. The downsweep begins at that point.

Downsweep and Catch

The mechanics of the downsweep can be seen best in Figures 18-1*g* and 18-1*h*. After entering the water, the hand sweeps down in a curvilinear path that ends at the catch position shown in Figure 18-1*h*. The arm is gradually flexed at the elbow during the downsweep, and the catch is made when the combination of downward motion and elbow flexion cause the elbow to ride up above the hand. The arm should flex approximately 40 degrees at the elbow during the downsweep so that the angle at the elbow is approximately 140 degrees when the catch is made. At that time, the hand and arm should be slightly outside the shoulder and facing back against the water. The palm should be pitched out and back. The characteristic position for the catch can be seen in Figure 18-1*b* for the left arm and Figure 18-1*h* for the right. The hand will be fairly deep, approximately 40 to 60 cm (15 to 24 inches) deep, when the catch is made (Schleihauf et al., 1988).

It is very important for swimmers to get their hand and forearm in alignment at the catch. Otherwise some propulsion will be lost during the insweep. If the arm is properly aligned, you should be able to draw a straight line from the elbow to the fingertips. *Swimmers must not try to push their hand back or sweep it in before the catch is made.*

Stroke patterns show that the hand also slides out somewhat during the downsweep. Swimmers should not emphasize this outward movement, however. It is a by-product of shoulder roll and occurs naturally. It has been my experience that swimmers generally sweep their hand out too wide if they stress this direction of the movement.

The downsweep is not a propulsive movement. One of its purposes is probably to prevent the recovery of the opposite arm from submerging the face while the swimmer inhales. This requires only a small amount of pressure from the arm as it travels down. The other purpose of the downsweep is, of course, to move the arm into position for the catch. The first propulsive movement, the insweep, begins at the moment the catch is made.

Insweep

The insweep is pictured in Figures 18-1*b* to 18-1*d* for the left arm and in Figures 18-1*h* through 18-1*j* for the right. Front views of the insweep are shown in Figures 18-2*c* and 18-2*d* for the right arm and in Figures 18-2*i* and 18-2*j* for the left. It is a semicircular sweep from the catch to a position under the body in which the hand travels down, in, and up until it is at or beyond the midline. The arm, which was flexed approximately 40 degrees at the elbow when the catch was made, flexes an additional 40 to 60 degrees throughout the insweep (see Figure 18-2*j*). Schleihauf and associates (1988) have reported measures of maximum elbow flexion between 82 and 104 degrees for a group of U.S. Olympic swimmers.

The palm of the hand should be rotated in *slowly* during the insweep until it is pitched in and up when the sweep ends. Hand speed should accelerate moderately from the start to finish of this motion. Hand velocities usually accelerate from approximately 1.5 m/sec to between 2.5 and 3.0 m/sec at the end of the insweep (Maglischo et al., 1986; Schleihauf et al., 1984).

Figure 18-3 illustrates how water is accelerated back during the insweep. The thumb side of the hand is the leading edge of the foil and the little-finger side the trailing edge as the swimmer's arm sweeps under his body. His hand should be pitched in as shown here. The relative direction of water flow is out and forward, opposite to the direction in which his hand is moving as it meets the leading edge of his hand. The shaded arrow, representing the relative flow of water, shows that this combination of direction and angle of attack cause the water to be displaced backward, imparting backward force to the water as it passes under the swimmer's palm from the thumb side to the little-finger side.

An important aspect of correct execution has to do with the speed of hand rotation from out to in during the insweep. A common mistake swimmers make is to rotate their palm in too quickly. This places the hand at too large an angle of attack during the second half of the movement. The hand should remain pitched out until it is midway through the sweep and should rotate in after it passes under the swimmer's elbow.

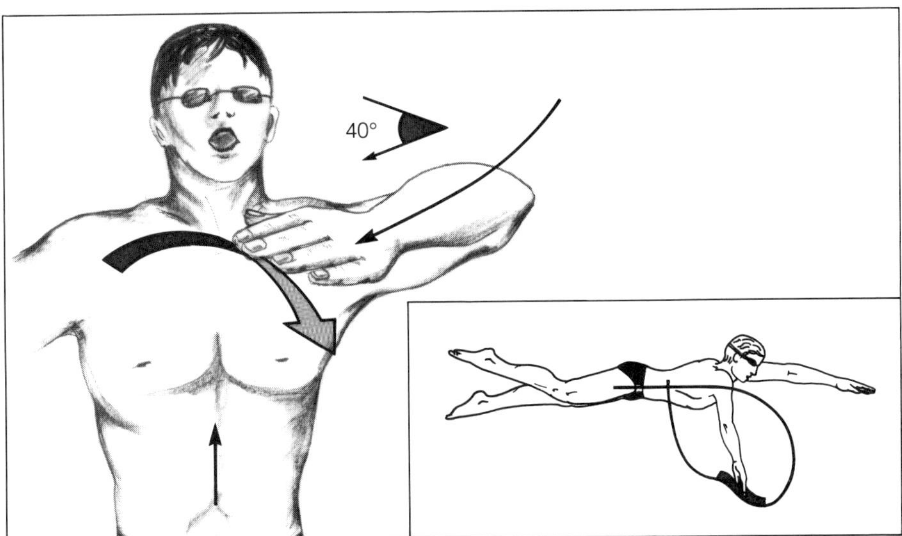

Figure 18-3. Propulsion during the second portion of the insweep.

Some swimmers sweep their hand in to the midline of their body, and others sweep well beyond their midline. Still others complete the insweep somewhere between the outer border and the midline of their body. Figure 18-4 illustrates these three insweep styles. The swimmer in Figure 18-4*a* uses a short insweep. The swimmer in Figure 18-4*b* illustrates a midline insweep, the most common style. The swimmer in Figure 18-4*c* is using a crossover insweep.

The distance the hand travels under the body probably depends on (1) the width of the hand at the catch and (2) the ability of a particular swimmer to maintain an effective angle of attack during the insweep. If the hand is wide at the catch, the swimmer will not have to sweep it beyond the midline to use the insweep over its effective propulsive range. Conversely, if the hand is inside the shoulder, the swimmer will have to sweep it beyond the midline toward the opposite side to use the insweep through an adequate range.

By the same token, if the hand is rotated in too soon, the angle of attack will become too great midway through the insweep and the swimmer will begin to lose propulsion. Consequently, a swimmer who feels that happening will shorten the insweep to get on to the next propulsive movement. On the other hand, a swimmer who maintains an effective angle of attack may sweep his hand in beyond the midline.

Many front crawl swimmers have used the crossover insweep effectively. Others have not. Although some swimmers increase propulsive force by sweeping across the midline, others may risk pushing their body out of lateral alignment by sweeping their hand across the body with a large angle of attack. Some care must be exercised when deciding whether to change swimmers from one style to another. The insweep should be shortened if their body wiggles from side to side when they sweep their hand across the midline. However, swimmers should not be forced to shorten their insweep if their body remains aligned and it feels comfortable.

Part of the force of the insweep is used to rotate the swimmer's body from side to side. The trade-off of propulsion for rotation is beneficial because this places the body in better alignment for the most propulsive phase of the underwater arm-

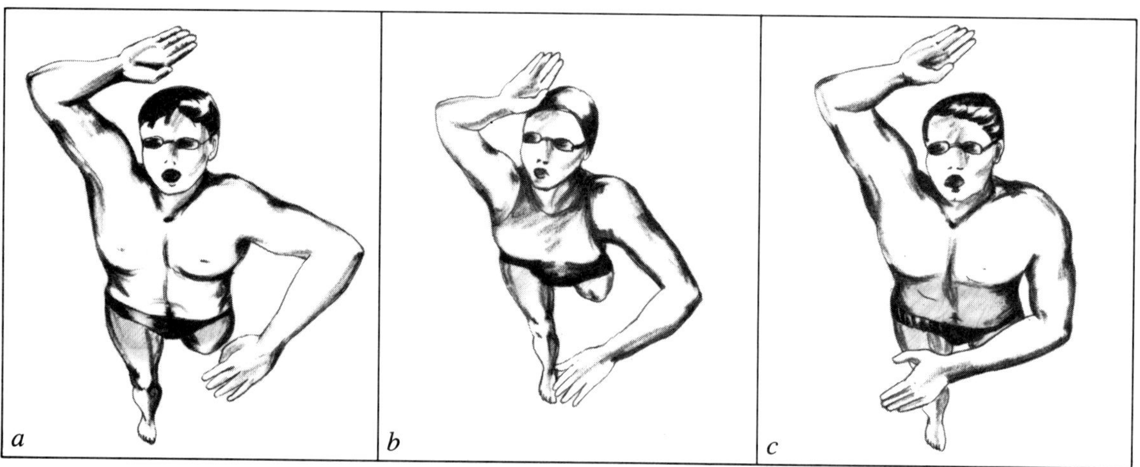

Figure 18-4. Three styles of insweep.

stroke—the upsweep. Most swimmers roll their body more to their breathing side and require a larger insweep to rotate their body back toward the other side. Thus, all swimmers sweep the hand of the arm opposite their breathing side across the midline, regardless of the insweep style they prefer for the breathing-side arm.

Upsweep

The upsweep is the second and final propulsive sweep of the front crawl stroke. Figures 18-1*k* through 18-1*m* show it best from a side view. It can also be seen from a front view in Figures 18-2*e* through 18-2*g*. It begins as the previous insweep is completed and continues until the swimmer's hand approaches his thigh. The movement is a semicircular sweep of the hand from underneath the swimmer's body and out, up, and back toward the surface of the water. The palm of the hand should rotate out quickly at the beginning of this sweep and remain pitched out and back throughout the movement. Although the arm should extend gradually at the elbow, the speed of extension should be such that the forearm remains flexed, with the underside of the forearm and palm of the hand facing back on the water until the propulsive phase of the sweep is completed.

When the hand approaches the thigh, the upsweep is completed. The swimmer should then release pressure on the water and rotate the palm in so that the hand can travel up and out of the water into the recovery with a minimum of resistance.

Hand speed should slow during the transition from insweep to upsweep. It should then accelerate rapidly throughout the remainder of this motion. The hand reaches its greatest velocity during this phase of the armstroke—between 3 and more than 6 m/sec (11 to 20 ft/sec) for most swimmers (Counsilman & Wasilak, 1982; Maglischo et al., 1986; Schleihauf et al., 1988).

Arm Extension There is a misconception that the arm extends rapidly during the upsweep. This notion is a remnant of the propulsive drag theory, when we thought that the hand was pushing back, not sweeping up. Actually, the amount of extension should be moderate. The swimmer's arm extends slightly, but not completely, during the upsweep. It still should be flexed approximately 60 degrees from the horizontal when this sweep is completed (see Figure 18-1*m*). The hand should remain in line with the forearm throughout the propulsive phase of the upsweep, and most of the effort should be expended in sweeping the arm up, not extending it back.

Stroking in this way permits swimmers to maintain a backward orientation with their forearm and hand so that they can displace water back for a longer time during the upsweep. That backward force can be continued with the hand even after the swimmer's forearm nears the surface if the hand remains pitched back (see Figure 18-1*m*).

If the arm were extended too rapidly, it would push up against the water at a large angle of attack during the second portion of this sweep. This is, in fact, one of the common mistakes that swimmers make during the upsweep; it causes their hips to submerge and it decelerates their forward speed.

Perhaps the most common reason for extending the elbow too much is to try to maintain propulsive force until the hand reaches the surface of the water. *Swimmers do not apply propulsive force to the surface of the water*. The propulsive phase of the upsweep is completed before the swimmer's hand reaches the surface. The arm begins moving forward and the hand and forearm will have traveled beyond an effective angle of attack when they pass the thigh. Any attempt to continue applying propulsive force after that time only decelerates forward speed. Skilled swimmers do not extend their elbow fully until after pressure on the water is released and the recovery has begun. Many do not extend it completely even then.

Backward Hand Orientation The success of the upsweep is, in large part, due to the ability of swimmers to keep their hand facing back during the final portion of the upsweep. If they do this, swimmers can maintain an angle of attack with their palm that will displace water back even after the orientation of their forearm is no longer adequate for this purpose. For this reason, swimmers should be coached to keep their palm facing back until the release is made.

Figure 18-5 illustrates the method for imparting backward force to the water during the upsweep. There are two parts to this sweep. The first, where the swimmer sweeps his hand out and back from underneath his body, is shown from an underneath view in Figure 18-5*a*. The hand should be pitched out and back, with the little-finger side as the leading edge of the hand-foil and the thumb side as the trailing edge. The relative direction of water flow is opposite to the direction in which the hand moves, so it travels in as it starts under the swimmer's palm. The outward inclination of the swimmer's palm causes the water to be displaced backward as it flows under the palm from the little-finger side to the thumb side.

The side view in Figure 18-5*b* shows how propulsion can be generated by the upward movements of the swimmer's arm during the second portion of the up-

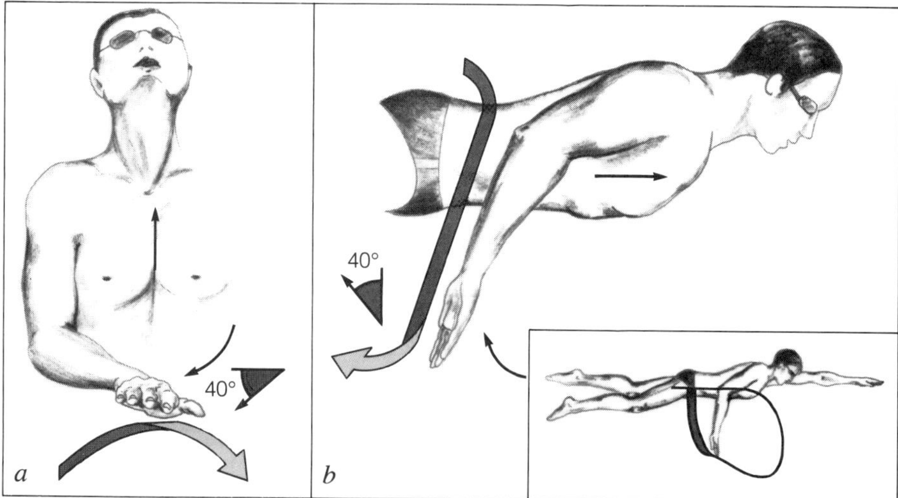

Figure 18-5. Propulsion during the upsweep. The two phases of this sweep are shown from an underneath view and a side view.

sweep. The swimmer's hand comes out from underneath his body and sweeps primarily in an upward direction. This changes its relative direction so that the water now flows down over the underside of his forearm, which becomes the leading edge, past the wrist and across the palm to the fingertips, which become the trailing edge. With the elbow gradually extending and the hand remaining pitched out and back, the arm and hand present an angle of attack that can displace water back and propel the swimmer forward. The shaded arrow shows how this combination of direction and angle of attack of the forearm and hand can displace the water back.

Although the upsweep has two parts, swimmers feel it as one continuous sweep, so it should be taught this way. Therefore, to simplify the propulsive nature of this complex movement, swimmers should be instructed to sweep their hand out, up, and back, with their hand pitched out and back. Their forearm, although extending somewhat, should remain flexed slightly throughout the movement.

Release and Recovery

The underwater portion of the release can be seen best from a front view in Figures 18-2*b* and 18-2*g* and from a side view in Figure 18-1*n*. Surface photos of the recovery appear in Figure 18-6. As mentioned, the arm recovery actually begins before the swimmer's hand leaves the water. The elbow leaves first and the swimmer begins to flex his arm to start it moving forward while his hand is still underwater. For this reason the swimmer should release pressure on the water when his hand reaches his thigh because it will be traveling forward and cannot create any more propulsion. This overlap between the end of the upsweep and the beginning of the recovery reduces the muscular effort required to overcome the arm's backward inertia so that it can begin moving forward into the recovery.

At the release, the palm should be turned in so that the hand can travel to the surface of the water on its edge, thus presenting the smallest possible surface area to the water and reducing the drag opposing the upward movement of the hand. Hand velocity decreases somewhat as it travels to the surface and the recovery gets underway.

The purpose of the recovery is to place the arm in position for another underwater stroke. While this is an important function, it is nonpropulsive, so the goals should be (1) to get the arm over the water with the least disruption of lateral alignment and (2) to provide a short period of reduced effort for the arm, shoulder, and trunk muscles. For these reasons, swimmers should try to relax their arm muscles during the recovery, using only enough effort to get the arm into the water in the proper relationship with the other arm. This does not require great speed or effort. Only moderate speed, minimal effort, and proper positioning.

In Figure 18-6, the swimmer is executing a *high-elbow recovery*. This is the most preferred type of recovery because the arm can travel over the surface with less lateral motion and because the entry can be made with a minimum of turbulence. There is one additional recovery style that has been used successfully by competitive swimmers—the *modified high-elbow recovery*.

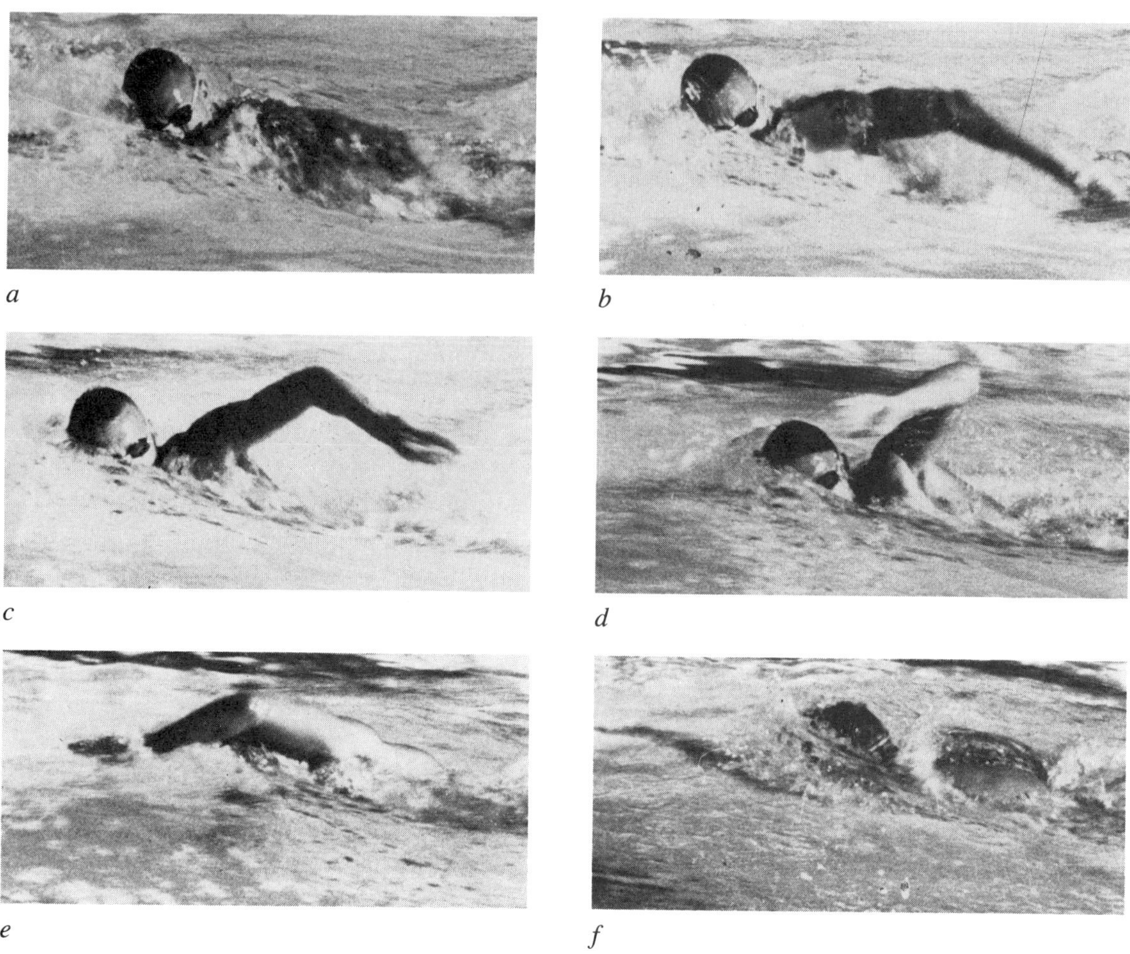

Figure 18-6. A surface view of the front crawl arm recovery. The swimmer is David Tittle, former NCAA Division II record holder for the 200-yd freestyle.

High-Elbow Recovery Figure 18-6*b* shows the swimmer's elbow leaving the water slightly flexed, with his hand on its side. The elbow continues to flex through the first half of the recovery as he brings his arm around and overhead (Figures 18-6*c* and 18-6*d*). He starts to extend his arm for the entry after his hand passes overhead (Figure 18-6*e*). His palm faces in during the first half of the recovery but rotates out as he reaches for the water so that the entry can be made with a minimum of turbulence. It is very important that swimmers keep their elbow high and that they do not begin extending their arm until it passes their shoulder (see Figure 18-6*d*). This puts their arm in the best position to enter the water cleanly.

The recovery should be as linear as possible to reduce the potential for disruption of lateral alignment, which occurs when the arm is swung out and around excessively. Alternately flexing and then extending the arm during the recovery keeps it from swinging out too wide.

Modified High-Elbow Recovery The difference between this and a regular high-elbow style is that the swimmer's arm is brought over the water in a higher arc. The arm is still bent as it leaves the water and remains flexed throughout the first half of the recovery. However, the alternating flexion and extension are not so great as in the high-elbow style. The arm tends to come out of the water slightly bent and then remains flexed approximately the same amount until the entry is made. Consequently, the hand and elbow are at nearly the same level during the first half of the recovery. However, swimmers reach forward for the entry in the same manner described for the high-elbow recovery after their hand passes their head.

Many sprinters use this recovery. It is probably more inertial and therefore faster without being fatiguing. Swimmers also tend to use this style on their breathing side more than on their nonbreathing side.

Timing the Arms

The two arms have a precise relationship to one another that is very important to fast swimming in the front crawl stroke. It is important because the alternating movements of the arms must be coordinated with body roll, and vice versa, to facilitate the application of propulsive force and to maintain the body in a streamlined position during each stroke cycle.

Where the armstroke is concerned, the most important coordinating event occurs when the arm in front enters the water as the other arm is completing its insweep (see Figure 18-1*d*). This allows the body to roll toward the stroking arm in preparation for its upsweep. It also permits the entering arm to stretch forward and streamlines the body while the upsweep is being performed (see Figures 18-2*e* through 18-2*g*).

Another important feature of this relationship is that the arm in front should not begin sweeping down until the other has completed its upsweep. This also permits the swimmer to stay streamlined during the upsweep. This will cause the swimmer to decelerate during the downsweep; however, this is apparently preferable to the reduction in propulsion that would occur if the broad surface of the front arm were being pushed forward against the water while the rear arm was sweeping up. The forward speed that is lost during the decelerative period between the end of the upsweep with the rear arm and the catch of the front arm is probably compensated by greater propulsion during the upsweep.

While this last point is true in middle-distance and distance races, the relationship between the stretch of one arm and upsweep of the other changes somewhat when swimmers are sprinting. Sprinters reduce the stretch and start the downsweep of one arm during the upsweep of the other. They do this so that they can catch and begin applying propulsive force with the arm in front almost immediately as the other arm releases pressure. While this reduces streamlining during the upsweep, it also increases speed by reducing the decelerative period between armstrokes. It also increases the energy cost, which probably explains why swimmers choose to sacrifice speed somewhat and conserve energy in longer races by stretching the arm out longer in front.

Stroke Patterns

Figure 18-7 illustrates stroke patterns for the front crawl from side, front, and underneath views. These particular stroke patterns are for a world-class freestyle sprinter, but they represent the patterns used by most front crawl swimmers at all race distances. They clearly show the extent to which front crawl swimmers use diagonal sculling motions in both lateral and vertical directions for propulsion.

The numbered dots on the stroke patterns designate where each phase of the stroke begins and ends. These patterns show the directions in which the hand is moving relative to the water. You can determine the three-dimensional nature of those motions by putting the patterns from any two views together.

Schleihauf and associates (1984) have reported that the most effective applications of propulsive force occur when the insweep and upsweep are made on a diagonal of 50 to 70 degrees. These diagonal lines of motion are sometimes difficult to grasp. Figure 18-8 may help illustrate this concept. The underneath view shows how the angle expressing the diagonality of these sweeps is measured during the insweep. A measure of diagonality for the upsweep can be seen in the side view.

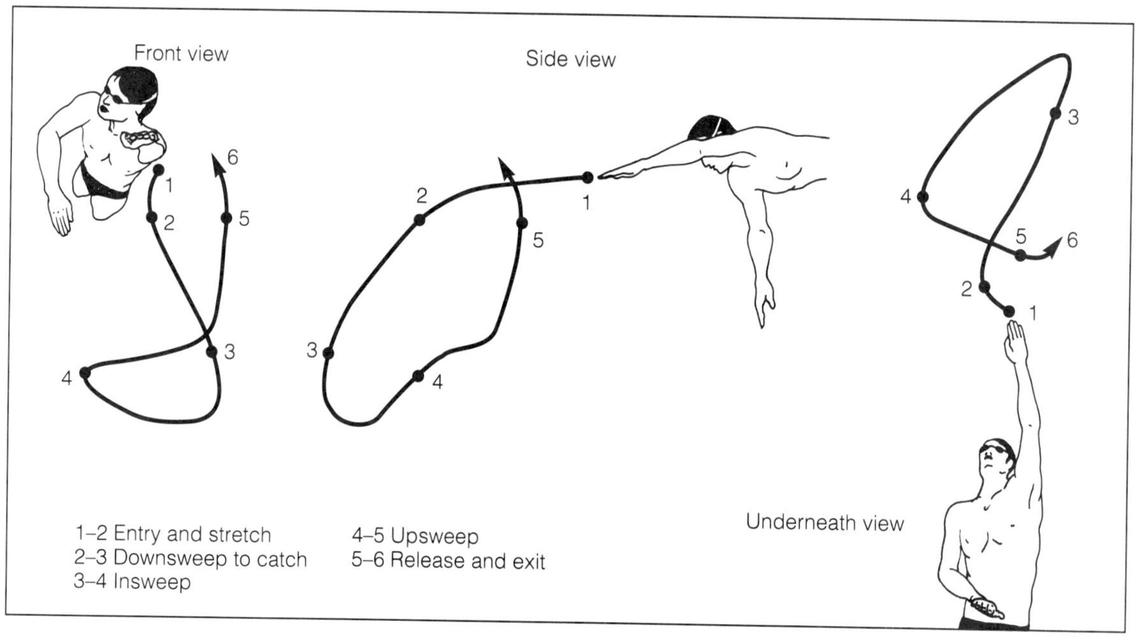

Figure 18-7. Typical front, side, and underneath stroke patterns for the front crawl stroke.

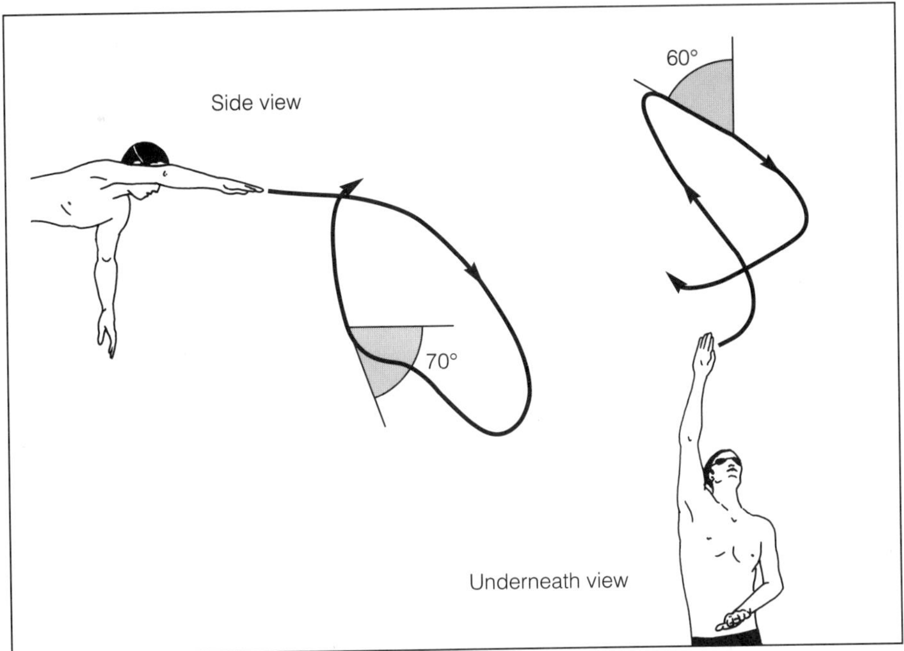

Figure 18-8. Measuring the diagonal nature of sweeps. (Adapted from Schleihauf et al., 1984)

The diagonal angle of the stroke is the angle formed between the forward component of the swimmer's motion and the direction in which the hand travels.

Lateral and vertical hand movements are another interesting aspect of these patterns. For freestyle swimmers on the 1984 U.S. Olympic Team, the patterns ranged in depth from 61 to 74 cm (24 to 31 inches). The length of lateral sweeps ranged between 29 and 45 cm (11 to 18 inches, Schleihauf et al., 1988).

FLUTTER KICK

The flutter kick consists of alternating diagonal sweeps of the legs. The primary direction in which the legs kick is up and down, so the movements are called *upbeats* and *downbeats*. These beats also contain lateral components, however. Figure 18-9 (p. 378) illustrates the flutter kick.

Downbeat

The downbeat of the right leg can be seen in Figures 18-9*a* through 18-9*d;* the downbeat of the left leg, in Figures 18-9*e* and 18-9*f*. Figure 18-10 illustrates a kick pattern. It depicts the direction of the big toe of the swimmer's foot during the one upbeat and one downbeat.

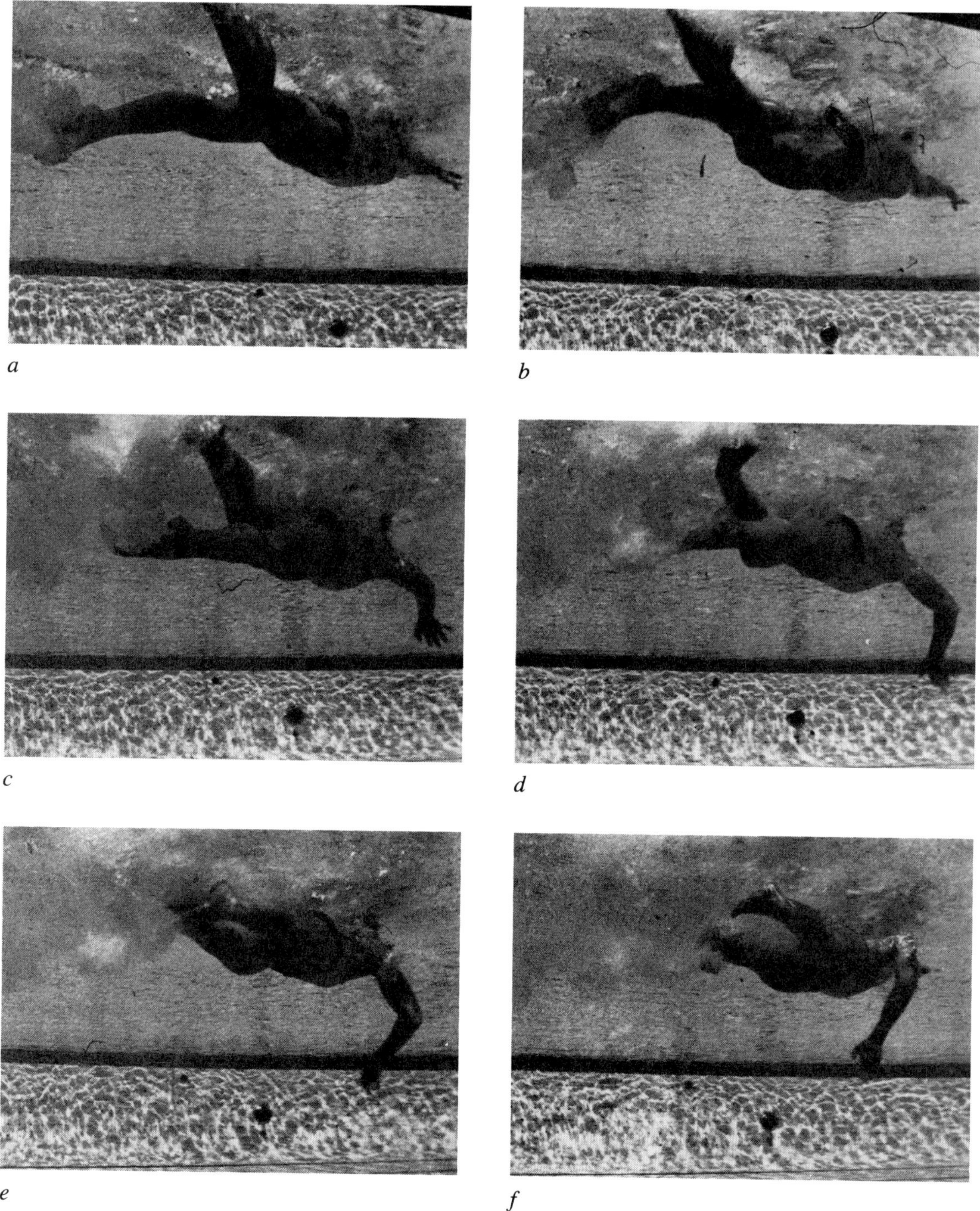

a *b* *c* *d* *e* *f*

Figure 18-9. The flutter kick.

The legs move in an alternating rhythm, with the downbeat of one taking place during the upbeat of the other. The downbeat is a whiplike movement that begins with flexion at the hip, followed by extension at the knee.

The downbeat actually begins during the previous upbeat. The leg flexes at the hip as it passes the body on its way up to the surface. The thigh begins to press down on the water while the lower leg, which should be relaxed, continues to be pushed up by the pressure of the water underneath it. This action overcomes the inertia of the previous upbeat, changing the direction of the leg to down without using excessive muscular effort.

The water pressure below the leg also pushes the foot into an extended position, with the toes pointed up (plantar flexed) and the foot turned in (inverted). Figure 18-9*a* illustrates this position best for the swimmer's left leg. Just after his foot nears the surface, the swimmer begins a rapid, downward extension of his lower leg and continues until the leg is completely extended and just below his body. The leg should kick down and laterally in the direction that the swimmer's body is rotating. The downbeat is executed in a whiplike motion, beginning with mild flexion at the hip and moving down the leg by extending the knee.

Upbeat

Figures 18-9*a* through 18-9*c* show the upbeat of the left leg; Figures 18-9*d* through 18-9*f*, the upbeat of the right leg. The beginning of the upbeat overlaps with the end of the preceding downbeat to overcome the inertia of changing leg direction from down to up. When swimmers extend their lower leg down, it has a reboundlike effect that pushes their thigh up. The thigh then pulls the lower leg up once it has completed its extension. The leg should sweep up, forward, and laterally, opposite to the direction in which the swimmer's body is turning.

The upbeat should be made with a straight leg. The pressure of the water pushing down on the leg keeps it extended and the foot in a natural position, midway between flexion and extension (see Figure 18-9*e*). The lower leg and foot should be relaxed throughout the upbeat and remain so until the knee begins extending during the next downbeat. This allows the water to position the leg properly. The upward movement of the entire leg is accomplished by the muscles that extend the hip joint. The upbeat ends when the leg passes the body on its way up. That is when the leg flexes at the hip for the next downbeat.

Inexperienced swimmers often work against the natural positioning effects of water pressure by flexing their leg at the knee during the upbeat. The effect of this and other mistakes are described later in this chapter.

Kick Width

The flutter kick cannot be too shallow or too deep. Body stabilization and propulsive force will be reduced if it is too shallow, and drag will be increased if it is too deep. At completion of the downbeat, the swimmer's foot should be just below his or her body line. Kicking deeper than this will not improve the propulsive and/or stabilizing effects of the kick but will increase the cross-sectional surface area presented

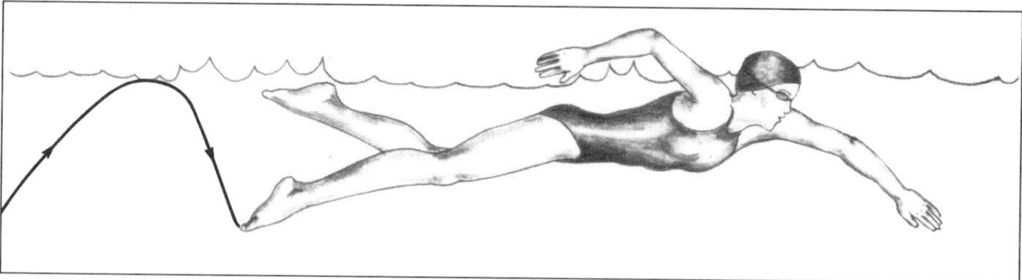

Figure 18-10. A kick pattern for the flutter kick.

to the water. Another reason for not kicking too deep is evident in the kick pattern shown in Figure 18-10. Notice that the foot travels forward near the end of a normal downbeat. If the downbeat is lengthened swimmers will be kicking forward against the water and this will reduce their forward speed. Kicking up too high will cause similar problems. Figure 18-10 shows that the legs move forward as well as up in the second portion of the upbeat. If this motion is made vigorously or if it is continued too long, the leg will push water up and forward, decelerating forward speed. This is a mistake that many poor kickers make.

The optimal width of the legs at their widest spread is not known, but it is probably between 50 and 80 cm (20 to 30 inches). Allen (1948) found that a kick width of approximately 30 cm (12 inches) was superior to a narrower kick of 15 cm (6 inches) for increasing propulsive force.

Diagonal Kicking

The lateral motion that occurs as the legs kick up and down probably assists in body rotation and stabilization. Body rotation is facilitated and lateral alignment can be preserved if one leg kicks in the same direction in which the swimmer's body is rolling while the other kicks in the opposite direction. That is, when the body rolls to the right, one leg should kick diagonally down and to the right while the other kicks diagonally up and to the left. These movements reverse when the body rolls toward the left side.

The usual practice of kicking with a board may be fine for improving leg endurance, but it inhibits diagonal kicking. Accordingly, most kicking drills should be done without a board so that the kick can be used in combination with body rotation. A drill for this purpose — *side kicking* — is described later in this chapter.

Should the Flutter Kick Be Used for Propulsion?

The fact that the flutter kick can be used for propulsion and stabilization was established in Chapter 17. The question here is whether front crawl swimmers *should* use it for that purpose. Adrian, Singh, and Karpovich (1966) have provided the most pertinent information concerning this matter. They measured the oxygen consumption of 12 competitive swimmers while they were kicking only, pulling only, and swimming full stroke. The swimmers used nearly four times more oxygen when kicking only as compared to pulling only. The oxygen requirement was 24.5 l when they kicked at a speed of 3.5 ft/sec (57 sec per 50 yd), compared to a requirement of only 7.01 when they pulled at the same speed. These results are supported by the work of other researchers (Astrand, 1978; Charbonnier et al., 1975; Holmer, 1974), all of whom found that kicking causes a considerable increase in the energy cost of swimming.

These data present a persuasive argument that swimmers should reduce the effort they expend in kicking to conserve energy, at least in middle-distance and distance races. In light of the disproportionately large energy requirement of the kick, it would seem wise to reduce the effort from the legs to the minimum required for support and stabilization in these races. By doing so, swimmers will delay fatigue so that they can swim a faster average pace for the entire race. The legs should be used for propulsion in sprint races and during the final sprint in middle-distance and distance races, however. This is when athletes need all of the propulsion they can get regardless of the energy cost.

TIMING OF THE ARMS AND LEGS

A kicking rhythm refers to the number of leg beats per stroke cycle (two armstrokes). World-class swimmers have used a variety of kicking rhythms successfully, including six-beat, two-beat, and four-beat rhythms. Of these, the six-beat kick seems to be most popular, although other styles have their advocates. The two-beat rhythm has been used primarily, but not exclusively, by male and female distance swimmers. Four-beat rhythms, although used less frequently, are still popular among a significant number of swimmers. Eight- and ten-beat rhythms have also been used on occasion, but were not successful and have been abandoned.

Six-Beat Kick

Figure 18-11 (p. 382) illustrates this rhythm. It incorporates three leg beats per armstroke, or six beats per stroke cycle. Actually, there are six kicks per armstroke because one leg kicks up as the other kicks down. However, it is common practice to refer to kick rhythms according to the number of downbeats only; thus, on this basis, there are three kicks per armstroke.

In this style, one downbeat is coordinated with each of the three sweeps in the underwater armstroke. The downsweep of one arm is coordinated with the downbeat of the leg on the same side (see Figure 18-11*a* for the right armstroke and Figure 18-11*d* for the left armstroke). The insweep is accompanied by a downbeat from the opposite leg (Figures 18-11*b* and 18-11*e*). The leg on the same side kicks down, once again, during the upsweep of the arms (Figures 18-11*c* and 18-11*f*).

The coordination between arm sweeps and leg beats is so precise that the beginning and end of each downbeat coincide exactly with the beginning and end of the corresponding arm sweep. Long sweeps require large kicks; however, the kick will be smaller when a corresponding sweep is used over a shorter distance.

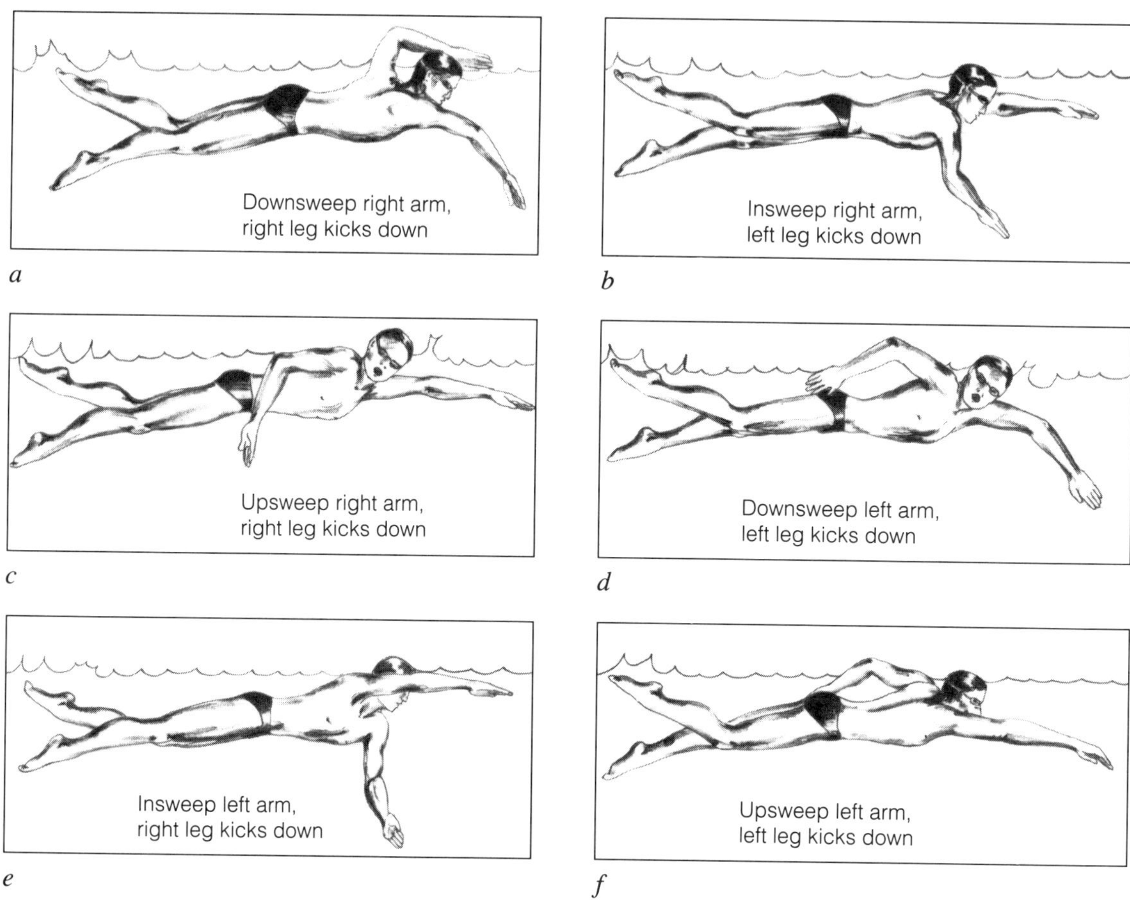

Figure 18-11. The six-beat kick.

This probably explains why many swimmers have what appear to be major and minor kicks during each stroke cycle.

The coordination of arms and legs that was just described is almost universal among six-beat kickers of any ability. It seems to be quite natural, and most swimmers perfect it through trial and error with little or no instruction. This timing probably contributes to the total propulsive force during each arm sweep. It also assists body roll and, thus, the maintenance of horizontal and lateral body alignment.

Straight Two-Beat Kick

Figure 18-12 illustrates the timing for the straight two-beat kick. The swimmer executes two downbeats per arm cycle, or one downbeat per armstroke. Each

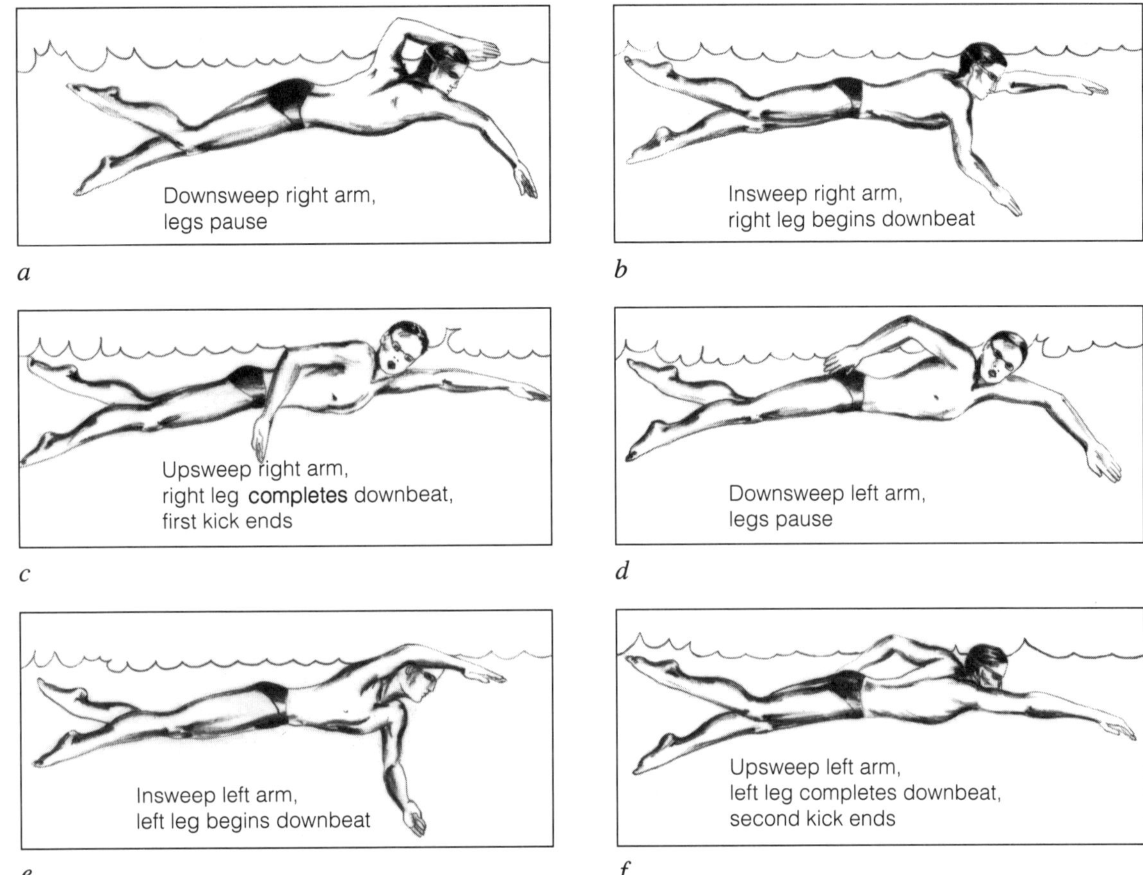

Figure 18-12. The straight two-beat kick.

downbeat accompanies the insweep and upsweep of the armstroke on the same side (see Figures 18-12*b* and 18-12*c* for the right armstroke and Figures 18-12*e* and 18-12*f* for the left). The opposite leg executes an upbeat at the same time. The legs hang, or remain stationary while the arm is recovered over the water and while it sweeps down during the next armstroke (see Figure 18-12*a* for the right armstroke and Figure 18-12*d* for the left).

The two-beat kick probably requires less energy than other rhythms, which may explain why it is preferred by many distance swimmers. Females also seem to gravitate toward this rhythm, perhaps because of greater buoyancy. Most males, because they are less buoyant, may require faster rhythms to keep their legs from sinking. Pendergast and coworkers (1977) reported that the legs of males tended to sink more readily than those of females. Watkins and Gordon (1983) reported that male swimmers could pull at only 80 percent of full-stroke speed when their legs were unsupported and that females could pull at 85 percent of full speed under the same conditions.

Swimmers who use a two-beat kick tend to modify the timing of their arms to compensate for the fact that they are not kicking during the downsweeps of the right and left arms. The first modification is a change in the stretch phase. Two-beat kickers stretch less and begin the downsweep sooner so that they can make a quick catch with the arm in front just as the arm behind completes its upsweep. They do this because they do not have a propulsive kick to fill in during the decelerative period between the end of the upsweep and the downsweep after a normal stretch.

Two-beat swimmers enter one arm slightly later in relationship to the other to facilitate their quick catch. They enter one arm when the upsweep, rather than the insweep, of the other begins. By doing so, the drag produced by the downsweep of the arm in front only interferes with the efforts of the stroking arm for a short time.

The second modification that two-beat swimmers generally make is to shorten the insweep. This modification is probably used because there is no kick from the opposite leg to counterbalance the insweep. Additionally, it allows them to get their stroking arm through the insweep quickly and into the upsweep before the recovering arm begins to sweep down.

Two-Beat Crossover Kick

Another kick style that is preferred by a significant number of male swimmers is the two-beat crossover kick. It is illustrated in Figure 18-13. There are really four kicks per stroke cycle in this style: two major downbeats and two minor crossover beats. The major beats are made during the insweep and upsweep of the corresponding armstrokes in the identical sequence that was described for the two-beat kick. The legs do not hang during the downsweep, as they did in the straight two-beat rhythm. Instead, the bottom leg kicks up and in and the top leg kicks down and over, causing them to cross midway through their respective beats. Swimmers complete the downsweep of their armstroke while this is happening and then uncross their legs in time to execute a major downbeat during the insweep and upsweep of the armstroke. The partial crossover beats take place during the downsweep of each arm, as shown in Figures 18-13*a* and 18-13*d*.

The leg that crosses over the top of the other will always be the one on the same side as the stroking arm. In Figure 18-13*a*, it is the right leg that crosses over the left while the right arm sweeps down; the left leg crosses over the right during the downsweep of the left arm in Figure 18-13*d*.

This rhythm appears to be a compromise between the energy-saving two-beat kick and the energy-expensive six-beat rhythm. Some swimmers, particularly less-buoyant males, may not find the two-beat kick vigorous enough to maintain horizontal and lateral alignment; however, a six-beat rhythm may require more energy than they can sustain for the race distance.

The two-beat crossover rhythm is also popular among swimmers who use lateral arm recoveries. Crossing the legs probably prevents the hips from swinging out in the same direction as the recovering arm is moving.

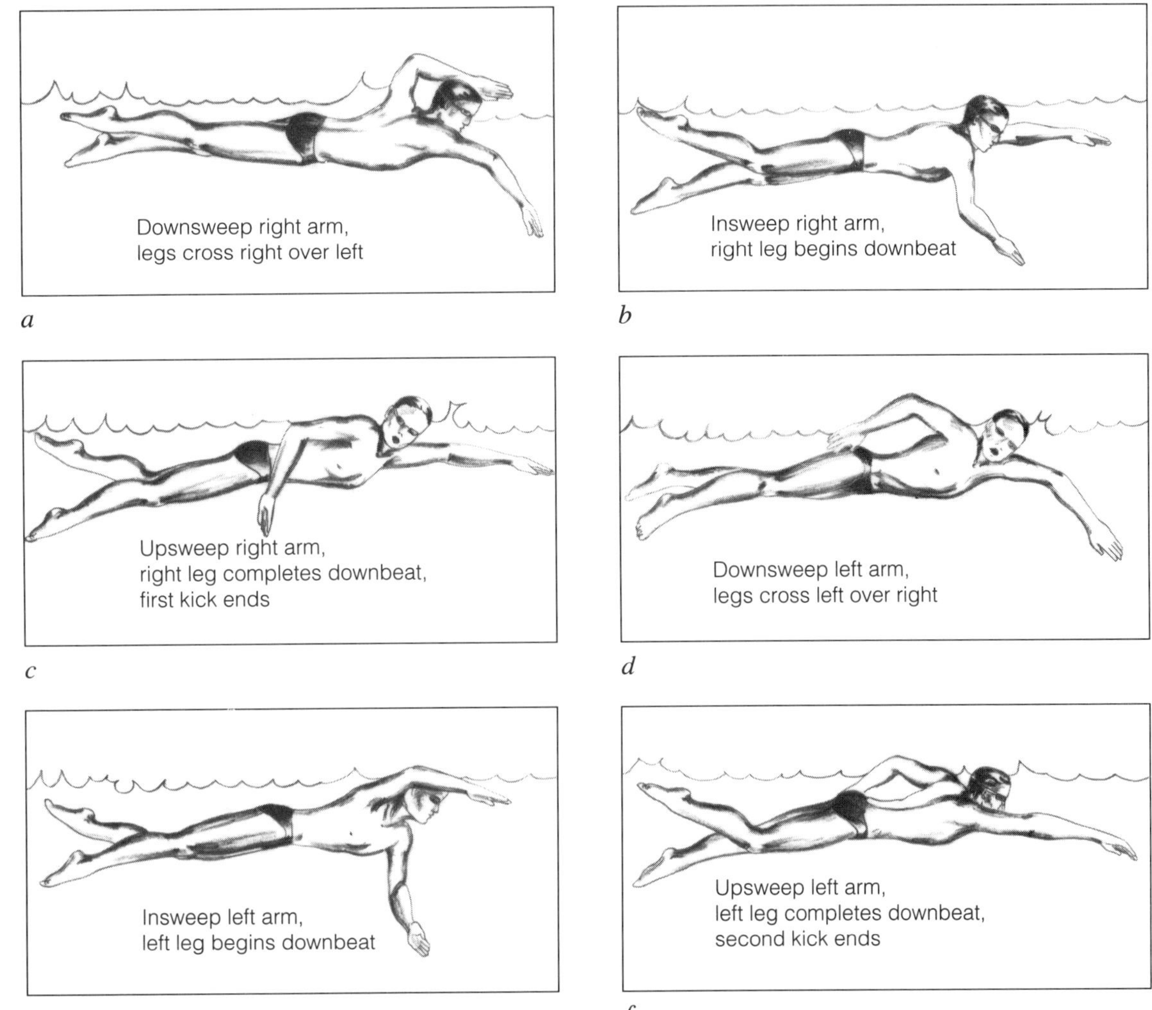

Figure 18-13. The two-beat crossover kick.

Straight Four-Beat Kick

Figure 18-14 (p. 386) shows a swimmer using a straight four-beat kick. This rhythm is really a combination of the six-beat and two-beat styles. The swimmer uses a two-beat rhythm during one armstroke (the right armstroke in Figure 18-14) and a six-beat rhythm during the other armstroke. Notice in Figures 18-14*a* through 18-14*c* that the swimmer executes only one downbeat with his right leg during his right armstroke. The downbeat takes place during the insweep and upsweep of that armstroke, just as it would with a two-beat rhythm. The swimmer kicks down three

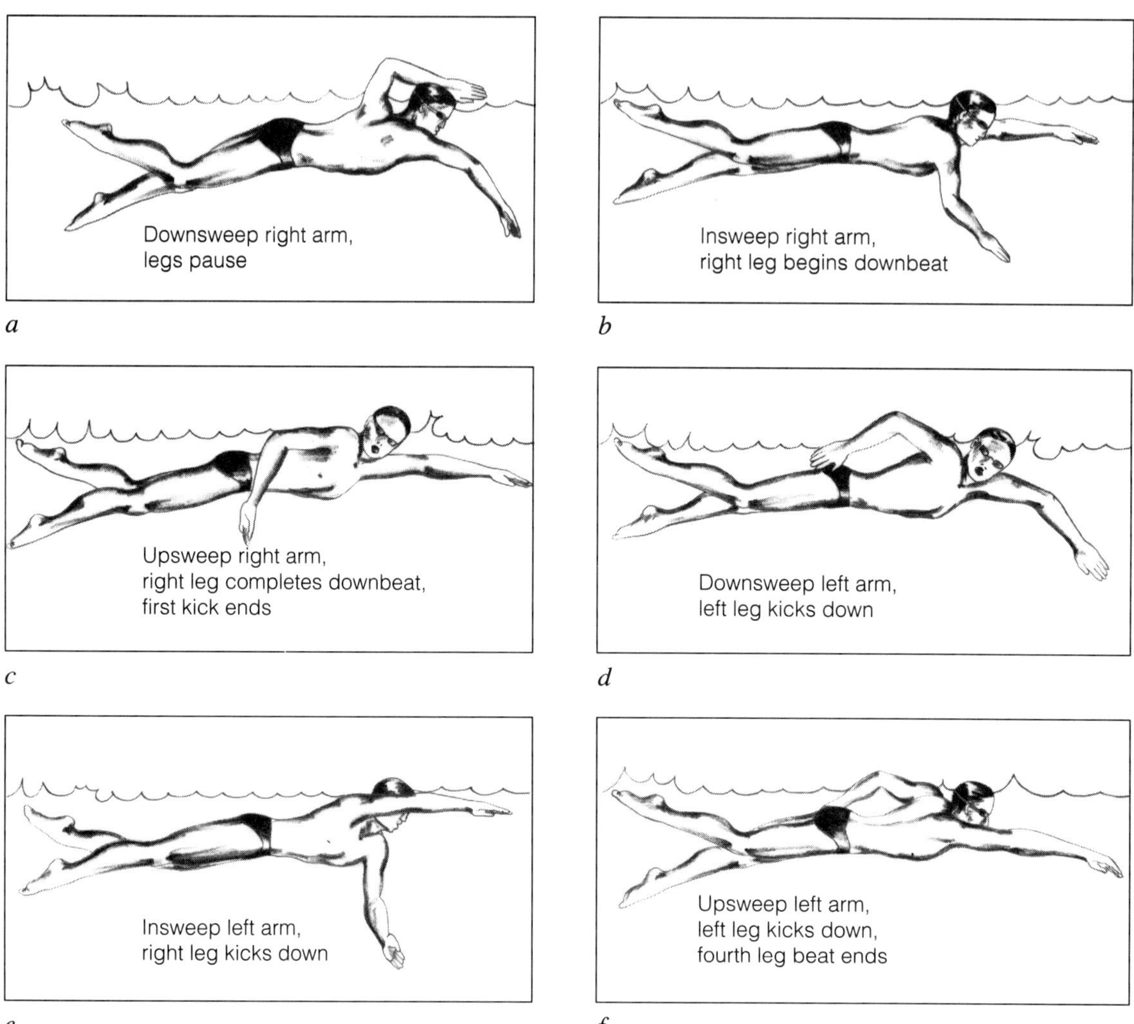

Figure 18-14. The straight four-beat kick.

times during the left armstroke, with each downbeat accompanying a sweep of the arms in the same rhythm described for the six-beat kick.

Four-Beat Crossover Kick

Figure 18-15 illustrates this rhythm. The difference between this rhythm and the four-beat kick comes during the downsweep on the side where the two-beat rhythm is used (the left side in Figure 18-15). The legs normally hang during this phase, however, with this rhythm, swimmers cross their legs, top over bottom, just as is done in a two-beat crossover kick (see Figure 18-15*d*). Swimmers then uncross their

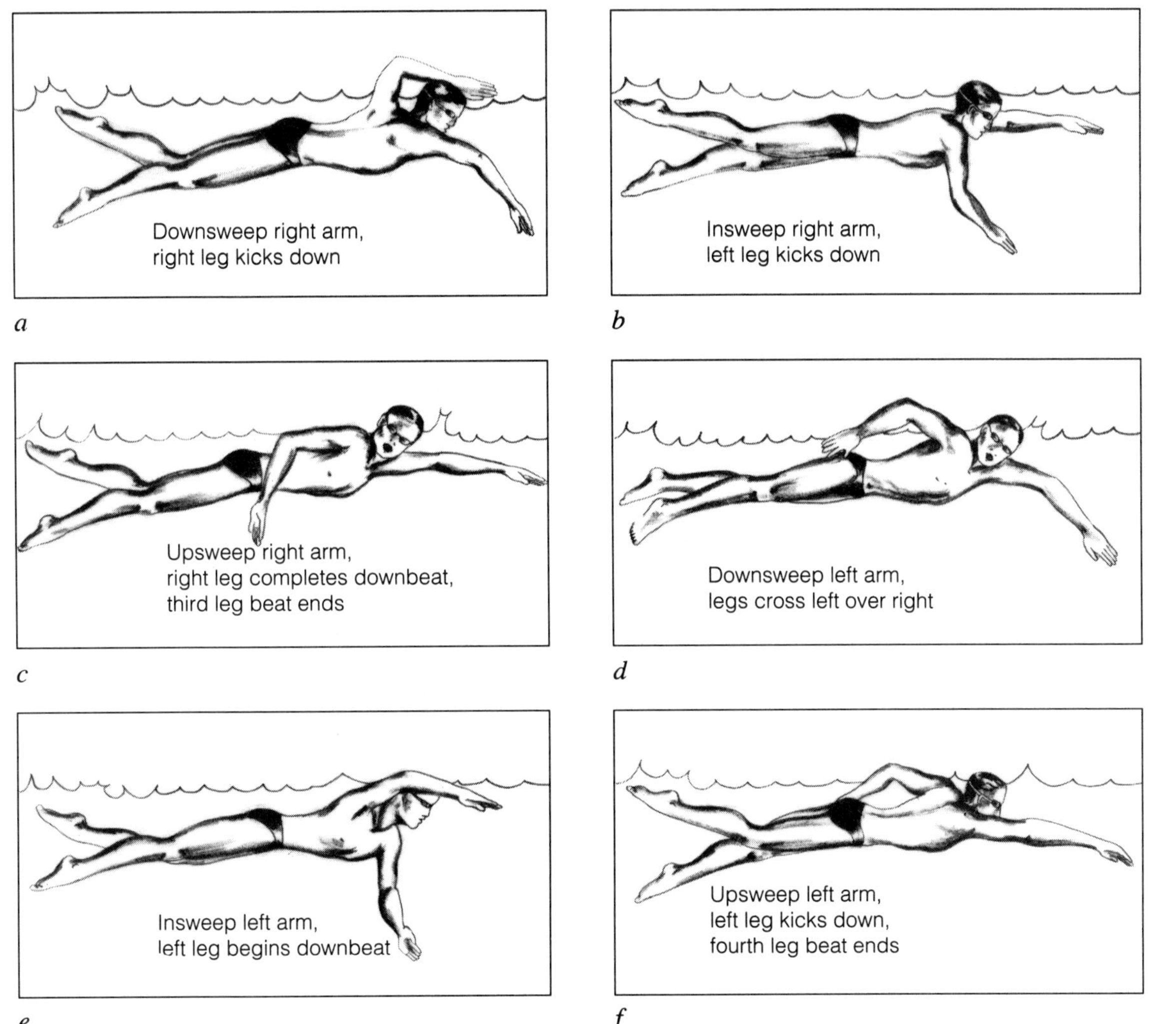

Figure 18-15. The four-beat crossover kick.

legs in time to kick down during the insweep and upsweep of the armstroke on that side.

Four-beat kickers who gravitate toward this style may use the crossover beat to counteract the disruptive effects of a lateral recovery on the nonbreathing side.

Which Rhythm Is Best?

It is tempting to recommend the six-beat rhythm as the best possible timing between arms and legs. The way these kicks coincide with the propulsive sweeps of the arms reminds one of a well-oiled piece of machinery. Nevertheless, many world-class swimmers have been successful at all distances using other rhythms, so the six-beat kick cannot be recommended for everyone.

Perhaps factors such as body build, specific muscular weakness, specific joint flexibility, and various physiological capacities make it more efficient for some swimmers to use fewer kicks per stroke cycle. In this regard, Persyn and his coworkers (1975) at the Leuven Institute in Belgium have reported the following results from a study of 62 national-level Belgian and Dutch swimmers:

1. Two-beat crossover kickers had longer legs.
2. Six-beat kickers had larger vital capacities, greater inward rotating ability at the hips, larger hands, and greater triceps and shoulder extension strength.
3. Six-beat kickers were able to kick faster for short distances.
4. Six-beat kickers' legs tended to sink more easily.

Swimmers with long legs may gravitate toward two-beat or four-beat rhythms because a six-beat kick would cause them to swim with a slow turnover rate. Swimmers with the characteristics mentioned in points 2 to 4 may prefer a six-beat rhythm for the following reasons. A larger vital capacity may partially offset the added energy cost of the six-beat kick. Inward rotation of the hips probably makes the kick more effective, and larger hands and greater strength in the triceps and shoulders allow for the longer stroke that is characteristic of six-beat swimmers. Faster kicking speeds undoubtedly mean that the propulsive potential of the kick is greater, and swimmers with marginal buoyancy may require faster leg rhythms to maintain horizontal alignment of the legs.

There is a final explanation for the use of two- and four-beat rhythms that has nothing to do with physical characteristics. The demands of training may have *encouraged* certain swimmers to develop energy-saving two- or four-beat rhythms early in their careers when their strokes were developing. We can only speculate that these swimmers might have been faster using six-beat kicks. Controlled research is needed to determine whether two- and four-beat rhythms are more efficient for some swimmers or whether the six-beat kick is the superior style for all.

BODY POSITION AND BREATHING

Body Position

As explained in Chapter 15, swimmers encounter less resistance when their bodies are streamlined horizontally and laterally. In the front crawl, the most likely time to upset these alignments is when swimmers turn their head to the side for a breath. Horizontal alignment is best evaluated from a side view, where the depth and inclination of the body are readily observable. The best way to evaluate lateral alignment is from underneath or overhead.

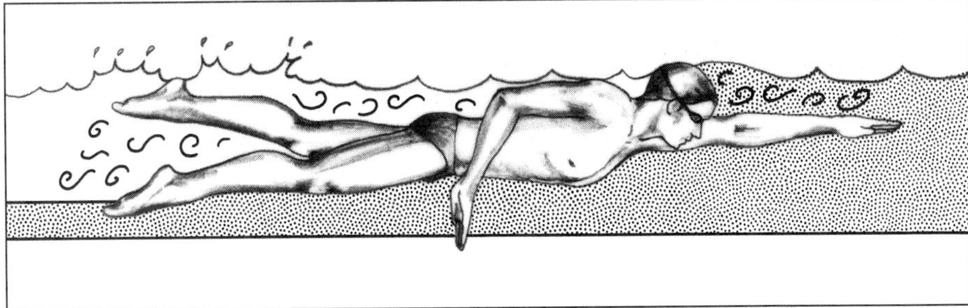

Figure 18-16. Good horizontal alignment.

Horizontal Alignment Good horizontal alignment is shown in Figure 18-16. The swimmer is nearly horizontal from head to feet, so his body presents a small frontal surface area to the water. Fewer streams of water molecules must be diverted as his body travels through them, so the pressure in front as well as the eddy currents behind are small and the amount of form drag should be minimal.

The keys to good horizontal alignment are (1) a natural head position, (2) a fairly straight back, and (3) a narrow kick. The face should be in the water, with the waterline somewhere between the hairline and the middle of the head. Swimmers should roll, not lift, their head to the side when they breathe, with one side of their face remaining in the water and with the waterline at about the middle of their head (see Figure 18-6*d*).

Swimmers should not attempt to hold their head unnaturally high or bury it excessively. Nor should they arch their back excessively to achieve a high body position. Swimming with the head held high will increase total drag 20 to 35 percent (Clarys, 1979).

The width of swimmers' kicks should be such that their feet just reach the surface on the upbeat and are only slightly below their body on the downbeat. Lack of buoyancy is not a significant hindrance to good horizontal alignment. Many great swimmers have been nonfloaters. When swimmers move through the water, the drag beneath their body increases buoyancy; consequently, it is possible for even nonfloaters to maintain good horizontal alignment once they get moving. Marginal floaters and nonfloaters may have to kick more to keep their legs horizontal than swimmers who possess more buoyancy. They will not need to kick deeper, however.

Lateral Alignment The swimmer in Figure 18-17 (p. 390) has his body in excellent lateral alignment. You could draw a straight line down the midline of his body from head to foot whether he was rolled to the right or to the left. Swimmers maintain good lateral alignment like this principally by rolling their body from side to side in time with the movements of their arms and shoulders.

Rolling is an indispensable aid to the maintenance of good lateral body alignment and drag reduction. The best front crawl swimmers continually rotate their body from side to side during each stroke cycle. In fact, they spend more time on their side than they spend in a flat position. Although it is possible to roll too much,

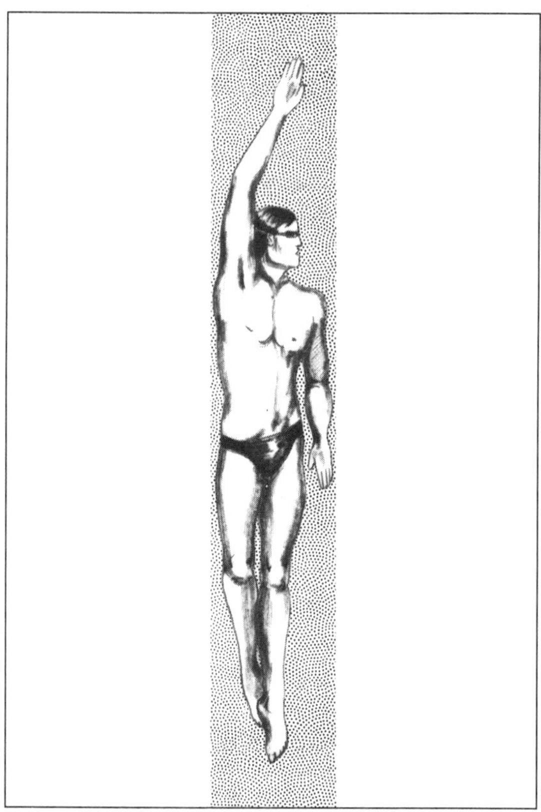

Figure 18-17. Good lateral alignment.

most swimmers roll too little. Front crawl swimmers should roll in the range of 30 to 40 degrees to each side (from a prone position). Gaines is rolling properly in Figure 18-2. Notice how much he rolls to the right in Figure 18-2*h*.

Rolling is, and should be, a natural reaction to swimmers' stroking movements. Swimmers should roll to the left when their left arm sweeps up, and they should roll to the right when their right arm sweeps up. Swimmers' bodies should follow the movements of their arms, rolling their shoulders, trunk, and legs as a unit. Otherwise, their hip and legs will swing from side to side.

Rolling also helps during the recovery to prevent the body from being pulled out of lateral alignment. The body should roll enough to bring each shoulder out of the water and keep it there during most of the recovery. Tittle, in Figure 18-6, is doing this very well. A *high* shoulder facilitates a high-elbow recovery. A low shoulder necessitates a low, lateral recovery that is potentially disruptive to lateral alignment.

Breathing

Head movements should be coordinated with body roll to reduce the tendency for swimmers to lift their head out of the water for a breath. Figure 18-6 shows the correct sequence for breathing. Tittle rotates his face toward the surface as the arm on that side sweeps up at the end of its underwater armstroke. He takes his breath during the first half of the recovery and returns his face to the water during the second half. Swimmers do the least amount of work when they rotate their head in coordination with the body roll.

In Figures 18-6*a* through 18-6*d,* Tittle's mouth does not appear to be above the surface because he is breathing at the base of a bow wave that was created around his head. This is the best way to breathe because it minimizes head lift.

Competitive swimmers should never hold their breath except in sprint races. They need a steady supply of oxygen to delay fatigue. They should breathe once during each stroke cycle in middle distance and distance races. Swimmers should begin to exhale immediately after inhaling. However, they must time that exhalation so that another breath is not needed before they have completed one stroke cycle. The exhalation should be very slow at first, letting just enough air escape from their mouth and nose to reduce thoracic pressure. Swimmers should continue exhaling slowly until their mouth is near the surface for the next inhalation, at which time they should exhale the remaining air in a rapid burst just as their mouth breaks through the surface. They should then take another breath and start the next cycle.

Inhalations should be larger than normal, but not excessive. Swimmers should not gasp for air. Practice and the demands of the race will train them to breathe in the most economical manner.

While the usual pattern is to breathe to one side only, some swimmers prefer breathing to both sides in a style called *alternate breathing*.

Alternate Breathing With this method, swimmers breathe twice during every three stroke cycles — breathing to the right on the first stroke cycle, to the left on the third, and not breathing during the second stroke cycle. Another style is to breathe twice to the left, complete a stroke cycle without a breath, and then breathe twice to the right. In this case, swimmers take four breaths during every five stroke cycles.

Alternate breathing has been used by many world-class swimmers, particularly females. The following advantages have been cited:

1. The stroke is more symmetrical. Alternate breathing encourages swimmers to roll their body equally to both sides, which increases body rotation and encourages a more effective armstroke and better streamlining.
2. Restricted breathing improves pulmonary diffusing capacity.
3. Swimmers can watch competitors on both sides.

The most compelling argument against alternate breathing is that the oxygen supply will be reduced in races, which will cause swimmers to fatigue sooner. The advantages in the list above must be weighed against this important disadvantage when deciding whether to use alternate breathing. In my experience, the strokes of some swimmers have been improved so dramatically by alternate breathing that they swam faster in spite of a reduced oxygen supply.

You can determine which swimmers fall into this category with a simple test procedure called experimental swims. Swimmers should complete a long set of repeats, totaling 2,000 to 4,000 m. They should use alternate breathing on the even-numbered swims and conventional breathing on the odd-numbered swims. Swimmers who are consistently faster on the even-numbered swims should consider using alternate breathing in races.

On the other hand, it may be advisable to train all young swimmers with alternate breathing. They may learn to roll better and swim more symmetrically when their strokes are evolving. They can switch to conventional breathing later, if they wish.

While some experienced swimmers may be able to correct stroke asymmetries by using alternate breathing in practice, it has been my experience that most return to their old styles almost immediately after conventional breathing is reinstated. The best way to change the stroke mechanics of experienced swimmers is to have them practice while using the same breathing techniques they plan to use in competition.

HAND AND BODY VELOCITY PATTERNS

Simply knowing the directions and angles of attack to use with the arms will not ensure fast swimming times. Swimmers must also apply propulsive efforts in the proper sequence. Body velocity and hand velocity patterns help us understand that sequence. Figure 18-18 illustrates ideal body velocity and hand velocity patterns for the front crawl. The data were collected while freestyler Carrie Stiensiefer was swimming at race speed.

The graph line at the bottom of Figure 18-18 illustrates the forward velocity of her center of gravity during one complete stroke cycle (two armstrokes). *It does not represent the upward and downward movements of her body*. The graph lines at the top show the velocity of her right and left hands during the underwater portions of one stroke cycle. These values represent the three-dimensional velocities of her hands, not simply their backward speeds. The nine swimmers drawn along the top of the graph correspond to the nine points on the velocity graph lines and show the portion of the stroke being completed.

Body Velocity Pattern

Stiensiefer's forward velocity pattern begins at point 1, corresponding to 0 time on the graph in Figure 18-18. Her right arm is about to begin its downsweep at that time. (It entered the water earlier and was stretched forward while she completed the propulsive phase of the left armstroke.) Her right arm sweeps down until the catch is made at point 2. Her forward velocity decelerates from 1.80 m/sec to 1.70 m/sec during the downsweep. This is normal because the downsweep is not a propulsive phase of the armstroke. Her forward velocity begins to accelerate at the catch and continues to increase during the insweep, between points 2 and 3, reaching a high of 1.80 m/sec as the insweep ends. The upsweep of her right armstroke is completed between points 3 and 4. There is a sudden loss of speed during the

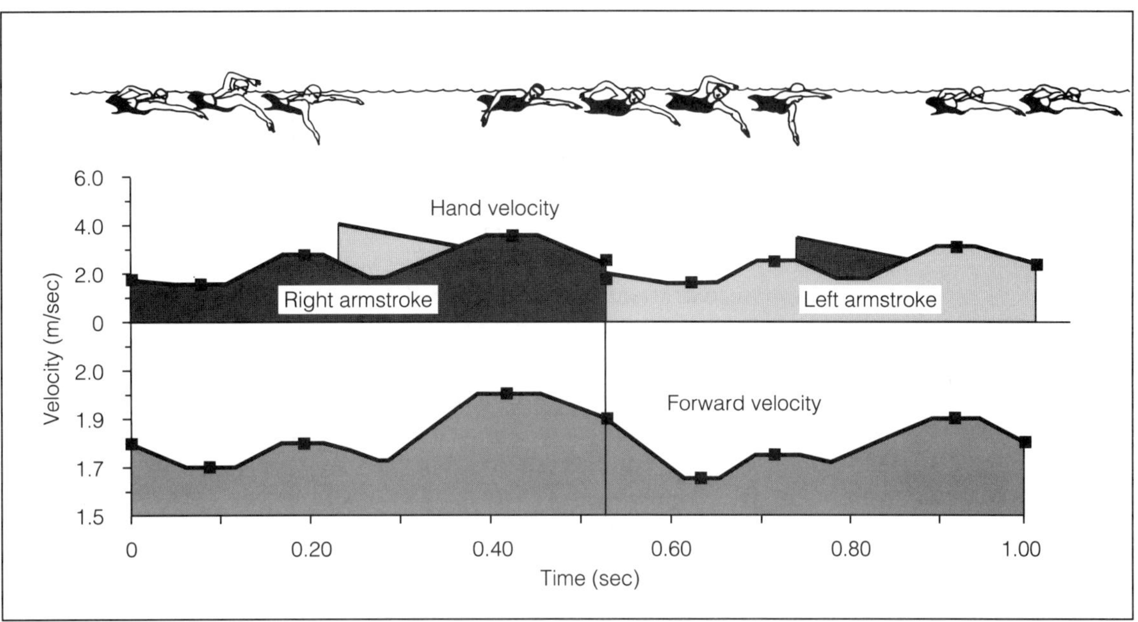

Figure 18-18. An example of body and hand velocity patterns for the front crawl stroke for swimmer Carrie Stiensiefer, cowinner of the 100-m freestyle at the 1984 Olympic Games.

transition between the insweep and upsweep, after which her forward velocity accelerates to a peak of 1.95 m/sec. This peak velocity is reached midway through the upsweep, and she begins decelerating as her hand approaches her thigh. At that time, she releases pressure on the water and starts the recovery of her right arm, which leaves the water at point 5.

Meanwhile her left arm entered the water when her right arm was at midstroke, and the left arm stretched forward during the upsweep of the right armstroke. She continues decelerating until the downsweep of her left hand has been completed at point 6, reaching a low velocity of 1.65 m/sec. Her forward velocity then accelerates to 1.75 m/sec during the insweep of her left arm, between points 6 and 7. The upsweep of the left armstroke is completed between points 7 and 8. As with the right arm, there is a sudden loss of speed during the transition from insweep to upsweep with the left arm. Her forward velocity then accelerates to a peak of 1.90 m/sec midway through the upsweep. This is followed by a slight deceleration to 1.80 m/sec until her hand leaves the water at point 9. One stroke cycle has been completed, and the next will begin at this point. One complete stroke cycle required approximately 1.10 seconds.

Hand Velocity Patterns

The hand velocity patterns are similar to those described in Chapter 16. Hand velocity decelerates during the downsweep of each arm until the catch is made, after which it accelerates moderately during the insweep. Hand velocity accelerates to its peak during the upsweep of each armstroke.

There are several interesting aspects of these hand and body velocity patterns that provide important insights into front crawl swimming.

1. *Swimmers should not begin propelling their body forward until they have completed approximately one-third of their underwater armstroke.* Notice in Figure 18-18 that the swimmer's forward speed does not begin to accelerate until approximately 0.10 second after she begins to sweep her right arm down. This is also .30 to .40 second after the arm has entered the water. I cannot state too strongly that *swimmers must wait until they have established a good catch before they apply force*.

2. *The deceleration of forward speed during the downsweep is a normal part of the stroke cycle and does not constitute a stroke defect.* Swimmers intuitively wait until the stroking arm has finished, or nearly finished, its propulsive movements before they begin sweeping down with the arm in front. As stated earlier, they apparently choose to maintain their front arm in a streamlined position while they are stroking with the other so that they do not increase drag. The gain in propulsion from the stroking arm evidently outweighs the subsequent period of deceleration during the downsweep of the front arm.

3. *Hand speed is not maximum for each arm until the upsweep.* Swimmers intuitively choose to save energy by making the insweep at something less than maximum effort, even though that sweep is propulsive. They save their greatest effort for the upsweep portion of each stroke.

4. *Hand velocity decelerates before a swimmer's hand leaves the water.* This provides good evidence that swimmers should not try to apply propulsive force all the way to the surface of the water. Notice in Figure 18-18 that the swimmer's hand velocity decelerates before it leaves the water and that her forward speed decelerates at the same time.

5. *There is a difference in the forward velocities generated by the right and left armstrokes.* The swimmer in Figure 18-18 gets more propulsion from her right arm than her left. Asymmetry of this type is characteristic of every swimmer we have tested. The left arm is usually, but not always, the least effective propelling agent. The valley for the left arm in Figure 18-18 is deeper and slightly longer than that of the right during their respective downsweeps. The propulsive peaks of the left arm are also lower in magnitude and shorter in duration than those of the right.

The reason or reasons for the propulsive differences between the right and left armstrokes are not known. The most obvious explanation would be that they are due to differences in strength between the right and left arms. I doubt the validity of this explanation, however. Various tests of arm strength, both specific and nonspecific, have not revealed that the less-propulsive arm is always the weaker of the two.

Another explanation has to do with body position. The less-propulsive arm is usually the one on the nonbreathing side. Therefore, swimmers may use some of the force from that arm to realign their body after breathing. A more plausible possibility is that they do not realign their body properly after breathing and, therefore, lose some propulsive force. A great number of swimmers fail to roll equally to the nonbreathing side. Consequently, it is very possible that poor realignment is at least partially responsible for the difference in propulsion between arms.

Contrary to this explanation, propulsive differences between the two arms have been found in the butterfly and breaststroke, where body rotation is not used. This fact leads me to believe that lateral dominance may be the principal factor that causes this asymmetry between swimmers' right and left armstrokes. Swimmers may develop a heightened kinesthetic sense in the arm that they have used most since birth. As a result, they may be able to stroke more correctly with it. This assumption is supported by underwater observations of swimmers that have shown that the dominant arm usually has fewer bubbles around it and appears to move through the various sweeps with greater precision.

In this same connection, swimmers may learn to rely on their dominant arm early in their career, when they are novices struggling up and down the pool. Consequently, they may develop a pattern of doing 55 to 60 percent of the work with their dominant arm. Once this habit becomes entrenched, they may continue to swim in the same way without realizing it.

Swimmers would improve their performances considerably if they could increase the propulsive force of their nondominant arm. For example, if the swimmer in Figure 18-18 could equal the average velocity or her right armstroke with her left, her time for 100 m would improve approximately 2.00 seconds. This has been demonstrated mathematically in the following equation:

100 meters ÷ 1.87 m/sec = 53.47 seconds

As you can see, the average velocity for the right armstroke is 1.87 m/sec; for the left, 1.75 m/sec. The difference is 0.12 m/sec. If she were able to average 1.87 m/sec with both arms, her time for 100 m would be 53.47, which is approximately 2.00 seconds faster than her winning time at the 1984 Olympic Games.

This difference is quite significant. It represents greater improvement than most experienced swimmers make during their entire collegiate careers, so efforts to improve the less-propulsive armstroke could pay big dividends. There is some question, however, as to whether lateral dominance and/or habit patterns can be corrected to the point where both arms contribute equally to propulsion. Nevertheless, swimmers should be able to improve the nondominant arm to some extent with the proper drills. I have three suggestions.

The first is to do some nondominant-arm swimming drills early in the season. One of the best is to make a fist with the dominant arm and swim with an open hand on the nondominant arm so that it carries most of the load. This may improve the sensitivity and/or endurance of that arm so that it becomes more effective.

The second suggestion is to concentrate on nearly equal rotation to the right and left sides. Swimmers should rotate toward their nonbreathing side enough to encourage a strong insweep and upsweep with the arm on that side.

The last suggestion is to encourage all young swimmers to use alternate breathing. This may encourage better use of the nondominant arm. Perhaps that arm will become more effective over the years, and swimmers can then use traditional breathing styles later in their career.

One-Peak and Two-Peak Velocity Patterns

Research with members of the 1984 U.S. Olympic Team showed that front crawl swimmers tended to fall into two categories according to the way they applied propulsive force (Maglischo et al., 1986; Schleihauf et al., 1988). Some had two peaks of acceleration during each underwater armstroke, and others had only one.

Two-Peak Pattern Figure 18-18 illustrated a two-peak pattern. The smaller of the two propulsive peaks occurred during the insweep of each armstroke; the larger peaks, during the upsweep. There was a short period, or valley, of deceleration between each peak.

One-Peak Pattern Figure 18-19 illustrates a one-peak velocity pattern. In this pattern, one large peak of forward velocity takes place during the insweep and upsweep of each armstroke. There is no decelerative period between the two sweeps, as there is with the two-peak style.

Swimmers who favor a one-peak style avoid the loss of velocity during the transition between the insweep and upsweep by using a small insweep. The insweep and upsweep become almost one continuous motion, with only a small change of direction from in to out under the swimmer's body. This allows the hand and body to accelerate steadily until both reach their peak velocities just before the hand releases pressure on the water.

You can usually tell two-peak swimmers from one-peak swimmers by the amount they sweep their hand under their body during the insweep. Two-peak

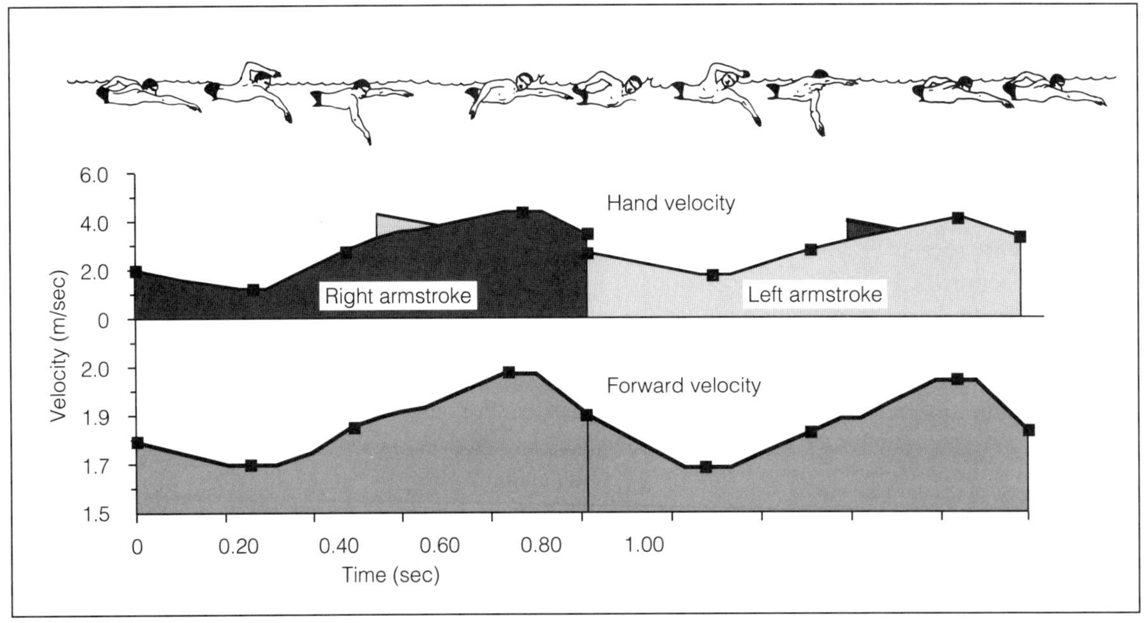

Figure 18-19. A one-peak velocity pattern for the front crawl stroke.

swimmers sweep their hand to the midline or beyond, yet one-peak swimmers do not bring their hand under their body quite as much.

You may be wondering if one style is superior to the other. That is not an easy judgment to make because both have been used by world-record holders. Matt Biondi was a two-peak swimmer, and Rowdy Gaines used a one-peak style; yet both were world-record holders and Olympic champions in the same event during their career.

The argument favoring a one-peak style rests on the absence of a decelerative period between the insweep and upsweep. Swimmers who use this style do not lose speed during the transition between these two propulsive phases. Still, the two-peak style has the potential to be more effective because propulsive force can be applied over a longer distance with less effort because of the increased diagonality of the stroke patterns. Two-peak swimmers should be able to find more undisturbed water to push against when they make major changes of direction during the transition from insweep to upsweep. Accordingly, they do not take as many strokes or accelerate their hands to the same extent as one-peak swimmers to gain the same propulsion.

Why do some swimmers select a one-peak style, and vice versa? The choice may be dictated by the kicking rhythm. Swimmers who use a greater number of kicks per stroke cycle may tend toward a two-peak style because it provides more time for kicking. There seems to be a tendency for one-peak swimmers to use minimal kicking styles. This is particularly true of females, who tend toward one-peak styles and two-beat kicks.

Another possibility is that one-peak swimmers might have been taught according to the drag propulsion theory early in their career. Consequently, they might have developed a style that minimized diagonal sculling. Most of the present world-class swimmers began their competitive career in the early 1970s, when this was the prevailing theory of propulsion. We can probably never determine if these swimmers might have been faster using a two-peak style because it may be too late to change a style that was developed over years of competition and hundreds of miles of training. However, it is probably wise to emphasize sculling when teaching young, developing swimmers because theoretical evidence tends to support the superiority of the two-peak style.

COMMON STROKE FAULTS

Some of the most common mistakes that swimmers make are described in this section to help readers diagnose stroke faults.

Armstroke Mistakes

Recovery and Entry Mistakes The most common mistakes that swimmers make during the arm recovery are (1) to use too much effort, (2) to swing their arm over the water low and wide, (3) to overreach, and (4) to underreach. The most common mistake during the entry is (5) to orient the hand incorrectly.

1. Maintaining a relaxed recovery is not easy for swimmers to do when they want to swim fast. Their natural reaction is to recover their arm over the water faster when they want to increase their speed. What they fail to realize is that their recovering arm is traveling a shorter distance and through a less-dense medium than the stroking arm. Consequently, the recovering arm will reach the entry position too early if it is accelerated. This will upset body rotation and stroking rhythm.

Swimmers who recover too fast usually shorten the upsweep of the stroking arm so that they can begin sweeping their recovering arm down almost immediately after it enters the water. This, in turn, shortens the most propulsive phase of their stroke. Furthermore, the force of the recovery may create unnecessary wave drag when their arm enters the water.

It is obvious that nothing is gained by recovering faster than necessary. Although it is true that swimmers use a faster stroke rate when they sprint, the mechanism for doing so is to shorten the stretch and to begin the downsweep more quickly. When this is done, one arm will naturally recover faster to maintain the proper relationship with the other. Even under these circumstances, the recovery should remain as inertial and relaxed as possible.

2. When swimmers recover their arm over the water low and wide, they usually pull their hips out of alignment in the opposite direction. The effect of this mistake is illustrated in Figure 18-20, which shows top views of two front crawl swimmers with good and poor lateral alignment. The swimmer in Figure 18-20*a* is

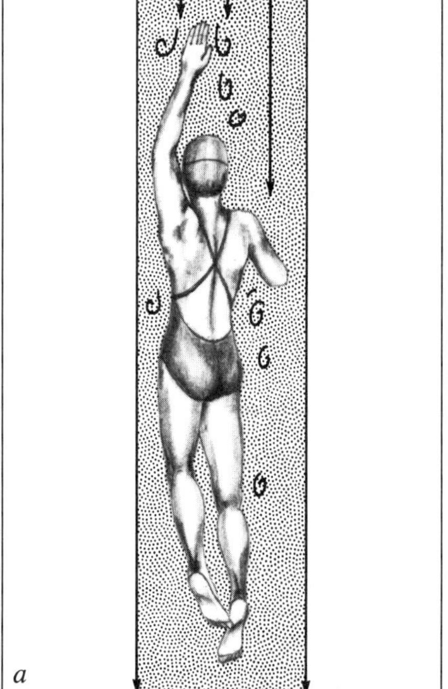

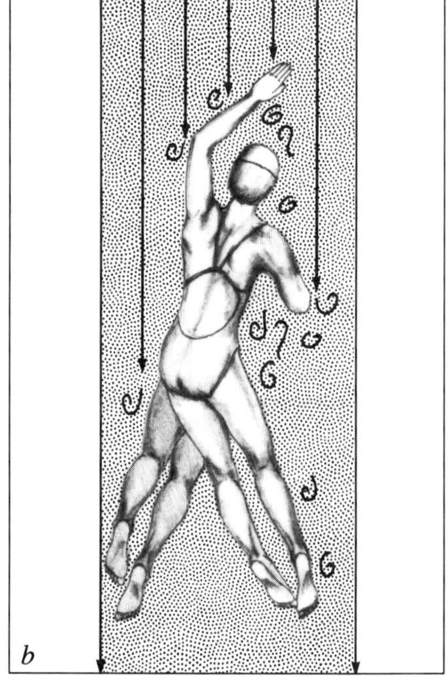

Figure 18-20. The effect of excessive side to side body movements on drag during the recovery.

streamlined, and the swimmer in Figure 18-20*b* is wiggling excessively from side to side. These side-to-side movements cause the latter swimmer to take up much more space in the water than the former. Additionally, the side-to-side movements of her body cause her to push water forward. Both actions will increase drag dramatically.

3. The mistake of *overreaching* takes place when swimmers extend their arm too much before entering it into the water. Figure 18-21 illustrates the effect of this mistake. This swimmer is overreaching by entering his entire arm at nearly the same time, smashing down onto a large column of water and creating a great deal of turbulence on top of and just beneath the water surface. This pushes big waves out in front of him that will decelerate his forward speed. Overreaching may result from simply trying to *reach out* too far with each stroke. More often, however, it occurs because swimmers fail to maintain a high-elbow position during the recovery. They begin reaching forward for the entry before their arm passes their shoulder, and this early reach causes their elbow and upper arm to drag forward through the water before their hand enters. Swimmers should be coached to maintain a high elbow throughout the first half of the recovery and to enter their hand before their arm is completely extended.

4. Underreaching is the opposite mistake. Figure 18-22 illustrates this effect. This swimmer makes his entry too close to his head. As a result, he puts his hand

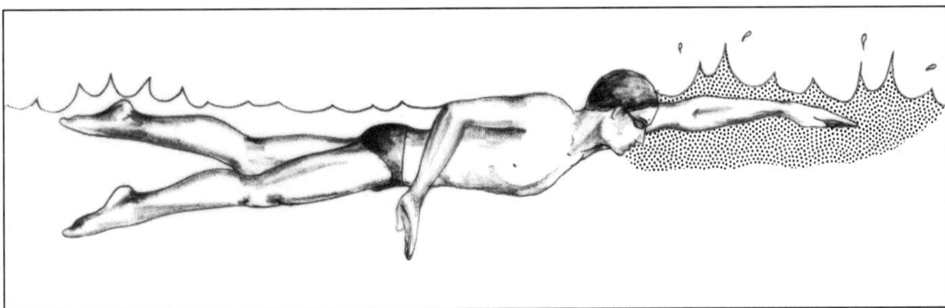

Figure 18-21. The effect of overreaching on drag during the entry.

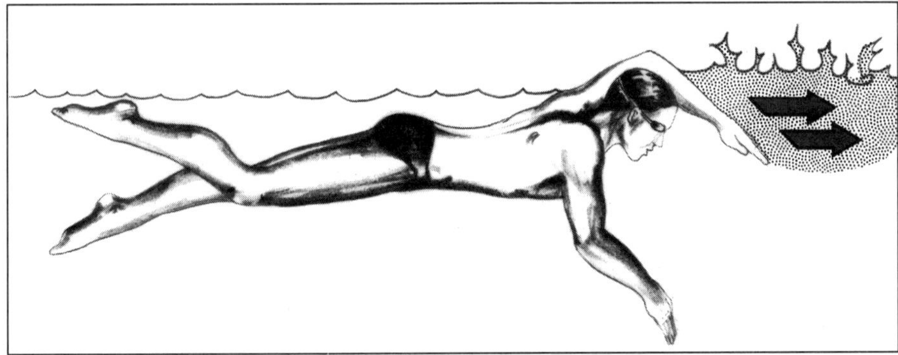

Figure 18-22. The effect of underreaching during the entry.

deep into the water almost immediately, causing him to push the broad upper surface of his hand and forearm forward against the water. This will create turbulence and decelerate his forward speed.

This style of entry was popular at one time because coaches believed that it placed the arm in a high-elbow position sooner after entry. We realize now that the entering arm should be stretched forward just under the surface of the water after it enters, where it should remain in alignment with the body until the rear arm has finished its propulsive phase.

5. In the past, experts believed that swimmers could make the catch faster by putting their hand into the water with their palm flat and their wrist flexed. This type of entry should be discouraged because there is a greater possibility that the broad surface of the back of the hand will push forward against the water. Figure 18-23 shows the effect of this mistake. Swimmers are better advised to enter their hand with their palm turned out slightly and in alignment with their arm. In this position, their hand can slice into the water with minimal resistance.

Downsweep Mistakes The most common mistakes are (1) to drop the elbow and (2) to slide the hand out too much.

1. The dropped elbow (which was described in Chapter 17 and illustrated in Figure 17-8) causes the forearm to face down early in the downsweep. If swimmers try to apply propulsive force, they will succeed only in pushing water down and decelerating their forward speed. They must wait until their elbow is above their hand before they attempt to apply propulsive force. This will orient the underside of their arm back against the water, where its diagonal sculling motion can displace water back, not down.

2. Although the hand should slide out a small amount during the downsweep, swimmers will delay the catch if they slide it out too much. They may also push some water to the side if they attempt to apply force, and this will disturb their lateral alignment.

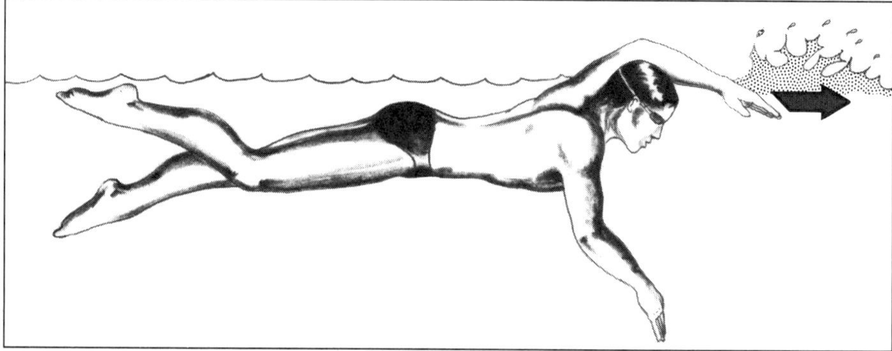

Figure 18-23. The effect of poor hand orientation during the entry.

Insweep Mistakes The most frequent errors that swimmers make are (1) to sweep their hand in without changing the pitch from out to in and (2) to pitch the hand in too soon and too much as it comes under their body.

1. Many swimmers simply do not comprehend using their hand like a propeller. They pitch their hand back at the catch and keep it in this position throughout the remainder of the underwater armstroke. Figure 18-24 illustrates the effect of making the insweep with the hand facing back. The underneath view of a freestyle swimmer shows that he keeps his hand facing back during the insweep so that the angle of attack is near zero its inward direction. You can see from the shaded arrow in the large drawing that water will pass under the swimmer's palm without changing directions. With their hand in this position, swimmers can only propel themselves forward if they push their hand directly back; it will not work if they sweep their hand in. Pushing back would only eliminate the insweep and shorten the propulsive phase of their stroke, so it would be better if they learned to scull across the water with their hand pitched in. The inset in Figure 18-24 shows a swimmer whose hand is pitched in correctly.

2. Another common mistake is the reverse of the one just described. In this case, swimmers pitch their hand in too much when they sweep it under their body, as shown in Figure 18-25. The pitch of the swimmer's hand is nearly perpendicular to the direction in which it is moving. With his hand at this large angle of attack, water will rebound from his hand in every direction, setting up a pattern of turbulence that will push his body sideward and reduce his forward speed.

Swimmers generally pitch their hand in too much because they start sweeping it in before the catch is made. Consequently, they rotate it past the most effective angle of attack too early in the insweep—that is, before it passes under their elbow.

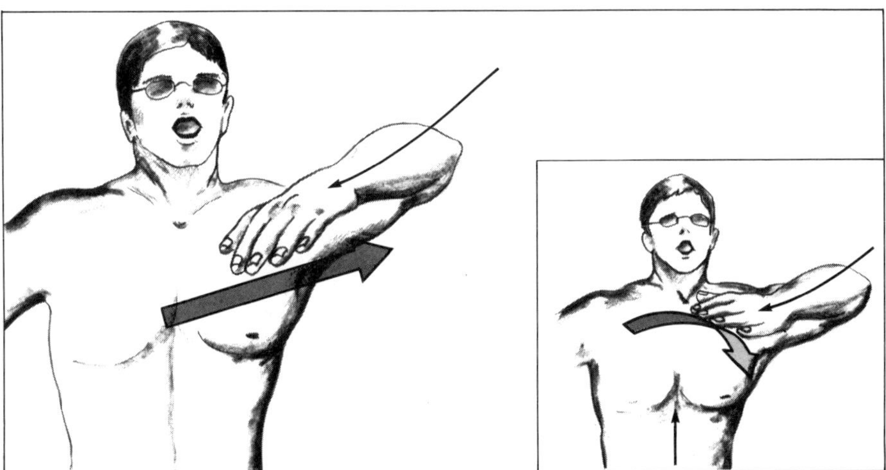

Figure 18-24. The effect of pitching the hand in too little during the insweep.

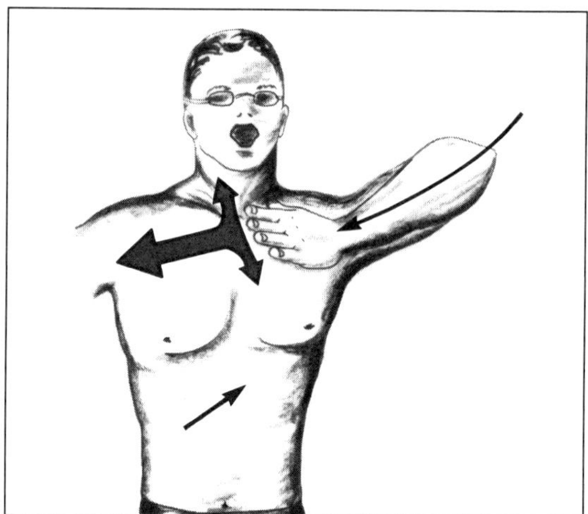

Figure 18-25. The effect of pitching the hand in too much during the insweep.

Most swimmers who make this mistake feel the loss of propulsion and cut the insweep short so that they can get into the upsweep.

Upsweep Mistakes In this phase of the armstroke, many swimmers extend their arm too rapidly at the elbow and try to push against the water until their hand reaches the surface. Both of these mistakes cause the same problem: the forearm and hand extend too early and too much so that they present an angle of attack that is nearly perpendicular to their upward direction through the water. That orientation will cause swimmers to push water up, rather than displace it back, and the effect will be to submerge their hips and decelerate their forward speed. Figure 18-26 shows a swimmer who is making this mistake.

Pushing up too long will cause the arm and hand to assume the same large angle of attack late in the upsweep, as shown in Figure 18-26. This will also push water

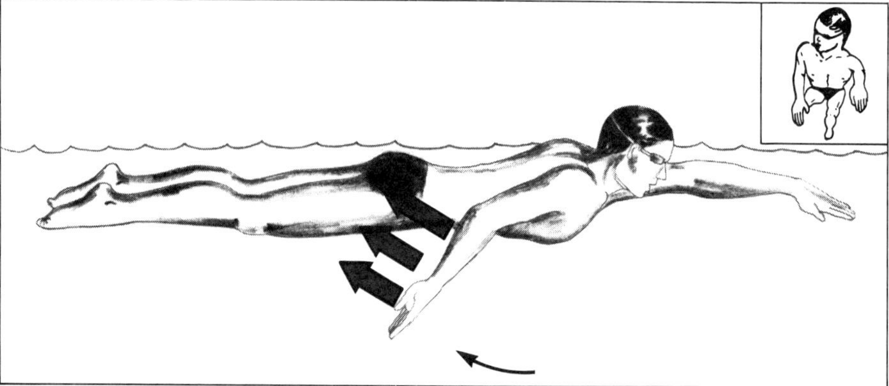

Figure 18-26. The effect of extending the arm too rapidly at the elbow during the upsweep.

up and reduce forward speed. Perhaps the most common reason for extending the elbow too much is to try to maintain propulsive force until the hand reaches the surface of the water. Skilled swimmers do not extend their elbow fully until after pressure on the water is released and the recovery has begun. Many do not extend it completely even then.

Swimmers should keep their arm flexed and their hand in line with their forearm throughout the propulsive phase of the upsweep. In addition, most of their effort should be expended in sweeping their arm up, not extending it back. Furthermore, their hand should release pressure on the water when it passes their thigh.

Kicking Mistakes

There are four mistakes that many swimmers make during the kick: (1) kicking too high, (2) kicking too deep, (3) bending the legs too much, and (4) extending the ankles too little.

1. Swimmers are kicking too high when their entire foot and part of their leg comes out of the water. Excessive upward movement of the leg may push the hips down.

2. When swimmers kick too deep, they increase frontal surface area unnecessarily. Swimmers' feet should be only slightly below their chest when they complete each downbeat.

3. Swimmers who bend their leg during the upbeat push the water forward with the underside of their lower leg. This, in turn, submerges their hips and decelerates their forward speed. (See Figure 17-18 for an illustration of this effect.)

4. The last mistake occurs because swimmers do not have adequate ankle extension ability. (See Figure 17-14, which contrasts the effect of good and poor ankle extension ability on propulsion.) Swimmers with above average ability to *point their toes up and back* have an advantage in that they can continue to displace water back for a longer time during the downbeat of the flutter kick. Robertson (1960) reported a significant positive relationship between the range of motion in the ankle joint and propulsive force during the flutter kick.

My experience has been that the best flutter kickers can extend their ankles 70 to 85 degrees from the vertical. Poor kickers usually score 50 degrees or less. A procedure for measuring ankle plantar flexing ability will be described in Chapter 24.

Timing Mistakes

The usual problems here are (1) to begin the downsweep too soon or (2) to stretch the arm too long. The effect of the first error was already described in the section on downsweep mistakes.

The effect of the second mistake, stretching too long, results in what is known as a *catch-up stroke*. The swimmer in Figure 18-27 is using a catch-up stroke. The term *catch up* is used because the relationship of the arms is such that one glides in an extended position in front of the swimmer until the other arm has entered the

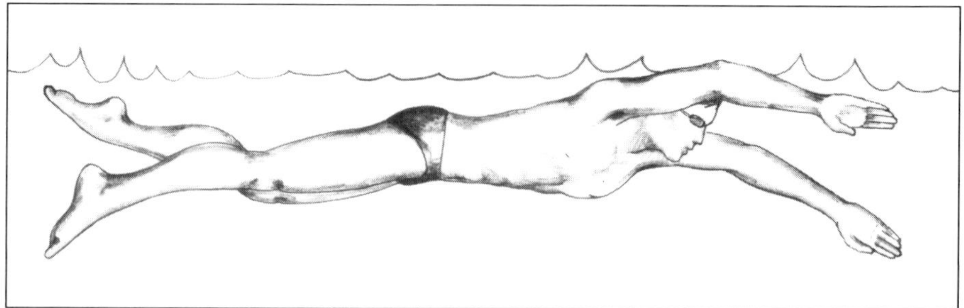

Figure 18-27. The catch-up stroke.

water and is also extending forward to the same position. In a sense, the entering arm is catching up with the one in front.

Catch-up timing was actually taught during the first half of the twentieth century. The theory was that this style provided a rest period for the arms. Counsilman (1968) argued convincingly against this theory when he stressed that gliding on one arm while the other was catching up was slower because the period of deceleration was lengthened between the end of the propulsive phase of the one arm and the beginning of the other. As a result of his writings, very few swimmers use this style today.

Unfortunately, some coaches have misinterpreted Counsilman's reasoning to mean that there should be no period of deceleration between the end of one propulsive phase and the beginning of the next. That is not possible. The stretch is necessary for streamlining for the reasons stated earlier.

Body Position

Horizontal Alignment The major mistakes are (1) trying to ride too high and (2) kicking too deep. In both cases, the body inclines down too much from the head to the feet, causing it to take up too much space in the water and increasing its resistance to forward progress. (See Figure 15-3 for an illustration of this mistake.)

The great swimmer Johnny Weismuller used to hydroplane while swimming the front crawl stroke (Bachrach, 1924), and his success influenced swimmers to arch their back and carry their head and shoulders high in the water for several decades thereafter. Today, however, we know that swimmers should try to remain in a horizontal position.

Fast sprinters seem to hydroplane over the water, but this is because their speed increases the drag under their body. That drag lifts them higher in the water in much the same way that a boat hydroplanes when its speed increases. All swimmers, even sprinters, ride lower in the water when they are swimming longer distances because there is less drag under their body to push it up. Conversely, all swimmers, including distance swimmers, ride higher when they sprint. Any attempt to augment this natural hydroplane would be foolhardy. Some stroking force would be wasted by attempting to hold the head and shoulders high in the water, and drag would be increased by the deep kick that would be required to maintain this high position.

Lateral Alignment Most of the mistakes that disrupt lateral alignment have to do with the armstroke and were discussed earlier. They are overreaching, recovering the arm wide to the side, and sweeping in with the hand at too great an angle of attack. These mistakes cause swimmers to *snake* down the pool.

Another way that swimmers can disrupt their lateral alignment is by pulling their head back when they breathe. Figure 18-28 shows this mistake from an underneath view. The swimmer in Figure 18-28*a* is breathing properly. The swimmer in Figure 18-28*b*, however, has pulled his head back to breathe, which causes his trunk to twist to the side. This, in turn, causes his hips to swing out to the opposite side and increases the space he takes up in the water.

Breathing Mistakes

The most frequent mistakes that swimmers make when they breathe are (1) turning their face too soon, (2) turning their face too late (late breathing), (3) lifting their

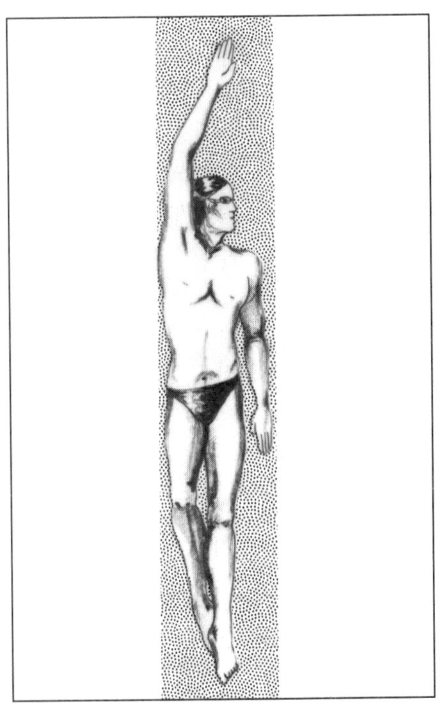

a

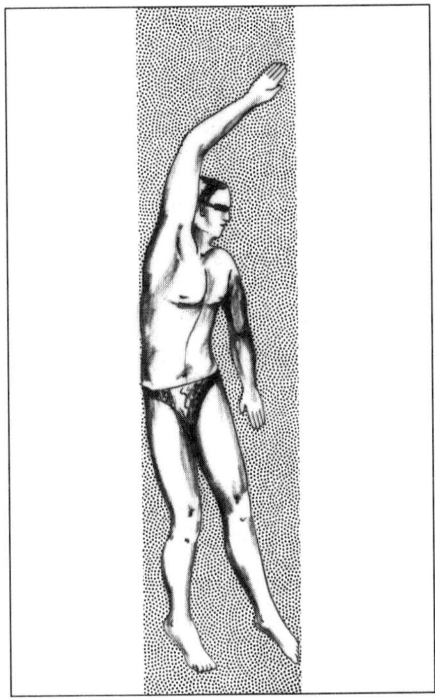

b

Figure 18-28. The effect on lateral alignment of pulling the head back during breathing.

head, (4) returning their head to the water too slowly, and (5) pulling their head back out of alignment. (The effect of the last mistake was described above.)

1. When swimmers try to breathe before the arm on the opposite side enters the water, they will interfere with their natural body rotation. Their body will actually rotate toward the breathing side when the arm on the other side is recovering. Consequently, they will pull it out of alignment. Most likely, they will cut the upsweep of the stroking arm short and rush the recovery of the opposite arm so that they can get their body rotated in the direction their head is turning. They must wait until their body naturally rotates toward the breathing side before they start turning their face in that direction.

The reason why some swimmers make this mistake is because they have been taught from an early age to breathe when the arm on the breathing side is stroking. They mistakenly interpret this to mean that they should start turning their head to the breathing side *when that stroke begins* instead of waiting until it is nearly completed. They should be taught to time the turn of their head with the stretch of the opposite arm.

2. Swimmers who turn their head too late usually have what is known as a *hitch* in their strokes. They inhale too late in the recovery. As a result, they hesitate with their recovering arm or they make a slow, high recovery on the breathing side to allow them time to breathe before beginning their rotation to the other side.

3. The third error, lifting the face from the water to breathe, is only seen occasionally and only with novice competitive swimmers. These swimmers usually try to swim without rolling their shoulders and have to lift their head forward to get their mouth out of the water. They should be taught to roll their body toward the breathing side and to leave their head in the water as they rotate their face to the side.

4. The mistake of not returning the head to the midline after breathing is common even among top-level swimmers. They either do not rotate their head back to the middle after breathing or they return it too slowly. In either event, they also do not rotate their body sufficiently toward the nonbreathing side. As mentioned earlier, this will force them to recover the arm on the nonbreathing side low and to the side.

However, an even more serious problem can result from not returning the head to the midline. It interferes with the upsweep of the armstroke because the hips must rotate up on the same side to perform that phase of the armstroke correctly. When they fail to rotate their hips up, swimmers must sweep their hand out too wide and that will cause them to extend their arm too much during the upsweep. (Figure 18-26 illustrated the effect of that mistake.) The angle of attack of the extended forearm and hand becomes too great and pushes water up more than back, causing a loss of propulsive force.

Swimmers should rotate their body back to the midline during the insweep so that they can then rotate toward the stroking arm as it sweeps up. This will improve propulsion from the upsweep because the arm can be positioned at a more effective angle of attack.

STROKE DRILLS

The sculling drills that were described in Chapter 17 are some of the best I have found for teaching the armstroke. Other good drills are described in this section.

Armstroke Drills

Stroke Pattern Drill A stroke pattern that is drawn relative to the body is one of the best methods for communicating the directions of the three sweeps in the underwater armstroke to swimmers of any age. Figure 18-29 displays a pattern for the front crawl. An underneath view has been used because it portrays the sweeps best.

Based on this illustration, the following are simple instructions for teaching the underwater armstroke for the front crawl. The hand moves in an *S* pattern under the body. It sweeps out in the first third (as it moves back toward the shoulder), in during the middle third (as it moves toward the chest), and out during the final third (as it moves toward the hip). The first curve is not propulsive and should be

Figure 18-29. A stroke pattern for the front crawl drawn relative to the swimmer's moving body.

performed gently. The hand gradually accelerates throughout the next two sweeps and reaches its fastest speed during the third. Swimmers will be using the correct angle of attack during each sweep if they keep the palm of their hand facing in the direction it is moving. Teaching swimmers to visualize this *S* pattern will go a long way toward helping them utilize the correct sculling movements when they swim the front crawl stroke.

Catch-up Drill Figure 18-30 illustrates this drill. Swimmers start in a prone position, with hands extended in front, right over left. They execute one complete armstroke with the left arm, placing it back over the right arm at the starting position. Next, they execute a stroke with the right arm, placing it back over the left arm to begin the sequence again. This drill is excellent because swimmers can focus their attention on stroking correctly with one arm at a time. It can also be done while holding a kickboard in front. The board should be held on the near end to allow enough space for complete stroking.

One-Arm Swimming Drill Here, athletes swim using only one arm at a time. The other arm stretches in front or it can extend back with the palm resting on the swimmer's thigh. The arm-in-front position is good when the arm on the breathing side is working. The arm-behind position is best when the opposite arm is being exercised. These positions cause the working arm to function more as it does in actual swimming because the body will be rotated in the correct directions. Swimmers should stroke with one arm for one or more lengths of the pool before switching arms. This can be done as a swimming or pulling drill.

One-Fist Swimming Drill The hand velocity graphs (Figures 18-18 and 18-19) showed that most swimmers have one arm that is less propulsive than the other. The one-fist drill helps to improve propulsive force with the "weak" arm. Primarily, it allows swimmers to overuse their nondominant arm in order to increase its propulsive contribution to the whole stroke. Athletes swim or pull any number of repeats with the hand of their nondominant arm open and the hand of their dominant arm in a fist.

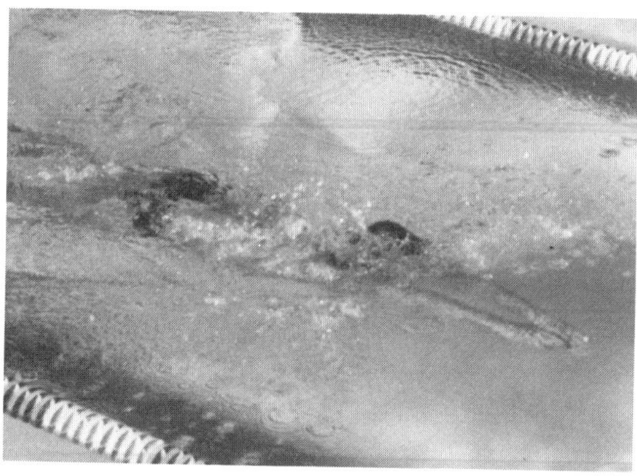

Figure 18-30. The catch-up drill done by Marcelo Menezes.

Recovery and Breathing Drills

The catch-up drill described in the previous section is excellent for improving recovery and breathing techniques as are the following drills.

Lane Swimming Drill Athletes swim down the pool with their shoulder touching a lane line. In this position, they have to recover their arm with a high elbow or it will get caught under the lane line. They should alternate swimming up and down the pool on the same side of the lane so that the drill is performed with both the right and left arms.

Dragging Fingers Drill This drill encourages a high-elbow recovery. Athletes swim or pull while dragging their fingers through the water during the recovery. Their elbow should be pointing up, and their fingers should be dragging forward in a straight line near the side of their body.

Sliding-Thumb Drill This drill is similar to the previous one, except that swimmers slide their thumb along their side to their armpit before reaching forward for the entry. It is also an excellent way to teach a high-elbow recovery.

Ear-Hesitation Drill This is yet another drill for teaching the high-elbow recovery. While swimming, athletes bring their thumb to their ear during the recovery and hesitate before reaching forward for the entry.

Timing Drill

Side-Kicking Drill This drill, illustrated in Figure 18-31, is excellent for teaching diagonal kicks. Swimmers kick down the pool on their side, with their lower arm extended overhead and the other arm extending back and resting against their thigh. After kicking four, six, eight, or some other designated number of times, they roll to the opposite side, reverse the positions of their arms, and repeat the sequence.

Figure 18-31. The side-kicking drill. The swimmer is Ondrej Bures.

The drill can be repeated any number of lengths. This drill can aid the process of learning six-beat timing by changing sides after every three kicks.

Experimental Swimming Drills

These drills were developed to test the effectiveness of stroke changes. The following procedure is used. Swimmers complete a set of repeats. They use their normal stroke on the odd-numbered repeats and a modified stroke on the even-numbered repeats. All of the repeats should be swum at the same effort. If a swimmer is faster on the even-numbered repeats, the modification may be a good one; if faster on the odd-numbered swims, the modification may be either undesirable or may require more time to master. Only one modification should be tested at a time. Otherwise, it will not be possible to pinpoint the reason for a swimmer's improvement or lack of it.

It is a good idea to count heart rates after each repeat and to record stroke rates or the number of strokes per length during the odd- and even-numbered swims. A reduction in any of these measures with no increase in time is a good sign that the modification is beneficial. If improved times are accompanied by an increased heart rate or a decreased distance per stroke, it probably means that an athlete was simply trying harder.

BREATHING PATTERNS

The breathing patterns that swimmers use are expressed in terms of the number of stroke cycles per breath. The most common pattern is one breath per stroke cycle. While most agree that this is the best pattern for races of 200 m and longer, many coaches recommend restricted breathing patterns for races of 25 to 100 yd/m. The dilemma facing a swimmer is that restricting their breathing too much will reduce their oxygen supply and may cause fatigue, whereas breathing too often may reduce their speed. Thus, it is important to determine the breathing pattern that is most effective for each race distance.

25 and 50 Races Swimmers usually restrict their breathing when they swim these distances because they believe that rotating their face to the side reduces propulsive force. Additionally, these distances are too short for oxygen deprivation to be a limiting factor.

Races of 25 yd/m are usually swum without breathing. Even 8-year-olds can be trained to swim these distances without breathing. Some athletes, teenage and older, can also race 50 yd/m without breathing, although most will take one to three breaths during the race. The breaths probably contribute very little to the muscles' energy supply, but they allow swimmers to expel carbon dioxide and reduce the distress caused by a buildup of that substance. Carbon dioxide buildup will create a compelling need to breathe long before the effects of oxygen deprivation are felt.

Swimmers in 50-yd/m events should experiment with one-, two-, and three-breath patterns to determine which produces the fastest time. These breathing patterns are used in the following ways.

Three-breath patterns The first breath is taken approximately 7 to 10 yd/m before the turn when a three-breath pattern is used in 50-yd or 50-m short-course races. The second breath should be taken on the final length, when the swimmer has completed approximately one-third of the distance. The third breath is taken when two-thirds of the distance has been completed.

The breaths can be taken at approximately the same positions in long-course races, except, of course, there is no turn. The first breath should be taken at the 20-m mark; the second, at the 30-m mark; and the third at the 40-m mark.

Two-breath patterns Swimmers use two different methods when they swim a 50-yd or 50-m short course. In the first method, the initial breath is taken 5 to 7 yards before the turn and the second breath at the halfway point of the second length. In the second method, the first length is swum without a breath and two breaths are taken during the second length. The first of these breaths is taken one-third of the way back, and the second is taken two-thirds of the way to the finish. Swimmers should breathe at the 20-m and 40-m marks in long-course races.

One-breath patterns There are also two methods that swimmers can use with this breathing style. In short-course races, the first breath can be taken 5 to 7 yards before the turn or on the final length about one-third of the way back. Swimmers should breathe at the 30-m or 40-m mark in long-course races.

Hypoxic training and other restricted-breathing sprinting drills are essential training elements for swimmers who want to use any of these breathing patterns. A two-breath pattern is recommended as the most effective way to swim the 50. With training, two breaths should be adequate for maintaining speed over this distance. An additional advantage in short-course races is that swimming the first length without breathing should improve speed and increase the likelihood of turning faster because swimmers will have the wall in view throughout most of the length and can adjust their strokes to hit the turn at full speed.

Preteen and early teen swimmers may find all of these breathing patterns too difficult to use because they require more time to complete their races. These swimmers should probably breathe once every two stroke cycles for the race distance.

100 Races Races of 100 yd and 100 m present a complex problem where breathing patterns are concerned. A compromise must be struck between increasing speed and delaying fatigue. A popular breathing pattern is to take one breath on the first 25, two on the second, and then one every second arm cycle for the remainder of the race. Some swimmers restrict their breathing even more during the second half of the race, breathing only three times during each of the last two lengths (or six times during the final 50 m if they are swimming long course).

I believe these patterns are too restrictive and cause swimmers to fatigue too early in the second half of the race. Most athletes will swim these events faster if they take more breaths during the first half to three-quarters of these races. It requires several seconds for oxygen to get from the lungs to the muscles. Therefore, the air that swimmers inhale during the first quarter of the race will be supplying oxygen to their muscles during the next quarter. The damage will already be done if athletes wait until they feel the need for a breath before taking one. Breathing early in the race should reduce the rate of fatigue and allow swimmers to complete the second half of the race faster. Their increased speed in later portions of the race should more than compensate for the small amount of time that may be sacrificed by breathing early.

Swimmers should experiment with the breathing patterns described in the following list until they find the one that suits them best:

1. Breathe every second cycle for the first quarter of the race and every cycle for the final three-quarters.
2. Breathe every second cycle for the first half of the race and every cycle thereafter.
3. Breathe every second cycle for the entire race.
4. Breathe every stroke cycle from start to finish.

Although many swimmers prefer the last method, most coaches feel that it is not the most effective breathing pattern to use in 100 races. Nevertheless, many great swims have been accomplished with this pattern. That is why it has been listed as one of the methods with which swimmers should experiment.

Regardless of the pattern preferred, swimmers should always swim the final 5 to 10 yd/m without breathing so that they can finish as fast as possible.

Drills should be used in the early season to help each swimmer find the most effective breathing pattern. The following experimental drill is recommended for this purpose. Athletes should swim a series of six or eight 50s at the end of a particularly strenuous practice session. The drill should be done at the end of practice so that swimmers are as fatigued as they are likely to be during the second half of a 100 race. The repeats should be swum at 100 pace. Swimmers should randomly alternate two or more of the recommended breathing patterns throughout the set of repeats. Coaches should keep a record of the times and breathing patterns used. The pattern that consistently produces the fastest times should be the one used in competition. If two or more patterns produce identical times, the one that allows for more frequent breathing should be used because that pattern will provide a greater oxygen supply.

Longer Races Although some may disagree, it is generally accepted that swimmers should breathe during every stroke cycle in races of 200 yd/m and longer. The increased oxygen supply will more than compensate for any increase in drag or decrease of propulsive force caused by frequent turning of the head.

CHAPTER 19

Butterfly

It was not until the mid 1950s that the butterfly became a separate competitive stroke. It began evolving from the breaststroke in the early 1930s. At that time, some swimmers found that they could swim breaststroke faster and still conform to the rules by using an over-water recovery. With the introduction of the butterfly armstroke, the breaststroke became one of the most interesting events in competitive swimming. Some competitors continued to swim the breaststroke underwater, as was the custom during those years. Others swam the "new" butterfly-breaststroke on the surface. Still others swam a combination of the two styles. In time, swimmers discovered that they could swim the butterfly-breaststroke faster if they used what we now know as the dolphin kick. This kick also conformed to the rules of breaststroke in use at that time because the legs moved simultaneously and in the same plane. Using the dolphin kick, the butterfly-breaststroke became so much faster than the conventional breaststroke that the butterfly was made a separate competitive stroke in 1955. The "invention" of the butterfly is credited to the swimmer Jack Sieg and his coach David Armbruster.

The butterfly stroke is described in this chapter by the same categories that were used to describe the front crawl stroke in Chapter 18.

ARMSTROKE

The butterfly armstroke consists of an outsweep, an upsweep, an insweep, a release, and a recovery. Underwater photos of the butterfly stroke are shown from a side view in Figure 19-1.

a *b* *c* *d* *e* *f*

Figure 19-1. Underwater sequence photos of the butterfly. The swimmer is Mary T., world-record holder for 100- and 200-m butterfly.

g h i j k l

Outsweep

This phase of the armstroke is shown in Figures 19-1*b* through 19-1*e*. The hands should enter the water in front of the body at shoulder width or slightly wider. The palms should face out slightly so that the hands slide into the water on their edges. They are then swept forward and out in a curvilinear path until they are outside the width of the shoulders. The palms should rotate out and back as the arms near the end of the outsweep.

After they enter the water, the hands should travel in and forward for a short time before circling out and forward. The hands should continue to circle out and forward until the arms are outside the shoulders and facing back against the water. This is when the catch is made, as shown in Figure 19-1*e*.

The palms should continue to rotate out during the outsweep, until they are facing out and back when the catch is made. The arms should flex gradually during the outsweep to aid in getting the undersides of the arms and the palms of the hands facing back on the water at the catch. The arms will flex through a range of 30 to 40 degrees until the catch is made. Any attempt to apply propulsive force before the hands are outside shoulder width and facing back will only result in pushing the water in unwanted directions. The hands and forearms should be aligned at the catch so that a straight line can be drawn from the fingertips to the elbows, and they should remain aligned throughout the subsequent insweep and upsweep.

The outsweep is not a propulsive movement. It should be a gentle stretching of the arms out and forward. Its purpose is to place the hands in position for the propulsive insweep that follows. Hand speed will decelerate after the entry, until the hands are barely moving at the catch.

The downbeat of the first dolphin kick of the stroke cycle facilitates the outsweep. That kick, which is made in conjunction with the outsweep, produces the undulation that pushes the arms out and forward. This action of the kick helps swimmers to overcome their inertia as they change the direction of their hands from in to out between the entry and catch. The change of arm direction from in to out can also be facilitated if the arms are flexed slightly at the elbows when they enter the water. Extending them at the elbows after the arms enter the water will change their direction from in to out so that their inward inertia can be overcome with less disruption of forward velocity. It is not essential for swimmers to flex their elbows during the recovery because the kick provides a means for overcoming the inertia when the hands change directions from in to out. Nevertheless, this change in direction can be completed with less muscular effort if the arms are extended immediately after they enter the water.

Insweep

The insweep is pictured in Figures 19-1*e* through 19-1*h*. It is the first of two propulsive sweeps in the butterfly armstroke. The insweep is a large semicircular movement of the arms from a wide position just beneath the surface of the water at the catch to a close together position underneath the body. It is accomplished by gradually bending the arms an additional 50 to 60 degrees until they are flexed between 90 and 100 degrees at the elbows when the hands come together. The elbows act like hubs of a wheel, with the hands rotating around them throughout the insweep.

The hands sweep out, down, and in until they are nearly together under the swimmer's body. The hands, which were facing out at the catch, are gradually rotated in during the insweep until they are pitched in and up when the movement ends. Figure 19-2 illustrates that pitch best from an underneath view. The hands accelerate moderately during the movement from approximately 2 m/sec (6 ft/sec) at the catch to speeds of approximately 3 to 4 m/sec (10 to 14 ft/sec) at the end of the insweep (Maglischo, 1984; Schleihauf et al., 1988).

Many swimmers sweep their hands in within a fraction of an inch of one another, like the athlete pictured in Figure 19-2. Others sweep them only slightly inside the confines of their trunk, like the swimmer in Figure 19-1*h*.

The width of the hands at the end of the outsweep is one factor that probably determines how far the hands are swept under the body. Swimmers who sweep out a longer distance naturally start the insweep with their hands farther apart. Consequently, they may be able to utilize the propulsive potential of the insweep without bringing their hands close together under their body. Another reason may have to do with a swimmer's affinity for using diagonal sculls. Good scullers sweep their hands in more diagonally, while poor swimmers shorten the inward movement of their hands and lengthen the upsweep. Because world-class butterfly swimmers have used both styles, the superior method cannot be identified positively, although diagonal sculling motions should be more efficient for the reasons mentioned in Chapter 16.

The insweep, as used in the butterfly, has two distinct parts where propulsion is concerned. The first is the downward portion and the second is the inward portion. Figures 19-3 and 19-4 show how propulsion is achieved during each of these two phases of the insweep. In the first portion, the hands sweep out, *down,* and back in the direction of the arrow above the swimmer's hand in Figure 19-3. His hands are

Figure 19-2. An underneath view of the insweep in the butterfly. This swimmer sweeps his hands in until they are together under his body.

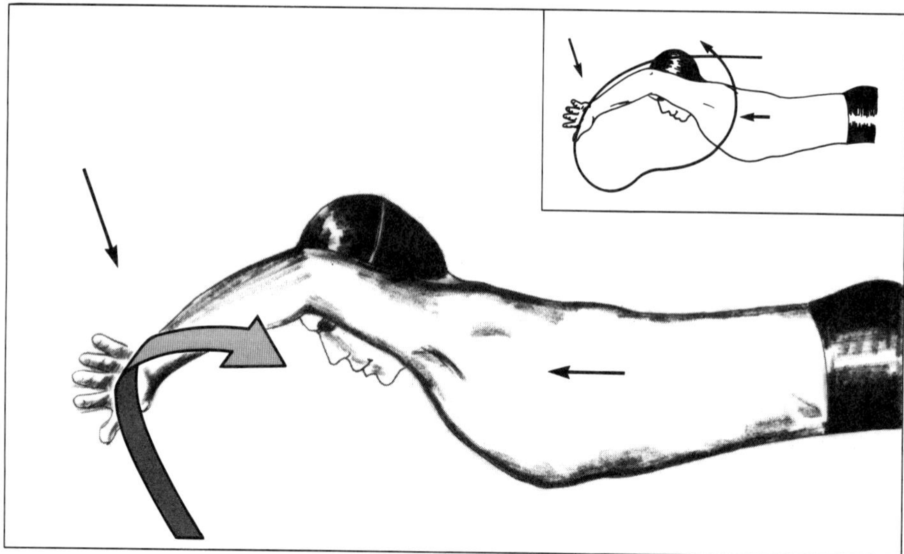

Figure 19-3. A side view of the first portion of the insweep, showing how propulsion can be generated.

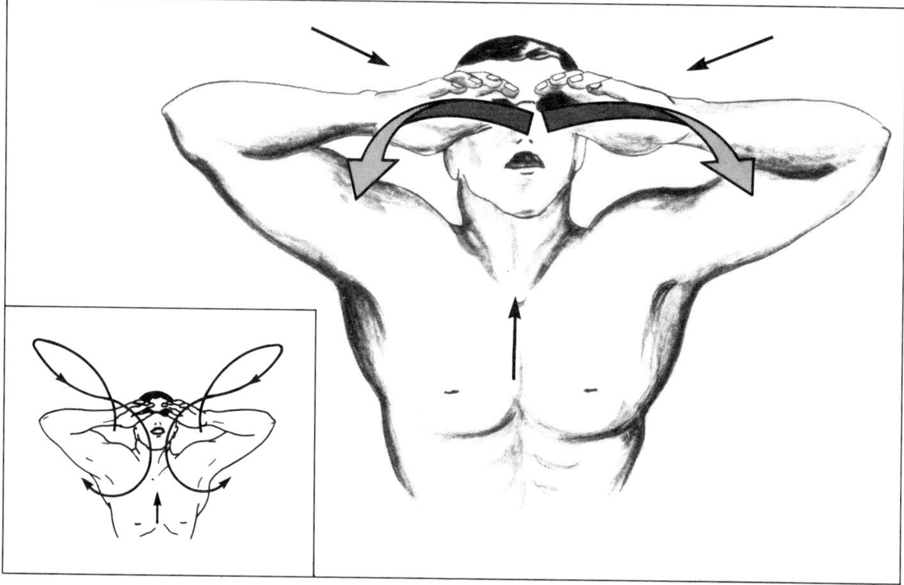

Figure 19-4. An underneath view of the insweep, showing how water is accelerated back as the swimmer's hands sweep in under his body.

correctly pitched out and back. In this position, the thumb sides are the leading edges of the hand-foils, and the little-finger sides are the trailing edges. You can see in Figure 19-3 that this combination of hand direction and angle of attack will displace water back under his palms from leading to trailing edges. The relative flow of water is upward as it passes the thumb sides of his hands, but their slight downward inclination causes the water to be displaced back as it travels under his palms toward the little-finger sides. This is shown by the change in direction of the shaded arrow passing under the swimmer's palm.

The direction in which the swimmer's hands are moving shifts inward during the second portion of the insweep, and hand pitch also changes until the palms are facing in and slightly upward during this phase. The underneath view in Figure 19-4 shows how this combination of direction and angle of attack will impart some backward force to the water during this portion of the insweep. Because his hands are pitched in while they sweep laterally across the water, the thumb sides are the leading edges and the little-finger sides the trailing edges of the hand-foils. The relative direction of water flow is outward as it meets the leading edges of the swimmer's hands. However, the inward pitch of his hands gradually changes the water direction to back as the water passes under the palms from the thumb sides toward the little-finger sides.

Swimmers *feel* the insweep as one semicircular propulsive motion, so it should be taught that way. Swimmers should think of the insweep as one circular sweep of their hands down and in under their body. Their hands should be pitched out when the insweep starts, and they should be pitched in and up when it is completed.

Upsweep

The upsweep is pictured in Figures 19-1*h* through 19-1*j*. It begins as the swimmer's hands come together near the end of the preceding insweep. At that point, the hands change directions and execute a semicircular sweep out, back, and up toward the surface of the water. The hands should rotate out and should remain pitched out and back during the upsweep. The undersides of the forearms should also maintain a backward orientation to the water throughout this motion, as shown in Figures 19-1*i* through 19-1*j*. Hand speed slows during the transition from insweep to upsweep and then accelerates until the hands release pressure on the water at the end of the movement. The release takes place when the hands pass the thighs during their upward path, at which time the recovery begins.

The arms should extend somewhat during the upsweep; however, they should still be flexed nearly 45 degrees when the release is made so that a backward orientation is maintained. Full extension should not take place until the recovery is underway.

As with the insweep, the upsweep feels like one continuous propulsive movement. Swimmers feel like they are sweeping their hands out, back and up, with their arms gradually extending and their palms pitched out and back. However, the upsweep has two distinct phases where propulsion is concerned, just as it did in the front crawl stroke. The underneath view in Figure 19-5 shows how propulsion is achieved during the first half of the upsweep when the hands sweep out from

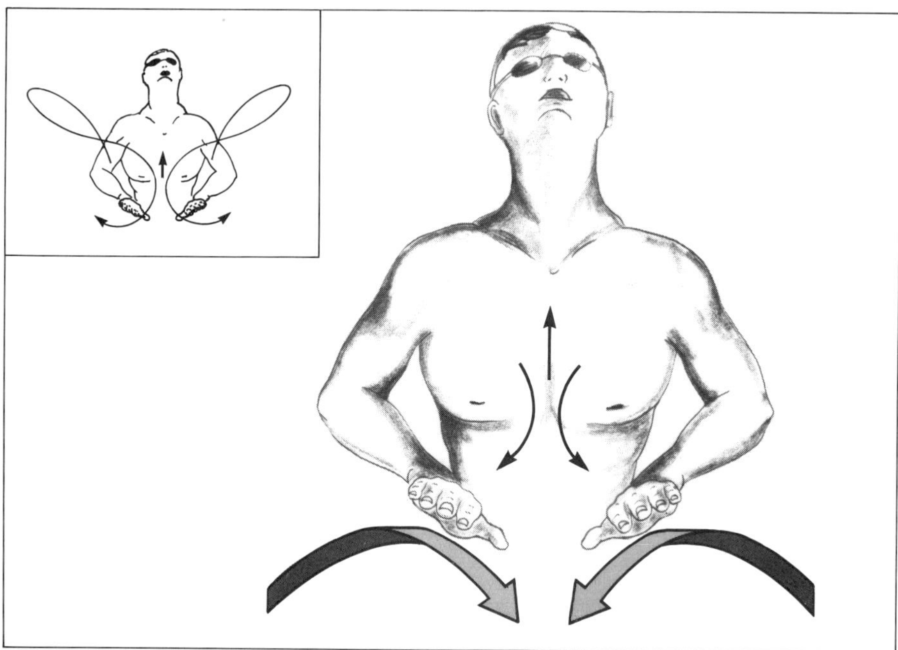

Figure 19-5. An underneath view of the first portion of the upsweep, showing how propulsion is produced.

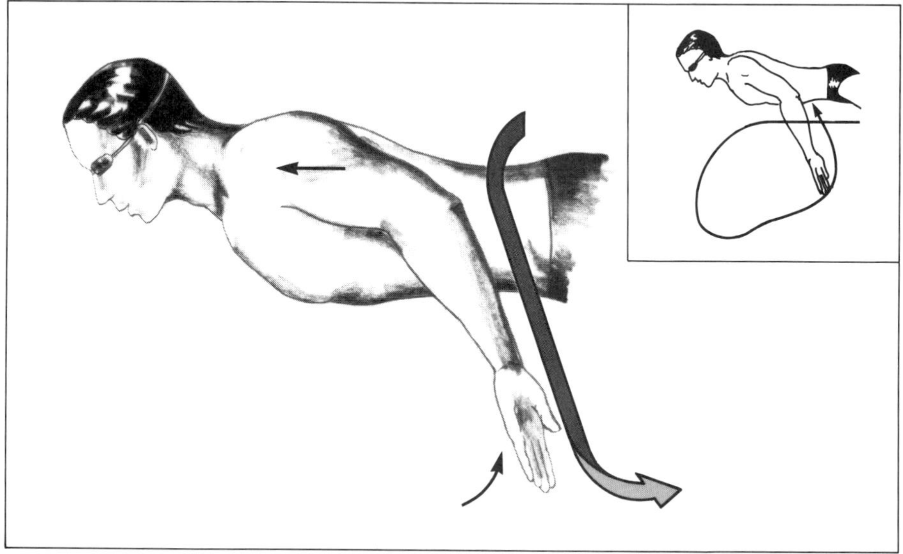

Figure 19-6. A side view of the upsweep, showing how water is displaced back by the upward movement of the swimmer's hands and arms.

underneath the body. The side view in Figure 19-6 illustrates how propulsion is generated during the final up-and-out portion of the upsweep.

In Figure 19-5, the swimmer's hands are sweeping back, out, and up from underneath his body in the first part of the upsweep. His palms are facing back and out, with the little-finger sides serving as the leading edges of his hand-foils and the thumb sides as the trailing edges. This outward pitch should impart some backward force to the water as the hands pass through it from the leading to the trailing edges.

The side view in Figure 19-6 shows how water is displaced back as the swimmer's hands sweep up toward the surface. With the swimmers' arms remaining flexed slightly at the elbows and his hands pitched out and back, the slight upward angle of attack will impart some backward force to the water as it passes down over the underside of his forearms and across his palms from the elbows to the little-finger edges. Gradual hyperextension of his hands at the wrists will allow him to maintain this angle of attack with his palm near the end of the upsweep when his forearms are leaving the water.

Sequence photos of the underwater armstroke of another world-class butterfly swimmer are shown from a front view in Figure 19-7 (p. 422) for your interest. She uses a somewhat different style, bringing her hands closer together under the body. Notice the excellent inward pitch of the hands in Figure 19-7*d*.

Release and Recovery

The release and beginning of the recovery can be seen from underneath in Figure 19-1*k*. Overhead views of the recovery are pictured in Figure 19-8 (p. 423), in which the swimmer is shown recovering his arms during both the breathing and non-breathing armstrokes.

As described earlier, the release is made before the hands reach the surface and before the arms are completely extended. The hands release pressure on the water when they pass the thighs by turning the palms in so that the hands can slide up and out of the water on edge and with a minimum of turbulence (see Figure 19-1*k*).

The arms, which were extending slowly during the upsweep, extend rapidly after the release (see Figure 19-8*b*). The arms leave the water traveling up, out, and forward. They continue circling over the water until they are in front of the shoulders, where the entry is made.

Some swimmers have been successful using a straight-arm recovery, where their arms leave the water completely extended and remain extended until after the entry is made. Others have achieved world class by flexing the elbows during the second half of the recovery. Still others have kept their arms flexed throughout the recovery. Either of the last two methods are recommended because, as mentioned, the entry can be made with elbows flexed to aid in overcoming their inertia during the change of arm direction from in to out as the outsweep begins.

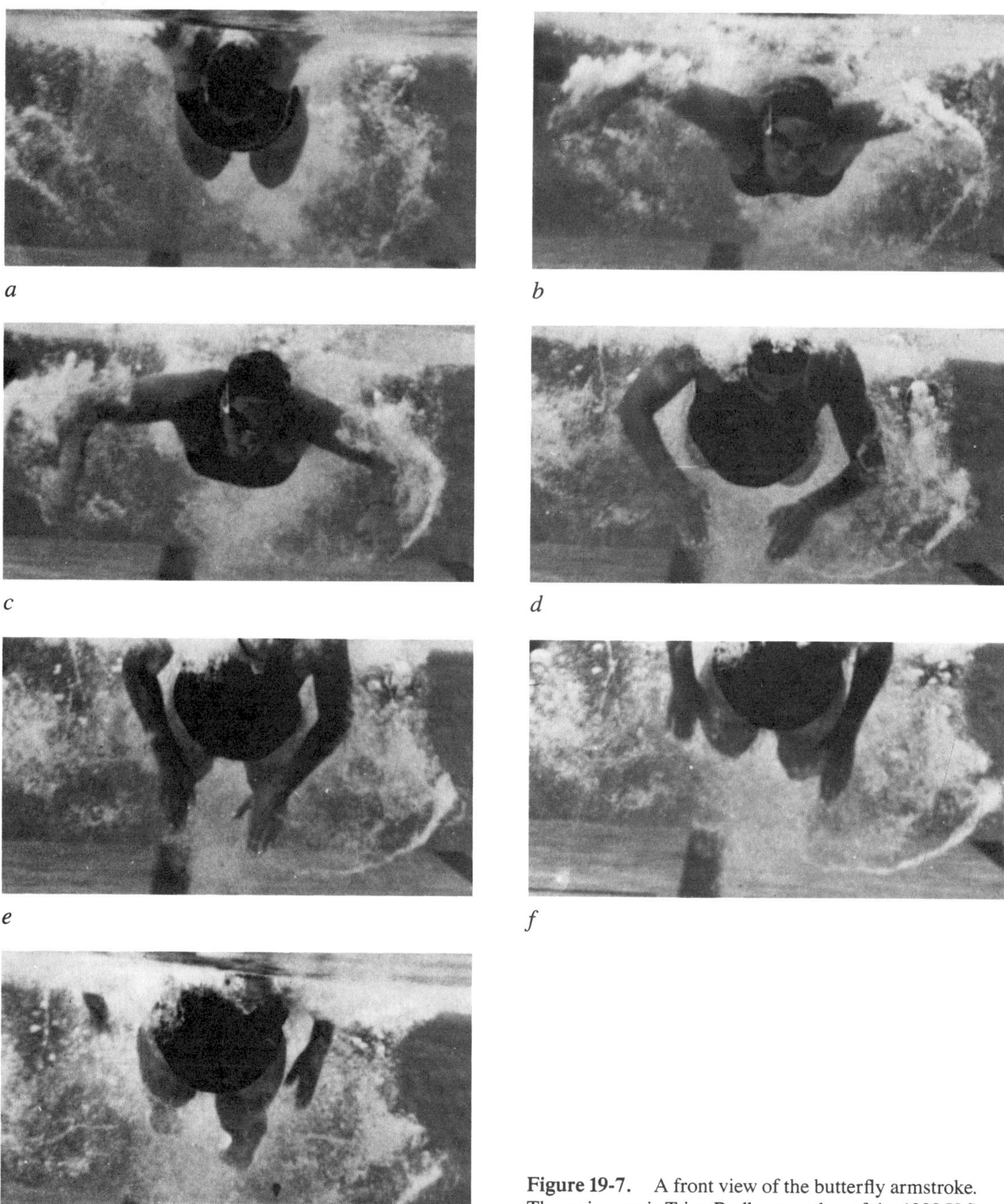

Figure 19-7. A front view of the butterfly armstroke. The swimmer is Trina Radke, member of the 1988 U.S. Olympic Swimming Team in the 200-m butterfly.

a *b* *c* *d* *e* *f* *g* *h*

Figure 19-8. A surface view of the butterfly arm recovery. The swimmer is David Santos, NCAA finalist in the 200-yd butterfly.

Swimmers' palms should remain facing in during the first half of the recovery (see Figure 19-8*b*) and they should be rotated out during the second half (see Figure 19-8*c*). The recovery should be made quickly, but it should not be rushed because swimmers need time to gets their legs in position for the downbeat of the first kick before their arms enter the water. Their arms should be relaxed as much as possible so that their muscles can get some rest; thus, swimmers should let the momentum of the upsweep carry their arms through most of the recovery, using only enough muscular effort to effect the changes of direction required.

Although the recovery is low and lateral, the arms should be carried high enough to remain clear of the water until the entry is made. If they are not high enough, the arms will drag forward through the water and increase wave drag. For this reason, it is advisable for butterfly swimmers to raise their shoulders out of the water high enough to allow their arms to recover without dragging through the water. Although butterfly swimmers have traditionally been taught to keep their shoulders in the water during the recovery, films and videotapes show that the majority of world-class swimmers have their shoulders out of the water during this phase of the stroke. The shoulder lift can be overdone, however. If the upward movement of the shoulders exceeds their forward motion, the trunk and legs will drop deeper in the water. Therefore, the shoulders should be carried over the water just high enough to permit the arms to recover forward without dragging through the water. Swimmers must be careful to keep their shoulders moving forward as well as up during the recovery.

Stroke Patterns

Figure 19-9 illustrates typical front, side, and underneath patterns for the butterfly armstroke. These patterns were drawn relative to the water. The outsweep occurs between points 1 and 2; the catch, at point 2; the insweep, between points 2 and 3; the upsweep, between points 3 and 4; and the release, at point 4. The swimmer's hands leave the water at point 5.

From the side, the butterfly pattern looks very much like the corresponding pattern for the front crawl stroke. The swimmers' hands sweep down in the beginning and up at the end. From front and underneath you can see that butterfly swimmers sweep their hands out to a considerable extent during the outsweep and that they use large diagonal sculls inward during the insweep. Schleihauf and associates (1988) collected data from members of the 1984 U.S. Olympic Swimming Team and found that the average depth the hands reached during the underwater armstroke was 59 cm (25 inches), with a range of 52 to 66 cm (20 to 26 inches) and that their average width was 47 cm (19 inches), with a range of 40 to 54 cm (16–21 inches).

There seem to be two distinct styles of butterfly in use. The difference is in the amount of diagonal motion that swimmers use during the insweep and upsweep portions of their underwater armstrokes. In one style, there is a considerable amount of side-to-side hand motion during the insweep and upsweep. In the second style, the hands move back to a greater extent. Schleihauf and coworkers (1988) reported an average diagonal angle of pull of 44 degrees for a group of U.S. Olympic swimmers during their underwater armstrokes. The range was 23 to 65 degrees,

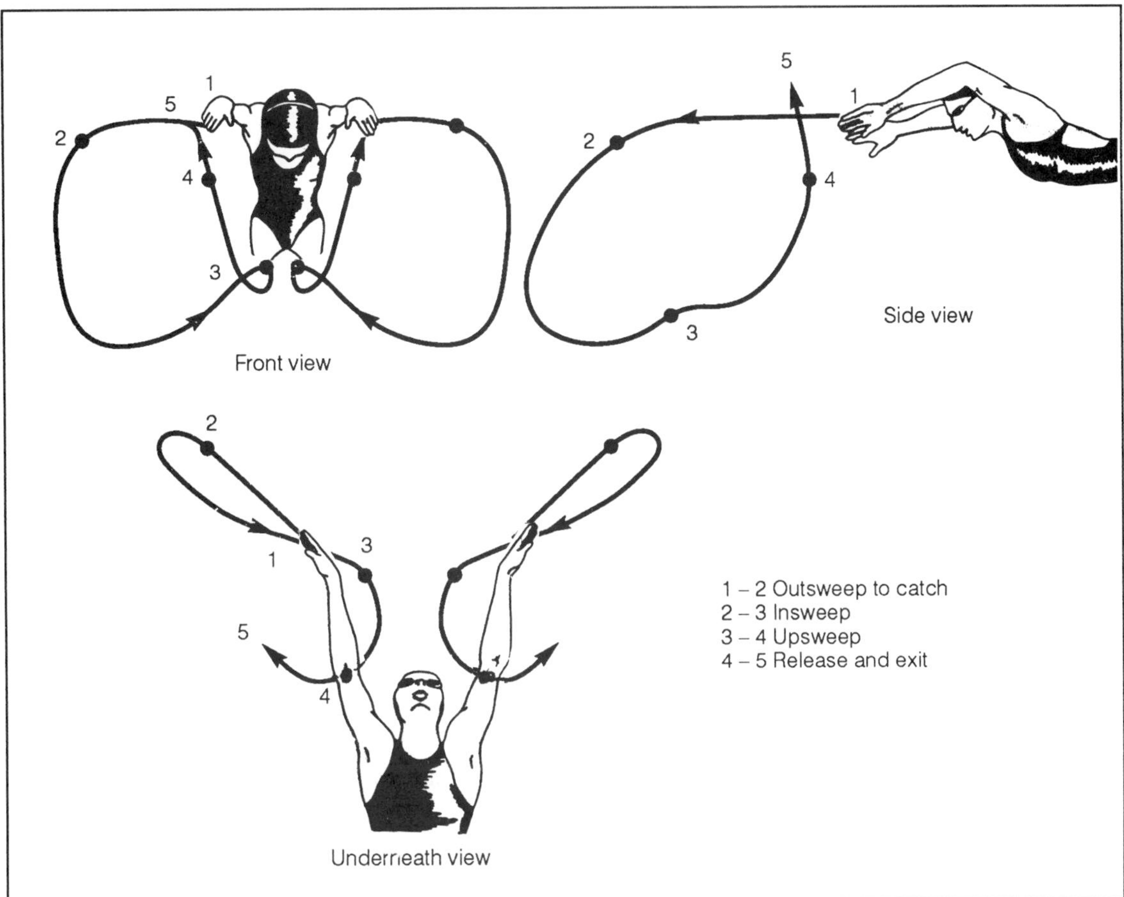

Figure 19-9. Front, side, and underneath views of stroke patterns for the butterfly.

however, indicating that some were sweeping their hands almost directly in and out and that others were moving their hands only slightly in and out. The style employing a great deal of side-to-side hand movement was illustrated in Figure 19-9. The underneath stroke pattern in Figure 19-10 (p. 426) displays the second style.

Swimmers who prefer the style shown in Figure 19-10 tend to utilize more drag force in the first portion of the upsweep, pushing their hands and, consequently, the water almost directly back under their body before sweeping them out and up toward the surface. The area where drag force predominates is between the two sets of arrows in Figure 19-10. The hands are used like paddles, and propulsion is drag dominated during the first portion of the upsweep, when swimmers push back in this manner.

World-class swimmers have used both styles effectively, so we can only conjecture as to which is the superior method. However, the application of physical laws favors the diagonal upsweep, the principal advantage being that swimmers can

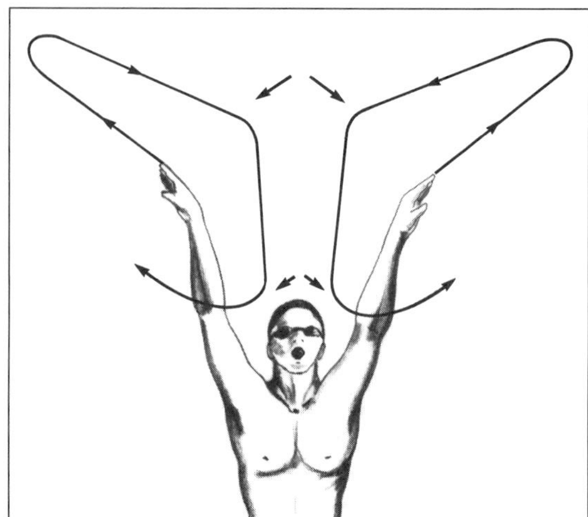

Figure 19-10. An underneath stroke pattern of butterfly, showing a "drag force" movement of the hands during the second half of the underwater armstroke. The phase of the stroke where drag force predominates is between the two pairs of arrows. The swimmer was Pablo Morales, world-record holder for 100-m butterfly.

achieve the same degree of propulsion with slower hand velocities and, thus, less effort.

DOLPHIN KICK

The kick used in butterfly is called a dolphin kick because the legs move as one unit, like the tail (fluke) of a dolphin. One dolphin kick consists of an upbeat and a downbeat, and swimmers execute two kicks during each stroke cycle, as shown in Figure 19-11.

Upbeat

Figures 19-11*a* and 19-11*b* show the upbeat of the first kick; Figures 19-11*d* through 19-11*f*, the upbeat of the second kick. Like the flutter kick, the dolphin kick is a whiplike motion in which one beat begins as the other nears completion in order to assist in overcoming the inertia of the legs as they change directions from down to up. The preceding downbeat starts a reboundlike reaction that pushes the thighs up to initiate the upbeat. Continued extension of the hips keeps the legs sweeping up until they pass above the swimmer's body, when the upbeat ends and the next downbeat begins (see Figures 19-11*b* and 19-11*g*).

The upbeat is made with the legs extended. The lower legs should be relaxed and passive so that the pressure of the water pushing down from above keeps them extended. Water pressure also pushes the swimmer's relaxed feet into a natural position midway between extension and flexion.

Downbeat

Figures 19-11*c* and 19-11*d* show the downbeat of the first kick; Figures 19-11*h* through 19-11*j*, the downbeat of the second kick. It is a whiplike motion that begins

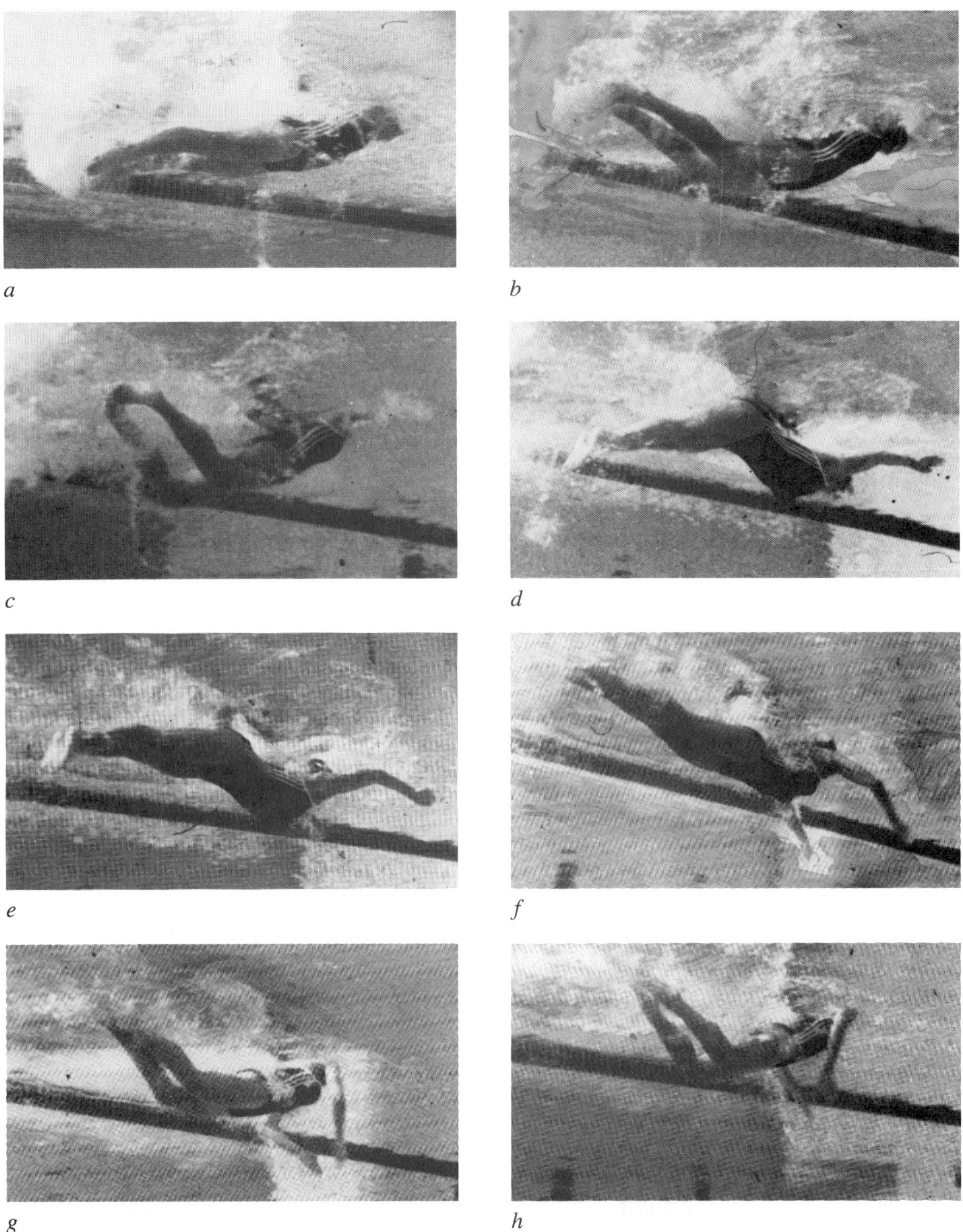

Figure 19-11. The dolphin kick of Mary T. (continued)

i

j

Figure 19-11. (continued)

by pushing the thighs down as the feet pass above the swimmers' body during the preceding upbeat. The water pressure, which is now pushing up from underneath, causes the lower legs to flex upward and pushes the feet up and in to an extended and pigeon-toed position (plantar flexed and inverted). This position of the feet can be seen best in Figure 19-11*c*. When the feet are at the surface, the lower legs kick vigorously downward until they are completely extended. The manner in which propulsive force can be generated during the downbeat of the dolphin kick was described in Chapter 17 in Figures 17-13 and 17-14.

The ability to extend the feet at the ankles is probably essential to an effective dolphin kick. Barthels and Adrian (1971) concluded that it was more important than strength. With good extension ability, the feet can remain facing up and back in a position to displace water back throughout the majority of the downbeat. Butterflyers should be able to extend their feet 70 to 85 degrees from the vertical. The procedure for measuring ankle extension ability will be described in Chapter 24.

Good dolphin kickers spread their knees at the beginning of the downbeat and then bring them together at the end (see Figures 19-11*c* and 19-11*d*). With the knees apart, the feet can be pitched in and up to a greater extent during the downbeat. The resulting inward rotation of the legs at the hips probably also adds to the force supplied during the downbeat.

TIMING THE ARMS AND LEGS

Figure 19-11 clearly illustrates the proper relationship between the two dolphin kicks and the various phases of the armstroke during each stroke cycle. The downbeat of the first kick should be made during the entry and outsweep of the arms, and the downbeat of the second kick should coincide with the upsweep of the underwater armstroke. This explanation, although correct, is an oversimplification of the complex timing between the arm and leg movements in this stroke.

The downbeat of the first kick should begin just before the hands enter the water (see Figure 19-11*a*). It should continue during the outsweep, ending just before the catch is made (see Figure 19-11*d*). Depending on the effectiveness of the first kick, it will either counteract the drag produced by the arms as they move forward and out against the water or propel the swimmer forward until the arms have made a catch.

The upbeat that follows takes place during the insweep of the arms (see Figures 19-11*e* through 19-11*f*). This movement improves streamlining during this propulsive phase of the armstroke by moving the legs up above the body and by bringing the hips down in alignment with the trunk. Of course, it also gets the legs in position for the next downbeat. Notice how streamlined Mary T's body is in Figure 19-11*e*. She is actually inclined downward somewhat from feet to head. This position is characteristic of many great butterfly swimmers during this phase of the stroke cycle. They seem to be traveling downhill. As you will see later, this streamlined position reduces drag and allows the arms to accelerate the body forward rapidly during this important phase of the stroke.

The downbeat of the second kick should be executed in time with the upsweep of the arms (see Figures 19-11*g* through 19-11*h*). That downbeat may assist in propelling swimmers. Even more important, however, it keeps the hips from being pulled down by the upward movements of the arms.

The next upbeat takes place during the arm recovery. This action performs the same two functions as did the upbeat of the first kick. It brings the legs up near the surface so that the body is more streamlined during this phase of the stroke, when the swimmer is decelerating rapidly, and it places the legs in position for the downbeat of the next kick. The correct body position during this phase of the stroke cycle can be seen best in Figure 19-11*h*. Notice how level Mary T's body remains during most of the arm recovery.

There is little doubt that the downbeat of the first kick can be propulsive. The downbeat of the second kick probably contributes somewhat to propulsion, but its main function is to support the swimmers' hips near the water surface. There is some controversy as to whether either upbeat is propulsive. I doubt that either is for the reasons given in Chapter 17 (Figure 17-17). Accordingly, upbeats should be made quickly, but gently, with the legs straight. The reboundlike force from the preceding downbeat should be used to bring the legs up, with only enough effort from the hip extensors to assist in keeping them moving once they start up.

Although not propulsive in itself, the upbeat may serve an indirect propulsive function. It was also mentioned in Chapter 17 that the downward and forward movement of the trunk may exert a backward force on the water that can propel a swimmer forward. If that is possible, the upbeat of the first kick will contribute to that propulsion by pushing the trunk down and by bringing the legs up in alignment with the body and reducing drag that would interfere with that propulsion.

Major and Minor Kicks?

For years, experts have debated whether one of the dolphin kicks is emphasized more than the other during each stroke cycle. They speak in terms of *major* and *minor* kicks, with opinions evenly divided over which of the two kicks in each stroke cycle — the first or second — is emphasized most. Figure 19-11 shows that the downbeat of the first kick is longer and elevates the hips more (see Figures 19-11*c* and 19-11*d*) and that the downbeat of the second kick is shorter and does not raise the body to the same extent (see Figures 19-11*f* and 19-11*g*). This gives the impression that the first kick is emphasized most. It might not be a good idea for swimmers to think in those terms, however. Both kicks serve different but important functions, and swimmers should probably feel that they are exerting equal amounts of effort during each. Any attempt to de-emphasize one of the kicks may upset a swimmer's rhythm.

Differences in body position, not effort, should cause the first kick to be longer and more propulsive. When the head is down during the first downbeat, the hips can travel up and forward for a longer distance. This permits them to kick down over a longer distance. The upbeat that follows is also longer in order to bring the hips down in alignment with the body. It appears to involve not only the legs and hips, but the lower back as well. Extension of the spine seems to be involved in bringing the legs up and lowering the hips. The downbeat of the second kick appears to be more *knee* oriented. The shoulders and trunk are elevated at the time it begins, so the hips cannot, and should not, pike as much when it is executed (see Figure 19-11*h*). If they did, the dolphin motion of the hips would push the head and shoulders down while swimmers tried to breathe.

The next upbeat, the one that coincides with the arm recovery, is also shorter. This is, once again, because the trunk is elevated and the lower legs cannot sweep up over as long a distance without pushing the head and shoulders down (see Figures 19-11*a* and 19-11*b*).

BODY POSITION AND BREATHING

Body Position

It is useless to talk of one body position for the butterfly because the body is constantly changing positions throughout each stroke cycle. There are, however, three positions the body assumes during each stroke cycle that play an important role in reducing drag. These can be seen best in the sequence of photographs in Figure 19-1.

First, the body should be as level as possible during the most propulsive phases of the armstroke — the insweep and the upsweep (see Figures 19-1*f* through 19-1*k*). This is accomplished by bringing the legs up during the insweep of the armstroke and by not kicking too deep during the upsweep.

Second, the hips should travel up and *forward* through the surface during the first downbeat (see Figures 19-1*d* and 19-1*e*). If this does not occur the kick has not been sufficiently propulsive nor has it served the function of streamlining the body.

Third, the force of the second kick should not be so great that it pushes the hips above the surface because that would interfere with the arm recovery. However, it must be strong enough to maintain the hips at the surface (see Figures 19-1*k* and 19-1*l*).

Breathing

Figures 19-8*a* through 19-8*c* show the correct sequence for breathing from a surface view. Figure 19-1 also provides some important information about this sequence from an underwater view.

The face should break through the surface of the water during the upsweep of the arms (see Figure 19-8*a*). Swimmers inhale to the front while completing that movement and during the first half of their arm recovery. The face drops back into the water during the second half of the recovery (see Figure 19-8*c*) and should remain in the water at the surface during the arm recovery of the nonbreathing strokes (see Figures 19-8*e* through 19-8*h*).

The preceding description is an oversimplification of the complex sequence of events that take place when swimmers raise their head out of the water to breathe. The breathing sequence actually begins during the outsweep of the armstroke, not during the upsweep, as just described. The sequence of events that leads to the face coming above the water for a breath can be seen best from an underwater view in Figure 19-1.

Swimmers are looking down when their arms enter the water (see Figure 19-1*b*). They must raise their head toward the surface during the outsweep and insweep (see Figures 19-1*c* through 19-1*h*) in order to get their face above the water during the upsweep of the armstroke. Their head should break through the surface at the end of the insweep (see Figure 19-1*h*), and it should remain above the surface, where a breath is taken during the upsweep and the first half of the arm recovery (see Figures 19-8*a* and 19-8*b*). An important point is that swimmers should drop their head underwater before their arms enter (see Figure 19-1*a*). This will assist swimmers in keeping their arms from dragging forward through the water during the second half of the recovery.

On the nonbreathing stroke (see Figures 19-8*e* through 19-8*h*), the head should be brought to the surface, even though the face remains underwater throughout the entire stroke cycle. Raising the head in this manner will allow the arms to recover over the water with more ease.

Breathing to the Side Some butterfly swimmers breathe to the side. They believe that the energy cost of lifting their head will be reduced if they rotate their face to the side, as is done in the front crawl. They also feel that it helps them maintain good horizontal alignment because the act of lifting their head forward to breathe tends to submerge their hips.

This reasoning is faulty because it overlooks an important difference between the butterfly and front crawl. Front crawl swimmers can roll their body to bring their face above the surface. Butterflyers must rotate their head *while their body is in a prone position*. The range of motion in their neck is usually too little to permit their mouth to come above the surface *unless* they elevate their head above the surface to begin with. Consequently, butterflyers who breathe to the side must lift their head and shoulders out of the water as much or more than swimmers who breathe to the front. Figure 19-12*a* shows a swimmer breathing to the side. Notice that his shoulders are just as high as those of the swimmer who is breathing to the front in Figure 19-12*b*.

a

b

Figure 19-12. Two breathing styles in the butterfly: to the side (*a*) and to the front (*b*).

There is one additional problem that swimmers could encounter when breathing to the side. They may rotate their body slightly toward the breathing side. This would probably reduce the propulsive force of the arm opposite the breathing side.

Breathing to the side is not recommended for the reasons stated. Breathing to the front is recommended, however, because it *fits* the simultaneous nature of the armstroke. The contribution from each arm should be greater when butterfly swimmers remain in a prone position as they breathe.

Breathing Frequency during Races Butterfly swimmers are usually advised *not* to breathe during every stroke cycle when they race because their hips and legs may drop deeper in the water when they breathe. The most common recommendation is to breathe once every two armstrokes in 100 races. This is referred to as a 1-and-1 breathing pattern. It is thought to strike a good compromise between the need to consume oxygen and the desire to maintain a horizontal body position.

Some coaches also recommend this breathing pattern for 200 races. However, others feel that it does not supply enough oxygen for longer races. They recommend patterns where breaths are taken for two or three consecutive strokes before a nonbreathing stroke is completed. These breathing frequencies are referred to as 2-and-1 and 3-and-1 patterns. The extra breathing strokes increase oxygen consumption, and the periodic nonbreathing strokes are used to regain horizontal alignment.

Despite this advice, many great butterfly swims have been completed where athletes breathed during every stroke cycle. This has been particularly true of 200 races, although some successful butterfly swimmers have also breathed this way in the 100 event.

Because there seems to be disagreement, each butterfly swimmer should determine his or her most effective breathing pattern by using a form of the experimental drill that was described in Chapter 18. The drill is performed as follows. Swimmers should complete a set of 12 or more 50 to 100 repeats on short or medium rest intervals. Breathing patterns should alternate from one repeat to the next, using 3-and-1, 2-and-1, 1-and-1, and every-stroke breathing patterns. The drill should be saved for the end of a training session, *when the swimmers are fatigued* as they would be in the second half of a race.

Swimmers should repeat this drill over several days, discarding the patterns that are obviously less effective until they find the one that is consistently faster. They should use that pattern in races. If there is no difference in speed between certain patterns, swimmers should use the one that provides the greatest oxygen supply.

HAND AND BODY VELOCITY PATTERNS

Figure 19-13 illustrates body and hand velocity patterns for butterfly swimmer Mary T. Meagher during one stroke cycle. The bottom graph depicts the forward velocity of her body, and the top graph depicts the three-dimensional velocity of her hands.

Body Velocity

Mary T's hands enter the water at point 1 (time 0). She is at her lowest velocity (1.6 m/sec) at this time because she has just completed her arm recovery. Her body accelerates forward to slightly over 2 m/sec as she kicks down and sweeps her arms out to the catch at point 2. This increase in forward speed is probably due to the kick, not the arms. There is a slight loss of velocity between the end of the downbeat of the first kick while she makes the catch and begins the propulsive phase of the insweep at point 2.

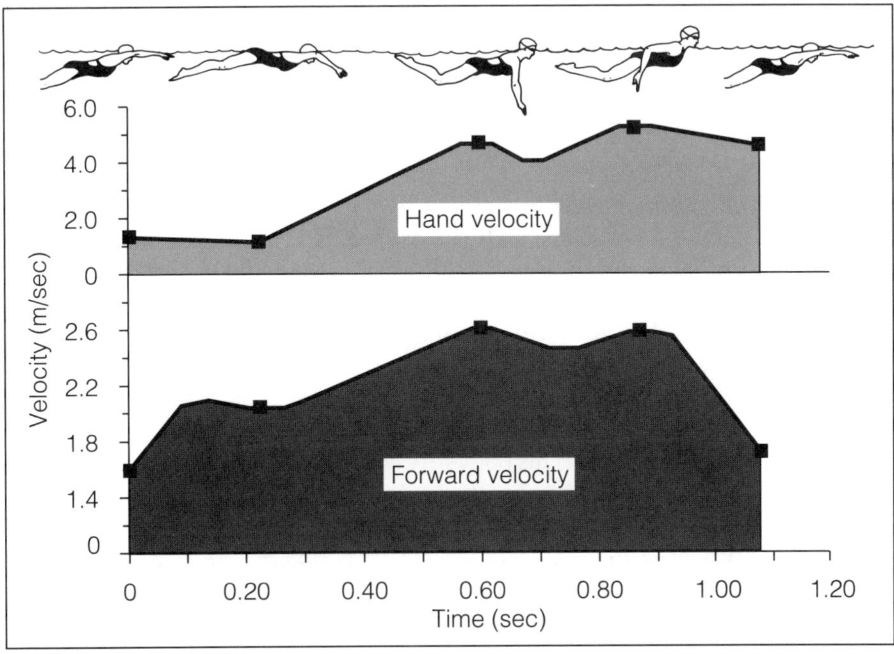

Figure 19-13. Hand and body velocity graphs for butterfly swimmer Mary T. Meagher measured at the 1984 U.S. Olympic Training Camp.

Her forward speed accelerates quite rapidly to a velocity of 2.6 m/sec during the insweep, between points 2 and 3. There is a small period of deceleration during the transition to the upsweep; however, when the upsweep gets underway, she once again accelerates her body to a velocity of nearly 2.6 m/sec at point 4. Her forward velocity begins to decelerate when she releases the water at point 4 and continues to decline until she begins kicking down just before her arms enter the water to being the next stroke cycle at point 5.

Hand Velocity

The accelerations and decelerations of her hands coincide with changes in her forward velocity, except during the outsweep, when her kick is propelling her forward. Her hands decelerate from the entry through the outsweep—points 1 to 2—until they are only being pushed forward by her body at the catch. This is followed by a rapid acceleration during the insweep between points 2 and 3. There is a slight deceleration as the hands change pitch from in to out during the transition from insweep to upsweep, after which her hands accelerate to their peak velocity of 5 m/sec at point 4. Hand velocity falls from the end of the upsweep until her hands leave the water at point 5, and it continues to decelerate during the recovery until the hands enter the water to begin the next stroke cycle.

Hand velocities typically reach speeds of 3 to 4 m/sec during the insweep and 4 to 5 m/sec during the upsweep for many world-class butterflyers (Maglischo, 1984; Schleihauf et al., 1988). Notice that Mary T's hand speed is nearly the same during the insweep and upsweep. She also attains approximately the same forward velocity during these two phases.

There are many facets of this velocity pattern that can furnish some insight as to why some butterfly swimmers reach world class and others do not. The body velocity graph in Figure 19-14 is provided for comparison purposes. It portrays some of the most common causes of reduced propulsion during the stroke cycle. The first and perhaps most important distinction is that *Mary T maintains a high level of forward velocity for nearly twice as long as the swimmer in Figure 19-14.* Her body accelerates forward at a high rate of speed for nearly 0.70 second during a stroke cycle that takes approximately 1.10 seconds to complete (see Figure 19-13). Most butterfly swimmers only accelerate forward for 0.30 to 0.40 second during each stroke cycle, as does the swimmer in Figure 19-14. This is probably because they are able to use only one of the propulsive arm sweeps (the insweep or upsweep) effectively. By contrast, the very best butterfly swimmers in the world achieve a sizable amount of propulsion from both sweeps. You can see that the swimmer in Figure 19-14 does not accelerate his body forward as much during the insweep even though he reaches nearly the same forward velocity as Mary T during the upsweep.

The second important difference can be seen during the arm recovery. *Mary T's forward velocity decelerates less and for a shorter period of time than the swimmer in Figure 19-14.* She decelerates to only 1.7 m/sec during this time (see Figure 19-13), yet the swimmer in Figure 19-14 decelerates to nearly 1.3 m/sec. Additionally, she completes the recovery in less than 0.20 second, yet the swimmer in Figure 19-14 requires nearly 0.40 second to recover his arms over the water. Also, underwater

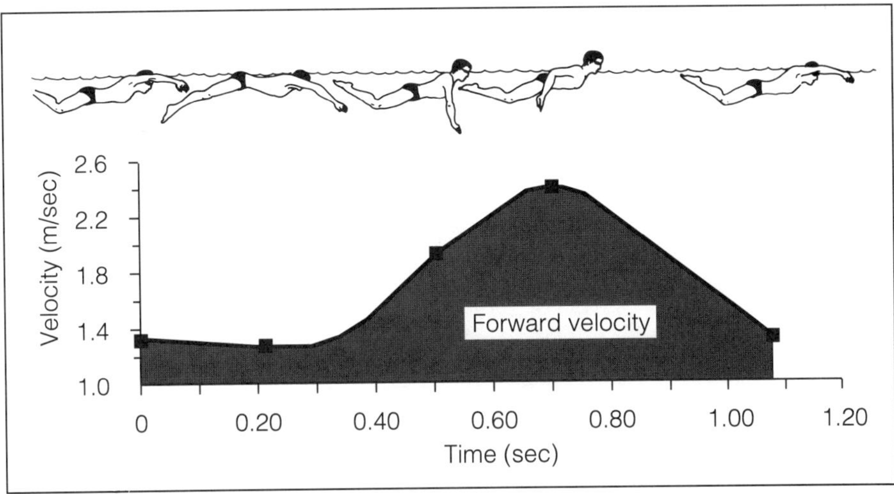

Figure 19-14. A forward velocity pattern for a butterfly swimmer.

films of the swimmer in Figure 19-14 showed that he did not maintain his body in a streamlined position during the recovery, which probably contributed to his greater loss of velocity during the arm recovery. He allowed his legs to *hang down* for a short time at the end of the downbeat of the second kick before sweeping them up. By comparison, Mary T's legs appeared to rebound up at the completion of that same downbeat.

A third difference can be seen during the interval between the end of the downbeat of the first kick and the catch. *The best butterfly swimmers, like Mary T, kick down while they sweep their arms out to the catch.* By doing so, the decelerative period between the end of the first kick and the beginning of the propulsive phases of the armstroke can be reduced to a minimum. You can see in Figure 19-13 that Mary T's forward velocity decelerates only slightly and for less than 0.20 second during this transition. This is because she coordinates the downbeat of her first kick with the outsweep of her arms. As a result, her kick accelerates her body forward until her arms are ready to take over at the catch. Contrast this with the swimmer in Figure 19-14 whose forward velocity continues to decelerate for nearly 0.40 second after his arms enter the water. This is because he completes his kick just after his hands enter the water and, with nothing to propel him forward, his body decelerates during the time he sweeps his arms out to the catch. This results in an additional loss of 0.4 m/sec in forward velocity at a time when his kick should have been accelerating his body forward.

Swimmers probably kick too early during the outsweep for two reasons:

1. They believe that they are covering more distance with each stroke when they stretch their arms forward, rather than out, as they kick.
2. They believe that propulsion begins when their arms start the outsweep instead of later, when the catch is made.

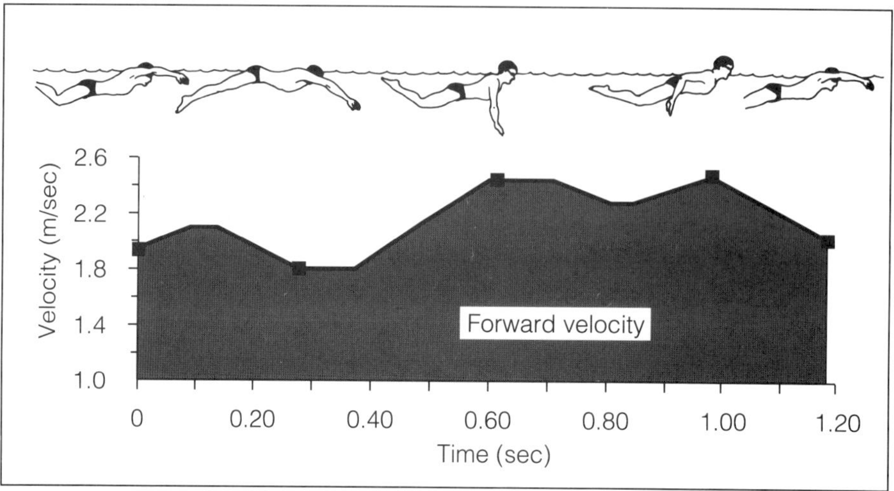

Figure 19-15. A forward velocity graph for Pablo Morales.

Figure 19-15 shows a forward velocity graph for world-record holder Pablo Morales to further substantiate the key differences between great and near-great butterfly swimmers. Please notice the similarities between this pattern and that of Mary T in Figure 19-13. Both swimmers maintain a propulsive peak of acceleration for nearly 0.70 second. Both decelerate only slightly during the arm recovery. Morales's velocity decreases only 0.50 m/sec during this time, which is actually less than Mary T decelerates during this same phase. Finally, both swimmers complete their arm recoveries in approximately 0.20 second. The only difference between the two velocity patterns is that Morales decelerates more than Mary T at the catch and during the first part of his insweep.

One-Peak and Two-Peak Velocity Patterns The velocity graphs in Figures 19-13 and 19-15 represent the style used by two of the best butterfly swimmers in the history of our sport. They are characterized by rapid acceleration during the insweep, with forward velocity maintained at nearly the same level during the upsweep. It is similar to the two-peak pattern described for the front crawl stroke, with one peak of forward speed taking place during the insweep and the other occurring during the upsweep of the armstroke. There is also a short period of deceleration during the transition between these two stroke phases, during which swimmers change the pitch and direction of their hands.

Many successful world-class butterfly swimmers have used another style where the upsweep is the most propulsive phase. It is represented in the velocity graph in Figure 19-16. This style is analogous to the one-peak velocity pattern described for the front crawl stroke.

The one-peak pattern is characterized by a gradual increase of forward velocity during the insweep and upsweep, with no period of deceleration during the transition between the two phases. It is generally used by swimmers with a wide pull.

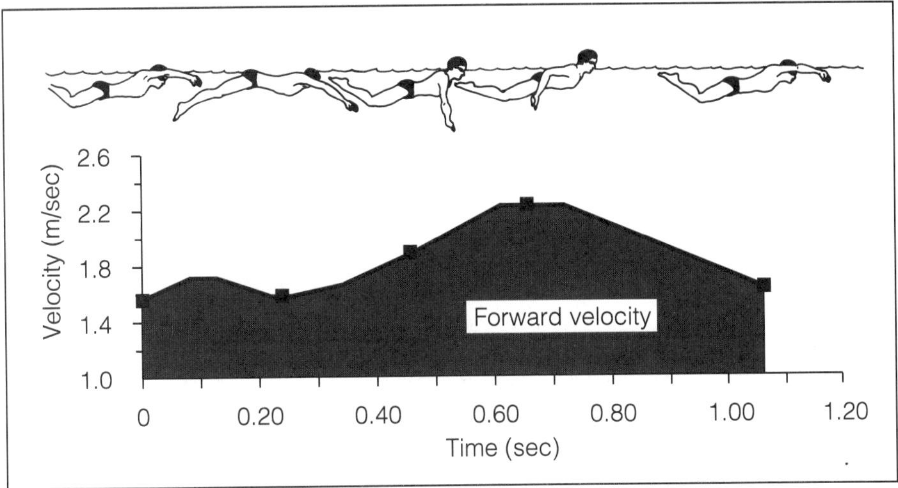

Figure 19-16. A velocity graph showing a one-peak pattern.

They tend to press their hands back more and in less during the insweep so that the transition from the insweep to the upsweep is barely noticeable. In other words, they tend to use less diagonal sculling during their underwater armstrokes.

COMMON STROKE FAULTS

Armstroke Mistakes

Outsweep and Insweep Mistakes Dropped elbows can easily occur during this phase if swimmers do not sweep their hands out wide enough before starting the insweep. Unlike freestyle swimmers, butterflyers cannot roll their body from side to side, so they must sweep their arms and hands out to the side until they are facing back against the water. If they begin pushing down with their hands and arms before they achieve a backward orientation, they will make the same mistake that freestylers make when they try to apply force too soon. Their hands and forearms will be perpendicular to the direction in which they are traveling, and they will push down against the water and thus decelerate their forward speed. Butterflyers must learn to wait until their hands are outside their shoulders, where they can achieve a backward orientation before they begin to sweep them in.

Figure 19-17 shows the velocity graph for a swimmer who is dropping his elbows. The period when he should be accelerating forward but does not is illustrated by the lightly shaded area. Figure 19-18 is a photo of the swimmer whose data were used to construct this graph. It shows him trying to sweep in too soon. Notice that his palms are facing down and that his elbows are dropped during the

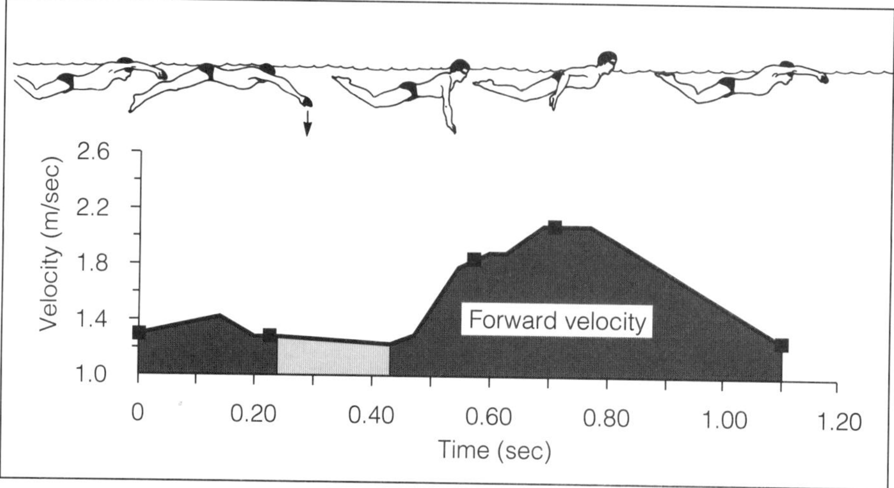

Figure 19-17. A velocity graph for a swimmer who pushes down with his arms too early during the outsweep.

Figure 19-18. A butterfly swimmer who is dropping his elbows.

outsweep. This photo shows the most common reason why butterflyers drop their elbows. The swimmer has *dived* his head too deep during the arm entry. As a result, he has to use the first third of his underwater armstroke to push his head to the surface.

Another common mistake that swimmers make during the outsweep is to press out too forcefully with their arms. This pushes water out and decelerates forward speed.

The usual mistake that swimmers make during the second half of the insweep is to keep their hands facing directly back. They should be pitched in slightly. When facing back, the angle of attack is too slight to impart backward force to the water

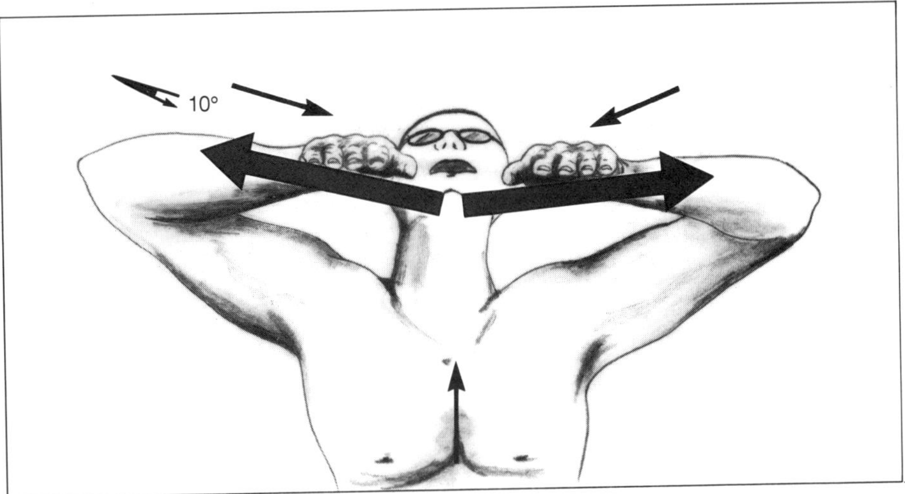

Figure 19-19. The effect of sweeping the hands in with too small an angle of attack.

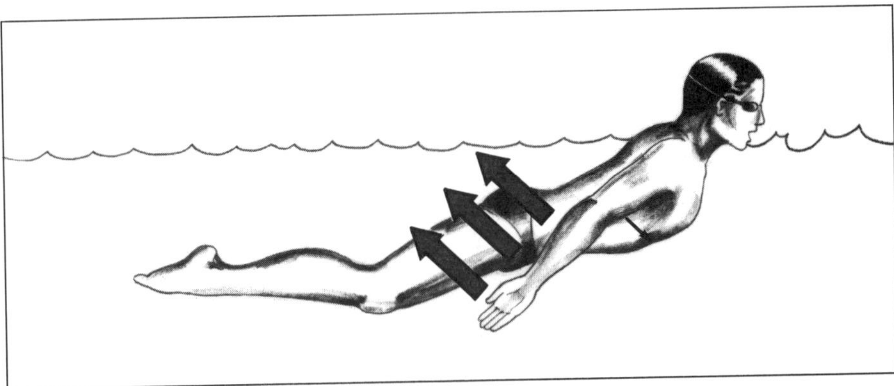

Figure 19-20. The effect of pushing up during the upsweep.

unless swimmers are pushing their hands back more than in; however, stroking this way shortens the insweep and, therefore, the entire propulsive phase of the armstroke. Figure 19-19 shows a swimmer making this mistake.

Upsweep Mistakes Once again, the mistakes are the same for the butterfly as were mentioned for the front crawl stroke in this phase of the underwater armstroke. Swimmers may extend their arms too rapidly at the elbows and, thus, push the water up rather than displace it back. They may also try to maintain propulsion until their hands reach the surface, which also results in pushing up against the water. Figure 19-20 illustrates the effect of these errors.

Swimmers should extend their elbows slowly during the upsweep, and complete extension should not occur until their arms recover over the water. Swimmers should also release pressure on the water and begin the recovery as their hands pass their thighs.

Recovery and Entry Mistakes The two most common mistakes are (1) to recover the arms too high and (2) to drag them through the water. The arms should swing laterally over the water during the recovery. Swimmers increase their energy cost when they recover their arms too high. Conversely, dragging their arms through the water increases drag considerably. The swimmer in Figure 19-21 is dragging his arms forward and *in* as they enter the water. This will push water forward and decelerate his forward speed. *After the entry is made, butterfly swimmers should immediately begin reaching their arms forward and out. Under no circumstances should they push their arms inward after they enter the water.*

Kicking Mistakes

The most frequent cause of a poor dolphin kick is lack of ankle extension ability and/or an inability to turn the feet in. Just as they do in freestyle swimming, these factors prevent butterfly swimmers from achieving a good angle of attack during the downbeat. Another frequent mistake is to kick too deep. A final mistake that is frequently made is to bend the knees too much during the upbeat. The effect of this mistake was illustrated in Figure 17-18.

Timing Mistakes

The most common timing mistake, which has already been mentioned, is to kick too early. A second mistake, which is really an extreme example of kicking too early, is the glide stroke.

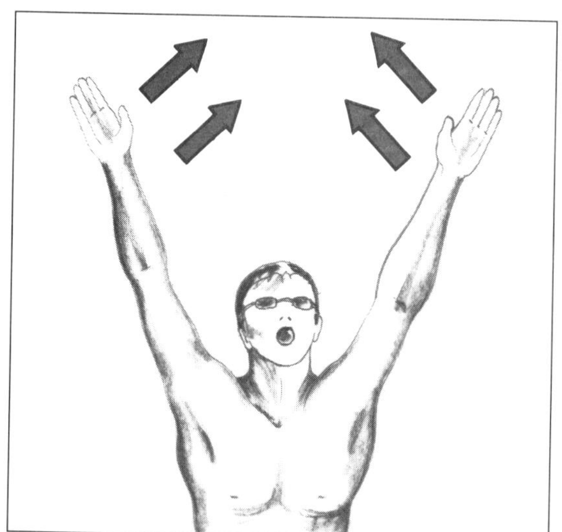

Figure 19-21. The effect of pushing the arms in through the water after the entry.

Glide Stroke This mistake occurs frequently when swimmers are learning the butterfly. They will stretch their arms forward after the entry and execute both kicks before starting the underwater arm stroke. With all of the kicking completed before arm propulsion begins, they will have no kick to counterbalance the upsweep of their armstroke and their hips will sink during this phase of the stroke. Butterfly swimmers must be coached to sweep their arms out immediately after they enter the water. A drill for correcting this problem—the stroke pattern drill—is described later in this chapter.

One-Kick Butterfly This is another mistake that swimmers make when first learning the butterfly. In reality, the one-kick butterfly is a 1½-kick butterfly because swimmers start but do not complete the downbeat of the second kick. This makes it difficult for them to maintain their hips near the surface and it increases form drag by inclining the position of their body.

The one-kick butterfly is difficult to correct because the solution is not as obvious as it seems. Simply telling swimmers to kick twice will not correct the problem. A short insweep of the arms is the culprit that sets in motion a chain of events that make it impossible for swimmers to finish their second kick. The upbeat of the first kick takes place during the insweep of the armstroke. If the insweep is too short, swimmers' legs will not have enough time to complete that upbeat until after the upsweep of their arms is well underway. As a result, they will only have time to execute a partial downbeat before their hands leave the water. This makes it appear that they are not kicking a second time.

One-kick butterflyers should be instructed to make a slower and longer insweep. This will give them time to get their legs in position for the second downbeat and should correct the problem.

Body Position Mistakes

Problems occur when swimmers undulate too little or too much. Too little undulation reduces propulsion because the hips and legs will sink if the "leg drive" is not sufficient to keep them elevated. Failure to undulate sufficiently is usually caused by starting the insweep of the arms too early and breathing too late. Both of these problems reduce undulation because they inhibit the upward movement of the hips. Swimmers may also undulate too little because they bend their knees excessively during the upbeat. This action inhibits undulation because it pulls their hips down.

Swimmers who undulate excessively are kicking too deep in an effort to raise their hips above the surface. Undulating excessively increases the space that swimmers take up in the water and the resistance of that water to their forward progress. Figure 19-22 compares adequate undulation with excessive undulation. The swimmer in Figure 19-22*a* is undulating properly. She is kicking deep enough to gain propulsion but not so deep as to increase drag unnecessarily. The swimmer in Figure 19-22*b* is kicking down excessively deep and taking up more space in the water than she should.

Excessive body undulation is frequently the result of being taught to dive up and down during the butterfly. Swimmers should not be taught to dive down

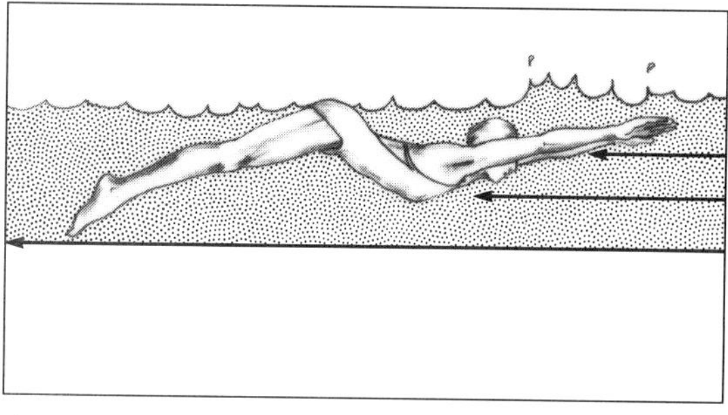

a

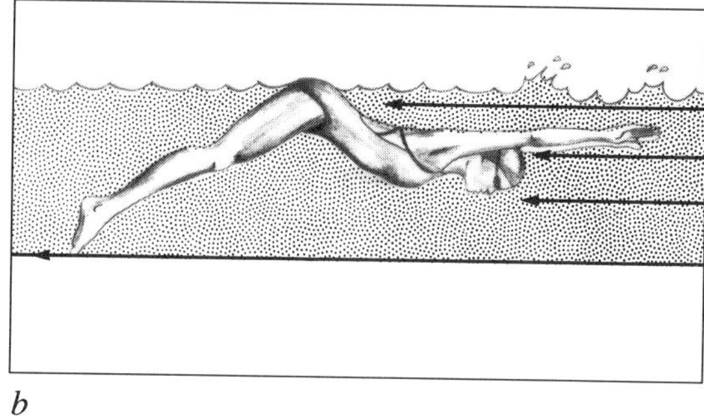

b

Figure 19-22. A comparison of adequate and excessive undulation in the butterfly.

excessively deep. Nor should they be taught to *pump* their hips up and down when they are learning the dolphin kick. The rise and fall of the hips should take place as a natural reaction to proper leg movements. They are an *effect* of the leg movements, not a *cause,* and should be taught as such.

Although one of the primary functions of the dolphin kick is to elevate and submerge the hips, swimmers must be careful not to overdo these up and down movements. When the kick is properly executed, the hips should flow up to and over the surface in a forward path during the first downbeat and fall just below the surface on the subsequent upbeat. The downbeat and upbeat of the second kick should merely cancel other forces and prevent the hips from moving vertically.

Breathing Mistakes

Mistakes in breathing take the form of staying too low in the water or coming too high out of the water. Other common mistakes are to breathe too early or too late.

Swimmers who stay too low in the water when they breathe will invariably drag their arms through the water during the last half of the recovery. Swimmers should not try to keep their shoulders in the water when they breathe. They must raise their head and shoulders high enough to recover without dragging their arms through the water.

Swimmers who breathe too early generally use a glide stroke. They glide after their arms enter the water and take a second kick while they lift their head to get a breath. These swimmers must be taught to keep their hands moving out into the outsweep after they enter the water.

When swimmers breathe too late, they develop a *hitch* in their strokes—that is, they hesitate to breathe before taking their hands out of the water at the end of the recovery. There are usually three causes for this mistake. The first is that swimmers may keep their head down too long during the outsweep and cannot get it above the surface for a breath before the upsweep is finished.

The second cause is that swimmers may finish the upsweep with their arms and hands extended too much. The large amount of downward force that they create requires them to kick very deep on the second downbeat to keep their body from sinking. As a result, their hips rise excessively above the water and they have to delay starting their arm recovery and head drop until their hips return below the surface.

The third cause for a hitch is that swimmers may turn their palms down before their hands leave the water. The change of position from up to down interrupts the movement of their arms and delays the start of the recovery.

STROKE DRILLS

Armstroke Drills

Sculling Drills The front, middle, and rear sculling drills that were described in Chapter 17 are excellent for this purpose.

Stroke Pattern Drills As with the front crawl, the movements of the arms can be communicated best with a stroke pattern drawn relative to a swimmer's moving body, such as the one in Figure 19-23. Swimmers enter their hands into the water at shoulder width (or slightly wider) and then trace a double-*S* pattern under their

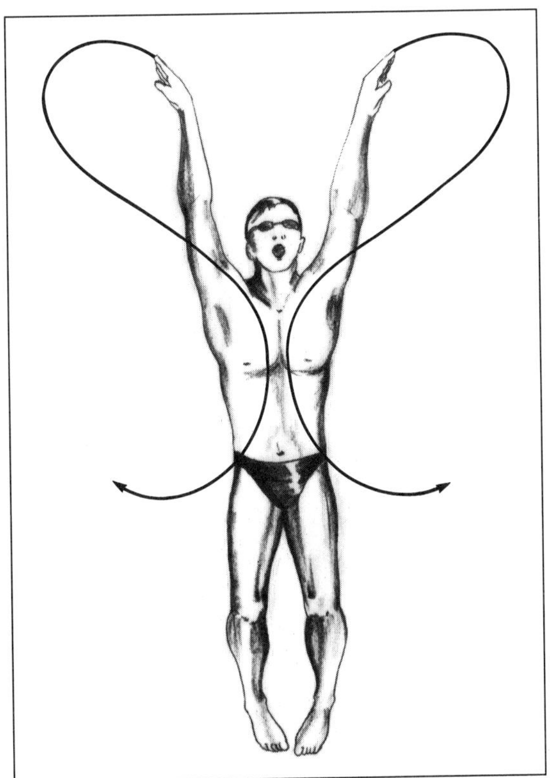

Figure 19-23. An underneath view of a stroke pattern for the butterfly drawn relative to the swimmer's moving body.

body. The outsweep corresponds to the first curve of the *S*; the insweep, to the middle curve; and the upsweep, to the final curve. A simple set of instructions would be to (1) sweep the hands out until they are outside the shoulders, (2) sweep them in under the chest until they are almost together, and (3) sweep them out, up, and back toward the surface of the water. The first curve of the *S* is not propulsive and should be made gently. Hand speed should accelerate gradually during the final two curves, reaching peak speed in the third curve. As is the case for freestyle swimmers, butterflyers who keep their palms facing in the direction they are moving relative to their bodies will be using the correct angle of attack during each sweep.

One-Fist Swimming Drill This is the same drill as was described for the front crawl, and it serves the same purpose. Primarily, it allows swimmers to overuse their nondominant arm in order to increase its propulsive contribution to the whole stroke. The athlete swims or pulls any number of repeats with the hand of the nondominant arm open and the hand of the dominant arm in a fist.

Kicking Drills

Board Kicking Drill This drill is good for improving the second kick; however, it does not provide enough body undulation to simulate the first kick. The head and trunk are elevated by the kickboard, and, in this relatively flat position, swimmers are not able to undulate enough to use their lower back, as they would during the first kick.

Underwater Kicking Drill This is a good drill for teaching the first kick. Swimmers imitate dolphins by kicking underwater with their hands back at their sides.

Kicking without a Board This is another good drill for teaching the first kick. Swimmers kick down the pool with their arms extended in front. They take a stroke and a breath after every third, sixth, or eighth kick. Swimmers will be able to undulate more without a board.

Back Kicking Drill Swimmers dolphin kick on their backs with their arms extended overhead. This is a good drill to teach swimmers how to open and close their legs during the kick so that they can position their legs and feet to deliver more propulsive force.

Side Kicking Drill Swimmers kick down the pool on their sides, with their hands back at their thighs. They can change sides after any specified number of kicks. Swimmers can undulate very well with their hands at their sides. The upbeat is performed more like the upbeat of the first kick when the drill is done this way. A variation on this drill is to kick with the hands overhead, which requires somewhat more lower back flexibility. This is an excellent drill for teaching swimmers to keep their legs straight during the upbeat.

Timing Drills

One-Arm Butterfly Drill This is a good drill for teaching swimmers to coordinate their kicks with their armstrokes. They swim butterfly down the pool using only one arm. The other arm remains back at their side. They breathe to the front as they would when swimming the butterfly. They should concentrate on kicking down once when they sweep their hand out and once when they sweep it up. This is also a very good drill for teaching the diagonal sweeps of the armstroke.

A variation on this drill is to switch arms after completing a specified number of strokes. In this case, the arm that is not stroking should be extended overhead. Another variation is to stroke a specified number of times with the right arm (for example, three times), an equal number of times with the left arm, and then to finish the pool length by swimming with both arms.

Fin Swimming Athletes who are new to the butterfly will be able to swim correctly for longer distances if they wear fins,which will provide them more time to practice the skills of the stroke before becoming fatigued.

Butterfly Pulling Drill This is a good drill for teaching swimmers to keep their arms moving out after the entry. They swim down the pool using a continuous armstroke while allowing their legs to "wave" behind them.

Butterfly pulling is also a good drill for teaching the two-kick timing. After doing this drill for a short time, swimmers will find that their legs naturally make two small, downward thrusts during each stroke cycle and that those thrusts occur in proper sequence with their arms. The next step is for swimmers to focus their attention on that rhythm so that it can be fine-tuned. The final step is to kick deeper without changing the rhythm.

CHAPTER 20

Back Crawl Stroke

The back crawl stroke, or backstroke, evolved from the inverted breaststroke. Over time, competitors found that they could swim faster and still comply with the rules by recovering their arms over the water in an alternating manner. The use of the flutter kick in this stroke also evolved because it was faster than the wedge kick.

From 1930 to 1960, backstroke swimmers used a style that was popularized by the great champion Adolph Kiefer. The underwater armstroke was executed just beneath the surface and to the side with a straight arm. Likewise, the recovery was made low and laterally with a straight arm. This style changed dramatically in the 1960s. With increasing use of underwater filming, experts realized that the most successful backstrokers of the day were using an *S*-type pulling pattern. Their arms were bending early in the stroke and extending later. In addition, the recovery was made straight overhead rather than to the side.

Today, the backstroke is very much like the front crawl, except that it is performed in a supine position. The arms stroke alternately, and there are six kicks per stroke cycle. Unlike the armstroke of the front crawl, the armstroke of the back crawl has three propulsive phases.

Dolphin kicking in the backstroke is a recent innovation that has improved the speed of many swimmers. The rules now permit a swimmer to dolphin kick underwater for 15 m after the start and after each turn. Although there have been no comparative studies to support this position, it is obvious that some backstrokers can travel faster by dolphin kicking underwater than by swimming backstroke on the surface. The reasons are not known but it may involve lessened drag, with the body completely submerged several feet below the surface turbulence. Swimmers with an affinity for the dolphin kick would do well to train themselves to use this technique over the full distance permitted by the rules. However, swimmers who are not good dolphin kickers probably gain no advantage whatsoever from using this technique.

This chapter presents the techniques for this stroke in an order that is slightly different from that of Chapters 18 and 19. The topic of stroke patterns is described first because it contains information that is important to an understanding of the propulsive components of the armstroke. After that, the topics are in the same order used in describing the front crawl and butterfly.

STROKE PATTERNS

Backstroke swimmers display more variations in their stroke patterns than swimmers in any of the other competitive strokes. The side, front, and underneath stroke patterns in Figure 20-1 (p. 448) illustrate what I think is the most effective three-dimensional pattern of hand movements.

Backstroke swimmers perform four sweeps during the underwater armstroke. These are followed by the release and exit of the arm and its recovery over the water. The sweeps have been termed *first downsweep, first upsweep, second downsweep,* and *second upsweep*. In Figure 20-1, the first downsweep takes place between points 1 and 2. The first upsweep, which is the first propulsive phase of the armstroke, occurs between points 2 and 3. The remaining two propulsive phases—the second downsweep and the second upsweep—occur between points 3 and 4 and points 4 and 5, respectively. The release and exit of the hand from the water are completed between points 5 and 6.

These patterns contain two elements that may surprise you. The first concerns the depth of the swimmer's hand during the second downsweep. Teachers of the typical *bent-arm* backstroke believe that swimmers push their hand back to their thigh during this phase. However, stroke patterns that have been drawn from films of world-class swimmers show that the most successful backstrokers sweep their hand down very deep below their thigh (Luedtke, 1986).

Additionally, it may surprise you that the second upsweep is included as a propulsive movement. This sweep has traditionally been considered the first part of the arm recovery. Contrary to this belief, however, measurements of propulsive force on members of the 1984 U.S. Olympic Swimming Team showed that some backstroke swimmers were gaining propulsion from this sweep (Luedtke, 1986; Maglischo et al., 1987; Maglischo, Maglischo, & Santos, 1987).

Figure 20-2 (p. 449) provides data on swimmer Betsy Mitchell, who is gaining propulsion from the second upsweep of her right hand. The propulsive force she creates with her right armstroke is listed on the vertical axis in kilograms. This graph is somewhat different from those shown in the two previous chapters. Those graphs displayed forward velocity, not propulsive force. *This graph displays her propulsive force. Nevertheless, the peaks in propulsive force should correspond to peaks in forward velocity*. The method developed by Schleihauf for estimating the propulsive force that swimmers produce with their hand and forearm was used in making these measurements (Schleihauf et al., 1984). Stroke phases are listed on

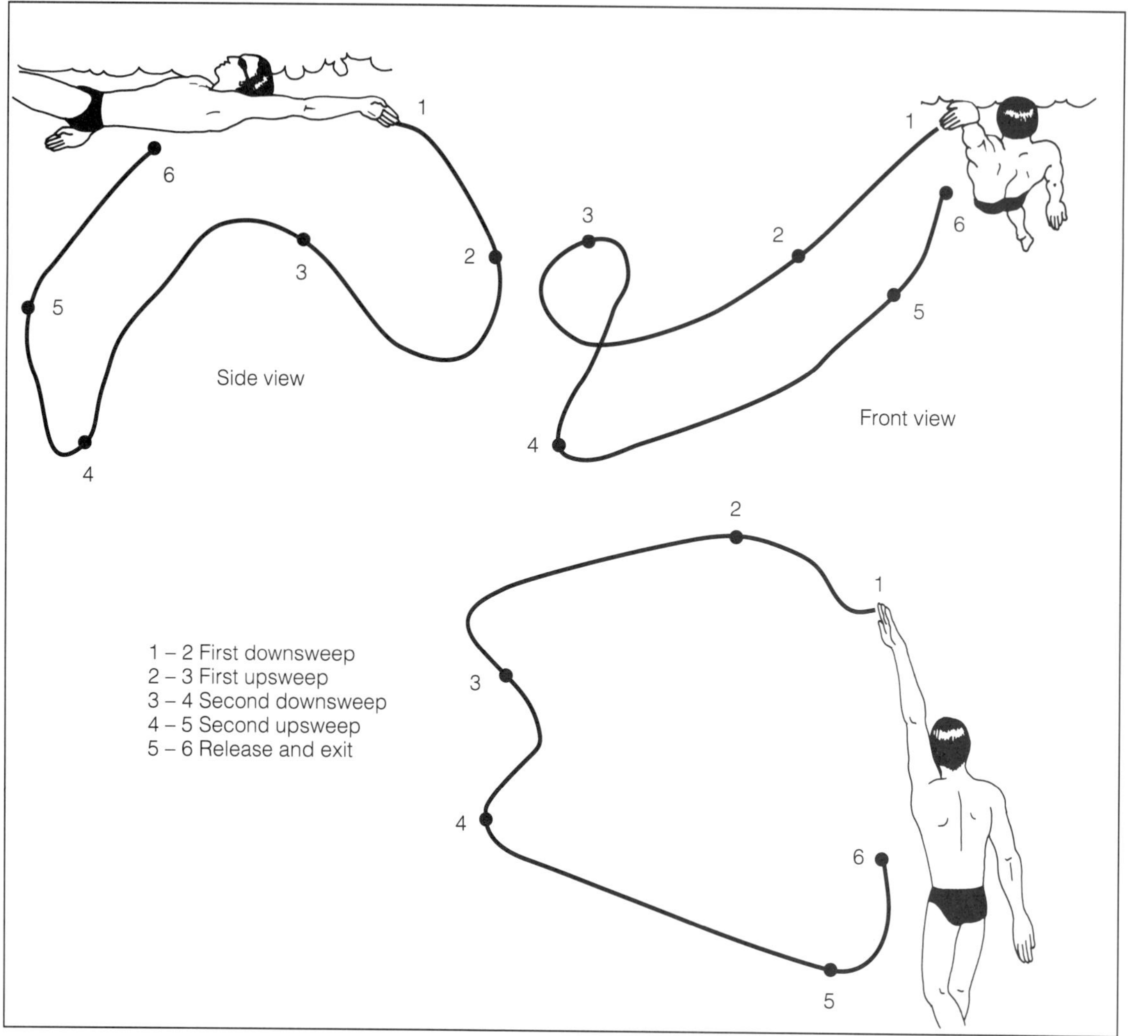

Figure 20-1. Side, front, and underneath views of the stroke patterns for the backstroke.

the horizontal axis. They are also shown on the side view stroke pattern at the top of the graph for reference purposes. The second upsweep is designated by the dotted line in the stroke pattern between points 4 and 5. The corresponding propulsive phase is indicated by the lightly shaded area on the propulsive force graph. Mitchell was swimming at 200-m speed when the films were taken.

The fact that the second upsweep is propulsive is shown by the peak of propulsive force that begins midway between points 4 and 5 on the force graph in Figure 20-2. Propulsion began midway through the second upsweep.

Figure 20-3 provides further proof that this phase of the armstroke can be propulsive. It shows hand and forearm propulsive force data gathered on another world-class backstroke swimmer, Jesse Vassallo. He gained more propulsion from

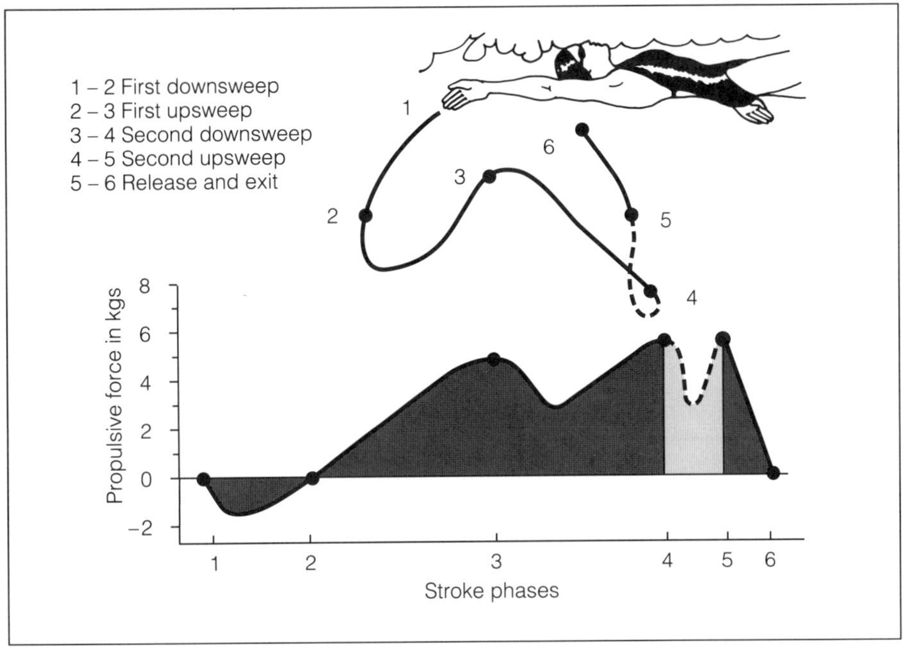

Figure 20-2. A propulsive force graph of the right armstroke for backstroker Betsy Mitchell, former world-record holder for the 200-m backstroke.

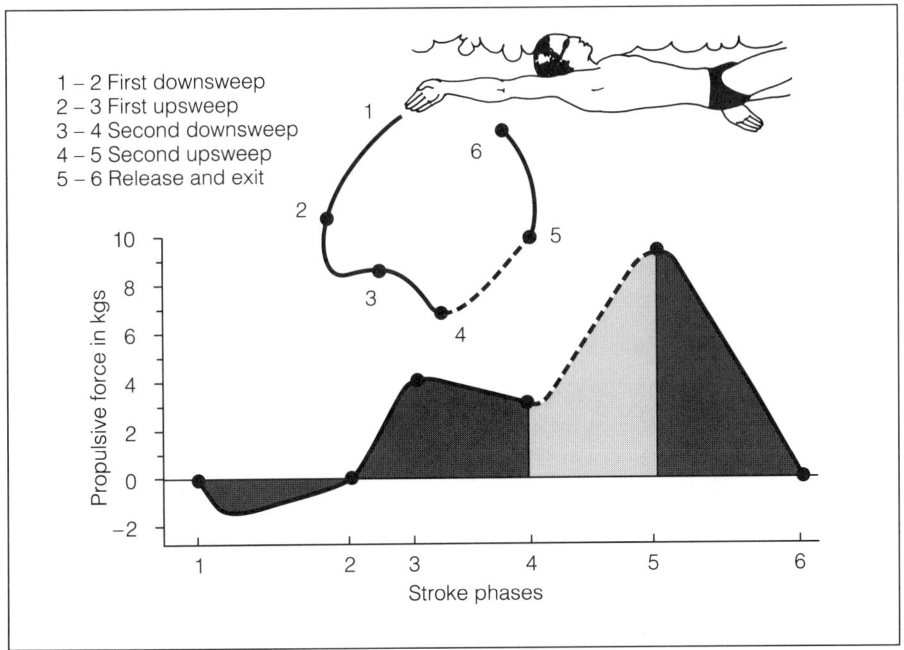

Figure 20-3. A propulsive force graph of the right armstroke for swimmer Jesse Vassallo, a member of the 1984 U.S. Olympic Swimming Team in the 200-m backstroke.

the second upsweep than any of the other U.S. Olympic swimmers that were studied in 1984 (Luedtke, 1986). Propulsive force generated during the second upsweep is indicated by the shaded area on the graph between points 4 and 5. The stroke pattern shows that his hand sweeps up and *back* during the time that force is produced.

The stroke pattern illustrated in Figure 20-3 does not represent the best way to swim backstroke. It is included merely to provide additional evidence that the second upsweep can be propulsive. The pattern displayed by Mitchell in Figure 20-2 is probably more efficient because she utilizes the first upsweep and second downsweep to a greater extent, and these phases of the stroke are potentially more propulsive. This fact notwithstanding, all swimmers would do well to use the second upsweep for propulsion as much as it can be used without shortening the propulsive sweeps that precede it.

Although they were not taught that this movement was propulsive, many swimmers have used it for this purpose unknowingly, suggesting that those swimmers with good feel for the water may have intuitively selected this style because it is superior.

ARMSTROKE

Underwater sequence photos of backstroker Bengt Baron's armstroke are displayed from a side view in Figure 20-4 and from an underneath view in Figure 20-5. Both sequences display important technical aspects of the stroke.

First Downsweep

The first downsweep of the right arm is pictured from a side view in Figures 20-4*a* and 20-4*b*. The first downsweep of Baron's left arm is shown in Figures 20-5*a* through 20-5*c*. Baron's arm enters the water fully extended and directly in front of his shoulder, with his palm facing out to the side. After the entry, he reaches down and out to the side until the underside of his arm and the palm of his hand are facing back against the water at the catch, which is made when his hand is near its deepest and widest point. Figure 20-4*b* shows the catch position of his right hand and arm. Excellent photos of the catch can also be seen from underneath in Figures 20-5*c* and 20-5*j*.

The hand is generally 45 to 60 cm deep (1½ to 2 ft) and approximately 60 cm (2 ft) wide of the shoulder at the catch (Schleihauf et al., 1988). The palm, which faces out at entry, rotates down slowly until it is pitched down and back when the catch is made. The arms should also flex gradually at the elbow during the first downsweep so that a backward orientation of the arm can be achieved when the catch is made. The arm flexes between 30 and 40 degrees during the downsweep, and the angle at the elbow is between 140 and 150 degrees when the catch is made. The hand should also be aligned with the forearm when the catch is made.

The hand enters the water traveling fairly fast, but its velocity decreases throughout the first downsweep until it is merely being pushed forward by the body when the catch is made.

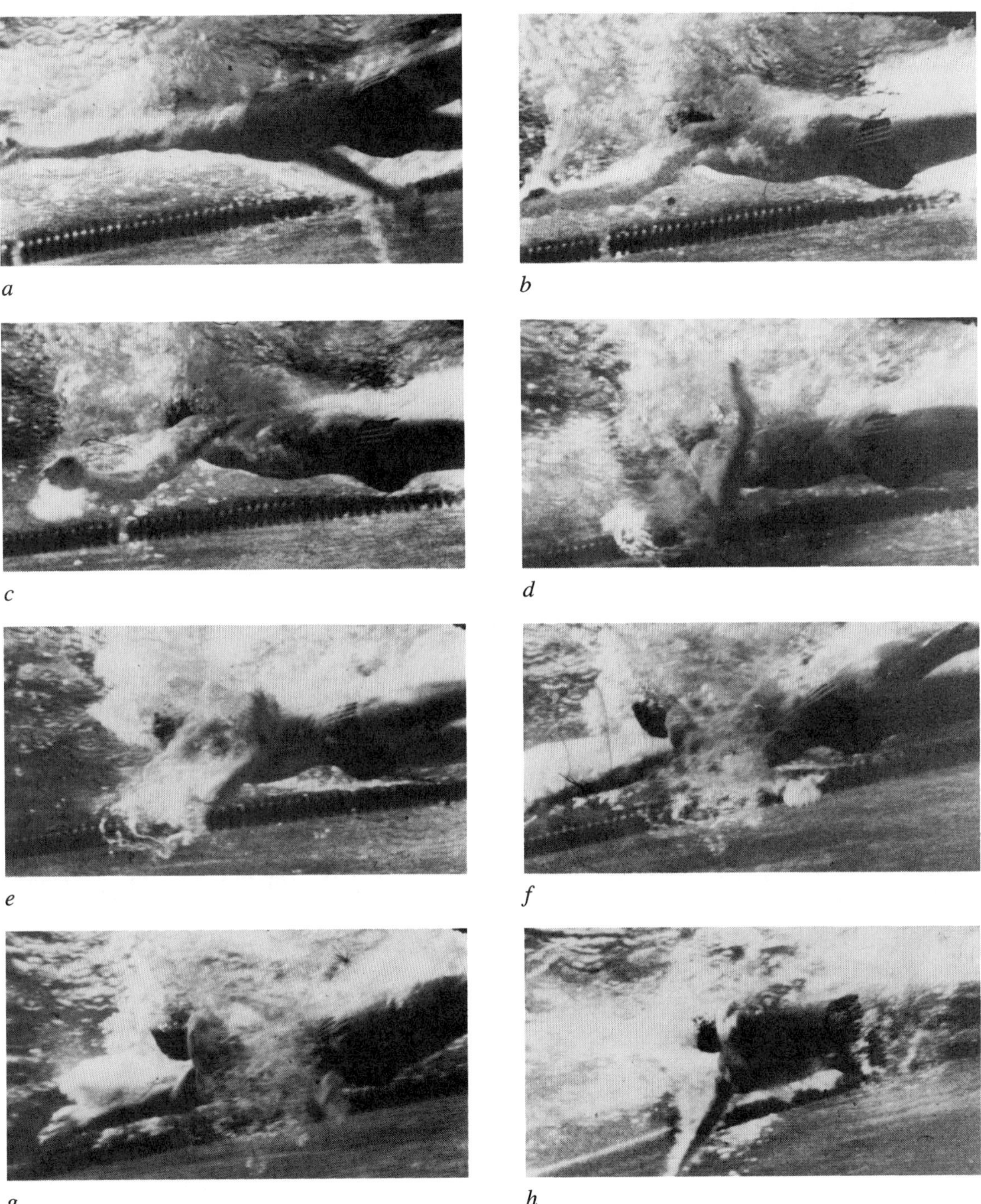

a *b* *c* *d* *e* *f* *g* *h*

Figure 20-4. A side view of the backstroke from underwater. The swimmer is Bengt Baron, gold medalist in the 100-m backstroke at the 1980 Olympic Games.

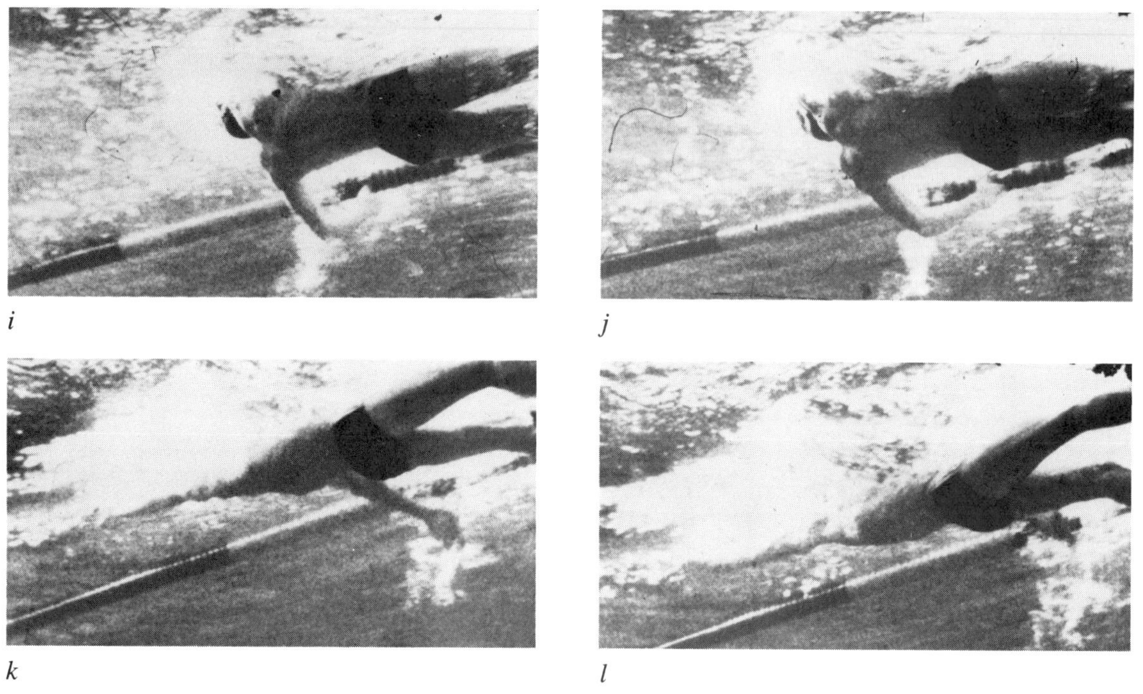

i *j* *k* *l*

Figure 20-4. (continued)

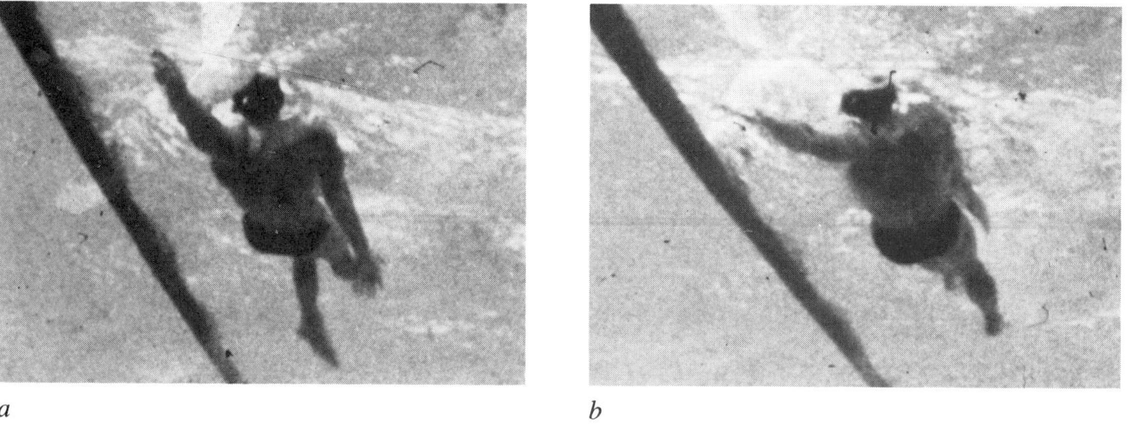

a *b*

Figure 20-5. An underneath view of Bengt Baron's backstroke.

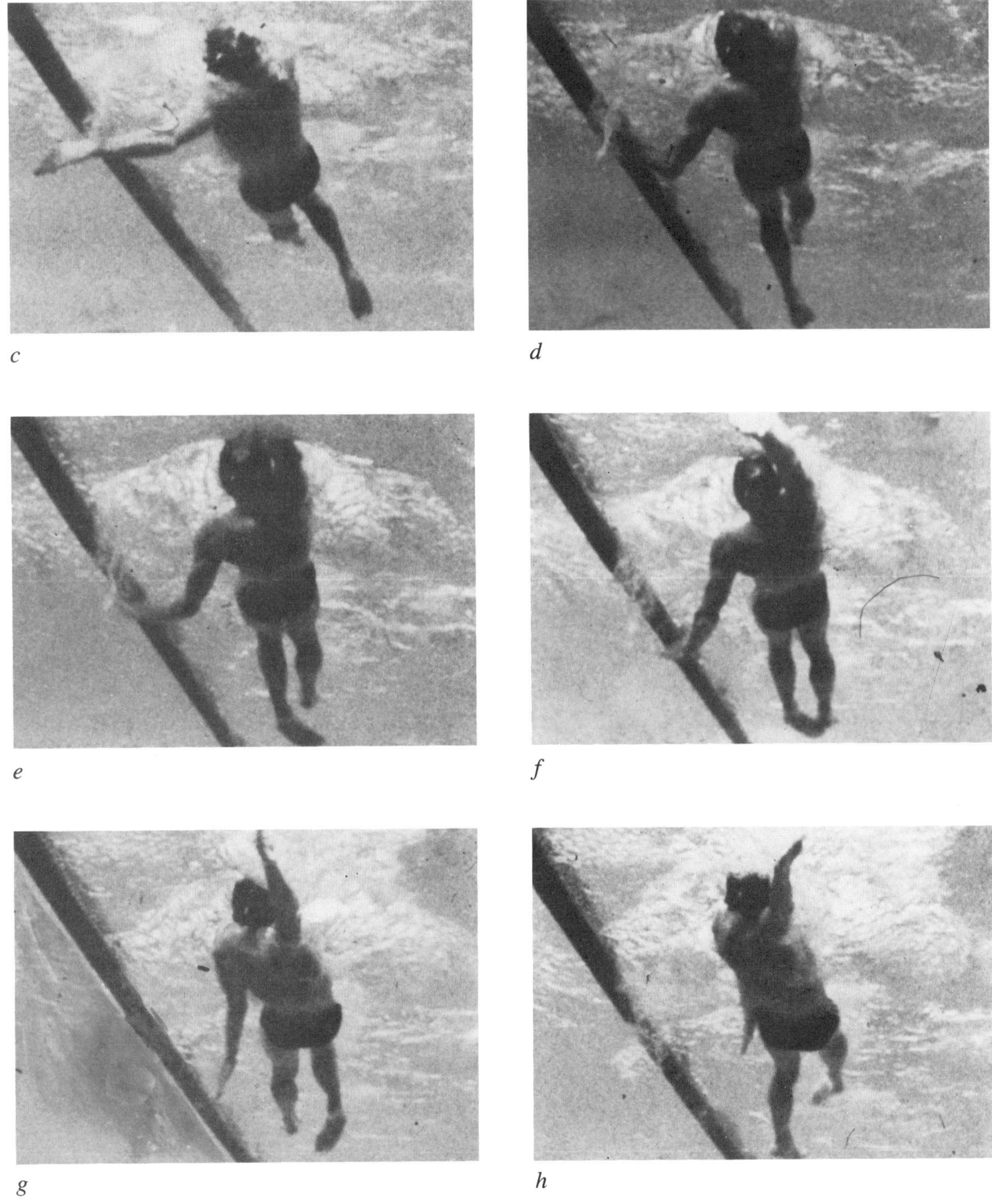

c

d

e

f

g

h

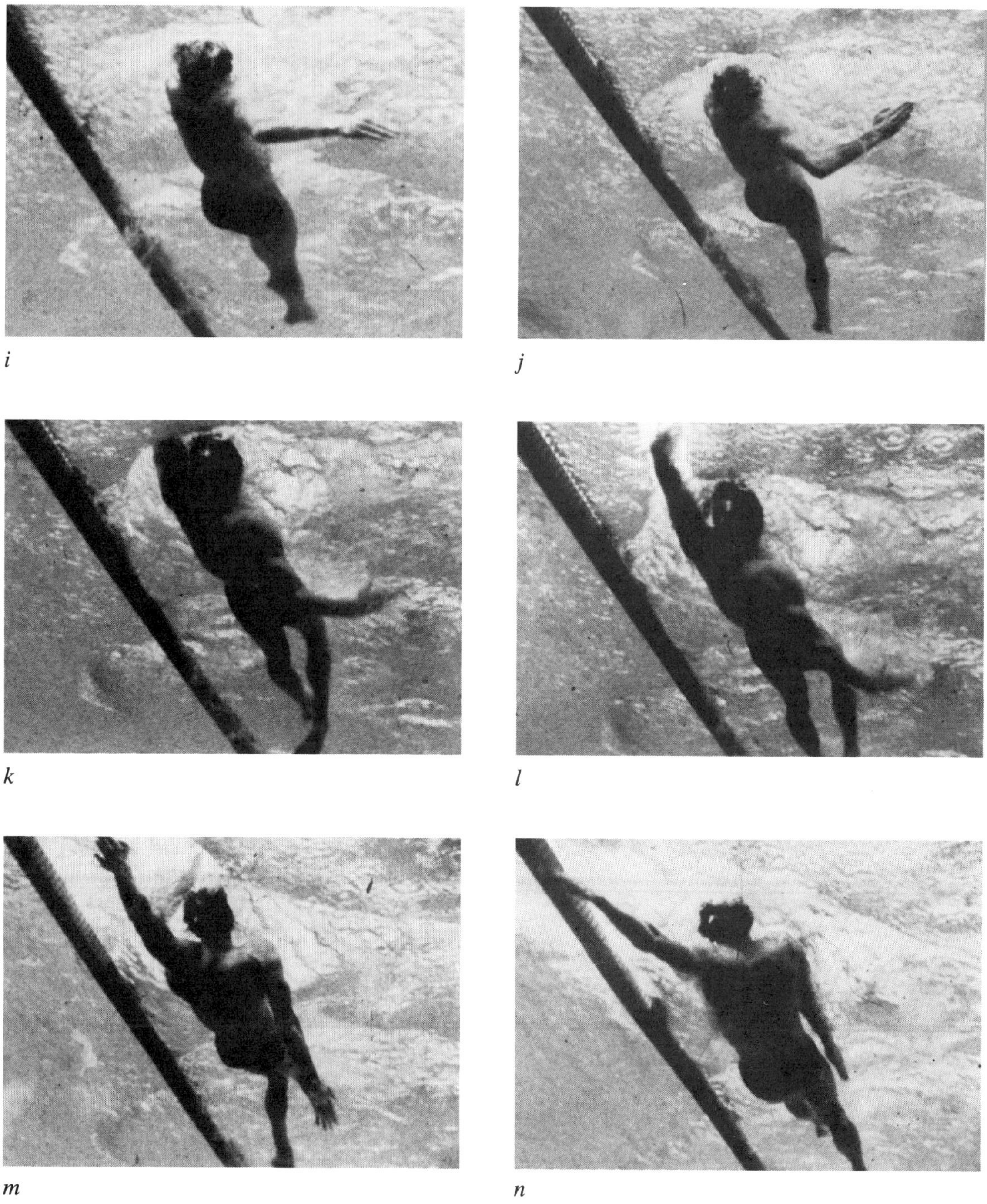

i *j* *k* *l* *m* *n*

Figure 20-5. (continued)

The first downsweep is not propulsive. Its primary purpose is to place the arm in position to apply propulsive force. It may also play a role in supporting the head and shoulders while the opposite arm is recovering over the water. Neither of these purposes requires any great expenditure of effort. Consequently, the first downsweep should feel like a gentle stretching motion.

As with other strokes, it is a common mistake for swimmers to begin pushing against the water immediately after their arm enters the water. They must be cautioned to wait until they reach the catch position before attempting to apply propulsive force. Any attempt to apply force while their arm is traveling down and out will only cause turbulence and decrease their forward speed.

First Upsweep

Baron is performing this phase of the underwater armstroke in Figures 20-4*b* through 20-4*d* and in Figures 20-5*c*, 20-5*d*, 20-5*j*, and 20-5*k*. It is the first propulsive phase of the underwater armstroke, and it begins at the catch. From there, the hand moves up and back in a semicircular sweep. The arm, which was slightly bent at the catch, continues flexing at the elbow throughout this stroke phase. The first upsweep ends when the arm is flexed through a range of between 50 and 60 degrees (Schleihauf et al., 1988) and is opposite the chest. The angle at the elbow is between 90 and 100 degrees when the first upsweep is nearing completion.

The palm should rotate from down to up during the first upsweep until it is pitched up and in when the movement has been completed (see Figure 20-4*d* and Figure 20-5*l*). This rotation must be gradual so that the hand remains at the most effective angle of attack for all parts of the first upsweep. The change to an upward pitch should not be made until the hand passes the elbow on its upward path, or some propulsion will be sacrificed. Figure 20-4*c* shows the point where the pitch of the hand should change from down to up.

Some swimmers sweep their hand up a long distance, yet others use a short upward motion. The choice probably depends on the way they were taught to swim as youngsters or their affinity for sculling versus pushing water back. The hand should remain aligned with the forearm throughout this sweep. Hand speed should accelerate moderately throughout the movement.

Figure 20-6 illustrates the method for generating propulsion during the second upsweep. With the swimmer's arm traveling up and back, the thumb side is the leading edge and the little-finger side is the trailing edge of the hand-foil. The relative flow of water, represented by the shaded arrow, will be in the opposite direction — down and forward — as the water meets his hand. The upward inclination of his hand will cause that water to be displaced back for a short time as it flows under his palm from the thumb side to the little-finger side. The water that is displaced back will create a counterforce of equal magnitude that will accelerate the swimmer's body forward.

If you can picture a backstroke swimmer in a face down position, you will see that the first upsweep of the back crawl is very similar to the insweep of the front crawl in the way that propulsive force is generated. Both are the middle sweeps of

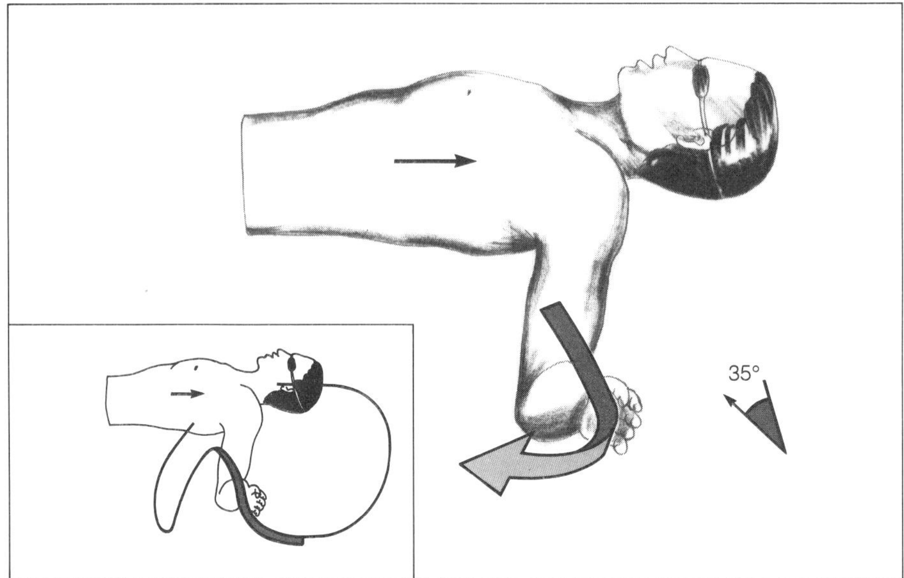

Figure 20-6. The method for generating propulsion during the upward portion of the first upsweep.

their respective armstrokes, and both are directed up and in, although backstrokers cannot sweep their hand under their body for obvious reasons. The pitch of the hand also imparts backward force to the water in similar ways in both strokes.

Second Downsweep

The second downsweep is shown in Figures 20-4*e* through 20-4*g*. It is also pictured for the left arm in Figures 20-5*d* through 20-5*g* and for the right arm in Figures 20-5*k* through 20-5*m*.

The second downsweep begins as the second upsweep is nearing completion. As the hand passes the top of the upsweep, the arm sweeps down and back until it is completely extended and well below the thigh. The hand should be approximately 30 cm (1 ft) deep when this sweep is completed (see Figure 20-4*g*).

Some swimmers also sweep their arm in toward their thigh during this phase of the stroke. I believe, however, that it is better for them to sweep it straight back or out to the side somewhat. The out and back direction of the second downsweep can be seen best in Figures 20-5*f*, 20-5*g*, 20-5*l*, and 20-5*m*. Notice that Baron's arms are wide of his hips when he completes this sweep.

Sweeping out may allow swimmers to use their forearm to greater advantage during the second downsweep. It also places their hand in position to make a propulsive second upsweep. Both of these advantages are discussed in greater detail later in this chapter.

The hand, which was pitched up and in at the end of the previous upsweep, should be rotated down and out during this sweep. The hand should be facing down toward the bottom of the pool when the second downsweep is completed. *The fingertips should remain facing to the side throughout the movement* (see Figures 20-4*f* and 20-4*m*). Swimmers should not turn their fingers up. This method was taught in the 1970s. However, underwater films show that the majority of world-class backstrokers keep their fingers facing to the side because it causes the angle of attack of their hand and forearm to be more effective for imparting backward force to the water as they sweep their arm down and back. Hand speed should decrease during the transition to the second downsweep and then accelerate rapidly throughout the movement.

Figure 20-7 shows how propulsion can be generated by the second downsweep. With the hand pitched down and out, the leading edge is the little-finger side and the thumb side is the trailing edge of the hand-foil as the swimmer sweeps his hand down. The relative flow of water will be up, opposite to the direction in which his arm is traveling. The shaded arrow shows how the downward inclination of the swimmer's palm will impart some backward force to the water that travels up under it from leading to trailing edges. The counterforce will accelerate the swimmer forward.

Second Upsweep

This final propulsive motion begins when the second downsweep is nearing completion. Baron is shown performing the second upsweep from a side view with his right arm in Figures 20-4*h* to 20-4*i* and with his left arm in Figures 20-4*l* and 20-4*m*.

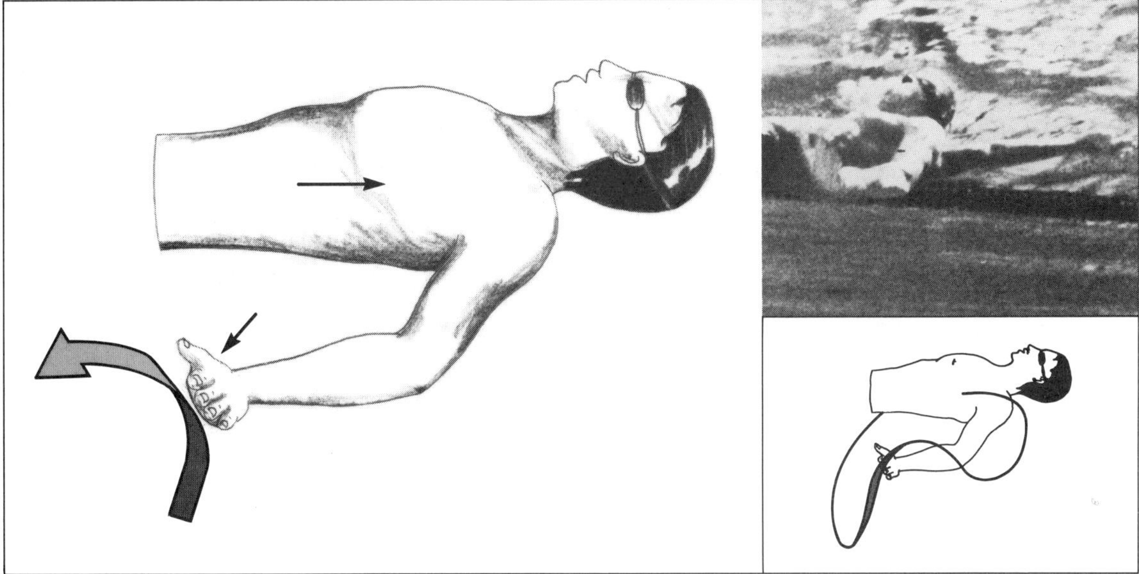

Figure 20-7. The method for generating propulsion during the second downsweep.

Once the second downsweep has been completed, the hand sweeps up, back, and in toward the surface. The second upsweep ends when the hand approaches the rear of the thigh. The arm should remain extended during this movement.

The position of the palm is the most important aspect of this movement. Swimmers who use this phase of the stroke for propulsion hyperextend their hand at the wrist so that their palm is pitched back and up, with their fingers pointing down toward the bottom of the pool. Figure 20-4*h* shows this position most clearly for the right hand; Figure 20-4*i*, for the left hand. This motion is very similar to the upsweep of the front crawl stroke and the butterfly, except, of course, that the swimmer is supine during the backstroke.

The hand decelerates during the transition from the second downsweep to the second upsweep and then accelerates rapidly until the second upsweep has been completed. Figure 20-8 shows how swimmers may displace water back during the second upsweep. The wrist edge is the leading edge and the fingertips the trailing edge as the hand travels up and in. The relative flow of water will start down and forward over the palm. However, with the swimmer's hand hyperextended at the wrist, that water will be displaced backward as it travels under his palm from wrist to fingertips, as shown by the shaded arrow.

The swimmer's forearm may also participate in displacing water back early in the second upsweep. Figure 20-8 shows that the forearm is also pitched back and up, at least during the first half of this movement. Swimmers who can hyperextend their arm at the elbow may have an advantage because they can maintain their forearm at a desirable angle of attack for a longer time during the second upsweep.

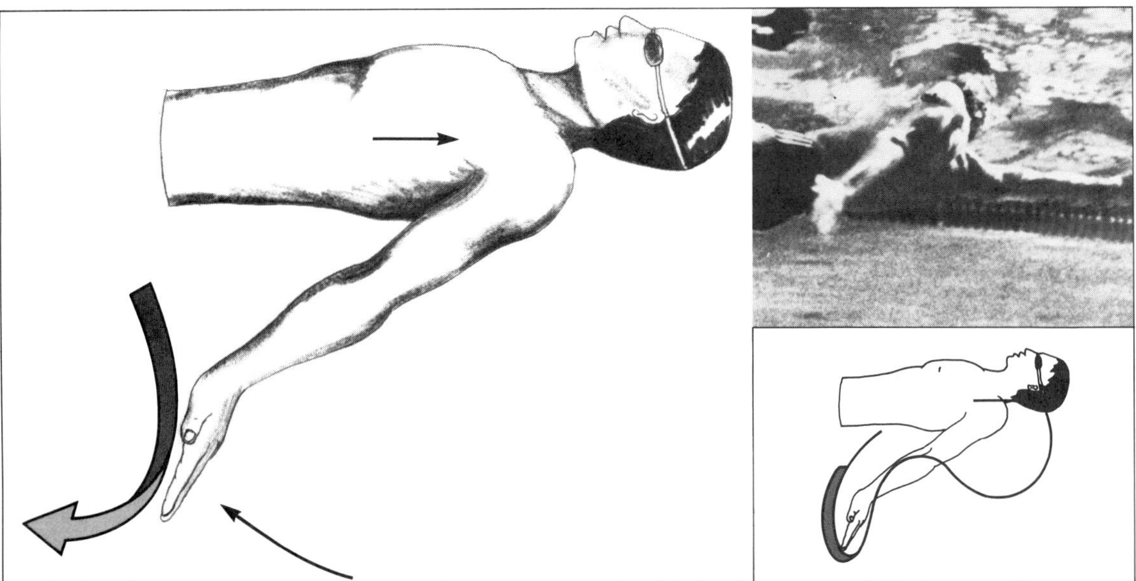

Figure 20-8. The method for displacing water back during the second upsweep.

This may explain why a great number of good backstroke swimmers possess this ability.

Swimmers who use the second upsweep for propulsion will be more effective if they use a wide stroke. They must sweep their hand *in* as well as up if they intend to use this sweep for a reasonable length of time. This point is discussed in greater detail later in this chapter.

Release, Recovery, and Entry

Figures 20-5*m* and *n* show an underneath view of the release and the first portion of the recovery. They are also displayed from the surface in Figure 20-9 (p. 460).

Swimmers release pressure on the water when their hand approaches the lower portions of their thigh, because their hand starts moving forward at that time and they cannot generate any propulsive force with it. They turn their palm in toward their body and slide their hand up out of the water on its edge to reduce its surface area and, thus, the resistance to its upward movement. The hand should leave the water *thumb first,* not little finger first, as some experts have suggested.

Hand speed decelerates markedly at the release. Body roll is primarily responsible for swinging the hand and arm up and out of the water. The upward movement of the shoulder also assists in lifting the arm on the same side out of the water with minimal effort.

After leaving the water, the arm travels through the air until the entry is made. The recovery should be made high and overhead (see Figure 20-9*c*), not low and to the side. A high, overhead recovery reduces any tendency for the arm to pull the hips and legs out of lateral alignment. The palm should face in during the first half and out during the second half of the recovery, making the change from in to out as the hand passes overhead and starts down for the entry (see Figures 20-9*e* through 20-9*g*). The entry of the hand should be made directly in advance of the shoulder on the same side (see Figure 20-9*h*).

The recovery should be made quickly but gently. The hand and arm should be relaxed as much as possible so that the muscles receive some rest between underwater armstrokes.

Backstrokers must recover with a straight arm; thus, their upper arm and forearm hit the water long before their hand enters. This produces wave drag. There is nothing backstroke swimmers can do to prevent this from happening. However, they can reduce it by carrying their recovering shoulder high. Rolling the body facilitates this. The shoulder of the recovering arm comes out of the water when swimmers roll toward the other side, allowing it and the upper arm to stay out of the water longer during the recovery (see Figures 20-9*d* through 20-9*f*).

Timing the Arms

The relationship of one arm to the other is best seen in the underneath sequence in Figure 20-5. The arms stroke in an alternating *windmill* fashion. The recovering arm should enter the water when the stroking arm is completing the second downsweep (see Figures 20-5*g* and 20-5*m* for the entries of the right and left arms,

a *b* *c* *d* *e* *f* *g* *h* *i*

Figure 20-9. A surface view of the backstroke arm release and recovery. The swimmer is Kristin Kuhlman, NCAA finalist in this stroke.

respectively). The first downsweep of the front arm should be made while the rear arm is executing its second upsweep so that propulsion can be maintained until the recovering arm has had time to sweep down to the catch position (see Figures 20-5*a* and 20-5*b* for the downsweep of the left arm and Figures 20-5*h* and 20-5*i* for the downsweep of the right arm).

Variations in Backstroke Styles

As mentioned, backstrokers show greater variety in their armstrokes than swimmers in other competitive styles. The variations seem to fall into two broad categories. In the first category are swimmers who use a deep catch versus those who use a shallow catch. In the second category, the two contrasting styles are the wide stroke and the narrow stroke.

Deep Versus Shallow Catch A shallow catch is being used by Baron in Figures 20-4 and 20-5. Figure 20-5*c* illustrates it best. The swimmer in Figure 20-10 is using a deep catch. Notice how her hand travels down much more and out less than Baron's.

The shallow catch results in a short sweep up simply because the hand is not very deep when the first upsweep begins. The front-view and side-view stroke patterns in Figures 20-11 and 20-12, respectively, illustrate this style for backstroker Theresa Andrews (p. 462). Notice in Figure 20-11 that Andrews sweeps her hand out to the side much more than she sweeps it down during the first downsweep. That sweep is indicated by the dashed line between points 1 and 2. She also sweeps her hand up only a short distance between the catch at point 2 and the top of the first upsweep at point 3, which is most evident in Figure 20-12.

Swimmers who use this style compensate for the short upward distance of the first upsweep by sweeping their hand back for a longer distance. This is what Andrews does between points 2 and 3 in Figure 20-12. This phase of her underwater armstroke is indicated by the dashed line between points 2 and 3. It should be noted that she does not have a propulsive second upsweep. Instead, she simply releases pressure on the water following the second downsweep, after which her hand travels up to the surface and exits from the water.

Figure 20-10. A swimmer using a deep catch.

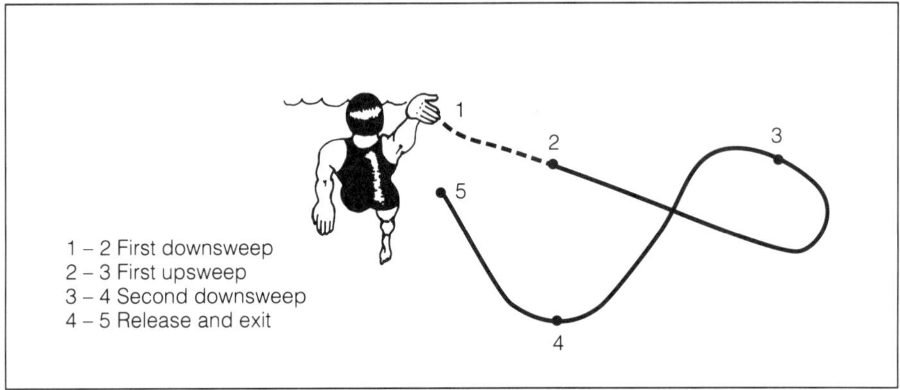

Figure 20-11. A front-view stroke pattern for Theresa Andrews, 1984 Olympic champion in the 100-m backstroke. She uses a wide catch and a short upsweep.

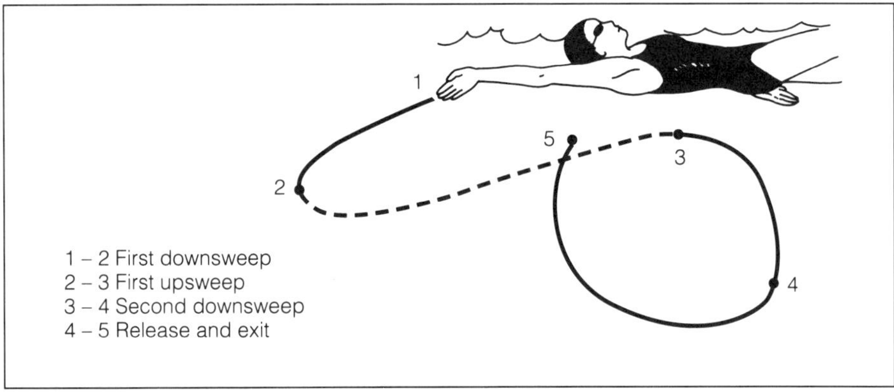

Figure 20-12. A side-view stroke pattern for Theresa Andrews. She sweeps her hand up only a short distance while using a long, backward path of motion.

The shallow catch is made by sweeping the hand out 65 to 75 cm (25 to 30 inches) and down a smaller amount, 50 to 60 cm (20 to 24 inches). By contrast, swimmers who use a deep catch usually sweep their hand out approximately 60 cm (24 inches) and down 60 to 70 cm (25 to 29 inches).

From a theoretical point of view, a deep catch and a long first upsweep should be most effective by allowing swimmers to apply propulsive force over a longer distance. All swimmers cannot use the deep catch effectively, however. They must have reasonably flexible shoulders and should be good scullers to use a deep catch and a long first upsweep. Those who do not have adequate ability to hyperflex their shoulders (reach down and back with their arms) usually end up rolling excessively and pushing down on the water during the first downsweep when they try to make a deep catch. Furthermore, if they are not good scullers, they will sweep their hand up over a long distance with little or no propulsion taking place. Swimmers in this category may lose more propulsion than they gain with the deep catch and long upsweep.

Swimmers should experiment with variations on the deep and shallow catch until they find the style that suits them best. The best technique for most may be a compromise between the two extremes.

Wide Versus Narrow Stroke Whether the stroke is wide or narrow has to do with the way swimmers perform the second downsweep. The narrow style is illustrated from a front view in Figure 20-13*a*. Notice that the swimmer's right hand is traveling *in* as well as down during the second downsweep. That phase of the stroke is indicated by the dashed line between points 3 and 4. Please notice that the swimmer illustrated in Figure 20-13*a* does not have a second upsweep phase in her stroke. A narrow stroke prevents swimmers from using a propulsive second upsweep because the second downsweep is completed so close to the body that swimmers cannot scull their hand in enough to use this phase of the stroke effectively.

The wide style is illustrated from a front view in Figure 20-13*b*. The dashed line between points 3 and 4 shows that this swimmer's hand is traveling *out* and down during the second downsweep. That swimmer can utilize a propulsive second upsweep.

As mentioned, swimmers traditionally have been taught to use the narrow style, the belief being that the propulsive phase of the stroke ended with the second

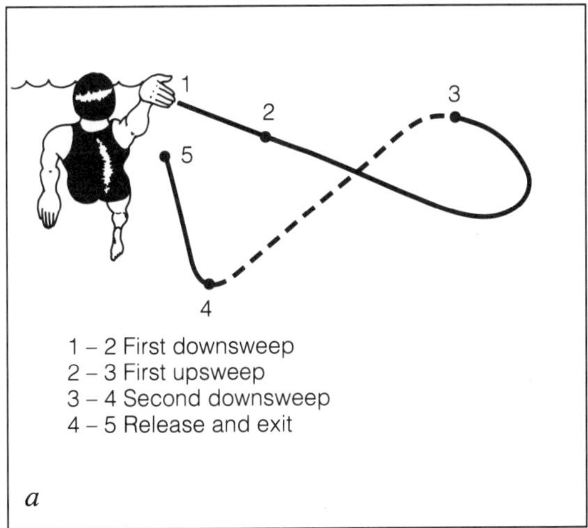

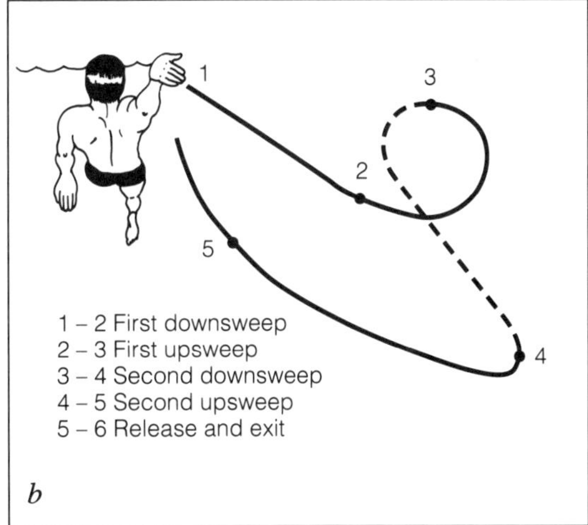

Figure 20-13. Two front-view stroke patterns for backstroke swimmers: one who sweeps her hand down and *in* during the second downsweep (*a*) and one who sweeps his hand down and *out* during the same phase of the armstroke (*b*).

downsweep. Consequently, swimmers were taught to bring their hand in toward their thigh so that it would be in position for the recovery. We realize now that swimmers can generate propulsive force as their hand travels up toward the surface and that they can generate more propulsion if their hand travels in as well as up. This is probably why swimmers who use a propulsive second upsweep tend toward the wide stroke.

A second advantage of sweeping the hand down and out may be that swimmers can position their hand and forearm to produce more propulsion during the second downsweep. Figure 20-14 illustrates why this may be true. The swimmers are shown from an overhead view. The swimmer in Figure 20-14*a* sweeps his arm down and in. This combination of direction and angle of attack will push water *in* and back, in the direction of the shaded arrows. Consequently, some of the propulsive force may be wasted pushing the swimmer's body to the side. By contrast, the swimmer in Figure 20-14*b* sweeps his hand down and out during the second downsweep. His forearm has a better backward orientation, which should allow him to displace water almost directly back and gain more propulsion.

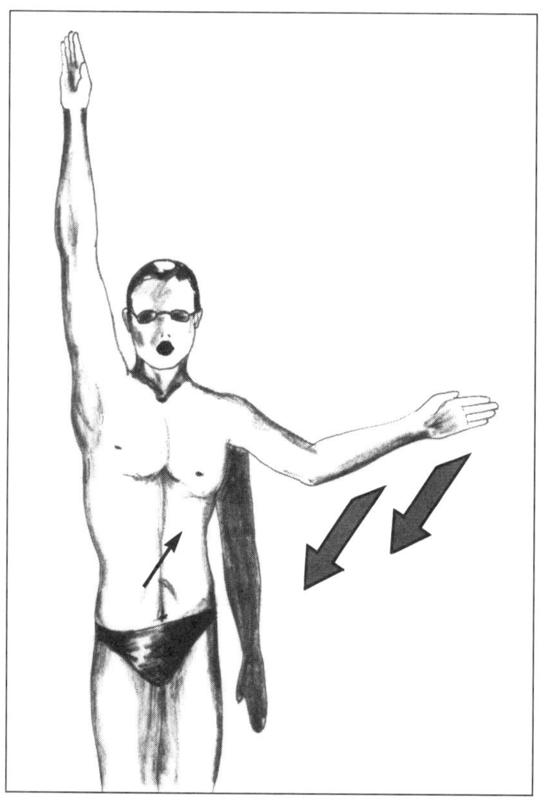

a

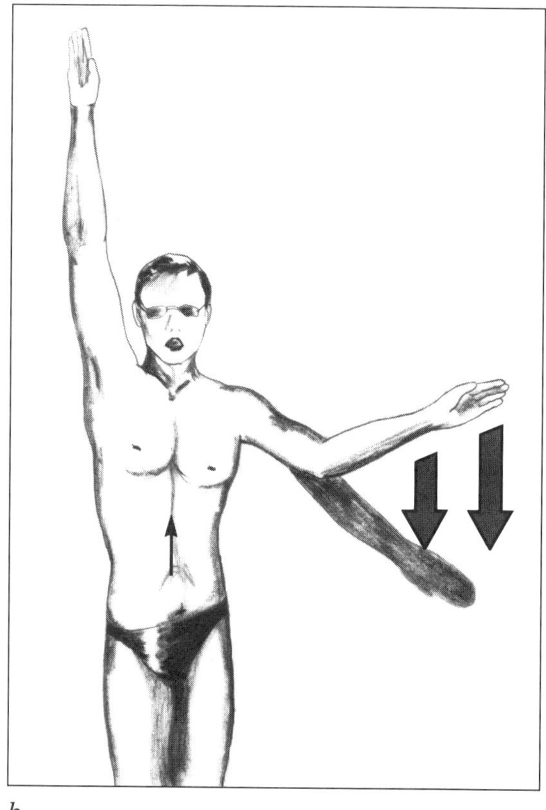

b

Figure 20-14. Overhead views of two swimmers executing the second downsweep.

As mentioned, swimmers who use a wide stroke will generally use a propulsive second upsweep, even though they may not be aware they are doing so. The superiority of the wide stroke cannot be supported with scientific data at the present time, but there are several theoretical reasons for recommending it. The most obvious is that total propulsive force should be increased if swimmers use three propulsive sweeps rather than two. An additional advantage is that the period of deceleration between the end of one underwater armstroke and the beginning of the next can be reduced if the second upsweep is propulsive. Generally, one arm does not enter the water until the other has completed its second downsweep in backstroke swimming, and the entering arm cannot generate propulsion until it sweeps down to the catch. This requires approximately 0.10 second. Swimmers will decelerate during that period if the second upsweep is not propulsive. However, a propulsive second upsweep will permit them to maintain a reasonable amount of forward speed with the arm behind while the overhead arm is traveling down to the catch position. Thus, the interval between the time when one arm stops delivering propulsive force and the other begins should be shortened to 0.03 or 0.05 second.

FLUTTER KICK

The flutter kick in the back crawl stroke is very similar to the one used in the front crawl. It consists of alternating diagonal thrusts of the legs called *upbeats* and *downbeats*. The upbeat is probably propulsive; the downbeat is not. Figure 20-15 illustrates mechanics of the flutter kick.

Upbeat

The upbeat is a whiplike extension of the leg that begins with flexion at the hip, followed by extension at the knee, and ending with partial flexion of the foot (the toes kick up and through the surface). Figure 20-15 illustrates the upbeat for the left leg.

The upbeat begins as the foot passes below the buttocks. At that point, the hip flexes to start the thigh moving up. In the meantime, the lower leg and foot are relaxed so that the water pressing down from above pushes the leg into a flexed position at the knee. Water pressing down on the top of the foot pushes it down and in so that the foot is plantar flexed and inverted. Figure 20-15*a* shows these positions of the lower leg and foot.

The thigh continues moving up until it passes above the hips (see Figure 20-15*b*), after which the leg extends rapidly, sweeping diagonally up toward the surface until it is completely extended just below the surface of the water (see Figure 20-15*c*). The foot is flexed at the very end of the upbeat to add a small amount of additional propulsion. If the upbeat is performed properly, the toes should break the surface of the water.

The leg flexes more during the upbeat in this stroke than in the corresponding downbeat of the front crawl stroke (approximately 10 degrees more). This is because the swimmer is in a supine position in which the leg can be flexed more without

a

b

c

Figure 20-15. The flutter kick in the backstroke.

increasing drag. The same amount of knee flexion would cause a swimmer's lower leg to travel above the surface of the water in the front crawl stroke.

The upbeat is probably the only propulsive phase of the kick. Chapter 17 described how this movement can displace water back (see Figure 17-15). The relative flow of water is down over the front surface of the swimmer's lower leg and foot. With the lower leg flexed and the foot extended, they assume an angle of attack that can impart some backward force to the water.

Downbeat

The downbeat is a reboundlike action that begins when the previous upbeat is nearing completion. Figure 20-15 illustrates the downbeat for the right leg.

The upward force of the extending lower leg starts the thigh of the same leg moving diagonally down while the lower leg and foot are traveling toward the surface. Once the previous upbeat is completed, a small amount of hip extension keeps the leg moving down as the downbeat gets underway. The leg travels down until it passes below the body line, which is when the next upbeat begins.

The leg is maintained in an extended position and the foot in a natural position between extension and flexion throughout the downbeat (see the left leg in Figures 20-15*a* and 20-15*b*). The pressure of the water pushing up from underneath the leg and foot keeps them in these positions. The downbeat is probably not propulsive because the leg is traveling down at too large an angle of attack to impart any backward force to the water. Consequently, swimmers should not kick down hard or unnecessarily fast.

Propulsion from the Flutter Kick

Backstroke competitions do not exceed 200 m; thus, in these short races, propulsion from the legs can contribute considerably more to success than it does in longer freestyle races. Backstroke swimmers almost universally use vigorous six-beat rhythms. This does not mean that backstrokers should kick their legs as hard as possible throughout entire races, however. The effort from the legs should be controlled until the final sprint in order to save energy. This is particularly true for distances of 200 yd and 200 m.

Stabilizing Role of the Flutter Kick

In addition to their propulsive contribution, the legs also play an important role in maintaining lateral and horizontal body alignment. Recoveries and the diagonal underwater sweeps of the arms can disrupt these alignments, and diagonal kicking probably acts to counterbalance these potentially damaging arm movements. The legs should kick in the general direction that the body rotates so that the diagonal nature of these leg beats can facilitate body roll and cancel tendencies for arm movements to push the body up, down, and to the side.

Dolphin Kicking

When the dolphin kick is used for a portion of each pool length, swimmers should push off the wall to a depth of 1 to 1.5 m (3 to 5 ft), where they can kick beneath the surface turbulence. Swimmers who use the dolphin kick should be sure to execute it correctly. The dolphin kick should be similar to the one described for butterfly except that the leg strokes should be shorter and faster. The motion should originate from the hips and lower spine. Swimmers' arms should be together overhead, with one hand on top of the other. Their head should be between their arms, and they should squeeze their ears with their shoulders to achieve a very streamlined position. They should make every effort to keep their arms, head, and shoulders from moving up and down. The dolphin kick should be performed from the lower back down through the hips and legs, with the upper torso, head, and arms remaining fairly motionless and streamlined.

Swimmers should begin angling upward as they near the point where they plan to surface. They should cease dolphin kicking and begin a flutter kick before they surface so that they will be stroking and kicking in the proper rhythm as their body comes through the surface. At the start and after each turn, the first armstroke should be taken just under the surface and it should bring the swimmer up through the surface at full stroking rhythm.

TIMING THE ARMS AND LEGS

Almost without exception, backstrokers use a six-beat timing in their races. There are six upbeats (and downbeats) of the legs during each stroke cycle, or three kicks per armstroke. These kicks are synchronized with the first three sweeps of the armstroke in much the same way that was described for the front crawl stroke. The fourth sweep—the second upsweep—of one arm takes place while the other arm executes its first downsweep, so one set of leg beats suffices for both of these arm sweeps.

Figure 20-16 shows a six-beat timing of the arms and legs. Beginning with the entry of the left arm, the sequence is as follows:

1. The left leg kicks up (and the right down) during the first downsweep of the left arm (see Figure 20-16*a*).
2. The right leg kicks up (and the left down) during the first upsweep of the left arm (see Figure 20-16*b*).
3. The left leg kicks up, once again, (and the right down) during the second downsweep of the left arm (see Figure 20-16*c*).

A similar, but opposite, sequence of arm and leg movements is repeated during the right armstroke (see Figures 20-16*d* through 20-16*f*). That is, (1) the right leg kicks up when the right arm executes its first downsweep; (2) the left leg kicks up during the right arm's first upsweep; and (3) the right leg kicks up again while the right arm completes its second downsweep.

The similarity between the timing of this stroke and the six-beat timing of the front crawl lends additional support to the theory that six-beat timing may be the most efficient method for both strokes, at least for distances of 200 m and less.

BODY POSITION AND BREATHING

Body Position

Backstrokers have problems maintaining lateral alignment because of their alternating armstrokes. Some also have a tendency to *sit* in the water, with their hips down and head up, which upsets their horizontal alignment.

Horizontal Alignment Good horizontal alignment is shown from an underwater view in Figure 20-4 and from a surface view in Figure 20-9. The body should be nearly horizontal with the surface of the water, with only a slight pike at the waist. This small bend enables swimmers to keep their thigh from breaking through the surface of the water during the upbeat of the kick. Swimmers should not bend excessively at the waist, however.

The back of the head should rest in the water, with the waterline passing just under the ears (the wake will cover the ears). The chin should be tucked slightly and the eyes should focus back and up (see Figure 20-9).

Figure 20-16. A six-beat timing sequence for the backstroke.

Lateral Alignment Good lateral alignment is shown from an underneath view in Figure 20-5. Figure 20-17 also illustrates good lateral alignment. In both figures, the swimmer's hips and legs remain within shoulder width at all times even though they are rolling from side to side.

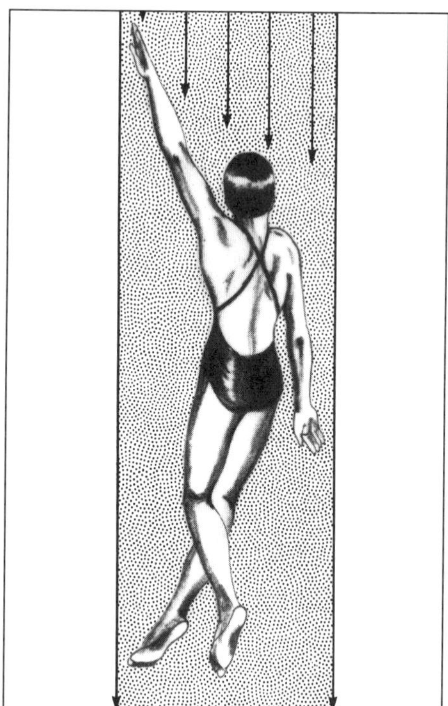

Figure 20-17. An underneath view showing good lateral alignment for the backstroke.

Backstrokers find it particularly difficult to maintain good lateral alignment because the sideward swings of their arm during its recovery over the water can pull their hips out in the same direction. If swimmers reach back behind their head for the entry, they can also pull their hips out of alignment. The best preventive measure where lateral alignment is concerned is for swimmers to roll their body in harmony with the movements of their arms.

Body Roll The alternate action of the arms in the back crawl causes one arm to be moving down while the other is traveling up. The trunk will naturally follow these arm movements. Consequently, it is very important for backstrokers to roll their body in the same directions their arms are moving if they want to prevent their hips and legs from swinging side to side. Any attempt to remain in a flat position while their arms and shoulders are sweeping down and up will cause countertorques that will throw their body out of alignment.

Although it is possible to roll too much, it is far more common for backstrokers to roll too little. Backstroke swimmers should roll approximately 45 degrees to each side. They should roll to the left as their left arm starts down for the water at the midpoint in its recovery, and they should continue rolling to the left as that arm completes its entry, first downsweep, and first upsweep. The legs should be kicking diagonally in the same direction (see Figures 20-5*a* through 20-5*e*). The roll toward the right side begins during the second downsweep of the left armstroke (and the entry of the opposite arm) and continues through the first half of the underwater stroke of the right arm (see Figures 20-5*f* through 20-5*k*). The legs should kick diagonally in the new direction to facilitate this roll.

If these rolling movements are timed properly, the body will stay in alignment, as though mounted on a skewer. Any body part that fails to roll in time with the others will be pulled out of alignment. The head is the only exception to this rule. The head should remain in a stationary position, with the eyes focused up and back.

Breathing

Unlike swimmers in the other competitive strokes, backstrokers do not submerge their face, so they do not need to inhale and exhale at specific times during the stroke cycle. Nevertheless, some coaches feel it is more efficient to establish a breathing rhythm that is coordinated with the arm movements during each stroke cycle. They recommend inhaling during one arm recovery and exhaling during the other. It may not be necessary to teach this or any rhythm, however. Because their face is out of the water and they can breathe at will, backstroke swimmers probably develop an efficient rhythm through trial and error.

HAND AND BODY VELOCITY PATTERNS

Figure 20-18 shows body and hand velocity patterns for the backstroke. The patterns are a composite of the best parts of several swimmers' strokes and, thus, depict what I believe are ideal patterns for this stroke.

The body velocity graph begins with the release of the left hand at point 1 (at the zero point on the time axis). The forward speed decelerates 0.10 to 0.20 m/sec (approximately .5 ft/sec) during the first downsweep while searching for the catch. The catch takes place at point 2. The forward speed accelerates after the catch and continues accelerating through the first upsweep (between points 2 and 3). There is a slight loss of speed during the transition from the first upsweep to the second downsweep, followed by another acceleration in forward velocity during the second downsweep (between points 3 and 4). Following this, there is a slight deceleration during the transition from the second downsweep to the second upsweep, after which forward velocity accelerates once again during the second sweep (between points 4 and 5). The right hand releases pressure on the water at point 5, and the forward speed decelerates until the left arm makes its catch at point 6. After that, accelerations and decelerations in forward speed follow the same pattern for the three propulsive sweeps of the left arm as were described for the right. Notice, however, that the velocity peaks tend to be somewhat lower and shorter and that the valleys are slightly deeper and longer for the left armstroke. These differences between the dominant (right) and nondominant (left) armstrokes are typical of most backstroke swimmers, as they are for freestyle swimmers. (Chapter 18 discussed the probable reasons for this asymmetry.)

The top graph of Figure 20-18 represents an ideal pattern of hand velocity for a one stroke cycle. As with other strokes, the peaks and valleys for hand velocity tend to mirror those for body velocity.

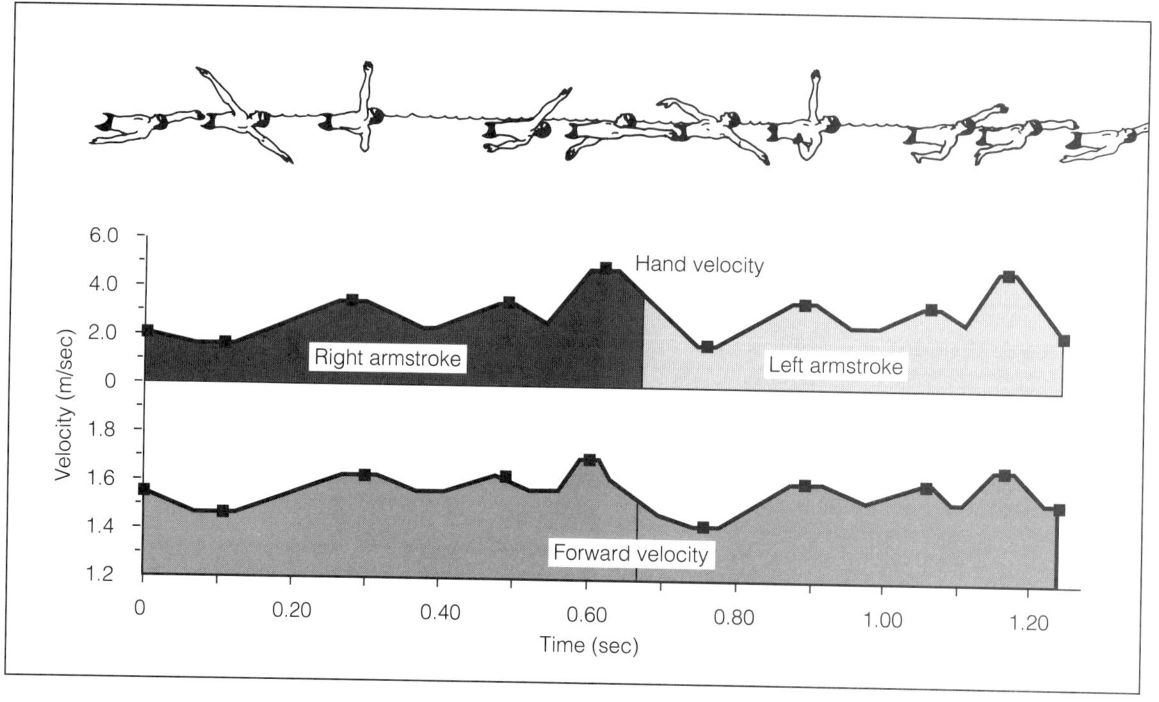

Figure 20-18. Ideal body and hand velocity patterns for a backstroke swimmer.

The hand enters the water traveling fairly fast, approximately 2.0 m/sec (7 ft/sec) at point 1. After entry, the hand slows down until it is traveling at approximately the same speed as the body when the catch is made at point 2. Once the catch is made, the hand accelerates in a three-peak pattern, with each peak corresponding to one of the three propulsive sweeps in the underwater armstroke. There are also decelerative periods during the transitions between each of these peaks, while the hand changes direction and pitch.

The right hand accelerates to approximately the same speeds—nearly 4 m/sec—during the first upsweep and second downsweep. It accelerates even more during the second upsweep, however, reaching a velocity of nearly 5 m/sec during this phase. Hand speed decelerates when the release is made and continues to decelerate through the recovery until it reaches the catch position for the next stroke. In the meantime, the left hand enters the water while the right completes its second downsweep. It decelerates until the catch is made. It then also accelerates in three peaks of velocity that correspond to the three propulsive sweeps of the armstroke.

The hand velocities shown in Figure 20-18 are typical of those measured for members of the 1984 U.S. Olympic Swimming Team. Hand velocities were generally between 3 and 3.5 m/sec (10 to 12 ft/sec) during the first upsweep and second downsweep (Schleihauf et al., 1988). The fastest hand velocities—4 to 4.5 m/sec

(12 to 15 ft/sec)—occurred during the second upsweep for those swimmers who used this part of their armstroke for propulsion (Luedtke, 1986).

Variations in Body Velocity Patterns

The example in Figure 20-18 was a three-peak velocity pattern. It should be noted that the majority of backstroke swimmers achieve only one or two propulsive peaks during each armstroke.

Two-Peak Velocity Pattern Figure 20-19 illustrates a typical two-peak body velocity pattern for backstroker Theresa Andrews. Only her right armstroke is shown. The propulsive peaks in her armstroke take place during the first upsweep and the second downsweep. There is no propulsive second upsweep. She simply moves from the second downsweep to the release and exit.

Many swimmers who use this style accelerate their body forward the most during the first upsweep. That propulsion is either maintained or reduced slightly during the second downsweep after a short transition period. Other swimmers achieve their greatest velocity during the second downsweep. For them, the previous upsweep is also propulsive but not to the same extent.

One-Peak Velocity Pattern Figure 20-20 illustrates another velocity pattern that is common among world-class backstroke swimmers. The swimmer is Tori Trees. Her forward velocity is also shown for the right underwater armstroke only. The

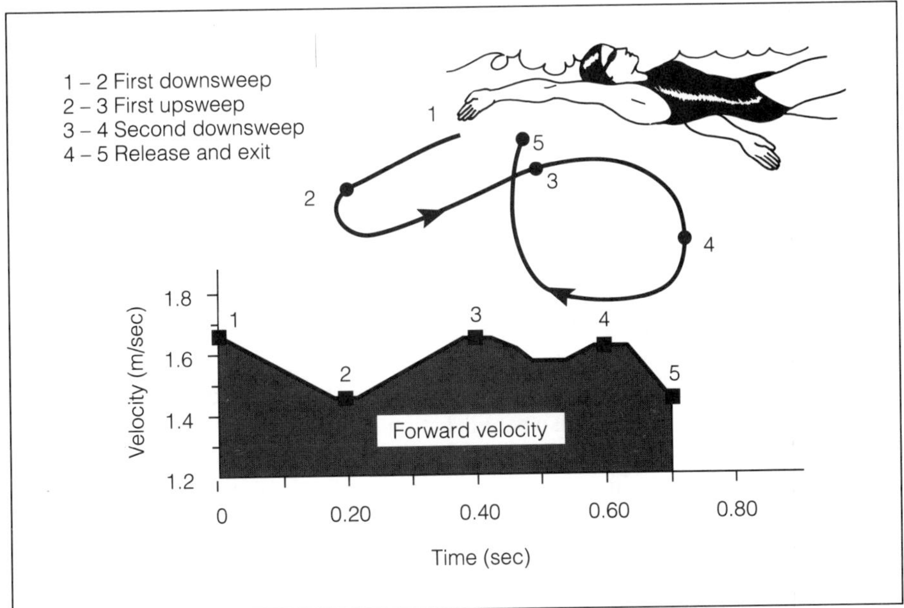

Figure 20-19. A two-peak velocity pattern for swimmer Theresa Andrews. Forward velocity is shown for her right armstroke only.

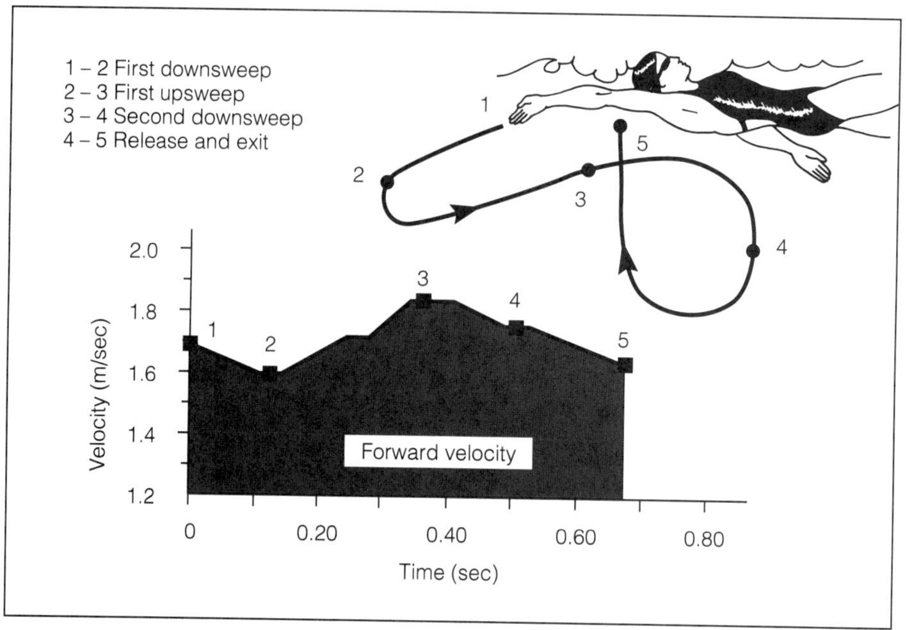

Figure 20-20. A one-peak velocity pattern for swimmer Tori Trees, 1984 Olympian in the 100-m backstroke.

velocity pattern begins when her right hand enters the water and ends when it leaves the water.

There is one major propulsive peak during the last portion of the first upsweep and the first portion of the second downsweep. Once again, there is no second upsweep phase. She goes from the second downsweep immediately into the release and exit phase.

This pattern, with minor variations, has been observed among a significant percentage (nearly 40 percent), of the U.S. Olympic swimmers studied in 1984 (Luedtke, 1986). It is typical of swimmers who use a shallow downsweep. Although their hand sweeps up and down somewhat, they tend to minimize movements in these directions and push their hand back to a much greater extent. They also do not change the angle of attack of their hand significantly once the catch is made. Essentially, one-peak swimmers *grab* a handful of water at the catch and fling it back toward their feet. The great amount of backward hand movement during the first upsweep and second downsweep direction in which their hand moves can be seen from the side-view stroke pattern at the top of Figure 20-20.

Although many swimmers have reached world class with this pattern, I believe that it is vastly inferior to the three-peak and two-peak patterns described earlier. The three-peak and two-peak patterns depend on sculling motions to a greater extent. Accordingly, they should be more efficient because swimmers should be able to accelerate more water back over a greater distance with less effort by making major changes in the directions and angles of attack of their hand two or three times during each underwater armstroke.

COMMON STROKE FAULTS

Armstroke Mistakes

First Downsweep Mistakes The most common mistake that swimmers make during this phase of the stroke is to attempt to apply force before their arm is deep enough and wide enough to make an effective catch. This mistake can take two forms: swimmers can (1) push water down or (2) push water to the side.

1. The deleterious effect of pushing water down is illustrated in Figure 20-21*a*. The shaded arrows represent the direction in which water is being moved by this swimmer. The solid arrow above the swimmer's head shows the direction in which his body will be moved. The shaded area on the stroke pattern in the inset shows the direction in which his arm is moving during this phase of the underwater stroke. That direction is also shown by the arrow above his hand. Pushing down on the water during the first downsweep will only push his body up and decelerate his forward speed. Swimmers who make this mistake usually bob up and down as each arm sweeps down.

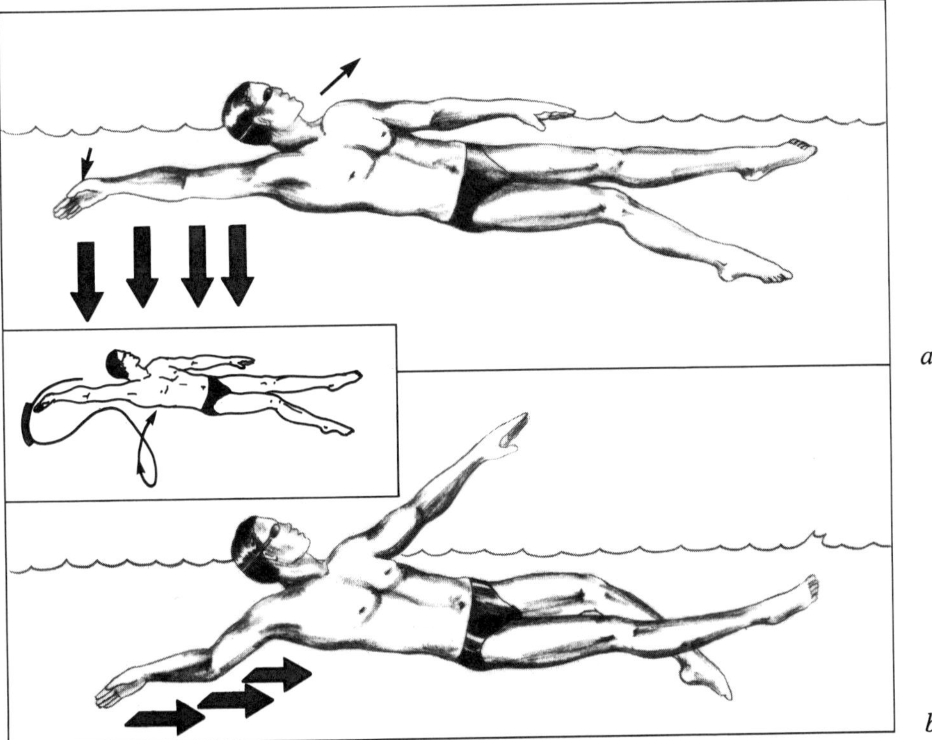

Figure 20-21. The effect of trying to apply force too early during the armstroke.

Figure 20-21*b* shows a swimmer who waits until his hand travels down sufficiently to achieve a backward orientation before attempting to apply force. As a result, he will displace water back in the direction of the arrows as he executes the second upsweep.

2. Swimmers who sweep their hand out to the side for a shallow catch can make a similar mistake. In this case, however, they push water to the side. Figure 20-22 illustrates this effect from an overhead view. In Figure 20-22*a*, the swimmer pushes out against the water while his arm and hand are moving to the side. As a result, he will displace water to the side, which will stall his forward speed and push his body out of lateral alignment. By contrast, the swimmer in Figure 20-22*b* waits until his arm has completed most of its outward movement before making the catch. You can see that his arm is facing back at this time so that he will be able to displace water back during subsequent sweeping motions.

Many swimmers find it difficult to wait until their arm has traveled down and out to the side before making a catch. They, understandably, get in a hurry when they feel the water building up around their arm during the recovery. Consequently, they start pushing against the water almost immediately when their hand enters. They flex their wrist immediately upon entry to get the palm of their hand facing back, giving them the mistaken impression that they are in position to push water

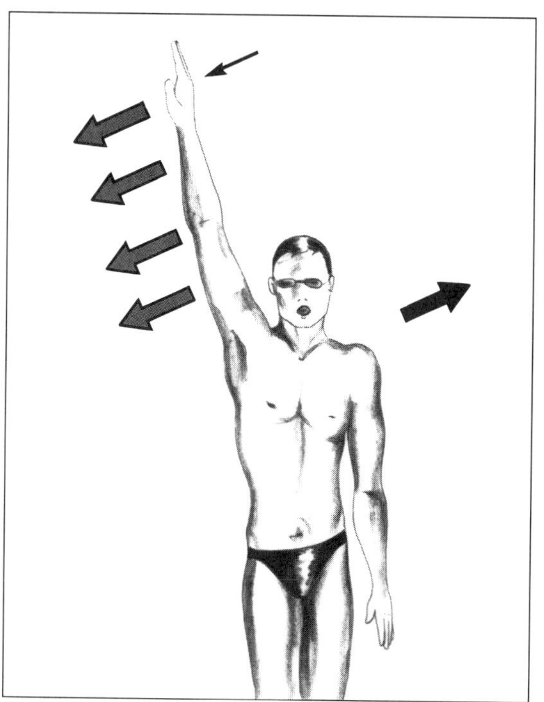

a

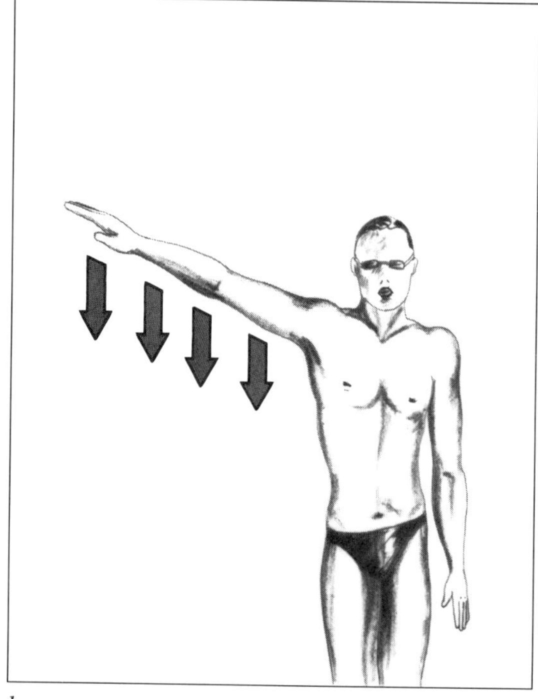

b

Figure 20-22. The effect of pushing water to the side during the first downsweep.

back. However, their hand and arm are actually traveling down and out at this time, so they can only push water in those directions with their arm in spite of the fact that their palm may be facing back. Before they try to apply force, backstroke swimmers must sweep their arm gently down and out to the side until the underside of their upper arm and forearm are facing back.

First Upsweep Mistakes The most common mistake that novice swimmers make in this phase of the armstroke is to keep their arm straight. This causes them to use their arm like an oar and push water to the side for a good portion of the motion. Swimmers must learn to bend their arm gradually throughout the first upsweep until it is flexed approximately 70 to 80 degrees at the elbow at the end of the movement.

The most common mistake that more experienced swimmers make is to fail to change the angle of attack of their hand. This results in an angle of attack that is very near zero degrees; thus, very little, if any, backward force is imparted to the water as swimmers sweep their hand up. Figure 20-23 shows a swimmer who is making this mistake. With his hand facing back at this slight angle of attack, the relative flow of water is not changed to any appreciable extent as it passes under his palm from the thumb to the little-finger sides.

Some swimmers commit the reverse of the mistake just described. That is, they rotate their palm up too much during the first upsweep. Figure 20-24 illustrates the effect of this error. This swimmer has his hand pitched up so much that it is nearly perpendicular to the direction in which it is moving. At this angle of attack, he will

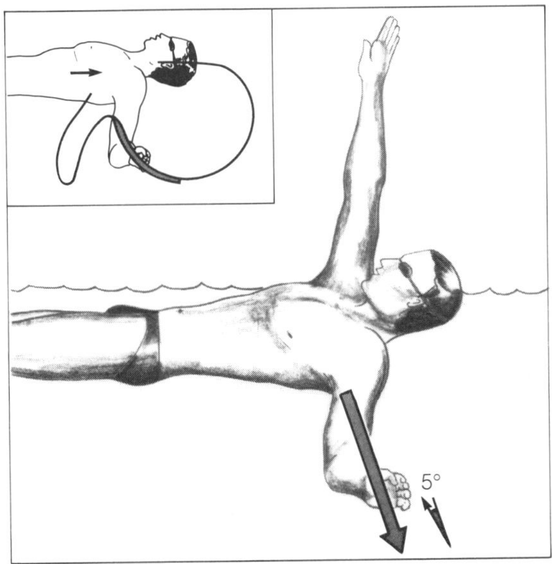

Figure 20-23. The effect of executing the first upsweep with a hand pitched near zero degrees to its direction of movement.

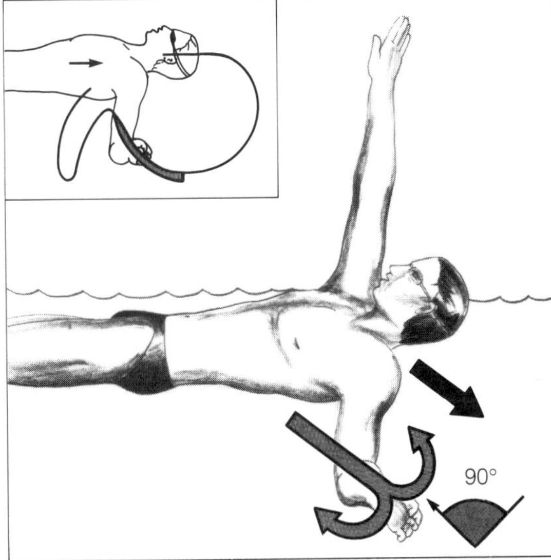

Figure 20-24. The effect of rotating the hand up too much during the first upsweep.

push water up with his hand until it becomes turbulent. Swimmers who make this mistake complain that their shoulder is being pulled down into the water when they sweep their hand up. They should have their hand facing back *and only slightly up* during this sweep. In addition, they should not change their hand from a downward to upward pitch until it passes their elbow on its way up.

Second Downsweep Mistakes The two most common mistakes have already been described. The first is for swimmers to sweep their hand back and in toward their thigh (see Figures 20-13*a* and 20-14*a*). The second is to perform the second downsweep with their fingertips pointing up.

Second Upsweep Mistakes Swimmers who use this phase of the armstroke for propulsion are prone to commit two mistakes. They may (1) pitch their hand up too much or (2) press against the water too long as their arm travels to the surface. Figure 20-25 illustrates the effects of both mistakes.

1. Most frequently, swimmers fail to hyperextend their hand sufficiently at the wrist and they sweep them up at too large an angle of attack, as shown by the

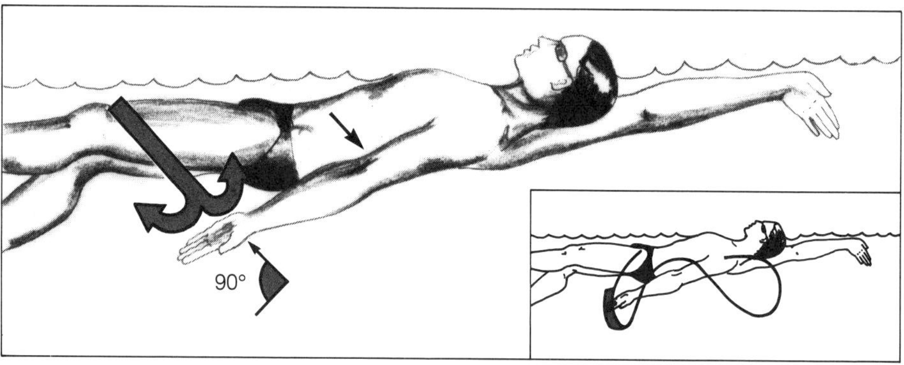

a

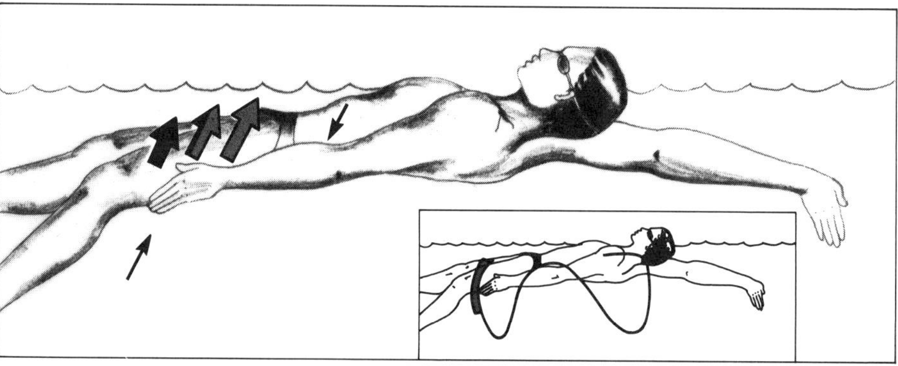

b

Figure 20-25. The effects of (*a*) pitching the hand up too much during the second upsweep and (*b*) continuing the motion for too long a distance.

swimmer in Figure 20-25*a*. With his palm almost perpendicular to the direction in which it is moving, water will be pushed up in the direction of the shaded arrow above his hand. In addition to sacrificing potential propulsion, the swimmer's hips will be submerged by this error, and his forward speed will be reduced.

2. The swimmer in Figure 20-25*b* is using the second upsweep over too long a distance. He is trying to apply propulsive force all the way to the surface of the water. This will be counterproductive because the backward inertia of the hand must be overcome during the second half of its trip to the surface so that it can begin moving forward into the recovery with no delay. This is done by completing the second upsweep in a curvilinear manner in which the hand begins moving forward as it passes the swimmer's leg. This circular direction change is shown in the stroke pattern inset at the bottom of this illustration. The hand will no longer be an effective propulsive agent when it starts moving forward because it cannot displace water in any direction but up. Backstrokers who use the second upsweep for propulsion should be cautioned to release pressure on the water and start the arm recovery when their hand nears the bottom portion of their thigh.

Release, Recovery, and Entry Mistakes There are two mistakes that are frequently seen during the release and exit of the hand from the water: (1) to bring the arm out of the water with the little finger up and the palm facing out and (2) to bring the hand out of the water with the palm facing down.

1. Turning the palm out will twist the humerus (the long bone of the upper arm) in its socket at the shoulder and cause unnecessary tension during the recovery. You can demonstrate this for yourself. Stand with your arm hanging down at your side with your palm facing in. Rotate your palm out and then lift it to the front until it is at shoulder height. You should feel a twisting motion that produces some tension in the shoulder. Now try lifting your arm overhead with your palm turned in. The tension should be gone.

The hand should leave the water thumb first. The first half of the arm recovery should be made with the swimmer's palm facing in, and the palm should not be turned out until the arm passes overhead.

2. When swimmers bring their hand out of the water with the palm facing down, there is a greater likelihood of increasing drag because they will be pushing up against the water with the broad surface of the back of their hand instead of its tapered edge.

Where the arm recovery is concerned, perhaps the most frequent mistake is to initiate it by lifting the hand from the water rather than rolling the shoulder up. Lifting the hand will submerge the shoulder on that side and cause the recovery to be made with more of the arm underwater for a longer period of time. This, of course, will increase wave drag as the arm pushes forward against the water.

The hand and arm should be relaxed after the release takes place and swimmers should allow their body roll to do as much of the work of bringing their arm over the water as possible. The recovery motion should be one of lifting and shrugging the shoulder, which will start the swimmer's arm moving forward over the water. With the body rolled to the side and the shoulder above the water, the swimmer's arm will remain clear of the water for a longer time during the recovery. In fact, the arm should not enter the water and push forward until it is almost in front of the shoulder.

Another common mistake during the recovery is to swing the arm low and to the side. The sideward movement of the arm will cause the hips to be pulled out in the same direction. This will, in turn, create a counterforce on the legs that will cause them to swing outside the body in the opposite direction. Consequently, the body will travel down the pool swinging from side to side and pushing water forward with the swinging legs. Backstroke arm recoveries should be made high and directly overhead with a minimum of sideward movement.

Some of the most common mistakes that swimmers make when they enter their hand into the water are (1) overreaching, (2) underreaching, (3) smashing the back of their hand down into the water, and (4) placing their fingertips in the water first.

1. When they overreach on the entry, swimmers swing their hand behind their head toward the other shoulder, which pulls their hips out of alignment in the opposite direction. (Figure 15-7 illustrated the effect of this mistake.)

2. When they underreach, backstroke swimmers put their hand in the water outside the shoulder on the same side. Swimmers were actually taught to put their arm into the water this way from 1930 to 1960. We realize now that entering the arm wide reduces the length of the propulsive phases of the armstroke.

To eliminate both underreaching and overreaching, swimmers should be coached to enter their hand somewhere between the middle of their head and the tip of the shoulder on the recovery side. A good teaching technique is to have swimmers imagine that they are lying on the face of a clock with their head pointing at twelve o'clock and their feet pointing at six o'clock. They then enter their right hand between eleven and twelve o'clock and their left hand between twelve and one o'clock.

3. Smashing the back of the hand into the water increases wave drag. The surface area presented to the water is considerably larger when the hand enters with the palm facing up rather than to the side. More water will be pushed forward, which will decelerate forward speed to a greater extent.

Figure 20-26 illustrates this mistake. The shaded area shows the wave drag produced by smashing the back of the hand into the water. Backstroke swimmers are best advised to slice their hand into the water on its side with the palm facing out so that a minimal surface area is presented to the water at entry.

4. The final mistake is usually made by novice swimmers, who try to enter their hand into the water before their arm. This is, no doubt, a carryover from the front crawl, in which a fingertips-first entry is desirable. It is not only undesirable in backstroke swimming, it is impossible to do without increasing drag and upsetting stroke rhythm. The swimmer in Figure 20-27 tries to enter his arm in this manner. He hyperextends his wrist and bends his arm in an attempt to place his hand into the water first. This awkward position causes him to push the palm of his hand forward against the water, which increases drag.

Swimmers who make this mistake usually display a hitch in their stroke. The hitch is a delay in beginning the first downsweep, which is caused by the need to

Figure 20-26. The effect of smashing the back of the hand into the water.

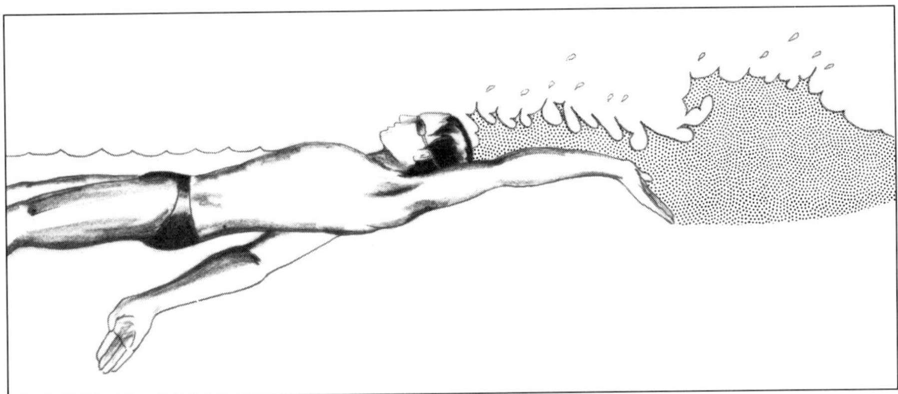

Figure 20-27. The effect of trying to place the hand into the water first during the entry.

straighten the arm and turn the palm out to the correct position so the first down-sweep can be performed.

This mistake usually occurs because swimmers fail to rotate toward the entering arm. They rotate too little or too late, so that their body is still inclined in the other direction when the arm is entering the water. Swimmers cannot turn the palm of their entering arm out if they remain rotated in the other direction, so they have no choice but to put their hand into the water with the palm facing up. Backstroke swimmers should be instructed to rotate toward the entering arm as it is traveling down for the entry.

Kicking Mistakes

The mistakes that swimmers make most often are (1) to pedal their legs and (2) to kick too deep. Additionally, (3) swimmers who cannot extend their feet and turn them in will not be fast kickers.

1. The detrimental effects of pedaling were described in Chapter 15 (see swimmer C in Figure 15-5). When swimmers' knees break the surface of the water during the kick, you can be sure that they are pedaling their legs. They push their thigh up and forward during the upbeat of the kick instead of extending it fully. In doing so, they exert a force that acts counter to their forward motion. They should be instructed to keep their knee underwater and to straighten their leg completely on the upbeat.

2. Figure 20-28 illustrates the effect of kicking too deep. The effect is an increase of form drag, because the cross-sectional area taken up by the body will increase due to the depth of the legs. The proper depth for the kick is approximately 45 cm (18 inches). Additionally, the thigh should not travel down below the hip during the downbeat. The lower leg may drop down below the body when the hip flexes on the upbeat, but this is not a stroke defect.

Swimmers who make this mistake tend to kick from the knee rather than from the hip and execute the downbeat of the kick with a flexed leg. The leg should be kept straight on the downbeat, and it should not bend until the pressure of the water above the leg forces it into a flexed position during the first portion of the next upbeat.

3. The same advice on ankle flexibility that was given in the previous two chapters applies to the kick in the backstroke. Swimmers should be able to extend

Figure 20-28. The effect on drag of kicking too deep.

their feet down and in at the ankles until they can move them through a range of 70 to 80 degrees from the vertical. This range is essential for fast kicking.

Body Position Mistakes

The most common mistakes are (1) swimming with the head too high and (2) piking excessively at the waist. A less common mistake is (3) swimming with the head pushed back into the water too deep.

1. Swimmers who hold their head too high generally have their body inclined down too much from head to feet so that form drag is increased. In addition, they need to use their arms and legs to support the high position of their head and, thus, increase form drag even more by pushing down with their arms during the first downsweep. They also kick too deep.

2. Frequently, these same athletes swim with their hips too low in the water because they pike excessively at the waist. This increases form drag. Figure 20-29 illustrates the effect of this mistake. The back crawl swimmer in Figure 20-29*b* has poor horizontal alignment, with her head too high and her hips too low. The swimmer in Figure 20-29*a* shows good horizontal alignment, with his body inclined down only slightly from head to hips. His kick works only through the effective propulsive range, without being excessively deep, and he maintains his head in a natural position, although it is flexed slightly at the neck. Consequently, he takes up less space in the water.

3. Some swimmers push their head back too deep in the water in a mistaken attempt to improve their horizontal alignment. This actually produces the opposite effect. They usually arch their back, thrusting their hips so near to the surface that their legs break through during the kick. In addition, they lose some sense of orientation because they are not able to see behind or to the side with their head in this position.

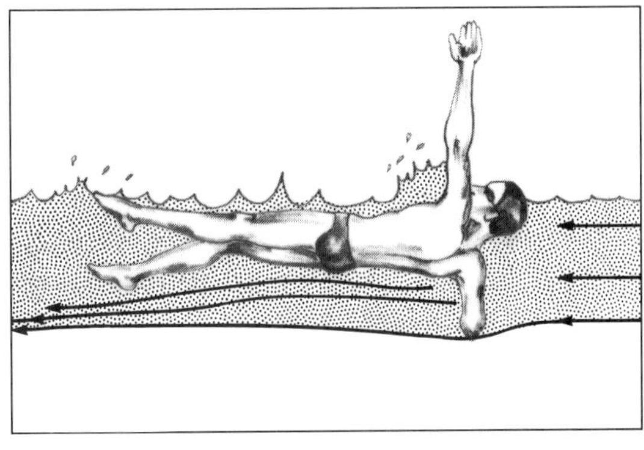

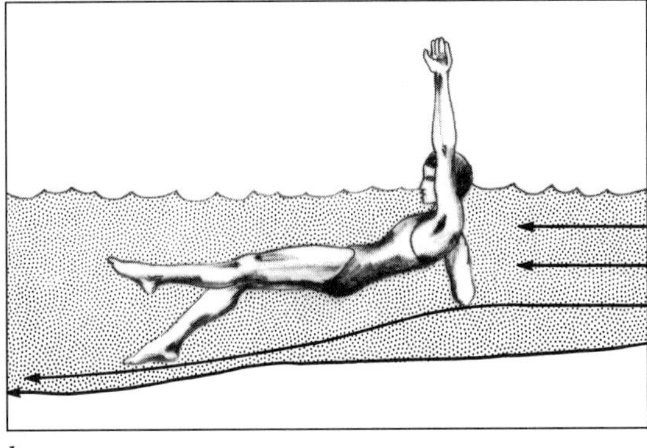

a *b*

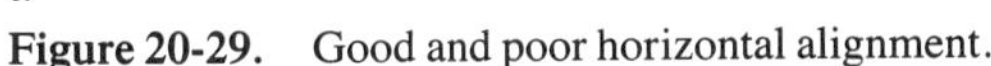

Figure 20-29. Good and poor horizontal alignment.

STROKE DRILLS

Armstroke Drills

Stroke Pattern Drill Tracing an *S* on its side is a good way to learn the arm directions for the underwater portion of the armstroke. Figure 20-30 illustrates a backstroke arm pattern that has been drawn relative to the swimmer's moving body. The *S* pattern is evident; however, an extra *tail* has been added to represent the second upsweep. This pattern could actually be likened more to the letter *W* than to an *S*.

The first curve corresponds to the first downsweep; the middle curve, to the first upsweep; the third curve, to the second downsweep; and the tail, to the second upsweep. Swimmers trace this pattern during their underwater armstrokes. Their palm should be facing in the direction it is moving during each portion of the stroke so that the correct angles of attack are used.

Sculling Drills The sweeps of the backstroke can be taught effectively by adapting the sculling drills that were described in Chapter 17.

Front sculling drill Figure 20-31 illustrates this drill. It is useful for teaching swimmers how to catch. This drill consists of a series of downward and upward sculling movements made in a continuous figure-eight pattern. The swimmer is shown at the completion of the downward scull in Figure 20-31*a*. Her hands are in nearly the same position they would reach at the catch. She is at the end of the scull up in Figure 20-31*b*. The drill can be done using the arms in an alternating or simultaneous manner.

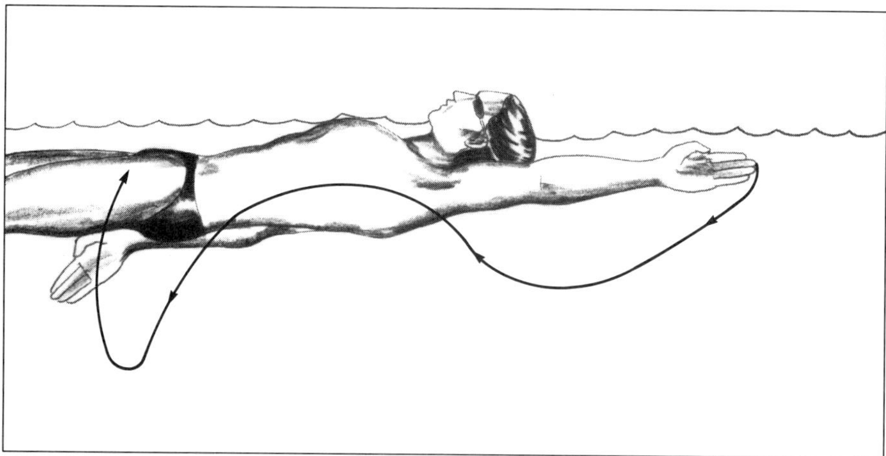

Figure 20-30. A stroke pattern for the backstroke drawn relative to the swimmer's moving body.

a

b

Figure 20-31. The front sculling drill for the backstroke.

a

b

Figure 20-32. The middle sculling drill for the backstroke.

The arms should extend somewhat but not completely on the scull down, and they should be flexed approximately 90 degrees on the scull up. The palms should rotate down approximately 30 degrees on the scull down, and they should rotate up about the same amount on the scull up. The leading edge of the hand should be the little-finger side on the scull down and the thumb side on the scull up.

Middle sculling drill This drill — illustrated in Figure 20-32 — combines elements of the first upsweep and the second downsweep. Swimmers scull up and down while keeping their hands between their shoulders and waist. Figure 20-32*a* shows the swimmer completing the scull up. She is sculling down in Figure 20-32*b*.

The elbows should be flexed and the hands should be near the surface of the water to begin the drill. The arms should flex at the elbows until they are almost at the surface of the water on the scull up, and they should extend until they are well below the body on the scull down. The fingertips should be pointing to the side for both the scull up and the scull down. The palms should be rotated down until they are facing the bottom of the pool at the end of the scull down, and they should be rotated up approximately 30 degrees on the scull up. The leading edges of the hand should be the little-finger sides on the scull down and the thumb sides on the scull up. The drill can be done using the arms alternately or simultaneously.

Rear sculling drill The purpose of this drill is to simulate the second downsweep and second upsweep. Swimmers scull their hands alternately down and up from a position near their waist. Figure 20-33*a* shows a swimmer at the midpoint of the scull down; Figure 20-33*b*, at the midpoint of the scull up.

Swimmers start in the same supine position, this time with their arms flexed slightly and their hands near the surface opposite their hips. From that position, swimmers scull their hands down, back, and out until they are completely extended below their thighs. They then scull their extended arms up and in toward the surface while maintaining a backward orientation with their palms. The scull up should be completed when their hands approach the rear of their thighs. Swimmers then flex their arms and bring them gently back toward their waist to begin the next scull down. Swimmers should not try to maintain propulsive force to the surface of the water on the scull up, as this will only push their body down.

The fingertips should be pointed to the side and the palms should rotate down until they are facing the bottom of the pool at the completion of the scull down. The little-finger sides are the leading edges and the thumb sides the trailing edges.

The hands should be hyperextended at the wrists and the palms facing back on the scull up. Figure 20-33*b* shows the position of the hands during the scull up. The wrists (or perhaps the elbows) are the leading edges of the arm-foils on the scull up, and the fingertips are the trailing edge.

Transition sculling drill The three sculling drills that were just described can be combined into a drill that will help swimmers make the transition from drills to

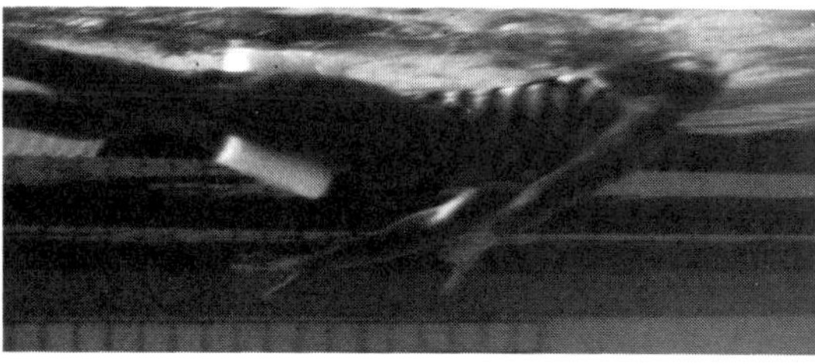

a

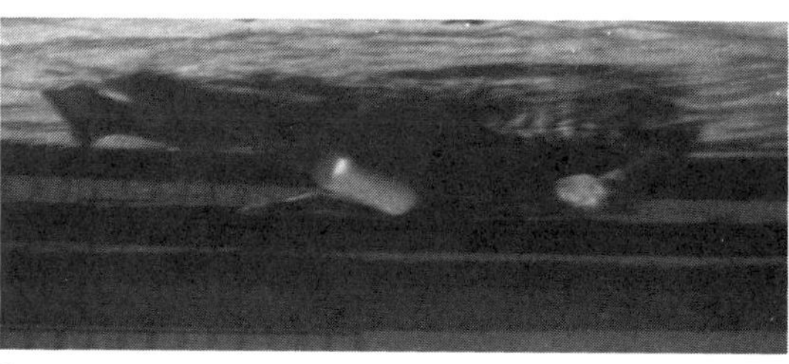

b

Figure 20-33. The rear sculling drill for the backstroke.

full-stroke swimming. It is a form of the elementary backstroke in which swimmers keep their hands underwater while they pull. Their legs should be supported by a pull buoy. Starting with a front scull, swimmers perform each of the three sculls in succession before recovering their arms (underwater) back to the front-sculling position to begin another cycle. The drill can be performed using the arms simultaneously or alternately.

One-Arm Swimming Drill Athletes swim repeats, stroking with one arm while keeping the other arm at their side. This is a good drill for the armstroke because swimmers can concentrate on the movements of one arm at a time.

It is also a good drill to teach swimmers to roll their body properly. After their arm enters the water, swimmers should roll their body toward it until the opposite shoulder *pops* up out of the water. They then roll toward the opposite side during the second downsweep and second upsweep until the shoulder of the stroking arm breaks the surface. The drill can be done as a pulling drill or a full-stroke drill.

Alternate-Arm Sidestroke Drill This drill helps swimmers learn to catch properly. Athletes swim down the pool, rolling from side to side while stroking alternately with the right and left arms. The arms remain underwater throughout the drill. Swimmers start on their right side, with their right arm extended overhead and underwater and the left arm back at their side. They slide their right arm down and out until they get the water behind it, and then they execute an underwater armstroke. They remain on their side facing toward the stroking arm during the first upsweep. After that, they rotate toward the other side while they complete the final two sweeps. In the meantime, they should slide the other arm forward underwater until it is extended overhead, after which they complete an identical stroke with it. Swimmers continue rolling from side to side, alternating armstrokes for any specified distance. This drill can be done with arms only or while kicking.

Half-Sidestroke Drill This drill helps swimmers learn to use the first upsweep of their underwater armstroke. Swimmers lie on their side with one arm stretched overhead and the other back at their side in a position similar to the glide position of the sidestroke. They then take a half-stroke by sweeping the arm that is overhead down and out to the catch and then up toward the surface. The movement is very much like the stroke of the forward arm in the sidestroke. When that arm nears the surface, it is recovered underwater and back to the starting position before executing another half-stroke. The arm should stroke continuously, with swimmers taking any specified number of strokes on one side before changing sides.

Finish Drill This drill is used to develop the second downsweep and second upsweep of the underwater armstroke. Swimmers lie on their back with both arms at their sides. All arm recoveries are made underwater as in the previous two drills. Swimmers slide the hand up opposite their chest and then sweep it down and up as they would when finishing the second downsweep and the second upsweep. The drill can be performed with the arms stroking alternately or simultaneously.

Second Upsweep Drill Athletes should swim down the pool on their back, with their arms extended at their sides and underwater. They scull the hand in and up as they would when executing the second upsweep and then return it to the starting position to repeat the motion in a continuous manner. The drill can be done using both hands simultaneously, or it can be done using the hands alternately to incorporate some body roll.

One-Fist Swimming Drill Swimming with the hand of the dominant arm in a fist encourages swimmers to use their nondominant arm more effectively in this stroke just as it did in the front crawl and butterfly.

Recovery Drills

Hesitation Drill Athletes swim a normal backstroke, with one exception: they stop their arm for an instant at the top of the recovery and turn their palm from in to out once or for any specified number of times before completing the recovery. Swimmers should concentrate on stopping their arm straight above their shoulder so that they turn their palm out at the proper time. The purpose of this drill is to teach a vertical recovery with a clean entry.

Double-Arm Backstroke Drill This drill is for swimmers who tend to overreach. They should swim backstroke while stroking simultaneously with both arms. It is impossible to overreach when swimmers recover their arms in this manner. Therefore, this drill may teach them the *feeling* of placing their arms in the water directly forward of their shoulders. It is also an excellent drill for teaching swimmers to use the four sweeps properly.

In-Out Drill This drill is useful for swimmers who recover their arms too low and laterally. It combats the tendency to swing the arm out during the first half of the recovery and in during the second half. In this drill, swimmers recover their arm up and in during the first half of the recovery and swing it out as it passes overhead and down for the entry.

Lane Swimming Drill This is another good drill for teaching a vertical recovery. Athletes swim down the pool with one shoulder next to the lane line. This forces them to recover that arm vertically, because it will get caught under the lane if they try to swing it to the side as it is leaving the water. Athletes should swim up and down the same side of the lane so that they can practice the drill with their left and right arms on alternate lengths.

Kicking and Body Position Drills

Side Kicking Drill Kicking on the side with one arm overhead and one arm at the side is an excellent way to improve diagonal kicking and body rotation. Swimmers should practice this drill with their body rotated toward the arm that is

Figure 20-34. The side kicking drill. The swimmer is Ondrej Bures, NCAA Division II record holder in three events.

stretched overhead. Figure 20-34 illustrates this drill. Swimmers should complete six, eight, ten, or any specified number of kicks in this position before changing sides.

Back Kicking Drill This drill is good for improving kicking endurance and power. It is also excellent for teaching swimmers to maintain a horizontal body position. The drill can be done with the arms at the sides or overhead. Kicking with the arms at the sides is easier and can be used with novice backstroke swimmers and those who have extremely weak kicks. Kicking with arms at the sides can also be good for improving body position if swimmers roll their shoulders from side to side as they kick.

Kicking with the arms overhead is more difficult. However, it helps swimmers to maintain a more horizontal body position, particularly if they tend to "sit" too deep in the water. Their arms should be stretched overhead and underwater, with their palms up and fingers interlocked while they kick.

One-Hand-Out Drill Swimmers kick down the pool on their side with one arm out of the water and directly above their shoulder. The other arm should be underwater at their side. Swimmers should roll toward the arm at their side. They can change sides after any specified number of kicks. This drill is excellent for improving the endurance and power of the flutter kick, because the kick must support the weight of the arm that is overhead.

Board Kicking Drill This is a good drill to correct a pedaling motion in the kick. Swimmers kick while holding a board lengthwise over their thighs. If the board bounces, they are pedaling and hitting it with their thighs and knees. The board will lie quietly if swimmers are kicking correctly. Figure 20-35 shows this drill.

Sponge Drill This drill is used for training backstroke swimmers to keep their head still. Swimmers place a small sponge on their forehead and swim down the pool while trying to keep the sponge from falling off. Swimmers can use coins or diving rings if a sponge is not available; however, diving bricks are not recommended.

Figure 20-35. The board kicking drill.

Dolphin Kicking Drills Swimmers who plan to dolphin kick on their back during a portion of their races need to learn the correct technique, and they need to train themselves to stay submerged for as much of the 15 m allowed per pool length as possible. Doing some backstroke kicking drills with the dolphin kick is an excellent way to develop the technique.

25, 50, and 75 sprints underwater These sprints are excellent for training swimmers to stay submerged. Performing them with fins is another excellent technique drill. Ten to twelve 25s, six to eight 50s, and three to four 75s are ideal for this purpose. The rest periods between repeats should be one to five minutes to allow swimmers sufficient recovery time to complete succeeding sprints with good quality.

Repeats combining dolphin and flutter kicking Repeats of any distance can be done in which swimmers dolphin kick for 15 m of each length and then come to the surface to use the flutter kick for the remainder of the pool length. It goes without saying that swimmers who plan to use the dolphin kick in races should train themselves to use it for the allowable distance in all of their practice swimming repeats.

CHAPTER 21

Breaststroke

The breaststroke has a rich competitive history. It was the first stroke used in competition after the Dark Ages, and all of the other strokes developed from it. At one time, the rules permitted swimmers to race underwater in breaststroke events, but that proved to be dangerous, as many athletes passed out from trying to stay underwater too long. The rules were changed in the late 1950s to ensure that most of the race was swum on the surface. Presently, swimmers are only allowed to stay underwater during one stroke cycle after the start and after each turn. After that, some part of their body, usually their head, must appear above the normal flat surface of the water once during each stroke cycle.

Breaststroke swimmers use a short semicircular armstroke and a kick that goes by various names, although it is most commonly called a *whip kick*. The breaststroke is the slowest of the competitive strokes. Although breaststrokers generate large forces during the propulsive phases of each stroke cycle, they also decelerate markedly each time they recover their legs to kick. This reduces their average velocity per stroke considerably below that of swimmers in the other styles. These huge intracyclic variations in forward velocity make the breaststroke the most rigorous of the competitive strokes.

Until recently, most experts believed that the breaststroke should be swum with a *flat* body position. An undulating style was introduced in the 1970s that involved moving the body in a dolphin motion somewhat like the butterfly. It is called by many names, including the *dolphin breaststroke* and the *European breaststroke*. The most common term at present is the *wave breaststroke*. This style was slow to catch on. However, the rule change that permitted swimmers to drop their head underwater during portions of each stroke cycle has accelerated its adoption. Because swimmers can lower their head between their arms, they can improve their streamlining during the kick phase of the stroke cycle. What they have also found is that they can reduce deceleration by elevating their head and trunk as they recover their legs. The first topic for this chapter is a comparison of the wave style and the flat style. After that, the mechanics of the stroke are discussed under the same headings that were used in the previous three chapters.

FLAT STYLE AND WAVE STYLE COMPARED

Figure 21-1 contrasts these two styles of breaststroke. The flat style is shown on the left and the wave style on the right. The flat style of breaststroke is characterized by a very horizontal body position, with the hips remaining at or near the surface throughout the stroke cycle. Breathing is accomplished by lifting and lowering the head so that the flat position of the trunk is not disturbed. In the wave style, the head *and shoulders* come up out of the water when swimmers breathe and the hips are lowered during the leg recovery.

The major differences between the two styles can be seen in Figures 21-1*c* and 21-1*d*. The flat-style breaststroker remains horizontal during the time he recovers his legs. His shoulders remain underwater, and his hips remain near the surface. By contrast, the shoulders of the wave-style breaststroker are out of the water, his hips are down, and his body is inclined down from shoulders to knees. Body positions are very similar for the two styles in all other phases of the stroke. Both swimmers remain very horizontal and streamlined during the propulsive phase of their armstrokes (see Figures 21-1*a* and 21-1*b*). They are also similar during the propulsive phase of their kicks (see Figure 21-1*e* of each style). The only other difference between the two can be seen in Figure 21-1*f* of each style. Wave-style breaststrokers tend to press their hips up slightly more at the end of the kick.

Proponents of the flat style argue that form drag is reduced and less energy is used because swimmers don't make extraneous movements up and down. This argument is open to question. Instead of creating more resistance to motion, form drag is probably reduced significantly when swimmers lower their hips because they can recover their lower legs without pushing their thighs forward against the water.

Figure 21-2 illustrates why this may be true. The swimmer in Figure 21-2*a* probably encounters more drag because he pushes his thighs down and forward against the water during his leg recovery. Velocity measurements of many flat-style breaststrokers have shown that their forward speed decelerates markedly when they recover their legs in this manner. This deceleration is depicted by the large valley at the end of the leg recovery in Figure 21-2*a*.

The swimmer in Figure 21-2*b* lowers his hips when he recovers his legs, and he raises his lower legs forward without pushing his thighs down. Because the lower legs are smaller and move forward behind the swimmer's trunk, they should not produce nearly as much drag as his larger thighs. Consequently, his velocity graph shows that he decelerates less and for a shorter period of time. Notice that the swimmer in Figure 21-2*a* decelerates to a low velocity of 0.20 m/sec and that the

Figure 21-1. A comparison of the flat style and the wave style of breaststroke.

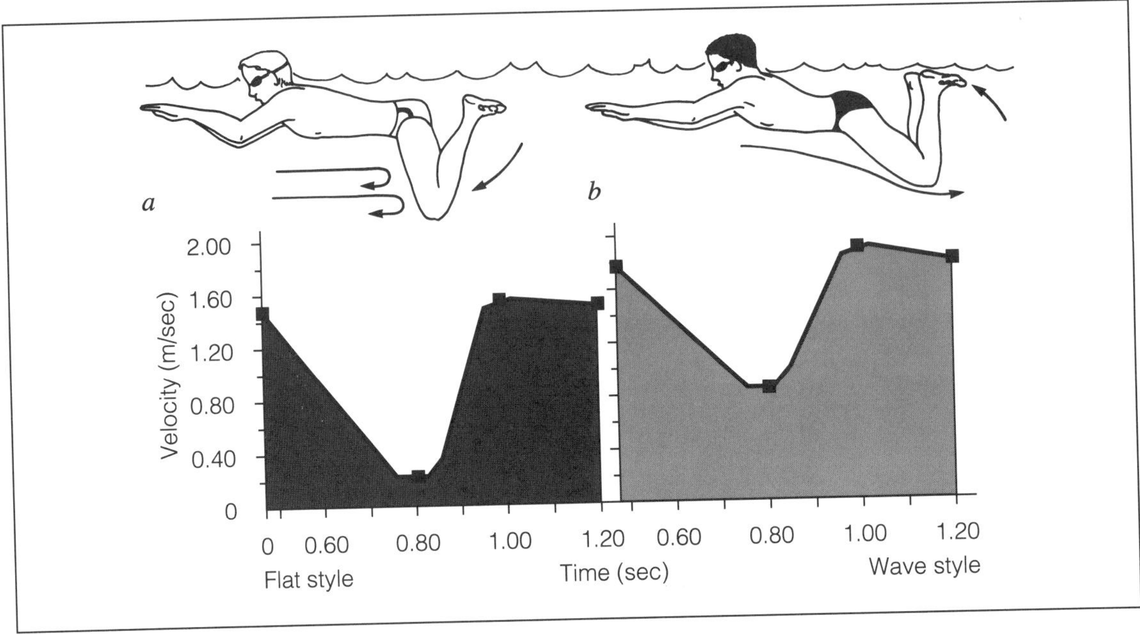

Figure 21-2. A comparison of resistive drag produced by the leg recoveries in the flat style (*a*) and the wave style (*b*) of breaststroke. Both swimmers are shown at the same point in the stroke cycle.

swimmer in Figure 21-2*b* decelerates to only 0.80 m/sec. When swimmers decelerate less during their leg recovery, their subsequent propulsive efforts should accelerate their body to faster speeds. This is illustrated by the higher velocities for the wave-style swimmer during the propulsive phase of his kick.

A second reason why the wave-style swimmer should encounter less drag is because he maintains a tapered shape with his trunk and legs during the leg recovery. His body is inclined down slightly from head to knees so that the flow of water can change directions gradually as it passes under his body. This is indicated by the arrow under the swimmer's body depicting the direction of water flow. The head and shoulders must be raised to lower the hips and achieve this tapered body position, which may explain why many skilled breaststrokers bring their shoulders out of the water when they recover their legs.

You may be thinking that swimmers could reduce resistive drag even more by remaining horizontal like the flat-style breaststroker and by recovering their legs with a minimum amount of hip flexion like the wave-style swimmer. This compromise is not possible. The feet of the wave-style swimmer would come out of the water if he tried to recover his legs while remaining flat. If the hips remain near the surface, breaststrokers cannot keep their feet underwater as they recover their legs *unless* they push their thighs down and forward. This can be seen by the fact that the thighs of the flat-style breaststroker in Figure 21-2*a* are almost perpendicular to his trunk. Wave-style breaststrokers, like the one in Figure 21-2*b*, are able to keep their feet underwater without pushing their thighs down and forward because they lower their hips. Contrary to popular belief, swimmers who recover their legs by lowering their hips do not drop their knees deeper into the water.

Another important reason why the wave style may be superior is because the upward movements of swimmers' shoulders are probably essential to a propulsive armstroke. The propulsive phase of the breaststroke armstroke is similar to the insweep of the butterfly, which is a large semicircular sweep *down* and in under the body. The swimmer in Figure 21-3*a* shows how propulsion is produced during the downward portion of that sweep. The angle of attack of the hands that imparts the most backward force to the water will also have a considerable drag component, as shown by the vector diagram. This drag force lifts the swimmer's shoulders up while the propulsive component accelerates his body forward. If the drag force were reduced, the propulsive force would also be reduced. This is shown in Figure 21-3*b*. This swimmer's hands are pitched at a very small angle of attack to the direction in which they are moving. Consequently, both the propulsive force and drag force will be reduced, because the water passes under his palm without changing direction to any great extent. This swimmer's shoulders will not rise, but neither will his body accelerate forward very much.

It seems, then, that the rise of the shoulders is a by-product of a propulsive insweep and should be encouraged rather than discouraged. Conversely, swimmers who keep their shoulders level during this part of the armstroke probably lose some propulsive force.

The final reason in favor of the wave style has to do with the possible propulsive effects of body undulation. The undulating movements of a wave-style breast-

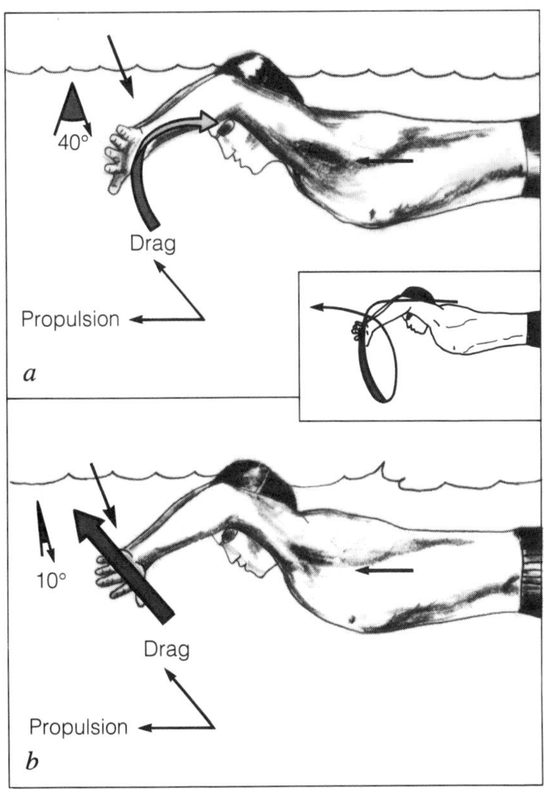

Figure 21-3. The effect of the hands' angle of attack on the upward movement of swimmers' shoulders during the wave style (*a*) and the flat style (*b*).

stroker's body may, as in butterfly, add to the total amount of propulsive force it can produce during each stroke cycle. This contribution to propulsive force during breaststroke swimming was described in Chapter 17 (see Figure 17-21). Swimmers may trap some water in the region of their hips when they pike slightly at the end of the kick and accelerate it back as they come down out of the piked position during the armstroke.

Swimmers should realize that the undulating motions of the wave style can be overdone. Effort will be wasted if they raise their head and trunk *excessively* high out of the water when they breathe, and drag will be increased if they *pump* their hips up and down like a butterflyer. Body undulation should be a by-product of the correct armstroke and kick. It should be sufficient to maximize propulsion without being excessive. The following guidelines should provide some help in determining if swimmers are undulating too much.

1. Undulation is excessive when the head and shoulders go up and down more than forward. The trunk should never be arching back when swimmers come out of the water.

2. Undulation is excessive if the hips rise more than a few inches above the surface of the water as swimmers kick. The downward sweeps of the legs should push the hips up to or slightly above the surface, but no more than this.

3. Undulation is excessive if the hands and head go more than a few inches underwater as the arms stretch forward. Swimmers who *dive* their hands and head down too deep will waste time and energy bringing them back to the surface. Swimmers should drop their head only slightly below the surface, and they should extend their arms only slightly down so that both are in line with the inclination of their trunk and legs. Figure 21-4 shows a wave-style breaststroker who is undulating correctly.

ARMSTROKE

Sequence photographs of the breaststroke armstroke are shown from a front view in Figure 21-5 (pp. 498–499) and from an underneath view in Figure 21-6 (pp. 500–501). The armstroke consists of an outsweep, insweep, and recovery. The insweep is the only propulsive phase of the armstroke.

Outsweep

Figures 21-5*a* through 21-5*c* and Figures 21-6*a* and 21-6*b* show the outsweep. This sweep is not propulsive. Its main purpose is to place the arms in position to produce propulsive force during the insweep that follows.

The outsweep begins by moving the arms out and forward when they near complete extension at the end of the recovery. The arms trace a semicircular path, sweeping out, forward, and slightly up until they pass outside the shoulders. There, they start circling down to make the catch. The catch position is shown in Figure 21-5*c* and Figure 21-6*b*. The arms should flex 30 to 40 degrees at the elbow during the latter portion of the outsweep so that the arms and hands can achieve a backward

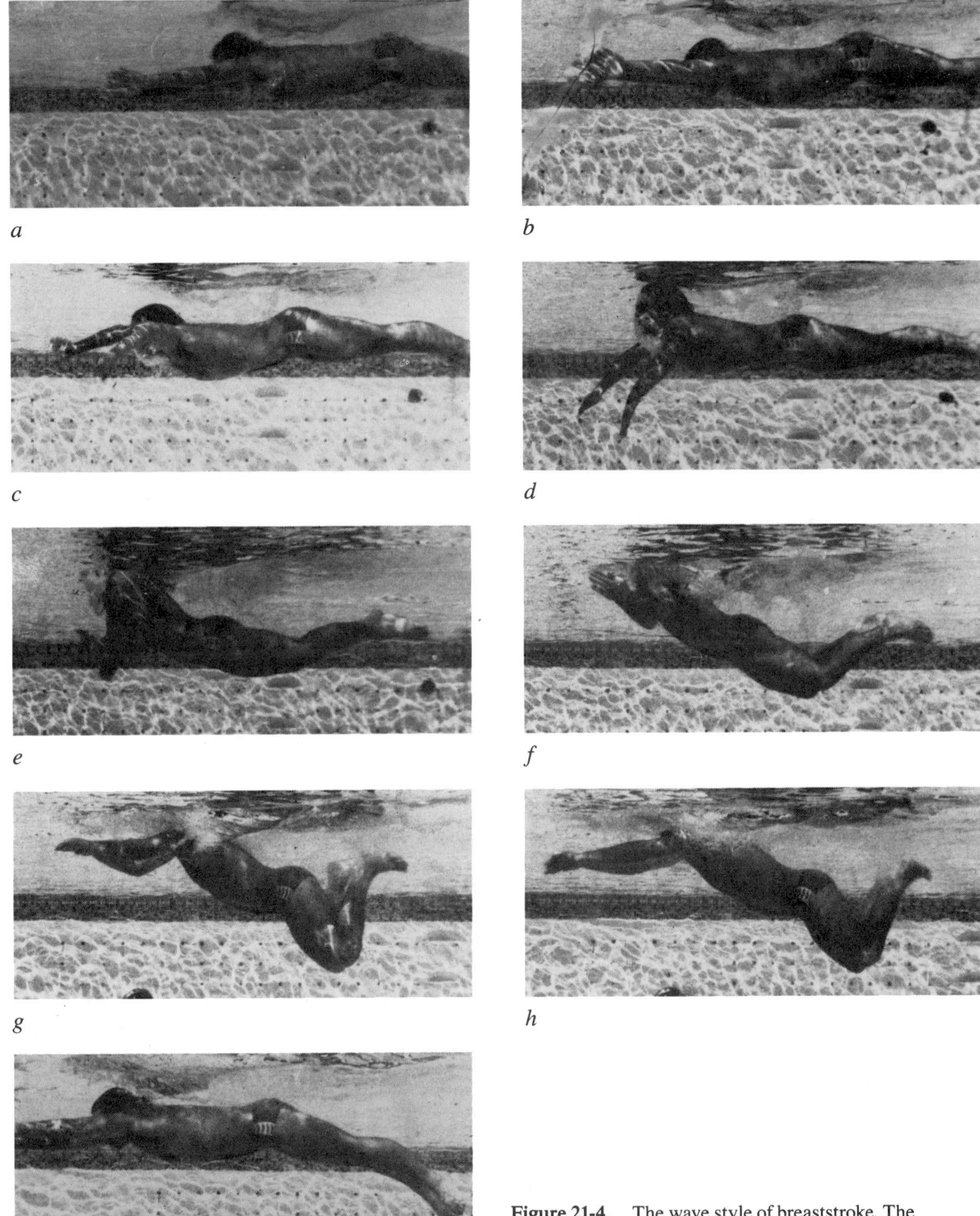

Figure 21-4. The wave style of breaststroke. The swimmer is Jim Johnson, former NCAA All-American and former Masters national record holder in the breaststroke.

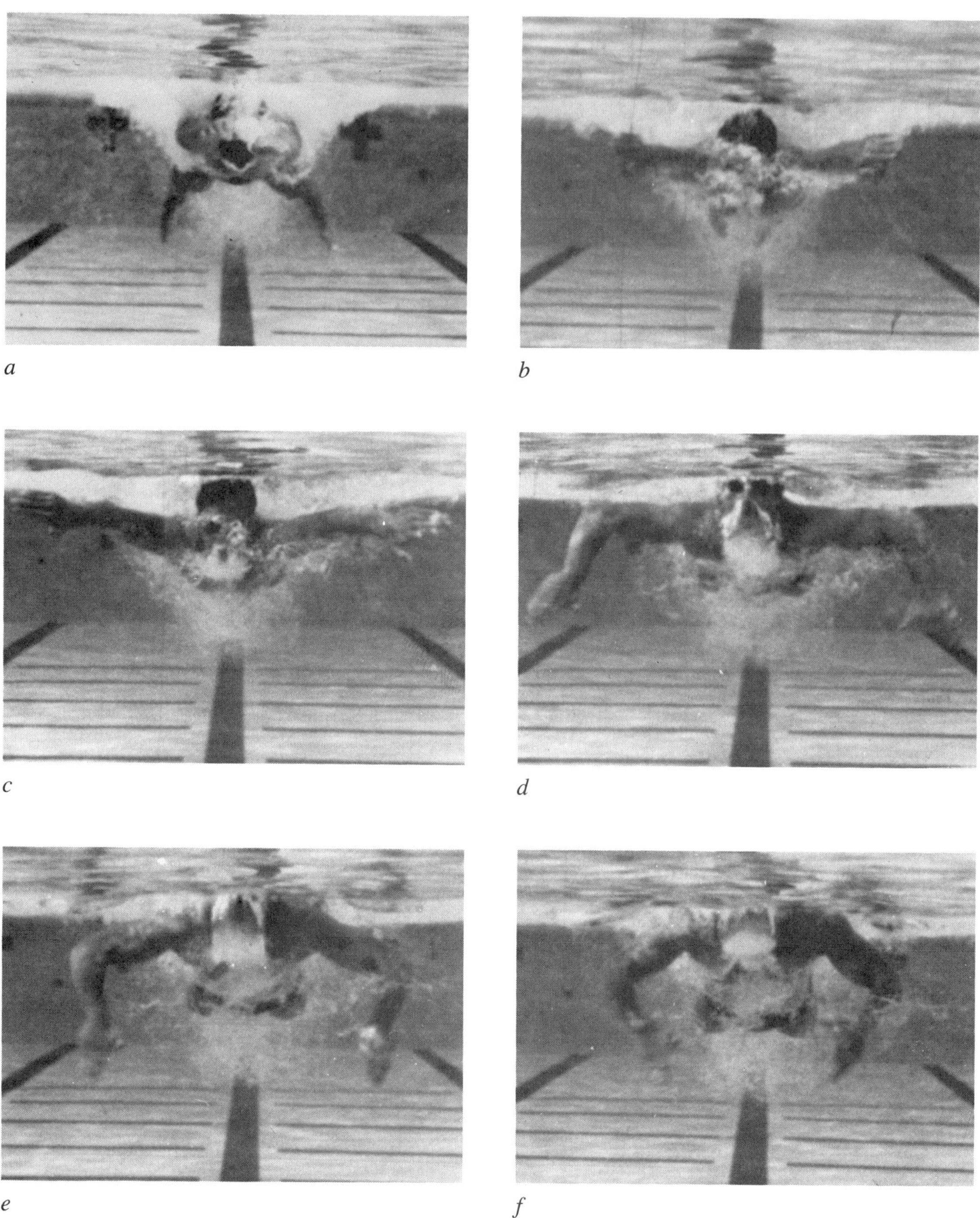

a *b* *c* *d* *e* *f*

Figure 21-5. A front view of the breaststroke. The swimmer is Roque Santos, who is world ranked in the breaststroke events.

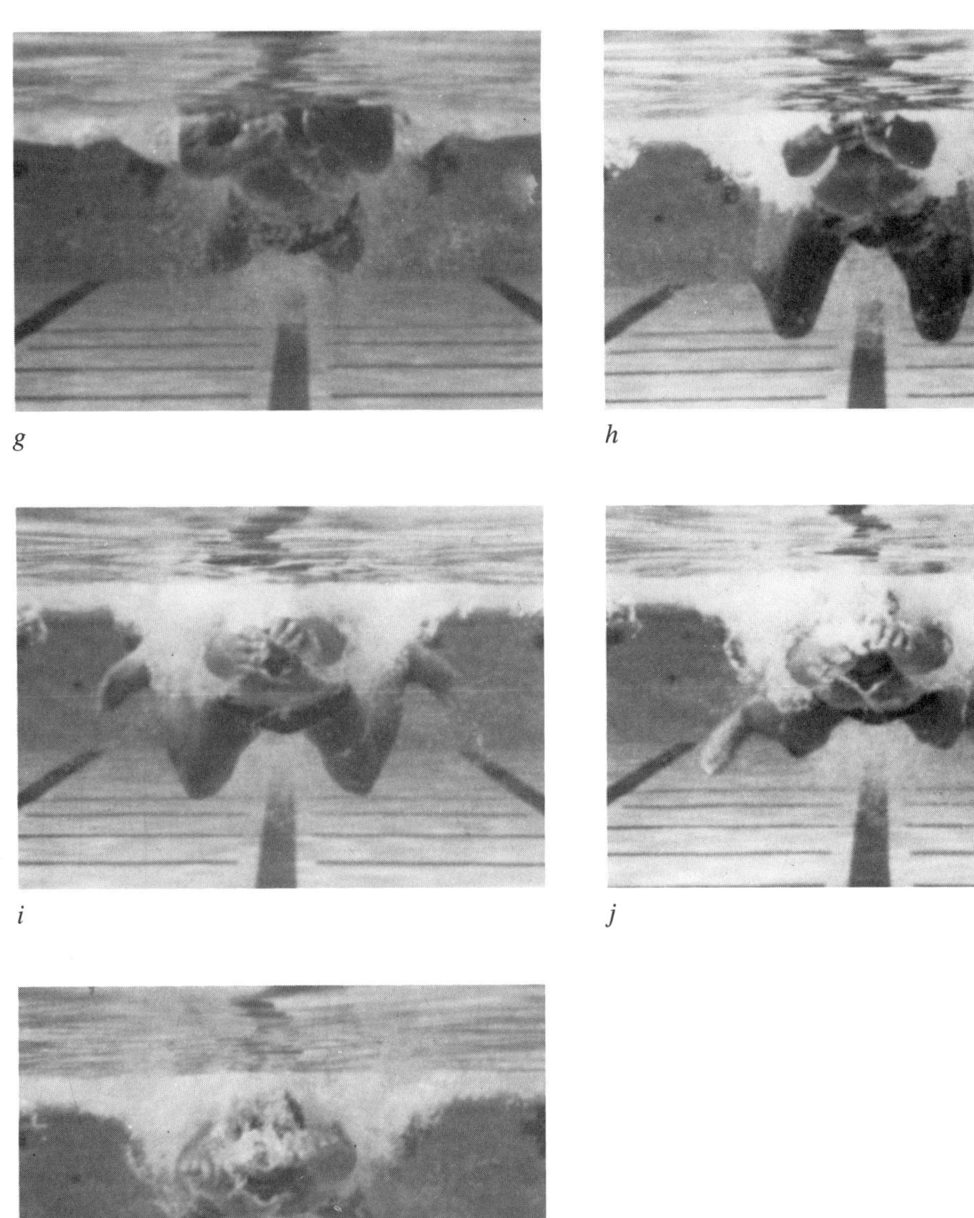

g h i j k

Figure 21-6. An underneath view of Roque Santos's breaststroke armstroke.

orientation at the catch. They must sweep out and down about 50 to 80 cm (20 to 30 inches) before attaining this orientation.

The palms are face down when the outsweep begins and rotate slowly out until they travel outside the shoulders and start down for the catch. They travel on edge, with the little fingers leading so that a smaller surface area (and, consequently, less resistance) is presented to the water. The hands should rotate out as they start down

g

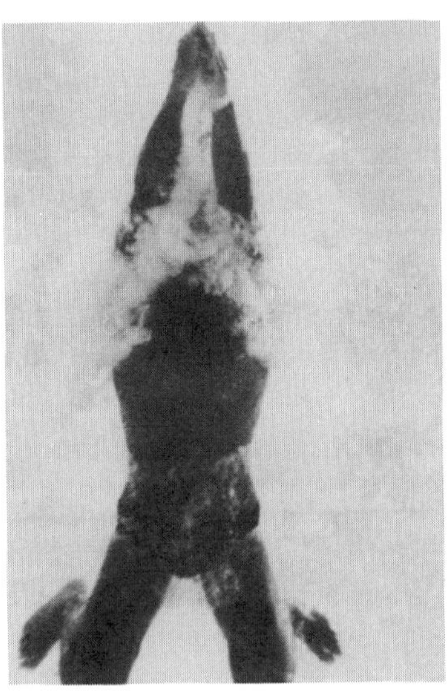
h

i

so that they are pitched out and back when the catch is made. Although swimmers may flex their wrists during the early portion of the outsweep, their hands and forearms should be aligned when the catch is made (see Figure 21-6*b*).

The hands will be traveling somewhat faster than the body during the transition from recovery to outsweep but will gradually decelerate during the outsweep until they are being pushed forward by the swimmer's body at the catch. The outsweep ends and the insweep begins when the swimmer's hands reach the catch.

Insweep

As mentioned, the insweep is *the* propulsive phase of the armstroke. It is pictured in Figures 21-5*c* through 21-5*f* and Figures 21-6*b* through 21-6*e*.

Once the catch is made, the arms move in a large semicircular sweep out, back, down, and in. The elbows remain high, and the hands and forearms rotate down and in around them. The insweep ends as the hands are coming together under the chest (see Figure 21-5*f* and Figure 21-6*e*). The arms gradually bend at the elbows throughout the insweep until they are flexed approximately 80 degrees when the movement ends. The palms, which were facing out at the catch, gradually rotate in throughout the insweep until they are facing in and back at its completion. As in the butterfly, the insweep of this stroke will be more propulsive if the hands remain facing out until they pass under the elbows. The point where hand pitch should change from in to out is shown in Figure 21-5*e* and Figure 21-6*d*.

After passing under the elbows, the hands continue rotating in until the insweep is completed. The hands should remain in line with the forearms throughout the insweep, and they should accelerate steadily throughout the movement, reaching their peak velocity just before the insweep ends.

Although the insweep feels like one continuous sweep, like the corresponding movement in the butterfly, it has two phases of propulsion: a downward and an inward phase. Figure 21-3*a* showed how water can be accelerated back during the first portion of the insweep. Figure 21-7 shows how water can be displaced back during the inward portion of the insweep.

In Figure 21-3*a*, the thumb sides of the hands were the leading edges and the little-finger sides the trailing edges as the hands swept down and back. They were pitched down slightly, causing the flow of water (which was up and forward when it met the leading edge) to be displaced back and to accelerate the swimmer forward, as the water traveled under the palms toward the trailing edge.

Figure 21-7 displays an underneath view of a swimmer who sweeps his hands back and in across the water during the second phase of the insweep. His hands are pitched in at an angle of attack of approximately 30 degrees. The leading edges of his hands are, once again, the thumb sides, and the little-finger sides are the trailing edges. The shaded arrows representing the relative direction of water flow show how this combination of direction and angle of attack can impart a backward force to the water traveling under his palms.

The hands will accelerate to their greatest extent during the insweep, often reaching velocities of 5 and 6 m/sec (15 to 20 ft/sec) during this phase of the armstroke. The insweep ends when the hands begin moving up and forward.

Recovery

Figures 21-5*f* through 21-5*k* and Figures 21-6*e* through 21-6*h* illustrate the recovery. It is one of the most controversial phases of the stroke cycle.

The recovery of the arms begins when the hands are approximately halfway through their inward motion (see Figure 21-5*f* and Figure 21-6*e*). They begin moving up and forward at that time, and no more propulsion can be gained from

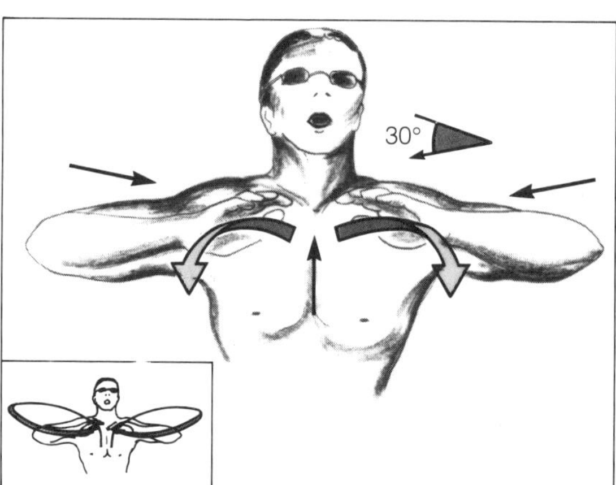

Figure 21-7. An underneath view of a breaststroke swimmer showing how water can be accelerated back during the second portion of the insweep.

them. Swimmers should release pressure on the water and *squeeze their arms down and in under their shoulders*. The elbow squeeze overcomes the backward inertia of the hands and starts them moving forward into the recovery. The hands should continue moving up and forward until they are near the surface in front of the face (see Figure 21-5*g* and Figure 21-6*f*). Once they near the surface, they are pushed forward just above or just below the surface of the water until the arms are almost completely extended (see Figures 21-5*h* through 21-5*j* and Figures 21-6*g* and 21-6*h*). At that point, the forward inertia of the hands is overcome as the arms complete their extension and start moving out into the next outsweep (see Figure 21-5*k* and Figure 21-6*i*). This reduces the muscular effort required to get the hands moving out as the outsweep begins.

The palms should rotate in and up and the elbows should come close together underneath the body as the hands travel toward the surface. The palms should be rotated down and the elbows should be held close together so that the arms form the shape of an arrow as they extend forward (see Figure 21-6*h*). Hand speed should remain fairly rapid throughout the recovery. However, that speed should decelerate as the arms start out.

Unique Aspects of the Recovery Some breaststroke swimmers prefer to recover their arms over the water, and others keep them underneath. Both styles have been used by successful swimmers.

The breaststroke swimmer in Figure 21-8 uses an over-the-water recovery. A recovery that is made over the water or near the surface is preferred to a deep recovery because the first two styles allow swimmers to remain in a streamlined position longer during their arm and leg recoveries. This point is discussed in detail later in the section on body position. A deep recovery causes swimmers to undulate too much as they reach forward. Furthermore, with their hands down too deep, swimmers waste time sweeping them *up* to the catch.

Although the arms should not be extended down too deep, a small amount of downward motion is necessary near the end of the recovery to streamline the body.

a

b

Figure 21-8. An over-the-water recovery. The swimmer is Marc Brown, NCAA Division II All-American in the breaststroke events.

The arms need to be in line with the body as they reach forward to begin the next outsweep, so the arms must extend down slightly because the trunk will be inclined down to some extent (see Figure 21-4*i*). To clarify this point, the arm recovery should be made over the water or along the surface, and the hands should extend down only when the recovery is nearly completed and the arms begin moving out into the outsweep.

Coaches often debate whether swimmers should rotate their palms up during the recovery. Although this motion is not in itself propulsive, it is a natural follow-through action that shows that the insweep was executed correctly. When the insweep is done properly, the palms will be rotating in and up very rapidly as the insweep nears completion. Consequently, the inertia of the hands will cause the palms to continue rotating up through the first portion of the recovery until they are actually facing up when the arms begin extending forward. The hands would need to decelerate during the insweep to prevent the palms from turning up, and this would actually sacrifice propulsion during the insweep to keep their palms from turning up.

Many swimmers are being taught to accelerate their hands forward during the recovery in a style that has been characterized as a *lunge*. Although we have not analyzed the strokes of athletes who use this technique, our data on other world-class swimmers show that they do not accelerate their arms during this phase. I suspect that swimmers appear to lunge forward because they begin the propulsive phase of their kick as they stretch their arms out.

Stroke Patterns

Breaststroke swimmers use diagonal sculls; however, the degree of diagonality is between 70 and 85 degrees rather than 30 to 60 degrees, as was the case in the other three competitive styles (Schleihauf et al., 1988). This means that breaststroke swimmers pull back less than swimmers in any of the other competitive styles. Nevertheless, some degree of backward hand movement is essential to success. The stroke patterns in Figure 21-9 illustrate the diagonal sculls in the breaststroke armstroke. The swimmer's stroke patterns are shown from front, side, and underneath views and were drawn relative to the water. The outsweep is indicated by the line between points 1 and 2 in the stroke patterns. The catch takes place at point 2. The insweep extends from points 2 to 3, and the recovery occurs between points 3 and 4. There are three important aspects of these stroke patterns.

1. The underneath view shows that the swimmer's hands begin sweeping out before they are completely extended. *There is no glide*. Although the glide has traditionally been taught, it is not used in competitive breaststroke swimming. However, there is a rest period for the arms as they stretch forward and out to the catch. As mentioned, the continuous movement of the hands out and forward near the end of the recovery is used to overcome inertia as they change directions.

2. The front view shows that the swimmer's hands sweep up slightly during the upsweep. Athletes do this to place their hands in position for a longer insweep. Because the rules now permit swimmers to drop their head underwater, their hands will travel down slightly during the recovery to maintain them in alignment with

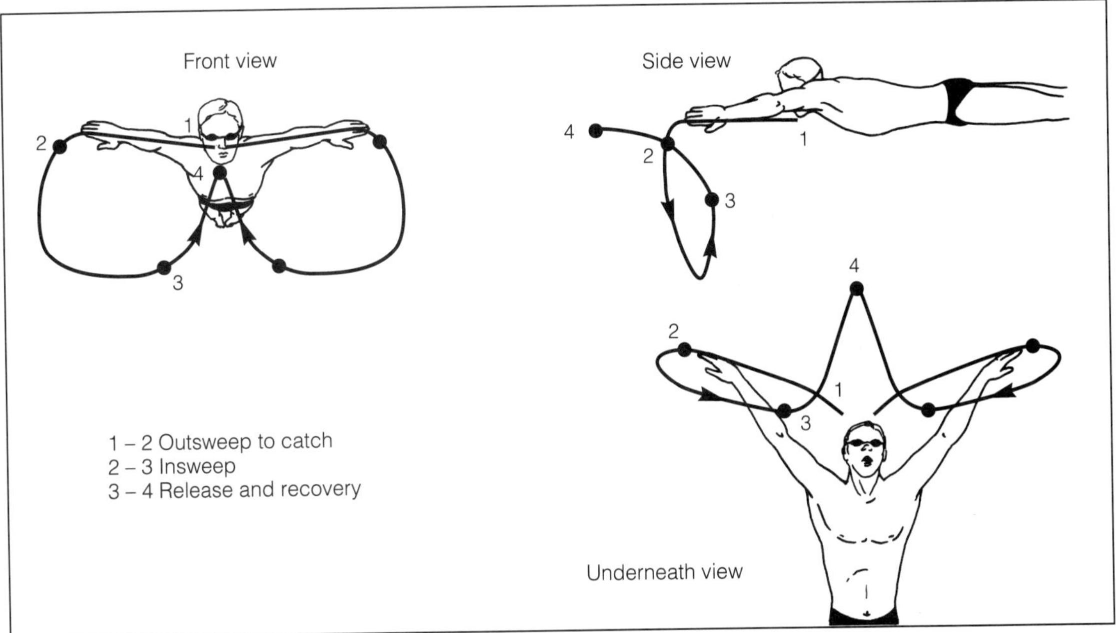

Figure 21-9. Front, side, and underneath stroke patterns for breaststroker Glenn Mills, former NCAA champion for the 200-yd event.

their body. This necessitates sweeping them up slightly during the outsweep so that they can make a more effective insweep.

3. The front view and side view show what to some may be a surprisingly large amount of downward motion during the first half of the insweep. Swimmers sweep their hands down nearly 60 cm (approximately 2 ft). They do not simply scull in and scull out. As mentioned, this downward portion is a very propulsive phase of the insweep and should not be minimized by sweeping the hands in too quickly.

Armstroke Variations There seem to be two distinct arm pulling styles in use by world-class swimmers today (Thayer et al., 1986). Some sweep their hands out and *forward* during the first portion of their armstroke and then in and *back* during the final portion. Figure 21-9 showed this pattern.

The second style is almost the direct opposite of the one just described. Swimmers sweep their hands out and *back* during the outsweep and in and *forward* during the insweep. Figure 21-10 (p. 506) illustrates this pattern from an underneath view.

The velocity graphs in Figure 21-11 (p. 506) show how propulsion is generated by the arms with both of these styles. The graph in Figure 21-11*a* shows what happens to forward velocity when the hands move forward during the outsweep and back during the insweep. Propulsion begins late in the outsweep and continues throughout the insweep.

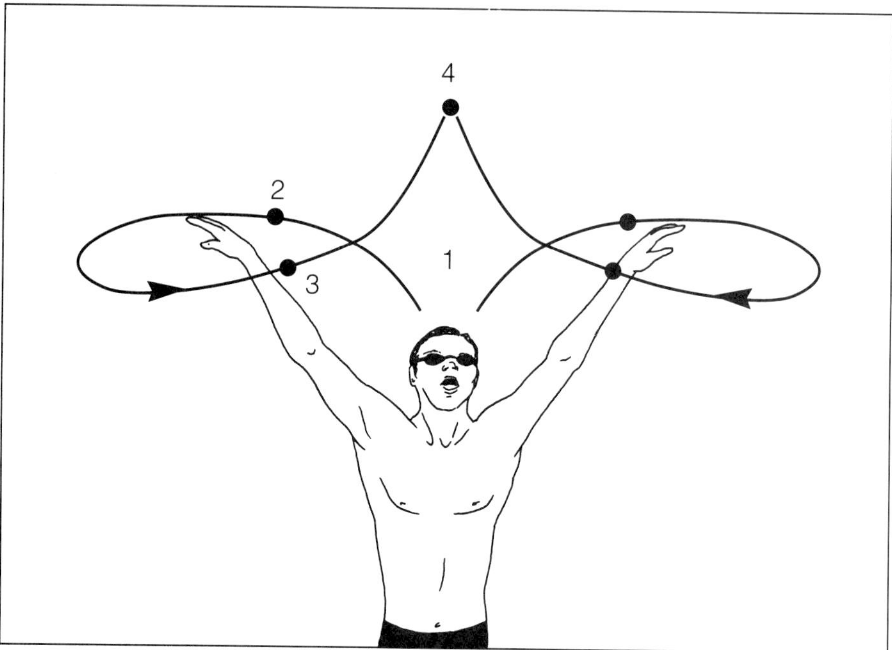

Figure 21-10. Another stroke pattern used by world-class breaststroke swimmers.

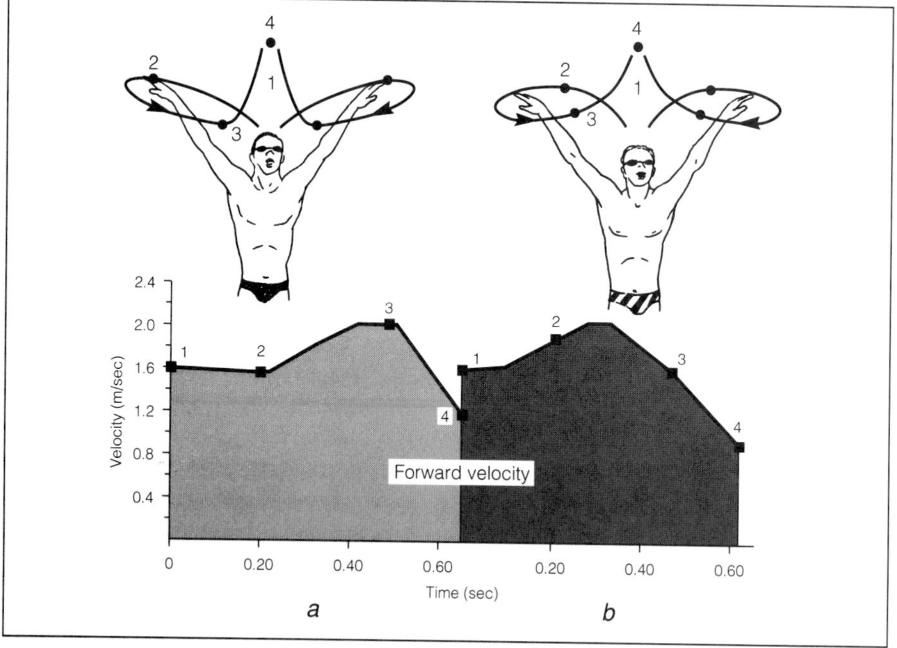

Figure 21-11. Propulsion during two types of breaststroke armstrokes.

The graph in Figure 21-11*b* depicts the effect on propulsion when the hands sweep out and back during the outsweep and in and forward during the insweep. Propulsion begins earlier (during the outsweep) and also terminates earlier (during the insweep). The point where forward velocity begins to decelerate is marked with a solid arrow on the stroke pattern.

Where propulsion is concerned, the differences in these styles can be summarized as follows:

1. The outsweep is nonpropulsive for the swimmer in Figure 21-11*a* because his hands are moving forward and cannot displace water back. The entire insweep is propulsive, however, because the swimmer keeps his hands moving in and back until they are almost together.

2. The second half of the outsweep is propulsive for the swimmer in Figure 21-11*b* because he begins moving his hands back during that phase. That propulsion continues through the first half of the insweep but terminates when his hands begin traveling forward during the second half of the insweep.

Although the distance over which propulsive force is applied may be the same in both styles, I suspect that the pattern in Figure 21-11*a* is potentially better because the swimmer reaches maximum forward velocity just before he begins to recover his legs. Because the leg recovery is the most potent retarding movement in this stroke, it follows that he may not decelerate as much when he recovers his legs if he is traveling faster as that phase of the stroke cycle begins. Conversely, the loss of velocity should be greater if a swimmer has already begun decelerating before the leg recovery begins.

Based on what was just said, it would seem reasonable to conclude that the best armstroke pattern would be one in which the hands moved out and *back* during the outsweep and in and back during the insweep; however, it is not possible to use such a pattern effectively. If swimmers swept their hands back during both the outsweep and insweep, their hands would be under their waist when the recovery began and the extra propulsion they achieved would probably be negated by the additional drag they would encounter during the recovery.

For the reasons stated, I recommend sweeping the hands *forward* and out during the outsweep, and *back* during the insweep. The most difficult aspect of stroking this way is in changing the direction of the hands from back to forward during the transition from the insweep to the recovery. Once again, the principle of overcoming inertia comes into play. Swimmers' hands will be moving back rather rapidly when the insweep is completed, so it will be necessary to overcome their backward inertia before they can begin moving forward. This is accomplished by squeezing the elbows down and in under the shoulders as the hands release pressure on the water. This movement of the arms will push the hands forward and up into the recovery.

Swimmers must be careful not to squeeze their elbows before the insweep ends or they will lose some propulsive force. They must also be careful that they do not simply drop their elbows back against their ribs. This will not change the direction in which their hands are moving. *They must squeeze their elbows down and in only.*

BREASTSTROKE KICK

Prior to 1960, the breaststroke kick was taught as a *wedge* action. Swimmers extended their legs in an inverted *V* and then attempted to *squirt* a wedge of water backward as they squeezed their legs together. Counsilman (1968) demonstrated the fallacy of the wedge kick when he showed that colored water placed between swimmers' legs did not squirt back when they squeezed their legs together. Coach James Counsilman and breaststroke swimmer Chet Jastremski then revolutionized the breaststroke kick with a narrow whip-style leg action that is used by most breaststrokers today. It has become known as the *whip kick*.

Initially, the whip kick was believed to be superior because water could be pushed back by extending the legs and using the soles of the feet like paddles. We realize now, however, that the feet (like the arms) scull in circular paths. Firby (1975) demonstrated the propellerlike capabilities of the feet in a unique way. He fashioned two plaster models of feet and joined them end to end to form a propeller with two blades as shown in Figure 21-12. The foot-propeller was attached to a toy boat by means of a rubber band. When the rubber band was wound up and released, the plaster feet propelled the boat forward by whirling around from side to side, in the same manner that an outboard motor would move when propelling a real boat.

The kick style that is used by most present-day world-class breaststrokers is really a diagonal propellerlike sweep of the legs, in which the feet scull out, down, and in as well as back. The soles of the feet are the primary propulsive surfaces, displacing water back like foils rather than pushing it back like paddles. Figure 21-5 shows the mechanics of the breaststroke kick from a front view. Figure 21-13 shows them from an underneath view. There are four phases: the recovery, the outsweep, the insweep, and the lift and glide.

Recovery

The recovery is shown in Figures 21-5*g* and 21-5*h* and Figures 21-13*a* and 21-13*b*. After completing the propulsive phase of the armstroke, the lower legs are brought

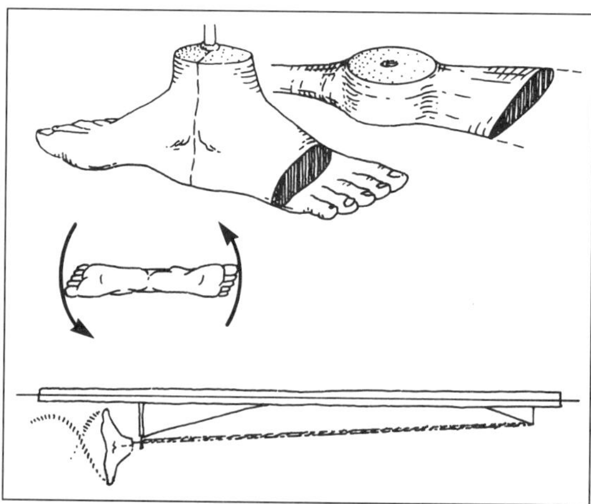

Figure 21-12. Firby's demonstration of the feet as propeller blades.

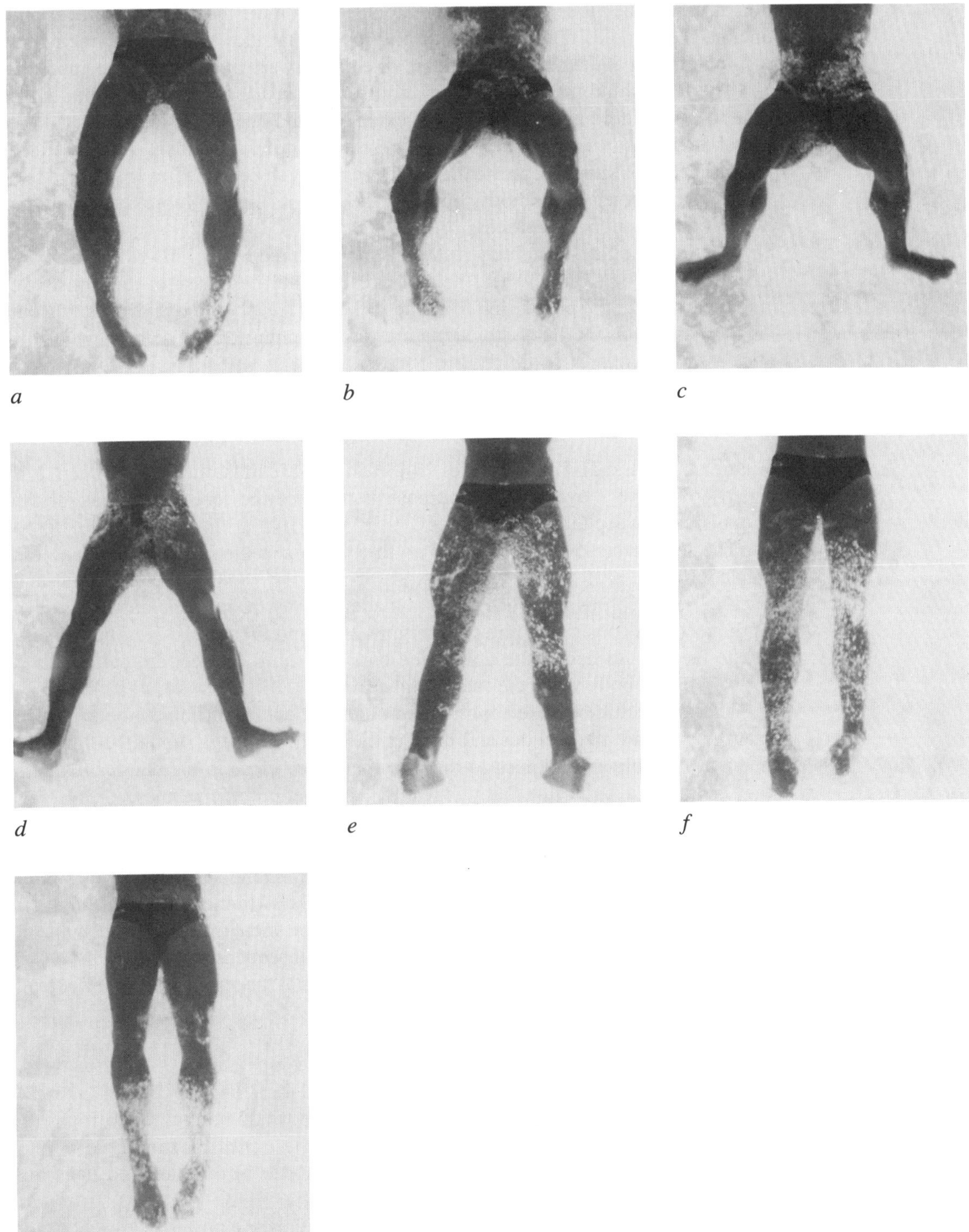

Figure 21-13. An underneath view of Roque Santos's breaststroke kick.

forward until they are very near the buttocks. Swimmers must drop their hips and incline their bodies down from head to hips so that they can recover their legs without flexing at the hips. The legs are brought forward by flexing at the knees.

The feet should travel almost directly forward *inside the confines of the hips*. The toes should be pointed back (feet extended) and held close together, and the lower legs should remain inside the hips throughout the movement to help reduce drag. The knees should separate during the recovery to keep the lower legs and feet inside the confines of the body, but they should not separate more than shoulder width or drag will be increased.

The legs should move fairly fast throughout the recovery. This will reduce the period of deceleration between the end of the propulsive phase of the armstroke and the beginning of propulsion from the kick. The feet should begin sweeping out as they approach the buttocks, signaling the beginning of the next phase of the kick—the outsweep.

Outsweep

Figures 21-5*h* and 21-5*i* and Figures 21-13*b* and 21-13*c* illustrate the outsweep. It is not a propulsive movement. Its purpose is to place the feet in position for the propulsive insweep that follows.

The legs circle out and forward as they approach the buttocks to make the transition from recovery to outsweep. After that, they continue circling out and back to the catch position. The catch is made midway through the outward sweep of the feet. This position is shown in Figure 21-5*i* and Figure 21-13*c*. The velocity of the feet should decelerate during the outsweep until the feet are being pulled forward by the body when the catch is made.

The feet should be flexed and rotated out at the ankles during the outsweep so that the soles are pitched out and back at the catch. The legs should be flexed as much as possible at the knees so that they pass very close to the buttocks, where they can make a high catch that will result in a longer propulsive phase.

Swimmers should flex their thighs slightly at the hips during the outsweep. Although it may seem so, there is no contradiction between this suggestion and the earlier recommendation to recover the legs without flexing at the hip. Underwater filming shows that nearly all world-class breaststroke swimmers flex their thighs at the hips during the outsweep. Although this action increases drag somewhat, it increases propulsive force even more during the subsequent insweep because two sets of muscles are used: those that extend the thighs at the hip and those that extend the legs at the knees.

The decelerative effect of flexing at the hips is not nearly as great as occurs with flat-style breaststrokers, who begin flexing at the hips earlier in the recovery. Consequently, they flex them to a greater extent and for a longer period of time. By contrast, swimmers who use the style described above do not pull their thighs up until they begin sweeping their legs out during the transition from recovery to outsweep. For this reason, the drag created is shorter in duration and does not decelerate forward speed as much.

Although a small amount of hip flexion is essential for a powerful kick, it is not necessary or desirable to pull the thighs up too much. Belokovsky and Ivanchenko

(1975) reported that more force was delivered when the thrust began with swimmers' hips flexed at 40 degrees than at angles that were closer to 90 degrees. They also reported that the range of hip flexion for wave-style breaststrokers was approximately 34 to 50 degrees and 60 to 90 degrees for flat-style swimmers.

Insweep

The insweep begins at the catch. Figures 21-5*i* through 21-5*k* and Figures 21-13*c* through 21-13*f* show this phase of the kick. The insweep is the only propulsive phase of the breaststroke kick.

The legs sweep down, back, and in until they are completely extended and nearly together behind the swimmer. The soles of the feet are rotated down and in until they are pitched in when the insweep has been completed (see Figure 21-13*f*).

The insweep ends just before the feet come together. As they come together, the feet overcome their downward inertia by releasing pressure on the water so that they can begin circling up toward a streamlined position near the surface for the glide. The velocity of the feet increases steadily throughout the insweep, with the peak velocity occurring just before the feet release pressure on the water to begin the lift.

The insweep of the kick actually has two distinct phases of propulsion. The first phase could be more correctly called a *downsweep* because the feet are traveling down and out. It is only during the second phase that they sweep in. Nevertheless, the insweep has been described as one motion because swimmers feel it as one continuous sweep of the legs. The propulsive mechanisms are discussed separately, however, to help readers understand them.

Figure 21-14 shows how propulsion is produced during the downward portion of the insweep. The feet should be facing out, and they should be rotating down as they sweep down and out. In this position, the leading edges of the feet are the big-

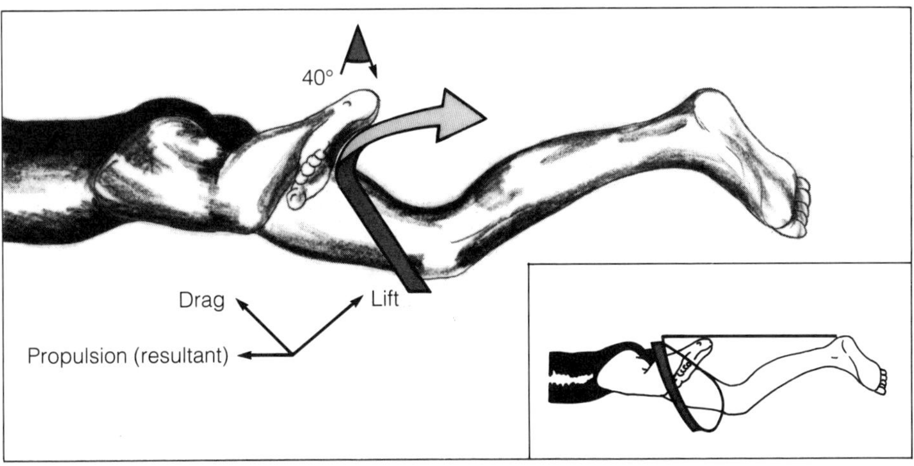

Figure 21-14. Propulsion during the downward portion of the insweep of the breaststroke kick.

toe sides and the trailing edges the little-toe sides. The relative flow of water is upward as it passes the leading edges of the swimmer's feet; however, as the shaded arrow shows, the downward inclination of the feet will impart some backward force to the water as it travels under the soles toward the trailing edges.

This first portion of the insweep continues until the legs are nearly extended. It is the most propulsive phase. The inward portion begins when the direction of the feet changes from down to in. The legs sweep in across the water until they are almost together. The feet continue to rotate down and in until the soles are facing in toward one another when the insweep is completed. Figure 21-15 shows this

Figure 21-15. A side view of the breaststroke kick showing the ideal position of the feet during the inward portion of the insweep.

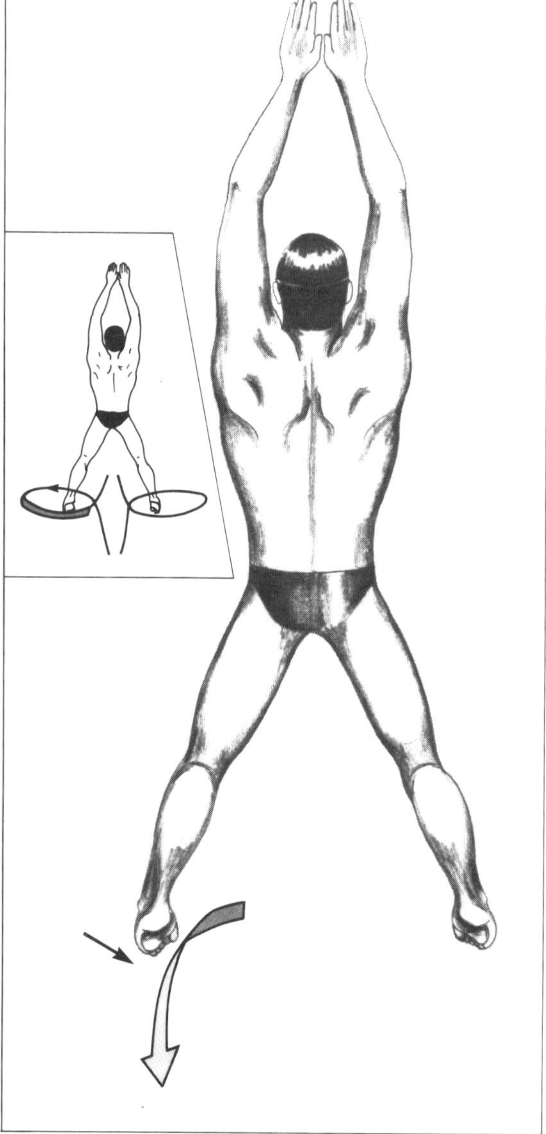

Figure 21-16. Propulsion during the inward portion of the insweep of the breaststroke kick.

position of the feet. Figure 21-16 depicts how foot position contributes to propulsion during the inward phase of the insweep.

The big-toe sides continue to function as the leading edges of the foot-propeller, and the little-toe sides remain the trailing edges, as they did in the previous phase. However, because they are traveling almost directly in across the water, the relative motion of water will be out across the soles of the swimmer's feet from the leading to the trailing edges. As you can see from the sweeping arrow in Figure 21-16, the inward pitch of the feet causes the water to be displaced back for a short time as it travels across the soles. The backward force imparted to the water should produce a counterforce that will accelerate the swimmer forward.

Where propulsion is concerned, the angle of attack of the feet is a very important and misunderstood feature of this phase of the insweep. To get propulsion during this phase of the kick, the feet must remain flexed at the ankles so that the toes are pointing toward the bottom of the pool and *the soles of the feet should be facing in*. Swimmers are commonly taught to point their toes back and to lift their legs to the surface as they sweep them across the water. However, they should delay these two actions until the insweep has been completed, or propulsion will be lost. The effect of this mistake is described later in the section on common stroke faults.

The latter portion of the insweep is less propulsive than the former portion, so it is possible to swim world-class times and even set world records without performing the second portion of the insweep as described. Nevertheless, those swimmers with the best breaststroke kicks generally complete the insweep with their feet flexed at the ankles and their soles facing in, as described here.

Leg Lift and Glide

The lift can be seen best in Figures 21-4*c* and 21-4*d*. It is really a continuation of the circular insweep. Beginning when the feet are nearly together and propulsion from the insweep is nearing completion, swimmers release pressure on the water and allow their legs to start up as their feet come together. The legs continue up until they are in line with the body and just beneath the surface. This is when the glide phase of the legs begins. The legs remain in a streamlined position during the propulsive phase of the armstroke so that they do not produce extra drag that detracts from the propulsive force being generated by the arms. The legs should be completely extended from hips to toes, with the feet extended back at the ankles. They should be held close together and in line with the trunk. The speed of the feet should decelerate during the lift until the legs are being pulled along by the body as the arms stroke.

Although some may disagree, the lift is probably *not* propulsive. Figure 21-17 shows that the legs move forward as well as up during the lift. This direction is shown by the arrow below the swimmer's feet. Propulsion could only be produced if the legs were sweeping directly up or, better still, up and back. When they travel up and forward in an extended position, the nearly perpendicular angle of attack of the legs succeeds only in pushing water up and forward, which exerts a counterforce that acts in a downward and backward direction against the swimmer's legs, decelerating forward speed. For this reason, swimmers should execute the lift gently, using it only to bring their legs up in line with their body.

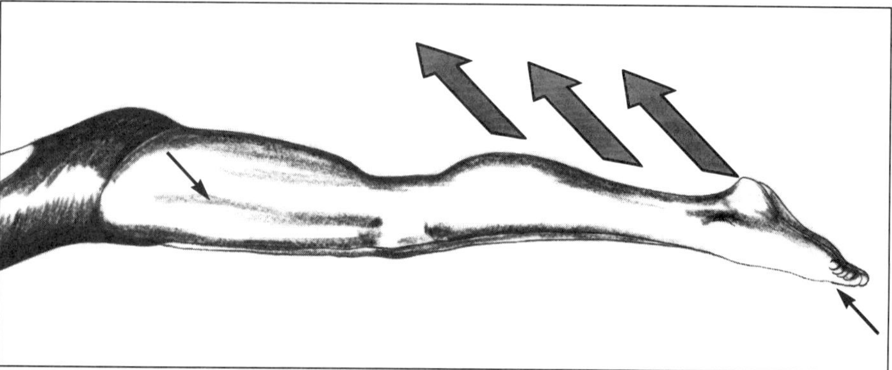

Figure 21-17. The leg lift in breaststroke swimming.

The Dolphin Motion: Good or Bad?

The hips will dolphin up slightly when swimmers perform the insweep correctly. Figure 21-4*i* shows this motion. This happens because some of the force that swimmers produce pushes their hips up when they sweep their legs down, just as the downward movement of their arms pushes their shoulders up during the insweep of the arms. The vector diagram in Figure 21-14 demonstrates why the hips elevate. In addition to producing a propulsive force, the downward movement of the legs also creates a drag force that is aimed up and forward. It is that component of force that elevates the hips. Propulsion would be reduced if the drag force were diminished. Consequently, the small dolphin action in the hips is a by-product of a good kick and should not be inhibited for the sake of maintaining a flat body position. Additionally, the slight pike at the hips may contribute to a small amount of propulsion when the trunk drops back in alignment with the body during the outsweep of the next armstroke.

Although a small dolphin motion is desirable during the kick, it is possible to overdo it. If swimmers concentrate too much on elevating their hips, they may kick down too deep and subsequently produce drag that slows their forward speed. Breaststrokers should not try to dolphin their hips like butterflyers. Their hips should dolphin only a small amount, and they should be moving forward much more than up when the dolphin is executed.

Ankle and Hip Flexibility

Several types of hip and ankle flexibility are probably essential to a good breaststroke kick. These include an ability to flex the feet and rotate them in and out (invert and evert the feet). Good flexibility in these directions should allow breaststroke swimmers to catch the water earlier during the outsweep of their kick so that they can lengthen the propulsive phase. They also allow swimmers to pitch their feet out in order to execute the succeeding insweep more effectively. The ability to rotate the legs in at the hips and out at the knee joints should also help in making an early catch during the outsweep of the kick and provide a better angle of attack for the feet during the succeeding insweep.

In a study that involved 178 subjects, Vervaecke and Persyn (1979) found that those who had the best breaststroke kicks maintained their feet in flexed and outwardly rotated positions longer than those with poor kicks. The poor kickers extended their feet much earlier during the insweep. The authors believed that a significantly greater ability to rotate the feet out accounted for the difference between the two groups. Surprisingly, they did not find a significant difference between the two groups in their ability to flex their feet at the ankles. These results were supported in a later study by Nimz and associates (1988).

Stretching exercises for the ankles and hips can usually be performed with no ill effects; however, it can be dangerous to stretch the knees outward, because their range of motion is very limited in this direction. So, although it may help the kick to stretch these joints, swimmers run the risk of precipitating knee injuries.

Kick Patterns

Figure 21-18 shows the directions in which swimmers' feet move during the breaststroke kick from front, side, and underneath views. The leg recovery begins at

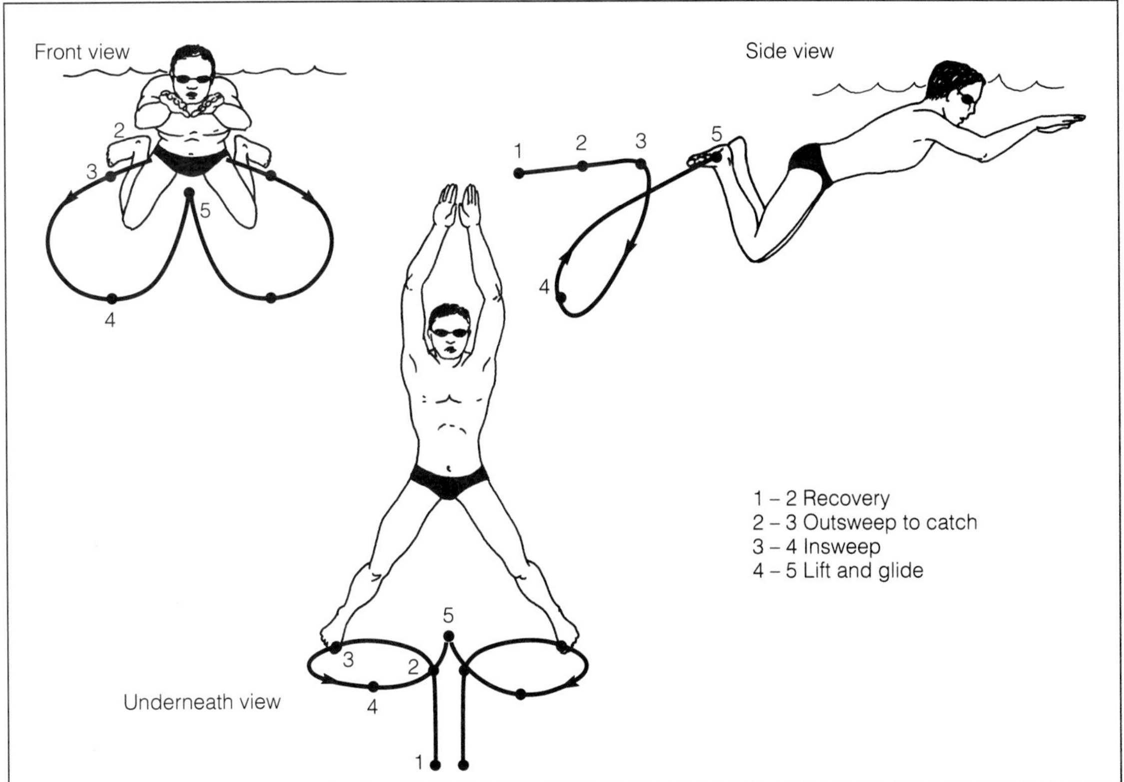

Figure 21-18. Front, side, and underneath views of breaststroke kick patterns drawn relative to the water. The swimmer is Bill Barrett, former NCAA champion in the 100-yd event.

point 1 and ends when the outsweep begins at point 2. The outsweep continues to point 3, where the catch is made. The insweep begins at point 3 and continues to point 4. The lift starts at point 4, and the legs are carried up to their glide position at point 5.

The front-view pattern shows clearly that the kick is a circular movement, in which the legs kick, out, down, in, and up. The side view shows how little they actually move back during the propulsive phases. Although swimmers feel as if they are extending their legs backward, these patterns show clearly that they rotate them down and in while their body is being pushed forward.

There are two important technical features illustrated by these kick patterns. The first concerns the amount that the legs sweep down. Swimmers' feet sweep down approximately the same distance as their armstrokes—about 50 to 60 cm (20 to 24 inches). This directional component lends support to the theory that propulsion from the breaststroke kick is the result of propellerlike, rather than paddlelike, movements of the feet.

The second feature is the difference between the patterns for the right and left legs. This asymmetry is typical of most breaststroke swimmers (Czabanski & Koszczyc, 1979). Just as one arm seems to be more effective than the other, so also do the legs differ in their propulsive efficiency. The left leg is usually the inferior limb (Czabanski, 1975). Reduced propulsion is indicated by the increased backward movement of the swimmer's left leg in the underneath view of Figure 21-18.

The three most logical explanations for asymmetry are (1) less strength in one leg relative to the other, (2) differences in the size of the two legs, or (3) greater range of motion in one leg relative to the other. Research indicates that the last explanation is the most likely of the three. Czabanski (1975) found that two groups of swimmers with good and poor breaststroke kicks did not score differently on tests of leg strength. Nimz and associates (1988) reported right-left differences between the legs in measures of knee-joint flexion and eversion (turning the feet out); however, they did not find any significant differences in measures of leg length, width, or circumference. These data suggest that exercises that increase the range of motion in the knee joints and possibly also the ankle joints may improve kicking speed.

Sore Knees

Coaches and breaststroke swimmers know what a serious problem sore knees can be. At the very least, valuable training time can be lost; at the worst, they can end a swimmer's career.

Sore knees are generally caused by chronic inflammation of the medial collateral ligaments and medial menisci that are located within these joints. These structures are shown in the inset drawing of the knee joint in Figure 21-19.

The medial collateral ligament connects the femur (the long bone in the upper leg) to the tibia (the bone on the inside of the lower leg). The medial meniscus is attached to the medial collateral ligament and runs between the femur and tibia. It is composed of cartilaginous connective tissue and cushions the articulation between these two bones.

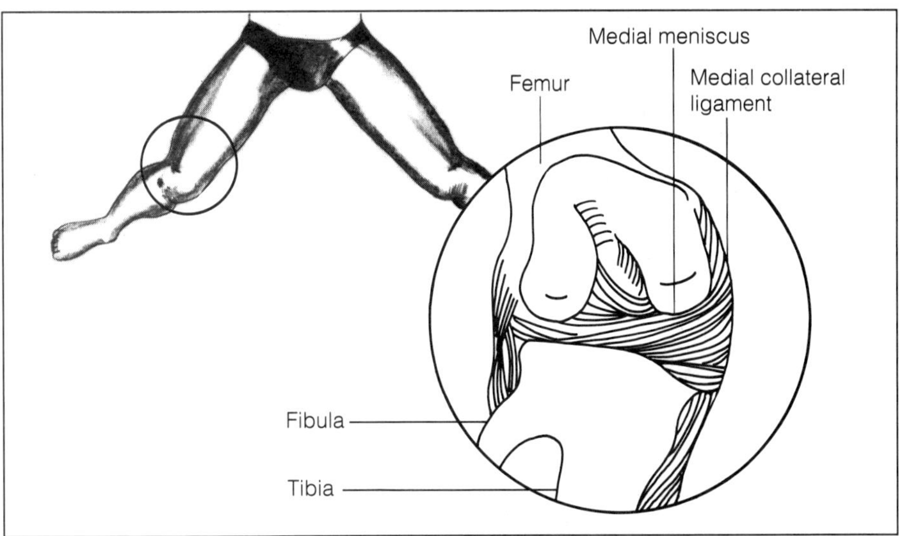

Figure 21-19. A drawing of the knee joint showing the medial collateral ligament and medial meniscus.

The outsweep and the first part of the insweep of the breaststroke kick exert a considerable amount of stress on these structures. When swimmers rotate their lower leg out, the head of the femur pushes in and the head of the tibia pulls out against the medial meniscus and the medial collateral ligament. In very severe cases, the ligament may be torn. At the same time, the medial meniscus may be compressed to the point that it tears away from the ligament. Most often, however, these structures become irritated and cause pain when swimmers are performing the breaststroke kick. The swimmer in Figure 21-19 is shown with his knee rotated out, where strain to these tissues is most likely to occur.

Knee pain and injury are common because the range of outward rotation at the knee joints is very limited in most humans; however, the ability to rotate the lower leg out at the knee is essential to a good breaststroke kick. Therefore, the breaststroke swimmer faces the dilemma of developing an effective kick at the risk of potential injury. Swimmers who can perform the kick without soreness and injury are very lucky. Others must curtail their kicking at the first sign of pain until that pain subsides.

Breaststrokers who are susceptible to sore knees may want to consider modifying their kick to remove some of the strain on the medial collateral ligaments and medial menisci. They can adopt a technique that reduces the amount of outward rotation by reducing the size of the outsweep and by pushing the feet back more than out during this phase of the kick. This reduces strain on the knee, but it also shortens the insweep and reduces the propulsive potential of the kick.

There is another technique that can reduce the incidence of sore knees without reducing the propulsive effectiveness of the kick as much. In this technique, swimmers recover their legs with their knees spread somewhat wider than recommended earlier. With their knees wide when the outsweep begins, swimmers can rotate their feet out a reasonable distance to the catch without requiring a significant amount of outward rotation at the knee joints. This modification should maintain the propellerlike characteristics of the kick without causing serious strain on the soft tissues of the knees. It will, however, increase drag because the knees will be slightly outside the body when the outsweep begins. Nevertheless, it is better than suffering sore knees. Obviously, swimmers should not turn their knees out any more than necessary to perform the outsweep without pain.

TIMING THE ARMS AND LEGS

There are three general styles of breaststroke timing that have been advocated by various swimming experts: continuous, glide, and overlap. When continuous timing is used, the armstroke begins immediately after the legs come together. With glide timing, there is a short interval between the completion of the kick and the beginning of the armstroke, when the swimmer is coasting, or gliding, along. In overlap timing, the armstroke begins before the propulsive phase of the kick has been completed.

The majority of coaches agree that glide timing is the least effective of the three methods because swimmers decelerate from the time the propulsive phase of their kick ends until the propulsive phase of their armstroke begins. The forward velocity chart in Figure 21-20 demonstrates the period of deceleration that occurs with glide timing. Notice the loss of velocity that takes place in the darkly shaded area while the swimmer is gliding. His velocity declines from 1.70 m/sec (5.5 ft/sec) to approximately 1.50 m/sec (5.0 ft/sec) during this phase. His forward velocity then decelerates even further to 1.40 m/sec (4 ft/sec) while he sweeps his arms out to the catch. The length of time between the end of the propulsive phase of this swimmer's kick and the beginning of the propulsive phase of his armstroke is nearly 0.40 second.

Some coaches believe that continuous timing can eliminate the gap between applications of force by the kick and armstroke that occurs with glide timing. It cannot, however, because the outsweep of the armstroke is not propulsive. Consequently, swimmers who use continuous timing also decelerate from the time they complete the propulsive phase of their kick until their arms reach the catch position during the outsweep, even though there was no glide phase. Although they should only decelerate for approximately 0.30 second, this still constitutes a significant reduction of forward velocity.

The best way to eliminate, or at least reduce, the period of deceleration between the *end of the propulsive phase of the kick and beginning of the propulsive phase of the armstroke* is to use overlap timing. The swimmer whose velocity is displayed in Figure 21-23 (p. 523) is using overlap timing. Compared to the swimmer's forward velocity in Figure 21-20, the swimmer's velocity in Figure 21-23 decelerates by a smaller amount (approximately 0.30 m/sec) and for a shorter period of time (0.15 second).

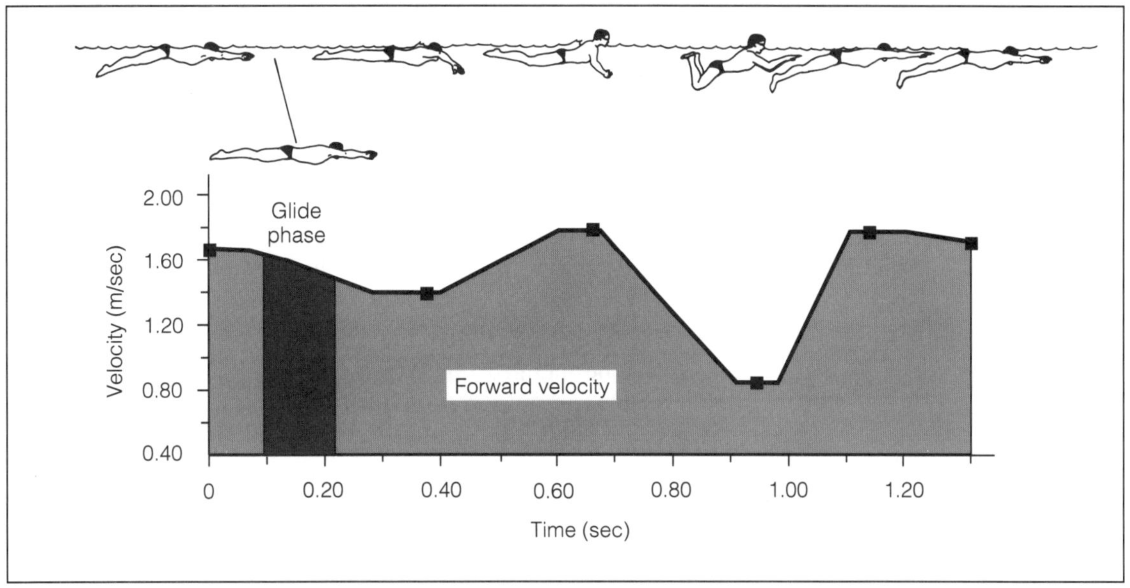

Figure 21-20. A forward velocity chart for a swimmer who is using glide timing.

The relationship between the kick and armstroke should be such that the arms make their catch almost immediately after the propulsive phase of the kick ends. This timing is accomplished by sweeping the arms out when the legs are sweeping in during the final portion of their insweep. Overlap timing can be seen from a front view in Figures 21-5*a* through 21-5*c*.

Swimmers with poor insweeps during the kick may need to use more overlap. Because the propulsive phase of their kick actually ends when the insweep of the legs begins, these swimmers will need to start sweeping their arms out a little earlier to get them to the catch before they lose too much forward velocity. Although their rapid turnover rate will increase the energy cost, it will probably be faster to swim this way than to save energy by taking fewer armstrokes with a slower average velocity per stroke.

BODY POSITION AND BREATHING

Body Position

As with the butterfly, it is useless to talk of one body position for the wave-style of breaststroke. There are two phases of the stroke cycle during which the body must be streamlined. These positions can be seen from a side view in Figure 21-4.

1. The trunk should be as horizontal as possible during the propulsive phases of the armstroke and kick (see Figures 21-4*c* and 21-4*d* for the armstroke and

Figure 21-4*i* for the kick). The trunk should be horizontal, with the hips near the surface and the legs in line with the body during the propulsive phases of the armstroke. The face should remain underwater until the propulsive phase of the armstroke is nearly completed and then break through the surface for a breath. Some swimmers are even inclined down from feet to head during the early portions of the armstroke (see Figure 21-4*c*). This downward inclination may even be more effective for reducing drag than a horizontal body position.

The trunk should be nearly horizontal, with the hips near the surface, the shoulders in the water, and the arms nearly extended during most of the propulsive phase of the kick. Now that the rules permit, the head should be underwater and between the extended arms during the thrust from the legs to improve streamlining.

2. The trunk should be inclined down from head to knees during the leg recovery. You should be able to draw a straight line from the shoulders to the knees until just before the outsweep of the kick begins (see Figures 21-4*f* through 21-4*h*).

Breathing

Breaststroke swimmers should breathe once during each stroke cycle regardless of the race distance. Breathing is such an integral part of the timing of this stroke that it aids, rather than interferes, with propulsion. Swimmers seem to lose their rhythm when they do not breathe and, in the case of wave-style breaststrokers, their head must be lifted so that they can recover their legs properly. The proper breathing sequence can be seen from the surface in Figure 21-21. Figure 21-5 shows the underneath sequence from a front view.

Swimmers should be looking down with their head tucked between their arms as their arms extend forward prior to beginning the armstroke (see Figure 21-5*a*). The face begins to lift toward the surface while the arms sweep out (see Figure 21-5*b*). The head should be on the surface when the catch is made (see Figure 21-5*c*).

After the head reaches the surface, the downward movement of the arms will complete the face lift so that the mouth will be above the surface as the arms sweep in. Swimmers breathe while their arms sweep up under their chin (see Figures 21-21*b* and 21-21*c*). After that, the head should lower into the water as the arms stretch forward (see Figures 21-21*d* and 21-21*e*). As mentioned, the head should be underwater between the arms, thus streamlining the upper body during the propulsive phases of the kick.

Swimmers should make certain that they continue to move forward while they are breathing. For this reason, they should not lift their head up and back. Rather, they should keep their head moving forward. A good teaching technique is for swimmers to keep their eyes focused down on the water directly in front of them as they breathe (see Figures 21-21*c* and 21-21*d*). Another technique for keeping the head moving forward is for swimmers to shrug their shoulders forward as they begin extending their arms forward and dropping their head toward the water.

The interrelationship between the leg recovery and the head drop is very important to success in the wave-style breaststroke. Swimmers can reduce drag considerably during the leg recovery by keeping their head and shoulders above the surface until their legs are completely recovered and the outsweep begins. This will

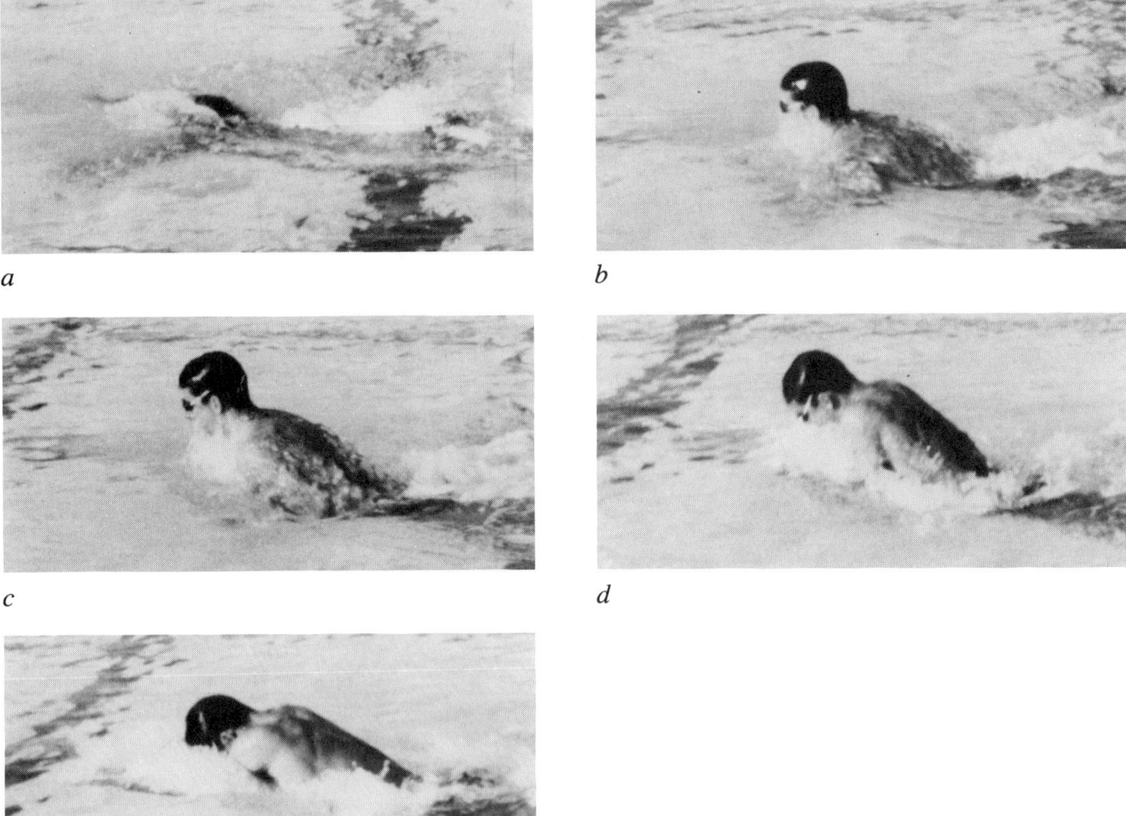

a *b* *c* *d* *e*

Figure 21-21. A surface view of breaststroker Roque Santos's breathing technique.

keep their hips submerged so that they can recover their legs forward without flexing at the hips. When swimmers lower their head and shoulders too early during the leg recovery, they have no choice but to flex at the hips and push their thighs down and forward to complete the recovery of their legs.

Figure 21-22 (p. 522) shows how swimmers can remain more streamlined when they use this style. The swimmer in Figure 21-22*a* has lowered his shoulders into the water too early during his leg recovery. This pushed his hips up near the surface so that he has to recover his legs by pushing his thighs down and forward against the water. This type of leg recovery will slow his forward velocity considerably.

The swimmer in Figure 21-22*b* keeps his shoulders above the water during the leg recovery, which maintains his body in an inclined position that reduces drag. With his hips down, he is able to bring his lower legs forward without flexing at the hips.

Recovering the arms over or at the surface of the water is a technique that allows swimmers to keep their trunk elevated and their hips down until their legs start

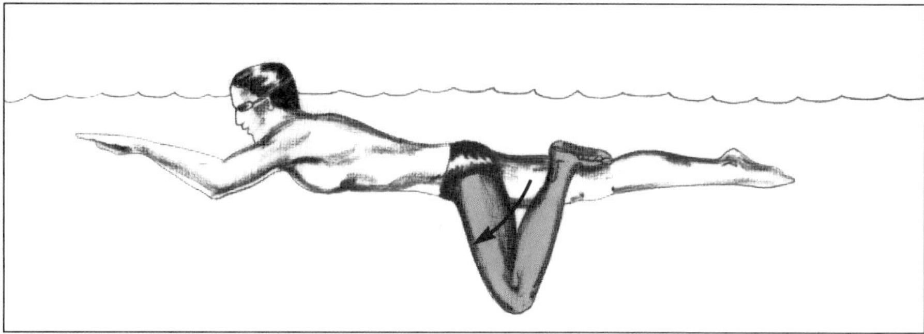

a

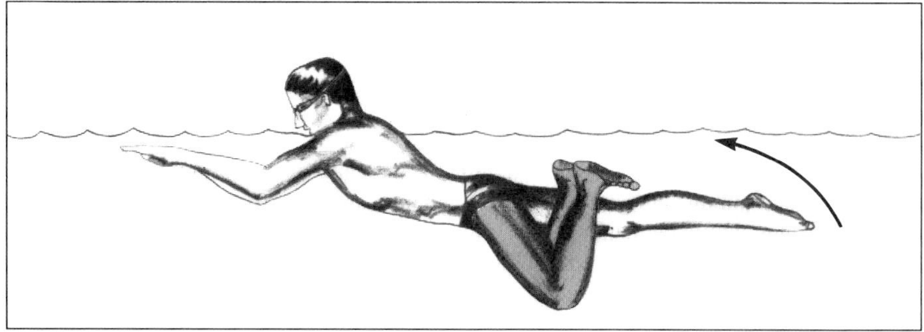

b

Figure 21-22. Two recovery styles in breaststroke.

sweeping out. Their head and shoulders stay above the surface longer when they recover this way. By contrast, when they recover underwater, their head and shoulders begin to drop under the surface while their feet are still traveling up. *Swimmers should not submerge their head until their hands are almost completely extended and their legs are beginning the outsweep* (see Figure 21-5*i*).

HAND, FOOT, AND BODY VELOCITY PATTERNS

Figure 21-23 shows excellent body, hand, and foot velocity graphs for a competitive breaststroke swimmer, Glenn Mills.

Body Velocity

Figure 21-23 shows Mills's forward velocity for one complete stroke cycle. He was swimming at 200 speed. The graph begins at point 1 (time 0 on the velocity graphs), as his arms start to sweep out near the end of their recovery. He is traveling forward at approximately 1.80 m/sec (5.80 ft/sec) at this time. The speed comes from his kick; his legs are sweeping in as his arms start out. Because of the timing between

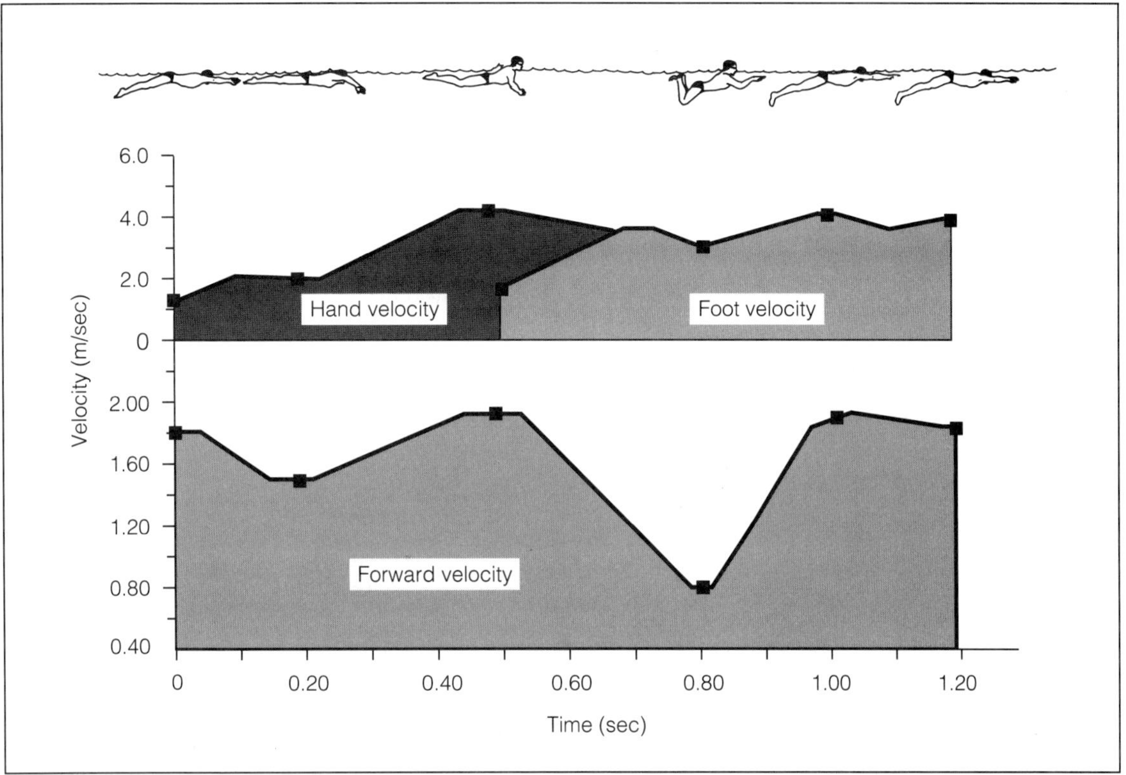

Figure 21-23. Hand, foot, and forward velocity graphs for breaststroker Glenn Mills.

the kick and armstroke, his speed only drops off slightly—to 1.50 m/sec (5 ft/sec)—while his arms sweep out to the catch at point 2.

After the catch, his forward velocity increases throughout the insweep of his armstroke, which takes place between points 2 and 3 of his forward velocity pattern. His forward velocity reaches a high of approximately 1.90 m/sec (6 ft/sec) just before he releases pressure on the water at the end of the insweep.

His forward speed decelerates markedly to approximately 0.80 m/sec (2.50 ft/sec) during the recovery of his arms and legs between points 3 and 4. The rate of deceleration is quite rapid and pronounced, because he is pushing both his legs and arms forward against the water. Most of the world-class breaststrokers we have studied decelerate to speeds of approximately 1.00 m/sec (3 ft/sec) during this time (Thayer et al., 1986). Some less-skilled breaststrokers actually stop moving forward for an instant near the end of the leg recovery (Craig, Boomer, & Skehan, 1988).

The swimmer in Figure 21-23 accelerates very rapidly from this valley of deceleration once the propulsive phase of his kick begins at point 4. He reaches his peak velocity about midway through the insweep, at point 5 and then maintains nearly that same speed until he releases pressure on the water with his feet at the end of this propulsive phase at point 6.

Most world-class breaststrokers reach similar peak velocities with their arms and legs. However, like Mills, they accelerate their body forward for a longer time with their arms than with their legs. Nevertheless, the kick is clearly the dominant propulsive agent in this stroke. In Figure 21-23, the swimmer's forward velocity increases nearly 1.00 m/sec during the kick. By contrast, it increases only 0.20 to 0.30 m/sec during the armstroke. Thus, swimmers do not accelerate their body forward as much with their arms as they do with their legs, even though peak velocities are similar during both phases of the stroke cycle.

The forward velocity pattern in Figure 21-23 provides important information about the techniques of breaststroke swimming. The most important concerns the valley of deceleration during the recovery. The major difference between world-class and less-successful breaststrokers takes place during this phase of the stroke cycle, rather than during the propulsive phases. World-class swimmers decelerate less, and they spend less time in this valley. The best swimmers do not decelerate much more than 1.00 m/sec during this time, and they do not spend more than 0.30 second in this valley. Less-skilled breaststrokers often decelerate 1.50 m/sec or more, and they will spend 0.40 to 0.60 second in the valley before completing their leg recovery.

Figure 21-24 shows a body velocity pattern for a female world-record holder in the breaststroke that contains a third propulsive phase that has only recently been identified (Mason, Patton, & Newton, 1989). Notice the middle propulsive peak—just after the swimmer begins to recover her arms and legs forward—that is repre-

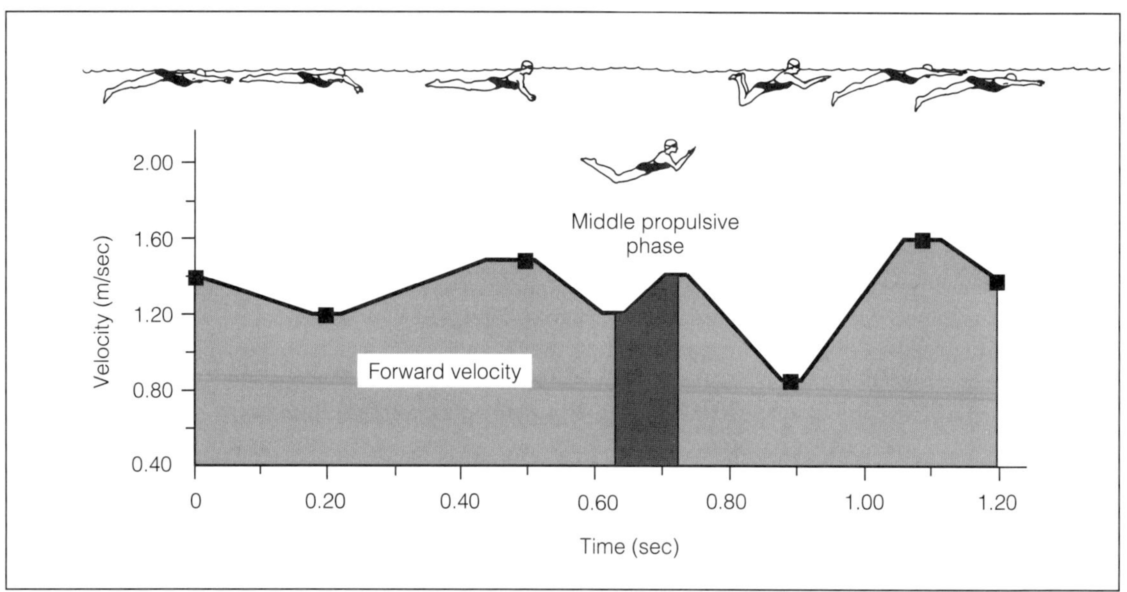

Figure 21-24. A velocity pattern for a world-record holder in the breaststroke. (Adapted from Mason, Patton, & Newton, 1989).

sented by the darkly shaded area on the velocity graph. The drawing shows the position of the swimmer's body during this phase.

Normally, the forward velocity would decelerate from the end of the armstroke (at point 3) to the beginning of the propulsive phase of the kick (at point 4). As you can see in Figure 21-24, however, this swimmer achieves a short period of acceleration at the beginning of her recovery phase.

After measuring the velocity of their centers of gravity, Mason and his colleagues (1989) reported that all members of a sample of nine national-level and world-class breaststrokers exhibited this third propulsive phase. They also said that it was most pronounced in the highest-ranking members of the group.

The interesting thing about this middle propulsive phase is that it takes place when both sets of limbs are in their recovery phases and, thus, could not be applying propulsive force against the water. This makes it difficult to ascertain the cause of the short period of acceleration that some swimmers achieve.

Mason and coworkers (1989) suggested that the middle propulsive phase might be due to the wave action of the water. They hypothesized that swimmers might be transferring momentum to the water by pushing their body against it as they accelerated forward during their armstroke. After the propulsive phase of the armstroke was completed and they began to decelerate, the wave of water that they created in front surged back, transferring its momentum to the swimmers and accelerating their body forward.

Although this explanation is possible, there are at least four others that may also account for this phenomenon. The picture of the world-record holder in Figure 21-25 can be used to illustrate the first and second explanations. The first may have to do with the way he keeps his body inclined forward during the recovery. You can see from the inclination of his head and shoulders, that he seems to keep his body moving *forward and down*. The second explanation may be that he reduces drag on his body by elevating his head and a good portion of his trunk above the water during the recovery phase.

A third explanation is that swimmers may accelerate their center of mass forward at the start of the recovery phase by rapidly shifting their arms and legs

Figure 21-25. World-record holder Mike Barrowman during the start of his arm and leg recoveries in the breaststroke.

forward. It is well known that the center of mass will shift in the direction in which the limbs are moving. Thus, when swimmers' arms — which travel back during the insweep — suddenly shift direction to forward during the recovery, their center of mass may shift forward as well. At the same time, their legs assist this shift by their rapid forward movement during the recovery.

The fourth explanation for the middle propulsive phase may be that some skilled breaststroke swimmers continue to accelerate their body forward with their arms as they sweep them up under their chin. Observations of videotape show that the middle propulsive phase occurs during this time. Swimmers who achieve it also appear to keep their palms pitched up and in and their hands moving in and up, rather than forward, when they sweep up toward the surface.

I believe that the forward shift of body parts during the recovery is the most probable explanation for the forward acceleration of the center of mass during the middle propulsive phase. It would behoove breaststroke swimmers to learn this technique because it will shorten the period of deceleration during the recovery. At present, the best advice that can be given for learning this technique is for swimmers to keep their head and shoulders moving down and forward and their arms moving forward as they execute the leg recovery.

Hand and Foot Velocities

Hand velocity is represented at the top left of Figure 21-23. The swimmer's hands are traveling at approximately the same speed as his body when they begin the outsweep at point 1 (time 0 in the hand velocity graph). They accelerate slightly during the outsweep and then slow until they are, once again, traveling at the same speed as the swimmer's body when the catch is made at point 2. Once the catch is made, hand speed accelerates rapidly throughout the insweep phase of the armstroke until the release takes place at point 3. The maximum velocity that the hands reach during the insweep more than doubles from their velocity at the catch (1.50 versus 3 to 5 m/sec). Hand speed starts decelerating when the recovery begins and continues declining until the catch is made for the next stroke cycle. As with other strokes, swimmers' changing hand velocities correspond to changes in their forward velocity during the armstroke.

Foot velocity is illustrated at the top right of Figure 21-23. The swimmer's legs are gliding motionless, being pulled forward by body velocity during the armstroke. His leg recovery begins immediately when the propulsive phase of his armstroke is completed at point 1 on the foot velocity graph. They are recovered rapidly, reaching a speed of approximately 3 m/sec (10 ft/sec) just before they start sweeping out. Their speed then decelerates during the outsweep until the catch is made at point 2 on the foot velocity graph. The feet accelerate rapidly again once the propulsive phase of the kick begins, and they continue to accelerate during the downward portion of the insweep, at point 3 on the foot velocity graph. Foot speed decelerates slightly while they change direction from out to in, after which they accelerate once again through the inward portion until the insweep is nearly completed at point 4 on the foot velocity graph. Peak velocities of 4.00 m/sec (13 ft/sec) are reached during both parts of the insweep. Once the propulsive phase of the kick has been completed, the legs decelerate while they are lifted toward the surface to the glide position.

The most surprising aspect of this foot velocity pattern is how fast the swimmer moves his feet during the recovery. He undoubtedly does this so that he can shorten the decelerative period while he recovers his legs and arms. Recovering the legs fast probably increases resistive drag; however, breaststrokers apparently prefer to reduce their speed rapidly for a short time instead of reducing it less rapidly for a longer time by recovering their legs slowly. The trade-off must be a good one where average velocity per stroke cycle is concerned. Even though swimmers recover their legs rapidly, they should *slip* them forward in a streamlined position so that they produce the least amount of drag while they travel forward.

Another important aspect of this foot velocity pattern is that the swimmer does not begin to recover his legs until the propulsive phase of his armstroke has been completed. I stress this point because some experts mistakenly believe that swimmers can reduce the decelerative period between the propulsive phases of their armstroke and kick if they start recovering their legs before they finish the propulsive phase with their arms. What they fail to realize is that the recovery movements of the legs reduce the propulsive efforts of the arms. Apparently, decelerating for a short time is preferable to losing propulsion from the arms, because all of the world-class breaststroke swimmers we have studied prefer to wait until the propulsive phase of their armstroke is completed before they recover their legs (Thayer et al., 1986). This trade-off, apparently, produces a greater average velocity per stroke cycle.

UNDERWATER ARMSTROKE

The rules permit breaststroke swimmers to take only one underwater stroke during each pool length — immediately after the start of the race and after each turn. After completing the underwater stroke, the head must break through the surface of the water before the hands reach the widest part of the next armstroke. The underwater armstroke is considerably more effective than surface strokes, so swimmers should practice until they can get every bit of available propulsion from it.

The underwater armstroke is similar to an exaggerated butterfly armstroke. It consists of an outsweep, an insweep, and an upsweep. There are also two glides: one before the stroke begins and one after it has been completed. The second glide is followed by a kick to the surface. The outsweep is a nonpropulsive movement that is used to place the arms in position for the delivery of propulsive force. The insweep and upsweep are propulsive. Figure 21-26 shows the underwater armstroke from a side view.

First Glide

After the pushoff or dive, swimmers hold a streamlined position until their speed begins to decelerate (see Figure 21-26*a*). The arms should be together and stretched

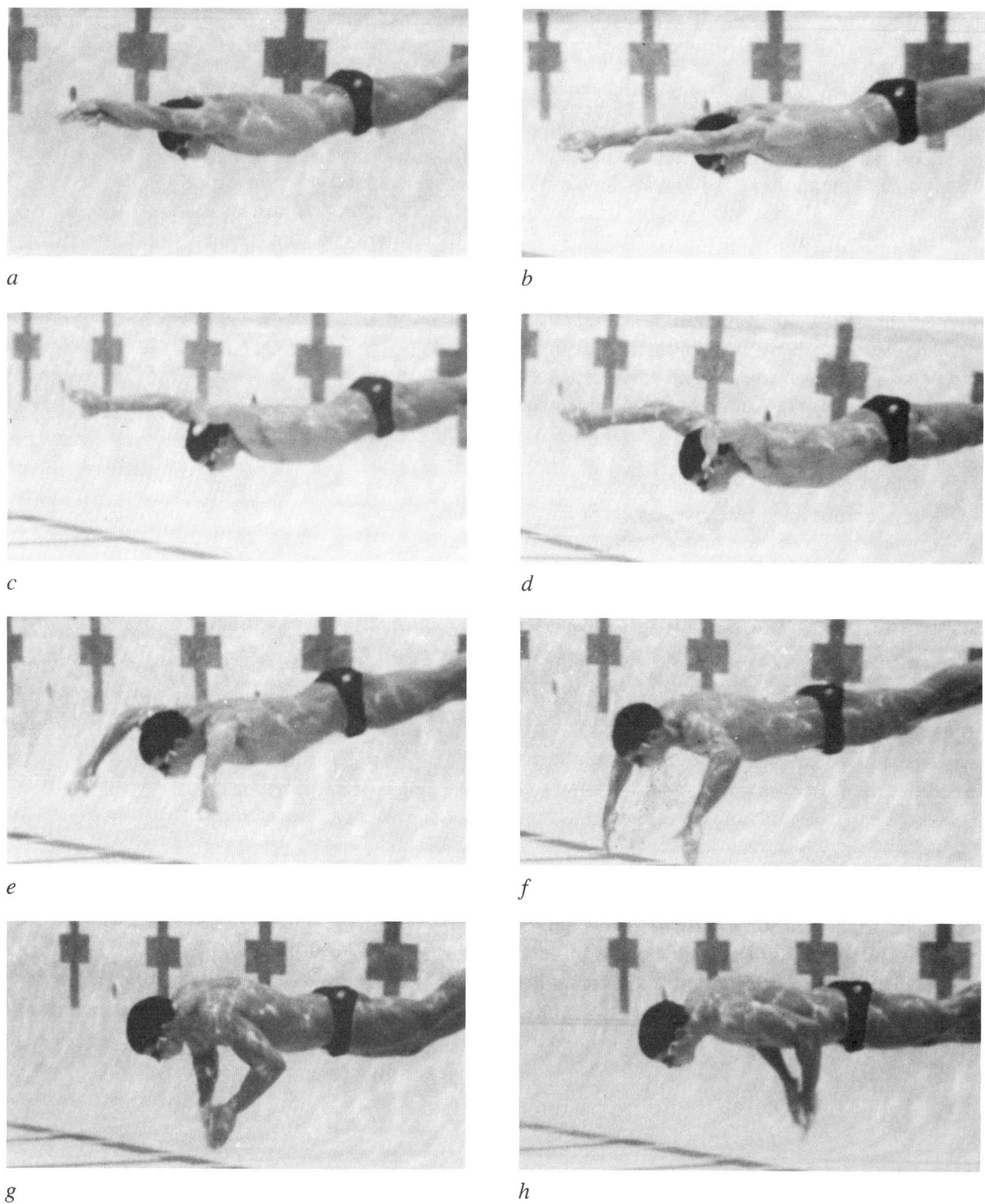

Figure 21-26. A side view of breaststroker Roque Santos's underwater armstroke.

i *j* *k* *l* *m* *n* *o*

tightly overhead during the glide. Placing one hand over the other helps in maintaining this position. The head should be between the arms, and the body should not sag or be piked at the waist. The legs should be held tightly together, with the toes extended back.

Outsweep

Figures 21-26*b* through 21-26*d* show the outsweep. As swimmers approach race speed, the arms sweep out and *up* until they are outside the shoulders and above the head, where the catch is made. The hands sweep up to position themselves for a longer and more propulsive insweep.

The arms flex after they pass outside the shoulders until they are facing back at the catch. The palms should be facing down when the outsweep begins, after which they should rotate out slowly until they are pitched out and back at the catch (see Figure 21-26*d*).

Swimmers should not push water to the side with their hands. The palms should be facing down when the outsweep begins and remain in this position until they are outside the shoulders. In this way, the hands slide out on their edges and encounter less drag during this nonpropulsive phase.

The hands accelerate slightly during the outsweep and then slow down at the catch. The outsweep is primarily a stretching motion to position the hands for an effective insweep.

Insweep

Figures 21-26*d* through 21-26*g* show the insweep. After the catch, the hands scull down, back, and in under the body with a large semicircular sweep that is like the insweep of the butterfly, only longer. The insweep is completed by gradually flexing the arms until they are bent nearly 90 degrees and they come together under the chest (see Figure 21-26*g*). The hands should rotate in gradually throughout the insweep until they are pitched in and up when the sweep is completed. Swimmers must be careful not to rotate their hands in too fast. Although they will be rotating in that direction, their palms should not be facing in until they pass under their elbows on their inward path.

The insweep has two propulsive phases—a downward portion and an inward portion—just as it does in the butterfly and regular breaststroke armstrokes. The only difference in the way that propulsion is generated is that this insweep is longer and more powerful than either of the other two. Hand velocity should increase moderately from the beginning to the end of the insweep.

Upsweep

Figures 21-26*g* through 21-26*j* show the upsweep. It begins as the previous insweep is being completed. The hands push out, up, and back until they are completely extended just above the thighs. The palms rotate out so that they are pitched out and back during the upsweep. The forearms and hands should maintain a backward orientation to the water as they sweep up.

The upsweep resembles the corresponding movement in butterfly until the hands approach the fronts of the thighs (see Figure 21-26*i*). At this point, the arms extend vigorously at the elbows and literally *throw* the water up and *away* from the thighs. The upsweep ends with the arms completely extended at the thighs. The palms should be just above the thighs and facing out (see Figure 21-26*j*). This final upward push is not for propulsive purposes but is used to keep the body submerged during the glide that follows.

The upsweep is the most propulsive phase of the underwater armstroke. The propulsion is produced in the same way as described for the butterfly. Hand velocity decelerates during the transition from insweep to upsweep, followed by a rapid acceleration to the end of the movement. Hand velocity should be maximum during the upsweep.

Second Glide

Once the upsweep is completed, the palms turn in and rest against the thighs to streamline body position. The body should remain in a streamlined position during the glide, with the arms extended and held close to the sides. The legs should be straight and held together with the toes extended back and up. The head should be in line with the body, and there should be no arch nor pike to the trunk. Figure 21-26*j* shows this glide position. The glide is very short, lasting only until the impetus of the upsweep begins to dissipate. Then swimmers recover their arms forward and kick to the surface.

Arm Recovery and Kick to the Surface

Figures 21-26*k* through 21-26*o* show this phase of the underwater armstroke. The arms recover forward under the chest. Swimmers then reach forward and kick their body up to the surface.

The arms slide forward underneath the body by flexing at the elbows, with the upper arms and elbows remaining close to the sides to reduce drag. The palms should face up as the hands approach the chest so that they can slip forward on their edges with a minimum of drag (see Figure 21-26*l*).

The arms begin to extend forward when they pass the head. They should extend in a streamlined position, with the elbows close and the palms facing one another. The arms continue to extend until they are completely straight in front. The palms should rotate down as they extend forward (see Figures 21-26*m* and 21-26*n*).

The legs also recover while the arms come up underneath the body (see Figures 21-26*l* and 21-26*m*). The legs kick powerfully when the arms extend forward toward the surface (see Figures 21-26*n* and 21-26*o*). The leg recovery should be as gentle as possible to reduce drag. Drag will also be reduced if the legs recover forward with very little hip flexion and if the knees stay reasonably close together within the confines of the body.

The head should break through the surface just before the kick is completed. The arms should begin sweeping out while the kick is being completed so that the hands are at the catch and ready to begin their propulsive phase when the head reaches the surface (see Figure 21-26*o*). *Swimmers should not glide to the surface.* They would decelerate too much if they did so. They should pull their head up and forward through the surface. This will bring them to the surface moving fast while also complying with the rules. Timing is critical. The arms should not pass their widest point in the stroke before the head reaches the surface. Testing has shown that *pulling up and through the surface* increases speed, as compared to gliding to the surface. Swimmers will be, on the average, 0.30 second faster from the turn to the time their head breaks through the surface. It can improve a swimmer's time by almost a full second in 100-yd and 200-m events and over 2.00 seconds in 200-yd events.

Once they reach the surface, swimmers should take their breath at the normal point in their armstroke — that is, while they are recovering their arms. *They should not interrupt the outsweep of their arms to catch a breath.*

COMMON STROKE FAULTS

Armstroke Mistakes

Outsweep Mistakes The most common mistakes are to make the sweep (1) too narrow, (2) too wide, or (3) too vigorously.

1. Swimmers who use a narrow outsweep press down and out rather than out and up, which causes them to push down on the water in the classic dropped-elbow position. Generally, swimmers who dive their head and arms excessively deep while they kick make this mistake because they must use their arms to lift their head to the surface for a breath. Swimmers should wait until their arms are wide enough to be facing back against the water before they start sweeping them down and in.

2. Swimmers pull too wide when they continue pressing straight back after the catch. Pushing back after the catch is propulsive but places the arms too far to the rear when the insweep begins so that swimmers must direct their arms *forward* during the insweep. In doing so, they sacrifice much of the propulsive force they could have produced during this phase of the armstroke. Swimmers should sweep their hands out and up, not out and down.

3. The final mistake that swimmers make during the outsweep is to sweep their arms out too vigorously. As indicated earlier, this only pushes water to the side and decelerates forward speed. The outsweep is nonpropulsive, so it should be made gently.

Insweep Mistakes The most common mistakes that swimmers make during this phase of the stroke are (1) to direct their hands *forward* and in and (2) to pitch the hands in too much.

1. Propulsive force drops off dramatically once swimmers begin moving their hands forward during the insweep. Consequently, they either terminate the insweep early or they waste time and effort performing a movement that is not propulsive. The illustration in Figure 21-27 shows why swimmers do not gain any propulsion when their hands move forward during the insweep.

Even though the swimmer's hands are pitched in, their forward direction of motion produces an angle of attack that is nearly zero degrees. With this combination of direction and angle of attack, little backward force will be imparted to the water as it passes outward under the swimmer's palms. As you can see, the direction of the shaded arrows remains unchanged, as compared to earlier drawings that showed water being displaced back.

The photo inset in Figure 21-27 shows a swimmer who has started moving his hands forward too early. Notice that his hands are pitched in much more than they should be. Notice also that his elbows are beginning to drop before his hands are inside them.

Propulsive force data from the swimmer pictured in the inset of Figure 21-27 were used to construct the velocity graph in Figure 21-28. The graph shows a loss of speed during the insweep of the armstroke. Notice that his forward velocity decelerates while his hand velocity is still increasing. This is a serious mistake. The swimmer is obviously wasting a considerable amount of muscular effort accelerating his hands in an effort to increase his speed while his forward velocity is actually decelerating.

There are two mistakes in teaching the armstroke that are responsible for this stroke fault. The first is a concern with keeping the elbows from going back behind

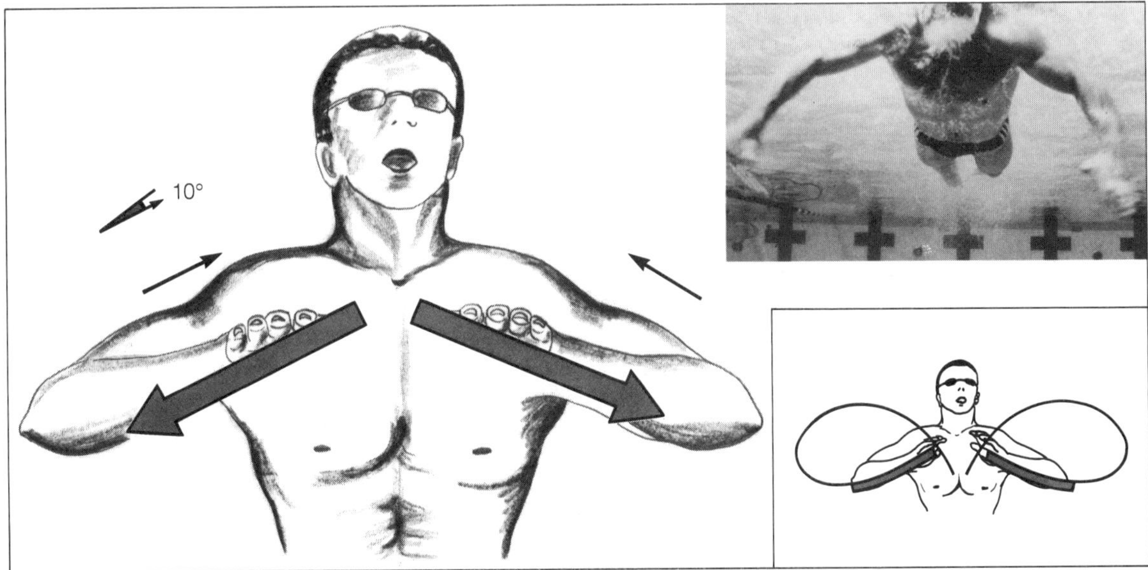

Figure 21-27. The effect of sweeping the hands forward during the insweep.

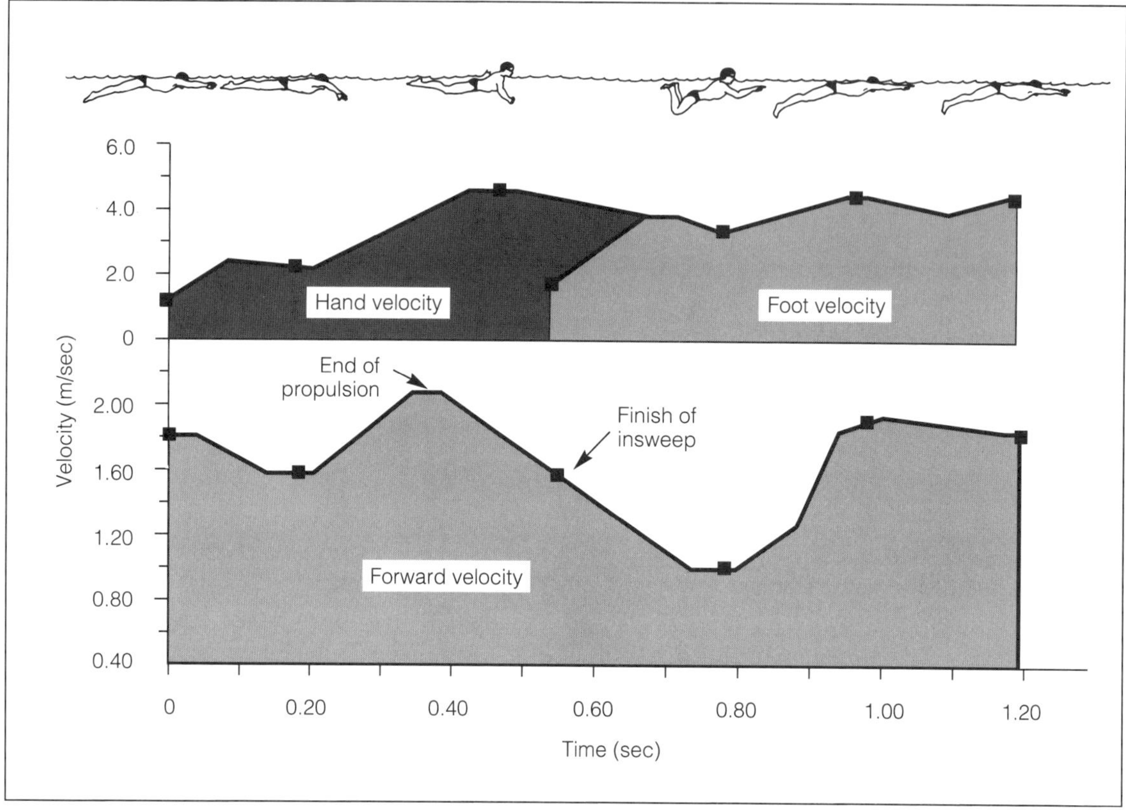

Figure 21-28. A velocity graph for a breaststroke swimmer who is losing propulsion during the insweep of his armstroke.

the shoulders, and the second regards an overemphasis on getting the hands out in front quickly during the arm recovery.

Swimmers have been told for years that they should not let their elbows come back behind their shoulders during the insweep or they will make the mistake of dropping their elbows. As a result, many swimmers sweep their hands forward during the insweep so that they can keep their elbows out in front of them. Actually, swimmers cannot make a propulsive insweep without having their elbows come back behind their shoulders. This does not necessarily mean that they are dropping their elbows.

Swimmers drop their elbows when they let them lead during the insweep. The swimmer in the inset photo of Figure 21-27 makes this mistake. His forearms are facing down at a large angle of attack as his hands sweep in. This action will merely push water down and slow his forward speed. By contrast, if swimmers keep their elbows high until their hands pass under them, they will not be dropping their elbows. Once the insweep nears completion, however, their elbows will quite naturally drop back behind their shoulders as they are squeezed down and in. *This is not a case of dropped elbows*. It is, instead, a natural reaction to an effective insweep. Notice in Figures 21-5*d* and 21-5*e* that the swimmer keeps his elbows up until after his hands have passed inside them. It is only after the propulsive phase of the insweep has been completed (in Figure 21-5*f*) that they drop back behind his shoulders.

The second technical error that causes swimmers to move their hands forward during the insweep is an attempt to get them out in front quickly during the recovery. Swimmers are often taught to accelerate their hands forward quickly during the recovery to keep them from getting *caught,* or hesitating, under their chin. Unfortunately, some swimmers accelerate their hands forward too soon. Although this gets their hands out in front quickly, it also causes a loss of propulsion during the insweep.

Another way to prevent this hesitation without losing propulsion during the insweep is for swimmers to squeeze their elbows down and forward quickly after their hands complete the insweep. This will change the direction of their hands from back to forward quickly. Consequently, they will be able to sweep their hands in and back during the insweep and still get them forward quickly during the recovery.

2. Figure 21-29 illustrates the effect of pitching the hands in too much. It causes a loss of propulsion for the same reasons that were described for the insweep of other strokes. The hands are pitched almost perpendicular to the directions in

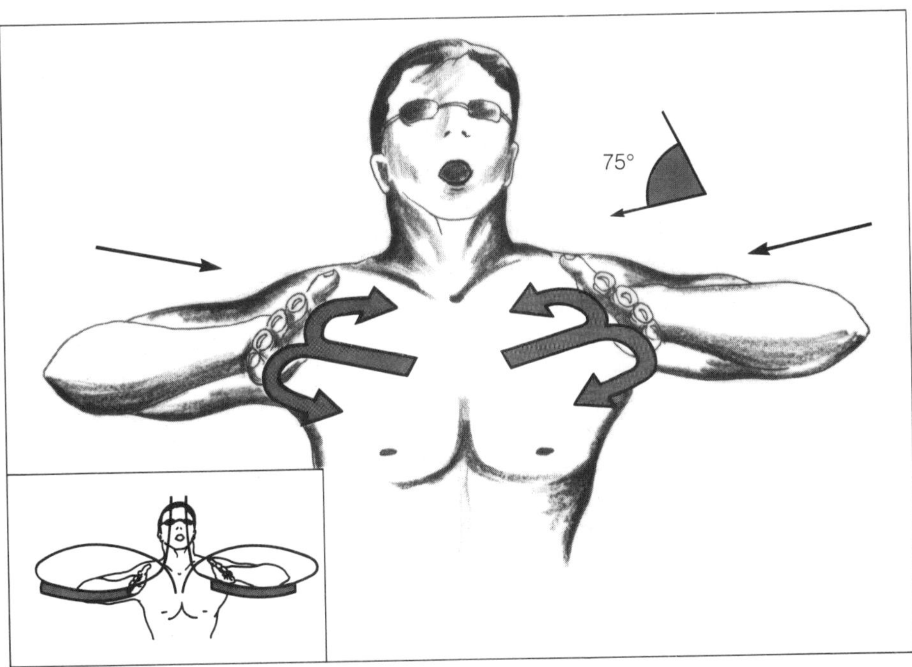

Figure 21-29. The effect of pitching the hands in too much during the insweep.

which they are traveling. Consequently, the water cannot be displaced back smoothly as it passes under the swimmer's palms. Instead, the water molecules rebound wildly inward, creating turbulence and a loss of propulsive force.

Recovery Mistakes The most common mistake during the recovery is for swimmers to push their hands forward with too much force, which causes a counterforce that decreases their forward velocity. Their hands should be slipped forward gently.

Another problem is lack of streamlining. Some swimmers recover their arms with their elbows wide. This increases the surface area of the arms that is pushing forward through the water. Many also have their palms down and wrists flexed so that the backs of their hands are pushing forward. Swimmers' arms should be close together, and their hands should be together, with their palms facing in during the first half of the recovery and rotating down during the second half.

The final problem is reaching down too much during the arm recovery. Swimmers' arms should be stretched forward in line with the direction in which their trunk is inclined. For a wave-style breaststroker, this will be forward and slightly down. For a flat-style breaststroker, it will be directly forward. Figure 21-30 shows a swimmer who is reaching down too much during the recovery. Notice that his arms are inclined down more than his trunk. (The angle of inclination of the swimmer's trunk is indicated by the arrow above his arms.) This position will increase frontal resistance. Furthermore, it will take the swimmer longer to get his arms up into position for the insweep.

Kicking Mistakes

Recovery Mistakes The most common mistake during this phase of the stroke, which has already been covered adequately, is for swimmers to push their thighs down and forward against the water (see Figure 21-2*a*). Another mistake is to recover with the knees and feet too wide in the fashion of the wedge kick. Swimmers' knees need to be slightly wider than their hips but not wider than shoulder width during the leg recovery. Form drag will increase if they are excessively wide.

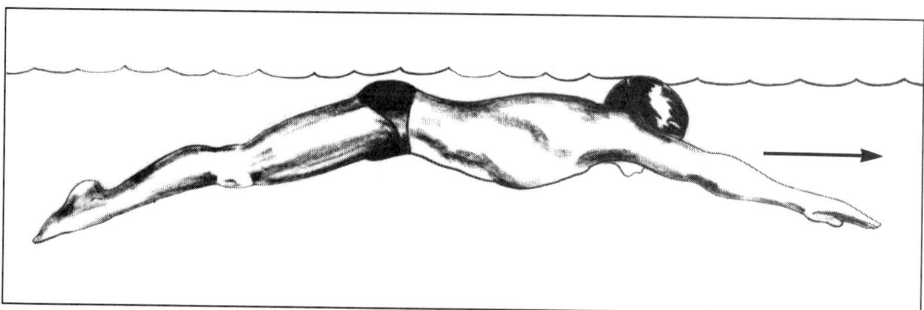

Figure 21-30. The effect of reaching down excessively during the arm recovery.

For this same reason, swimmers' feet should stay inside their hips until the recovery is nearly completed and the outsweep begins.

Outsweep Mistakes The mistake made most often during this phase is pitching the feet incorrectly. Some swimmers do not possess the rotational flexibility at their knee and ankle joints to turn their feet out sufficiently for an effective outsweep. As mentioned, these swimmers should do special stretching exercises to increase flexibility in these joints. Some of these exercises are listed in Chapter 24.

Insweep and Lift Mistakes Because they were taught incorrectly or because they lack rotational ability in their knees and ankles and cannot keep their feet flexed during the insweep, many swimmers extend their feet back and lift them too early during the insweep. These mistakes will cause swimmers to lose some propulsive force by terminating the insweep too early. In addition, these mistakes push water up toward the surface and produce a counterforce that will push the legs down and decelerate forward speed. The effect of these mistakes are shown in Figure 21-31. *Swimmers should not point their toes back and lift their legs to the surface until their feet are nearly together*. Instead, they should keep their feet traveling down and in across the water. The soles of their feet should be facing inward throughout this movement.

A second mistake during the insweep is for swimmers to push their feet directly back. The insweep should be a propellerlike sweep in which the feet rotate down and in. Only drag force is used when the feet push directly back. Consequently, both the amount of propulsive force and the length of time over which it can be applied will be reduced.

The last mistake is to delay the leg lift after the insweep has been completed. Figure 21-32 illustrates the effect of this mistake. The swimmer's legs hang down, increasing the space his body takes up in the water and, consequently, the form drag he encounters.

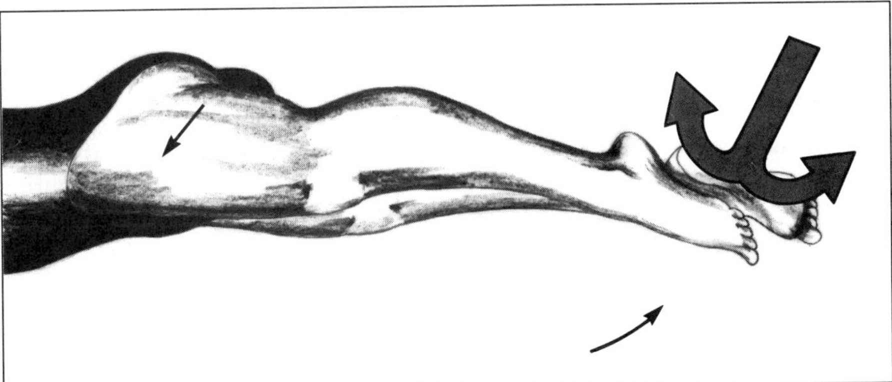

Figure 21-31. The effect of completing the insweep by extending the feet back and pushing the legs up.

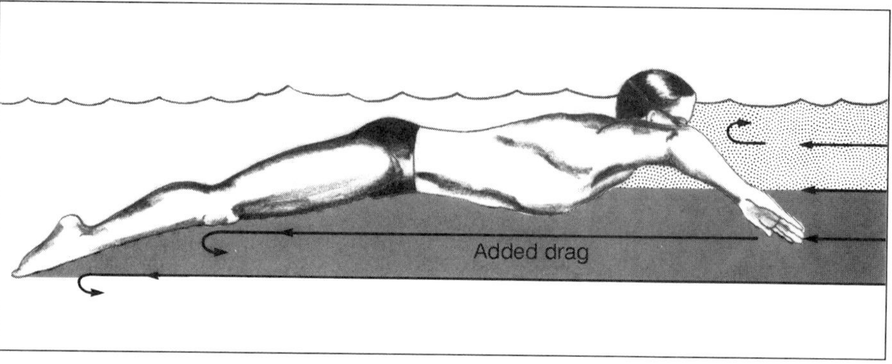

Figure 21-32. The effect of delaying the lift at the end of the propulsive phase of the kick.

Timing Mistakes

Two major errors in this area are to use glide timing and continuous timing. Both were covered earlier on pages 518–519. Another mistake that was mentioned is for swimmers to recover their legs during the propulsive phase of their armstroke. When this happens, the legs act as brakes, reducing the forward propulsion being generated by the arms.

Body Position Mistakes

Most of these mistakes have also been covered. I believe that the wave-style breaststroke is vastly superior from the standpoint of increasing propulsive force and reducing drag; thus, trying to remain flat during the stroke cycle is a mistake. Nevertheless, it is possible to overdo the undulation of the wave style so that the body travels up and down too much. A serious mistake in either style is for swimmers to be poorly streamlined during the propulsive phases of the armstroke and kick.

Breathing Mistakes

The mistake that swimmers make most frequently is to breathe too early. They breathe during the outsweep of their armstroke, which reduces streamlining during a phase of the armstroke in which the swimmer is already decelerating. Breathing at this time also causes swimmers to push down with their arms during the outsweep to provide support for their head. Swimmers should breathe at the end of the insweep, when their head and shoulders are at their highest point so that very little additional effort is needed to raise their face above the water to take a breath.

Another mistake is to lift the head too high out of the water when breathing. Swimmers who make this mistake actually force their head and shoulders up and back. This also decelerates their forward speed. Swimmers should move their body up and forward when they breathe.

I mentioned earlier that a new rule permits swimmers to put their head underwater during much of the stroke cycle. Swimmers should take advantage of this rule and put their head underwater in line with their arms as they kick. They should not keep their head above the surface because this will reduce streamlining. Swimmers who use this technique must not bury their head below their arms, nor should they dive down excessively in order to submerge their head. Their head should be between their arms and in line with their trunk. They must also begin lifting their head for the surface as their arms sweep out. They do not want to keep it down after the catch, or they will have to use an inordinate amount of force during the first portion of the insweep to lift it.

Most breaststroke swimmers fail to continue moving forward or change the directions of their limbs quickly enough to accelerate their body forward as they breathe. They seem to bring their head and shoulders up and somewhat back, as the swimmer in Figure 21-33 is doing. In addition, they are often slow in bringing their hands and legs forward when their recovery begins.

Underwater Armstroke Mistakes

Glide Mistakes The glides should never be so long that swimmers decelerate below race speed before they begin their underwater armstroke or before they begin kicking to the surface. Any extra distance they travel will actually add time to their races if their velocity falls below race speed during the glide.

Conversely, it is senseless for swimmers to begin their underwater armstroke while their body is traveling faster than race speed. Swimmers must learn to sense when it is time to begin their underwater armstroke and their kick to the surface. They should glide less in 100 races and more in 200 races.

Outsweep, Insweep, and Upsweep Mistakes The four most common technical errors made during the underwater armstroke are (1) a narrow outsweep, (2) a short insweep, (3) pushing up too much, and (4) pushing up too little during the upsweep.

Figure 21-33. The effect of lifting the head up and back while breathing.

1. Swimmers make the same mistake in the underwater armstroke that was described for the surface armstroke when they do not sweep their arms out wide enough. They push down on the water, raising their body to the surface more than propelling it forward.

2. With a short insweep, swimmers push their hands back too much and in too little. This is a by-product of drag propulsion teaching and reduces the length of time over which swimmers can apply propulsive force during their underwater armstrokes.

3. Swimmers who push up too much during the upsweep cause their arms to extend back faster than they travel up. As a result, their arms are extended while they are still underneath their body. In this position, they can only push up, not back, against the water. Pushing up will keep them submerged, but it will not propel them forward to any great extent.

4. Many swimmers also commit the opposite mistake during the upsweep of their underwater armstroke. That is, they push up too little. They stop their underwater armstroke before their hands pass up above their legs, terminating this propulsive phase prematurely and causing them to surface too quickly. Swimmers' arms should always travel up above their thighs during the upsweep.

Recovery and Kick-to-the-Surface Mistakes Most of the mistakes swimmers make in this part of the stroke have already been mentioned. The major one—gliding to the surface—was covered adequately earlier on pages 531–532. Recovering the arms with the elbows wide and the hands away from the body, extending the arms forward while they are wide apart, flexing the hips too much during the leg recovery, and making both the arm and leg recoveries with too much speed and effort are other common errors that were covered earlier in the section on the underwater armstroke.

One additional mistake is to begin the leg recovery too early. Some swimmers recover their legs as soon as they begin recovering their arms toward the surface. Consequently, they recover their legs slowly for a long period of time, which increases their deceleration during this phase of the underwater armstroke. Swimmers should begin to recover their legs as their arms reach forward. This will give them plenty of time to get their legs in position for the kick to the surface and will not produce drag for as long a period.

STROKE DRILLS

Armstroke Drills

The front and middle sculling drills that were described in Chapter 17 are excellent for learning the breaststroke armstroke. The following are some other good drills.

Stroke Pattern Drills There is no one pattern that makes a good vehicle for teaching the arm movements of the breaststroke. An underneath stroke pattern gives the impression that the hands sweep only out and in. It does not show the important downward portion of the insweep. Side-view stroke patterns do not emphasize the importance of the outward and inward movements of the arms sufficiently. A front view is better than the other two; although it does not really *fit* with the sensations that swimmers experience when they pull, it shows movement in all three directions.

One-Fist Pulling Drill This drill is designed to improve the pull of swimmers' nondominant arms. Swimmers pull or swim repeats with the hand of the dominant arm in a fist and the hand of the nondominant arm open.

Vertical Sculling Drills This drill is excellent for developing the insweep. It can take two forms. Swimmers assume a vertical position in deep water for both. In the first drill, they scull with a diving brick held between their legs. This forces them to keep steady pressure on the water while sculling in and out. In the second drill, they emphasize only the scull in and try to bring their head and shoulders out of the water as high as possible with each stroke. They need not use a weight in the second drill, but they should cross their legs at the ankles to prevent them from assisting in lifting their body out of the water.

Out-Slow, In-Fast Drill Swimmers pull in a horizontal position during this drill. They sweep out slowly and gently until the water is behind their arms and then scull in fast and hard. This is an excellent drill for teaching swimmers how to make a good catch and to emphasize the phase of the armstroke where propulsive force belongs—that is, in the insweep.

Crossing Hands Drill Again, swimmers pull in a horizontal position. They cross their hands at the wrists every time they sweep them in. This is a good drill for athletes who rotate their hands in too quickly during the insweep. When they are forced to extend the sweep longer, they rotate their hands in more slowly so that they can maintain an effective angle of attack later in the insweep.

Kicking Drills

Distance-Per-Kick Drill Swimmers travel down the pool using the fewest number of kicks possible. They can do the drill with a kickboard or without. This drill encourages swimmers to maximize the propulsive phase of their kick and to streamline their trunk and legs during the glide. They should be reminded to lift their legs up in line with their body during the glide.

Dolphin Kick Drill This drill can also be done using a breastroke kick with or without a kickboard. Swimmers emphasize pressing their hips up and forward over the water with each kick. The drill emphasizes the downward portion of the kick and is good for swimmers who need to learn how to scull their feet down and in.

Back Kicking Drill Swimmers practice the breaststroke kick while on their back. Their arms should be extended overhead and lying in the water with the palms up.

Figure 21-34. Marcelo Menezes, NCAA Division II All-American in the breaststroke, doing the breaststroke kick on his back.

Figure 21-35. The hands-back kicking drill performed by Mindi Bach.

This drill, shown in Figure 21-34, helps swimmers learn to kick without pulling their thighs up.

Hands-Back Kicking Drill Swimmers kick down the pool without a board. Their arms extend behind them, and their hands rest beside their hips near the surface of the water. Swimmers touch their feet to their hands each time they recover their legs. This drill is good for teaching swimmers to recover their legs without flexing at the hips. It can also be very good for teaching body position if swimmers (1) raise their head and lower their hips to breathe during the leg recovery and (2) lower their head and shoulders into a streamlined position underwater before they execute the propulsive phase of the kick. Figure 21-35 shows a swimmer doing this drill.

Leg Recovery Drill Swimmers kick with their arms together and extended forward and concentrate on keeping their body moving forward during the leg recovery. Swimmers should *shrug* their shoulders forward as they bring their legs up and drop their head underwater to streamline as they kick. They should also concentrate on flexing their legs properly during the recovery.

Body Position and Timing Drills

Kick and Stretch Drill Swimmers kick without a board executing a half armstroke with each kick. After the outsweep, and without completing the insweep of the armstroke, they extend their arms in front of their body so that they remain streamlined while they recover their legs and execute a kick. They should begin sweeping their arms out again as they execute the insweep of that kick. This is a good drill to teach the overlap timing.

Lineup Drill Once again, swimmers kick without a board. This time, however, they concentrate on getting their head down between their arms and their body streamlined as they execute the propulsive phase of their kick. They should push down with their hands or use a very small sculling motion to get a breath during their leg recovery. The obvious purpose of this drill is to teach swimmers to streamline their body during the propulsive phase of their kick.

Dolphin Pull Drill Swimmers use a dolphin kick while they pull without a buoy or tube. The timing is one dolphin kick per arm pull. Swimmers kick while their arms are sweeping out. This drill helps swimmers get a feeling for the wave-style breaststroke. The dolphin motion should not be excessive. Swimmers' hips should rise only slightly above the surface when they kick down and their hands and head should not lower too deep into the water as they pull.

Two Pulls, One Kick Drill This is a modification of the previous drill and is used for the same purpose. Swimmers execute several continuous series of three stroke cycles. They use dolphin kicks during the first two arm pulls of each series and a breaststroke kick during the third arm pull.

Underwater Armstroke Drills

Double Pulldown Drill Athletes swim repeats doing two underwater armstrokes after each turn before they come to the surface. This drill helps swimmers develop the ability to stay underwater during the armstroke.

Distance Pulldown Drill Swimmers try to get the maximum distance possible on each underwater armstroke before they surface. This is a good drill for teaching swimmers to maximize the propulsive elements of their underwater armstroke and to streamline their body during turns. They must be cautioned not to *stretch* their pulldowns for these distances during races.

Speed Pulldown Drill This drill is used to counteract the overlong glide that may develop from the previous drill. Time swimmers from when they touch the wall to begin their turns until they reach some specified point in the pool after the turn and underwater armstroke. That spot should be just after the place where they usually surface.

CHAPTER 22

Starts, Turns, and Finishes

In these days of crowded pools and high-mileage training programs, athletes spend very little time perfecting the techniques of starting, turning, and finishing. This is a serious oversight. Start times account for approximately 25 percent of the total time spent swimming 25 races; 10 percent, swimming 50 races; and 5 percent, swimming 100 races. Freestyle swimmers spend between 20 and 38 percent of their time turning in short-course races that range from 50 yd/m to 1,650 yd, respectively. Breaststrokers in short-course 200 races spend a whopping 39 percent of their time turning and completing their underwater armstrokes (Thayer & Hay, 1984). It can be said that swimmers in all short-course events spend approximately one-fourth to one-third of their time turning in all but the longest races.

Data gathered over several years indicate that, on the average, improving the start can reduce race times by at least 0.10 second and that improving turns can decrease race times by at least 0.20 second per pool length. Improving the finish can reduce race times by at least an additional 0.10 second. So, just two hours of practice per week on these techniques could improve a swimmer's short-course 50 time by at least 0.40 second. It could mean a minimum reduction of 0.80 second in a 100-yd race, because there are two additional turns. Improvements in longer races could be even more dramatic. For example, improving turns could reduce a swimmer's time by as much as 5 seconds in 1,500-m races and by 12 seconds over distances of 1,650 yd.

The significance of these improvements is evidenced by the fact that only 0.34 second separated the first- and sixth-place finishers in the 50-yd freestyle at the Men's 1988 NCAA Division I Championships. In the 1,650, 15 seconds separated first- and seventh-place finishers at the same meet. Certainly, practicing starts, turns, and finishes is time well spent.

STANDING STARTS

Many starting styles have been used over the years. Initially, swimmers took a starting position with their arms extended back. They soon found that they could get their body moving toward the water faster by starting with their arms forward and then swinging them back. This technique became known as the *straight-backswing start*. It was later replaced by a faster, circular backswing. Circling the arms back enabled swimmers to overcome the backward inertia of their arms in a circular manner so that they could then swing them forward with greater speed and increase forward velocity during the flight. The circular backswing has now been replaced by an even faster method—the *grab start*. This start was introduced by Hanauer in the late 1960s and has rapidly gained in popularity since that time (Hanauer, 1967).

Several research studies have verified that the grab start is faster than other methods (Bowers & Cavanaugh, 1975; Cavanaugh, Palmgren, & Kerr, 1975; Jorgenson 1971; Michaels, 1973; Roffer & Nelson, 1972; Thorsen, 1975; Van Slooten, 1973; Winters, 1968). Swimmers can get their body moving toward the water faster by pulling against the starting platform than they can by swinging their arms backward. However, they decelerate more quickly once they enter the water without the momentum from the armswing. Nevertheless, studies show that swimmers who use the grab start are usually faster, even though they lose some speed during the glide. For example, Thorsen (1975) found that horizontal and vertical velocities were greater with the circular backswing start, yet the grab start was faster by 0.10 second to the point of entry. Bowers and Cavanaugh (1975) reported that swimmers left the block 0.17 second faster on the average when they used the grab start as compared to the circular backswing method, which accounted for practically all of the difference in time between the two starts at a point 10 yards down the pool.

Another important change in starting technique is known by various names, the two most common being the *pike start* and *scoop start*. In this style, swimmers travel through the air in a high arc, often piking (bending) at the waist so that they enter the water at a very steep angle. Prior to the advent of this style, swimmers were advised to dive almost straight out and to enter the water at a very slight angle. Figure 22-1 (p. 546) illustrates the differences between the two dives.

The major advantage of the pike start is that swimmers encounter less drag at the point of entry. Consequently, they travel faster during the glide underwater. In Figure 22-1, the swimmer's body hits the water in several places at once with a flat start, which should cause her to decelerate quite rapidly during the glide. With the pike start, the swimmer's body enters the water at a more steep angle so that it slips underwater with less turbulence. This should allow her to glide much faster once she is underwater.

A word of caution regarding the pike start: Several accidents have been reported in which swimmers hit their face and head on the bottom when they attempted this

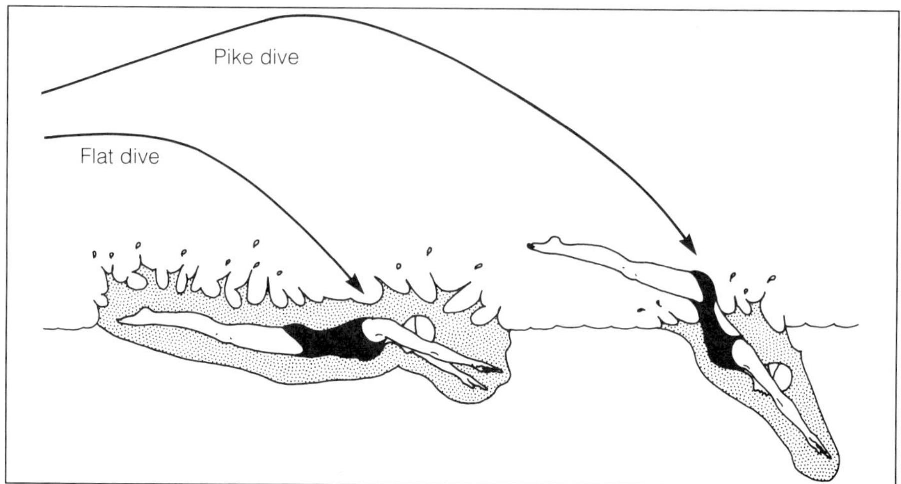

Figure 22-1. A comparison of the pike start and the flat start.

dive in shallow pools. A small number of these swimmers suffered serious neck injuries that left them paralyzed. The depth that swimmers reached with the pike start varied from 3 to 5 ft (1.0 to 1.7 m) in a study by Counsilman and associates (1988). *This dive should not be attempted in pools that are less than 6 feet deep.*

Another recent adaptation of the grab start is the *track start*. The major difference between this and the pike start occurs in the preparatory position on the starting platform. Swimmers place one foot near the rear of the block, whereas both feet are over the front edge of the starting block for the traditional grab start. The two major advantages of the track start follow:

1. Swimmers may get into the water faster because their center of mass travels almost straight forward beyond the starting platform until it reaches the point where it begins falling toward the water. With the pike start, their center of mass travels up a greater distance after leaving the block and then down into the water, perhaps increasing the time it takes for swimmers to reach the entry position.

2. Swimmers' legs may deliver a greater forward thrust with two impulses rather than one.

To date, there have been three studies comparing the track and grab starts. In one, there was no difference in speed for a distance of 5, 10, and 12.5 yd (Counsilman, Counsilman, Nomura, & Endo, 1988). In another study, swimmers left the block significantly faster with the track start, but there was no difference in time between it and the regular grab start for a distance of 5 m (approximately 16 yd) (Ayalon, Van Gheluwe, & Kanitz, 1975). In a third study, the track start was significantly slower than the grab start for a distance of 5.5 m (approximately 18 yd) (Zatsiorsky, Bulgakova, & Chaplinsky, 1979).

Apparently, the jury is still out on the track start. Swimmers who use this style seem to *get off the block* faster, but they enter the water at a somewhat flatter angle and lose time during the glide. By contrast, swimmers who use the conventional starting position (both feet at the edge of the block) are slower leaving the block but enter the water at an angle that permits a faster glide.

Although some successful athletes have used the track start effectively, I believe that the pike start is potentially better. It allows swimmers to enter the water more streamlined so that they can glide faster underwater. Both Guimares and Hay (1985) and Zatsiorsky and his associates (1979) have reported that the gliding speed after entry accounts for most of the difference in starting times. Zatsiorsky and coworkers reported a significant relationship of 0.94 second between starting speed and gliding speed. By comparison, the correlation between starting speed and speed off the block was 0.60 second.

It should be mentioned, however, that the track start is clearly superior for preventing false starts. Swimmers have a more stable position on the platform and are not as likely to lose their balance if they pull early.

Pike Start

Figure 22-2 (pp. 548–549) shows the pike start. These drawings show an *ideal* technique from above and from under the water. Figure 22-3 (p. 550) also provides a "real-life" photographic perspective, although the underwater portion is not visible. For descriptive purposes, the pike start is divided into (1) the preparatory position, (2) the pull, (3) the drive from the block, (4) the flight, (5) the entry, (6) the glide, and (7) the pullout.

Preparatory Position Figure 22-2*a* illustrates the preparatory position. Swimmers should stand at the rear of the starting platform until the starter gives them permission to assume the preparatory position by saying, Take your marks. After that command, swimmers assume a preparatory position in which the toes of both feet grip the front edge of the starting platform. Their feet should be approximately shoulder width, because this position permits a stronger leg drive than one in which the feet are outside the shoulders or positioned close together. Swimmers grasp the front edge of the starting platform with the first and second joints of their fingers. Their hands may be either inside or outside their feet, because neither method has proven superior to the other. Their knees should be flexed approximately 30 to 40 degrees, and their elbows should be flexed slightly. Their head should be down, and they should look at the water just beyond the starting platform. Swimmers should lean forward in the preparatory position, and they should maintain themselves just on balance by holding onto the block with their hands.

Swimmers are generally asked to bend their knees more and to keep their heads up higher. The knee and head positions that I describe are different from those usually recommended for the following reasons: With their legs flexed less, swimmers' hips remain closer to the front edge of the starting platform. This is desirable because one of the most important determinants in getting off the block quickly is the speed with which the center of mass can be moved beyond the front edge of the starting platform. The center of mass is the balance point of the body and is located

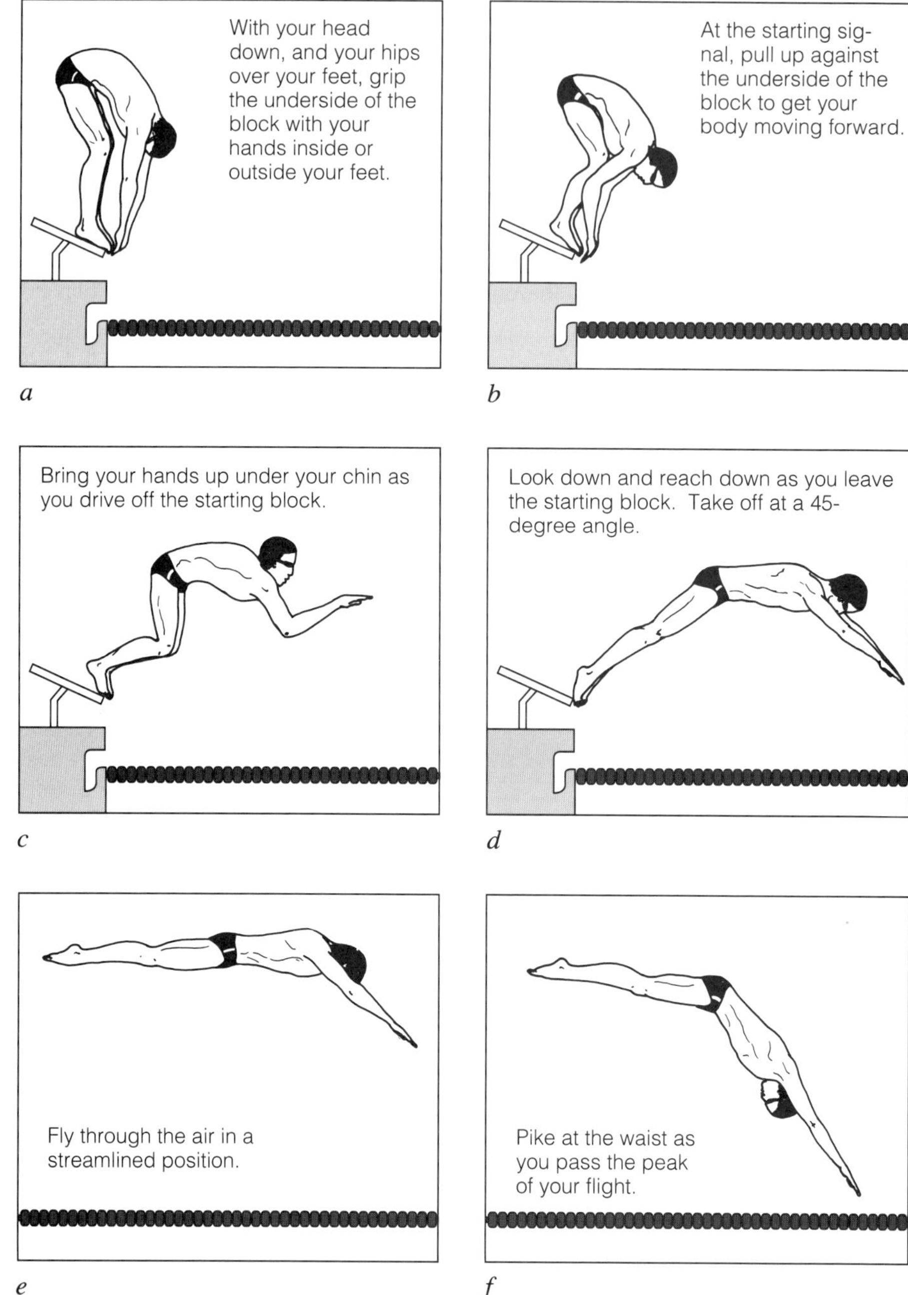

Figure 22-2. The pike start.

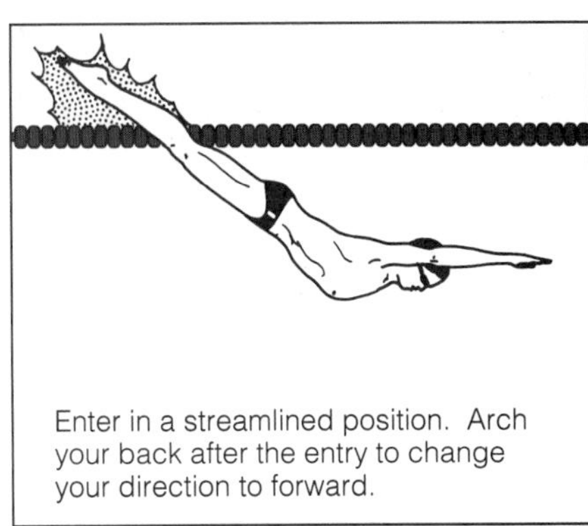

Enter in a streamlined position. Arch your back after the entry to change your direction to forward.

g

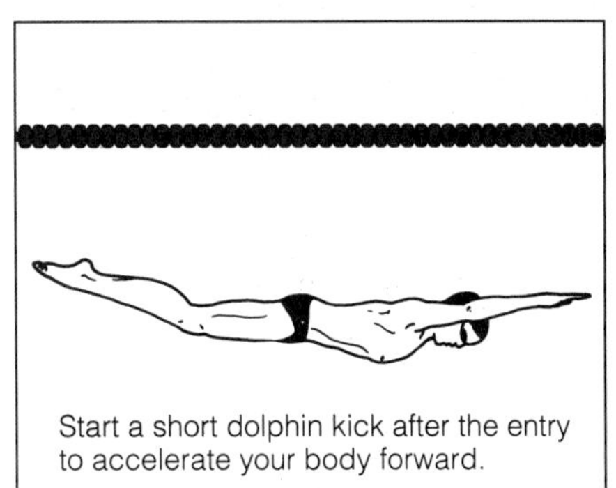

Start a short dolphin kick after the entry to accelerate your body forward.

h

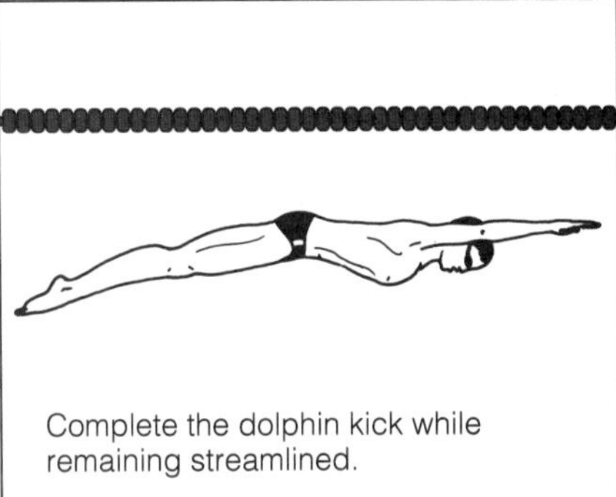

Complete the dolphin kick while remaining streamlined.

i

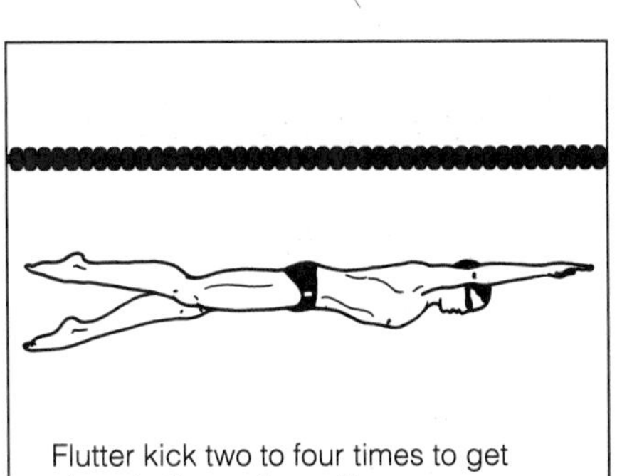

Flutter kick two to four times to get close to the surface. Keep your head down and remain streamlined.

j

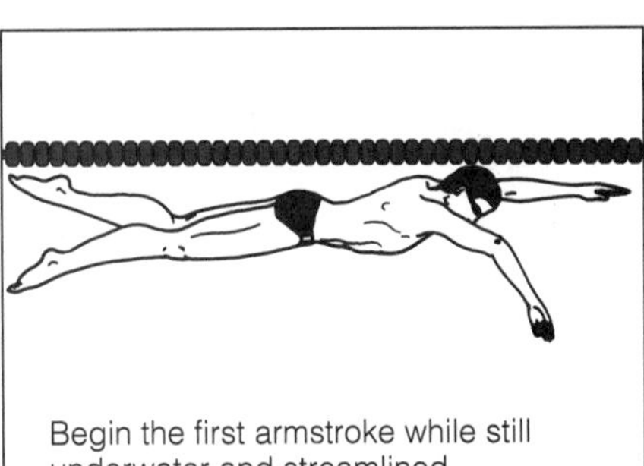

Begin the first armstroke while still underwater and streamlined.

k

Complete the first armstroke as your head breaks through the surface. Don't breathe on the first stroke after the start in sprint races.

l

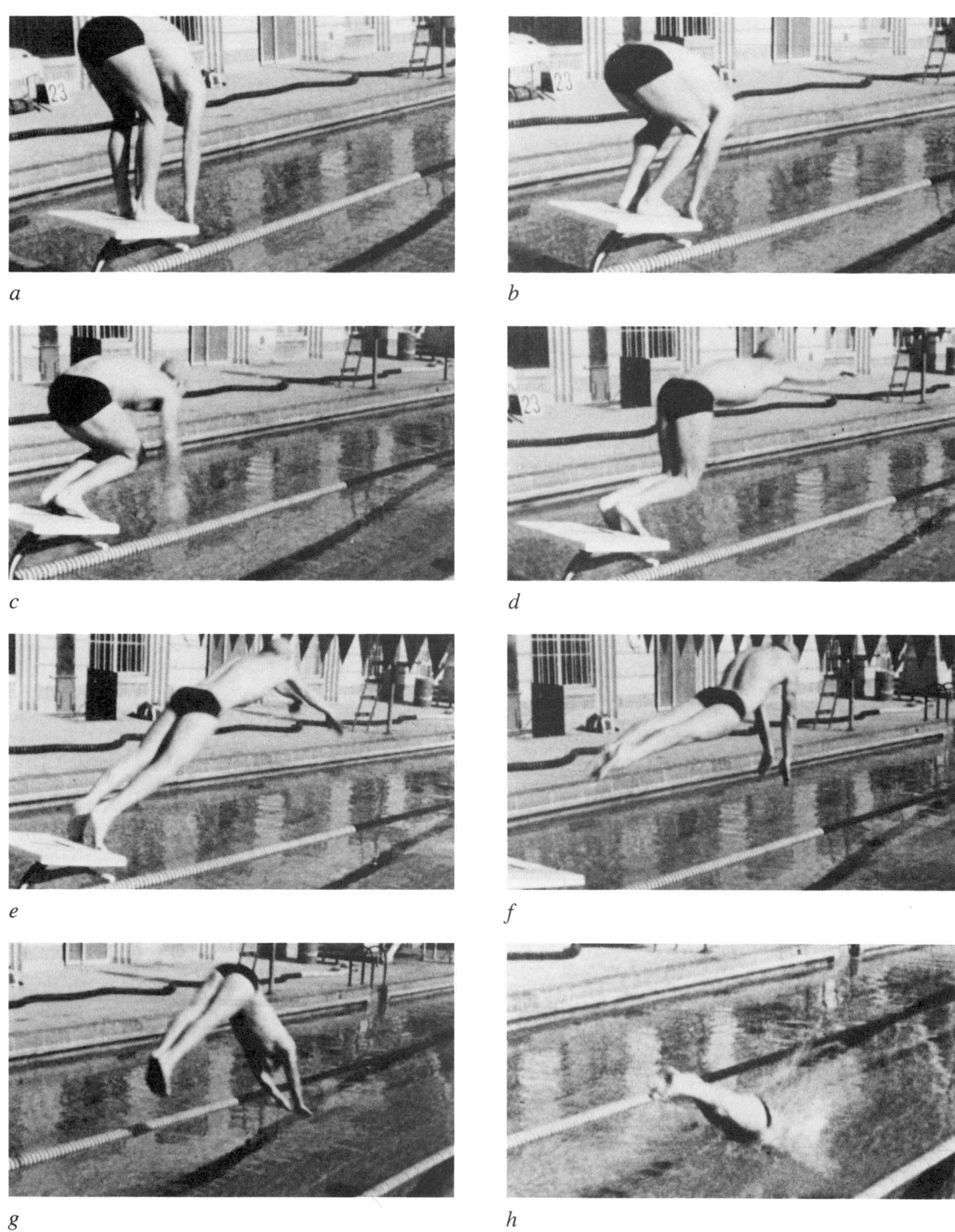

Figure 22-3. Sequence photos of a swimmer performing a pike start.

in the hip area. However, its location shifts slightly each time swimmers rearrange their body parts. A deep crouch places the center of mass farther back behind the feet than a preparatory position in which the hips are up and over the feet, thus, requiring additional time to move the center of mass beyond the front edge of the starting block.

Figure 22-4 compares the position of the center of mass for these two preparatory positions. In Figure 22-4*b*, the swimmer assumes a deep crouch. The swimmer in Figure 22-4*a* has his legs flexed less. You can see that the center of mass tends to be farther back behind the front edge of the platform when a deep crouch is used.

The position of the head also plays a role in the position of the center of mass on the starting platform. When it is down, as it is in Figure 22-4*a*, the center of mass tends to shift forward slightly. When the head is looking up, as it is in Figure 22-4*b*, the position of the center of mass shifts back slightly.

Pull At the sound of the starting signal, swimmers should *pull up* against the starting platform (see Figure 22-2*b*). This pulls the hips and the center of gravity down and forward beyond the front edge of the starting platform so that they begin falling toward the water. Pulling in this direction also flexes the knees and hips so that swimmers can thrust their body forward rapidly with their legs once they are in position to do so. *Swimmers should not push back against the starting platform with their hands*. This will result in a slower speed off the block.

There is no need for swimmers to use a long or powerful arm pull to get their body in motion. This will not add speed or force to the dive. All they need to do is to get their body moving forward, and gravity will take over.

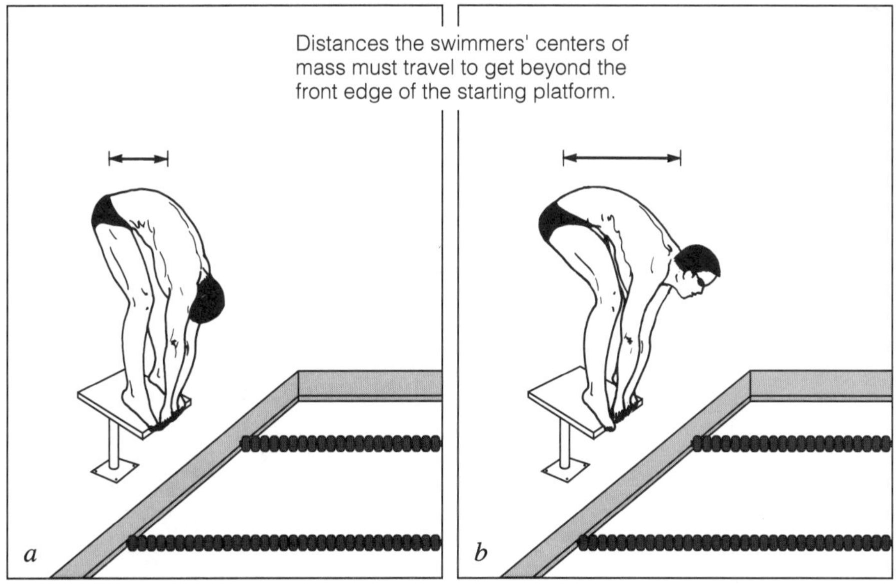

Figure 22-4. A comparison of the position of the center of mass in two preparatory positions for the standing start.

Drive from the Block Figures 22-2*c* and 22-2*d* illustrate this phase of the start. Swimmers should release the front of the starting platform immediately when their body starts moving forward. They will fall down and forward until their knees are flexed approximately 80 degrees, at which time they begin extending their legs as they drive from the starting platform. The leg drive is executed by a powerful extension at the hips and knee joints, followed by an extension of the feet at the ankles.

When their hands release the block, swimmers should extend their arms forward in a semicircular path until they are pointing at the area where they wish to enter the water. Their arms should bend rapidly during the first half of the movement to bring them up under the chin as they fall forward. They should then extend their arms rapidly forward and down as they extend their legs during the second half of the drive.

The head should follow the movements of the arms, looking up and then down. Swimmers should time their head movements so that they are *looking down as they extend their legs* and before they leave the starting platform.

The angle of takeoff from feet to hips should be approximately 35 to 40 degrees from the top edge of the starting block (see Figure 22-2*d*). This angle will give swimmers the arc-like trajectory they need for a clean entry.

Flight After leaving the starting platform, swimmers travel through the air with their trunk in a piked position (see Figures 22-2*e* and 22-2*f*). Swimmers achieve the pike position at the top of the flight by driving their arms forward and *down* and *by looking down* as they leave the block. This technique causes their upper body to begin moving down for the water as their hips and legs continue up over the peak of the flight. After their body passes that peak, swimmers pull their legs up in line with their trunk to streamline their entire body as it enters the water.

Entry Swimmers should try to enter their entire body into the water through the same *hole* they opened with their hands. The entry is shown in Figure 22-2*g*. It is also shown from behind in Figure 22-5, which clearly shows how the body enters through the same hole made by the hands and head.

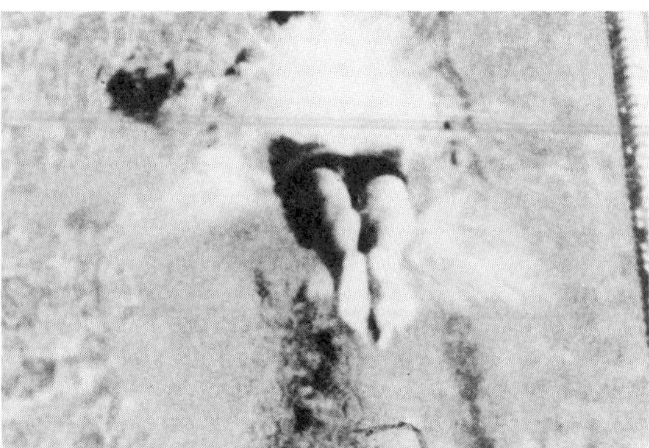

Figure 22-5. A view from behind of a swimmer entering the water with a pike start.

The body should be streamlined during the entry. The arms should be fully extended and together, preferably with one hand on top of the other. The head should be between the arms. The legs should be fully extended and together, with the toes extended back (pointed), and there should be no arch or pike at the waist. The angle of entry should be approximately 30 to 40 degrees from the surface of the water (Beritzhoff, 1974).

Although swimmers will be streamlined if they enter the water in the manner just described, this steep angle will cause them to plunge too deep beneath the surface unless they make some adjustments to change the direction in which their body is traveling immediately after it enters the water. They accomplish this directional change from down and forward to forward and up after entering by snapping their legs down in a dolphin kicking motion and, at the same time, by lifting their head and hands toward the surface (see Figures 22-2*g* through 22-2*i*). The timing of these actions will vary according to how quickly swimmers wish to reach the surface. In shorter races, they will begin as their body enters the water. In longer races, they will wait until after their body is nearly submerged. The only exception takes place in the breaststroke, in which swimmers purposely glide deeper underwater in preparation for their underwater armstroke.

Glide After the entry, swimmers should glide for a short time in the most streamlined position possible. Their head should remain down between their arms. Their arms should be extended overhead and held tightly together, with one hand on top of the other. Their legs should be extended and together, with their toes extended back. Swimmers should not arch their back or pike at their waist. *The glide should be extended until swimmers are approaching the velocity of the race.* They will lose time and waste muscular effort accelerating their body back to race speed if they glide too long. Swimmers should glide for only a short time in sprint races, yet they should hold the glide position for a somewhat greater length of time for longer races.

Pullout In butterfly and front crawl races, swimmers should begin kicking just before they decelerate to race velocity. Their upper body should remain streamlined during these kicks, with their head down between their extended arms (see Figure 22-2*j*). Two dolphin kicks or two to four flutter kicks should bring them close to the surface, where they can begin their underwater pullout and recover their arms over the water with no delay.

Swimmers should begin their first armstroke when they near the surface, and their head should break through the surface as it is being completed. That armstroke should be a powerful sweep back that brings them up through the surface traveling forward at race speed. Their head should remain down during the underwater stroke, and they should not look up until they feel it break through the surface (see Figures 22-2*k* and 22-2*l*). Swimmers should pull and kick themselves diagonally to the surface so that they reach it traveling forward more than up.

Swimmers should not delay in attaining the proper stroke rhythm for the race once they reach the surface. Breathing and looking around are two of the most common causes for such delays. For this reason, it is best for swimmers of freestyle and butterfly events to delay breathing until the end of the first stroke. They should wait even longer in sprint events. Breaststroke swimmers take one underwater armstroke after the start and breathe as their head comes through the surface. Breaststrokers should be sure that they surface before their arms reach the widest point during the second armstroke.

I want to elaborate on the movement of the head during the pike start because this is, perhaps, the *key* technique in achieving a streamlined entry. As mentioned, swimmers must begin looking down at the instant their feet leave the starting platform. Lowering their head establishes a downward trajectory for their upper body during the flight so that they can pike and lift their legs in time to enter their entire body in the same spot. Many swimmers look ahead during their flight through the air and cannot execute a pike start effectively.

Figure 22-6 shows the entry for a swimmer who keeps his head up during the flight. As a consequence, he passes the peak of the flight with his trunk angled up, which causes him to pike on the way down. He does not have time to get his legs up behind him for a streamlined entry, so he enters the water in a piked position, with his legs behind his trunk and dragging forward through the water. This will, of course, increase drag and slow his glide underwater.

Track Start

Figure 22-7 illustrates the track start. The major differences between this start and the pike start are in the preparatory position and the angle of takeoff. Figure 22-7*a* illustrates the preparatory position. The obvious difference is that one foot is behind the other. Figure 22-7*d* shows the angle of takeoff. Notice that it is much flatter than the takeoff angle for the pike start.

While waiting for the starting signal, swimmers place the toes of one foot over the front edge and press the other foot back against the incline of the starting platform. Their head should be down, and they should grip the front edge of the

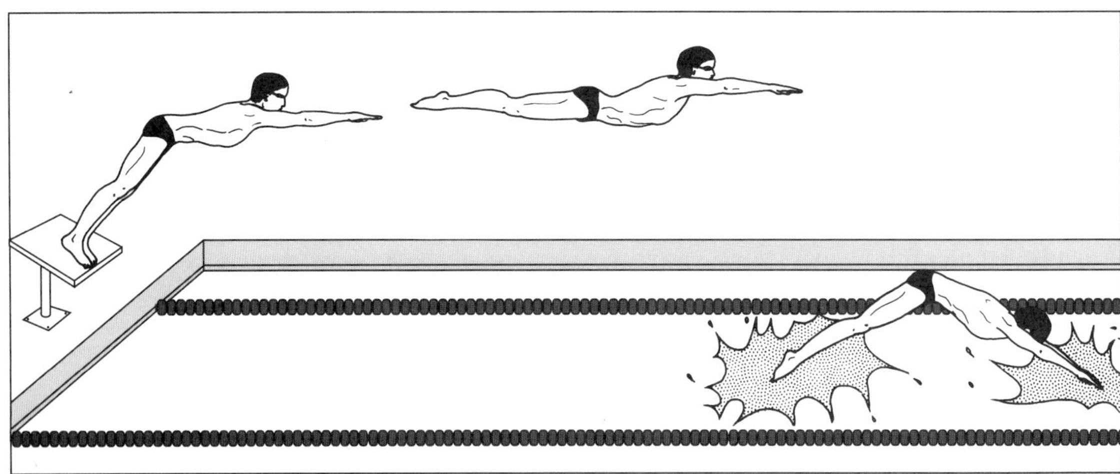

Figure 22-6. The effect of keeping the head up too long during the flight.

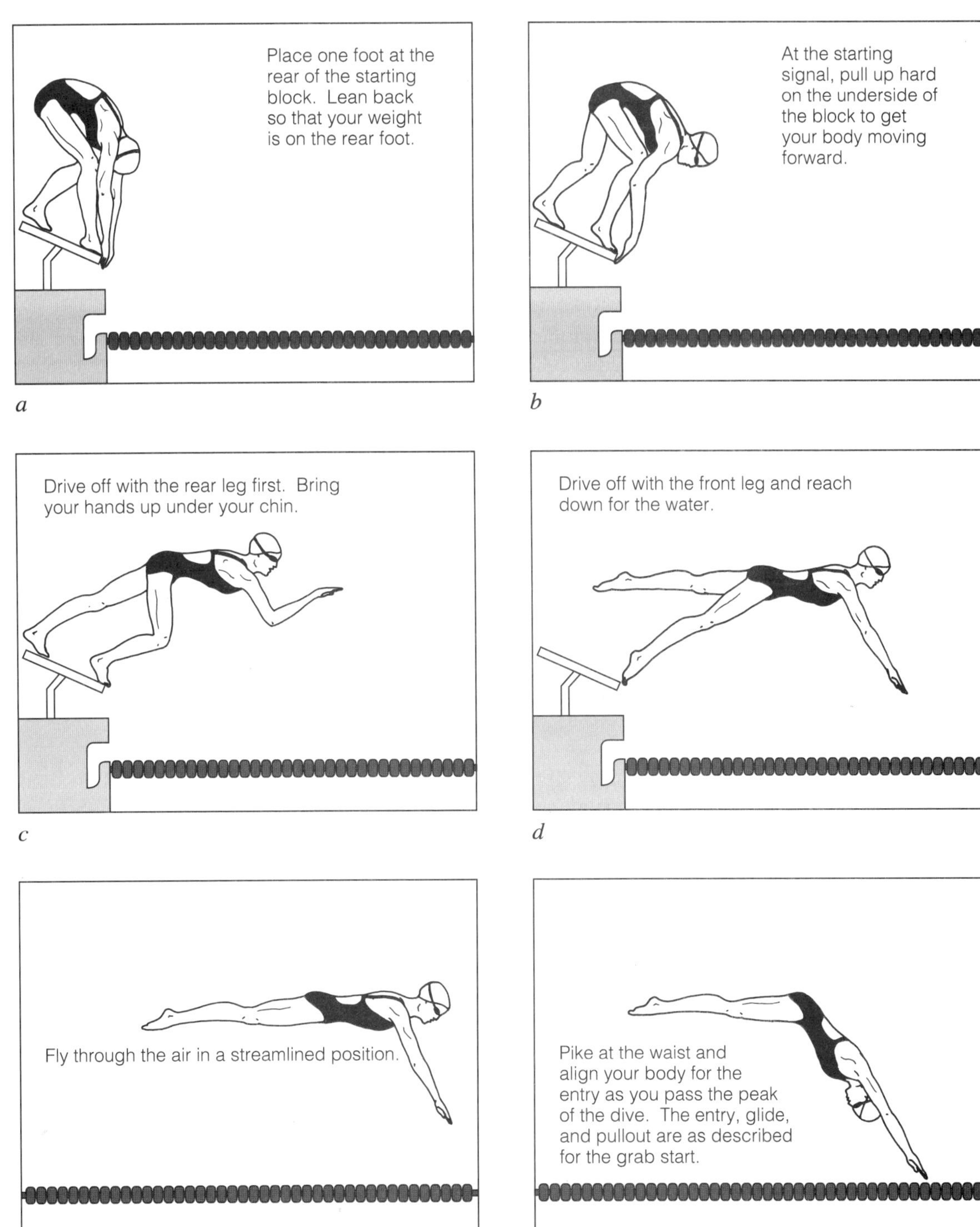

Figure 22-7. The track start.

block with both hands. They should lean back, with their *weight on the ball of the rear foot*. When the starting signal sounds, swimmers pull their body down and forward with their hands to start them falling for the water. When their hips are outside the front edge of the block, they let go with their hands and shoot their arms forward in the same semicircular arc described for the pike start (see Figures 22-2*c* and 22-2*d*). In the meantime, they drive off the block by extending their rear leg first and then immediately extending their front leg (see Figures 22-7*c* and 22-7*d*).

When swimmers leave the starting platform they fly through the air in an arc that is somewhat flatter than the arc of the pike start (see Figures 22-2*e* and 22-2*f*). This makes it almost impossible for their body to enter the water in one spot. Nevertheless, they should try for the cleanest, most streamlined entry possible. As in the pike start, swimmers should look up when pulling their body forward, and they should look down when their feet are leaving the block. They should probably pike slightly at the waist during the flight in order to achieve a better angle of entry.

Swimmers who use the track start should try for the steepest angle of takeoff that is compatible with their low position at the start. They do not want to drive off the block at a large angle, however, because their center of mass will rise too high during the flight through the air and that will negate the advantage of moving it rapidly and horizontally forward. The glide and pullout should be the same as described for the pike start.

Faster Reactions to the Starting Signal

Reaction time is the interval between the starting signal and the swimmer's first movement. That interval of time can be shortened by concentrating only on the starting signal.

Henry and Rogers (1960) have shown that concentrating on the starting signal rather than the starting movements produces faster reaction times. They believed that this happens because the brain functions like a computer by reacting more slowly when it is required to process more information. In other words, swimmers take longer to react after the starting signal has sounded if they are thinking about the myriad movements they will execute during the dive. If they concentrate only on the starting signal, their reaction time should be shortened because they can let the start "unfold" automatically. Measurements for several athletes indicate that the difference in speed is in the neighborhood of 0.03 to 0.06 second.

To use this technique successfully, swimmers must learn the mechanics of the start so thoroughly that they can perform them almost perfectly without conscious thought. It would do no good to react fast and dive poorly. The time gained in reacting would be lost several times over during the flight through the air and the glide under the water. Consequently, swimmers cannot concentrate only on the starting signal until they learn to dive correctly. In the meantime, they can improve their reaction time by reducing the number of self-instructions to the absolute minimum needed to perform a reasonably good dive. Reaction time should improve somewhat if swimmers concentrate only on those elements in the dive that are incorrect, rather than the entire sequence of movements.

RELAY STARTS

In relay races, the rules permit the second, third, and fourth swimmers to be in motion on the starting platform before their incoming teammates have finished their segment of the race. Their toes must still be in contact with the platform when the incoming swimmer touches the wall, or the relay can be disqualified. Because they can be in motion before the incoming swimmer touches the wall, the outgoing swimmers can gain an advantage of 0.60 to 1.00 second over a signaled start. Consequently, three swimmers with good relay starts could swim a time that is 2 to 3 seconds faster than the sum of their best flat-start times. This could easily make a difference of two or more places in today's closely contested championship meets, and it could frequently be the deciding factor in dual-meet victories. Good relay starts could improve a team's total by as much as 14 points in dual meets; with five relays in championship meets, the amount could be considerably more. For this reason, swimmers should practice relay starts until they can regularly leave the block as early as possible without being disqualified.

The conventional grab start or track start should *not* be used on relays, except by the lead-off swimmer. A circular-backswing start is preferable because it provides greater speed through the air. Circling the arms backward and then forward adds additional momentum to the dive, which allows swimmers to get out farther before entering the water and glide faster after entering it. Contrary to the belief of some, circling the arms *does not* delay getting in motion, because the outgoing swimmer can start his or her armswing before the incoming swimmer touches the wall. Figure 22-8 (p. 558) illustrates a circular-backswing relay start.

Proper timing of the armswing is critical so that the outgoing swimmer gains the maximum possible advantage without leaving the starting platform too early. Consequently, the outgoing swimmer must make judgments based on his incoming teammate's speed and distance from the wall. In relays, the usual practice is to begin the *windup* (the circular backswing of the arms) after the incoming swimmer's head crosses the *T* of the black lane marker on the bottom of the pool. From that point, it should require *one arm recovery,* approximately 0.60 second for the incoming swimmer to touch the wall (see Figure 22-8*b*). It requires about the same time for the outgoing swimmer's feet to leave the block once his arms start in motion.

Consequently, the outgoing swimmer should coordinate his armswing with the final recovery of the incoming swimmer. The timing should be as follows: In backstroke, butterfly, and freestyle races, the outgoing swimmer should establish a recovery rhythm for the incoming swimmer by moving (pumping) his arms slightly in time with the arm recovery of the incoming swimmer as he approaches the *T* at the end of the lane marker. That is, the outgoing swimmer should move his arms back and forth slightly as the incoming swimmer recovers his arm(s) over the water. Once the incoming swimmer's head crosses the *T,* the outgoing swimmer should coordinate his circular backswing with the final recovery of the incoming swimmer's arms. The outgoing swimmer should follow that recovery in by swinging his arms back in the first part of the circular backswing as the incoming swimmer's arms recover forward. The outgoing swimmer should then swing his arms forward

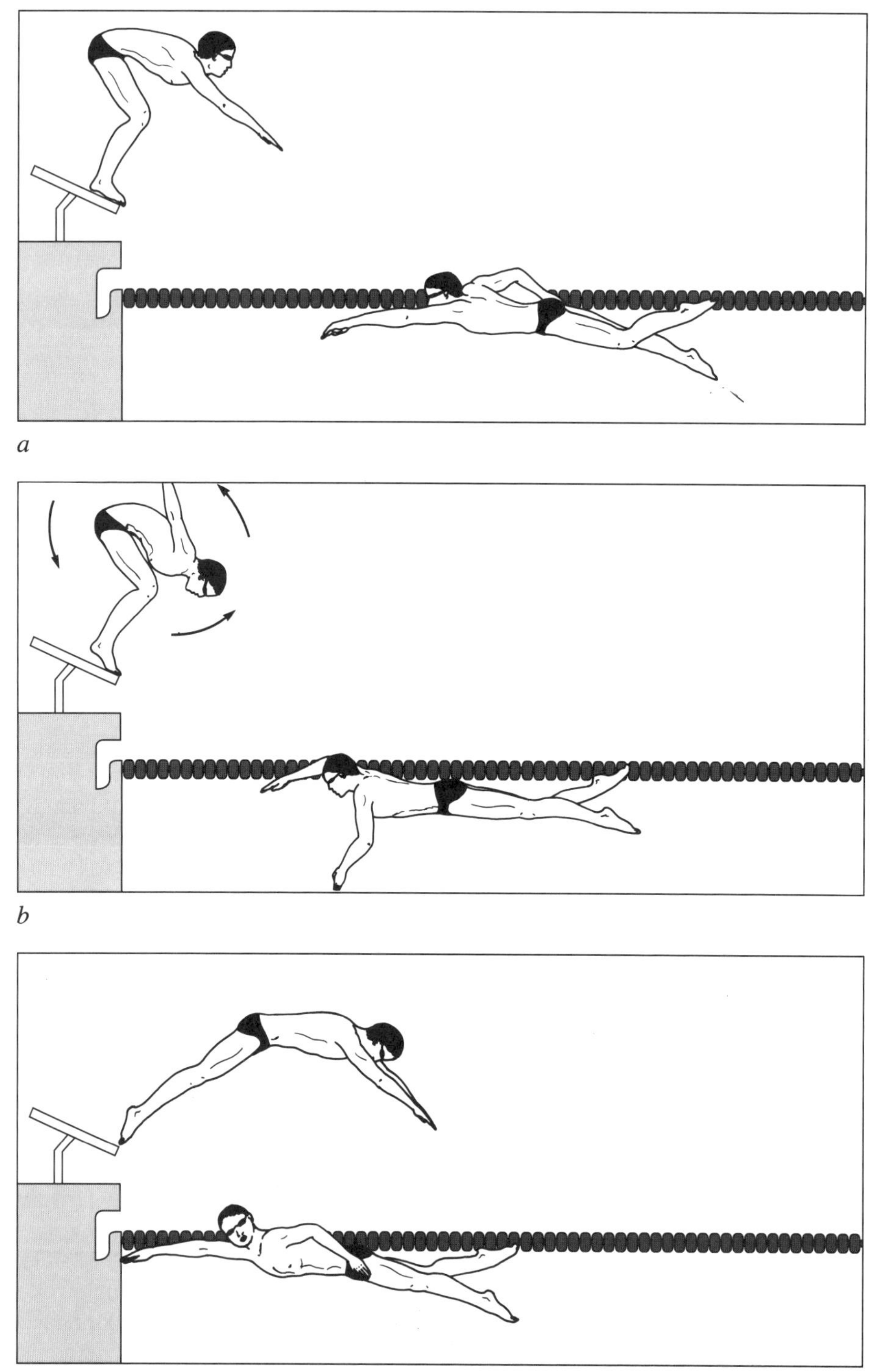

Figure 22-8. A circular-backswing relay start.

as the incoming swimmer's hand(s) enters the water and stretches for the wall (see Figure 22-8*b*). The outgoing swimmer should be in the act of pushing off the block as the incoming swimmer touches the wall (see Figure 22-8*c*).

In the medley relays, the manner in which butterfly swimmers time their relay starts from incoming breaststrokers is quite similar, except for the fact that the breaststroker's last arm recovery will be made underwater. The outgoing swimmer, once again, should move his arms back in time with the arm recovery of the incoming swimmer as the latter approaches the *T* at the end of the lane line. The armswing of the outgoing butterflyer is made in time with the final forward arm recovery of the incoming breaststroker. The outgoing butterflyer should wait for the breaststroker's head to reach the highest point in his breathing cycle as he approaches the *T*. The breaststroker's arms will be under his chin at that time and ready to stretch forward to touch the wall. The outgoing butterflyer should swing his arms back in time with the incoming breaststroker's reach forward. The outgoing butterflyer should then swing his arms forward and dive off the starting platform when the incoming swimmer completes his reach for the wall.

Step-Through Relay Start

A recent development in relay starting has been the use of a *step-through* method. With this technique, the swimmer waits with both feet at the *rear edge* of the starting platform. Similar to the timing for the relay start just described, when the incoming swimmer's head passes the *T*, the outgoing swimmer steps forward with one foot and executes a circular-backswing start in time with the final arm recovery of the incoming swimmer. The drive off the starting platform is made in the manner of a track start, with the outgoing swimmer pushing off the rear inclined portion of the platform with one foot followed immediately by the other foot pushing off the front edge with the toes.

Proponents of the step-through method believe that swimmers can gain additional momentum as they leave the block because their body weight will shift forward as they execute the circular armswing. This advantage seems doubtful. Outgoing swimmers can shift their body weight forward with conventional methods just as effectively as with the step-through start because they are permitted to be in motion before the incoming swimmer touches the wall. Furthermore, an important advantage of the conventional relay start is that it does not require such precise timing. Consequently, the possibility of *jumping* on relays should be lessened with a conventional relay start.

BACKSTROKE START

Short-course and long-course rules have now been standardized so that swimmers must have their feet entirely underwater in the preparatory position for all backstroke races. This rule change will probably eliminate the stand-up backstroke start that was used so successfully when short-course rules allowed swimmers to stand in the gutter. All swimmers will now have to push off from the flat end of the wall, making it more difficult to drive their body over the water. Figure 22-9 (pp. 560–561) and Figure 22-10 (p. 562) show the backstroke start.

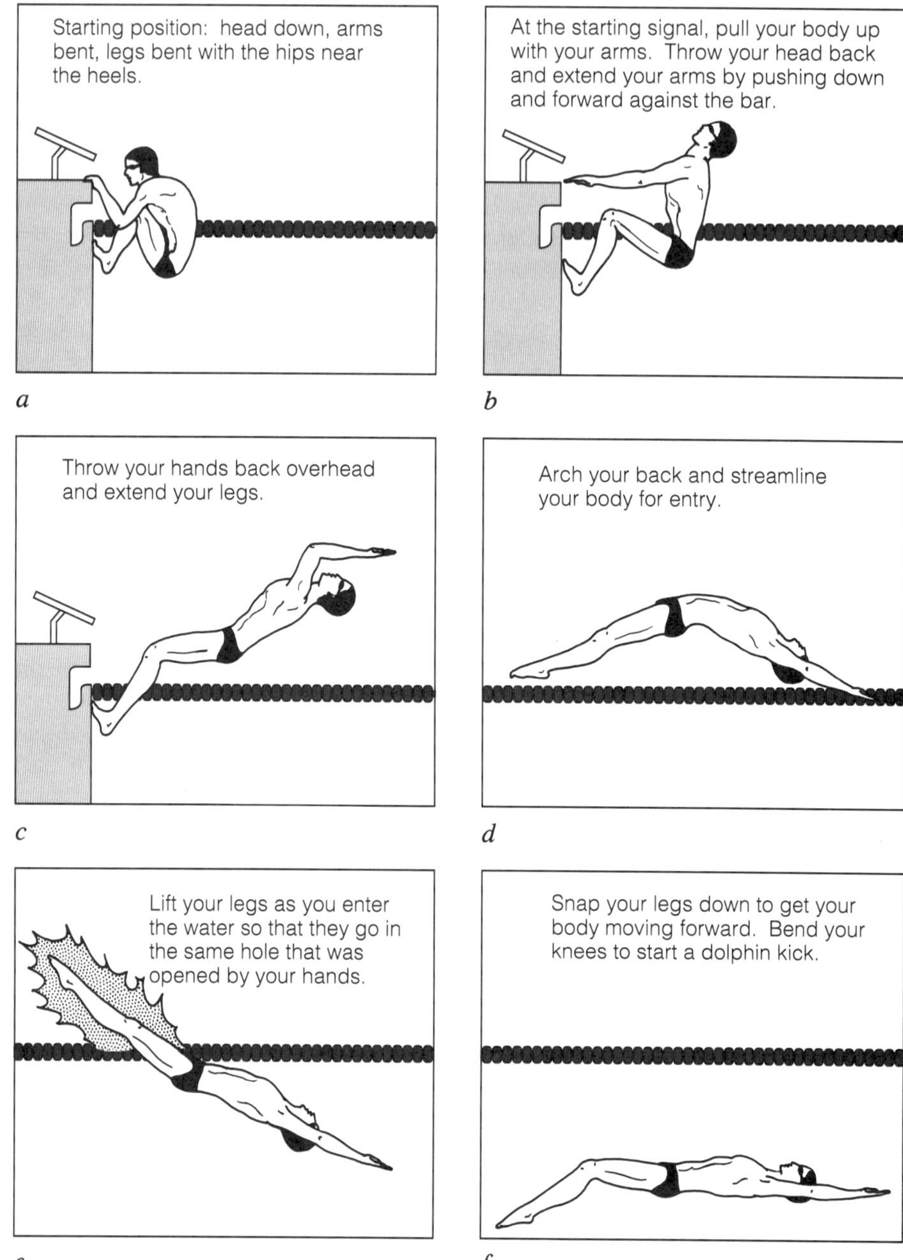

Figure 22-9. The backstroke start.

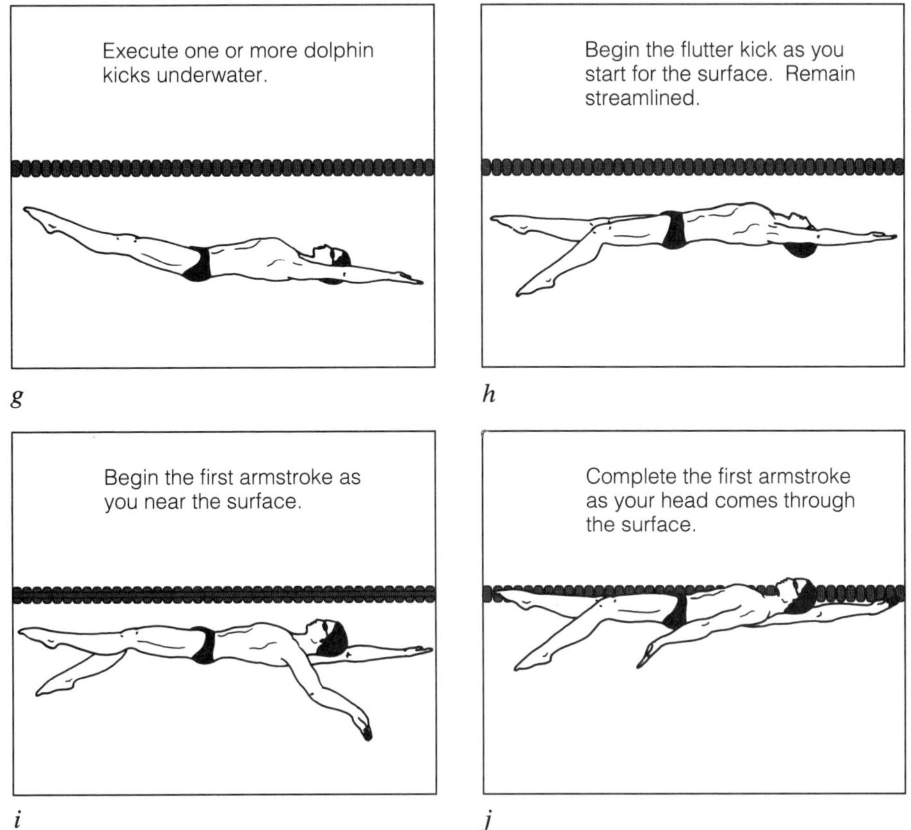

Preparatory Position

While waiting for the command, Take your marks, swimmers should be in the water facing the wall and gripping the backstroke bar with both hands. Their feet should be entirely underwater and in contact with the end of the wall. The balls of their feet and their toes should be against the wall, and their heels should be away from the wall. Their legs should be bent and their hips in the water.

Swimmers should pull themselves into a crouched position when commanded to take their marks. Their head should be down, and they should be looking at the gutter in front. Their arms should be flexed at the elbows, and their elbows should be in against their sides. Their hips should be as high as possible without removing their feet from the wall (see Figure 22-9*a*). Their feet should be entirely underwater, with their buttocks close to their heels.

Some swimmers have their feet together on the wall, yet others prefer to use a staggered position, with one foot slightly below the other. Research has not resolved this issue, so swimmers should try both foot placements and select the one that seems best.

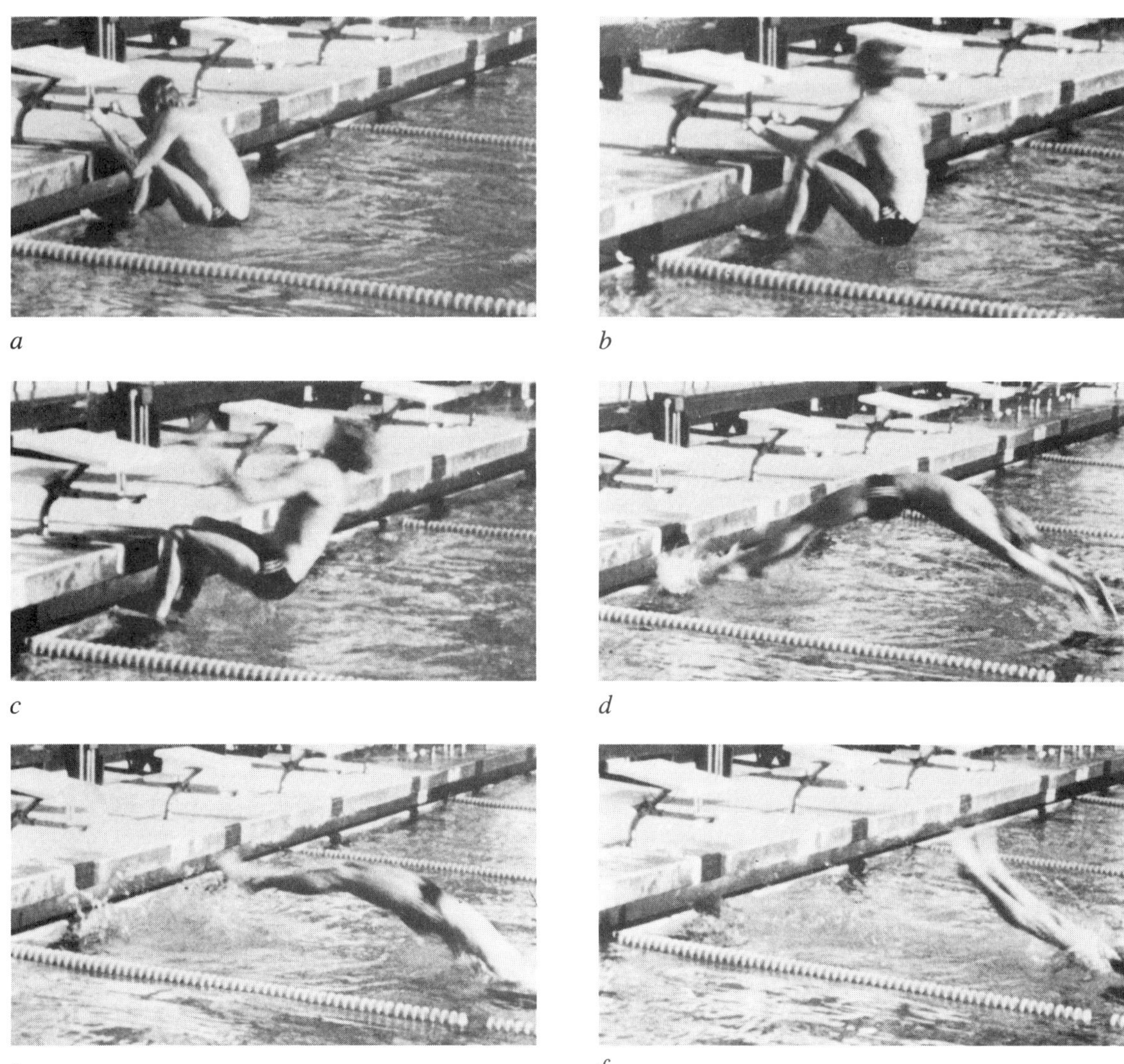

a *b* *c* *d* *e* *f* *g*

Figure 22-10. Swimmer Bengt Baron performing the backstroke start.

Drive from the Wall

When the starting signal sounds, swimmers should throw their head up and back and look for the opposite end of the pool. Simultaneously, they should push their body up and back by pushing down and forward against the bar with their hands (see Figure 22-9*b*). Once their body is in motion, swimmers should release the bar and bring their arms over their head as quickly as possible. At the same time, they should push their body up and away from the wall with their legs (see Figure 22-9*c*). The leg drive is accomplished by a powerful extension at the knees followed by an extension of the feet.

Swimmer's arms should be thrown *up and back overhead* (as shown in Figure 22-11), not around to the side as has been traditionally taught. Their arms should bend during the first half of the swing overhead, and they should extend during the second half, as they reach back and down for the entry. That extension should take place concurrently as their legs extend from the wall to add momentum and streamlining to the dive.

There are at least two reasons for recommending that backstrokers swing their arms overhead rather than around to the side.

1. Swimmers' arms will get overhead faster so that their body can be lined up from fingertips to toes as their feet leave the wall. In the other method, their arms travel sideward while their legs are extending. This will not add to their momentum.

2. An overhead armswing encourages a higher arc and a greater back arch during the flight. This should, in turn, provide for a more streamlined entry.

Flight

The body should travel through the air in an arc, with the back arched, the head facing back, and the arms extended overhead. The legs should also be extended and together, with the feet extended at the ankles (see Figure 22-9*d*).

Swimmers should endeavor to have their entire body out of the water during the flight, although this is difficult to do because of their low position in the water in the preparatory position. Nevertheless, if they get a reasonably high angle of takeoff and they arch their back sufficiently during the drive from the wall, they should be

Figure 22-11. A swimmer throwing his hands over his head during the backstroke start.

able to keep their lower legs and feet from dragging through the water during most of the flight.

Entry

Figure 22-9*e* illustrates this phase of the backstroke start. The entry should be made in a streamlined position, with the arms extended and together. The head should be between the arms, with the legs and feet remaining in an extended position. The angle of entry should be such that the hands enter first, followed by the head, trunk, and, finally, the legs. It would be ideal for the entire body, including the legs and the feet, to enter the same spot through which the hands first entered the water. This is difficult to accomplish because the swimmer is so near the water during the flight through the air. For this reason, the hips and legs usually enter the water slightly behind the point where the hands entered. Nevertheless, swimmers can reduce drag considerably by lifting their legs to a piked position as they enter. This will permit their legs to enter in nearly the same spot as their hips. The leg lift is accomplished by a contraction of the hip flexors. It is shown in Figure 22-9*e* and Figure 22-10*f*.

Glide and Dolphin Kick

After entering the water, swimmers should bring their legs down sharply to change the direction of their body from down to forward. Several quick dolphin kicks will assist in making this change of direction (see Figures 22-9*f* and 22-9*g*). The arms should be straight from the fingertips to the shoulders. The back of one hand should be in the palm of the other. The head should be between the arms.

A sizable number of backstroke swimmers have begun using a dolphin kick during the underwater phase of this start. International rules now permit them to do so for up to 15 m. Those with good dolphin kicks should take advantage of this rule change and kick as much of the 15 m underwater as possible before surfacing.

Pullout

After several dolphin kicks, swimmers should begin flutterkicking and take one underwater armstroke that brings them to the surface (see Figures 22-9*i* and 22-9*j*). They should not lift their head from a streamlined position until they reach the surface. Once on the surface, swimmers should establish the stroking frequency for the race as quickly as possible.

The back arch and head movements in this start control its success to a great extent, so I want to elaborate on them. As stated earlier, swimmers must throw their head up and back as they drive from the wall; however, they should not fly through the air with their head up. They must arch their back and start their head down *before their feet leave the wall* (see Figure 22-9*c*). These head movements provide the proper angle of takeoff and sufficient arch to the back to allow for a streamlined entry. Swimmers will most certainly land flat on their back if their head remains up and their back is not arched until after their feet leave the wall.

Common Mistakes

Two of the most common problems in the backstroke start have already been mentioned: (1) dragging the legs through the water during the flight and (2) landing flat on the back during the entry. There is a drill that can help correct these problems. Lay a small piece of rope across the lane at the point where the swimmers' hips should reach the peak of their flight. Swimmers then try to do backstroke starts over the rope without touching it.

Two final mistakes that many backstroke swimmers make are (1) lifting their head out of a streamlined position during the glide and (2) gliding to the surface before beginning their armstroke. The additional drag created by the loss of streamlining when they lift their head early will, of course, decelerate forward velocity during the glide. Kicking rather than stroking to the surface will cause them to decelerate well below race speed before beginning their armstroke.

TURNS

Turns for freestyle, backstroke, butterfly, and breaststroke races are described in this section. The turns used while changing from one stroke to the next in individual medley races are also covered.

Freestyle Flip Turn

There seem to be two styles of freestyle flip turns in use. The techniques of both are similar, except that swimmers push off on their side in one and they push off on their back in the other. The latter turn is described here. I believe that it is the faster method.

Figure 22-12 (pp. 566–567) shows a swimmer executing that turn correctly. It is a forward somersault with approximately a one-eighth twist of the body toward a prone position followed by a pushoff from the wall. Swimmers rotate the remaining seven-eighths to a prone position during the glide. The sequence of this turn is described under the following heading: (1) approach, (2) turn, (3) pushoff, (4) glide, and (5) pullout.

Approach Figure 22-12*a* shows the swimmer approaching the wall. She actually begins the turn while taking her final armstroke into the wall. Most swimmers begin that final armstroke 1.70 to 2.00 m (5.50 to 6.50 ft) from the wall (Chow, Hay, Wilson, & Imel, 1984). Sprinters tend to start the turn sooner, probably because they are traveling into the wall faster.

Swimmers should sight the wall from several strokes away in order to make modifications in their approach that will take them into the turn with no loss of speed. It is very important to maintain race speed on the approach, because an advantage can be gained over competitors, most of whom will slow down to anticipate the turn.

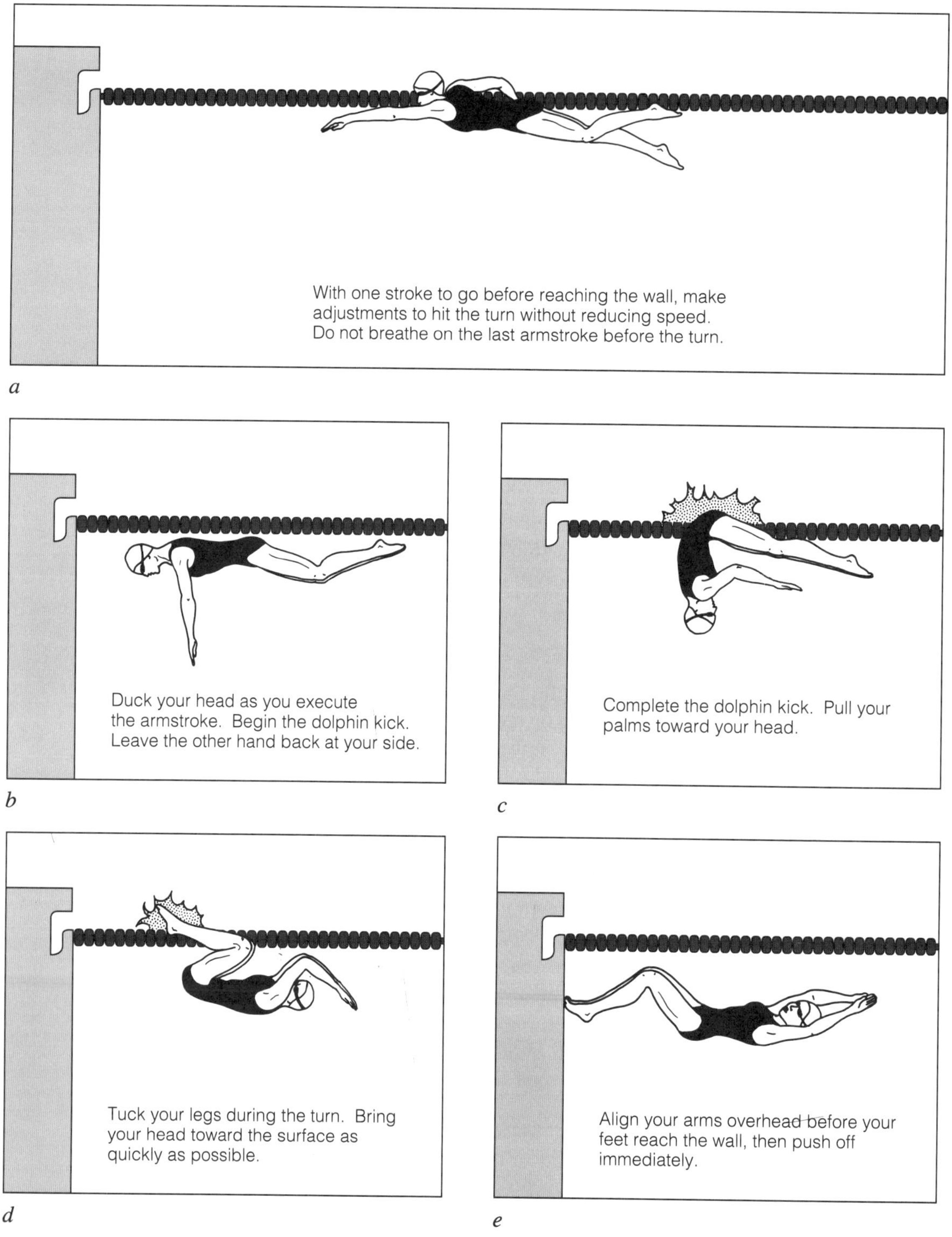

With one stroke to go before reaching the wall, make adjustments to hit the turn without reducing speed. Do not breathe on the last armstroke before the turn.

a

Duck your head as you execute the armstroke. Begin the dolphin kick. Leave the other hand back at your side.

b

Complete the dolphin kick. Pull your palms toward your head.

c

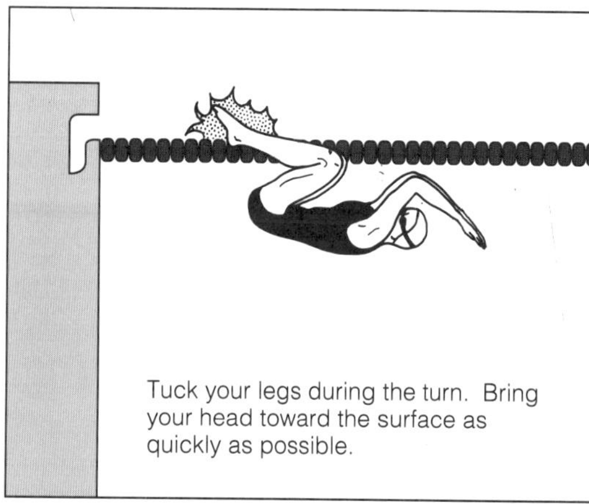

d

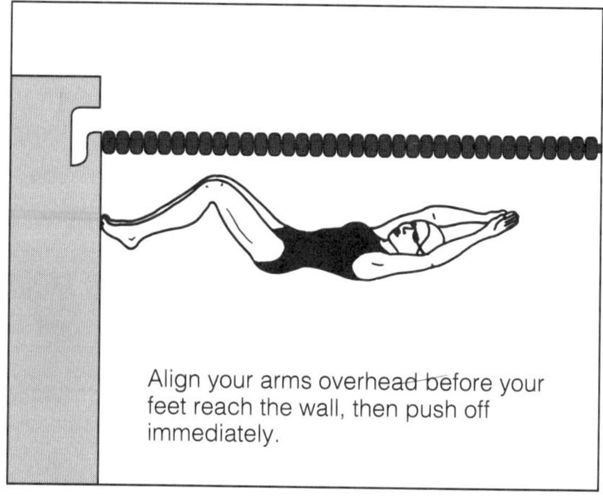

e

Figure 22-12. The freestyle flip turn.

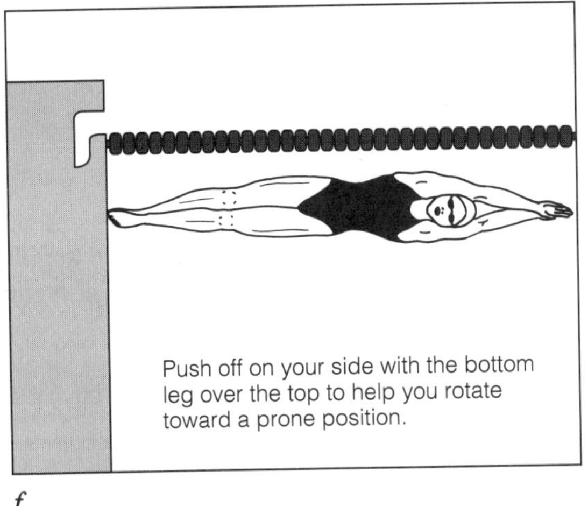
Push off on your side with the bottom leg over the top to help you rotate toward a prone position.

f

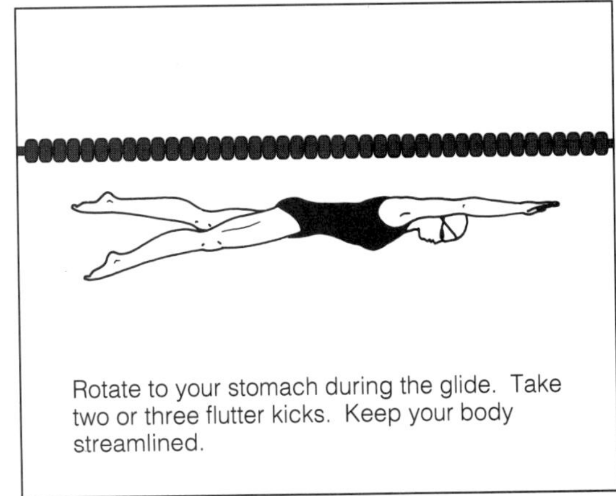
Rotate to your stomach during the glide. Take two or three flutter kicks. Keep your body streamlined.

g

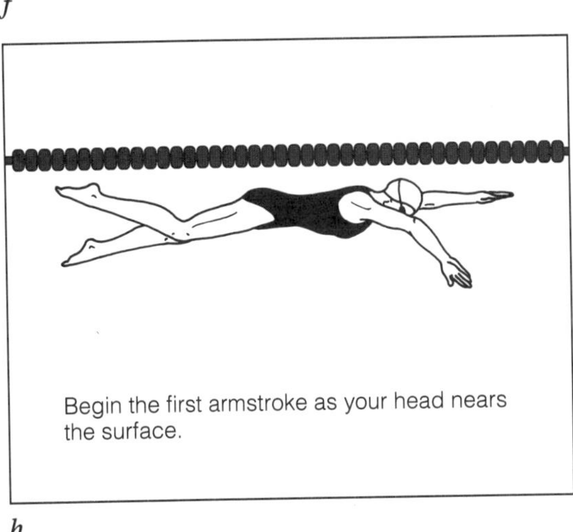
Begin the first armstroke as your head nears the surface.

h

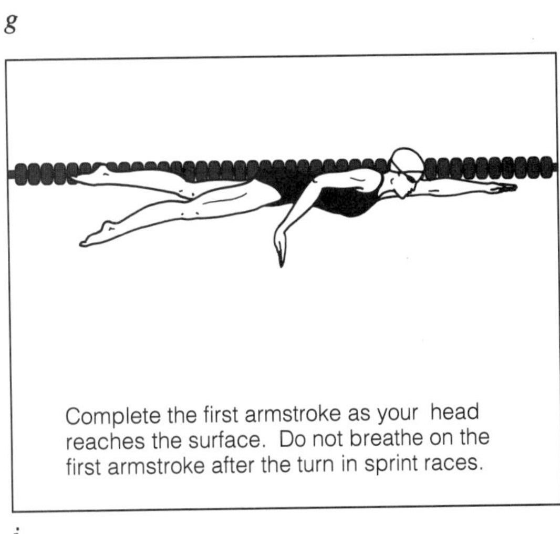
Complete the first armstroke as your head reaches the surface. Do not breathe on the first armstroke after the turn in sprint races.

i

Turn Figures 22-12*b* through 22-12*f* show the actual mechanics of the turn. The swimmer leaves her opposite arm in the water back at her hip when she begins the final armstroke prior to the turn. She pulls the forward arm back to her other hip during the final armstroke and begins somersaulting over during that arm pull. Her eyes focus on the wall at the beginning of that stroke, but she ducks her head and follows that arm back once it is underway.

The swimmer executes a small dolphin kick during the final armstroke to assist in pushing her hips up over the water (see Figures 22-12*b* and 22-12*c*). She continues somersaulting nearly straight over until her head comes up between her arms (see Figure 22-12*d*). Her legs are tucked as her feet travel over the water so that she can somersault faster.

Her hands, which were back at her hips during the first portion of the somersault, turn palms down and press down against the water to help pull her head toward the surface (see Figures 22-12*c* and 22-12*d*). Her head comes up between her arms before her feet reach the wall so that her body is aligned and ready for the pushoff at the instant her feet make contact. Her feet are planted on the wall with the toes facing up and slightly out in the same direction her body is facing (see Figure 22-12*e*).

Pushoff The swimmer's feet hit the wall at a depth of approximately 30 to 40 cm (12 to 15 inches). Her legs are flexed nearly 90 degrees at the hips and beyond 90 degrees at the knees when her feet make contact (see Figure 22-12*e*). She begins extending her legs immediately when contact is made. She rotates to a prone position during the pushoff and the glide that follows (see Figures 22-12*f* and 22-12*g*). The drive off the wall should be powerful. The swimmer extends her arms and legs simultaneously to add impetus to the pushoff. The pushoff should be made horizontally, *not upward*.

Although the pushoff is made mostly on the back, swimmers should rotate to the side as they drive off the wall. This can be accomplished by turning the head slightly to one side as the feet are coming into the wall (see Figure 22-12*c*). This provides the one-eighth twist that starts the rotation toward a prone position during the pushoff and glide. Swimmers may rotate to either side they prefer. However, most turn their head away from the arm that was used to stroke into the turn, as does the swimmer in Figure 22-12. This places swimmers facing slightly toward the opposite side as they push off the wall.

Glide Figures 22-12*f* and 22-12*g* illustrate the gliding position. The swimmer glides in a streamlined position as she rotates toward a prone position. Her legs assist the rotation. She crosses the top leg over the bottom leg when she leaves the wall (see Figure 22-12*f*). During the glide, she brings the top leg down and the bottom leg up to help rotate her body to a prone position.

The swimmer is traveling faster than race speed when she leaves the wall, but she decelerates very quickly soon after. Consequently, she should glide for a short time only, until she approaches race speed. At that point, she will take two or three flutter kicks to bring her body close to the surface, where she can start the pullout (see Figure 22-12*g*).

Pullout The swimmer begins her pullout when she feels that one underwater armstroke will bring her head up through the surface. She times that armstroke so that her head breaks through the surface when she is midway through it. She remains streamlined, with her head down until it breaks through the surface. After that, she raises her head to a normal swimming position (see Figures 22-12*h* and 22-12*i*).

Common Mistakes There are several errors that some swimmers make when executing this turn: (1) turning in a piked position, (2) throwing their legs over the water, (3) failing to align their body before their feet reach the wall, (4) pushing up toward the surface, (5) breathing in and out of the turn, (6) gliding into turns, (7) pushing off in a poorly streamlined position, and (8) gliding too long or too little after the turn.

1. Experts disagree about the relative speed of turning in a piked position versus a tucked position. The pike turn was very popular at one time because of the mistaken belief that straight legs traveled over the water faster than bent legs. Actually the reverse is true. The tuck turn is much faster (Ward, 1976). Swimmers' feet travel over the water more quickly in a tucked position for the same reason that divers somersault faster in tucked positions: Their axis of rotation is reduced. In addition, with the legs bent, swimmers' feet move back instead of down as they make contact with the wall. This permits a faster pushoff, because the legs can be preparing to extend before they make contact.

2. Swimmers who thrust their legs over almost invariably arch their back to lift their legs out of the water. Consequently, their body is not aligned when their feet reach the wall and swimmers must waste time aligning their body before they can push off. Swimmers who throw their legs over the water usually reach the wall in the position shown in Figure 22-13. A time analysis of this swimmer's turn revealed that he wasted 0.41 second aligning his body before he could begin to push off.

Many swimmers believe that they must throw their legs into the wall to make a fast turn. This usually slows the turn rather than speeds it up. The speed of the turn is really controlled by how quickly swimmers can rotate their head around and up in line with their body. For this reason, they should move their head through the turn and up toward the surface as quickly as possible. If they do this, their legs will follow, tumbling over very rapidly. They will not need to thrust their legs over the surface to increase that speed.

3. Many swimmers make the mistake of pulling one of their arms toward the wall when they somersault over the water, and they end up with that arm back at their waist when their feet reach the wall. They then waste valuable time bringing the arm back overhead before they can push off. Both arms should remain back as swimmers somersault over so that both arms are overhead and aligned with the body when their feet reach the wall.

4. When swimmers push off the wall with their body inclined up toward the surface, both the speed and distance of the pushoff are reduced. Swimmers should push off in a horizontal position so that they can glide under the wake they created

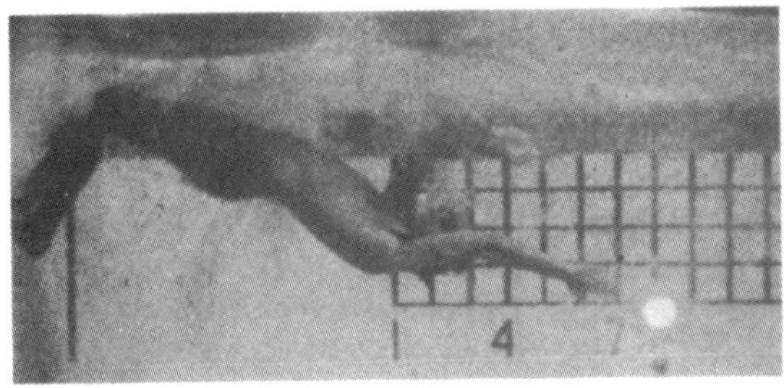

a

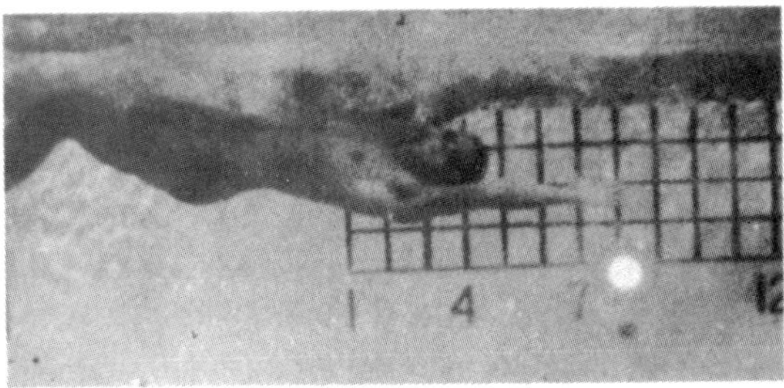

b

Figure 22-13. A swimmer who makes the mistake of thrusting his legs over the water.

going into the turn. The pressure of the water underneath their body and their kicks will bring them to the surface at the proper time.

5. *Swimmers should never breathe during the armstroke that carries them into the turn.* This causes them to delay in somersaulting over. I'm surprised how many athletes make this mistake, even those at the world-class level. These swimmers could easily improve their times by 0.10 to 0.20 second per turn if they did not try to catch a breath while turning. That could mean an improvement of 3 to 4 seconds in long-course 1,500-m races and more than double that amount in short-course races of 1,500 m or 1,650 yd.

The other part of this issue concerns when to breathe coming out of the turn. The most popular technique is to delay the first breath at least until the second armstroke after the turn. The wisdom behind this technique is that breathing on the first stroke after the turn causes a hesitation and subsequent delay in achieving race stroke rhythms. A popular technique for avoiding this problem has been to take the first stroke out of the turn with the arm that is opposite the breathing side. This forces swimmers to delay breathing until the second armstroke.

The original research that fostered this technique of delaying the breath until the second armstroke was flawed, however, because it failed to take into account the effects of fatigue (Ransom, 1973). It has never been shown that the turning times for swimmers in longer races would be affected by breathing on the first stroke. In fact, Ransom recommended that if a breath were needed it would be better to breathe immediately after the turn than before it.

Unfortunately, this technique of delaying the first breath after the turn has spawned a generation of swimmers who make the first mistake mentioned in this category—breathing as they go into the turn. They do this so that they can get enough air to delay the first breath coming out of the turn. I believe that swimmers lose more time when they delay their somersault by breathing as they start the turn than would be lost by breathing on the first stroke after the turn. In fact, swimmers can be taught to breathe on the first stroke without hesitating so that no time is lost at either end of the turn.

Breathing on the first stroke after the turn should help delay fatigue, particularly in longer races. There will be a period of approximately 3 to 5 seconds during which swimmers do not exchange air if they don't take a breath on the last stroke going into the turn and delay breathing until the second stroke coming out (Thayer & Hay, 1984). Because front crawl swimmers generally take a breath approximately every second during middle-distance and distance races, holding their breath longer than necessary during turns may cause them to fatigue earlier.

In races of 400 m and longer, swimmers should probably breathe on the first stroke out of each turn. This may even be a good technique to use in 200 races. However, it may be faster to breathe on the second stroke after the turn in 100 races, provided, of course, that *swimmers do not delay their somersault to breathe before going into the turn*.

6. *Swimmers should not glide into the turn.* Athletes must swim into the turn. There should be no delay between the end of the final armstroke and the beginning of the somersault. In fact, the somersault should begin before that armstroke is completed. Swimmers who glide into the turn will decelerate from the time they complete their last armstroke until their feet reach the wall. Accordingly, their total turn time will be slowed.

7. Many swimmers push off in poorly streamlined positions. Swimmers who make this error arch their back and drop their abdomen. They have their hands and legs apart and their head up. It is easy to see how such a body position increases drag. With practice, swimmers can quickly correct most of these errors in streamlining. They can learn to align their body and hold their hands and legs together in an extended position. Correcting the head position is another matter, however. The head-up position is a nearly universal error, because swimmers look forward on the pushoff so that they can keep their goggles from filling with water. They may do this literally thousands of times in practice, so it is no wonder that it becomes a habit that carries over into competition. Time should be spent conditioning swimmers to keep their head down on the pushoff when the most important meets of the season approach.

8. A final problem associated with turns in this and other strokes is that swimmers frequently lose time by gliding too long or too little after they push off the wall. By gliding too long, they allow their body to decelerate below race speed, so additional time and energy are required to regain that speed. By gliding too little, they literally *spin their wheels* when they begin the pullout too soon. They will be traveling so fast that their arms cannot accelerate them further. Thus, their stroking movements will increase form drag without adding any propulsive force.

Swimmers should begin their first armstroke when they feel themselves approaching race velocity. They should never let their speed decelerate below that of the race just for the sake of gaining additional distance during the glide. Nor should they begin stroking too early. Streamlining will increase gliding distances so that swimmers can glide further without losing speed.

Rollover Backstroke Turn

A recent rule change has allowed backstroke swimmers to turn without first touching the wall with their hand. This has made obsolete the variety of turning styles that swimmers used in this stroke. Following is the new FINA (Fédération Internationale de Natation Amateur) rule on backstroke turns:

> Upon completion of each length, some part of the swimmer must touch the wall. During the turn the shoulders may turn past the vertical toward the breast. If the swimmer turns past the vertical, such motion must be part of a continuous turning action and the swimmer must return to a position on the back before the feet leave the wall.

The most common interpretation of this rule is that swimmers can leave the position on their back as they begin the final arm recovery of each length. They may then take one stroke while in a prone position as they somersault into the turn, provided the turn is executed as one continuous motion. A hand touch is not required. It is sufficient if any part of the swimmer's body touches the wall during the turn.

All swimmers should take advantage of the no-hand-touch provision. It allows swimmers to start turning earlier during each length of the pool and it undoubtedly permits them to somersault over more quickly. The rollover turn that has been developed in response to this rule change is described in this section.

The rollover backstroke turn has only been used in competition for a short time; therefore, it will be some time before innovative and intuitive swimmers demonstrate the best technique(s) to us. This, together with the fact that rule interpretations may change as the turn is used in more major competitions, could mean that the following description may not stand the test of time. These observations, notwithstanding, I believe that the turn illustrated in Figure 22-14 is the fastest method within the present interpretation of the new rule.

Approach The prerequisite to making any good backstroke turn is for swimmers to judge their distance from the wall with a minimum of looking around. They should use the backstroke flags to determine when they are approaching the turn and then count the number of strokes needed before they should begin rotating to a prone position. For most teenage and senior swimmers, that will be two or three armstrokes after they pass the backstroke flags.

Ideally, it is best to swim into the turn without looking for the wall beforehand. The new rule makes this much easier for all swimmers to do. Because swimmers can begin the turn one stroke cycle from the wall, they no longer need to worry about hitting their arm or head against the wall. Also, should they misjudge the turn slightly, they can make adjustments while they are in a prone position during the last armstroke that will take them into the wall properly.

Rotation to a Prone Position As mentioned, the turn should begin one stroke cycle from the wall. The underwater portion of the first of these armstrokes begins with the swimmer on his back, as shown in Figure 22-14*a*. The swimmer begins rotating toward the pulling arm to a prone position once that armstroke is underway. In the meantime, his other arm recovers over the water in a manner similar to the high-elbow recovery of the front crawl stroke (see Figure 22-14*b*). The swimmer is in a completely prone position as the stroking arm comes under his chest and as the other arm enters the water (see Figure 22-14*c*).

Turn Once a prone position is reached, the turn is executed like a freestyle flip, except, of course, that the swimmer stays on his back after the pushoff. The swimmer makes a strong upsweep during his first armstroke of the cycle and then leaves that arm at his side. He sights the wall at this time to assist in making any adjustments that may be required to bring his feet to the wall quickly. The swimmer then completes a full front crawl underwater armstroke with the other arm. Midway through that stroke, he tucks his head to his chest and executes a dolphin kick to assist in getting his hips over the water (see Figure 22-14*d*).

Once both hands are back at his sides, the swimmer turns his palms toward the bottom and uses them to pull his head up and his feet over (see Figure 22-14*e*). Both hands meet overhead before the swimmer's feet reach the wall. His head is

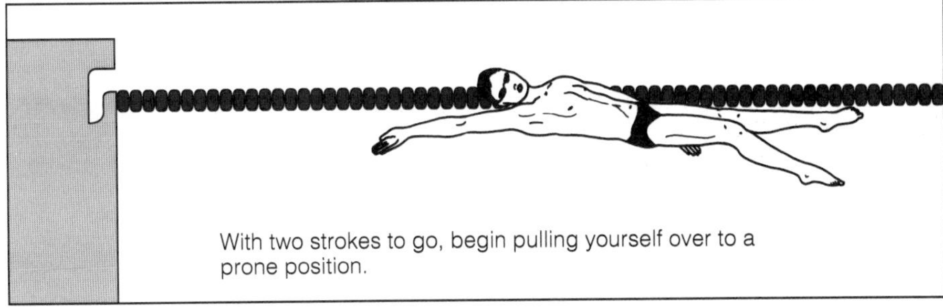

a

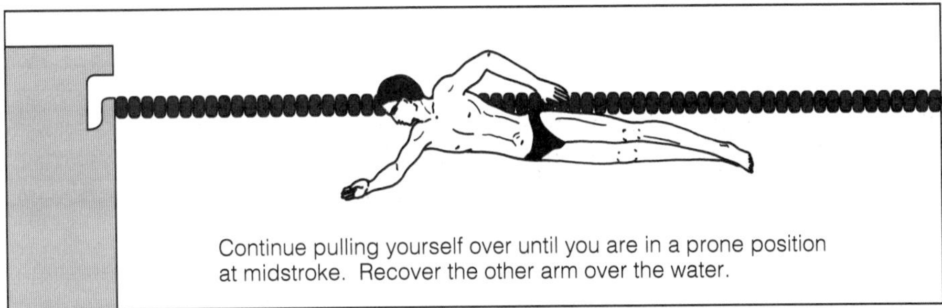

b

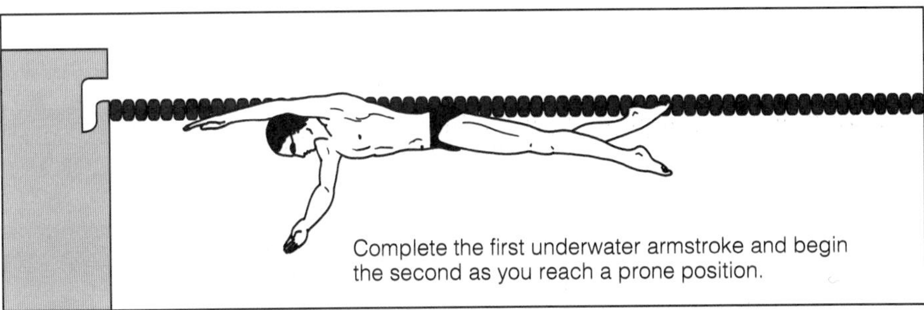

c

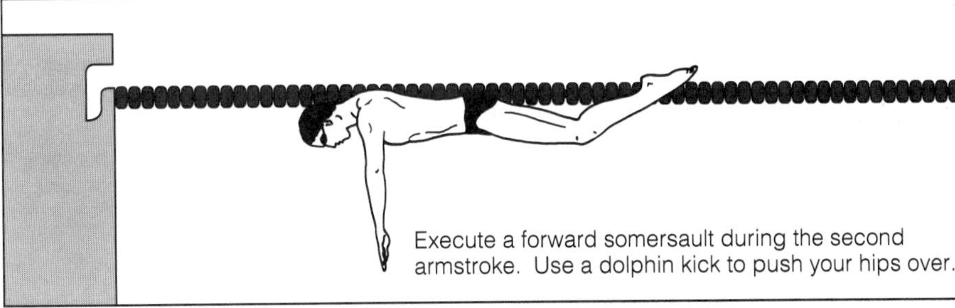

d

Figure 22-14. The rollover backstroke turn.

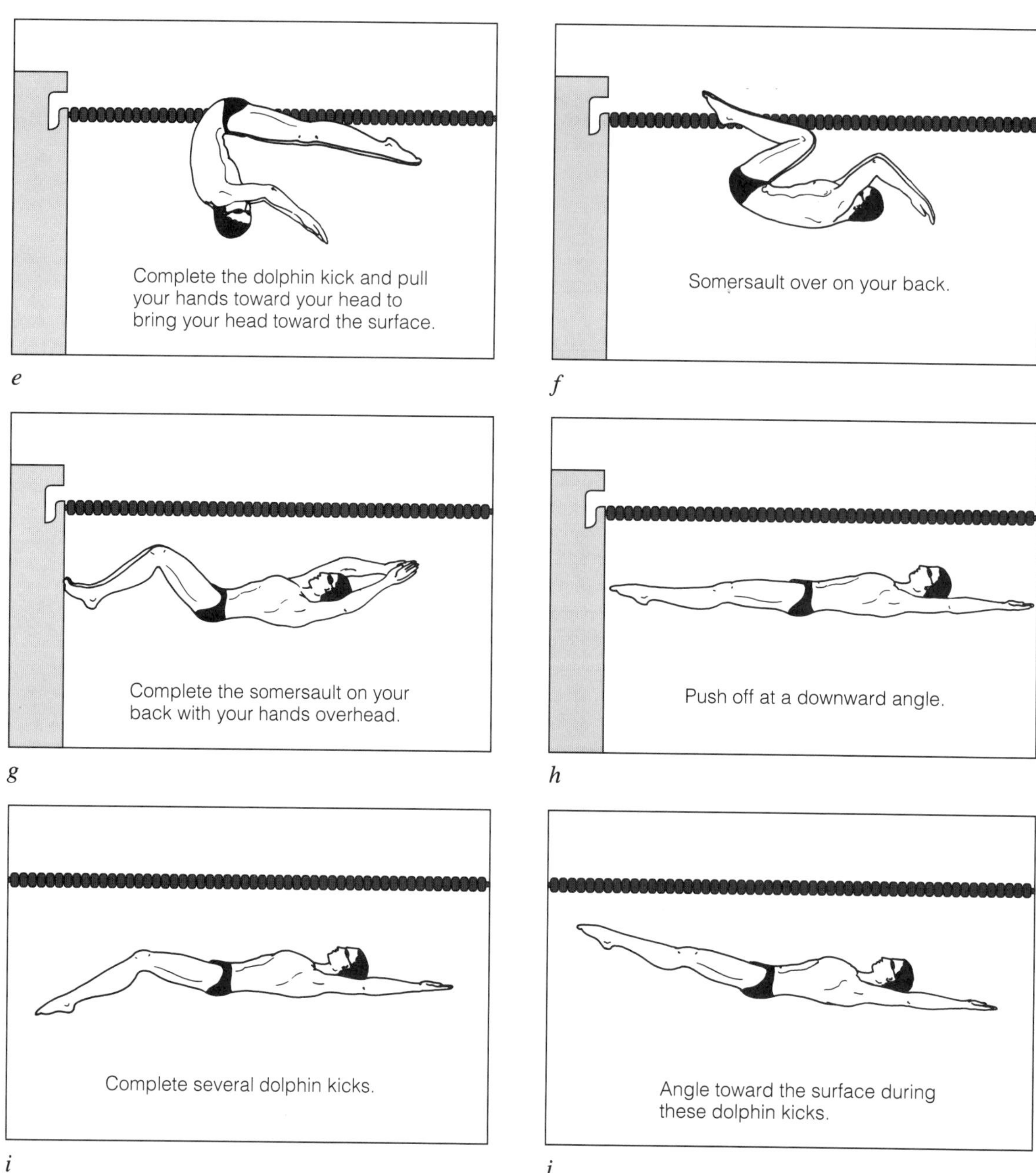

Figure 22-14. (continued)

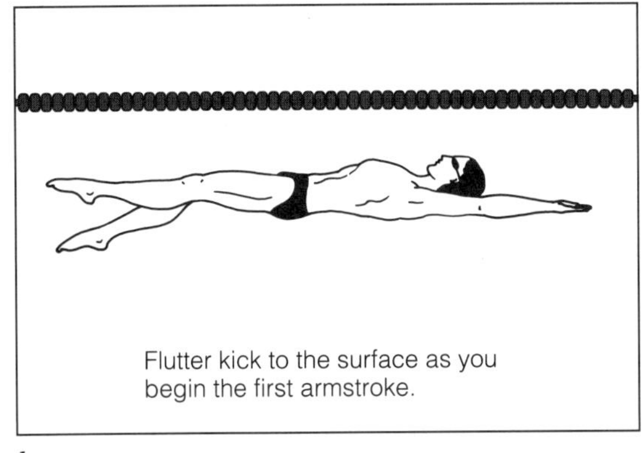

Flutter kick to the surface as you begin the first armstroke.

k

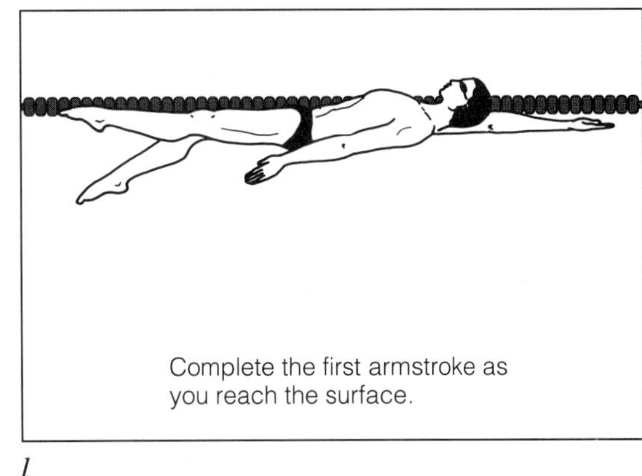

Complete the first armstroke as you reach the surface.

l

back between his arms and he has his upper body and arms aligned so that he can push off with no delay once his feet make contact (see Figure 22-14*f*). His feet are planted on the wall several inches below the surface so that he can make a deep pushoff that will facilitate the use of the dolphin kick.

Pushoff His arms and legs extend simultaneously as he drives off the wall on his back. He pushes off in a slightly downward direction to glide under the surface turbulence and to keep his body deeper during the dolphin kick (see Figure 22-14*h*). His body is streamlined from head to toes during the glide.

Dolphin Kick After gliding a short distance, the swimmer begins dolphin kicking. Swimmers with good kicks are advised to take several dolphin kicks after the pushoff, traveling as much of the allowable distance as possible underwater in this manner (see Figures 22-14*i* and 22-14*j*). Swimmers with weak kicks may prefer not to use dolphin kicks. In that case, they should take two to four flutter kicks and begin their arm pull to the surface.

Pullout The swimmer begins flutter kicking as he starts pulling himself toward the surface (see Figure 22-14*k*). After two to four flutter kicks, he begins an underwater armstroke that brings his head up and through the surface (see Figure 22-14*l*). His head remains streamlined (in line with the other arm) until it reaches the surface. The swimmer should not delay in establishing the proper stroke frequency for the race once he reaches the surface.

Some swimmers glide to the surface before they begin stroking, and they decelerate markedly by doing so. Another common mistake is for swimmers to begin the pullout before they have kicked their body close to the surface. Consequently, they complete the underwater portion of the armstroke too early and must glide until they reach the surface before they can recover the arm over the water and start the next stroke. Swimmers should pull their body up through the surface.

Butterfly and Breaststroke Turns

The turns that swimmers use in the butterfly and the breaststroke are almost identical, with the exception that breaststrokers angle their pushoffs deeper because of their underwater pulldown. Figure 22-15 illustrates the butterfly turn. Figure 22-16 (p. 579) provides a surface view of the breaststroke turn.

Previously, short-course swimmers were permitted to anticipate the turn by lowering one shoulder as they reached for the wall. The rules have now been standardized so that swimmers must touch the wall in a prone position with the shoulders level. They must also touch the wall with both hands simultaneously. After the touch, they turn on their side and push off the wall, rotating to a prone position while they are leaving the wall and during the glide that follows. According to the rules, swimmers must be in a prone position from the start of their first stroke after the turn.

Approach Figure 22-15*a* illustrates the approach. The swimmer focuses on the wall as he approaches so that he can adjust his strokes to reach the wall as he extends his arms forward during the recovery. He makes the final kick powerfully in order to hit the wall with as much momentum as possible. That momentum will help him get his body moving in the opposite direction faster by providing a reboundlike action off the wall. Ideally, he wants to make contact with the wall just as the propulsive phase of his kick is ending. If he must glide to the wall, he should begin drawing his legs under him as he glides so that the turn is underway when contact is made.

Turn Once contact is made, the swimmer releases one hand from the wall and heads it in the other direction as quickly as possible. He does this by bending his arm and pulling his elbow into his ribs (see Figure 22-15*c*). He turns his body toward the side of the arm that is pulled back. In the meantime, he grasps the gutter (if one is available) with the other hand and pulls his hips and legs forward into the wall by flexing that arm.

The swimmer brings his legs up directly underneath his body in a tightly tucked position and holds them close together with one foot on top of the other to reduce drag and increase their speed into the wall (see Figure 22-15*c*). The feeling is one of pulling the knees tightly into the gut.

The swimmer raises his head out of the water as he pulls his legs under him. Once his legs pass under his body, he shoves his head away from the wall by extending the contact arm. No part of the swimmer's body is in contact with the wall during this phase of the turn (see Figure 22-15*d*). Nevertheless, the momentum he develops when he pushes his trunk away produces a counterforce that drives his legs into the wall. The swimmer takes a breath while he pushes his body away from the wall.

He completes the turn on his side. He brings the arm that was used to push his head away from the wall over the water in a position similar to that of a high-elbow recovery. He follows that arm with his eyes over the water so that the arm and head enter together. This sequence of events occurs between Figures 22-15*c* and 22-15*e*. The swimmer then drops underwater on his side and remains on his side until the pushoff is underway.

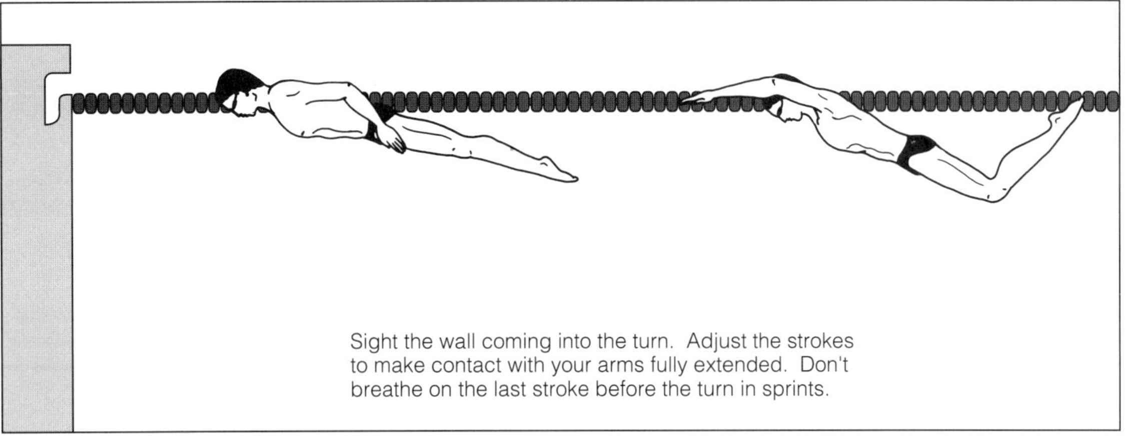

a

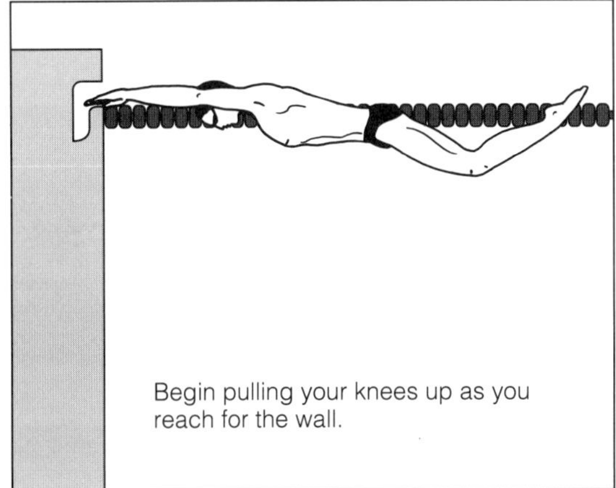

b

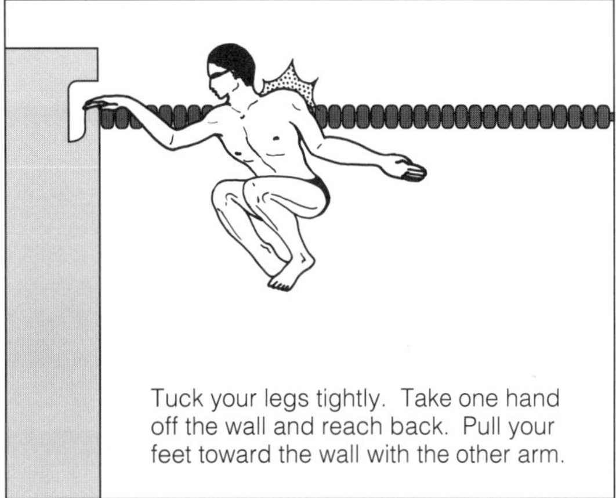

c

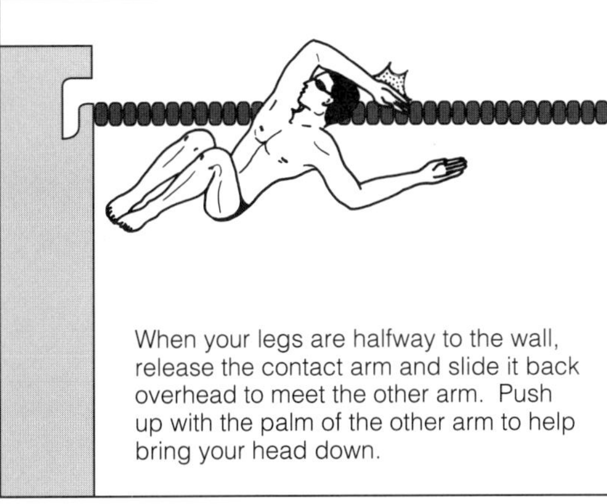

d

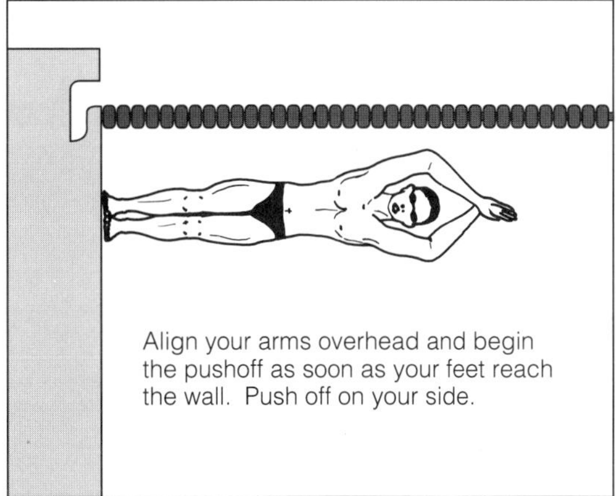

e

Figure 22-15. The butterfly turn.

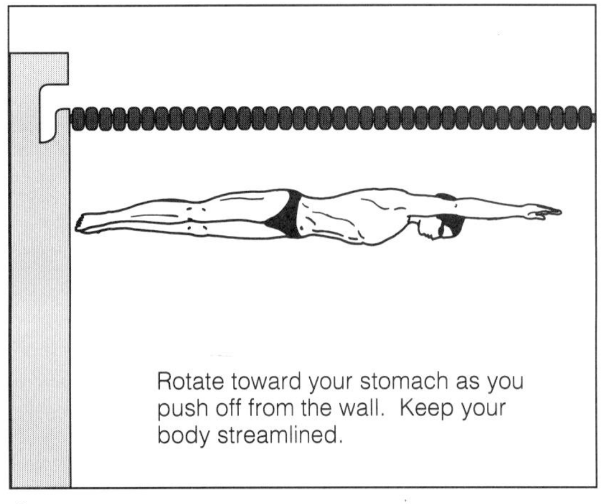

Rotate toward your stomach as you push off from the wall. Keep your body streamlined.

f

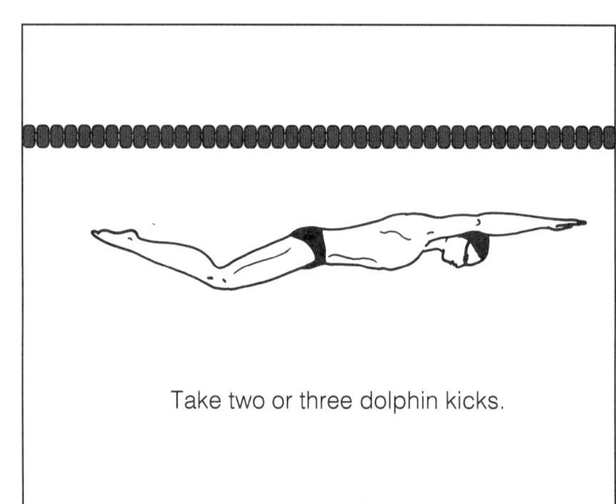

Take two or three dolphin kicks.

g

Keep your body streamlined while dolphin kicking.

h

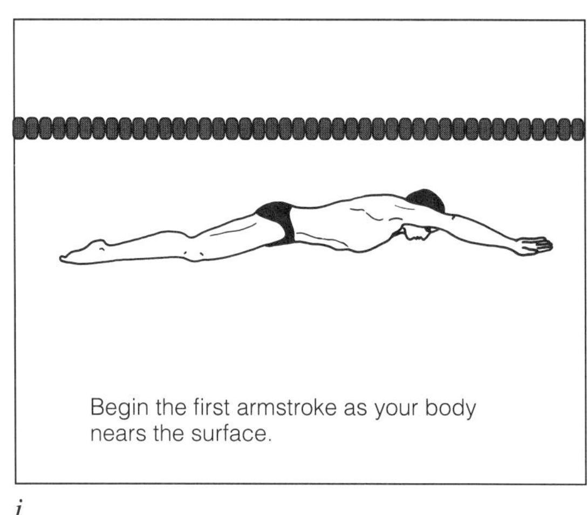

Begin the first armstroke as your body nears the surface.

i

Complete the first armstroke as your head comes through the surface. Don't breathe on the first armstroke in sprint races.

j

Figure 22-15. (continued)

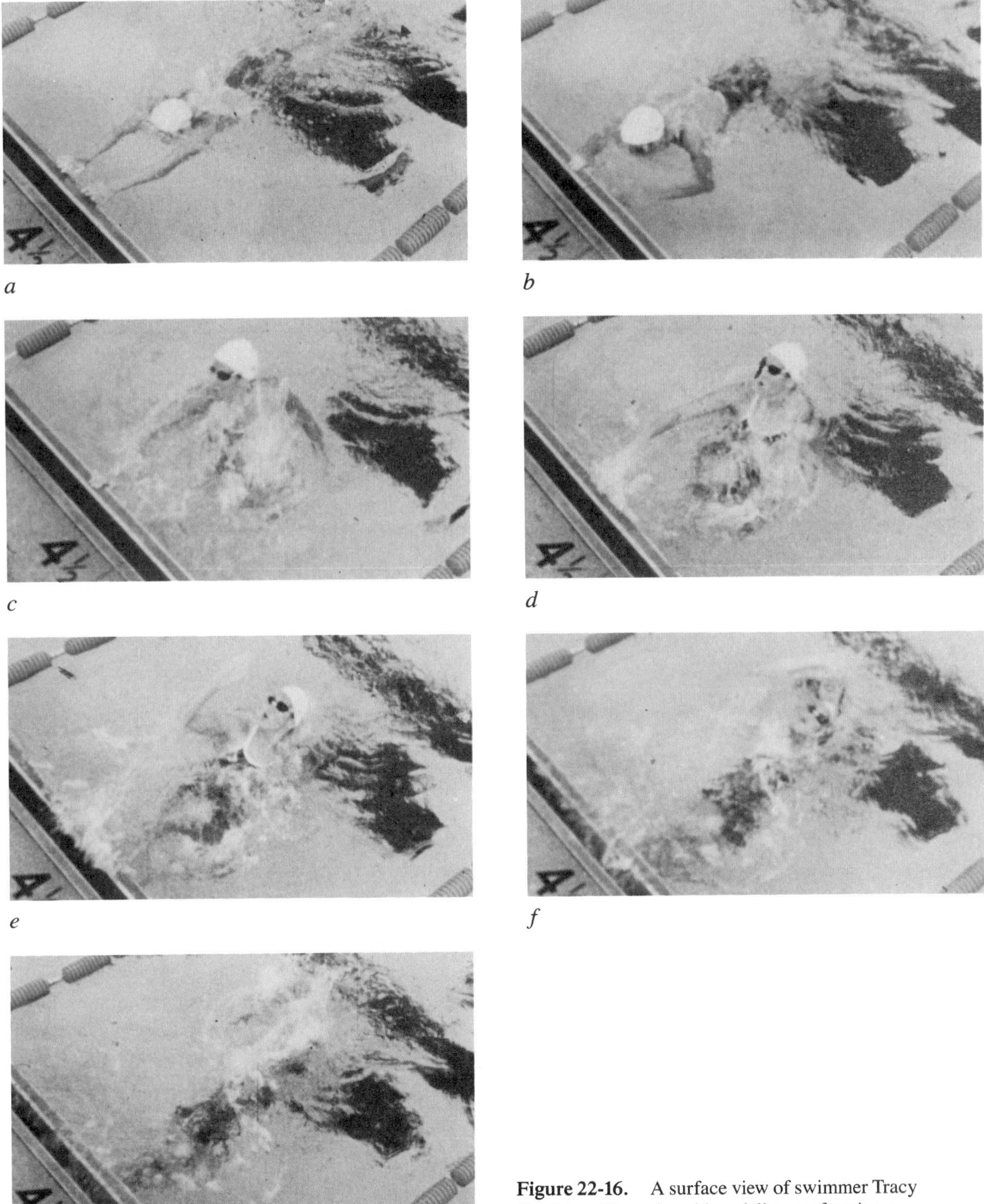

Figure 22-16. A surface view of swimmer Tracy Caulkins, Olympic gold medalist, performing a breaststroke turn.

While all of this is going on, the arm that was pulled into his ribs extends forward underwater to meet the other overhead. This arm also helps to pull the swimmer's body down into the water faster by turning the palm up and pushing up with it (see Figure 22-15*d*).

Referring to the surface photographs in Figure 22-16, notice the breaststroker's high-elbow recovery and the way she places her hand into the water behind her head. Notice also that she continues looking at the wall until she drops underwater (see Figures 22-16*e* and 22-16*f*). This keeps her from turning to a prone position during the turn, which is a common mistake.

Pushoff Swimmers should try to have both hands overhead and their body aligned when their feet reach the wall. They can then push off immediately. Figure 22-15*e* shows the swimmer in the act of pushing off. His feet are planted on the wall with the toes facing sideward and about 45 to 50 cm (18 to 20 inches) underwater. He makes the pushoff on his side. He pushes vigorously against the wall with his feet, extending his legs and driving his body away from the wall. He extends his arms simultaneously to provide additional impetus. He rotates toward a prone position during the pushoff (see Figure 22-15*f*). His feet leave the wall with one over the top of the other. He then completes the rotation to a prone position by bringing his top leg down over the bottom leg during the glide.

Although swimmers should attempt to align their body as well as possible when their feet reach the wall, it is not possible to align it perfectly. Generally, the head will be underwater and one arm will be extending down and forward into the water when the feet make contact. *Swimmers should not waste time aligning their body perfectly before pushing off.* They can always complete the alignment during the pushoff. This may affect the streamlining of their pushoff somewhat; nevertheless, the time they save getting off the wall will more than compensate for this loss of streamlining and will give them a faster time off the wall and out to the point where they surface.

Glide and Pullout Butterfly swimmers should push off horizontally, yet breaststrokers should angle the pushoff down so that they can glide deeper, where their underwater pulldown and glide can be performed more effectively. Swimmers in both strokes should glide in a streamlined position until they feel that they are approaching race speed. At that point, butterfly swimmers should execute two or three dolphin kicks and begin an armstroke that will bring them up through the surface traveling forward (see Figures 22-15*g* through 22-15*j*). They may wait until the second stroke to breathe in sprint events. In 200 races, they should take a breath at the end of the first underwater armstroke.

Breaststroke swimmers should execute an underwater armstroke and kick to the surface. This technique was described in Chapter 21.

One of the most important techniques of a fast turn bears repeating: Swimmers must push their head and trunk away from the wall before their feet reach it. If the turn is executed in this way, swimmers can get both hands overhead and their body nearly aligned for the pushoff immediately when their feet reach the wall. If they keep their hand on the wall until their feet are almost in contact, as many swimmers do, they will lose valuable time bringing that arm over the water and aligning their body before they can begin the pushoff.

Turning on a Flat Wall The mechanics of the turn change only slightly when no gutter is available to grasp. Swimmers touch the flat wall with their fingertips. After touching the wall, they pull one arm quickly back into their ribs as described previously. In the meantime, they let their body ride into the wall by flexing the other arm and placing the palm of that hand against the wall, with the fingers pointing up and diagonally toward the side of the turn. At the same time, they should tuck their legs tightly into their stomach. Once their legs pass underneath their body, they push their body away from the wall with the palm of their contact hand. They then bring that arm over the water in a high-elbow fashion and execute the remainder of the turn as described earlier.

Common Mistakes The most common mistakes that swimmers make are (1) pulling their body too high out of the water, (2) turning their body to a prone position before pushing off, (3) pushing off too near the surface of the water, and (4) double breathing while hanging on the wall.

1. Bringing the head and shoulders too high out of the water is time consuming and requires unnecessary muscular effort. Swimmers who make this mistake usually grab the gutter and pull themselves in and *up* before pushing their body away from the wall. They should simply pull their body toward the wall and then push it back without making any attempt to lift it up. Faster turns are achieved if swimmers fall nearly straight back from the wall, with their head and shoulders close to the surface. Although it is true that their upper body will rise somewhat as they pull their legs into the wall and even more as they push back with their arms, they should not attempt to lift them any higher.

2. Swimmers will slow their descent if they fail to remain on their side as they drop underwater. Figure 22-17 (p. 582) illustrates the effect of this mistake. It slows the turn in at least two ways. The swimmer in Figure 22-17 has spent additional time in the actual turn at the wall by rotating his body toward a prone position before pushing off. Furthermore, his trunk is nearly flat during its descent and will create more drag as it drops underwater. Swimmers should execute the turn on their side to reduce the time and surface area as they drop underwater. They should be coached to plant their feet on the wall with the toes pointed sideward and to keep looking to the side until they have begun pushing off.

3. Swimmers usually push off too near the surface because they hold onto the wall too long and do not get their trunk and arms underwater before their feet are planted on the wall. As a result, they push off while part of their body is still above the water. The increased form and wave drag they produce will cause them to decelerate rapidly during the glide. They can correct this mistake by getting their hand off the wall and started overhead as soon as their feet pass under their body.

Another reason many swimmers push off on the surface is that they try to throw both arms over the water simultaneously. Some experts have mistakenly advocated this method as a faster way to turn. The speed of the turn is determined by the quickness with which swimmers can get their legs to the wall. Throwing both hands

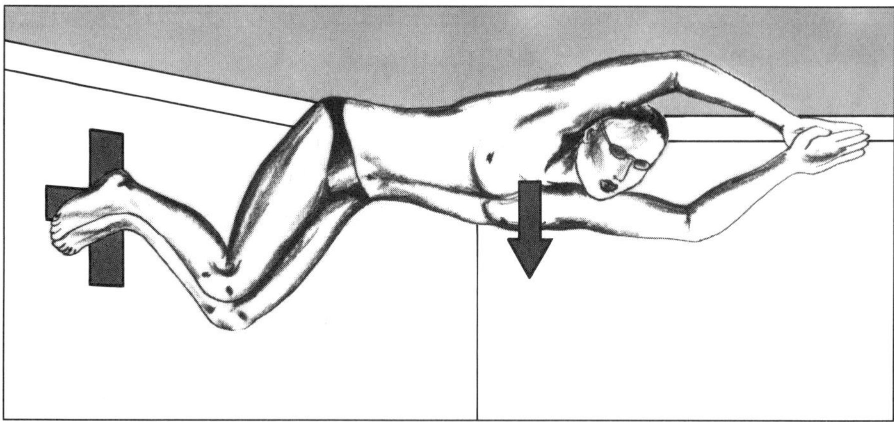

Figure 22-17. The effect of dropping underwater in a partially prone position during butterfly and breaststroke turns.

away from the wall immediately will not get their feet to the wall any faster. Furthermore, swimmers will be poorly streamlined during the pushoff if they turn in this way.

4. The final mistake is to double breathe. Many swimmers lift their head and breathe immediately when they touch the wall and then breathe again as their head comes over the water. The first breath delays their turn because they hang onto the wall with both hands until it has been completed instead of taking one hand off immediately. They should breathe only once, as they drop their head back over the water.

Individual Medley Turns

Turns are often neglected in these events. Practicing them could improve a swimmer's time by at least 1.00 second over the 200 distance and by almost 2.00 seconds for 400 m. The following changeovers are required in the IM: (1) from butterfly to backstroke, (2) from backstroke to breaststroke (the most complex of the turns), and (3) from breaststroke to freestyle.

Changeover from Butterfly to Backstroke Figure 22-18 illustrates this turn, which is not very much different from the regular butterfly turn. Swimmers must make contact by touching with both hands simultaneously and with the shoulders level (see Figure 22-18*a*). After that, the turn they execute is identical to the one described for butterfly until the pushoff (see Figures 22-18*b* and 22-18*c*). Swimmers rotate toward their back as they push off so that they comply with the rules for backstroke swimming which require that their shoulders be beyond the vertical toward their back when their feet leave the wall. They complete the rotation into a perfectly supine position during the glide. Once they are in a supine position, they

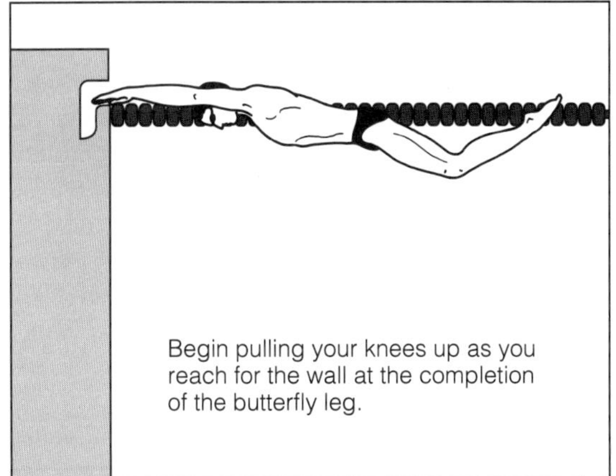

a

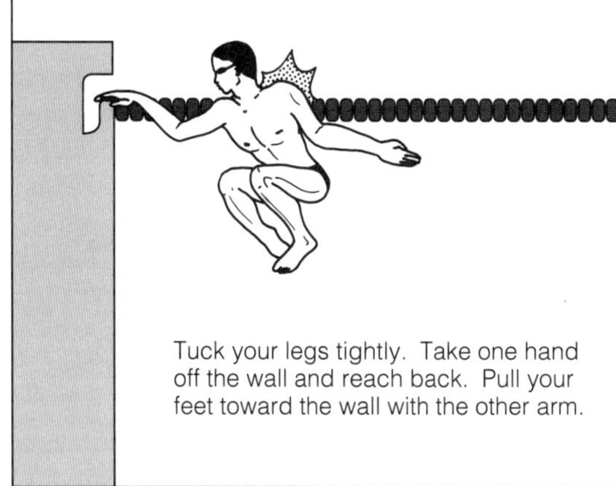

b

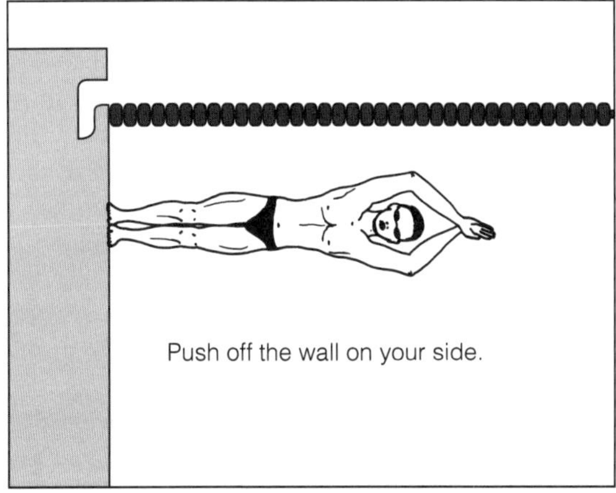

c

Rotate toward your back as you leave the wall. Be sure that your shoulders are beyond the vertical toward your back before your feet leave the wall.

d

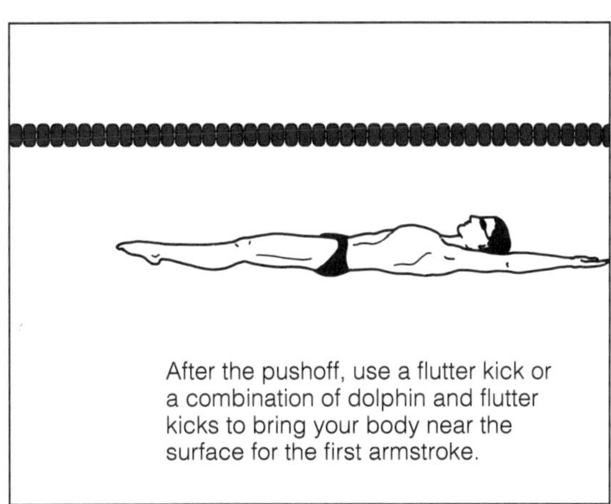

e

Figure 22-18. The changeover turn from butterfly to backstroke.

can flutter kick toward the surface or use a combination of dolphin and flutter kicks to get their body near the surface for the first armstroke.

This turn is far faster than the methods of diving back or dropping straight back that some swimmers use. Methods that incorporate diving back or pushing off completely on the back are slower because it takes longer for swimmers to get their feet to the wall and to align their body before pushing off.

Changeover from Backstroke to Breaststroke Because the rules do not permit a backstroke rollover turn in this changeover, swimmers use one of four different types of turns here: an open turn, a somersault turn, a modification of the Naber turn, or a modification of the old backstroke roll turn, which is, perhaps, the fastest method.

The open turn is the most popular of these methods, although it is probably also the slowest. The reason it is so popular may be that most swimmers do not practice the more complicated turns often enough to become proficient with them and they lose their sense of orientation as they perform them. That problem can be overcome with practice, and the additional speed can pay big dividends in races.

Open turn Figure 22-19 illustrates the open turn. This turn can be used most easily when there are gutters to grasp; however, it is difficult to do against a flat wall.

The backstroke flags should be used to judge the approach to the wall in this and the other changeover turns from backstroke to breaststroke. The swimmer reaches back on the last stroke and grasps the gutter while turning toward his contact arm. After gripping the gutter, he pulls his legs down and forward into the wall while moving his head and shoulders in the opposite direction over the water. His legs should be tucked tightly and he should remain on his side throughout the turn (see Figures 22-19*a* and 22-19*b*).

The free arm, which was back at his hip when the turn began, remains extended forward with the palm up and is used to pull his head and trunk underwater in the last portion of the turn. This happens between Figures 22-19*b* and 22-19*c*.

Once his feet pass underneath his body, he removes his contact arm from the wall and brings it forward over the water with a high elbow, in the same manner described for a breaststroke turn. His head follows that arm over the water, and he drops underwater on his side with one shoulder directly above the other. Swimmers should try to have their body aligned with both hands overhead and underwater before their feet reach the wall.

As in other open turns, the swimmer pushes off immediately when his feet reach the wall. (If the body is not perfectly aligned at this time, swimmers can align it during the pushoff.) He rotates toward a prone position as he pushes off the wall at a slightly downward angle (see Figure 22-19*d*). He then glides in a streamlined position until he decelerates almost to race speed, which is when the underwater armstroke is taken.

When the open turn is done against a flat wall, swimmers have to glide in, plant their palm against the wall, and then push away as they do in butterfly and breaststroke turns. They should make contact at water level, with their fingers facing in toward their body. They can then ride this arm in by letting their elbow bend as they flex their legs and bring them under their body toward the wall. When their

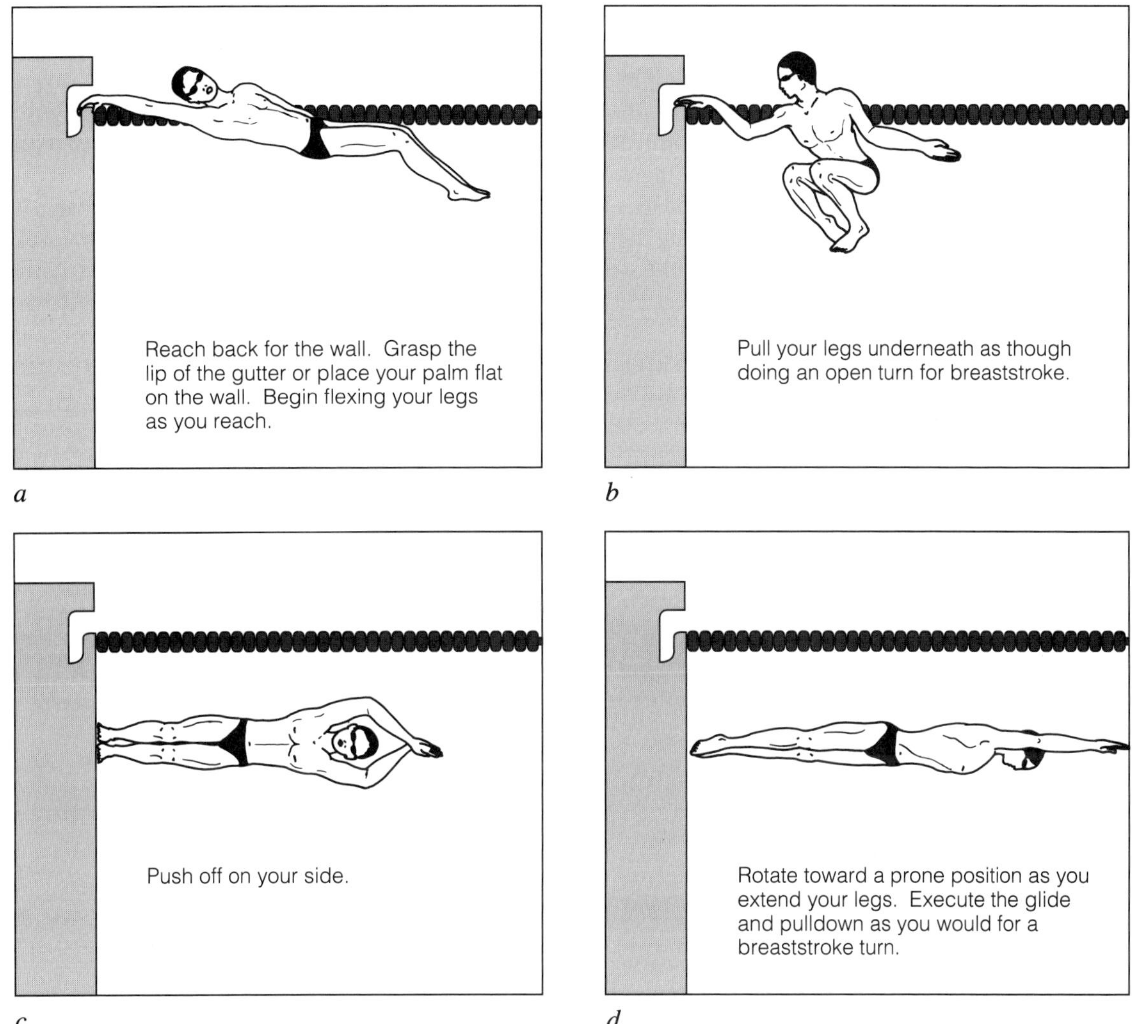

Figure 22-19. The open turn used in the changeover from backstroke to breaststroke.

legs pass under their body, they should push their head away from the wall by extending the contact arm. After that, the mechanics of the turn are the same as those just described.

The advantage of the open turn is that swimmers can get a breath that will last them through the glide and underwater armstroke. They also seem to have an easier time maintaining a sense of orientation. Many swimmers prefer this turn for these reasons. However, as I indicated earlier, the remaining turns should be faster if swimmers practice them.

Somersault turn Figure 22-20 illustrates this method of changing over from backstroke to breaststroke. Upon approaching the turn, the swimmer dives back into the wall as he completes his last arm recovery so that he can somersault over in a tucked position without breaking the rhythm of the approach (see Figure 22-20*b*). His contact arm swings straight over the top and touches fairly deep, with the palm flat and the fingers pointing down (see Figure 22-20*a*).

The contact arm pushes back and up against the wall to help the swimmer rotate his body around during the first half of the somersault. The swimmer then releases the contact arm from the wall as his feet pass over his head and brings it quickly up under his body to meet the other above his head. He does this by flexing his arm and sliding it up under his chest and then extending it forward. He tries to get that hand overhead before his feet reach the wall.

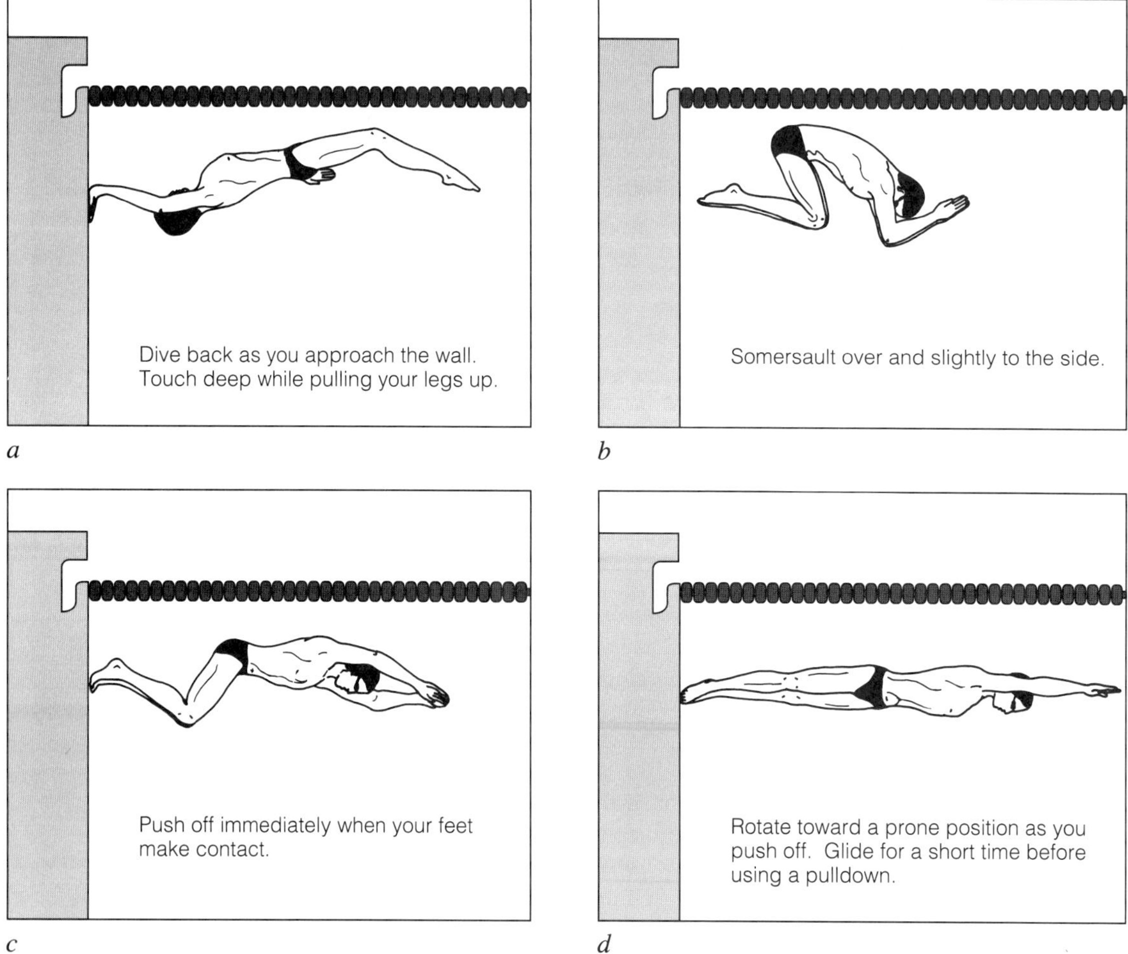

Figure 22-20. The somersault turn used in the changeover from backstroke to breaststroke.

In the meantime, his noncontact arm, which is back at his hips as his other arm makes contact with the wall, is used to help him complete the second half of his somersault into the wall. He does this by turning the palm of that hand down and pushing it down toward his head, which is coming up toward the surface. This helps pull his head and trunk up into alignment with his legs for the pushoff. The palm of that hand ends up just above his head when the somersault has been completed (see Figure 22-20*c*).

Reaching back on the approach causes his body to twist slightly during the somersault, so he ends up in a semiprone position when his feet reach the wall. As a result, his feet are planted on the wall with the toes pointing to the side. His legs are bent in preparation for the pushoff (see Figure 22-20*c*).

He pushes off without delay once his feet reach the wall. The pushoff is made partially on his side, with his arms and legs extending simultaneously (see Figure 22-20*c*). As with other turns, he rotates toward his stomach while pushing off from the wall (see Figure 22-20*d*). The pushoff is angled slightly downward in order for the swimmer to get deep enough for the underwater armstroke. After the push-off, he glides until he approaches race speed, when the breaststroke pulldown commences.

Modified Naber turn The great backstroke swimmer John Naber popularized a style of backstroke turn that was a combination of the old spin turn and the open turn. It allowed swimmers to take a breath while using a fast spinning motion during the turn. Although the no-hand touch rule in backstroke swimming has made this turn obsolete for that stroke, a modification of it can be used effectively in the changeover from backstroke to breaststroke.

Figure 22-21 illustrates the modified Naber turn. The swimmer makes contact with the wall by reaching back over his shoulder and underneath it toward the other side. The hand is placed on the wall close to the surface. He should reach back and make contact with the wall with his hand—approximately 15 to 20 cm (6 to 8 inches) deep—with his fingers pointing in toward his body (see Figure 22-21*a*). *The swimmer should not grab the gutter, even if one is available.*

His legs start bending as he reaches for the wall so that the spin is already initiated when contact is made with his hand. Once the touch is made, the swimmer rides into the wall by bending his contact arm. In the meantime, he continues lifting his legs out of the water by flexing them at the hips and knees (see Figure 22-21*b*). His legs tuck as tightly as possible to clear the water and to speed their rotation into the wall. They may drag through the water somewhat, although the swimmer should make every effort to prevent this from happening. In the meantime, his head comes up above the surface so he can lean his head and trunk back, which helps in getting his legs out and over the water (see Figure 22-21*b*). Swimmers should spin in a clockwise direction if contact is made with their right arm and counterclockwise if made with their left arm.

When his legs pass his body, the swimmer pushes his head away from the wall with his contact arm. He then brings that arm over and down into the water with a high elbow, where it meets the other in preparation for the pushoff (see Figure 22-21*c*). From there, the turn resembles the method described for breaststroke. The

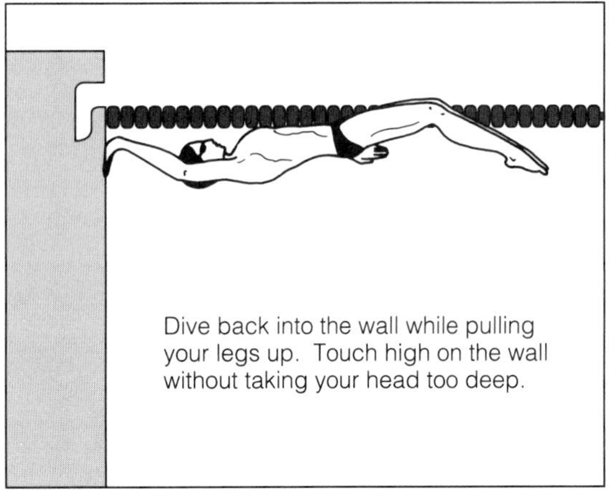

a

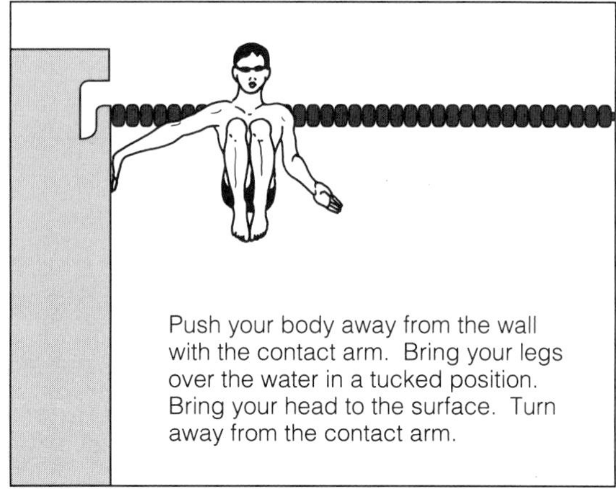

b

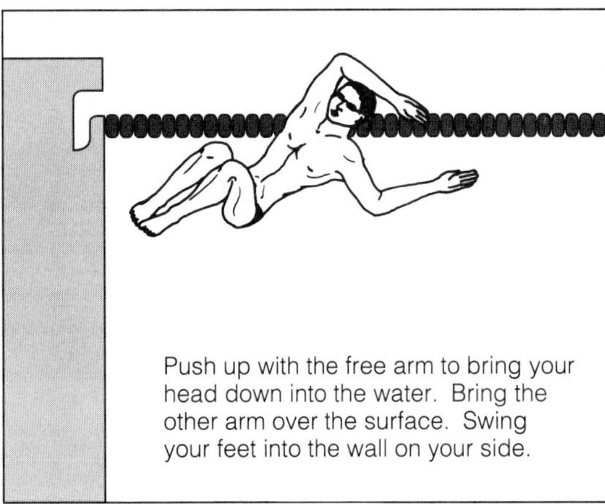

c

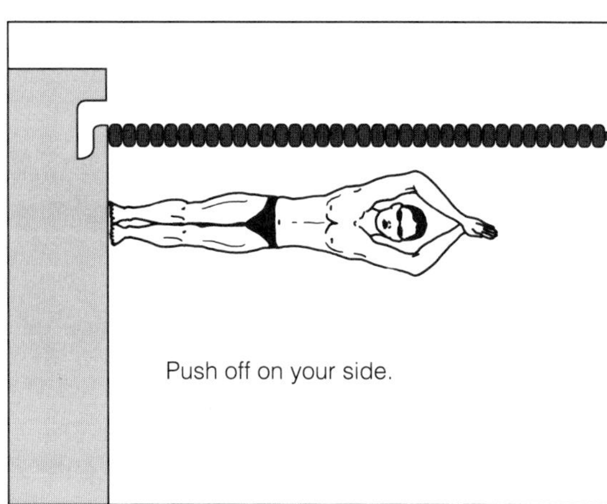

d

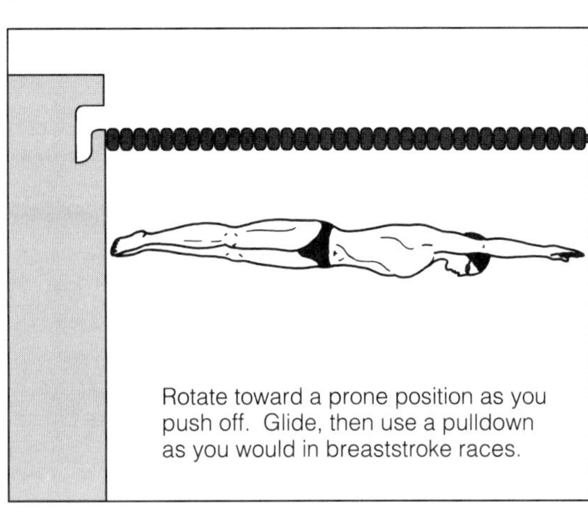

e

Figure 22-21. The modified Naber turn used in the changeover from backstroke to breaststroke.

swimmer's head follows his arm over the water and he drops underwater on his side, with one shoulder directly above the other.

The palm of his noncontact arm, which was back at his hip when the turn began, is turned up toward the surface and used to help pull his head underwater when his body is dropping beneath the surface.

The swimmer is on his side when the pushoff begins. He rotates toward a prone position during the pushoff and glide that follows (see Figures 22-21*d* and 22-21*e*).

The major problem that swimmers have when learning this turn is to spin to the side too much. The turn should be made in the vertical plane. The key techniques for doing it successfully are (1) to continue looking sideward throughout the turn and (2) to move the upper shoulder almost directly forward toward the water as the contact arm is traveling over the surface. If swimmers make a turn that resembles the backstroke spin turn, they will decelerate their speed considerably.

Modified roll turn Until the recent rule change that allowed the rollover turn, the roll turn was the fastest method in backstroke swimming. With modifications, it can be the fastest method for the changeover from backstroke to breaststroke.

Figure 22-22 (p. 590) illustrates the modified roll turn. The swimmer rolls on his side and reaches behind his head for the wall on the last armstroke before contact is made. However, he must be careful that he does not turn over beyond the vertical toward a prone position before touching the wall. The touch is made fairly deep, behind the opposite shoulder, with the palm flat against the wall and the fingers pointing diagonally down and out. Once the touch is made, he continues to roll toward a prone position as he somersaults over (see Figures 22-22*a* through 22-22*c*). He does not roll completely, however. Instead, he remains on his side as his head comes up toward the surface in order to prepare himself for a breaststroke pushoff when his feet reach the wall (see Figure 22-22*c*). He then pushes off the wall on his side and rotates toward a prone position as he leaves the wall (see Figures 22-22*d* and 22-22*e*).

Changeover from Breaststroke to Freestyle Figure 22-23 (p. 591) illustrates this turn. It is almost identical to the turn used in the changeover from butterfly to backstroke until the pushoff. In this turn, the swimmer begins the pushoff on his side and rotates to a prone position during the pushoff and the glide that follows.

The pullout is performed as described for a freestyle turn. The swimmer takes two to four flutter kicks until he nears the surface, at which time he takes one arm stroke to bring his body up and through the surface and into stroke rhythm. He may breathe as he completes that stroke, provided it does not cause any delay in achieving the proper stroke rate.

FINISHING RACES

Many races have been lost because swimmers glided to the finish. However, races have also been lost because swimmers took more strokes than needed to reach the wall. The techniques of finishing races should be practiced until swimmers can consistently accelerate to the finish with a minimal glide and no extra strokes. In all

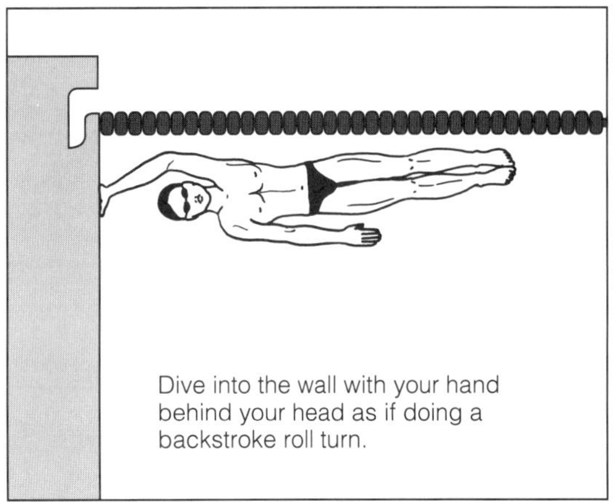

a

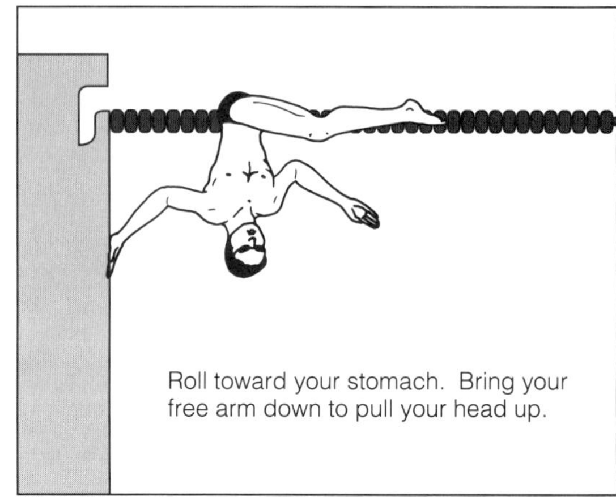

b

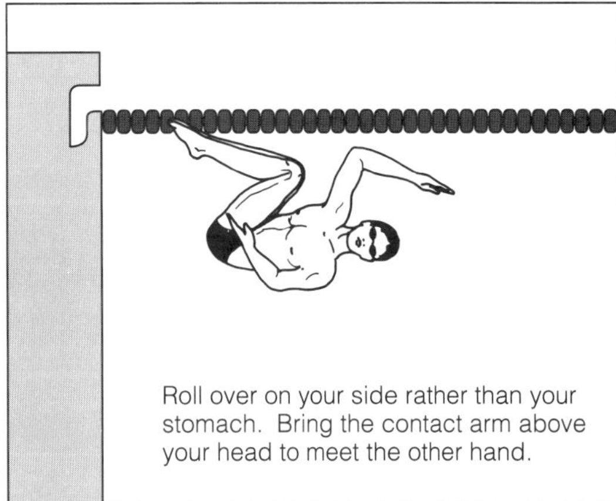

c

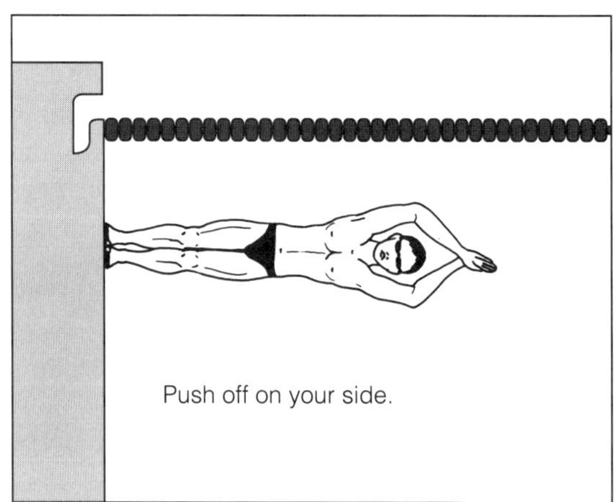

d

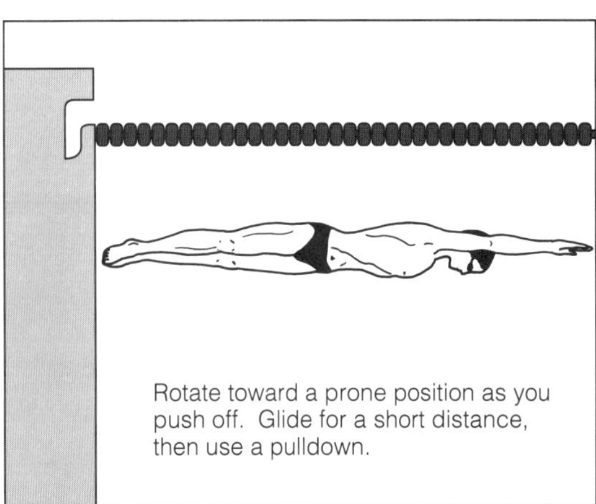

e

Figure 22-22. The modified roll turn used in the changeover from backstroke to breaststroke.

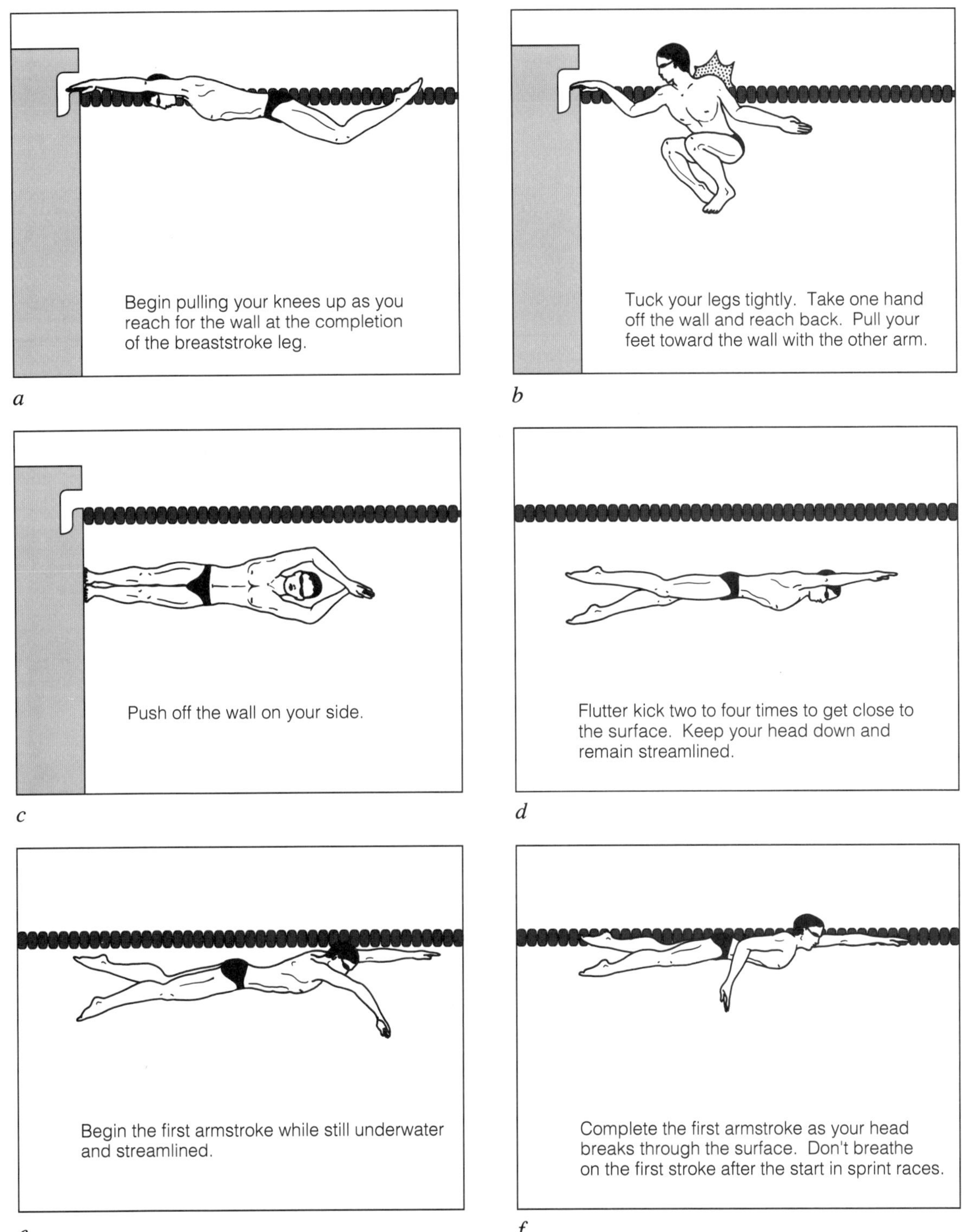

Figure 22-23. The changeover turn from breaststroke to freestyle.

swimming styles, swimmers should lunge for the wall without lifting their head or splashing water. Their arm(s) should be fully extended, and they should touch the pad near the surface of the water with their fingertips. Some skills for finishing races are described in this section.

Freestyle Finishes

The advent of electronic timing systems has made obsolete the once popular method of looking up and splashing water into the wall at the finish of races in order to fool judges into believing that the touch had been made before the swimmer's hand actually made contact with the wall. Electronic timing has eliminated the need for this deception, and swimmers must now touch the timing pad to win races. The fastest way to do this is by *jabbing* the arm straight forward into the pad. The swimmer in Figure 22-24 finishes in this manner.

For most swimmers, the finishing touch is made at the completion of a normal high-elbow recovery. The jab finish is a faster modification of that style. It is performed in the following manner.

When swimmers judge that the next arm recovery will bring their hand into contact with the wall, they *accelerate the speed of that recovery* and bring their arm rapidly over the water in the normal high-elbow manner. However, they should

Figure 22-24. The finishing technique for freestyle races.

not slide it down into the water and forward to the pad; instead, they should extend it quickly forward *at water level* to hit the touchpad. They should also *lean* into that recovery to give added reach to their arm. This is done by looking away from the recovering arm and by stretching their body in the direction of that arm. At the same time, they should accelerate their body toward the wall as rapidly as possible with the underwater stroke of the other arm and their kick.

The touch should be made with the fingers outstretched, rather than with a flat palm, in order to decrease the distance the arm must travel. *The face should remain in the water during the reach*. Lifting the head will shorten the reach and decelerate the speed into the wall.

Ideally, the touch should be made when the arm reaches full extension. If the touch is made with a bent arm, an extra stroke was taken. This will increase a race time by 0.20 to 0.30 second.

Swimmers should not glide into the wall if their arm does not make contact at full extension. Neither should they take another stroke. They should continue stretching and continue kicking until their hand reaches the pad. Kicking will get their hand to the wall faster than either gliding or taking another armstroke. Of course, this advice only applies when swimmers have misjudged the finish by *less than one armstroke*. It will be faster to bring the other arm over the water if they are one or more armstrokes from the wall.

Butterfly Finishes

Figure 22-25 illustrates the finishing technique for butterfly races. Because a two-hand touch is required, the lunge must be made with both arms simultaneously. The last few armstrokes should be the most powerful of the race, and swimmers should accelerate their hands into the touchpad on the last recovery. They should also make this recovery with flexed elbows and jab their hands into the wall. This will shorten the distance their hands must travel. While reaching for the wall, they should accelerate their kick to push their body forward at a faster speed than they would travel if they glided over the last few yards or meters. Their face should be in the water, and they should stretch every fiber of their body forward in order to reach the wall as quickly as possible.

If they misjudge the finish and find themselves less than an armstroke from the wall, butterflyers should continue stretching and kicking until they reach it. An additional half stroke will, as in freestyle races, take more time than stretching to the finish. If they are more than one armstroke from the wall, they should, of course, take another stroke to reach the finish.

Breaststroke Finishes

Swimmers in this stroke should also lunge for the finish with both hands simultaneously. The final few armstrokes and the final recovery should be accelerated so that their arms can slice forward as quickly as possible. They should not breathe on the last armstroke before the finish so that they can accelerate into the wall even faster. They will gain several extra centimeters of reach if their face remains in the water as they stretch for the pad.

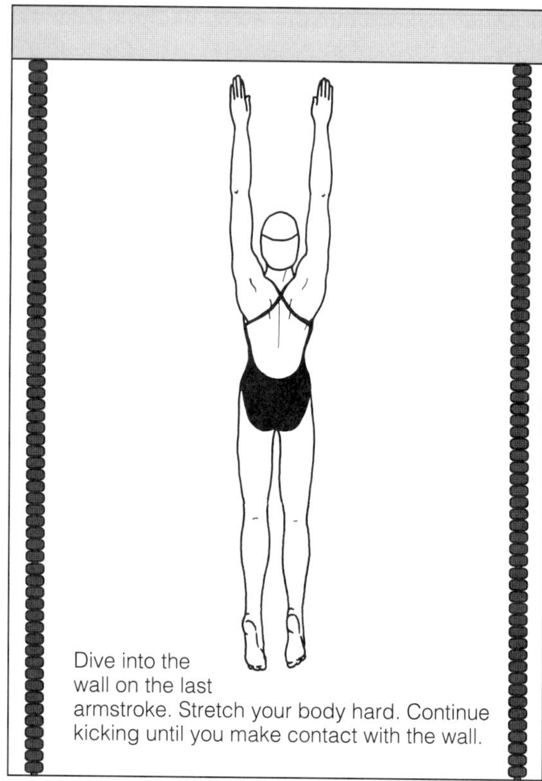

Figure 22-25. The finishing technique for butterfly races.

The final kick should be very strong in order to accelerate their body to the finish. If the reach is slightly short, they should stretch for the wall. A partial stroke will require more time than simply stretching and gliding in. They should only take an extra halfstroke if they find themselves so far from the wall that they will lose time by gliding. It seldom happens that swimmers misjudge the finish by more than a few centimeters, however.

Backstroke Finishes

In the backstroke, swimmers should count the number of strokes they will need to take in order to cover the distance from the flags to the wall. Figure 22-26 illustrates the backstroke finish. When backstroke swimmers determine that one more arm recovery will bring their hand into contact with the wall, they should accelerate that recovery and jab their hand back into the pad. The jab is accomplished by flexing their arm forward after it leaves the water and then extending it rapidly into the touchpad at water level, *not underwater* (see Figures 22-26*a* and 22-26*b*). Reaching in this way is faster than a normal vertical recovery with a straight arm. Swimmers should rotate their body toward the finishing arm in order to increase

a

b

Figure 22-26. The finishing technique for backstroke races.

the reach, and they should stretch hard for the finish. They should stretch their head toward the wall and look to the side toward the finishing arm to aid the stretch (see Figure 22-26*b*). Swimmers should stroke powerfully with the other arm while kicking vigorously to avoid gliding into the wall. Contact should be made with the fingertips near water level.

Ideally, the hand should make contact with the wall at the instant the arm reaches its full extension. However, if the touch is misjudged, the best strategy is to continue stretching and kicking until the fingers reach the pad. This advice, of course, applies only to finishes that have been misjudged by less than one armstroke.

Breathing During the Final Sprint

Breathing during the final sprint to the wall should have no effect on speed in backstroke races for obvious reasons. In the breaststroke, breathing seems to be necessary to stroke rhythm and, therefore, should not be restricted until the lunge for the finish takes place. The situation is different in butterfly and freestyle races, however. Turning or lifting the head for a breath will definitely slow a swimmer's speed during the final sprint. So, in these events, swimmers should be trained to swim as much of the final 25 yd/m as they can tolerate without taking a breath. The additional speed they achieve will compensate for the strain and fatigue. There is no longer any need to conserve energy during the final sprint to the wall, and the only thing that is important is getting to the finish as fast as possible.

The usual practice is to train swimmers not to breathe once they pass the backstroke flags at the finishing end of the pool. With practice, it may be possible to train them to hold their breath for longer periods with no loss in speed. However, swimmers must never restrict their breathing for such a long period that they lose speed over the final few yards or meters of races. They should practice breath-holding finishes during competitions and practices until they know how much of the final portion of the race they can sprint without breathing and *without losing speed*.

Part III

GUIDELINES FOR COMPETITION, DRYLAND TRAINING, AND NUTRITION

The first chapter in this section, Chapter 23, discusses the techniques of pacing, strategy, and warming up. It also considers the benefits of massage and hyperventilating before races and the importance of swimming down to postcompetition recovery.

Chapter 24 discusses the topics of strength, power, and flexibility and critiques the various modes of resistance training. Training procedures with regard to frequency, numbers of sets and number of repetitions are also suggested and methods for cycling the resistance program are described.

Chapter 24 also discusses stretching—an often-overlooked aspect of training. The joints in which swimmers can benefit from improved ranges of motion are listed and the relative merits of the various methods for improving range of motion (ballistic, dynamic, held-stretch, and partner-assisted stretching) and methods for proprioceptive neuromuscular facilitation (PNF) are described. Measuring flexibility is the final topic of this chapter.

Nutrition is the focus of the final chapter. The first part of Chapter 25 contains information on the caloric and nutritional needs of swimmers. Special dietary practices that may enhance training and competition are spotlighted in the next part of this chapter, including the number of meals athletes should eat each day, the premeet meals, postcompetition meals, and carbohydrate loading. The latest research on high-energy snacks immediately before, during, and after training and competition are also covered. The relationship of body fat to swimming performance, the dangers of dieting during hard training, and ergogenic aids are the final topics of Chapter 25.

CHAPTER 23

Guidelines for Competition

The topics of pacing, race strategy, warming up, massage, hyperventilation, and swimming down all bear on a swimmer's success in competition. These topics are discussed in this chapter.

PACING

Pacing is a misunderstood and frequently neglected part of many training programs. This is unfortunate, because a race that is paced properly is generally 0.50 second faster per 100 yd/m than one that is poorly paced. Pacing involves swimming the first half to three-quarters of a race slower than possible so that the remainder of the race can be swum faster.

When athletes fail to pace races properly, they accumulate excessive amounts of lactic acid early in the races. The subsequent acidosis that occurs reduces the rate of energy metabolism, causing swimmers to lose stroking power, coordination, and speed. In swimming terms, the athletes *die*. Consequently, their time for the latter portions of races will be so slow that the advantage they gained by swimming fast earlier will be negated. Pacing is particularly noticeable in races of 400 m and longer. The 100 and 200 events should also be paced, although some people continue to think of them as sprints.

Races of 100 and 200 yd/m should be paced, regardless of the fact that well-trained athletes do not experience severe acidosis until they have swum all out for 40 to 45 seconds. This is because they begin to lose speed even before acidosis becomes severe. Actually, the effects of progressing acidosis begin to reduce the rate of anaerobic glycolysis and, consequently, swimming speed after approximately 15 seconds of all-out effort (Jacobs et al., 1983; Song et al., 1988).

Swimming slower in the early stages of a race reduces the rate of anaerobic metabolism, so lactic acid accumulates more slowly and acidosis is delayed. Consequently, athletes who pace the early stages of a race find that they can swim the later stages considerably faster. Most often, their speed over the last portion more than compensates for their slower speed in the beginning so that the total time for the race ends up being faster.

There are three general race plans that swimmers use: even pacing, fast-slow pacing, and slow-fast pacing, or negative-split pacing. Research has shown that fast-slow pacing is the least effective of the three methods but has been inconclusive concerning the relative superiority of the remaining two methods (Mathews, Bowers, Fox, & Wilgus, 1963; Robinson, Robinson, Montoye, & Bullard, 1958).

Thirty years of studying the paces of world and national championship races has yielded similar conclusions. Most athletes have used even-pace plans during these swims, although there is a small but growing number who have used negative-split patterns in recent years. Fast-slow pacing has seldom been used effectively in outstanding swims, even at distances of 100 yd/m.

Some representative world- and national-record splits for each race distance are presented later in this section to illustrate the even-pace and negative-split plans that various swimmers have used. The pace plans, whether negative-split or even-pace, have been so similar for various race distances, that I feel justified in stating that they represent the best methods for swimming those races. When swimmers of both sexes from different parts of the world and even from different eras pace their most outstanding races in nearly the same manner, the conclusion seems inescapable that the methods they used are worth emulating.

There are some unique aspects of swimming races that require explanation before these pace patterns can be understood. The first two concern the advantage gained by the start and the influence of turns.

Effect of Starts and Turns

In swimming, the start will cause the first split to be 1 to 2 seconds faster than later splits, even though athletes swim at a constant velocity throughout. Turns add to the difference between the first and later splits. The later portions of breaststroke and butterfly races begin with a turn that will add nearly 1 second to the split time as compared to the first split that began with a start. Accordingly, when an athlete is swimming at a constant velocity, the first split of butterfly and breaststroke races will be 2 to 3 seconds faster than later splits. By contrast, the first splits of freestyle and backstroke races will be 1 to 2 seconds faster than later splits because they include the turn.

When these relationships are maintained, the swimmer is even-pacing. For example, if early splits of butterfly and breaststroke races are 4 or more seconds faster than later splits, swimmers are using a fast-slow pace plan. They are even-splitting if the first splits are only 2 to 3 seconds faster than later splits, and they are negative-splitting if the early portions of the race are only 1 to 2 seconds faster than later splits. Because splits are taken from a foot touch in freestyle and backstroke races, the first split will be 3 or more seconds faster than later splits if swimmers are using a fast-slow pace plan. They are even-pacing if the first split is 1 to 2 seconds faster than later splits, and they are negative-splitting if the first split is even or slightly slower than later splits.

Effect of the Final Sprint

Another unique aspect of swim pacing concerns the split for the last 50 or 100 yd/m of races. It is usually slightly faster than earlier splits in a well-paced race. This is known as a good finishing kick. The fact that the time for the final 50 or 100 yd/m of a race may be faster than earlier portions does not necessarily mean that swimmers were using a negative-split pace plan. If all other portions of the race were swum at a constant speed, then an even-pace plan was used.

An example may help to clarify the points I have just made about the influence of starts and turns and the effect of the final sprint. Suppose a female swimmer with a best time of 1:58.0 for 200-m freestyle completed the first half of the race in 58.50 seconds and the second half in 59.50 seconds. Her drop-off (or difference in time between the first and second 100 of the race) was 1.0 second; therefore, she even-paced the race. This is true even though her splits were 28.50, 30.00, 30.00, and 29.50. This is because the first three splits were swum at a constant velocity when the influence of the start is taken into account. If that same swimmer completed the race with 50 splits of 29.00, 30.00, 29.50, and 29.50, she would be negative-splitting even though her 100 splits were 59.00 and 59.00. This is because her final two splits were swum at a faster velocity than the first two when the influence of the start was removed.

Taking Races Out

The phrase *taking races out* usually refers to the speed of the first quarter to first half of the race. The ideal pace for going out will be the slowest speed that athletes can swim and still be in position to win or achieve their goal time. One way to estimate the proper early speeds for certain races has been to compare the first split of great swims to a particular swimmer's best time for that same distance. These comparisons have shown a very consistent difference between best times and split times for a particular race distance during world- and national-record swims.

Using the earlier example of the female athlete who swam 200 meters in 1:58.0 with splits of 58.50 and 59.50, if that swimmer had a best time of 56.00 seconds for 100 m, she would be swimming the first half of the race 2.5 seconds slower than her best time. As you will learn later, swimming the first split 2 to 3 seconds over best time for 100 m is the correct way to pace the first half of a 200-m race.

Although the times for early world- and national-record swims were considerably slower than those of today, the difference between the time for the first split and a swimmer's best time for the same distance has remained very similar over the years, as have the drop-off time from the first to later splits of races. For example, Frank Heckl won the 200-yd freestyle at the 1971 U.S. Short Course Nationals in a time of 1:40.55. His split at 100 yd was 48.80, which was 3.24 seconds slower than his winning time in the 100-yd freestyle (45.56) at that same meet. His drop-off from the first to second 100 of the 200 swim was 2.90 seconds (48.80 – 51.70). Compare this with Matt Biondi's 1987 American record time of 1:33.03 in this same event. That race was swum with splits of 45.34 and 47.69, and Biondi's time for the 100-yd freestyle was an American-record 41.80 at the same meet. Almost identically to Heckl, Biondi swam the first 100 of the 200 event 3.54 seconds slower than his best time for 100 yd, and his drop-off was 2.35. The following box compares these two splits.

A Comparison of American-Record 200-yd Freestyles

Best time for 100 yd	Frank Heckl—45.56 1971	Matt Biondi—41.80 1987
Splits for 200 swims	48.80 (+3.24) 51.70 (+ 2.90)	45.34 (+3.54) 47.69 (+2.35)
	1:40.50	1:33.03

The best pace plans for certain races can be learned by studying the splits of world- and national-record swims. I have listed examples of such splits in the following sections. The pace plans for these swims are similar to those I have observed over the past three decades. Splits are listed for both long-course and short-course competitions. Where known, a swimmer's best time for a distance equal to an early split of the race is listed as a guide for the relative time that should be used going out. A knowledge of the difference between all-out speed and going-out speed in a particular race can help in counseling swimmers and establishing realistic goals. For example, a swimmer with a best time of 54.00 seconds for the 100-m freestyle could not be expected to swim 1:50.00 for 200 m. He would have to swim the first 100 m of the race under his best time. That swimmer should be counseled to attempt a time of 1:56.00 by going out in 57.00 and coming back in 59.00. Following are descriptions of the pace plans for each event that have been used most frequently in outstanding swims.

100 Events: Long Course and Short Course

100-m and 100-yd Freestyle Events Splits for representative world and American records are shown on page 603. In the 100-m event, you can see that Biondi took his race out approximately 1.0 off his best times for 50 m at the time and brought it back with a drop-off of 1.86 seconds. Thompson, on the other hand, took her 100-m race out 1.62 seconds slower than her time for 50 m and brought it back with a drop-off of only 0.84 second.

Jenny Thompson—54.48 1992 world record 100 m Time for 50 m = 25.20			Matt Biondi—48.42 1988 world record 100 m Time for 50 m =· 22.14		
Distance	Cumulative Time	Split Time	Distance	Cumulative Time	Split Time
50	26.82	26.82	50	23.28	23.28
100	54.48	27.66	100	48.42	25.14
		Drop-off = +0.84			Drop-off = +1.86
Jenny Thompson—47.61 1992 American record 100 yd Time for 50 yd = 22.14			**Matt Biondi—41.80** 1987 American record 100 yd Time for 50 yd = 19.15		
50	22.87	22.87	50	20.25	20.25
100	47.61	24.74	100	41.80	21.55
		Drop-off = +1.87			Drop-off = 1.30

Representative Splits for World and American Records for 100-m and 100-yd Freestyle Swims

Over 100 yd, the difference between the best time and the first 50 should be approximately 1.10 to 1.50 seconds, and the swimmers should be able to bring the race home with a drop-off of 1.0 to 1.5 seconds. Thompson's 100-yd race was taken out somewhat too fast, which accounts for her drop-off of 1.87 seconds.

Analysis of the pace for 100-yd/m freestyle events indicates that swimmers use even pacing. They go out fast, but not as fast as possible. They appear to reduce their speed for the first 50 by approximately 0.40 to 0.60 second even though the actual time is usually a little over 1.00 second slower than their times for 50 yd or 50 m. This is because the split for the first 50 is taken when the swimmers feet are on the wall after the turn, whereas the time for 50 yd/m results from a hand touch with no turn included. The drop-off time from the first to the second 50 indicates that the swimmers are maintaining nearly the same velocity on the second half of the race as the first, when you consider that they gained the advantage of starting out of the water on the first half.

The splits for a previous American-record swim by Rowdy Gaines are listed on page 604 and show how a short-course 100 event is paced by 25s. He is out slightly faster than I have recommended (0.68 over his best time for 50 yd). Consequently, his drop-off is slightly greater from the first to the second 50 (2.02 seconds). Please notice, however, that the split for the last 25 yd of the race is slightly slower than the second and third split times. This is characteristic of most short-course 100 swims. Athletes tend to slow down slightly on the final 25 of 100 races. This is probably because a good 100 swim requires a fast (but not too fast) first 25 for swimmers to be competitive and/or to stay ahead of the turbulence. It is probably better for swimmers in these races to get out fast even though they may drop off slightly more at the end than it is for them to swim too slow in the beginning and try to catch up later.

Rowdy Gaines Previous American Record 100 yd Best time for 50 yd = 19.50			
Distance	Cumulative Time	Split Time	Drop-off by 25's
25	9.68	9.68	
50	20.18	10.50	+0.82
75	31.13	10.95	+0.45
100	42.38 (22.20)	11.25	+0.30
Drop-off from first to second 100 = +2.02			

Splits for a Previous American-Record 100-yd Freestyle Swim by Rowdy Gaines

100-m and 100-yd Butterfly Events Splits for world- and American-record 100 butterfly swims are listed below. Unfortunately, 50 times are not available for these record holders or for swimmers in the 100 backstroke and breaststroke events that will be discussed next. Nevertheless, I would assume from personal experience that swimmers in the butterfly events also swim the first 50 m/yd approximately 0.50 second slower than their fastest possible speed for that distance. The expected drop-off in these events should be approximately 2.50 to 3.00 seconds for 100-m events and 2.40 to 2.60 seconds for 100-yd events. I suspect that the drop-off times for Morales and Ahmann-Leighton are slightly greater than should be expected. Morales was quoted as saying that he was out a little too fast on his world-record 100-m swim (Crouse, 1986).

Mary T. Meagher—57.93 1981 world record 100 m				**Pablo Morales—52.84** 1986 world record 100 m			
Distance	Cumulative Time	Split Time	Drop-off	Distance	Cumulative Time	Split Time	Drop-off
50	27.75	27.75		50	24.59	24.59	
100	57.93	30.18	+2.43	100	52.84	28.25	+3.66
Chrissy Ahmann-Leighton—51.75 1992 American record 100 yd				**Pablo Morales—46.26** 1986 American record 100 yd			
50	24.18	24.18		50	21.66	21.66	
100	51.75	27.57	+3.39	100	46.26	24.60	+2.94

Representative Splits for World and American Records for 100-m and 100-yd Butterfly Swims

Below are some representative 25 splits that can be used as a reference for swimming short-course 100 butterflys. They are from a previous U.S.-Open-record and NCAA-record swim by Per Arvidsson. Notice that his drop-off from the first to the second 50 yd is 2.61 seconds. Notice also that the final 25 is slightly slower than the second and third 25 splits just as it was for 100-yd freestyle events.

Per Arvidsson—47.39 Previous 1980 U.S. Open record 100 yd			
Distance	Cumulative Time	Split Time	Drop-off by 25's
25	10.26	10.26	
50	22.39	12.13	+1.87
75	34.46	12.07	−0.06
100	47.39 (25.00)	12.93	+0.86
Drop-off from first to second 100 = +2.61			

Splits for a U.S.-Open-record 100-yd Butterfly Swim by Per Arvidsson

100-m and 100-yd Breaststroke Events The record times and splits for these events are listed below. The drop-off from the first to the second half of these races is somewhat greater than in the other competitive strokes. It is generally in the neighborhood of 3.50 to 4.00 seconds for long-course 100-m events and 2.80 to

Silke Horner–1:07.91 1987 world record 100 m				**Norbert Rozsa** 1991 world record 100 m			
Distance	Cumulative Time	Split Time	Drop-off	Distance	Cumulative Time	Split Time	Drop-off
50	32.00	32.00		50	28.67	28.67	
100	1:07.91	35.91	+3.91	100	1:01.29	32.62	+3.95
Tracey McFarlane—1:00.51 1988 U.S. Open record 100 yd				**Steve Lundquist—52.48** 1983 American record 100 yd			
50	28.63	28.63		50	24.80	24.80	
100	1:00.51	31.88	+3.25	100	52.48	27.68	+2.88

Representative Splits for World, American, and U.S. Open Records for 100-m and 100-yd Breaststroke Swims

3.30 seconds for short-course swims. I suspect that the drop-off is greater for breaststrokers because of the work their legs must do to accelerate their body forward after each recovery. Because the muscular involvement is much greater when the legs are working hard, it stands to reason that breaststroke swimmers fatigue more quickly. For this reason, breaststrokers should probably take their 100 races out somewhat slower than swimmers in other strokes. Although most swimmers seem to hold back about 0.50 second during the first 50 in 100 races, it might be better to hold back somewhat more, perhaps 0.70 to 0.80 second.

Listed below are 25-yd splits for an NCAA-Championship swim by John Moffet. They show the same pattern as in other 100 events, with a somewhat slower final 25 yards.

John Moffet—53.62
1985 NCAA champion 100 yd

Distance	Cumulative Time	Split Time	Drop-off
25	11.71	11.71	
50	25.29	13.58	+1.87
75	38.96	13.67	+0.09
100	53.62 (28.33)	14.66	+0.99

Drop-off from first to second 50 = +3.04

Splits for an NCAA-Championship 100-yd Breaststroke Swim by John Moffett

100-m and 100-yd Backstroke Events Times and splits from world- and American-record swims in these events are listed on page 607.

It is probably best for swimmers in these events to slow the first 50 approximately 1.00 second from the fastest speed that is possible (including the turn). The drop-off from the first to the second half of these races should be similar to those in freestyle races now that the no-hand touch is being required at the turn. This assumes, of course, that the split for the first 50 is taken when the swimmers' feet reach the wall. Backstrokers do not gain as great an advantage on the start as swimmers in other strokes. With the split taken later in the turn, the drop-off from the first to the second 50 of these races will be 1.5 seconds or less. Rouse's split for 100 m was taken to a hand touch; however, if a foot touch had been used, his drop-off would have been in the neighborhood of 1.20 seconds.

Pace Plans for 100 Events Summarized In long-course 100 events, the usual pattern is to pace the first 50 m approximately 0.50 to 0.60 second slower than an all-out effort for that distance. The difference is generally 1.00 second for free-

Kristina Egerszegi—1:00.21 1991 world record 100 m				Jeff Rouse—53.86 1992 world record 100 m			
Distance	Cumulative Time	Split Time	Drop-off	Distance	Cumulative Time	Split Time	Drop-off
50	29.82	29.82		50	26.32	26.32	
100	1:00.31	30.39	+0.57	100	53.86	27.54	+2.16
Lea Loveless—52.79 1992 American record 100 yd Time for 50 yd = 24.67				**Jeff Rouse—46.12** 1992 American record 100 yd Time for 50 yd = 21.48			
50	25.73	25.73		50	22.38	22.38	
100	52.79	27.06	+1.33	100	46.12	23.74	+1.36

Representative Splits for 100-m and 100-yd Backstroke Events in Which the No-Hand-Touch Rule Was in Effect

stylers and backstrokers, because their split for the first 50 m includes a turn. The drop-off in the second half of freestyle and backstroke races should be in the neighborhood of 1.50 to 2.00 seconds (Egerszegi's swim was an exception). In butterfly, it should be 2.50 to 3.00 seconds. In breaststroke, it may be slightly greater—3.50 to 4.00 seconds.

In short-course races, the best plan appears to be for athletes to swim the first 25 approximately 0.50 to 0.60 second slower than could be swum for an all-out sprint. The next two 25s should be nearly identical in speed and approximately 2.00 seconds slower than the first 25 in all strokes except freestyle and backstroke. The difference should be approximately 1.00 second in those strokes because turns are included in the splits. The final 25 yd should be 0.50 to 1.00 second slower than the middle two splits.

The expected drop-off from the first to the second 50 of short-course races should probably be 0.50 second less than for long-course events; that is, 1.00 to 1.50 seconds for freestyle and backstroke events, 2.00 to 2.50 seconds for butterfly, and 3.00 to 3.50 seconds for breaststroke.

50-m and 50-yd Freestyle Events

This is one event on the program that should not be paced; however, it must be swum with skill. Swimmers cannot simply flail their arms and expect a fast time. The splits for Matt Biondi's American- and NCAA-record 50-yd freestyle swim are listed on page 608 as a guide to determine what the difference in time between the first and second half of short-course 50 races should be. He swam the first 25, including the turn and planting his feet on the wall, in 9.15 seconds and the second 25 in 10.00 seconds. So, his drop-off from the first to the second length of the race was 0.85 second.

Matt Biondi 1987 American record 50 yd			
Distance	Cumulative Time	Split Time	Drop-off
25	9.15	9.15	
50	19.15	10.00	+0.85

Splits for an American-record 50-yd Freestyle Swim by Matt Biondi

200 Events: Long Course and Short Course

200-m and 200-yd Freestyle Events Most 200 swimmers use an even pace. Splits for two American-record 200-yd freestyle swims and two world-record 200-m swims are listed below.

Heike Friedrich—1:57.55 1986 world record 200 m Time for 100 m = 56.16			
Distance	Cumulative Time	Split Time	Drop-off
50			
100	58.36*	58.36	
150			
200	1:57.55	59.19	+0.83
Drop-off from first to second 100 = +0.83			

Giorgio Lamberti 1989 world record 200 m Time for 100 m = 49.24			
Distance	Cumulative Time	Split Time	Drop-off
50	25.14	25.14	
100	52.42	27.88	+2.74
150	1:19.74	27.32	−0.56
200	1:46.69 (54.27)	26.95	−0.37
Drop-off from first to second 100 = +1.85			

Nicole Haislett—1:43.28 1992 American record 200 yd Time for 100 yd = 48.23			
Distance	Cumulative Time	Split Time	Drop-off
50	24.48	24.48	
100	50.58	26.10	+1.62
150	1:16.99	26.41	+0.31
200	1:43.28 (52.70)	26.29	−0.12
Drop-off from first to second 100 = +2.12			

Matt Biondi—1:33.03 1987 American record 200 yd Time for 100 yd = 41.80			
Distance	Cumulative Time	Split Time	Drop-off
50	21.92	21.92	
100	45.34	23.42	+1.50
150	1:09.15	23.81	+0.39
200	1:33.03 (47.69)	23.88	+0.07
Drop-off from first to second 100 = 2.35			

*Times for 50 splits were not available

Representative Splits for World and American Records for 200-m and 200-yd Freestyle Swims

Swimmers in 200 freestyle events swim the first 100 approximately 2.00 to 3.00 seconds slower than their best 100 time, and their drop-off is generally 1.00 to 2.00 seconds during the next 100. The pace by 50s is as follows. The first 50 is approximately 2.00 to 2.50 seconds slower than a swimmer's best 50 time. If a swimmer's best time for 50 yd/m is not known, another guide is for the athlete to swim the first 50 of the 200 about 1.50 to 2.00 seconds slower than he or she swims the first 50 of a 100 race. The second and third 50s are even-paced and are approximately 1.50 to 2.00 seconds slower than the first. The final 50 is equal to, or sometimes slightly faster than, the middle two.

There is a tendency in some 200-m freestyle races for athletes to swim the first 100 m at a slower relative speed than they might swim during the first half of 200-yd races. This is probably because they fatigue more quickly when they have fewer turns. Several excellent 200-m swims have been done with a slight negative-split pattern.

200-m and 200-yd Butterfly Events These events should also be even-paced, although there is a trend for several swimmers to use a fast-slow pace. The splits for representative American-record 200-yd and world-record 200-m butterfly swims are listed below.

Mary T. Meagher—2:05.96 1981 world record 200 m Time for 100 m = 57.93				**Melvin Stewart—1:55.69** 1990 world record 200 m Time for 100 m = 54.06			
Distance	Cumulative Time	Split Time	Drop-off	Distance	Cumulative Time	Split Time	Drop-off
50	29.53	29.53		50	26.34	26.34	
100	1:01.41	31.88	+2.35	100	55.60	29.26	+2.92
150	1:33.69	32.28	+0.40	150	1:25.44	29.84	+0.58
200	2:05.96 (1:04.55)	32.27	−0.01	200	1:55.69 (1:00.09)	30.25	+0.41
Drop-off from first to second 100 = +3.14				Drop-off from first to second 100 = +4.49			
Mary T. Meagher—1:52.99 1981 American record 200 yd Time for 100 yd = 52.42				**Melvin Stewart—1:41.78** 1991 American record 200 yd Time for 100 yd = 47.64			
50	25.90	25.90		50	22.99	22.99	
100	54.43	28.53	+2.63	100	48.38	25.39	+2.40
150	1:23.37	28.94	+0.41	150	1:14.58	26.20	+0.81
200	1:52.99 (58.56)	29.62	+0.68	200	1:41.78 (53.40)	27.20	+1.00
Drop-off from first to second 100 = +4.13				Drop-off from first to second 100 = +5.02			

Representative Splits for World and American Records for 200-m and 200-yd Butterfly Swims

Butterfly swimmers usually hold back more than freestylers when they go out. Their drop-off is also slightly greater from the first to the second half of the race because the second split includes a turn. Meagher's world-record splits for 200 m exemplify what I have observed to be the best pacing plan for these races over the years. The first 100 should be approximately 3.00 seconds slower than the swimmer's best time for that distance. The second 100 should be approximately 3.00 seconds slower than the first.

The record swims by Stewart and the 200-yd swim by Meagher are taken out a little too fast—approximately 2.00 to 2.50 seconds over their best times for 100 yd/m. Consequently, their drop-off is also greater—4.00 to 5.00 seconds. I think the times for all three of these swims might have been faster if the athletes had swum the first 100 yd/m slightly slower. It is possible, however, that some swimmers need to go out only 2.00 seconds off their best time to swim a fast race. They should expect a drop-off of 4.00 to 5.00 seconds when they do this, however.

By 50s, the 200 race is paced so that the first split is approximately 1.50 to 2.00 seconds slower than the time for the first 50 of a particular swimmer's 100 race. The next two 50s should be swum at nearly the same velocity, but the time will be approximately 2.50 seconds slower than the first 50. The last 50 of the race should be swum at the same speed or slightly faster than the previous two 50 splits.

200-m and 200-yd Breaststroke Events Most successful swimmers in these events swim an even-paced race. Times and splits for world- and American-record long- and short-course swims are listed below.

Anita Nall—2:25.35
1992 world record 200 m
Time for 100 m = 1:09.29

Distance	Cumulative Time	Split Time	Drop-off
50	33.19	33.19	
100	1:10.19	37.00	+3.81
150	1:47.53	37.34	+0.34
200	2:25.35 (1:15.16)	37.82	+0.48

Drop-off from first to second 100 = +4.97

Michael Barrowman—2:10.16
1992 world record 200 m
Time for 100 m = 1:02.12

Distance	Cumulative Time	Split Time	Drop-off
50	30.43	30.43	
100	1:03.91	33.48	+3.05
150	1:37.12	33.21	−0.27
200	2:10.16 (1:06.25)	33.04	+0.17

Drop-off from first to second 100 = +3.22

Mary Ellen Blanchard —2:09.06
1989 American record 200 yd
Time for 100 yd = 1:00.66

Distance	Cumulative Time	Split Time	Drop-off
50	30.07	30.07	
100	1:03.08	33.01	+2.94
150	1:35.61	32.53	−0.48
200	2:09.06 (1:05.98)	33.45	+0.92

Drop-off from first to second 100 = +2.90

Michael Barrowman—1:53.77
1990 American record 200 yd
Time for 100 yd = 53.77

Distance	Cumulative Time	Split Time	Drop-off
50	26.27	26.27	
100	55.26	28.99	+2.72
150	1:24.31	29.05	+0.06
200	1:53.77 (58.51)	29.46	+0.41

Drop-off from first to second 100 = +3.25

Representative Splits for World and American Records for 200-m and 200-yd Breaststroke Swims

The splits for both of Barrowman's races and Blanchard's short course race represent what I believe is the best pace plans for these events. Athletes should swim the first 100 yd/m approximately 2.00 to 3.00 seconds slower than their fastest 100 time. The drop-off on the second 100 should be 3.00 to 4.00 seconds. This is slightly greater than the drop-off in other events. The reason, as I said earlier, is probably because the legs must work so much harder in the breaststroke than they do in other strokes.

When the pace is broken down by 50s, you can see that breaststrokers tend to go out somewhat faster than swimmers in other strokes. They generally swim the first 50 yd/m about 1.00 second slower than the time they swim in the first half of a 100 race. There may be two reasons for this: (1) swimmers in these events may rely more on early speed because they are going to fatigue more than swimmers in other events; or (2) the nature of breaststroke is such that the difference between the top speed and cruising speed is not as great as in other competitive strokes. I suspect, however, that they could be somewhat faster on the second half of the race if they slowed the first 50 yd/m down so that it was between 1.50 to 2.00 seconds slower than their speed for the first 50 of 100 events.

As was the case in other 200 events, velocities on the second and third 50s are nearly identical and are 2.50 to 3.00 seconds slower than their time for the first 50 yd/m. The final 50 should be nearly the same speed as the others. Breaststrokers usually do not swim this 50 faster than the second and third splits. In fact, there is generally a slight drop-off.

200-m and 200-yd Backstroke Events Times and splits for world- and American-record swims are shown on page 612. The first 100 should be 2.00 to 3.00 seconds slower than top speed for that distance. The drop-off from the first to second 100 should probably be 1.00 to 2.00 seconds.

For pacing the race by 50s, the first split should be 1.00 to 1.50 seconds slower than the first half of 100 races. The next two 50s should be swum approximately 1.20 to 1.50 seconds slower than the first. The final 50 should be at least as fast as the middle two, or slightly faster.

Pace Plans for 200 Events Summarized The pacing plans are very similar for all 200 butterfly and breaststroke events. The first 100 yd/m should usually be 2.00 to 3.00 seconds slower than a swimmer's best time for 100 yd/m. The drop-off in the second 100 should be 3.00 to 4.00 seconds.

In freestyle and backstroke events, the first 100 should be approximately 2.00 seconds slower than a swimmer's best time for that distance. The drop-off from the first to the second 100 should be between 1.50 and 2.50 seconds.

When the pace is examined by 50s, the paces for all events becomes more similar. The time for the first 50 yd/m should be 2.00 to 3.00 seconds slower than the time for the first half of their respective 100 races. The next two 50s should be swum at the same relative velocity but should be approximately 1.50 to 2.00 seconds slower than the first because they do not benefit from a start and because they include turns. The difference between the first and later 50s should be slightly less in freestyle events—1.50 to 2.00 seconds—and should be even less in backstroke—1.20 to 1.50 seconds—because swimmers start in the water. The final 50

Kristina Egerszegi—2:06.62 1991 world record 200 m Time for 100 m = 1:00.31				**Martin Lopez-Zubero—1:56.57** 1991 world record 200 m Time for 100 m = 55.30			
Distance	Cumulative Time	Split Time	Drop-off	Distance	Cumulative Time	Split Time	Drop-off
50	30.55	30.55		50	28.29	28.29	
100	1:02.34	31.79	+1.24	100	58.08	29.79	+1.50
150	1:34.79	32.45	+0.66	150	1:27.50	29.42	−0.37
200	2:06.62 (1:04.28)	31.83	−0.62	200	1:56.57 (58.49)	29.07	−0.35
Drop-off from first to second 100 = +1.94				Drop-off from first to second 100 = +0.41			
Whitney Hedgepeth—1:52.98 1992 American record 200 yd Time for 100 yd = Not available				**Jeff Rouse—1:40.64** 1992 American record 200 yd Time for 100 yd = 46.12			
50	27.32	27.32		50	23.87	23.87	
100	55.89	28.57	+1.25	100	49.21	25.34	+1.47
150	1:24.76	28.87	+0.30	150	1:14.76	25.55	+0.21
200	1:52.98 (57.09)	28.22	−0.65	200	1:40.64 (51.43)	25.88	+0.33
Drop-off from first to second 100 = +1.20				Drop-off from first to second 100 = +2.22			

Representative Splits for World and American Records for 200-m and 200-yd Backstroke Swims

yd/m should be at the same speed or slightly faster than the middle two splits, although it may be slightly slower in breaststroke and butterfly events.

400-m and 500-yd Freestyle Events

The splits for world, American, and U.S. Open records in these events are listed opposite. Swimmers generally even-pace the first 300 m of 400 events and the first 400 yd of 500 events. They then finish with a *big sprint,* saving enough energy to swim the final 100 m faster than the previous two or three splits. The remarkable swim by Evans is a notable exception. It is a negative split. That swim notwithstanding, most world-record 400-m swims have been even-paced until the final 100 m. Most athletes swim the first 200 yd/m of these races approximately 3.00 to 6.00 seconds slower than their best times for these 200 events.

The 500-yd races of Evans and Wojdat are good examples of even-paced swims. Their velocities were nearly constant for the first 400 m when you take into account the advantage they gained on the dive during the first 100 yd. They then increased their pace so that the final 100 yd was as fast or faster than the first. Actually, most of that speed occurred over the final 50 yd, with only a slight increase from 400 to 450 yd.

The 400 m swim by Evans is an example of negative-split pacing and is very similar to the plan used by former world-record holder Tracey Wickham. Evans's

Janet Evans—4:03.85 1988 world record 400 m Time for 200 m = 1:59 to 2:00*			
Distance	Cumulative Time	Split Time	Drop-off
100	59.99	59.99	
200	2:02.14	1:02.15	+2.16
300	3:03.40	1:01.26	−0.89
400	4:03.85 (2:01.71)	1:00.45	−0.81
Drop-off from first to second 200 = −0.43			

Evgueni Sadovyi—3:45.00 1992 world record 400 m Time for 200 m = 1:46.70			
Distance	Cumulative Time	Split Time	Drop-off
100	54.61	54.61	
200	1:52.74	58.13	+3.52
300	3:50.38	57.64	−0.49
400	3:45.00 (1:52.26)	54.62	−3.02
Drop-off from first to second 200 = −0.48			

Janet Evans—4:34.39 1990 American record 500 yd Time for 200 yd = 1:46. +*			
Distance	Cumulative Time	Split Time	Drop-off
100	53.48	53.48	
200	1:48.90	55.42	+1.94
300	2:44.40	55.50	+0.08
400	3:40.19 (1:51.29)	55.79	+0.29
500	4:34.39	54.20	−1.59
Drop-off from first to second 200 = +2.39			

Artur Wojdat—4:12.24 1989 U.S. Open record 500 yd Time for 200 yd = 1:33.82			
Distance	Cumulative Time	Split Time	Drop-off
100	49.55	49.55	
200	1:40.44	50.89	+1.34
300	2:31.89	51.45	+0.56
400	3:22.81 (1:42.37)	50.92	−0.53
500	4:12.24	49.43	−1.49
Drop-off from first to second 200 = +1.93			

*Estimated 200 time

Representative Splits for World, American, and U.S. Open Records for 400-m and 500-yd Freestyle Swims

best time for 200 m is not known. We could assume, however, that she was probably capable of swimming at least 1:59.00 seconds for that distance at the time of her record 400-m swim. So, she was probably in the neighborhood of 3.00 seconds slower than her best time for 200 m going out, and she swam the second half of the race slightly faster than the first (2:02.14 versus 2:01.71). Her first two 100-m splits were swum at a constant velocity. That velocity increased during the third 100 and increased even more on the final 100.

It seems from these excellent times that 400-m swimmers must be very conscious of pace. Some will swim well by even-pacing, yet others prefer to negative-split. Swimmers should try both methods to determine which works best. For an even-pacer, the first 200 m should be swum in a controlled manner at a comfortable and constant speed that is approximately 3.00 seconds slower than his or her best time for 200 m. The third 100 m should be swum at the same velocity as the previous two, and the final 100 m should be swum faster than the middle two.

Going-out speed for the first 200 m can be about 4.00 to 5.00 seconds slower than a best time for a negative-split swimmer. The third 100 m should be swum at a slightly faster speed, with the last 100 m swum at nearly the same speed as the first.

Actually, whether even-pacing or negative-splitting, the speed for the seventh 50 should be approximately the same as the speed for the third 100, with enough energy saved for a very fast final sprint over the last 50 m.

Swimmers in 500-yd freestyle events seem to prefer even-pacing over negative-splitting, possibly because, with more turns, they swim less of the total distance and can afford to swim faster early in the race. Regardless of this fact, 500 swimmers also save enough energy to make the final 100 yd faster than any of the previous splits except the first. As in the 400-m event, the split for the final 100 yd should be very similar to the time for the first 100 yd of the race.

The splits for Wojdat are nearly ideal for 500 races. His first 200 yd is approximately 6.00 to 7.00 seconds slower than his fastest time for a 200-yd swim. The second 200 segment is swum approximately 2.00 seconds slower, but only because it began from a pushoff rather than a standing start. Actually, it is swum at the same constant velocity as the first 200 yd. Swimming speed is increased slightly on the next 50 yd, followed by a final 50 sprint that is swum at a relatively faster velocity than any other segment of the race.

If we break the race down into 100-yd segments, the first 100 yd should be approximately 4.00 to 5.00 seconds slower than a swimmer's best time for 100 yd. The next four 100 splits should be swum at a constant speed that is 1.50 to 2.00 seconds slower than the time for the first 100 yd. The final 100 yd should be swum in approximately the same time as the first 100 split of the race.

The 500 swim by Evans is outstanding in that she can take the first 200 yd out only 2.00 to 3.00 seconds slower than her best estimated time for 200 yards. And, she can maintain nearly the same speed for the remainder of the race. Most swimmers have not been able to take this race out at such fast relative speeds and still maintain their pace, so I would not recommend this as the best way to pace the race. It may only work for those persons who are exceptional distance swimmers, like Evans.

800-m and 1,000-yd Freestyle Events

An even pace throughout with a fast finish seems to be preferred by swimmers in these events just as it was for 400-m and 500-yd events. Splits for Evans's and Perkins's world-record 800-m swim are listed opposite. They represent the usual pattern for this and 1,000-yd events.

The first 200 and 400 m of 800 races should be approximately 4.00 to 6.00 seconds slower than a swimmer's best times for these distances. Considering the race by 100s, the first and last 100 splits of these events should be nearly identical. The splits from 100 to 700 m should be within 0.50 second of one another and approximately 2.00 to 3.00 seconds slower than the split for the first 100.

The same pattern is followed in 1,000-yd swims. The splits at 200 and 500 yd should be between 4.00 and 5.00 seconds slower than a swimmer's best time for those distances, and the other splits should be 2.00 to 3.00 seconds slower than the first and fairly constant until the final sprint.

Janet Evans—8:16.22
1989 world record 800 m
Time for 200 m = 1:59 to 2:00*
Time for 400 m = 4:03.85

Distance	Cumulative Time	Split Time	Drop-off
100	1:00.20	1:00.20	
200	2:02.53	1:02.33	+2.13
300	3:05.12	1:02.59	+0.26
400	4:07.92	1:02.80	+0.21
500	5:10.27	1:02.35	−0.45
600	6:12.82	1:02.55	+0.20
700	7:15.54	1:02.72	+0.17
800	8:16.22 (4:08.30)	1:00.68	−2.04

Drop-off from first to second 400 = +0.38

*Estimated 200 time

Kieren Perkins
1992 world record 800 m
Time for 200 m = 1:48.92
Time for 400 m = 3:46.47

Distance	Cumulative Time	Split Time	Drop-off
100	55:92	55.92	
200	1:53.83	57.91	+1.99
300	2:52.79	58.96	+1.05
400	3:52.06	57.27	−1.69
500	4:51.10	59.04	+1.77
600	5:50.29	59.19	+0.15
700	6:49.69	59.40	+0.21
800	7:46.60 (3:54.54)	56.91	−2.49

Drop-off from first to second 400 = +2.48

Splits for World-Record 800-m Swims by Janet Evans and Kieren Perkins

1,500-m and 1,650-yd Freestyle Events

Most distance swimmers even-pace until the final 100 or 200 yd/m, when they increase their speed. They then sprint to the finish over the final 50 yd/m. The splits for world-record 1,500-m swims and American-record 1,650-yd swims are presented on page 616.

The athletes try to swim each segment in about the same time in these races. This pattern is exemplified by Evans's and Perkin's great world-record swims for 1,500 m and Kostoff's American-record 1,650-yd swim.

The going-out speed for the 1,500 and 1,650 races should be approximately 7.00 to 10.00 seconds slower than a swimmer's best time for 400 m or 500 yd. Most of that difference takes place in the first 200 yd/m, which should be 6.00 to 8.00 seconds slower than a swimmer's best time for that distance. Energy should be saved so that the final 100 yd/m of either event can be swum in approximately the same time as the first 100-yd/m segment.

The pace for Kostoff's 1,650-yd swim is also listed by 100 splits. You can see that after the first 100 his splits do not generally differ by more than 0.50 second until he begins picking up the pace in the final 150 to 200 yd. The first 100 yd/m, because of the benefit of the dive, should be approximately 1.50 to 2.00 seconds faster than the other 100 segments, even though it is swum at the same constant velocity.

Janet Evans—15:52.10 1988 world record 1,500 m Time for 400 m = 4:03.85				**Janet Evans—15:44.98** 1988 American record 1,650 yd Time for 500 yd = 4:38.82			
Distance	Cumulative Time	Split Time	Drop-off	Distance	Cumulative Time	Split Time	Drop-off
By 400s				By 500s			
400	4:11.70	4:11.70		500	4:42.38	4:42.38	
800	8:26.52	4:14.82	+3.12	1000	9:31.52	4:49.15	+6.77
1200	12:42.00	4:15.48	+0.66	1500	14:20.08	4:48.56	−0.59
1500	15:52.10	3:10.10		1650	15:44.98	1:24.90	
Kieren Perkins—14:48.40 1992 world record 1,500 m Time for 400 m = 3:46.47				**Jeff Kostoff—14:37.87** 1986 American record 1,650 yd Best time for 500 yd = 4:16.39			
By 400s				By 500s			
400	3:52.43	3:52.43		500	4:25.27	4:25.27	
800	7:51.15	3:58.72	+6.29	1000	8:52.04	4:26.77	+1.50
1200	11:50.96	3:59.81	+1.09	1500	13:19.94	4:27.90	+1.13
1500	14:48.40	2:57.44		1650	14:37.87	1:17.93	
By 100s							
100	51:91	51.91					
200	1:45.47	53.56	+1.65				
300	2:38.69	53.22	−0.34				
400	3:32.02	53.53					
500	4:25.27	53.25					
600	5:18.60	53.33					
700	6:11.56	52.96					
800	7:04.81	53.25					
900	7:58.47	53.66					
1000	8:52.04	53.57					
1100	9:45.51	53.47					
1200	10:38.94	53.43					
1300	11:32.47	53.53					
1400	12:26.18	53.71					
1500	13:19.94	53.76					
1600	14:12.45	52.49					
1650	14:37.87	25.42					

Representative Splits for World and American Records for 1,500-m and 1,650-yd Freestyle Swims

Individual Medley Events

It is difficult to calculate the best pace patterns for individual medleys with drop-off times; those times are inconclusive because the strokes change during each quarter of the race. Nevertheless, the length of these events makes it imperative that swimmers use some form of pacing. The approach I have taken to determine the best pace for each of these races has been to compare each leg of the two individual medley events to a particular swimmer's best time for the same stroke and distance.

200-m and 200-yd Individual Medley Events Splits for world- and American-record swims are listed below. The paces that are recommended are based on my own experiences with swimmers in these events.

Tamas Darnyi—1:59.36 1991 world record 200 m				**Lin Li—2:11.65** 1992 world record 200 m			
Distance	Cumulative Time	Split Time	Drop-off	Distance	Cumulative Time	Split Time	Drop-off
50	26.84	26.84		50	28.68	28.68	
100	56.80	29.96	+3.12	100	1:02.05	33.37	+4.49
150	1:31.65	34.85	+4.89	150	1:40.77	38.72	+5.35
200	1:59.36	27.71	−7.14	200	2:11.65	30.88	−7.84
Summer Sanders—1:55.45 1992 American record 200 yd				**Martin Lopez-Zubero—1:44.01** 1991 U.S. Open record 200 yd			
50	25.08	25.08		50	22.98	22.98	
100	54.59	29.51	+4.43	100	48.11	25.13	+2.15
150	1:27.70	33.11	+3.60	150	1:19.01	30.90	+5.77
200	1:55.45	27.75	−5.36	200	1:44.01	25.00	−5.90

Representative Splits for World, American, and U.S. Open Records for 200-m and 200-yd Individual Medley Swims

Athletes who swim 200-individual medley events usually complete the first 50 yd/m of butterfly about 1.00 second slower than an all-out sprint for the same distance. The backstroke split is approximately 3.00 seconds slower than the best time for 50 yd/m of that stroke. The breaststroke is 5.00 to 6.00 seconds slower, and the freestyle is approximately 4.00 seconds slower.

Another way to look at these events is according to the differences between the times for each segment. These differences will not be exactly the same for all swimmers because of differing levels of skill in certain strokes. However, the times are remarkably similar from swimmer to swimmer, even considering that complicating factor.

The backstroke split will usually be 3.00 to 4.00 seconds slower than the butterfly. The breaststroke will usually be 4.00 to 5.00 seconds slower than the backstroke. The freestyle split will usually be 6.00 to 7.00 seconds faster than the time for the breaststroke segment, and it will be very similar to the time for the butterfly leg of the race. These same relationships between segments hold true for both long-course and short-course events.

400-m and 400-yd Individual Medley Events The splits for current world- and American-record holders are listed below. The first leg of both the long-course and short-course races should be approximately 2.50 to 3.00 seconds slower than a swimmer's fastest time for 100 yd/m of butterfly. The backstroke and freestyle legs should be 6.00 to 7.00 seconds slower than a swimmer's best times for those strokes and distances. The breaststroke leg should generally be 8.00 to 10.00 seconds slower than a swimmer's best time. The freestyle time is also similar to the time for the opening butterfly leg in this event just as it was for the 200 individual medley.

Petra Schneider—4:36.10 1982 world record 400 m				**Tamas Darnyi—4:12.36** 1991 world record 400 m			
Distance	Cumulative Time	Split Time	Drop-off	Distance	Cumulative Time	Split Time	Drop-off
100	1:02.42	1:02.42		100	59.10	59.10	
200	2:12.16	1:09.66	+7.24	200	2:02.57	1:03.47	+4.37
300	3:33.16	1:21.00	+11.34	300	3:14.72	1:12.15	+8.68
400	4:36.10	1:02.84	−18.16	400	4:12.36	57.54	−14.61
Summer Sanders—4:02.28 1992 American record 400 yd				**David Wharton—3:42.23** 1988 American record 400 yd			
100	54.87	54.87		100	50.85	50.85	
200	1:57.39	1:02.52	+7.65	200	1:49.00	58.15	+7.30
300	3:05.92	1:08.53	+6.01	300	2:52.34	1:03.34	+5.19
400	4:02.28	56.36	−12.17	400	3:42.23	49.89	−13.45

Representative Splits for World and American Records for 400-m and 400-yd Individual Medley Swims

A swimmer with nearly equal ability in all strokes would swim the backstroke leg of this event 4.00 to 5.00 seconds slower than the time for the opening butterfly leg. The breaststroke would be 10.00 to 12.00 seconds slower than the backstroke leg, and the finishing freestyle leg would be 14.00 to 15.00 seconds faster than the breaststroke segment. Once again, these relationships seem to be true for both long-course and short-course 400 individual medleys.

Teaching Swimmers to Pace

Underdistance repeats and broken swims are the best vehicles to use for teaching swimmers how to pace. Swimmers should be able to repeat swims of one-quarter the race distance or less within 0.20 to 0.50 second of their ideal pace by the time their most important meets are scheduled.

The pace for taking a race out should be practiced with a block start for greater accuracy. Paced swims for the middle portions of races should begin from a turn so that the time accurately reflects the true pace. The time should, of course, be taken from a hand touch for butterfly and breaststroke events and from a foot touch for freestyle and backstroke events.

Stroke Rates

In addition to their influence on improving speed, stroke rates can also be used to teach pacing. In fact, learning to control one's stroke rate is the quickest and easiest way to learn pacing. Swimmers increase their stroke rate when they swim faster and reduce it when they swim slower. They can learn very quickly, therefore, to swim an even pace by maintaining a constant stroke rate. Of course, implicit in this recommendation is the presumption that stroke length is optimal and remains constant at a particular stroke rate. This is not always the case, particularly when swimmers become fatigued in the later portion of a race. Their stroke length usually decreases somewhat at that time, and their stroke rate increases compensatorily so that they can maintain a constant speed. Pai and associates (1984) reported that stroke rates increased an average of 6.3 percent in the second half of races. This amounts to an increase of 2 or 3 stroke cycles per minute (stroke cycle/min).

With this information in mind, the first step is to determine the combination of stroke rate and stroke length that is optimal for each swimmer for certain races. This does not always mean that a swimmer should stroke at the slowest rate with the longest possible stroke. The relationship between stroke rate, stroke length, and swimming speed is a complex one, as illustrated in Figure 23-1 (p. 620). It shows that the fastest speeds occur at some optimal combination of stroke rate and stroke length.

The hypothetical swimmer in this figure has a best time of 4:08.00 for 400 m of freestyle, which she achieves with a stroke rate of 42 stroke cycle/min and a stroke length of 2.3 m/stroke cycle. She is capable of stroking faster, but if she does, her length will drop dramatically and so will her speed. Conversely, she can take longer strokes; however, this will cause her rate to decline too much and she will lose speed.

The relationship between stroke rate and stroke length is such that maximum or minimum values in either will produce slow times, yet the fastest speeds result from some optimal combination of the two (Craig & Pendergast, 1979; Pai, Hay, Wilson, & Thayer, 1981). A long stroke length is only possible at a very slow stroke rate. Conversely, stroke length necessarily decreases as stroke rate increases. One job of the coach is to help athletes find the optimal combination of each that will allow them to swim at a desired speed with the least energy expenditure. The optimal combination of rate and length is undoubtedly somewhat different for each

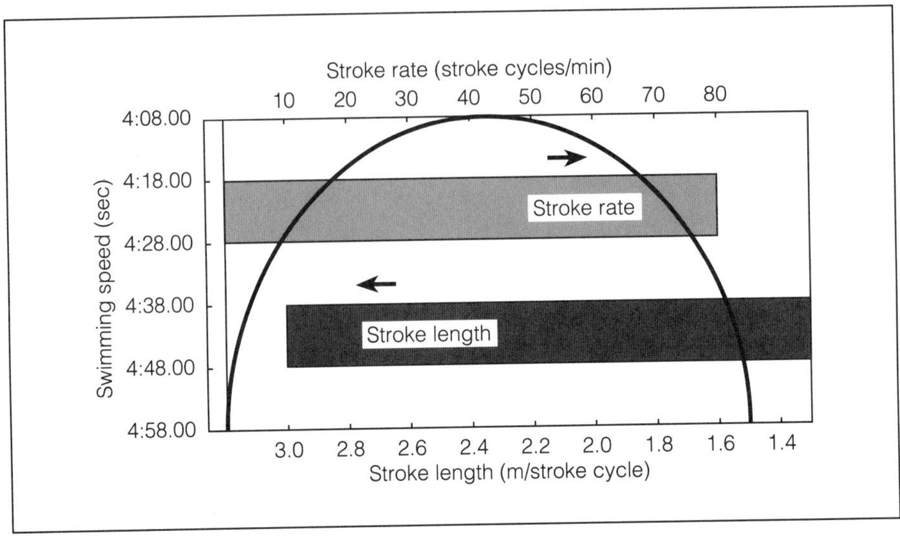

Figure 23-1. The relationship of stroke rate and stroke length to swimming speed.

swimmer in a particular event. Nevertheless, the range of difference is small enough to make generalizations concerning the best rates for each event.

Craig and his colleagues (1985) have reported the range of stroke rates and stroke lengths for finalists at the 1984 U.S. Olympic Trials. The ranges for stroke rates agree with those I calculated for members of the 1987 NCAA Men's Swimming Championship and both male and female finalists in the 1988 Olympic Games. They are listed in Table 23-1 as guides for senior swimmers. Stroke cycles per 50 m and 50 yd have also been estimated from the stroke length data to simplify the use of this information when training swimmers. Allowances have been made for gliding time after turns, and, in the case of the 50-m freestyle, for gliding time after the start.

The stroke rates and lengths listed in Table 23-1 are for very high level senior swimmers. Most swimmers who hope to compete internationally need to fit within these ranges, although there have been some very successful exceptions. Both Michael Gross and Matt Biondi have used noticeably slower stroke rates in their events and Janet Evans uses a rate in the 54 to 56 range in her distance races. Taller swimmers usually have longer strokes at any race distance (Weiss et al., 1988). You can expect that swimmers with excellent kicks and swimmers with very large hands probably also use a slower stroke rate and that smaller swimmers with less effective kicks compensate for a shorter stroke length by increasing their stroke rate (Grimston & Hay, 1984).

The energy required to swim a particular speed can usually be reduced by increasing stroke length and decreasing stroke rate within reasonable limits. However, the energy cost can be inordinately high when an athlete exerts a great deal of muscular force over an unusually long stroking distance, even if the rate is low.

Table 23-1. The Range of Stroke Rates and Stroke Lengths and Approximate Stroke Cycles Per 50 m and 50 yd* for Male and Female National and World-class Swimmers

Events	Stroke Rates (stroke cycle/min)	Stroke Lengths (m/stroke cycle)	Approximate Strokes/50 m	Approximate Strokes/50 yd
Women				
50 freestyle	60–64	1.90–2.06	19–21**	18–20**
100 freestyle	53–56	1.91–2.20	19–23	20–22
200 freestyle	48–52	1.90–2.02	22–23	19–20
400/500 freestyle	45–52	1.81–2.05	22–25	18–20
800/1,000 freestyle	Not available			
1,500/1,650 freestyle	50–53	1.79–1.85	24–25	21–22
100 backstroke	44–49	1.90–2.07	22–24	18–19***
200 backstroke	40–43	2.08–2.22	20–22	17–18***
100 breaststroke	44–53	1.56–1.90	21–26	15–18
200 breaststroke	42–44	1.70–1.84	22–24	15–17
100 butterfly	54–57	1.69–1.90	24–27	19–22
200 butterfly	50–54	1.67–1.77	25–26	22–23
Men				
50 freestyle	65–70	2.05–2.15	18–20**	17–18**
100 freestyle	50–54	2.14–2.30	19–21	15–17
200 freestyle	48–50	2.31–2.39	19–20	15–16
400/500 freestyle	42–45	2.20–2.42	18–20	15–19
800/1,000 freestyle	41–44	Not available		
1,500/1,650 freestyle	40–43	2.27–2.37	19–20	15–16
100 backstroke	48–51	1.82–1.96	22–23	17–19***
200 backstroke	42–49	1.90–2.10	21–23	17–19***
100 breaststroke	50–55	1.64–1.74	23–24	14–15
200 breaststroke	40–45	1.88–2.18	19–21	13–15
100 butterfly	50–55	2.01–2.20	21–22	17–18
200 butterfly	50–55	1.75–2.00	23–25	18–20

Sources: Craig, Skehan, Pawelczyk, & Boomer, 1985; Maglischo, 1991.

*Stroke cycles per 50 m and 50 yd are adjusted for turn and glide distances.

**Includes start for 50-m long course and start and turn for 50-yd short course.

***Does not include dolphin kick.

Conversely, energy expenditure can sometimes be reduced by stroking faster with less force. As proof of this, distance swimmers tend to use a slower stroke rate and a shorter stroke length than sprinters (Weiss et al., 1988), possibly because lower force output per stroke conserves energy in long races. Sprinting, on the other hand, requires the application of maximum force, because conservation of energy is not as great a consideration for sprinters as it is for distance swimmers. This may be why sprinters tend to use both a longer stroke and a faster rate.

The ideal stroke rate for each swimmer can be determined in a number of ways. One of the best is to swim underdistance practice repeats at present race speeds while using various combinations of stroke rate and stroke length. Evaluations can be made from the times for these repeats, the increase in immediate postswim and recovery heart rate, and a swimmer's subjective sensation of effort. Some procedures for measuring stroke rate and stroke length were described in Chapter 5 in the section on sprint training.

Another method for determining the optimal stroke rate is to count it during competition. When it varies from competition to competition in the same event, the rate that produces the best time is probably closest to a particular swimmer's optimum.

Surprisingly, an optimal stroke rate generally does not change for a particular race distance when swimmers shave and taper. Stroke length increases as they rest and particularly after they shave, but stroke rate does not change appreciably. Although a few swimmers' rate may increase when they rest and shave, stroke rates usually do not decrease under these conditions.

Once the optimal combination of rate and length has been determined, races can be paced efficiently by learning to control and maintain that combination for nearly the entire race distance. It is surprising how few swimmers are conscious of this relationship between maintaining a constant stroke rate and energy expenditure. In terms of energy use, it should be most economical to swim at a constant stroke rate throughout a race rather than to vary the rate from segment to segment. The way our body uses energy is analogous to the way automobiles consume gas. You can drive a particular distance at a constant rate of, say, 40 mph and use a small amount of gas, or you can drive the same distance at the same average rate by varying speeds between 35 and 55 mph and use much more gas. Swimmers must learn to cover their race distances in the most economical manner, that is, with a constant stroke rate.

Figure 23-2 shows the typical changes in stroke rate that swimmers use in races. A 200 race is used as the example, but these changes are typical of other race distances.

Athletes generally swim the first one-fourth to one-third of a race with a stroke rate that is faster than average before settling into a very efficient rate through the middle portion. The rate during the middle portion generally represents the optimal combination of rate and length for that particular race distance. The rate increases during the final sprint so that it is, once again, above average.

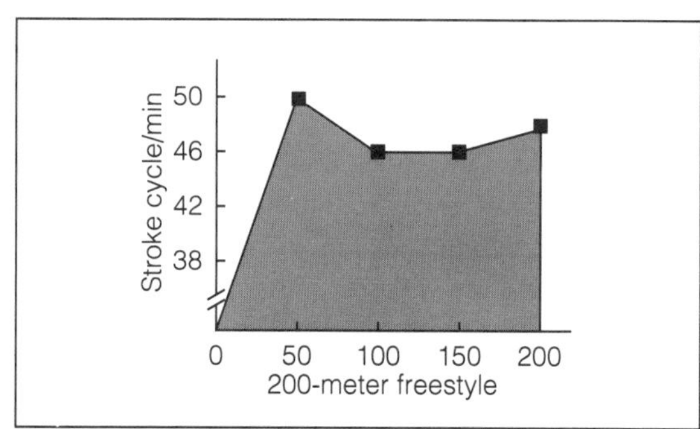

Figure 23-2. Typical stroke rate changes during a race.

It would probably be more economical in terms of energy expenditure for swimmers to start a race at the same stroke rate that they will use through the middle portion and then to maintain that rate until the final sprint. A fast rate early in a race probably increases energy cost for the first 50 m inordinately, causing an increase in lactic acid production that will contribute to an earlier onset of acidosis and slower speed later in the race. The shrill sound of the starting signal and the exhilaration of hitting the water at the beginning of a race makes it very difficult for swimmers to control their stroke rate, nevertheless, the savings in energy makes it wise to do so.

It should make for faster times if swimmers began their races at a constant rate that could be maintained until the final sprint. At that point, the rate should increase, say, by 2 or 3 stroke cycles/min.

Two other mistakes that swimmers make where stroke rates are concerned are (1) to start a race with a rate that they cannot maintain, and (2) to increase their stroke rate inordinately during their final sprint. Figure 23-3 illustrates both of these mistakes.

The most common mistake is for swimmers to begin with a rate that is too high to maintain for the entire race. Consequently, both their rate and swimming speed decline progressively throughout the race. This pattern occurs when swimmers take a race out too fast and simply cannot maintain their speed at the end. It usually results in a poor performance.

Some swimmers make the second mistake of increasing their stroke rate too much at the end of a race. Swimmers who increase their rate inordinately in their desire to finish a race fast also reduce their stroke length so much that their speed suffers. Athletes who swim this way usually pace the race too fast in the first and middle portions and become so fatigued that stroke length deteriorates rapidly in the last stages. They try in vain to compensate for this reduction in length with a faster rate but usually swim slower.

Another reason for an inordinate increase in the stroke rate during the final sprint is that some athletes believe that they can swim faster by moving their arms as fast as possible. Unfortunately, if their rate is too fast, stroke length will suffer and they will swim the final portion of the race at a slower speed even if they are not fatigued. As mentioned, an increase in rate of 2 or 3 stroke cycles/min is probably ideal for most races.

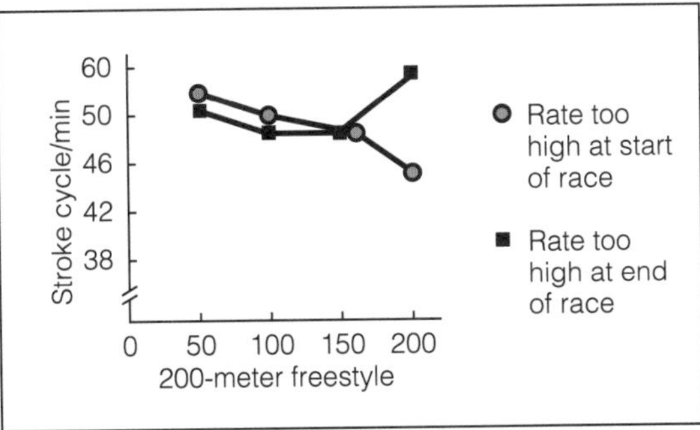

Figure 23-3. Two common stroke rate mistakes that swimmers make.

STRATEGY

Although pacing usually results in faster times, those times will not always win races. Races between swimmers with similar times are often won by one competitor who makes an unexpected move that upsets another competitor's race plan. In addition to pacing, swimmers should also learn offensive and defensive strategies for racing. They should know when to make unexpected moves that will upset their opponents, and they should learn how to counter when opponents swim a race in an unforeseen manner. Following are descriptions of some of the most common offensive tactics that swimmers use in races.

Offensive Tactics

Going out Faster Than Expected This tactic works well against opponents who are inexperienced and those who have a strong finishing sprint. Inexperienced swimmers may become demoralized when another swimmer takes an early lead. Fast finishers will not be able to bring the race home quickly if they are forced to go out faster than they had planned and become fatigued.

Going out Slower Than Expected This tactic is useful against opponents who tend to go out fast, because they are not strong finishers. Swimming slow at the beginning of a race may fool an opponent into swimming slower than he planned. As a result, both swimmers will reach the final segment less fatigued than usual. In this case, the one with the fastest sprint should win the race.

A Fast Breakaway Sprint in the Middle of a Race This is a good tactic to use against opponents who tend to give up when they are behind. A sprint somewhere in the middle of a race may demoralize opponents into thinking that they have no chance. A swimmer who sprints away may not swim the last portion of a race as quickly when using this strategy, but she may not need to because her opponents may have given up.

Taking the Lead There is an advantage to taking the lead in pools that tend to be turbulent. This is particularly true in butterfly races. Swimming in the wake of competitors increases the energy that a swimmer must expend to combat wave drag. In such cases, an athlete should swim slightly faster than planned in order to stay ahead of competitors, instead of swimming through their wakes. When the pace seems too fast to take the lead, the swimmer should remain as close as possible to the leaders to reduce the amount of wake through which he must swim.

Drafting The final piece of advice concerns *drafting* in races. Swimmers will tell you that drafting reduces the energy cost for a particular race because they are pulled along by their competitors. Accordingly, an athlete will swim along one side of her lane just behind her nearest competitor in an adjacent lane trying to fit into the low pressure area in the wake behind the leader so that she is sucked along somewhat toward the high pressure area in front of the leading swimmer. There is no scientific evidence to support this practice, yet the experience of many swimmers suggests that drafting reduces the energy cost for the trailing swimmer, leaving her with more speed to overtake her competitor during the final sprint.

Defensive Tactics

Following are some defensive strategies that can be used to counter some of the offensive tactics just described.

When a Competitor Goes Out Faster Than Expected A swimmer should stay close enough to overtake an opponent, even if it means swimming faster than planned. The opponent will have to work hard to stay ahead and may become quite fatigued later; consequently, the trailing swimmer uses less energy and may be able to take the lead when his opponent starts to tire.

When a Competitor Goes Out Slower Than Expected A swimmer should not be afraid to take the lead when this happens. Some swimmers are so devoted to negative-splitting that they expect to be behind in the early stage of a race and thus refuse to take the lead, even when the pace is too slow. A swimmer should know her race pace well enough that she cannot be fooled into making this mistake. Otherwise, she may find herself outsprinted at the end by a faster but less-enduring opponent if she does not build an early lead when the pace is too slow.

When a Competitor Makes a Breakaway Sprint in the Middle of a Race A swimmer should not let a competitor sprint away from him, even if the pace seems too fast. An opponent may become encouraged if he can get away. On the other hand, he may become discouraged if he fails to get away, and the swimmer who stays close may be able to overtake him and win the race.

The three defensive tactics just described usually work best when two competitors of equal or nearly equal ability are racing; however, they may sometimes work against opponents with superior speed for the reasons that were indicated. One of the best training procedures for preparing swimmers to utilize offensive and defensive strategies during competition is to purposely have them swim some practice repeats at speeds that are both faster and slower than their planned paces for certain races. By swimming faster, they will learn how much they can deviate from these paces without hampering their ability to maintain a reasonably fast speed during the final part of a race. Swimming slower than race pace in practice will help them realize when they are being maneuvered into a pace that is too slow in the early portion of a race.

When a Competitor Is Drafting Defensively, a swimmer should try to swim in the center of her lane so that competitors cannot *draft off her wake*. When an opponent tries this technique, the leading swimmer should move to the other side of her lane to prevent it. That move should take place during a turn, when the swimmer can change sides without increasing the distance she swims.

WARMING UP

The value of warming up was controversial at the time the first edition of this book was written. Recent works tend to support this practice, however.

Reasons for Warming Up

From a physiological point of view, there are at least five very good reasons for preceding any performance with a mild warm-up:

1. Muscles should contract faster and relax more completely.
2. Mechanical efficiency should improve because of decreased resistance to movement in the muscles and joints.
3. The rate of blood flow should increase.
4. Hemoglobin should release more oxygen for diffusion into the muscles.
5. Myoglobin should transport oxygen across the cells faster as muscle temperature increases.

Some other reasons for warming up follow:

6. Stretching joints should increase flexibility and thus improve stroking efficiency.
7. A good warm-up can provide a rehearsal effect. Swimmers can refine stroke techniques, starts, and turns for an upcoming competition, and they can practice paces and stroke rates for various events during the warm-up so that they can go into their races knowing exactly how they should feel when they try to swim a particular speed.
8. Swimmers can become accustomed to their surroundings during the warm-up. Each new pool has a different feel and distinctive problems and various identifying landmarks (such as backstroke flags) that swimmers use to gauge their position during a race.
9. Another reason for warming up is to provide time for mental rehearsal. It can be a time during which swimmers practice mental imagery. They can plan their races and become focused on those aspects of their performance that will lead to success while swimming easily down the pool or while swimming sprint and paced swims.

The final reason for warming up is, perhaps, the most important—to prevent illness and injury. There is a very compelling study that points to the necessity for using warm-up procedures with Masters swimmers. It shows the presence of abnormal electrocardiographic tracings in middle-aged subjects who were subjected to strenuous exercise without a proper warm-up (Barnard et al., 1973). These researchers reported that warming up reduced the incidence of abnormal ECG readings during exercise. Abnormal ECG recordings had previously been recorded on 31 of 44 middle-aged men who were free of symptoms of coronary artery disease when they exercised without warming up. Only 2 of the men exhibited abnormal ECG's after warming up.

An additional benefit of warming up was also reported in this study: blood pressure was lower for some of the men during the run preceded by warming up. These same men had an unusually high blood pressure during the run that *was not preceded by a warm-up*. Systolic blood pressure increased to 168 mm Hg in 7 of the men after running without a warm-up. After warming up, their systolic blood pressure increased to only 140 mm Hg during the run.

Apparently, the oxygen supply to the heart can be inadequate during a sudden increase in effort that is not preceded by a warm-up. This, in turn, can increase the risk of heart attack for persons with advanced narrowing of their coronary arteries. Warming up is advantageous for all of us, but because of the potential danger of heart failure, it should be required of all middle-aged and older swimmers.

Warm-up Procedures

There are several questions about warm-up procedures that need to be answered before an intelligent protocol can be established. These concern warm-up intensity, length, and nearness to competition.

Intensity At one time, the prevailing opinion was that warming up was only effective if it was vigorous enough to raise muscle temperature (deVries, 1974). However, some recent studies have shown that vigorous warm-ups impair performance because of the precompetition fatigue they cause (DeBruyn-Prevost & Lefebvre, 1980; Genovely & Stanford, 1982). Hermiston and O'Brien (1972) came to this conclusion when they tested a group of subjects for a treadmill-simulated 220-yd run following 10 minutes of warm-up at 60 percent $\dot{V}O_2$max. The oxygen cost of the run was increased following that warm-up as compared to a run that had been completed after warming up at an intensity of 30 percent of $\dot{V}O_2$max.

Research now suggests that warm-ups be performed with moderate effort to encourage blood flow and heating of the skin and surface blood vessels without being so vigorous as to cause fatigue. The ideal intensity seems to be between 30 and 50 percent of $\dot{V}O_2$max, which is similar to easy efforts at 20 to 40 percent of maximum speed. (Chwalbinska-Moneta & Hanninen, 1989; Ingjer & Strommer, 1979; Martin, Robinson, Wiegman, & Aulick, 1975). In one study (Chwalbinska-Moneta & Hanninen, 1989), subjects were able to increase their workload by an average of 5 percent following a 10-minute warm-up at 40 percent of $\dot{V}O_2$max.

While this low intensity may be best physiologically, some vigorous swimming is required for rehearsal purposes during a warm-up. It should be minimal, however, and it should be completed at least 20 minutes before a swimmer's first event to provide adequate time for removal of any lactic acid that may have accumulated.

Length There is very little information that can help in answering this question. The warm-up that produced a 5-percent increase in work at the 4-mmol threshold lasted only 10 minutes. DeVries (1974) recommends a duration of 15 to 30 minutes.

Nearness to Competition The vigorous portion of the warm-up—sprints and pace work—should be completed about 15 to 30 minutes before the event. This will provide more than adequate recovery time for any drop in muscle pH that may have occurred. The less-vigorous portions of the warm-up should be continued until at least 5 minutes before competition, although swimming easy until the event is called to the blocks may even be more beneficial.

Protocol In addition to increasing blood flow and oxygen consumption, swimmers should include activities that improve their ranges of motion, stroke mechanics, pace, and focus on the race. The following procedures are suggested by the available research and the reported experiences of successful coaches and athletes.

1. *Stretching* Prior to entering the water, athletes should spend 5 or 10 minutes doing some flexibility exercises. They should pay particular attention to increasing the range of motion in the joints that are important to swimmers: the ankles, shoulders, lower back, and, for breaststrokers, the groin and knees.

2. *Easy swimming* Swimmers should spend 10 to 20 minutes swimming easy at approximately 20- to 40-percent effort. Swimming, pulling, kicking, and stroke drills should be included. Swimmers should practice these drills until they feel very loose, efficient, and powerful. This is a good time for them to mentally rehearse their races. They should plan their paces, any offensive strategies that they intend to use, and their procedures for countering any defensive strategies that their opponents may use. They should see themselves swimming their races properly and successfully. They should concentrate intently, narrowing their focus to the races at hand and blocking out any extraneous factors that may interfere with their goals.

3. *Starts and turns* Swimmers should practice these during the warm-up until they feel confident that they will be able to do them well in their races. They should also practice relay starts if they are swimming on a relay.

4. *Pace and sprint swims* Athletes should swim some 25, 50, or 100 repeats at race pace to increase their sensitivity to the kinesthetic cues associated with those speeds. These repeats should be swum both off the block and from the wall so that they have the paces for both the first and second splits of races firmly under control. They should pay close attention to the stroke rate and stroke length they will use for each different event.

   The usual ritual of swimming a few 25 sprints is really not necessary unless an athlete is swimming a 50 or 100 event. Nevertheless, many swimmers like to sprint fast before competing, and Astrand and Rodahl (1977) have indicated that sprinting during the warm-up has a beneficial effect on sprint events. However, swimmers should complete these vigorous portions of the warm-up at least 15 to 30 minutes before the first race.

5. *Maintaining the warm-up effect* It is a good idea for swimmers to reenter the water about 5 or 10 minutes before race time and to swim easily at 20- to 40-percent effort until the race is called to the blocks. This will maintain *surface heating* without causing fatigue. By doing this, swimmers' physiological mechanisms will respond faster when the race begins, and they will be able to swim farther and faster before becoming fatigued.

The following box summarizes the warm-up procedures just described.

Suggested Warm-up Procedures

1. Stretch the ankles, shoulders, lower back, and knees (breaststrokers) for 5 or 10 minutes.
2. Swim long and easy for 10 to 20 minutes. This is a good time for practicing stroke drills.
3. Practice starts and turns.
4. Swim 25s, 50s, or 100s at race pace, or sprint 25s.
5. Swim down long and easy for 2 to 5 minutes. Finish 15 to 30 minutes before race time.
6. Reenter the water 5 or 10 minutes before race time and swim easy until called to the block.

MASSAGE AND HYPERVENTILATION

Massage and hyperventilation are two precompetition rituals that some swimmers depend on to improve their performances.

Massage

The prerace massage or rubdown has become increasingly popular among swimmers. Research reports concerning the benefits of this procedure have been contradictory, however (Asmussen & Boje, 1945; Karpovich, 1965; Schmid, 1947), forcing us to use empirical judgments to evaluate the possible beneficial effects of this procedure. In theory, massage should be beneficial for the following reasons:

1. The heat generated from the palms and the friction of the hands can increase muscle temperature.
2. The manipulation of the athlete's limbs should increase flexibility.
3. The relaxing combination of increased body heat and joint manipulation may reduce muscle tension and prerace anxiety.
4. Massage should facilitate postrace recovery because, when performed properly, it increases diffusion of the waste products of energy metabolism from the muscles to the bloodstream, where they can be transported to other parts of the body and metabolized.

Obviously, the potential benefits of massage are considerable; therefore, I would advise including it in the precompetition ritual.

Hyperventilation

Many swimmers and coaches believe that taking several deep breaths while waiting for races to start aids performance. There is some physiological support for this practice, although not for the reasons usually stated.

Hyperventilation *does not* improve performance by increasing the oxygen supply before a race. The oxygen that is inhaled before the race cannot be stored. Instead, it is simply exhaled with the next breath. However, hyperventilation is beneficial because it reduces the carbon dioxide level of the blood, so athletes do not feel the need to breathe until late in the race. It is carbon dioxide accumulation and not oxygen deprivation that precipitates the feeling of breathlessness and the need for air that swimmers experience during races. The carbon dioxide content of the blood and, thus, the need to breathe can be reduced by taking several long, forced exhalations immediately prior to competition. Once the carbon dioxide content of their blood has been reduced, sprinters are able to swim 50 races and even the first half of 100 races with fewer breaths.

Swimmers should begin hyperventilating while waiting behind the block and continue as they step to the back of the starting platform. They should take large, but not massive, inhalations, followed by very long and complete exhalations. Five or six such exhalations should be sufficient. They should not overdo it, however. Athletes can become dizzy or they may even faint from too much hyperventilating.

Swimmers should not hold their breath after hyperventilating; instead, they should breathe normally when they are called to their mark. At the starting signal, they should take one large breath as they dive into the water. That breath, plus the reduction in carbon dioxide from hyperventilating, should allow them to swim farther before feeling the need to breathe.

Although hyperventilating should provide some benefit in 25, 50, and even 100 races, it probably has no beneficial effect in longer races. Swimmers should begin breathing in a normal rhythm just after diving into the water in these races. Consequently, there is no need for them to hold their breath at anytime during the race until just before finishing.

SWIMMING DOWN

This is one of the most important postrace (and posttraining) procedures for swimmers and one that is most often neglected. Athletes should always swim easy for 800 to 1,200 yd/m (10 to 20 minutes) after a race. This will increase their recovery rate. In fact, several studies have shown that swimmers recover twice as fast if they do so (Bond et al., 1987; Bonen & Belcastro, 1976; Krukau, Volker, & Liesen, 1987).

Figure 5-5 illustrated the accelerated rate of recovery that takes place during mild exercise. It is reproduced here as Figure 23-4. As you can see, blood lactate was reduced to near resting levels in 30 minutes when some mild exercise was performed. It required 60 minutes to produce the same reduction when the athletes simply rested without exercising.

Recovery is more rapid during mild exercise because the removal of lactic acid is accomplished through a mechanism called the *muscle pump*. The contraction of the muscles exerts a squeezing effect on the veins, which pushes blood back to the heart at an accelerated rate, where the excess lactate can be removed and metabolized by cardiac muscle fibers. In addition, the elevated rate of flow causes more

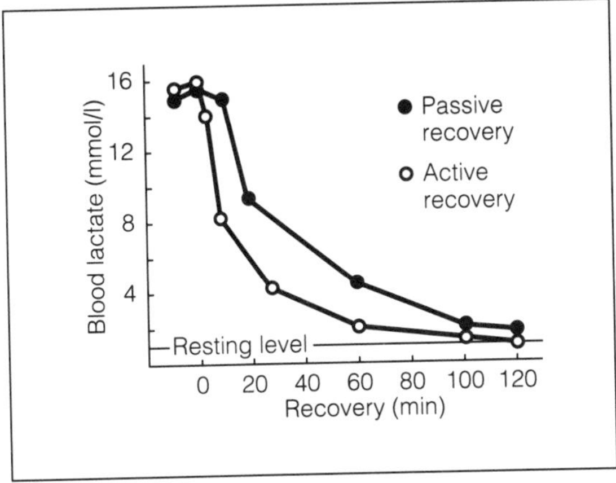

Figure 23-4. The effects of active recovery and passive recovery on the removal of blood lactic acid.

blood to reach the lungs, where it will give up its carbon dioxide and take on oxygen. The oxygen can then be transported to the muscles, where it will increase the rate of lactic acid removal by aiding in the metabolism of that substance to glucose.

Figure 23-4 shows that the major portion of the recovery can be completed within the first 10 to 20 minutes; thus, muscle pH is probably normalized, or nearly so, in that length of time. For this reason, 10 to 20 minutes is the recommended length for recovery swims. It is very difficult to get athletes to swim for this long after a race when their teammates are swimming other events and awards are being given. Nevertheless, they should be strongly encouraged to do so because the potential benefits are so great.

The speed during the swim-down should be sufficient to maintain a high rate of blood flow without causing additional muscle glycogen use and lactic acid production. Well-conditioned athletes can probably swim up to 50 percent of their maximum speed without producing additional lactic acid, although athletes will intuitively choose the proper speed for swimming down if left to their own devices (Bonen & Belcastro, 1976).

CHAPTER 24

Strength, Power, and Flexibility

During the past four decades, we have witnessed a complete turnaround in thinking about the importance of resistance training to swimmers. In the 1950s, swimmers were warned that lifting weights would build bulky muscles and decrease flexibility. An excellent study by Massey and Chaudet (1956) debunked this myth. These researchers demonstrated that weight trainers and body builders were actually more flexible than the general population. Their results were later supported in a study in which Olympic weight lifters were second only to gymnasts in flexibility among a large group of Olympic athletes from a variety of sports (Jensen & Fisher, 1975). Because of these studies and others like them, attitudes toward resistance training have changed so much that experts now believe that swimmers *must* engage in resistance training if they wish to be successful.

Despite this change in thinking, there have been few well controlled pieces of research that substantiated the connection between weight training and improved athletic performances until recently. In a study involving swimmers, Strass (1988) reported improvements of 0.04 to 0.08 m/sec in average swimming velocity over 50 m after resistance training. This amounts to a reduction of 0.50 to 1.00 second for the time to cover that distance. The belief that these improvements were the result of greater ability to apply force was evidenced by the fact that the subjects reduced their stroke rates by approximately 2 stroke cycle/min and increased their stroke length an average of 0.13 m/stroke cycle (5 inches). The training program consisted of heavy-resistance, nonspecific weight training exercises for the swimming muscles (arm extensors), and the subjects were instructed to make each repetition as explosively as possible. A control group of swimmers who went through regular swim training but did not take part in resistance training did not improve significantly in swimming speed or any measure of stroke efficiency.

Hickson and coworkers (1988) reported that participation in a resistance program designed to improve the strength of leg muscles resulted in average improvements of 47 percent in endurance time to exhaustion for a group of subjects that cycled and 12 percent for a group that ran. Muscle strength increased 40 percent during the training program. This is certainly evidence of a significant improvement in performance consequent to heavy-resistance training. Some methods for improving strength are discussed in this chapter.

INCREASING MUSCULAR STRENGTH

At one time, we believed that increases in strength occurred simply because muscles became larger. Although the potential for force development is certainly greater when there is more protein material to contract, that is only one avenue for strength improvement. There is another that involves a learning effect that allows the nervous system to stimulate (recruit) muscle fibers more efficiently for the job at hand. In this case, the number of contracting muscle fibers increases and their sequence of contraction improves so that more force can be exerted. Both avenues for strength improvement—increased muscle size and improved neuromuscular recruitment—are important; however, the methods for training each are somewhat different.

Improvements in strength that are not related to increased muscle size are thought to occur because the nervous system removes inhibitory influences, allowing more muscle fibers to contract. The inhibitory influence of the nervous system probably protects against breaking bones and tearing connective tissue. There is always more strength available in our muscles than we can use because we are not able to contract all of the muscle fibers within a particular muscle at one moment in time. Substantiation for this theory comes from stories we have all heard of incredible feats of strength performed by people during times of great stress. In one such case, a nine-year-old boy lifted a car weighing 4,100 pounds to free his father, who was trapped underneath. The boy weighed just 65 pounds (Wilmore & Costill, 1988).

The rapid strength increases that occur during the early weeks of resistance training are probably due to better neuromuscular recruitment. The effect of increased muscle size on strength appears to take place later in training. The repetitive use of large numbers of muscle fibers apparently causes them to take on more protein, so they become larger and, thus, capable of exerting more force. This process is called *hypertrophy*. The potential for force development is certainly greater when there is more protein material to contract.

The amount of hypertrophy can vary tremendously. Some persons possess a genetic predisposition toward large increases in muscle size, yet others can make only modest gains. In one study, the range of increase in muscle size among a group of subjects undergoing heavy-resistance training was 3 to 49 percent (MacDougall et al., 1979). Most men *and women* need not be concerned about increasing muscle size so much that they become bulky, however. Most persons do not possess the genetic predisposition to *bulk up*. Those few athletes who do tend to become bulky can concentrate more on stroke-simulating exercises and spend less time with nonspecific heavy-resistance training so that they can improve strength without increasing muscle tissue inordinately.

The implications of this information are that swimmers should spend the early portion of their season doing nonspecific resistance training to increase muscle size and strength. They should spend the latter portion of the season performing stroke-simulated exercises against resistance both on land and in water in order to train the nervous system to recruit the raw material (larger muscle fibers) that was developed earlier. If by chance time constraints or lack of equipment should force swimmers to choose between traditional forms of weight training and stroke-simulated exercises, they should select the latter because they enhance the learning effect and increase muscle size, although they probably do not achieve quite the same increases in muscle size as might have been realized through the addition of heavy-resistance training.

Relationships between Strength, Power, and Swimming Speed

Research has verified that powerful swimmers are faster (Costill, King, Holdren, & Hargreaves, 1983). The two components of power are muscular force and speed of movement. Both play equally important roles. Stronger athletes will not necessarily swim faster if they cannot apply their force at a fast rate. By the same token, swimmers with a fast stroke rate will not win a race unless they can apply a reasonable amount of force.

The relationship between strength and power is such that one increases as the other decreases. Figure 24-1 illustrates this connection. A large application of force is only possible at a slow rate of speed, because the resistance that must be moved

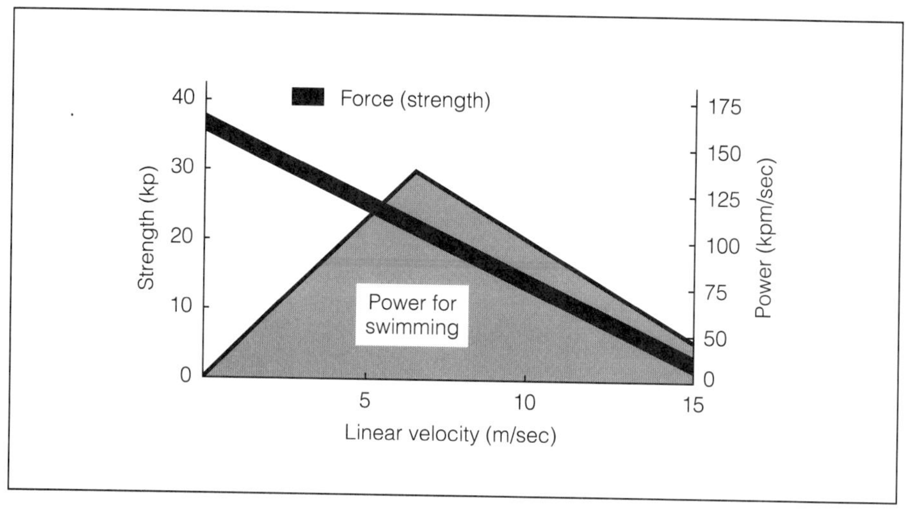

Figure 24-1. The relationship among strength, power, and speed of movement.

is so great. By the same token, fast movement is only possible when resistance to motion is minimal. Consequently, the power for forward acceleration is greatest when swimmers use some optimal combination of muscular force and turnover rate.

The strength component of power plays a dominant role when the resistance to be overcome is great. The speed component becomes more important when the resistance is less, as in water. For example, a person who tries to do one repetition of a bench press with a maximum weight may take several seconds to push the weight from his or her chest to arms' length. This is because the resistance of the weight is so great that it can only be moved slowly. Nevertheless, the power that is being generated is quite large because of the tremendous amount of force being applied to overcome the heavy weight.

Power is calculated by multiplying the muscular force times the distance over which it is being applied and then by dividing the product by the length of time required for that application. These relationships are expressed by the formulas in the following box. The athlete in this example is applying 50 kiloponds (kp) of force (about 110 pounds) over a distance of 1.2 m (3 ft, 11 in) in 1.00 second, so his power is equal to 60 kpm/sec (429 ft/lb/sec).

Calculating Power

$$\text{Power} = \frac{\text{Force} \times \text{Distance}}{\text{Time}}$$

$$\text{Power} = 60 \text{ kpm/sec} = \frac{50 \text{ kp} \times 1.2 \text{ m}}{1.00 \text{ sec}}$$

Assuming his stroking distance remains the same, the athlete in this example can improve his power output by increasing the force component and by decreasing the time component as shown in the following box. He can double his power output per stroke by doubling his stroking force or by increasing his turnover rate. Obviously, it should be easier for him to double his strength than to double his turnover rate. Hence, the reason that improving strength is so important to performance.

Increasing Power

$$\text{Original power} = \frac{50 \text{ kp} \times 1.2 \text{ m}}{1.00 \text{ sec}} = 60 \text{ kpm/sec}$$

By increasing force:

$$\frac{100 \text{ kp} \times 1.2 \text{ m}}{1.00 \text{ sec}} = 120 \text{ kpm/sec}$$

By reducing time

$$\frac{50 \text{ kp} \times 1.2 \text{ m}}{0.50 \text{ sec}} = 120 \text{ kp m/sec}$$

However, recent studies have shown a high degree of specificity between strength and its speed of application.

Training Speed and Strength Improvement Strength and speed seem to function as an entity rather than two separate components of power. The classic study by Moffroid and Whipple (1970) demonstrated this function quite convincingly. Table 24-1 lists the results of that study. These researchers trained two groups of subjects with leg extensions on a Cybex apparatus. Group 1 trained at a low rate of speed (6 rpm), and group 2 trained at a fast rate (18 rpm). Subjects in both groups were tested for leg force (referred to as *peak torque*) at a variety of speeds that were both faster and slower than their training speed. The interesting feature of the study was that subjects improved most at their particular training speed. They also improved significantly at slower speeds; however, their improvements at higher speeds were negligible. The slow-trained group improved their peak torque most at their training speed of 6 rpm. By contrast, their improvement at the faster speed—18 rpm—was not as great as that of the subjects in group 2, who had trained at this faster rate.

The results of this and other studies demonstrate that swimmers should train with fast movements if they want to improve their power for fast movements (Costill et al., 1978; Davis et al., 1986; Perrin, Lephart, & Weltman, 1987). Some studies, however, have shown a slightly different relationship between strength improvement and training speed. They have demonstrated a carryover to both slower and faster speeds when training was performed at some speed in the middle of the possible range of speeds. Miyashita and Kanehisa (1983) reported that training at a speed of 180 degrees per second (d/sec) seemed to improve performance at both slower and faster speeds, and Timm (1987) reported improvements at speeds that were above or below 120 d/sec of the training speed.

One of the important items to consider in any program for improving swimming power, then, is that the exercises approximate stroking speed. Unfortunately, that

Table 24-1. A Comparison of Mean Increases for Peak Torque of the Quadriceps Muscles

Test Velocity	Group 1 (6 rpm)	Group 2 (18 rpm)	Group 3 (control)
0 rpm	28.6	21.8	14.1
3 rmp	35.4	16.8	3.0
6 rpm*	47.1	24.8	8.3
9 rpm	14.5	14.5	8.4
12 rpm	14.1	17.5	6.9
15 rmp	10.8	12.3	4.8
18 rpm**	8.4	15.6	2.0

Source: Moffroid & Whipple, 1970.

*Training speed for group 1.

**Training speed for group 2.

is an almost impossible task. Swimmers do not move their arms through the water at a constant rate. Their underwater armstrokes consist of pulses of speed, with the hands decelerating and accelerating with every major change of direction. In certain portions of the stroke cycle, the hands travel as fast as 6 m/sec (20 ft/sec); at other times, they move at only 1.5 m/sec (5 ft/sec) (Maglischo et al., 1986). The average velocity of the hands is generally in the neighborhood of 3 m/sec, yet they seldom travel at that speed during the stroke cycle.

Resistance Training Methods

Various training methods have been used to increase the muscular strength of swimmers, including isometric exercises, isotonic training, isokinetic training, and variable-resistance training. There is an ongoing debate concerning the relative merits of these methods. Each is critiqued in the following sections.

Isometrics This is a form of training in which muscles contract against resistance without moving through a range of motion. The resistance can be supplied by other muscles or immovable objects. Figure 24-2 shows an athlete doing a partner-assisted isometric triceps extension. He is contracting his triceps by attempting to extend his arms against the resistance supplied by his partner.

Early reports suggesting that isometric training could improve overall strength were apparently premature (Hettinger & Muller, 1953). Later research showed that isometric exercises could increase strength, but only within a small range of degrees from the angle used for training. Doubt was also expressed that the strength developed by isometric exercises could be used to improve power for athletic performance.

Regardless of these shortcomings, there are situations in which isometric exercises can be helpful. When other forms of resistance training are not available,

Figure 24-2. Rodrigo Messias (*right*) performing a partner-assisted isometric triceps extension. The resistance is supplied by Rasmus Jensen (*left*), who is doing an isometric biceps curl.

isometrics can be used to increase muscular size and strength (Kanehisa & Miyashita, 1983; Meyers, 1967). Later, that strength can be used to improve stroking power during specific in-water resistance training.

Isotonic Training This category is a catchall for training procedures that embrace exercising a joint through a particular range of motion. The types of isotonic programs in use are (1) constant-resistance training, (2) variable-resistance training, (3) isokinetic training, and (4) eccentric training.

Constant-resistance versus variable-resistance training Constant-resistance training refers to traditional forms of *free-weight training* with barbells and dumbbells. Surprisingly, the resistance is really not constant in this method of training. Although the weight is constant, the resistance changes from the beginning to the end of a particular exercise because of momentum. Resistance is greatest when a weight is motionless. Once the athlete gets it moving, ballistic motion causes that weight to decrease somewhat. At the same time, the weight is easier to move through certain parts of the total range of motion than others because of greater mechanical efficiency.

The criticism of constant-resistance training is that it does not fully overload muscles. The heaviest weight that can be used in an exercise is the one that can be moved through the weakest point in the range of motion. Consequently, the weight will provide an overload in the weakest portion, but the resistance may not be great enough to overload the stronger portions in the range of motion.

Variable-resistance training methods were developed to counter this weakness. The exercises are done on machines that are specially designed to increase resistance throughout the range of motion. They attempt to match those increases to the average changes in strength throughout a particular exercise. Although these averages cannot possibly match the available force of every individual, they do provide a greater overload throughout the range of motion than can be supplied by constant-resistance training. Some of the variable-resistance machines use stacks of weight that are moved by camshafts or levers to increase the load as the stacks travel upward. The Nautilus machines are devices that use camshafts, and the Universal Gym and others utilize levers.

On a theoretical basis, variable-resistance training seems to be a superior training form. Research has not verified this superiority, however. At this point, it appears that athletes can get equally good results with either constant-resistance or variable-resistance methods.

Isokinetic training This method has also been called *accommodating-resistance training* because it is designed to provide a perfect match between the resistance and the strength of the athlete at each point in the range of motion. The machines that have been designed around this principle control the speed of movement so that the exercise can only be performed at a preset velocity. The theory behind isokinetic training is that force is exerted against the object at a faster rate than it moves. Consequently, if athletes apply all or most of the force they have available while attempting to accelerate the object, they will overload their muscles maximally at each point in the range of motion. Accordingly, the resistance of the object, be it a handle at the end of a rope or a bar, will always match (or accommodate itself) to the force that is being applied against it. With some isokinetic training devices, the velocity is adjustable, so athletes can match their training rates to competition rates of joint movement.

Isokinetic training was touted as *the* answer to the weaknesses of both constant-resistance and variable-resistance methods, because athletes could achieve a maximum overload at every point in the entire range of motion of an exercise at speeds that mimicked those used in competition. Unfortunately, this method has not proved as effective in practice as in theory. Isokinetic training has one glaring weakness: athletes must be highly motivated to achieve maximum overloads. They will only reap the benefits of maximum overload throughout the complete range of motion if they push against the resistive device *with all of the force they have available*. They can, if they wish, push against it with less than maximum force and still complete the exercise because the resistive device will keep moving once it is in motion.

Athletes may use less than maximum force against isokinetic devices, not because they are lazy but because they have no monitoring device to provide them with motivating *feedback*. For this reason, the most effective isokinetic devices have some type of measuring instrument that tells athletes how many pounds or kiloponds of force they are producing. The mini-gym and biokinetic swim bench are two devices that incorporate measurement with accommodating-resistance training.

Although isokinetic devices show great promise for strength and power development, they have not been proven superior in their present form. Athletes who use constant-resistance and variable-resistance forms of training can achieve similar or better results because once they select a particular resistance they are committed to moving it through the complete range.

One important point in favor of isokinetic training is that athletes do not become sore when they train with these devices. Although the cause of muscle soreness is not known, the prevailing theory is that it results from torn and injured muscle tissue, which may occur less frequently with isokinetic training than with other forms of resistance training.

Eccentric training This form of training consists of controlling the descent of a weight that is being returned to the starting position. It is technically referred to as *controlled lengthening of muscles* as opposed to concentric training, which involves controlled shortening. The main advantage of eccentric training is that greater amounts of resistance can be handled; thus, the strength benefits are believed to be greater.

Most studies have shown that eccentric training is at least as effective as other forms of resistance training, and some have reported even greater gains through the use of this method (Fleck & Kraemer, 1987). There is one major disadvantage to this form of training where swimmers are concerned, however. Unlike athletes in other sports, swimmers seldom make powerful movements that are eccentric in nature. Other disadvantages are (1) that eccentric training can be very dangerous for athletes because of the heavy weights they use and (2) that eccentric training causes greater amounts of muscle soreness, which could signal greater tissue damage.

Plyometrics This form of exercise has recently become quite popular for training the legs of swimmers. The procedure usually involves jumping from a small height (a box), landing on the ground with the knees and hips flexed, and then executing a quick and powerful rebound jump into the air. The second jump is sometimes used to reach the top of another box or simply to return to the ground. The supposed advantage of this method lies in the fact that the elastic recoil of the muscles during the landing can be used to increase the force and power generated during the jump. As athletes become stronger, some experts suggest increasing resistance by jumping from and to greater heights. Carrying weights in the hands or in a backpack while jumping is another method for increasing resistance.

The major drawback to plyometric training is the danger of injury. Supporters of the method say that plyometrics are no more dangerous than other forms of training when done correctly; however, the potential for incorrect performance is considerably greater with these exercises. Orthopedic surgeons report treating a growing number of injuries resulting from the use of plyometrics (American Coach, 1988), and Brooks and Fahey (1984) have reported cases of two world-class track athletes, one a former world-record holder in the shot put and the other an American record holder in the discus, who developed serious knee injuries following plyometric training.

There seems little doubt that isometric training is the least effective of the methods in use today, with eccentric training and plyometric training close behind where swimmers are concerned. Of the remaining methods, all have been reported to produce similar increases in muscle size. Motor performance improvements have been reported with constant-resistance, variable-resistance, and isokinetic training, although fast-speed isokinetic training may be somewhat more effective for this purpose. Table 24-2 lists the results of a study by Smith and Melton (1981) comparing variable-resistance and isokinetic methods. You can see that the vertical jump, standing long jump, and 40-yd dash were all improved significantly more by high-speed isokinetic training than by variable-resistance training or low-speed isokinetic training.

Table 24-2. Comparisons of Variable-Resistance, High-Speed Isokinetic, and Slow-Speed Isokinetic Training for Improvements of Motor Performance

	Percentage of Improvement		
Test	*Variable-Resistance Training*	*High-Speed Isokinetic Training*	*Low-Speed Isokinetic Training*
Vertical jump	1.6	5.4	3.9
Standing long jump	.3	9.1	.4
40-yd dash	− 1.4	− 10.1	+ 1.1

Source: Smith & Melton, 1981.

Free Weights

The term *free weights* refers to standard weight training exercises that are performed with barbells and dumbbells rather than machines. There is a belief in some circles that lifting free weights is superior to other methods of resistance training for improving athletic performance because lifting free weights requires speed and agility as well as muscular strength and because the necessity to balance these weights during lifting strengthens larger groups of muscles, leading to greater improvements of total body power.

The research on this matter is equivocal at the present time, without having proved or disproved the superiority of free weights. I doubt that it is an important issue where swimmers are concerned because they do not use the explosive movements of other sports and because their movements are so different from standard free-weight exercises that the transfer of power, balance, and agility is probably negligible.

Free weights are not recommended for one other very important reason. The possibility of injury is greater with free weights than with machines. Although the incidence of injury is small in well-supervised resistance training programs of any type, machines are potentially safer than free weights. With machines, the chance of injury from dropping a weight during an exercise is reduced to zero, as is the possibility of injury from plates being dropped inadvertently by someone else. Coaches and swimmers should consider themselves very lucky if they have access to the various machines designed for resistance training.

Circuit Training

This may be the best resistance training procedure for swimmers to use. It involves performing a series of exercises in a preselected sequence. Usually, six to ten exercises are selected. They can be arranged to provide a *set-type* effect by exercising the same muscle group two or three times in succession, or they can be placed to alternately exercise muscle groups. The number of repetitions and sets are standardized for each station, and the rest period between sets and stations should be regulated so that athletes can work in groups of two to four before moving on to the next station.

Circuit training is an excellent form of resistance training because large groups can be moved through a program in a short time with minimal waiting between stations. When the group is too large for the number of pieces of equipment, supplemental stations can be added in which calisthenics, cords, or stretching exercises are performed. Circuits should generally contain between 6 and 12 stations and require 20 to 40 minutes to complete.

Resistance Training Procedures

All strength training is based on progressive overload. As strength increases, the resistance must also increase to continue overloading the muscles so that strength will increase even more. The earliest example of the application of this principle comes from Greek mythology. A young boy in ancient Greece, Milo of Crotona, wanted to become the strongest man in the world, so he began lifting a baby bull on his shoulders each day and carrying it around the pasture. He continued doing this until the bull was fully grown. Milo's muscles grew stronger as the bull became larger, and he went on to become an Olympic champion.

The most obvious way for modern-day athletes to apply the progressive-resistance principle is to add more weight each time they become capable of doing so. Sets and repetitions are used to determine when it is time to make such increases. Typical programs involve a specific resistance exercise that is executed for a particular number of repetitions (times) and a particular number of sets (groups of repetitions). The speed of performance is also monitored in some programs.

Sets and Repetitions for Constant-Resistance and Variable-Resistance Programs The majority of studies have shown that 4 to 8 repetitions for 3 or more sets is optimal for improving muscular strength. Programs in which up to 12 repetitions have been used have also been very effective. No differences in strength gains were found between programs including as few as 3 sets of 10 repetitions and as many as 15 sets of 10 repetitions (Davies et al., 1986).

Large amounts of resistance can be used in leg exercises; consequently, the possibility of injuring the back, hips, or knees is greater. For this reason, more repetitions are recommended for training the lower limbs so that athletes can achieve an overload with less weight and, thus, less likelihood of injury.

The progressive-resistance principle is applied to training in the following manner. Athletes select a resistance for a particular exercise that requires almost maximum effort over 4, or in the case of the legs 8, repetitions. They then perform the exercise with that weight for three sets during each session, trying to do at least 1 more repetition with each training session until they are able to do 8 or 12 repetitions with the starting weight. At that point, they know they have become stronger, so they add 5 or 10 additional pounds and begin once again with 4 or 8 repetitions. They should rest 2 to 3 minutes between sets for recovery. The method just described is known as the *double progressive system*.

Sets and Repetitions for Isokinetic Training Very few studies have been concerned with the different combination of sets and repetitions needed for isokinetic training. Three sets of 8 to 12 repetitions appears to be optimal in those few that have been conducted.

Resistance The most important factor in any resistance program that is designed to increase muscular strength is the amount of force that athletes apply. The number of repetitions and sets they perform are secondary to the resistance they must overcome. More than any other factor, the resistance creates an overload on muscles. Combinations of sets and repetitions are used as guides that tell athletes when it is safe to increase resistance. For developing muscular strength, the resistance should be between 70 to 90 percent of the maximum resistance that can be moved for one repetition (Bompa, 1983). Power is improved best with resistance in the range of 30 to 80 percent of maximum.

Frequency Most experts agree that training three days per week is optimal, although both two and five days per week have been used effectively (Braith et al., 1989). The program should require 30 to 45 minutes and include 6 to 12 exercises. The following box summarizes the recommended procedures for heavy-resistance training and isokinetic training.

Procedures for Heavy-Resistance Training and Isokinetic Training

Heavy Resistance Training

1. Frequency: 3 to 5 days per week
2. Sets: 3 to 5
3. Repetitions: upper body, 4 to 8; legs, 8 to 12

Isokinetic Training

1. Frequency: 3 to 5 days per week
2. Sets: 3 to 5
3. Repetitions: 8 to 12

Exercise Selection The exercises that should be performed are those that work the major muscle groups that swimmers use to propel themselves through the water. They should also mimic swimming movements as much as possible. The major muscle groups used in stroking include those that bring the arms from a position overhead to the hips. They are the pectoralis major muscles of the chest, the latissimus dorsi, rhomboid, and trapezius muscles of the back, and the frontal (anterior) deltoids of the shoulders.

The inward sweeps of the arms are accomplished by the biceps, brachialis, brachioradialis, and supinator muscles of the upper arm and forearm as well as the teres major and minor of the upper back. The muscles that sweep the arms out and up from under the body are the middle and posterior deltoids. The triceps and anconeus are the primary muscles involved in extending the arms at the elbows.

The various kicking motions of the four competitive strokes are accomplished by contractions of the knee extensor and the hip flexor and extensor muscles. The knee extensors are the quadriceps (rectus femoris, vastus intermedius, vastus medialis, and vastus lateralis). The psoas major, iliacus, and pectineus flex the hips. The hip extensor muscles are the hamstrings (biceps femoris, semitendinosus, and

Table 24-3. Resistance Training Exercises

Joints or Body Parts Involved	Exercises
Shoulder for downsweep and upsweep:	Lat machine pulldowns to the front and behind the neck, upright rows, bent-over rowing, seated rows, straight-arm pullovers, bent-arm pullovers, bench press, chins, incline bench press, decline bench press, pulleys, shoulder shrugs, swim bench.
for insweep:	Lying lateral raises, side pulleys.
Upper arm	Curls, triceps extensions.
Forearms	Forearm curls, wrist curls.
Lower back	Back hyperextensions, dead lifts.
Abdomen	Sit-ups, side twists.
Hips and knees	Leg curls, leg extensions, leg presses, half-squats.
Ankles	Calf raises.
Adductors	Adductors with pulleys, adductor machine, ball squeezes.

semimebranosus) and gluteus maximus. Breaststrokers also require strength in the adductor muscles, which are responsible for squeezing the legs together during the propulsive phase of their kick. These muscles are the adductor brevis, adductor longus, adductor magnus, and gracilis. In addition to the muscles involved in hip and knee extension, starts and turns require powerful extensions of the ankles, which are made possible by the gastrocnemius, soleus, and plantaris muscles.

The abdominal muscles (the rectus abdominus), the internal and external obliques on the sides of the abdominal area, and the erector spinae muscles of the middle and lower back stabilize the trunk during stroking and kicking motions.

Table 24-3 lists some of the best resistance exercises for these muscles. Some very popular exercises—military presses, dips, and push-ups—are not included because they are not recommended for swimmers. These exercises can cause friction between the head of the humerus and the tendons of the shoulder, which may exacerbate or, perhaps, precipitate tendinitis.

To establish a resistance training program, athletes should select 6 to 12 of the exercises in Table 24-3, making sure that they cover all of the major muscle groups in the arms, trunk, and legs.

Cycling Resistance Training Programs The exercises in a resistance program should be changed every three to four weeks to discourage plateaus. A good resistance program should be conducted in stages that shift the emphasis from the development of nonspecific strength to the development of specific stroking power during the course of the season. The following box lists the suggested stages for cycling resistance training.

Suggested Stages for Resistance Training

1. Preparation: 2 to 4 weeks
2. Muscular strength: 3 to 12 weeks
3. Muscular power and endurance: 3 to 6 weeks

The first stage should be for preparation and should last two to four weeks. The exercises should be nonspecific and should work all of the large muscle groups of the body. Start with one set of 10 to 15 repetitions and progress to three sets of 8 to 12 repetitions throughout this period.

The purpose of the second stage is to increase muscular strength. It can last from three weeks to three months. The repetitions should be reduced to between 4 and 8, utilizing three or more sets. The primary purpose should be to perform the exercises against gradually increasing amounts of resistance throughout this period.

The emphasis during the third stage should be on the improvement of muscular power or, if preferred, muscular endurance. This is the time to use in-water resistance training and stroke-simulating land training with swim benches, trolleys, and mini-gyms. The exercises should be as specific as possible to swimming, and they should be performed at or near actual swimming stroke rates. The resistance should be reduced from the previous stage to accommodate more and faster repetitions. The number of repetitions should increase to between 10 and 20 in sets of three to five. Work periods of 5 to 15 seconds can also be used in sets of three to five.

Can Heavy-Resistance Training Reduce Endurance?

Although some studies have suggested that strength training reduces aerobic capacity (Gollnick et al., 1972; Nelson et al., 1984; Tesch, Hakkinen, & Komi, 1985), the majority show no negative effect when athletes engage in resistance and endurance training simultaneously (Dudley & Djamil, 1985; Hickson et al., 1988; Jacobs, Sale, & MacDougall, 1987; MacDougall et al., 1987). The possibility that heavy-resistance training may interfere with improvements of aerobic capacity should not be dismissed, however. The subjects in many of the studies in which simultaneous strength and endurance training were compared were untrained when the research began. Consequently, these subjects would be expected to improve dramatically in both strength and aerobic capacity during the training period. Antagonistic effects of simultaneous strength and endurance training, if they occurred, would not be expected to show up until these subjects had become well trained.

I believe the possibility of reducing endurance with simultaneous strength training is sufficient to warrant caution among groups of well-trained athletes. For this reason, it may be advisable to confine attempts to increase muscle strength and size to periods when aerobic training is not being emphasized, such as during the early season and during breaks from training. The emphasis should be on specific power training during periods of the season when aerobic training is being stressed.

FLEXIBILITY TRAINING

The relationship between flexibility and swimming success has not been substantiated by research, yet I believe that it plays a very important role. Listed below are some of the reasons why an increased range of motion in certain joints should contribute to faster times:

1. It should allow propulsive force to be applied over a longer time.
2. It should facilitate arm recovery and kicking movements that do not disturb horizontal and lateral body alignment.
3. It may diminish the energy cost and increase swimming speed by reducing intramuscular resistance to motion.

Hortobagyi and associates (1985) hypothesized this last effect from a study of runners who participated in a stretching program. After seven weeks, the runners showed an increase in stride frequency and muscle relaxation time. They were also able to reach peak force more rapidly during maximum efforts against heavy resistance, and they could contract their muscles faster when the resistance was light.

Improving Joint Flexibility

A large range of motion in the ankles, shoulders, and lower back should be most advantageous to swimmers. Breaststroke swimmers may also profit from improved flexibility in the adductor muscles of the groin, the outward rotators of the knees, and the knee extensors of the upper leg. The importance of improving flexibility in each of these areas is discussed in the following sections.

Ankles Freestyle, butterfly, and backstroke swimmers who possess greater ankle extension flexibility should be able to maintain their feet in a position to displace water back for a longer period of time during the downbeat of their kick (upbeat in backstroke). Swimmers in these strokes also need to be able to turn the soles of their feet inward (inversion). This improves their ability to position their feet to displace water back during the downbeat of the flutter and dolphin kicks and the upbeat of the back crawl flutter kick.

Propulsion during the breaststroke kick depends on having a good range of motion in a flexing direction (dorsiflexion) in the ankles. If breaststroke swimmers can flex their ankles enough to maintain a backward and outward angle of attack during the outsweep of the kick, they should be able to *catch* the water sooner and apply force longer during the subsequent insweep.

Breaststrokers also need to be able to invert and evert their feet at the ankles. That is, they should be able to turn the soles of their feet in and out with ease. The outward motion helps them get a good angle of attack during the outsweep of the kick, and the inward rotation provides a more propulsive position during the insweep.

Shoulders We are all aware of the importance of shoulder flexibility to the arm recovery in the freestyle, butterfly, and backstroke. A high-elbow recovery in freestyle reduces the potential for the arm to pull the body out of lateral alignment as it swings over the water. The backward range of motion of the arm at the shoulder joint (horizontal extension) is, to a great extent, responsible for the effectiveness of a high-elbow recovery. Butterfly swimmers need flexibility in the same movement to avoid dragging their arms through the water during the recovery. The ability to hyperflex the arm overhead at the shoulder joint is needed by backstrokers to ensure a recovery that does not disrupt later alignment.

A dropped elbow during the propulsive phase of the various underwater armstrokes may be caused by a less than average ability to rotate the upper arm inward at the shoulder joint. Inward rotation allows swimmers to get their elbow above their hand early in the stroke cycle, allowing them to make a catch and begin applying propulsive force sooner. Nevertheless, it should be mentioned that many world-record swimmers have used a deep catch very successfully.

Lower Back The dolphin motion of the breaststroke and butterfly is probably inhibited by a less than average ability to hyperextend the lower back. As you can see from Figure 24-3, the ability of a butterfly swimmer to swim efficiently depends to a great extent on her ability to hyperextend her lower back. Breaststrokers also need good lower back flexibility as they execute their arm and leg recoveries, as you can see in Figure 24-4.

Knees, Legs, and Groin Flexibility in these joints is a decided advantage to breaststrokers. They are able to displace water back more effectively if they can rotate their lower legs out as they start the outsweep of their kick. This same

Figure 24-3. A butterfly swimmer hyperextending her lower back as she brings her legs up after the first kick.

Figure 24-4. A breaststroke swimmer hyperextending her lower back as she begins her leg recovery.

outward rotation pulls on the adductor muscles of the groin and can cause soreness if these muscles are tight and inflexible.

Some breaststrokers also need to stretch their quadriceps so that they can flex their knees and bring their feet as close to their buttocks as possible during the leg recovery. This provides a longer propulsive phase during the kick.

A word of caution is needed because flexibility exercises for the knee joints can be potentially dangerous. Outward rotation is limited at the knees in most people because stability is required at these joints during many land activities. For this reason, an attempt to increase the range of motion in this direction could result in a loss of stability or injury while participating in sports on land.

Stretching Can Be Dangerous

Stretching ligaments and tendons is only safe within limits. A joint's resistance to stretch provides a protective mechanism. This resistance reduces the chance of the joint becoming overextended to the point where the collagen that forms ligaments and tendons and the muscle fibers themselves are torn apart. Sprains, strains, and tears are types of injuries that can result from forcing muscles and connective tissue beyond their present state of extensibility. Flexibility exercises should be aimed at stretching the connective tissue within muscles but not the tendons and ligaments.

Two of the most outspoken critics of improper stretching are Richard Dominguez and Robert Gajda (1982). They claim that more patients become injured from stretching exercises than from lack of flexibility. They warn that we are engaging in a potentially beneficial, yet dangerous form of exercise when we prescribe stretching programs for swimmers. For this reason, stretching exercises should be administered with special care; swimmers should stretch only to the point at which resistance is felt. They should be cautioned to improve their ranges of motion slowly and carefully, without attempting the usual superoverload they use in other aspects of training. Additionally, stretching exercises that are potentially dangerous should be eliminated from programs. Figure 24-5 shows two of the most dangerous shoulder exercises. Both of these exercises and others like them force the heads of the long bones in the arms (the humerus) forward against the tendons and ligaments

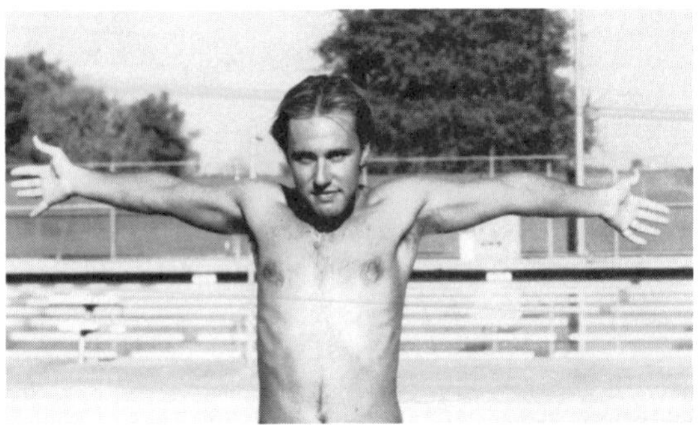

Figure 24-5. Two stretching exercises that should be avoided.

that surround the shoulder joints. These are the same tendons and ligaments that become chronically inflamed when swimmers develop tendinitis. Consequently, it would be best to avoid any exercises that precipitate or exacerbate this condition.

Stretching exercises should also be avoided for the knees and hips. Although an improved ability to rotate the lower legs out while they are in a flexed position is a decided advantage in breaststroke, the potential for long-term damage is too great to recommend any special exercises for these joints. Some degree of compensation for less than adequate ability to rotate the lower legs out can be achieved by separating the knees to shoulder width or slightly wider just prior to beginning the outsweep of the breaststroke kick. This will increase the range of outward motion of the lower legs somewhat and reduce the stress on the hips and knee joints.

Training Methods

Several types of stretching exercises have been used over the years. The following are the most popular.

Ballistic Stretching This involves moving joints rapidly and powerfully from one end of their range of motion to the other.

Held Stretching This is the opposite of ballistic stretching. Joints are moved gently and slowly to the limit of their range and then held there for 5 to 60 seconds.

Partner-Assisted Stretching These are static stretching exercises in which another person provides the stretching force. The partner's efforts permit a greater degree of stretch than could be achieved individually.

Slow-Dynamic Stretching This is a reduced-speed version of ballistic stretching. Joints are moved slowly rather than quickly through a range of motion. Slow-dynamic stretching can be combined with held stretching by holding for five or more seconds at the extended end of the range.

Contract-Relax Stretching This is an outgrowth of proprioceptive neuromuscular facilitation (PNF) techniques. It is based on the belief that muscles relax more completely and permit a greater range of motion when they are contracted beforehand. For example, in a contract-relax method for improving ankle extension ability, athletes flex their feet at the ankles and hold them in this position for five to ten seconds with an isometric contraction. They then release the contraction and extend their feet at the ankles.

Contract-relax methods can be enhanced by performing exercises with a partner. First, the partner resists the flexed isometric contraction so that more force must be applied by the person doing the stretching. The partner then pushes the other person's feet into extension to increase the range of movement.

Although all of these methods have their advocates, research has not shown one to be superior to the others (Beaulieu, 1980). It seems that any exercise that stretches a joint will increase its range of motion, with the degree of stretch playing a more important role than the mode of training. However, two of these stretching methods are potentially more dangerous than the others and should be avoided.

Ballistic methods are considered the most dangerous of all. To perform ballistic stretches, athletes must contract the muscles on one side of a joint rapidly and powerfully in order to move the body part in that direction. These powerful contractions and the speed of the movement make it difficult to control the motion once it is underway. Thus, there is a greater risk of tearing connective tissue. The danger of violently exceeding the present range of motion in joints is ever-present with ballistic stretching exercises like toe touches, arm swings, duck walks, hurdler stretches, and others.

Partner-assisted stretching is the other dangerous method. There is no doubt that a greater range of motion can be achieved with the help of a partner. However, there is always the possibility that an enthusiastic athlete who is very strong may stretch a partner's muscles and tendons beyond the breaking point. In particular, partner-assisted stretches for the shoulders and lower back should be avoided. This advice notwithstanding, I recommend some partner-assisted stretching exercises for the ankles later in this chapter because they are safe and very effective.

Held stretching and slow-dynamic stretching are relatively safe if the movement is stopped at the point where resistance is felt and *not continued until pain is felt*. Contract-relax stretching is best done *without* a partner to reduce the possibility of injury.

Training Procedures

Flexibility can be increased quickly, but it can also be lost quickly. Stretching for a few minutes can increase the range of motion in joints by five to ten degrees or more. However, the change will not be permanent. Most of the increase will be gone by the next day. Reasonably long lasting changes in flexibility may take several weeks to produce. Once produced, however, they can be maintained by moving the joint through its new range of motion just a few times each day.

The overload and progressive-resistance principles must be applied with stretching exercises just as they are in other forms of training. They must be applied without pain, however. Athletes should not force joints beyond the point where resistance is felt. As the weeks go by, they should wait for the range to lengthen before stretching the joint further.

As was the case when the first edition of this book was written, research has not yet determined optimal weekly frequency, duration, numbers of sets, and numbers of repetitions. Therefore, the suggestions I make are based on the opinions of experts.

Frequency and Duration Most experts continue to recommend daily stretching for 10 to 20 minutes.

Sets and Repetitions Recommendations concerning the number of repetitions range from 10 to 15. The number of sets recommended are between three and six (Beaulieu, 1980; Bompa, 1983; Harre, 1982).

Duration of Held Stretching and Contract-Relax Stretching Recommendations have ranged from 6 to 60 seconds. I agree with Jerome (1987) that long stretches held for 20 to 30 seconds are a waste of time. The training effect probably occurs in the first few seconds after the limit of the range of motion is reached. In support of this belief, Hortobagyi and colleagues (1985) reported significant improvements after seven weeks of training three times per week with two repetitions that were held for 10 seconds each.

Age and Flexibility Training The need for flexibility training may increase as swimmers become older. Flexibility is greatest during childhood and gradually decreases after puberty. Women are more flexible than men at all ages, but their ranges of motion also decline after puberty.

Time of the Season and Flexibility Training The time to emphasize flexibility training is during the preparation and general endurance periods of the season so that swimmers are able to incorporate their increased ranges of motion into their strokes, starts, and turns.

Static Versus Dynamic Flexibility The stretching method(s) for a swimming program should reflect the kind of flexibility that swimmers need, whether static or dynamic. *Static flexibility* refers to the total range of motion in a joint. *Dynamic flexibility* applies to the ease with which a joint can be moved through a portion of the range.

The common belief has always been that any person who possesses good static flexibility will also be superior in dynamic flexibility. This assumption could be in error considering the specific nature of other training effects. It is very possible that dynamic flexibility exercises may be best for joints that must move easily through an average range of motion and that static training is best for joints in which a large range of motion is required. In this regard, slow-dynamic stretching exercises may be best for the shoulders, lower back, groin, knees, and quadriceps. During swimming, movements in all of these joints are caused by muscles contracting on one side and relaxing on the other. The dynamic range of motion in these joints should improve most with exercises that involve patterns of muscular contraction and relaxation similar to those used in swimming.

The ankles present a different situation entirely. Water pressure pushes the feet into positions of extension and inversion during the flutter and dolphin kicks and into flexed and everted positions during the breaststroke kick. Muscular contraction should play no role in extending the range of motion in these joints, because it will increase the energy cost of swimming unnecessarily. Therefore, static methods, particularly partner-assisted stretching, are probably best suited for improving the range of motion in these joints. The partner applies pressure against the foot to push it into extension and inversion or flexion and eversion just as the feet are moved into these positions by water pressure when athletes are swimming. Swimmers who are being stretched should relax the muscles around their ankles and let their feet be stretched to the greatest possible extent in the directions dictated by the exercise.

The possibility of injury from partner-assisted stretching should be slight in this case. The ankle joint is so strong that there is very little chance of a partner causing connective tissue tears. Nevertheless, there is certainly a danger of loosening the ankles to the point that they are more easily injured during land activities. However, these injuries are usually not as serious as those to the knee, and the benefits of a powerful kick are probably worth the potential risk. Each coach and athlete will have to make the decision whether to use partner-assisted stretching for the ankles. I would not recommend starting these exercises until a swimmer reaches the senior ranks, however, because children tend to spend more time running and jumping and are, therefore, more susceptible to ankle injuries.

The box below summarizes suggested procedures for flexibility training.

Suggested Procedures for Flexibility Training

1. Frequency: daily
2. Sets: 3 to 6
3. Repetitions: 10 to 15
4. Hold time: 6 to 10 seconds
5. Type: static stretching for ankles, slow-dynamic stretching for all other joints

Exercises for Increasing Flexibility

Figures 24-6 through 24-37 illustrate various flexibility exercises. All should be performed with a combination of slow-dynamic and held stretching methods. The body part should first be moved slowly through a range of motion and then held at the extreme end for six to ten seconds. Each exercise should be repeated ten to fifteen times and should be performed for three to six sets daily.

Shoulder Flexibility Exercises

1. *Shoulder Stretches* In Figure 24-6 the swimmer moves his arm through the range of motion used in the crawl stroke recovery, trying to work near the end of the range of motion for horizontal extension of the shoulder. The swimmer then repeats the exercise with the other arm. The same exercise can be done using butterfly and backstroke recovery movements.
2. *Towel Stretches* The swimmer in Figure 24-7 uses a towel to pull the arm that is flexed overhead down the back.
3. *Elbow Stretches* The exercise in Figure 24-8 is also for the front crawl and butterfly recoveries. With his elbows bent and his hands behind his head, the swimmer tries to push his elbows up and back.

4. *Elbow Pulls* The swimmer in Figure 24-9 grasps the elbow of one arm with his other hand and pulls it in and up. The swimmer holds this position and then repeats the exercise on the other arm.
5. *Arm Swings* For the final shoulder exercise for the freestyle and butterfly, the swimmer in Figure 24-10 swings his arms overhead in slow, gentle circles that encompass the total range of motion of his shoulder joints.

Figure 24-6. Shoulder stretches performed by Don Justice.

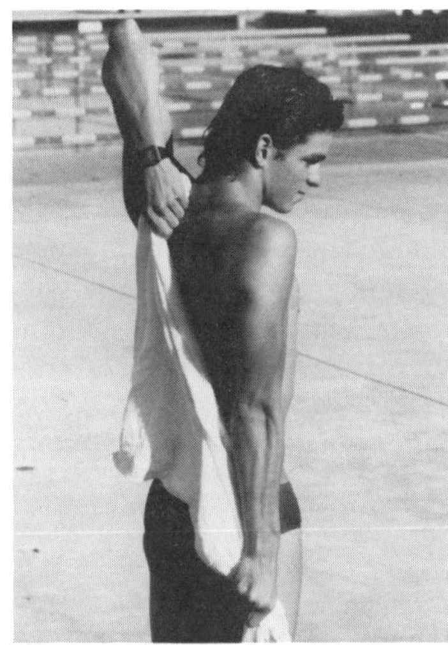

Figure 24-7. Towel stretches performed by Marcelo Menezes.

Figure 24-8. Elbow stretches performed by Rodrigo Messias.

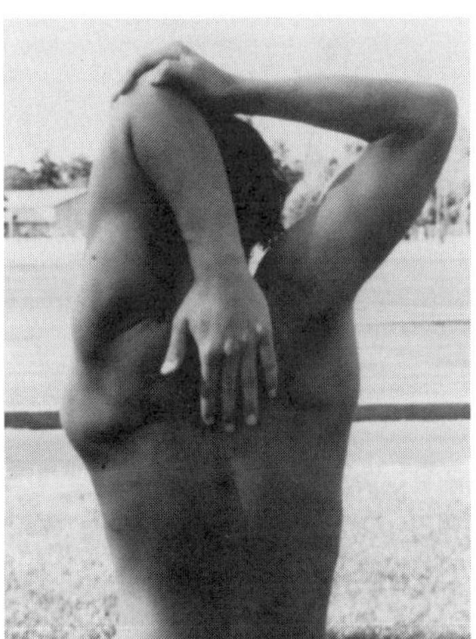

Figure 24-9. Elbow pulls performed by Matt Kowta.

Figure 24-10. Arm swings performed by Don Justice.

The exercises in Figures 24-11 through 24-13 are for the backstroke arm recovery.

6. *Overhead Arm Stretches* In Figure 24-11, the swimmer stands with his arms stretched overhead and hands together. He then pushes his arms back to the limit of his range of motion and holds.
7. *Bent-over Arm Stretches* The same exercise is shown in a bent-over position, using an object such as the one shown in Figure 24-12.
8. *Lying Arm Stretches* Figure 24-13 shows a similar exercise to the two previous stretches. The swimmer is in a supine position while holding light weights.

Lower Back Flexibility Exercises

1. *Back Arches* In Figure 24-14, the swimmer lies face down with his hands clasped behind his head. A partner may be used to hold his legs down. He then raises his head and trunk as high as possible off the ground and holds.
2. *Leg Arches* In Figure 24-15, the swimmer lifts his legs from a prone position while a partner holds his shoulders down.
3. *Back-bend Push-ups* Figure 24-16 shows this exercise. The swimmer starts on her back, with her legs bent and her palms flat against the ground under her

Figure 24-11. Overhead arm stretches performed by Derek Robinson.

Figure 24-12. Bent-over arm stretches performed by Neil Naramore.

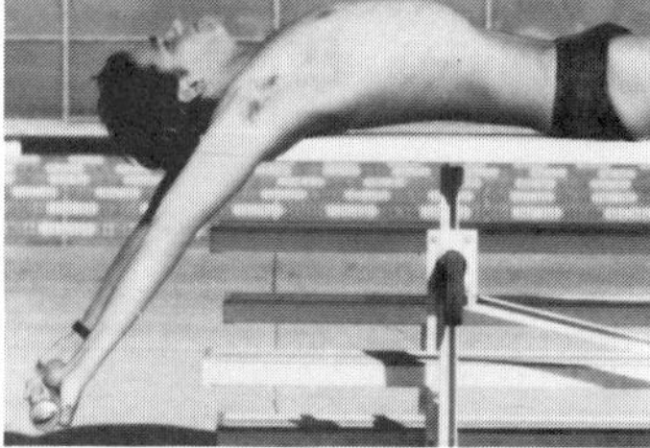

Figure 24-13. Lying arm stretches performed by Marcelo Menezes.

Figure 24-14. Back arches performed by Neil Naramore and assisted by Derek Robinson.

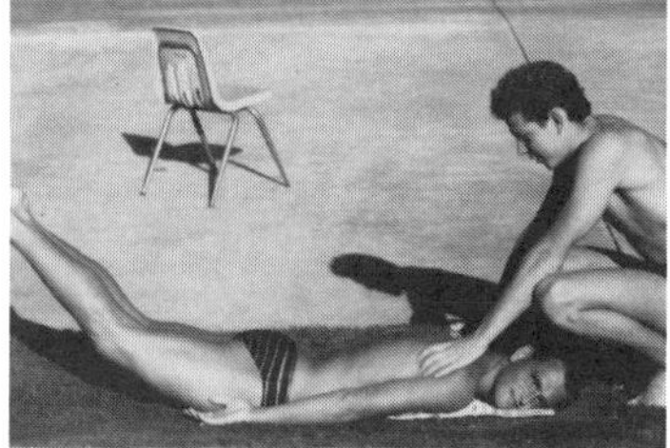

Figure 24-15. Leg arches performed by Ondreij Bures and assisted by Rasmus Jensen.

Figure 24-16. Back-bend push-ups performed by Mindi Bach.

shoulders. From this position, she pushes her body up as high as it will go and holds.

4. *Push-backs* Figure 24-17 shows another very simple stretching exercise for the lower back. From a prone position with his palms behind his lower back, the swimmer stretches his head and shoulders up and back as far as possible and holds.
5. *Head Lifts* In Figure 24-18, the swimmer lies face down with his hands underneath his shoulders as if in position to do a push-up. He then pushes his head and chest up and back while keeping his legs on the ground.
6. *Ankle Pulls* The exercise in Figure 24-19 is an excellent advanced maneuver. Lying face down, the swimmer reaches back and grasps his ankles. He then lifts his head and shoulders off the ground while pulling his ankles up and back.

Groin Flexibility Exercises

1. *Palm Touches* In Figure 24-20, the swimmer stands with feet wide apart. He then reaches down and touches the ground in front, slowly stretching his feet out as far as he can while bending forward.
2. *Leg Pulls* In Figure 24-21, while lying on his side, the swimmer grasps one ankle and pulls his foot up and back. He then repeats the exercise on the other leg.
3. *Sitting Leg Stretches* Figure 24-22 shows a swimmer seated with his legs apart. From this position he grasps his ankles and bends forward as far as he can.

Figure 24-17. Push-backs performed by Neil Naramore.

Figure 24-18. Head lifts performed by Frederic Pollizzi.

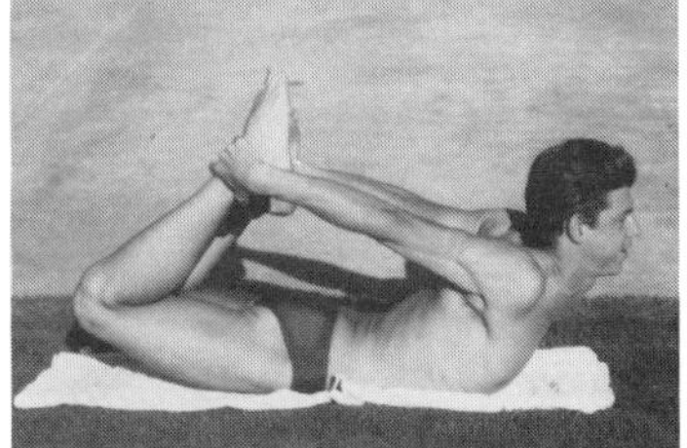

Figure 24-19. Ankle pulls performed by Rasmus Jensen.

Figure 24-20. Palm touches performed by Rasmus Jensen.

Figure 24-21. Leg pulls performed by Ondreij Bures.

Figure 24-22. Sitting leg stretches performed by Rasmus Jensen.

4. *Knee Pushes* The exercise in Figure 24-23 is also done from a sitting position, this time with the feet together and the knees bent and apart. The swimmer pushes down on his knees, trying to press them to the ground.
5. *Groin Stretches* The exercise in Figure 24-24 is done from a standing position. The swimmer slides one leg out while flexing the knee of the other leg and squatting down. He should keep his trunk in an upright position throughout. After holding this position for a short time, he repeats the exercise with his other leg.

Quadriceps Flexibility Exercises

1. *Lying Leg Flexors* In Figure 24-25, from a prone position, the swimmer bends his knees, trying to bring his feet up and back until they are in contact with his buttocks.
2. *Standing Leg Flexors* The exercise in Figure 24-26 is done from a standing position. The swimmer flexes one leg back and grabs his foot, pulling it up and forward toward his buttocks.
3. *Towel Leg Flexors* The exercise just described can also be done with a towel as shown in Figure 24-27.

Ankle Flexibility Exercises

The exercises in Figures 24-28 through 24-36 should be done using the held-stretching or partner-stretching procedures.

1. *Cross-legged Sitting Ankle Stretches* In Figure 24-28, the swimmer sits cross-legged and grasps one foot and pulls it into an extended and inverted position. He holds this position and then repeats the exercise with the other foot.
2. *Cross-legged Sitting Ankle Stretches for Breaststrokers* Breaststrokers use the same procedure, except they push their foot into a flexed and everted position as shown in Figure 24-29.
3. *Straight-leg Sitting Ankle Stretches* The swimmer in Figure 24-30 sits and extends his toes down and in as much as possible.
4. *Straight-leg Sitting Ankle Stretches for Breaststrokers* The breaststroke swimmer in Figure 24-31 pulls his toes back and turns the soles of his feet out as much as possible.
5. *Towel Ankle Stretches* The exercise in Figure 24-32 is also a good way for breaststrokers to increase ankle flexion ability. The swimmer uses a towel to pull his feet back.
6. *Toe Pushes* Another ankle stretching exercise for breaststrokers is pictured in Figure 24-33. The swimmer leans forward against a wall. Keeping his feet flat on the ground, he backs away from the wall as far as possible and then pushes against the ground with his toes and the balls of his feet. This exercise is best done in a straddled-leg position, with one foot forward and the other back.
7. *Sit on Ankles* The exercise pictured in Figure 24-34 is for improving ankle extension ability. The swimmer kneels, with his feet and ankles behind him. He then leans back on his ankles and tries to touch his head and shoulders to the ground behind him.

Figure 24-23. Knee pushes performed by Rasmus Jensen.

Figure 24-24. Groin stretches performed by Marcelo Menezes.

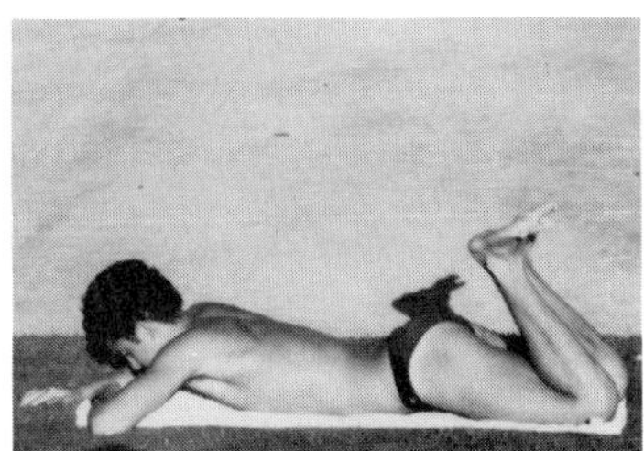

Figure 24-25. Lying leg flexors performed by Rodrigo Messias.

Figure 24-26. Standing leg flexors performed by Derek Robinson.

Figure 24-27. Towel leg flexors performed by Ondreij Bures.

Figure 24-28. Cross-legged sitting ankle stretches performed by Rasmus Jensen.

Figure 24-29. Cross-legged sitting ankle stretches for breaststrokers performed by Marcelo Menezes.

Figure 24-30. Straight-leg sitting ankle stretches performed by Frederic Pollizzi.

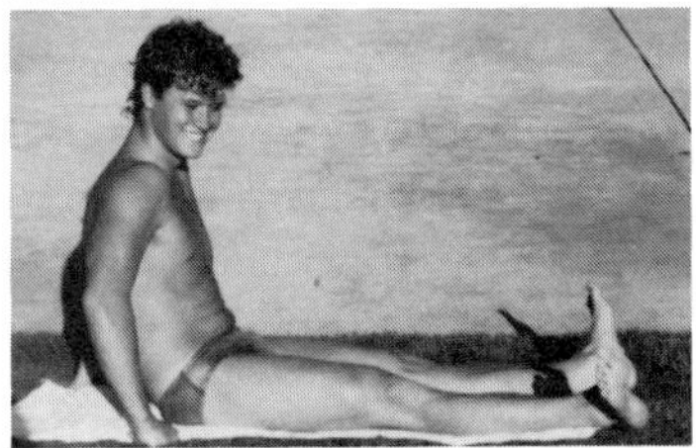

Figure 24-31. Straight-leg sitting ankle stretches for breaststrokers performed by Neil Naramore.

Figure 24-32. Towel ankle stretches performed by Don Justice.

Figure 24-33. Toe pushes performed by Marcelo Menezes.

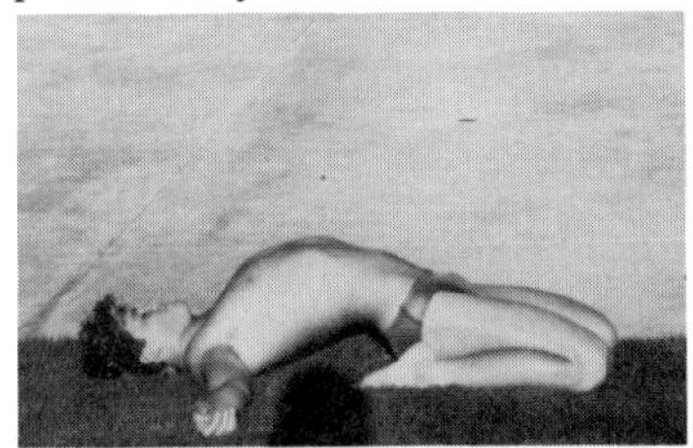

Figure 24-34. Sit on ankles performed by Neil Naramore.

8. *Partner-Assisted Ankle Stretches* The exercises in Figures 24-35 and 24-36 are two of the most effective for increasing the range of motion in the ankle joints. Swimmers sit facing one another with their legs outstretched. Each swimmer grasps one of the other's ankles. They then either push that ankle into extension and inversion (as shown in Figure 24-35) or flexion and eversion (as shown in Figure 24-36). They then repeat the respective exercises on the other foot.
9. *Partner-Assisted Ankle Pushes* Figure 24-37 shows another excellent exercise for breaststrokers. One swimmer lies on his stomach with his heel pulled up to his buttocks. The partner then presses his feet out to the side.

Measuring Flexibility

Periodic measurements of flexibility are important because they motivate swimmers by permitting them to evaluate their progress. Cureton (1941) developed some tests of shoulder and lower back flexibility that are ideal for this purpose because they do not require expensive equipment or lengthy training. I have developed some ankle flexibility tests that have these same advantages.

Shoulder Flexion Figure 24-38 illustrates the procedure for evaluating shoulder flexion. The swimmer lies in a prone position with his chin touching the floor or mat and stretches his arms forward. On a signal, he lifts his arms as high as possible without lifting his chin from the floor. His score is the distance from the floor to his fingertips. This distance can be measured with a ruler, or a yardstick can also be mounted on a wall or stand to make the measurements easier to perform. Backstrokers should score better than other swimmers on this test.

Shoulder Extension Figure 24-39 illustrates the procedure for this test. The swimmer stands and holds her arms at shoulder height with the palms facing forward. On a signal, she presses her arms back as far as possible while keeping them at shoulder height. Her palms should remain facing forward. The distance between the centers of her wrists are measured. Freestyle and butterfly swimmers should score well on this test.

Back Hyperextension Figure 24-40 illustrates this test. The swimmer lies face down on the ground with his hands clasped behind his neck. A partner should hold his legs down. On a signal, he lifts his head and chest as high as possible from the ground. A yardstick measures the distance from the floor to the sternal notch at the base of his neck. Butterflyers and breaststrokers should score high on this test.

All of the tests that were just described are influenced by height and the relative size of limbs. For this reason, scores cannot be compared from athlete to athlete. They are very effective for evaluating individual improvements, however.

Ankle Flexibility The usual procedure for evaluating ankle flexibility is to measure the total range of motion in the ankle joint, from flexion to extension. This method is not recommended for swimmers, however, because athletes with excellent ankle extension ability may score high even if their ankle flexing ability is very

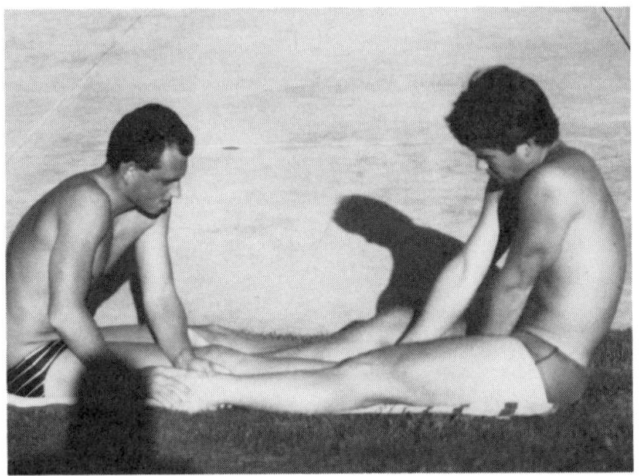

Figure 24-35. Partner-assisted ankle stretches performed by Ondreij Bures and Derek Robinson.

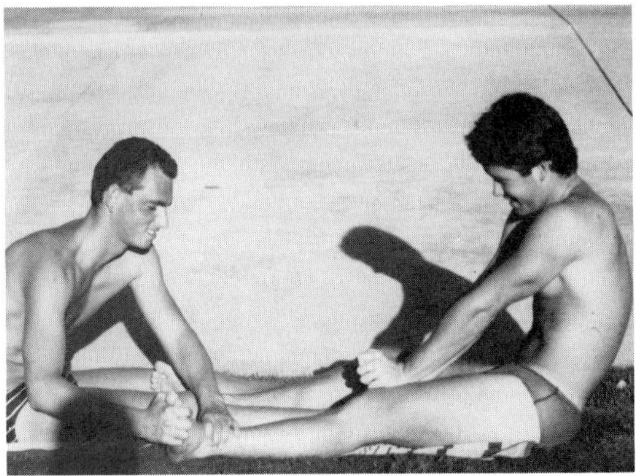

Figure 24-36. Partner-assisted ankle stretches for the breaststroke.

Figure 24-37. Partner-assisted ankle pushes performed by Rodrigo Messias and assisted by Marcelo Menezes.

Figure 24-38. Procedure for measuring shoulder flexion.

Figure 24-39. Procedure for measuring shoulder extension.

Figure 24-40. Procedure for measuring back hyperextension. The swimmer being tested is Don Justice. Rodrigo Messias is holding his legs and Rasmus Jensen is taking the measurement.

Figure 24-41. Procedure for measuring ankle extension ability.

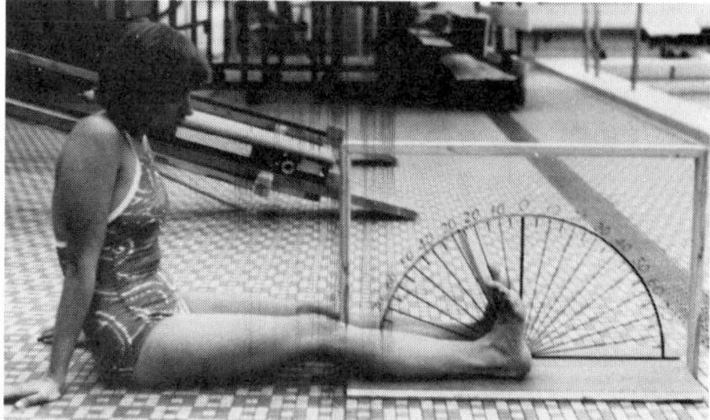

Figure 24-42. Procedure for measuring ankle flexion ability.

poor and vice versa. It is best to measure the ranges of flexion and extension separately. Freestyle, backstroke, and butterfly swimmers should excel in extension ability; breaststrokers should be superior on tests of ankle flexion.

Figures 24-41 and 24-42 illustrate tests for measuring ankle flexibility. The measurements can be taken with the homemade protractor shown. It has a movable indicator bolted at the bottom for recording the scores. The line representing 90 degrees should be marked as the zero point, with markers at 2- to 5-degree increments emanating from this point in both directions.

Ankle extension Ankle extension ability is measured according to the procedure shown in Figure 24-41. The swimmer is seated with her palms on the ground behind her. She begins with her feet near the zero (90-degree) mark on the plexiglass protractor and her heels pressing against the base of the line indicating the perpendicular. To measure, she extends her ankles forward as far as possible without moving her heels. The marker measures the alignment from her heels to the balls of her feet, *not her toes*.

Ankle flexion A similar procedure is used to measure ankle flexion ability. The swimmer in Figure 24-42 begins with her heels on the zero mark, once again. This time she pulls her feet back as far as possible without moving her heels. The marker is moved and aligned from her heels through the balls of her feet, and the measurement is read off the protractor in degrees.

Separate flexibility measurements should be taken on the left and right ankles, because most athletes have one ankle that is more flexible than the other. A good score for ankle extension is 70 degrees and above. Average scores are in the 60-degree range, and poor scores are below 60 degrees. A good ankle flexion score for breaststrokers is 20 degrees or higher. Average scores are in the 12- to 15-degree range. A score of 9 degrees and less indicate very low ankle flexion ability. The following box summarizes these scores. A breaststroker should strive for scores above 24 degrees and swimmers in other strokes should try to achieve scores above 75 degrees.

Scores for Ankle Flexion and Extension

Ankle Extension	Ankle Flexion
Good: greater than 70 degrees	Good: greater than 20 degrees
Average: 60 degrees	Average: 12 to 15 degrees
Poor: less than 60 degrees	Poor: less than 9 degrees

Foot inversion and eversion These two movements of the feet have not received the attention they deserve. The ability to turn the feet out (eversion) and in (inversion) is extremely important to breaststrokers. In fact, one study reported that movements in these directions are even more important to breaststroke kicking than ankle flexing ability (Daly, Persyn, Van Tilborgh, & Riemaker, 1988). Foot inversion ability is also important to swimmers in the other competitive strokes. Freestyle, butterfly, and backstroke swimmers who can turn their feet in can maintain a more effective angle for displacing water back for a longer period of time during the propulsive phase of their kick. Figures 24-43 and 24-44 illustrate methods for measuring foot inversion and eversion flexibility.

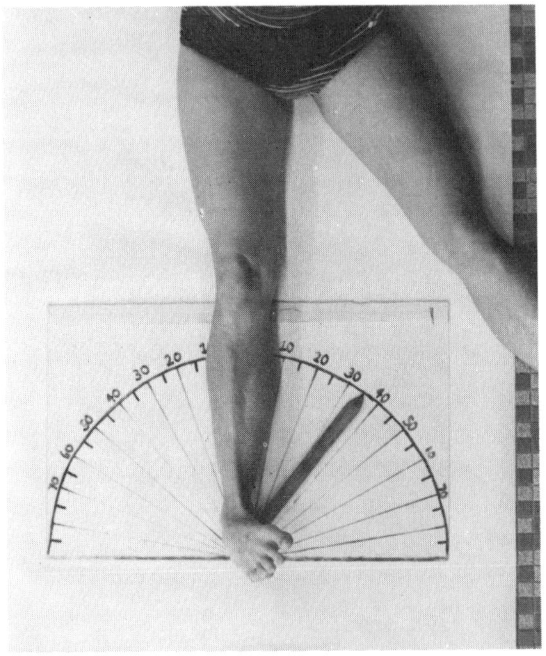

Figure 24-43. Procedure for measuring ankle inversion.

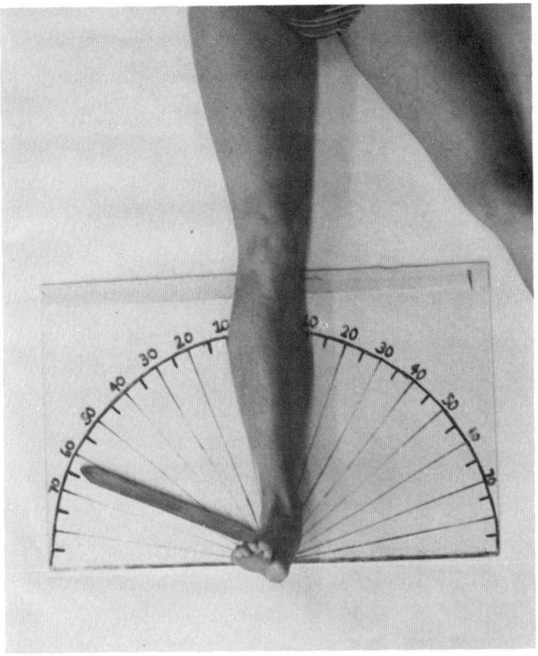

Figure 24-44. Procedure for measuring ankle eversion.

The same protractor device that was used for measuring ankle extension and flexion can be used for these measurements. A small protractor can also be used effectively. The range of motion should be measured on each foot separately.

The swimmer starts in a seated position with the protractor underneath her foot and her heel on the zero (90-degree) mark. The sole of her foot should face forward. To measure inversion, she turns her foot in as far as possible without bending her knee or removing her heel from the zero point (see Figure 24-43). Measure the distance traveled in degrees from the ball of the foot on the little-toe side through the ball of the foot on the big toe side.

Eversion is measured as pictured in Figure 24-44. In this case, the swimmer turns her foot out as much as possible. The measurement is taken according to the number of degrees the ball of her foot moves on the little-toe side. Measure through the ball of the foot from the zero line on the big-toe side through the little-toe side.

CHAPTER

25

Diets for Training and Competition

A swimmer's potential is established by heredity and realized through proper training. Good nutrition is the element that can make that realization possible or prevent it from happening. The food that we eat supplies the fuel to keep our body's engine running during exercise. Like an automobile, the body must have enough fuel to take it where it wants to go. However, it is not enough to simply have a *full tank* of fuel. The fuel must contain the best possible combination of ingredients so that the engine runs as efficiently as possible and does not break down before the trip is completed. In other words, athletes require enough fuel to keep their body functioning, and that fuel must be of high quality so that their body performs well. Consequently, good nutrition supersedes training because it is essential for proper training to take place.

Most swimmers eat diets that are characteristic of their culture, even though their dietary requirements are usually quite different from those of the average person in that culture. The typical diet in most cultures is too high in fat and too low in carbohydrates to meet the energy needs of swimmers in training. Also, much of the food comes from fast-food chains, where sizable portions of vitamin and mineral content have been lost in preparation.

Some athletes think that they can make up for poor nutrition with dietary supplements. I am always amazed at swimmers who eat donuts and coffee rather than cereal and juice for breakfast and then pop high-protein tablets and vitamin pills. Some athletes believe false advertisements for "super foods" that claim to enhance performance. Some even believe that they can substitute these foods for training. They soon find out that they are wrong. Claims are made faster than they can be investigated, and this leaves consumers easy prey to charlatans who promote substances whose benefits have neither been proved nor disproved.

Sensible daily food choices and prudent supplementation provide our body with the fuel it needs for training and competition. Beyond these practices, there are other procedures that can enhance the energy for training and competition. Those that can enhance a swimmer's ability to train involve the number of meals they eat each day and their use of energy-supplying drinks during training. Nutritional practices that may improve competitive performance include the premeet meal, the postcompetition meal, special quick-energy foods, and carbohydrate loading.

There are many substances that have been touted to improve performance over the years. They are collectively known as *ergogenic aids* because they are thought to increase work output. The popular ones are reviewed later in this chapter. Most are no help at all, and some may actually be dangerous to your health. Yet there are just a few that could possibly improve performance.

Many coaches are overly concerned about the effects of body weight on swimming performance. Body fat and weight control are not really problems for athletes. In fact, coaches and parents who blow these issues out of proportion may be doing their athletes a serious disservice.

The final section of this chapter is concerned with practices that can be detrimental to health and performance. These include lack of proper rest and sleep, the use of drugs, alcohol, and tobacco, and the practice of fasting before important competitions.

CALORIC NEEDS

All of our normal daily activities require energy. Simply living requires energy. The amount of energy needed for various daily activities is measured in calories. The number of calories we need each day to stay alive, even if we never got out of bed, is known as our *basal metabolic rate (BMR)*. It differs from person to person, depending on the size of their body and their body composition. Large bodies and bodies with more muscle require a larger number of calories for maintenance than do small bodies or those with a greater amount of fat tissue. Average values for teenage and young adult males and females are 2,100 and 1,800 calories per day, respectively. Children actually burn more calories than adults in a basal state, but their bodies are smaller, so their BMRs are less. They are in the range of 1,600 to 1,700 calories per day with no difference between boys and girls. The following box summarizes these figures.

Daily activities such as running, walking, cycling, swim training, and even eating require energy and, thus, increase the daily caloric expenditure above the BMR. The amount of increase depends on the intensity and duration of the activities. For most persons, the increased energy requirement is in the neighborhood of 800 to 1,000 calories per day. The energy required for swim training has been calculated between 6 and 10 calories per minute, so competitive swimmers can add another 300 to 500 calories per training hour to this total. Table 25-1 lists approximate caloric expenditures for male and female swimmers from various age groups.

Average Basal Metabolic Rates (BMR) for Young Adults and Children

Basal metabolic rate (BMR) = The minimum number of calories required to sustain life

Average Values

Young adult males: 2,100 calories/day

Young adult females: 1,800 calories/day

Children: 1,600 to 1,700 calories/day

The values in Table 25-1 are only estimates for average-sized persons in the various age groups. Children who are much larger or smaller than average may have somewhat different caloric expenditures, as will those with anxious and placid temperaments and those with more or less muscle tissue. Nevertheless, these values provide a starting point for estimating the caloric expenditures of male and female swimmers from the various age categories.

Table 25-1. Estimated Daily Caloric Expenditures for Children, Teenage, and Adult Swimmers

Sex and Age Range	Pretraining Daily Caloric Requirement (calories/day)	Estimated Increase with Training (calories/day)		
		1 hour/day	*2 hours/day*	*4 hours/day*
Males				
10 and under	1,800–2,000	2,100–2,500		
11–12	2,000–2,200	2,300–2,700	2,600–3,000	
13–14	2,200–2,400	2,800–3,200	3,100–3,600	3,600–4,300
15–18	2,600–3,000	3,000–3,500	3,400–3,800	3,800–5,000
18–25	2,700–3,200	3,000–3,600	3,400–4,000	4,000–5,400
30–40	2,400–2,600	2,700–3,100	3,000–3,600	
40–50	2,300–2,500	2,600–3,000	2,900–3,500	
50–70	2,200–2,400	2,500–2,800	2,800–3,200	
Females				
10 and under	2,100–2,300	2,400–2,600		
11–12	2,200–2,400	2,500–2,800	2,700–3,000	
13–14	2,300–2,500	2,600–2,900	2,900–3,100	3,500–4,200
15–18	2,300–2,500	2,600–2,900	2,900–3,100	3,500–4,200
18–25	2,200–2,400	2,500–2,800	2,800–3,200	3,400–4,000
26–40	2,100–2,300	2,400–2,700	2,700–3,100	
40–50	2,000–2,200	2,200–2,600	2,500–3,000	
50–70	1,900–2,100	2,100–2,500	2,300–2,800	

NUTRITIONAL NEEDS

Carbohydrates, fats, protein, water, vitamins, and minerals constitute the categories of nutrients needed by all persons, including athletes.

Carbohydrates

As described in Chapter 1, carbohydrates are the foods that are most easily digested for storage as glycogen in the muscles and liver. As such, they provide the most readily available source of energy for vigorous training and competition.

Carbohydrates are found in the body in three forms: monosaccharides, disaccharides, and polysaccharides. Monosaccharides are the simple sugars glucose, fructose, and galactose. They are called monosaccharides because they cannot be converted to a simpler form. Glucose, more commonly known as simple sugar, is the form used for ATP recycling. The glucose molecule consists of 6 atoms of carbon, 12 of hydrogen, and 6 of oxygen. Figure 25-1 illustrates the chemical structure of a glucose molecule.

Common table sugar, or sucrose, is classified as a disaccharide because it is made up of glucose and fructose molecules. Starches are considered polysaccharides because they contain 11 or more molecules of simple sugars arranged in complex chains. In other words, starchy foods such as bread and cereal are simply chains of glucose and other simple sugars.

Athletes who train twice per day need 8 to 10 grams of carbohydrate per kilogram of body weight per day (8 to 10 g/kg/d) to replace the carbohydrates they lose from their muscles. For most teenage and senior swimmers, this amounts to between 500 to 800 grams of carbohydrates per day. In other words, athletes need to consume between 2,000 and 3,200 calories per day in the form of carbohydrates. Table 25-2 summarizes this information for athletes of various weights.

Most of the carbohydrates should consist of starch forms: breads, grains, pasta, and starchy vegetables such as potatoes and beets. The consumption of sugar forms, such as baked goods, candy, and carbonated beverages, should be reduced considerably. Sugar provides just as much carbohydrate as starch, but it usually contains fewer vitamins and minerals. Additionally, sugar forms of carbohydrate tend to cause a rapid increase in blood glucose followed by a compensatory drop about two hours later that causes a feeling of lethargy; yet starch forms of carbohydrates produce a smaller but longer lasting blood glucose increase that maintains a high level for a longer period.

Fats

Fats are important nutrients that perform many necessary functions in the body. Fats are needed for rebuilding cell membranes, skin, and nerve fibers. They are

$$C_6 H_{12} O_6$$

Figure 25-1. The chemical structure of a glucose molecule.

Table 25-2. Recommended Daily Carbohydrate Consumption for Athletes of Various Weights in Hard Training*

Body Weight (lb)	Caloric Intake per Day	Carbohydrates (calories)	Carbohydrates (g)
100	2,800	1,800	450
150	4,200	2,700	675
180	5,000	3,250	818

Source: Sherman & Maglischo, 1992.

*Based on maintaining a carbohydrate intake of 10 g/kg/d and 65 percent of the daily caloric intake as carbohydrates.

also involved in the synthesis of certain hormones. The fat-soluble vitamins A, D, E, and K are transported in combination with fats. Fats are also a major source of energy for living. They provide almost 70 percent of the total energy we use at rest.

Fats contain the same structural elements as carbohydrates, except they are linked together in different patterns. There are three types of fats: saturated, unsaturated, and polyunsaturated. Saturated fats come from animal sources and dairy foods. Triglycerides are the primary saturated fats, and they are also the major storage form of fat in our bodies. More than 99 percent of our fat consists of triglycerides. Triglycerides are made up of one cluster of glycerol and three clusters of fatty acids. The carbon atoms in triglycerides join with two hydrogen atoms at each available binding site. When this occurs, they are called *saturated* because they contain as many hydrogen atoms as is chemically possible. Figure 25-2 shows the chemical structure of a typical saturated fat.

The danger of ingesting large amounts of saturated fats is that they tend to harden and adhere to the interior of blood vessels, where, in time, they may obstruct blood flow to the point where certain forms of coronary heart disease become severe.

Unsaturated fats come from vegetable oils. They have fewer hydrogen-binding sites along the carbon chain because some of the carbon atoms are joined in double bonds. They are classified as *unsaturated* because hydrogen atoms are not present at every possible binding site. The degree to which they are unsaturated is determined by the number of carbon bonds that do not contain hydrogen. A fat is considered to be *monounsaturated* if there is only one spot along the chain at which a hydrogen atom does not bind. When hydrogen does not join with two or more double bonds along the carbon chain, the fat is called *polyunsaturated*. Figure 25-3 shows the chemical structure of a typical unsaturated fat.

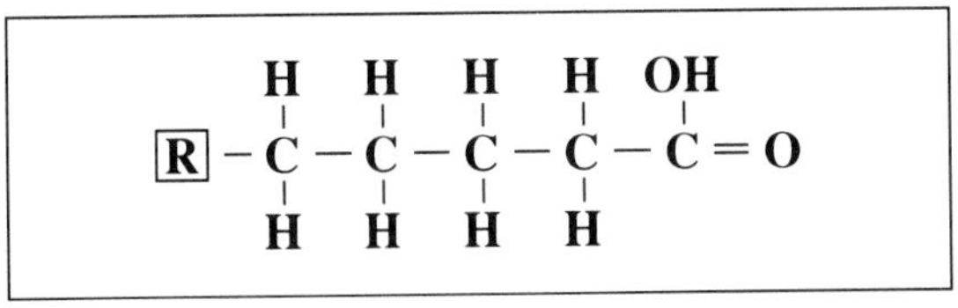

```
        H   H   H   H   OH
        |   |   |   |   |
   [R]- C - C - C - C - C = O
        |   |   |   |
        H   H   H   H
```

Figure 25-2. The chemical structure of a typical saturated fat. (Adapted from McArdle, Katch, & Katch, 1991)

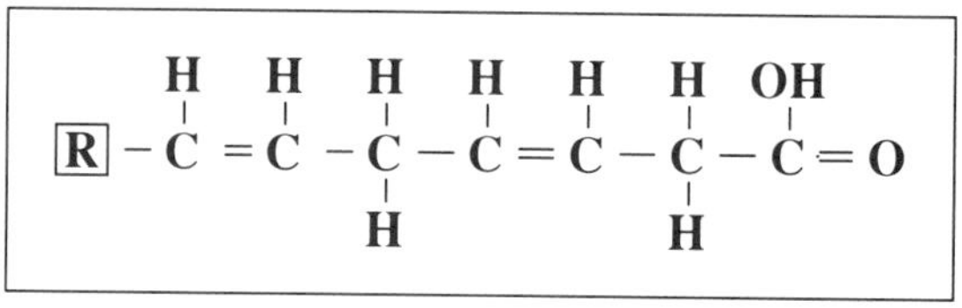

$$
\begin{array}{ccccccccccccccc}
 & & H & & H & & H & & H & & H & & H & & OH \\
 & & | & & | & & | & & | & & | & & | & & | \\
\boxed{R} & - & C & = & C & - & C & - & C & = & C & - & C & - & C = O \\
 & & & & & & | & & & & & & | & & \\
 & & & & & & H & & & & & & H & &
\end{array}
$$

Figure 25-3. The chemical structure of a typical unsaturated fat. (Adapted from McArdle, Katch, & Katch, 1991)

Unsaturated and polyunsaturated fats remain liquid at body temperature and are easily transported throughout the body without hardening in the arteries. Therefore, they are not believed to present a potential health risk.

Athletes need about 50 to 100 g, or 450 to 950 calories, of fat per day depending on their age, size, and time spent in training (1 g of fat = 9 calories). This amounts to between 15 and 20 percent of the calories they consume each day. Most Americans and many persons from other countries presently consume 40 to 50 percent of their daily calories in the form of fats, and much of this consists of saturated fats. Most of the fat that athletes eat should be in unsaturated and polyunsaturated forms. Many swimmers need to cut their fat consumption in half to reduce their intake to the recommended range. This means fewer desserts, less ice cream, and a reduction in red meat and candy.

Proteins

There are several reasons why proteins are important. Muscle tissue is composed of protein. So are the mitochondria and myoglobin in muscle cells. Hemoglobin—the oxygen-carrying substance in the blood—is also composed of protein. Proteins are also one of the most important buffers in the body. All of the more than 2,000 different enzymes that catalyze chemical reactions and many of the hormones that regulate body functions are also made up of proteins. In addition to their other functions, proteins can donate small amounts of energy for recycling ATP during exercise. All of these functions make proteins a valuable material for aerobic and anaerobic exercise.

Like carbohydrates and fats, proteins are constructed of carbon, hydrogen, and oxygen atoms. Unlike the other two nutrients, proteins also contain nitrogen, sulfur, phosphorus, and iron. The structural units of proteins are amino acids. They are combined in a variety of ways to form the thousands of different proteins used in the body. There are more than 20 known amino acids, 9 of which are considered essential because they cannot be synthesized in the body. Essential amino acids must be supplied through the diet.

Amino acids have a limited life span in the human body. They can last for several days or up to a few months before they must be replaced by "new" amino acids through the diet or from other tissues. Consequently, swimmers need a constant and adequate supply of the essential amino acids to rebuild muscle tissue and maintain progress in training.

Essential amino acids can be found in both plant and animal foods. However, meat, fish, poultry, eggs, and milk tend to be better sources than plants because they contain *complete proteins*—that is, all of the 9 essential amino acids are contained in each of these foods. Plant sources are usually lacking in one or more of the essential amino acids and, thus, are considered *incomplete* sources of protein. Approximately 15 to 20 percent of the calories that swimmers consume each day should be high in protein content.

Do Swimmers Need Additional Amounts of Protein? The RDA for adults has been established at .80 gram of protein per kilogram of body weight (g/kg). A slightly greater value of 1.0 g/kg has been established for teenagers because they grow so rapidly. However, several studies have shown that an intake of approximately 1.5 g/kg is needed to support endurance exercise (Friedman & Lemon, 1985, 1989) and that more than 2.0 to 3.0 g/kg per day may be needed for muscle building (Marable et al., 1979). In one study, subjects experienced greater increases in muscle size when their diets were supplemented with additional protein (Consolazio et al., 1975), and the rate of improvement for subjects on protein supplements was greater for both anaerobic work and aerobic work in two others (Sharp, 1991; Sharp et al., 1988).

The elevated caloric intake of athletes should be able to supply the additional protein they need if their diets are well balanced. That is often not the case, however, because most ingest a large portion of those extra calories as fats and carbohydrates. The typical protein intake of female swimmers is between 50 and 60 g per day (van Erp-Baart et al., 1989a). They need approximately 80 to 180 g of protein each day to meet the requirement of 1.50 to 3.00 g/kg, assuming a body weight of between 45 and 60 kg (100 to 130 lb). Males weighing between 68 and 84 kg (150 to 185 lb) need 100 to 250 g of protein each day. Their typical daily intake has been reported to be in the neighborhood of 80 to 100 g (van Erp-Baart et al., 1989a).

The addition of 30 to 150 g (120 to 600 calories) of protein foods daily should meet an athlete's elevated training needs. More will not produce better results. Most of the increase should come from the diet, although some can also be supplied by supplements. Protein foods or supplements should contain substantial amounts of glutamate and branched-chain amino acids for best results. Branched-chain amino acids have been shown to have muscle-building properties, and both glutamate and branched-chain amino acids may reduce the formation of lactic acid (Sharp, 1991).

Too Much of a Good Thing? Although small amounts of protein supplementation are recommended, caution is advised against overdoing it. An overabundance of proteins may tax the ability of the kidneys to remove the excess nitrogen. Proteins also contain purines, which produce waste products when metabolized in the body. There is concern that these waste products may collect in the joints, causing gout or arthritis when abnormally large amounts are circulating in the blood.

A final caution against the overuse of protein concerns red meats. If athletes eat large amounts of red meat as a solution to protein supplementation, they will probably consume too much saturated fat. Protein intake should be increased by consuming more fish, poultry, eggs, milk, peas, beans, or amino acid supplements, *not red meat*. For example, an 8-oz glass of milk has a similar amino acid content to 2 oz of red meat, and ½ cup of peas or beans is equivalent to 1 oz of red meat in protein content.

Table 25-3 summarizes the information on the carbohydrate, fat, and protein needs of swimmers in training. The daily quantities of each that are needed are listed as grams, calories, and percentages.

Water

We usually take water for granted. However, next to oxygen, it is the most important substance we consume. Approximately 60 percent of our body weight comes from water. Two-thirds of that amount is found inside the cells, bathing their contents. In fact, 70 percent of the weight of a muscle cell comes from its water content. Water in this form is called *intracellular fluid*. The remaining water fills spaces outside the cells and is called *extracellular fluid*. Blood plasma is primarily water with some bits of protein. Lymph fluid and synovial fluid in the joints are also largely water.

Water makes most of our life processes possible. It serves four primary functions. It prevents the concentrations of certain chemicals and elements in the body from becoming too great by keeping them in solution. It transports substances from place to place within the body. It provides a cooling effect, and it lubricates the joints.

The need for body water replacement exceeds 2.5 l per day for swimmers who are training. It is nearly impossible to estimate the exact amount, however, because of the large number of factors that can affect water loss. As a general rule, swimmers should probably drink 6 to 10 glasses of water or other liquids such as fruit juices and milk each day.

Vitamins

Although they do not furnish energy or build tissue, vitamins are organic compounds that serve as catalysts for these processes through their actions on metabolic enzymes. They cannot be manufactured in the cells of the body; therefore, they must be consumed on a regular basis. Fourteen different vitamins have been discovered to date. Their chemical structures have been analyzed, their functions in the human body have been classified, and, in most cases, the recommended amounts that are needed daily have been established.

Vitamins are classified in two groups: water soluble and fat soluble. Water-soluble vitamins are not stored in the body. They are transported in body fluids to

Table 25-3. Daily Carbohydrate, Fat, and Protein Needs of Normal-Sized Teenage and Adult Competitive Swimmers

	Grams	Calories	Percentage
Carbohydrates	500–800	2,000–3,200	65–70
Fats	50–100	450–900	15–20
Proteins	100–200	400–800	15–20

sites where they can be used if needed. Excesses are excreted in the urine and feces each day. The B-complex vitamins and vitamin C are water soluble, as are niacin, pantothenic acid, folacin (vitamin M), biotin (vitamin H), and choline.

Fat-soluble vitamins are also transported to body sites where they are needed. In this case, however, excess amounts are stored in fat tissue, sometimes for years. Vitamins A, D, E, and K are fat soluble.

Table 25-4 lists the RDAs for the various vitamins, their functions in the human body, and the foods that contain them.

Table 25-4. Vitamins: Their RDAs, Function, and Sources

Vitamin	RDA	Functions	Sources
Vitamin A	1 mg	Essential for good vision, the normal growth of bones and teeth, and healthy skin. Protects against colds and infections.	Fish, milk, (carotene) orange, green, and yellow vegetables, and fruits.
B-complex vitamins:			
Vitamin B_1 (thiamine)	1.5 mg	Important for fat, carbohydrate, and protein metabolism.	Cereals, eggs, milk, beef, poultry, potatoes, beans, and peas.
Vitamin B_2 (riboflavin)	1.8 mg	Aids in fat, carbohydrate, and protein metabolism.	Milk, eggs, cheese, cereals, grains, meat, and green leafy vegetables.
Niacin	20 mg	Important for the proper digestion of foods. Also needed in aerobic metabolism, particularly the metabolism of fats. Deficiencies may cause depression.	Milk, lean meat, fish, eggs, liver, potatoes, poultry, peas, green and yellow beans, and peanuts.
Vitamin B_6 (pyridoxine)	2 mg	Aids in protein and fat metabolism.	Meat, grains, peas, oats, rice, corn, milk, lettuce, fish, tomatoes, spinach, green beans, and peas.
Folic acid (folacin)	0.40 mg	Important for the production of red and white blood cells in bone marrow. Also important for protein metabolism.	Liver, fresh green vegetables, lean beef, whole wheat cereals, beans, and potatoes.
Pantothenic acid	10 mg	Important for fat, carbohydrate, and protein metabolism and for the formation of hemoglobin.	Liver, eggs, fish, broccoli, potatoes, cauliflower, lean beef, skim milk, and tomatoes.
Vitamin B_{12} (cobalamin)	0.05 mg	Important for digestion, proper bone growth, and the repair of nerve tissue. Involved in the formation of red blood cells and in fat, carbohydrate, and protein metabolism.	Liver, meat, fish, poultry, milk, and dairy products.

(*continued*)

Table 25-4. Vitamins: Their RDAs, Function, and Sources (continued)

Vitamin	RDA	Functions	Sources
Choline	Not established; the usual intake is 500–900 mg	Involved in fat metabolism and in muscular contraction.	Eggs, lean meat, beans, and peas.
Biotin	0.10–0.20 mg	Involved in fat and carbohydrate metabolism.	Liver, chicken, fish, corn, spinach, and peas.
Vitamin C (ascorbic acid)	60 mg	Important for the metabolism of muscle tissue and for bone growth. In adequate quantities, considered to be a stress-relieving vitamin by aiding in the proper functioning of the adrenal gland. Also believed to aid in the utilization of oxygen, the production of red blood cells, and the prevention of respiratory infections. Improves recovery time and prevents fatigue.	Citrus fruits, melons, tomatoes, cabbage, leafy vegetables, and potatoes.
Vitamin D	0.01 mg	Important for the formation of bones and teeth.	Liver, butter, eggs, fish, and sunlight.
Vitamin E (tocopherol)	25–30 mg	Believed to aid in the production of red blood cells. Also enhances activity of vitamins A and C.	Wheat germ oil, corn, lettuce, whole grain cereals, eggs, rice, green leafy vegetables, vegetable oils, milk, and dairy products.
Vitamin K	0.03 mg	Appears to be necessary for blood clotting.	Green leafy vegetables and egg yolk.

Minerals

Unlike vitamins, which are organic, minerals are metallic, inorganic elements. Our bodies contain more than 20 minerals, 17 of which are classified as essential to life. Some minerals—such as zinc, iodine, and chloride—are needed for the synthesis of hormones. Others function as carrier systems. For example, iron in hemoglobin and myoglobin carries oxygen to the tissues of the body. Still others are electrolytes (electrically charged ions) that are used to create the electrical energy our bodies need to transmit nerve impulses and initiate muscular contraction. Sodium, chloride, potassium, and calcium are essential to nerve transmission and muscular contraction. Potassium is a primary regulator of the acid-base balance. The minerals calcium and phosphorus also form a large portion of our bones and other hard tissues. In fact, approximately 4 percent of our body weight is composed of minerals.

Minerals are classified as *macrominerals* or *microminerals*. Macrominerals are present in large quantities in our bodies — 100 mg or more. Microminerals, or the trace elements, are needed in smaller amounts.

The minerals known to be needed in relatively large amounts in the human diet are calcium, phosphorus, potassium, sodium, chloride, and magnesium. Sulfur is also part of this group, although the need for it is met by amino acids. The trace elements are iron, manganese, copper, zinc, cobalt, chromium, selenium, iodine, molybdenum, nickel, and fluoride. Table 25-5 (pp. 674–675) lists these minerals, their functions in the human body, their RDAs, and the foods that contain them.

Vitamin-Mineral Supplements Deficiencies of certain vitamins and minerals can affect performance adversely. In one study, subjects were purposely fed diets low in the B-complex vitamins for eight weeks to produce a deficiency (van der Beek et al., 1984). Work required to reach the anaerobic threshold was increased by 24 percent, and maximum oxygen consumption ($\dot{V}O_2max$) declined by 16 percent by the eighth week. Two weeks of supplementation improved subjects' scores on these measures but did not bring them back to the levels they had attained before the deficiencies were induced. Apparently, vitamin-mineral deficiencies develop over a long period of time and require an equally long time to correct; consequently, athletes should take every reasonable precaution to prevent them.

Athletes undoubtedly require more than the RDA of those vitamins and minerals that are involved in energy metabolism and tissue regeneration and repair. However, prevailing opinion is that the augmented caloric intake of an athlete's diet will supply those additional quantities. This may not be true, however. There are indications that the average diet of Americans does not contain adequate amounts of certain vitamins and minerals. The *First Health and Nutrition Examination Survey* (U.S. Department of Health, Education, and Welfare, 1976) and the *Nationwide Food Consumption Survey* (U.S. Department of Agriculture, 1977–1978) have shown that up to 40 percent of Americans' diets are deficient in one or more vitamins and minerals. This is undoubtedly due to the tremendous increase in the number of meals being eaten at fast-food restaurants, where the vitamin-mineral content is removed during preparation. The quality of food in these restaurants is frequently low despite claims to the contrary. Furthermore, many use cereal fillers that add bulk and calories, but not nutrition.

With this information in mind, there are two very good reasons to assume that athletes need vitamin-mineral supplements: (1) the vast majority obtain a large number of their additional calories from fast-food restaurants; and (2) many female athletes diet while they train so that their caloric intake does not even supply enough calories to match their output (van Erp-Baart et al., 1989a, 1989b). For these reasons, supplementation seems advisable purely as a precautionary measure.

A word of caution is necessary, however. Ingesting unusually large amounts of certain vitamins and minerals — a practice known as *megadosing* — can be dangerous in at least two ways. The first danger is that, over several months, fat-soluble vitamins can accumulate to toxic amounts that could, at the least, cause illness or, at the worst, death. The second danger is that many athletes believe that supplements take care of their nutritional requirements and that they do not need to

Table 25-5. Minerals: Their RDAs, Functions, and Sources

Mineral	RDA	Functions	Sources
Iron	10–18 mg	Essential for the formation of hemoglobin and myoglobin and for the transportation of oxygen.	Liver, lean meat, fish, poultry, green leafy vegetables, dried beans, peas, breads, cereals, fruit, and eggs.
Calcium	800–1,200 mg	Important for the formation of bones and teeth. Essential for nerve impulse transmission and muscular contraction. Also encourages blood clotting and the maintenance of proper water balance.	Milk, dairy products, and green leafy vegetables.
Phosphorus	800–1,200 mg	Important for the formation of bones and teeth. Needed for the formation of cell membranes. Important to the acid-base balance through its action as a buffer. An important constituent of ATP and CP. Also important for metabolism. Many B-complex vitamins function only in combination with phosphorus.	Meat, poultry, fish, milk, cheese, eggs, nuts, beans, and peas.
Sodium	1–3 g	Important for the maintenance of normal water balance and acid-base balance. Essential for muscular contraction.	Table salt, seafood, meat, milk, and eggs.
Chloride	1–3 g	Aids in the regulation of acid-base balance and enzyme function.	Table salt, seafood, meat, milk, and eggs.
Potassium	2–5 g	Important for the maintenance of normal water balance and acid-base balance. Important for muscular contraction.	Fruits, milk, meat, cereals, vegetables, peas, and beans.
Magnesium	350 mg	Activates enzymes involved in glucose and protein metabolism.	Nuts, peas, beans, cereals, and green leafy vegetables.
Zinc	15 mg	Needed for normal growth and repair of muscle tissue. Participates with insulin in glucose metabolism. Activates many enzymes involved with muscular contraction. Needed for normal sex gland development.	Milk, liver, wheat bran, meat, and shellfish.
Chromium	0.05–0.20 mg	Involved in glucose and fat metabolism	Corn oil, whole grain cereals, and meat.
Copper	3 mg	Important for the formation of red blood cells. Constituent of enzymes involved with iron metabolism. Involved in the maintenance of the myelin sheaths of nerve fibers.	Liver, shellfish, whole grains, peas, beans, nuts, meat, poultry, fish, and dried fruits.

Table 25-5. Minerals: Their RDAs, Functions, and Sources (continued)

Mineral	RDA	Functions	Sources
Sulfur	Provided by amino acids	Important for carbohydrate metabolism. Needed in muscle tissues, tendons, and cartilage and for the maintenance of skin and hair.	Meat, fish, poultry, eggs, milk, cheese, peas, beans, and nuts.
Flouride	2–4 mg	Needed for the growth and maintenance of bones and teeth.	Water, rice, soybeans, and green leafy vegetables.
Cobalt	0.1 mg in combination with vitamin B_{12}	Essential to the normal function of all cells, particularly those of the bones, nervous system, and digestive system.	Liver, poultry, and milk. Found in vitamin B_{12}.
Manganese	3–5 mg	Essential to the function of most enzymes. Needed for the formation of most tissues, particularly bones.	Beets, bran, nuts, peas, beans, fruits, and lettuce.
Iodine	0.15 mg	Needed for proper thyroid function.	Table salt, seafood, water, and vegetables.
Molybdenum	0.15–0.50 mg	Constituent of many enzymes involved in iron absorption.	Peas, beans, cereal, grains, green leafy vegetables, milk, and meat.
Selenium	0.05–0.20 mg	Involved in fat metabolism in association with vitamin E.	Grains, meat, milk, vegetables, and onions.

consume well-balanced diets of nutritious foods each day. In such cases, they may not consume the daily quantities of carbohydrates, fats, proteins, and liquids that they need.

Athletes should view vitamin-mineral supplements as safeguards, not quick-energy foods that can improve their performances. Although vitamin-mineral supplements can prevent deficiencies that could hamper performance, *they will not improve performance if athletes consume excess amounts*. Let me reiterate: *I am not advocating megadosing or the use of vitamin-mineral supplements in place of good nutrition*. Preventing deficiencies is the only reason for recommending supplementation.

Guidelines for Supplementation Table 25-6 (p. 676) lists the vitamins and minerals that may need to be supplemented to prevent deficiencies. The amounts of each that should provide an adequate *and safe* level of supplementation are also listed. Keep this information in mind when selecting a supplement.

The vitamins and minerals that athletes need in greater-than-normal amounts are the B-complex vitamins, vitamin C, vitamin E, beta-carotene, iron, calcium, zinc, chromium, manganese, and selenium. Women appear to need iron and calcium more than men because they lose more of these minerals from their body each month and because of the potential for greater deficiencies. Magnesium is another mineral that may be needed more by women than men for this same reason. There

Table 25-6. What To Look for in a Vitamin-Mineral Supplement

Vitamin or Mineral	Suggested Daily Supplementation	
Vitamins		
B-complex vitamins		
Thiamine (B_1)	20–25 mg	
Riboflavin (B_2)	2–4 mg (possibly needed only by women)	
Pyridoxine (B_6)*	4–6 mg	
Folacin*	2–4 mg	
Cobalamin (B_{12})	2–4 mg	
Pantothenic acid	10–15 mg	
Vitamin C	400–1,000 mg	
Vitamin E	400–1,000 I.U.	
Beta-carotene	5,000–8,000 I.U.	
Minerals	*Females*	*Males*
Iron	100–150 mg	20–50 mg
Calcium**	1,000 mg	500 mg
Magnesium	200–300 mg	50–100 mg
Zinc	10–20 mg	10–20 mg
Manganese	1–2 mg	1–2 mg
Chromium	1 mg	1 mg
Selenium	0.20–0.50 mg	0.20–0.50 mg
Iodine	0.10–0.20 mg	0.10–0.20 mg

*Females using oral contraceptives may have to double the amounts shown here.
**Amenorrheic females may require 1,500 mg.

also appears to be an increased need for the B-complex vitamin folacin in women who use oral contraceptives.

With this in mind, a good vitamin-mineral supplement should contain most of the B-complex vitamins, particularly thiamine (B_1), riboflavin (B_2), pyridoxine (B_6), pantothenic acid, folacin, and cobalamin (B_{12}). Daily amounts of 20 to 25 mg of thiamine may be needed, but the other B-complex vitamins can probably be supplemented with daily amounts of 2 to 6 mg. An exception is pantothenic acid, which should probably be supplemented by 10 to 15 mg per day. Men may not need to supplement with riboflavin. Women who use oral contraceptives are advised to supplement their diets with 8 to 12 mg of pyridoxine (B_6) and 4 to 8 mg of folacin each day.

Many athletes supplement their diet with too much vitamin C because of all the publicity it has received. There is no need to supplement with more than 100 to 150 mg per day.

The fat-soluble vitamins should not be supplemented because, as explained earlier, they are stored in the body and can become toxic if megadoses are taken over a long time. Choose a supplement that has minimum amounts of vitamins A, D, E, and K. Small amounts of these vitamins will not cause toxicity or illness. The amounts required to reach toxic levels are far beyond the usual quantities that would accumulate from taking one or two vitamin-mineral tablets each day. It has been estimated, for example, that daily supplements of 200 and 300 times the RDA for these vitamins is required to produce toxicity.

Iron and calcium are the two most important minerals that should be included in a program of supplementation. Females may need 100 to 150 mg of additional iron each day and 1,000 mg of additional calcium. Women who are not menstruating regularly are advised to increase their daily calcium intake to 1,500 mg. This may require consuming additional sources of calcium, such as milk, because most vitamin-mineral supplements do not contain this amount. The amounts that will safeguard males against deficiencies are 20 to 50 mg of iron and 500 mg of calcium.

Magnesium is another mineral that may be needed in greater quantities by females than by males. Women who have a daily caloric intake below 3,000 calories may not be consuming enough magnesium. Therefore, a daily supplement of 200 to 300 mg is recommended.

The other minerals that should be included in a daily supplement are zinc (10 to 20 mg), manganese (1 to 2 mg), chromium (1 mg), selenium (0.20 to 0.50 mg), and possibly iodine (0.10 to 0.20 mg), if it is not included in drinking water.

Based on the information presented, the eating habits of most swimmers need to change from that of the general population so that they eat 800 to 1,200 fewer calories per day in the form of fats. Their caloric intake of protein should increase by 100 to 200 calories per day, and their consumption of starch forms of carbohydrates should increase by 600 to 1,000 calories per day.

They should drink 6 to 10 glasses of water or some nutritious liquid daily. Diet or sugared soft drinks are not recommended because they have little, if any, nutritional value.

THE FIVE FOOD GROUPS: A GUIDE TO INTELLIGENT FOOD SELECTION

As mentioned previously, athletes should never make the mistake of thinking that vitamin-mineral supplements obviate the need for an adequate daily intake of carbohydrates, fats, proteins, and fluids. The U.S. Department of Agriculture has suggested a simplified process for making food choices that will result in good nutrition. The earlier form of this plan was popularized as the "basic four food groups." That plan has now been revised to include five food groups (U.S. Department of Agriculture & U.S. Department of Health and Human Services, 1990). The major differences between this and the earlier plan are (1) that fruits and vegetables are now two groups rather than one, with more servings of each recommended because of their importance to sound nutrition, and (2) that considerably more servings are recommended from the cereals and grain group because they are high in the complex carbohydrates, which serve as our principle source of energy for physical activity. The five food groups consist of the following:

1. Cereals and grain products
2. Fruits
3. Vegetables
4. Milk and milk products
5. Meat, poultry, and fish

Table 25-7 lists the foods contained in each group, the suggested daily servings, and the nutrients they supply. The first number listed for daily servings represents the recommended minimum for nonathletes. The second number represents the additional needs of adult swimmers in hard training. Younger athletes and those who are training less should ingest a number of servings somewhere above the minimum suggested for nonathletes but below the amount recommended for adult athletes. For athletes, you'll notice that the largest servings are recommended in the cereal and grain group because of the carbohydrates they contain. A small number of additional servings are recommended from the fruit, vegetable, and meat groups

Table 25-7. The Five Food Groups

Group	Foods Included	Suggested Daily Servings	Nutrients
Cereals and grains	Wheat, barley, corn, oats, rice, bread, cereals, macaroni, pasta, and grits.	6 to 15 servings (a serving equals 1 slice of bread or ½ cup of cereal, spaghetti, etc.).	Carbohydrates, protein, thiamin, riboflavin, niacin, and iron.
Fruits	Apples, pears, bananas, oranges, figs, pineapples, grapes, and juices.	2 to 6 servings (a serving equals 1 medium apple, orange, etc. or ¾ cup of juice).	Carbohydrates, vitamin A, vitamin C, folacin, and various minerals.
Vegetables	Lettuce, broccoli, green and yellow beans, peas, carrots, potatoes, and corn.	3 to 7 servings (a serving equals 1 cup of raw leafy greens or ½ cup of other kinds of vegetables).	Carbohydrates, protein, vitamin A, vitamin C, B-complex vitamins, folacin, and various minerals.
Milk and milk products	Milk, cheese, yogurt, ice milk.	2 to 4 servings (a serving equals 1 cup of milk or yogurt or 1½ oz of cheese).	Protein, fat, calcium, riboflavin, and vitamin D.
Meat, poultry, fish and other high-protein products	Beef, pork, veal, lamb, game, fish, poultry, shellfish, eggs, peas, beans, lentils, peanuts, and nuts.	2 to 4 servings (a serving equals 3.5 oz).	Protein, fat, thiamin, iron, niacin, and riboflavin.

because of the vitamins, minerals, and protein they supply to athletes in training. The intake of foods that are high in fats should remain at the suggested minimum levels for nonathletes.

Swimmers should avoid whole milk, fats, and oils because they are high in saturated fats and cholesterol. Instead, they should choose skim or lowfat milk and fat-free or lowfat yogurt and cheese. One cup of whole milk has 8 g of fat versus 5 g of fat for an equal amount of lowfat milk. Swimmers should use fat and saturated oils sparingly in cooking and avoid salad dressings made with saturated oils. They should also keep their consumption of butter, margarine, and mayonnaise to a minimum. One tablespoon of each of these contains 10 to 11 g of fat.

Athletes should maintain a low consumption of foods with high sugar contents, choosing instead starch forms of carbohydrates. Foods that contain large amounts of sugar supply energy but are low in nutrients. Cereal and grain products supply just as much energy and a considerably greater number of vitamins and minerals, as well as needed fiber.

Salt should also be used in moderation. Although both sodium and chloride are essential nutrients, most persons consume more than they need. Large intakes of sodium have been linked to high blood pressure. Although most age group swimmers and young adult competitors certainly require more of these nutrients than nonathletes, it would be better if they did not develop an appetite for heavily salted foods because of the greater risk of heart disease they might incur in later years. Many foods and drinks, particularly sports drinks, contain enough sodium and chloride to meet athlete's needs without increasing their use of salt.

VEGETARIAN DIETS

There is a trend for many athletes to increase their consumption of vegetables and reduce their intake of red meat. This is a desirable trend because it reduces the intake of saturated fats in the process. Additionally, diets that are high in vegetables usually contain more carbohydrates. Vegetables are also rich in potassium and magnesium — minerals that are important to energy metabolism.

However, performances can suffer if the nutrients in meat are not provided by other foods. In two recent studies, approximately one-third of the athletes surveyed described their diets as vegetarian or semivegetarian (Barr, 1986; Slavin, McNamara, & Lutter, 1986). Athletes on poorly planned vegetarian diets are at risk for eating disorders, inadequate repair of muscle tissue, weak bones, and amenorrhea. Because meats are readily available sources of complete protein (they contain all of the essential amino acids), a reduced intake of this food group can also reduce the protein available for tissue growth and repair. When meat is eliminated from the diet, iron absorption may also be reduced, increasing the risk of anemia because a valuable source of the readily available heme iron has been eliminated. Zinc is another nutrient that is often deficient in vegetarian diets. Diets of strict vegetarians also tend to be lower in calcium, vitamin B_{12}, and vitamin D unless they include milk, dairy products, and dark green leafy vegetables. Female vegetarians tend to lose more estrogen in their feces than nonvegetarians, which may alter their menstrual cycles (Golden et al., 1982; Schultz, Wilcox, Spuehler, & Howie, 1987). Additionally, swimmers in hard training may find it difficult to eat enough to meet their energy needs on a purely vegetarian diet.

Semivegetarians can ensure an adequate intake of complete proteins and iron by eating fish and poultry. Another possible solution is to eat more milk and eggs. Eggs are rated highest in protein quality, because the mixture and quantity of essential amino acids is considered the best found in any food. Milk is ranked third on the list behind fish and just ahead of beef. A final solution is to use a daily protein supplement that contains all of the essential amino acids.

Although it is certainly possible for swimmers to eliminate all meats and other animal products from their diets without incurring protein, vitamin, and mineral deficiencies, strict vegetarians have to choose their foods with great care to guard against such deficiencies. They must become students of protein nutrition, being careful to include wide varieties of peas, beans, nuts, whole grains, dried fruits, and dark green vegetables in their diets in order to get all of the essential amino acids they need each day. Although these foods are all incomplete sources of protein, they can provide all of the essential amino acids if eaten in various combinations each day. For example, cereals are deficient in lysine, and legumes are deficient in sulfur amino acids. Consequently, meals prepared with legume and grain combinations, such as beans and brown rice, can provide complete sources of these proteins.

DIETARY PRACTICES THAT CAN ENHANCE TRAINING

Making the proper food choices provides for the storage of fuels that athletes use in training, yet there are certain dietary practices that can make those fuels more readily available. The number of meals that athletes eat each day can have a bearing on fuel availability, and research has demonstrated the benefits of using high-energy foods and carbohydrate beverages immediately before, during, and immediately after training sessions.

Eating Four to Six Meals Per Day

Swimmers who are training twice per day should eat four to six small meals rather than three larger ones each day, because eating at more frequent intervals helps maintain blood glucose at a high level and also helps replace muscle glycogen faster from one training session to the next. Blood glucose tends to fall within two to three hours after eating; consequently, eating more frequently than once every five or six hours should maintain blood glucose at a higher level so that more can enter the muscles for storage. Furthermore, swimmers that eat a high-carbohydrate meal within one to two hours after training enhance their rate of liver and muscle glycogen replacement.

Because most swimmers snack frequently throughout the day, you may question the advisability of eating more than three major meals. However, the problem with snacking is that the wrong kinds of foods are usually consumed. The typical swimmer will hit the candy or soda machine in the lobby of the swimming pool immediately after training and choose foods that contain large amounts of sugar and fat and practically no vitamin or mineral content. It would be much better for them to have a nutritious snack of foods that are high in complex carbohydrates, vitamins, and minerals and low in sugar and fat.

Swimmers must be careful that the practice of eating four to six times daily does not lead to a corresponding caloric increase. Rather, the usual number of calories needed to meet the demands of training should be spread over four to six meals per day instead of three. The following plan is recommended for this purpose.

Meals 1 and 2 When swimmers are training twice per day, they should consume 300 to 500 calories of a liquid or semiliquid carbohydrate substance before morning training. This can be followed by a normal breakfast after training.

Meals 3 and 4 The noontime meal should contain fewer calories than usual, with the missing calories consumed at a midafternoon snack scheduled an hour or two before training. That snack should also include complex carbohydrates, perhaps in the form of a sandwich and fruit.

Meals 5 and 6 A somewhat smaller than normal supper and an evening snack one or two hours before retiring should complete the day. The evening snack provides for a higher blood glucose level overnight.

High-Carbohydrate Snacks and Drinks before, during, and after Training

The importance of maintaining an adequate level of muscle glycogen has been stressed repeatedly. The difficulty in doing so, of course from the fact that swimmers who train twice per day never have 24 hours between sessions for the complete replacement of all of the glycogen they use. Thus, athletes frequently train when their muscle glycogen supply is low. At these times, they run the risk of combusting muscle protein for energy. Taking high-carbohydrate snacks before or during training can provide glucose when muscle glycogen is low. High-carbohydrate snacks immediately after training can encourage more rapid replacement of muscle glycogen.

Work output and performance improved markedly in studies in which subjects were fed carbohydrate solutions before and during training (Neufer et al., 1987; Sherman, Peden, & Wright, 1991). In one study, work time to exhaustion was improved an average of 17 percent (134 to 157 minutes; Norris, Davis, & Lonnet, 1989). In another study, performances during an 80-mile bicycle race were improved an average of 5 percent (253 to 241 minutes) by using high-carbohydrate solutions during the race (Seifert, Langenfeld, Rudge, & Buchert, 1986). The reason provided for these improvements was that the carbohydrate solutions maintained blood glucose at a higher level during the exercise so that more was available to the muscles for energy. This has the effect of maintaining a supply of glucose to the muscles late in the training and in races, when muscle glycogen supplies are running low. In fact, the major improvements in performance in such tests are always seen in the last half of the effort (Wilmore & Costill, 1988).

Swimmers should be able to gain benefits similar to those gained by runners and cyclers from using carbohydrate drinks and snacks before or during training. More blood glucose will be available, which should allow them to train at an average faster speed during the entire two or more hours of a typical training session.

High-Carbohydrate Snacks before Training

Consuming 100 to 400 g of some high-carbohydrate substance in solid form or 150 to 200 ml (4 to 8 oz) of a high-carbohydrate drink within one to two hours of training should increase an athlete's subsequent work output. Candy bars and drinks containing only sugar are not the best sources for snacks. Complex or starchy forms of carbohydrates, such as cereals and grains, or drinks containing glucose or some other easily digested form of carbohydrate are preferred because they are more nutritious and because they produce a longer-lasting insulin effect that can maintain blood glucose at a high level for a longer time. When they compared the effects of preexercise snacks of sugar and starch forms of carbohydrates on performances, Thomas and colleagues (1989) reported that, although both substances caused improvements, the group that used complex carbohydrates improved slightly more.

High-Carbohydrate Drinks during Training

Research has shown consistent and significant improvements in work output when subjects consumed high-carbohydrate drinks during exercise. Although nearly any liquid substance that contains carbohydrates will help maintain blood glucose at a reasonably high level, there are some that work better than others. The four rules that should govern your choice are the following:

1. The drink should contain enough carbohydrate to maintain blood glucose at a high level during training.
2. It should contain some sodium chloride (salt) to stimulate glucose uptake.
3. It should be easily digested so that it can reach the muscles as quickly as possible.
4. It should be palatable.

Regarding the first requirement, it appears that swimmers need to consume approximately 50 to 60 g of carbohydrates each hour (about 2 to 3 oz) to maintain blood glucose at a high level (Maughan, 1991). In this respect, small amounts of liquid taken at frequent intervals seem to maintain blood glucose better than one large drink taken before training. A large drink will deliver a sizable amount of glucose to the blood in a short time, but that supply will also be consumed quite rapidly. Several smaller drinks at frequent intervals will provide a level of blood glucose that is initially lower but will be maintained for the duration of the session. Consequently, it is recommended that approximately 100 to 200 ml of a carbohydrate solution (about 4 to 6 oz) be provided every 20 minutes.

The solution should contain approximately 5 to 10 percent of its volume as glucose, sucrose, or maltodextrins in order to supply the 50 to 60 g per hour that are required (Mitchell et al., 1989). This means that each liter should contain about 100 to 140 g (4 to 6 oz) of one of these carbohydrate substances. Each liter should also contain between 20 and 50 mmol of sodium chloride to comply with the second requirement.

Glucose, sucrose, and maltodextrins are preferred over fructose because of their greater digestibility. In fact, glucose polymer solutions appear to empty from the stomach faster than solutions of free glucose. Fructose is not recommended because it has been shown to cause vomiting and diarrhea (Maughan, 1991; Murray et al.; 1989, Paul, Seifert, Eddy, & Murray, 1988).

There are three misconceptions about sports drinks that should be cleared up. Previous reports indicated that weaker concentrations of glucose (2.5-percent solutions) were emptied from the stomach faster than stronger concentrations (Foster, Costill, & Fink, 1980). That doesn't appear to be true, however. Recent research has shown that concentrations up to 10 percent leave the stomach just as rapidly as plain water while supplying more glucose (Murray et al., 1989; Owen, Kregel, Wall, & Gisofi, 1986). Although it was once believed that cold drinks emptied from the stomach faster than warm drinks, recent evidence suggests that the temperature of drinks has little, if any effect, on the length of time required to get carbohydrate solutions into the bloodstream (McArthur & Feldman, 1989).

The final misconception concerning these drinks is that they should have an electrolyte concentration similar to that of sweat. There is really no need to include electrolytes in a high-carbohydrate solution. The amounts of electrolytes lost in sweat are minute compared to the amount that remains in the body during training. Consequently, electrolytes actually become more concentrated during training. Sodium chloride is the only electrolyte recommended because of its effect on glucose absorption, not because it is lost in sweat.

Providing carbohydrate solutions to a team of swimmers during training can be an expensive proposition. However, the benefits are worth the expense. Athletes will be able to train more intensely on a frequent basis, and they will be less likely to become overtrained from glycogen depletion and subsequent consumption of their own muscle protein.

It would be a good idea for swimmers to purchase a sports bottle that they can fill with a carbohydrate solution before going to training. This can be left on the deck beside their lane, where they can drink from it whenever they desire.

High-Carbohydrate Snacks after Training

The rate of muscle glycogen replacement will increase considerably if athletes consume a high-carbohydrate snack within one to two hours after training. On the other hand, the rate of replacement will be reduced by 33 percent if they wait more than two hours after training to consume this snack (Ivy, Katz et al, 1988; MacDougall, Ward, Sale, & Sutton, 1977). Consumption of 150 to 300 g of some easily digested form of carbohydrate is recommended. Another solution to replacing the energy supply is to eat frequent smaller snacks totaling 40 to 80 g of carbohydrate per hour for four hours after training. This procedure appears to cause an even more rapid rate of muscle glycogen replacement (Ivy, Katz et al., 1988; Ivy, Lee, Broznick, & Reed, 1988). Glucose in sugar or starch forms also results in more rapid replacement than similar quantities of fructose (Sherman & Maglischo, 1992).

DIETARY PRACTICES THAT MAY IMPROVE PERFORMANCE IN MEETS

Eating Two to Three Days Prior to Competition

The meals that athletes eat one to three days prior to competition are actually more important to performance than the precompetition meal, because they contain the foods that will be stored as muscle glycogen and then used in the competition. Athletes should enter important meets with muscle glycogen storage at normal levels or higher. To accomplish this, swimmers should increase the carbohydrate content of their meals two or three days prior to the meet and continue this pattern until the competition begins. They should reduce the fat and protein content of these meals so that caloric intake is not excessive.

If the meet is an important one, both the quantity and intensity of training should be reduced to maintenance levels to prevent a reduction of muscle glycogen before meet time. If it is not a meet that requires special preparation, the additional carbohydrate intake may protect swimmers from complete depletion during hard training so that some muscle glycogen will be available for competition.

The Premeet Meal

Actually, the premeet meal has very little to do with improving performance. Its main functions are to reduce hunger and, in some cases, to provide a ritual for psyching up before a competition. Above all, these meals should not interfere with athletes' efforts. They should not cause them to enter a meet with a full stomach or a feeling of nausea. A sensible premeet meal should meet the following criteria:

1. It should be small and easily digested so that athletes do not go into competition with a full stomach.
2. The food should be familiar to the swimmers and not heavily spiced or cooked in a way that causes digestive distress.

Five hundred to 600 calories of some bland form of complex carbohydrates fill the bill perfectly for a premeet meal. They are quickly digested and can be poured into the blood quickly to replace the muscle glycogen used during competition. Fats and proteins are digested more slowly; therefore fried foods and large quantities of meat should be avoided. Large amounts of high-fiber foods are also not recommended because they may cause intestinal discomfort. Toast, muffins, pancakes, waffles, and noodles are much better choices. Pizza, spaghetti, tacos, and burritos have also been recommended because of their carbohydrate content, but they are not good choices because they also contain considerable amounts of fat and protein and because the spices used in their preparation may cause nausea or diarrhea.

Liquid supplements also make excellent premeet meals because they leave the stomach rapidly. Several commercial preparations are available in both powder and solution forms. They provide balanced nutrition and an adequate, but not excessive, number of calories, and they satiate swimmers' appetites.

If the premeet meal contains a sizable amount of solid food, it should be eaten at least three hours before the meet. Liquid solutions can be consumed anywhere from two hours to five minutes prior to competing and even during breaks in the competition. The following box lists suggestions for the premeet meal.

Suggestions for the Premeet Meal

1. It should contain 500 to 600 calories, mostly in carbohydrate form (60 to 70 percent).
2. Easily digested starch forms of carbohydrates are best. Avoid fried and heavily spiced foods.
3. It should be eaten approximately three hours before competition, although it can be consumed later than this with no ill effects if it is in the form of a liquid solution.

Quick-Energy Snacks before Competition

In the first edition of this book, I reported that the common practice of eating candy or other foods containing high levels of sugar prior to competition could be detrimental to performance. It was suggested that sugar consumed immediately before competition might cause a drop in blood glucose that could reduce the potential for endurance work. It was also suggested that the immediate increase in insulin secretion and subsequent glucose uptake by the muscles following a high-carbohydrate snack would result in a compensatory drop in both that could limit glucose availability to the muscles during exercise.

It now appears that these assumptions were incorrect. Recent studies show that eating an easily digestible source of carbohydrates immediately before competition does not have a detrimental effect. In one study, eating one or two candy bars 30 minutes before a long ride did not hurt or help performance (Alberici, Farrell, Kris-Etherton, & Shively, 1989). Blood insulin levels were higher when the exercise began and did not fall below normal values during the work period. The demand for energy during exercise apparently prevents a decline in insulin and a subsequent drop in blood glucose. Consequently, eating easily digested sources of sugar (candy bars, high-energy drinks, and so on) immediately before competition does not seem to aid or hinder performance in most swimming events.

The Postcompetition Meal

The need for a high-carbohydrate meal or several high-carbohydrate snacks immediately following competition has not received the attention it deserves in the literature on athletic nutrition. The attitude has been that what an athlete eats after the race is not important. Although the postcompetition meal has no bearing on the competition that has just concluded, it is significant for athletes who must compete or train within a short time afterward. High-carbohydrate snacks similar to those that were suggested after training will encourage faster replacement of muscle glycogen.

Research has shown that as few as four races can deplete some muscle fibers of glycogen (MacDougall, Ward, Sale, & Sutton, 1977). Thus, some carbohydrate foods taken immediately after a morning preliminary session may provide partial repletion by afternoon. By the same token, foods eaten soon after an afternoon or evening competition will provide more rapid repletion for the events of the following day.

The timing of postcompetition meals or snacks can be critical, because, as mentioned previously, muscle glycogen replacement is faster when food is eaten within the first two hours after exercise (Ivy, Katz, et al., 1988). The postcompetition meal should contain 500 to 800 calories, mostly in the form of easily digested carbohydrates. This food should pass through the stomach and begin reaching the muscles for storage within one hour, and a significant amount should be stored after two or three hours. Several carbohydrate snacks similar to those recommended for posttraining can also provide the glucose needed for energy replacement. A liquid source of carbohydrates is preferred because it can be digested faster. Fruit juices and commercial carbohydrate powders or solutions are ideal for this purpose. It is probably a good idea for swimmers to drink one or two glasses of these between competitive sessions as a precaution against depleting muscle glycogen. Following is a list of readily available foods that are high in carbohydrates. They should be consumed in preference to candy and bakery products because of the nutrients they contain.

Bread	Skim milk	Cereal
Muffins	Potatoes	Apples
Bananas	Orange juice	Pineapple juice
Baked beans	Pretzels	Crackers
Peaches	Pineapple	Apricots
Oranges	Chow Mein	
Macaroni	Bagels	

Fasting before Competition

This is one of the most senseless fads to appear in competitive sports. Some persons have reasoned that eliminating food for 12 or more hours before competition mobilizes metabolic mechanisms so that more energy is available for races. Others also believe that fasting produces a cleansing effect that makes an athlete's body function as though it had just had a tune-up. Neither of these assumptions has any basis in fact. Performances worsened by 50 to 100 percent in studies in which this theory was tested (Loy et al., 1986; Nieman, Carlson, & Brandstater, 1987).

Carbohydrate Loading

The practice of carbohydrate loading is based on the research of Bergstrom and his associates (1967), who showed that a sequence of dietary manipulation and exercise caused muscles to store twice their normal amount of glycogen. This increase resulted in improvements of 33 percent in work time to exhaustion.

The original loading procedure required three weeks, during which athletes first depleted muscle glycogen reserves with exercise and a low-carbohydrate diet. The explanation provided for the extraordinary increase in muscle glycogen was that the initial depletion increased the activity of enzymes involved in glycogen formation, causing the muscles to store almost twice as much glycogen when it became available later in the process.

Although effective, several problems resulted from the use of this lengthy loading procedure. The most serious of these was a symptom akin to withdrawal during the second week of low-carbohydrate eating. Athletes became listless and depressed, and their performances in training were so poor that many lost confidence in their ability to compete. The result was that they performed poorly in the subsequent event. It was also suggested that some endurance might have been lost by training hard when the muscles were depleted of glycogen.

Because of these problems and as a result of additional research, the three-week procedure was modified to a one-week plan. This procedure, although requiring less time, created problems that were similar to those experienced during the three-week regimen. Athletes lacked energy and became depressed during the early part of the week and were concerned that they might lose endurance.

Research that is now available indicates that the process of carbohydrate loading can be equally effective if athletes skip the low-carbohydrate phase and just rest and increase their intake of carbohydrates for two to four days prior to competition (Sherman, Costill, Fink, & Miller, 1981). The results of this research have been reproduced in Figure 25-4. The two lines represent the modified (three-day) regimen and the classical (one-week) regimen. In the classical regimen, the muscles were depleted of glycogen and a low-carbohydrate diet (350 g/day) was eaten during the first four days of the week and a high-carbohydrate diet was eaten during the

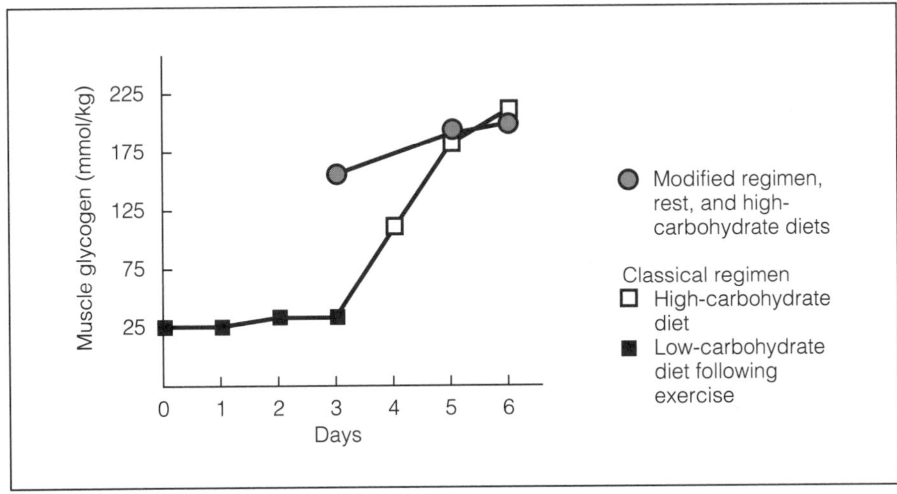

Figure 25-4. Comparison of two methods for carbohydrate loading. (Sherman, Costill, Fink, & Miller, 1981)

final three days. The subjects simply increased their carbohydrate intake for three days with the modified regimen. You can see that the total amount of glycogen stored in the muscles was the same with the modified plan as with the classical plan.

One way to tell if swimmers are getting a carbohydrate loading effect is by weighing them each day during the rest period. If they gain two to four pounds in just a few days, you can be sure that additional amounts of glycogen are being stored in their muscles. Large amounts of water are stored with glycogen in the muscles at a ratio of three grams of water for each gram of glycogen. Hence, a sudden weight increase over one to three days means that carbohydrate loading has taken place.

The practice of carbohydrate loading may have little or no value for swimming competition, even though it provides more muscle glycogen. Although studies have consistently shown improvements in events requiring more than 60 minutes (Bergstrom, Hermansen, Hultman, & Saltin, 1967; Wilson & Cureton, 1984), no decrements in performance have been reported in events of shorter duration unless muscle glycogen supplies were low before the competition began (Jacobs, Kaiser, & Tesch, 1982; Wooton & Williams, 1984). In the study by Jacobs and associates, decrements were not reported until 50 percent of the fibers in muscles were depleted of their glycogen content.

The longest swimming event requires only 14 to 20 minutes, and most events take 5 minutes or less to complete. Although individual fibers within muscles can be depleted in as little as 5 minutes, the speed required to do so is well beyond that which could be maintained in these races. Consequently, it is doubtful that athletes could completely empty any muscle fibers in competitive swimming events, with the possible exception of the 1,500-m and 1,650-yd freestyles. The possibility of depletion occurring in shorter events is only imminent when swimmers enter a competition with muscles that are already partially depleted of glycogen from previous events or from training.

Although carbohydrate loading may not be necessary, it would be a prudent precautionary measure for swimmers to enter important competitions with their muscles' glycogen supply replenished to at least normal levels. Then, there would be no chance that partial glycogen depletion could hurt their efforts. Therefore, the ingestion of high-carbohydrate meals for 3 or 4 days prior to competition is recommended.

BODY FAT: STOP WORRYING ABOUT IT

There has been a huge interest shown in measuring the body composition of swimmers since the early 1980s. The belief has been that increasing the muscle tissue of men and reducing the body fat of women would help each sex swim faster. There is considerable truth to the first part of this statement, but very little to the last.

It is doubtful that swimmers who are training for two hours or more each day would be carrying excess fat on their body. Their daily caloric expenditure is so large that they undoubtedly use all of the calories they consume to replace their energy supply and repair tissues. In fact, the caloric demands of training are usually so great that the major problem is *preventing* weight loss. Therefore, dieting during training will more than likely reduce caloric intake below output and severely reduce a swimmer's capacity to perform.

Heredity is probably the major determinant of body fat. We inherit a certain body type from our parents and grandparents that includes a particular amount of fat. Although we can certainly increase this amount by eating too much food and exercising too little, we probably cannot reduce it beyond the hereditary minimum without serious consequences.

The average male carries approximately 15 percent of his body weight as fat. Three percent of that amount is known as essential fat, because it is needed to maintain normal life processes. Essential fat is stored in the brain, spinal cord, various organs, and cell membranes. We cannot rid our bodies of essential fat, nor should we attempt to do so by dieting.

The body fat of male swimmers is well below the average of 15 percent because of the extensive amount of training they do. Most world-class male swimmers carry between 6 and 10 percent of their weight as body fat, with heredity being the primary determinant of an individual swimmer's placement within this range. The body will not give up additional fat once it reaches its hereditary limit, except during severe starvation. When dieting results in low muscle glycogen and glucose supplies, athletes burn muscle tissue to reduce the loss of fat, which causes devastating consequences: they lose endurance and power, and their performance worsens considerably.

The average female carries between 24 and 25 percent of her body weight as fat. The amount of essential fat is considerably higher than that found in males. Some experts estimate the essential fat content of females at 12 percent (Behnke, 1969)—a figure that may be too high, because the body fat percentages of some female distance swimmers have been measured at 10 percent and below (Wilmore & Costill, 1988).

Estimates of body fat among world-class female swimmers have generally been between 15 and 20 percent (Heusner, 1985). It is important to understand that some swimmers may perform better at the high end of this range because of hereditary predispositions to store more body fat.

The time when we are most prone to mislabel female swimmers as overweight is when they go through puberty and accumulate additional body fat. There have been several reports of mature female swimmers being asked, or required, to reduce their body fat percentages to 16 percent *and below* simply because that was the low end of the range found among female Olympians. This practice is not recommended. There are some female swimmers who may appear overweight due to their hereditary predisposition to store more fat. It would be a mistake to ask these swimmers to lose weight, because many may already be energy-efficient. We have evidence that many female swimmers maintain a caloric intake that is below their output (van Erp-Baart et al., 1989a), so it is a good bet that many are already in a negative-energy balance. Consequently, special diets are not needed. In fact, most female swimmers should be encouraged to eat more.

We should stop using body composition measures to estimate the body fat percentages of female swimmers. It is a dangerous practice that can have dire consequences. One of the worst consequences of an overconcern with body weight is the surfacing of a latent tendency toward bulimia or anorexia nervosa, which are very serious eating and behavior disorders that can result in early death. See Chapter 14 for a more complete discussion of these topics. Body composition measures should only be used to estimate changes in muscle tissue. An increase in muscle tissue will provide more strength, which should increase power and swimming speed.

INCREASING MUSCLE TISSUE: THE KEY TO IMPROVED SWIMMING

Increasing muscle tissue should improve power and, consequently, swimming speed for members of both sexes, yet it may be more beneficial to females than males. Strength per kilogram is the same for both sexes and may even be greater for females in the leg muscles. Nevertheless, females generally have smaller amounts of muscle tissue than men, and this may be the single most important reason for the differences in speed between the two sexes. Consequently, female swimmers should work very hard to increase the size of their swimming muscles. Stager and colleagues (1984) found that the 100-yd freestyle times for a group of female swimmers were significantly related to their lean body weights. *There was no relationship between speed and body fat percentage.*

Female swimmers need to be encouraged to gain muscle tissue. They do not need to be concerned about getting too bulky. It requires considerable time and dedication to increase muscle tissue even a small amount, because muscles simply do not grow that fast. Females, as well as males, should understand that they cannot increase muscle size simply by exercising. Although the stimulation of heavy-resistance training and sprinting are required to encourage muscle growth, caloric intake also plays a role.

It requires 2,500 additional calories beyond those needed for maintenance and training to gain .5 kg (1 lb) of muscle (Smith, 1977). This additional caloric intake should be spread over one or two weeks at the rate of approximately 100 to 300 calories per day to provide time for muscle growth rather than the formation of additional fat. Consuming large amounts of food each day will only provide calories faster than they can be used to build muscle, and the additional amount will be deposited as fat.

Athletes should plan for a maximum gain of 1 kg of muscle tissue every few weeks. Most of the additional calories consumed during these periods should be in the form of foods that are high in complete proteins (containing all of the essential amino acids). High-protein supplements alone will not suffice; they may even produce a satiating effect that will reduce the number of calories that athletes eat every day.

The use of anabolic steroids for increasing muscle tissue is not recommended for both ethical and health reasons. Anabolic steroids are synthetic derivatives of the hormone testosterone, which has both anabolic and androgenic effects. The anabolic effect refers to the fact that they encourage muscle growth. The androgenic effect has to do with the development of male secondary sex characteristics. In females, these are the growth of unwanted facial hair and a deepening of the voice. In males, anabolic steroids can cause atrophy of the testicles, a reduced production of sperm, and prostate gland enlargement. For both sexes, there is increased risk for liver cancer, hepatitis, and coronary heart disease. There has also been recent evidence of weakened immune systems among body builders using anabolic steroids (Williams, 1989). Less severe but, nevertheless, unwanted symptoms are acne, baldness, and swelling due to excess storage of body water. Some of these symptoms are irreversible in females.

Human growth hormone has been used as a substitute for anabolic steroids because it is not as easily detected during drug testing at competition sites and because it is believed to be safer. This hormone is secreted by the pituitary gland and aids in the growth and development of body tissue. Although there is very little information about any potentially harmful side effects of human growth hormone, it is known that excess production by the pituitary causes acromegaly—a condition marked by a progressive enlargement of the face, hands, and feet.

Human growth hormone was originally synthesized for use by children whose pituitary glands did not produce sufficient amounts of growth hormone. Unfortunately, its use by body builders and athletes has reduced its supply and has driven the price so high that it is no longer readily available or affordable for bona fide medical purposes. The use of human growth hormone for muscle building is not recommended for ethical reasons and because the potential dangers of its use have not been adequately investigated.

THE DANGER OF DIETING DURING HARD TRAINING

When swimmers diet during training, they run the risk of depleting muscle glycogen supplies, which will cause them to metabolize additional protein (Lemon & Mullin, 1980). At the very least, this may cause some swimmers to lose significant amounts of muscle tissue, with concomitant reductions in strength and endurance.

Unfortunately, there will always be swimmers who report for training in an overweight condition. They face the difficult task of training hard, improving their performance, and losing fat, all at the same time. There is no way they can accomplish the first two if they diet. Luckily, it is possible for swimmers to lose a sufficient amount of weight without reducing their caloric intake below their daily expenditure. If they are patient, the training-induced need for muscle hypertrophy will cause some of the foods they eat to be used for this purpose, and the additional energy that is needed for training will be supplied by stored fat. Consequently, body composition should return to normal training levels within four to eight weeks without dieting if a swimmer is willing to wait it out.

Swimmers should make every effort to maintain their in-training body composition during breaks from training and enforced absences. Engaging in some maintenance activity is recommended in order to prevent muscle atrophy and the resulting loss of power. Swimmers should be sure to start the season within 1 to 3 kg (2 to 6 lb) of their usual training weight. When weight gains do occur in the off-season, they should diet before the regular season begins so that they can report for training within the recommended 1 to 3 kg of their ideal body weight.

Females should consider running, cycling, or low-impact aerobics during the off-season as methods for preventing gains in fat weight or for reducing fat after breaks in training. For some unexplained reason, land activities seem to prevent greater gains and cause greater losses of fat weight than water training of similar duration and intensity.

During breaks in training, swimmers should reduce their caloric intake to match their lowered caloric expenditure, and they should exercise to maintain muscular hypertrophy. Weight training would be good for this purpose, but participation in other sports and games will also suffice.

Swimmers should also reduce their caloric intake drastically when they are laid up with an illness or injury, and they should perform some type of resistance exercise for unaffected body parts. Isometric exercises will work if other methods cannot be used.

ERGOGENIC AIDS

Ergogenic aids are substances that can improve work output simply by ingesting them. Some are chemicals, and others are foods. They can be administered in pill and liquid form and, in one case, as a gas. A large variety have been used by athletes over the years. Most of these have no value. Some have caused athletes considerable discomfort, and others have even been life threatening. However, there are a few that may actually improve performance under certain circumstances. Some of the more common ergogenic aids are discussed in the following sections.

Amphetamines

These are prescription drugs that stimulate the central nervous system. They are used most commonly as appetite suppressants by members of the general population. Athletes have used them to combat fatigue and improve endurance. They are referred to as *pep pills, uppers, bennies, greenies,* and *dexies,* to name a few terms.

Amphetamines seem to reduce sensations of fatigue and, in doing so, may reduce the inhibiting effects of pain that limit some athletes. Several studies have reported improvements in endurance, strength, and reaction time with their use; however, it has never been clear whether these effects were due to improved physiological mechanisms or to the power of suggestion. In many studies, the ergogenic effect was greater with poorly trained athletes, whereas well-trained athletes did not necessarily perform better (Ivy, 1983).

The potential dangers of amphetamines outweigh their possible benefits. Serious injuries and even deaths have occurred when athletes pushed themselves beyond normal exhaustion under the influence of amphetamines. This was probably because the amphetamines did not improve physiological capacity; instead, they probably masked the sensations of fatigue. Amphetamines can be toxic when taken in too large quantities, and they can also be addictive.

Ephedrine

This substance was once used in prescription form by many asthmatic sufferers. Today, its use has been banned in competition because of its stimulant properties. It operates much like amphetamines and may improve performance for the same reasons.

Caffeine

Caffeine is a stimulant with a much weaker effect than that of amphetamines. Nevertheless, excessive use has been banned for major competitions because of its possible ergogenic properties. The upper limit for allowable competition is 15 micrograms per milliliter of urine. This would be the equivalent of five or six cups of coffee taken over a short time.

One of the major ergogenic effects of caffeine concerns fat metabolism. It stimulates the release of fatty acids so that more can be used for energy. This, in turn, reduces the rate of muscle glycogen depletion and has been found in some studies to improve performance for long-distance events. However, all of the events in these studies were far in excess of the longest swimming event. Consequently, it is doubtful that swimmers experience any ergogenic effect from drinking coffee or ingesting other substances that contain caffeine before competing.

Oxygen

Regardless of the number of football and basketball players you may have seen inhaling pure oxygen on the sidelines during games, this practice does not improve their ability to perform. Inhaling pure oxygen before competition gained popularity during the 1936 Olympic Games, when the Japanese swimmers, who swept every event but one, inhaled oxygen before their races. This set off a flurry of research on the ergogenic effects of oxygen, and early studies were nearly unanimous in reporting improvements of performance. It was later found, however, that these improvements resulted from placebo effects when one clever scientist switched the labels on tanks of air and oxygen so that subjects who thought they were breathing pure oxygen were only breathing normal room air from a tank. Their performances improved just as much as when they were actually breathing pure oxygen (Wilmore, 1972).

Oxygen cannot be stored in the body before competition and used after the race has begun. Any oxygen that is inhaled prior to a competition is usually exhaled before the race begins or shortly thereafter. Breathing pure oxygen immediately after races is another unnecessary practice, because it does not improve recovery time. The content of oxygen in normal room air is sufficient to completely saturate the blood; thus, no greater concentration is needed either before or after races.

The only situation in which breathing pure oxygen could actually benefit performance would be during the race itself. Saturation is not always maximum when large amounts of air are being moved in and out of the body quickly during competition; therefore, a greater concentration of oxygen would provide a greater driving force and push more of this gas into the blood and carry it to the muscles.

This matter is academic, however. It is obviously not possible for swimmers to compete with a tank of oxygen on their back or to stop at each turn to inhale oxygen from a stationary tank.

Bee Pollen, Honey, and Tiger's Milk

There is no factual basis for the supposed ergogenic properties of these substances. Bee pollen became popular when the results of one very poorly controlled study with track athletes was used by advertisers to demonstrate its effectiveness. Ergogenic benefits were not reported in a number of later studies, however (Chandler, 1985).

Bee pollen is a mixture of various vitamins, minerals, amino acids, and other organic compounds. As such, it could be used as a vitamin-mineral supplement or perhaps as an additional source of protein, but nothing more.

Honey and tiger's milk contain carbohydrates. Consuming them before competition may benefit athletes in long events, during which high levels of blood glucose can supplement muscle glycogen. However, they should not be any more effective than other foods that are high in carbohydrates. Because all competitive swimming races are relatively short, swimmers with substantial amounts of glycogen stored in their muscles will not derive any benefit from using these substances before races.

Octacosanol

This is an ingredient of wheat germ oil. Many persons believed it was octacosanol rather than vitamin E that improved endurance in the early studies by Cureton (1955) that recommended wheat germ oil as a performance enhancer. It is doubtful that either substance was ergogenic, however. Williams (1989) concluded that using octacosanol and wheat germ oil as dietary supplements did not improve performance after reviewing over 35 studies in which they were administered.

Vitamin B_{15}

This substance is really not a vitamin because it has no known function in humans. What is known as vitamin B_{15} is really calcium pangamate—an amino acid. Its supposed ergogenic properties are doubtful because they were inferred from questionable research with rats.

Aspartates

Aspartic acid is an amino acid that forms one of the links between carbohydrate and protein metabolism. In this role, it provides a means for reducing lactic acid production by providing another avenue for the removal of pyruvic acid. The ergogenic value of this substance is based on early research that suggested that it relieved fatigue in older persons when taken in combination with potassium and magnesium. Some studies with rats (Rosen, Blumenthal, & Agersborg, 1962) and humans (Fallis, Wilson, Tetreault, & La Sagna, 1963) showed improved performances in aerobic and anaerobic endurance, but others could not duplicate these results (Consolazio, Nelson, Matoush, & Isaac, 1964).

Interest in research with aspartic acid waned for several years after the study by Consolazio and associates. Recently, however, a study with trained athletes showed that performance time to exhaustion improved by 12 minutes by ingesting 10 mg of potassium-magnesium aspartate over a 24-hour period prior to being tested (Wesson, McNaughton, Davies, & Tristam, 1988). More research needs to be done before the ergogenic properties of aspartates can be substantiated. However, they may be beneficial, and, most importantly, they are not banned substances.

Aspartates are considered foods, not drugs. Consequently, the decision to use them is an ethical one. There is no danger with sensible doses, although there have been some incidences of digestive upset reported.

Soda Loading

This is another ergogenic aid that may be beneficial. At present, however, the results of studies have been equivocal as to its effect on performance.

Soda loading involves ingesting a bicarbonate of soda solution before competition. The rationale for this practice is as follows: Soda is alkaline, so consuming it before an event will increase the pH of the blood. If the pH of the blood becomes greater than that of the muscles, more lactic acid will be caused to leave the muscles. With less lactic acid accumulating in the muscles, athletes will be able to sustain a higher rate of anaerobic metabolism without a large drop in pH.

This rationale appears to have some basis in fact. Most of the studies in which performance improved by soda loading showed that blood pH was, indeed, increased by this practice. They also showed that the amount of blood lactic acid was higher after maximum efforts than it was during control trials. Improvements were in the range of 2 to 3 percent over periods of one to nine minutes (Pate, Smith, Lambert, & Rocchio, 1985; Pfefferle & Wilkinson, 1988).

The ergogenic effects of alkaline substances, if they occur, probably have little effect on events of 100 m and less because there is not enough time for a significant amount of lactic acid to get out of the muscles during the length of time required to complete these races. The major benefits should be realized during events of 200 yd/m to 400 m and 500 yd.

Another interesting aspect of soda loading has been its effect on recovery and subsequent efforts. Horswill and colleagues (1988) had ten swimmers perform five 100-yd swims on a two-minute rest interval after soda loading and during normal, unloaded conditions. Improvements were noted after soda loading, but only on the fourth and fifth swims. Times were approximately 0.75 second faster on the last two swims for the group that used soda loading. Their times were similar to those of the control group on the first three swims. Blood lactate and pH were higher after each of the five swims as well, suggesting that lactic acid was getting out of the muscles faster during the rest periods between time trials. Knowles and coworkers (1989) reported similar results with a group of adolescent swimmers who performed a comparable repeat set.

Any beneficial effect on performance that may result from soda loading depends on using the proper dosage and administering it sufficiently in advance of the competition to provide time for the soda to get into the blood. An adequate dose is between 200 and 300 milligrams of sodium bicarbonate (baking soda) per kilogram of body weight. This amounts to approximately 15 to 16 g for women and 20 to 21 g for most men. Three or 4 teaspoons of baking soda mixed with a large glass of water or juice will supply this amount. It should be taken 1 to 1½ hours before competition.

There are some negative aspects of soda loading. It causes diarrhea in some persons, and it can also produce alkalosis if the doses are too great. The symptoms of alkalosis are pain, a feeling of weakness and, possibly, muscle spasms. An alternative method for soda loading is to eat foods that are high in alkalinity before competition. Fruits and fruit juices are good for this purpose.

Phosphate Loading

Phosphorus has been suggested as an alternative to soda loading because it is alkaline and because it is related to the enzymes and high-energy substances stored in muscles. Furthermore, it is essential for the optimal functioning of several B-complex vitamins. Phosphate loading is believed to improve endurance performance by increasing oxygen consumption during exercise through its effect on the B-complex vitamins.

Unlike soda loading, it is recommended that phosphates be administered over several days prior to competition. Some persons have even suggested that phosphate be provided as a daily supplement. One commercial phosphate product—*Stim-o-stam*—has been produced for use as a supplement.

A recent study reported an increase of both $\dot{V}O_2$max and work performed at the anaerobic threshold when supplements of 1,000 mg of sodium tribasic phosphate were administered four times per day for six days. Times for a 5-mile run were reduced by an average of 12 seconds (Miller, Kreider, & Williams, 1989). Several other studies have failed to verify the ergogenic properties of this substance, however (Williams, 1989). At present, the findings on phosphate loading, like those of soda loading, are inconclusive.

Carnitine

Carnitine is an organic compound produced in the body. It functions as part of the enzyme carnitine palmityl transferase, which is involved in the release of fatty acids so that they can enter Krebs cycle and be used for energy. The major effect of using this substance is believed to be an increased consumption of fat during training and long-distance races so that muscle glycogen is spared for later use.

The ergogenic properties of carnitine appear doubtful, in spite of its popularity. In well-controlled studies in which placebo effects were monitored, supplementation with this substance did not reduce blood lactate levels or increase the amount of energy derived from fat during long work efforts (Williams, 1989).

Dihydroxyacetone and Pyruvate (DHAP)

This substance is involved in glycogen storage, so it has been suggested that supplementation might improve the glycogen supply in muscles. Although research on this is too sparse to form an opinion concerning its ergogenic properties, daily supplements totaling 400 calories improved time to exhaustion from 66 to 79 minutes after seven days in one study (Stanko et al., 1989).

Alcohol, Drugs, and Tobacco

Despite some reports to the contrary, all of these substances can have detrimental effects on performance. The fact that all are potentially addictive should be reason enough to eliminate their use. Addictions can have horrifying effects, including loss of family, friends, livelihood, health, and sanity.

Alcohol The moderate use of alcohol should not affect performance if consumed well in advance of training or competition. Alcohol can be metabolized and, thus, eliminated from the body after several hours. It has no known ergogenic properties, however, and it can be detrimental if used immediately before contests. The belief that a beer before competition will relax athletes is a myth. A small amount of alcohol will not reduce anxiety, and large amounts will override concentration and motor coordination.

Although each of us has a different degree of tolerance to the inebriating effects of alcohol, some studies have reported that the alcohol in one mixed drink or a glass of beer slows reaction time and impairs judgment in a large percentage of the population and that hangovers, even 24 hours later, can cause visual disturbances, loss of coordination, intestinal upset, and impaired judgment (Williams, 1989).

Dehydration can also be a problem after alcohol use. Alcohol acts as a diuretic and causes frequent urination, which can result in a temporary water and electrolyte imbalance when used in excessive amounts. Dehydration may also occur when persons experience diarrhea and vomiting after excessive alcohol consumption.

Alcohol is the number one drug problem in the United States and in many other countries. Although moderate amounts pose no problem for most, a small but significant number of people are prone to addiction, including children and teenagers. Once addicted, the need for alcohol supersedes almost all other aspects of their lives. Their performances suffer in the pool as well as in school and in their various occupations. Their diets usually suffer, and they develop a number of deficiencies, which can lead to impaired brain function and the appearance of several diseases. The chance of becoming seriously injured or of injuring others is always increased when people drive while inebriated. For these reasons, more than its effect on performance, the use of alcohol cannot be recommended for athletes.

Drugs Research has shown that smoking marijuana immediately before competition reduces endurance and impairs motor coordination and judgment. Likewise, cocaine and crack cocaine will not benefit performance and may impair it if used immediately before training or competition for the same reasons.

Bracken and associates (1988) reported that rats became exhausted quicker while running when they were given cocaine (20 milligrams per kilogram of body weight) 20 minutes before exercise. In a later study (Bracken, Bracken, Winder, & Conlee, 1989), these same researchers showed that glycogen depletion was more severe in the fast-twitch muscles of rats receiving cocaine as compared to a control group that performed the same exercise. Blood lactate values for the rats receiving cocaine were, on the average, 10.5 mmol/l, yet the same work produced an average value of only 2.4 mmol/l in members of a control group.

Even the occasional use of cocaine, marijuana, and other drugs should not be condoned, for athletes or anyone else, because of their addictive effects. Addictions can develop rapidly and have the same detrimental effects and consequences as those of excessive alcohol use.

Tobacco Smoking cigarettes increases resistance to breathing and decreases oxygen consumption. Because most smokers are addicted to nicotine, they are never very long between cigarettes. Consequently, smokers undoubtedly experience these effects during competition. Fortunately, the number of smokers has declined significantly in the last few years, so very few athletes still indulge this habit.

Unfortunately, some athletes have switched to smokeless tobacco (or chewing tobacco) to reduce the effect of nicotine on their airway resistance and oxygen supply. Some baseball players even believe that it improves their reaction times. There is no evidence of this. In addition, there are tremendous health risks associated with the use of smokeless tobacco, including cancer of the mouth and throat. Chewing tobacco is a practice that should definitely be discouraged.

References

Part I

Adams, W. C., Bernauer, E. M., Dill, D. B., & Bomar, J. B., Jr. (1975). Effect of equivalent sea-level and altitude training on $\dot{V}O_2$max and running performance. *Journal of Applied Physiology, 39*(2), 262–266.

Aftergood, L., & Alfin-Slater, R. B. (1980). Women and nutrition. *Contemporary Nutrition*. [Booklet]. *5*(3). General Mills, Inc.

Afrasiabi, R., & Spector, S. L. (1991). Exercise-induced asthma. *Physician and Sportsmedicine, 19*(5), 49–62.

Ahlborg, G., Hagenfeldt, L., & Wahren, J. (1974). Influence of lactate infusion on glucose during prolonged exercise in man. *Journal of Clinical Investigation, 53,* 1080–1090.

Anderson, D. E., & Sharp, R. L. (1990). Effects of muscle glycogen depletion on protein catabolism during exercise. [Abstract]. *Medicine and Science in Sports and Exercise, 22*(2), S59.

Arcos, J. C., Sohal, R. S., Sun, S., Argus, M. F., & Burch, G. E. (1968). Changes in ultra structure and respiratory control in mitochondria of rat muscle hypertrophied by exercise. *Experimental and Molecular Biology, 8,* 49–65.

Astrand, P. O., & Rodahl, K. (1977). *Textbook of Work Physiology.* New York: McGraw-Hill.

Baker, E. R. (1981). Menstrual dysfunction and hormonal status in athletic women: a review. *Fertility and Sterility, 36,* 691–696.

Baldwin, K. M., Klinkerfuss, G. H., Terjung, R. L., Mole, P. A., & Holloszy, J. O. (1972). Respiratory capacity of white, red and intermediate muscle: adaptive response to exercise. *American Journal of Physiology, 222,* 373–378.

Baldwin, K. M., Winder, W. W., Terjung, R. L., & Holloszy, J. O. (1973). Glycolytic enzymes in red, white and intermediate skeletal muscle: adaptation to exercise. *American Journal of Physiology, 225,* 962–966.

Balke, B. (1964). Work capacity and its limiting factors at high altitude. In *Physiological Effects of High Altitude* (pp. 223–247). New York: Macmillan.

Balke, B. (1973) The development of higher oxygen intake through training. In J. Keul (Ed.), *Limiting Factors of Physical Performance* (pp. 267–280). Stuttgart, Germany: Georg Thieme Verlag.

Balke, B., Nagle, F. J., & Daniels, J. T. (1965). Altitude and maximum performance in work and sport activity. *Journal of American Medical Association, 194,* 646–649.

Ballard, F. J., & Tomas, F. M. (1983). 3-Methylhistadine as a measure of skeletal muscle protein breakdown in human subjects: the case for its continued use. *Clinical Science, 65,* 209–215.

Bannister, E. W., & Woo, W. (1978). Effects of simulated altitude training on aerobic and anaerobic power. *European Journal of Applied Physiology, 38,* 55–69.

Bar-Or, O. (1985). Some notes on physiological and medical considerations for exercise and training of children. In R. A. Binkhorst, H. C. G. Kemper, & W. H. M. Saris (Eds.), *International Series on Sport Sciences: Vol. 15. Children and Exercise XI* (pp. 346–353). Champaign, IL: Human Kinetics.

Bar-Or, O. (1989). Trainability of the prepubescent child. *Physician and Sportsmedicine, 17*(5), 65–82.

Belcastro, A. N., & Bonen, A. (1975). Lactic acid removal rates during controlled and uncontrolled recovery exercise. *Journal of Applied Physiology, 39,* 932–937.

Bell, R. D., MacDougall, J. D., Billeter, R., & Howald, H. (1980). Muscle fiber types and morphometric analysis of skeletal muscle in six-year-old children. *Medicine and Science in Sports and Exercise, 12*(1), 28–31.

Bellew, K. M., Burke, E. J., & Jensen, B. E. (1983). Ratings of perceived exertion at anaerobic threshold in males and females. [Abstract]. In *Abstracts of Research Papers,* p. 10. Reston, VA: AAHPERD.

Beltz, J. D., Costill, D. L., Thomas, R., Fink, W. J., & Kirwan, J. P. (1988). Energy demands of interval training for competitive swimming. *Journal of Swimming Research, 4*(3), 5–9.

Benton, J. W. (1983). Epiphyseal fractures in sports. *Physician and Sportsmedicine, 10,* 63–71.

Bergstrom, J., Hermansen, L., Hultman, D., & Saltin, B. (1967). Diet, muscle glycogen and physical performance. *Acta Physiologica Scandinavica, 71,* 140–150.

Beunen, G., & Malina, R. M. (1988). Growth and physical performance relative to the timing of the adolescent spurt. In K. B. Pandolf (Ed.), *Exercise and Sports Sciences Reviews* (Vol. 16, pp. 503–540). New York: Macmillan.

Bird, S. (1988). Modifying cruise intervals for high school swimmers. In J. Leonard (Ed.), *ASCA Twentieth Annual World Clinic Yearbook* (pp. 139–144). Ft. Lauderdale: American Swimming Coaches Association.

Blimpkie, C., Ramsay, J., Sale, D., MacDougall, J., Smith, K., & Garner, S. (1988). Resistance training, muscle morphology and contractile properties in prepubertal boys. [Abstract]. *Medicine and Science in Sports and Exercise, 20*(2), S9.

Bompa, T. O. (1983). *Theory and Methodology of Training*. Dubuque, IA: Kendall/Hunt.

Bond, V., Adams, R., Gresham, K., Tearney, R., Capraroia, M., Ruff, W., Gregory, H., & Stoddard, A. (1987). Effects of active and passive recovery on lactic acid removal and subsequent muscle function. [Abstract]. *Medicine and Science in Sports and Exercise, 19*(2), S35.

Bonen, A., McDermott, J. C., & Hutber, C. A. (1989). Carbohydrate metabolism in skeletal muscle: an update of current concepts. *International Journal of Sports Medicine, 6*(10), 385–401.

Booth, F. W., & Holloszy, J. O. (1977). Cytochrome c turnover in rat skeletal muscle. *Journal of Biological Chemistry, 252,* 416–419.

Bovens, A. P. M., Keizer, H. A., & Kuipers, H. (1985). Muscle glycogen synthesis in dependence of liquid and solid meals. [Abstract]. *Medicine and Science in Sports and Exercise, 17*(2), 205.

Bower, D. (1985). Cruise intervals—further applications. In T. F. Welsh (Ed.), *1985 ASCA World Clinic Yearbook* (pp. 131–140). Fort Lauderdale: American Swimming Coaches Association.

Brady, T. A., Cahill, B., & Bodnar, L. (1982). Weight training related injuries. *American Journal of Sports Medicine, 10,* 1–5.

Brodal, P., Ingjer, F., & Hermansen, L. (1976). Capillary supply of skeletal muscle fibers in untrained and endurance trained men. *Acta Physiologica Scandinavica, (Suppl. 440),* 178, 296.

Brooke, M. H., & Kaiser, K. K. (1970). Muscle fiber types: how many and what kinds. *Archives of Neurology, 23,* 369–379.

Brooks, G. A. (1986). The lactate shuttle during exercise and recovery. *Medicine and Science in Sports and Exercise, 18*(3), 360–368.

Brooks, G. A. (1987). Amino acid and protein metabolism during exercise, and recovery. *Medicine and Science in Sports and Exercise, 19*(5), S150–156.

Brooks, G. A., & Fahey, T. D. (1984). *Exercise Physiology: Human Bioenergetics and Its Applications.* New York: John Wiley.

Brooks, G. A., & Roth, D. A. (1989). Characteristics of the lactate transporter in muscle. [Abstract]. *Medicine and Science in Sports and Exercise, 21*(2), S35.

Brooks, S. M., Sanborn, C. F., Albrecht, B. H., & Wagner, W. W., Jr. (1984). Athletic amenorrhea: the role of diet. [Abstract]. *Medicine and Science in Sports and Exercise, 16*(2), S117.

Brown, A. G., McCartney, N., Moroz, D., Sale, D. G., Garner, S. A., & MacDougall, J. D.

(1988). Strength training effects in aging. [Abstract]. *Medicine and Science in Sports and Exercise, 20*(2), S80.

Brynteson, P., & Sinning, W. E. (1973). The effects of training frequencies on the retention of cardiovascular fitness. *Medicine and Science in Sports and Exercise, 5,* 29–33.

Bunc, V., Heller, J., Sprynarova, S., & Zdanowicz, R. (1986). Comparison of the anaerobic threshold and mechanical efficiency of running in young and adult athletes. *International Journal of Sports Medicine, 7*(3), 156–160.

Buskirk, E. R., Kollias, J., Akers, R. F., Prokop, E. K., & Reategui, E. P. (1967). Maximal performance at altitude and on return from altitude in conditioned runners. *Journal of Applied Physiology, 23,* 259–266.

Busse, M. W., Maassen, N., & Boning, D. (1987). The work load-lactate-curve: measure of endurance capacity or criterion of muscle glycogen storage? [Abstract]. *International Journal of Sports Medicine, 8*(2), 140.

Campbell, C. J., Bonen, A., Kirby, R. L., & Belcastro, A. N. (1979). Muscle fiber composition and performance capacities of women. *Medicine and Science in Sports and Exercise, 11*(3), 260–265.

Cann, C. E., Martin, M. C., Genant, H. K., & Jaffe, R. B. (1984). Decreased spinal mineral content in amenorrheic women. *Journal of American Medical Association, 251,* 626–629.

Carlile, F. (1966). *Forbes Carlile on Swimming*. London: Pelham.

Carlile, F., & Carlile, U. (1978). *New Directions in Scientific Training*. Sydney, Australia: Authors.

Carrow, R., Brown, R., & Van Huss, W. (1967). Fiber sizes and capillary to fiber ratios in skeletal muscles of exercised rats. *Anatomical Record, 159,* 33–38.

Cazorla, G., Dufort, C., Montpetit, R. R., & Cevetti, J. P. (1983). The influence of active recovery on blood lactate disappearance after supramaximal swimming. In A. P. Hollander, P. A. Huijing, & G. de Groot (Eds.), *International Series on Sport Sciences: Vol. 14. Biomechanics and Medicine in Swimming* (pp. 244–250). Champaign, IL: Human Kinetics.

Cellini, M., Vitiello, P., Nagliati, A., Ziglio, P. G., Martinelli, S., Ballarin, E., & Conconi, F. (1986). Noninvasive determination of the anaerobic threshold in swimming. *International Journal of Sports Medicine, 7*(6), 347–351.

Chance, B., Sapega, A., Sokolov, D., Eleff, S., Leigh, J. S., Graham, T., Armstrong, J., & Warnell, R. (1983). Fatigue in retrospect and prospect: $^{31}{}_{P}$NMR studies of exercise performance. In H. G. Knuttgen, J. A. Vogel, & J. Poortmans, *International Series on Sport Sciences: Vol. 13. Biochemistry of Exercise* (pp. 895–908). Champaign, IL: Human Kinetics.

Cheetham, M. E., Boobis, L. H., Brooks, S., & Williams, C. (1986). Human muscle metabolism during sprint running. *Journal of Applied Physiology, 6*(1), 54–60.

Clausen, J. P. (1973). Muscle blood flow during exercise and its significance for maximal performance. In J. Keul (Ed.), *Limiting Factors of Physical Performance* (pp. 253–265). Stuttgart, Germany: Georg Thieme Verlag.

Clausen, J. P., Klausen, K., Rasmussen, B., & Trap-Jensen, J. (1971). Effect of selective arm and leg training on cardiac output and regional blood flow. *Acta Physiologica Scandinavica, 82,* 35–36a.

Clement, D., Taunton, J., McKenzie, D., Lyster, D., Wiley, J., & Sawchuck, L. (1984). Iron absorption in iron-deficient endurance trained females. [Abstract]. *Medicine and Science in Sports and Exercise, 16*(2), 164.

Clement, L. M., Jenkins, R. R., Ciccone, C. D., Frye, P. A., & Thomas, D. P. (1985). Effects of menstrual cycle phase on selected performance variables in athletes and non-athletes. [Abstract]. *Medicine and Science in Sports and Exercise, 17*(2), 208.

Coen, B., Urhausen, A., & Kindermann, W. (1988). Value of the Conconi test for determination of the anaerobic threshold. [Abstract]. *International Journal of Sports Medicine, 9*(5), 372.

Colgan, M. (1986). Effects of multinutrient supplementation on athletic performance. In F. I. Katch (Ed.), *Sport, Health and Nutrition* (pp. 21–50). Champaign, IL: Human Kinetics.

Conconi, F., Ferrari, M., Ziglio, P. G., Droghetti, P., & Codeca, L. (1982). Determination of the anaerobic threshold by a noninvasive field test in runners. *Journal of Applied Physiology, 52,* 869–873.

Consolazio, C. F., Matoushi, L. O., Nelson, R. A., Hardings, R. S., & Canham, J. E. (1963). Excretion of sodium, potassium, magnesium, and iron in human sweat and the relation of each to balance and requirements. *Journal of Nutrition, 79,* 407–415.

Cooter-Mowbray, A. (1978). Effects of iron supplementation and activity on serum iron depletion and hemoglobin levels in female athletes. *Research Quarterly, 49,* 114–117.

Costill, D. L. (1978). Adaptations in skeletal muscle during training for sprint and endurance swimming. In B. Eriksson & B. Furberg, (Eds.), *Swimming Medicine IV* (pp. 233–248). Baltimore: University Park Press.

Costill, D. L. (1986). *Inside Running: Basics of Sports Physiology.* Indianapolis: Benchmark Press.

Costill, D. L., Bowers, R., Branam, G., & Sparks, K. (1971). Muscle glycogen utilization during prolonged exercise on successive days. *Journal of Applied Physiology, 31,* 834–838.

Costill, D. L., Daniels, J., Evans, W., Fink, W. J., Krahenbuhl, G., & Saltin, B. (1976). Skeletal muscle enzymes and fiber composition of male and female track athletes. *Journal of Applied Physiology, 40,* 149–153.

Costill, D. L., Fink, W. J., Getchell, L. H., Ivy, J. L., & Witzman, F. A. (1979). Lipid metabolism in skeletal muscle of endurance-trained males and females. *Journal of Applied Physiology, 47,* 787–791.

Costill, D. L., Fink, W. J., Hargreaves, M., King, D. S., & Thomas, R. (1985). Metabolic characteristics of skeletal muscles during detraining from competitive swimming. *Medicine and Science in Sports and Exercise, 17*(3), 339–343.

Costill, D. L., Fink, W. J., & Pollock, M. (1976). Muscle fiber composition and enzyme activities of elite distance runners. *Medicine and Science in Sports and Exercise, 8,* 96–100.

Costill, D. L., Flynn, M. G., Kirwan, J. P., Houmard, J. A., Mitchell, J. B., Thomas, R., & Park, S. H. (1988). Effects of repeated days of intensified training on muscle glycogen and swimming performance. *Medicine and Science in Sports and Exercise, 20*(3), 249–254.

Costill, D. L., Gollnick, P. D., Jansson, E., Saltin, B., & Stein, E. (1973). Glycogen depletion patterns in human muscle fibers during distance running. *Acta Physiologica Scandinavica, 89,* 374–383.

Costill, D. L., King, D. S., Thomas, R., & Hargreaves, M. (1985). Effects of reduced training on muscular power in swimmers. *Physician and Sportsmedicine, 13,* 94–101.

Costill, D. L., Maglischo, E. W., & Richardson, A. B. (1992). *Swimming.* Oxford, England: Blackwell Scientific Publications.

Costill, D. L., Sherman, W. M., Fink, W. J., Maresh, C., Witten, M., & Miller, J. M. (1981). The role of dietary carbohydrates in muscle glycogen resynthesis after strenuous running. *American Journal of Clinical Nutrition, 34,* 1831–1836.

Coyle, E. F., Martin, W. H., III, Bloomfield, S. A., Lowry, O. H., & Holloszy, J. O. (1985). Effects of detraining on responses to submaximal exercise. *Journal of Applied Physiology, 59*(3), 853–859.

Coyle, E. F., Martin, W. H., & Holloszy, J. O. (1983). Cardiovascular and metabolic rates of detraining. [Abstract]. *Medicine and Science in Sports and Exercise, 15,* 158.

Craig, A. B., Jr. (1978). Fallacies of hypoxic training in swimming. In J. Terauds & E. W. Bedingfield (Eds.) *International Series on Sport Sciences: Vol. 8. Swimming III* (pp. 235–239). Baltimore: University Park Press.

Craig, A. B. & Pendergast, D. R. (1979). Relationship of stroke rate, distance per stroke and velocity in competition swimming. *Medicine and Science in Sports and Exercise, 11,* 28–283.

Craig, A. B., Skehan, P. L., Pawelczyk, J. A., & Boomer, W. L. (1985). Velocity, stroke rate, and distance per stroke during elite swimming competition. *Medicine and Science in Sports and Exercise, 17*(6), 625–634.

Cumming, G. R., Hastman, L., McCort, J., & McCullough, S. (1980). High serum lactates do occur in young children after maximal work. *International Journal of Sports Medicine, 1,* 66–69.

Cunningham, D. A., & Faulkner, J. A. (1969). The effect of training on aerobic and anaerobic metabolism during a short exhaustive run. *Medicine and Science in Sports and Exercise, 1,* 65–69.

Cunningham, D. A., & Paterson, D. H. (1988). Physiological characteristics of young active boys. In E. W. Brown & C. F. Branta (Eds.), *Competitive Sports for Children and Youth: An Overview of Research and Issues* (pp. 159–169). Champaign, IL: Human Kinetics.

Cureton, K. J., Collins, M. A., Hill, D. W., & McElhannon, F. M., Jr. (1988). Muscle hypertrophy in men and women. *Medicine and Science in Sports and Exercise, 20*(4), 338–344.

Danforth, W. H. (1965). Activation of glycolytic pathway in muscle. In B. Chance & R. W. Estabrook, *Control of Energy Metabolism* (pp. 287–297). New York: Academic Press.

Daniels, J., Daniels, N., Rinehardt, K., & Nye, S. (1987). Effects of altitude exposure on female swimmers. [Abstract]. *Medicine and Science in Sports and Exercise, 19*(2), S65.

Daniels, J., & Oldridge, N. (1970). The effects of alternate exposure to altitude and sea level on world-class middle distance runners. *Medicine and Science in Sports and Exercise, 2*, 107–112.

Daniels, J., Troup, J., & Telander, T. (1989). The effects of altitude training on sea-level swimming performance. [Abstract]. In J. P. Troup (Ed.), *Winning Spirit: Instructional Series* (p. 92). Colorado: United States Swimming.

Darabos, B., Bulbulian, R., & Wilcox, A. R. (1984). Aerobic and anaerobic measures in distance running performance of trained athletes. [Abstract]. *Medicine and Science in Sports and Exercise, 16*(2), 177.

Davies, C. T. M., Knibbs, A. V., & Musgrove, J. (1970). The rate of lactic acid removal in relation to different baselines of recovery exercise. *Int. Z. Angew. Physiol. 28*, 155–161.

Davis, J. A., Frank, M. H., Whipp, B. J., & Wasserman, K. (1979). Anaerobic threshold alterations caused by endurance training in middle-aged men. *Journal of Applied Physiology, 46*(6), 1039–1046.

DeMello, J. J., Cureton, K. J., Boineau, R. E., & Singh, M. (1987). Ratings of perceived exertion at the lactate threshold in trained and untrained men and women. *Medicine and Science in Sports and Exercise, 19*(4), 354–362.

Denis, C., Fouquet, R., Poty, P., Geyssant, A., & Lacour, J. R. (1982). Effect of 40 weeks of endurance training on the anaerobic threshold. *International Journal of Sports Medicine, 3*(4), 208–214.

Dicker, S. G., Lofthus, G. K., Thornton, N. W., & Brooks, G. A. (1980). Respiratory and heart rate responses to tethered controlled frequency swimming. *Medicine and Science in Sports and Exercise, 12*, 20–23.

Dill, D. B., & Adams, W. C. (1971). Maximal oxygen uptake at sea level and at 3,090-m altitude in high school champion runners. *Journal of Applied Physiology, 30*, 854–859.

Dintiman, G. B. (1984). *How to Run Faster.* New York: Leisure Press.

Dintiman, G. B., & Ward, R. D. (1988). *Sport Speed*. Champaign, IL: Human Kinetics, Leisure Press.

DiVico, P., Simon, J., Lichtman, S., & Gutin, B. (1989). Objectivity and reliability of the lactate breakpoint. [Abstract]. *Medicine and Science in Sports and Exercise, 21*(2), S22.

Dohm, G. L., Israel, R. G., Breedlove, R. L., Williams, R. T., & Askew, E. W. (1985). Biphasic changes in 3-methylhistidine excretions in humans after exercise. *American Journal of Physiology, 248:* E588–E592.

Dohm, G. L., Williams, R. T., Kasperek, G. J., & van Rig, A. M. (1982). Increased excretion of urea and N^{τ}-methylhistidine by rats and humans after a bout of exercise. *Journal of Applied Physiology, 52*, 27–33.

Doll, E. (1973). Oxygen pressure and content in the blood during physical exercise and hypoxia. In J. Keul (Ed.), *Limiting Factors of Physical Performance* (pp. 201–211). Stuttgart, Germany: George Thieme Verlag.

Dominguez, R. H. (1980). Shoulder pain in swimmers. *Physician and Sports Medicine, 8*(7), 37–42.

Donovan, C. M., & Brooks, G. A. (1983). Endurance training affects lactate clearance, not lactate production. *American Journal of Physiology, Endocrinology and Metabolism, 7:* E83–E92.

Dressendorfer, R. H., Wade, C. E., & Schaff, J. H. (1985). Increased morning heart rate in runners: a valid sign of overtraining? *Physician and Sportsmedicine, 13*, 77–86.

Drinkwater, B. L. (1984a). Athletic amenorrhea: a review. *American Academy of Physical Education Papers, Exercise and Health, 17,* 120–131.

Drinkwater, B. L. (1984b). Women and exercise: physiological aspects. In R. L. Terjung (Ed.), *Exercise and Sport Sciences Reviews* (Vol. 12, pp. 21–51). MA: D. C. Heath and Co.

Drinkwater, B. L., & Horvath, S. M. (1972). Detraining in young women. *Medicine and Science in Sports and Exercise, 4,* 91–95.

Drinkwater, B. L., Nilson, K., Chestnut, C. H., III, Bremmer, W. J., Shainholtz, S., & Southworth, M. B. (1984). Bone mineral content of amenorrheic and eumenorrheic athletes. *The New England Journal of Medicine, 311,* 277–281.

Dudley, G. A., Abraham, W. M., & Terjung, R. L. (1982). Influence of exercise intensity and duration on biochemical adaptations in skeletal muscle. *Journal of Applied Physiology, 53*(4), 844–850.

Dudley, G. A., & Djamil, R. (1985). Incompatibility of endurance and strength training modes of exercise. [Abstract]. *Medicine and Science in Sports and Exercise, 17*(2), 184.

Dummer, G. M., Rosen, L. W., Heusner, W. W., Roberts, P. J., & Counsilman, J. E. (1987). Pathogenic weight-control behaviors of young competitive swimmers. *Physician and Sportsmedicine, 15*(5), 75–85.

duPlessis, M. P., Smit, P. J., duPlessis, L. A. S., Geyer, H. J., Mathews, G., & Louw, H. N. J. (1986). The composition of muscle fibers in a group of adolescents. In R. A. Binkhorst, H. C. G. Kemper, & W. H. M. Saris (Eds.) *International Series on Sport Sciences: Vol. 15. Children and Exercise XI* (pp. 323–328). Champaign, IL: Human Kinetics.

Eddy, D. O., Sparks, K. L., & Adelizi, D. A. (1977). The effects of continuous and interval training in women and men. *European Journal of Applied Physiology, 37,* 83–92.

Edington, D. W., & Edgerton, V. R. (1976). *The Biology of Physical Activity.* Boston: Houghton-Mifflin.

Eriksson, B. O., Golnick, P. D., & Saltin, B. (1973). Muscle metabolites and enzyme activities after training in boys 11–13 years old. *Acta Physiologica Scandinavica, 87,* 485–497.

Evans, W. J., Meredith, C. N., Frontera, W. R., Hughes, V. A., & Fisher, E. C. (1987). Effects of aerobic training in young and old subjects. [Abstract]. *Medicine and Science in Sports and Exercise, 19*(2), S45.

Farrell, P. A., Wilmore, J. H., Coyle, E. F., Billings, J. E., & Costill, D. L. (1979). Plasma lactate accumulation and distance running performance. *Medicine and Science in Sports and Exercise, 11,* 338–344.

Faulkner, J. A., Daniels, J. T., & Balke, B. (1967). Effects of training at moderate altitude on physical performance capacity. *Journal of Applied Physiology, 23,* 85–89.

Faulkner, J. A., Kollias, J., Favour, C. B., Buskirk, E. R., & Balke, B. (1968). Maximum aerobic capacity and running performance at altitude. *Journal of Applied Physiology, 24,* 685–691.

Favier, R. J., Constable, S. H., Chen, M., & Holloszy, J. O. (1986). Endurance training reduces lactate production. *Journal of Applied Physiology, 6,* 885–889.

Feicht, C. B., Johnson, T. S., Martin, B. J., Sparks, K. E., & Wagner, W. W., Jr. (1978). Secondary amenorrhea in athletes. *Lancet, 2,* 1145–1146.

Felig, P., & Wahren, J. (1971). Amino acid metabolism in exercising man. *Journal of Clinical Investigation, 50,* 2703–2714.

Felig, P., & Wahren, J. (1975). Fuel homeostasis in exercise. *Physician and Sportsmedicine, 293*(21), 1078 — 1084.

Ferris, D., Pizza, F., Wygand, J., & Otto, R. M. (1989). Seasonal comparison of anaerobic and aerobic power outputs in United States swimming class 2A swimmers. [Abstract]. *Medicine and Science in Sports and Exercise, 21*(2), S104.

Firman, R., & Maglischo, E. W. (1986). Verification of Cruise Intervals. Unpublished data.

Fitts, R. H., Booth, F. W., Winder, W. W., & Holloszy, J. O. (1975). Skeletal muscle respiratory capacity, endurance, and glycogen utilization. *American Journal of Physiology, 228,* 1029–1033.

Fitts, R. H., Costill, D. L., & Gardetto, P. R. (1989). Effect of swim exercise training on human muscle fiber function. *Journal of Applied Physiology, 66*(1), 465–475.

Fox, E. L., & Mathews, D. K. (1981). *The Physiological Basis of Physical Education and Athletics*. Philadelphia: Saunders.

Fric, J., Jr., Fric, J., Boldt, F., Stoboy, H., Meller, W., Feldt, F., & Drygas, W. (1988). Reproducibility of post-exercise lactate and anaerobic threshold. *International Journal of Sports Medicine, 9*(5), 310–312.

Frisch, R. E., & McArthur, J. W. (1974). Menstrual cycles: fatness as a determinant of minimum weight for height necessary for their maintenance or onset. *Science, 185*, 949–951.

Frisch, R. E., & Revelle, R. (1971a). Height and weight at menarche and a hypothesis of critical body weights and adolescent events. *Science, 169*, 397–399.

Frisch, R. E., & Revelle, R. (1971b). Height and weight at menarche and a hypothesis of menarche. *Archives of Disease in Childhood, 46*, 695–701.

Frisch, R. E., & Revelle, R. (1971c). The height and weight of girls and boys at the time of initiation of the adolescent growth spurt in height and weight and relationship to menarche. *Human Biology, 43*, 140–159.

Frohlich, J., Urhausen, A., Seul, U., & Kindermann, W. (1988). Effect of low and high carbohydrate diet on lactate kinetics. [Abstract]. *International Journal of Sports Medicine, 9*(5), 361.

Frontera, W. R., Meredith, C. N., Reilly, K. O., Knuttgen, H., & Evans, W. J. (1987). Strength training in older men. [Abstract]. *Medicine and Science in Sports and Exercise, 19*(2), S44.

Gaesser, G. A., & Poole, D. C. (1988). Blood lactate during exercise: time course of training adaptation in humans. *International Journal of Sports Medicine, 9*(9), 284–288.

Gergley, T., McArdle, W., DeJesus, P., Toner, M., Jacobowitz, S., & Spina, P. (1984). Specificity of arm training on aerobic power during swimming and running. *Medicine and Science in Sports and Exercise, 16*(4), 349–354.

Glina, J. C., Caiozzo, V. J., Bielen, R. J., Prietto, C. A., & McMaster, W. C. (1984). Anaerobic threshold for leg cycling and arm cranking. [Abstract]. *Medicine and Science in Sports and Exercise, 16*(2), 109.

Goldspink, D. F., Garlick, P. J., & McNurian, M. A. (1983). Protein turnover measured in vivo and in vitro in muscles undergoing compensatory growth and subsequent denervation atrophy. *Biochemical Journal, 210*, 84–98.

Gollnick, P. D., Armstrong, R. B., Saltin, B., Saubert, C. W., IV, Sembrowich, W. L., & Shepherd, R. E. (1973). Effects of training on enzyme activity and fiber composition of human skeletal muscle. *Journal of Applied Physiology, 34*, 107–111.

Gollnick, P. D., Armstrong, R. B., Sembrowich, W. L., Shepard, W. L., & Saltin, B. (1973). Glycogen depletion patterns in human skeletal muscle fibers after heavy exercise. *Journal of Applied Physiology, 34*, 615–618.

Gollnick, P. D., & Hermansen, L. (1973). Biochemical adaptations to exercise: anaerobic metabolism. In J. Wilmore (Ed.), *Exercise and Sports Sciences Reviews, Vol. 1* (pp. 1–44). New York: Academic Press.

Gollnick, P. D., Parsons, D., Riedy, M., & Moore, R. L. (1983). Fiber number and size in overloaded chicken anterior latissimus dorsi muscle. *Journal of Applied Physiology, 54*, 1292–1297.

Gollnick, P. D., Timson, B. F., Moore, R. L., & Riedy, M. (1981). Muscular enlargement and number of fibers in skeletal muscles of rats. *Journal of Applied Physiology, 50*: 936–943.

Gong, Henry, Jr. (1992). Breathing easy: exercise despite asthma. *Physician and Sportsmedicine, 20*(3), 158–167.

Gonyea, W. J., Ericson, G. C., & Bonde-Peterson, F. (1977). Skeletal muscle fiber splitting induced by weight lifting exercise in cats. *Acta Physiologica Scandinavica, 19*, 105–109.

Gonyea, W. J., Sale, D. G., Gonyea, F. B., & Mikesky, A. (1986). Exercise induced increases in muscle fiber number. *European Journal of Applied Physiology, 55*, 137–141.

Good, V. (1973). *Effects of isokinetic exercise program on sprint swimming performance of college women*. Unpublished master's thesis, California State University, Chico.

Graves, J. M., Pollock, M., Leggett, S., Braith, R., & Carpenter, D. (1988). Effect of reduced training frequency on muscle strength. *International Journal of Sports Medicine, 9*(5), 316–319.

Green, H. J., Klug, G. A., Reichmann, H., Seedorf, U., Wiehrer, W., & Pette, D. (1984). Exercise-induced fibre transitions with regard to myosin, parvalbimin and sarcoplasmic reticulum in muscles of the rat. *Pflugers Archives 400,* 432–438.

Greipp, J. F. (1985). Swimmer's shoulder: the influence of flexibility and weight training. *Physician and Sportsmedicine, 13*(8), 92–106.

Griess, M., Teftbut, U., Braumann, K-M, Bosse, M. W., & Maassen, N. (1988). [Abstract]. A new method to determine the "Maxlass" workload. *International Journal of Sports Medicine, 9*(5), 379.

Grover, R. F., Weil, J. V., & Reeves, J. T. (1986). Cardiovascular adaptation to exercise at high altitude. In K. B. Pandolf (Ed.), *Exercise and Sports Sciences Reviews, Vol. 14* (pp. 269–302). New York: Macmillan.

Gullstrand, L. (1984). The use of science in improving swimming performance. In J. L. Cramer (Ed.), *How to Develop Olympic Level Swimmers,* pp. 63–69. Helsinki, Finland: International Sports Media.

Gullstrand, L. (1985). Tapering. In T. F. Welsh (Ed.), *ASCA World Clinic Yearbook* (pp. 15–19). Fort Lauderdale: American Swimming Coaches Association.

Gullstrand, L., & Holmer, I. (1983). Physiological characteristics of champion swimmers during a five-year follow-up period. In P. A. Huijing & G. de Groot (Eds.), *Biomechanics and Medicine in Swimming* (pp. 258–262). Champaign, IL: Human Kinetics.

Gumbs, V. L. (1982). Bilateral distal radius and ulnar fracture in weight-lifters. *American Journal of Sports Medicine, 10,* 375–379.

Guyton, A. C. (1964). *Textbook of Medical Physiology.* Philadelphia: Saunders.

Hagberg, J. M., Allen, W. K., Seals, D. R., Hurley, B. F., Ehsani, A. A., & Holloszy, J. O. (1985). A hemodynamic comparison of young and older endurance athletes during exercise. *Journal of Applied Physiology, 58*(6), 2041–2046.

Hagberg, J. M., & Coyle, E. R. (1983). Physiological determinants of endurance performance as studied in competitive racewalkers. *Medicine and Science in Sports and Exercise, 15,* 287–289.

Hagberg, J. M., Graves, J. E., Limacher, M., Woods, D. R., Leggett, S., Connie, C., Gruber, J., & Pollock, M. L. (1989). Cardiovascular responses of 70–79 year old men and women to endurance and strength training. [Abstract]. *Medicine and Science in Sports and Exercise, 21*(2), S95.

Hagerman, F. C., Hikida, R. S., Staron, R. S., Sherman, W. M., & Costill, D. L. (1984). Muscle damage in marathon runners. *Physician and Sportsmedicine, 12,* 39–48.

Hall-Jurkowski, J. E., Jones, N. L., Toews, C. J., & Sutton, J. R. (1981). Effects of menstrual cycle on blood lactate, O_2 delivery, and performance during exercise. *Journal of Applied Physiology, 51*(6), 1493–1499.

Hardman, A. E., & Williams, C. (1983). Single leg maximum oxygen uptake and endurance performance before and after short-term training. *International Journal of Sports Medicine, 5*(Suppl.), 122–123.

Harms, S. J., & Hickson, R. C. (1983). Skeletal muscle mitochondria and myoglobin, endurance, and intensity of training. *Journal of Applied Physiology, 54*(3), 798–802.

Harre, D. (Ed.). (1982). *Principles of Sports Training.* Berlin: Sportverlag.

Hasson, S. M., & Barnes, W. S. (1986). Peak power output and fatigue during brief bicycle ergometric exercise. [Abstract]. *Medicine and Science in Sports and Exercise, 18*(2), S7.

Hays, G. W., Davis, J. M., & Lamb, D. R. (1984). Increased pain tolerance in rats following strenuous exercise: effects of Nalonone. [Abstract]. *Medicine and Science in Sports and Exercise, 16*(2), 156.

Heck, H., Mader, A., Hess, G., Mucke, S., Miller, R., & Hollmann, W. (1985). Justification of the 4-mmol/l lactate threshold. *International Journal of Sports Medicine, 6*(3), 117–130.

Heck, H., Reinhards, G., Mader, A., & Hollmann, W. (1987). Maximal lactate steady state and anaerobic threshold in children. [Abstract]. *International Journal of Sports Medicine, 8*(2), 141–142.

Heck, H., Tiberi, M., Beckers, K., Lammerschmidt, W., Pruin, E., & Hollmann, W. (1988). Lactic acid concentration during bicycle-ergometer exercise with preselected percentages of the Conconi-threshold. [Abstract]. *International Journal of Sports Medicine, 9*(5), 367.

Heigenhauser, G. J. F., & Lindinger, M. T. (1986). Effects of hypoxia on exercise performance and skeletal muscle metabolism in swimming rats. [Abstract]. *Medicine and Science in Sports and Exercise, 18*(2), S74.

Hellwig, T., Liesen, H., Mader, A., & Hollmann, W. (1988). Possible means of sprint-specific performance diagnostics and training support using blood lactate concentration. [Abstract]. *International Journal of Sports Medicine, 9*(5), 387–388.

Henneman, E., & Olson, C. B. (1965). Relation between structure and function in the design of skeletal muscle. *Journal of Neurophysiology, 28,* 581–598.

Hermansen, L., & Osnes, J. B. (1972). Blood and muscle pH after maximal exercise in man. *Journal of Applied Physiology, 32,* 304–308.

Hermansen, L., & Stensvold, I. (1972). Production and removal of lactate during exercise in man. *Acta Physiologica Scandinavica, 86,* 191–201.

Hermansen, L., & Wachlova, M. (1971). Capillary density of skeletal muscle in well-trained and untrained men. *Journal of Applied Physiology, 30,* 860–863.

Heusner, W. W. (1985). *Body composition of Olympic male and female swimmers.* Report, presented at the U.S. Swimming Sports Medicine Meeting, Phoenix, AZ.

Hickson, R. C. (1980). Interference of strength development by simultaneously training for strength and endurance. *European Journal of Applied Physiology, 45,* 255–263.

Hickson, R. C. (1981). Skeletal muscle cytochrome c and myoglobin, endurance, and frequency of training. *Journal of Applied Physiology, 51*(3), 746–749.

Hickson, R. C., Dvorak, B. A., Corostiaga, E. M., Kurowski, T. T., & Foster, C. (1988). Strength training and performance in endurance trained subjects. [Abstract]. *Medicine and Science in Sports and Exercise, 20*(2), S86.

Hickson, R. C., Foster, C., Pollock, M. L., Galassi, T. M., & Rich, S. (1985). Reduced training intensities and loss of aerobic power, endurance, and cardiac growth. *Journal of Applied Physiology, 58*(2), 492–499.

Hickson, R. C., Hagberg, J. M., Ehsani, A. A., & Holloszy, J. O. (1981). Time course of the adaptive responses of aerobic power and heart rate to training. *Medicine and Science in Sports and Exercise, 13*(1), 17–20.

Hickson, R. C., Kanakis, C., Jr., Davis, J. R., Moore, A. M., & Rich, S. (1982). Reduced training duration effects on aerobic power, endurance, and cardiac growth. *Journal of Applied Physiology, 53*(1), 225–229.

Hickson, R. C., & Rosenkoetter, M. A. (1981a). Reduced training frequencies and maintenance of increased aerobic power. *Medicine and Science in Sports and Exercise, 13*(1), 13–16.

Hickson, R. C., & Rosenkoetter, M.A. (1981b). Separate turnover of cytochrome c and myoglobin in the red types of skeletal muscle. *American Journal of Physiology, 241 (Cell Physiology, 10),* C140–C144.

Hirche, H., Hombach, V., Langohr, H. D., Wacker, U., & Busse, J. (1975). Lactic acid permeation rate in working gastrocnemii of dogs during metabolic alkalosis and acidosis. *Pflugers Archives, 356:* 209–222.

Hoffman, T., Stauffer, R. W., & Jackson, A. S. (1979). Sex differences in strength. *American Journal of Sports Medicine, 7,* 265–267.

Hollman, W., Rost, R., Liesen, H., Dufaux, B., Heck, B., & Mader, A. (1981). Assessment of different forms of physical activity with respect to preventive and rehabilitative cardiology. *International Journal of Sports Medicine, 2,* 67–80.

Holloszy, J. O. (1973). Biochemical adaptations to exercise: aerobic metabolism. In J. Wilmore (Ed.), *Exercise and Sports Sciences Reviews, Vol. 1* (pp. 45–71). New York: Academic Press.

Holloszy, J. O. (1975). Adaptation of skeletal muscle to endurance exercise. *Medicine and Science in Sports and Exercise, 7*(3), 155–164.

Holloszy, J. O., Dalsky, G. P., Nemeth, P. M., Hurley, B. F., Martin, W. H., III, & Hagberg, J. M. (1986). Utilization of fat as substrate during exercise: effects of training. In B. Saltin (Ed.), *International Series on Sport Sciences: Vol. 16. Biochemistry of Exercise VI* (pp. 183–190). Champaign, IL: Human Kinetics.

Holloszy, J. O., Mole, P. A., Baldwin, K. M., & Terjung, R. L. (1973). Exercise induced enzymatic adaptations in muscle. In J. Keul (Ed.), *Limiting Factors of Physical Performance* (pp. 66–80). Stuttgart, Germany: Georg Thieme Verlag.

Holloszy, J. O., Oscai, L. B., Don, I. J., & Mole, P. A. (1970). Mitochondrial citric acid cycle and related enzymes: adaptive response to exercise. *Biochem. Biophys. Res. Commun. 40,* 1368–1373.

Holloszy, J. O., Smith, E. K., Vining, M., & Adams, S. (1985). Effect of voluntary exercise on longevity of rats. *Journal of Applied Physiology, 59,* 826–831.

Holmer, I. (1974). Physiology of swimming man. *Acta Physiologica Scandinavica, (Suppl. 407),* 1–55.

Horswill, C. A., Layman, D. K., Boileau, R. A., Williams, B. T., & Massey, B. H. (1988). Excretion of 3-methylhistidine and hydroxyproline following acute weight-training exercise. *International Journal of Sports Medicine, 9*(4), 245–248.

Houmard, J. A., Kirwan, J. P., Flynn, M. G., & Mitchell, J. B. (1989). Effect of reduced training on submaximal and maximal running responses. *International Journal of Sports Medicine, 10*(1), 30–33.

Houston, M. E. (1978). Metabolic responses to exercise with special reference to training and competition in swimming. In B. Eriksson & B. Furberg (Eds.), *International Series on Sport Sciences: Vol. 6. Swimming Medicine IV* (pp. 207–232). Baltimore: University Park Press.

Houston, M. E., & Thomson, J. A. (1977). The response of endurance adapted adults to intense anaerobic training. *European Journal of Applied Physiology, 36,* 207–213.

Howald, H. (1975). Ultrastructural adaptation of skeletal muscles to prolonged physical exercise. In H. Howald & J. R. Poortmans (Eds.), *Metabolic Adaptations to Prolonged Physical Exercise* (pp. 372–383). Basel, Switzerland: Birkhauser Verlag.

Hultman, E., & Sahlin, K. (1981). Acid-base balance during exercise. In R. S. Hutton & D. I. Miller (Eds.), *Exercise and Sport Sciences Reviews, Vol. 8.* (pp. 41–128). Philadelphia: Franklin Institute Press.

Hurley, B. F., Nemeth, P. M., Martin, W. H., III, Dalsky, G. P., Hagberg, J. M., & Holloszy, J. O. (1985). The effects of endurance exercise training on intramuscular substrate use during prolonged submaximal exercise. [Abstract]. *Medicine and Science in Sports and Exercise, 17,* 259–260.

Hutinger, P. (1970). *Comparison of isokinetic, isotonic, and isometric developed strength to speed in swimming the crawl stroke.* Unpublished doctoral dissertation, Indiana University.

Inbar, O., & Bar-Or, O. (1986). Anaerobic characteristics in male children and adolescents. *Medicine and Science in Sports and Exercise, 18*(3), 264–269.

Israel, S. (1963). Das Akute Entlastungssyndrom. *Theorie und Praxis der Korperkulter. 12.* Cited in: T. Bompa (1983), *Theory and Methodology of Training.* Dubuque, IA: Kendall/Hunt.

Ivy, J. L., Chi, M. M. Y., Hintz, C. S., Sherman, W. M., Hellendall, R. P., & Lowry, O. H. (1987). Muscle fiber recruitment during a lactate threshold test. [Abstract]. *Medicine and Science in Sports and Exercise, 19*(2), S35.

Ivy, J. L., Withers, R. T., Van Handel, P. J., Elger, D. H., & Costill, D. L. (1980). Muscle respiratory capacity and fiber type as determinants of the lactate threshold. *Journal of Applied Physiology, 48,* 523–527.

Iwaoka, K., Fuchi, T., Higuchi, M., & Kobayashi, S. (1988). Blood lactate accumulation during exercise in older endurance runners. *International Journal of Sports Medicine, 9*(4), 253–256.

Jacobs, I. (1981). Lactate concentrations after short, maximal exercise at various glycogen levels. *Acta Physiologica Scandinavica, 111,* 465–469.

Jacobs, I. (1986). Blood lactate: Implications for training and sports performance. *Sports Medicine, 3*: 10–25.

Jacobs, I., Bar-Or, O., Dotan, R., Karlsson, J., & Tesch, P. (1983). Changes in muscle ATP, CP, glycogen, and lactate after performance of the Wingate anaerobic test. In H. G. Knuttgen, A. Vogel, & J. Poortmans (Eds.), *International Series on Sports Sciences: Vol. 13. Biochemistry of Exercise* (pp. 234–238). Champaign, IL: Human Kinetics.

Jacobs, I., Esbjornsson, M., Sylven, C., Holm, I., & Jansson, E. (1987). Sprint training effect on muscle myoglobin, enzymes, fiber types, and blood lactates. *Medicine and Science in Sports and Exercise, 19*(4), 368–374.

Jacobs, I., & Kaiser, P. (1982). Lactate in blood, mixed skeletal muscle, and FT or ST fibres during cycle exercise in man. *Acta Physiologica Scandinavica, 114,* 461–466.

Jacobs, I., Kaiser, P., & Tesch, P. (1982). The effects of glycogen exhaustion on maximal short-term performance. In P. V. Komi (Ed.), *Exercise and Sport Biology* (pp. 103–108). Champaign, IL: Human Kinetics.

Jacobs, I., Sale, D., & MacDougall, J. D. (1987). Combined strength and endurance training effects on muscle enzymatic and histochemical characteristics. [Abstract]. *Medicine and Science in Sports and Exercise, 19*(2), S88.

Jang, K. T., Flynn, M. G., Costill, D. L., Kirwan, J. P., Houmard, J. A., Mitchell, J. B., & D'Acquisto, L. J. (1987). Energy balance in competitive swimmers and runners. *Journal of Swimming Research, 3*(1), 19–23.

Jansson, E., Sjodin, B., & Tesch, P. (1978). Changes in muscle fibre type distribution in man after physical training. *Acta Physiologica Scandinavica, 104,* 235–237.

Jansson, E., Sylven, C., & Nordevang, E. (1982). Myoglobin in the quadriceps femoris muscle of competitive cyclists and untrained men. *Acta Physiologica Scandinavica, 114,* 627–629.

Jones, N. L., & Ehrsam, R. E. (1982). The anaerobic threshold. In R. L. Terjung (Ed.), *Exercise and Sport Sciences Reviews: Vol. 10* (pp. 49–83). Syracuse, NY: The Franklin Institute.

Jorfeldt, L., Juhlin-Dannfelt, A., & Karlsson, J. (1978). Lactate release in relation to tissue lactate in human skeletal muscle during exercise. *Journal of Applied Physiology, 44*(3), 350–352.

Kaijser, L. (1973). Oxygen supply as a limiting factor in physical performance. In J. Keul (Ed.), *Limiting Factors of Physical Performance* (pp. 145–155). Stuttgart, Germany: Georg Thieme Verlag.

Karikosk, O. (1983). Altitude problems. *Modern Athlete and Coach. 21*(2), 25–27.

Karlsson, J., & Jacobs, I. (1982). Onset of blood lactate accumulation during muscular exercise as a threshold concept. I. Theoretical considerations. *International Journal of Sports Medicine, 3,* 190–201.

Karlsson, J., Nordesjo, L-O., Jorfeldt, L., & Saltin, B. (1972). Muscle lactate, ATP and CP levels during exercise after physical training in man. *Journal of Applied Physiology, 33,* 199–203.

Karvonen, J., Peltola, E., & Saarla, J. (1986). The effect of sprint training performed in a hypoxic environment on specific performance capacity. *Journal of Sports Medicine, 26,* 219–224.

Katz, R. M. (1986). Prevention with and without the use of medications for exercise-induced asthma. *Medicine and Science in Sports and Exercise, 18*(3), 331–333.

Katz, R. M. (1989). Exercise-induced asthma/other allergic reactions in the athlete. *Allergy Proceedings, 10*(3), 203–208.

Kaufman, D. A., & Hall, D. C. (1985). Effects of physical conditioning on health of pregnant women and their offspring. [Abstract]. *Medicine and Science in Sports and Exercise, 17*(2), 215.

Kemper, H. C. G., Verschuur, R., & Ritmeester, J. W. (1986). Maximal aerobic power in early and late maturing teenagers. In J. Rutenfranz, R. Mocellin, & F. Klimt (Eds.), *International Series on Sport Sciences: Vol. 17. Children and Exercise XII* (pp. 213–225). Champaign, IL: Human Kinetics.

Kennedy, J. C., & Hawkins, R. J. (1974). Swimmer's shoulder. *Physician and Sportsmedicine, 2,* 34–38.

Keul, J., Doll, E., & Keppler, D. (1972). *Energy Metabolism of Human Muscle.* Baltimore: University Park Press.

Keul, J., Simon, G., Berg, A., Dickhuth, H-H., Goertler, I., & Kubel, R. (1979). Bestimmung der individuellen anaeroben schwelle zur leistungsbewertung und trainingsgestaltung. *Dtsch Z Sportmed. 30,* 212–218. Cited in H. Stegmann & W. Kindermann (1982) *International Journal of Sports Medicine, 3,* 105–110.

Kieper, C. (1983). Effects of endurance training on acid-base status and pulmonary ventilation. *European Journal of Applied Physiology, 51,* 295–302.

Kiessling, K. H., Piehl, K., & Lundquist, C. G. (1971). Effect of physical training on ultrastructural features in human skeletal muscle. In B. Pernow & B. Saltin (Eds.), *Muscle Metabolism During Exercise* (pp. 97–101). New York: Plenum.

Kindermann, W. (1987). Metabolism and hormonal behaviour in aerobic and anaerobic exercise. [Abstract]. *International Journal of Sports Medicine, 8*(2), 147–148.

Kindermann, W., Huber, G., & Keul, J. (1975). Anaerobic capacity in children and adolescents in comparison to adults. *Sportarzi Sportmed 6,* 112–115. Cited in O. Inbar & O. Bar-Or (1986), Anaerobic characteristics in male children and adolescents. *Medicine and Science in Sports and Exercise, 18*(3), 264–269.

Kindermann, W., Simon, G., & Keul, J. (1979). The significance of the aerobic-anaerobic transition for the determination of work load intensities during endurance training. *European Journal of Applied Physiology, 42,* 25–34.

Kirwan, J. P., Costill, D. L., Flynn, M. G., Mitchell, J. B., Fink, W. J., Neufer, P. D., & Houmard, J. A. (1988). Physiological responses to successive days of intense training in competitive swimmers. *Medicine and Science in Sports and Exercise, 20*(3), 255–259.

Klausen, K., Anderson, L. A., & Pelle, I. (1981). Adaptive changes in work capacity, skeletal muscle capillarization and enzyme levels during training and detraining. *Acta Physiologica Scandinavica, 113,* 9–16.

Klausen, K., Dill, D. B., & Horvath, S. M. (1970). Exercise at ambient and high oxygen pressure at high altitude and sea level. *Journal of Applied Physiology, 29,* 456–463.

Komi, P. V., & Karlsson, J. (1978). Skeletal muscle fibre types, enzyme activities and physical performance in young males and females. *Acta Physiologica Scandinavica, 103,* 210–218.

Koshkin, Igor. (1984). The training program that developed Salnikov. In J. L. Cramer (Ed.), *How to Develop Olympic Level Swimmers: Scientific and Practical Foundations* (pp. 109–117). Helsinki, Finland: International Sports Media.

Krahenbuhl, G. S., Morgan, D. W., & Pangrazi, R. P. (1989). Longitudinal changes in distance-running performance of young males. *International Journal of Sports Medicine, 10*(2), 92–96.

Kruger, J., Mortier, R., Heck, H., & Hollmann, W. (1988). Relationship between the Conconi-threshold and lactic-acid at endurance workload on the turning crank ergometer. [Abstract]. *International Journal of Sports Medicine, 9*(5), 367.

Krukau, M., Volker, K., & Leisen, H. (1987). The influence of sport-specific and sport-unspecific recovery on lactate behaviour after anaerobic swimming. [Abstract]. *International Journal of Sports Medicine, 8*(2), 142.

Kumagi, S., Tanaka, K., Matsuura, Y., Matsuzak, A., Hirakoba, K., & Asano, K. (1982). Relationship of the anaerobic threshold with the 5 km, 10 km, and 10 mile races. *European Journal of Applied Physiology, 49,* 13–23.

Kutsar, K. (1983). Some aspects of altitude training. *Modern Athlete and Coach, 21*(2), 27–28.

LaFontaine, T. P., Londeree, B. R., & Spath, W. K. (1981). The maximal steady state versus selected running events. *Medicine and Science in Sports and Exercise, 13*(3), 190–192.

Lahiri, S. (1974). Physiological responses and adaptations to high altitude. In D. Robertshaw (Ed.), *Environmental Physiology* (pp. 271–311). London: Butterworths.

Lamanca, J., & Haymes, E. (1989). Effects of dietary iron supplementation on endurance. [Abstract]. *Medicine and Science in Sports and Exercise, 21*(2), S77.

Lamb, D. R. (1978). *Physiology of Exercise: Responses and Adaptations.* New York: Macmillan.

Lamb, D. R., Rinehardt, K. F., Bartels, R. L., Sherman, W. M., & Snook, J. T. (1990). Dietary carbohydrate and intensity of interval swim training. *American Journal of Clinical Nutrition, 52,* 1058–1063.

Laughlin, T. (1989). Here's Boomer. *Swimming World, 30*(7), 45–49.

Laurent, G. J., & Milward, D. J. (1980). Protein turnover during skeletal muscle hypertrophy. *Federation Proceedings, 39,* 42–47.

Lemon, P. W. R., & Mullin, J. P. (1980). Effect of initial muscle glycogen levels on protein catabolism during exercise. *Journal of Applied Physiology, 48,* 624–629.

Lemon, P. W. R., Yarasheski, K. E., & Dolny, D. G. (1984). The importance of protein for athletes. *Sports Medicine, 1,* 474–478.

Letzelter, H., & Freitag, W. (1983). Stroke length and stroke frequency variations in men's and women's 100-m freestyle swimming. In A. P. Hollander, P. A. Huijing, & G. de Groot (Eds.), *International Series on Sport Sciences: Vol. 14. Biomechanics and Medicine in Swimming* (pp. 315–322). Champaign, IL: Human Kinetics.

Lindberg, J. S., Fears, W. B., Hunt, M. M., Powell, M. R., Boll, D., & Wade, C. E. (1984). Exercise-induced amenorrhea and bone density. *Annals of Internal Medicine, 101,* 647–649.

Lindinger, M. I., Galea, V., Heigenhauser, G. J. F., & Green, H. J. (1990). Duration of endurance training affects lactate release and production. [Abstract]. *Medicine and Science in Sports and Exercise, 22*(2), S8.

Loftin, M., Boileau, R. A., Massey, B. H., & Lohman, T. G. (1988). Effect of arm training on central and peripheral circulatory function. *Medicine and Science in Sports and Exercise, 20*(2), 136–141.

Loucks, A. B. (1988). Osteoporosis prevention begins in childhood. In E. W. Brown & C. F. Braun (Eds.), *Competitive Sports for Children and Youth: An Overview of Research and Issues* (pp. 213–223). Champaign, IL: Human Kinetics.

Loy, S. F., & Segel, L. D. (1988). 31P-NMR of rat thigh muscle: effect of sprint and endurance training. [Abstract]. *Medicine and Science in Sports and Exercise, 20*(2), S65.

Luthi, J. M., Howald, H., Claassen, H., Rosler, K., Vock, P., & Hoppeler, H. (1986). Structural changes in skeletal muscle tissue with heavy-resistance exercise. *International Journal of Sports Medicine, 7*(3), 123–127.

Lutter, J. M., & Cushman, S. (1982). Menstrual patterns in female runners. *Physician and Sportsmedicine, 10*(9), 60–72.

MacDougall, J. D. (1986a). Morphological changes in human skeletal muscle following strength training and immobilization. In N. I. Jones, N. McCartney, & A. J. McComas (Eds.), *Human Muscle Power* (pp. 269–285). Champaign, IL: Human Kinetics.

MacDougall, J. D. (1986b). Adaptability of muscle to strength training—A cellular approach. In B. Saltin (Ed.), *International Series on Sport Sciences: Vol. 16. Biochemistry of Exercise VI* (pp. 501–513). Champaign, IL: Human Kinetics.

MacDougall, J. D., Elder, G. C., Sale, D. G., Moroz, J. R., & Sutton, J. R. (1980). Effects of strength training and immobilization on human muscle fibers. *European Journal of Applied Physiology, 43,* 25–34.

MacDougall, J. D., Sale, D. G., Alway, S. E., & Sutton, J. R. (1984). Muscle fiber number in biceps brachii in body builders and control subjects. *Journal of Applied Physiology, 57*(5), 1399–1403.

MacDougall, J. D., Sale, D., Jacobs, I., Garner, S., Moroz, D., & McMaster, D. (1987). Concurrent strength and endurance training do not impede gains in $\dot{V}O_2max$. [Abstract]. *Medicine and Science in Sports and Exercise, 19*(2), S87.

MacDougall, J. D., Ward, G. R., Sale, D. G., & Sutton, J. R. (1975). Muscle glycogen repletion after high intensity intermittent exercise. *Journal of Applied Physiology, 42,* 129–132.

MacDougall, J. D., Ward, G. R., Sale, D. G., & Sutton, J R. (1977). Biochemical adaptation of human skeletal muscle to heavy resistance training and immobilization. *Journal of Applied Physiology, 43,* 700–703.

Macek, M. (1986). Aerobic and anaerobic energy output in children. In J. Rutenfranz, R. Mocellin, & F. Klimt (Eds.), *International Series on Sport Sciences: Vol. 17. Children and Exercise XII* (pp. 3–9). Champaign, IL: Human Kinetics.

Macek, M., & Vavra, J. (1985). Anaerobic threshold in children. In R. A. Binkhorst, H. C. G. Kemper, & W. H. M. Saris (Eds.), *International Series on Sport Sciences: Vol. 15. Children and Exercise XI* (pp. 110–113). Champaign IL: Human Kinetics.

Mader, A., Heck, H., & Hollmann, W. (1976). Evaluation of lactic acid anaerobic energy contribution by determination of post-exercise lactic acid concentration of ear capillary blood in middle distance runners and swimmers. In F. Landing & W. Orban (Eds.), *Exercise Physiology* (pp. 187–199). Miami: Symposia Specialists.

Madsen, O., & Lohberg, M. (1987). The lowdown on lactates. *Swimming Technique, 24*(1), 21–26.

Madsen, O., & Olbrecht, J. (1983). Specifics of aerobic training. In R. M. Ousley (Ed.), *ASCA World Clinic Yearbook* (pp. 15–29). Fort Lauderdale: American Swimming Coaches Association.

Madsen, O., & Wilke, K. (1983). A comprehensive multi-year training plan. In R. M. Ousley (Ed.), *ASCA World Clinic Yearbook* (pp. 47–62). Fort Lauderdale: American Swimming Coaches Association.

Magel, J. R., Foglia, G. F., McArdle, W. D., Gutin, B., Pechar, G., & Katch, F. I. (1975). Specificity of swim training on maximum oxygen uptake. *Journal of Applied Physiology, 38*(1), 151–155.

Maglischo, E. W. (1987). [Stroke rates of swimmers at the Men's 1987 NCAA Swimming Championships]. Unpublished data.

Maglischo, E. W. (1988). [Blood lactate values after detraining]. Unpublished observation.

Maglischo, E. W. (1989a). [Comparison of threshold paces predicted from blood testing and the swimming step test]. Unpublished data.

Maglischo, E. W. (1989b). [Peak blood lactate before and after tapering]. Unpublished data.

Maglischo, E. W. (1990). [Flexibility losses during detraining from competitive swimming]. Unpublished data.

Maglischo, E. W., & Daland, P. (1987). *Observations of the 1987 European Swimming Championships.* Written report presented to United States Swimming.

Maglischo, C. W., Maglischo, E. W., Sharp, R. L., Zier, D. J., & Katz, A. (1984). Tethered and nontethered crawl swimming. In J. Terauds, K. Barthels, E. Kreighbaum, R. Mann, & J. Crakes (Eds.), *Proceedings of ISBS: Sports Biomechanics* (pp. 163–176). Del Mar, CA: Academic Publishers.

Maglischo, E. W., Maglischo, C. W., Zier, D. J., Santos, T. R. (1985). The effect of sprint-assisted and sprint-resisted swimming on stroke mechanics. *Journal of Swimming Research, 1*(2), 27–33.

Maher, J. T., Jones, L. G., & Hartley, L. H. (1974). Effects of high-altitude exposure on submaximal endurance capacity of men. *Journal of Applied Physiology, 37*(6), 895–898.

Marcus, R., Cann, C., Madvig, P., Minkoff, J., Goddard, M., Bayer, M., Martin, M., Gaudani, L., Haskell, W., & Genant, H. (1985). Menstrual function and bone mass in elite women distance runners. *Annals of Internal Medicine, 102,* 158–163.

Martin, A. D., & Houston, C. S. (1987). Osteoporosis, calcium, and physical activity. *Canadian Medical Association Journal, 136*(6), 587–593.

Mason, T. A. (1970). Is weight lifting deleterious to the spines of young people? *British Journal of Sports Medicine, 5,* 54–56.

Mathews, D. K., & Fox, E. L. (1976). *The Physiological Basis of Physical Education and Athletics.* Philadelphia: W. B. Saunders.

Matveev, L. P., Kalinin, V. K., & Ozolin, N. N. (1974). *Characteristics of Athletic Shape and Methods of Rationalizing the Structure of the Competitive Phase* (pp. 4–23). Moscow: Scientific Research Collection.

McArdle, W. D., Katch, F. I., & Katch, V. L. (1981). *Exercise Physiology: Energy, Nutrition, and Human Performance* (2nd ed.). Philadelphia: Lea & Febiger.

McArdle, W. D., Katch, F. I., & Katch, V. L. (1991). *Exercise Physiology: Energy, Nutrition, and Human Performance* (3rd ed.). Philadelphia: Lea & Febiger.

McArdle, W. D., Magel, J. R., DeLuca, D. J., Toner, M., & Chase, J. M. (1978). Specificity of run training on $\dot{V}O_2$max and heart rate changes during running and swimming. *Medicine and Science in Sports and Exercise, 10*(1), 16–20.

McCarthy, P. (1989). Wheezing and breezing through exercise-induced asthma. *Physician and Sportsmedicine, 17*(7), 125–130.

McKenzie, D. C., & Mavrogiannis, A. (1986). Changes in the lactate inflection point with prolonged aerobic exercise. [Abstract]. *Medicine and Science in Sports and Exercise, 18*(2), S22.

McKenzie, D. C., Parkhouse, W. S., Rhodes, E. C., Hochochka, P. W., Ovalle, W. K., Mommsen, T. P., & Shinn, S. L. (1983). Skeletal muscle buffering capacity in elite athletes. In H. G. Knuttgen, J. A. Vogel, & J. Poortmans (Eds.), *International Series on Sport Sciences: Vol. 13. Biochemistry of Exercise* (pp. 584–589). Champaign, IL: Human Kinetics.

McLellan, T. M., & Jacobs, I. (1989). The influence of active recovery on the individual anaerobic threshold. [Abstract]. *Medicine and Science in Sports and Exercise, 21*(2), S22.

McMurray, R. G., Ben-Ezra, V., Forsythe, W. A., & Smith, A. T. (1985). Responses of endurance-trained subjects to caloric deficits induced by diet or exercise. *Medicine and Science in Sports and Exercise, 17*(5), 574–579.

McNair, D. M., Lorr, M., & Droppleman, L. F. (1971). *Profile of Mood States Manual.* San Diego: Educational and Industrial Testing Service.

Medbo, J. I., & Burgers, S. (1990). Effect of training on the anaerobic capacity. *Medicine and Science in Sports and Exercise, 22*(4), 501–507.

Micheli, L. J. (1988a). The incidence of injuries in children's sports: a medical perspective. In E. W. Brown & C. F. Branta (Eds.), *Competitive Sports for Children and Youth: An Overview of Research and Issues* (pp. 279–284). Champaign, IL: Human Kinetics.

Micheli, L. J. (1988b). Strength training in the young athlete. In E. W. Brown & C. F. Branta (Eds.), *Competitive Sports for Children and Youth: An Overview of Research and Issues* (pp. 99–105). Champaign, IL: Human Kinetics.

Mikesell, K. A., & Dudley, G. A. (1984). Influence of intense endurance training on aerobic power of competitive distance runners. *Medicine and Science in Sports and Exercise, 16*(4), 371–375.

Millard, M., Zauner, C., Cade, R., & Reese, R. (1985). Serum CPK levels in male and female world class swimmers during a season of training. *Journal of Swimming Research, 1*(2), 12–16.

Miller, K., Telander, T., Heppes, L., & Troup, J. P. (1989). Alterations in swimming economy following intense training periods. In J. Troup (Ed.), *Winning Spirit Instructional Series.* Colorado Springs: U.S. Swimming.

Miller, R. E., & Mason, J. W. (1964). Changes in 17-hydroxycorticosteroid excretion related to increased muscular work. In *Medical Aspects of Stress in the Military Climate* (pp. 137–151). Washington, DC: Walter Reed Army Institute of Research.

Mitchell, M., Brynes, W., & Mazzeo, R. (1989). Effects of age and endurance training on skeletal muscle morphology. [Abstract]. *Medicine and Science in Sports and Exercise, 21*(2), S63.

Mizuno, M., Juel, C., Bro-Rasmussen, T., Mygind, E., Schibye, B., Rasmussen, B., & Saltin, B. (1990). Limb skeletal muscle adaptation in athletes after training at altitude. *Journal of Applied Physiology, 68,* 496–502.

Moffroid, M. T., & Whipple, R. H. (1970). Specificity of speed to exercise. *Physical Therapy, 50,* 1692–1700.

Mole, P. A., Baldwin, K. M., Terjung, R. L., & Holloszy, J. O. (1973). Enzymatic pathways of pyruvate metabolism in skeletal muscle: adaptations to exercise. *American Journal of Physiology, 224,* 50–54.

Montpetit, R., Duvallet, A., Cazorla, G., & Smith, H. (1987). The relative stability of maximal aerobic power in elite swimmers and its relation to training performance. *Journal of Swimming Research, 3*(1), 15–18.

Morgan, T. E., Cobb, L. A., Short, F. A., Ross, R., & Gunn, D. R. (1971). Effect of long-term exercise on human muscle mitochondria. In B. Pernow & B. Saltin (Eds.), *Muscle Metabolism During Exercise* (pp. 87–95). New York: Plenum Books.

Morgan, W. P. (1985). Affective beneficence of vigorous physical activity. *Medicine and Science in Sports and Exercise, 17,* 94–100.

Morgan, W. P., Brown, D. R., Raglin, J. S., O'Connor, P. J., & Ellickson, K. A. (1987). Physiological monitoring of overtraining and staleness. *British Journal of Sports Medicine, 21*(3), 107–114.

Morgan, W. P., Costill, D. L., Flynn, M. G., Raglin, J. S., & O'Connor, P. J. (1988). Mood disturbance following increased training in swimmers. *Medicine and Science in Sports and Exercise, 20*(4), 408–414.

Munn, K. (1981). Effects of exercise on the range of motion in elderly subjects. In E. Smith & R. Serfass (Eds.), *Exercise and Aging: The Scientific Basis* (pp. 167–186). Hillside, NJ: Enslow Publishers.

Myerson, M., Gutin, B., Warren, M., May, M., Contento, I., Lee, M., Pierson, R., & Sunyer, F. P. I. (1987). Energy Balance of amenorrheic and eumenorrheic runners. [Abstract]. *Medicine and Science in Sports and Exercise, 19*(2), S37.

Nakamura, Y., Takei, Y., Mutoh, Y., & Miyashita, M. (1985). Specificity of exercise duration for anaerobic type training. [Abstract]. *Medicine and Science in Sports and Exercise, 17*(2), 268.

Nelson, A. G., Conlee, R. K., Arnall, D. A., Loy, S. F., & Sylvester, L. J. (1984). Adaptations to simultaneous training for strength and endurance. 1984. [Abstract]. *Medicine and Science in Sports and Exercise, 16*(2), 184.

Neufer, P. D., Costill, D. L., Fielding, R. A., Flynn, M. G., & Kirwan, J. P. (1988). Changes during reduced training. *Swimming Technique, 24*(4), 21–24.

Newhouse, I. J., & Clement, D. B. (1988). Iron status in athletes. *Sports Medicine, 56 (Annual Update),* 337–352.

Newhouse, I. J., Clement, D. B., Taunton, J. E., & McKenzie, D. C. (1989). The effects of perlatent/latent iron deficiency on physical work capacity. *Medicine and Science in Sports and Exercise, 21*(3), 263–268.

Nygaard, E. (1980). Number of fibres in skeletal muscle of man. [Abstract]. *Muscle and Nerve, 3,* 268.

Nygaard, E. (1982). Skeletal muscle fibre capillarization in young women. *Acta Physiologica Scandinavica, 112,* 299–304.

Nygaard, E., & Nielsen, E. (1978). Skeletal muscle fiber capillarization with extreme endurance exercise in man. In B. Eriksson & B. Furberg (Eds.), *International Series on Sport Sciences: Vol. 6. Swimming Medicine IV* (pp. 282–296). Baltimore: University Park Press.

O'Connor, J., Beld, K., & Skinner, J. (1987). Effects of brief high-intensity anaerobic training. [Abstract]. *Medicine and Science in Sports and Exercise, 19*(2), S61.

O'Connor, P. J., Morgan, W. P., Raglin, J. S., Barksdale, C. M., & Kalin, N. H. (1989). Selected psychoendocrine responses to overtraining. [Abstract]. *Medicine and Science in Sports and Exercise, 21*(2), S50.

Olbrecht, J., Mader, A., Heck, H., & Hollman, W. (1988). Relation between lactate and swimming speed depending on the test conditions (pool length, before and after endurance training, AM versus PM, qualifications and finals, relay or individual races). [Abstract]. *International Journal of Sports Medicine, 9*(5), 379.

Olbrecht, J., Madsen, O., Mader, A., Liesen, H., & Hollmann, W. (1985). Relationship between swimming velocity and lactic acid concentration during continuous and intermittent training exercise. *International Journal of Sports Medicine, 6*(2), 74–77.

Ozolin, N. G. (1971). Sovremennaia systema sportivnoi trenirovsky [Athlete's training system for competition]. Moscow: *Phyyzkultura I Sport.* Cited in T. Bompa (1983). *Theory and Methodology of Training*. Dubuque, IA: Kendall/Hunt.

Pate, R. R., Baldwin, C., Sientz, C., Miller, B., & Burgess, W. (1986). Iron status of female runners. [Abstract]. *Medicine and Science in Sports and Exercise, 18*(2), S55.

Pate, R. R., Dover, E. V., Fronsoe, M., Pu, J., & Lambert, M. (1984). Effects of exercise training on plasma ferritin in women. [Abstract]. *Medicine and Science in Sports and Exercise, 16*(2), 178.

Pate, R. R., Maguire, M., & Van Wyke, J. (1979). Dietary iron supplementation in women athletes. *Physician and Sportsmedicine, 7,* 81–88.

Paterson, D. H., & Cunningham, D. A. (1985). Development of anaerobic capacity in early and late maturing boys. In R. A. Blinkhorst, H. C. G. Kemper, & W. H. M. Saris (Eds.), *International Series on Sport Sciences: Vol. 15. Children and Exercise XI* (pp. 119–128). Champaign, IL: Human Kinetics.

Pattengale, P. K., & Holloszy, J. O. (1967). Augmentation of skeletal muscle myoglobin by a program of treadmill running. *American Journal of Physiology, 213,* 783–785.

Paulsson, L. E. (1984). Developing sprint champions through strength training and other tricks. In J. L. Cramer (Ed.), *How to Develop Olympic Level Swimmers: Scientific and Practical Foundations* (pp. 138–159). Helsinki, Finland: International Sports Media.

Pechar, G. S., McArdle, W. D., Katch, F. I., Magel, J. R., & DeLuca, J. (1974). Specificity of cardiorespiratory adaptation to bicycle and treadmill training. *Journal of Applied Physiology, 36*(6), 753–756.

Pelliccia, A., & DiNucci, G. B. (1987). Anemia in swimmers: Fact or fiction? Study of hematologic and iron status in male and female top-level swimmers. *International Journal of Sports Medicine, 8*(3), 227–230.

Pendergast, D. R., diPrampero, P. E., Craig, A. B., Sr., & Rennie, D. W. (1978). The influence of selected biomechanical factors on the energy cost of swimming. In B. Eriksson & B. Furberg (Eds.), *International Series on Sport Sciences: Vol. 6. Swimming Medicine IV* (pp. 367–378). Baltimore: University Park Press.

Pette, D., & Staudte, H. W. (1973). Differences between red and white muscles. In J. Keul (Ed.), *Limiting Factors of Physical Performance* (pp. 23–33). Stuttgart, Germany: Georg Thieme Verlag.

Pfeiffer, H. (1988, October). *Theoretical and practical aspects for the planning in sports swimming at top level.* Paper presented at the Schicting Congres Venlo, Venlo, The Netherlands.

Pollock, M. L., Foster, C., Knapp, D., Rod, J. L., & Schmidt, D. H. (in press). Effect of age and training on aerobic capacity and body composition of master athletes. *Journal of Applied Physiology.*

Purvis, J. W., & Cureton, K. (1981). Ratings of perceived exertion at anaerobic threshold. *Ergonomics, 24,* 295–300.

Raglin, J. S., & Morgan, W. P. (1989). Development of a scale to measure training-induced distress. [Abstract]. *Medicine and Science in Sports and Exercise, 21*(2), S50.

Radha, E., & Bessman, S. P. (1983). Effect of exercise on protein degradation: 3-methylhistidine and creatinine excretion. *Biochemical Medicine, 29,* 96–100.

Rahkila, P., & Rusko, H. (1982). Effect of high altitude training on muscle enzyme activities and physical performance characteristics of cross-country skiers. In P. V. Komi (Ed.), *Exercise and Sport Biology* (pp. 143–151). Champaign, IL: Human Kinetics.

Reeves, J. T., Grover, R. F., & Cohn, J. E. (1967). Regulation of ventilation during exercise at 10,200 ft in athletes born at low altitude. *Journal of Applied Physiology, 22,* 546–554.

Refsum, H. E., Gjessing, L. R., & Stromme, S. B. (1979). Changes in plasma amino acid distribution and urine amino acid excretion during prolonged heavy exercise. *Scandinavian Journal of Clinical Laboratory Investigation, 39,* 407–413.

Relman, A. (1972). Metabolic consequences of acid-base disorders. *Kidney International, 1,* 347–359.

Rennie, M. J., & Millward, D. J. (1983). 3-Methylhistidine excretion and the urinary 3-methylhistidine/creatine ratios are poor indicators of skeletal muscle protein breakdown. *Clinical Science, 65,* 217–225.

Ribeiro, J. P., Fielding, R. A., Hughes, V., Black, A., Bochese, M. A., & Knuttgen, H. G. (1985). Heart rate break point may coincide with the anaerobic and not the aerobic threshold. *International Journal of Sports Medicine, 6*(4), 220–224.

Risser, W. L., Lee, E. J., Poindexter, H. B. W., West, M. S., Pivarnik, J. M., Risser, J. M. H., & Hickson, J. F. (1988). Iron deficiency in female athletes: its prevalence and impact on performance. *Medicine and Science in Sports and Exercise, 20*(2), 116–121.

Robergs, R. A., Chwalbinska-Moneta, J., Costill, D. L., & Fink, W. J. (1989). Threshold for muscle lactate accumulation during progressive exercise. [Abstract]. *Medicine and Science in Sports and Exercise, 21*(2), S24.

Robinson, S., & Harmon, P. M. (1941). The lactic acid mechanism and certain properties of the blood in relation to training. *American Journal of Physiology, 132,* 757–769.

Rogol, A. D. (1988). Pubertal development in endurance-trained female athletes. In E. W. Brown & C. F. Branta (Eds.), *Competitive Sports for Children and Youth: An Overview of Research and Issues* (pp. 173–193). Champaign, IL: Human Kinetics.

Rohrs, D. M., Stager, J. M., & Harris, A. (1989). A new technique for evaluating anaerobic power and capacity in competitive swimmers. [Abstract]. *Medicine and Science in Sports and Exercise, 21*(2), S27.

Ross, D. T. (1973). *Selected training procedures for the development of arm extensor strength and swimming speed of the sprint crawl stroke.* Unpublished master's thesis, University of Oregon.

Rotstein, A., Dotan, R., Bar-Or, O., & Tenenbaum, G. (1986). Effect of training on anaerobic threshold, maximal aerobic power and anaerobic performance of preadolescent boys. *International Journal of Sports Medicine, 7*(5), 281–286.

Rowe, E., Maglischo, E. W., & Lytle, D. E. (1977). The use of swim fins for the development of sprint swimming speed. *Swimming Technique, 14,* 73–76.

Rowland, T. W. (1985). Aerobic response to endurance training in prepubescent children: a critical analysis. *Medicine and Science in Sports and Exercise, 17*(5), 493–497.

Rowland, T. W., Deisroth, M., & Kelleher, J. F. (1987). The effect of iron therapy on the exercise capacity of non-anemic iron deficient female high school runners. [Abstract]. *Medicine and Science in Sports and Exercise, 19*(2), S20.

Rutenfranz, J. (1985). Long-term effects of excessive training procedures on young athletes. In R. A. Binkhorst, H. C. G. Kemper, & W. H. M. Saris (Eds.), *International Series on Sport Sciences: Vol. 15. Children and Exercise XI* (pp. 354–357). Champaign, IL: Human Kinetics.

Ruud, J. S. (1990). *Iron and Physical Performance: Implications for Athletes.* Omaha: International Center for Sports Nutrition.

Ryan, J. R., & Salciccioli, G. G. (1976). Fracture of the distal radial epiphysis in adolescent weight lifters. *American Journal of Sports Medicine, 4,* 26–27.

Sahlin, K., Harris, R. C., Nylind, B., & Hultman, E. (1976). Lactate content and pH in muscle samples obtained after dynamic exercise. *Pflugers Archives, 367,* 143–149.

Sale, D. G. (1986). Neural adaptation in strength and power training. In N. L. Jones, N. McCartney, & A. J. McComas (Eds.), *Human Muscle Power* (pp. 289–305). Champaign, IL: Human Kinetics.

Sale, D., Jacobs, I., Moroa, D., MacDougall, D., & Garner, S. (1988). Comparison of two regimes of combined strength and endurance training. [Abstract]. *Medicine and Science in Sports and Exercise, 20*(2), S9.

Salo, D. C. (1986). Sprint training can affect endurance performance. In J. Leonard (Ed.), *1986 ASCA World Clinic Yearbook* (pp. 73–76). Fort Lauderdale: American Swimming Coaches Association.

Salo, D. C. (1988). Specifics of high-intensity training. *Swimming World, 29*(7), 21.

Saltin, B. (1967). Aerobic and anaerobic work capacity at an altitude of 2,250 meters. In R. F. Goddard (Ed.), *The Effects of Altitude on Physical Performance* (pp. 97–101). Chicago: Athletic Institute.

Saltin, B. (1973). Oxygen transport by the circulatory system during exercise in man. In J. Keul (Ed.), *Limiting Factors of Physical Performance* (pp. 235–251). Stuttgart, Germany: Georg Thieme Verlag.

Saltin, B. (1975). Adaptive changes in carbohydrate metabolism with exercise. In H. Howald & J. R. Poortmans (Eds.), *Metabolic Adaptations to Prolonged Physical Exercise* (pp. 94–100). Basel: Birkhauser Verlag.

Saltin, B., Blomquist, B., Mitchell, J. H., Johnson, R. L., Jr., Wildenthal, K., & Chapman, C. B. (1968). Response to submaximal and maximal exercise after bed rest and training. *Circulation, 38*(Suppl.) *7,* 1–78.

Saltin, B., & Gollnick, P. D. (1983). Skeletal muscle adaptability: Significance for metabolism and performance. In L. D. Peachey, R. H. Adrian, & S. R. Geiger (Eds.), *Handbook of Physiology* (pp. 555–632). Baltimore: Waverly Press.

Saltin, B., Grover, R. F., Blomqvist, C. G., Hartley, I. H., & Johnson, R. L., Jr. (1968). Maximal oxygen uptake and cardiac output after 2 weeks at 4,300 m. *Journal of Applied Physiology, 25,* 400–409.

Saltin, B., & Karlsson, J. (1971a). Muscle ATP, CP, and lactate during exercise after physical conditioning. In B. Pernow & B. Saltin (Eds.), *Muscle Metabolism During Exercise* (pp. 395–399). New York: Plenum.

Saltin, B., & Karlsson, J. (1971b). Muscle glycogen utilization during work of different intensities. In B. Pernow & B. Saltin (Eds.), *Muscle Metabolism During Exercise* (pp. 289–299). New York: Plenum.

Saltin, B., Nazar, K., Costill, D. L., Stein, E., Jansson, E., Essen, B., & Gollnick, P. (1976). The nature of the training response: peripheral and central adaptations to one-legged exercise. *Acta Physiologica Scandinavica, 96,* 289–305.

Sanborn, C. F., Martin, B. J., & Wagner, W. W. (1982). Is athletic amenorrhea specific to runners? *American Journal of Obstetrics and Gynecology, 143,* 859–861.

Sapega, A. A., Sokolow, D. P., Grahm, T. J., & Chance, B. (1988). Phosphorus nuclear magnetic resonance: a non-invasive technique for the study of muscle bioenergetics during exercise. *Medicine and Science in Sports and Exercise, 19*(4), 410–420.

Saris, W. H. M., & Brouns, F. (1986). Nutritional concerns for the young athlete. In J. Rutenfranz, R. Mocellin, & F. Klimt (Eds.), *International Series on Sport Sciences: Vol. 17. Children and Exercise* (pp. 11–18). Champaign, IL: Human Kinetics.

Saris, W. H. M., Noordeloos, A. M., Ringnalda, B. E. M., Van't Hof, M. A., & Binkhorst, R. A. (1985). Reference values for aerobic power of healthy 4 to 18 year-old Dutch children preliminary results. In R. A. Binkhorst, H. C. G. Kemper, & W. H. M. Saris (Eds.), *International Series on Sport Sciences: Vol. 15. Children and Exercise* (pp. 151–160). Champaign, IL: Human Kinetics.

Schottelius, B. A., & Schottelius, D. D. (1973). *Textbook of Physiology.* Saint Louis: Mosby.

Schubert, M. (1977). Blood testing and training of distance swimmers. In B. M. Ousley (Ed.), 1976 *ASCA World Clinic Yearbook* (pp. 71–86). Fort Lauderdale: American Swimming Coaches Association.

Schwartz, B., Cumming, D. C., Riodan, E., Selye, M., Yen, S. S. C., & Rebar, R. W. (1981). Exercise-associated amenorrhea: a distinct entity? *American Journal of Obstetrics and Gynecology, 141,* 662–670.

Schwarzkopf, R., McKenzie, R., Tatham, G., & Keller, K. (1986). The effects of iron supplementation on female endurance athletes. [Abstract]. *Medicine and Science in Sports and Exercise, 18*(2), S55.

Selby, G. B., & Eichner, E. R. (1985). Intravascular hemolysis and iron depletion in distance swimmers. [Abstract]. *Medicine and Science in Sports and Exercise, 17*(2), 293.

Selye, H. (1956). *The Stress of Life.* New York: McGraw-Hill.

Serresse, O., Lortie, G., Bouchard, C., & Boulay, M. R. (1988). Estimation of the contribution of the various energy systems during maximal work of short duration. *International Journal of Sports Medicine, 9*(6), 456–460.

Sewall, L., & Micheli, L. J. (1984). Strength development in children. *Medicine and Science in Sports and Exercise, 16,* 158.

Shangold, M. M., & Levine, H. S. (1982). The effect of marathon training upon menstrual function. *American Journal of Obstetrics and Gynecology, 143,* 862–869.

Sharp, R. L. (1984). Use of blood lactates in training. In T. F. Welsh (Ed.), *1984 ASCA World Clinic Yearbook* (pp. 87–92). Ft. Lauderdale: American Swimming Coaches Association.

Sharp, R. L. (1986). Muscle strength and power as related to competitive swimming. *Journal of Swimming Research, 2*(2), 5–10.

Sharp, R. L., & Costill, D. L. (1982). Force, work and power: what they mean to the competitive swimmer. *Swimming World, 23,* 41–43.

Sharp, R. L., Costill, D. L., Fink, W. J., & King, D. S. (1983). The effects of eight weeks of sprint training on the buffer capacity of muscle in man. [Abstract]. *Medicine and Science in Sports and Exercise, 15,* 116.

Sharp, R. L., Costill, D. L., Fink, W. J., & King, D. S. (1986). Effects of eight weeks of bicycle ergometer sprint training on human muscle buffer capacity. *International Journal of Sports Medicine, 7*(1), 13–17.

Sharp, R. L., Costill, D. L., & King, D. S. (1983). *Power characteristics of swimmers at the 1982 U.S. Senior National Long Course Swimming Championships.* Research report submitted to the American Swimming Coaches Association. Referenced in R. L. Sharp. (1986). Muscle strength and power as related to competitive swimming. *Journal of Swimming Research, 2*(2), 5–10.

Sharp, R. L., Ness, R. J., Hackney, A. C., & Runyan, W. S. (1989). Compatibility of aerobic and anaerobic adaptations to training in man. [Abstract]. *Medicine and Science in Sports and Exercise, 21*(2), S76.

Sharp, R. L., Troup, J. P., & Costill, D. L. (1982). Relationship between power and sprint freestyle swimming. *Medicine and Science in Sports and Exercise, 14,* 53–56.

Sharp, R. L., Troup, J. P., Richardson, A. B., & Stanford, P. D. (1984). Blood lactate profiles of 1984 Olympic swimmers: comparison with sub-elite collegiate swimmers. [Abstract]. *Medicine and Science in Sports and Exercise, 16*(2), 193.

Sharp, R. L., Vitelli, C. A., Costill, D. L., & Thomas, R. (1984). Comparison between blood lactate and heart rate profiles during a season of competitive swim training. *Journal of Swimming Research, 1*(1), 17–20.

Sharrat, M. T. (1982). Training limitations at altitude. *Sportsmedicine Gazette, 14*(1), 5–7.

Sherif, M., Harvey, O. J., White, B. J., Hood, W. R., & Sherif, C. W. (1961). *Intergroup Conflict and Cooperation: The Robber's Cave Experiment.* Norman, OK: University of Oklahoma Book Exchange.

Sherman, W. M., & Maglischo, E. W. (1991). Minimizing chronic athletic fatigue among swimmers: special emphasis on nutrition. *Sports Science Exchange, 4*(35). Chicago, IL: Gatorade Sports Science Institute.

Simmons, R., & Shepard, R. J. (1972). The influence of training over the distribution of cardiac output. In A. W. Taylor (Ed.), *Training: Scientific Basis and Application* (pp. 131–138). Springfield, IL: Charles J. Thomas.

Simon, G., Berg, A., Dickhuth, H. H., Simon-Alt, A., & Keul, J. (1981). Bestimmung der anaeroben schwelle in abhangigkeit vom alter und von die leistungfahigkeit. Dtsch. Z Sportmed. *32,* 7–14. Referenced in Stegmann, H., & Kindermann, W. (1982). Comparison of prolonged exercise tests at the individual anaerobic threshold and the fixed anaerobic threshold of 4 mmol.1-1 lactate. *International Journal of Sports Medicine, 3,* 105–110.

Simon, J., Segal, K. R., & Jaffe, L. A. (1987). Exercise prescription based on perceived exertion versus heart rate in middle-aged women. [Abstract]. *Medicine and Science in Sports and Exercise, 19*(2), S14.

Simoneau, J. A., Lortie, G., Boulay, M. R., Marcotte, M., Thibault, M. C., & Bouchard, C. (1986). Inheritance of human skeletal muscle and anaerobic capacity adaptation to high intensity training. *International Journal of Sports Medicine, 7*(3), 167–171.

Simonsen, J. C., Sherman, W. M., Lamb, D. R., Dernbach, A. R., Doyle, J. A., & Strauss, R. (1991). Dietary carbohydrate, muscle glycogen, and power output during rowing training. *Journal of Applied Physiology, 70*(4), 1500–1505.

Sjodin, B. (1982). The relationships among running economy, aerobic power, muscle power, and onset of blood lactate accumulation in young boys (11–15 years). In P. V. Komi (Ed.), *International Series on Sport Sciences: Vol. 12. Exercise and Sport Biology* (pp. 57–60). Baltimore: University Park Press.

Sjodin, B., & Jacobs, I. (1981). Onset of blood lactate accumulation and marathon running performance. *International Journal of Sports Medicine, 2,* 23–26.

Sjodin, B., Schele, R., & Karlsson, J. (1982). The physiological background of onset of blood lactate accumulation (OBLA). In P. V. Komi (Ed.), *International Series on Sport Sciences: Vol. 12. Exercise and Sport Biology* (pp. 43–56). Champaign, IL: Human Kinetics.

Sly, R. M. (1986). History of exercise-induced asthma. *Medicine and Science in Sports and Exercise, 18*(3), 314–317.

Snyder, A. C., Dvorak, L. L., & Roepke, J. B. (1987). Dietary patterns and iron parameters of middle aged female runners. [Abstract]. *Medicine and Science in Sports and Exercise, 19*(2), S38.

Song, T. K., Serressee, O., Ama, P., Theriault, J., & Boulay, M. R. (1988). Effects of three anaerobic tests on venous blood values. [Abstract]. *Medicine and Science in Sports and Exercise, 20*(2), S39.

Stachenfeld, N. S., Gleim, G. W., Nicholas, J. A., & Coplan, N. L. (1988). Variation in Borg scale at lactate threshold. [Abstract]. *Medicine and Science in Sports and Exercise, 20*(2), S21.

Stager, J. M., & Cordain, L. (1984). Relationship of body composition in female swimmers. *Journal of Swimming Research, 1*(1), 21–26.

Stager, J. M., Cordain, L., Malley, J., & Stickler, J. (1985). Arterial desaturation during arm exercise with controlled frequency breathing. [Abstract]. *Medicine and Science in Sports and Exercise, 17*(2), 227.

Stainsby, W. N. (1973). Oxygen tensions in muscle. In J. Keul (Ed.), *Limiting Factors of Physical Performance* (pp. 137–145). Stuttgart, Germany: Georg Thieme Verlag.

Stanford, P. D., Williams, D. J., Sharp, R. L., & Bevan, L. (1985). Effect of reduced breathing frequency during exercise on blood gases and acid-base balance. [Abstract]. *Medicine and Science in Sports and Exercise, 17*(2), 228.

Stegmann, H., & Kindermann, W. (1982). Comparison of prolonged exercise tests at the individual anaerobic threshold and the fixed anaerobic threshold of 4 mmol.l-1 lactate. *International Journal of Sports Medicine, 3,* 105–110.

Stegmann, H., Kindermann, W., & Schnabel, A. (1981). Lactate kinetics and individual anaerobic threshold. *International Journal of Sports Medicine, 2,* 160–165.

Stein, T. P., Schulter, M. D., & Diamond, C. E. (1983). Nutrition protein turnover and physical activity in young women. *American Journal of Clinical Nutrition, 38,* 223–228.

Stewart, J. G., Ahlquist, D. A., McGill, D. B., Ilstrup, D. M., Schwartz, S., & Owen, R. A. (1984). Gastrointestinal blood loss and anemia in runners. *Annals of Internal Medicine, 100*(6), 843–845.

Stray-Gunderson, J., Videman, T., & Snell, P. G. (1986). Changes in selected objective parameters during overtraining. [Abstract]. *Medicine and Science in Sports and Exercise, 18*(2), S54–S55.

Suominen, H., Heikkinen, E., Parkatti, T., Forsberg, S., & Kiiskinen, A. (1980). Effects of lifelong physical training on functional aging in men. *Scandinavian Journal of Social Medicine, 14*(Suppl.): 225–240.

Suurnakki, T., Ilmarinen, J., Nygard, C-H., Komi, P. V., & Karlsson, J. (1986). Anaerobic strain in children during a cross-country skiing competition. In R. Rutenfranz, R. Mocellin, & F. Klimt (Eds.), *International Series on Sport Sciences, Vol. 17. Children and Exercise XII* (pp. 67–75). Champaign, IL: Human Kinetics.

Svarc, V., & Novak, J. (1975). The changes of acid-base balance during interval swimming training in trained and untrained men. In H. Howald & J. R. Poortmans (Eds.), *Metabolic Adaptations to Prolonged Physical Exercise* (pp. 73–77). Basel: Birkhauser Verlag.

Svedenhag, J., Henriksson, J., & Sylven, C. (1983). Dissociation of training effects on skeletal muscle mitochondrial enzymes and myoglobin in man. *Acta Physiologica Scandinavica, 117,* 213–218.

Symons, J. D., & Jacobs, I. A. (1989). High-intensity exercise performance is not impaired by low intramuscular glycogen. *Medicine and Science in Sports and Exercise, 21*(5), 550–557.

Taguchi, S., Hata, Y., Itoh, K., & Itoh, M. (1984). Effects of swimming training and hypobaric hypoxia on biochemical and histochemical profiles of skeletal muscles in rats. [Abstract]. *Medicine and Science in Sports and Exercise, 16*(2), 146.

Tamayo, M., Sucec, A., Phillips, W., Buono, M., Laubach, +L., & Frey, + +M. (1984). The Wingate anaerobic power test, peak blood lactate, and maximal oxygen uptake in elite volleyball players: a validation study. [Abstract]. *Medicine and Science in Sports and Exercise, 16*(2), 126.

Tanaka, H., & Shindo, M. (1985). Running velocity at blood lactate threshold of boys aged 6–15 years compared with untrained and trained young males. *International Journal of Sports Medicine, 6*(2), 90–94.

Tarnopolsky, M. A., MacDougall, J. D., & Atkinson, S. A. (1988). Influence of protein intake and training status on nitrogen balance and lean mass. *Journal of Applied Physiology, 64,* 187–193.

Tegtbur, U., Griess, M., Braumann, K. M., Busse, M. W., & Maasen, W. (1988). A method for determining the endurance capacity of runners. [Abstract]. *International Journal of Sports Medicine, 9*(5), 387.

Tenny, S. M. (1968). Physiological adaptations to life at high altitude. In Jokl (Ed.), *Medicine and Sport: Vol. 1. Exercise and Altitude* (pp. 60–70). Basel: S. Karger.

Terrados, N., Melichna, J., Sylven, C., Jansson, E., & Kaijser, L. (1988). Effects of training at simulated altitude on performance and muscle metabolic capacity in competitive road cyclists. *European Journal of Applied Physiology, 57,* 203–209.

Tesch, P. A., Hakkinen, K., & Komi, P. V. (1985). The effect of strength training and detraining on various enzyme activities. [Abstract]. *Medicine and Science in Sports and Exercise, 17*(2), 245.

Thomson, J. A., Green, H. J., & Houston, M. E. (1979). Muscle glycogen depletion patterns in fast twitch fibre subgroups of man during submaximal and supramaximal exercise. *Pflugers Archives, 379,* 105–108.

Thorland, W., Johnson, G., Housh, T., Tharp, G., & Cisar, C. (1988). Generality of strength & power in young male runners. [Abstract]. *Medicine and Science in Sports and Exercise, 20*(2), S67.

Tiberi, M., Bohle, E., Zimmermann, E., Heck, H., & Hollmann, W. (1988). Comparative examination between Conconi- and Lactate thresholds on the treadmill by middle distance runners. [Abstract]. *International Journal of Sports Medicine, 9*(5), 372.

Timson, B. F., Bowlin, B. K., Dudenhoeffer, G. A., & George, J. B. (1985). Fiber number, area, and composition of mouse soleus muscle following enlargement. *Journal of Applied Physiology, 58,* 619–624.

Troup, J. P. (1989a). Training limits. *Research Updates* (p. 6). Colorado Springs: United States Swimming.

Troup, J. P. (1989b). Interim training periods. *Research Updates* (p. 9). Colorado Springs: United States Swimming.

Troup, J. P. (1989c). Detraining. *Research Updates* (p. 10). Colorado Springs: United States Swimming.

Troup, J. P., Bradley, P. W., Hall, R. R., & Van Handel, P. J. (1985). The effects of fatigue and recovery on muscle function following high intensity training. [Abstract]. *Medicine and Science in Sports and Exercise, 17*(2), 194.

Troup, J. P., & Daniels, J. T. (1986). Swimming economy: an introductory review. *Journal of Swimming Research, 2*(1), 5–9.

Troup, J. P., & House, J. W. (1989). *Sports Participation & Exercise-Induced Asthma.* Pamphlet prepared by United States Swimming, Colorado Springs.

Troup, J. P., Plyley, M. J., Sharp, R. L., & Costill, D. L. (1981, August). Development of peak performance: Strength training and tapering. *Swimming World.*

Ui, M. (1966). A role of phosphofructokinase in pH-dependent regulation of glycolysis. *Biochemica et Biophysica Acta, 124,* 310–322.

Urhausen, A., Kullmer, T., & Kindermann, W. (1987). The influence of an intense training and competition period upon the anabolic-catabolic hormonal relationship in rowers. [Abstract]. *International Journal of Sports Medicine, 8*(2), 149.

van Erp-Baart, A. M. J., Saris, W. H. M., Binkhorst, R. A., Vos, J. A., & Elvers, J. W. H. (1989). Nationwide survey on nutritional habits in elite athletes: Part II. Mineral and vitamin intake. *International Journal of Sports Medicine, 10* (Suppl. 1), S11–S16.

Van Handel, P. J., Katz, A., Morrow, J. R., Troup, J. P., Daniels, J. T., & Bradley, P. W. (1988). Aerobic economy and competitive swimming performance of U.S. elite swimmers. In B. E. Ungerechts, K. Wilke, & K. Reischle (Eds.), *International Series on Sports Sciences: Vol. 18. Swimming Science* (pp. 295–303). Champaign, IL: Human Kinetics.

VanNess, J. M., & Town, G. P. (1989). Controlled frequency breathing does not alter blood lactate levels in competitive swimmers. [Abstract]. *Medicine and Science in Sports and Exercise, 21*(2), S104.

Veller, O. D. (1968). Studies on sweat loss of nutrients. Iron content of whole body sweat and its association with other sweat constituents, serum iron levels, hematological indices, body surface area and sweat rate. *Scandinavian Journal of Clinical Investigation, 1,* 157–167.

Weicker, H., Bert, H., Rettenmeier, A., Oettinger, U., Hagele, H., & Keilholz, U. (1983). Alanine formation during maximal short-term exercise. In H. G. Knuttgen, J. A. Vogel, & J. Poortmans (Eds.), *International Series on Sport Sciences: Vol. 13. Biochemistry of Exercise* (pp. 385–394). Champaign, IL: Human Kinetics.

Weight, L. M., & Noakes, T. D. (1987). Is running an analog of anorexia? A survey of the incidence of eating disorders in female distance runners. *Medicine and Science in Sports and Exercise, 19*(3), 213–217.

Weihe, W. H. (1967). Time course of acclimatization to high altitude. In *The Effects of Altitude on Physical Performance* (pp. 33–35). Chicago: The Athletic Institute.

Weiss, M., Bouws, N. E., & Weicker, H. (1988). Comparison between the 30-minutes-test and the 300 m step-test according to Simon in the women's national swimming team. [Abstract]. *International Journal of Sports Medicine, 9*(5), 379.

Weiss, M., Reischle, K., Bouws, N., Simon, G., & Weicker, H. (1988). Relationship of blood lactate accumulation to stroke rate and distance per stroke in top female swimmers. In B. E. Ungerechts, K. Wilke, & K. Reischle (Eds.), *International Series on Sports Sciences, Vol. 18. Swimming Science V* (pp. 295–303). Champaign, IL: Human Kinetics.

Wells, C. L. (1985). *Women, Sport & Performance.* Champaign, IL: Human Kinetics.

Wells, C. L., & Plowman, S. A. (1988). Relationship between training, menarche, and amenorrhea. In E. W. Brown & C. F. Branta (Eds.), *Competitive Sports for Children and Youth: An Overview of Research and Issues* (pp. 195–211). Champaign, IL: Human Kinetics.

Weltman, A., Janney, C., Rians, C. B., Strand, K., Berg, B., Tippit, S., Wise, J., Cahill, B. R., & Katch, F. I. (1986). The effects of hydraulic resistance strength training in pre-pubertal males. *Medicine and Science in Sports and Exercise, 18,* 629–638.

Weyman, M., Reybrouck, T., Stijns, H., & Knops, J. (1985). Influence of age and sex on the ventilatory anaerobic threshold in children. In R. A. Binkhorst, H. C. G. Kemper, & W. H. M. Saris (Eds.), *International Series on Sport Sciences: Vol. 15. Children and Exercise XI* (pp. 114–118). Champaign, IL: Human Kinetics.

Wilke, K., & Madsen, O. (1983). *Coaching the Young Swimmer.* London: Pelham Books.

Wilmore, J. H., & Costill, D. L. (1988). *Training for Sport and Activity: The Physiological Basis of the Conditioning Process.* Dubuque, IA: Wm. C. Brown Publishers.

Winder, W. W., Hickson, R. C., Hagberg, J. M., Ehsani, A. A., & McLane, J. A. (1979). Training induced changes in hormonal and metabolic responses to submaximal exercise. *Journal of Applied Physiology, 46*(4), 766–771.

Wolfe, R. R. (1987). Does exercise stimulate protein breakdown in humans? Isotropic approaches to the problem. *Medicine and Science in Sports and Exercise, 19*(5), S172–S178.

Wong, S., & McKenzie, D. C. (1985). Fitness and pregnancy. [Abstract]. *Medicine and Science in Sports and Exercise, 17*(2), 208.

Wyndham, C. H., Strydom, W. B., van Renisburg, A. J., & Benade, A. J. S. (1969). Physiological requirements for world class running performance in endurance running. *South African Medical Journal, 43,* 996–1002.

Yakolev, N. N. (1950). The order of biochemical changes in muscle training and breaking of training. (Russ) *Fziol. J. 36,* 744. Cited in J. Keul, E. Doll, & D. Keppler (Eds.), *Energy Metabolism of Human Muscle.* Baltimore: University Park Press, 1972.

Yamamoto, Y., Mutoh, Y., Kobayashi, H., & Miyashita, M. (1985). The effects of controlled respiration rate on metabolic responses to submaximal intermittent exercise. [Abstract]. *Medicine and Science in Sports and Exercise, 17*(2), 230.

Yates, A., Leefkey, K., & Shisslak, C. M. (1983). Running—An analogue of anorexia? *New England Journal of Medicine, 308,* 251–255.

Yoshida, T., Chida, M., Ichioka, M., & Suda, Y. (1987). Blood lactate parameters related to aerobic capacity and endurance performance. *European Journal of Applied Physiology, 56,* 7–11.

Yoshimura, H., Inone, T., Yamada, T., & Shiraki, K. (1980). Anemia during hard physical training (sports anemia) and its causal mechanism with special reference to protein nutrition. *World Review of Nutrition and Diet, 35,* 1–86.

Young, A. J., Evans, W. J., Fisher, E. C., Sharp, R. L., Costill, D. L., & Maher, J. T. (1984). Skeletal muscle metabolism of sea-level natives following short-term high-altitude residence. *European Journal of Applied Physiology, 52,* 463–466.

Young, V. R., & Munro, H. N. (1978). N-methylhistidine (3-methylhistidine) and muscle protein turnover. An overview. *Federation Proceedings, 37,* 2291–2300.

Part II

Adrian, M., Singh, M., & Karpovich, P. (1966). Energy cost of the leg kick, arm stroke and whole stroke. *Journal of Applied Physiology, 21,* 1763–1766.

Allen, R. H. (1948). A study of the leg stroke in swimming the crawl stroke. Unpublished master's thesis, State University of Iowa.

Alley, L. E. (1952). An analysis of water resistance and propulsion in swimming the crawl stroke. *Research Quarterly, 23,* 253–270.

Astrand, P. (1978). Aerobic power in swimming. In B. Eriksson & B. Furberg (Eds.), *International Series on Sports Sciences: Vol. 6. Swimming Medicine IV* (pp. 127–131). Baltimore: University Park Press.

Astrand, P. O., & Rodahl, K. (1977). *Textbook of Work Physiology.* San Francisco: McGraw-Hill.

Aviation Research Associates. (1943). *How Planes Fly.* New York: Harper and Row.

Ayalon, A., Van Gheluwe, B., & Kanitz, M. (1975). A comparison of four styles of racing start in swimming. In L. Lewillie & J. P. Clarys (Eds.), *International Series on Sport Sciences: Vol. 2. Swimming II* (pp. 233–240). Baltimore: University Park Press.

Bachman, J. C. (1969). A comparison of hand positions in swimming freestyle. *Swimming Technique, 6*(3), 72–73.

Bachrach, W. (1924). *The Outline of Swimming*. Chicago: Bradwell.

Barna, P. S. (1969). *Fluid Mechanics for Engineers.* New York: Plenum Press.

Barthels, K. M., & Adrian, M. J. (1971). Variability in the dolphin kick under four conditions. In L. Lewillie & J. P. Clarys (Eds.), *First International Symposium on Biomechanics in Swimming, Waterpolo and Diving Proceedings* (pp. 105–108). Brussels: Universitie Libre de Bruxelles Laboratoire de L'effort.

Barthels, K., & Adrian, M. J. (1974). Three dimensional spatial hand patterns of skilled butterfly swimmers. In J. P. Clarys & L. Lewillie (Eds.), *International Series on Sport Sciences: Vol. 2. Swimming II* (pp. 154–160). Baltimore: University Park Press.

Becker, T. (1984). Coaches Guide to Bicepital Tendonitis. In T. F. Welsh (Ed.), *ASCA World Clinic Yearbook*. (pp. 19–24). Fort Lauderdale: American Swimming Coaches Association.

Belokovsky, V., & Ivanchenko, E. (1975). A hydrokinetic apparatus for the study and improvement of leg movements in the breaststroke. In L. Lewillie & J. P. Clarys (Eds.), *International Series on Sport Sciences: Vol. 2. Swimming II* (pp. 64–69). Baltimore: University Park Press.

Bergen, P. (1978). Breaststroke. In R. M. Ousley (Ed.), *ASCA World Clinic Yearbook* (pp. 99–106). Fort Lauderdale: American Swimming Coaches Association.

Beritzhoff, S. T. (1974). *The relative effectiveness of two breaststroke starting techniques among selected intercollegiate swimmers.* Unpublished master's thesis, California State University, Chico.

Bober, T., & Czabanski, B. (1975). Changes in breaststroke technique under different speed conditions. In L. Lewillie & J. P. Clarys (Eds.), *International Series on Sport Sciences: Vol. 2. Swimming II* (pp. 188–193). Baltimore: University Park Press.

Bowers, J. E., & Cavanaugh, P. R. (1975). A biomechanical comparison of the grab and conventional sprint starts in competitive swimming. In L. Lewillie & J. P. Clarys (Eds.), *International Series on Sport Sciences: Vol. 2. Swimming II* (pp. 225–232). Baltimore: University Park Press.

Brown, R. M., & Counsilman, J. E. (1971). The role of lift in propelling swimmers. In J. M. Cooper (Ed.), *Biomechanics* (pp. 179–188). Chicago: Athletic Institute.

Bucher, W. (1975). The influence of the leg kick and the arm stroke on the total speed during the crawl stroke. In L. Lewillie & J. P. Clarys (Eds.), *International Series on Sport Sciences: Vol. 2. Swimming II* (pp. 180–187). Baltimore: University Park Press.

Cavanaugh, P. R., Palmgren, J. V., & Kerr, B. A. (1975). A device to measure forces at the hand during the grab start in swimming. In L. Lewillie & J. P. Clarys (Eds.), *International Series on Sport Sciences: Vol. 2. Swimming II* (pp. 43–50). Baltimore: University Park Press.

Chadwick, A. W. (1967). *A cinematographical analysis of ten breaststroke swimmers, including certain strength and anatomical measures.* Unpublished master's thesis, Michigan State University, East Lansing.

Charbonnier, J. P., Lacour, J. P., Rigffal, J., & Flandrois, R. (1975). Experimental study of the performance of competitive swimmers. *Journal of Applied Physiology, 34,* 157–167.

Chow, J. W., Hay, J. G., Wilson, B. D., & Imel, C. (1984). Turning techniques of elite swimmers. *Journal of Sports Sciences, 2,* 241–255.

Clarys, J. P. (1979). Human morphology and hydrodynamics. In J. Terauds & E. W. Bedingfield (Eds.), *International Series on Sport Sciences: Vol. 8. Swimming III* (pp. 3–41). Baltimore: University Park Press.

Clarys, J. P., & Jiskoot, J. (1975). Total resistance of selected body positions in the front crawl. In L. Lewillie & J. P. Clarys (Eds.), *International Series on Sport Sciences: Vol. 2. Swimming II* (pp. 110–117). Baltimore: University Park Press.

Colwin, C. (1984). Fluid dynamics: Vortex circulation in swimming propulsion. In T. F. Welsh (Ed.), *ASCA World Clinic Yearbook* (pp. 38–46). Fort Lauderdale: American Swimming Coaches Association.

Colwin, C. (1985a, July/August). Essential fluid dynamics of swimming propulsion. *ASCA Newsletter,* pp. 22–27.

Colwin, C. (1985b, September/October). Practical application of flow analysis as a coaching tool. *ASCA Newsletter,* pp. 5–8.

Counsilman, J. E. (1955). Forces in swimming two types of crawl stroke. *Research Quarterly, 26*(2), 127–139.

Counsilman, J. E. (1968). *The Science of Swimming*. Englewood Cliffs, NJ: Prentice-Hall.

Counsilman, J. E. (1977). *Competitive Swimming Manual for Coaches and Swimmers.* Bloomington, IN: Counsilman Co.

Counsilman, J. E., Counsilman, B. E., Nomura, T., & Endo, M. (1988). Three types of grab starts for competitive swimming. In B. E. Ungerechts, K. Wilke, & K. Reischle (Eds.), *International Series on Sport Sciences: Vol. 18. Swimming Science V* (pp. 81–91). Champaign, IL: Human Kinetics.

Counsilman, J., & Wasilak, J. (1982). The importance of hand speed and hand acceleration. In R. M. Ousley (Ed.), *1981 ASCA World Clinic Yearbook* (pp. 41–45). Fort Lauderdale: American Swimming Coaches Association.

Craig, A. B., Jr., Boomer, W. L., & Skehan, P. L. (1988). Patterns of velocity in breaststroke swimming. In B. Ungerechts, K. Wilke, & K. Reischle (Eds.), *International Series on Sport Sciences: Vol. 18. Swimming Science V* (pp. 73–77). Champaign, IL: Human Kinetics.

Crist, J. M. (1979). An analytical comparison between two types of butterfly pull patterns: the crossover and the keyhole. *Swimming Technique 15*(4), 110–117.

Cureton, T. K. (1930). Relationship of respiration to speed efficiency in swimming. *Research Quarterly, 1*(1), 66.

Czabanski, B. (1975). Asymmetry of the lower limbs in breaststroke swimming. In L. Lewillie & J. P. Clarys (Eds.), *International Series on Sport Sciences: Vol. 2. Swimming II* (pp. 207–213). Baltimore: University Park Press.

Czabanski, B., & Koszczyc, T. (1979). Relationship between stroke asymmetry and speed of breaststroke swimming. In J. Terauds & E. W. Bedingfield (Eds.), *International Series on Sport Sciences: Vol. 8. Swimming III* (pp. 148–152). Baltimore: University Park Press.

Daly, D., Persyn, U., Van Tilborgh, L., & Riemaker, D. (1988). Estimation of sprint performances in the breaststroke from body characteristics. In B. Ungerechts, K. Wilkie, & K. Reischle (Eds.), *International Series on Sport Sciences: Vol. 18. Swimming Science V* (pp. 101–107). Champaign, IL: Human Kinetics.

de Groot, G., & van Ingen Schenau, G. J. (1988). Fundamental mechanics applied to swimming technique and propelling efficiency. In B. Ungerechts, K. Wilkie, & K. Reischle (Eds.), *International Series on Sport Sciences: Vol. 18. Swimming Science V* (pp. 17–29). Champaign, IL: Human Kinetics.

Disch, J. G., Hosler, W. W., & Bloom, J. A. (1979). Effects of weight, height, and reach on the performance of the conventional and grab starts in swimming. In J. Terauds & E. W. Bedingfield (Eds.), *International Series on Sport Sciences: Vol. 8. Swimming III* (pp. 215–221). Baltimore: University Park Press.

Dubois, A. B., Cavagna, G. A., & Fox, R. S. (1974). Pressure distribution on the body surface of swimming fish. *European Journal of Biology, 60,* 581–591.

Firby, H. (1975). *Howard Firby on Swimming*. London: Pelham Books.

Gibson, G., & Holt, L. E. (1976). A cinema-computer analysis of selected starting techniques. *Swimming Technique, 13,* 75–76, 79.

Groves, R., & Roberts, J. A. (1972). A further investigation of the optimum angle of projection for the racing start in swimming. *Research Quarterly, 43*(2), 167–174.

Guimares, A. C. S., & Hay, J. G. (1985). A mechanical analysis of the grab starting technique in swimming. *International Journal of Sports Biomechanics, 1,* 25–35.

Haljand, R. (1984). A new scientific approach to analyzing swimming technique. In J. L. Cramer (Ed.), *How to Develop Olympic Level Swimmers: Scientific and Practical Foundations* (pp. 72–105). Helsinki, Finland: Int. Sports Media.

Hanauer, E. (1967). The grab start. *Swimming World, 8,* 5, 42.

Hanauer, E. S. (1972). Grab start faster than conventional start. *Swimming World, 13,* 8–9, 54–55.

Hay, J. G. (1985). *The Biomechanics of Sports Techniques*. Englewood Cliffs, NJ: Prentice-Hall.

Hay, J. G. (1986). The status of research on the biomechanics of swimming. In J. G. Hay (Ed.), *Starting, Stroking & Turning*. (pp. 53–76). Iowa City: Biomechanics Laboratory, University of Iowa.

Hay, J. G., & Thayer, A. (1989). Flow visualization of competitive swimming techniques: the tufts method. *Journal of Biomechanics, 22*(1), 11–19.

Healey, J. H. (1970). *A comparative study to determine the relationship between plantar flexion at the ankle joint and success in selected skills in swimming*. Unpublished doctoral dissertation. University of Utah, Salt Lake City, Utah.

Hendrickson, C. B. (1949). *Effect of development of foot flexibility on learning the flutter kick*. Unpublished master's thesis, University of Wisconsin, Madison.

Henry, F. M., & Rogers, D. E. (1960). Increased response latency for complicated movements and a 'Memory Drum' theory of neuromotor reaction. *Research Quarterly, 31,* 448–458.

Hinrichs, R. (1986). Biomechanics of butterfly. In T. Johnston, J. Woolger, & D. Scheider (Eds.), *ASCA World Clinic Yearbook* (p. 94). Fort Lauderdale: American Swimming Coaches Association.

Hollander, A. P., de Groot, G., van Ingen Schneau, G. J., Kahman, R., & Toussaint, H. M. (1988). Contributions of the legs to propulsion in front crawl swimming. In B. Ungerechts, K. Wilkie, & R. Reischle (Eds.), *International Series on Sport Sciences: Vol. 18. Swimming Science V* (pp. 39–43). Champaign, IL: Human Kinetics.

Holmer, I. (1974). Energy cost of the arm stroke, leg kick and the whole stroke in competitive swimming style. *Journal of Applied Physiology, 33,* 105–118.

Jensen, R. K., & McIlwain, J. (1979). Modeling lower extremity forces in the dolphin kick. In J. Terauds and E. W. Bedingfield (Eds.), *International Series on Sport Sciences: Vol. 8. Swimming III* (pp. 137–147). Baltimore: University Park Press.

Jiskoot, J., & Clarys, J. P. (1975). Body resistance on and under the water surface. In L. Lewillie & J. P. Clarys (Eds.), *International Series on Sport Sciences: Vol. 2. Swimming II* (pp. 105–109). Baltimore: University Park Press.

Jorgenson, L. W. (1971). *A cinematographical and descriptive comparison of three selected freestyle racing starts in competitive swimming*. Unpublished doctoral dissertation, Louisiana State University, Baton Rouge.

Kennedy, J. C. (1978). Orthopaedic manifestations. In B. Eriksson & B. Furberg (Eds.), *International Series on Sport Sciences: Vol. 6. Swimming Medicine IV* (pp. 94–97). Baltimore: University Park Press.

Koehler, J. A. (1987). *Bernoulli, bah or how aircraft fly*. Unpublished manuscript, University of Saskatchewan, Saskatoon.

Kornecki, S., & Bober, T. (1978). Extreme velocities of a swimming cycle as a technique criterion. In B. Eriksson & B. Furberg (Eds.), *International Series on Sport Sciences: Vol. 6. Swimming Medicine IV* (pp. 402–407). Baltimore: University Park Press.

Krahenbuhl, G. S., Plummer, R. F., & Gaintner, G. L. (1975). Motor and sensory set effects of grab-start times of champion female swimmers. *Research Quarterly, 46*(4), 441–446.

Kreighbaum, E., & Barthels, K. M. (1985). *Biomechanics: A Qualitative Approach for Studying Human Motion*. Minneapolis: Burgess Publishing.

LaRue, R. J. (1983). A biomechanical comparison of the grab start and the track start in competitive swimming. *AAHPERD, Abstracts of Research Papers, 1*, 20.

Lewis, S. (1980). Comparison of five swimming start techniques. *Swimming Technique, 16*, 124–128.

Lighthill, J. (1969). Hydrodynamics of aquatic animal propulsion. *Annual Review of Fluid Mechanics, 1*, 413–446.

Luedtke, D. (1986). Backstroke biomechanics. In T. Johnston, J. Woolger, & D. Scheider (Eds.), *ASCA World Clinic Yearbook* (p. 95). Fort Lauderdale: American Swimming Coaches Association.

Maglischo, E. W. (1984). A 3-dimensional cinematographical analysis of competitive swimming strokes. In R. M. Ousley (Ed.), *1983 ASCA World Clinic Yearbook* (pp. 1–14). Fort Lauderdale: American Swimming Coaches Association.

Maglischo, C. W., Maglischo, E. W., Higgins, J., Hinrichs, R., Luedtke, D., Schleihauf, R. E., & Thayer, A. (1986). A biomechanical analysis of the 1984 U.S. Olympic swimming team: the distance freestylers. *Journal of Swimming Research, 2*(3), 12–16.

Maglischo, C. W., Maglischo, E. W., Luedtke, D., Schleihauf, R. E., Higgins, J., Thayer, A., & Hinrichs, R. (1987). The swimmer: A study of propulsion and drag. *SOMA 2*(2), 40–44.

Maglischo, C. W., Maglischo, E. W., & Santos, T. R. (1987). The relationship between the forward velocity of the center of gravity and the hip in the four competitive strokes. *Journal of Swimming Research 3*(2), 11–17.

Mason, B. R., Patton, S. G., & Newton, A. P. (1989). Propulsion in breaststroke swimming. In W. E. Morrison (Ed.), *Proceedings of the VII International Symposium on Biomechanics in Sports* (pp. 257–267). Melbourne, Australia: Footscray Institute of Technology.

Michaels, R. A. (1973). A time distance comparison of the conventional and the grab start. *Swimming Technique, 10*, 16–17.

Miller, J. A., Hay, J. G., & Wilson, B. D. (1984). Starting techniques of elite swimmers. *Journal of Sports Sciences, 2*, 213–223.

Nagy, J. (1989). From a technical angle: Breaking down the technical elements of the wave-action breaststroke. *Swimming Technique, 26*(2), 16–19.

Nimz, R., Rader, U., Wilkie, K., & Skipka, W. (1988). The relationship of anthropometric measures to different types of breaststroke kicks. In B. Ungerechts, K. Wilkie, & K. Reischle (Eds.), *International Series on Sport Sciences: Vol. 18. Swimming Science V* (pp. 115–119). Champaign, IL: Human Kinetics.

Northrip, J. W., Logan, G. A., & McKinney, W. C. (1974). *Introduction to Biomechanic Analysis of Sport*. Dubuque, IA: Wm. C. Brown.

Pai, Y. (1986). A hydrodynamic study of the oscillation motion in swimming. In J. G. Hay (Ed.), *Starting, Stroking & Turning* (pp. 145–150). Iowa City: Biomechanics Laboratory, University of Iowa.

Pendergast, D. R., diPrampero, P. E., Craig, A. B., Wilson, D. R., & Rennie, D. W. (1977). Quantitative analysis of the front crawl in men and women. *Journal of Applied Physiology, 43*, 475–479.

Persyn, U., De Maeyer, J., & Vervaecke, H. (1975). Investigation of hydrodynamic determinants of competitive swimming strokes. In L. Lewillie & J. P. Clarys (Eds.), *International Series on Sport Sciences: Vol. 2. Swimming II*. (pp. 214–222). Baltimore: University Park Press.

Persyn, U., Van Tilborgh, L., Daly, D., Colman, V., Vijfvinkel, D. J., & Verhetsel, D. (1988). Computerized evaluation and advice in swimming. In B. Ungerechts, K. Wilkie, & K. Reischle (Eds.), *International Series on Sport Sciences: Vol. 18. Swimming Science V* (pp. 341–349). Champaign, IL: Human Kinetics.

Persyn, U., Vervaecke, H., & Verhetsel, D. (1983). Factors influencing stroke mechanics and speed in swimming butterfly. In H. Matsui & K. Koybayashi (Eds.), *International Series on Sport Sciences: Biomechanics VIII-B* (pp. 833–841). Champaign, IL: Human Kinetics.

Pfeifer, H. (1984). Some selected problems of technique and training in backstroke swimming. In J. L. Cramer (Ed.), *How to Develop Olympic Level Swimmers* (pp. 160–179). Helsinki, Finland: International Sports Media.

Plagenhoff, S. (1971). *Patterns of Human Motion*. Englewood Cliffs, NJ: Prentice-Hall.

Ransom, G. G. (1973). The no breather flip turn. *Swimming Technique, 10,* 70–82.

Reischle, K. (1979). A kinematic investigation of movement patterns in swimming with photo-optical methods. In J. Terauds & E. W. Bedingfield (Eds.), *International Series on Sport Sciences: Vol. 8. Swimming III* (pp. 97–104). Baltimore: University Park Press.

Remmonds, P., & Bartlett, R. M. (1981). Effects of finger separation. *Swimming Technique, 18*(1), 28–30.

Robertson, D. F. (1960). Relationship of strength of selected muscle groups and ankle flexibility to the flutter kick in swimming. Unpublished master's thesis, State University of Iowa. Iowa City.

Roffer, B. J., & Nelson, R. C. (1972). The grab start is faster. *Swimming Technique, 8,* 101–102.

Rouse, H. (1946). *Elementary Mechanics of Fluids*. New York: Dover.

Schleihauf, R. E., Jr. (1986). Biomechanics. In T. Johnston, J. Woolger, & D. Scheider (Eds.), *ASCA World Clinic Yearbook* (pp. 88–93). Fort Lauderdale: American Swimming Coaches Association.

Schleihauf, R. E., Jr. (1974). A biomechanical analysis of freestyle. *Swimming Technique, 11,* 88–96.

Schleihauf, R. E., Jr. (1976). A hydrodynamic analysis of breaststroke pulling efficiency. *Swimming Technique, 12,* 100–105.

Schleihauf, R. E., Jr. (1978). Swimming propulsion: a hydrodynamic analysis. In B. Ousley (Ed.), *1977 ASCA World Clinic Yearbook* (pp. 49–86). Fort Lauderdale: American Swimming Coaches Association.

Schleihauf, R. E., Gray, L., & DeRose, J. (1983). Three-dimensional analysis of hand propulsion in the sprint front crawl stroke. In A. P. Hollander, P. A. Huijing, & G. de Groot (Eds.), *International Series on Sport Sciences: Vol. 14. Biomechanics and Medicine in Swimming* (pp. 173–183). Champaign, IL: Human Kinetics.

Schleihauf, R. E., Higgins, J., Hinrichs, R., Luedtke, D., Maglischo, C., Maglischo, E., & Thayer, A. (1984). Biomechanics of swimming propulsion. In T. F. Welsh (Ed.), *ASCA World Clinic Yearbook* (pp. 19–24). Fort Lauderdale: American Swimming Coaches Association.

Schleihauf, R. E., Higgins, J. R., Hinrichs, R., Luedtke, D., Maglischo, C., Maglischo, E. W., & Thayer, A. (1988). Propulsive techniques: front crawl stroke, butterfly, backstroke and breaststroke. In B. Ungerechts, K. Wilkie, & K. Reischle (Eds.), *International Series on Sport Sciences: Vol. 18. Swimming Science V* (pp. 53–60). Champaign, IL: Human Kinetics.

Sharp, R. L., & Costill, D. L. (1989). Influence of body hair removal on physiological responses during breaststroke swimming. *Medicine and Science in Sports and Exercise, 21*(5), 576–580.

Sharp, R. L., Hackney, A. C., Cain, S. M., & Ness, R. J. (1988). The effect of shaving down on the physiologic cost of freestyle swimming. *Journal of Swimming Research, 4*(1), 9–13.

Silvia, C. E. (1970). *Manual and Lesson Plans for Basic Swimming, Water Stunts, Lifesaving, Springboard Diving, Skin and Scuba Diving*. Springfield, MA: author.

Sprigings, E. J., & Koehler, J. A. (1990). The choice between Bernoulli's or Newton's model in predicting dynamic lift. *International Journal of Sports Biomechanics, 6*(3), 235–245.

Stratten, G. (1970). A comparison of three backstroke starts. *Swimming Technique, 7,* 55–60.

Thayer, A. L., & Hay, J. G. (1984). Motivating start and turn improvement. *Swimming Technique, 20*(4), 17–20.

Thayer, A., Schleihauf, R. E., Higgins, R. E., Hinrichs, J. R., Luedtke, D. L., Maglischo, C. W., & Maglischo, E. W. (1986). A hydrodynamic analysis of breaststroke swimmers. In J. G. Hay (Ed.), *Starting, Stroking & Turning* (pp. 131–143). Iowa City: Biomechanics Laboratory, Department of Exercise Science, University of Iowa.

Thorsen, E. A. (1975). Comparison of the conventional and grab start in swimming. *Tidsofkroft fur Legenspuelset, 39,* 130–138.

Toussaint, H. M. (1988). *Mechanics and Energetics of Swimming*. Amsterdam: published by the author.

Toussaint, H. M., de Groot, G., Savelberg, H. H. C. M., Vervoorn, K., Hollander, A. P., & van Ingen Schneau, G. J. (1988). Active drag related to velocity in male and female swimmers. *Journal of Biomechanics, 21,* 435–438.

Toussaint, H. M., van der Helm, F. C. T., Elzerman, J. R., Hollander, A. P., de Groot, G., & van Ingen Schneau, G. J. (1983). A power balance applied to swimming. In J. P. Hollander, P. A. Huijing, & G. de Groot (Eds.), *International Series on Sport Sciences: Vol. 14. Biomechanics and Medicine in Swimming* (pp. 165–172). Champaign, IL: Human Kinetics.

Ungerechts, B. E. (1983). A comparison of the movements of the rear parts of dolphin and butterfly swimmers. In A. P. Hollander, P. A. Huijing, & G. de Groot (Eds.), *International Series on Sport Sciences: Vol. 14. Biomechanics and Medicine in Swimming* (pp. 215–221). Champaign, IL: Human Kinetics.

Ungerechts, B. E. (1988). The relation of peak body acceleration to phases of movements in swimming. In B. Ungerechts, K. Wilkie, & K. Reischle (Eds.), *International Series on Sport Sciences: Vol. 18. Swimming Science V* (pp. 61–66). Champaign, IL: Human Kinetics.

Van Slooten, P. H. (1973). An analysis of two forward swim starts using cinematography. *Swimming Technique, 10,* 85–88.

Van Tilborgh, L., Willens, E. J., & Persyn, U. (1988). Evaluation of breaststroke propulsion and resistance-resultant impulses from film analysis. In B. Ungerechts, K. Wilkie, & K. Reischle (Eds.), *International Series on Sport Sciences: Vol. 18. Swimming Science V* (pp. 67–71). Champaign, IL: Human Kinetics.

Vervaecke, H. U. B., & Persyn, U. J. J. (1979). Effectiveness of the breaststroke leg movement in relation to selected time-space, anthropometric, flexibility, and force data. In J. Terauds & E. W. Bedingfield (Eds.), *International Series on Sport Sciences: Vol. 8. Swimming III* (pp. 320–328). Baltimore: University Park Press.

Ward, T. A. (1976). A cinematographical comparison of two turns. *Swimming Technique, 13*(1), 4–6.

Watkins, J., & Gordon, A. T. (1983). The effects of leg action on performance in the sprint front crawl stroke. In A. P. Hollander, P. A. Huijing, & G. de Groot (Eds.), *International Series on Sport Sciences: Vol. 14. Biomechanics and Medicine in Swimming* (pp. 310–314). Champaign, IL: Human Kinetics.

Wilson, D. S., & Marino, G. W. (1983). Kinematic analysis of three starts. *Swimming Technique, 19,* 30–34.

Winters, C. N. (1968). A comparison of the grip start in competitive swimming. Unpublished master's thesis. Southeast Missouri State College, Cape Girardeau.

Wood, T. C. (1978). A fluid dynamic analysis of the propulsive potential of the hand and forearm in swimming. In J. Terauds & E. W. Bedingfield (Eds.), *International Series on Sport Sciences: Vol. 8. Swimming III* (pp. 62–69). Baltimore: University Park Press.

Zatsiorsky, V. M., Bulgakova, N. Zh., & Chaplinsky, N. M. (1979). Biomechanical analysis of starting techniques in swimming. In J. Terauds & E. W. Bedingfield (Eds.), *International Series on Sport Sciences: Vol. 8. Swimming III* (pp. 199–206). Baltimore: University Park Press.

Part III

Alberici, J. C., Farrell, P. A., Kris-Etherton, P. M., & Shively, C. A. (1989). Effects of preexercise candy bar ingestion on substrate utilization and performance in trained cyclists. [Abstract]. *Medicine and Science in Sports and Exercise, 21*(2), S47.

Alta, M. J. (1988). *Science of Stretching*. Champaign, IL: Human Kinetics.

American Coach. (1988). The plyometrics debate (editorial), p. 10.

Asmussen, E., & Boje, O. (1945). Body temperature and capacity for work. *Acta Physiologica Scandinavica, 10,* 1–22.

Astrand, P. O., & Rodahl, K. (1977). *Textbook of Work Physiology.* New York: McGraw-Hill.

Barnard, R. J., Gardner, G. W., Diaco, N. V., MacAlpin, R. M., & Kattus, A. A. (1973). Cardiovascular responses to sudden strenuous exercise—heart rate, blood pressure, and ECG. *Journal of Applied Physiology, 34*(6), 833–837.

Barr, S. I. (1986). Nutrition knowledge and selected nutritional practices of female recreational athletes. *Journal of Nutritional Education, 18*(4), 167–174.

Beaulieu, J. E. (1980). *Stretching for All Sports*. Pasadena, CA: The Athletic Press.

Becker, J., & Braumann, K. (1988). The anaerobic performance after orally taken bicarbonate. [Abstract]. *International Journal of Sports Medicine, 9*(5), 363.

Behnke, A. R. (1969). New concepts in height-weight relationships. In N. Wilson (Ed.), *Obesity*. Philadelphia: F. A. Davis.

Bergstrom, J., Hermansen, L., Hultman, D., & Saltin, B. (1967). Muscle glycogen and physical performance. *Acta Physiologica Scandinavica, 71,* 140–150.

Bompa, T. (1983). *Theory and Methodology of Training*. Dubuque, IA: Kendall/Hunt.

Bond, V., Adams, R., Gresham, K., Tearney, R., Caprarola, M., Ruff, W., Gregory, H., & Stoddard, A. (1987). Effects of active and passive recovery on lactic acid removal and subsequent muscle function. [Abstract]. *Medicine and Science in Sports and Exercise, 19*(2), S35.

Bonen, A., & Belcastro, A. N. (1976). Comparison of self-selected recovery methods on lactic acid removal rates. *Medicine and Science in Sports and Exercise, 8*(3), 176–178.

Bourne, G. H. (1968). Nutrition and exercise. In H. B. Falls (Ed.), *Exercise Physiology* (pp. 155–171). New York: Academic Press.

Boven, A. P. M., Keizer, H. A., & Kuipers, H. (1985). Muscle glycogen synthesis rate in dependence of liquid and solid meals. [Abstract]. *Medicine and Science in Sports and Exercise, 17*(2), 205.

Bracken, M. E., Bracken, D. R., Nelson, A. G., & Conlee, R. K. (1988). The effect of cocaine on exercise endurance and glycogen use in the rat. *Journal of Applied Physiology, 64,* 884–887.

Bracken, M. E., Bracken, D. R., Winder, W. W., & Conlee, R. K. (1989). Effect of various doses of cocaine on endurance capacity in rats. *Journal of Applied Physiology, 66*(1), 377–383.

Braith, R. W., Graves, J. E., Pollock, M. L., Leggett, S. L., Carpenter, D. M., & Colvin, A. B. (1989). Comparison of 2 vs. 3 days/week of variable resistance training during 10- and 18-week programs. *International Journal of Sports Medicine, 6*(10), 450–454.

Brooks, G. A., & Fahey, T. D. (1984). *Exercise Physiology: Human Bioenergetics and Its Applications*. New York: John Wiley.

Brouns, F., Rehrer, N. J., Saris, H. M., Beckers, E., Menheere, P., & ten-Hoor, F. (1989). Effects of carbohydrate intake during warming-up on the regulation of blood glucose during exercise. *International Journal of Sports Medicine, 10,* S68–S75.

Chandler, J. V. (1985). The effect of bee pollen on physiological performance. [Abstract]. *Medicine and Science in Sports and Exercise, 17*(2), 287.

Chwalbinska-Moneta, J., & Hanninen, O. (1989). Effect of active warming-up on thermoregulatory, circulatory, and metabolic responses to incremental exercise in endurance-trained athletes. *International Journal of Sports Medicine, 10*(1), 25–29.

Consolazio, C. F., Johnson, H. L., Nelson, R. A., Dramise, J. G., & Skala, J. H. (1975). Protein metabolism during intensive physical training in the young adult. *American Journal of Clinical Nutrition, 28,* 29–35.

Consolazio, C. F., Nelson, R. A., Matoush, L. O., & Isaac, G. J. (1964). Effects of aspartic acid salts (Mg + K) on physical performance of men. *Journal of Applied Physiology, 19,* 257–261.

Costill, D. L. (1989). Sports drinks: Limitations of gastric emptying. *Sports Medicine Digest, 11*(5), 4.

Costill, D. L., Coyle, E. F., Fink, W. J., Lesmes, G. R., & Witzman, F. A. (1978). Adaptations in skeletal muscle following strength training. *Journal of Applied Physiology, 46,* 96–99.

Costill, D. L., King, D. S., Holdren, A., & Hargreaves, M. (1983). Swimming speed vs. swimming power. *Swimming Technique, 20*(1), 20–22.

Craig, A. B., & Pendergast, D. R. (1979). Relationship of stroke rate, distance per stroke and velocity in competition swimming. *Medicine and Science in Sports and Exercise, 11,* 278–283.

Craig, A. B., Skehan, P. L., Pawelczyk, J. A., & Boomer, W. L. (1985). Velocity, stroke rate, and distance per stroke during elite swimming competition. *Medicine and Science in Sports and Exercise, 17*(6), 625–634.

Crouse, K. (1986). The Matt and Pablo Show. *Swimming World, 27*(8), 31–36.

Cureton, T. K. (1941). Flexibility as an aspect of physical fitness. *Research Quarterly, 12,* 381–390.

Cureton, T. K. (1955). Wheat germ oil, the "wonder fuel." *Scholastic Coach, 24,* 36–37, 67–68.

Daly, D., Persyn, U., Van Tilborgh, L., & Riemaker, D. (1988). Estimation of sprint performances in the breaststroke from body characteristics. In B. E. Ungerechts, K. Wilke, & K. Reischle (Eds.), *International Series on Sport Sciences, Vol. 18. Swimming Science V* (pp. 101–107). Champaign, IL: Human Kinetics.

Davies, G. J., Bendle, S. R., Wood, K. L., Rowinski, M. J., & Price, S. (1986). The optimal number of repetitions to be used with isokinetic training to increase peak torque to body weight ratios. [Abstract]. *Medicine and Science in Sports and Exercise, 18*(2), S32.

DeBruyn-Prevost, P., & Lefebvre, F. (1980). The effects of various warming-up intensities and durations during a short maximal anaerobic exercise. *European Journal of Applied Physiology, 43,* 101–108.

deVries, H. A. (1974). Warm-up: Its values and efficient utilization. In L. Percival (Ed.), *Proceedings: International Symposium on the Art and Science of Coaching: Vol. 2* (pp. 207–213). Ontario, Canada: F.I. Productions.

Dominguez, R. H., & Gajda, R. S. (1982). *Total Body Training*. New York: Scribner.

Dudley, G. A., & Djamil, R. (1985). Incompatibility of endurance and strength training modes of exercise. [Abstract]. *Medicine and Science in Sports and Exercise, 17*(2), 184.

Duffy, D., & Conlee, R. (1986). Effects of phosphate loading on leg power and high intensity treadmill exercise. *Medicine and Science in Sports and Exercise, 18,* 674–677.

Fallis, N., Wilson, W. R., Tetreault, L. L., & La Sagna, L. (1963). Effect of potassium and magnesium aspartates on athletic performance. *Journal of American Medical Association, 185*(2), 129.

Fielding, R. A., Costill, D. L., Fink, W. J., King, D. S., Hargreaves, M., & Kovaleski, J. E. (1985). Effect of carbohydrate feeding frequencies and dosage on muscle glycogen use during exercise. *Medicine and Science in Sports and Exercise, 17,* 472–476.

Fleck, S. J., & Kraemer, W. J. (1987). *Designing Resistance Training Programs.* Champaign, IL: Human Kinetics.

Friedman, J. E., & Lemon, P. W. R. (1985). Effect of protein intake and endurance exercise on daily protein requirements. [Abstract]. *Medicine and Science in Sports and Exercise, 17*(2), 232–232.

Friedman, J. E., & Lemon, P. W. R. (1989). Effect of chronic endurance exercise on retention of dietary protein. *International Journal of Sports Medicine, 10*(2), 118–223.

Foster, C., Costill, D. L., & Fink, W. J. (1980). Gastric emptying characteristics of glucose and glucose polymers. *Research Quarterly, 51,* 299–305.

Genovely, H., & Stanford, B. A. (1982). Effects of prolonged warm-up above and below the anaerobic threshold on maximal performance. *European Journal of Applied Physiology, 48,* 323–330.

Golden, B. R., Adlercreutz, H., Gorsuch, S. L., Warram, J. H., Dwyer, J. T., Swenson, L., & Woods, M. N. (1982). Estrogen excretion patterns and plasma levels in vegetarian and omnivorous women. *New England Journal of Medicine, 307*(25), 1542–1547.

Gollnick, P. D., Armstrong, R. B., Saubert, C. W., Piehl, K., & Saltin, B. (1972). Enzyme activity and fiber composition in skeletal muscle of untrained and trained men. *Journal of Applied Physiology, 33,* 312–319.

Grimston, S. K., & Hay, J. G. (1984). The relationship among anthropometric and stroking characteristics of male varsity swimmers. [Abstract]. *Medicine and Science in Sports and Exercise, 16*(2), 159.

Haas, R. (1986). *Eat to Succeed.* New York: Rawson Associates.

Harre, D. (1982). *Principles of Sports Training*. Berlin: Sportverlag.

Hermiston, R. T., & O'Brien, M. E. (1972). The effects of three types of warm-up on the total oxygen cost of a short treadmill run. In A. W. Taylor (Ed.), *Training: Scientific Basis and Application* (pp. 70–75). Springfield, IL: Charles C. Thomas.

Hettinger, T., & Muller, E. A. (1953). Muskelleistung and Muskeltraining. *Arbeitsphysiologie, 15,* 111–126.

Heusner, W. W. (1985). *Body composition of Olympic male and female swimmers.* Report presented at the U.S. Swimming Sports Medicine Meeting, Phoenix, AZ.

Hickson, R. C., Dvorak, B. A., Corostiaga, E. M., Kurowski, T. T., & Foster, C. (1988). Strength training and performance in endurance trained subjects. [Abstract]. *Medicine and Science in Sports and Exercise, 20*(2), S86.

Horswill, C. A., Gao, J., Costill, D. L., & Park, S. H. (1988). Oral $NaHCO_3$ improves performance in interval swimming. [Abstract]. *Medicine and Science in Sports and Exercise, 20*(2), S3.

Horswill, C. A., Hickner, R. C., Scott, J. R., Costill, D. L., & Gould, D. (1990). Weight loss, dietary carbohydrate modifications, and high intensity, physical performance. *Medicine and Science in Sports and Exercise, 22*(4), 470–476.

Hortobagyi, T., Faludi, J., Tihanyi, J., & Merkely, B. (1985). Effects of intense "stretching"-flexibility training on the range of motion of the hip joint. *International Journal of Sports Medicine, 6*(6), 317–321.

Ingjer, F., & Strommer, S. B. (1979). Effects of active, passive, or no warm-up on the physiological responses to heavy exercise. *European Journal of Applied Physiology, 40,* 273–282.

Ivy, J. L. (1983). Amphetamines. In M. Williams (Ed.), *Ergogenic Aids in Sports* (pp. 101–127). Champaign, IL: Human Kinetics.

Ivy, J. L., Katz, A. L., Cutler, C. L., Sherman, W. M., & Coyle, E. F. (1988). Muscle glycogen synthesis after exercise: effect of time of carbohydrate ingestion. *Journal of Applied Physiology, 64,* 1480–1485.

Ivy, J. L., Lee, M. C., Broznick, J. T., & Reed, M. J. (1988). Muscle glycogen storage after different amounts of carbohydrate ingestion. *Journal of Applied Physiology, 65,* 2018–2023.

Jacobs, I., Bar-Or, O., Dotan, R., Karlsson, J., & Tesch, P. (1983). Changes in muscle ATP, CP, glycogen, and lactate after performance of the Wingate anaerobic test. In H. G. Knuttgen, J. A. Vogel, & J. Poortmans (Eds.), *International Series on Sport Sciences: Vol. 13. Biochemistry of Exercise* (pp. 234–238). Champaign, IL: Human Kinetics.

Jacobs, I., Kaiser, P., & Tesch, P. (1982). The effects of glycogen exhaustion on maximal short-term performance. In P. V. Komi (Ed.), *Exercise and Sport Biology* (pp. 103–108). Champaign, IL: Human Kinetics.

Jacobs, I., Sale, D., & MacDougall, J. D. (1987). Combined strength and endurance training effects on muscle enzymatic and histochemical characteristics. [Abstract]. *Medicine and Science in Sports and Exercise, 19*(2), S88.

Jang, K. T., Flynn, M. G., Costill, D. L., Kirwan, J. P., Houmard, J. A., Mitchell, J. B., & D'Acquisto, L. J. (1987). Energy balance in competitive swimmers and runners. *Journal of Swimming Research, 3*(1), 19–23.

Jensen, C. R., & Fisher, A. G. (1972). *Scientific Basis of Athletic Training*. Philadelphia: Lea & Febiger.

Jensen, C. R., & Fisher, A. G. (1975). *Scientific Basis of Athletic Conditioning* (2nd ed.). Philadelphia: Lea & Febiger.

Jerome, J. (1987). *Staying Supple: The Bountiful Pleasures of Stretching*. New York: Bantam.

Kanehisa, H., & Miyashita, M. (1983). Effects of isometric and isokinetic muscle training on static strength and dynamic power. *European Journal of Applied Physiology, 50,* 365–371.

Karpovich, P. V. (1965). *Physiology of Muscular Activity.* Philadelphia: W. B. Saunders.

Keul, J., Doll, E., & Keppler, D. (1972). *Energy Metabolism of Human Muscle.* Baltimore: University Park Press.

Knowles, R., Otto, R. M., Wygand, J., Taylor, D., Lagerman, L., & Ferris, D. (1989). The effect of sodium bicarbonate ingestion on sprint performance of adolescent swimmers. [Abstract]. *Medicine and Science in Sports and Exercise, 21*(2), S48.

Krukau, M., Volker, K., & Liesen, H. (1987). The influence of sport-specific and sport-unspecific recovery on lactate behaviour after anaerobic swimming. [Abstract]. *International Journal of Sports Medicine, 8*(2), 142.

Lamb, D. R., Baur, T. S., Brodowicz, G. R., Blair, C. S., & Corrigan, D. L. (1986). Consumption of carbohydrate, electrolytes, and acid buffers: Effects on brief, high intensity exercise performance. *Activities Report of the Research and Development Associates, 38,* 44–52.

Leatt, P. B., & Jacobs, I. (1986). Effects of glucose polymer ingestion on muscle glycogen utilization during a soccer match. [Abstract]. *Medicine and Science in Sports and Exercise, 18*(2), S6.

Lemon, P. W. R. (1987). Protein and exercise: Update 1987. *Medicine and Science in Sports and Exercise, 19*(5 Suppl.), S179–S190.

Lemon, P. W. R., & Mullin, J. P. (1980). Effect of initial muscle glycogen levels on protein catabolism during exercise. *Journal of Applied Physiology, 48,* 624–628.

Loy, S., Conlee, R., Winder, W., Nelson, A., Arnall, D., & Fisher, G. (1986). Effects of a 24-h fast on cycling endurance time. [Abstract]. *Medicine and Science in Sports and Exercise, 18*(2), S12–S13.

MacDougall, J. D., Sale, D. G., Elder, G. C. B., Sutton, J. R., & Howald, H. (1979). Mitochondrial volume density in human skeletal muscle following heavy resistance training. *Medicine and Science in Sports and Exercise, 11,* 164–166.

MacDougall, J. D., Sale, D., Jacobs, I., Garner, S., Moroz, D., & McMaster, D. (1987). Concurrent strength and endurance training do not impede gains in $\dot{V}O_2$max. [Abstract]. *Medicine and Science in Sports and Exercise, 19*(2), S87.

MacDougall, J. D., Ward, G. R., Sale, D. G., & Sutton, J. R. (1977). Muscle glycogen repletion after high-intensity intermittent exercise. *Journal of Applied Physiology, 42,* 129–132.

Maglischo, E. W. (1991). [Stroke rates for national and international swimmers]. Unpublished research.

Maglischo, C. W., Maglischo, E. W., Higgins, J., Hinrichs, R., Luedtke, D., Schleihauf, R. E., & Thayer, A. (1986). A biomechanical analysis of the 1984 U.S. Olympic swimming team: the distance freestylers. *Journal of Swimming Research, 2*(3), 12–16.

Marable, N. L., Hickson, J. F., Korslund, M. K., Herbert, W. G., Desjardins, R. F., & Thye, F. W. (1979). Urinary nitrogen excretion as influenced by a muscle-building exercise program and protein intake variation. *Nutrition Reports International, 19,* 795–805.

Martin, B. J., Robinson, S., Wiegman, D. L., & Aulick, L. H. (1975). Effect of warm-up on metabolic responses to strenuous exercise. *Medicine and Science in Sports and Exercise, 7,* 146–149.

Massey, B. H., & Chaudet, N. L. (1956). Effects of heavy resistance exercise on range of joint movement in young male adults. *Research Quarterly, 27,* 41–51.

Mathews, D. K., Bowers, R., Fox, E., & Wilgus, W. (1963). Aerobic and anaerobic work efficiency. *Research Quarterly, 34*, 356–360.

Maughan, R. (1991). Carbohydrate-electrolyte solutions during prolonged exercise. In D. R. Lamb & M. L. Williams (Eds.), *Perspectives in Exercise Science and Sports Medicine: Vol. 4. Ergogenics: The enhancement of performance in exercise and sport.* Indianapolis, IN: Benchmark.

McArdle, W. D., Katch, F. I., & Katch, V. L. (1981). *Exercise Physiology: Energy, Nutrition, and Human Performance.* Philadelphia, PA: Lea & Febiger.

McArthur, K. E., & Feldman, M. (1989). Gastric acid secretion, gastrin release, and gastric temperature in humans as affected by liquid meal temperature. *American Journal of Clinical Nutrition, 49,* 51–54.

Meyers, C. R. (1967). Effect of two isometric routines on strength, size and endurance in exercised and non-exercised arms. *Research Quarterly, 38,* 430–440.

Miller, G. W., Kreider, R. B., & Williams, M. H. (1989). Effects of phosphate loading on maximal and five mile run performance. [Abstract]. *Medicine and Science in Sports and Exercise, 17*(2), 200.

Mitchell, J. B., Costill, D. L., Houmard, J. A., Fink, W. J., Robergs, R. A., Pascoe, D. D., & Davis, J. A. (1989). Gastric emptying: influence of prolonged exercise and carbohydrate concentration. *Medicine and Science in Sports and Exercise, 21*(3), 269–274.

Miyashita, M., & Kanehisa, H. (1983). Effects of isokinetic, isotonic, and swim training on swimming performance. In A. P. Hollander, P. A. Huijing, & G. de Groot (Eds.), *International Series on Sport Sciences: Vol. 14. Biomechanics and Medicine in Swimming* (pp. 329–334). Champaign, IL: Human Kinetics.

Moffroid, M. T., & Whipple, R. H. (1970). Specificity of speed of exercise. *Physical Therapy, 50,* 1692–1700.

Murray, R., Paul, G. L., Seifert, J. G., Eddy, D. E., & Halaby, G. A. (1989). The effects of glucose, fructose, and sucrose ingestion during exercise. *Medicine and Science in Sports and Exercise, 21*(3), 275–282.

Nash, H. (1988). L-carnitine: unproven as an ergogenic aid. *Physician and Sportsmedicine, 16*(3), 74–75.

Nelson, A. G., Conlee, R. K., Arnall, D. A., Loy, S. F., & Sylvester, L. J. (1984). Adaptations to simultaneous training for strength and endurance. [Abstract]. *Medicine and Science in Sports and Exercise, 16*(2), 184.

Neufer, P. D., Costill, D. L., Fink, W. J., Kirwan, J. P., Fielding, R. A., & Flynn, M. G. (1987). Improvements in exercise performance: effects of carbohydrate feedings and diet. *Journal of Applied Physiology, 62,* 983–988.

Nieman, D. C., Carlson, K. A., & Brandstater, M. E. (1987). Running endurance in 27-hour fasted males. [Abstract]. *Medicine and Science in Sports and Exercise, 19*(2), S43.

Norris, J., Davis, M., & Lonnett, M. (1989). Oxidation of ingested glucose during exercise. [Abstract]. *Medicine and Science in Sports and Exercise, 21*(2), S44.

O'Keefe, K. A., Keith, R. E., Blessing, D. L., Wilson, G. D., & Young, K. L. (1987). Dietary carbohydrates and female endurance performance. [Abstract]. *Medicine and Science in Sports and Exercise, 19*(2), S38.

Owen, M. D., Kregel, K. C., Wall, P. T., & Gisolfi, C. V. (1986). Effects of ingesting carbohydrate beverages during exercise in the heat. *Medicine and Science in Sports and Exercise, 18,* 568–575.

Pai, Y., Hay, J. G., Wilson, B. D., & Thayer, A. L. (1984). Stroking techniques of elite swimmers. [Abstract]. *Medicine and Science in Sports and Exercise, 16*(2), 159.

Paul, G. L., Seifert, J. G., Eddy, D. E., & Murray, R. (1988). Sensory response to carbohydrate beverages consumed during exercise. [Abstract]. *Medicine and Science in Sports and Exercise, 20*(2), S25.

Pate, R. R., Smith, P. E., Lambert, M. I., & Rocchio, M. L. (1985). Effect of orally administered sodium bicarbonate on performance of high intensity exercise. [Abstract]. *Medicine and Science in Sports and Exercise, 17*(2), 200.

Peden, C., Sherman, W. M., & D'Acquisto, L. (1989). 1 h preexercise carbohydrate meals enhance performance. [Abstract]. *Medicine and Science in Sports and Exercise, 21*(2), S59.

Perrin, D. H., Lephart, S. M., & Weltman, A. (1987). Specificity of isokinetic training on quadriceps and hamstring peak torque, torque acceleration energy, power and work in intercollegiate lacrosse players. [Abstract]. *Medicine and Science in Sports and Exercise, 19*(2), S88.

Pfefferle, K. P., & Wilkinson, J. G. (1988). Induced alkalosis and submaximal cycling in trained and untrained men. [Abstract]. *Medicine and Science in Sports and Exercise, 20*(2), S25.

Pitts, G. C., Consolazio, F. C., & Johnson, R. E. (1944). Dietary protein and physical fitness in temperature and hot climates. *Journal of Nutrition, 27,* 497–508.

Pizzo, A. (1961). [The influence different preworkout breakfasts have on blood sugar levels of competitive swimmers]. Unpublished research, Indiana University, Bloomington. Cited in C. R. Jensen & A. G. Fisher (Eds.), *Scientific Basis of Athletic Conditioning*. Philadelphia: Lea & Febiger, 1975.

Rasch, P. J., Hamby, J. W., & Burns, H. J. (1969). Protein dietary supplementation and physical performance. *Medicine and Science in Sports and Exercise, 1,* 195–199.

Rasch, P. J., & Peirson, W. R. (1962). Effect of a protein dietary supplement on muscular strength and hypertrophy. *American Journal of Clinical Nutrition, 11,* 530–532.

Robinson, S., Robinson, D. L., Montoye, R. I. J., & Bullard, R. W. (1958). Fatigue and efficiency of men during exhausting runs. *Journal of Applied Physiology, 12,* 197–201.

Rosen, H., Blumenthal, A., & Agersborg, H. P. K. (1962). Effects of the potassium and magnesium salts of aspartic acid on metabolic exhaustion. *Journal of Pharmaceutical Science, 51,* 592–593.

Sale, D., Jacobs, I., Moroa, D., MacDougall, J. D., & Garner, S. (1988). Comparison of two regimes of combined strength and endurance training. [Abstract]. *Medicine and Science in Sports and Exercise, 20*(2), S9.

Schmid, L. (1947). Increase in Body Output by Warming-up. *Casop. Lek. Cesk, 86,* 950.

Schultz, T. D., Wilcox, R. B., Spuehler, J. M., & Howie, B. J. (1987). Dietary and hormonal interrelationships in premenopausal women: evidence for a relationship between dietary nutrients and plasma prolactic levels. *American Journal of Clinical Nutrition, 46,* 905–911.

Seifert, J. G., Langenfeld, M. E., Rudge, S. J., & Buchert, R. J. (1986). Effects of glucose polymer ingestion on ultraendurance bicycling performance. [Abstract]. *Medicine and Science in Sports and Exercise, 18*(2), S5–S6.

Sharp, R. L. (1986). Muscle strength and power related to competitive swimming. *Journal of Swimming Research, 2*(2), 5–10.

Sharp, R. L. (1991). Effects of dietary supplementation with MAXXON on adaptations to combined aerobic and anaerobic cycling. *International Journal of Sports Nutrition,* in review.

Sharp, R. L., Costill, D. L., & King, D. S. (1983). Power characteristics of swimmers at the 1982 U.S. senior national long course swimming championships. Research report submitted to the American Swimming Coaches Association, Fort Lauderdale.

Sharp, R. L., Hackney, A., Runyan, W., Kim, Y., & Ness, R. (1988). Effect of a protein supplement on adaptations to combined aerobic and anaerobic training. [Abstract]. *Medicine and Science in Sports and Exercise, 20*(2), S3.

Sharp, R. L., Ness, R. J., Hackney, A. C., & Runyan, W. S. (1989). Compatibility of aerobic and anaerobic adaptations to training in man. [Abstract]. *Medicine and Science in Sports and Exercise, 21*(2), S76.

Sharp, R. L., Troup, J. P., & Costill, D. L. (1982). Relationship between power and sprint freestyle swimming. *Medicine and Science in Sports and Exercise, 14,* 53–56.

Sherman, W. M. (1983). Carbohydrates, muscle glycogen, and muscle glycogen supercompensation. In M. H. Williams (Ed.), *Ergogenic Aids in Sports* (pp. 3–26). Champaign, IL: Human Kinetics.

Sherman, W. M., Costill, D. L., Fink, W. J., & Miller, J. M. (1981). Effects of exercise-diet manipulation on muscle glycogen and its subsequent utilization during performance. *International Journal of Sports Medicine, 2,* 1–15.

Sherman, W. M., & Maglischo, E. W. (1992). Minimizing athletic fatigue among swimmers: special emphasis on nutrition. *Sports Science Exchange, 4*(35), Chicago: Gatorade Sports Science Institute.

Sherman, W. M., Peden, M. C., & Wright, D. A. (1991). Carbohydrate feedings 1 h before exercise improves cycling performance. *American Journal of Clinical Nutrition,* in press.

Slavin, J. L., McNamara, E. A., & Lutter, J. M. (1986). Nutritional practices of women cyclists, including recreational riders and elite racers. In F. I. Katch (Ed.), *Sport, Health and Nutrition* (pp. 107–111). Champaign, IL: Human Kinetics.

Smith, M. J., & Melton, P. (1981). Isokinetic versus isotonic variable resistance training. *American Journal of Sports Medicine, 9,* 275–279.

Smith, N. J. (1977). Gaining and losing weight in athletics. In E. J. Burke (Ed.), *Toward an Understanding of Human Performance* (pp. 48–50). Ithaca, NY: Mouvement Publications.

Song, T. K., Serresse, O., Ama, P., Theriault, G. J., & Boulay, M. R. (1988). Effects of three anaerobic tests on venous blood values. [Abstract]. *Medicine and Science in Sports and Exercise, 20*(2), S39.

Stager, J. M., Cordain, L., & Becker, T. J. (1984). Relationship of body composition to swimming performance in female swimmers. *Journal of Swimming Research, 1*(1), 21–26.

Stanko, R. T., Robertson, R. J., Galbreath, R. W., Reilly, J. J., Greenwalt, K. D., & Goss, F. L. (1989). Effect of dihydroxyacetone and pyruvate on leg endurance. [Abstract]. *Medicine and Science in Sports and Exercise, 23*(2), S44.

Strass, D. (1988). Effects of maximal strength training on sprint performance of competitive swimmers. In B. E. Ungerechts, K. Wilke, & K. Reischle (Eds.), *International Series on Sport Sciences, Vol. 18. Swimming Science V* (pp. 149–156). Champaign, IL: Human Kinetics.

Tesch, P. A., Hakkinen, K., & Komi, P. V. (1985). The effect of strength training and detraining on various enzyme activities. *Medicine and Science in Sports and Exercise, 2,* 245.

Thomas, D. E., Brotherhood, J., & Brand, J. C. (1989). Pre-game low glycemic index meal provides advantage before prolonged strenuous exercise. [Abstract]. *Medicine and Science in Sports and Exercise, 21*(2), S59.

Timm, K. E. (1987). Investigation of exercise effect overflow from speed-specific isokinetic activity. [Abstract]. *Medicine and Science in Sports and Exercise, 19*(2), S88.

U.S. Department of Agriculture. (1977–1978). *Nationwide Food Consumption Survey, 1977–1978* (preliminary report No. 2). Washington, DC.

U.S. Department of Agriculture & U.S. Department of Health and Human Services. (1990). *Dietary Guidelines for Americans* (3rd ed.). (Pamphlet).

U.S. Department of Health, Education, and Welfare. (1976). *Hanes I* (First health and nutrition examination survey, United States 1971–72) publication 76-1219-1. Rockville, MD: author.

van der Beek, E. J., van Dokkum, W., Schrijver, J., Wesstra, J. A., van de Weerd, H., & Hermus, R. J. J. (1984). Effect of marginal vitamin intake on physical performance in man. *International Journal of Sports Medicine, 5*(Suppl.), 28–34.

van Erp-Baart, A. M. J., Saris, W. H. M., Binkhorst, R. A., Vos, J. A., & Elvers, J. W. H. (1989a). Nationwide survey on nutritional habits in elite athletes: Part I. Energy, carbohydrate, protein, and fat intake. *International Journal of Sports Medicine, 10*(Suppl. 1), S3–S10.

van Erp-Baart, A. M. J., Saris, W. H. M., Binkhorst, R. A., Vos, J. A., & Elvers, J. W. H. (1989b). Nationwide survey on nutritional habits in elite athletes: Part II. Mineral and vitamin intake. *International Journal of Sports Medicine, 10*(Suppl. 1), S11–S16.

Weiss, M., Reischle, K., Bouws, N., Simon, G., & Weicker, H. (1988). Relationship of blood lactate accumulation to stroke rate and distance per stroke in top female swimmers. In B. E. Ungerechts, K. Wilke, & K. Reischle (Eds.), *International Series on Sport Sciences: Vol. 18. Swimming Science V* (pp. 295–303). Champaign, IL: Human Kinetics.

Welham, W. C., & Behnke, A. R. (1942). The specific gravity of healthy men. *Journal of the American Medical Association, 118,* 498–501.

Wesson, M., McNaughton, L., Davies, P., & Tristram, S. (1988). Effects of oral administration of aspartic salts on the endurance capacity of trained athletes. *Research Quarterly, 59*(3), 234–239.

Williams, M. H. (1989). *Beyond Training: How Athletes Enhance Performance Legally and Illegally.* Champaign, IL: Leisure Press.

Wilmore, J. H. (1972). Oxygen. In W. P. Morgan (Ed.), *Ergogenic Aids and Muscular Performance* (pp. 321–342). New York: Academic.

Wilmore, J. H., & Costill, D. L. (1988). *Training for Sport and Activity: The Physiological Basis of the Conditioning Process.* Dubuque, IA: Wm. C. Brown.

Wilson, G. E., & Cureton, K. J. (1984). Effects of glycogen depletion and glycogen loading on anaerobic threshold and distance running performance. [Abstract]. *Medicine and Science in Sports and Exercise, 16*(2), 190.

Wooton, S. A., & Williams, C. (1984). Influence of carbohydrate-status on performance during maximal exercise. *International Journal of Sports Medicine, 5*(Suppl.), 126–127.

INDEX

Note: Lower-case f *following a page number refers to a figure; lower-case* t *refers to a table.*

ACKNOWLEDGMENTS

Page 13 From D. R. Lamb, *Physiology of Exercise: Responses and Adaptations*. Copyright © 1978 Macmillan Publishing Co.
Page 14 From Edgerton/Edgerton, *The Biology of Physical Activity*, 1976.
Pages 24, 32, 99, 291 From J. H. Wilmore and D. C. Costill, *Training for Sport and Physical Activity: The Physiological Basis of the Conditioning Process*, 3e. Copyright © 1988 Wm. C. Brown, Dubuque, Iowa. All rights reserved. Reprinted by permission.
Pages 24, 69, 70 From Edward L. Fox, Richard W. Bowers, and Merle L. Foss, *The Physiological Basis of Physical Education and Athletics*, 4e. Copyright © 1971, 1976, 1981, and 1988 by W. B. Saunders Company. Reprinted by permission of Wm. C. Brown Publishers, Dubuque, Iowa. All rights reserved.
Page 31 From M. E. Houston, "Metabolic Responses to Exercise with Special Reference to Training and Competition in Swimming," *Swimming Medicine IV*, ed. B. Eriksson and B. Furberg, p. 222, fig. 4, by permission of the author and the publisher University Park Press, 1978.
Pages 40, 67 From P. Astrand and K. Rodahl, *Textbook of Work Physiology*. Copyright © 1977 McGraw-Hill Publishing Company.
Page 78 From Jorfeldt et al., *Journal of Applied Physiology* 44(3) 1978.
Page 108 From Fitts et al., *Journal of Applied Physiology* 66(1): 472.
Page 168 From *Journal of Swimming Research* 1(1) 17–20.
Page 244 From *Journal of Swimming Research* 1(2) 14.
Page 246 From W. P. Morgan et al., "Mood disturbance following increased training in swimmers," *Medicine and Science in Sports and Exercise* 20(4), 412.
Page 279 From A. D. Rogol, "Pubertal development in endurance-trained female athletes," *Competitive Sports for Children and Youth*, (eds.) Brown and Banta. Reprinted by permission.
Page 286 From Dumner et al., "Pathogenic Weight-Control Behaviors," *The Physician and Sportsmedicine*, May 1987.
Page 310 From J. G. Hay and A. M. Thayer, "Flow Visualization of Competitive Swimming Techniques. The Tufts Method." Fig. 3, p. 208 in *Starting, Stroking and Turning*, James G. Hay (ed.), 1986. Reprinted by permission of the editor.
Page 356 From "Propelling efficiency of front crawl swimming" by H. Toussaint, *Journal of Applied Physiology* 65(6): 2506–2512, 1988.
Page 508 Reprinted from H. Firby, *Howard Firby on Swimming*, Pelham Books, 1975, p. 75, by permission of Pelham Books Ltd.
Page 640 From *American Journal of Sports Medicine*, 1981, 9:275–270. Reprinted with permission.
Pages 667, 668 From *Exercise Physiology, Energy, Nutrition, and Human Performance*, 3e, 1991, Lea & Febiger. Reprinted by permission of the author.
Page 687 From "Effects of exercise-diet manipulation on muscle glycogen and its subsequent utilization during performance," *Journal of Sports Medicine* 2:1–15, 1981.